Solutions Manual

Chapters 1-17

Accounting 25e

or

Financial Accounting 13e

Carl S. Warren

Professor Emeritus of Accounting
University of Georgia, Athens

James M. Reeve

Professor Emeritus of Accounting
University of Tennessee, Knoxville

Jonathan E. Duchac

Professor of Accounting
Wake Forest University

 SOUTH-WESTERN
CENGAGE Learning·

Australia • Brazil • Japan • Korea • Mexico • Singapore • Spain • United Kingdom • United States

ISBN-13: 978-1-285-07443-6

ISBN-10: 1-285-07443-2

South-Western Cengage Learning
5191 Natorp Boulevard
Mason, OH 45040
USA

Cengage Learning is a leading provider of customized learning solutions with office locations around the globe, including Singapore, the United Kingdom, Australia, Mexico, Brazil, and Japan. Locate your local office at: **international.cengage.com/region**.

Cengage Learning products are represented in Canada by Nelson Education, Ltd.

For your course and learning solutions, visit **www.cengage.com**.

Purchase any of our products at your local college store or at our preferred online store **www.CengageBrain.com**.

Printed in the United States of America
1 2 3 4 5 6 7   16 15 14 13 12

CONTENTS

CHAPTER 1
INTRODUCTION TO ACCOUNTING AND BUSINESS

DISCUSSION QUESTIONS

1. Some users of accounting information include managers, employees, investors, creditors, customers, and the government.

2. The role of accounting is to provide information for managers to use in operating the business. In addition, accounting provides information to others to use in assessing the economic performance and condition of the business.

3. The corporate form allows the company to obtain large amounts of resources by issuing stock. For this reason, most companies that require large investments in property, plant, and equipment are organized as corporations.

4. No. The business entity concept limits the recording of economic data to transactions directly affecting the activities of the business. The payment of the interest of $4,500 is a personal transaction of Josh Reilly and should not be recorded by Dispatch Delivery Service.

5. The land should be recorded at its cost of $167,500 to Reliable Repair Service. This is consistent with the cost concept.

6. a. No. The offer of $2,000,000 and the increase in the assessed value should not be recognized in the accounting records.

   b. Cash would increase by $2,125,000, land would decrease by $900,000, and owner's equity would increase by $1,225,000.

7. An account receivable is a claim against a customer for goods or services sold. An account payable is an amount owed to a creditor for goods or services purchased. Therefore, an account receivable in the records of the seller is an account payable in the records of the purchaser.

8. (b) The business realized net income of $91,000 ($679,000 – $588,000).

9. (a) The business incurred a net loss of $75,000 ($640,000 – $715,000).

10. (a) Net income or net loss
    (b) Owner's equity at the end of the period
    (c) Cash at the end of the period

© 2014 Cengage Learning. All Rights Reserved. May not be scanned, copied or duplicated, or posted to a publicly accessible website, in whole or in part.

PRACTICE EXERCISES

PE 1–1A

$345,000. Under the cost concept, the land should be recorded at the cost to Integrity Repair Service.

PE 1–1B

$437,500. Under the cost concept, the land should be recorded at the cost to Higgins Repair Service.

PE 1–2A

a.
$$A = L + OE$$
$$\$942{,}000 = \$584{,}000 \quad + OE$$
$$OE = \$358{,}000$$

b.
$$A = L + OE$$
$$+\$113{,}000 = +\$44{,}000 \quad + OE$$
$$OE = +\$69{,}000$$
OE on December 31, 2014 =
$$\$427{,}000 = \$358{,}000 \quad + \quad \$69{,}000$$

PE 1–2B

a.
$$A = L + OE$$
$$\$395{,}000 = \$97{,}000 \quad + OE$$
$$OE = \$298{,}000$$

b.
$$A = L + OE$$
$$-\$65{,}000 = +\$36{,}000 \quad + OE$$
$$OE = -\$101{,}000$$
OE on December 31, 2014 =
$$\$197{,}000 = \$298{,}000 \quad - \quad \$101{,}000$$

PE 1–3A

(2) Asset (Cash) decreases by $3,750;
Liability (Accounts Payable) decreases by $3,750.

(3) Asset (Accounts Receivable) increases by $22,400;
Revenue (Delivery Service Fees) increases by $22,400.

(4) Asset (Cash) increases by $11,300;
Asset (Accounts Receivable) decreases by $11,300.

(5) Asset (Cash) decreases by $6,000;
Asset (Gates Deeter, Drawing) increases by $6,000.

nse) increases by $4,850;
...$4,850.

...s by $2,100;
...able) increases by $2,100.

...eivable) increases by $14,700;
...Service Fees) increases by $14,700.

...reases by $8,200;
...s Receivable) decreases by $8,200.

.–4A

SUNSET TRAVEL SERVICE		
Income Statement		
For the Year Ended April 30, 2014		
Fees earned		$1,673,000
Expenses:		
Wages expense	$660,000	
Office expense	488,000	
Miscellaneous expense	34,000	
Total expenses		1,182,000
Net income		$ 491,000

PE 1–4B

SENTINEL TRAVEL SERVICE		
Income Statement		
For the Year Ended August 31, 2014		
Fees earned		$750,000
Expenses:		
Wages expense	$450,000	
Office expense	295,000	
Miscellaneous expense	12,000	
Total expenses		757,000
Net loss		$ (7,000)

PE 1–5A

SUNSET TRAVEL SERVICE		
Statement of Owner's Equity		
For the Year Ended April 30, 2014		
Craig Daws, capital, May 1, 2013		$3
Additional investment by owner during year	$ 75,000	
Net income for the year	491,000	
	$566,000	
Less withdrawals	66,000	
Increase in owner's equity		500,000
Craig Daws, capital, April 30, 2014		$800,000

PE 1–5B

SENTINEL TRAVEL SERVICE		
Statement of Owner's Equity		
For the Year Ended August 31, 2014		
Barb Schroeder, capital, September 1, 2013		$380,000
Additional investment by owner during year	$36,000	
Net loss for the year	(7,000)	
	$29,000	
Less withdrawals	18,000	
Increase in owner's equity		11,000
Barb Schroeder, capital, August 31, 2014		$391,000

PE 1–6A

SUNSET TRAVEL SERVICE			
Balance Sheet			
April 30, 2014			
Assets		Liabilities	
Cash	$274,000	Accounts payable	$ 61,000
Accounts receivable	124,000		
Supplies	13,000	Owner's Equity	
Land	450,000	Craig Daws, capital	800,000
		Total liabilities and	
Total assets	$861,000	owner's equity	$861,000

PE 1–6B

SENTINEL TRAVEL SERVICE			
Balance Sheet			
August 31, 2014			
Assets		**Liabilities**	
Cash	$ 45,400	Accounts payable	$ 44,600
Accounts receivable	75,500		
Supplies	4,700	**Owner's Equity**	
Land	310,000	Barb Schroeder, capital	391,000
		Total liabilities and	
Total assets	$435,600	owner's equity	$435,600

PE 1–7A

SUNSET TRAVEL SERVICE		
Statement of Cash Flows		
For the Year Ended April 30, 2014		
Cash flows from operating activities:		
Cash received from customers	$ 1,500,000	
Deduct cash payments for operating expenses	(1,215,000)	
Net cash flows from operating activities		$ 285,000
Cash flows used for investing activities:		
Cash payments for purchase of land		(240,000)
Cash flows from financing activities:		
Cash received from owner as investment	$ 75,000	
Deduct cash withdrawals by owner	(66,000)	
Net cash flows from financing activities		9,000
Net increase in cash during year		$ 54,000
Cash as of May 1, 2013		220,000
Cash as of April 30, 2014		$ 274,000

PE 1–7B

SENTINEL TRAVEL SERVICE Statement of Cash Flows For the Year Ended August 31, 2014		
Cash flows from operating activities:		
Cash received from customers	$ 734,000	
Deduct cash payments for operating expenses	(745,600)	
Net cash flows used for operating activities		$(11,600)
Cash flows used for investing activities:		
Cash payments for purchase of land		(50,000)
Cash flows from financing activities:		
Cash received from owner as investment	$ 36,000	
Deduct cash withdrawals by owner	(18,000)	
Net cash flows from financing activities		18,000
Net decrease in cash during year		$(43,600)
Cash as of September 1, 2013		89,000
Cash as of August 31, 2014		$ 45,400

PE 1–8A

a.

	Dec. 31, 2014	Dec. 31, 2013
Total liabilities..	$547,800	$518,000
Total owner's equity...	$415,000	$370,000
Ratio of liabilities to owner's equity................................	1.32 *	1.40 **

 * $547,800 ÷ $415,000
 ** $518,000 ÷ $370,000

b. **Decreased**

PE 1–8B

a.

	Dec. 31, 2014	Dec. 31, 2013
Total liabilities...	$4,085,000	$2,880,000
Total owner's equity...	$4,300,000	$3,600,000
Ratio of liabilities to owner's equity................................	0.95 *	0.80 **

 * $4,085,000 ÷ $4,300,000
 ** $2,880,000 ÷ $3,600,000

b. **Increased**

EXERCISES

Ex. 1–1

a.

1.	manufacturing	6.	manufacturing	11.	service
2.	manufacturing	7.	service	12.	service
3.	manufacturing	8.	service	13.	manufacturing
4.	service	9.	manufacturing	14.	service
5.	merchandise	10.	merchandise	15.	merchandise

b.   The accounting equation is relevant to all companies. It serves as the basis of the accounting information system.

Ex. 1–2

As in many ethics issues, there is no one right answer. Oftentimes, disclosing only what is legally required may not be enough. In this case, it would be best for the company's chief executive officer to disclose both reports to the county representatives. In doing so, the chief executive officer could point out any flaws or deficiencies in the fired researcher's report.

Ex. 1–3

a.

1.	M	5.	O	9.	X
2.	L	6.	O	10.	O
3.	O	7.	X		
4.	M	8.	L		

b.   A business transaction is an economic event or condition that directly changes an entity's financial condition or results of operations.

Ex. 1–4

Peet's Coffee & Tea's owners' equity: $209 – $36 = $173
Starbucks' owners' equity: $6,386 – $2,711 = $3,675

Ex. 1–5

Dollar Tree's owners' equity: $2,381 – $922 = $1,459
Target's owners' equity: $43,705 – $28,218 = $15,487

Ex. 1–6

a. $456,100 ($118,000 + $338,100)

b. $355,010 ($766,750 – $411,740)

c. $2,072,200 ($3,250,300 – $1,178,100)

Ex. 1–7

a. $775,000 ($1,250,000 – $475,000)

b. $890,000 ($775,000 + $225,000 – $110,000)

c. $385,000 ($775,000 – $300,000 – $90,000)

d. $1,460,000 ($775,000 + $550,000 + $135,000)

e.   Net income: $350,000 ($1,500,000 – $375,000 – $775,000)

Ex. 1–8

a.   (2) liability

b.   (1) asset

c.   (3) owner's equity (revenue)

d.   (1) asset

e.   (1) asset

f.   (3) owner's equity (expense)

Ex. 1–9

a.   Increases assets and increases owner's equity.

b.   Decreases assets and decreases owner's equity.

c.   Increases assets and decreases assets.

d.   Increases assets and increases liabilities.

e.   Increases assets and increases owner's equity.

Ex. 1–10

a.   (1)   Total assets increased $260,000 ($440,000 – $180,000).

    (2)   No change in liabilities.

    (3)   Owner's equity increased $260,000.

b.   (1)   Total assets decreased $69,000.

    (2)   Total liabilities decreased $69,000.

    (3)   No change in owner's equity.

c.   No, it is false that a transaction always affects at least two elements (Assets, Liabilities, or Owner's Equity) of the accounting equation. Some transactions affect only one element of the accounting equation. For example, purchasing supplies for cash only affects assets.

Ex. 1–11

1. (b) decrease
2. (a) increase
3. (b) decrease
4. (a) increase

Ex. 1–12

1. c	6. c
2. a	7. d
3. e	8. a
4. e	9. e
5. c	10. e

Ex. 1–13

a. (1) Provided catering services for cash, $33,000.
   (2) Purchase of land for cash, $20,000.
   (3) Payment of cash for expenses, $24,000.
   (4) Purchase of supplies on account, $1,000.
   (5) Withdrawal of cash by owner, $3,000.
   (6) Payment of cash to creditors, $6,000.
   (7) Recognition of cost of supplies used, $1,800.

b. – $20,000 ($10,000 – $30,000)
c. $4,200 (–$3,000 + $33,000 – $25,800)
d. $7,200 ($33,000 – $25,800)
e. $4,200 ($7,200 – $3,000)

Ex. 1–14

No. It would be incorrect to say that the business had incurred a net loss of $8,000. The excess of the withdrawals over the net income for the period is a decrease in the amount of owner's equity in the business.

Ex. 1–15

Juliet

Owner's equity at end of year ($1,125,000 – $500,000)................................	$625,000
Deduct owner's equity at beginning of year ($600,000 – $150,000).................	450,000
Net income (increase in owner's equity)...	$175,000

Kilo

Increase in owner's equity (as determined for Juliet)..................................	$175,000
Add withdrawals..	55,000
Net income...	$230,000

Lima

Increase in owner's equity (as determined for Juliet)..................................	$175,000
Deduct additional investment..	100,000
Net income...	$ 75,000

Mike

Increase in owner's equity (as determined for Juliet)..................................	$175,000
Deduct additional investment..	100,000
	$ 75,000
Add withdrawals..	55,000
Net income...	$130,000

Ex. 1–16
Balance sheet items: 1, 2, 4, 5, 6, 10

Ex. 1–17
Income statement items: 3, 7, 8, 9

Ex. 1–18

a.

INFRA-SYSTEMS COMPANY		
Statement of Owner's Equity		
For the Month Ended November 30, 2014		
Lori Izzo, capital, November 1, 2014		$400,000
Net income for November	$275,000	
Less withdrawals	40,000	
Increase in owner's equity		235,000
Lori Izzo, capital, November 30, 2014		$635,000

b. The statement of owner's equity is prepared before the November 30, 2014, balance sheet because Lori Izzo, Capital as of November 30, 2014, is needed for the balance sheet.

Ex. 1–19

EXPLORATION SERVICES		
Income Statement		
For the Month Ended March 31, 2014		
Fees earned		$1,100,000
Expenses:		
Wages expense	$715,000	
Rent expense	80,000	
Supplies expense	9,000	
Miscellaneous expense	12,000	
Total expenses		816,000
Net income		$ 284,000

Ex. 1–20

In each case, solve for a single unknown, using the following equation:

Owner's Equity (beginning) + Investments – Withdrawals + Revenues – Expenses = Owner's Equity (ending)

Freeman

Owner's equity at end of year ($1,260,000 – $330,000)........................	$930,000
Owner's equity at beginning of year ($900,000 – $360,000)...................	540,000
Increase in owner's equity...	$390,000
Deduct increase due to net income ($570,000 – $240,000)...................	330,000
	$ 60,000
Add withdrawals...	75,000
Additional investment in the business................................. (a)	$135,000

Heyward

Owner's equity at end of year ($675,000 – $220,000)........................	$455,000
Owner's equity at beginning of year ($490,000 – $260,000)...................	230,000
Increase in owner's equity...	$225,000
Add withdrawals...	32,000
	$257,000
Deduct additional investment...	150,000
Increase due to net income...	$107,000
Add expenses...	128,000
Revenue... (b)	$235,000

Jones

Owner's equity at end of year ($100,000 – $80,000)...........................	$ 20,000
Owner's equity at beginning of year ($115,000 – $81,000)...................	34,000
Decrease in owner's equity...	$ (14,000)
Deduct decrease due to net loss ($115,000 – $122,500)......................	7,500
	$ (6,500)
Deduct additional investment...	10,000
Withdrawals from the business... (c)	$ (16,500)

Ramirez

Owner's equity at end of year ($270,000 – $136,000)........................	$134,000
Add decrease due to net loss ($115,000 – $128,000).........................	13,000
	$147,000
Add withdrawals...	39,000
Owner's equity at beginning of year..	$186,000
Deduct additional investment...	55,000
	$131,000
Add liabilities at beginning of year...	120,000
Assets at beginning of year.. (d)	$251,000

Ex. 1–21

a.

EBONY INTERIORS Balance Sheet February 28, 2014			
Assets		**Liabilities**	
Cash	$ 320,000	Accounts payable	$ 310,000
Accounts receivable	800,000		
Supplies	30,000	**Owner's Equity**	
		Justin Berk, capital	840,000
		Total liabilities and	
Total assets	$1,150,000	owner's equity	$1,150,000

EBONY INTERIORS Balance Sheet March 31, 2014			
Assets		**Liabilities**	
Cash	$ 380,000	Accounts payable	$ 400,000
Accounts receivable	960,000		
Supplies	35,000	**Owner's Equity**	
		Justin Berk, capital	975,000
		Total liabilities and	
Total assets	$1,375,000	owner's equity	$1,375,000

b.

Owner's equity, March 31	$975,000
Owner's equity, February 28	840,000
Net income	$135,000

c.

Owner's equity, March 31	$975,000
Owner's equity, February 28	840,000
Increase in owner's equity	$135,000
Add withdrawal	50,000
Net income	$185,000

Ex. 1–22

a. Balance sheet: 1, 2, 3, 4, 6, 7, 8, 9, 10, 11, 13
    Income statement: 5, 12, 14, 15

b. Yes, an item can appear on more than one financial statement. For example, cash appears on both the balance sheet and statement of cash flows. However, the same item cannot appear on both the income statement and balance sheet.

c. Yes, the accounting equation is relevant to all companies, including Exxon Mobil Corporation.

Ex. 1–23

1. (a) operating activity
2. (a) operating activity
3. (b) investing activity
4. (c) financing activity

Ex. 1–24

ETHOS CONSULTING GROUP Statement of Cash Flows For the Year Ended May 31, 2014		
Cash flows from operating activities:		
Cash received from customers	$637,500	
Deduct cash payments for operating expenses	475,000	
Net cash flows from operating activities		$162,500
Cash flows used for investing activities:		
Cash payments for purchase of land		(90,000)
Cash flows from financing activities:		
Cash received from owner as investment	$ 62,500	
Deduct cash withdrawals by owner	17,500	
Net cash flows from financing activities		45,000
Net decrease in cash during year		$117,500
Cash as of June 1, 2013		58,000
Cash as of May 31, 2014		$175,500

Ex. 1–25

1. All financial statements should contain the name of the business in their heading. The statement of owner's equity is incorrectly headed as "Omar Farah" rather than We-Sell Realty. The heading of the balance sheet needs the name of the business.

2. The income statement and statement of owner's equity cover a period of time and should be labeled "For the Month Ended August 31, 2014."

3. The year in the heading for the statement of owner's equity should be 2014 rather than 2013.

4. The balance sheet should be labeled "August 31, 2014," rather than "For the Month Ended August 31, 2014."

5. In the income statement, the miscellaneous expense amount should be listed as the last expense.

6. In the income statement, the total expenses are incorrectly subtracted from the sales commissions, resulting in an incorrect net income amount. The correct net income should be $24,150. This also affects the statement of owner's equity and the amount of Omar Farah, Capital, that appears on the balance sheet.

7. In the statement of owner's equity, the additional investment should be added first to Omar Farah, capital, as of August 1, 2014. The net income should be presented next, followed by the amount of withdrawals, which is subtracted from the net income to yield a net increase in owner's equity.

8. Accounts payable should be listed as a liability on the balance sheet.

9. Accounts receivable and supplies should be listed as assets on the balance sheet.

10. The balance sheet assets should equal the sum of the liabilities and owner's equity.

Ex. 1–25 (Concluded)

Corrected financial statements appear as follows:

WE-SELL REALTY		
Income Statement		
For the Month Ended August 31, 2014		
Sales commissions		$140,000
Expenses:		
Office salaries expense	$87,000	
Rent expense	18,000	
Automobile expense	7,500	
Supplies expense	1,150	
Miscellaneous expense	2,200	
Total expenses		115,850
Net income		$ 24,150

WE-SELL REALTY		
Statement of Owner's Equity		
For the Month Ended August 31, 2014		
Omar Farah, capital, August 1, 2014		$ 0
Investment on August 1, 2014	$15,000	
Net income for August	24,150	
	$39,150	
Less withdrawals during August	10,000	
Increase in owner's equity		29,150
Omar Farah, capital, August 31, 2014		$29,150

WE-SELL REALTY			
Balance Sheet			
August 31, 2014			
Assets		**Liabilities**	
Cash	$ 8,900	Accounts payable	$22,350
Accounts receivable	38,600		
Supplies	4,000	**Owner's Equity**	
		Omar Farah, capital	29,150
		Total liabilities and	
Total assets	$51,500	owner's equity	$51,500

Ex. 1–26

a.   Year 2: $21,236 ($40,125 – $18,889)
     Year 1: $21,484 ($40,877 – $19,393)

b.   Year 2: 1.12 ($21,236 ÷ $18,889)
     Year 1: 1.11 ($21,484 ÷ $19,393)

c.   The ratio of liabilities to stockholders' equity increased from 1.11 to 1.12
     indicating a slight increase in risk for creditors from Year 1 to Year 2.

Ex. 1–27

a.   Year 2: $18,112 ($33,699 – $15,587)
     Year 1: $19,069 ($33,005 – $13,936)

b.   Year 2: 0.86 ($15,587 ÷ $18,112)
     Year 1: 0.73 ($13,936 ÷ $19,069)

c.   The risk for creditors has increased from 0.73 in Year 1 to 0.86 in Year 2. In
     both years, creditors have less at stake in Lowe's than do stockholders,
     since the ratio is less than 1.

d.   Lowe's ratio of liabilities to stockholders' equity is less than 1. In comparison,
     The Home Depot's ratio of liabilities to stockholders' equity is greater than 1
     for Year 2 and Year 1. Thus, the creditors of The Home Depot are more at risk
     than are the creditors of Lowe's.

PROBLEMS

Prob. 1–1A

1.

	Cash	+	Accts. Rec.	+	Supplies	=	Accts. Payable	+	Bret Eisen, Capital	−	Bret Eisen, Drawing	+	Fees Earned	−	Rent Expense	−	Salaries Expense	−	Supplies Expense	−	Auto Exp.	−	Misc. Exp.
(a)	+ 30,000							+	30,000														
(b)				+	1,200		+ 1,200																
Bal.	30,000				1,200		1,200		30,000														
(c)	+ 7,200											+	7,200										
Bal.	37,200				1,200		1,200		30,000				7,200										
(d)	− 3,000													−	3,000								
Bal.	34,200				1,200		1,200		30,000				7,200		3,000								
(e)	− 750						− 750																
Bal.	33,450				1,200		450		30,000				7,200		3,000								
(f)			+ 5,000									+	5,000										
Bal.	33,450		5,000		1,200		450		30,000				12,200		3,000								
(g)	− 900																				− 600		− 300
Bal.	32,550		5,000		1,200		450		30,000				12,200		3,000						600		300
(h)	− 1,800																− 1,800						
Bal.	30,750		5,000		1,200		450		30,000				12,200		3,000		1,800				600		300
(i)					− 500														− 500				
Bal.	30,750		5,000		700		450		30,000				12,200		3,000		1,800		500		600		300
(j)	− 1,500									−	1,500												
Bal.	29,250		5,000		700		450		30,000		1,500		12,200		3,000		1,800		500		600		300

Headers (spanning): **Assets** (Cash + Accts. Rec. + Supplies); **= Liabilities +** (Accts. Payable); **Owner's Equity** (Bret Eisen, Capital − Bret Eisen, Drawing + Fees Earned − Rent Expense − Salaries Expense − Supplies Expense − Auto Exp. − Misc. Exp.)

2. Owner's equity is the right of owners to the assets of the business. These rights are increased by owner's investments and revenues and decreased by owner's withdrawals and expenses.

3. $6,000 ($12,200 − $3,000 − $1,800 − $500 − $600 − $300)

4. June's transactions increased Bret Eisen's capital by $34,500 ($30,000 + $6,000 − $1,500), which is the initial capital investment of $30,000 plus June's net income of $6,000 less Bret Eisen's withdrawals of $1,500.

Prob. 1–2A

1.

ORIENTAL TRAVEL AGENCY Income Statement For the Year Ended December 31, 2014		
Fees earned		$1,100,000
Expenses:		
Wages expense	$490,000	
Rent expense	150,000	
Utilities expense	79,000	
Supplies expense	14,000	
Miscellaneous expense	7,000	
Total expenses		740,000
Net income		$ 360,000

2.

ORIENTAL TRAVEL AGENCY Statement of Owner's Equity For the Year Ended December 31, 2014		
Sung Kim, capital, January 1, 2014		$450,000
Net income for the year	$360,000	
Less withdrawals	25,000	
Increase in owner's equity		335,000
Sung Kim, capital, December 31, 2014		$785,000

3.

ORIENTAL TRAVEL AGENCY Balance Sheet December 31, 2014			
Assets		**Liabilities**	
Cash	$210,000	Accounts payable	$115,000
Accounts receivable	370,000		
Supplies	20,000		
Land	300,000	**Owner's Equity**	
		Sung Kim, capital	785,000
		Total liabilities and	
Total assets	$900,000	owner's equity	$900,000

4.   Sung Kim, Capital of $785,000

Prob. 1–3A

1.

RELIANCE FINANCIAL SERVICES		
Income Statement		
For the Month Ended July 31, 2014		
Fees earned		$144,500
Expenses:		
Salaries expense	$55,000	
Rent expense	33,000	
Auto expense	16,000	
Supplies expense	4,500	
Miscellaneous expense	4,800	
Total expenses		113,300
Net income		$ 31,200

2.

RELIANCE FINANCIAL SERVICES		
Statement of Owner's Equity		
For the Month Ended July 31, 2014		
Seth Feye, capital, July 1, 2014		$ 0
Investment on July 1, 2014	$50,000	
Net income for July	31,200	
	$81,200	
Less withdrawals	15,000	
Increase in owner's equity		66,200
Seth Feye, capital, July 31, 2014		$66,200

3.

RELIANCE FINANCIAL SERVICES			
Balance Sheet			
July 31, 2014			
Assets		**Liabilities**	
Cash	$32,600	Accounts payable	$ 3,400
Accounts receivable	34,500		
Supplies	2,500	**Owner's Equity**	
		Seth Feye, capital	66,200
		Total liabilities and	
Total assets	$69,600	owner's equity	$69,600

Prob. 1–3A (Concluded)

4.   **(Optional)**

RELIANCE FINANCIAL SERVICES Statement of Cash Flows For the Month Ended July 31, 2014		
Cash flows from operating activities:		
Cash received from customers	$110,000	
Deduct cash payments for expenses		
and payments to creditors*	112,400	
Net cash flows used for operating activities		$ (2,400)
Cash flows from investing activities		0
Cash flows from financing activities:		
Cash received as owner's investment	$ 50,000	
Deduct cash withdrawal by owner	15,000	
Net cash flows from financing activities		35,000
Net increase in cash and July 31, 2014, cash balance		$ 32,600

* $3,600 + $33,000 + $20,800 + $55,000; these amounts are taken from the cash
column shown in the problem.

Prob. 1–4A

1.

	Assets		=	Liabilities	+	Owner's Equity								
	Cash	+ Supplies	=	Accts. Payable	+	Kevin Bosley, Capital	− Kevin Bosley, Drawing	+ Sales Comm.	− Rent Exp.	− Salaries Exp.	− Auto Exp.	− Supplies Exp.	− Misc. Exp.
(a)	+ 18,000				+	18,000							
(b)		+ 3,200		+ 3,200									
Bal.	18,000	3,200		3,200		18,000							
(c)	− 1,800			− 1,800									
Bal.	16,200	3,200		1,400		18,000							
(d)	+ 36,750							+ 36,750					
Bal.	52,950	3,200		1,400		18,000		36,750					
(e)	− 4,000								− 4,000				
Bal.	48,950	3,200		1,400		18,000		36,750	− 4,000				
(f)	− 3,000						− 3,000						
Bal.	45,950	3,200		1,400		18,000	− 3,000	36,750	− 4,000				
(g)	− 3,700										− 2,500		− 1,200
Bal.	42,250	3,200		1,400		18,000	− 3,000	36,750	− 4,000		− 2,500		− 1,200
(h)	− 3,750									− 3,750			
Bal.	38,500	3,200		1,400		18,000	− 3,000	36,750	− 4,000	− 3,750	− 2,500		− 1,200
(i)		− 1,650										− 1,650	
Bal.	38,500	1,550		1,400		18,000	− 3,000	36,750	− 4,000	− 3,750	− 2,500	− 1,650	− 1,200

Prob. 1–4A (Concluded)

2.

SUNRISE REALTY Income Statement For the Month Ended October 31, 2014		
Sales commissions		$36,750
Expenses:		
Rent expense	$4,000	
Salaries expense	3,750	
Automobile expense	2,500	
Supplies expense	1,650	
Miscellaneous expense	1,200	
Total expenses		13,100
Net income		$23,650

SUNRISE REALTY Statement of Owner's Equity For the Month Ended October 31, 2014		
Kevin Bosley, capital, October 1, 2014		$ 0
Investment on October 1, 2014	$18,000	
Net income for October	23,650	
	$41,650	
Less withdrawals	3,000	
Increase in owner's equity		38,650
Kevin Bosley, capital, October 31, 2014		$38,650

SUNRISE REALTY Balance Sheet October 31, 2014			
Assets		Liabilities	
Cash	$38,500	Accounts payable	$ 1,400
Supplies	1,550		
		Owner's Equity	
		Kevin Bosley, capital	38,650
		Total liabilities and	
Total assets	$40,050	owner's equity	$40,050

Prob. 1–5A

1.

Assets					=	Liabilities	+	Owner's Equity
Cash	+	Accounts Receivable	+ Supplies +	Land	=	Accounts Payable	+	Joel Palk, Capital
$45,000	+	$93,000	+ $7,000 +	$75,000	=	$40,000	+	Joel Palk, Capital
				$220,000	=	$40,000	+	Joel Palk, Capital
				$180,000	=	Joel Palk, Capital		

Prob. 1–5A (Continued)

2.

			Assets			=	Liabilities +	Owner's Equity		
	Cash	+	Accts. Rec.	+ Supplies +	Land	=	Accts. Payable	+ Joel Palk, Capital	–	Joel Palk, Drawing
Bal.	45,000		93,000	7,000	75,000		40,000	180,000		
(a)	+ 35,000							+ 35,000		
Bal.	80,000		93,000	7,000	75,000		40,000	215,000		
(b)	– 50,000				+ 50,000					
Bal.	30,000		93,000	7,000	125,000		40,000	215,000		
(c)	+ 32,125									
Bal.	62,125		93,000	7,000	125,000		40,000	215,000		
(d)	– 6,000									
Bal.	56,125		93,000	7,000	125,000		40,000	215,000		
(e)				+ 2,500			+ 2,500			
Bal.	56,125		93,000	9,500	125,000		42,500	215,000		
(f)	– 22,800						– 22,800			
Bal.	33,325		93,000	9,500	125,000		19,700	215,000		
(g)			+ 84,750							
Bal.	33,325		177,750	9,500	125,000		19,700	215,000		
(h)							+ 29,500			
Bal.	33,325		177,750	9,500	125,000		49,200	215,000		
(i)	– 14,000									
Bal.	19,325		177,750	9,500	125,000		49,200	215,000		
(j)	+ 88,000		– 88,000							
Bal.	107,325		89,750	9,500	125,000		49,200	215,000		
(k)				– 3,600						
Bal.	107,325		89,750	5,900	125,000		49,200	215,000		
(l)	– 12,000								–	12,000
Bal.	95,325		89,750	5,900	125,000		49,200	215,000	–	12,000

Prob. 1–5A (Continued)

Owner's Equity (Continued)

	+	Dry Cleaning Revenue	–	Dry Cleaning Exp.	–	Wages Exp.	–	Rent Exp.	–	Supplies Exp.	–	Truck Exp.	–	Utilities Exp.	–	Misc. Exp.
Bal.																
(a)																
Bal.																
(b)																
Bal.																
(c)	+	32,125														
Bal.		32,125														
(d)							–	6,000								
Bal.		32,125						–	6,000							
(e)																
Bal.		32,125						–	6,000							
(f)																
Bal.		32,125						–	6,000							
(g)	+	84,750														
Bal.		116,875						–	6,000							
(h)			–	29,500												
Bal.		116,875	–	29,500				–	6,000							
(i)							–	7,500					–	2,500	–	1,300	–	2,700
Bal.		116,875	–	29,500	–	7,500	–	6,000			–	2,500	–	1,300	–	2,700
(j)																
Bal.		116,875	–	29,500	–	7,500	–	6,000			–	2,500	–	1,300	–	2,700
(k)									–	3,600						
Bal.		116,875	–	29,500	–	7,500	–	6,000	–	3,600	–	2,500	–	1,300	–	2,700
(l)																
Bal.		116,875	–	29,500	–	7,500	–	6,000	–	3,600	–	2,500	–	1,300	–	2,700

Prob. 1–5A (Continued)

3.

D'LITE DRY CLEANERS Income Statement For the Month Ended July 31, 2014		
Dry cleaning revenue		$116,875
Expenses:		
Dry cleaning expense	$29,500	
Wages expense	7,500	
Rent expense	6,000	
Supplies expense	3,600	
Truck expense	2,500	
Utilities expense	1,300	
Miscellaneous expense	2,700	
Total expenses		53,100
Net income		$ 63,775

D'LITE DRY CLEANERS Statement of Owner's Equity For the Month Ended July 31, 2014		
Joel Palk, capital, July 1, 2014		$180,000
Additional investment during July	$35,000	
Net income for July	63,775	
	$98,775	
Less withdrawals	12,000	
Increase in owner's equity		86,775
Joel Palk, capital, July 31, 2014		$266,775

D'LITE DRY CLEANERS Balance Sheet July 31, 2014			
Assets		Liabilities	
Cash	$ 95,325	Accounts payable	$ 49,200
Accounts receivable	89,750		
Supplies	5,900	Owner's Equity	
Land	125,000	Joel Palk, capital	266,775
		Total liabilities and	
Total assets	$315,975	owner's equity	$315,975

Prob. 1–5A (Concluded)

4.   **(Optional)**

D'LITE DRY CLEANERS Statement of Cash Flows For the Month Ended July 31, 2014		
Cash flows from operating activities:		
Cash received from customers*	$120,125	
Deduct cash payments for expenses		
and payments to creditors**	42,800	
Net cash flows from operating activities		$ 77,325
Cash flows used for investing activities:		
Purchase of land		(50,000)
Cash flows from financing activities:		
Cash received as owner's investment	$ 35,000	
Deduct cash withdrawal by owner	12,000	
Net cash flows from financing activities		23,000
Net Increase in cash during July		$ 50,325
Cash balance, July 1, 2014		45,000
Cash balance, July 31, 2014		$ 95,325

  * $32,125 + $88,000; These amounts are taken from the cash column of the spreadsheet in Part 2.

 ** $6,000 + $22,800 + $14,000; These amounts are taken from the cash column of the spreadsheet in Part 2.

Prob. 1–6A

a. Fees earned, $750,000 ($275,000 + $475,000)

b. Supplies expense, $30,000 ($475,000 − $300,000 − $100,000 − $20,000 − $25,000)

c. Dakota Rowe, capital, April 1, 2014, $0; Wolverine Realty was organized on April 1, 2014.

d. Net income for April, $275,000 from income statement

e. $650,000 ($375,000 + $275,000)

f. Increase in owner's equity, $525,000 ($650,000 − $125,000)

g. Dakota Rowe, capital, April 30, 2014, $525,000

h. Total assets, $625,000 ($462,500 + $12,500 + $150,000)

i. Dakota Rowe, capital, $525,000 ($625,000 − $100,000); same as (g)

j. Total liabilities and owner's equity, $625,000 ($100,000 + $525,000)

k. Cash received from customers, $750,000 ($387,500 + $362,500); this is the same as fees earned (a) since there are no accounts receivable.

l. Net cash flows from operating activities, $362,500 ($750,000 − $387,500)

m. Cash payments for acquisition of land, ($150,000)

n. Cash received as owner's investment, $375,000

o. Cash withdrawal by owner, ($125,000)

p. Net cash flows from financing activities, $250,000 ($375,000 − $125,000)

q. Net cash flow and April 30, 2014, cash balance, $462,500 ($362,500 − $150,000 + $250,000); also the cash balance on the balance sheet.

Prob. 1–1B

1.

	Assets			=	Liabilities +	Owner's Equity							
	Cash +	Accts. Rec. +	Supplies =		Accts. Payable +	Amy Austin, Capital –	Amy Austin, Drawing +	Fees Earned –	Rent Expense –	Salaries Expense –	Supplies Expense –	Auto Exp. –	Misc. Exp.
(a)	+ 50,000					+ 50,000							
(b)			+ 4,000		+ 4,000								
Bal.	50,000		4,000		4,000	50,000							
(c)	– 2,300				– 2,300								
Bal.	47,700		4,000		1,700	50,000							
(d)	+ 13,800							+ 13,800					
Bal.	61,500		4,000		1,700	50,000		13,800					
(e)	– 5,000								– 5,000				
Bal.	56,500		4,000		1,700	50,000		13,800	5,000				
(f)	– 1,450											– 1,150	– 300
Bal.	55,050		4,000		1,700	50,000		13,800	5,000			1,150	300
(g)	– 2,500									– 2,500			
Bal.	52,550		4,000		1,700	50,000		13,800	5,000	2,500		1,150	300
(h)			– 1,300								– 1,300		
Bal.	52,550		2,700		1,700	50,000		13,800	5,000	2,500	1,300	1,150	300
(i)		+ 12,500						+ 12,500					
Bal.	52,550	12,500	2,700		1,700	50,000		26,300	5,000	2,500	1,300	1,150	300
(j)	– 3,900						– 3,900						
Bal.	48,650	12,500	2,700		1,700	50,000	3,900	26,300	5,000	2,500	1,300	1,150	300

2. Owner's equity is the right of owners to the assets of the business. These rights are increased by owner's investments and revenues and decreased by owner's withdrawals and expenses.

3. $16,050 ($26,300 – $5,000 – $2,500 – $1,300 – $1,150 – $300)

4. March's transactions increased Amy Austin's capital by $62,150 ($50,000 + $16,050 – $3,900), which is the initial investment of $50,000 plus the excess of March's net income of $16,050 over Amy Austin's withdrawals of $3,900.

1-30

Prob. 1–2B

1.

WILDERNESS TRAVEL SERVICE Income Statement For the Year Ended April 30, 2014		
Fees earned		$875,000
Expenses:		
Wages expense	$525,000	
Rent expense	75,000	
Utilities expense	38,000	
Supplies expense	12,000	
Taxes expense	10,000	
Miscellaneous expense	15,000	
Total expenses		675,000
Net income		$200,000

2.

WILDERNESS TRAVEL SERVICE Statement of Owner's Equity For the Year Ended April 30, 2014		
Harper Borg, capital, May 1, 2013		$180,000
Net income for the year	$200,000	
Less withdrawals	40,000	
Increase in owner's equity		160,000
Harper Borg, capital, April 30, 2014		$340,000

3.

WILDERNESS TRAVEL SERVICE Balance Sheet April 30, 2014			
Assets		**Liabilities**	
Cash	$146,000	Accounts payable	$ 25,000
Accounts receivable	210,000		
Supplies	9,000	**Owner's Equity**	
		Harper Borg, capital	340,000
		Total liabilities and	
Total assets	$365,000	owner's equity	$365,000

4.   Net income of $200,000

Prob. 1–3B

1.

BRONCO CONSULTING		
Income Statement		
For the Month Ended August 31, 2014		
Fees earned		$125,000
Expenses:		
Salaries expense	$58,000	
Rent expense	27,000	
Auto expense	15,500	
Supplies expense	6,100	
Miscellaneous expense	7,500	
Total expenses		114,100
Net income		$ 10,900

2.

BRONCO CONSULTING		
Statement of Owner's Equity		
For the Month Ended August 31, 2014		
Jose Loder, capital, August 1, 2014		$ 0
Investment on August 1, 2014	$75,000	
Net income for August	10,900	
	$85,900	
Less withdrawals	15,000	
Increase in owner's equity		70,900
Jose Loder, capital, August 31, 2014		$70,900

3.

BRONCO CONSULTING			
Balance Sheet			
August 31, 2014			
Assets		Liabilities	
Cash	$38,000	Accounts payable	$ 3,000
Accounts receivable	33,000		
Supplies	2,900	Owner's Equity	
		Jose Loder, capital	70,900
		Total liabilities and	
Total assets	$73,900	owner's equity	$73,900

Prob. 1–3B (Concluded)

4.   (Optional)

BRONCO CONSULTING Statement of Cash Flows For the Month Ended August 31, 2014		
Cash flows from operating activities:		
Cash received from customers	$ 92,000	
Deduct cash payments for expenses		
and payments to creditors*	114,000	
Net cash flows used for operating activities		$(22,000)
Cash flows from investing activities		0
Cash flows from financing activities:		
Cash received as owner's investment	$ 75,000	
Deduct cash withdrawal by owner	15,000	
Net cash flows from financing activities		60,000
Net increase in cash and August 31, 2014, cash balance		$ 38,000

* $27,000 + $6,000 + $23,000 + $58,000; These amounts are taken from the
cash column shown in the problem.

Prob. 1–4B

1.

| | Assets | | = Liabilities + | Owner's Equity | | | | | | | |
	Cash	+ Supplies	= Accts. Payable	+ Maria Adams, Capital	− Maria Adams, Drawing	+ Sales Comm.	− Rent Exp.	− Salaries Exp.	− Auto Exp.	− Supplies Exp.	− Misc. Exp.
(a)	+ 24,000			+ 24,000							
(b)	− 3,600						− 3,600				
Bal.	20,400			24,000			3,600				
(c)	− 1,950								− 1,350		− 600
Bal.	18,450			24,000			3,600		− 1,350		− 600
(d)		+ 1,200	+ 1,200								
Bal.	18,450	1,200	1,200	24,000			3,600		− 1,350		− 600
(e)	+ 19,800					+ 19,800					
Bal.	38,250	1,200	1,200	24,000		19,800	3,600		− 1,350		− 600
(f)	− 750		− 750								
Bal.	37,500	1,200	450	24,000		19,800	3,600		− 1,350		− 600
(g)	− 2,500							− 2,500			
Bal.	35,000	1,200	450	24,000		19,800	3,600	− 2,500	− 1,350		− 600
(h)	− 3,500				− 3,500						
Bal.	31,500	1,200	450	24,000	− 3,500	19,800	3,600	− 2,500	− 1,350		− 600
(i)		− 900								− 900	
Bal.	31,500	300	450	24,000	− 3,500	19,800	3,600	− 2,500	− 1,350	− 900	− 600

Prob. 1–4B (Concluded)

2.

CUSTOM REALTY Income Statement For the Month Ended April 30, 2014		
Sales commissions		$19,800
Expenses:		
Rent expense	$3,600	
Salaries expense	2,500	
Automobile expense	1,350	
Supplies expense	900	
Miscellaneous expense	600	
Total expenses		8,950
Net income		$10,850

CUSTOM REALTY Statement of Owner's Equity For the Month Ended April 30, 2014		
Maria Adams, capital, April 1, 2014		$ 0
Investment on April 1, 2014	$24,000	
Net income for April	10,850	
	$34,850	
Less withdrawals	3,500	
Increase in owner's equity		31,350
Maria Adams, capital, April 30, 2014		$31,350

CUSTOM REALTY Balance Sheet April 30, 2014			
Assets		Liabilities	
Cash	$31,500	Accounts payable	$ 450
Supplies	300		
		Owner's Equity	
		Maria Adams, capital	31,350
		Total liabilities and	
Total assets	$31,800	owner's equity	$31,800

Prob. 1–5B

1.

Assets								=	Liabilities	+	Owner's Equity
Cash	+	Accounts Receivable	+	Supplies	+	Land		=	Accounts Payable	+	Beverly Zahn, Capital
$39,000	+	$80,000	+	$11,000	+	$50,000		=	$31,500	+	Beverly Zahn, Capital
						$180,000		=	$31,500	+	Beverly Zahn, Capital
						$148,500		=			Beverly Zahn, Capital

Prob. 1–5B (Continued)

2.

		Assets			=	Liabilities	+	Owner's Equity	
	Cash	+ Accts. Rec.	+ Supplies	+ Land	=	Accts. Payable	+	Beverly Zahn, Capital	− Beverly Zahn, Drawing
Bal.	39,000	80,000	11,000	50,000		31,500		148,500	
(a)	+ 21,000							+ 21,000	
Bal.	60,000	80,000	11,000	50,000		31,500		169,500	
(b)	− 35,000			+ 35,000					
Bal.	25,000	80,000	11,000	85,000		31,500		169,500	
(c)	− 4,000								
Bal.	21,000	80,000	11,000	85,000		31,500		169,500	
(d)		+ 72,000							
Bal.	21,000	152,000	11,000	85,000		31,500		169,500	
(e)	− 20,000					− 20,000			
Bal.	$1,000	152,000	11,000	85,000		11,500		169,500	
(f)			+ 8,000			+ 8,000			
Bal.	$1,000	152,000	19,000	85,000		19,500		169,500	
(g)	+ 38,000								
Bal.	39,000	152,000	19,000	85,000		19,500		169,500	
(h)	+ 77,000	− 77,000							
Bal.	116,000	75,000	19,000	85,000		19,500		169,500	
(i)						+ 29,450			
Bal.	116,000	75,000	19,000	85,000		48,950		169,500	
(j)	− 29,200								
Bal.	86,800	75,000	19,000	85,000		48,950		169,500	
(k)			− 7,200						
Bal.	86,800	75,000	11,800	85,000		48,950		169,500	
(l)	− 5,000								− 5,000
Bal.	81,800	75,000	11,800	85,000		48,950		169,500	− 5,000

Prob. 1–5B (Continued)

Owner's Equity (Continued)

	+	Dry Cleaning Revenue	–	Dry Cleaning Exp.	–	Wages Exp.	–	Supplies Exp.	–	Rent Exp.	–	Truck Exp.	–	Utilities Exp.	–	Misc. Exp.
Bal.																
(a)																
Bal.																
(b)																
Bal.																
(c)										–	4,000					
Bal.										–	4,000					
(d)	+	72,000														
Bal.		72,000								–	4,000					
(e)																
Bal.		72,000								–	4,000					
(f)																
Bal.		72,000								–	4,000					
(g)	+	38,000														
Bal.		110,000								–	4,000					
(h)																
Bal.		110,000								–	4,000					
(i)			–	29,450												
Bal.		110,000	–	29,450						–	4,000					
(j)					–	24,000						–	2,100	–	1,800	–	1,300
Bal.		110,000	–	29,450	–	24,000				–	4,000	–	2,100	–	1,800	–	1,300
(k)							–	7,200								
Bal.		110,000	–	29,450	–	24,000	–	7,200	–	4,000	–	2,100	–	1,800	–	1,300
(l)																
Bal.		110,000	–	29,450	–	24,000	–	7,200	–	4,000	–	2,100	–	1,800	–	1,300

Prob. 1–5B (Continued)

3.

BEV'S DRY CLEANERS Income Statement For the Month Ended November 30, 2014		
Dry cleaning revenue		$110,000
Expenses:		
Dry cleaning expense	$29,450	
Wages expense	24,000	
Supplies expense	7,200	
Rent expense	4,000	
Truck expense	2,100	
Utilities expense	1,800	
Miscellaneous expense	1,300	
Total expenses		69,850
Net income		$ 40,150

BEV'S DRY CLEANERS Statement of Owner's Equity For the Month Ended November 30, 2014		
Beverly Zahn, capital, November 1, 2014		$148,500
Additional investment during November	$21,000	
Net income for November	40,150	
	$61,150	
Less withdrawals	5,000	
Increase in owner's equity		56,150
Beverly Zahn, capital, November 30, 2014		$204,650

BEV'S DRY CLEANERS Balance Sheet November 30, 2014			
Assets		**Liabilities**	
Cash	$ 81,800	Accounts payable	$ 48,950
Accounts receivable	75,000		
Supplies	11,800	**Owner's Equity**	
Land	85,000	Beverly Zahn, capital	204,650
		Total liabilities and	
Total assets	$253,600	owner's equity	$253,600

Prob. 1–5B (Concluded)

4.   (Optional)

BEV'S DRY CLEANERS Statement of Cash Flows For the Month Ended November 30, 2014		
Cash flows from operating activities:		
Cash received from customers*	$115,000	
Deduct cash payments for expenses		
and payments to creditors**	53,200	
Net cash flows from operating activities		$61,800
Cash flows used for investing activities:		
Purchase of land		(35,000)
Cash flows from financing activities:		
Cash received as owner's investment	$21,000	
Deduct cash withdrawal by owner	5,000	
Net cash flows from financing activities		16,000
Net increase in cash during November		$42,800
Cash balance, November 1, 2014		39,000
Cash balance, November 30, 2014		$81,800

  * $38,000 + $77,000; these amounts are taken from the cash column of the
    spreadsheet in Part 2.

 ** $4,000 + $20,000 + $29,200; these amounts are taken from the cash column
    of the spreadsheet in Part 2.

Prob. 1–6B

a. Wages expense, $203,200 ($288,000 – $48,000 – $17,600 – $14,400 – $4,800)

b. Net income, $112,000 ($400,000 – $288,000)

c. LuAnn Martin, capital, May 1, 2014, $0; Atlas Realty was organized on May 1, 2014.

d. Investment on May 1, 2014, $160,000; from statement of cash flows.

e. Net income for May, $112,000; from (b)

f. $272,000 ($160,000 + $112,000)

g. Withdrawals, $64,000; from statement of cash flows.

h. Increase in owner's equity, $208,000 ($272,000 – $64,000)

i. LuAnn Martin, capital, May 31, 2014, $208,000

j. Land, $120,000; from statement of cash flows.

k. Total assets, $256,000 ($123,200 + $12,800 + $120,000)

l. LuAnn Martin, capital, $208,000

m. Total liabilities and owner's equity, $256,000 ($48,000 + $208,000)

n. Cash received from customers, $400,000; this is the same as fees earned since there are no accounts receivable.

o. Net cash flows from operating activities, $147,200 ($400,000 – $252,800)

p. Net cash flows from financing activities, $96,000 ($160,000 – $64,000)

q. Net cash flows and May 31, 2014, cash balance, $123,200 ($147,200 – $120,000 + $96,000); also, the cash balance on the balance sheet.

CONTINUING PROBLEM

1.

		Assets			= Liabilities +		Owner's Equity		
	Cash	+	Accts. Rec.	+ Supplies =	Accts. Payable	+ Peyton Smith, Capital	– Peyton Smith, Drawing	+ Fees Earned
June 1	+ 4,000					+ 4,000		
June 2	+ 3,500							+ 3,500
Bal.	7,500					4,000		3,500
June 2	– 800							
Bal.	6,700					4,000		3,500
June 4				+ 350	+ 350			
Bal.	6,700			350	350	4,000		3,500
June 6	– 500							
Bal.	6,200			350	350	4,000		3,500
June 8	– 675							
Bal.	5,525			350	350	4,000		3,500
June 12	– 350							
Bal.	5,175			350	350	4,000		3,500
June 13	– 100				– 100			
Bal.	5,075			350	250	4,000		3,500
June 16	+ 300							+ 300
Bal.	5,375			350	250	4,000		3,800
June 22		+ 1,000						+ 1,000
Bal.	5,375	1,000		350	250	4,000		4,800
June 25	+ 500							+ 500
Bal.	5,875	1,000		350	250	4,000		5,300
June 29	– 240							
Bal.	5,635	1,000		350	250	4,000		5,300
June 30	+ 900							+ 900
Bal.	6,535	1,000		350	250	4,000		6,200
June 30	– 400							
Bal.	6,135	1,000		350	250	4,000		6,200
June 30	– 300							
Bal.	5,835	1,000		350	250	4,000		6,200
June 30				– 180				
Bal.	5,835	1,000		170	250	4,000		6,200
June 30	– 415							
Bal.	5,420	1,000		170	250	4,000		6,200
June 30	– 1,000							
Bal.	4,420	1,000		170	250	4,000		6,200
June 30	– 500						– 500	
Bal.	3,920	1,000		170	250	4,000	– 500	6,200

Continuing Problem (Continued)

Owner's Equity (Continued)

		Music Exp.		Office Rent Exp.		Equip. Rent Exp.		Advertising Exp.		Wages Exp.		Utilities Exp.		Supplies Exp.		Misc. Exp.
June	1															
June	2															
Bal.																
June	2			–	800											
Bal.				–	800											
June	4															
Bal.				–	800											
June	6							–	500							
Bal.				–	800			–	500							
June	8					–	675									
Bal.				–	800	–	675	–	500							
June	12	–	350													
Bal.		–	350	–	800	–	675	–	500							
June	13															
Bal.		–	350	–	800	–	675	–	500							
June	16															
Bal.		–	350	–	800	–	675	–	500							
June	22															
Bal.		–	350	–	800	–	675	–	500							
June	25															
Bal.		–	350	–	800	–	675	–	500							
June	29	–	240													
Bal.		–	590	–	800	–	675	–	500							
June	30															
Bal.		–	590	–	800	–	675	–	500							
June	30									–	400					
Bal.		–	590	–	800	–	675	–	500	–	400					
June	30											–	300			
Bal.		–	590	–	800	–	675	–	500	–	400	–	300			
June	30													–	180	
Bal.		–	590	–	800	–	675	–	500	–	400	–	300	–	180	
June	30															–	415
Bal.		–	590	–	800	–	675	–	500	–	400	–	300	–	180	–	415
June	30	–	1,000													
Bal.		–	1,590	–	800	–	675	–	500	–	400	–	300	–	180	–	415
June	30															
Bal.		–	1,590	–	800	–	675	–	500	–	400	–	300	–	180	–	415

Continuing Problem (Concluded)

2.

PS MUSIC Income Statement For the Month Ended June 30, 2014		
Fees earned:		$6,200
Expenses:		
Music expense	$1,590	
Office rent expense	800	
Equipment rent expense	675	
Advertising expense	500	
Wages expense	400	
Utilities expense	300	
Supplies expense	180	
Miscellaneous expense	415	
Total expenses		4,860
Net income		$1,340

3.

PS MUSIC Statement of Owner's Equity For the Month Ended June 30, 2014		
Peyton Smith, capital, June 1, 2014		$ 0
Investment on June 1, 2014	$4,000	
Net income for June	1,340	
	$5,340	
Less withdrawals	500	
Increase in owner's equity		4,840
Peyton Smith, capital, June 30, 2014		$4,840

4.

PS MUSIC Balance Sheet June 30, 2014			
Assets		**Liabilities**	
Cash	$3,920	Accounts payable	$ 250
Accounts receivable	1,000		
Supplies	170	**Owner's Equity**	
		Peyton Smith, capital	4,840
		Total liabilities and	
Total assets	$5,090	owner's equity	$5,090

CASES & PROJECTS

CP 1–1

1. Acceptable professional conduct requires that Colleen Fernandez supply First Federal Bank with all the relevant financial statements necessary for the bank to make an informed decision. Therefore, Colleen should provide the complete set of financial statements. These can be supplemented with a discussion of the net loss in the past year or other data explaining why granting the loan is a good investment by the bank.

2. a. Owners are generally willing to provide bankers with information about the operating and financial condition of the business, such as the following:

    - Operating Information:
        - Description of business operations
        - Results of past operations
        - Preliminary results of current operations
        - Plans for future operations

    - Financial Condition:
        - List of assets and liabilities (balance sheet)
        - Estimated current values of assets
        - Owner's personal investment in the business
        - Owner's commitment to invest additional funds in the business

    Owners are normally reluctant to provide the following types of information to bankers:

    - *Proprietary Operating Information.* Such information, which might hurt the business if it becomes known by competitors, might include special processes used by the business or future plans to expand operations into areas that are not currently served by a competitor.

    - *Personal Financial Information.* Owners may have little choice here because banks often require owners of small businesses to pledge their personal assets as security for a business loan. Personal financial information requested by bankers often includes the owner's net worth, salary, and other income. In addition, bankers usually request information about factors that might affect the personal financial condition of the owner. For example, a pending divorce by the owner might significantly affect the owner's personal wealth.

    b. Bankers typically want as much information as possible about the ability of the business and the owner to repay the loan with interest. Examples of such information are described above.

    c. Both bankers and business owners share the common interest of the business doing well and being successful. If the business is successful, the bankers will receive their loan payments on time with interest, and the owners will increase their personal wealth.

CP 1–2

The difference in the two bank balances, $55,000 ($80,000 – $25,000), may not be pure profit from an accounting perspective. To determine the accounting profit for the six-month period, the revenues for the period would need to be matched with the related expenses. The revenues minus the expenses would indicate whether the business generated net income (profit) or a net loss for the period. Using only the difference between the two bank account balances ignores such factors as amounts due from customers (receivables), liabilities (accounts payable) that need to be paid for wages or other operating expenses, additional investments that Dr. Cousins may have made in the business during the period, or withdrawals during the period that Dr. Cousins might have taken for personal reasons unrelated to the business.

Some businesses that have few, if any, receivables or payables may use a "cash" basis of accounting. The cash basis of accounting ignores receivables and payables because they are assumed to be insignificant in amount. However, even with the cash basis of accounting, additional investments during the period and any withdrawals during the period have to be considered in determining the net income (profit) or net loss for the period.

CP 1-3

1.

	Assets		= Liabilities +	Owner's Equity						
	Cash	+ Supplies	= Accts. Payable	+ Lisa Duncan, Capital	− Lisa Duncan, Drawing	+ Fees Earned	− Salaries Expense	− Rent Expense	− Supplies Expense	− Misc. Exp.
(a)	+ 950			+ 950						
(b)	− 300	+ 300								
Bal.	650	300		950						
(c)	− 275							− 275		
Bal.	375	300		950				275		
(d)	− 100		+ 150					− 250		
Bal.	275	300	150	950				525		
(e)	+ 1,750					+ 1,750				
Bal.	2,025	300	150	950		1,750		525		
(f)	+ 600					+ 600				
Bal.	2,625	300	150	950		2,350		525		
(g)	− 800						− 800			
Bal.	1,825	300	150	950		2,350	800	525		
(h)	− 290									− 290
Bal.	1,535	300	150	950		2,350	800	525		290
(i)	+ 1,300					+ 1,300				
Bal.	2,835	300	150	950		3,650	800	525		290
(j)		− 120							− 120	
Bal.	2,835	180	150	950		3,650	800	525	120	290
(k)	− 400				− 400					
Bal.	2,435	180	150	950	400	3,650	800	525	120	290

CP 1–3 (Continued)

2.

SERVE-N-VOLLEY		
Income Statement		
For the Month Ended September 30, 2014		
Fees earned:		$3,650
Expenses:		
Salaries expense	$800	
Rent expense	525	
Supplies expense	120	
Miscellaneous expense	290	
Total expenses		1,735
Net income		$1,915

3.

SERVE-N-VOLLEY		
Statement of Owner's Equity		
For the Month Ended September 30, 2014		
Lisa Duncan, capital, September 1, 2014		$ 0
Investment on September 1, 2014	$ 950	
Net income for September	1,915	
	$2,865	
Less withdrawals	400	
Increase in owner's equity		2,465
Lisa Duncan, capital, September 30, 2014		$2,465

4.

SERVE-N-VOLLEY			
Balance Sheet			
September 30, 2014			
Assets		**Liabilities**	
Cash	$2,435	Accounts payable	$ 150
Supplies	180		
		Owner's Equity	
		Lisa Duncan, capital	2,465
		Total liabilities and	
Total assets	$2,615	owner's equity	$2,615

CP 1–3 (Concluded)

5.   a.   Serve-N-Volley would provide Lisa with $715 more income per month than working as a waitress. This amount is computed as follows:

Net income of Serve-N-Volley, per month..	$1,915
Earnings as waitress, per month:	
30 hours per week × $10 per hour × 4 weeks.................................	1,200
Difference...	$ 715

   b.   Other factors that Lisa should consider before discussing a long-term arrangement with the Phoenix Tennis Club include the following:

Llsa should consider whether the results of operations for September are indicative of what to expect each month. For example, Lisa should consider whether club members will continue to request lessons or use the ball machine during the fall months when interest in tennis may slacken. Lisa should evaluate whether the additional income of $715 per month from Serve-N-Volley is worth the risk being taken and the effort being expended.

Lisa should also consider how much her investment in Serve-N-Volley could have earned if invested elsewhere. For example, if the initial investment of $950 had been invested to earn a rate of return of 6% per year, it would have earned $4.75 in September, or $57 for the year.

Note to Instructors: Numerous other considerations could be mentioned by students, such as the ability of Lisa to withdraw cash from Serve-N-Volley for personal use. For example, some of her investment in Serve-N-Volley will be in the form of supplies (tennis balls, etc.), which are readily convertible to cash. The objective of this case is not to mention all possible considerations but, rather, to encourage students to begin thinking about the use of accounting information in making business decisions.

CP 1–4

Note to Instructors: The purpose of this activity is to familiarize students with the certification requirements and their online availability. You might use this as an opportunity to discuss the advantages and disadvantages of careers in public accounting (CPA), management accounting (CMA), and internal auditing (CIA).

The following Web sites provide useful information (such as starting salaries, etc.) for students on careers in accounting:

American Institute of Certified Public Accountants (AICPA)
   http://www.aicpa.org/becomeacpa/faqs/pages/faqs.aspx

Institute of Certified Management Accountants (IMA)
   http://imanet.org/ima_home.aspx

Institute of Internal Auditors (IIA)
   http://www.theiia.org/theiia/about-the-profession/about-the-internal-audit-profession/

CP 1–5

	First Year	Second Year	Third Year
Net cash flows from operating activities	negative	positive	positive
Net cash flows from investing activities	negative	negative	negative
Net cash flows from financing activities	positive	positive	positive

Start-up companies normally experience negative net cash flows from operating activities; however, Amazon.com was able to generate positive net cash flows from operations by its second year. Start-up companies normally have negative net cash flows from investing activities as they build up their infrastructure through purchases of property, plant, and equipment. This was the case with Amazon.com for each of its first three years. Likewise, start-up companies normally have positive net cash flows from financing activities from raising capital. This is also the case for Amazon.com. Also, start-up companies normally have positive cash flows from financing activities—activities from raising capital.

CP 1–6

As can be seen from the balance sheet data in the case, Enron was financed largely by debt as compared to equity. Specifically, Enron's stockholders' equity represented only 17.5% ($11,470 ÷ $65,503) of Enron's total assets. The remainder of Enron's total assets, 82.5%, was financed by debt. When a company is financed largely by debt, it is said to be highly leveraged.

In late 2001 and early 2002, allegations arose as to possible misstatements of Enron's financial statements. These allegations revolved around the use of "special purpose entities" (partnerships) and related party transactions. The use of special purpose entities allowed Enron to hide a significant amount of additional debt off its balance sheet. The result was that Enron's total assets were even more financed by debt than the balance sheet indicated.

After the allegations of misstatements became public, Enron's stock rapidly declined and the company filed for bankruptcy. Subsequently, numerous lawsuits were filed against the company and its management. In addition, the Securities and Exchange Commission, the Justice Department, and Congress launched investigations into Enron. As a result, several of Enron's top executives faced criminal prosecution and were sentenced to prison.

Note to Instructors: The role of the auditors and board of directors of Enron also might be discussed. Note, however, that these topics are not covered in Chapter 1 but in later chapters.

CHAPTER 2
ANALYZING TRANSACTIONS

DISCUSSION QUESTIONS

1. An account is a form designed to record changes in a particular asset, liability, owner's equity, revenue, or expense. A ledger is a group of related accounts.

2. The terms *debit* and *credit* may signify either an increase or a decrease, depending upon the nature of the account. For example, debits signify an increase in asset and expense accounts but a decrease in liability, owner's capital, and revenue accounts.

3. **a.** Assuming no errors have occurred, the credit balance in the cash account resulted from drawing checks for $1,850 in excess of the amount of cash on deposit.

    b. The $1,850 credit balance in the cash account as of December 31 is a liability owed to the bank. It is usually referred to as an "overdraft" and should be classified on the balance sheet as a liability.

4. **a.** The revenue was earned in October.

    b. (1) Debit Accounts Receivable and credit Fees Earned or another appropriately titled revenue account in October.

    (2) Debit Cash and credit Accounts Receivable in November.

5. No. Errors may have been made that had the same erroneous effect on both debits and credits, such as failure to record and/or post a transaction, recording the same transaction more than once, and posting a transaction correctly but to the wrong account.

6. The listing of $9,800 is a transposition; the listing of $100 is a slide.

7. **a.** No. Because the same error occurred on both the debit side and the credit side of the trial balance, the trial balance would not be out of balance.

    b. Yes. The trial balance would not balance. The error would cause the debit total of the trial balance to exceed the credit total by $90.

8. **a.** The equality of the trial balance would not be affected.

    b. On the income statement, total operating expenses (salary expense) would be overstated by $7,500, and net income would be understated by $7,500. On the statement of owner's equity, the beginning and ending capital would be correct. However, net income and withdrawals would be understated by $7,500. These understatements offset one another, and, thus, ending owner's equity is correct. The balance sheet is not affected by the error.

9. **a.** The equality of the trial balance would not be affected.

    b. On the income statement, revenues (fees earned) would be overstated by $300,000, and net income would be overstated by $300,000. On the statement of owner's equity, the beginning capital would be correct. However, net income and ending capital would be overstated by $300,000. The balance sheet total assets is correct. However, liabilities (notes payable) is understated by $300,000, and owner's equity is overstated by $300,000. The understatement of liabilities is offset by the overstatement of owner's equity, and, thus, total liabilities and owner's equity is correct.

10. **a.** From the viewpoint of Surety Storage, the balance of the checking account represents an asset.

    b. From the viewpoint of Ada Savings Bank, the balance of the checking account represents a liability.

PRACTICE EXERCISES

PE 2–1A

1. Debit and credit entries, normal debit balance
2. Credit entries only, normal credit balance
3. Debit and credit entries, normal credit balance
4. Credit entries only, normal credit balance
5. Credit entries only, normal credit balance
6. Debit entries only, normal debit balance

PE 2–1B

1. Debit and credit entries, normal credit balance
2. Debit and credit entries, normal debit balance
3. Debit entries only, normal debit balance
4. Debit entries only, normal debit balance
5. Debit entries only, normal debit balance
6. Credit entries only, normal credit balance

PE 2–2A

Feb.	12	Office Equipment	18,000	
		Cash		7,000
		Accounts Payable		11,000

PE 2–2B

Sept.	30	Office Supplies	2,500	
		Cash		800
		Accounts Payable		1,700

PE 2–3A

July	9	Accounts Receivable	12,000	
		Fees Earned		12,000

PE 2–3B

Aug.	13	Cash	9,000	
		Fees Earned		9,000

PE 2–4A

Jan.	25	Jay Nolan, Drawing	16,000	
		Cash		16,000

PE 2–4B

June	30	Dawn Pierce, Drawing	11,500	
		Cash		11,500

PE 2–5A

Using the following T account, solve for the amount of cash receipts (indicated by ? below).

	Cash		
Feb. 1 Bal.	14,750	93,400	Cash payments
Cash receipts	?		
Feb. 28 Bal.	15,200		

$15,200 = $14,750 + Cash receipts – $93,400
Cash receipts = $15,200 + $93,400 – $14,750 = $93,850

PE 2–5B

Using the following T account, solve for the amount of supplies expense (indicated by ? below).

	Supplies		
Aug. 1 Bal.	1,025	?	Supplies expense
Supplies purchased	3,110		
Aug. 31 Bal.	1,324		

$1,324 = $1,025 + $3,110 – Supplies expense
Supplies expense = $1,025 + $3,110 – $1,324 = $2,811

PE 2–6A

a.   The totals are unequal. The credit total is lower by $900 ($5,400 – $4,500).

b.   The totals are equal since both the debit and credit entries were journalized and posted for $720.

c.   The totals are unequal. The debit total is higher by $3,200 ($1,600 + $1,600).

PE 2–6B

a.   The totals are equal since both the debit and credit entries were journalized and posted for $12,900.

b.   The totals are unequal. The credit total is higher by $1,656 ($1,840 – $184).

c.   The totals are unequal. The debit total is higher by $4,500 ($8,300 – $3,800).

PE 2–7A

a.

Utilities Expense	7,300	
Miscellaneous Expense		7,300
Utilities Expense	7,300	
Cash		7,300

Note: The first entry in (a) reverses the incorrect entry, and the second entry records the correct entry. These two entries could also be combined into one entry as shown below; however, preparing two entries would make it easier for someone to understand later what happened and why the entries were necessary.

Utilities Expense	14,600	
Miscellaneous Expense		7,300
Cash		7,300

b.

Accounts Payable	6,100	
Accounts Receivable		6,100

PE 2–7B

a.

Cash	8,400	
Accounts Receivable		8,400

b.

Supplies	2,500	
Office Equipment		2,500
Supplies	2,500	
Accounts Payable		2,500

Note: The first entry in (b) reverses the incorrect entry, and the second entry records the correct entry. These two entries could also be combined into one entry as shown below; however, preparing two entries would make it easier for someone to understand later what happened and why the entries were necessary.

Supplies	5,000	
Office Equipment		2,500
Accounts Payable		2,500

PE 2–8A

Fuller Company Income Statements For Years Ended December 31			Increase/(Decrease)	
	2014	2013	Amount	Percent
Fees earned	$680,000	$850,000	$(170,000)	−20.0%
Operating expenses	541,875	637,500	(95,625)	−15.0%
Net income	$138,125	$212,500	$ (74,375)	−35.0%

PE 2–8B

Paragon Company Income Statements For Years Ended December 31			Increase/(Decrease)	
	2014	2013	Amount	Percent
Fees earned	$1,416,000	$1,200,000	$216,000	18.0%
Operating expenses	1,044,000	900,000	144,000	16.0%
Net income	$ 372,000	$ 300,000	$ 72,000	24.0%

EXERCISES

Ex. 2–1

Balance Sheet Accounts	Income Statement Accounts

Assets

Revenue

Flight Equipment

Cargo and Mail Revenue

Purchase Deposits for Flight Equipment[a]

Passenger Revenue

Spare Parts and Supplies

Liabilities

Expenses

Accounts Payable

Aircraft Fuel Expense

Air Traffic Liability[b]

Commissions (Expense)[c]

Landing Fees (Expense)[d]

Owner's Equity

None

[a] Advance payments (deposits) on aircraft to be delivered in the future
[b] Passenger ticket sales not yet recognized as revenue
[c] Commissions paid to travel agents
[d] Fees paid to airports for landing rights

Ex. 2–2

Account	Account Number
Accounts Payable	21
Accounts Receivable	12
Cash	11
Fees Earned	41
Gina Kissel, Capital	31
Gina Kissel, Drawing	32
Land	13
Miscellaneous Expense	53
Supplies Expense	52
Wages Expense	51

Note: Expense accounts are normally listed in order of magnitude from largest to smallest with Miscellaneous Expense always listed last. Since Wages Expense is normally larger than Supplies Expense, Wages Expense is listed as account number 51 and Supplies Expense as account number 52.

Ex. 2–3

| Balance Sheet Accounts | Income Statement Accounts |

1. Assets
11 Cash
12 Accounts Receivable
13 Supplies
14 Prepaid Insurance
15 Equipment

2. Liabilities
21 Accounts Payable
22 Unearned Rent

3. Owner's Equity
31 Ivy Bishop, Capital
32 Ivy Bishop, Drawing

4. Revenue
41 Fees Earned

5. Expenses
51 Wages Expense
52 Rent Expense
53 Supplies Expense
59 Miscellaneous Expense

Note: The order of some of the accounts within the major classifications is somewhat arbitrary, as in accounts 13–14, accounts 21–22, and accounts 51–53. In a new business, the order of magnitude of balances in such accounts is not determinable in advance. The magnitude may also vary from period to period.

Ex. 2–4

a.	debit	g.	debit
b.	credit	h.	credit
c.	credit	i.	debit
d.	credit	j.	credit
e.	debit	k.	debit
f.	credit	l.	debit

Ex. 2–5
1. debit and credit entries (c)
2. debit and credit entries (c)
3. debit and credit entries (c)
4. credit entries only (b)
5. debit entries only (a)
6. debit entries only (a)
7. debit entries only (a)

Ex. 2–6

a.	Liability—credit	e.	Asset—debit
b.	Asset—debit	f.	Revenue—credit
c.	Owner's equity (Amanda Whitmore, Capital)—credit	g.	Asset—debit
		h.	Expense—debit
d.	Owner's equity (Amanda Whitmore, Drawing)—debit	i.	Asset—debit
		j.	Expense—debit

Ex. 2–7

2014				
July	1	Rent Expense	3,200	
		Cash		3,200
	3	Advertising Expense	750	
		Cash		750
	5	Supplies	1,300	
		Cash		1,300
	6	Office Equipment	12,500	
		Accounts Payable		12,500
	10	Cash	11,400	
		Accounts Receivable		11,400
	15	Accounts Payable	1,175	
		Cash		1,175
	27	Miscellaneous Expense	600	
		Cash		600
	30	Utilities Expense	180	
		Cash		180
	31	Accounts Receivable	33,760	
		Fees Earned		33,760
	31	Utilities Expense	1,300	
		Cash		1,300
	31	Dennis Isberg, Drawing	4,000	
		Cash		4,000

Ex. 2–8

a.

		JOURNAL		Page	19

Date		Description	Post. Ref.	Debit	Credit
2014		**Adjusting Entries**			
May	22	Supplies	15	6,180	
		Accounts Payable	21		6,180
		Purchased supplies on account.			

b., c., d.

Account: **Supplies**   Account No.   15

Date		Item	Post. Ref.	Debit	Credit	Balance Debit	Balance Credit
2014							
May	1	Balance	✓			1,500	
	22		19	6,180		7,680	

Account: **Accounts Payable**   Account No.   21

Date		Item	Post. Ref.	Debit	Credit	Balance Debit	Balance Credit
2014							
May	1	Balance	✓				16,750
	22		19		6,180		22,930

e.   Yes, the rules of debit and credit apply to all companies.

Ex. 2–9

a.	(1)	Accounts Receivable	48,600	
		Fees Earned		48,600
	(2)	Supplies	1,975	
		Accounts Payable		1,975
	(3)	Cash	31,400	
		Accounts Receivable		31,400
	(4)	Accounts Payable	1,350	
		Cash		1,350

Ex. 2–9 (Concluded)

b.

	Cash		
(3)	31,400	(4)	1,350

	Accounts Payable		
(4)	1,350	(2)	1,975

	Supplies	
(2)	1,975	

Fees Earned		
	(1)	48,600

	Accounts Receivable		
(1)	48,600	(3)	31,400

c. No. A credit balance in Accounts Receivable could occur if a customer overpaid his or her account. Regardless, the credit balance should be investigated to verify that an error has not occurred.

Ex. 2–10

a. The increase of $140,000 ($515,000 – $375,000) in the cash account does not indicate net income of that amount. Net income is the net change in all assets and liabilities from operating (revenue and expense) transactions.

b. $60,000 ($200,000 – $140,000)

or

Cash	
X	375,000
515,000	
200,000	

X + $515,000 – $375,000 = $200,000
X = $200,000 – $515,000 + $375,000
X = $60,000

Ex. 2–11

a.

	Accounts Payable		
		Mar. 1	X
	276,500		261,000
		Mar. 31	76,000

$X + \$261,000 - \$276,500 = \$76,000$
$X = \$76,000 + \$276,500 - \$261,000$
$X = \$91,500$

b.

Accounts Receivable			
July 1	49,000		525,000
	X		
July 31	61,500		

$\$49,000 + X - \$525,000 = \$61,500$
$X = \$61,500 + \$525,000 - \$49,000$
$X = \$537,500$

c.

Cash			
Sept. 1	28,440		X
	112,100		
Sept. 30	33,200		

$\$28,440 + \$112,100 - X = \$33,200$
$X = \$28,440 + \$112,100 - \$33,200$
$X = \$107,340$

Ex. 2–12

a.   Debit (negative) balance of $16,000 ($314,000 – $10,000 – $320,000). This negative balance means that the liabilities of Waters' business exceed the assets.

b.   Yes. The balance sheet prepared at December 31 will balance, with Terrace Waters, Capital, being reported in the owner's equity section as a negative $16,000.

Ex. 2–13

a. and b.

	Account Debited		Account Credited	
Transaction	Type	Effect	Type	Effect
(1)	asset	+	owner's equity	+
(2)	asset	+	asset	–
(3)	asset	+	asset	–
			liability	+
(4)	expense	+	asset	–
(5)	asset	+	revenue	+
(6)	liability	–	asset	–
(7)	asset	+	asset	–
(8)	expense	+	asset	–
(9)	drawing	+	asset	–

Ex. 2–14

(1)	Cash	75,000	
	Luis Chavez, Capital		75,000
(2)	Supplies	4,000	
	Cash		4,000
(3)	Equipment	25,000	
	Accounts Payable		22,000
	Cash		3,000
(4)	Operating Expenses	2,700	
	Cash		2,700
(5)	Accounts Receivable	19,500	
	Service Revenue		19,500
(6)	Accounts Payable	9,000	
	Cash		9,000
(7)	Cash	11,000	
	Accounts Receivable		11,000
(8)	Operating Expenses	2,000	
	Supplies		2,000
(9)	Luis Chavez, Drawing	5,000	
	Cash		5,000

© 2014 Cengage Learning. All Rights Reserved. May not be scanned, copied or duplicated, or posted to a publicly accessible website, in whole or in part.

Ex. 2–15

a.

GRAND CANYON TOURS CO. Unadjusted Trial Balance April 30, 2014		
	Debit Balances	Credit Balances
Cash	62,300	
Accounts Receivable	8,500	
Supplies	2,000	
Equipment	25,000	
Accounts Payable		13,000
Luis Chavez, Capital		75,000
Luis Chavez, Drawing	5,000	
Service Revenue		19,500
Operating Expenses	4,700	
	107,500	107,500

b.   Net income, $14,800 ($19,500 – $4,700)

Ex. 2–16

LEAF CO. Unadjusted Trial Balance December 31, 2014		
	Debit Balances	Credit Balances
Cash	13,500*	
Accounts Receivable	38,100	
Supplies	3,200	
Prepaid insurance	6,400	
Land	40,000	
Accounts Payable		23,500
Unearned Rent		13,500
Notes Payable		50,000
Dan Leafdale, Capital		50,000
Dan Leafdale, Drawing	16,000	
Fees Earned		538,000
Wages Expense	476,800	
Rent Expense	36,000	
Utilities Expense	18,000	
Supplies Expense	9,000	
Insurance Expense	6,000	
Miscellaneous Expense	12,000	
	675,000	675,000

*$13,500 = $675,000 – $12,000 – $6,000 – $9,000 – $18,000 – $36,000 – $476,800 – $16,000
– $40,000 – $6,400 – 3,200 – $38,100

Ex. 2–17

Inequality of trial balance totals would be caused by errors described in (c) and (e). For (c), the debit total would exceed the credit total by $9,900 ($4,950 + $4,950). For (e), the credit total would exceed the debit total by $17,100 ($19,000 – $1,900).

Errors (b), (d), and (e) would require correcting entries. Although it is not a correcting entry, the entry that was not made in (a) should also be entered in the journal.

Ex. 2–18

RANGER CO. Unadjusted Trial Balance August 31, 2014		
	Debit Balances	Credit Balances
Cash	15,500	
Accounts Receivable	46,750	
Prepaid Insurance	12,000	
Equipment	190,000	
Accounts Payable		24,600
Unearned Rent		5,400
Carmen Meeks, Capital		110,000
Carmen Meeks, Drawing	13,000	
Service Revenue		385,000
Wages Expense	213,000	
Advertising Expense	16,350	
Miscellaneous Expense	18,400	
	525,000	525,000

Ex. 2–19

Error	(a) Out of Balance	(b) Difference	(c) Larger Total
1.	yes	$6,000	debit
2.	no	—	—
3.	yes	5,400	credit
4.	yes	480	debit
5.	no	—	—
6.	yes	90	credit
7.	yes	360	credit

Ex. 2–20

1. The Debit column total is added incorrectly. The sum is $890,700 rather than $1,189,300.

2. The trial balance should be dated "July 31, 2014," not "For the Month Ending July 31, 2014."

3. The Accounts Receivable balance should be in the Debit column.

4. The Accounts Payable balance should be in the Credit column.

5. The Samuel Parson, Drawing, balance should be in the Debit column.

6. The Advertising Expense balance should be in the Debit column.

A corrected trial balance would be as follows:

MASCOT CO. Unadjusted Trial Balance July 31, 2014		
	Debit Balances	Credit Balances
Cash	36,000	
Accounts Receivable	112,600	
Prepaid Insurance	18,000	
Equipment	375,000	
Accounts Payable		53,300
Salaries Payable		7,500
Samuel Parson, Capital		297,200
Samuel Parson, Drawing	17,000	
Service Revenue		682,000
Salary Expense	396,800	
Advertising Expense	73,000	
Miscellaneous Expense	11,600	
	1,040,000	1,040,000

Ex. 2–21

a.	Prepaid Rent	13,550	
	Cash		13,550
b.	Ron Sutin, Drawing	14,000	
	Wages Expense		14,000

Ex. 2–22

a.

Cash	17,600	
Fees Earned		8,800
Accounts Receivable		8,800

b.

Accounts Payable*	1,760	
Supplies Expense		1,760

Supplies	1,760	
Cash		1,760

* The first entry reverses the original entry. The second entry is the entry that should have been made initially.

Ex. 2–23

a. 1. Revenue:
$2,033 million increase ($67,390 – $65,357)
3.1% increase ($2,033 ÷ $65,357)

2. Operating expenses:
$1,454 million increase ($62,138 – $60,684)
2.4% increase ($1,454 ÷ $60,684)

3. Operating income:
$579 million increase ($5,252 – $4,673)
12.4% increase ($579 ÷ $4,673)

b. During the recent year, revenue increased by 3.1%, while operating expenses increased by only 2.4%. As a result, operating income increased by 12.4%, a favorable trend from the prior year.

Ex. 2–24

a. 1. Revenue:
        $13,764 million increase ($421,849 – $408,085)
        3.4% increase ($13,764 ÷ $408,085)

    2. Operating expenses:
        $12,224 million increase ($396,307 – $384,083)
        3.2% increase ($12,224 ÷ $384,083)

    3. Operating expenses:
        $1,540 million increase ($25,542 – $24,002)
        6.4% increase ($1,540 ÷ $24,002)

b. During the recent year, revenue increased by 3.4%, while operating expenses increased by 3.2%. As a result, operating income increased by 6.4%, a favorable trend from the prior year.

c. Because of the size differences between Target and Walmart (Walmart has over 6 times the revenue), it is best to compare the two companies on the basis of percent changes. Target and Walmart increased their revenue from the prior year by approximately the same percent (3.1% for Target and 3.4% for Walmart). However, Target's operating expenses increased by only 2.4% compared to Walmart's 3.2% increase. As a result, Target's operating income increased by 12.4% compared to Walmart's 6.4% increase. Based upon this analysis, it appears that Target was better able to control its operating expenses as its revenue increased than was Walmart.

PROBLEMS

Prob. 2–1A

1. and 2.

Cash			
(a)	25,000	(b)	2,750
(g)	11,150	(c)	4,000
		(e)	1,600
		(f)	2,400
		(h)	300
		(i)	3,500
		(j)	550
		(m)	2,200
		(n)	815
Bal.	18,035		

Equipment	
(d)	9,000

Notes Payable			
(j)	550	(c)	26,000
		Bal.	25,450

Accounts Payable			
(i)	3,500	(d)	9,000
		(k)	1,500
		Bal.	7,000

Accounts Receivable	
(l)	17,300

Lynn Cantwell, Capital			
		(a)	25,000

Supplies	
(e)	1,600

Professional Fees			
		(g)	11,150
		(l)	17,300
		Bal.	28,450

Prepaid Insurance	
(f)	2,400

Rent Expense	
(b)	2,750

Automobiles	
(c)	30,000

Salary Expense	
(m)	2,200

Blueprint Expense	
(k)	1,500

Automobile Expense	
(n)	815

Miscellaneous Expense	
(h)	300

Prob. 2–1A (Concluded)

3.

LYNN CANTWELL, ARCHITECT Unadjusted Trial Balance July 31, 2014	Debit Balances	Credit Balances
Cash	18,035	
Accounts Receivable	17,300	
Supplies	1,600	
Prepaid Insurance	2,400	
Automobiles	30,000	
Equipment	9,000	
Notes Payable		25,450
Accounts Payable		7,000
Lynn Cantwell, Capital		25,000
Professional Fees		28,450
Rent Expense	2,750	
Salary Expense	2,200	
Blueprint Expense	1,500	
Automobile Expense	815	
Miscellaneous Expense	300	
	85,900	85,900

4. Net income, $20,885 ($28,450 – $2,750 – $2,200 – $1,500 – $815 – $300)

Prob. 2–2A

1. (a)

Cash	23,500	
Alicia Masingale, Capital		23,500

(b)

Rent Expense	4,000	
Cash		4,000

(c)

Supplies	1,800	
Accounts Payable		1,800

(d)

Accounts Payable	675	
Cash		675

(e)

Cash	16,750	
Sales Commissions		16,750

(f)

Automobile Expense	1,000	
Miscellaneous Expense	800	
Cash		1,800

(g)

Office Salaries Expense	2,150	
Cash		2,150

(h)

Supplies Expense	925	
Supplies		925

(i)

Alicia Masingale, Drawing	1,600	
Cash		1,600

Prob. 2–2A (Continued)

2.

	Cash					Sales Commissions	
(a)	23,500	(b)	4,000			(e)	16,750
(e)	16,750	(d)	675				
		(f)	1,800			Rent Expense	
		(g)	2,150		(b)	4,000	
		(i)	1,600				
Bal.	30,025						

	Supplies					Office Salaries Expense	
(c)	1,800	(h)	925		(g)	2,150	
Bal.	875						

	Accounts Payable					Automobile Expense	
(d)	675	(c)	1,800		(f)	1,000	
		Bal.	1,125				

	Alicia Masingale, Capital					Supplies Expense	
		(a)	23,500		(h)	925	

	Alicia Masingale, Drawing					Miscellaneous Expense	
(i)	1,600				(f)	800	

Prob. 2–2A (Concluded)

3.

LEOPARD REALTY Unadjusted Trial Balance January 31, 2014	Debit Balances	Credit Balances
Cash	30,025	
Supplies	875	
Accounts Payable		1,125
Alicia Masingale, Capital		23,500
Alicia Masingale, Drawing	1,600	
Sales Commissions		16,750
Rent Expense	4,000	
Office Salaries Expense	2,150	
Automobile Expense	1,000	
Supplies Expense	925	
Miscellaneous Expense	800	
	41,375	41,375

4. a. $16,750

 b. $8,875 ($4,000 + $2,150 + $1,000 + $925 + $800)

 c. $7,875 ($16,750 – $8,875)

5. $29,775, which is the initial investment of $23,500 plus the excess of net income of $7,875 over the withdrawals of $1,600.

Prob. 2–3A

1.

JOURNAL Page 1

Date	Description	Post. Ref.	Debit	Credit
2014				
June 1	Cash	11	21,500	
	Ellie Hopkins, Capital	31		21,500
1	Rent Expense	53	4,200	
	Cash	11		4,200
6	Equipment	16	8,500	
	Accounts Payable	22		8,500
8	Truck	18	28,000	
	Cash	11		3,000
	Notes Payable	21		25,000
10	Supplies	13	1,800	
	Cash	11		1,800
12	Cash	11	9,000	
	Fees Earned	41		9,000
15	Prepaid Insurance	14	2,700	
	Cash	11		2,700
23	Accounts Receivable	12	13,650	
	Fees Earned	41		13,650
24	Truck Expense	55	975	
	Accounts Payable	22		975

JOURNAL Page 2

Date	Description	Post. Ref.	Debit	Credit
2014				
June 29	Utilities Expense	54	2,480	
	Cash	11		2,480
29	Miscellaneous Expense	59	750	
	Cash	11		750

Prob. 2–3A (Continued)

30	Cash	11	7,800	
	Accounts Receivable	12		7,800
30	Wages Expense	51	5,100	
	Cash	11		5,100
30	Accounts Payable	22	4,250	
	Cash	11		4,250
30	Ellie Hopkins, Drawing	32	3,000	
	Cash	11		3,000

2.

GENERAL LEDGER

Account: Cash   Account No. 11

Date		Item	Post. Ref.	Debit	Credit	Balance Debit	Balance Credit
2014							
June	1		1	21,500		21,500	
	1		1		4,200	17,300	
	8		1		3,000	14,300	
	10		1		1,800	12,500	
	12		1	9,000		21,500	
	15		1		2,700	18,800	
	29		2		2,480	16,320	
	29		2		750	15,570	
	30		2	7,800		23,370	
	30		2		5,100	18,270	
	30		2		4,250	14,020	
	30		2		3,000	11,020	

Account: Accounts Receivable   Account No. 12

Date		Item	Post. Ref.	Debit	Credit	Balance Debit	Balance Credit
2014							
June	23		1	13,650		13,650	
	30		2		7,800	5,850	

Prob. 2–3A (Continued)

Account: __Supplies__   Account No. __13__

Date		Item	Post. Ref.	Debit	Credit	Balance Debit	Balance Credit
2014							
June	10		1	1,800		1,800	

Account: Prepaid Insurance   Account No. __14__

Date		Item	Post. Ref.	Debit	Credit	Balance Debit	Balance Credit
2014							
June	15		1	2,700		2,700	

Account: Equipment   Account No. __16__

Date		Item	Post. Ref.	Debit	Credit	Balance Debit	Balance Credit
2014							
June	6		1	8,500		8,500	

Account: Truck   Account No. __18__

Date		Item	Post. Ref.	Debit	Credit	Balance Debit	Balance Credit
2014							
June	8		1	28,000		28,000	

Account: Notes Payable   Account No. __21__

Date		Item	Post. Ref.	Debit	Credit	Balance Debit	Balance Credit
2014							
June	8		1		25,000		25,000

Account: Accounts Payable   Account No. __22__

Date		Item	Post. Ref.	Debit	Credit	Balance Debit	Balance Credit
2014							
June	6		1		8,500		8,500
	24		1		975		9,475
	30		2	4,250			5,225

Prob. 2–3A (Continued)

Account: **Ellie Hopkins, Capital**   Account No.   **31**

Date		Item	Post. Ref.	Debit	Credit	Balance Debit	Balance Credit
2014							
June	1		1		21,500		21,500

Account: **Ellie Hopkins, Drawing**   Account No.   **32**

Date		Item	Post. Ref.	Debit	Credit	Balance Debit	Balance Credit
2014							
June	30		2	3,000		3,000	

Account: **Fees Earned**   Account No.   **41**

Date		Item	Post. Ref.	Debit	Credit	Balance Debit	Balance Credit
2014							
June	12		1		9,000		9,000
	23		1		13,650		22,650

Account: **Wages Expense**   Account No.   **51**

Date		Item	Post. Ref.	Debit	Credit	Balance Debit	Balance Credit
2014							
June	30		2	5,100		5,100	

Account: **Rent Expense**   Account No.   **53**

Date		Item	Post. Ref.	Debit	Credit	Balance Debit	Balance Credit
2014							
June	1		1	4,200		4,200	

Account: **Utilities Expense**   Account No.   **54**

Date		Item	Post. Ref.	Debit	Credit	Balance Debit	Balance Credit
2014							
June	29		2	2,480		2,480	

Prob. 2–3A (Continued)

Account: **Truck Expense**   Account No. 55

Date		Item	Post. Ref.	Debit	Credit	Balance Debit	Balance Credit
2014							
June	24		1	975		975	

Account: **Miscellaneous Expense**   Account No. 59

Date		Item	Post. Ref.	Debit	Credit	Balance Debit	Balance Credit
2014							
June	29		2	750		750	

Prob. 2–3A (Concluded)

3.

FIRST-CLASS DESIGNS Unadjusted Trial Balance June 30, 2014	Debit Balances	Credit Balances
Cash	11,020	
Accounts Receivable	5,850	
Supplies	1,800	
Prepaid Insurance	2,700	
Equipment	8,500	
Truck	28,000	
Notes Payable		25,000
Accounts Payable		5,225
Ellie Hopkins, Capital		21,500
Ellie Hopkins, Drawing	3,000	
Fees Earned		22,650
Wages Expense	5,100	
Rent Expense	4,200	
Utilities Expense	2,480	
Truck Expense	975	
Miscellaneous Expense	750	
	74,375	74,375

4. $9,145 ($22,650 – $5,100 – $4,200 – $2,480 – $975 – $750)

5. As will be discussed in Chapter 3, various adjustments are normally required at the end of the accounting period. For example, adjustments for supplies used, insurance expired, and depreciation would probably be required.

Note to Instructors: At this point, students have not been exposed to depreciation, but some insightful students might recognize the need for recording supplies used and insurance expired. You might use this as an opportunity to discuss what is coming in Chapter 3.

Prob. 2–4A

2. and 3.

JOURNAL   Page _____ 18

Date		Description	Post. Ref.	Debit	Credit
2014					
Apr.	1	Rent Expense	52	6,500	
		Cash	11		6,500
	2	Office Supplies	14	2,300	
		Accounts Payable	21		2,300
	5	Prepaid Insurance	13	6,000	
		Cash	11		6,000
	10	Cash	11	52,300	
		Accounts Receivable	12		52,300
	15	Land	16	200,000	
		Cash	11		30,000
		Notes Payable	23		170,000
	17	Accounts Payable	21	6,450	
		Cash	11		6,450
	20	Accounts Payable	21	325	
		Office Supplies	14		325
	23	Advertising Expense	53	4,300	
		Cash	11		4,300

JOURNAL   Page _____ 19

Date		Description	Post. Ref.	Debit	Credit
2014					
Apr.	27	Cash	11	2,500	
		Salary and Commission Expense	51		2,500
	28	Automobile Expense	54	1,500	
		Cash	11		1,500
	29	Miscellaneous Expense	59	1,400	
		Cash	11		1,400

Prob. 2–4A (Continued)

∧∧

30	Accounts Receivable		12	57,000	
	Fees Earned		41		57,000
30	Salary and Commission Expense		51	11,900	
	Cash		11		11,900
30	Lester Wagner, Drawing		32	4,000	
	Cash		11		4,000
30	Cash		11	10,000	
	Unearned Rent		22		10,000

1. and 3.

GENERAL LEDGER

Account: **Cash**　　　　　　　　　　　　　　　Account No. **11**

Date		Item	Post. Ref.	Debit	Credit	Balance Debit	Balance Credit
2014							
Apr.	1	Balance	✓			26,300	
	1		18		6,500	19,800	
	5		18		6,000	13,800	
	10		18	52,300		66,100	
	15		18		30,000	36,100	
	17		18		6,450	29,650	
	23		18		4,300	25,350	
	27		19	2,500		27,850	
	28		19		1,500	26,350	
	29		19		1,400	24,950	
	30		19		11,900	13,050	
	30		19		4,000	9,050	
	30		19	10,000		19,050	

Account: **Accounts Receivable**　　　　　　　　Account No. **12**

Date		Item	Post. Ref.	Debit	Credit	Balance Debit	Balance Credit
2014							
Apr.	1	Balance	✓			61,500	
	10		18		52,300	9,200	
	30		19	57,000		66,200	

Prob. 2–4A (Continued)

Account: Prepaid Insurance   Account No.   13

Date		Item	Post. Ref.	Debit	Credit	Balance Debit	Balance Credit
2014							
Apr.	1	Balance	✓			3,000	
	5		18	6,000		9,000	

Account: Office Supplies   Account No.   14

Date		Item	Post. Ref.	Debit	Credit	Balance Debit	Balance Credit
2014							
Apr.	1	Balance	✓			1,800	
	2		18	2,300		4,100	
	20		18		325	3,775	

Account: Land   Account No.   16

Date		Item	Post. Ref.	Debit	Credit	Balance Debit	Balance Credit
2014							
Apr.	15		18	200,000		200,000	

Account: Accounts Payable   Account No.   21

Date		Item	Post. Ref.	Debit	Credit	Balance Debit	Balance Credit
2014							
Apr.	1	Balance	✓				14,000
	2		18		2,300		16,300
	17		18	6,450			9,850
	20		18	325			9,525

Account: Unearned Rent   Account No.   22

Date		Item	Post. Ref.	Debit	Credit	Balance Debit	Balance Credit
2014							
Apr.	30		19		10,000		10,000

Account: Notes Payable   Account No.   23

Date		Item	Post. Ref.	Debit	Credit	Balance Debit	Balance Credit
2014							
Apr.	15		18		170,000		170,000

Prob. 2–4A (Continued)

Account: Lester Wagner, Capital   **Account No.** 31

Date		Item	Post. Ref.	Debit	Credit	Balance Debit	Balance Credit
2014							
Apr.	1	Balance	✓				46,000

Account: Lester Wagner, Drawing   **Account No.** 32

Date		Item	Post. Ref.	Debit	Credit	Balance Debit	Balance Credit
2014							
Apr.	1	Balance	✓			2,000	
	30		19	4,000		6,000	

Account: Fees Earned   **Account No.** 41

Date		Item	Post. Ref.	Debit	Credit	Balance Debit	Balance Credit
2014							
Apr.	1	Balance	✓				240,000
	30		19		57,000		297,000

Account: Salary and Commission Expense   **Account No.** 51

Date		Item	Post. Ref.	Debit	Credit	Balance Debit	Balance Credit
2014							
Apr.	1	Balance	✓			148,200	
	27		19		2,500	145,700	
	30		19	11,900		157,600	

Account: Rent Expense   **Account No.** 52

Date		Item	Post. Ref.	Debit	Credit	Balance Debit	Balance Credit
2014							
Apr.	1	Balance	✓			30,000	
	1		18	6,500		36,500	

Account: Advertising Expense   **Account No.** 53

Date		Item	Post. Ref.	Debit	Credit	Balance Debit	Balance Credit
2014							
Apr.	1	Balance	✓			17,800	
	23		18	4,300		22,100	

Prob. 2–4A (Continued)

Account: **Automobile Expense**   Account No.   **54**

Date		Item	Post. Ref.	Debit	Credit	Balance Debit	Balance Credit
2014							
Apr.	1	Balance	✓			5,500	
	28		19	1,500		7,000	

Account: **Miscellaneous Expense**   Account No.   **59**

Date		Item	Post. Ref.	Debit	Credit	Balance Debit	Balance Credit
2014							
Apr.	1	Balance	✓			3,900	
	29		19	1,400		5,300	

4.

ELITE REALTY Unadjusted Trial Balance April 30, 2014	Debit Balances	Credit Balances
Cash	19,050	
Accounts Receivable	66,200	
Prepaid Insurance	9,000	
Office Supplies	3,775	
Land	200,000	
Accounts Payable		9,525
Unearned Rent		10,000
Notes Payable		170,000
Lester Wagner, Capital		46,000
Lester Wagner, Drawing	6,000	
Fees Earned		297,000
Salary and Commission Expense	157,600	
Rent Expense	36,500	
Advertising Expense	22,100	
Automobile Expense	7,000	
Miscellaneous Expense	5,300	
	532,525	532,525

Prob. 2–4A (Concluded)

5. (a) **The unadjusted trial balance in (4) still balances, since the debits equaled the credits in the original journal entry.**

    (b) **The correcting entry for $7,200 ($19,100 – $11,900) would be as follows:**

JOURNAL

Page   19

Date		Description	Post. Ref.	Debit	Credit
2014					
Apr.	30	Salary and Commission Expense	51	7,200	
		Cash	11		7,200

    (c) **Transposition**

Prob. 2–5A

1.

THE COLBY GROUP Unadjusted Trial Balance August 31, 2014	Debit Balances	Credit Balances
Cash*	22,400	
Accounts Receivable	48,000	
Supplies	8,750	
Prepaid Insurance	4,300	
Equipment	196,000	
Notes Payable		117,600
Accounts Payable		30,800
Terry Colby, Capital		122,150
Terry Colby, Drawing	63,000	
Fees Earned		454,450
Wages Expense	270,000	
Rent Expense	58,100	
Advertising Expense	25,200	
Gas, Electricity, and Water Expense	24,150	
Miscellaneous Expense	5,100	
	725,000	725,000

* $17,300 + $6,000 (a) – $900 (b)

2. No. The trial balance indicates only that the debits and credits are equal. Any errors that have the same effect on debits and credits will not affect the balancing of the trial balance.

Prob. 2–1B

1. and 2.

Cash			
(a)	18,000	(b)	2,500
(g)	12,000	(c)	3,150
		(d)	1,450
		(f)	2,400
		(h)	1,800
		(i)	375
		(l)	2,800
		(m)	200
		(n)	300
		(o)	550
Bal.	14,475		

Accounts Receivable	
(k)	15,650

Supplies	
(d)	1,450

Prepaid Insurance	
(f)	2,400

Automobiles	
(b)	19,500

Equipment	
(e)	6,500

Notes Payable			
(n)	300	(b)	17,000
		Bal.	16,700

Accounts Payable			
(h)	1,800	(e)	6,500
		(j)	2,500
		Bal.	7,200

Ken Jones, Capital			
		(a)	18,000

Professional Fees			
		(g)	12,000
		(k)	15,650
		Bal.	27,650

Rent Expense	
(c)	3,150

Salary Expense	
(l)	2,800

Blueprint Expense	
(j)	2,500

Automobile Expense	
(o)	550

Miscellaneous Expense		
(i)	375	
(m)	200	
Bal.	575	

Prob. 2–1B (Concluded)

3.

	Debit Balances	Credit Balances
KEN JONES, ARCHITECT Unadjusted Trial Balance April 30, 2014		
Cash	14,475	
Accounts Receivable	15,650	
Supplies	1,450	
Prepaid Insurance	2,400	
Automobiles	19,500	
Equipment	6,500	
Notes Payable		16,700
Accounts Payable		7,200
Ken Jones, Capital		18,000
Professional Fees		27,650
Rent Expense	3,150	
Salary Expense	2,800	
Blueprint Expense	2,500	
Automobile Expense	550	
Miscellaneous Expense	575	
	69,550	69,550

4.   Net income, $18,075 ($27,650 – $3,150 – $2,800 – $2,500 – $550 – $575)

Prob. 2–2B

1. **(a)**

Cash	17,500	
Rafael Masey, Capital		17,500

(b)

Supplies	2,300	
Accounts Payable		2,300

(c)

Cash	13,300	
Sales Commissions		13,300

(d)

Rent Expense	3,000	
Cash		3,000

(e)

Accounts Payable	1,150	
Cash		1,150

(f)

Rafael Masey, Drawing	1,800	
Cash		1,800

(g)

Automobile Expense	1,500	
Miscellaneous Expense	400	
Cash		1,900

(h)

Office Salaries Expense	2,800	
Cash		2,800

(i)

Supplies Expense	1,050	
Supplies		1,050

Prob. 2–2B (Continued)

2.

	Cash					Sales Commissions	
(a)	17,500	(d)	3,000			(c)	13,300
(c)	13,300	(e)	1,150				
		(f)	1,800			Rent Expense	
		(g)	1,900	(d)	3,000		
		(h)	2,800				
Bal.	20,150						

	Supplies					Office Salaries Expense	
(b)	2,300	(i)	1,050	(h)	2,800		
Bal.	1,250						

	Accounts Payable					Automobile Expense	
(e)	1,150	(b)	2,300	(g)	1,500		
		Bal.	1,150				

	Rafael Masey, Capital					Supplies Expense	
		(a)	17,500	(i)	1,050		

	Rafael Masey, Drawing					Miscellaneous Expense	
(f)	1,800			(g)	400		

Prob. 2–2B (Concluded)

3.

PLANET REALTY Unadjusted Trial Balance August 31, 2014	Debit Balances	Credit Balances
Cash	20,150	
Supplies	1,250	
Accounts Payable		1,150
Rafael Masey, Capital		17,500
Rafael Masey, Drawing	1,800	
Sales Commissions		13,300
Rent Expense	3,000	
Office Salaries Expense	2,800	
Automobile Expense	1,500	
Supplies Expense	1,050	
Miscellaneous Expense	400	
	31,950	31,950

4. a. $13,300
    b. $8,750 ($3,000 + $2,800 + $1,500 + $1,050 + $400)
    c. $4,550 ($13,300 – $8,750)

5. $20,250, which is the initial investment of $17,500 plus the excess of net income of $4,550 over the withdrawals of $1,800.

Prob. 2–3B

1.

JOURNAL   Page _____ 1

Date		Description	Post. Ref.	Debit	Credit
2014					
Oct.	1	Cash	11	18,000	
		Jay Pryor, Capital	31		18,000
	4	Rent Expense	53	3,000	
		Cash	11		3,000
	10	Truck	18	23,750	
		Cash	11		3,750
		Notes Payable	21		20,000
	13	Equipment	16	10,500	
		Accounts Payable	22		10,500
	14	Supplies	13	2,100	
		Cash	11		2,100
	15	Prepaid Insurance	14	3,600	
		Cash	11		3,600
	15	Cash	11	8,950	
		Fees Earned	41		8,950

JOURNAL   Page _____ 2

Date		Description	Post. Ref.	Debit	Credit
2014					
Oct.	21	Accounts Payable	22	2,000	
		Cash	11		2,000
	24	Accounts Receivable	12	14,150	
		Fees Earned	41		14,150
	26	Truck Expense	55	700	
		Accounts Payable	22		700
	27	Utilities Expense	54	2,240	
		Cash	11		2,240

Prob. 2–3B (Continued)

∧∧

	27	Miscellaneous Expense	59	1,100	
		Cash	11		1,100
	29	Cash	11	7,600	
		Accounts Receivable	12		7,600
	30	Wages Expense	51	4,800	
		Cash	11		4,800
	31	Jay Pryor, Drawing	32	3,500	
		Cash	11		3,500

2.

GENERAL LEDGER

Account: **Cash**   Account No.   11

Date		Item	Post. Ref.	Debit	Credit	Balance Debit	Balance Credit
2014							
Oct.	1		1	18,000		18,000	
	4		1		3,000	15,000	
	10		1		3,750	11,250	
	14		1		2,100	9,150	
	15		1		3,600	5,550	
	15		1	8,950		14,500	
	21		2		2,000	12,500	
	27		2		2,240	10,260	
	27		2		1,100	9,160	
	29		2	7,600		16,760	
	30		2		4,800	11,960	
	31		2		3,500	8,460	

Account: **Accounts Receivable**   Account No.   12

Date		Item	Post. Ref.	Debit	Credit	Balance Debit	Balance Credit
2014							
Oct.	24		2	14,150		14,150	
	29		2		7,600	6,550	

Prob. 2–3B (Continued)

Account: **Supplies**   Account No. **13**

Date		Item	Post. Ref.	Debit	Credit	Balance Debit	Balance Credit
2014							
Oct.	14		1	2,100		2,100	

Account: **Prepaid Insurance**   Account No. **14**

Date		Item	Post. Ref.	Debit	Credit	Balance Debit	Balance Credit
2014							
Oct.	15		1	3,600		3,600	

Account: **Equipment**   Account No. **16**

Date		Item	Post. Ref.	Debit	Credit	Balance Debit	Balance Credit
2014							
Oct.	13		1	10,500		10,500	

Account: **Truck**   Account No. **18**

Date		Item	Post. Ref.	Debit	Credit	Balance Debit	Balance Credit
2014							
Oct.	10		1	23,750		23,750	

Account: **Notes Payable**   Account No. **21**

Date		Item	Post. Ref.	Debit	Credit	Balance Debit	Balance Credit
2014							
Oct.	10		1		20,000		20,000

Account: **Accounts Payable**   Account No. **22**

Date		Item	Post. Ref.	Debit	Credit	Balance Debit	Balance Credit
2014							
Oct.	13		1		10,500		10,500
	21		2	2,000			8,500
	26		2		700		9,200

Prob. 2–3B (Continued)

Account: **Jay Pryor, Capital**   Account No. ___31___

Date		Item	Post. Ref.	Debit	Credit	Balance Debit	Balance Credit
2014							
Oct.	1		1		18,000		18,000

Account: **Jay Pryor, Drawing**   Account No. ___32___

Date		Item	Post. Ref.	Debit	Credit	Balance Debit	Balance Credit
2014							
Oct.	31		2	3,500		3,500	

Account: **Fees Earned**   Account No. ___41___

Date		Item	Post. Ref.	Debit	Credit	Balance Debit	Balance Credit
2014							
Oct.	15		1		8,950		8,950
	24		2		14,150		23,100

Account: **Wages Expense**   Account No. ___51___

Date		Item	Post. Ref.	Debit	Credit	Balance Debit	Balance Credit
2014							
Oct.	30		2	4,800		4,800	

Account: **Rent Expense**   Account No. ___53___

Date		Item	Post. Ref.	Debit	Credit	Balance Debit	Balance Credit
2014							
Oct.	4		1	3,000		3,000	

Account: **Utilities Expense**   Account No. ___54___

Date		Item	Post. Ref.	Debit	Credit	Balance Debit	Balance Credit
2014							
Oct.	27		2	2,240		2,240	

Prob. 2–3B (Continued)

Account: **Truck Expense**   Account No. **55**

Date		Item	Post. Ref.	Debit	Credit	Balance Debit	Balance Credit
2014							
Oct.	26		2	700		700	

Account: **Miscellaneous Expense**   Account No. **59**

Date		Item	Post. Ref.	Debit	Credit	Balance Debit	Balance Credit
2014							
Oct.	27		2	1,100		1,100	

Prob. 2–3B (Concluded)

3.

PIONEER DESIGNS Unadjusted Trial Balance October 31, 2014	Debit Balances	Credit Balances
Cash	8,460	
Accounts Receivable	6,550	
Supplies	2,100	
Prepaid Insurance	3,600	
Equipment	10,500	
Truck	23,750	
Notes Payable		20,000
Accounts Payable		9,200
Jay Pryor, Capital		18,000
Jay Pryor, Drawing	3,500	
Fees Earned		23,100
Wages Expense	4,800	
Rent Expense	3,000	
Utilities Expense	2,240	
Truck Expense	700	
Miscellaneous Expense	1,100	
	70,300	70,300

4. $11,260 ($23,100 – $4,800 – $3,000 – $2,240 – $700 – $1,100)

5. As will be discussed in Chapter 3, various adjustments are normally required at the end of the accounting period. For example, adjustments for supplies used, insurance expired, and depreciation would probably be required.

Note to Instructors: At this point, students have not been exposed to depreciation, but some insightful students might recognize the need for recording supplies used and insurance expired. You might use this as an opportunity to discuss what is coming in Chapter 3.

Prob. 2–4B

2. and 3.

JOURNAL   Page _____ 18

Date		Description	Post. Ref.	Debit	Credit
2014					
Aug.	1	Office Supplies	14	3,150	
		Accounts Payable	21		3,150
	2	Rent Expense	52	7,200	
		Cash	11		7,200
	3	Cash	11	83,900	
		Accounts Receivable	12		83,900
	5	Prepaid Insurance	13	12,000	
		Cash	11		12,000
	9	Accounts Payable	21	400	
		Office Supplies	14		400
	17	Advertising Expense	53	8,000	
		Cash	11		8,000
	23	Accounts Payable	21	13,750	
		Cash	11		13,750

JOURNAL   Page _____ 19

Date		Description	Post. Ref.	Debit	Credit
2014					
Aug.	29	Miscellaneous Expense	59	1,700	
		Cash	11		1,700
	30	Automobile Expense	54	2,500	
		Cash	11		2,500
	31	Cash	11	2,000	
		Salary and Commission Expense	51		2,000
	31	Salary and Commission Expense	51	53,000	
		Cash	11		53,000

Prob. 2–4B (Continued)

^^

	31	Accounts Receivable	12	183,500	
		Fees Earned	41		183,500
	31	Land	16	75,000	
		Cash	11		7,500
		Notes Payable	23		67,500
	31	Cindy Getman, Drawing	32	1,000	
		Cash	11		1,000
	31	Cash	11	5,000	
		Unearned Rent	22		5,000

1. and 3.

GENERAL LEDGER

Account: **Cash**   Account No. **11**

			Post.			Balance	
Date		Item	Ref.	Debit	Credit	Debit	Credit
2014							
Aug.	1	Balance	✓			52,500	
	2		18		7,200	45,300	
	3		18	83,900		129,200	
	5		18		12,000	117,200	
	17		18		8,000	109,200	
	23		18		13,750	95,450	
	29		19		1,700	93,750	
	30		19		2,500	91,250	
	31		19	2,000		93,250	
	31		19		53,000	40,250	
	31		19		7,500	32,750	
	31		19		1,000	31,750	
	31		19	5,000		36,750	

Account: **Accounts Receivable**   Account No. **12**

			Post.			Balance	
Date		Item	Ref.	Debit	Credit	Debit	Credit
2014							
Aug.	1	Balance	✓			100,100	
	3		18		83,900	16,200	
	31		19	183,500		199,700	

Prob. 2–4B (Continued)

Account: **Prepaid Insurance**   Account No. **13**

Date		Item	Post. Ref.	Debit	Credit	Balance Debit	Balance Credit
2014							
Aug.	1	Balance	✓			12,600	
	5		18	12,000		24,600	

Account: **Office Supplies**   Account No. **14**

Date		Item	Post. Ref.	Debit	Credit	Balance Debit	Balance Credit
2014							
Aug.	1	Balance	✓			2,800	
	1		18	3,150		5,950	
	9		18		400	5,550	

Account: **Land**   Account No. **16**

Date		Item	Post. Ref.	Debit	Credit	Balance Debit	Balance Credit
2014							
Aug.	31		19	75,000		75,000	

Account: **Accounts Payable**   Account No. **21**

Date		Item	Post. Ref.	Debit	Credit	Balance Debit	Balance Credit
2014							
Aug.	1	Balance	✓				21,000
	1		18		3,150		24,150
	9		18	400			23,750
	23		18	13,750			10,000

Account: **Unearned Rent**   Account No. **22**

Date		Item	Post. Ref.	Debit	Credit	Balance Debit	Balance Credit
2014							
Aug.	31		19		5,000		5,000

Account: **Notes Payable**   Account No. **23**

Date		Item	Post. Ref.	Debit	Credit	Balance Debit	Balance Credit
2014							
Aug.	31		19		67,500		67,500

Prob. 2–4B (Continued)

Account: **Cindy Getman, Capital**　　　　　　　　　Account No. ____ 31

Date		Item	Post. Ref.	Debit	Credit	Balance Debit	Balance Credit
2014							
Aug.	1	Balance	✓				87,500

Account: **Cindy Getman, Drawing**　　　　　　　　　Account No. ____ 32

Date		Item	Post. Ref.	Debit	Credit	Balance Debit	Balance Credit
2014							
Aug.	1	Balance	✓			44,800	
	31		19	1,000		45,800	

Account: **Fees Earned**　　　　　　　　　Account No. ____ 41

Date		Item	Post. Ref.	Debit	Credit	Balance Debit	Balance Credit
2014							
Aug.	1	Balance	✓				591,500
	31		19		183,500		775,000

Account: **Salary and Commission Expense**　　　　　　　　　Account No. ____ 51

Date		Item	Post. Ref.	Debit	Credit	Balance Debit	Balance Credit
2014							
Aug.	1	Balance	✓			385,000	
	31		19		2,000	383,000	
	31		19	53,000		436,000	

Account: **Rent Expense**　　　　　　　　　Account No. ____ 52

Date		Item	Post. Ref.	Debit	Credit	Balance Debit	Balance Credit
2014							
Aug.	1	Balance	✓			49,000	
	2		18	7,200		56,200	

Account: **Advertising Expense**　　　　　　　　　Account No. ____ 53

Date		Item	Post. Ref.	Debit	Credit	Balance Debit	Balance Credit
2014							
Aug.	1	Balance	✓			32,200	
	17		18	8,000		40,200	

Prob. 2–4B (Continued)

Account: **Automobile Expense**   Account No. **54**

Date		Item	Post. Ref.	Debit	Credit	Balance Debit	Balance Credit
2014							
Aug.	1	Balance	✓			15,750	
	30		19	2,500		18,250	

Account: **Miscellaneous Expense**   Account No. **59**

Date		Item	Post. Ref.	Debit	Credit	Balance Debit	Balance Credit
2014							
Aug.	1	Balance	✓			5,250	
	29		19	1,700		6,950	

4.

VALLEY REALTY Unadjusted Trial Balance August 31, 2014	Debit Balances	Credit Balances
Cash	36,750	
Accounts Receivable	199,700	
Prepaid Insurance	24,600	
Office Supplies	5,550	
Land	75,000	
Accounts Payable		10,000
Unearned Rent		5,000
Notes Payable		67,500
Cindy Getman, Capital		87,500
Cindy Getman, Drawing	45,800	
Fees Earned		775,000
Salary and Commission Expense	436,000	
Rent Expense	56,200	
Advertising Expense	40,200	
Automobile Expense	18,250	
Miscellaneous Expense	6,950	
	945,000	945,000

Prob. 2–4B (Concluded)

5.   (a) The unadjusted trial balance in (4) still balances, since the debits equaled
the credits in the original journal entry.

   (b) The correcting entry for $9,000 ($10,000 – $1,000) would be as follows:

JOURNAL   Page _____ 19

Date		Description	Post. Ref.	Debit	Credit
2014					
Aug.	31	Cindy Getman, Drawing	32	9,000	
		Cash	11		9,000

   (c) Slide

Prob. 2–5B

1.

TECH SUPPORT SERVICES Unadjusted Trial Balance January 31, 2014	Debit Balances	Credit Balances
Cash*	20,250	
Accounts Receivable	56,400	
Supplies	6,750	
Prepaid Insurance	9,600	
Equipment	162,000	
Notes Payable		54,000
Accounts Payable		16,650
Thad Engelberg, Capital		107,850
Thad Engelberg, Drawing	39,000	
Fees Earned		534,000
Wages Expense	306,000	
Rent Expense	62,550	
Advertising Expense	28,350	
Gas, Electricity, and Water Expense	17,000	
Miscellaneous Expense	4,600	
	712,500	712,500

* $25,550 – $8,000 (a) + $2,700 (b)

2.   No. The trial balance indicates only that the debits and credits are equal.
Any errors that have the same effect on debits and credits will not affect the
balancing of the trial balance.

CONTINUING PROBLEM

2. and 3.

		JOURNAL			Page _____ 1

Date		Description	Post. Ref.	Debit	Credit
2014					
July	1	Cash	11	5,000	
		Peyton Smith, Capital	31		5,000
	1	Office Rent Expense	51	1,750	
		Cash	11		1,750
	1	Prepaid Insurance	15	2,700	
		Cash	11		2,700
	2	Cash	11	1,000	
		Accounts Receivable	12		1,000
	3	Cash	11	7,200	
		Unearned Revenue	23		7,200
	3	Accounts Payable	21	250	
		Cash	11		250
	4	Miscellaneous Expense	59	900	
		Cash	11		900
	5	Office Equipment	17	7,500	
		Accounts Payable	21		7,500
	8	Advertising Expense	55	200	
		Cash	11		200
	11	Cash	11	1,000	
		Fees Earned	41		1,000
	13	Equipment Rent Expense	52	700	
		Cash	11		700
	14	Wages Expense	50	1,200	
		Cash	11		1,200

Continuing Problem (Continued)

2. and 3.

JOURNAL   Page _____ 2

Date		Description	Post. Ref.	Debit	Credit
2014					
July	16	Cash	11	2,000	
		Fees Earned	41		2,000
	18	Supplies	14	850	
		Accounts Payable	21		850
	21	Music Expense	54	620	
		Cash	11		620
	22	Advertising Expense	55	800	
		Cash	11		800
	23	Cash	11	750	
		Accounts Receivable	12	1,750	
		Fees Earned	41		2,500
	27	Utilities Expense	53	915	
		Cash	11		915
	28	Wages Expense	50	1,200	
		Cash	11		1,200
	29	Miscellaneous Expense	59	540	
		Cash	11		540
	30	Cash	11	500	
		Accounts Receivable	12	1,000	
		Fees Earned	41		1,500
	31	Cash	11	3,000	
		Fees Earned	41		3,000
	31	Music Expense	54	1,400	
		Cash	11		1,400
	31	Peyton Smith, Drawing	32	1,250	
		Cash	11		1,250

Continuing Problem (Continued)

1. and 3.

Account: __Cash__   Account No. ____11

Date		Item	Post. Ref.	Debit	Credit	Balance Debit	Balance Credit
2014							
July	1	Balance	✓			3,920	
	1		1	5,000		8,920	
	1		1		1,750	7,170	
	1		1		2,700	4,470	
	2		1	1,000		5,470	
	3		1	7,200		12,670	
	3		1		250	12,420	
	4		1		900	11,520	
	8		1		200	11,320	
	11		1	1,000		12,320	
	13		1		700	11,620	
	14		1		1,200	10,420	
	16		2	2,000		12,420	
	21		2		620	11,800	
	22		2		800	11,000	
	23		2	750		11,750	
	27		2		915	10,835	
	28		2		1,200	9,635	
	29		2		540	9,095	
	30		2	500		9,595	
	31		2	3,000		12,595	
	31		2		1,400	11,195	
	31		2		1,250	9,945	

Account: __Accounts Receivable__   Account No. ____12

Date		Item	Post. Ref.	Debit	Credit	Balance Debit	Balance Credit
2014							
July	1	Balance	✓			1,000	
	2		1		1,000	—	—
	23		2	1,750		1,750	
	30		2	1,000		2,750	

Continuing Problem (Continued)

Account: Supplies   **Account No.** 14

Date		Item	Post. Ref.	Debit	Credit	Balance Debit	Balance Credit
2014							
July	1	Balance	✓			170	
	18		2	850		1,020	

Account: Prepaid Insurance   **Account No.** 15

Date		Item	Post. Ref.	Debit	Credit	Balance Debit	Balance Credit
2014							
July	1		1	2,700		2,700	

Account: Office Equipment   **Account No.** 17

Date		Item	Post. Ref.	Debit	Credit	Balance Debit	Balance Credit
2014							
July	5		1	7,500		7,500	

Account: Accounts Payable   **Account No.** 21

Date		Item	Post. Ref.	Debit	Credit	Balance Debit	Balance Credit
2014							
July	1	Balance	✓				250
	3		1	250		—	—
	5		1		7,500		7,500
	18		2		850		8,350

Account: Unearned Revenue   **Account No.** 23

Date		Item	Post. Ref.	Debit	Credit	Balance Debit	Balance Credit
2014							
July	3		1		7,200		7,200

Account: Peyton Smith, Capital   **Account No.** 31

Date		Item	Post. Ref.	Debit	Credit	Balance Debit	Balance Credit
2014							
July	1	Balance	✓				4,000
	1		1		5,000		9,000

Continuing Problem (Continued)

Account: Peyton Smith, Drawing   Account No. 32

Date		Item	Post. Ref.	Debit	Credit	Balance Debit	Balance Credit
2014							
July	1	Balance	✓			500	
	31		2	1,250		1,750	

Account: Fees Earned   Account No. 41

Date		Item	Post. Ref.	Debit	Credit	Balance Debit	Balance Credit
2014							
July	1	Balance	✓				6,200
	11		1		1,000		7,200
	16		2		2,000		9,200
	23		2		2,500		11,700
	30		2		1,500		13,200
	31		2		3,000		16,200

Account: Wages Expense   Account No. 50

Date		Item	Post. Ref.	Debit	Credit	Balance Debit	Balance Credit
2014							
July	1	Balance	✓			400	
	14		1	1,200		1,600	
	28		2	1,200		2,800	

Account: Office Rent Expense   Account No. 51

Date		Item	Post. Ref.	Debit	Credit	Balance Debit	Balance Credit
2014							
July	1	Balance	✓			800	
	1		1	1,750		2,550	

Account: Equipment Rent Expense   Account No. 52

Date		Item	Post. Ref.	Debit	Credit	Balance Debit	Balance Credit
2014							
July	1	Balance	✓			675	
	13		1	700		1,375	

Continuing Problem (Continued)

Account: **Utilities Expense**   Account No.   **53**

Date		Item	Post. Ref.	Debit	Credit	Balance	
						Debit	Credit
2014							
July	1	Balance	✓			300	
	27		2	915		1,215	

Account: **Music Expense**   Account No.   **54**

Date		Item	Post. Ref.	Debit	Credit	Balance	
						Debit	Credit
2014							
July	1	Balance	✓			1,590	
	21		2	620		2,210	
	31		2	1,400		3,610	

Account: **Advertising Expense**   Account No.   **55**

Date		Item	Post. Ref.	Debit	Credit	Balance	
						Debit	Credit
2014							
July	1	Balance	✓			500	
	8		1	200		700	
	22		2	800		1,500	

Account: **Supplies Expense**   Account No.   **56**

Date		Item	Post. Ref.	Debit	Credit	Balance	
						Debit	Credit
2014							
July	1	Balance	✓			180	

Account: **Miscellaneous Expense**   Account No.   **59**

Date		Item	Post. Ref.	Debit	Credit	Balance	
						Debit	Credit
2014							
July	1	Balance	✓			415	
	4		1	900		1,315	
	29		2	540		1,855	

Continuing Problem (Concluded)

4.

PS MUSIC Unadjusted Trial Balance July 31, 2014	Debit Balances	Credit Balances
Cash	9,945	
Accounts Receivable	2,750	
Supplies	1,020	
Prepaid Insurance	2,700	
Office Equipment	7,500	
Accounts Payable		8,350
Unearned Revenue		7,200
Peyton Smith, Capital		9,000
Peyton Smith, Drawing	1,750	
Fees Earned		16,200
Music Expense	3,610	
Wages Expense	2,800	
Office Rent Expense	2,550	
Advertising Expense	1,500	
Equipment Rent Expense	1,375	
Utilities Expense	1,215	
Supplies Expense	180	
Miscellaneous Expense	1,855	
	40,750	40,750

CASES & PROJECTS

CP 2–1

Acceptable ethical conduct requires that Gil look for the difference. If Gil cannot find the difference within a reasonable amount of time, he should confer with his supervisor as to what action should be taken so that the financial statements can be prepared by the 5 o'clock deadline. Gil's responsibility to his employer is to act with integrity, objectivity, and due care, so that users of the financial statements will not be misled.

CP 2–2

The following general journal entry should be used to record the receipt of tuition payments received in advance of classes:

Cash...	XXXX	
Unearned Tuition Deposits...		XXXX

Cash is an asset account, and Unearned Tuition Deposits is a liability account. As the classes are taught throughout the term, the unearned tuition deposits become earned revenue.

CP 2–3

The journal is called the book of original entry. It provides a time-ordered history of the transactions that have occurred for the firm. This time-ordered history is very important because it allows one to trace ledger account balances back to the original transactions that created those balances. This is called an "audit trail." If the firm recorded transactions by posting to ledgers directly, it would be nearly impossible to reconstruct actual transactions. The debits and credits would all be separated and accumulated into the ledger balances. Once the transactions become part of the ledger balances, the original transactions would be lost. That is, there would be no audit trail, and any errors that might occur in recording transactions would be almost impossible to trace. Thus, firms first record transaction debits and credits in a journal. These transactions are then posted to the ledger to update the account balances. The journal and ledger are linked using posting references. This allows an analyst to trace the transaction flow forward or backward, depending on the need.

CP 2–4

1. The rules of debit and credit must be memorized. Dot is correct in that the rules of debit and credit could be reversed as long as everyone accepted and abided by the rules. However, the important point is that everyone accepts the rules as the way in which transactions should be recorded. This generates uniformity across the accounting profession and reduces errors and confusion. Since the current rules of debit and credit have been used for centuries, Dot should adapt to the current rules of debit and credit, rather than devise her own.

    The primary reason that all accounts do not have the same rules for increases and decreases is for control of the recording process. The double-entry accounting system, which includes both (1) the rules of debit and credit and (2) the accounting equation, guarantees that (1) debits always equal credits and (2) assets always equal liabilities plus owner's equity. If all increases in the account were recorded by debits, then the control that debits always equal credits would be removed. In addition, the control that the normal balance of assets is a debit would also be removed. The accounting equation would still hold, but the control over recording transactions would be weakened.

    Dot is correct that we could call the left and right sides of an account different terms, such as "LE" or "RE." Again, centuries of tradition dictate the current terminology used. One might note, however, that in Latin, *debere* (debit) means left and *credere* (credit) means right.

2. The accounting system may be designed to capture information about the buying habits of various customers or vendors, such as the quantity normally ordered, average amount ordered, number of returns, etc. Thus, in a sense, there can be other "sides" of (information about) a transaction that are recorded by the accounting system. Such information would be viewed as supplemental to the basic double-entry accounting system.

CP 2–5

a. Although the titles and numbers of accounts may differ, depending on how expenses are classified, the following accounts would be adequate for recording transaction data for Eagle Caddy Service:

Balance Sheet Accounts		Income Statement Accounts	
1. Assets		**4. Revenue**	
11	Cash	41	Service Revenue
12	Accounts Receivable		
13	Supplies		**5. Expenses**
		51	Rent Expense
2. Liabilities		52	Supplies Expense
21	Accounts Payable	53	Wages Expense
		54	Utilities Expense
3. Owner's Equity		55	Miscellaneous Expense
31	Cory Neece, Capital		
32	Cory Neece, Drawing		

b.

EAGLE CADDY SERVICE Income Statement For Month Ended June 30, 2014		
Service revenue		$11,400
Expenses:		
Rent expense	$3,500	
Supplies expense	1,925	
Wages expense	850	
Utilities expense	340	
Miscellaneous expense	395	
Total expenses		7,010
Net income		$ 4,390

Note to Instructors: Students may have prepared slightly different income statements, depending upon the titles of the major expense classifications chosen. Regardless of the classification of expenses, however, the total sales, total expenses, and net income should be as presented above.

T accounts are not required for the preparation of the income statement of Eagle Caddy Service. The following presentation illustrates one solution using T accounts. Alternative solutions are possible if students used different accounts. In presenting the following T account solution, instructors may wish to emphasize the advantages of using T accounts (or a journal and four-column accounts) when a large number of transactions must be recorded.

CP 2–5 (Continued)

		Cash		11
2014			2014	
June	1	2,000	June 1	500
	15	5,400	2	750
	30	4,200	3	600
	30	1,500	17	1,000
			20	2,400
			28	395
			30	340
			30	850
Bal.		6,265		

		Accounts Receivable		12
2014			2014	
June	25	1,800	June 30	1,500
Bal.		300		

		Supplies		13
2014			2014	
June	2	750	June 30	1,925
	7	1,000		
	22	850		
Bal.		675		

		Accounts Payable		21
2014			2014	
June	17	1,000	June 3	2,400
	20	2,400	7	1,000
			22	850
			Bal.	850

	Cory Neece, Capital		31
		2014	
		June 1	2,000

	Service Revenue		41
		2014	
		June 15	5,400
		25	1,800
		30	4,200
		Bal.	11,400

		Rent Expense		51
2014				
June	1	500		
	3	3,000		
Bal.		3,500		

		Supplies Expense		52
2014				
June	30	1,925		

		Wages Expense		53
2014				
June	30	850		

		Utilities Expense		54
2014				
June	30	340		

		Miscellaneous Expense		55
2014				
June	28	395		

CP 2–5 (Concluded)

c.   **$6,265, computed in the following manner:**

Cash receipts:

Initial investment..	$2,000	
Cash sales..	9,600	
Collections on accounts..	1,500	
Total cash receipts during June................................		$13,100

Cash disbursements:

Rent expense ($500 + $600 + $2,400).............................	$3,500	
Supplies purchased for cash...	750	
Wages expense...	850	
Payment for supplies on account..................................	1,000	
Utilities expense...	340	
Miscellaneous expense..	395	
Total cash disbursements during June......................		6,835
Cash on hand according to records*.....................................		$ 6,265

* If the student used T accounts in completing part (b), or this part, this amount ($6,265) should agree with the balance of the cash account.

d.   **The difference of $90 ($6,265 – $6,175) between the cash on hand according to records ($6,265) and the cash on hand according to the count ($6,175) could be due to many factors, including errors in the record keeping and withdrawals made by Cory.**

CP 2–6

Note to Instructors: **The purpose of this activity is to familiarize students with the job opportunities available in accounting or in fields that require (or prefer) the employee to have some knowledge of accounting.**

An example of an advertisement for an accounting job is shown on the next page.

Source: CareerBuilders.com

CP 2–6 (Continued)

ACCOUNTING MANAGER
Accountants One

JOB SNAPSHOT:

Location: North East metro Atlanta area, GA

Base Pay: $60,000–$65,000/Year

Other Pay: Excellent corporate benefits!

Employee Type: Full-Time

Industry: Manufacturing

Manages Others: Yes

Job Type: Accounting

Education: 4-Year Degree

Experience: 3 to 8 years

Travel: None

Relocation Covered: No

Post Date: 5/9/2011

Contact Information

Contact:

Phone: 555-395-6969

Ref ID: RD5694

DESCRIPTION:

A growing and well-established Atlanta company has asked us to recruit an Accounting Manager. This person will report to the Controller and be responsible for all day-to-day management of the department.

ESSENTIAL FUNCTIONS:

- Provide management with timely and accurate data and reports
- Responsible for accuracy of accounting entries, monthly P & L and Balance Sheets
- Perform analysis of financial reports and performance
- Personally conduct and manage collection activities
- Process biweekly employee payroll in an accurate and timely manner
- Supervise, train, and develop Accounts Payable Coordinator and additional accounting staff as necessary
- Interact with vendors and customers in a payables and receivables management process
- Initiate bank wires and ACH transfers
- Interact with internal and external auditors in completing audits
- Perform other duties as assigned

REQUIREMENTS:

- BS degree in Accounting, successful completion of CPA exams is a plus. Minimum 3 years experience as an accounting manager or supervisor in a manufacturing environment is absolutely required! Working knowledge of Microsoft Dynamics 10.0 is very strongly preferred!
- Exceptional analytical and problem-solving abilities
- Must be well-versed in the financial aspects of inventory as well as state and federal financial regulations
- Must possess the ability to professionally interact with internal and external customers
- Excellent written and verbal communication skills
- Proficient knowledge of Excel and Word
- Experience with EXACT software as well as LOTUS Notes would be a plus
- Ability to analyze financial data and prepare financial reports, statements, and projections

CLIENT IS INTERVIEWING FOR AN IMMEDIATE HIRE!

NO CALLS PLEASE, AND LOCAL CANDIDATES ONLY need apply by emailing confidential resume as soon as possible. All qualified will be contacted immediately.

CP 2–6 (Continued)
An example of a job advertisement requiring accounting knowledge is as follows:
Source: CareerBuilders.com

EAST REGION FINANCIAL INSTITUTIONS DIRECTOR
Jefferson Wells

JOB SNAPSHOT:

Location: Atlanta, GA 30301	Experience: Not Specified
Employee Type: Full-Time	Travel: Up to 50%
Industry: Accounting—Finance	Post Date: 5/17/2011
Manages Others: Yes	Contact Information
Job Type: Accounting	Ref ID: 1294

DESCRIPTION:

Directors at Jefferson Wells are crucial to our success. They bring a wealth of experience and knowledge to our various service offerings and are responsible for ensuring the development and execution of the strategic plan for their respective market. Their goal is to drive the development of the Solution Area with the goal of significant growth and profitability. They provide technical expertise and leverage a network of clients and contacts. The Director plays a critical role in the leadership and development of our Engagement Managers and Professional Consultants.

Directors create and implement the Marketing Operating Plan, as well as create revenue strategies to meet revenue targets. They drive development and execution of effective client solutions to key targets. Directors work closely with Business Development Managers on proposals and business development calls. Directors serve as the business advisor to clients to ensure quality assurance standards are met. They manage, direct, and monitor multiple client services teams on client engagements. They maintain strong communication with clients to manage expectations, ensure client satisfaction and adherence to deadlines. Other key success factors include:

- Solid history of excellent performance, management capability, and revenue growth
- Proven ability to drive a business including selling, work plan development, proposal writing, and overseeing service delivery
- Management experience of a large group of professionals of 10 or more, with demonstrated history of building a solution area—hiring, training, and mentoring
- Demonstrated ability in developing meaningful client relationships, and capacity to bring and leverage relationships to Jefferson Wells

The East Region Financial Institutions Director works under the general supervision of the East Region Vice President and has a dotted line relationship to the Managing Directors in the region. This Director will be recognized as a financial institution industry leader with expertise in the areas of commercial and residential loan origination/servicing, deposit operations, and the corresponding GAAP accounting requirements as well as regulatory compliance. He/she will be accountable for overseeing the following projects/activities at Jefferson Wells' financial institution clients in one or all of the following areas:

- Regulatory Compliance including Loan Compliance and BSA/AML
- Troubled Debt Restructuring
- Enterprise Risk Management
- Loan Reviews (Commercial and/or Consumer) and Credit Risk
- FAS 15 and FAS 114
- Foreclosure Application Processing
- Loss Mitigation
- Financial Process Documentation and Improvement
- Policy and Procedure Development

CP 2–6 (Concluded)

Jefferson Wells (www.jeffersonwells.com) delivers professional services in the areas of internal audit and controls, technology risk management, tax, and finance and accounting-related services. The firm's unique, agile structure aligns experienced professionals with proven processes to deliver pragmatic and cost-effective results. Headquartered in Milwaukee, Jefferson Wells serves clients, including Fortune 500 and Global 1000 companies, from offices worldwide. Jefferson Wells is an independently operating, wholly owned subsidiary of Manpower Inc. (NYSE: MAN).

Jefferson Wells is an Equal Opportunity Employer.

REQUIREMENTS:

- Minimum 12 years or more of clearly progressive, professional development in the general area of accounting services/internal auditing, including a mix of public accounting and managerial level financial institution industry experience
- Bachelor's degree in accounting
- CPA, CIA, and/or MBA preferred
- Consulting delivery experience
- Strong leadership skills
- Senior-level internal compliance experience within a large financial institution
- Willingness and ability to travel

CHAPTER 3
THE ADJUSTING PROCESS

DISCUSSION QUESTIONS

1. **a.** Under cash-basis accounting, revenues are reported in the period in which cash is received and expenses are reported in the period in which cash is paid.

   b. Under accrual-basis accounting, revenues are reported in the period in which they are earned and expenses are reported in the same period as the revenues to which they relate.

2. The matching concept is related to the accrual basis of accounting.

3. Adjusting entries are necessary at the end of an accounting period to bring the ledger up to date.

4. Adjusting entries bring the ledger up to date as a normal part of the accounting cycle. Correcting entries correct errors in the ledger.

5. Four different categories of adjusting entries include prepaid expenses (deferred expenses), unearned revenues (deferred revenues), accrued expenses (accrued liabilities), and accrued revenues (accrued assets).

6. Statement (a): Increases the balance of a revenue account.

7. Statement (b): Increases the balance of an expense account.

8. Yes, because every adjusting entry affects expenses or revenues.

9. **a.** The rights acquired represent an asset.

   b. The justification for debiting Rent Expense is that when the ledger is summarized in a trial balance at the end of the month and statements are prepared, the rent will have become an expense. Hence, no adjusting entry will be necessary.

10. **a.** The portion of the cost of a fixed asset deducted from revenue of the period is debited to Depreciation Expense. It is the expired cost for the period. The reduction in the fixed asset account is recorded by a credit to Accumulated Depreciation rather than to the fixed asset account. The use of the contra asset account facilitates the presentation of original cost and accumulated depreciation on the balance sheet.

    b. Depreciation Expense—debit balance; Accumulated Depreciation—credit balance.

    c. No, it is not customary for the balances of the two accounts to be equal in amount.

    d. Depreciation Expense appears on the income statement; Accumulated Depreciation appears on the balance sheet.

PRACTICE EXERCISES

PE 3–1A

a.	Yes	c.	No	e.	Yes
b.	No	d.	Yes	f.	Yes

PE 3–1B

a.	No	c.	Yes	e.	No
b.	No	d.	No	f.	Yes

PE 3–2A

a.	Unearned revenue	c.	Accrued revenue
b.	Prepaid expense	d.	Accrued expense

PE 3–2B

a.	Unearned revenue	c.	Accrued expense
b.	Accrued revenue	d.	Prepaid expense

PE 3–3A

Supplies Expense	4,250	
Supplies		4,250
Supplies used ($1,975 + $4,125 − $1,850).		

PE 3–3B

Insurance Expense	15,140	
Prepaid Insurance		15,140
Insurance expired ($9,600 + $12,900 − $7,360).		

PE 3–4A

Unearned Fees	44,825	
Fees Earned		44,825
Fees earned ($78,500 − $33,675).		

PE 3–4B

Unearned Rent	11,025	
Rent Revenue		11,025
Rent earned [($18,900 ÷ 12 months) × 7 months].		

PE 3–5A

Accounts Receivable	12,840	
Fees Earned		12,840
Accrued fees.		

PE 3–5B

Accounts Receivable	17,555	
Fees Earned		17,555
Accrued fees.		

PE 3–6A

Salaries Expense	9,750	
Salaries Payable		9,750
Accrued salaries [($16,250 ÷ 5 days) × 3 days].		

PE 3–6B

Salaries Expense	23,000	
Salaries Payable		23,000
Accrued salaries [($27,600 ÷ 6 days) × 5 days].		

PE 3–7A

Depreciation Expense	9,100	
Accumulated Depreciation—Equipment		9,100
Depreciation on equipment.		

PE 3–7B

Depreciation Expense	7,700	
Accumulated Depreciation—Equipment		7,700
Depreciation on equipment.		

PE 3–8A

a. Revenues were understated by $44,500.

b. Expenses were understated by $13,100 ($5,800 + $7,300).

c. Net income was understated by $31,400 ($44,500 – $13,100).

PE 3–8B

a. Revenues were understated by $6,600.

b. Expenses were understated by $10,400 ($1,400 + $9,000).

c. Net income was overstated by $3,800 ($10,400 – $6,600).

PE 3–9A

a. The totals are unequal. The debit total is higher by $900 ($9,800 – $8,900).

b. The totals are equal, since the adjusting entry was omitted.

PE 3–9B

a. The totals are equal even though the credit should have been to Wages Payable instead of Accounts Payable.

b. The totals are unequal. The credit total is higher by $27 ($1,152 – $1,125).

PE 3–10A

a.

HEMLOCK COMPANY Income Statements For Years Ended December 31				
	2014		2013	
	Amount	Percent	Amount	Percent
Fees earned	$725,000	100%	$615,000	100%
Operating expenses	435,000	60%	356,700	58%
Operating income	$290,000	40%	$258,300	42%

b. An unfavorable trend of increasing operating expenses and decreasing operating income is indicated.

PE 3–10B

a.

CORNEA COMPANY Income Statements For Years Ended December 31				
	2014		2013	
	Amount	Percent	Amount	Percent
Fees earned	$1,640,000	100%	$1,300,000	100%
Operating expenses	869,200	53%	715,000	55%
Operating income	$ 770,800	47%	$ 585,000	45%

b. A favorable trend of decreasing operating expenses and increasing operating income is indicated.

EXERCISES

Ex. 3–1

1.	Prepaid expense	5.	Unearned revenue
2.	Accrued revenue	6.	Prepaid expense
3.	Unearned revenue	7.	Accrued expense
4.	Accrued expense	8.	Accrued expense

Ex. 3–2

Account	Answer
Accounts Receivable.............................	Normally requires adjustment (AR).
Cash..	Does not normally require adjustment.
Interest Expense...................................	Normally requires adjustment (AE).
Interest Receivable...............................	Normally requires adjustment (AR).
Johann Atkins, Capital...........................	Does not normally require adjustment.
Land..	Does not normally require adjustment.
Office Equipment...................................	Does not normally require adjustment.
Prepaid Rent..	Normally requires adjustment (PE).
Supplies..	Normally requires adjustment (PE).
Unearned Fees.....................................	Normally requires adjustment (UR).
Wages Expense....................................	Normally requires adjustment (AE).

Ex. 3–3

Supplies Expense	1,559	
Supplies		1,559
Supplies used ($2,389 – $830).		

Ex. 3–4

$5,810 ($1,560 + $4,250).

Ex. 3–5

a. Insurance expense (or expenses) will be understated. Net income will be overstated.

b. Prepaid insurance (or assets) will be overstated. Owner's equity will be overstated.

Ex. 3–6

a.
Insurance Expense	16,450	
Prepaid Insurance		16,450
Insurance expired.		

b.
Insurance Expense	16,450	
Prepaid Insurance		16,450
Insurance expired ($21,700 – $5,250).		

Ex. 3–7

a.
Insurance Expense	16,400	
Prepaid Insurance		16,400
Insurance expired ($12,000 + $18,000 – $13,600).		

b.
Insurance Expense	16,400	
Prepaid Insurance		16,400
Insurance expired.		

Ex. 3–8

Unearned Fees	25,200	
Fees Earned		25,200
Fees earned ($37,500 – $12,300).		

Ex. 3–9

a.   Rent revenue (or revenues) will be understated. Net income will be understated.

b.   Unearned rent (liabilities) will be overstated. Owner's equity at the end of the period will be understated.

Ex. 3–10

a.
Accounts Receivable	8,450	
Fees Earned		8,450
Accrued fees.		

b.   No. If the cash basis of accounting is used, revenues are recognized only when the cash is received. Therefore, earned but unbilled revenues would not be recognized in the accounts, and no adjusting entry would be necessary.

Ex. 3–11

a.	Unearned Fees	71,600	
	Fees Earned		71,600
	Unearned fees earned during year.		

b.	Accounts Receivable	47,400	
	Fees Earned		47,400
	Accrued fees earned.		

Ex. 3–12

a.   Fees earned (or revenues) will be understated. Net income will be understated.

b.   Accounts (fees) receivable (or assets) will be understated. Owner's equity will be understated.

Ex. 3–13

a.	Salaries Expense	7,050	
	Salaries Payable		7,050
	Accrued salaries [($11,750 ÷ 5 days) × 3 days].		

b.	Salaries Expense	9,400	
	Salaries Payable		9,400
	Accrued salaries [($11,750 ÷ 5 days) × 4 days].		

Ex. 3–14

$66,075 ($73,250 – $7,175)

Ex. 3–15

a.   Salary expense (or expenses) will be understated. Net income will be overstated.

b.   Salaries payable (or liabilities) will be understated. Owner's equity will be overstated.

Ex. 3–16

a.   Salary expense (or expenses) will be overstated. Net income will be understated.

b.   The balance sheet will be correct. This is because salaries payable has been satisfied, and the net income errors have offset each other. Thus, owner's equity is correct.

Ex. 3–17

a.

Taxes Expense	21,600	
Prepaid Taxes		21,600
Prepaid taxes expired [($28,800 ÷ 12 months) × 9 months].		
Taxes Expense	49,800	
Taxes Payable		49,800
Accrued taxes.		

b. $71,400 ($21,600 + $49,800)

Ex. 3–18

Depreciation Expense	6,760	
Accumulated Depreciation—Equipment		6,760
Depreciation on equipment.		

Ex. 3–19

a. $650,000 ($1,375,000 – $725,000)

b.   No. Depreciation is an allocation of the cost of the equipment to the periods benefiting from its use. It does not necessarily relate to value or loss of value.

Ex. 3–20

a. $7,630 million ($16,259 – $8,629)

b.   No. Depreciation is an allocation method, not a valuation method. That is, depreciation allocates the cost of a fixed asset over its useful life. Depreciation does not attempt to measure market values, which may vary significantly from year to year.

Ex. 3–21

Income: $3,947 million ($2,054 + $1,893)

Ex. 3–22

a. $560 million

b.   45.1% ($560 ÷ $1,242)

Ex. 3–23

		Error (a)		Error (b)	
		Over-stated	Under-stated	Over-stated	Under-stated
1.	Revenue for the year would be.................	$ 0	$23,250	$ 0	$ 0
2.	Expenses for the year would be................	0	0	0	4,000
3.	Net income for the year would be..............	0	23,250	4,000	0
4.	Assets at August 31 would be..................	0	0	0	0
5.	Liabilities at August 31 would be..............	23,250	0	0	4,000
6.	Owner's equity at August 31 would be.......	0	23,250	4,000	0

Ex. 3–24

$132,900 ($113,650 + $23,250 – $4,000)

Ex. 3–25

a.

Depreciation Expense	13,900	
Accumulated Depreciation—Equipment		13,900
Depreciation on equipment.		

b. (1) Depreciation expense would be understated. Net income would be overstated.

(2) Accumulated depreciation would be understated, and total assets would be overstated. Owner's equity would be overstated.

Ex. 3–26

1.	Accounts Receivable	3	
	Fees Earned		3
	Accrued fees earned.		

2.	Supplies Expense	1	
	Supplies		1
	Supplies used.		

3.	Insurance Expense	6	
	Prepaid Insurance		6
	Insurance expired.		

4.	Depreciation Expense	2	
	Accumulated Depreciation—Equipment		2
	Equipment depreciation.		

5.	Wages Expense	1	
	Wages Payable		1
	Accrued wages.		

Ex. 3–27

1. The accountant debited Accounts Receivable for $5,000 but did not credit Laundry Revenue. This adjusting entry represents accrued laundry revenue.

2. The accountant debited rather than credited Laundry Supplies for $3,000.

3. The accountant credited the prepaid insurance account for $3,600, but debited the insurance expense account for only $600.

4. The accountant credited Laundry Equipment for the depreciation expense of $13,000, instead of crediting the accumulated depreciation account.

5. The accountant did not debit Wages Expense for $1,000.

The corrected adjusted trial balance is shown below.

EVA'S LAUNDRY Adjusted Trial Balance May 31, 2014		
	Debit Balances	**Credit Balances**
Cash	7,500	
Accounts Receivable	23,250	
Laundry Supplies	750	
Prepaid Insurance	1,600	
Laundry Equipment	190,000	
Accumulated Depreciation—Laundry Equipment		61,000
Accounts Payable		9,600
Wages Payable		1,000
Eva Bruns, Capital		110,300
Eva Bruns, Drawing	28,775	
Laundry Revenue		187,100
Wages Expense	50,200	
Rent Expense	25,575	
Utilities Expense	18,500	
Depreciation Expense	13,000	
Laundry Supplies Expense	3,000	
Insurance Expense	3,600	
Miscellaneous Expense	3,250	
	369,000	369,000

Ex. 3–28

a. $420 million increase ($1,907 − $1,487)

   28.2% ($420 ÷ $1,487) increase

b. Year 2: 10.0% ($1,907 ÷ $19,014)
   Year 1: 7.8% ($1,487 ÷ $19,176)

c. The net income increased during Year 2 by $420 million from Year 1. Net income as a percent of net sales also increased from 7.8% in Year 1 to 10.0% in Year 2. Both of these results are favorable trends for Nike.

Ex. 3–29

a. Dell Inc.

	Amount	Percent
Net sales	$61,494	100.0%
Cost of goods sold	(50,098)	81.5%
Operating expenses	(7,963)	12.9%
Operating income (loss)	$ 3,433	5.6%

b. Hewlett-Packard Company (HP)

	Amount	Percent
Net sales	$126,033	100.0%
Cost of goods sold	(96,089)	76.2%
Operating expenses	(18,465)	14.7%
Operating income (loss)	$ 11,479	9.1%

c. Hewlett-Packard (HP) is more profitable than Dell. Specifically, HP's cost of goods sold of 76.2% is 5.3% (81.5% − 76.2%) less than Dell's cost of goods sold. This is partially offset by HP's higher operating expenses of 14.7% as compared to Dell's operating expenses of 12.9%. The net result is that HP generates an operating income of 9.1% of sales, while Dell generates operating income of 5.6% of sales. Dell must improve its operations if it is to remain competitive with HP.

PROBLEMS

Prob. 3–1A

1. a.

Supplies Expense	4,680	
Supplies		4,680
Supplies used ($6,880 – $2,200).		

b.

Unearned Rent	2,300	
Rent Revenue		2,300
Rent earned ($9,200 ÷ 4 months).		

c.

Wages Expense	1,850	
Wages Payable		1,850
Accrued wages.		

d.

Accounts Receivable	11,700	
Fees Earned		11,700
Accrued fees earned.		

e.

Depreciation Expense	3,500	
Accumulated Depreciation—Office Equipment		3,500
Depreciation expense.		

2. Adjusting entries are a planned part of the accounting process to update the accounts. Correcting entries are not planned, but arise only when necessary to correct errors.

Prob. 3–2A

1.

a.

Accounts Receivable	9,150	
Fees Earned		9,150
Accrued fees earned.		

b.

Supplies Expense	2,325	
Supplies		2,325
Supplies used ($3,000 – $675).		

c.

Rent Expense	5,000	
Prepaid Rent		5,000
Prepaid rent expired.		

d.

Depreciation Expense	3,300	
Accumulated Depreciation—Equipment		3,300
Equipment depreciation.		

e.

Unearned Fees	7,500	
Fees Earned		7,500
Fees earned ($10,500 – $3,000).		

f.

Wages Expense	3,100	
Wages Payable		3,100
Accrued wages.		

2. Fees Earned would be understated by $9,150; Wages Expense would be understated by $3,100; and net income would be understated by $6,050 ($9,150 – $3,100).

3. Accounts Receivable would be understated by $9,150; total assets would be understated by $9,150; Wages Payable would be understated by $3,100; total liabilities would be understated by $3,100; owner's capital would be understated by $6,050 ($9,150 – $3,100); and total liabilities and owner's equity would be understated by $9,150 ($3,100 + $6,050).

4. There is no effect on the "Net increase or decrease in cash" on the statement of cash flows, since adjusting entries do not affect cash.

Prob. 3–3A

1.

a.	Accounts Receivable	12,700	
	Fees Earned		12,700
	Accrued fees earned.		

b.	Supplies Expense	17,425	
	Supplies		17,425
	Supplies used ($21,600 – $4,175).		

c.	Depreciation Expense	7,400	
	Accumulated Depreciation—Equipment		7,400
	Equipment depreciation.		

d.	Unearned Fees	14,200	
	Fees Earned		14,200
	Fees earned.		

e.	Wages Expense	1,100	
	Wages Payable		1,100
	Accrued wages.		

2.

Revenues........................	$393,000	
Expenses........................	301,800	($126,000 + $96,000 + $69,000 + $10,800)
Net Income....................	$ 91,200	

3.

Revenues........................	$419,900	($393,000 + $12,700 + $14,200)
Expenses........................	327,725	($301,800 + $17,425 + $7,400 + $1,100)
Net Income....................	$ 92,175	

4. The effect of the adjusting entries on Amy Wolf, Capital is the difference in net income in (2) and (3) of $975 ($92,175 – $91,200), which increases Amy Wolf, Capital.

Prob. 3–4A

2014				
Nov.	30	Supplies Expense	8,850	
		Supplies		8,850
		Supplies used ($11,250 – $2,400).		
	30	Insurance Expense	10,400	
		Prepaid Insurance		10,400
		Insurance expired ($14,250 – $3,850).		
	30	Depreciation Expense—Equipment	11,600	
		Accumulated Depreciation—Equipment		11,600
		Equipment depreciation		
		($106,100 – $94,500).		
	30	Depreciation Expense—Automobiles	7,300	
		Accumulated Depreciation—Automobiles		7,300
		Automobile depreciation		
		($62,050 – $54,750).		
	30	Utilities Expense	1,200	
		Accounts Payable		1,200
		Accrued utilities expense		
		($26,130 – $24,930, or $14,100 – $12,900).		
	30	Salary Expense	8,100	
		Salaries Payable		8,100
		Accrued salary ($525,000 – $516,900).		
	30	Unearned Service Fees	9,000	
		Service Fees Earned		9,000
		Service fees earned ($18,000 – $9,000, or		
		$742,800 – $733,800).		

Prob. 3–5A

1.

a.	Insurance Expense	1,800	
	Prepaid Insurance		1,800
	Insurance expired ($7,200 – $5,400).		

b.	Supplies Expense	1,605	
	Supplies		1,605
	Supplies used ($1,980 – $375).		

c.	Depreciation Expense—Building	6,000	
	Accumulated Depreciation—Building		6,000
	Building depreciation.		

d.	Depreciation Expense—Equipment	3,000	
	Accumulated Depreciation—Equipment		3,000
	Equipment depreciation.		

e.	Unearned Rent	5,400	
	Rent Revenue		5,400
	Rent revenue earned ($6,750 – $1,350).		

f.	Salaries and Wages Expense	2,900	
	Salaries and Wages Payable		2,900
	Accrued salaries and wages.		

g.	Accounts Receivable	18,600	
	Fees Earned		18,600
	Accrued fees earned.		

Prob. 3–5A (Concluded)

2.

DICKENS COMPANY Adjusted Trial Balance October 31, 2014		
	Debit Balances	Credit Balances
Cash	7,500	
Accounts Receivable	57,000	
Prepaid Insurance	5,400	
Supplies	375	
Land	112,500	
Building	150,250	
Accumulated Depreciation—Building		93,550
Equipment	135,300	
Accumulated Depreciation—Equipment		100,950
Accounts Payable		12,150
Unearned Rent		1,350
Salaries and Wages Payable		2,900
Monica Baker, Capital		221,000
Monica Baker, Drawing	15,000	
Fees Earned		343,200
Rent Revenue		5,400
Salaries and Wages Expense	196,270	
Utilities Expense	42,375	
Advertising Expense	22,800	
Repairs Expense	17,250	
Depreciation Expense—Building	6,000	
Depreciation Expense—Equipment	3,000	
Insurance Expense	1,800	
Supplies Expense	1,605	
Miscellaneous Expense	6,075	
	780,500	780,500

Prob. 3–6A

1.

a.

Supplies Expense	2,750	
Supplies		2,750
Supplies used.		

b.

Accounts Receivable	23,700	
Fees Earned		23,700
Accrued fees earned.		

c.

Depreciation Expense	1,800	
Accumulated Depreciation—Equipment		1,800
Equipment depreciation.		

d.

Wages Expense	1,400	
Wages Payable		1,400
Accrued wages.		

2.

	Net Income	Total Assets	=	Total Liabilities	+	Total Owner's Equity
Reported amounts	$120,000	$750,000		$300,000		$450,000
Corrections:						
Adjustment (a)	–2,750	–2,750		0		–2,750
Adjustment (b)	+23,700	+23,700		0		+23,700
Adjustment (c)	–1,800	–1,800		0		–1,800
Adjustment (d)	–1,400	0		+1,400		–1,400
Corrected amounts	$137,750	$769,150		$301,400		$467,750

Prob. 3–1B

1.

a.

Accounts Receivable	19,750	
Fees Earned		19,750
Accrued fees earned.		

b.

Supplies Expense	8,150	
Supplies		8,150
Supplies used ($12,300 – $4,150).		

c.

Wages Expense	2,700	
Wages Payable		2,700
Accrued wages.		

d.

Unearned Rent	3,000	
Rent Revenue		3,000
Rent earned ($9,000 ÷ 3 months).		

e.

Depreciation Expense	3,200	
Accumulated Depreciation—Equipment		3,200
Depreciation expense.		

2. Adjusting entries are a planned part of the accounting process to update the accounts. Correcting entries are not planned, but arise only when necessary to correct errors.

Prob. 3–2B

1.

a.

Supplies Expense	2,620	
Supplies		2,620
Supplies used ($3,170 – $550).		

b.

Depreciation Expense	1,675	
Accumulated Depreciation—Equipment		1,675
Depreciation for year.		

c.

Rent Expense	8,500	
Prepaid Rent		8,500
Rent expired.		

d.

Wages Expense	2,000	
Wages Payable		2,000
Accrued wages.		

e.

Unearned Fees	6,000	
Fees Earned		6,000
Fees earned ($10,000 – $4,000).		

f.

Accounts Receivable	5,380	
Fees Earned		5,380
Accrued fees.		

2. Fees Earned would be understated by $6,000; Depreciation Expense would be understated by $1,675; and net income would be understated by $4,325 ($6,000 – $1,675).

3. Accumulated Depreciation—Equipment would be understated by $1,675; total assets would be overstated by $1,675; Unearned Fees would be overstated by $6,000; total liabilities would be overstated by $6,000; owner's capital would be understated by $4,325 ($6,000 – $1,675); and total liabilities and owner's equity would be overstated by $1,675 ($6,000 – $4,325).

4. There is no effect on the "Net increase or decrease in cash" on the statement of cash flows, since adjusting entries do not affect cash.

Prob. 3–3B

1.

a.

Supplies Expense	5,820	
Supplies		5,820
Supplies used ($7,200 – $1,380).		

b.

Accounts Receivable	3,900	
Fees Earned		3,900
Accrued fees earned.		

c.

Depreciation Expense	3,000	
Accumulated Depreciation—Equipment		3,000
Equipment depreciation.		

d.

Wages Expense	2,475	
Wages Payable		2,475
Accrued wages.		

e.

Unearned Fees	14,140	
Fees Earned		14,140
Fees earned.		

2.   Revenues........................ $305,800
        Expenses........................ 261,800 ($157,800 + $55,000 + $42,000 + $7,000)
        Net Income..................... $ 44,000

3.   Revenues........................ $323,840 ($305,800 + $3,900 + $14,140)
        Expenses........................ 273,095 ($261,800 + $5,820 + $3,000 + $2,475)
        Net Income..................... $ 50,745

4. The effect of the adjusting entries on Diana Keck, Capital is the difference
in net income in (3) and (2) of $6,745 ($50,745 – $44,000), which would increase
Diana Keck, Capital.

Prob. 3–4B

2014				
Mar.	31	Supplies Expense	4,025	
		Supplies		4,025
		Supplies used ($6,200 – $2,175).		
	31	Insurance Expense	7,850	
		Prepaid Insurance		7,850
		Insurance expired ($9,000 – $1,150).		
	31	Depreciation Expense—Buildings	9,500	
		Accumulated Depreciation—Buildings		9,500
		Depreciation ($61,000 – $51,500).		
	31	Depreciation Expense—Trucks	5,000	
		Accumulated Depreciation—Trucks		5,000
		Depreciation ($17,000 – $12,000).		
	31	Utilities Expense	1,830	
		Accounts Payable		1,830
		Accrued utilities expense		
		($8,750 – $6,920, or $8,030 – $6,200).		
	31	Salary Expense	1,400	
		Salaries Payable		1,400
		Accrued salaries ($81,400 – $80,000).		
	31	Unearned Service Fees	6,650	
		Service Fees Earned		6,650
		Service fees earned ($10,500 – $3,850, or		
		$169,330 – $162,680).		

Prob. 3–5B

1.

a.	Depreciation Expense—Building	6,400	
	Accumulated Depreciation—Building		6,400
	Building depreciation.		

b.	Depreciation Expense—Equipment	2,800	
	Accumulated Depreciation—Equipment		2,800
	Equipment depreciation.		

c.	Salaries and Wages Expense	900	
	Salaries and Wages Payable		900
	Accrued salaries and wages.		

d.	Insurance Expense	4,500	
	Prepaid Insurance		4,500
	Insurance expired ($6,000 – $1,500).		

e.	Accounts Receivable	10,200	
	Fees Earned		10,200
	Accrued fees earned.		

f.	Supplies Expense	1,110	
	Supplies		1,110
	Supplies used ($1,725 – $615).		

g.	Unearned Rent	3,300	
	Rent Revenue		3,300
	Rent revenue earned ($3,600 – $300).		

Prob. 3–5B (Concluded)

2.

REECE FINANCIAL SERVICES CO. Adjusted Trial Balance July 31, 2014		
	Debit Balances	Credit Balances
Cash	10,200	
Accounts Receivable	44,950	
Prepaid Insurance	1,500	
Supplies	615	
Land	50,000	
Building	155,750	
Accumulated Depreciation—Building		69,250
Equipment	45,000	
Accumulated Depreciation—Equipment		20,450
Accounts Payable		3,750
Unearned Rent		300
Salaries and Wages Payable		900
Joni Reece, Capital		153,550
Joni Reece, Drawing	8,000	
Fees Earned		168,800
Rent Revenue		3,300
Salaries and Wages Expense	57,750	
Utilities Expense	14,100	
Advertising Expense	7,500	
Depreciation Expense—Building	6,400	
Repairs Expense	6,100	
Insurance Expense	4,500	
Depreciation Expense—Equipment	2,800	
Supplies Expense	1,110	
Miscellaneous Expense	4,025	
	420,300	420,300

Prob. 3–6B

1.

a.

Accounts Receivable	31,900	
Fees Earned		31,900
Accrued fees earned.		

b.

Depreciation Expense	7,500	
Accumulated Depreciation—Equipment		7,500
Equipment depreciation.		

c.

Wages Expense	5,200	
Wages Payable		5,200
Accrued wages.		

d.

Supplies Expense	3,000	
Supplies		3,000
Supplies used.		

2.

	Net Income	Total Assets	=	Total Liabilities	+	Total Owner's Equity
Reported amounts	$112,500	$650,000		$225,000		$425,000
Corrections:						
Adjustment (a)	+31,900	+31,900		0		+31,900
Adjustment (b)	–7,500	–7,500		0		–7,500
Adjustment (c)	–5,200	0		+5,200		–5,200
Adjustment (d)	–3,000	–3,000		0		–3,000
Corrected amounts	$128,700	$671,400		$230,200		$441,200

CONTINUING PROBLEM

1.

JOURNAL

Page _____ 3

Date		Description	Post. Ref.	Debit	Credit
2014		**Adjusting Entries**			
July	31	Accounts Receivable	12	1,400	
		Fees Earned	41		1,400
		Accrued fees earned (115 hrs. –			
		80 hrs.) × $40 = $1,400.			
	31	Supplies Expense	56	745	
		Supplies	14		745
		Supplies used ($1,020 – $275).			
	31	Insurance Expense	57	225	
		Prepaid Insurance	15		225
		Insurance expired ($2,700 ÷			
		12 months) = $225 per month.			
	31	Depreciation Expense	58	50	
		Accum. Depr.—Office Equipment	18		50
		Office equipment depreciation.			
	31	Unearned Revenue	23	3,600	
		Fees Earned	41		3,600
		Fees earned ($7,200 ÷ 2 months).			
	31	Wages Expense	50	140	
		Wages Payable	22		140
		Accrued wages.			

3-28

Continuing Problem (Continued)

2.

Account: **Cash**   Account No. **11**

Date		Item	Post. Ref.	Debit	Credit	Balance Debit	Balance Credit
2014							
July	1	Balance	✓			3,920	
	1		1	5,000		8,920	
	1		1		1,750	7,170	
	1		1		2,700	4,470	
	2		1	1,000		5,470	
	3		1	7,200		12,670	
	3		1		250	12,420	
	4		1		900	11,520	
	8		1		200	11,320	
	11		1	1,000		12,320	
	13		1		700	11,620	
	14		1		1,200	10,420	
	16		2	2,000		12,420	
	21		2		620	11,800	
	22		2		800	11,000	
	23		2	750		11,750	
	27		2		915	10,835	
	28		2		1,200	9,635	
	29		2		540	9,095	
	30		2	500		9,595	
	31		2	3,000		12,595	
	31		2		1,400	11,195	
	31		2		1,250	9,945	

Account: **Accounts Receivable**   Account No. **12**

Date		Item	Post. Ref.	Debit	Credit	Balance Debit	Balance Credit
2014							
July	1	Balance	✓			1,000	
	2		1		1,000	—	—
	23		2	1,750		1,750	
	30		2	1,000		2,750	
	31	Adjusting	3	1,400		4,150	

Continuing Problem (Continued)

Account: **Supplies**   Account No. **14**

Date		Item	Post. Ref.	Debit	Credit	Balance Debit	Balance Credit
2014							
July	1	Balance	✓			170	
	18		2	850		1,020	
	31	Adjusting	3		745	275	

Account: **Prepaid Insurance**   Account No. **15**

Date		Item	Post. Ref.	Debit	Credit	Balance Debit	Balance Credit
2014							
July	1		1	2,700		2,700	
	31	Adjusting	3		225	2,475	

Account: **Office Equipment**   Account No. **17**

Date		Item	Post. Ref.	Debit	Credit	Balance Debit	Balance Credit
2014							
July	5		1	7,500		7,500	

Account: **Accumulated Depreciation—Office Equipment**   Account No. **18**

Date		Item	Post. Ref.	Debit	Credit	Balance Debit	Balance Credit
2014							
July	31	Adjusting	3		50		50

Account: **Accounts Payable**   Account No. **21**

Date		Item	Post. Ref.	Debit	Credit	Balance Debit	Balance Credit
2014							
July	1	Balance	✓				250
	3		1	250		—	—
	5		1		7,500		7,500
	18		2		850		8,350

Account: **Wages Payable**   Account No. **22**

Date		Item	Post. Ref.	Debit	Credit	Balance Debit	Balance Credit
2014							
July	31	Adjusting	3		140		140

Continuing Problem (Continued)

Account: **Unearned Revenue**   Account No.   **23**

Date		Item	Post. Ref.	Debit	Credit	Balance Debit	Balance Credit
2014							
July	3		1		7,200		7,200
	31	Adjusting	3	3,600			3,600

Account: **Peyton Smith, Capital**   Account No.   **31**

Date		Item	Post. Ref.	Debit	Credit	Balance Debit	Balance Credit
2014							
July	1	Balance	✓				4,000
	1		1		5,000		9,000

Account: **Peyton Smith, Drawing**   Account No.   **32**

Date		Item	Post. Ref.	Debit	Credit	Balance Debit	Balance Credit
2014							
July	1	Balance	✓			500	
	31		2	1,250		1,750	

Account: **Income Summary**   Account No.   **33**

Date		Item	Post. Ref.	Debit	Credit	Balance Debit	Balance Credit

(This account is not used in Chapter 3.)

Account: **Fees Earned**   Account No.   **41**

Date		Item	Post. Ref.	Debit	Credit	Balance Debit	Balance Credit
2014							
July	1	Balance	✓				6,200
	11		1		1,000		7,200
	16		2		2,000		9,200
	23		2		2,500		11,700
	30		2		1,500		13,200
	31		2		3,000		16,200
	31	Adjusting	3		1,400		17,600
	31	Adjusting	3		3,600		21,200

Continuing Problem (Continued)

Account: **Wages Expense**   Account No.   **50**

Date		Item	Post. Ref.	Debit	Credit	Balance	
						Debit	Credit
2014							
July	1	Balance	✓			400	
	14		1	1,200		1,600	
	28		2	1,200		2,800	
	31	Adjusting	3	140		2,940	

Account: **Office Rent Expense**   Account No.   **51**

Date		Item	Post. Ref.	Debit	Credit	Balance	
						Debit	Credit
2014							
July	1	Balance	✓			800	
	1		1	1,750		2,550	

Account: **Equipment Rent Expense**   Account No.   **52**

Date		Item	Post. Ref.	Debit	Credit	Balance	
						Debit	Credit
2014							
July	1	Balance	✓			675	
	13		1	700		1,375	

Account: **Utilities Expense**   Account No.   **53**

Date		Item	Post. Ref.	Debit	Credit	Balance	
						Debit	Credit
2014							
July	1	Balance	✓			300	
	27		2	915		1,215	

Account: **Music Expense**   Account No.   **54**

Date		Item	Post. Ref.	Debit	Credit	Balance	
						Debit	Credit
2014							
July	1	Balance	✓			1,590	
	21		2	620		2,210	
	31		2	1,400		3,610	

Continuing Problem (Continued)

Account: Advertising Expense   **Account No.** 55

Date		Item	Post. Ref.	Debit	Credit	Balance Debit	Balance Credit
2014							
July	1	Balance	✓			500	
	8		1	200		700	
	22		2	800		1,500	

Account: Supplies Expense   **Account No.** 56

Date		Item	Post. Ref.	Debit	Credit	Balance Debit	Balance Credit
2014							
July	1	Balance	✓			180	
	31	Adjusting	3	745		925	

Account: Insurance Expense   **Account No.** 57

Date		Item	Post. Ref.	Debit	Credit	Balance Debit	Balance Credit
2014							
July	31	Adjusting	3	225		225	

Account: Depreciation Expense   **Account No.** 58

Date		Item	Post. Ref.	Debit	Credit	Balance Debit	Balance Credit
2014							
July	31	Adjusting	3	50		50	

Account: Miscellaneous Expense   **Account No.** 59

Date		Item	Post. Ref.	Debit	Credit	Balance Debit	Balance Credit
2014							
July	1	Balance	✓			415	
	4		1	900		1,315	
	29		2	540		1,855	

Continuing Problem (Concluded)

3.

PS MUSIC Adjusted Trial Balance July 31, 2014		
	Debit Balances	Credit Balances
Cash	9,945	
Accounts Receivable	4,150	
Supplies	275	
Prepaid Insurance	2,475	
Office Equipment	7,500	
Accumulated Depreciation—Office Equipment		50
Accounts Payable		8,350
Wages Payable		140
Unearned Revenue		3,600
Peyton Smith, Capital		9,000
Peyton Smith, Drawing	1,750	
Fees Earned		21,200
Music Expense	3,610	
Wages Expense	2,940	
Office Rent Expense	2,550	
Advertising Expense	1,500	
Equipment Rent Expense	1,375	
Utilities Expense	1,215	
Supplies Expense	925	
Insurance Expense	225	
Depreciation Expense	50	
Miscellaneous Expense	1,855	
	42,340	42,340

CASES & PROJECTS

CP 3–1

It is acceptable for Daryl to prepare the financial statements for Squid Realty Co. on an accrual basis. The revision of the financial statements to include the accrual of the $30,000 commission as of December 28, 2013, would not be appropriate. Most real estate contracts include contingencies that can void the contract. Such contingencies include obtaining a loan, appraisals, environmental studies, and inspection results. In other words, Daryl can only be sure of earning the commission on January 5, 2014, when the attorney formally records the transfer of the property to the buyer, and Daryl may disclose the pending sale and related commission in a note to the financial statements. Indicating on the loan application to Free Spirit Bank that Squid Realty Co. has not been rejected previously for credit is unethical and unprofessional, and intentionally filing false loan documents is illegal.

CP 3–2

The cost of the warranty repairs, $1,650, should be recognized as an expense of 2014 in order to properly match revenues from the sale of the truck with the related expenses. Since the cost of the actual repairs will not be known at the time of sale (2014), Ford Motor Company would estimate warranty costs and expenses at the end of 2014 using its past warranty (repair) history with the Ford 350F. This estimate would be recorded in the accounts through use of an adjusting entry. The adjusting entry would debit Warranty Expense and credit Estimated Warranty Payable, a liability account.

CP 3–3

Revenue is normally recorded when the services are provided or when the goods are delivered (title passes) to the buyer. By waiting until after the services are provided, the expenses of providing the services can be more accurately measured and matched against the related revenues. Also, at this point, the provider of the services has a right to demand payment for the services if payment hasn't already been received.

Airlines, such as Delta Air Lines, normally record revenue from ticket sales after completing a flight. At this point, the boarding passes, which have been collected from the passengers, represent revenue to the airline. In addition, the expenses related to each flight, such as landing fees and fuel, would have been incurred and would be accurately measured.

Note to Instructors: The following points might also be worth discussing:

(1)   The receipt of revenue from customers in advance of a flight represents unearned revenues to the airline. For example, the purchase of discount tickets, which often requires prepayment months in advance of the actual flight, is unearned revenue to the airline.

(2)   At the end of the airline's accounting period, it would have adjusting entries related to such items as the following:

- Accrued wages for employees

- Depreciation on airplanes, terminal buildings, etc.

- Unearned revenues (described above)

- Accrued income from transporting freight, etc.

- Accrued income from other airlines
  (When a flight is delayed or canceled, airlines often accept passengers from other airlines and then later collect the revenue from the other airline.)

- Prepaid expenses related to insurance, etc.

CP 3–4

a. There are several indications that adjusting entries were not recorded before the financial statements were prepared, including:

   1. All expenses on the income statement are identified as "paid" items and not as "expenses."

   2. No expense is reported on the income statement for depreciation, and no accumulated depreciation is reported on the balance sheet.

   3. No supplies, accounts payable, or wages payable are reported on the balance sheet.

b. Likely accounts requiring adjustment include:

   1. Accumulated Depreciation—Truck for depreciation expense.
   2. Supplies (paid) expense for supplies on hand.
   3. Insurance (paid) expense for unexpired insurance.
   4. Wages accrued.
   5. Utilities accrued.

CP 3–5

Note to Instructors: The purpose of this activity is to familiarize students with behaviors that are common in codes of conduct. In addition, this activity addresses an actual ethical dilemma for students related to doing their homework. Consider asking students to look up your school's Student Code of Conduct and discuss its implications for the behaviors described in this case. An excerpt from one such Honor Code is shown below.

> Students must share the responsibility for creating and maintaining an atmosphere of honesty and integrity. Students should be aware that personal experience in completing assigned work is essential to learning. Permitting others to prepare their work, using published or unpublished summaries as a substitute for studying required materials, or giving or receiving unauthorized assistance in the preparation of work to be submitted are directly contrary to the honest process of learning. Students who are aware that others in a course are cheating or otherwise acting dishonestly have the responsibility to inform the professor and/or bring an accusation to the Honor Council.
>
>   http://smu.edu/studentlife/studenthandbook/pcl_05_hc.asp

Southern Methodist University, The Honor Code, http://smu.edu/studentlife/studenthandbook.

CHAPTER 4
COMPLETING THE ACCOUNTING CYCLE

DISCUSSION QUESTIONS

1. The end-of-period spreadsheet illustrates the flow of accounting information from the unadjusted trial balance into the adjusted trial balance and into the financial statements. In doing so, the spreadsheet illustrates the impact of the adjustments on the financial statements.

2. **a.** Current assets are composed of cash and other assets that may reasonably be expected to be realized in cash or sold or used up, usually within one year or less, through the normal operations of the business.

   b. Property, plant, and equipment is composed of assets that are used in the business and that are of a permanent or relatively fixed nature.

3. Current liabilities are liabilities that will be due within a short time (usually one year or less) and that are to be paid out of current assets. Liabilities that will not be due for a comparatively long time (usually more than one year) are called long-term liabilities.

4. Revenue, expense, and drawing accounts are generally referred to as temporary accounts.

5. Closing entries are necessary at the end of an accounting period (1) to transfer the balances in temporary accounts to permanent accounts and (2) to prepare the temporary accounts for use in recording transactions for the next accounting period.

6. Adjusting entries bring the accounts up to date, while closing entries reduce the revenue, expense, and drawing accounts to zero balances for use in recording transactions for the next accounting period.

7. The purpose of the post-closing trial balance is to make sure that the ledger is in balance at the beginning of the next period.

8. **a.** The financial statements are the most important output of the accounting cycle.

   b. Yes, all companies have an accounting cycle that begins with analyzing and journalizing transactions and ends with a post-closing trial balance. However, companies may differ in how they implement the steps in the accounting cycle. For example, while most companies use computerized accounting systems, some companies may use manual systems.

9. The natural business year is the fiscal year that ends when business activities have reached the lowest point in the annual operating cycle.

10. All the companies listed are general merchandisers whose busiest time of the year is during the holiday season, which extends through most of December. Traditionally, the lowest point of business activity for general merchandisers will be near the end of January and the beginning of February. Thus, these companies have chosen their natural business year for their fiscal year.

PRACTICE EXERCISES

PE 4–1A

1. Balance sheet
2. Income statement
3. Statement of owner's equity
4. Balance sheet
5. Income statement
6. Income statement
7. Balance sheet
8. Balance sheet

PE 4–1B

1. Balance sheet
2. Balance sheet
3. Income statement
4. Income statement
5. Balance sheet
6. Balance sheet
7. Statement of owner's equity
8. Income statement

PE 4–2A

Daffodil Advertising Services Statement of Owner's Equity For the Year Ended December 31, 2013		
Francis Matthews, capital, January 1, 2013		$475,000
Additional investment during 2013	$ 50,000	
Net income	139,500	
	$189,500	
Less withdrawals	30,000	
Increase in owner's equity		159,500
Francis Matthews, capital, December 31, 2013		$634,500

PE 4–2B

Grab Bag Delivery Services Statement of Owner's Equity For the Year Ended December 31, 2013		
Blake Knudson, capital, January 1, 2013		$918,000
Net loss	$43,500	
Add withdrawals	15,000	
Decrease in owner's equity		58,500
Blake Knudson, capital, December 31, 2013		$859,500

PE 4–3A

1. Property, plant, and equipment
2. Owner's equity
3. Long-term liability
4. Current asset
5. Current liability
6. Current asset
7. Current liability
8. Current liability

PE 4–3B

1. Current liability
2. Current asset
3. Property, plant, and equipment
4. Current asset
5. Owner's equity
6. Long-term liability
7. Current asset
8. Current liability

PE 4–4A

		Closing Entries		
Aug.	31	Fees Earned	880,000	
		Income Summary		880,000
	31	Income Summary	629,000	
		Wages Expense		524,000
		Rent Expense		80,000
		Supplies Expense		16,000
		Miscellaneous Expense		9,000
	31	Income Summary	251,000	
		Rita Sands, Capital		251,000
	31	Rita Sands, Capital	55,000	
		Rita Sands, Drawing		55,000

PE 4–4B

		Closing Entries		
Apr.	30	Fees Earned	356,500	
		Income Summary		356,500
	30	Income Summary	363,600	
		Wages Expense		283,100
		Rent Expense		56,000
		Supplies Expense		11,500
		Miscellaneous Expense		13,000
	30	Felix Godwin, Capital	7,100	
		Income Summary		7,100
	30	Felix Godwin, Capital	10,500	
		Felix Godwin, Drawing		10,500

PE 4–5A

The following two steps are missing: (1) posting the transactions to the ledger and (2) the preparation of the financial statements. Transactions should be posted to the ledger after step (a). The financial statements should be prepared after step (f).

PE 4–5B

The following two steps are missing: (1) assembling and analyzing adjustment data and (2) journalizing and posting the closing entries. The adjustment data should be assembled and analyzed after step (c). The closing entries should be journalized and posted to the ledger after step (g).

PE 4–6A

a.

	2014	2013
Current assets.............	$1,467,000	$1,269,000
Current liabilitites........	815,000	675,000
Working capital............	$ 652,000	$ 594,000
Current ratio...............	1.80	1.88
	($1,467,000 ÷ $815,000)	($1,269,000 ÷ $675,000)

b. The change from 1.88 to 1.80 indicates an unfavorable trend.

PE 4–6B

a.

	2014	2013
Current assets..................	$1,586,250	$1,210,000
Current liabilitites..............	705,000	550,000
Working capital.................	$ 881,250	$ 660,000
Current ratio....................	2.25	2.20
	($1,586,250 ÷ $705,000)	($1,210,000 ÷ $550,000)

b.   The change from 2.20 to 2.25 indicates a favorable trend.

EXERCISES

Ex. 4–1

1. **Income statement: 5, 8, 9**
2. **Statement of owner's equity: 4**
3. **Balance sheet: 1, 2, 3, 6, 7, 10**

Ex. 4–2

a. **Asset: 1, 2, 5, 6, 10**
b. **Liability: 9, 12**
c. **Revenue: 3, 7**
d. **Expense: 4, 8, 11**

Ex. 4–3

HOLISM CONSULTING
Income Statement
For the Year Ended May 31, 2014

Fees earned		$175,200
Expenses:		
Salary expense	$70,500	
Supplies expense	6,000	
Depreciation expense	4,800	
Miscellaneous expense	7,400	
Total expenses		88,700
Net income		$ 86,500

HOLISM CONSULTING
Statement of Owner's Equity
For the Year Ended May 31, 2014

Scott Cutler, capital, June 1, 2013		$ 90,400
Net income	$86,500	
Less withdrawals	12,000	
Increase in owner's equity		74,500
Scott Cutler, capital, May 31, 2014		$164,900

HOLISM CONSULTING
Balance Sheet
May 31, 2014

Assets			Liabilities		
Current assets:			Current liabilities:		
Cash	$38,000		Accounts payable	$24,400	
Accounts receivable	90,000		Salaries payable	1,500	
Supplies	3,600		Total liabilities		$ 25,900
Total current assets		$131,600			
Property, plant, and					
equipment:					
Office equipment	$74,000				
Less accum. depr.	14,800		Owner's Equity		
Total property, plant,			Scott Cutler, capital		164,900
and equipment		59,200	Total liabilities and		
Total assets		$190,800	owner's equity		$190,800

Ex. 4–4

OLYMPIA CONSULTING Income Statement For the Year Ended April 30, 2014		
Fees earned		$60,000
Expenses:		
Salary expense	$32,450	
Supplies expense	1,800	
Depreciation expense	750	
Miscellaneous expense	1,500	
Total expenses		36,500
Net income		$23,500

OLYMPIA CONSULTING Statement of Owner's Equity For the Year Ended April 30, 2014		
Raul Hann, capital, May 1, 2013		$ 82,200
Net income	$23,500	
Less withdrawals	2,000	
Increase in owner's equity		21,500
Raul Hann, capital, April 30, 2014		$103,700

OLYMPIA CONSULTING Balance Sheet April 30, 2014					
Assets			**Liabilities**		
Current assets:			Current liabilities:		
Cash	$27,500		Accounts payable	$3,300	
Accounts receivable	53,500		Salaries payable	450	
Supplies	1,200		Total liabilities		$ 3,750
Total current assets		$ 82,200			
Property, plant, and					
equipment:					
Office equipment	$30,500				
Less accum. depr.	5,250		**Owner's Equity**		
Total property, plant,			Raul Hann, capital		103,700
and equipment		25,250	Total liabilities and		
Total assets		$107,450	owner's equity		$107,450

Ex. 4–5

SHANGHAI MESSENGER SERVICE		
Income Statement		
For the Year Ended September 30, 2014		
Fees earned		$440,000
Expenses:		
Salaries expense	$265,150	
Rent expense	36,000	
Utilities expense	28,500	
Depreciation expense	7,250	
Supplies expense	2,200	
Insurance expense	1,200	
Miscellaneous expense	7,100	
Total expenses		347,400
Net income		$ 92,600

Ex. 4–6

VEGGIE HEALTH SERVICES CO.		
Income Statement		
For the Year Ended February 28, 2014		
Service revenue		$270,900
Expenses:		
Wages expense	$213,100	
Rent expense	42,000	
Utilities expense	17,600	
Depreciation expense	9,000	
Insurance expense	4,000	
Supplies expense	3,000	
Miscellaneous expense	6,000	
Total expenses		294,700
Net loss		$ (23,800)

Ex. 4–7

a.

FEDEX CORPORATION Income Statement For the Year Ended May 31, 2011 (in millions)		
Revenues		$39,304
Expenses:		
Salaries and employee benefits	$15,276	
Purchased transportation	5,674	
Fuel	4,151	
Rentals and landing fees	2,462	
Maintenance and repairs	1,979	
Depreciation	1,973	
Provision for income taxes	813	
Other expense (income) net	5,524	
Total expenses		37,852
Net income		$ 1,452

b.   The income statements are very similar. The actual statement includes some additional expense and income classifications. For example, the actual statement reports Income Before Income Taxes and Provision for Income Taxes separately. In addition, the "Other expense (income) net" in the text is a summary of several items from the Web site, including Intercompany charges, Interest expense, and Interest income.

Ex. 4–8

WELL SYSTEMS CO. Statement of Owner's Equity For the Year Ended October 31, 2014		
Wendy McGee, capital, November 1, 2013		$475,000
Net income	$90,000	
Less withdrawals	48,000	
Increase in owner's equity		42,000
Wendy McGee, capital, October 31, 2014		$517,000

Ex. 4–9

WEIRD SPORTS Statement of Owner's Equity For the Year Ended June 30, 2014		
Paige Demar, capital, July 1, 2013		$115,800
Net loss	$20,900	
Plus withdrawals	24,000	
Decrease in owner's equity		44,900
Paige Demar, capital, June 30, 2014		$ 70,900

Ex. 4–10

a.   Current asset: 1, 3, 5, 6

b.   Property, plant, and equipment: 2, 4

Ex. 4–11

Since current liabilities are usually due within one year, $15,000 ($1,250 × 12 months) would be reported as a current liability on the balance sheet. The remainder of $360,000 ($375,000 – $15,000) would be reported as a long-term liability on the balance sheet.

Ex. 4-12

LABRADOR WEIGHT LOSS CO.
Balance Sheet
June 30, 2014

Assets			Liabilities		
Current assets:			Current liabilities:		
Cash*	$ 37,500		Accounts payable	$18,500	
Accounts receivable	78,250		Salaries payable	8,500	
Supplies	5,350		Unearned fees	9,000	
Prepaid insurance	19,200		Total liabilities		$ 36,000
Prepaid rent	18,000				
Total current assets		$158,300			
Property, plant, and equipment:					
Land		$290,000	Owner's Equity		
Equipment	$300,000				
Less accumulated depreciation	103,300	196,700	Shi Deng, capital		609,000
Total property, plant, and equipment		486,700	Total liabilities and owner's		
Total assets		$645,000	equity		$645,000

*$37,500 = $645,000 − $486,700 − $18,000 − $19,200 − $5,350 − $78,250

4-12

Ex. 4–13

1. The date of the statement should be "August 31, 2014" and not "For the Year Ended August 31, 2014."

2. Accounts payable should be a current liability.

3. Land should be classified as property, plant, and equipment.

4. "Accumulated depreciation" should be deducted from the related fixed asset.

5. An adding error was made in determining the amount of the total property, plant, and equipment.

6. Accounts receivable should be a current asset.

7. Net income should be reported on the income statement and statement of owner's equity.

8. Wages payable should be a current liability.

A corrected balance sheet would be as follows:

Ex. 4–13 (Concluded)

LABYRINTH SERVICES CO.
Balance Sheet
August 31, 2014

Assets				Liabilities			
Current assets:				Current liabilities:			
Cash		$ 18,500		Accounts payable		$31,300	
Accounts receivable		41,400		Wages payable		6,500	
Supplies		6,500		Total liabilities			$ 37,800
Prepaid insurance		16,600					
Total current assets			$ 83,000				
Property, plant, and equipment:				Owner's Equity			
Land		$225,000		Ruben Daniel, capital			587,200
Building	$400,000						
Less accumulated depreciation	155,000	245,000					
Equipment	$ 97,000						
Less accumulated depreciation	25,000	72,000					
Total property, plant, and equipment			542,000	Total liabilities and owner's equity			$625,000
Total assets			$625,000				

Ex. 4–14

c.   **Depreciation Expense—Equipment**

g.   **Fees Earned**

j.   **Supplies Expense**

k.   **Wages Expense**

Note: Ernie Hale, Drawing is closed to Ernie Hale, Capital rather than to Income Summary.

Ex. 4–15

The income summary account is used to close the revenue and expense accounts, and it aids in detecting and correcting errors. The $1,190,500 represents expense account balances, and the $1,476,300 represents revenue account balances that have been closed. In this case, the company had net income of $285,800 ($1,476,300 – $1,190,500).

Ex. 4–16

a.

Income Summary	122,650	
Darcy Lewis, Capital		122,650
($613,400 – $490,750).		
Darcy Lewis, Capital	55,000	
Darcy Lewis, Drawing		55,000

b. $901,250   ($833,600 + $122,650 – $55,000)

Ex. 4–17

		Closing Entries		
July	31	Fees Earned	337,900	
		Income Summary		337,900
	31	Income Summary	362,000	
		Wages Expense		277,500
		Rent Expense		54,000
		Supplies Expense		14,300
		Miscellaneous Expense		16,200
	31	Gail Sabatini, Capital	24,100	
		Income Summary		24,100
	31	Gail Sabatini, Capital	45,000	
		Gail Sabatini, Drawing		45,000

Ex. 4–18

a. Accounts Payable
b. Accumulated Depreciation
c. Casey Ryan, Capital
e. Cash
h. Office Equipment
j. Salaries Payable
k. Supplies

Ex. 4–19

IGLOO TREASURES CO. Post-Closing Trial Balance January 31, 2014	Debit Balances	Credit Balances
Cash	21,350	
Accounts Receivable	56,700	
Supplies	7,500	
Equipment	74,450	
Accumulated Depreciation—Equipment		12,400
Accounts Payable		29,600
Salaries Payable		3,200
Unearned Rent		11,000
Nicole O'Brien, Capital		103,800
	160,000	160,000

Ex. 4–20

1. h
2. g
3. f
4. c
5. i
6. d
7. b
8. a
9. e
10. j

Ex. 4–21

a.

	December 31	
	Year 2	Year 1
Current assets...............	$555,850	$448,000
Current liabilitites..........	149,147	120,162
Working capital.............	$406,703	$327,838
Current ratio.................	3.73	3.73
	($555,850 ÷ $149,147)	($448,000 ÷ $120,162)

b. Under Armour's working capital increased by $78,865 ($406,703 – $327,838) during Year 2. The current ratio remained the same at 3.73 in Year 1 and Year 2. A current ratio of 3.73 indicates a strong solvency position. Thus, short-term creditors should not be concerned about receiving payment from Under Armour.

Ex. 4–22

a.

	Year 2	Year 1
Current assets...............	$2,756,400	$2,035,800
Current liabilitites..........	1,779,100	1,581,000
Working capital.............	$ 977,300	$ 454,800
Current ratio.................	1.55	1.29
	($2,756,400 ÷ $1,779,100)	($2,035,800 ÷ $1,581,000)

b. Starbucks' working capital improved (increased) from Year 1 to Year 2 by $522,500 ($977,300 – $454,800). Starbucks' current ratio also improved (increased) from 1.29 in Year 1 to 1.55 in Year 2. The improved working capital and current ratio indicate that short-term creditors should not be concerned about receiving payment from Starbucks.

Appendix Ex. 4–23

1. i   6. f
2. a   7. j
3. g   8. e
4. d   9. h
5. c   10. b

Appendix Ex. 4-24

ALERT SECURITY SERVICES CO.
End-of-Period Spreadsheet (Work Sheet)
For the Year Ended October 31, 2014

Account Title	Unadjusted Trial Balance Debit	Unadjusted Trial Balance Credit	Adjustments Debit	Adjustments Credit	Adjusted Trial Balance Debit	Adjusted Trial Balance Credit
Cash	12				12	
Accounts Receivable	90		(a) 13		103	
Supplies	8			(b) 4	4	
Prepaid Insurance	12			(c) 10	2	
Land	190				190	
Equipment	50				50	
Accum. Depr.—Equipment		4		(d) 3		7
Accounts Payable		36				36
Wages Payable		0		(e) 1		1
Brenda Schultz, Capital		260				260
Brenda Schultz, Drawing	8				8	
Fees Earned		200		(a) 13		213
Wages Expense	110		(e) 1		111	
Rent Expense	12				12	
Insurance Expense	0		(c) 10		10	
Utilities Expense	6				6	
Supplies Expense	0		(b) 4		4	
Depreciation Expense	0		(d) 3		3	
Miscellaneous Expense	2				2	
Totals	500	500	31	31	517	517

Appendix Ex. 4-25

ALERT SECURITY SERVICES CO.
End-of-Period Spreadsheet (Work Sheet)
For the Year Ended October 31, 2014

Account Title	Adjusted Trial Balance		Income Statement		Balance Sheet	
	Debit	Credit	Debit	Credit	Debit	Credit
Cash	12				12	
Accounts Receivable	103				103	
Supplies	4				4	
Prepaid Insurance	2				2	
Land	190				190	
Equipment	50				50	
Accum. Depr.—Equipment		7				7
Accounts Payable		36				36
Wages Payable		1				1
Brenda Schultz, Capital		260				260
Brenda Schultz, Drawing	8				8	
Fees Earned		213		213		
Wages Expense	111		111			
Rent Expense	12		12			
Insurance Expense	10		10			
Utilities Expense	6		6			
Supplies Expense	4		4			
Depreciation Expense	3		3			
Miscellaneous Expense	2		2			
Totals	517	517	148	213	369	304
Net income (loss)			65			65
			213	213	369	369

4-19

Appendix Ex. 4–26

ALERT SECURITY SERVICES CO. Income Statement For the Year Ended October 31, 2014		
Fees earned		$213
Expenses:		
Wages expense	$111	
Rent expense	12	
Insurance expense	10	
Utilities expense	6	
Supplies expense	4	
Depreciation expense	3	
Miscellaneous expense	2	
Total expenses		148
Net income		$ 65

ALERT SECURITY SERVICES CO. Statement of Owner's Equity For the Year Ended October 31, 2014		
Brenda Schultz, capital, November 1, 2013		$260
Net income	$65	
Less withdrawals	8	
Increase in owner's equity		57
Brenda Schultz, capital, October 31, 2014		$317

Appendix Ex. 4–26 (Concluded)

ALERT SECURITY SERVICES CO.
Balance Sheet
October 31, 2014

Assets			Liabilities		
Current assets:			**Current liabilities:**		
Cash	$ 12		Accounts payable	$36	
Accounts receivable	103		Wages payable	1	
Supplies	4		**Total liabilities**		$ 37
Prepaid insurance	2				
Total current assets		$121			
Property, plant, and equipment:					
Land		$190	**Owner's Equity**		
Equipment	$50				
Less accumulated depreciation	7	43	Brenda Schultz, capital		317
Total property, plant, and equipment		233	Total liabilities and owner's equity		$354
Total assets		$354			

4-21

Appendix Ex. 4–27

2014			Adjusting Entries		
Oct.		31	Accounts Receivable	13	
			Fees Earned		13
			Accrued fees.		
		31	Supplies Expense	4	
			Supplies		4
			Supplies used ($8 – $4).		
		31	Insurance Expense	10	
			Prepaid Insurance		10
			Insurance expired.		
		31	Depreciation Expense	3	
			Accumulated Depreciation—Equipment		3
			Equipment depreciation.		
		31	Wages Expense	1	
			Wages Payable		1
			Accrued wages.		

Appendix Ex. 4–28

2014			Closing Entries		
Oct.		31	Fees Earned	213	
			Income Summary		213
		31	Income Summary	148	
			Wages Expense		111
			Rent Expense		12
			Insurance Expense		10
			Utilities Expense		6
			Supplies Expense		4
			Depreciation Expense		3
			Miscellaneous Expense		2
		31	Income Summary	65	
			Brenda Schultz, Capital		65
		31	Brenda Schultz, Capital	8	
			Brenda Schultz, Drawing		8

PROBLEMS

Prob. 4–1A

1.

WATCHDOG COMPANY Income Statement For the Year Ended July 31, 2014		
Fees earned	$368,100	
Rent revenue	1,000	
Total revenues		$369,100
Expenses:		
Salaries and wages expense	$164,900	
Advertising expense	21,700	
Utilities expense	11,400	
Repairs expense	8,850	
Depreciation expense—equipment	4,200	
Insurance expense	2,500	
Supplies expense	1,830	
Depreciation expense—building	1,600	
Miscellaneous expense	4,320	
Total expenses		221,300
Net income		$147,800

2.

WATCHDOG COMPANY Statement of Owner's Equity For the Year Ended July 31, 2014		
Ted Hickman, capital, August 1, 2013		$203,100
Net income for the year	$147,800	
Less withdrawals	10,000	
Increase in owner's equity		137,800
Ted Hickman, capital, July 31, 2014		$340,900

Prob. 4–1A (Continued)

3.

WATCHDOG COMPANY
Balance Sheet
July 31, 2014

Assets				Liabilities			
Current assets:				**Current liabilities:**			
Cash		$ 10,800		Accounts payable		$15,700	
Accounts receivable		43,300		Salaries and wages payable		1,800	
Prepaid insurance		1,700		Unearned rent		1,100	
Supplies		900		Total liabilities			$ 18,600
Total current assets			$ 56,700				
Property, plant, and equipment:				**Owner's Equity**			
Land		$ 98,000		Ted Hickman, capital			340,900
Building	$400,000						
Less accumulated depreciation	206,900	193,100					
Equipment	$101,000						
Less accumulated depreciation	89,300	11,700					
Total property, plant, and equipment			302,800	Total liabilities and owner's			
Total assets			$359,500	equity			$359,500

Prob. 4–1A (Concluded)

4.

2014		Closing Entries		
July	31	Fees Earned	368,100	
		Rent Revenue	1,000	
		Income Summary		369,100
	31	Income Summary	221,300	
		Salaries and Wages Expense		164,900
		Advertising Expense		21,700
		Utilities Expense		11,400
		Repairs Expense		8,850
		Depreciation Expense—Equipment		4,200
		Insurance Expense		2,500
		Supplies Expense		1,830
		Depreciation Expense—Building		1,600
		Miscellaneous Expense		4,320
	31	Income Summary	147,800	
		Ted Hickman, Capital		147,800
	31	Ted Hickman, Capital	10,000	
		Ted Hickman, Drawing		10,000

5.

WATCHDOG COMPANY
Post-Closing Trial Balance
July 31, 2014

	Debit Balances	Credit Balances
Cash	10,800	
Accounts Receivable	43,300	
Prepaid Insurance	1,700	
Supplies	900	
Land	98,000	
Building	400,000	
Accumulated Depreciation—Building		206,900
Equipment	101,000	
Accumulated Depreciation—Equipment		89,300
Accounts Payable		15,700
Salaries and Wages Payable		1,800
Unearned Rent		1,100
Ted Hickman, Capital		340,900
	655,700	655,700

Prob. 4–2A

1.

IRONSIDE SECURITY SERVICES Income Statement For the Year Ended April 30, 2014		
Revenues:		
Service fees	$480,000	
Rent revenue	25,000	
Total revenues		$505,000
Expenses:		
Salaries expense	$336,000	
Rent expense	62,500	
Supplies expense	12,000	
Depreciation expense—building	6,000	
Utilities expense	4,400	
Repairs expense	3,200	
Insurance expense	2,800	
Miscellaneous expense	5,100	
Total expenses		432,000
Net income		$ 73,000

IRONSIDE SECURITY SERVICES Statement of Owner's Equity For the Year Ended April 30, 2014		
Don Chadwell, capital, May 1, 2013		$179,300
Net income for the year	$73,000	
Less withdrawals	10,000	
Increase in owner's equity		63,000
Don Chadwell, capital, April 30, 2014		$242,300

Prob. 4–2A (Continued)

IRONSIDE SECURITY SERVICES
Balance Sheet
April 30, 2014

Assets			Liabilities		
Current assets:			Current liabilities:		
Cash	$18,000		Accounts payable	$6,000	
Accounts receivable	37,200		Salaries payable	1,500	
Supplies	7,500		Unearned rent	3,000	
Prepaid insurance	4,800		Total liabilities		$ 10,500
Total current assets		$ 67,500			
Property, plant, and equipment:			Owner's Equity		
Building	$240,500		Don Chadwell, capital		242,300
Less accum. depreciation	55,200				
Total property, plant, and building		185,300	Total liabilities and owner's equity		$252,800
Total assets		$252,800			

Prob. 4–2A (Concluded)

2.

2014			Closing Entries		
Apr.	30	Service Fees		480,000	
		Rent Revenue		25,000	
		Income Summary			505,000
	30	Income Summary		432,000	
		Salaries Expense			336,000
		Rent Expense			62,500
		Supplies Expense			12,000
		Depreciation Expense—Building			6,000
		Utilities Expense			4,400
		Repairs Expense			3,200
		Insurance Expense			2,800
		Miscellaneous Expense			5,100
	30	Income Summary		73,000	
		Don Chadwell, Capital			73,000
	30	Don Chadwell, Capital		10,000	
		Don Chadwell, Drawing			10,000

3. $37,500 ($47,500 – $10,000) net loss. The $47,500 decrease is caused by the $10,000 withdrawals and a $37,500 net loss.

Prob. 4–3A

1., 3., and 6.

Cash

June	30	Bal.	11,000			

Laundry Supplies

June	30	Bal.	21,500	June	30	Adj.	17,900
	30	Adj. Bal.	3,600				

Prepaid Insurance

June	30	Bal.	9,600	June	30	Adj.	5,700
	30	Adj. Bal.	3,900				

Laundry Equipment

June	30	Bal.	232,600			

Accumulated Depreciation

		June	30	Bal.	125,400
			30	Adj.	6,500
			30	Adj. Bal.	131,900

Accounts Payable

		June	30	Bal.	11,800

Wages Payable

		June	30	Adj.	1,100

Sophie Perez, Capital

June	30	Clos.	10,000	June	30	Bal.	105,600
					30	Clos.	10,700
					30	Bal.	106,300

Sophie Perez, Drawing

June	30	Bal.	10,000	June	30	Clos.	10,000

Prob. 4–3A (Continued)

Income Summary

June	30	Clos.	221,500	June	30	Clos.	232,200
		Clos.	10,700				

Laundry Revenue

June	30	Clos.	232,200	June	30	Bal.	232,200

Wages Expense

June	30	Bal.	125,200	June	30	Clos.	126,300
	30	Adj.	1,100				
	30	Adj. Bal.	126,300				

Rent Expense

June	30	Bal.	40,000	June	30	Clos.	40,000

Utilities Expense

June	30	Bal.	19,700	June	30	Clos.	19,700

Laundry Supplies Expense

June	30	Adj.	17,900	June	30	Clos.	17,900

Depreciation Expense

June	30	Adj.	6,500	June	30	Clos.	6,500

Insurance Expense

June	30	Adj.	5,700	June	30	Clos.	5,700

Miscellaneous Expense

June	30	Bal.	5,400	June	30	Clos.	5,400

Prob. 4–3A (Continued)

2. Optional (Appendix)

EPICENTER LAUNDRY
End-of-Period Spreadsheet (Work Sheet)
For the Year Ended June 30, 2014

Account Title	Unadjusted Trial Balance		Adjustments		Adjusted Trial Balance		Income Statement		Balance Sheet	
	Debit	Credit	Debit	Credit	Debit	Credit	Debit	Credit	Debit	Credit
Cash	11,000				11,000				11,000	
Laundry Supplies	21,500			(a) 17,900	3,600				3,600	
Prepaid Insurance	9,600			(b) 5,700	3,900				3,900	
Laundry Equipment	232,600				232,600				232,600	
Accum. Depreciation		125,400		(c) 6,500		131,900				131,900
Accounts Payable		11,800				11,800				11,800
Wages Payable				(d) 1,100		1,100				1,100
Sophie Perez, Capital		105,600				105,600				105,600
Sophie Perez, Drawing	10,000				10,000				10,000	
Laundry Revenue		232,200				232,200		232,200		
Wages Expense	125,200		(d) 1,100		126,300		126,300			
Rent Expense	40,000				40,000		40,000			
Utilities Expense	19,700				19,700		19,700			
Laundry Supplies Exp.			(a) 17,900		17,900		17,900			
Depreciation Expense			(c) 6,500		6,500		6,500			
Insurance Expense			(b) 5,700		5,700		5,700			
Miscellaneous Expense	5,400				5,400		5,400			
	475,000	475,000	31,200	31,200	482,600	482,600	221,500	232,200	261,100	250,400
Net income							10,700			10,700
							232,200	232,200	261,100	261,100

Prob. 4–3A (Continued)

3.

			Adjusting Entries		
2014					
June	30		Laundry Supplies Expense	17,900	
			Laundry Supplies		17,900
			Supplies used ($21,500 – $3,600).		
	30		Insurance Expense	5,700	
			Prepaid Insurance		5,700
			Insurance expired.		
	30		Depreciation Expense	6,500	
			Accumulated Depreciation		6,500
			Equipment depreciation.		
	30		Wages Expense	1,100	
			Wages Payable		1,100
			Accrued wages.		

4.

EPICENTER LAUNDRY
Adjusted Trial Balance
June 30, 2014

	Debit Balances	Credit Balances
Cash	11,000	
Laundry Supplies	3,600	
Prepaid Insurance	3,900	
Laundry Equipment	232,600	
Accumulated Depreciation		131,900
Accounts Payable		11,800
Wages Payable		1,100
Sophie Perez, Capital		105,600
Sophie Perez, Drawing	10,000	
Laundry Revenue		232,200
Wages Expense	126,300	
Rent Expense	40,000	
Utilities Expense	19,700	
Laundry Supplies Expense	17,900	
Depreciation Expense	6,500	
Insurance Expense	5,700	
Miscellaneous Expense	5,400	
	482,600	482,600

Prob. 4–3A (Continued)

5.

EPICENTER LAUNDRY		
Income Statement		
For the Year Ended June 30, 2014		
Laundry revenue		$232,200
Expenses:		
Wages expense	$126,300	
Rent expense	40,000	
Utilities expense	19,700	
Laundry supplies expense	17,900	
Depreciation expense	6,500	
Insurance expense	5,700	
Miscellaneous expense	5,400	
Total expenses		221,500
Net income		$ 10,700

EPICENTER LAUNDRY		
Statement of Owner's Equity		
For the Year Ended June 30, 2014		
Sophie Perez, capital, July 1, 2013		$105,600
Net income for the year	$10,700	
Less withdrawals	10,000	
Increase in owner's equity		700
Sophie Perez, capital, June 30, 2014		$106,300

Prob. 4–3A (Continued)

EPICENTER LAUNDRY
Balance Sheet
June 30, 2014

Assets			Liabilities		
Current assets:			**Current liabilities:**		
Cash	$ 11,000		Accounts payable	$11,800	
Laundry supplies	3,600		Wages payable	1,100	
Prepaid insurance	3,900		Total liabilities		$ 12,900
Total current assets		$ 18,500			
Property, plant, and equipment:					
Laundry equipment	$232,600		**Owner's Equity**		
Less accum. depreciation	131,900		Sophie Perez, capital		106,300
Total property, plant, and equipment		100,700	Total liabilities and owner's equity		$119,200
Total assets		$119,200			

Prob. 4–3A (Concluded)

6.

			Closing Entries		
2014					
June	30		Laundry Revenue	232,200	
			Income Summary		232,200
	30		Income Summary	221,500	
			Wages Expense		126,300
			Rent Expense		40,000
			Utilities Expense		19,700
			Laundry Supplies Expense		17,900
			Depreciation Expense		6,500
			Insurance Expense		5,700
			Miscellaneous Expense		5,400
	30		Income Summary	10,700	
			Sophie Perez, Capital		10,700
	30		Sophie Perez Capital	10,000	
			Sophie Perez, Drawing		10,000

7.

EPICENTER LAUNDRY		
Post-Closing Trial Balance		
June 30, 2014		
	Debit Balances	Credit Balances
Cash	11,000	
Laundry Supplies	3,600	
Prepaid Insurance	3,900	
Laundry Equipment	232,600	
Accumulated Depreciation		131,900
Accounts Payable		11,800
Wages Payable		1,100
Sophie Perez, Capital		106,300
	251,100	251,100

Prob. 4–4A

1., 3., and 6.

Account: **Cash**   Account No. **11**

Date		Item	Post. Ref.	Debit	Credit	Balance Debit	Balance Credit
2014							
Mar.	31	Balance	✓			12,000	

Account: **Supplies**   Account No. **13**

Date		Item	Post. Ref.	Debit	Credit	Balance Debit	Balance Credit
2014							
Mar.	31	Balance	✓			30,000	
	31	Adjusting	26		22,500	7,500	

Account: **Prepaid Insurance**   Account No. **14**

Date		Item	Post. Ref.	Debit	Credit	Balance Debit	Balance Credit
2014							
Mar.	31	Balance	✓			3,600	
	31	Adjusting	26		1,800	1,800	

Account: **Equipment**   Account No. **16**

Date		Item	Post. Ref.	Debit	Credit	Balance Debit	Balance Credit
2014							
Mar.	31	Balance	✓			110,000	

Account: **Accumulated Depreciation—Equipment**   Account No. **17**

Date		Item	Post. Ref.	Debit	Credit	Balance Debit	Balance Credit
2014							
Mar.	31	Balance	✓				25,000
	31	Adjusting	26		8,350		33,350

Account: **Trucks**   Account No. **18**

Date		Item	Post. Ref.	Debit	Credit	Balance Debit	Balance Credit
2014							
Mar.	31	Balance	✓			60,000	

Prob. 4–4A (Continued)

Account: **Accumulated Depreciation—Trucks**　　　Account No. **19**

Date		Item	Post. Ref.	Debit	Credit	Balance Debit	Balance Credit
2014							
Mar.	31	Balance	✓				15,000
	31	Adjusting	26		6,200		21,200

Account: **Accounts Payable**　　　Account No. **21**

Date		Item	Post. Ref.	Debit	Credit	Balance Debit	Balance Credit
2014							
Mar.	31	Balance	✓				4,000

Account: **Wages Payable**　　　Account No. **22**

Date		Item	Post. Ref.	Debit	Credit	Balance Debit	Balance Credit
2014							
Mar.	31	Adjusting	26		600		600

Account: **Kaya Tarango, Capital**　　　Account No. **31**

Date		Item	Post. Ref.	Debit	Credit	Balance Debit	Balance Credit
2014							
Mar.	31	Balance	✓				96,000
	31	Closing	27		51,150		147,150
	31	Closing	27	15,000			132,150

Account: **Kaya Tarango, Drawing**　　　Account No. **32**

Date		Item	Post. Ref.	Debit	Credit	Balance Debit	Balance Credit
2014							
Mar.	31	Balance	✓			15,000	
	31	Closing	27		15,000	—	—

Prob. 4–4A (Continued)

Account: **Income Summary**   Account No.   **33**

Date		Item	Post. Ref.	Debit	Credit	Balance	
						Debit	Credit
2014							
Mar.	31	Closing	27		160,000		160,000
	31	Closing	27	108,850			51,150
	31	Closing	27	51,150		—	—

Account: **Service Revenue**   Account No.   **41**

Date		Item	Post. Ref.	Debit	Credit	Balance	
						Debit	Credit
2014							
Mar.	31	Balance	✓				160,000
	31	Closing	27	160,000		—	—

Account: **Wages Expense**   Account No.   **51**

Date		Item	Post. Ref.	Debit	Credit	Balance	
						Debit	Credit
2014							
Mar.	31	Balance	✓			45,000	
	31	Adjusting	26	600		45,600	
	31	Closing	27		45,600	—	—

Account: **Supplies Expense**   Account No.   **52**

Date		Item	Post. Ref.	Debit	Credit	Balance	
						Debit	Credit
2014							
Mar.	31	Adjusting	26	22,500		22,500	
	31	Closing	27		22,500	—	—

Account: **Rent Expense**   Account No.   **53**

Date		Item	Post. Ref.	Debit	Credit	Balance	
						Debit	Credit
2014							
Mar.	31	Balance	✓			10,600	
	31	Closing	27		10,600	—	—

Prob. 4–4A (Continued)

Account: **Truck Expense**   Account No. **54**

Date		Item	Post. Ref.	Debit	Credit	Balance Debit	Balance Credit
2014							
Mar.	31	Balance	✓			9,000	
	31	Closing	27		9,000	—	—

Account: **Depreciation Expense—Equipment**   Account No. **55**

Date		Item	Post. Ref.	Debit	Credit	Balance Debit	Balance Credit
2014							
Mar.	31	Adjusting	26	8,350		8,350	
	31	Closing	27		8,350	—	—

Account: **Depreciation Expense—Trucks**   Account No. **56**

Date		Item	Post. Ref.	Debit	Credit	Balance Debit	Balance Credit
2014							
Mar.	31	Adjusting	26	6,200		6,200	
	31	Closing	27		6,200	—	—

Account: **Insurance Expense**   Account No. **57**

Date		Item	Post. Ref.	Debit	Credit	Balance Debit	Balance Credit
2014							
Mar.	31	Adjusting	26	1,800		1,800	
	31	Closing	27		1,800	—	—

Account: **Miscellaneous Expense**   Account No. **59**

Date		Item	Post. Ref.	Debit	Credit	Balance Debit	Balance Credit
2014							
Mar.	31	Balance	✓			4,800	
	31	Closing	27		4,800	—	—

Prob. 4-4A (Continued)

2. **Optional (Appendix)**

LAKOTA FREIGHT CO.
End-of-Period Spreadsheet (Work Sheet)
For the Year Ended March 31, 2014

Account Title	Unadjusted Trial Balance Debit	Unadjusted Trial Balance Credit	Adjustments Debit	Adjustments Credit	Adjusted Trial Balance Debit	Adjusted Trial Balance Credit	Income Statement Debit	Income Statement Credit	Balance Sheet Debit	Balance Sheet Credit
Cash	12,000				12,000				12,000	
Supplies	30,000			(a) 22,500	7,500				7,500	
Prepaid Insurance	3,600			(b) 1,800	1,800				1,800	
Equipment	110,000				110,000				110,000	
Accum. Depr.—Equip.		25,000		(c) 8,350		33,350				33,350
Trucks	60,000				60,000				60,000	
Accum. Depr.—Trucks		15,000		(d) 6,200		21,200				21,200
Accounts Payable		4,000				4,000				4,000
Wages Payable				(e) 600		600				600
Kaya Tarango, Capital		96,000				96,000				96,000
Kaya Tarango, Drawing	15,000				15,000				15,000	
Service Revenue		160,000				160,000		160,000		
Wages Expense	45,000		(e) 600		45,600		45,600			
Supplies Expense			(a) 22,500		22,500		22,500			
Rent Expense	10,600				10,600		10,600			
Truck Expense	9,000				9,000		9,000			
Depr. Exp.—Equipment			(c) 8,350		8,350		8,350			
Depr. Exp.—Trucks			(d) 6,200		6,200		6,200			
Insurance Expense			(b) 1,800		1,800		1,800			
Miscellaneous Expense	4,800				4,800		4,800			
	300,000	300,000	39,450	39,450	315,150	315,150	108,850	160,000	206,300	155,150
Net income							51,150			51,150
							160,000	160,000	206,300	206,300

Prob. 4–4A (Continued)

3.

JOURNAL

Page _____ 26

Date			Post. Ref.	Debit	Credit
2014		**Adjusting Entries**			
Mar.	31	Supplies Expense	52	22,500	
		Supplies	13		22,500
		Supplies used ($30,000 – $7,500).			
	31	Insurance Expense	57	1,800	
		Prepaid Insurance	14		1,800
		Insurance expired.			
	31	Depreciation Expense—Equipment	55	8,350	
		Accumulated Depr.—Equipment	17		8,350
		Equipment depreciation.			
	31	Depreciation Expense—Trucks	56	6,200	
		Accumulated Depr.—Trucks	19		6,200
		Truck depreciation.			
	31	Wages Expense	51	600	
		Wages Payable	22		600
		Accrued wages.			

Prob. 4–4A (Continued)

4.

LAKOTA FREIGHT CO. Adjusted Trial Balance March 31, 2014	Debit Balances	Credit Balances
Cash	12,000	
Supplies	7,500	
Prepaid Insurance	1,800	
Equipment	110,000	
Accumulated Depreciation—Equipment		33,350
Trucks	60,000	
Accumulated Depreciation—Trucks		21,200
Accounts Payable		4,000
Wages Payable		600
Kaya Tarango, Capital		96,000
Kaya Tarango, Drawing	15,000	
Service Revenue		160,000
Wages Expense	45,600	
Supplies Expense	22,500	
Rent Expense	10,600	
Truck Expense	9,000	
Depreciation Expense—Equipment	8,350	
Depreciation Expense—Trucks	6,200	
Insurance Expense	1,800	
Miscellaneous Expense	4,800	
	315,150	315,150

Prob. 4–4A (Continued)

5.

LAKOTA FREIGHT CO. Income Statement For the Year Ended March 31, 2014		
Service revenue		$160,000
Expenses:		
Wages expense	$45,600	
Supplies expense	22,500	
Rent expense	10,600	
Truck expense	9,000	
Depreciation expense—equipment	8,350	
Depreciation expense—trucks	6,200	
Insurance expense	1,800	
Miscellaneous expense	4,800	
Total expenses		108,850
Net income		$ 51,150

LAKOTA FREIGHT CO. Statement of Owner's Equity For the Year Ended March 31, 2014		
Kaya Tarango, capital, April 1, 2013		$ 96,000
Net income for the year	$51,150	
Less withdrawals	15,000	
Increase in owner's equity		36,150
Kaya Tarango, capital, March 31, 2014		$132,150

Prob. 4–4A (Continued)

LAKOTA FREIGHT CO.
Balance Sheet
March 31, 2014

Assets				Liabilities		
Current assets:				Current liabilities:		
Cash		$12,000		Accounts payable	$4,000	
Supplies		7,500		Wages payable	600	
Prepaid insurance		1,800		Total liabilities		$ 4,600
Total current assets			$ 21,300			
Property, plant, and equipment:				Owner's Equity		
Equipment	$110,000			Kaya Tarango, capital		132,150
Less accum. depreciation	33,350	$76,650				
Trucks	$ 60,000					
Less accum. depreciation	21,200	38,800				
Total property, plant, and equipment			115,450	Total liabilities and owner's		
Total assets			$136,750	equity		$136,750

Prob. 4–4A (Concluded)

6.

			Post. Ref.	Debit	Credit
Date					
2014		**Closing Entries**			
Mar.	31	Service Revenue	41	160,000	
		Income Summary	33		160,000
	31	Income Summary	33	108,850	
		Wages Expense	51		45,600
		Supplies Expense	52		22,500
		Rent Expense	53		10,600
		Truck Expense	54		9,000
		Depreciation Expense—Equipment	55		8,350
		Depreciation Expense—Trucks	56		6,200
		Insurance Expense	57		1,800
		Miscellaneous Expense	59		4,800
	31	Income Summary	33	51,150	
		Kaya Tarango, Capital	31		51,150
	31	Kaya Tarango, Capital	31	15,000	
		Kaya Tarango, Drawing	32		15,000

JOURNAL   Page ____27____

7.

LAKOTA FREIGHT CO.
Post-Closing Trial Balance
March 31, 2014

	Debit Balances	Credit Balances
Cash	12,000	
Supplies	7,500	
Prepaid Insurance	1,800	
Equipment	110,000	
Accumulated Depreciation—Equipment		33,350
Trucks	60,000	
Accumulated Depreciation—Trucks		21,200
Accounts Payable		4,000
Wages Payable		600
Kaya Tarango, Capital		132,150
	191,300	191,300

Prob. 4–5A

1. and 2.

JOURNAL   Page _____ 1

Date			Post. Ref.	Debit	Credit
2014					
July	1	Cash	11	13,500	
		Accounts Receivable	12	20,800	
		Supplies	14	3,200	
		Office Equipment	18	7,500	
		Steffy Lopez, Capital	31		45,000
	1	Prepaid Rent	15	4,800	
		Cash	11		4,800
	2	Prepaid Insurance	16	4,500	
		Cash	11		4,500
	4	Cash	11	5,500	
		Unearned Fees	23		5,500
	5	Office Equipment	18	6,500	
		Accounts Payable	21		6,500
	6	Cash	11	15,300	
		Accounts Receivable	12		15,300
	10	Miscellaneous Expense	59	400	
		Cash	11		400
	12	Accounts Payable	21	5,200	
		Cash	11		5,200
	12	Accounts Receivable	12	13,300	
		Fees Earned	41		13,300
	14	Salary Expense	51	1,750	
		Cash	11		1,750

Prob. 4–5A (Continued)

JOURNAL   Page _____ 2

Date			Post. Ref.	Debit	Credit
2014					
July	17	Cash	11	9,450	
		Fees Earned	41		9,450
	18	Supplies	14	600	
		Cash	11		600
	20	Accounts Receivable	12	6,650	
		Fees Earned	41		6,650
	24	Cash	11	4,000	
		Fees Earned	41		4,000
	26	Cash	11	12,000	
		Accounts Receivable	12		12,000
	27	Salary Expense	51	1,750	
		Cash	11		1,750
	29	Miscellaneous Expense	59	325	
		Cash	11		325
	31	Miscellaneous Expense	59	675	
		Cash	11		675
	31	Cash	11	5,200	
		Fees Earned	41		5,200
	31	Accounts Receivable	12	3,000	
		Fees Earned	41		3,000
	31	Steffy Lopez, Drawing	32	12,500	
		Cash	11		12,500

4-47

Prob. 4–5A (Continued)
2., 6., and 9.

Account: **Cash**   Account No.   **11**

Date		Item	Post. Ref.	Debit	Credit	Balance	
						Debit	Credit
2014							
July	1		1	13,500		13,500	
	1		1		4,800	8,700	
	2		1		4,500	4,200	
	4		1	5,500		9,700	
	6		1	15,300		25,000	
	10		1		400	24,600	
	12		1		5,200	19,400	
	14		1		1,750	17,650	
	17		2	9,450		27,100	
	18		2		600	26,500	
	24		2	4,000		30,500	
	26		2	12,000		42,500	
	27		2		1,750	40,750	
	29		2		325	40,425	
	31		2		675	39,750	
	31		2	5,200		44,950	
	31		2		12,500	32,450	

Account: **Accounts Receivable**   Account No.   **12**

Date		Item	Post. Ref.	Debit	Credit	Balance	
						Debit	Credit
2014							
July	1		1	20,800		20,800	
	6		1		15,300	5,500	
	12		1	13,300		18,800	
	20		2	6,650		25,450	
	26		2		12,000	13,450	
	31		2	3,000		16,450	

Account: **Supplies**   Account No.   **14**

Date		Item	Post. Ref.	Debit	Credit	Balance	
						Debit	Credit
2014							
July	1		1	3,200		3,200	
	18		2	600		3,800	
	31	Adjusting	3		2,275	1,525	

Prob. 4–5A (Continued)

Account: **Prepaid Rent**   Account No. ___15___

Date		Item	Post. Ref.	Debit	Credit	Balance Debit	Balance Credit
2014							
July	1		1	4,800		4,800	
	31	Adjusting	3		2,400	2,400	

Account: **Prepaid Insurance**   Account No. ___16___

Date		Item	Post. Ref.	Debit	Credit	Balance Debit	Balance Credit
2014							
July	2		1	4,500		4,500	
	31	Adjusting	3		375	4,125	

Account: **Office Equipment**   Account No. ___18___

Date		Item	Post. Ref.	Debit	Credit	Balance Debit	Balance Credit
2014							
July	1		1	7,500		7,500	
	5		1	6,500		14,000	

Account: **Accumulated Depreciation**   Account No. ___19___

Date		Item	Post. Ref.	Debit	Credit	Balance Debit	Balance Credit
2014							
July	31	Adjusting	3		750		750

Account: **Accounts Payable**   Account No. ___21___

Date		Item	Post. Ref.	Debit	Credit	Balance Debit	Balance Credit
2014							
July	5		1		6,500		6,500
	12		1	5,200			1,300

Account: **Salaries Payable**   Account No. ___22___

Date		Item	Post. Ref.	Debit	Credit	Balance Debit	Balance Credit
2014							
July	31	Adjusting	3		175		175

Prob. 4–5A (Continued)

Account: **Unearned Fees**   Account No. _____ **23**

Date		Item	Post. Ref.	Debit	Credit	Balance Debit	Balance Credit
2014							
July	4		1		5,500		5,500
	31	Adjusting	3	2,750			2,750

Account: **Steffy Lopez, Capital**   Account No. _____ **31**

Date		Item	Post. Ref.	Debit	Credit	Balance Debit	Balance Credit
2014							
July	1		1		45,000		45,000
	31	Closing	4		33,475		78,475
	31	Closing	4	12,500			65,975

Account: **Steffy Lopez, Drawing**   Account No. _____ **32**

Date		Item	Post. Ref.	Debit	Credit	Balance Debit	Balance Credit
2014							
July	31		2	12,500		12,500	
	31	Closing	4		12,500	—	—

Account: **Income Summary**   Account No. _____ **33**

Date		Item	Post. Ref.	Debit	Credit	Balance Debit	Balance Credit
2014							
July	31	Closing	4		44,350		44,350
	31	Closing	4	10,875			33,475
	31	Closing	4	33,475		—	—

Prob. 4–5A (Continued)

Account: **Fees Earned**   Account No. **41**

Date		Item	Post. Ref.	Debit	Credit	Balance Debit	Balance Credit
2014							
July	12		1		13,300		13,300
	17		2		9,450		22,750
	20		2		6,650		29,400
	24		2		4,000		33,400
	31		2		5,200		38,600
	31		2		3,000		41,600
	31	Adjusting	3		2,750		44,350
	31	Closing	4	44,350		—	—

Account: **Salary Expense**   Account No. **51**

Date		Item	Post. Ref.	Debit	Credit	Balance Debit	Balance Credit
2014							
July	14		1	1,750		1,750	
	27		2	1,750		3,500	
	31	Adjusting	3	175		3,675	
	31	Closing	4		3,675	—	—

Account: **Rent Expense**   Account No. **52**

Date		Item	Post. Ref.	Debit	Credit	Balance Debit	Balance Credit
2014							
July	31	Adjusting	3	2,400		2,400	
	31	Closing	4		2,400	—	—

Account: **Supplies Expense**   Account No. **53**

Date		Item	Post. Ref.	Debit	Credit	Balance Debit	Balance Credit
2014							
July	31	Adjusting	3	2,275		2,275	
	31	Closing	4		2,275	—	—

Prob. 4–5A (Continued)

Account: **Depreciation Expense**   Account No.   **54**

Date		Item	Post. Ref.	Debit	Credit	Balance Debit	Balance Credit
2014							
July	31	Adjusting	3	750		750	
	31	Closing	4		750	—	—

Account: **Insurance Expense**   Account No.   **55**

Date		Item	Post. Ref.	Debit	Credit	Balance Debit	Balance Credit
2014							
July	31	Adjusting	3	375		375	
	31	Closing	4		375	—	—

Account: **Miscellaneous Expense**   Account No.   **59**

Date		Item	Post. Ref.	Debit	Credit	Balance Debit	Balance Credit
2014							
July	10		1	400		400	
	29		2	325		725	
	31		2	675		1,400	
	31	Closing	4		1,400	—	—

Prob. 4–5A (Continued)

3.

DIAMOND CONSULTING Unadjusted Trial Balance July 31, 2014		
	Debit Balances	Credit Balances
Cash	32,450	
Accounts Receivable	16,450	
Supplies	3,800	
Prepaid Rent	4,800	
Prepaid Insurance	4,500	
Office Equipment	14,000	
Accumulated Depreciation		0
Accounts Payable		1,300
Salaries Payable		0
Unearned Fees		5,500
Steffy Lopez, Capital		45,000
Steffy Lopez, Drawing	12,500	
Fees Earned		41,600
Salary Expense	3,500	
Rent Expense	0	
Supplies Expense	0	
Depreciation Expense	0	
Insurance Expense	0	
Miscellaneous Expense	1,400	
	93,400	93,400

Prob. 4–5A (Continued)

5.   Optional (Appendix)

DIAMOND CONSULTING
End-of-Period Spreadsheet (Work Sheet)
For the Month Ended July 31, 2014

Account Title	Unadjusted Trial Balance Debit	Unadjusted Trial Balance Credit	Adjustments Debit	Adjustments Credit	Adjusted Trial Balance Debit	Adjusted Trial Balance Credit	Income Statement Debit	Income Statement Credit	Balance Sheet Debit	Balance Sheet Credit
Cash	32,450				32,450				32,450	
Accounts Receivable	16,450				16,450				16,450	
Supplies	3,800			(b) 2,275	1,525				1,525	
Prepaid Rent	4,800			(e) 2,400	2,400				2,400	
Prepaid Insurance	4,500			(a) 375	4,125				4,125	
Office Equipment	14,000				14,000				14,000	
Accum. Depreciation				(c) 750		750				750
Accounts Payable		1,300				1,300				1,300
Salaries Payable				(d) 175		175				175
Unearned Fees		5,500	(f) 2,750			2,750				2,750
Steffy Lopez, Capital		45,000				45,000				45,000
Steffy Lopez, Drawing	12,500				12,500				12,500	
Fees Earned		41,600		(f) 2,750		44,350		44,350		
Salary Expense	3,500		(d) 175		3,675		3,675			
Rent Expense			(e) 2,400		2,400		2,400			
Supplies Expense			(b) 2,275		2,275		2,275			
Depreciation Expense			(c) 750		750		750			
Insurance Expense			(a) 375		375		375			
Miscellaneous Expense	1,400				1,400		1,400			
	93,400	93,400	8,725	8,725	94,325	94,325	10,875	44,350	83,450	49,975
Net income							33,475			33,475
							44,350	44,350	83,450	83,450

Prob. 4–5A (Continued)

6.

			Post. Ref.	Debit	Credit
Date					
2014		**Adjusting Entries**			
July	31	Insurance Expense	55	375	
		Prepaid Insurance	16		375
		Insurance expired.			
	31	Supplies Expense	53	2,275	
		Supplies	14		2,275
		Supplies used ($3,800 – $1,525).			
	31	Depreciation Expense	54	750	
		Accumulated Depreciation	19		750
		Equipment depreciation.			
	31	Salary Expense	51	175	
		Salaries Payable	22		175
		Accrued salaries.			
	31	Rent Expense	52	2,400	
		Prepaid Rent	15		2,400
		Rent expired.			
	31	Unearned Fees	23	2,750	
		Fees Earned	41		2,750
		Unearned fees earned			
		($5,500 – $2,750).			

JOURNAL   Page _____ 3

Prob. 4–5A (Continued)

7.

DIAMOND CONSULTING Adjusted Trial Balance July 31, 2014	Debit Balances	Credit Balances
Cash	32,450	
Accounts Receivable	16,450	
Supplies	1,525	
Prepaid Rent	2,400	
Prepaid Insurance	4,125	
Office Equipment	14,000	
Accumulated Depreciation		750
Accounts Payable		1,300
Salaries Payable		175
Unearned Fees		2,750
Steffy Lopez, Capital		45,000
Steffy Lopez, Drawing	12,500	
Fees Earned		44,350
Salary Expense	3,675	
Rent Expense	2,400	
Supplies Expense	2,275	
Depreciation Expense	750	
Insurance Expense	375	
Miscellaneous Expense	1,400	
	94,325	94,325

Prob. 4–5A (Continued)

8.

DIAMOND CONSULTING Income Statement For the Month Ended July 31, 2014		
Fees earned		$44,350
Expenses:		
Salary expense	$3,675	
Rent expense	2,400	
Supplies expense	2,275	
Depreciation expense	750	
Insurance Expense	375	
Miscellaneous expense	1,400	
Total expenses		10,875
Net income		$33,475

DIAMOND CONSULTING Statement of Owner's Equity For the Month Ended July 31, 2014		
Steffy Lopez, capital, July 1, 2014		$ 0
Investments during month	$45,000	
Net income	33,475	
	$78,475	
Less withdrawals	12,500	
Increase in owner's equity		65,975
Steffy Lopez, capital, July 31, 2014		$65,975

Prob. 4-5A (Continued)

DIAMOND CONSULTING
Balance Sheet
July 31, 2014

Assets			Liabilities		
Current assets:			Current liabilities:		
Cash	$32,450		Accounts payable	$1,300	
Accounts receivable	16,450		Salaries payable	175	
Supplies	1,525		Unearned fees	2,750	
Prepaid rent	2,400		Total liabilities		$ 4,225
Prepaid insurance	4,125				
Total current assets		$56,950			
Property, plant, and equipment:			Owner's Equity		
Office equipment	$14,000		Steffy Lopez, capital		65,975
Less accum. depreciation	750				
Total property, plant, and equipment		13,250	Total liabilities and owner's equity		$70,200
Total assets		$70,200			

Prob. 4–5A (Concluded)

9.

			Post. Ref.	Debit	Credit
Date		JOURNAL			Page ___ 4
2014		**Closing Entries**			
July	31	Fees Earned	41	44,350	
		Income Summary	33		44,350
	31	Income Summary	33	10,875	
		Salary Expense	51		3,675
		Rent Expense	52		2,400
		Supplies Expense	53		2,275
		Depreciation Expense	54		750
		Insurance Expense	55		375
		Miscellaneous Expense	59		1,400
	31	Income Summary	33	33,475	
		Steffy Lopez, Capital	31		33,475
	31	Steffy Lopez, Capital	31	78,475	
		Steffy Lopez, Drawing	32		78,475

10.

DIAMOND CONSULTING
Post-Closing Trial Balance
July 31, 2014

	Debit Balances	Credit Balances
Cash	32,450	
Accounts Receivable	16,450	
Supplies	1,525	
Prepaid Rent	2,400	
Prepaid Insurance	4,125	
Office Equipment	14,000	
Accumulated Depreciation		750
Accounts Payable		1,300
Salaries Payable		175
Unearned Fees		2,750
Steffy Lopez, Capital		65,975
	70,950	70,950

Prob. 4–1B

1.

LAST CHANCE COMPANY Income Statement For the Year Ended June 30, 2014		
Revenues:		
Fees earned	$283,750	
Rent revenue	3,000	
Total revenues		$286,750
Expenses:		
Salaries and wages expense	$147,000	
Advertising expense	86,800	
Utilities expense	30,000	
Travel expense	18,750	
Depreciation expense—equipment	4,550	
Depreciation expense—building	3,000	
Supplies expense	1,500	
Insurance expense	1,300	
Miscellaneous expense	5,875	
Total expenses		298,775
Net loss		$ 12,025

2.

LAST CHANCE COMPANY Statement of Owner's Equity For the Year Ended June 30, 2014		
Tami Garrigan, capital, July 1, 2013		$361,300
Net loss for the year	$12,025	
Add withdrawals	20,000	
Decrease in owner's equity		32,025
Tami Garrigan, capital, June 30, 2014		$329,275

Prob. 4–1B (Continued)

3.

LAST CHANCE COMPANY
Balance Sheet
June 30, 2014

Assets			Liabilities		
Current assets:			**Current liabilities:**		
Cash		$ 5,100	Accounts payable	$9,750	
Accounts receivable		26,500	Salaries and wages payable	1,900	
Prepaid insurance		2,300	Unearned rent	1,500	
Supplies		525	Total liabilities		$ 13,150
Total current assets		$ 34,425			
Property, plant, and equipment:			**Owner's Equity**		
Land		$ 80,000			
Building	$340,000		Tami Garrigan, capital		329,275
Less accum. depreciation	193,000	147,000			
Equipment	$140,000				
Less accum. depreciation	59,000	81,000			
Total property, plant, and equipment		308,000	Total liabilities and owner's equity		$342,425
Total assets		$342,425			

Prob. 4–1B (Concluded)

4.

2014					
June	30	Fees Earned		283,750	
		Rent Revenue		3,000	
		Income Summary			286,750
	30	Income Summary		298,775	
		Salaries and Wages Expense			147,000
		Advertising Expense			86,800
		Utilities Expense			30,000
		Travel Expense			18,750
		Depreciation Expense—Equipment			4,550
		Depreciation Expense—Building			3,000
		Supplies Expense			1,500
		Insurance Expense			1,300
		Miscellaneous Expense			5,875
	30	Tami Garrigan, Capital		12,025	
		Income Summary			12,025
	30	Tami Garrigan, Capital		20,000	
		Tami Garrigan, Drawing			20,000

5.

LAST CHANCE COMPANY Post-Closing Trial Balance June 30, 2014	Debit Balances	Credit Balances
Cash	5,100	
Accounts Receivable	26,500	
Prepaid Insurance	2,300	
Supplies	525	
Land	80,000	
Building	340,000	
Accumulated Depreciation—Building		193,000
Equipment	140,000	
Accumulated Depreciation—Equipment		59,000
Accounts Payable		9,750
Salaries and Wages Payable		1,900
Unearned Rent		1,500
Tami Garrigan, Capital		329,275
	594,425	594,425

Prob. 4–2B

1.

THE GORMAN GROUP Income Statement For the Year Ended October 31, 2014		
Revenues:		
Service fees	$468,000	
Rent revenue	5,000	
Total revenues		$473,000
Expenses:		
Salaries expense	$291,000	
Depreciation expense—equipment	17,500	
Rent expense	15,500	
Supplies expense	9,000	
Utilities expense	8,500	
Depreciation expense—buildings	6,600	
Repairs expense	3,450	
Insurance expense	3,000	
Miscellaneous expense	5,450	
Total expenses		360,000
Net income		$113,000

THE GORMAN GROUP Statement of Owner's Equity For the Year Ended October 31, 2014		
Nicole Gorman, capital, November 1, 2013		$220,000
Net income for the year	$113,000	
Less withdrawals	20,000	
Increase in owner's equity		93,000
Nicole Gorman, capital, October 31, 2014		$313,000

Prob. 4–2B (Continued)

THE GORMAN GROUP
Balance Sheet
October 31, 2014

Assets			Liabilities		
Current assets:			Current liabilities:		
Cash		$ 11,000	Accounts payable	$33,300	
Accounts receivable		28,150	Salaries payable	3,300	
Supplies		6,350	Unearned rent	1,500	
Prepaid insurance		9,500	Total liabilities		$ 38,100
Total current assets		$ 55,000			
Property, plant, and equipment:			Owner's Equity		
Land		$ 75,000			
Buildings	$250,000		Nicole Gorman, capital		313,000
Less accum. depreciation	117,200	132,800			
Equipment	$240,000				
Less accum. depreciation	151,700	88,300			
Total property, plant, and equipment		296,100	Total liabilities and owner's		
Total assets		$351,100	equity		$351,100

Prob. 4–2B (Concluded)

2.

2014			Closing Entries		
Oct.	31	Service Fees		468,000	
		Rent Revenue		5,000	
		Income Summary			473,000
	31	Income Summary		360,000	
		Salaries Expense			291,000
		Depreciation Expense—Equipment			17,500
		Rent Expense			15,500
		Supplies Expense			9,000
		Utilities Expense			8,500
		Depreciation Expense—Buildings			6,600
		Repairs Expense			3,450
		Insurance Expense			3,000
		Miscellaneous Expense			5,450
	31	Income Summary		113,000	
		Nicole Gorman, Capital			113,000
	31	Nicole Gorman, Capital		20,000	
		Nicole Gorman, Drawing			20,000

3. $135,000 ($115,000 + $20,000) net income. The $115,000 increase is caused by the net income of $135,000 less the $20,000 withdrawals.

Prob. 4–3B

1., 3., and 6.

Cash

Aug.	31	Bal.	3,800					

Laundry Supplies

Aug.	31	Bal.	9,000	Aug.	31	Adj.	7,000
	31	Adj. Bal.	2,000				

Prepaid Insurance

Aug.	31	Bal.	6,000	Aug.	31	Adj.	5,300
	31	Adj. Bal.	700				

Laundry Equipment

Aug.	31	Bal.	180,800					

Accumulated Depreciation

				Aug.	31	Bal.	49,200
					31	Adj.	8,150
					31	Adj. Bal.	57,350

Accounts Payable

				Aug.	31	Bal.	7,800

Wages Payable

				Aug.	31	Adj.	2,200

Bobbi Downey, Capital

Aug.	31	Clos.	2,400	Aug.	31	Bal.	95,000
					31	Clos.	27,350
					31	Bal.	119,950

Bobbi Downey, Drawing

Aug.	31	Bal.	2,400	Aug.	31	Clos.	2,400

Prob. 4–3B (Continued)

Income Summary

Aug.	31	Clos.	220,650	Aug.	31	Clos.	248,000
		Clos.	27,350				

Laundry Revenue

Aug.	31	Clos.	248,000	Aug.	31	Bal.	248,000

Wages Expense

Aug.	31	Bal.	135,800	Aug.	31	Clos.	138,000
	31	Adj.	2,200				
	31	Adj. Bal.	138,000				

Rent Expense

Aug.	31	Bal.	43,200	Aug.	31	Clos.	43,200

Utilities Expense

Aug.	31	Bal.	16,000	Aug.	31	Clos.	16,000

Depreciation Expense

Aug.	31	Adj.	8,150	Aug.	31	Clos.	8,150

Laundry Supplies Expense

Aug.	31	Adj.	7,000	Aug.	31	Clos.	7,000

Insurance Expense

Aug.	31	Adj.	5,300	Aug.	31	Clos.	5,300

Miscellaneous Expense

Aug.	31	Bal.	3,000	Aug.	31	Clos.	3,000

Prob. 4–3B (Continued)

2. Optional (Appendix)

LA MESA LAUNDRY
End-of-Period Spreadsheet (Work Sheet)
For the Year Ended August 31, 2014

Account Title	Unadjusted Trial Balance Debit	Unadjusted Trial Balance Credit	Adjustments Debit	Adjustments Credit	Adjusted Trial Balance Debit	Adjusted Trial Balance Credit	Income Statement Debit	Income Statement Credit	Balance Sheet Debit	Balance Sheet Credit
Cash	3,800				3,800				3,800	
Laundry Supplies	9,000			(c) 7,000	2,000				2,000	
Prepaid Insurance	6,000			(d) 5,300	700				700	
Laundry Equipment	180,800				180,800				180,800	
Accum. Depreciation		49,200		(b) 8,150		57,350				57,350
Accounts Payable		7,800				7,800				7,800
Wages Payable				(a) 2,200		2,200				2,200
Bobbi Downey, Capital		95,000				95,000				95,000
Bobbi Downey, Drawing	2,400				2,400				2,400	
Laundry Revenue		248,000				248,000		248,000		
Wages Expense	135,800		(a) 2,200		138,000		138,000			
Rent Expense	43,200				43,200		43,200			
Utilities Expense	16,000				16,000		16,000			
Depreciation Expense			(b) 8,150		8,150		8,150			
Laundry Supplies Exp.			(c) 7,000		7,000		7,000			
Insurance Expense			(b) 5,300		5,300		5,300			
Miscellaneous Expense	3,000				3,000		3,000			
	400,000	400,000	22,650	22,650	410,350	410,350	220,650	248,000	189,700	162,350
Net income							27,350			27,350
							248,000	248,000	189,700	189,700

Prob. 4–3B (Continued)

3.

		Adjusting Entries		
2014				
Aug.	31	Wages Expense	2,200	
		Wages Payable		2,200
		Accrued wages.		
	31	Depreciation Expense	8,150	
		Accumulated Depreciation		8,150
		Equipment depreciation.		
	31	Laundry Supplies Expense	7,000	
		Laundry Supplies		7,000
		Supplies used ($9,000 – $2,000).		
	31	Insurance Expense	5,300	
		Prepaid Insurance		5,300
		Insurance expired.		

4.

LA MESA LAUNDRY Adjusted Trial Balance August 31, 2014		
	Debit Balances	Credit Balances
Cash	3,800	
Laundry Supplies	2,000	
Prepaid Insurance	700	
Laundry Equipment	180,800	
Accumulated Depreciation		57,350
Accounts Payable		7,800
Wages Payable		2,200
Bobbi Downey, Capital		95,000
Bobbi Downey, Drawing	2,400	
Laundry Revenue		248,000
Wages Expense	138,000	
Rent Expense	43,200	
Utilities Expense	16,000	
Depreciation Expense	8,150	
Laundry Supplies Expense	7,000	
Insurance Expense	5,300	
Miscellaneous Expense	3,000	
	410,350	410,350

Prob. 4–3B (Continued)

5.

LA MESA LAUNDRY Income Statement For the Year Ended August 31, 2014		
Laundry revenue		$248,000
Expenses:		
Wages expense	$138,000	
Rent expense	43,200	
Utilities expense	16,000	
Depreciation expense	8,150	
Laundry supplies expense	7,000	
Insurance expense	5,300	
Miscellaneous expense	3,000	
Total expenses		220,650
Net income		$ 27,350

LA MESA LAUNDRY Statement of Owner's Equity For the Year Ended August 31, 2014		
Bobbi Downey, capital, September 1, 2013		$ 95,000
Net income for the year	$27,350	
Less withdrawals	2,400	
Increase in owner's equity		24,950
Bobbi Downey, capital, August 31, 2014		$119,950

Prob. 4–3B (Continued)

LA MESA LAUNDRY
Balance Sheet
August 31, 2014

Assets		
Current assets:		
Cash	$ 3,800	
Laundry supplies	2,000	
Prepaid insurance	700	
Total current assets		$ 6,500
Property, plant, and equipment:		
Laundry equipment	$180,800	
Less accum. depreciation	57,350	
Total property, plant, and equipment		123,450
Total assets		$129,950

Liabilities		
Current liabilities:		
Accounts payable	$7,800	
Wages payable	2,200	
Total liabilities		$ 10,000
Owner's Equity		
Bobbi Downey, capital		119,950
Total liabilities and owner's equity		$129,950

Prob. 4–3B (Concluded)

6.

			Closing Entries		
2014					
Aug.	31	Laundry Revenue		248,000	
			Income Summary		248,000
	31	Income Summary		220,650	
			Wages Expense		138,000
			Rent Expense		43,200
			Utilities Expense		16,000
			Depreciation Expense		8,150
			Laundry Supplies Expense		7,000
			Insurance Expense		5,300
			Miscellaneous Expense		3,000
	31	Income Summary		27,350	
			Bobbi Downey, Capital		27,350
	31	Bobbi Downey, Capital		2,400	
			Bobbi Downey, Drawing		2,400

7.

LA MESA LAUNDRY Post-Closing Trial Balance August 31, 2014		
	Debit Balances	Credit Balances
Cash	3,800	
Laundry Supplies	2,000	
Prepaid Insurance	700	
Laundry Equipment	180,800	
Accumulated Depreciation		57,350
Accounts Payable		7,800
Wages Payable		2,200
Bobbi Downey, Capital		119,950
	187,300	187,300

Prob. 4–4B

1., 3., and 6.

Account: __Cash__   Account No. _____ 11

Date		Item	Post. Ref.	Debit	Credit	Balance Debit	Balance Credit
2014							
Jan.	31	Balance	✓			13,100	

Account: __Supplies__   Account No. _____ 13

Date		Item	Post. Ref.	Debit	Credit	Balance Debit	Balance Credit
2014							
Jan.	31	Balance	✓			8,000	
	31	Adjusting	26		5,150	2,850	

Account: __Prepaid Insurance__   Account No. _____ 14

Date		Item	Post. Ref.	Debit	Credit	Balance Debit	Balance Credit
2014							
Jan.	31	Balance	✓			7,500	
	31	Adjusting	26		3,150	4,350	

Account: __Equipment__   Account No. _____ 16

Date		Item	Post. Ref.	Debit	Credit	Balance Debit	Balance Credit
2014							
Jan.	31	Balance	✓			113,000	

Account: __Accumulated Depreciation—Equipment__   Account No. _____ 17

Date		Item	Post. Ref.	Debit	Credit	Balance Debit	Balance Credit
2014							
Jan.	31	Balance	✓				12,000
	31	Adjusting	26		5,250		17,250

Account: __Trucks__   Account No. _____ 18

Date		Item	Post. Ref.	Debit	Credit	Balance Debit	Balance Credit
2014							
Jan.	31	Balance	✓			90,000	

Prob. 4–4B (Continued)

Account: **Accumulated Depreciation—Trucks**   Account No. **19**

Date		Item	Post. Ref.	Debit	Credit	Balance Debit	Balance Credit
2014							
Jan.	31	Balance	✓				27,100
	31	Adjusting	26		4,000		31,100

Account: **Accounts Payable**   Account No. **21**

Date		Item	Post. Ref.	Debit	Credit	Balance Debit	Balance Credit
2014							
Jan.	31	Balance	✓				4,500

Account: **Wages Payable**   Account No. **22**

Date		Item	Post. Ref.	Debit	Credit	Balance Debit	Balance Credit
2014							
Jan.	31	Adjusting	26		900		900

Account: **Jeanne McQuay, Capital**   Account No. **31**

Date		Item	Post. Ref.	Debit	Credit	Balance Debit	Balance Credit
2014							
Jan.	31	Balance	✓				126,400
	31	Closing	27		46,150		172,550
	31	Closing	27	3,000			169,550

Account: **Jeanne McQuay, Drawing**   Account No. **32**

Date		Item	Post. Ref.	Debit	Credit	Balance Debit	Balance Credit
2014							
Jan.	31	Balance	✓			3,000	
	31	Closing	27		3,000	—	—

Prob. 4–4B (Continued)

Account: **Income Summary**   Account No. ___**33**___

Date		Item	Post. Ref.	Debit	Credit	Balance Debit	Balance Credit
2014							
Jan.	31	Closing	27		155,000		155,000
	31	Closing	27	108,850			46,150
	31	Closing	27	46,150		—	—

Account: **Service Revenue**   Account No. ___**41**___

Date		Item	Post. Ref.	Debit	Credit	Balance Debit	Balance Credit
2014							
Jan.	31	Balance	✓				155,000
	31	Closing	27	155,000		—	—

Account: **Wages Expense**   Account No. ___**51**___

Date		Item	Post. Ref.	Debit	Credit	Balance Debit	Balance Credit
2014							
Jan.	31	Balance	✓			72,000	
	31	Adjusting	26	900		72,900	
	31	Closing	27		72,900	—	—

Account: **Rent Expense**   Account No. ___**52**___

Date		Item	Post. Ref.	Debit	Credit	Balance Debit	Balance Credit
2014							
Jan.	31	Balance	✓			7,600	
	31	Closing	27		7,600	—	—

Account: **Truck Expense**   Account No. ___**53**___

Date		Item	Post. Ref.	Debit	Credit	Balance Debit	Balance Credit
2014							
Jan.	31	Balance	✓			5,350	
	31	Closing	27		5,350	—	—

Prob. 4–4B (Continued)

Account: **Depreciation Expense—Equipment**   Account No.   **54**

Date		Item	Post. Ref.	Debit	Credit	Balance Debit	Balance Credit
2014							
Jan.	31	Adjusting	26	5,250		5,250	
	31	Closing	27		5,250	—	—

Account: **Supplies Expense**   Account No.   **55**

Date		Item	Post. Ref.	Debit	Credit	Balance Debit	Balance Credit
2014							
Jan.	31	Adjusting	26	5,150		5,150	
	31	Closing	27		5,150	—	—

Account: **Depreciation Expense—Trucks**   Account No.   **56**

Date		Item	Post. Ref.	Debit	Credit	Balance Debit	Balance Credit
2014							
Jan.	31	Adjusting	26	4,000		4,000	
	31	Closing	27		4,000	—	—

Account: **Insurance Expense**   Account No.   **57**

Date		Item	Post. Ref.	Debit	Credit	Balance Debit	Balance Credit
2014							
Jan.	31	Adjusting	26	3,150		3,150	
	31	Closing	27		3,150	—	—

Account: **Miscellaneous Expense**   Account No.   **59**

Date		Item	Post. Ref.	Debit	Credit	Balance Debit	Balance Credit
2014							
Jan.	31	Balance	✓			5,450	
	31	Closing	27		5,450	—	—

Prob. 4-4B (Continued)

2. Optional (Appendix)

RECESSIVE INTERIORS
End-of-Period Spreadsheet (Work Sheet)
For the Year Ended January 31, 2014

Account Title	Unadjusted Trial Balance Debit	Unadjusted Trial Balance Credit	Adjustments Debit	Adjustments Credit	Adjusted Trial Balance Debit	Adjusted Trial Balance Credit	Income Statement Debit	Income Statement Credit	Balance Sheet Debit	Balance Sheet Credit
Cash	13,100				13,100				13,100	
Supplies	8,000			(a) 5,150	2,850				2,850	
Prepaid Insurance	7,500			(b) 3,150	4,350				4,350	
Equipment	113,000				113,000				113,000	
Accum. Depr.—Equipment		12,000		(c) 5,250		17,250				17,250
Trucks	90,000				90,000				90,000	
Accum. Depr.—Trucks		27,100		(d) 4,000		31,100				31,100
Accounts Payable		4,500				4,500				4,500
Wages Payable				(e) 900		900				900
Jeanne McQuay, Capital		126,400				126,400				126,400
Jeanne McQuay, Drawing	3,000				3,000				3,000	
Service Revenue		155,000				155,000		155,000		
Wages Expense	72,000		(e) 900		72,900		72,900			
Rent Expense	7,600				7,600		7,600			
Truck Expense	5,350				5,350		5,350			
Depr. Exp.—Equipment			(c) 5,250		5,250		5,250			
Supplies Expense			(a) 5,150		5,150		5,150			
Depr. Exp.—Trucks			(d) 4,000		4,000		4,000			
Insurance Expense			(b) 3,150		3,150		3,150			
Miscellaneous Expense	5,450				5,450		5,450			
	325,000	325,000	18,450	18,450	335,150	335,150	108,850	155,000	226,300	180,150
Net income							46,150			46,150
							155,000	155,000	226,300	226,300

Prob. 4–4B (Continued)

3.

JOURNAL   Page _____ 26

Date			Post. Ref.	Debit	Credit
2014		Adjusting Entries			
Jan.	31	Supplies Expense	55	5,150	
		Supplies	13		5,150
		Supplies used ($8,000 – $2,850).			
	31	Insurance Expense	57	3,150	
		Prepaid Insurance	14		3,150
		Insurance expired.			
	31	Depreciation Expense—Equipment	54	5,250	
		Accumulated Depr.—Equipment	17		5,250
		Equipment depreciation.			
	31	Depreciation Expense—Trucks	56	4,000	
		Accumulated Depr.—Trucks	19		4,000
		Truck depreciation.			
	31	Wages Expense	51	900	
		Wages Payable	22		900
		Accrued wages.			

Prob. 4–4B (Continued)

4.

RECESSIVE INTERIORS Adjusted Trial Balance January 31, 2014	Debit Balances	Credit Balances
Cash	13,100	
Supplies	2,850	
Prepaid Insurance	4,350	
Equipment	113,000	
Accumulated Depreciation—Equipment		17,250
Trucks	90,000	
Accumulated Depreciation—Trucks		31,100
Accounts Payable		4,500
Wages Payable		900
Jeanne McQuay, Capital		126,400
Jeanne McQuay, Drawing	3,000	
Service Revenue		155,000
Wages Expense	72,900	
Rent Expense	7,600	
Truck Expense	5,350	
Depreciation Expense—Equipment	5,250	
Supplies Expense	5,150	
Depreciation Expense—Trucks	4,000	
Insurance Expense	3,150	
Miscellaneous Expense	5,450	
	335,150	335,150

Prob. 4–4B (Continued)

5.

RECESSIVE INTERIORS Income Statement For the Year Ended January 31, 2014		
Service revenue		$155,000
Expenses:		
Wages expense	$72,900	
Rent expense	7,600	
Truck expense	5,350	
Depreciation expense—equipment	5,250	
Supplies expense	5,150	
Depreciation expense—trucks	4,000	
Insurance expense	3,150	
Miscellaneous expense	5,450	
Total expenses		108,850
Net income		$ 46,150

RECESSIVE INTERIORS Statement of Owner's Equity For the Year Ended January 31, 2014		
Jeanne McQuay, capital, February 1, 2013		$126,400
Net income for the year	$46,150	
Less withdrawals	3,000	
Increase in owner's equity		43,150
Jeanne McQuay, capital, January 31, 2014		$169,550

Prob. 4–4B (Continued)

RECESSIVE INTERIORS
Balance Sheet
January 31, 2014

Assets					Liabilities			
Current assets:					**Current liabilities:**			
Cash		$13,100			Accounts payable	$4,500		
Supplies		2,850			Wages payable	900		
Prepaid insurance		4,350			Total liabilities			$ 5,400
Total current assets			$ 20,300					
Property, plant, and equipment:					**Owner's Equity**			
Equipment	$113,000				Jeanne McQuay, capital			169,550
Less accum. depreciation	17,250	$95,750						
Trucks	$ 90,000							
Less accum. depreciation	31,100	58,900						
Total property, plant, and equipment			154,650		Total liabilities and owner's			
Total assets			$174,950		equity			$174,950

Prob. 4–4B (Concluded)

6.

JOURNAL   Page _____ 27

Date			Post. Ref.	Debit	Credit
2014		**Closing Entries**			
Jan.	31	Service Revenue	41	155,000	
		Income Summary	33		155,000
	31	Income Summary	33	108,850	
		Wages Expense	51		72,900
		Rent Expense	52		7,600
		Truck Expense	53		5,350
		Depreciation Expense—Equipment	54		5,250
		Supplies Expense	55		5,150
		Depreciation Expense—Trucks	56		4,000
		Insurance Expense	57		3,150
		Miscellaneous Expense	59		5,450
	31	Income Summary	33	46,150	
		Jeanne McQuay, Capital	31		46,150
	31	Jeanne McQuay, Capital	31	3,000	
		Jeanne McQuay, Drawing	32		3,000

7.

RECESSIVE INTERIORS
Post-Closing Trial Balance
January 31, 2014

	Debit Balances	Credit Balances
Cash	13,100	
Supplies	2,850	
Prepaid Insurance	4,350	
Equipment	113,000	
Accumulated Depreciation—Equipment		17,250
Trucks	90,000	
Accumulated Depreciation—Trucks		31,100
Accounts Payable		4,500
Wages Payable		900
Jeanne McQuay, Capital		169,550
	223,300	223,300

4-82

Prob. 4–5B

1. and 2.

JOURNAL   Page _____ **1**

Date			Post. Ref.	Debit	Credit
2014					
Apr.	1	Cash	11	20,000	
		Accounts Receivable	12	14,700	
		Supplies	14	3,300	
		Office Equipment	18	12,000	
		Jeff Horton, Capital	31		50,000
	1	Prepaid Rent	15	6,000	
		Cash	11		6,000
	2	Prepaid Insurance	16	4,200	
		Cash	11		4,200
	4	Cash	11	9,400	
		Unearned Fees	23		9,400
	5	Office Equipment	18	8,000	
		Accounts Payable	21		8,000
	6	Cash	11	11,700	
		Accounts Receivable	12		11,700
	10	Miscellaneous Expense	59	350	
		Cash	11		350
	12	Accounts Payable	21	6,400	
		Cash	11		6,400
	12	Accounts Receivable	12	21,900	
		Fees Earned	41		21,900
	14	Salary Expense	51	1,650	
		Cash	11		1,650

Prob. 4–5B (Continued)

JOURNAL

Page _____ 2

Date			Post. Ref.	Debit	Credit
2014					
Apr.	17	Cash	11	6,600	
		Fees Earned	41		6,600
	18	Supplies	14	725	
		Cash	11		725
	20	Accounts Receivable	12	16,800	
		Fees Earned	41		16,800
	24	Cash	11	4,450	
		Fees Earned	41		4,450
	26	Cash	11	26,500	
		Accounts Receivable	12		26,500
	27	Salary Expense	51	1,650	
		Cash	11		1,650
	29	Miscellaneous Expense	59	540	
		Cash	11		540
	30	Miscellaneous Expense	59	760	
		Cash	11		760
	30	Cash	11	5,160	
		Fees Earned	41		5,160
	30	Accounts Receivable	12	2,590	
		Fees Earned	41		2,590
	30	Jeff Horton, Drawing	32	18,000	
		Cash	11		18,000

4-84

Prob. 4–5B (Continued)

2., 6., and 9.

Account: **Cash**　　　　　　　　　　　Account No.　　**11**

Date		Item	Post. Ref.	Debit	Credit	Balance Debit	Balance Credit
2014							
Apr.	1		1	20,000		20,000	
	1		1		6,000	14,000	
	2		1		4,200	9,800	
	4		1	9,400		19,200	
	6		1	11,700		30,900	
	10		1		350	30,550	
	12		1		6,400	24,150	
	14		1		1,650	22,500	
	17		2	6,600		29,100	
	18		2		725	28,375	
	24		2	4,450		32,825	
	26		2	26,500		59,325	
	27		2		1,650	57,675	
	29		2		540	57,135	
	30		2		760	56,375	
	30		2	5,160		61,535	
	30		2		18,000	43,535	

Account: **Accounts Receivable**　　　　　　Account No.　　**12**

Date		Item	Post. Ref.	Debit	Credit	Balance Debit	Balance Credit
2014							
Apr.	1		1	14,700		14,700	
	6		1		11,700	3,000	
	12		1	21,900		24,900	
	20		2	16,800		41,700	
	26		2		26,500	15,200	
	30		2	2,590		17,790	

Account: **Supplies**　　　　　　　　　Account No.　　**14**

Date		Item	Post. Ref.	Debit	Credit	Balance Debit	Balance Credit
2014							
Apr.	1		1	3,300		3,300	
	18		2	725		4,025	
	30	Adjusting	3		2,800	1,225	

Prob. 4–5B (Continued)

Account: **Prepaid Rent** Account No. **15**

Date		Item	Post. Ref.	Debit	Credit	Balance Debit	Balance Credit
2014							
Apr.	1		1	6,000		6,000	
	30	Adjusting	3		2,000	4,000	

Account: **Prepaid Insurance** Account No. **16**

Date		Item	Post. Ref.	Debit	Credit	Balance Debit	Balance Credit
2014							
Apr.	2		1	4,200		4,200	
	30	Adjusting	3		350	3,850	

Account: **Office Equipment** Account No. **18**

Date		Item	Post. Ref.	Debit	Credit	Balance Debit	Balance Credit
2014							
Apr.	1		1	12,000		12,000	
	5		1	8,000		20,000	

Account: **Accumulated Depreciation** Account No. **19**

Date		Item	Post. Ref.	Debit	Credit	Balance Debit	Balance Credit
2014							
Apr.	30	Adjusting	3		400		400

Account: **Accounts Payable** Account No. **21**

Date		Item	Post. Ref.	Debit	Credit	Balance Debit	Balance Credit
2014							
Apr.	5		1		8,000		8,000
	12		1	6,400			1,600

Account: **Salaries Payable** Account No. **22**

Date		Item	Post. Ref.	Debit	Credit	Balance Debit	Balance Credit
2014							
Apr.	30	Adjusting	3		275		275

Prob. 4–5B (Continued)

Account: **Unearned Fees**   Account No.   **23**

Date		Item	Post. Ref.	Debit	Credit	Balance Debit	Balance Credit
2014							
Apr.	4		1		9,400		9,400
	30	Adjusting	3	7,050			2,350

Account: **Jeff Horton, Capital**   Account No.   **31**

Date		Item	Post. Ref.	Debit	Credit	Balance Debit	Balance Credit
2014							
Apr.	1		1		50,000		50,000
	30	Closing	4		53,775		103,775
	30	Closing	4	18,000			85,775

Account: **Jeff Horton, Drawing**   Account No.   **32**

Date		Item	Post. Ref.	Debit	Credit	Balance Debit	Balance Credit
2014							
Apr.	30		2	18,000		18,000	
	30	Closing	4		18,000	—	—

Account: **Income Summary**   Account No.   **33**

Date		Item	Post. Ref.	Debit	Credit	Balance Debit	Balance Credit
2014							
Apr.	30	Closing	4		64,550		64,550
	30	Closing	4	10,775			53,775
	30	Closing	4	53,775		—	—

Prob. 4–5B (Continued)

Account: **Fees Earned**   Account No. **41**

Date		Item	Post. Ref.	Debit	Credit	Balance Debit	Balance Credit
2014							
Apr.	12		1		21,900		21,900
	17		2		6,600		28,500
	20		2		16,800		45,300
	24		2		4,450		49,750
	30		2		5,160		54,910
	30		2		2,590		57,500
	30	Adjusting	3		7,050		64,550
	30	Closing	4	64,550		—	—

Account: **Salary Expense**   Account No. **51**

Date		Item	Post. Ref.	Debit	Credit	Balance Debit	Balance Credit
2014							
Apr.	14		1	1,650		1,650	
	27		2	1,650		3,300	
	30	Adjusting	3	275		3,575	
	30	Closing	4		3,575	—	—

Account: **Supplies Expense**   Account No. **52**

Date		Item	Post. Ref.	Debit	Credit	Balance Debit	Balance Credit
2014							
Apr.	30	Adjusting	3	2,800		2,800	
	30	Closing	4		2,800	—	—

Account: **Rent Expense**   Account No. **53**

Date		Item	Post. Ref.	Debit	Credit	Balance Debit	Balance Credit
2014							
Apr.	30	Adjusting	3	2,000		2,000	
	30	Closing	4		2,000	—	—

Prob. 4–5B (Continued)

Account: **Depreciation Expense**   Account No. **54**

Date		Item	Post. Ref.	Debit	Credit	Balance Debit	Balance Credit
2014							
Apr.	30	Adjusting	3	400		400	
	30	Closing	4		400	—	—

Account: **Insurance Expense**   Account No. **55**

Date		Item	Post. Ref.	Debit	Credit	Balance Debit	Balance Credit
2014							
Apr.	30	Adjusting	3	350		350	
	30	Closing	4		350	—	—

Account: **Miscellaneous Expense**   Account No. **59**

Date		Item	Post. Ref.	Debit	Credit	Balance Debit	Balance Credit
2014							
Apr.	10		1	350		350	
	29		2	540		890	
	30		2	760		1,650	
	30	Closing	4		1,650	—	—

Prob. 4–5B (Continued)

3.

ROSEBUD CONSULTING Unadjusted Trial Balance April 30, 2014	Debit Balances	Credit Balances
Cash	43,535	
Accounts Receivable	17,790	
Supplies	4,025	
Prepaid Rent	6,000	
Prepaid Insurance	4,200	
Office Equipment	20,000	
Accumulated Depreciation		0
Accounts Payable		1,600
Salaries Payable		0
Unearned Fees		9,400
Jeff Horton, Capital		50,000
Jeff Horton, Drawing	18,000	
Fees Earned		57,500
Salary Expense	3,300	
Supplies Expense	0	
Rent Expense	0	
Depreciation Expense	0	
Insurance Expense	0	
Miscellaneous Expense	1,650	
	118,500	118,500

Prob. 4–5B (Continued)

5.   Optional (Appendix)

ROSEBUD CONSULTING
End-of-Period Spreadsheet (Work Sheet)
For the Month Ended April 30, 2014

Account Title	Unadjusted Trial Balance Debit	Unadjusted Trial Balance Credit	Adjustments Debit		Adjustments Credit		Adjusted Trial Balance Debit	Adjusted Trial Balance Credit	Income Statement Debit	Income Statement Credit	Balance Sheet Debit	Balance Sheet Credit
Cash	43,535						43,535				43,535	
Accounts Receivable	17,790						17,790				17,790	
Supplies	4,025				(b)	2,800	1,225				1,225	
Prepaid Rent	6,000				(e)	2,000	4,000				4,000	
Prepaid Insurance	4,200				(a)	350	3,850				3,850	
Office Equipment	20,000						20,000				20,000	
Accum. Depreciation					(c)	400		400				400
Accounts Payable		1,600						1,600				1,600
Salaries Payable					(d)	275		275				275
Unearned Fees		9,400	(f)	7,050				2,350				2,350
Jeff Horton, Capital		50,000						50,000				50,000
Jeff Horton, Drawing	18,000						18,000				18,000	
Fees Earned		57,500			(f)	7,050		64,550		64,550		
Salary Expense	3,300		(d)	275			3,575		3,575			
Supplies Expense			(b)	2,800			2,800		2,800			
Rent Expense			(e)	2,000			2,000		2,000			
Depreciation Expense			(c)	400			400		400			
Insurance Expense			(a)	350			350		350			
Miscellaneous Expense	1,650						1,650		1,650			
	118,500	118,500		12,875		12,875	119,175	119,175	10,775	64,550	108,400	54,625
Net income									53,775			53,775
									64,550	64,550	108,400	108,400

Prob. 4–5B (Continued)

6.   **JOURNAL**   Page _____ 3

Date		Post. Ref.	Debit	Credit
2014	**Adjusting Entries**			
Apr.	30 Insurance Expense	55	350	
	Prepaid Insurance	16		350
	Insurance expired.			
	30 Supplies Expense	52	2,800	
	Supplies	14		2,800
	Supplies used ($4,025 – $1,225).			
	30 Depreciation Expense	54	400	
	Accumulated Depreciation	19		400
	Equipment depreciation.			
	30 Salary Expense	51	275	
	Salaries Payable	22		275
	Accrued salaries.			
	30 Rent Expense	53	2,000	
	Prepaid Rent	15		2,000
	Rent expired.			
	30 Unearned Fees	23	7,050	
	Fees Earned	41		7,050
	Unearned fees earned			
	($9,400 – $2,350).			

4-92

Prob. 4–5B (Continued)

7.

ROSEBUD CONSULTING Adjusted Trial Balance April 30, 2014	Debit Balances	Credit Balances
Cash	43,535	
Accounts Receivable	17,790	
Supplies	1,225	
Prepaid Rent	4,000	
Prepaid Insurance	3,850	
Office Equipment	20,000	
Accumulated Depreciation		400
Accounts Payable		1,600
Salaries Payable		275
Unearned Fees		2,350
Jeff Horton, Capital		50,000
Jeff Horton, Drawing	18,000	
Fees Earned		64,550
Salary Expense	3,575	
Supplies Expense	2,800	
Rent Expense	2,000	
Depreciation Expense	400	
Insurance Expense	350	
Miscellaneous Expense	1,650	
	119,175	119,175

Prob. 4–5B (Continued)

8.

ROSEBUD CONSULTING		
Income Statement		
For the Month Ended April 30, 2014		
Fees earned		$64,550
Expenses:		
Salary expense	$3,575	
Supplies expense	2,800	
Rent expense	2,000	
Depreciation expense	400	
Insurance expense	350	
Miscellaneous expense	1,650	
Total expenses		10,775
Net income		$53,775

ROSEBUD CONSULTING		
Statement of Owner's Equity		
For the Month Ended April 30, 2014		
Jeff Horton, capital, April 1, 2014		$ 0
Investment during month	$ 50,000	
Net income	53,775	
	$103,775	
Less withdrawals	18,000	
Increase in owner's equity		85,775
Jeff Horton, capital, April 30, 2014		$85,775

Prob. 4–5B (Continued)

ROSEBUD CONSULTING
Balance Sheet
April 30, 2014

Assets			Liabilities		
Current assets:			Current liabilities:		
Cash	$43,535		Accounts payable	$1,600	
Accounts receivable	17,790		Salaries payable	275	
Supplies	1,225		Unearned fees	2,350	
Prepaid rent	4,000		Total liabilities		$ 4,225
Prepaid insurance	3,850				
Total current assets		$70,400			
Property, plant, and equipment:			Owner's Equity		
Office equipment	$20,000		Jeff Horton, capital		85,775
Less accum. depreciation	400				
Total property, plant, and equipment		19,600	Total liabilities and owner's		
Total assets		$90,000	equity		$90,000

Prob. 4–5B (Concluded)

9.

JOURNAL

Page _____ 4

Date			Post. Ref.	Debit	Credit
2014		**Closing Entries**			
Apr.	30	Fees Earned	41	64,550	
		Income Summary	33		64,550
	30	Income Summary	33	10,775	
		Salary Expense	51		3,575
		Supplies Expense	52		2,800
		Rent Expense	53		2,000
		Depreciation Expense	54		400
		Insurance Expense	55		350
		Miscellaneous Expense	59		1,650
	30	Income Summary	33	53,775	
		Jeff Horton, Capital	31		53,775
	30	Jeff Horton, Capital	31	103,775	
		Jeff Horton, Drawing	32		103,775

10.

ROSEBUD CONSULTING Post-Closing Trial Balance April 30, 2014	Debit Balances	Credit Balances
Cash	43,535	
Accounts Receivable	17,790	
Supplies	1,225	
Prepaid Rent	4,000	
Prepaid Insurance	3,850	
Office Equipment	20,000	
Accumulated Depreciation		400
Accounts Payable		1,600
Salaries Payable		275
Unearned Fees		2,350
Jeff Horton, Capital		85,775
	90,400	90,400

CONTINUING PROBLEM

1. Optional (Appendix)

PS MUSIC
End-of-Period Spreadsheet (Work Sheet)
For the Two Months Ended July 31, 2014

Account Title	Unadjusted Trial Balance Debit	Unadjusted Trial Balance Credit	Adjustments Debit	Adjustments Credit	Adjusted Trial Balance Debit	Adjusted Trial Balance Credit	Income Statement Debit	Income Statement Credit	Balance Sheet Debit	Balance Sheet Credit
Cash	9,945				9,945				9,945	
Accounts Receivable	2,750		(a) 1,400		4,150				4,150	
Supplies	1,020			(b) 745	275				275	
Prepaid Insurance	2,700			(c) 225	2,475				2,475	
Office Equipment	7,500				7,500				7,500	
Accum. Depr.—Off. Equip.				(d) 50		50				50
Accounts Payable		8,350				8,350				8,350
Wages Payable				(f) 140		140				140
Unearned Revenue		7,200	(e) 3,600			3,600				3,600
Peyton Smith, Capital		9,000				9,000				9,000
Peyton Smith, Drawing	1,750				1,750				1,750	
Fees Earned		16,200		(a) 1,400		21,200		21,200		
				(e) 3,600						
Music Expense	3,610				3,610		3,610			
Wages Expense	2,800		(f) 140		2,940		2,940			
Office Rent Expense	2,550				2,550		2,550			
Advertising Expense	1,500				1,500		1,500			
Equip. Rent Expense	1,375				1,375		1,375			
Utilities Expense	1,215				1,215		1,215			
Supplies Expense	180		(b) 745		925		925			
Insurance Expense			(c) 225		225		225			
Depreciation Expense			(d) 50		50		50			
Miscellaneous Expense	1,855				1,855		1,855			
	40,750	40,750	6,160	6,160	42,340	42,340	16,245	21,200	26,095	21,140
Net income							4,955			4,955
							21,200	21,200	26,095	26,095

Continuing Problem (Continued)

2.

PS MUSIC Income Statement For the Two Months Ended July 31, 2014		
Fees earned		$21,200
Expenses:		
Music expense	$3,610	
Wages expense	2,940	
Office rent expense	2,550	
Advertising expense	1,500	
Equipment rent expense	1,375	
Utilities expense	1,215	
Supplies expense	925	
Insurance expense	225	
Depreciation expense	50	
Miscellaneous expense	1,855	
Total expenses		16,245
Net income		$ 4,955

PS MUSIC Statement of Owner's Equity For the Two Months Ended July 31, 2014		
Peyton Smith, capital, June 1, 2014		$ 0
Investment during month	$ 9,000	
Net income	4,955	
	$13,955	
Less withdrawals	1,750	
Increase in owner's equity		12,205
Peyton Smith, capital, July 31, 2014		$12,205

Continuing Problem (Continued)

PS MUSIC
Balance Sheet
July 31, 2014

Assets		
Current assets:		
Cash	$9,945	
Accounts receivable	4,150	
Supplies	275	
Prepaid insurance	2,475	
Total current assets		$16,845
Property, plant, and equipment:		
Office equipment	$7,500	
Less accum. depreciation	50	
Total property, plant, and equipment		7,450
Total assets		$24,295

Liabilities		
Current liabilities:		
Accounts payable	$8,350	
Wages payable	140	
Unearned revenue	3,600	
Total liabilities		$12,090
Owner's Equity		
Peyton Smith, capital		12,205
Total liabilities and owner's equity		$24,295

Continuing Problem (Continued)

3.   JOURNAL   Page _____ 4

Date			Post. Ref.	Debit	Credit
2014		**Closing Entries**			
July	31	Fees Earned	41	21,200	
		Income Summary	33		21,200
	31	Income Summary	33	16,245	
		Wages Expense	50		2,940
		Office Rent Expense	51		2,550
		Equipment Rent Expense	52		1,375
		Utilities Expense	53		1,215
		Music Expense	54		3,610
		Advertising Expense	55		1,500
		Supplies Expense	56		925
		Insurance Expense	57		225
		Depreciation Expense	58		50
		Miscellaneous Expense	59		1,855
	31	Income Summary	33	4,955	
		Peyton Smith, Capital	31		4,955
	31	Peyton Smith, Capital	31	13,955	
		Peyton Smith, Drawing	32		13,955

4-100

Continuing Problem (Continued)

Account: **Cash**   Account No.   **11**

Date		Item	Post. Ref.	Debit	Credit	Balance Debit	Balance Credit
2014							
July	1	Balance	✓			3,920	
	1		1	5,000		8,920	
	1		1		1,750	7,170	
	1		1		2,700	4,470	
	2		1	1,000		5,470	
	3		1	7,200		12,670	
	3		1		250	12,420	
	4		1		900	11,520	
	8		1		200	11,320	
	11		1	1,000		12,320	
	13		1		700	11,620	
	14		1		1,200	10,420	
	16		2	2,000		12,420	
	21		2		620	11,800	
	22		2		800	11,000	
	23		2	750		11,750	
	27		2		915	10,835	
	28		2		1,200	9,635	
	29		2		540	9,095	
	30		2	500		9,595	
	31		2	3,000		12,595	
	31		2		1,400	11,195	
	31		2		1,250	9,945	

Account: **Accounts Receivable**   Account No.   **12**

Date		Item	Post. Ref.	Debit	Credit	Balance Debit	Balance Credit
2014							
July	1	Balance	✓			1,000	
	2		1		1,000	—	—
	23		2	1,750		1,750	
	30		2	1,000		2,750	
	31	Adjusting	3	1,400		4,150	

Continuing Problem (Continued)

Account: **Supplies**   Account No. **14**

Date		Item	Post. Ref.	Debit	Credit	Balance Debit	Balance Credit
2014							
July	1	Balance	✓			170	
	18		2	850		1,020	
	31	Adjusting	3		745	275	

Account: **Prepaid Insurance**   Account No. **15**

Date		Item	Post. Ref.	Debit	Credit	Balance Debit	Balance Credit
2014							
July	1		1	2,700		2,700	
	31	Adjusting	3		225	2,475	

Account: **Office Equipment**   Account No. **17**

Date		Item	Post. Ref.	Debit	Credit	Balance Debit	Balance Credit
2014							
July	5		1	7,500		7,500	

Account: **Accumulated Depreciation—Office Equipment**   Account No. **18**

Date		Item	Post. Ref.	Debit	Credit	Balance Debit	Balance Credit
2014							
July	31	Adjusting	3		50		50

Account: **Accounts Payable**   Account No. **21**

Date		Item	Post. Ref.	Debit	Credit	Balance Debit	Balance Credit
2014							
July	1	Balance	✓				250
	3		1	250		—	—
	5		1		7,500		7,500
	18		2		850		8,350

Continuing Problem (Continued)

Account: Wages Payable   Account No. 22

Date		Item	Post. Ref.	Debit	Credit	Balance Debit	Balance Credit
2014							
July	31	Adjusting	3		140		140

Account: Unearned Revenue   Account No. 23

Date		Item	Post. Ref.	Debit	Credit	Balance Debit	Balance Credit
2014							
July	3		1		7,200		7,200
	31	Adjusting	3	3,600			3,600

Account: Peyton Smith, Capital   Account No. 31

Date		Item	Post. Ref.	Debit	Credit	Balance Debit	Balance Credit
2014							
July	1	Balance	✓				4,000
	1		1		5,000		9,000
	31	Closing	4		4,955		13,955
	31	Closing	4	1,750			12,205

Account: Peyton Smith, Drawing   Account No. 32

Date		Item	Post. Ref.	Debit	Credit	Balance Debit	Balance Credit
2014							
July	1	Balance	✓			500	
	31		2	1,250		1,750	
	31	Closing	4		1,750	—	—

Account: Income Summary   Account No. 33

Date		Item	Post. Ref.	Debit	Credit	Balance Debit	Balance Credit
2014							
July	31	Closing	4		21,200		21,200
	31	Closing	4	16,245			4,955
	31	Closing	4	4,955		—	—

Continuing Problem (Continued)

Account: Fees Earned   **Account No.** 41

Date		Item	Post. Ref.	Debit	Credit	Balance Debit	Balance Credit
2014							
July	1	Balance	✓				6,200
	11		1		1,000		7,200
	16		2		2,000		9,200
	23		2		2,500		11,700
	30		2		1,500		13,200
	31		2		3,000		16,200
	31	Adjusting	3		1,400		17,600
	31	Adjusting	3		3,600		21,200
	31	Closing	4	21,200		—	—

Account: Wages Expense   **Account No.** 50

Date		Item	Post. Ref.	Debit	Credit	Balance Debit	Balance Credit
2014							
July	1	Balance	✓			400	
	14		1	1,200		1,600	
	28		2	1,200		2,800	
	31	Adjusting	3	140		2,940	
	31	Closing	4		2,940	—	—

Account: Office Rent Expense   **Account No.** 51

Date		Item	Post. Ref.	Debit	Credit	Balance Debit	Balance Credit
2014							
July	1	Balance	✓			800	
	1		1	1,750		2,550	
	31	Closing	4		2,550	—	—

Account: Equipment Rent Expense   **Account No.** 52

Date		Item	Post. Ref.	Debit	Credit	Balance Debit	Balance Credit
2012							
July	1	Balance	✓			675	
	13		1	700		1,375	
	31	Closing	4		1,375	—	—

Continuing Problem (Continued)

Account: Utilities Expense **Account No.** 53

Date		Item	Post. Ref.	Debit	Credit	Balance Debit	Balance Credit
2014							
July	1	Balance	✓			300	
	27		2	915		1,215	
	31	Closing	4		1,215	—	—

Account: Music Expense **Account No.** 54

Date		Item	Post. Ref.	Debit	Credit	Balance Debit	Balance Credit
2014							
July	1	Balance	✓			1,590	
	21		2	620		2,210	
	31		2	1,400		3,610	
	31	Closing	4		3,610	—	—

Account: Advertising Expense **Account No.** 55

Date		Item	Post. Ref.	Debit	Credit	Balance Debit	Balance Credit
2014							
July	1	Balance	✓			500	
	8		1	200		700	
	22		2	800		1,500	
	31	Closing	4		1,500	—	—

Account: Supplies Expense **Account No.** 56

Date		Item	Post. Ref.	Debit	Credit	Balance Debit	Balance Credit
2014							
July	1	Balance	✓			180	
	31	Adjusting	3	745		925	
	31	Closing	4		925	—	—

Continuing Problem (Continued)

Account: **Insurance Expense**   Account No.   57

Date		Item	Post. Ref.	Debit	Credit	Balance Debit	Balance Credit
2014							
July	31	Adjusting	3	225		225	
	31	Closing	4		225	—	—

Account: **Depreciation Expense**   Account No.   58

Date		Item	Post. Ref.	Debit	Credit	Balance Debit	Balance Credit
2014							
July	31	Adjusting	3	50		50	
	31	Closing	4		50	—	—

Account: **Miscellaneous Expense**   Account No.   59

Date		Item	Post. Ref.	Debit	Credit	Balance Debit	Balance Credit
2014							
July	1	Balance	✓			415	
	4		1	900		1,315	
	29		2	540		1,855	
	31	Closing	4		1,855	—	—

Continuing Problem (Concluded)

4.

PS MUSIC Post-Closing Trial Balance July 31, 2014	Debit Balances	Credit Balances
Cash	9,945	
Accounts Receivable	4,150	
Supplies	275	
Prepaid Insurance	2,475	
Office Equipment	7,500	
Accumulated Depreciation—Office Equipment		50
Accounts Payable		8,350
Wages Payable		140
Unearned Revenue		3,600
Peyton Smith, Capital		12,205
	24,345	24,345

COMPREHENSIVE PROBLEM 1

1. and 2.

JOURNAL

Page _____ 5

Date			Post. Ref.	Debit	Credit
2014					
May	3	Cash	11	4,500	
		Unearned Fees	23		4,500
	5	Cash	11	2,450	
		Accounts Receivable	12		2,450
	9	Miscellaneous Expense	59	225	
		Cash	11		225
	13	Accounts Payable	21	640	
		Cash	11		640
	15	Accounts Receivable	12	9,180	
		Fees Earned	41		9,180
	16	Salary Expense	51	630	
		Salaries Payable	22	120	
		Cash	11		750
	17	Cash	11	8,360	
		Fees Earned	41		8,360

Comp. Prob. 1 (Continued)

JOURNAL   Page _____ **6**

Date			Post. Ref.	Debit	Credit
2014					
May	20	Supplies	14	735	
		Accounts Payable	21		735
	21	Accounts Receivable	12	4,820	
		Fees Earned	41		4,820
	25	Cash	11	7,900	
		Fees Earned	41		7,900
	27	Cash	11	9,520	
		Accounts Receivable	12		9,520
	28	Salary Expense	51	750	
		Cash	11		750
	30	Miscellaneous Expense	59	260	
		Cash	11		260
	31	Miscellaneous Expense	59	810	
		Cash	11		810
	31	Cash	11	3,300	
		Fees Earned	41		3,300
	31	Accounts Receivable	12	2,650	
		Fees Earned	41		2,650
	31	Kelly Pitney, Drawing	32	10,500	
		Cash	11		10,500

4-109

Comp. Prob. 1 (Continued)

2., 6., and 9.

Account: **Cash**   Account No.   **11**

Date		Item	Post. Ref.	Debit	Credit	Balance Debit	Credit
2014							
May	1	Balance	✓			22,100	
	3		5	4,500		26,600	
	5		5	2,450		29,050	
	9		5		225	28,825	
	13		5		640	28,185	
	16		5		750	27,435	
	17		5	8,360		35,795	
	25		6	7,900		43,695	
	27		6	9,520		53,215	
	28		6		750	52,465	
	30		6		260	52,205	
	31		6		810	51,395	
	31		6	3,300		54,695	
	31		6		10,500	44,195	

Account: **Accounts Receivable**   Account No.   **12**

Date		Item	Post. Ref.	Debit	Credit	Balance Debit	Credit
2014							
May	1	Balance	✓			3,400	
	5		5		2,450	950	
	15		5	9,180		10,130	
	21		6	4,820		14,950	
	27		6		9,520	5,430	
	31		6	2,650		8,080	

Account: **Supplies**   Account No.   **14**

Date		Item	Post. Ref.	Debit	Credit	Balance Debit	Credit
2014							
May	1	Balance	✓			1,350	
	20		6	735		2,085	
	31	Adjusting	7		1,370	715	

Comp. Prob. 1 (Continued)

Account: **Prepaid Rent**   Account No. **15**

Date		Item	Post. Ref.	Debit	Credit	Balance Debit	Balance Credit
2014							
May	1	Balance	✓			3,200	
	31	Adjusting	7		1,600	1,600	

Account: **Prepaid Insurance**   Account No. **16**

Date		Item	Post. Ref.	Debit	Credit	Balance Debit	Balance Credit
2014							
May	1	Balance	✓			1,500	
	31	Adjusting	7		275	1,225	

Account: **Office Equipment**   Account No. **18**

Date		Item	Post. Ref.	Debit	Credit	Balance Debit	Balance Credit
2014							
May	1	Balance	✓			14,500	

Account: **Accumulated Depreciation**   Account No. **19**

Date		Item	Post. Ref.	Debit	Credit	Balance Debit	Balance Credit
2014							
May	1	Balance	✓				330
	31	Adjusting	7		330		660

Account: **Accounts Payable**   Account No. **21**

Date		Item	Post. Ref.	Debit	Credit	Balance Debit	Balance Credit
2014							
May	1	Balance	✓				800
	13		5	640			160
	20		6		735		895

Account: **Salaries Payable**   Account No. **22**

Date		Item	Post. Ref.	Debit	Credit	Balance Debit	Balance Credit
2014							
May	1	Balance	✓				120
	16		5	120			—
	31	Adjusting	7		325		325

4-111

Comp. Prob. 1 (Continued)

Account: __Unearned Fees__   Account No. __23__

Date		Item	Post. Ref.	Debit	Credit	Balance Debit	Balance Credit
2014							
May	1	Balance	✓				2,500
	3		5		4,500		7,000
	31	Adjusting	7	3,790			3,210

Account: __Kelly Pitney, Capital__   Account No. __31__

Date		Item	Post. Ref.	Debit	Credit	Balance Debit	Balance Credit
2014							
May	1	Balance	✓				42,300
	31	Closing	8		33,425		75,725
	31	Closing	8	10,500			65,225

Account: __Kelly Pitney, Drawing__   Account No. __32__

Date		Item	Post. Ref.	Debit	Credit	Balance Debit	Balance Credit
2014							
May	31		6	10,500		10,500	
	31	Closing	8		10,500	—	—

Account: __Income Summary__   Account No. __33__

Date		Item	Post. Ref.	Debit	Credit	Balance Debit	Balance Credit
2014							
May	31	Closing	8		40,000		40,000
	31	Closing	8	6,575			33,425
	31	Closing	8	33,425		—	—

Comp. Prob. 1 (Continued)

Account: **Fees Earned**   Account No. **41**

Date		Item	Post. Ref.	Debit	Credit	Balance Debit	Balance Credit
2014							
May	15		5		9,180		9,180
	17		5		8,360		17,540
	21		6		4,820		22,360
	25		6		7,900		30,260
	31		6		3,300		33,560
	31		6		2,650		36,210
	31	Adjusting	7		3,790		40,000
	31	Closing	8	40,000		—	—

Account: **Salary Expense**   Account No. **51**

Date		Item	Post. Ref.	Debit	Credit	Balance Debit	Balance Credit
2014							
May	16		5	630		630	
	28		6	750		1,380	
	31	Adjusting	7	325		1,705	
	31	Closing	8		1,705	—	—

Account: **Rent Expense**   Account No. **52**

Date		Item	Post. Ref.	Debit	Credit	Balance Debit	Balance Credit
2014							
May	31	Adjusting	7	1,600		1,600	
	31	Closing	8		1,600	—	—

Account: **Supplies Expense**   Account No. **53**

Date		Item	Post. Ref.	Debit	Credit	Balance Debit	Balance Credit
2014							
May	31	Adjusting	7	1,370		1,370	
	31	Closing	8		1,370	—	—

Comp. Prob. 1 (Continued)

Account: **Depreciation Expense**   Account No. **54**

Date		Item	Post. Ref.	Debit	Credit	Balance Debit	Balance Credit
2014							
May	31	Adjusting	7	330		330	
	31	Closing	8		330	—	—

Account: **Insurance Expense**   Account No. **55**

Date		Item	Post. Ref.	Debit	Credit	Balance Debit	Balance Credit
2014							
May	31	Adjusting	7	275		275	
	31	Closing	8		275	—	—

Account: **Miscellaneous Expense**   Account No. **59**

Date		Item	Post. Ref.	Debit	Credit	Balance Debit	Balance Credit
2014							
May	9		5	225		225	
	30		6	260		485	
	31		6	810		1,295	
	31	Closing	8		1,295	—	—

Comp. Prob. 1 (Continued)

3.

KELLY CONSULTING Unadjusted Trial Balance May 31, 2014	Debit Balances	Credit Balances
Cash	44,195	
Accounts Receivable	8,080	
Supplies	2,085	
Prepaid Rent	3,200	
Prepaid Insurance	1,500	
Office Equipment	14,500	
Accumulated Depreciation		330
Accounts Payable		895
Salaries Payable		0
Unearned Fees		7,000
Kelly Pitney, Capital		42,300
Kelly Pitney, Drawing	10,500	
Fees Earned		36,210
Salary Expense	1,380	
Rent Expense	0	
Supplies Expense	0	
Depreciation Expense	0	
Insurance Expense	0	
Miscellaneous Expense	1,295	
	86,735	86,735

Comp. Prob. 1 (Continued)

5.   Optional (Appendix)

KELLY CONSULTING
End-of-Period Spreadsheet (Work Sheet)
For the Month Ended May 31, 2014

Account Title	Unadjusted Trial Balance Debit	Credit	Adjustments Debit	Credit	Adjusted Trial Balance Debit	Credit	Income Statement Debit	Credit	Balance Sheet Debit	Credit
Cash	44,195				44,195				44,195	
Accounts Receivable	8,080				8,080				8,080	
Supplies	2,085			(b) 1,370	715				715	
Prepaid Rent	3,200			(e) 1,600	1,600				1,600	
Prepaid Insurance	1,500			(a) 275	1,225				1,225	
Office Equipment	14,500				14,500				14,500	
Accum. Depreciation		330		(c) 330		660				660
Accounts Payable		895				895				895
Salaries Payable				(d) 325		325				325
Unearned Fees		7,000	(f) 3,790			3,210				3,210
Kelly Pitney, Capital		42,300				42,300				42,300
Kelly Pitney, Drawing	10,500				10,500				10,500	
Fees Earned		36,210		(f) 3,790		40,000		40,000		
Salary Expense	1,380		(d) 325		1,705		1,705			
Rent Expense			(e) 1,600		1,600		1,600			
Supplies Expense			(b) 1,370		1,370		1,370			
Depreciation Expense			(c) 330		330		330			
Insurance Expense			(a) 275		275		275			
Miscellaneous Expense	1,295				1,295		1,295			
	86,735	86,735	7,690	7,690	87,390	87,390	6,575	40,000	80,815	47,390
Net income							33,425			33,425
							40,000	40,000	80,815	80,815

Comp. Prob. 1 (Continued)

6.   **JOURNAL**   Page _____ 7

Date			Post. Ref.	Debit	Credit
2014		**Adjusting Entries**			
May	31	Insurance Expense	55	275	
		Prepaid Insurance	16		275
		Insurance expired.			
	31	Supplies Expense	53	1,370	
		Supplies	14		1,370
		Supplies used ($2,085 – $715).			
	31	Depreciation Expense	54	330	
		Accumulated Depreciation	19		330
		Equipment depreciation.			
	31	Salary Expense	51	325	
		Salaries Payable	22		325
		Accrued salaries.			
	31	Rent Expense	52	1,600	
		Prepaid Rent	15		1,600
		Rent expired.			
	31	Unearned Fees	23	3,790	
		Fees Earned	41		3,790
		Unearned fees ($7,000 – $3,210).			

Comp. Prob. 1 (Continued)

7.

KELLY CONSULTING Adjusted Trial Balance May 31, 2014		
	Debit Balances	Credit Balances
Cash	44,195	
Accounts Receivable	8,080	
Supplies	715	
Prepaid Rent	1,600	
Prepaid Insurance	1,225	
Office Equipment	14,500	
Accumulated Depreciation		660
Accounts Payable		895
Salaries Payable		325
Unearned Fees		3,210
Kelly Pitney, Capital		42,300
Kelly Pitney, Drawing	10,500	
Fees Earned		40,000
Salary Expense	1,705	
Rent Expense	1,600	
Supplies Expense	1,370	
Depreciation Expense	330	
Insurance Expense	275	
Miscellaneous Expense	1,295	
	87,390	87,390

Comp. Prob. 1 (Continued)

8.

KELLY CONSULTING		
Income Statement		
For the Month Ended May 31, 2014		
Fees earned		$40,000
Expenses:		
Salary expense	$1,705	
Rent expense	1,600	
Supplies expense	1,370	
Depreciation expense	330	
Insurance expense	275	
Miscellaneous expense	1,295	
Total expenses		6,575
Net income		$33,425

KELLY CONSULTING		
Statement of Owner's Equity		
For the Month Ended May 31, 2014		
Kelly Pitney, capital, May 1, 2014		$42,300
Net income for the month	$33,425	
Less withdrawals	10,500	
Increase in owner's equity		22,925
Kelly Pitney, capital, May 31, 2014		$65,225

Comp. Prob. 1 (Continued)

KELLY CONSULTING
Balance Sheet
May 31, 2014

Assets			Liabilities		
Current assets:			**Current liabilities:**		
Cash	$44,195		Accounts payable	$ 895	
Accounts receivable	8,080		Salaries payable	325	
Supplies	715		Unearned fees	3,210	
Prepaid rent	1,600		Total liabilities		$ 4,430
Prepaid insurance	1,225				
Total current assets		$55,815			
Property, plant, and equipment:			**Owner's Equity**		
Office equipment	$14,500		Kelly Pitney, capital		65,225
Less accum. depreciation	660				
Total property, plant, and equipment		13,840	Total liabilities and owner's equity		$69,655
Total assets		$69,655			

CHAPTER 4   Completing the Accounting Cycle

© 2014 Cengage Learning. All Rights Reserved. May not be scanned, copied or duplicated, or posted to a publicly accessible website, in whole or in part.

Comp. Prob. 1 (Concluded)

9.

JOURNAL   Page _____ 8

Date			Post. Ref.	Debit	Credit
2014		**Closing Entries**			
May	31	Fees Earned	41	40,000	
		Income Summary	33		40,000
	31	Income Summary	33	6,575	
		Salary Expense	51		1,705
		Rent Expense	52		1,600
		Supplies Expense	53		1,370
		Depreciation Expense	54		330
		Insurance Expense	55		275
		Miscellaneous Expense	59		1,295
	31	Income Summary	33	33,425	
		Kelly Pitney, Capital	31		33,425
	31	Kelly Pitney, Capital	31	10,500	
		Kelly Pitney, Drawing	32		10,500

10.

KELLY CONSULTING
Post-Closing Trial Balance
May 31, 2014

	Debit Balances	Credit Balances
Cash	44,195	
Accounts Receivable	8,080	
Supplies	715	
Prepaid Rent	1,600	
Prepaid Insurance	1,225	
Office Equipment	14,500	
Accumulated Depreciation		660
Accounts Payable		895
Salaries Payable		325
Unearned Fees		3,210
Kelly Pitney, Capital		65,225
	70,315	70,315

CASES & PROJECTS

CP 4–1

It is unacceptable to prepare financial statements in such a way that users of the statements would be misled. The July 31, 2014, balance sheet of Picasso Graphics could be misleading in two ways. First, the account receivable from Becky should be segregated and reported separately from trade (customer) receivables. Such receivables are normally reported as "officer receivables" or "other receivables" and accompanied by a note disclosing the nature of the receivable. Such disclosure is required for what are termed "related-party transactions." Second, given that the receivable has been outstanding since January 2012, it is questionable whether the receivable from Becky should be classified as a current asset. Pablo could justify the classification as "current" if Becky has agreed to a written schedule for repaying within the next year. Alternatively, the receivable could be classified as current if it has been converted to a note receivable with a specific due date within the next year.

In summary, because of the preceding issues, it appears that Pablo is not behaving in a professional manner. *Note:* It is a criminal offense to submit false or misleading documents to a bank in applying for a loan.

CP 4–2

1. (a) With the decreasing cost of computers and related software, Main Street Co. may find it desirable to computerize its financial reporting system. In many cases, the computerization of a manual accounting system reduces the overall cost of the accounting function.

    (b) A computerized accounting system would allow for eliminating the end-of-period spreadsheet (work sheet) and, thus, financial statements could be prepared with "a push of a button." However, adjustment data would still need to be recorded at the end of the accounting period before the financial statements could be prepared.

    (c) In designing a computerized financial reporting (accounting) system, it is essential that proper accounting principles, concepts, and procedures be followed. At a minimum, basic controls such as the use of the double-entry accounting system should be included. For example, debits must equal credits for all transactions, and assets must equal liabilities plus owner's equity. In addition, the system should be designed to detect obvious errors, such as a credit (minus) balance for supplies or prepaid insurance. In other words, to design an adequate financial reporting system, a computer programmer must have a thorough understanding of accounting and the accounting cycle.

    Note: Numerous accounting software packages, similar to the Cengage Learning General Ledger software package accompanying this text, are available. Therefore, it would probably be better for Main Street Co. to purchase an existing accounting software package rather than trying to design its own.

2. Supplies cannot have a credit balance, since the supplies account is an asset account. A business cannot have a "negative" asset. Thus, the only way that a credit balance could have occurred in Supplies is the result of an error in recording one or more transactions.

CP 4–3

1. A set of financial statements provides useful information concerning the economic condition of a company. For example, the balance sheet describes the financial condition of the company as of a given date and is useful in assessing the company's financial soundness and liquidity. The income statement describes the results of operations for a period and indicates the profitability of the company. The statement of owner's equity describes the changes in the owner's interest in the company for a period. Each of these statements is useful in evaluating whether to extend credit to the company.

2. The following adjustments might be necessary before an accurate set of financial statements could be prepared:

    No supplies expense is shown. The supplies account should be adjusted for the supplies used during the year.

    No depreciation expense is shown for the building or equipment accounts. An adjusting entry should be prepared for depreciation expense on each of these assets.

    An inquiry should be made as to whether any accrued expenses, such as wages or utilities, exist at the end of the year.

    An inquiry should be made as to whether any prepaid expenses, such as rent or insurance, exist at the end of the year.

    An inquiry should be made as to whether the owner withdrew any funds from the company during the year. No drawing account is shown in the "Statement of Accounts."

    The following items should be relabeled for greater clarity:

    Billings Due from Others—Accounts Receivable
    Amounts Owed to Others—Accounts Payable
    Investment in Business—Joan Whalen, Capital
    Other Expenses—Miscellaneous Expense

    Note to Instructors: The preceding items are not intended to include all adjustments that might exist in the Statement of Accounts. The possible adjustments listed include only items that have been covered in Chapters 1–4. For example, uncollectible accounts expense (discussed in a later chapter) is not mentioned.

CP 4–3 (Concluded)

3. In general, the decision to extend a loan is based on an assessment of the profitability and riskiness of the loan. Although the financial statements provide useful data for this purpose, other factors such as the following might also be significant:

    The due date and payment terms of the loan.

    Security for the loan. For example, whether Joan Whalen is willing to pledge personal assets in support of the loan will affect the riskiness of the loan.

    The intended use of the loan. For example, if the loan is to purchase real estate (possibly for a future building site), the real estate could be used as security for the loan.

    The projected profitability of the company.

CP 4–4

The purpose of this activity is to familiarize students with the information (assets, liabilities, and owner's equity) that a balance sheet provides about a company. Consider emphasizing the similarities and differences among different company balance sheets. For example, while all companies have cash in their balance sheets, companies in different industries will have different types of assets. Likewise, while all companies have accounts payable in their balance sheets, companies often are financed using different types of liabilities. At this point in the course, we have not covered corporations. Thus, consider deferring any discussion of different capital structures until after Chapter 13.

CHAPTER 5
ACCOUNTING SYSTEMS

DISCUSS[ ]ESTIONS

[handwritten: Subsidiary Ledger]
[handwritten: C = CASH]
[handwritten: R = Revenue]
[handwritten: CR = CASH Revenu]
[handwritten: CR 46 =]
[handwritten: Cash Revenuy]
[handwritten: Pg 46 of CASH]
[handwritten: Receipt JRNL]
[handwritten: P = Purchase Journal]
[handwritten: CP = cash payment JRNL]

1. The individual accounts receivable ledger[   ] information on the status of individual customer accounts, w[   ] [ ]ctions. Managers need to know which customers owe money, h[   ] amount owed has been outstanding.

2. The major advantages of the use of spe[   ] n record-keeping expenses and a reduction of record-kee[   ]

3. a. 400
    b. None

4. a. 400
    b. 1

5. a. Sometime following the end of t[   ] gs may happen: (1) an overdue notice will be received from Kel[   ] received from Kelley Co., informing the buyer of the over[   ] the error will be discovered at the time of making payment if the[   ] he time the check is being written.)

    b. The schedule of accounts pay[   ] lance of the accounts payable account. The error might als[   ] voice is paid.

    c. The creditor will call the at[   ] balance of $800.

    d. The error will become ev[   ] ss at the end of the month. The total debits in the purchases j[   ] edits by $3,600.

6. a. Purchases journal   payments journal
    b. Cash payments journal   payments journal
    c. Purchases journal

7. An electronic form is a software window that provides the inputs for a particular transaction. For example, a check form provides the inputs (payee, amount, date) for a cash payment transaction. An electronic invoice provides the inputs (customer, amount sold, item sold) for recording revenues earned on account.

8. The use of controlling accounts to verify the accuracy of subsidiary accounts is used in a manual system. In a computerized system, it is assumed that the computer will accurately sum the individual transactions in the subsidiary accounts in determining the aggregate balance.

9. For automated systems that use electronic forms, the special journals are not used to record original transactions. Rather, electronic forms capture the original transaction detail from an invoice, for example, and automatically post the transaction details to the appropriate ledger accounts.

10. E-commerce can be used by a business to conduct transactions directly with customers. Thus, an order can be received directly from the customer's Internet input and cash can be received from the credit card. Many times, the cash is received prior to actually shipping the product, resulting in a faster revenue/collection cycle. Reducing paperwork throughout the cycle also improves the efficiency of the process. For example, all of the accounting transactions can be fed automatically from the initial Internet-based inputs.

PRACTICE EXERCISES

PE 5–1A

REVENUE JOURNAL

Date		Invoice No.	Account Debited	Post. Ref.	Accounts Rec. Dr. Fees Earned Cr.
Nov.	7	121	Drew Co.		290
	17	122	Triple A Inc.		470
	23	123	Whaley Co.		610

PE 5–1B

REVENUE JOURNAL

Date		Invoice No.	Account Debited	Post. Ref.	Accounts Rec. Dr. Fees Earned Cr.
Apr.	6	78	Lemon Co.		1,240
	11	79	Hitchcock Inc.		2,570
	19	80	Fletcher Inc.		990

PE 5–2A

May   20. Collected cash of $100 from Matrix Communications Inc. (Invoice No. 527). Amount posted from page 106 of the cash receipts journal.

27. Provided $90 of services on account to Matrix Communications Inc., itemized on Invoice No. 579. Amount posted from page 92 of the revenue journal.

PE 5–2B

Aug.   10. Provided $750 services on account to Moravian Products Inc., itemized on Invoice No. 119. Amount posted from page 24 of the revenue journal.

17. Collected cash of $610 from Moravian Products Inc. (Invoice No. 106). Amount posted from page 46 of the cash receipts journal.

PE 5–3A

PURCHASES JOURNAL

Date		Account Credited	Post. Ref.	Accounts Payable Cr.	Party Supplies Dr.	Other Accounts Dr.	Post. Ref.	Amount
Feb.	11	Celebration Supplies Inc.		440	440			
	14	Fun 4 All Supplies Inc.		290	290			
	27	Office Space Inc.		2,350		Office Furniture		2,350

PE 5–3B

PURCHASES JOURNAL

Date		Account Credited	Post. Ref.	Accounts Payable Cr.	Office Supplies Dr.	Other Accounts Dr.	Post. Ref.	Amount
Nov.	6	Carry Out Supply Inc.		330	330			
	14	Zell Computer Inc.		1,950		Office Equipment		1,950
	22	Carry Out Supply Inc.		195	195			

PE 5–4A

Dec.   11.   Made purchases of $2,340 on account from Martin Computer Services Inc. (Invoice No. 75). Amount posted from page 8 of the purchases journal.

          19.   Paid $5,540 to Martin Computer Services Inc. on account (Invoice No. 43). Amount posted from page 46 of the cash payments journal.

PE 5–4B

Jan.   11.   Paid $64 to Colonial Inc. on account (Invoice No. 122). Amount posted from page 71 of the cash payments journal.

          26.   Made purchases of $72 on account from Colonial Inc. (Invoice No. 139). Amount posted from page 55 of the purchases journal.

PE 5–5A

Horizontal analysis:

	2014	2013	Increase/(Decrease) Amount	Percent
Retail	$110,000	$ 92,000	$ 18,000	19.6%
Wholesale	140,000	164,000	(24,000)	−14.6%
Total revenue	$250,000	$256,000	$ (6,000)	−2.3%

Vertical analysis:

	2014 Amount	Percent	2013 Amount	Percent
Retail	$110,000	44.0%	$ 92,000	35.9%
Wholesale	140,000	56.0%	164,000	64.1%
Total revenue	$250,000	100.0%	$256,000	100.0%

PE 5–5B

Horizontal analysis:

	2014	2013	Increase/(Decrease)	
			Amount	Percent
Camping	$280,000	$240,000	$ 40,000	16.7%
Fishing	140,000	160,000	(20,000)	−12.5%
Total revenue	$420,000	$400,000	$ 20,000	5.0%

Vertical analysis:

	2014		2013	
	Amount	Percent	Amount	Percent
Camping	$280,000	66.7%	$240,000	60.0%
Fishing	140,000	33.3%	160,000	40.0%
Total revenue	$420,000	100.0%	$400,000	100.0%

EXERCISES

Ex. 5–1

1.   **General ledger accounts:** (e)
2.   **Subsidiary ledger accounts:** (a), (b), (c), (d)

Ex. 5–2

a., b., and c.

Accounts Receivable

Mar.	1 Bal.	480
Mar.	31	6,795
Mar.	31 Bal.	7,275

Eco-Systems

Mar.	20	1,700
Mar.	31 Bal.	1,700

Hazmat Safety Co.

Mar.	1	2,875
Mar.	31 Bal.	2,875

Masco Co.

Mar.	10	980
Mar.	31 Bal.	980

Sunrise Enterprises

Mar.	1 Bal.	480
Mar.	27	1,240
Mar.	31 Bal.	1,720

d.

ZETA SERVICES INC. Accounts Receivable Customer Balances March 31, 2014	
Eco-Systems	$1,700
Hazmat Safety Co.	2,875
Masco Co.	980
Sunrise Enterprises	1,720
Total accounts receivable	$7,275

Ex. 5–3

a. Cash receipts journal
b. General journal
c. Cash receipts journal
d. General journal (not a revenue transaction)
e. Cash receipts journal

f. Cash receipts journal
g. General journal
h. Cash receipts journal
i. Cash receipts journal
j. Revenue journal

Ex. 5–4

a. General journal
b. Cash payments journal
c. Cash payments journal
d. Cash payments journal
e. General journal

f. General journal
g. Purchases journal
h. Purchases journal
i. Purchases journal
j. Cash payments journal
k. General journal

Ex. 5–5

Apr. 3. Provided service on account; posted from revenue journal page 44.

6. Granted an invoice adjustment or corrected an error related to sale of April 3; posted from general journal page 11. This does not represent a collection of cash, since the credit was not posted from the cash receipts journal.

24. Received cash for balance due; posted from cash receipts journal page 81.

Ex. 5–6

a.

REVENUE JOURNAL

Date		Invoice No.	Account Debited	Post. Ref.	Accounts Rec. Dr. Fees Earned Cr.
Sept.	2	201	Triple Play Corp.		380
	3	202	Mid States Inc.		295
	14	203	Triple Play Corp.		320
	22	204	Rose Co.		650
	30				1,645

b. $1,645   Debit to Accounts Receivable [from revenue journal column total in (a)].

$1,645   Credit to Fees Earned [from revenue journal column total in (a)].

c. $ 320   ($0 + $380 + $320 – $380)

Ex. 5–7

a. and b.

Aladdin Co.					Borman Co.			
May	1 Bal.	505			May	4	1,670	
	14	1,140				22	3,150	
Bal.		1,645			Bal.		4,820	

Life Star Inc.			
May	9	2,870	
Bal.		2,870	

c.

Accounts Receivable					Fees Earned			
May	1 Bal.	505				May	31	8,830
	31	8,830				Bal.		8,830
Bal.		9,335						

d.

EVERGREEN CONSULTING INC. Accounts Receivable Customer Balances May 31, 2014	
Aladdin Co.	$1,645
Borman Co.	4,820
Life Star Inc.	2,870
Total accounts receivable	$9,335

The total in the schedule above agrees with the T account balance for the accounts receivable controlling account in part (c).

e.   A computerized system would likely use an electronic form specially designed for recording sales transactions, such as an electronic invoice form. The transaction details would be input into the form fields and submitted. Once submitted, the transaction would be saved and automatically posted as a debit to the individual customer account receivable and a credit to the revenue account. There would be no control totals posted to a controlling account.

Ex. 5–8

FANTASY PRODUCTIONS INC. Accounts Receivable Customer Balances July 31, 2014	
Amber Communications Inc.	$3,940
Crowne Studios Inc.	1,250
Franklin Broadcasting Co.	2,200
Gold Coast Media Inc.	0
Total accounts receivable	$7,390

Accounts Receivable (Controlling)	
Balance, July 1, 2014	$ 3,670
Total debits (from revenue journal)	13,640
Total credits (from cash receipts journal)	(9,920)
Balance, July 31, 2014	$ 7,390

Ex. 5–9

REVENUE JOURNAL   Page ____ 8

Date		Invoice No.	Account Debited	Post. Ref.	Accounts Rec. Dr. Fees Earned Cr.
2014					
Oct.	2	512	Albany Co.	✓	670
	8	513	Gabriel Co.	✓	275
	12	514	Ells Inc.	✓	840
	22	515	Electronic Central Inc.	✓	150
	31				1,935

CASH RECEIPTS JOURNAL   Page ____ 12

Date		Account Credited	Post. Ref.	Fees Earned Cr.	Accts. Rec. Cr.	Cash Dr.
2014						
Oct.	4	CMI Inc.	✓		215	215
	19	Ells Inc.	✓		475	475
	27	Fees Earned		145		145
	29	Albany Co.	✓		670	670
	31	Fees Earned		90		90
	31			235	1,360	1,595

Ex. 5–10

a.

| | | REVENUE JOURNAL | | Page | 19 |

Date	Invoice No.	Account Debited	Post. Ref.	Accounts Rec. Dr. Fees Earned Cr.
2014				
Dec. 3	622	Palace Corp.	✓	2,340
8	623	Sunny Style Inc.	✓	1,690
18	624	Amex Services Inc.	✓	2,750
28	625	Veritas Co.	✓	980
31		Total		7,760

| | CASH RECEIPTS JOURNAL | | | | Page | 25 |

Date	Account Credited	Post. Ref.	Fees Earned Cr.	Accts. Rec. Cr.	Cash Dr.
2014					
Dec. 5	Champion Co.	✓		880	880
12	Veritas Co.	✓		1,130	1,130
23	Palace Corp.	✓		2,340	2,340
30	Fees Earned		80		80
31	Total		80	4,350	4,430

b.

AUTUMN COVE INC.	
Accounts Receivable Customer Balances	
December 31, 2014	
Amex Services Inc.	$2,750
Sunny Style Inc.	1,690
Veritas Co.	980
Total accounts receivable	$5,420

The total of the customer accounts on December 31, 2014, $5,420, equals the balance of the accounts receivable controlling account, shown as follows:

Accounts Receivable				
Dec. 1 Bal.	2,010	Dec. 31	4,350	
31	7,760			
Dec. 31 Bal.	5,420			

Ex. 5–10 (Concluded)

c.   The accounts receivable subsidiary ledger is needed to track customer services provided on account and customer collections. Without the subsidiary ledger, it would not be possible for Autumn Cove Inc. to know who owes how much for services rendered. Furthermore, without the subsidiary ledger, it would be impossible to manage collections from individual customers.

Ex. 5–11

1.   General ledger account: (b), (f), (h), (j), (k), (l)
2.   Subsidiary ledger account: (a), (c), (d), (e), (g), (i)
3.   No posting required: (m)

Ex. 5–12

1.   General ledger account: (a), (c), (e), (f), (g), (i), (k), (l)
2.   Subsidiary ledger account: (b), (d), (h)
3.   No posting required: (j)

Ex. 5–13

May   6.   Purchased services, supplies, equipment, or other commodities on account; posted from purchases journal page 44.

        14.   Received an invoice adjustment or corrected an error related to purchase of May 6; posted from general journal page 12. (A payment would be recorded in the cash payments journal.)

        16.   Paid balance owed; posted from cash payments journal page 23.

Ex. 5–14

a.

PURCHASES JOURNAL

Date		Account Credited	Post. Ref.	Accounts Payable Cr.	Office Supplies Dr.	Other Accounts Dr.	Post. Ref.	Amount
June	4	Office Universe Inc.		490	490			
	9	Tek Village, Inc.		2,790		Office Equipment		2,790
	16	Office Universe Inc.		140	140			
	21	Paper-to-Go Inc.		225	225			
	30	Total		3,645	855			2,790

b. $3,645   Credit to Accounts Payable [from purchases journal column total in (a)].

   $855   Debit to Office Supplies [from purchases journal column total in (a)].

c. $140 ($0 + $490 + $140 − $490)

Ex. 5–15

a. and b.

Enviro-Wash Supplies Inc.		
Jan.	4	570
	26	350
Bal.		920

Little Co.		
Jan.	1 Bal.	410
	15	290
Bal.		700

Office Mate Inc.		
Jan.	19	3,050
Bal.		3,050

c.

Accounts Payable			
	Jan.	1 Bal.	410
		31	4,260
	Bal.		4,670

Cleaning Supplies		
Jan.	31	1,210
Bal.		1,210

d.

WALLACE WINDOW CLEANERS INC. Accounts Payable Creditor Balances January 31, 2014	
Enviro-Wash Supplies Inc.	$ 920
Little Co.	700
Office Mate Inc.	3,050
Total supplier account balances	$4,670

The total in the schedule above agrees with the T account balance for the accounts payable control account in (c).

e. A computerized system would likely use an electronic form specially designed for recording purchase transactions. The transaction details would be input into the form fields and submitted. Once submitted, the transaction would be saved and automatically posted as a debit to an appropriate asset account and a credit to the individual creditor accounts payable account. There would be no control totals posted to a controlling account.

Ex. 5–16

OUT OF EDEN LANDSCAPING CO.	
Accounts Payable Creditor Balances	
April 30, 2014	
Augusta Sod Co.	$ 6,010
Concrete Equipment Co.	4,550
Home Centers Lumber Co.	7,810
Schott's Fertilizer	0
Total accounts payable	$18,370

Accounts Payable	
(Controlling)	
Balance, April 1, 2014	$ 1,990
Total credits (from purchases journal)	23,790
Total debits (from cash payments journal)	(7,410)
Balance, April 30, 2014	$18,370

Ex. 5–17

PURCHASES JOURNAL

Page 36

Date		Account Credited	Post. Ref.	Accounts Payable Cr.	Cleaning Supplies Dr.	Other Accounts Dr.	Post. Ref.	Amount
2014								
Mar.	3	Sani-Fresh Products Inc.	✓	190	190			
	12	Porter Products Inc.	✓	320	320			
	18	Liquid Klean Supplies Inc.	✓	245	245			
	20	Bowman Laundry Service	✓	130		Laundry Service Expense	53	130
	31			885	755			130
				(21)	(14)			

CASH PAYMENTS JOURNAL

Page 41

Date		Ck. No.	Account Debited	Post. Ref.	Other Accounts Dr.	Accounts Payable Dr.	Cash Cr.
2014							
Mar.	1	57	Liquid Klean Supplies Inc.	✓		325	325
	8	58	Equipment	18	2,850		2,850
	15	59	Bowman Laundry Service	✓		150	150
	26	60	Sani-Fresh Products Inc.	✓		190	190
	31	61	Salary Expense	51	5,900		5,900
	31				8,750	665	9,415
						(21)	(11)

Ex. 5–18

a.

PURCHASES JOURNAL

Page 16

Date		Account Credited	Post. Ref.	Accounts Payable Cr.	Pet Supplies Dr.	Other Accounts Dr.	Post. Ref.	Amount
2014								
June	4	Best Friend Supplies Inc.	✓	255	255			
	13	Poodle Pals Inc.	✓	710	710			
	19	Office Helper Inc.	✓	2,670		Office Equipment	18	2,670
	27	Meow Mart Inc.	✓	400	400			
	30			4,035	1,365			2,670
				(21)	(14)			

CASH PAYMENTS JOURNAL

Page 22

Date		Ck. No.	Account Debited	Post. Ref.	Other Accounts Dr.	Accounts Payable Dr.	Cash Cr.
2014							
June	6	345	Labradore Inc.	✓		360	360
	18	346	Meow Mart Inc.	✓		240	240
	23	347	Best Friend Supplies Inc.	✓		255	255
	30	348	Cleaning Expense	54	65		65
	30				65	855	920
						(21)	(11)

5-17

Ex. 5–18 (Concluded)

b.

HAPPY TAILS INC. Accounts Payable Creditor Balances June 30, 2014	
Meow Mart Inc.	$ 400
Poodle Pals Inc.	710
Office Helper Inc.	2,670
Total creditor (supplier) accounts	$3,780

The total of the creditor accounts on June 30, 2014, $3,780, equals the
balance of the accounts payable controlling account, shown as follows:

Accounts Payable

June	30		855	June	1 Bal.	600
					30	4,035
				Bal.		3,780

c. Happy Tails Inc. uses a subsidiary ledger for accounts payable to track its credit
purchases and payments to the individual supplier. This is needed so that it
knows how much it owes to each individual supplier. Without the subsidiary
ledger, it would be difficult for it to accurately pay suppliers for the amount
owed in a timely manner.

Ex. 5–19

a. Two errors were made in balancing the accounts in the subsidiary ledger:

(1) The Castle Chemical Supplies Inc. transaction of March 9 should have
resulted in a balance of $14,300 instead of $14,000, and the account
balance at March 12 should have been $14,000 instead of $13,700. The
account balance at March 20 should have been $8,200 instead of $7,900.

(2) The Hudson Bay Minerals Co. transaction of March 25 should have resulted
in a balance of $2,700 instead of $1,700.

Ex. 5–19 (Concluded)

b.

KLONDIKE ASSAY SERVICES INC. Accounts Payable Creditor Balances March 31, 2014	
C. D. Greer and Son	$15,750
Castle Chemical Supplies Inc.	8,200
Cutler and Powell	7,800
Hudson Bay Minerals Co.	2,700
Valley Power	3,150
Total accounts payable	$37,600

Ex. 5–20

Revenue journal: (c)

Cash receipts journal: (a)

Purchases journal: (d)

Cash payments journal: (b)

General journal: (e)

Ex. 5–21

1.   The Cash column is for debits (not credits).

2.   The Other Accounts column is for credits (not debits).

3.   A better order of columns would be to place the Other Accounts Cr. column to the left of the Fees Earned Cr. column.

A recommended and corrected cash receipts journal is as follows:

CASH RECEIPTS JOURNAL   Page ____ 12

Date	Account Credited	Post. Ref.	Other Accounts Cr.	Fees Earned Cr.	Accts. Rec. Cr.	Cash Dr.

Ex. 5–22

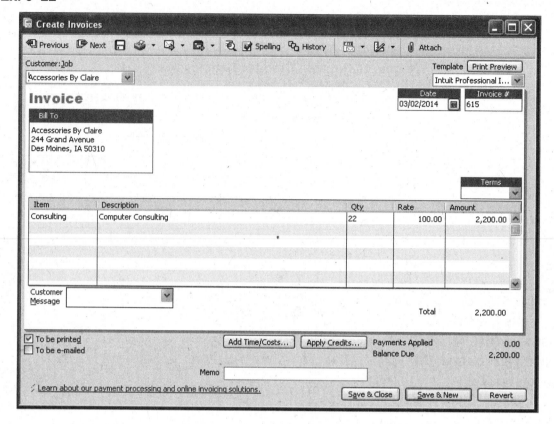

a.   In the electronic invoice form from QuickBooks® shown above, typical
     fields for data input can be identified as follows:

     1.   Customer name and address
     2.   Date and invoice number
     3.   Description of item sold
     4.   Amount of revenue

b.   The customer Accounts Receivable is debited, and Fees Earned is credited.
     A computerized accounting system does not require posting to a separate
     accounts receivable control account. In this case, the total accounts receivable
     reported on the balance sheet is merely the sum of the balances of the individual
     customer account balances. That is, the accounts receivable account summarizes
     the customer accounts automatically.

Ex. 5–22 (Concluded)

c.   Controlling accounts are not posted at the end of the month in a computerized accounting system. In addition, special journals are not normally used to accumulate transactions. Transactions are recorded through data input into electronic forms (or for infrequent transactions, by an electronic general journal). Balances of affected accounts are automatically posted and updated from the information recorded on the form. If desired, the computer can provide a printout of the monthly transaction history for a particular account, which provides the same information as a journal. In addition, the controlling account is not separately posted. In a manual system, separate posting to the controlling account provides additional control by reconciling the controlling account balance against the sum of the individual customer account balances. However, in a computerized accounting system, there are no separate postings to a controlling account because the computer is not going to make posting or mathematical errors. Therefore, there is no need for the additional control provided by posting a journal total to a controlling account.

Ex. 5–23

a.   iTunes is an example of a B2C, or business-to-consumer e-commerce application. The B, or business, is Apple. The C, or consumers, would mostly be individuals who purchase digital products from the download store.

b.

Cash	12	
Fees Earned		12

c.   The cash receipts journal is used to record debits to Cash from cash sales or collections on account.

d.   The electronic invoice form can be used for either transactions on account, as illustrated in the chapter, or for cash sales. The invoice form used for sales on account is different from the one used for cash sales. The latter invoice form makes a debit to Cash, rather than a debit to a customer account.

e.   Sales made on B2C e-commerce transactions are computerized transactions, so a special journal is inappropriate. On an e-commerce site, the consumer inputs the transaction information on the Web page; thus, there is no need for a separate electronic form for re-entering the same information to record the sale. Essentially, the e-commerce application is the form that originates the sales transaction inside the accounting system. Accounting transactions flow directly from the shopping cart information directly into the accounting system.

Ex. 5–24

a.	Amazon.com	B2C. Sells books, DVDs, and other products to individual consumers.
b.	Dell Inc.	B2C and B2B. Sells computer products to both individuals and corporations. Its site separates individual and corporate sales.
c.	DuPont	B2B. Specialty chemicals. DuPont Direct® is its B2B Web application.
d.	Intuit Inc.	B2C and B2B. Arranges its site for both individuals and businesses, since its products are divided this way.
e.	L.L. Bean, Inc.	B2C. Consumer clothes e-retailer.
f.	W.W. Grainger, Inc.	B2B. Sells maintenance, repair, and operating supplies to manufacturing companies.

Ex. 5–25

a. Horizontal analysis:

	Recent Year (in millions)	Prior Year (in millions)	Increase/(Decrease)	
			Amount	Percent
United States	$ 7,560	$7,061	$499	7.1%
International	2,289	1,914	375	19.6%
Global consumer products	707	674	33	4.9%
Total revenues	$10,556	$9,649	$907	9.4%

b. Vertical analysis:

	Recent Year		Prior Year	
	Amount	Percent	Amount	Percent
United States	$ 7,560	71.6%	$7,061	73.2%
International	2,289	21.7%	1,914	19.8%
Global consumer products	707	6.7%	674	7.0%
Total revenues	$10,556	100.0%	$9,649	100.0%

Ex. 5–25 (Concluded)

c. The horizontal analysis indicates that the total revenues of Starbucks increased by over 9% (9.4%) from the prior year to the recent year. This increase is explained by improvements in consumer confidence experienced during this time. Starbucks was positively impacted because its product is both premium priced and discretionary. Thus, as economic times improved, consumers increased consumption and/or chose more expensive options. Revenues increased by 19.6% internationally, versus 7.1% in the United States. Higher international growth may be the result of more store openings internationally, than in the United States. Global consumer products (segment that sells Starbucks-licensed products) had the lowest growth between the two years. The vertical analysis indicates that the percent of U.S. revenues to total revenues decreased from 73.2% in the prior year to 71.6% in the recent year. In this same period, the percent of international revenues to total revenues increased from 19.8% in the prior year to 21.7% in the recent year. Both analyses indicate that Starbucks' international operations grew more than did the U.S. operations during the two-year period.

Ex. 5–26

a.

Major Product Segments	For a Recent Year (in millions)	Percent
Filmed Entertainment	$ 7,631	23.3%
Television	4,228	12.9%
Cable Network Programming	7,038	21.5%
Direct Broadcast Satellite Television	3,802	11.6%
Magazines and Inserts	1,192	3.6%
Newspapers and Information Services	6,087	18.6%
Book Publishing	1,269	3.9%
Other	1,531	4.7%
Total revenues	$32,778	100.0%

b.   News Corporation is very diversified. The Filmed Entertainment segment has the largest percent of revenues to total revenues at 23.3%. This is a low percent for a single segment, suggesting little concentration. In addition, four additional segments have a percent of revenues to total revenues in excess of 10% (Television, Cable Network Programming, Direct Broadcast Satellite Television, and Newspapers and Information Services). The three smallest segments total 12.2% (3.6% + 3.9% + 4.7%) of revenues to total revenues. Overall, News Corporation is a highly diversified entertainment company, deriving significant revenues from multiple sources.

Ex. 5–27

a. **Horizontal analysis:**

	Year 2 (in millions)	Year 1 (in millions)	Increase/(Decrease) Amount	Percent
United States	$ 8,112	$ 7,944	$ 168	2.1%
Europe	9,569	9,274	295	3.2%
APMEA	5,065	4,337	728	16.8%
Other Countries & Corporate	1,328	1,190	138	11.6%
Total revenues	$24,074	$22,745	$1,329	5.8%

b. **Vertical analysis:**

	Year 2 Amount (in millions)	Percent	Year 1 Amount (in millions)	Percent
United States	$ 8,112	33.7%	$ 7,944	34.9%
Europe	9,569	39.8%	9,274	40.8%
APMEA	5,065	21.0%	4,337	19.1%
Other Countries & Corporate	1,328	5.5%	1,190	5.2%
Total revenues	$24,074	100.0%	$22,745	100.0%

c. The United States (U.S.) segment revenues increased 2.1% from Year 1 to Year 2, while Europe, APMEA, and Other Countries & Corporate increased 3.2%, 16.8%, and 11.6%, respectively. The higher growth rate in the smaller regions is the result of growing from a smaller base of revenue. The vertical analysis indicates that the U.S. and Europe declined from 34.9% to 33.7% of total revenues, and 40.8% to 39.8% of total revenues, respectively, while APMEA increased from 19.1% to 21.0% of total revenues. The vertical analysis is consistent with the horizontal analysis, showing modest revenue increases in the U.S. and Europe and stronger increases in APMEA. The growth in APMEA is likely due to restaurant unit growth in this part of the world.

PROBLEMS

Prob. 5–1A

1. and 2.

REVENUE JOURNAL   Page _____ 1

Date		Invoice No.	Account Debited	Post. Ref.	Accounts Rec. Dr. Fees Earned Cr.
2014					
May	21	1	J. Dunlop	✓	90
	22	2	K. Tisdale	✓	320
	24	3	T. Patrick	✓	75
	27	4	F. Mintz	✓	190
	30	5	D. Chase	✓	145
	30	6	K. Tisdale	✓	115
	31	7	T. Patrick	✓	85
	31				1,020
					(12) (41)

JOURNAL   Page _____ 1

Date		Description	Post. Ref.	Debit	Credit
2014					
May	25	Supplies	13	200	
		Fees Earned	41		200

Prob. 5–1A (Continued)

ACCOUNTS RECEIVABLE SUBSIDIARY LEDGER

Name: **D. Chase**

Date		Item	Post. Ref.	Debit	Credit	Balance
2014						
May	30		R1	145		145

Name: **J. Dunlop**

Date		Item	Post. Ref.	Debit	Credit	Balance
2014						
May	21		R1	90		90

Name: **F. Mintz**

Date		Item	Post. Ref.	Debit	Credit	Balance
2014						
May	27		R1	190		190

Name: **T. Patrick**

Date		Item	Post. Ref.	Debit	Credit	Balance
2014						
May	24		R1	75		75
	31		R1	85		160

Name: **K. Tisdale**

Date		Item	Post. Ref.	Debit	Credit	Balance
2014						
May	22		R1	320		320
	30		R1	115		435

Prob. 5–1A (Concluded)

GENERAL LEDGER

Account: **Accounts Receivable**   Account No. **12**

Date		Item	Post. Ref.	Debit	Credit	Balance Debit	Balance Credit
2014							
May	31		R1	1,020		1,020	

Account: **Supplies**   Account No. **13**

Date		Item	Post. Ref.	Debit	Credit	Balance Debit	Balance Credit
2014							
May	25		J1	200		200	

Account: **Fees Earned**   Account No. **41**

Date		Item	Post. Ref.	Debit	Credit	Balance Debit	Balance Credit
2014							
May	25		J1		200		200
	31		R1		1,020		1,220

3. a. $1,020 ($145 + $90 + $190 + $160 + $435)
    b. $1,020

4. The computerized system is much more efficient. Each sales transaction
    would be entered into an electronic invoice form. The postings to the accounts
    receivable subsidiary and fees earned ledgers would be automatic. Also, all
    sums and totals in the subsidiary ledgers are calculated automatically. There
    would be no separate postings to an accounts receivable control account,
    because there would be no need to verify the accuracy of account totals. There
    would not be a math or posting error. The computerized system would also
    provide management current customer account balance information, since the
    postings are automatic.

Prob. 5–2A

1. and 5.

GENERAL LEDGER

Account: **Cash**   Account No. **11**

Date		Item	Post. Ref.	Debit	Credit	Balance Debit	Balance Credit
2014							
Sept.	1	Balance	✓			11,350	
	30		CR36	33,650		45,000	

Account: **Accounts Receivable**   Account No. **12**

Date		Item	Post. Ref.	Debit	Credit	Balance Debit	Balance Credit
2014							
Sept.	1	Balance	✓			14,340	
	25		J1		2,500	11,840	
	30		R40	24,350		36,190	
	30		CR36		21,680	14,510	

Account: **Notes Receivable**   Account No. **14**

Date		Item	Post. Ref.	Debit	Credit	Balance Debit	Balance Credit
2014							
Sept.	1	Balance	✓			6,000	
	25		J1	2,500		8,500	

Account: **Fees Earned**   Account No. **41**

Date		Item	Post. Ref.	Debit	Credit	Balance Debit	Balance Credit
2014							
Sept.	30		R40		24,350		24,350
	30		CR36		11,970		36,320

Prob. 5–2A (Continued)

2. and 4.

ACCOUNTS RECEIVABLE SUBSIDIARY LEDGER

Name: Mendez Co.

Date		Item	Post. Ref.	Debit	Credit	Balance
2014						
Sept.	1	Balance	✓			8,230
	5		CR36		8,230	—
	22		R40	7,590		7,590

Name: Nickle Co.

Date		Item	Post. Ref.	Debit	Credit	Balance
2014						
Sept.	2		R40	5,200		5,200
	19		CR36		5,200	—

Name: Rahal Co.

Date		Item	Post. Ref.	Debit	Credit	Balance
2014						
Sept.	1	Balance	✓			6,110
	6		R40	2,140		8,250
	15		CR36		6,110	2,140
	16		R40	6,000		8,140
	20		CR36		2,140	6,000

Name: Shilo Co.

Date		Item	Post. Ref.	Debit	Credit	Balance
2014						
Sept.	13		R40	3,420		3,420
	25		J1		2,500	920

Prob. 5–2A (Continued)

3., 4., and 5.

REVENUE JOURNAL   Page _____ 40

Date		Invoice No.	Account Debited	Post. Ref.	Accounts Rec. Dr. Fees Earned Cr.
2014					
Sept.	2	793	Nickle Co.	✓	5,200
	6	794	Rahal Co.	✓	2,140
	13	795	Shilo Co.	✓	3,420
	16	796	Rahal Co.	✓	6,000
	22	797	Mendez Co.	✓	7,590
	30				24,350
					(12) (41)

CASH RECEIPTS JOURNAL   Page _____ 36

Date		Account Credited	Post. Ref.	Fees Earned Cr.	Accts. Rec. Cr.	Cash Dr.
2014						
Sept.	5	Mendez Co.	✓		8,230	8,230
	15	Rahal Co.	✓		6,110	6,110
	19	Nickle Co.	✓		5,200	5,200
	20	Rahal Co.	✓		2,140	2,140
	30	Fees Earned		11,970		11,970
	30			11,970	21,680	33,650
				(41)	(12)	(11)

JOURNAL   Page _____ 1

Date		Description	Post. Ref.	Debit	Credit
2014					
Sept.	25	Notes Receivable	14	2,500	
		Accounts Receivable—Shilo Co.	12/✓		2,500

The subsidiary account of Shilo Co. must also be posted for a $2,500 credit.

5-31

Prob. 5–2A (Concluded)

6. The sum of the customer balances is in agreement with the controlling account. Both have balances of $14,510 ($7,590 + $6,000 + $920).

7. In an automated system, individual sales transactions are posted automatically to the general ledger at the time of the original transaction. Thus, there is no need to post summary totals to the general ledger accounts. The accounts receivable account reported on the balance sheet is often merely the sum of the individual customer accounts.

Prob. 5–3A

1. and 4.

GENERAL LEDGER

Account: **Field Supplies**   Account No. **14**

Date		Item	Post. Ref.	Debit	Credit	Balance Debit	Balance Credit
2014							
Oct.	1	Balance	✓			5,920	
	31		P30	11,930		17,850	

Account: **Office Supplies**   Account No. **15**

Date		Item	Post. Ref.	Debit	Credit	Balance Debit	Balance Credit
2014							
Oct.	1	Balance	✓			750	
	31		P30	1,030		1,780	

Account: **Office Equipment**   Account No. **18**

Date		Item	Post. Ref.	Debit	Credit	Balance Debit	Balance Credit
2014							
Oct.	1	Balance	✓			12,300	
	5		P30	3,980		16,280	

Account: **Accounts Payable**   Account No. **21**

Date		Item	Post. Ref.	Debit	Credit	Balance Debit	Balance Credit
2014							
Oct.	1	Balance	✓				1,170
	31		P30		16,940		18,110

Prob. 5–3A (Continued)

2. and 3.

ACCOUNTS PAYABLE SUBSIDIARY LEDGER

Name: Executive Office Supply Co.

Date		Item	Post. Ref.	Debit	Credit	Balance
2014						
Oct.	1	Balance	✓			390
	9		P30		320	710
	29		P30		310	1,020

Name: Meade Co.

Date		Item	Post. Ref.	Debit	Credit	Balance
2014						
Oct.	1	Balance	✓			780
	2		P30		400	1,180

Name: Omni Co.

Date		Item	Post. Ref.	Debit	Credit	Balance
2014						
Oct.	14		P30		2,940	2,940
	24		P30		3,880	6,820
	31		P30		1,800	8,620

Name: Peach Computers Co.

Date		Item	Post. Ref.	Debit	Credit	Balance
2014						
Oct.	5		P30		3,980	3,980

Name: Yamura Co.

Date		Item	Post. Ref.	Debit	Credit	Balance
2014						
Oct.	13		P30		1,420	1,420
	17		P30		1,890	3,310

Prob. 5–3A (Concluded)

3. and 4.

PURCHASES JOURNAL

Date	Account Credited	Post. Ref.	Accounts Payable Cr.	Field Supplies Dr.	Office Supplies Dr.	Other Accounts Dr.	Post. Ref.	Amount
2014								
Oct. 2	Meade Co.	✓	400		400			
5	Peach Computers Co.	✓	3,980			Office Equipment	18	3,980
9	Executive Office Supply Co.	✓	320		320			
13	Yamura Co.	✓	1,420	1,420				
14	Omni Co.	✓	2,940	2,940				
17	Yamura Co.	✓	1,890	1,890				
24	Omni Co.	✓	3,880	3,880				
29	Executive Office Supply Co.	✓	310		310			
31	Omni Co.	✓	1,800	1,800				
31			16,940	11,930	1,030			3,980
			(21)	(14)	(15)			(✓)

5. a. $18,110 ($1,020 + $1,180 + $8,620 + $3,980 + $3,310)
    b. $18,110

6. Supply chain management e-commerce applications are used to plan and coordinate transactions with suppliers.

Prob. 5–4A

1., 2., and 3.

PURCHASES JOURNAL

Date		Account Credited	Post. Ref.	Accounts Payable Cr.	Field Supplies Dr.	Office Supplies Dr.	Other Accounts Dr.	Post. Ref.	Amount
2014									
June	16	Hydro Supply Co.	✓	4,920	4,920				
	16	Pure Aqua Equipment Co.	✓	19,500			Field Equipment	17	19,500
	17	Best Office Supply Co.	✓	465		465			
	23	Best Office Supply Co.	✓	620		620			
	30	Hydro Supply Co.	✓	7,300	7,300				
	30	Pure Aqua Equipment Co.	✓	5,600	1,200		Field Equipment	17	4,400
	30			38,405	13,420	1,085			23,900
				(21)	(14)	(15)			(✓)

Prob. 5–4A (Continued)

CASH PAYMENTS JOURNAL   Page _____ 1

Date		Ck. No.	Account Debited	Post. Ref.	Other Accounts Dr.	Accounts Payable Dr.	Cash Cr.
2014							
June	16	1	Rent Expense	71	2,900		2,900
	19	2	Field Supplies	14	3,080		3,080
			Office Supplies	15	350		350
	23	3	Land	19	120,000		120,000
	24	4	Hydro Supply Co.	✓		4,920	4,920
	26	5	Pure Aqua Equip. Co.	✓		19,500	19,500
	30	6	Best Office Supply Co.	✓		465	465
	30	7	Salary Expense	61	26,800		26,800
	30		Total		153,130	24,885	178,015
					(✓)	(21)	(11)

1. and 2.

JOURNAL   Page _____ 1

Date		Description	Post. Ref.	Debit	Credit
2014					
June	30	Land	19	10,000	
		Field Equipment	17		10,000

Prob. 5–4A (Continued)

1.

ACCOUNTS PAYABLE SUBSIDIARY LEDGER

Name: __Best Office Supply Co.__

Date		Item	Post. Ref.	Debit	Credit	Balance
2014						
June	17		P1		465	465
	23		P1		620	1,085
	30		CP1	465		620

Name: __Hydro Supply Co.__

Date		Item	Post. Ref.	Debit	Credit	Balance
2014						
June	16		P1		4,920	4,920
	24		CP1	4,920		—
	30		P1		7,300	7,300

Name: __Pure Aqua Equipment Co.__

Date		Item	Post. Ref.	Debit	Credit	Balance
2014						
June	16		P1		19,500	19,500
	26		CP1	19,500		—
	30		P1		5,600	5,600

Prob. 5–4A (Continued)

2. and 3.

GENERAL LEDGER

Account: Cash   Account No. ___11___

Date		Item	Post. Ref.	Debit	Credit	Balance Debit	Balance Credit
2014							
June	30		CP1		178,015		178,015

Account: Field Supplies   Account No. ___14___

Date		Item	Post. Ref.	Debit	Credit	Balance Debit	Balance Credit
2014							
June	19		CP1	3,080		3,080	
	30		P1	13,420		16,500	

Account: Office Supplies   Account No. ___15___

Date		Item	Post. Ref.	Debit	Credit	Balance Debit	Balance Credit
2014							
June	19		CP1	350		350	
	30		P1	1,085		1,435	

Account: Field Equipment   Account No. ___17___

Date		Item	Post. Ref.	Debit	Credit	Balance Debit	Balance Credit
2014							
June	16		P1	19,500		19,500	
	30		P1	4,400		23,900	
	30		J1		10,000	13,900	

Account: Land   Account No. ___19___

Date		Item	Post. Ref.	Debit	Credit	Balance Debit	Balance Credit
2014							
June	23		CP1	120,000		120,000	
	30		J1	10,000		130,000	

Prob. 5–4A (Concluded)

Account: **Accounts Payable**   Account No.   **21**

Date		Item	Post. Ref.	Debit	Credit	Balance Debit	Balance Credit
2014							
June	30		P1		38,405		38,405
	30		CP1	24,885			13,520

Account: **Salary Expense**   Account No.   **61**

Date		Item	Post. Ref.	Debit	Credit	Balance Debit	Balance Credit
2014							
June	30		CP1	26,800		26,800	

Account: **Rent Expense**   Account No.   **71**

Date		Item	Post. Ref.	Debit	Credit	Balance Debit	Balance Credit
2014							
June	16		CP1	2,900		2,900	

4.

SWEETWATER WATER TESTING SERVICE Accounts Payable Creditor Balances June 30, 2014	
Best Office Supply Co.	$ 620
Hydro Supply Co.	7,300
Pure Aqua Equipment Co.	5,600
Total accounts payable*	$13,520

* The total of the schedule of accounts payable is equal to the balance of the accounts
payable control account.

5. A subsidiary ledger for the field equipment would allow the company to track
    each individual piece of equipment with respect to cost, location, useful life,
    and other data. Such information would be useful for safeguarding equipment
    and determining depreciation.

Prob. 5–5A

1., 3., and 4.

GENERAL LEDGER

Account: Cash   **Account No.** 11

Date		Item	Post. Ref.	Debit	Credit	Balance Debit	Balance Credit
2014							
Dec.	1	Balance	✓			160,900	
	31		CR31	57,430		218,330	
	31		CP34		125,350	92,980	

Account: Accounts Receivable   **Account No.** 12

Date		Item	Post. Ref.	Debit	Credit	Balance Debit	Balance Credit
2014							
Dec.	1	Balance	✓			14,050	
	31		R35	21,920		35,970	
	31		CR31		16,030	19,940	

Account: Maintenance Supplies   **Account No.** 14

Date		Item	Post. Ref.	Debit	Credit	Balance Debit	Balance Credit
2014							
Dec.	1	Balance	✓			10,850	
	20		J1		3,600	7,250	
	31		P37	3,250		10,500	

Account: Office Supplies   **Account No.** 15

Date		Item	Post. Ref.	Debit	Credit	Balance Debit	Balance Credit
2014							
Dec.	1	Balance	✓			4,900	
	31		CP34	310		5,210	
	31		P37	765		5,975	

Account: Office Equipment   **Account No.** 16

Date		Item	Post. Ref.	Debit	Credit	Balance Debit	Balance Credit
2014							
Dec.	1	Balance	✓			28,500	
	6		P37	4,800		33,300	

Prob. 5–5A (Continued)

Account: **Accumulated Depreciation—Office Equipment**   Account No.   **17**

Date		Item	Post. Ref.	Debit	Credit	Balance Debit	Balance Credit
2014							
Dec.	1	Balance	✓				6,900

Account: **Vehicles**   Account No.   **18**

Date		Item	Post. Ref.	Debit	Credit	Balance Debit	Balance Credit
2014							
Dec.	1	Balance	✓			95,900	
	5		P37	39,500		135,400	
	16		CP34	40,900		176,300	

Account: **Accumulated Depreciation—Vehicles**   Account No.   **19**

Date		Item	Post. Ref.	Debit	Credit	Balance Debit	Balance Credit
2014							
Dec.	1	Balance	✓				14,700

Account: **Accounts Payable**   Account No.   **21**

Date		Item	Post. Ref.	Debit	Credit	Balance Debit	Balance Credit
2014							
Dec.	1	Balance	✓				4,250
	31		P37		48,315		52,565
	31		CP34	48,550			4,015

Account: **S. Holmes, Capital**   Account No.   **31**

Date		Item	Post. Ref.	Debit	Credit	Balance Debit	Balance Credit
2014							
Dec.	1	Balance	✓				289,250

Account: **S. Holmes, Drawing**   Account No.   **32**

Date		Item	Post. Ref.	Debit	Credit	Balance Debit	Balance Credit
2014							
Dec.	24		CP34	3,200		3,200	

Prob. 5–5A (Continued)

Account: **Fees Earned**   Account No.   **41**

Date		Item	Post. Ref.	Debit	Credit	Balance Debit	Balance Credit
2014							
Dec.	16		CR31		21,700		21,700
	31		CR31		19,700		41,400
	31		R35		21,920		63,320

Account: **Driver Salaries Expense**   Account No.   **51**

Date		Item	Post. Ref.	Debit	Credit	Balance Debit	Balance Credit
2014							
Dec.	30		CP34	16,900		16,900	

Account: **Maintenance Supplies Expense**   Account No.   **52**

Date		Item	Post. Ref.	Debit	Credit	Balance Debit	Balance Credit
2014							
Dec.	20		J1	3,600		3,600	

Account: **Fuel Expense**   Account No.   **53**

Date		Item	Post. Ref.	Debit	Credit	Balance Debit	Balance Credit
2014							
Dec.	9		CP34	800		800	

Account: **Office Salaries Expense**   Account No.   **61**

Date		Item	Post. Ref.	Debit	Credit	Balance Debit	Balance Credit
2014							
Dec.	30		CP34	7,600		7,600	

Account: **Rent Expense**   Account No.   **62**

Date		Item	Post. Ref.	Debit	Credit	Balance Debit	Balance Credit
2014							
Dec.	1		CP34	4,500		4,500	

Prob. 5–5A (Continued)

Account: **Advertising Expense**   Account No.   63

Date		Item	Post. Ref.	Debit	Credit	Balance	
						Debit	Credit
2014							
Dec.	20		CP34	1,990		1,990	

Account: **Miscellaneous Administrative Expense**   Account No.   64

Date		Item	Post. Ref.	Debit	Credit	Balance	
						Debit	Credit
2014							
Dec.	17		CP34	600		600	

Prob. 5–5A (Continued)

2. and 4.

PURCHASES JOURNAL

Date		Account Credited	Post. Ref.	Accounts Payable Cr.	Maintenance Supplies Dr.	Office Supplies Dr.	Other Accounts Dr.	Post. Ref.	Amount
2014									
Dec.	5	Boston Transportation	✓	39,500			Vehicles	18	39,500
	6	Austin Computer Co.	✓	4,800			Office Equipment	16	4,800
	18	Essential Supply Co.	✓	1,750	1,750				
	19	McClain Co.	✓	1,825	1,500	325			
	23	Office To Go Inc.	✓	440		440			
	31			48,315	3,250	765			44,300
				(21)	(14)	(15)			(✓)

CASH RECEIPTS JOURNAL

Date		Account Credited	Post. Ref.	Other Accounts Cr.	Accounts Receivable Cr.	Cash Dr.
2014						
Dec.	3	Trimble Co.	✓		5,100	5,100
	10	Sing Co.	✓		4,850	4,850
	12	Capps Co.	✓		1,980	1,980
	16	Fees Earned	41	21,700		21,700
	25	Trimble Co.	✓		4,100	4,100
	31	Fees Earned	41	19,700		19,700
	31			41,400	16,030	57,430
				(✓)	(12)	(11)

Prob. 5–5A (Continued)

2. and 4.

REVENUE JOURNAL   Page 35

Date		Invoice No.	Account Debited	Post. Ref.	Accounts Rec. Dr. Fees Earned Cr.
2014					
Dec.	2	940	Capps Co.	✓	1,980
	6	941	Dawar Co.	✓	5,680
	10	942	Joy Co.	✓	2,140
	24	943	Sing Co.	✓	6,400
	25	944	Dawar Co.	✓	5,720
	31				21,920
					(12) (41)

CASH PAYMENTS JOURNAL   Page 34

Date		Ck. No.	Account Debited	Post. Ref.	Other Accounts Dr.	Accounts Payable Dr.	Cash Cr.
2014							
Dec.	1	610	Rent Expense	62	4,500		4,500
	9	611	Fuel Expense	53	800		800
	10	612	Office To Go Inc.	✓		360	360
	11	613	Essential Supply Co.	✓		3,240	3,240
	11	614	Porter Co.	✓		650	650
	13	615	Boston Transportation	✓		39,500	39,500
	16	616	Vehicles	18	40,900		40,900
	17	617	Misc. Admin. Expense	64	600		600
	20	618	Advertising Expense	63	1,990		1,990
	24	619	S. Holmes, Drawing	32	3,200		3,200
	26	620	Austin Computer Co.	✓		4,800	4,800
	30	621	Driver Salaries Exp.	51	16,900		16,900
			Office Salaries Exp.	61	7,600		7,600
	31	622	Office Supplies	15	310		310
	31				76,800	48,550	125,350
					(✓)	(21)	(11)

Prob. 5–5A (Concluded)

3.

		JOURNAL			Page 1
Date		Description	Post. Ref.	Debit	Credit
2014					
Dec.	20	Maintenance Supplies Expense	52	3,600	
		Maintenance Supplies	14		3,600

5.

REVERE COURIER COMPANY Unadjusted Trial Balance December 31, 2014		
	Debit Balances	Credit Balances
Cash	92,980	
Accounts Receivable	19,940	
Maintenance Supplies	10,500	
Office Supplies	5,975	
Office Equipment	33,300	
Accumulated Depreciation—Office Equipment		6,900
Vehicles	176,300	
Accumulated Depreciation—Vehicles		14,700
Accounts Payable		4,015
S. Holmes, Capital		289,250
S. Holmes, Drawing	3,200	
Fees Earned		63,320
Driver Salaries Expense	16,900	
Office Salaries Expense	7,600	
Rent Expense	4,500	
Maintenance Supplies Expense	3,600	
Advertising Expense	1,990	
Fuel Expense	800	
Miscellaneous Administrative Expense	600	
	378,185	378,185

Prob. 5–1B

1. and 2.

REVENUE JOURNAL   Page _____ 1

Date		Invoice No.	Account Debited	Post. Ref.	Accounts Rec. Dr. Fees Earned Cr.
2014					
Jan.	18	1	Murphy Co.	✓	490
	20	2	Qwik-Mart Co.	✓	340
	24	3	Hopkins Co.	✓	750
	27	4	Carson Co.	✓	680
	28	5	Amber Waves Co.	✓	120
	30	6	Qwik-Mart Co.	✓	200
	31	7	Hopkins Co.	✓	295
	31				2,875
					(12) (41)

JOURNAL   Page _____ 1

Date		Description	Post. Ref.	Debit	Credit
2014					
Jan.	28	Supplies	14	100	
		Fees Earned	41		100

Prob. 5–1B (Continued)

ACCOUNTS RECEIVABLE SUBSIDIARY LEDGER

Name: **Amber Waves Co.**

Date		Item	Post. Ref.	Debit	Credit	Balance
2014						
Jan.	28		R1	120		120

Name: **Carson Co.**

Date		Item	Post. Ref.	Debit	Credit	Balance
2014						
Jan.	27		R1	680		680

Name: **Hopkins Co.**

Date		Item	Post. Ref.	Debit	Credit	Balance
2014						
Jan.	24		R1	750		750
	31		R1	295		1,045

Name: **Murphy Co.**

Date		Item	Post. Ref.	Debit	Credit	Balance
2014						
Jan.	18		R1	490		490

Name: **Qwik-Mart Co.**

Date		Item	Post. Ref.	Debit	Credit	Balance
2014						
Jan.	20		R1	340		340
	30		R1	200		540

Prob. 5–1B (Concluded)

GENERAL LEDGER

Account: Accounts Receivable   Account No.   12

Date		Item	Post. Ref.	Debit	Credit	Balance	
						Debit	Credit
2014							
Jan.	31		R1	2,875		2,875	

Account: Supplies   Account No.   14

Date		Item	Post. Ref.	Debit	Credit	Balance	
						Debit	Credit
2014							
Jan.	28		J1	100		100	

Account: Fees Earned   Account No.   41

Date		Item	Post. Ref.	Debit	Credit	Balance	
						Debit	Credit
2014							
Jan.	28		J1		100		100
	31		R1		2,875		2,975

3.   a. $2,875 ($120 + $680 + $1,045 + $490 + $540)
     b. $2,875

4.   The computerized system is much more efficient. Each sales transaction would be entered into an electronic invoice form. The postings to the accounts receivable subsidiary and fees earned ledgers would be automatic. Also, all sums and totals in the subsidiary ledgers are calculated automatically. There would be no separate postings to an accounts receivable control account, because there would be no need to verify the accuracy of account totals. There would not be a math or posting error. The computerized system would also provide management current customer account balance information, since the postings are automatic.

Prob. 5–2B

1. and 5.

GENERAL LEDGER

Account: Cash   **Account No.** 11

Date		Item	Post. Ref.	Debit	Credit	Balance Debit	Balance Credit
2014							
June	1	Balance	✓			18,340	
	30		CR36	9,270		27,610	

Account: Accounts Receivable   **Account No.** 12

Date		Item	Post. Ref.	Debit	Credit	Balance Debit	Balance Credit
2014							
June	1	Balance	✓			2,650	
	30		J1		1,800	850	
	30		R40	6,200		7,050	
	30		CR36		4,750	2,300	

Account: Office Equipment   **Account No.** 18

Date		Item	Post. Ref.	Debit	Credit	Balance Debit	Balance Credit
2014							
June	1	Balance	✓			34,700	
	30		J1	1,800		36,500	

Account: Fees Earned   **Account No.** 41

Date		Item	Post. Ref.	Debit	Credit	Balance Debit	Balance Credit
2014							
June	30		R40		6,200		6,200
	30		CR36		4,520		10,720

Prob. 5–2B (Continued)

2. and 4.

ACCOUNTS RECEIVABLE SUBSIDIARY LEDGER

Name: Auto-Flex Co.

Date		Item	Post. Ref.	Debit	Credit	Balance
2014						
June	1	Balance	✓			1,670
	3		CR36		1,670	—
	23		R40	860		860

Name: Cooper Development Co.

Date		Item	Post. Ref.	Debit	Credit	Balance
2014						
June	1	Balance	✓			980
	7		R40	670		1,650
	14		CR36		980	670
	16		R40	400		1,070
	20		CR36		670	400

Name: Ridge Communities

Date		Item	Post. Ref.	Debit	Credit	Balance
2014						
June	10		R40	2,840		2,840
	30		J1		1,800	1,040

Name: Yee Co.

Date		Item	Post. Ref.	Debit	Credit	Balance
2014						
June	2		R40	1,430		1,430
	18		CR36		1,430	—

Prob. 5–2B (Continued)

3., 4., and 5.

REVENUE JOURNAL   Page _____ 40

Date		Invoice No.	Account Debited	Post. Ref.	Accounts Rec. Dr. Fees Earned Cr.
2014					
June	2	717	Yee Co.	✓	1,430
	7	718	Cooper Development Co.	✓	670
	10	719	Ridge Communities	✓	2,840
	16	720	Cooper Development Co.	✓	400
	23	721	Auto-Flex Co.	✓	860
	30				6,200
					(12) (41)

CASH RECEIPTS JOURNAL   Page _____ 36

Date		Account Credited	Post. Ref.	Fees Earned Cr.	Accts. Rec. Cr.	Cash Dr.
2014						
June	3	Auto-Flex Co.	✓		1,670	1,670
	14	Cooper Development Co.	✓		980	980
	18	Yee Co.	✓		1,430	1,430
	20	Cooper Development Co.	✓		670	670
	30	Fees Earned		4,520		4,520
	30			4,520	4,750	9,270
				(41)	(12)	(11)

JOURNAL   Page _____ 1

Date		Description	Post. Ref.	Debit	Credit
2014					
June	30	Office Equipment	18	1,800	
		Accounts Receivable—Ridge			
		Communities	12/✓		1,800

The subsidiary account for Ridge Communities must also be posted for an $1,800 credit.

Prob. 5–2B (Concluded)

6. The sum of the customer balances is in agreement with the controlling account. Both have balances of $2,300 ($860 + $400 + $1,040).

7. In an automated system, individual sales transactions are posted automatically to the general ledger at the time of the original transaction. Thus, there is no need to post summary totals to the general ledger accounts. The accounts receivable account reported on the balance sheet is often merely the sum of the individual customer accounts.

Prob. 5–3B

1. and 4.

GENERAL LEDGER

Account: Field Supplies   Account No.   14

Date		Item	Post. Ref.	Debit	Credit	Balance Debit	Balance Credit
2014							
May	1	Balance	✓			6,200	
	31		P30	16,900		23,100	

Account: Office Supplies   Account No.   15

Date		Item	Post. Ref.	Debit	Credit	Balance Debit	Balance Credit
2014							
May	1	Balance	✓			1,490	
	31		P30	1,105		2,595	

Account: Office Equipment   Account No.   18

Date		Item	Post. Ref.	Debit	Credit	Balance Debit	Balance Credit
2014							
May	1	Balance	✓			19,400	
	19		P30	8,150		27,550	

Account: Accounts Payable   Account No.   21

Date		Item	Post. Ref.	Debit	Credit	Balance Debit	Balance Credit
2014							
May	1	Balance	✓				5,145
	31		P30		26,155		31,300

Prob. 5–3B (Continued)

2. and 4.

ACCOUNTS PAYABLE SUBSIDIARY LEDGER

Name: **Accu-Vision Supply Co.**

Date		Item	Post. Ref.	Debit	Credit	Balance
2014						
May	1	Balance	✓			3,900
	19		P30		8,150	12,050

Name: **J-Mart Co.**

Date		Item	Post. Ref.	Debit	Credit	Balance
2014						
May	1	Balance	✓			730
	15		P30		500	1,230
	26		P30		265	1,495

Name: **Lassiter Co.**

Date		Item	Post. Ref.	Debit	Credit	Balance
2014						
May	1	Balance	✓			515
	3		P30		340	855

Name: **Tri Cities Supplies**

Date		Item	Post. Ref.	Debit	Credit	Balance
2014						
May	8		P30		4,500	4,500
	23		P30		2,450	6,950
	30		P30		3,040	9,990

Name: **Wendell Co.**

Date		Item	Post. Ref.	Debit	Credit	Balance
2014						
May	1		P30		3,240	3,240
	12		P30		3,670	6,910

Prob. 5–3B (Concluded)

3. and 4.

PURCHASES JOURNAL

Date		Account Credited	Post. Ref.	Accounts Payable Cr.	Field Supplies Dr.	Office Supplies Dr.	Other Accounts Dr.	Post. Ref.	Amount
2014									
May	1	Wendell Co.	✓	3,240	3,240				
	3	Lassiter Co.	✓	340		340			
	8	Tri Cities Supplies	✓	4,500	4,500				
	12	Wendell Co.	✓	3,670	3,670				
	15	J-Mart Co.	✓	500		500			
	19	Accu-Vision Supply Co.	✓	8,150			Office Equipment	18	8,150
	23	Tri Cities Supplies	✓	2,450	2,450				
	26	J-Mart Co.	✓	265		265			
	30	Tri Cities Supplies	✓	3,040	3,040				
	31			26,155	16,900	1,105			8,150
				(21)	(14)	(15)			(✓)

5. a. $31,300 ($12,050 + $1,495 + $855 + $9,990 + $6,910)

    b. $31,300

6. Supply chain management e-commerce applications are used to plan and coordinate transactions with suppliers.

Prob. 5–4B

1., 2., and 3.

PURCHASES JOURNAL

Date		Account Credited	Post. Ref.	Accounts Payable Cr.	Field Supplies Dr.	Office Supplies Dr.	Other Accounts Dr.	Post. Ref.	Amount
2014									
Oct.	16	Petro Services Inc.	✓	32,600			Field Equipment	17	32,600
	17	Midland Supply Co.	✓	9,780	9,780				
	20	A-One Office Supply Co.	✓	1,320		1,320			
	28	A-One Office Supply Co.	✓	3,670		3,670			
	30	Petro Services Inc.	✓	30,800	25,300		Office Equipment	18	5,500
	30	Midland Supply Co.	✓	12,450	12,450				
	31			90,620	47,530	4,990			38,100
				(21)	(14)	(15)			(✓)

Prob. 5–4B (Continued)

1. and 2.

			JOURNAL			Page	1

Date		Description	Post. Ref.	Debit	Credit
2014					
Oct.	31	Prepaid Rent	16	15,000	
		Field Equipment	17		15,000

1., 2., and 3.

CASH PAYMENTS JOURNAL Page 1

Date		Ck. No.	Account Debited	Post. Ref.	Other Accounts Dr.	Accounts Payable Dr.	Cash Cr.
2014							
Oct.	16	1	Rent Expense	71	7,000		7,000
	18	2	Field Supplies	14	4,570		4,570
			Office Supplies	15	650		650
	24	3	Petro Services Inc.	✓		32,600	32,600
	26	4	Midland Supply Co.	✓		9,780	9,780
	28	5	Land	19	240,000		240,000
	30	6	A-One Office Supply Co.	✓		1,320	1,320
	31	7	Salary Expense	61	32,000		32,000
	31				284,220	43,700	327,920
					(✓)	(21)	(11)

Prob. 5–4B (Continued)

1.

ACCOUNTS PAYABLE SUBSIDIARY LEDGER

Name: **A-One Office Supply Co.**

Date		Item	Post. Ref.	Debit	Credit	Balance
2014						
Oct.	20		P1		1,320	1,320
	28		P1		3,670	4,990
	30		CP1	1,320		3,670

Name: **Midland Supply Co.**

Date		Item	Post. Ref.	Debit	Credit	Balance
2014						
Oct.	17		P1		9,780	9,780
	26		CP1	9,780		—
	30		P1		12,450	12,450

Name: **Petro Services Inc.**

Date		Item	Post. Ref.	Debit	Credit	Balance
2014						
Oct.	16		P1		32,600	32,600
	24		CP1	32,600		—
	30		P1		30,800	30,800

Prob. 5–4B (Continued)

2. and 3.

GENERAL LEDGER

Account: **Cash**   Account No.   **11**

Date		Item	Post. Ref.	Debit	Credit	Balance	
						Debit	Credit
2014							
Oct.	31		CP1		327,920		327,920

Account: **Field Supplies**   Account No.   **14**

Date		Item	Post. Ref.	Debit	Credit	Balance	
						Debit	Credit
2014							
Oct.	18		CP1	4,570		4,570	
	31		P1	47,530		52,100	

Account: **Office Supplies**   Account No.   **15**

Date		Item	Post. Ref.	Debit	Credit	Balance	
						Debit	Credit
2014							
Oct.	18		CP1	650		650	
	31		P1	4,990		5,640	

Account: **Prepaid Rent**   Account No.   **16**

Date		Item	Post. Ref.	Debit	Credit	Balance	
						Debit	Credit
2014							
Oct.	31		J1	15,000		15,000	

Account: **Field Equipment**   Account No.   **17**

Date		Item	Post. Ref.	Debit	Credit	Balance	
						Debit	Credit
2014							
Oct.	16		P1	32,600		32,600	
	31		J1		15,000	17,600	

Account: **Office Equipment**   Account No.   **18**

Date		Item	Post. Ref.	Debit	Credit	Balance	
						Debit	Credit
2014							
Oct.	31		P1	5,500		5,500	

Prob. 5–4B (Concluded)

Account: __Land__   Account No. ___19___

Date		Item	Post. Ref.	Debit	Credit	Balance Debit	Balance Credit
2014							
Oct.	28		CP1	240,000		240,000	

Account: __Accounts Payable__   Account No. ___21___

Date		Item	Post. Ref.	Debit	Credit	Balance Debit	Balance Credit
2014							
Oct.	31		P1		90,620		90,620
	31		CP1	43,700			46,920

Account: __Salary Expense__   Account No. ___61___

Date		Item	Post. Ref.	Debit	Credit	Balance Debit	Balance Credit
2014							
Oct.	31		CP1	32,000		32,000	

Account: __Rent Expense__   Account No. ___71___

Date		Item	Post. Ref.	Debit	Credit	Balance Debit	Balance Credit
2014							
Oct.	16		CP1	7,000		7,000	

4.

WEST TEXAS EXPLORATION CO. Accounts Payable Creditor Balances October 31, 2014	
A-One Office Supply Co.	$ 3,670
Midland Supply Co.	12,450
Petro Services Inc.	30,800
Total accounts payable*	$46,920

* The total of the schedule of accounts payable is equal to the balance of the accounts payable control account.

5. A subsidiary ledger for the field equipment would allow the company to track each individual piece of equipment with respect to cost, location, useful life, and other data. Such information would be useful for safeguarding equipment and determining depreciation.

Prob. 5–5B

1., 3., and 4.

GENERAL LEDGER

Account: Cash   **Account No.** 11

Date		Item	Post. Ref.	Debit	Credit	Balance Debit	Balance Credit
2014							
Mar.	1	Balance	✓			65,200	
	31		CR31	96,050		161,250	
	31		CP34		135,365	25,885	

Account: Accounts Receivable   **Account No.** 12

Date		Item	Post. Ref.	Debit	Credit	Balance Debit	Balance Credit
2014							
Mar.	1	Balance	✓			31,950	
	31		R35	39,540		71,490	
	31		CR31		38,950	32,540	

Account: Maintenance Supplies   **Account No.** 14

Date		Item	Post. Ref.	Debit	Credit	Balance Debit	Balance Credit
2014							
Mar.	1	Balance	✓			7,240	
	20		J1		4,400	2,840	
	31		P37	5,070		7,910	

Account: Office Supplies   **Account No.** 15

Date		Item	Post. Ref.	Debit	Credit	Balance Debit	Balance Credit
2014							
Mar.	1	Balance	✓			3,690	
	31		CP34	600		4,290	
	31		P37	2,490		6,780	

Account: Office Equipment   **Account No.** 16

Date		Item	Post. Ref.	Debit	Credit	Balance Debit	Balance Credit
2014							
Mar.	1	Balance	✓			17,300	
	3		P37	1,570		18,870	

Prob. 5–5B (Continued)

Account: **Accumulated Depreciation—Office Equipment**   Account No. **17**

Date		Item	Post. Ref.	Debit	Credit	Balance Debit	Balance Credit
2014							
Mar.	1	Balance	✓				4,250

Account: **Vehicles**   Account No. **18**

Date		Item	Post. Ref.	Debit	Credit	Balance Debit	Balance Credit
2014							
Mar.	1	Balance	✓			62,400	
	2		P37	26,900		89,300	
	16		CP34	28,500		117,800	

Account: **Accumulated Depreciation—Vehicles**   Account No. **19**

Date		Item	Post. Ref.	Debit	Credit	Balance Debit	Balance Credit
2014							
Mar.	1	Balance	✓				17,800

Account: **Accounts Payable**   Account No. **21**

Date		Item	Post. Ref.	Debit	Credit	Balance Debit	Balance Credit
2014							
Mar.	1	Balance	✓				2,755
	31		P37		36,030		38,785
	31		CP34	31,225			7,560

Account: **J. Wu, Capital**   Account No. **31**

Date		Item	Post. Ref.	Debit	Credit	Balance Debit	Balance Credit
2014							
Mar.	1	Balance	✓				162,975

Account: **J. Wu, Drawing**   Account No. **32**

Date		Item	Post. Ref.	Debit	Credit	Balance Debit	Balance Credit
2014							
Mar.	27		CP34	4,000		4,000	

Prob. 5–5B (Continued)

Account: **Fees Earned**   Account No. **41**

Date		Item	Post. Ref.	Debit	Credit	Balance Debit	Balance Credit
2014							
Mar.	16		CR31		26,800		26,800
	31		CR31		29,400		56,200
	31		R35		39,540		95,740

Account: **Rent Revenue**   Account No. **42**

Date		Item	Post. Ref.	Debit	Credit	Balance Debit	Balance Credit
2014							
Mar.	18		CR31		900		900

Account: **Driver Salaries Expense**   Account No. **51**

Date		Item	Post. Ref.	Debit	Credit	Balance Debit	Balance Credit
2014							
Mar.	30		CP34	33,300		33,300	

Account: **Maintenance Supplies Expense**   Account No. **52**

Date		Item	Post. Ref.	Debit	Credit	Balance Debit	Balance Credit
2014							
Mar.	20		J1	4,400		4,400	

Account: **Fuel Expense**   Account No. **53**

Date		Item	Post. Ref.	Debit	Credit	Balance Debit	Balance Credit
2014							
Mar.	9		CP34	820		820	

Account: **Office Salaries Expense**   Account No. **61**

Date		Item	Post. Ref.	Debit	Credit	Balance Debit	Balance Credit
2014							
Mar.	31		CP34	21,200		21,200	

Prob. 5–5B (Continued)

Account: __Rent Expense__   Account No. _____ 62

Date		Item	Post. Ref.	Debit	Credit	Balance	
						Debit	Credit
2014							
Mar.	1		CP34	2,450		2,450	

Account: __Advertising Expense__   Account No. _____ 63

Date		Item	Post. Ref.	Debit	Credit	Balance	
						Debit	Credit
2014							
Mar.	20		CP34	8,590		8,590	

Account: __Miscellaneous Administrative Expense__   Account No. _____ 64

Date		Item	Post. Ref.	Debit	Credit	Balance	
						Debit	Credit
2014							
Mar.	17		CP34	4,680		4,680	

Prob. 5–5B (Continued)

2. and 4.

PURCHASES JOURNAL

Date		Account Credited	Post. Ref.	Accounts Payable Cr.	Maintenance Supplies Dr.	Office Supplies Dr.	Other Accounts Dr.	Post. Ref.	Amount
2014									
Mar.	2	McIntyre Sales Co.	✓	26,900			Vehicles	18	26,900
	3	Office Mate Inc.	✓	1,570			Office Equipment	16	1,570
	18	Bastille Co.	✓	2,430	2,430				
	19	Master Supply Co.	✓	4,140	2,640	1,500			
	21	Office City	✓	990		990			
	31			36,030	5,070	2,490			28,470
				(21)	(14)	(15)			(✓)

CASH RECEIPTS JOURNAL

Date		Account Credited	Post. Ref.	Other Accounts Cr.	Accounts Receivable Cr.	Cash Dr.
2014						
Mar.	6	Chavez Co.	✓		7,950	7,950
	10	Sajeev Co.	✓		10,000	10,000
	12	Ellis Co.	✓		7,000	7,000
	16	Fees Earned	41	26,800		26,800
	18	Rent Revenue	42	900		900
	25	Chavez Co.	✓		14,000	14,000
	31	Fees Earned	41	29,400		29,400
				57,100	38,950	96,050
				(✓)	(12)	(11)

Prob. 5–5B (Continued)

2. and 4.

REVENUE JOURNAL   Page _____ 35

Date		Invoice No.	Account Debited	Post. Ref.	Accounts Rec. Dr. Fees Earned Cr.
2014					
Mar.	5	91	Ellis Co.	✓	7,000
	7	92	Trent Co.	✓	9,840
	11	93	Jarvis Co.	✓	7,200
	24	94	Sajeev Co.	✓	9,200
	25	95	Trent Co.	✓	6,300
	31				39,540
					(41) (12)

CASH PAYMENTS JOURNAL   Page _____ 34

Date		Ck. No.	Account Debited	Post. Ref.	Other Accounts Dr.	Accounts Payable Dr.	Cash Cr.
2014							
Mar.	1	205	Rent Expense	62	2,450		2,450
	9	206	Fuel Expense	53	820		820
	10	207	Office City	✓		450	450
	10	208	Bastille Co.	✓		1,890	1,890
	11	209	Porter Co.	✓		415	415
	13	210	McIntyre Sales Co.	✓		26,900	26,900
	16	211	Vehicles	18	28,500		28,500
	17	212	Misc. Admin. Expense	64	4,680		4,680
	20	213	Advertising Expense	63	8,590		8,590
	26	214	Office Mate Inc.	✓		1,570	1,570
	27	215	J. Wu, Drawing	32	4,000		4,000
	30	216	Driver Salaries Expense	51	33,300		33,300
	31	217	Office Salaries Expense	61	21,200		21,200
	31	218	Office Supplies	15	600		600
	31				104,140	31,225	135,365
					(✓)	(21)	(11)

Prob. 5–5B (Concluded)

3.

				JOURNAL		Page	1

Date			Description	Post. Ref.	Debit	Credit
2014						
Mar.	20		Maintenance Supplies Expense	52	4,400	
			Maintenance Supplies	14		4,400

5.

AM EXPRESS COMPANY Unadjusted Trial Balance March 31, 2014		
	Debit Balances	Credit Balances
Cash	25,885	
Accounts Receivable	32,540	
Maintenance Supplies	7,910	
Office Supplies	6,780	
Office Equipment	18,870	
Accumulated Depreciation—Office Equipment		4,250
Vehicles	117,800	
Accumulated Depreciation—Vehicles		17,800
Accounts Payable		7,560
J. Wu, Capital		162,975
J. Wu, Drawing	4,000	
Fees Earned		95,740
Rent Revenue		900
Driver Salaries Expense	33,300	
Office Salaries Expense	21,200	
Advertising Expense	8,590	
Maintenance Supplies Expense	4,400	
Rent Expense	2,450	
Fuel Expense	820	
Miscellaneous Administrative Expense	4,680	
	289,225	289,225

CASES & PROJECTS

CP 5–1

a. The half-price offer is a normal business practice, so long as it is not the result of price collusion with other competitors or considered "unfair pricing" according to federal statutes. Many businesses will offer low initial offers to entice customers to a subscription service. For example, cable and satellite companies will often offer premium channels, such as HBO, for free for the first several months of service. The business objective of low initial pricing is to demonstrate the value of the service so that customers will elect to continue the service at the full subscription price. Thus, there is nothing inherently unethical about such a practice, and it would be considered a fairly typical business practice.

b. Customer "lock in" can be unethical if it is the result of price fixing or acquiring competitors in order to achieve monopolistic concentration within an industry. However, in this case, the customer lock in is a function and nature of the product. Namely, the data that are created by the product cannot be easily migrated to another application. Note, Netbooks is not denying the customer ownership of the data; rather it is making it costly to switch. Such lock in is not considered an unethical business practice. Indeed, we see such lock in characteristics in many settings. For example:

   • Razor blades are designed to be used only by the handle of the manufacturer. Thus, customers become locked in to the razor blades of the handle manufacturer. This is such a common strategy in many arenas that it has been termed the "razor blade strategy."

   • Movie theaters prevent customers from walking in with refreshments, thus locking theater goers in to the popcorn and refreshment stand of the theater. Theater pricing of refreshments reflects this lock in.

   • Sony designs video games so that they only work on its Play Station® equipment. Therefore, the games are locked in to the consoles. This allows Sony and its licensees to limit and control competition for games.

   • Many manufacturers control replacement parts for equipment by custom designing the parts. Customers then become locked into the original manufacturer for replacement parts.

   • Apple Computer's iTunes can only be played on an iTunes compatible player. Thus, Apple reduces competition for songs for its player and locks customers into its music platform. Apple employs the same lock in strategy for its Mac operating system.

CP 5–2

Kyle is missing some of the principal benefits of the computerized system. There are three primary advantages of a computerized system. First, the computerized system is much more efficient and accurate at transaction processing. In the computerized system, once the transaction data have been input, the information is simultaneously recorded in the electronic journal (file) and posted to the ledger accounts. This saves a significant amount of time in recording and posting transactions. Second, the computerized environment is less prone to mathematical, posting, and recording errors. The computer does not make these types of mistakes. Thus, the computerized environment should require less time correcting errors. Third, the computerized system provides more timely information to management because account balances are always kept current. Under the manual system, ledger accounts will only be as current as the latest posting date, but the computerized system posts every transaction when it is journalized or recorded on a form. Thus, management has more current information with which to make decisions.

As an additional note, Kyle may be reacting out of some fear of the unknown. This is a common reaction to change. Thus, Kyle may be overreacting to the new computer environment because it will require significant change in the way the job is done as compared to the manual approach.

CP 5–3

a.   The accounts receivable and accounts payable accounts consist of transactions with individual customers and creditors (suppliers). In both cases, the subsidiary ledger tracks what is collectible from customers or owed to suppliers. Thus, the subsidiary ledger is required for tracking the collection and payment process to individual customers and suppliers, respectively.

b.   The equipment account could use a subsidiary ledger. The subsidiary ledger for equipment would track individual items of equipment, including their cost, location, and useful lives. The subsidiary ledger would be useful for determining equipment depreciation and safeguarding equipment assets.

CP 5–4

1.   Special journals are used to reduce the processing time and expense to record transactions. A special journal is usually created when a specific type of transaction occurs frequently enough so that the use of the traditional two-column journal becomes cumbersome. The frequency of transactions for Omni Care would probably justify the following special journals:

>   Purchases journal
>   Cash payments journal
>   Revenue journal
>   Cash receipts journal

Note to Instructors: The number and nature of the special journals to be established for Omni Care involve judgment. Differences of opinion may exist as to whether all the preceding special journals are necessary or cost-efficient. You may wish to use this time to comment further on the costs of establishing special journals and the potential benefits of reducing the processing time to record transactions.

CP 5-4 (Concluded)

2.

PURCHASES JOURNAL

Page _____ 1

Date	Account Credited	Post. Ref.	Accounts Payable Cr.	Medical Supplies Dr.	Office Supplies Dr.	Other Accounts Dr.	Post. Ref.	Amount

REVENUE JOURNAL

Page _____ 1

Date	Account Debited	Invoice No.	Post. Ref.	Accounts Rec. Dr. Fees Earned Cr.

3. The business should maintain subsidiary ledgers for customer accounts receivable, supplier accounts payable, and medical equipment.

CP 5–5

MEMORANDUM

To: Senior Management
From: Student
Re: Internet-based (cloud computing) accounting software

A new approach to automating our accounting requirements is now available. It is called Internet-based accounting using a cloud computing provider. Rather than purchasing our accounting software and loading it on our own computers, Internet-based accounting software is rented and resides on the provider's computers. Our data, along with the accounting software, stay with the provider. There are several advantages to this approach.

1.   We don't need to administer the application or data on our own computers. This becomes the job of the service provider, thus saving us computer system personnel costs. All we need is a desktop computer and browser to use the software.

2.   Our people can work with our data anytime or anyplace. We don't need to rely on our own internal computer network for accounting-related work. Instead, this product is available on the Internet. This means that we can enter transactions and access our accounting data from anywhere in the world, rather than having to be plugged into our corporate network. This also will save us network support costs.

3.   We never need to purchase and load software upgrades. All upgrades are provided on the provider's server when they are available. Thus, we are always using the latest version.

4.   Providers promise a highly secure environment for our data.

5.   An Internet-based accounting system should help us when passing data, such as orders, between ourselves and our customers and suppliers.

There are also a number of disadvantages we need to consider.

1.   The cost of the software is recurring. Thus, we are trading off the recurring costs of maintaining our system infrastructure for the recurring cost of the service. A financial analysis should be conducted to determine if the service is cost effective.

2.   The Internet can be slow. During busy times, we may experience slow response times.

3.   Our data physically reside with the service provider. Thus, we don't control the security of our own data; the provider does. Our data are our lifeblood, so confidence in the provider's controls is paramount.

4.   Once we begin, we will become "locked in" to the provider. It will be hard to change our mind at a later date. However, this is also true for purchased software to some extent.

CP 5–6

Note to Instructors: While the list of functions and services can be quite large, the key services are identified below. The purpose of these services will be fairly advanced for most students. The activity asks for a listing rather than an explanation because most students would have very limited experience by which to provide much explanation. Use this case to demonstrate the scope and basic nature of these application tools.

Selected JDA Supply Chain Management Solutions

- Demand management
- Factory planning and scheduling
- Merchandise operations
- Supplier relationship management
- Transportation and logistics management
- Space and category management
- Visibility, collaboration, and performance management
- Inventory optimization
- Planning on demand
- Replenishment and fulfillment
- Customer order management

Selected Salesforce.com Customer Relationship Management Solutions

- Provide the sales force with real-time information about all customer contacts with the firm in order to improve the effectiveness of the sales call
- Provide real-time forecast estimation and accumulation tools
- Support promotion plans and integrate the plans with forecasting and manufacturing
- Decision tools for evaluating marketing campaign effectiveness
- Tools to support call center responsiveness

CHAPTER 6
ACCOUNTING FOR MERCHANDISING BUSINESSES

DISCUSSION QUESTIONS

1. Merchandising businesses acquire merchandise for resale to customers. It is the selling of merchandise, instead of a service, that makes the activities of a merchandising business different from the activities of a service business.

2. Yes. Gross profit is the excess of (net) sales over cost of merchandise sold. A net loss arises when operating expenses exceed gross profit. Therefore, a business can earn a gross profit but incur operating expenses in excess of this gross profit and end up with a net loss.

3. The date of sale as shown by the date of the invoice or bill.

4. a. 1% discount allowed if paid within 15 days of date of invoice; entire amount of invoice due within 60 days of date of invoice.

   b. Payment due within 30 days of date of invoice.

   c. Payment due by the end of the month in which the sale was made.

5. Sales to customers who use MasterCard or VISA cards are recorded as cash sales.

6. a. A credit memo issued by the seller of merchandise indicates the amount for which the buyer's account is to be credited (credit to Accounts Receivable) and the reason for the sales return or allowance.

   b. A debit memo issued by the buyer of merchandise indicates the amount for which the seller's account is to be debited (debit to Accounts Payable) and the reason for the purchases return or allowance.

7. a. The buyer

   b. The seller

8. Examples of such accounts include the following: Sales, Sales Discounts, Sales Returns and Allowances, Cost of Merchandise Sold, Merchandise Inventory.

9. Cost of Merchandise Sold would be debited; Merchandise Inventory would be credited.

10. Loss from Merchandise Inventory Shrinkage would be debited.

PRACTICE EXERCISES

PE 6–1A

a. $700,000 ($450,000 + $1,350,000 – $1,100,000)

PE 6–1B

a. $126,000 ($18,300 + $295,700 – $188,000)

PE 6–2A

a. $8,526. Purchase of $12,650 less the return of $3,950 less the discount of $174 [($12,650 – $3,950) × 2%)].

b.   Merchandise Inventory

PE 6–2B

a. $56,925. Purchase of $65,000 less the return of $7,500 less the discount of $575 [($65,000 – $7,500) × 1%].

b.   Accounts Payable

PE 6–3A

a.

Accounts Receivable	41,100	
Sales		41,100
Cost of Merchandise Sold	26,750	
Merchandise Inventory		26,750

b.

Cash	40,278	
Sales Discounts	822	
Accounts Receivable		41,100

PE 6–3B

a.

Accounts Receivable	92,500	
Sales		92,500
Cost of Merchandise Sold	55,500	
Merchandise Inventory		55,500

b.

Cash	91,575	
Sales Discounts	925	
Accounts Receivable		92,500

PE 6–4A

a. **$161,400. Purchase of $180,000 less return of $20,000 less the discount of $1,600 [($180,000 – $20,000) × 1%] plus $3,000 of shipping.**

b. **$77,420. Purchase of $88,000 less return of $9,000 less the discount of $1,580 [($88,000 – $9,000) × 2%].**

PE 6–4B

a. **$31,680. Purchase of $36,000 less return of $4,000 less the discount of $320 [($36,000 – $4,000) × 1%].**

b. **$42,025. Purchase of $44,900 less return of $2,400 less the discount of $850 [($44,900 – $2,400) × 2%] plus $375 of shipping.**

PE 6–5A

Sundance Co. journal entries:

Cash ($16,800 – $3,800 – $260)	12,740	
Sales Discounts [($16,800 – $3,800) × 2%]	260	
Accounts Receivable—Butterfield Co. ($16,800 – $3,800)		13,000

Butterfield Co. journal entries:

Accounts Payable—Sundance Co. ($16,800 – $3,800)	13,000	
Merchandise Inventory [($16,800 – $3,800) × 2%]		260
Cash ($16,800 – $3,800 – $260)		12,740

PE 6–5B

Shore Co. journal entries:

Cash ($112,000 – $2,240 + $1,800)	111,560	
Sales Discounts ($112,000 × 2%)	2,240	
Accounts Receivable—Blue Star Co. ($112,000 + $1,800)		113,800

Blue Star Co. journal entries:

Accounts Payable—Shore Co. ($112,000 + $1,800)	113,800	
Merchandise Inventory ($112,000 × 2%)		2,240
Cash ($112,000 – $2,240 + $1,800)		111,560

PE 6–6A

Apr.	30	Cost of Merchandise Sold	13,750	
		Merchandise Inventory		13,750
		Inventory shrinkage ($890,000 – $876,250).		

PE 6–6B

Dec.	31	Cost of Merchandise Sold	23,250	
		Merchandise Inventory		23,250
		Inventory shrinkage ($1,333,150 – $1,309,900).		

PE 6–7A

a.

	2014	2013
Ratio of net sales to assets	3.4*	3.5**

* $1,734,000 ÷ [($480,000 + $540,000) ÷ 2]
** $1,645,000 ÷ [($460,000 + $480,000) ÷ 2]

b. The change from 3.5 to 3.4 indicates an unfavorable trend in using assets to generate sales.

PE 6–7B

a.

	2014	2013
Ratio of net sales to assets	2.4*	2.2**

* $1,884,000 ÷ [($770,000 + $800,000) ÷ 2]
** $1,562,000 ÷ [($650,000 + $770,000) ÷ 2]

b. The change from 2.2 to 2.4 indicates a favorable trend in using assets to generate sales.

EXERCISES

Ex. 6–1

a. $931,000 ($2,450,000 – $1,519,000)

b. 38% ($931,000 ÷ $2,450,000)

c. No. If operating expenses are less than gross profit, there will be a net income. On the other hand, if operating expenses exceed gross profit, there will be a net loss.

Ex. 6–2

$37,635 million ($50,272 million – $12,637 million)

Ex. 6–3

a. $28,215 {Purchase of $34,900, less return of $6,400, less discount of $285 [($34,900 – $6,400) × 1%]}

b. Merchandise Inventory

Ex. 6–4

The offer of Supplier Two is lower than the offer of Supplier One. Details are as follows:

	Supplier One	Supplier Two
List price	$100,000	$99,750
Less discount	1,000	1,995
	$ 99,000	$97,755
Freight		975
	$ 99,000	$98,730

Ex. 6–5

(1) Purchased merchandise on account at a cost of $21,000.

(2) Paid freight, $300.

(3) An allowance or return of merchandise was granted by the creditor, $4,000.

(4) Paid the balance due within the discount period: debited Accounts Payable, $17,000, and credited Merchandise Inventory for the amount of the discount, $170, and Cash, $16,830.

Ex. 6–6

a.

Merchandise Inventory	60,000	
Accounts Payable		60,000

b.

Accounts Payable	12,000	
Merchandise Inventory		12,000

c.

Accounts Payable	48,000	
Cash		47,040
Merchandise Inventory		960

Ex. 6–7

a.

Merchandise Inventory	71,500	
Accounts Payable—Sitwell Co.		71,500

b.

Accounts Payable—Sitwell Co.	71,500	
Cash		70,785
Merchandise Inventory		715

c.

Accounts Payable*—SitwellCo.	13,365	
Merchandise Inventory		13,365

d.

Merchandise Inventory	9,000	
Accounts Payable—SitwellCo.		9,000

e.

Cash	4,365	
Accounts Payable—Sitwell Co.		4,365

* *Note:* The debit of $13,500 to Accounts Payable in entry (c) is the amount of cash refund due from Sitwell Co. It is computed as the amount that was paid for the returned merchandise, $13,500, less the purchase discount of $135 ($13,500 × 1%). The credit to Accounts Payable of $9,000 in entry (d) reduces the debit balance in the account to $4,365, which is the amount of the cash refund in entry (e). The alternative entries below yield the same final results.

c.

Accounts Receivable—Sitwell Co.	13,365	
Merchandise Inventory		13,365

d.

Merchandise Inventory	9,000	
Accounts Payable—Sitwell Co.		9,000

e.

Cash	4,365	
Accounts Payable—Sitwell Co.	9,000	
Accounts Receivable—Sitwell Co.		13,365

Ex. 6–8

a.	Cash	45,000	
	Sales		45,000
	Cost of Merchandise Sold	27,000	
	Merchandise Inventory		27,000
b.	Accounts Receivable	115,000	
	Sales		115,000
	Cost of Merchandise Sold	69,000	
	Merchandise Inventory		69,000
c.	Cash	130,000	
	Sales		130,000
	Cost of Merchandise Sold	78,000	
	Merchandise Inventory		78,000
d.	Cash	100,000	
	Sales		100,000
	Cost of Merchandise Sold	60,000	
	Merchandise Inventory		60,000
e.	Credit Card Expense	9,200	
	Cash		9,200

Ex. 6–9

It was acceptable to debit Sales for the $55,000. However, using Sales Returns and Allowances assists management in monitoring the amount of returns so that quick action can be taken if returns become excessive.

Accounts Receivable should also have been credited for $55,000. In addition, Cost of Merchandise Sold should only have been credited for the cost of the merchandise sold, not the selling price. Merchandise Inventory should also have been debited for the cost of the merchandise returned. The entries to correctly record the returns would have been as follows:

Sales (or Sales Returns and Allowances)	55,000	
Accounts Receivable		55,000
Merchandise Inventory	33,000	
Cost of Merchandise Sold		33,000

Ex. 6–10

a. $27,440 [$28,000 – ($28,000 × 2%)]

b.

Sales Returns and Allowances	28,000	
Sales Discounts		560
Cash		27,440

b.

Merchandise Inventory	16,800	
Cost of Merchandise Sold		16,800

Ex. 6–11

(1) Sold merchandise on account, $42,000.

(2) Recorded the cost of the merchandise sold and reduced the merchandise inventory account, $25,200.

(3) Accepted a return of merchandise and granted an allowance, $2,000.

(4) Updated the merchandise inventory account for the cost of the merchandise returned, $1,200.

(5) Received the balance due within the discount period, $39,200. [Sale of $42,000, less return of $2,000, less discount of $800 (2% × $40,000).]

Ex. 6–12

a. $24,000
b. $24,425
c. $480 ($24,000 × 2%)
d. $23,945 ($24,425 – $480)

Ex. 6–13

a. $49,600 ($52,300 – $2,700)
b. $13,136 [($14,800 – $1,600) – ($13,200 × 2%) + $200]
c. $17,622 [($19,100 – $1,300) – ($17,800 × 1%)]
d. $6,352 [($6,700 – $300) – ($6,400 × 2%) + $80]
e. $22,374 [$22,600 – ($22,600 × 1%)]

Ex. 6–14

a.

Accounts Receivable—Belarus Co.	64,300	
Sales		64,300
Cost of Merchandise Sold	38,000	
Merchandise Inventory		38,000

b.

Sales Returns and Allowances	13,300	
Accounts Receivable—Belarus Co.		13,300
Merchandise Inventory	8,000	
Cost of Merchandise Sold		8,000

c.

Cash	49,980	
Sales Discounts	1,020	
Accounts Receivable—Belarus Co.		51,000

Ex. 6–15

a.

Merchandise Inventory	64,300	
Accounts Payable—Sombrero Co.		64,300

b.

Accounts Payable—Sombrero Co.	13,300	
Merchandise Inventory		13,300

c.

Accounts Payable—Sombrero Co.	51,000	
Cash		49,980
Merchandise Inventory		1,020

Ex. 6–16

Balance Sheet Accounts			Income Statement Accounts		
100	**Assets**		**400**	**Revenues**	
	110	Cash		410	Sales
	112	Accounts Receivable		411	Sales Returns and Allowances
	114	Merchandise Inventory		412	Sales Discounts
	115	Store Supplies	**500**	**Expenses**	
	116	Office Supplies		510	Cost of Merchandise Sold
	117	Prepaid Insurance		520	Sales Salaries Expense
	120	Land		521	Advertising Expense
	123	Store Equipment		522	Depreciation Expense— Store Equipment
	124	Accumulated Depreciation— Store Equipment		523	Store Supplies Expense
	125	Office Equipment		524	Delivery Expense
	126	Accumulated Depreciation— Office Equipment		529	Miscellaneous Selling Expense
200	**Liabilities**			530	Office Salaries Expense
	210	Accounts Payable		531	Rent Expense
	211	Salaries Payable		532	Depreciation Expense— Office Equipment
	212	Notes Payable		533	Insurance Expense
300	**Owner's Equity**			534	Office Supplies Expense
	310	Kailey Garner, Capital		539	Miscellaneous Administrative Expense
	311	Kailey Garner, Drawing	**600**	**Other Expense**	
	312	Income Summary		610	Interest Expense

Note: The order and number of some of the accounts within subclassifications is somewhat arbitrary, as in accounts 115–117, accounts 520–524, and accounts 530–534. For example, in a new business, the order of magnitude expense account balances often cannot be determined in advance. The magnitude may also vary from period to period.

Ex. 6–17

a.   At the time of sale

b. $36,000

c. $38,880 [$36,000 + ($36,000 × 8%)]

d.   Sales Tax Payable

Ex. 6–18

a.

Accounts Receivable	23,730	
Sales		22,600
Sales Tax Payable ($22,600 × 5%)		1,130
Cost of Merchandise Sold	13,600	
Merchandise Inventory		13,600

b.

Sales Tax Payable	51,668	
Cash		51,668

Ex. 6–19

a.   debit

b.   debit

c.   debit

d.   credit

e.   debit

f.   debit

g.   credit

Ex. 6–20

a.   Net sales: $6,865,000 ($8,135,000 – $795,000 – $475,000)

b.   Gross profit: $1,765,000 ($6,865,000 – $5,100,000)

c.   No, there could be other income and expense items that could affect the amount of net income.

Ex. 6–21

a.   Selling expense, (1), (2), (7), (8)
b.   Administrative expense, (3), (5), (6)
c.   Other expense, (4)

Ex. 6–22

a. $20,250 ($525,000 – $41,350 – $463,400)

b. $379,900 ($463,400 – $83,500)

c. $687,500 ($733,000 – $28,000 – $17,500)

d. $277,500 ($687,500 – $410,000)

e. $45,000 ($1,440,000 – $100,000 – $1,295,000)

f. $1,020,000 ($1,295,000 – $275,000)

g. $1,650,000 ($1,500,000 + $85,000 + $65,000)

h. $1,500,000 ($900,000 + $600,000)

Ex. 6–23

a.

FOLDAWAY FURNISHINGS COMPANY Income Statement For the Year Ended February 28, 2014			
Revenue from sales:			
Sales		$2,850,000	
Less: Sales returns and allow.	$90,000		
Sales discounts	25,000	115,000	
Net sales			$2,735,000
Cost of merchandise sold			1,641,000
Gross profit			$1,094,000
Expenses:			
Selling expenses		$ 300,000	
Administrative expenses		290,000	
Total expenses			590,000
Income from operations			$ 504,000
Other expense:			
Interest expense			29,000
Net income			$ 475,000

b. The major advantage of the multiple-step form of income statement is that relationships such as gross profit to sales are indicated. The major disadvantages are that it is more complex and the total revenues and expenses are not indicated, as is the case in the single-step income statement.

Ex. 6–24

1. Sales returns and allowances and sales discounts should be deducted from (not added to) sales.

2. Sales returns and allowances and sales discounts should be deducted from sales to yield "net sales" (not gross sales).

3. Deducting the cost of merchandise sold from net sales yields gross profit.

4. Deducting the total expenses from gross profit would yield income from operations (or operating income).

5. Interest revenue should be reported under the caption "Other income" and should be added to income from operations to arrive at net income.

6. The final amount on the income statement should be labeled net income, not gross profit.

A correct income statement would be as follows:

CURBSTONE COMPANY Income Statement For the Year Ended August 31, 2014			
Revenue from sales:			
Sales		$9,132,000	
Less: Sales returns and allowances	$422,000		
Sales discounts	115,000	537,000	
Net sales			$8,595,000
Cost of merchandise sold			6,110,000
Gross profit			$2,485,000
Expenses:			
Selling expenses		$ 800,000	
Administrative expenses		575,000	
Delivery expense		425,000	
Total expenses			1,800,000
Income from operations			$ 685,000
Other income:			
Interest revenue			45,000
Net income			$ 730,000

Ex. 6–25

CUMMERBUND COMPANY Income Statement For the Year Ended June 30, 2014		
Revenues:		
Net sales		$3,750,000
Rent revenue		125,000
Total revenues		$3,875,000
Expenses:		
Cost of merchandise sold	$2,400,000	
Selling expenses	550,000	
Administrative expenses	420,000	
Interest expense	30,000	
Total expenses		3,400,000
Net income		$ 475,000

Ex. 6–26

Cost of Merchandise Sold	14,450	
Merchandise Inventory		14,450
Inventory shrinkage ($1,498,200 – $1,483,750).		

Ex. 6–27

(b) Advertising Expense
(c) Cost of Merchandise Sold
(e) Sales
(f) Sales Discounts
(g) Sales Returns and Allowances
(i) Supplies Expense

Note: (j) Valery Lavine, Drawing is closed to Valery Lavine, Capital, *not* Income Summary.

Ex. 6–28

2014			Closing Entries		
Feb.	28	Sales		2,850,000	
			Income Summary		2,850,000
	28	Income Summary		2,375,000	
			Sales Discounts		25,000
			Sales Returns and Allowances		90,000
			Cost of Merchandise Sold		1,641,000
			Selling Expenses		300,000
			Administrative Expenses		290,000
			Interest Expense		29,000
	28	Income Summary		475,000	
			Lonnie Clemente, Capital		475,000
	28	Lonnie Clemente, Capital		50,000	
			Lonnie Clemente, Drawing		50,000

Ex. 6–29

2014			Closing Entries		
Oct.	31	Sales		1,375,000	
			Income Summary		1,375,000
	31	Income Summary		1,145,000	
			Administrative Expenses		300,000
			Cost of Merchandise Sold		650,000
			Interest Expense		10,000
			Sales Discounts		20,000
			Sales Returns and Allowances		13,000
			Selling Expenses		140,000
			Store Supplies Expense		12,000
	31	Income Summary		230,000	
			Jordan Davenport, Capital		230,000
	31	Jordan Davenport, Capital		25,000	
			Jordan Davenport, Drawing		25,000

Ex. 6–30

a.   Year 2: 1.68 {$67,997 ÷ [($40,125 + $40,877) ÷ 2]}
      Year 1: 1.61 {$66,176 ÷ [($40,877 + $41,164) ÷ 2]}

b.   These analyses indicate an increase in the effectiveness in the use of the assets to generate profits. A comparison with similar companies or industry averages would be helpful in making a more definitive statement on the effectiveness of the use of the assets.

Ex. 6–31

a.   3.53 {$82,189 ÷ [($23,505 + $23,126) ÷ 2]}

b.   Although Kroger and Tiffany are both retail stores, Tiffany sells jewelry using a much longer operating cycle than Kroger uses selling groceries. Thus, Kroger is able to generate $3.53 of sales for every dollar of assets. Tiffany, however, is only able to generate $0.85 in sales per dollar of assets. This difference is reasonable when one considers the sales rate for jewelry and the cost of holding jewelry inventory, relative to groceries. Fortunately, Tiffany is able to offset its longer operating cycle, relative to groceries, with higher gross profits, relative to groceries.

Note to Instructors: For a recent year, Kroger's gross profit percentage (gross profit divided by revenues) was 22.2%, while Tiffany's gross profit percentage was 59.1%. Kroger's ratio of net income to revenues was 1.4%, while Tiffany's ratio of net income to revenues was 11.9%.

Appendix Ex. 6–32

a.   Purchases discounts, purchases returns and allowances
b.   Freight in
c.   Merchandise available for sale
d.   Merchandise inventory (ending)

Appendix Ex. 6–33

a.   Cost of merchandise sold:

Merchandise inventory, May 1, 2013			$ 380,000
Purchases		$3,800,000	
Less: Purchases returns and			
allowances	$150,000		
Purchases discounts	80,000	230,000	
Net purchases		$3,570,000	
Add freight in		16,600	
Cost of merchandise purchased			3,586,600
Merchandise available for sale			$3,966,600
Less merchandise inventory, April 30, 2014			415,000
Cost of merchandise sold			$3,551,600

b. $2,298,400 ($5,850,000 – $3,551,600)

c.   No. Gross profit would be the same if the perpetual inventory system was used.

Appendix Ex. 6–34

Cost of merchandise sold:

Merchandise inventory, November 1			$ 28,000
Purchases		$475,000	
Less: Purchases returns and			
allowances	$15,000		
Purchases discounts	9,000	24,000	
Net purchases		$451,000	
Add freight in		7,000	
Cost of merchandise purchased			458,000
Merchandise available for sale			$486,000
Less merchandise inventory, November 30			31,500
Cost of merchandise sold			$454,500

Appendix Ex. 6–35

Cost of merchandise sold:

Merchandise inventory, July 1			$ 190,850
Purchases		$1,126,000	
Less: Purchases returns and			
allowances	$46,000		
Purchases discounts	23,000	69,000	
Net purchases		$1,057,000	
Add freight in		17,500	
Cost of merchandise purchased			1,074,500
Merchandise available for sale			$1,265,350
Less merchandise inventory, July 31			160,450
Cost of merchandise sold			$1,104,900

Appendix Ex. 6–36

1. The schedule should begin with the June 1, 2013, not the May 31, 2014, merchandise inventory.

2. Purchases returns and allowances and purchases discounts should be deducted from (not added to) purchases.

3. The result of subtracting purchases returns and allowances and purchases discounts from purchases should be labeled "net purchases."

4. Freight in should be added to net purchases to yield cost of merchandise purchased.

5. The merchandise inventory at May 31, 2014, should be deducted from merchandise available for sale to yield cost of merchandise sold.

    A correct cost of merchandise sold section is as follows:

Cost of merchandise sold:

Merchandise inventory, June 1, 2013			$ 91,300
Purchases		$1,110,000	
Less: Purchases returns and			
allowances	$55,000		
Purchases discounts	30,000	85,000	
Net purchases		$1,025,000	
Add freight in		22,000	
Cost of merchandise purchased			1,047,000
Merchandise available for sale			$1,138,300
Less merchandise inventory, May 31, 2014			105,000
Cost of merchandise sold			$1,033,300

Appendix Ex. 6–37

(a) credit

(b) debit

(c) debit

(d) credit

(e) debit

(f) credit

(g) credit

Appendix Ex. 6–38

Jan.	2	Purchases	18,200	
		Accounts Payable		18,200
	5	Freight In	190	
		Cash		190
	6	Accounts Payable	2,750	
		Purchases Returns and Allowances		2,750
	13	Accounts Receivable	37,300	
		Sales		37,300
	15	Delivery Expense	215	
		Cash		215
	17	Accounts Payable	15,450	
		Purchases Discounts		309
		Cash		15,141
	23	Cash	36,927	
		Sales Discounts	373	
		Accounts Receivable		37,300

Appendix Ex. 6–39

Jan.					
Jan.	2	Merchandise Inventory	18,200	
		Accounts Payable		18,200
	5	Merchandise Inventory	190	
		Cash		190
	6	Accounts Payable	2,750	
		Merchandise Inventory		2,750
	13	Accounts Receivable	37,300	
		Sales		37,300
	13	Cost of Merchandise Sold	22,400	
		Merchandise Inventory		22,400
	15	Delivery Expense	215	
		Cash		215
	17	Accounts Payable	15,450	
		Merchandise Inventory		309
		Cash		15,141
	23	Cash	36,927	
		Sales Discounts	373	
		Accounts Receivable		37,300

Appendix Ex. 6–40

			Closing Entries		
Dec.		31	Merchandise Inventory	460,000	
			Sales	2,300,000	
			Purchases Discounts	35,000	
			Purchases Returns and Allowances	45,000	
			Income Summary		2,840,000
		31	Income Summary	2,665,000	
			Merchandise Inventory		375,000
			Sales Discounts		30,000
			Sales Returns and Allowances		50,000
			Purchases		1,760,000
			Freight In		17,000
			Salaries Expense		375,000
			Advertising Expense		36,000
			Depreciation Expense		13,000
			Miscellaneous Expense		9,000
		31	Income Summary	175,000	
			Pat Kirwan, Capital		175,000
		31	Pat Kirwan, Capital	65,000	
			Pat Kirwan, Drawing		65,000

PROBLEMS

Prob. 6–1A

Oct.				
	1	Merchandise Inventory	14,448	
		Accounts Payable—UK Imports Co.		14,448
	3	Merchandise Inventory	10,170	
		Accounts Payable—Hoagie Co.		10,170
	4	Merchandise Inventory	13,650	
		Accounts Payable—Taco Co.		13,650
	6	Accounts Payable—Taco Co.	4,550	
		Merchandise Inventory		4,550
	13	Accounts Payable—Hoagie Co.	10,170	
		Cash		9,971
		Merchandise Inventory		199
	14	Accounts Payable—Taco Co.	9,100	
		Cash		8,918
		Merchandise Inventory		182
	19	Merchandise Inventory	27,300	
		Accounts Payable—Veggie Co.		27,300
	19	Merchandise Inventory	400	
		Cash		400
	20	Merchandise Inventory	22,000	
		Accounts Payable—Caesar Salad Co.		22,000
	30	Accounts Payable—Caesar Salad Co.	22,000	
		Cash		21,780
		Merchandise Inventory		220
	31	Accounts Payable—UK Imports Co.	14,448	
		Cash		14,448
	31	Accounts Payable—Veggie Co.	27,300	
		Cash		27,300

Prob. 6–2A

Mar.	2	Accounts Receivable—Equinox Co.	18,900	
		Sales		18,900
	2	Cost of Merchandise Sold	13,300	
		Merchandise Inventory		13,300
	3	Cash	12,031	
		Sales		11,350
		Sales Tax Payable		681
	3	Cost of Merchandise Sold	7,000	
		Merchandise Inventory		7,000
	4	Accounts Receivable—Empire Co.	55,400	
		Sales		55,400
	4	Cost of Merchandise Sold	33,200	
		Merchandise Inventory		33,200
	5	Cash	31,800	
		Sales		30,000
		Sales Tax Payable		1,800
	5	Cost of Merchandise Sold	19,400	
		Merchandise Inventory		19,400
	12	Cash	18,711	
		Sales Discounts	189	
		Accounts Receivable—Equinox Co.		18,900
	14	Cash	13,700	
		Sales		13,700
	14	Cost of Merchandise Sold	8,350	
		Merchandise Inventory		8,350
	16	Accounts Receivable—Targhee Co.	27,500	
		Sales		27,500
	16	Cost of Merchandise Sold	16,000	
		Merchandise Inventory		16,000

Prob. 6–2A (Concluded)

Mar.	18	Sales Returns and Allowances	4,800	
		Accounts Receivable—Targhee Co.		4,800
	18	Merchandise Inventory	2,900	
		Cost of Merchandise Sold		2,900
	19	Accounts Receivable—Vista Co.	8,250	
		Sales		8,250
	19	Accounts Receivable—Vista Co.	75	
		Cash		75
	19	Cost of Merchandise Sold	5,000	
		Merchandise Inventory		5,000
	26	Cash	22,473	
		Sales Discounts	227	
		Accounts Receivable—Targhee Co.		22,700
	28	Cash	8,160	
		Sales Discounts	165	
		Accounts Receivable—Vista Co.		8,325
	31	Cash	55,400	
		Accounts Receivable—Empire Co.		55,400
	31	Delivery Expense	5,600	
		Cash		5,600
Apr.	3	Credit Card Expense	940	
		Cash		940
	15	Sales Tax Payable	6,544	
		Cash		6,544

Prob. 6–3A

Nov.	3	Merchandise Inventory	63,750	
		Accounts Payable—Moonlight Co.		63,750
		[$85,000 – ($85,000 × 25%)] = $63,750.		
	4	Cash	37,680	
		Sales		37,680
	4	Cost of Merchandise Sold	22,600	
		Merchandise Inventory		22,600
	5	Merchandise Inventory	48,310	
		Accounts Payable—Papoose Creek Co.		48,310
	6	Accounts Payable—Moonlight Co.	13,500	
		Merchandise Inventory		13,500
	11	Accounts Receivable—Quinn Co.	15,600	
		Sales		15,600
		[$24,000 – ($24,000 × 35%)] = $15,600.		
	11	Cost of Merchandise Sold	9,400	
		Merchandise Inventory		9,400
	13	Accounts Payable—Moonlight Co.	50,250	
		Cash		49,245
		Merchandise Inventory		1,005
	14	Cash	236,000	
		Sales		236,000
	14	Cost of Merchandise Sold	140,000	
		Merchandise Inventory		140,000
	15	Accounts Payable—Papoose Creek Co.	48,310	
		Cash		47,360
		Merchandise Inventory		950
	21	Cash	15,444	
		Sales Discounts	156	
		Accounts Receivable—Quinn Co.		15,600

Prob. 6–3A (Concluded)

Nov.	24	Accounts Receivable—Rabel Co.	56,900	
		Sales		56,900
	24	Cost of Merchandise Sold	34,000	
		Merchandise Inventory		34,000
	28	Credit Card Expense	3,540	
		Cash		3,540
	30	Sales Returns and Allowances	8,400	
		Accounts Receivable—Rabel Co.		8,400
	30	Merchandise Inventory	5,000	
		Cost of Merchandise Sold		5,000

Prob. 6–4A

1.

Aug.	1	Accounts Receivable—Beartooth Co.	48,000	
		Sales		48,000
	1	Cost of Merchandise Sold	28,800	
		Merchandise Inventory		28,800
	2	Delivery Expense	1,150	
		Cash		1,150
	5	Accounts Receivable—Beartooth Co.	66,000	
		Sales		66,000
	5	Cost of Merchandise Sold	40,000	
		Merchandise Inventory		40,000
	6	Sales Returns and Allowances	10,500	
		Accounts Receivable—Beartooth Co.		10,500
	6	Merchandise Inventory	6,300	
		Cost of Merchandise Sold		6,300
	15	Accounts Receivable—Beartooth Co.	58,700	
		Sales		58,700
	15	Accounts Receivable—Beartooth Co.	1,675	
		Cash		1,675
	15	Cost of Merchandise Sold	35,000	
		Merchandise Inventory		35,000
	16	Cash	36,750	
		Sales Discounts	750	
		Accounts Receivable—Beartooth Co.		37,500
	25	Cash	59,788	
		Sales Discounts	587	
		Accounts Receivable—Beartooth Co.		60,375
	31	Cash	66,000	
		Accounts Receivable—Beartooth Co.		66,000

Prob. 6–4A (Concluded)

2.

Aug.	1	Merchandise Inventory	48,000	
		Accounts Payable—Summit Company		48,000
	5	Merchandise Inventory	66,000	
		Accounts Payable—Summit Company		66,000
	6	Accounts Payable—Summit Company	10,500	
		Merchandise Inventory		10,500
	9	Merchandise Inventory	2,300	
		Cash		2,300
	15	Merchandise Inventory	60,375	
		Accounts Payable—Summit Company		60,375
		$58,700 + $1,675 = $60,375.		
	16	Accounts Payable—Summit Company	37,500	
		Cash		36,750
		Merchandise Inventory		750
	25	Accounts Payable—Summit Company	60,375	
		Cash		59,788
		Merchandise Inventory		587
	31	Accounts Payable—Summit Company	66,000	
		Cash		66,000

Prob. 6–5A

1.

GLOUCESTER CO. Income Statement For the Year Ended August 31, 2014			
Revenue from sales:			
Sales		$4,576,000	
Less: Sales returns and allowances	$ 31,000		
Sales discounts	28,000	59,000	
Net sales			$4,517,000
Cost of merchandise sold			2,650,000
Gross profit			$1,867,000
Expenses:			
Selling expenses:			
Sales salaries expense	$745,000		
Advertising expense	205,000		
Depreciation expense—store equipment	40,000		
Miscellaneous selling expense	18,000		
Total selling expenses		$1,008,000	
Administrative expenses:			
Office salaries expense	$410,000		
Rent expense	60,000		
Depreciation expense—office equipment	30,000		
Insurance expense	18,000		
Office supplies expense	11,000		
Miscellaneous administrative expense	8,000		
Total administrative expenses		537,000	
Total operating expenses			1,545,000
Income from operations			$ 322,000
Other expense:			
Interest expense			12,000
Net income			$ 310,000

Prob. 6–5A (Continued)

2.

GLOUCESTER CO. Statement of Owner's Equity For the Year Ended August 31, 2014		
Mia Reynolds, capital, September 1, 2013		$675,000
Net income for the year	$310,000	
Less withdrawals	75,000	
Increase in owner's equity		235,000
Mia Reynolds, capital, August 31, 2014		$910,000

Prob. 6–5A (Continued)

3.

GLOUCESTER CO. Balance Sheet August 31, 2014			
Assets			
Current assets:			
Cash		$125,000	
Accounts receivable		335,000	
Merchandise inventory		380,000	
Office supplies		12,000	
Prepaid insurance		9,000	
Total current assets			$ 861,000
Property, plant, and equipment:			
Office equipment	$275,000		
Less accumulated depreciation	187,000	$ 88,000	
Store equipment	$859,000		
Less accumulated depreciation	293,000	566,000	
Total property, plant, and equipment			654,000
Total assets			$1,515,000
Liabilities			
Current liabilities:			
Accounts payable		$193,000	
Salaries payable		12,000	
Note payable (current portion)		16,000	
Total current liabilities			$ 221,000
Long-term liabilities:			
Note payable (final payment due 2037)			384,000
Total liabilities			$ 605,000
Owner's Equity			
Mia Reynolds, capital			910,000
Total liabilities and owner's equity			$1,515,000

Prob. 6–5A (Concluded)

4. a. The multiple-step form of income statement contains various sections for revenues and expenses, with intermediate balances, and concludes with net income. In the single-step form, the total of all expenses is deducted from the total of all revenues. There are no intermediate balances.

    b. In the report form of balance sheet, the assets, liabilities, and owner's equity are presented in that order in a downward sequence. In the account form, the assets are listed on the left-hand side, and the liabilities and owner's equity are listed on the right-hand side.

Prob. 6–6A

1.

GLOUCESTER CO. Income Statement For the Year Ended August 31, 2014		
Revenues:		
Net sales		$4,517,000
Expenses:		
Cost of merchandise sold	$2,650,000	
Selling expenses	1,008,000	
Administrative expenses	537,000	
Interest expense	12,000	
Total expenses		4,207,000
Net income		$ 310,000

2.

GLOUCESTER CO. Statement of Owner's Equity For the Year Ended August 31, 2014		
Mia Reynolds, capital, September 1, 2013		$675,000
Net income for the year	$310,000	
Less withdrawals	75,000	
Increase in owner's equity		235,000
Mia Reynolds, capital, August 31, 2014		$910,000

Prob. 6–6A (Continued)

3.

GLOUCESTER CO.
Balance Sheet
August 31, 2014

Assets

Current assets:			
Cash		$125,000	
Accounts receivable		335,000	
Merchandise inventory		380,000	
Office supplies		12,000	
Prepaid insurance		9,000	
Total current assets			$ 861,000
Property, plant, and equipment:			
Office equipment	$275,000		
Less accumulated depreciation	187,000	$ 88,000	
Store equipment	$859,000		
Less accumulated depreciation	293,000	566,000	
Total property, plant, and equipment			654,000
Total assets			$1,515,000

Liabilities

Current liabilities:			
Accounts payable	$193,000		
Salaries payable	12,000		
Notes payable (current portion)	16,000		
Total current liabilities			$ 221,000
Long-term liabilities:			
Notes payable (final payment due 2037)			384,000
Total liabilities			$ 605,000

Owner's Equity

Mia Reynolds, capital			910,000
Total liabilities and owner's equity			$1,515,000

Prob. 6–6A (Concluded)

4.

2014			Closing Entries		
Aug.	31		Sales	4,576,000	
			Income Summary		4,576,000
	31		Income Summary	4,266,000	
			Sales Returns and Allowances		31,000
			Sales Discounts		28,000
			Cost of Merchandise Sold		2,650,000
			Sales Salaries Expense		745,000
			Advertising Expense		205,000
			Depreciation Expense—Store Equipment		40,000
			Miscellaneous Selling Expense		18,000
			Office Salaries Expense		410,000
			Rent Expense		60,000
			Depreciation Expense—Office Equipment		30,000
			Insurance Expense		18,000
			Office Supplies Expense		11,000
			Miscellaneous Administrative Expense		8,000
			Interest Expense		12,000
	31		Income Summary	310,000	
			Mia Reynolds, Capital		310,000
	31		Mia Reynolds, Capital	75,000	
			Mia Reynolds, Drawing		75,000

Appendix Prob. 6–7A

Oct.				
	1	Purchases	14,448	
		Accounts Payable—UK Imports Co.		14,448
	3	Purchases	9,950	
		Freight In	220	
		Accounts Payable—Hoagie Co.		10,170
	4	Purchases	13,650	
		Accounts Payable—Taco Co.		13,650
	6	Accounts Payable—Taco Co.	4,550	
		Purchases Returns and Allowances		4,550
	13	Accounts Payable—Hoagie Co.	10,170	
		Cash		9,971
		Purchases Discounts		199
	14	Accounts Payable—Taco Co.	9,100	
		Cash		8,918
		Purchases Discounts		182
	19	Purchases	27,300	
		Accounts Payable—Veggie Co.		27,300
	19	Freight In	400	
		Cash		400
	20	Purchases	22,000	
		Accounts Payable—Caesar Salad Co.		22,000
	30	Accounts Payable—Caesar Salad Co.	22,000	
		Cash		21,780
		Purchases Discounts		220
	31	Accounts Payable—UK Imports Co.	14,448	
		Cash		14,448
	31	Accounts Payable—Veggie Co.	27,300	
		Cash		27,300

Appendix Prob. 6–8A

Nov.				
Nov.	3	Purchases	63,750	
		Accounts Payable—Moonlight Co.		63,750
		[$85,000 – ($85,000 × 25%)] = $63,750.		
	4	Cash	37,680	
		Sales		37,680
	5	Purchases	47,500	
		Freight In	810	
		Accounts Payable—Papoose Creek Co.		48,310
	6	Accounts Payable—Moonlight Co.	13,500	
		Purchases Returns and Allowances		13,500
	11	Accounts Receivable—Quinn Co.	15,600	
		Sales		15,600
		[$24,000 – ($24,000 × 35%)] = $15,600.		
	13	Accounts Payable—Moonlight Co.	50,250	
		Cash		49,245
		Purchases Discounts		1,005
	14	Cash	236,000	
		Sales		236,000
	15	Accounts Payable—Papoose Creek Co.	48,310	
		Cash		47,360
		Purchases Discounts		950
	21	Cash	15,444	
		Sales Discounts	156	
		Accounts Receivable—Quinn Co.		15,600
	24	Accounts Receivable—Rabel Co.	56,900	
		Sales		56,900
	28	Credit Card Expense	3,540	
		Cash		3,540
	30	Sales Returns and Allowances	8,400	
		Accounts Receivable—Rabel Co.		8,400

Appendix Prob. 6–9A

1.

Aug.				
Aug.	1	Accounts Receivable—Beartooth Co.	48,000	
		Sales		48,000
	2	Delivery Expense	1,150	
		Cash		1,150
	5	Accounts Receivable—Beartooth Co.	66,000	
		Sales		66,000
	6	Sales Returns and Allowances	10,500	
		Accounts Receivable—Beartooth Co.		10,500
	15	Accounts Receivable—Beartooth Co.	58,700	
		Sales		58,700
	15	Accounts Receivable—Beartooth Co.	1,675	
		Cash		1,675
	16	Cash	36,750	
		Sales Discounts	750	
		Accounts Receivable—Beartooth Co.		37,500
	25	Cash	59,788	
		Sales Discounts	587	
		Accounts Receivable—Beartooth Co.		60,375
	31	Cash	66,000	
		Accounts Receivable—Beartooth Co.		66,000

Appendix Prob. 6–9A (Concluded)

2.

Aug.					
Aug.	1	Purchases		48,000	
		Accounts Payable—Summit Company			48,000
	5	Purchases		66,000	
		Accounts Payable—Summit Company			66,000
	6	Accounts Payable—Summit Company		10,500	
		Purchases Returns and Allowances			10,500
	9	Freight In		2,300	
		Cash			2,300
	15	Purchases		58,700	
		Freight In		1,675	
		Accounts Payable—Summit Company			60,375
	16	Accounts Payable—Summit Company		37,500	
		Cash			36,750
		Purchases Discounts			750
	25	Accounts Payable—Summit Company		60,375	
		Cash			59,788
		Purchases Discounts			587
	31	Accounts Payable—Summit Company		66,000	
		Cash			66,000

Appendix Prob. 6–10A

1. Periodic inventory system. Wyman Company uses a periodic inventory system since it maintains accounts for purchases, purchases returns and allowances, purchases discounts, and freight in.

2. See page 6-42.

Appendix Prob. 6–10A (Continued)

2.

WYMAN COMPANY			
Income Statement			
For the Year Ended December 31, 2014			
Revenue from sales:			
Sales		$3,355,000	
Less: Sales returns and allowances	$ 46,000		
Sales discounts	29,000	75,000	
Net sales			$3,280,000
Cost of merchandise sold:			
Merchandise inventory, January 1, 2014		$ 257,000	
Purchases	$2,650,000		
Less: Purchases returns and allowances	93,000		
Purchases discounts	37,000		
Net purchases	$2,520,000		
Add freight in	48,000		
Cost of merchandise purchased		2,568,000	
Cost of merchandise available for sale		$2,825,000	
Less merchandise inventory,		305,000	
December 31, 2014			
Cost of merchandise sold			2,520,000
Gross profit			$ 760,000
Expenses:			
Selling expenses:			
Sales salaries expense	$ 300,000		
Advertising expense	45,000		
Delivery expense	9,000		
Depreciation expense—store equipment	6,000		
Miscellaneous selling expense	12,000		
Total selling expenses		$ 372,000	
Administrative expenses:			
Office salaries expense	$ 175,000		
Rent expense	28,000		
Insurance expense	3,000		
Office supplies expense	2,000		
Depreciation expense—office equipment	1,500		
Miscellaneous administrative expense	3,500		
Total administrative expenses		213,000	
Total operating expenses			585,000
Income from operations			$ 175,000
Other income and expense:			
Rent revenue		$ 7,000	
Less interest expense		2,000	5,000
Net income			$ 180,000

Appendix Prob. 6–10A (Concluded)

3.

Merchandise Inventory	305,000	
Sales	3,355,000	
Purchases Returns and Allowances	93,000	
Purchases Discounts	37,000	
Rent Revenue	7,000	
Income Summary		3,797,000
Income Summary	3,617,000	
Merchandise Inventory		257,000
Sales Returns and Allowances		46,000
Sales Discounts		29,000
Purchases		2,650,000
Freight In		48,000
Sales Salaries Expense		300,000
Advertising Expense		45,000
Delivery Expense		9,000
Depreciation Expense—Store Equipment		6,000
Miscellaneous Selling Expense		12,000
Office Salaries Expense		175,000
Rent Expense		28,000
Insurance Expense		3,000
Office Supplies Expense		2,000
Depreciation Expense—Office Equipment		1,500
Miscellaneous Administrative Expense		3,500
Interest Expense		2,000
Income Summary	180,000	
Shirley Wyman, Capital		180,000
Shirley Wyman, Capital	25,000	
Shirley Wyman, Drawing		25,000

4. $180,000. The same net income as under the periodic inventory system.

Prob. 6–1B

Mar.	1	Merchandise Inventory	43,900	
		Accounts Payable—Haas Co.		43,900
	5	Merchandise Inventory	19,175	
		Accounts Payable—Whitman Co.		19,175
	10	Accounts Payable—Haas Co.	43,900	
		Cash		43,035
		Merchandise Inventory		865
	13	Merchandise Inventory	15,550	
		Accounts Payable—Jost Co.		15,550
	14	Accounts Payable—Jost Co.	3,750	
		Merchandise Inventory		3,750
	18	Merchandise Inventory	13,560	
		Accounts Payable—Fairhurst Company		13,560
	18	Merchandise Inventory	140	
		Cash		140
	19	Merchandise Inventory	6,500	
		Accounts Payable—Bickle Co.		6,500
	23	Accounts Payable—Jost Co.	11,800	
		Cash		11,564
		Merchandise Inventory		236
	29	Accounts Payable—Bickle Co.	6,500	
		Cash		6,370
		Merchandise Inventory		130
	31	Accounts Payable—Fairhurst Company	13,560	
		Cash		13,560
	31	Accounts Payable—Whitman Co.	19,175	
		Cash		19,175

Prob. 6–2B

July	1	Accounts Receivable—Landscapes Co.	33,450	
		Sales		33,450
	1	Cost of Merchandise Sold	20,000	
		Merchandise Inventory		20,000
	2	Cash	92,880	
		Sales		86,000
		Sales Tax Payable		6,880
	2	Cost of Merchandise Sold	51,600	
		Merchandise Inventory		51,600
	5	Accounts Receivable—Peacock Company	17,500	
		Sales		17,500
	5	Cost of Merchandise Sold	10,000	
		Merchandise Inventory		10,000
	8	Cash	120,960	
		Sales		112,000
		Sales Tax Payable		8,960
	8	Cost of Merchandise Sold	67,200	
		Merchandise Inventory		67,200
	13	Cash	96,000	
		Sales		96,000
	13	Cost of Merchandise Sold	57,600	
		Merchandise Inventory		57,600
	14	Accounts Receivable—Loeb Co.	16,000	
		Sales		16,000
	14	Cost of Merchandise Sold	9,000	
		Merchandise Inventory		9,000
	15	Cash	17,325	
		Sales Discounts	175	
		Accounts Receivable—Peacock Company		17,500

Prob. 6–2B (Concluded)

July	16	Sales Returns and Allowances	3,000	
		Accounts Receivable—Loeb Co.		3,000
	16	Merchandise Inventory	1,800	
		Cost of Merchandise Sold		1,800
	18	Accounts Receivable—Jennings Company	11,350	
		Sales		11,350
	18	Accounts Receivable—Jennings Company	475	
		Cash		475
	18	Cost of Merchandise Sold	6,800	
		Merchandise Inventory		6,800
	24	Cash	12,870	
		Sales Discounts	130	
		Accounts Receivable—Loeb Co.		13,000
	28	Cash	11,598	
		Sales Discounts	227	
		Accounts Receivable—Jennings Company		11,825
	31	Delivery Expense	8,550	
		Cash		8,550
	31	Cash	33,450	
		Accounts Receivable—Landscapes Co.		33,450
Aug.	3	Credit Card Expense	3,770	
		Cash		3,770
	10	Sales Tax Payable	41,260	
		Cash		41,260

Prob. 6–3B

July	3	Merchandise Inventory	62,650	
		Accounts Payable—Hamling Co.		62,650
		[$72,000 – ($72,000 × 15%)] = $61,200.		
		$61,200 + $1,450 = $62,650.		
	5	Merchandise Inventory	33,450	
		Accounts Payable—Kester Co.		33,450
	6	Accounts Receivable—Parsley Co.	30,150	
		Sales		30,150
		[$45,000 – ($45,000 × 33%)] = $30,150.		
	6	Cost of Merchandise Sold	25,000	
		Merchandise Inventory		25,000
	7	Accounts Payable—Kester Co.	6,850	
		Merchandise Inventory		6,850
	13	Accounts Payable—Hamling Co.	62,650	
		Cash		61,426
		Merchandise Inventory		1,224
	15	Accounts Payable—Kester Co.	26,600	
		Cash		26,068
		Merchandise Inventory		532
	16	Cash	29,547	
		Sales Discounts	603	
		Accounts Receivable—Parsley Co.		30,150
	19	Cash	108,000	
		Sales		108,000
	19	Cost of Merchandise Sold	64,800	
		Merchandise Inventory		64,800
	22	Accounts Receivable—Tabor Co.	16,650	
		Sales		16,650
	22	Cost of Merchandise Sold	10,000	
		Merchandise Inventory		10,000

Prob. 6–3B (Concluded)

July	23	Cash	91,200	
		Sales		91,200
	23	Cost of Merchandise Sold	55,000	
		Merchandise Inventory		55,000
	28	Sales Returns and Allowances	3,600	
		Accounts Receivable—Tabor Co.		3,600
	28	Merchandise Inventory	2,000	
		Cost of Merchandise Sold		2,000
	31	Credit Card Expense	1,650	
		Cash		1,650

Prob. 6–4B

1.

Apr.				
Apr.	2	Accounts Receivable—Bird Company	32,000	
		Sales		32,000
	2	Accounts Receivable—Bird Company	330	
		Cash		330
	2	Cost of Merchandise Sold	19,200	
		Merchandise Inventory		19,200
	8	Accounts Receivable—Bird Company	49,500	
		Sales		49,500
	8	Cost of Merchandise Sold	29,700	
		Merchandise Inventory		29,700
	8	Delivery Expense	710	
		Cash		710
	12	Sales Returns and Allowances	7,500	
		Accounts Receivable—Bird Company		7,500
	12	Merchandise Inventory	4,800	
		Cost of Merchandise Sold		4,800
	12	Cash	31,690	
		Sales Discounts	640	
		Accounts Receivable—Bird Company		32,330
	23	Cash	41,580	
		Sales Discounts	420	
		Accounts Receivable—Bird Company		42,000
	24	Accounts Receivable—Bird Company	67,350	
		Sales		67,350
	24	Cost of Merchandise Sold	40,400	
		Merchandise Inventory		40,400
	30	Cash	67,350	
		Accounts Receivable—Bird Company		67,350

Prob. 6–4B (Concluded)

2.

Apr.				
Apr.	2	Merchandise Inventory	32,330	
		Accounts Payable—Swan Company		32,330
		$32,000 + $330 = $32,330.		
	8	Merchandise Inventory	49,500	
		Accounts Payable—Swan Company		49,500
	12	Accounts Payable—Swan Company	7,500	
		Merchandise Inventory		7,500
	12	Accounts Payable—Swan Company	32,330	
		Cash		31,690
		Merchandise Inventory		640
	23	Accounts Payable—Swan Company	42,000	
		Cash		41,580
		Merchandise Inventory		420
	24	Merchandise Inventory	67,350	
		Accounts Payable—Swan Company		67,350
	26	Merchandise Inventory	875	
		Cash		875
	30	Accounts Payable—Swan Company	67,350	
		Cash		67,350

Prob. 6–5B

1.

KANPUR CO. Income Statement For the Year Ended June 30, 2014			
Revenue from sales:			
Sales		$9,175,000	
Less: Sales returns and allowances	$160,000		
Sales discounts	90,000	250,000	
Net sales			$8,925,000
Cost of merchandise sold			5,620,000
Gross profit			$3,305,000
Expenses:			
Selling expenses:			
Sales salaries expense	$850,000		
Advertising expense	420,000		
Depreciation expense—store equipment	33,000		
Miscellaneous selling expense	18,000		
Total selling expenses		$1,321,000	
Administrative expenses:			
Office salaries expense	$540,000		
Rent expense	48,000		
Insurance expense	24,000		
Depreciation expense—office equipment	10,000		
Office supplies expense	4,000		
Miscellaneous administrative expense	6,000		
Total administrative expenses		632,000	
Total operating expenses			1,953,000
Income from operations			$1,352,000
Other expense:			
Interest expense			12,000
Net income			$1,340,000

Prob. 6–5B (Continued)

2.

KANPUR CO. Statement of Owner's Equity For the Year Ended June 30, 2014		
Gerri Faber, capital, July 1, 2013		$ 431,000
Net income for the year	$1,340,000	
Less withdrawals	300,000	
Increase in owner's equity		1,040,000
Gerri Faber, capital, June 30, 2014		$1,471,000

Prob. 6–5B (Continued)

3.

KANPUR CO. Balance Sheet June 30, 2014			
Assets			
Current assets:			
Cash		$ 92,000	
Accounts receivable		450,000	
Merchandise inventory		375,000	
Office supplies		10,000	
Prepaid insurance		12,000	
Total current assets			$ 939,000
Property, plant, and equipment:			
Office equipment	$220,000		
Less accumulated depreciation	58,000	$162,000	
Store equipment	$650,000		
Less accumulated depreciation	87,500	562,500	
Total property, plant, and equipment			724,500
Total assets			$1,663,500
Liabilities			
Current liabilities:			
Accounts payable		$ 48,500	
Salaries payable		4,000	
Note payable (current portion)		7,000	
Total current liabilities			$ 59,500
Long-term liabilities:			
Note payable (final payment due 2032)			133,000
Total liabilities			$ 192,500
Owner's Equity			
Gerri Faber, capital			1,471,000
Total liabilities and owner's equity			$1,663,500

Prob. 6–5B (Concluded)

4.   a.   **The multiple-step form of income statement contains various sections for revenues and expenses, with intermediate balances, and concludes with net income. In the single-step form, the total of all expenses is deducted from the total of all revenues. There are no intermediate balances.**

      b.   **In the report form of balance sheet, the assets, liabilities, and owner's equity are presented in that order in a downward sequence. In the account form, the assets are listed on the left-hand side, and the liabilities and owner's equity are listed on the right-hand side.**

Prob. 6–6B

1.

KANPUR CO. Income Statement For the Year Ended June 30, 2014		
Revenues:		
Net sales		$8,925,000
Expenses:		
Cost of merchandise sold	$5,620,000	
Selling expenses	1,321,000	
Administrative expenses	632,000	
Interest expense	12,000	
Total expenses		7,585,000
Net income		$1,340,000

2.

KANPUR CO. Statement of Owner's Equity For the Year Ended June 30, 2014		
Gerri Faber, capital, July 1, 2013		$ 431,000
Net income for the year	$1,340,000	
Less withdrawals	300,000	
Increase in owner's equity		1,040,000
Gerri Faber, capital, June 30, 2014		$1,471,000

Prob. 6–6B (Continued)

3.

KANPUR CO.
Balance Sheet
June 30, 2014

Assets				Liabilities			
Current assets:				**Current liabilities:**			
Cash		$ 92,000		Accounts payable	$48,500		
Accounts receivable		450,000		Salaries payable	4,000		
Merchandise inventory		375,000		Notes payable (current portion)	7,000		
Office supplies		10,000		Total current liabilities		$ 59,500	
Prepaid insurance		12,000		**Long-term liabilities:**			
Total current assets			$ 939,000	Notes payable (final payment			
Property, plant, and equipment:				due 2032)		133,000	
Office equipment	$220,000			Total liabilities		$ 192,500	
Less accum. depreciation	58,000	$162,000		**Owner's Equity**			
Store equipment	$650,000			Gerri Faber, capital		1,471,000	
Less accum. depreciation	87,500	562,500					
Total property, plant, and							
equipment			724,500				
Total assets			$1,663,500	Total liabilities and owner's equity		$1,663,500	

Prob. 6–6B (Concluded)

4.

2014		Closing Entries		
June	30	Sales	9,175,000	
		Income Summary		9,175,000
	30	Income Summary	7,835,000	
		Sales Returns and Allowances		160,000
		Sales Discounts		90,000
		Cost of Merchandise Sold		5,620,000
		Sales Salaries Expense		850,000
		Advertising Expense		420,000
		Depreciation Expense—Store Equipment		33,000
		Miscellaneous Selling Expense		18,000
		Office Salaries Expense		540,000
		Rent Expense		48,000
		Insurance Expense		24,000
		Depreciation Expense—Office Equipment		10,000
		Office Supplies Expense		4,000
		Miscellaneous Administrative Expense		6,000
		Interest Expense		12,000
	30	Income Summary	1,340,000	
		Gerri Faber, Capital		1,340,000
	30	Gerri Faber, Capital	300,000	
		Gerri Faber, Drawing		300,000

Appendix Prob. 6–7B

Mar.	1	Purchases	43,250	
		Freight In	650	
		Accounts Payable—Haas Co.		43,900
	5	Purchases	19,175	
		Accounts Payable—Whitman Co.		19,175
	10	Accounts Payable—Haas Co.	43,900	
		Cash		43,035
		Purchases Discounts		865
	13	Purchases	15,550	
		Accounts Payable—Jost Co.		15,550
	14	Accounts Payable—Jost Co.	3,750	
		Purchases Returns and Allowances		3,750
	18	Purchases	13,560	
		Accounts Payable—Fairhurst Company		13,560
	18	Freight In	140	
		Cash		140
	19	Purchases	6,500	
		Accounts Payable—Bickle Co.		6,500
	23	Accounts Payable—Jost Co.	11,800	
		Cash		11,564
		Purchases Discounts		236
	29	Accounts Payable—Bickle Co.	6,500	
		Cash		6,370
		Purchases Discounts		130
	31	Accounts Payable—Fairhurst Company	13,560	
		Cash		13,560
	31	Accounts Payable—Whitman Co.	19,175	
		Cash		19,175

Appendix Prob. 6–8B

July	3	Purchases	61,200	
		Freight In	1,450	
		Accounts Payable—Hamling Co.		62,650
		[$72,000 – ($72,000 × 15%)] = $61,200.		
	5	Purchases	33,450	
		Accounts Payable—Kester Co.		33,450
	6	Accounts Receivable—Parsley Co.	30,150	
		Sales		30,150
		[$45,000 – ($45,000 × 33%)] = $30,150.		
	7	Accounts Payable—Kester Co.	6,850	
		Purchases Returns and Allowances		6,850
	13	Accounts Payable—Hamling Co.	62,650	
		Cash		61,426
		Purchases Discounts		1,224
	15	Accounts Payable—Kester Co.	26,600	
		Cash		26,068
		Purchases Discounts		532
	16	Cash	29,547	
		Sales Discounts	603	
		Accounts Receivable—Parsley Co.		30,150
	19	Cash	108,000	
		Sales		108,000
	22	Accounts Receivable—Tabor Co.	16,650	
		Sales		16,650
	23	Cash	91,200	
		Sales		91,200
	28	Sales Returns and Allowances	3,600	
		Accounts Receivable—Tabor Co.		3,600
	31	Credit Card Expense	1,650	
		Cash		1,650

Appendix Prob. 6–9B

1.

Apr.				
Apr.	2	Accounts Receivable—Bird Company	32,000	
		Sales		32,000
	2	Accounts Receivable—Bird Company	330	
		Cash		330
	8	Accounts Receivable—Bird Company	49,500	
		Sales		49,500
	8	Delivery Expense	710	
		Cash		710
	12	Sales Returns and Allowances	7,500	
		Accounts Receivable—Bird Company		7,500
	12	Cash	31,690	
		Sales Discounts	640	
		Accounts Receivable—Bird Company		32,330
	23	Cash	41,580	
		Sales Discounts	420	
		Accounts Receivable—Bird Company		42,000
	24	Accounts Receivable—Bird Company	67,350	
		Sales		67,350
	30	Cash	67,350	
		Accounts Receivable—Bird Company		67,350

Appendix Prob. 6–9B (Concluded)

2.

Apr.	2	Purchases	32,000	
		Freight In	330	
		Accounts Payable—Swan Company		32,330
	8	Purchases	49,500	
		Accounts Payable—Swan Company		49,500
	12	Accounts Payable—Swan Company	7,500	
		Purchases Returns and Allowances		7,500
	12	Accounts Payable—Swan Company	32,330	
		Cash		31,690
		Purchases Discounts		640
	23	Accounts Payable—Swan Company	42,000	
		Cash		41,580
		Purchases Discounts		420
	24	Purchases	67,350	
		Accounts Payable—Swan Company		67,350
	26	Freight In	875	
		Cash		875
	30	Accounts Payable—Swan Company	67,350	
		Cash		67,350

Appendix Prob. 6–10B

1. Periodic inventory system. Simkins Company uses a periodic inventory
    system since it maintains accounts for purchases, purchases returns and
    allowances, purchases discounts, and freight in.

2. See page 6-63.

Appendix Prob. 6–10B (Continued)

2.

SIMKINS COMPANY			
Income Statement			
For the Year Ended June 30, 2014			
Revenue from sales:			
Sales		$6,748,000	
Less: Sales returns and allowances	$ 92,000		
Sales discounts	66,000	158,000	
Net sales			$6,590,000
Cost of merchandise sold:			
Merchandise inventory, July 1, 2013		$ 415,000	
Purchases	$4,100,000		
Less: Purchases returns and allowances	32,000		
Purchases discounts	13,000		
Net purchases	$4,055,000		
Add freight in	45,000		
Cost of merchandise purchased		4,100,000	
Cost of merchandise available for sale		$4,515,000	
Less merchandise inventory,		508,000	
June 30, 2014			
Cost of merchandise sold			4,007,000
Gross profit			$2,583,000
Expenses:			
Selling expenses:			
Sales salaries expense	$ 580,000		
Advertising expense	315,000		
Delivery expense	18,000		
Depreciation expense—store equipment	12,000		
Miscellaneous selling expense	28,000		
Total selling expenses		$ 953,000	
Administrative expenses:			
Office salaries expense	$ 375,000		
Rent expense	43,000		
Insurance expense	17,000		
Office supplies expense	5,000		
Depreciation expense—office equipment	4,000		
Miscellaneous administrative expense	16,000		
Total administrative expenses		460,000	
Total operating expenses			1,413,000
Income from operations			$1,170,000
Other income and expense:			
Rent revenue		$ 32,500	
Less interest expense		2,500	30,000
Net income			$1,200,000

Appendix Prob. 6–10B (Concluded)

3.

Closing Entries		
Merchandise Inventory	508,000	
Sales	6,748,000	
Purchases Returns and Allowances	32,000	
Purchases Discounts	13,000	
Rent Revenue	32,500	
Income Summary		7,333,500
Income Summary	6,133,500	
Merchandise Inventory		415,000
Sales Returns and Allowances		92,000
Sales Discounts		66,000
Purchases		4,100,000
Freight In		45,000
Sales Salaries Expense		580,000
Advertising Expense		315,000
Delivery Expense		18,000
Depreciation Expense—Store Equipment		12,000
Miscellaneous Selling Expense		28,000
Office Salaries Expense		375,000
Rent Expense		43,000
Insurance Expense		17,000
Office Supplies Expense		5,000
Depreciation Expense—Office Equipment		4,000
Miscellaneous Administrative Expense		16,000
Interest Expense		2,500
Income Summary	1,200,000	
Amy Gant, Capital		1,200,000
Amy Gant, Capital	275,000	
Amy Gant, Drawing		275,000

4. $1,200,000. The same net income as under the periodic inventory system.

COMPREHENSIVE PROBLEM 2

1., 2., 6., and 9.

Account: **Cash**   Account No. **110**

Date		Item	Post. Ref.	Debit	Credit	Balance Debit	Balance Credit
2014							
May	1	Balance	✓			83,600	
	1		20		5,000		
	4		20		600		
	7		20	22,300			
	10		20	54,000			
	13		20		35,280		
	15		20		11,000		
	16		20	53,900			
	19		20		18,700		
	19		20		33,450		
	21		21		2,300		
	21		21	42,900			
	26		21		7,500		
	28		21		85,000		
	29		21		2,400		
	30		21	111,200			
	31		21		82,170	84,500	

Account: **Accounts Receivable**   Account No. **112**

Date		Item	Post. Ref.	Debit	Credit	Balance Debit	Balance Credit
2014							
May	1	Balance	✓			233,900	
	6		20	68,500			
	7		20		22,300		
	14		20		13,500		
	16		20		55,000		
	20		21	110,000			
	21		21	2,300			
	21		21		42,900		
	30		21	78,750			
	30		21		112,300	247,450	

Comp. Problem 2 (Continued)

Account: **Merchandise Inventory**   Account No. **115**

Date		Item	Post. Ref.	Debit	Credit	Balance Debit	Balance Credit
2014							
May	1	Balance	✓			602,400	
	3		20	36,000			
	4		20	600			
	6		20		41,000		
	10		20		32,000		
	13		20		720		
	14		20	8,000			
	19		20	18,700			
	20		21		70,000		
	21		21	88,000			
	24		21		5,000		
	26		21	4,800			
	30		21		47,000		
	31		21		830	561,950	
	31	Adjusting	22		11,950	550,000	

Account: **Prepaid Insurance**   Account No. **116**

Date		Item	Post. Ref.	Debit	Credit	Balance Debit	Balance Credit
2014							
May	1	Balance	✓			16,800	
	31	Adjusting	22		12,000	4,800	

Account: **Store Supplies**   Account No. **117**

Date		Item	Post. Ref.	Debit	Credit	Balance Debit	Balance Credit
2014							
May	1	Balance	✓			11,400	
	29		21	2,400		13,800	
	31	Adjusting	22		9,800	4,000	

Account: **Store Equipment**   Account No. **123**

Date		Item	Post. Ref.	Debit	Credit	Balance Debit	Balance Credit
2014							
May	1	Balance	✓			569,500	

Comp. Problem 2 (Continued)

Account: **Accumulated Depreciation—Store Equipment**   Account No. ___124___

Date		Item	Post. Ref.	Debit	Credit	Balance Debit	Balance Credit
2014							
May	1	Balance	✓				56,700
	31	Adjusting	22		14,000		70,700

Account: **Accounts Payable**   Account No. ___210___

Date		Item	Post. Ref.	Debit	Credit	Balance Debit	Balance Credit
2014							
May	1	Balance	✓				96,600
	3		20		36,000		
	13		20	36,000			
	19		20	33,450			
	21		21		88,000		
	24		21	5,000			
	31		21	83,000			63,150

Account: **Salaries Payable**   Account No. ___211___

Date		Item	Post. Ref.	Debit	Credit	Balance Debit	Balance Credit
2014							
May	31	Adjusting	22		13,600		13,600

Account: **Lynn Tolley, Capital**   Account No. ___310___

Date		Item	Post. Ref.	Debit	Credit	Balance Debit	Balance Credit
2013							
June	1	Balance	✓				685,300
2014							
May	31	Closing	23		762,500		
	31	Closing	23	135,000			1,312,800

Account: **Lynn Tolley, Drawing**   Account No. ___311___

Date		Item	Post. Ref.	Debit	Credit	Balance Debit	Balance Credit
2014							
May	1	Balance	✓			135,000	
	31	Closing	23		135,000	—	—

Comp. Problem 2 (Continued)

Account: __Income Summary__   Account No. ___312___

Date		Item	Post. Ref.	Debit	Credit	Balance Debit	Balance Credit
2014							
May	31	Closing	23		5,532,350		
	31	Closing	23	4,769,850			762,500
	31	Closing	23	762,500		—	—

Account: __Sales__   Account No. ___410___

Date		Item	Post. Ref.	Debit	Credit	Balance Debit	Balance Credit
2014							
May	1	Balance	✓				5,221,100
	6		20		68,500		
	10		20		54,000		
	20		21		110,000		
	30		21		78,750		5,532,350
	31	Closing	23	5,532,350		—	—

Account: __Sales Returns and Allowances__   Account No. ___411___

Date		Item	Post. Ref.	Debit	Credit	Balance Debit	Balance Credit
2014							
May	1	Balance	✓			92,700	
	14		20	13,500			
	26		21	7,500		113,700	
	31	Closing	23		113,700	—	—

Account: __Sales Discounts__   Account No. ___412___

Date		Item	Post. Ref.	Debit	Credit	Balance Debit	Balance Credit
2014							
May	1	Balance	✓			59,400	
	16		20	1,100			
	30		21	1,100		61,600	
	31	Closing	23		61,600	—	—

Comp. Problem 2 (Continued)

Account: **Cost of Merchandise Sold**   Account No. _____ **510**

Date		Item	Post. Ref.	Debit	Credit	Balance Debit	Balance Credit
2014							
May	1	Balance	✓			2,823,000	
	6		20	41,000			
	10		20	32,000			
	14		20		8,000		
	20		21	70,000			
	26		21		4,800		
	30		21	47,000		3,000,200	
	31	Adjusting	22	11,950		3,012,150	
	31	Closing	23		3,012,150	—	—

Account: **Sales Salaries Expense**   Account No. _____ **520**

Date		Item	Post. Ref.	Debit	Credit	Balance Debit	Balance Credit
2014							
May	1	Balance	✓			664,800	
	28		21	56,000		720,800	
	31	Adjusting	22	7,000		727,800	
	31	Closing	23		727,800	—	—

Account: **Advertising Expense**   Account No. _____ **521**

Date		Item	Post. Ref.	Debit	Credit	Balance Debit	Balance Credit
2014							
May	1	Balance	✓			281,000	
	15		20	11,000		292,000	
	31	Closing	23		292,000	—	—

Account: **Depreciation Expense**   Account No. _____ **522**

Date		Item	Post. Ref.	Debit	Credit	Balance Debit	Balance Credit
2014							
May	31	Adjusting	22	14,000		14,000	
	31	Closing	23		14,000	—	—

Comp. Problem 2 (Continued)

Account: **Stores Supplies Expense**   Account No. **523**

Date		Item	Post. Ref.	Debit	Credit	Balance Debit	Balance Credit
2014							
May	31	Adjusting	22	9,800		9,800	
	31	Closing	23		9,800	—	—

Account: **Miscellaneous Selling Expense**   Account No. **529**

Date		Item	Post. Ref.	Debit	Credit	Balance Debit	Balance Credit
2014							
May	1	Balance	✓			12,600	
	31	Closing	23		12,600	—	—

Account: **Office Salaries Expense**   Account No. **530**

Date		Item	Post. Ref.	Debit	Credit	Balance Debit	Balance Credit
2014							
May	1	Balance	✓			382,100	
	28		21	29,000		411,100	
	31	Adjusting	22	6,600		417,700	
	31	Closing	23		417,700	—	—

Account: **Rent Expense**   Account No. **531**

Date		Item	Post. Ref.	Debit	Credit	Balance Debit	Balance Credit
2014							
May	1	Balance	✓			83,700	
	1		20	5,000		88,700	
	31	Closing	23		88,700	—	—

Account: **Insurance Expense**   Account No. **532**

Date		Item	Post. Ref.	Debit	Credit	Balance Debit	Balance Credit
2014							
May	31	Adjusting	22	12,000		12,000	
	31	Closing	23		12,000	—	—

Comp. Problem 2 (Continued)

Account: **Miscellaneous Administrative Expense**   **Account No.** **539**

Date		Item	Post. Ref.	Debit	Credit	Balance Debit	Balance Credit
2014							
May	1	Balance	✓			7,800	
	31	Closing	23		7,800	—	—

Comp. Problem 2 (Continued)

1. and 2.
JOURNAL
Page _____ 20

Date			Post. Ref.	Debit	Credit
2014					
May	1	Rent Expense	531	5,000	
		Cash	110		5,000
	3	Merchandise Inventory	115	36,000	
		Accounts Payable—Martin Co.	210		36,000
	4	Merchandise Inventory	115	600	
		Cash	110		600
	6	Accounts Receivable—Korman Co.	112	68,500	
		Sales	410		68,500
	6	Cost of Merchandise Sold	510	41,000	
		Merchandise Inventory	115		41,000
	7	Cash	110	22,300	
		Accounts Receivable—Halstad Co.	112		22,300
	10	Cash	110	54,000	
		Sales	410		54,000
	10	Cost of Merchandise Sold	510	32,000	
		Merchandise Inventory	115		32,000
	13	Accounts Payable—Martin Co.	210	36,000	
		Cash	110		35,280
		Merchandise Inventory	115		720
	14	Sales Returns and Allowances	411	13,500	
		Accounts Receivable—Korman Co.	112		13,500
	14	Merchandise Inventory	115	8,000	
		Cost of Merchandise Sold	510		8,000
	15	Advertising Expense	521	11,000	
		Cash	110		11,000
	16	Cash	110	53,900	
		Sales Discounts	412	1,100	
		Accounts Receivable—Korman Co.	112		55,000
	19	Merchandise Inventory	115	18,700	
		Cash	110		18,700
	19	Accounts Payable—Buttons Co.	210	33,450	
		Cash	110		33,450

6-72

Comp. Problem 2 (Continued)

JOURNAL   Page _____ **21**

Date		Post. Ref.	Debit	Credit
2014				
May	20 Accounts Receivable—Crescent Co.	112	110,000	
	Sales	410		110,000
	20 Cost of Merchandise Sold	510	70,000	
	Merchandise Inventory	115		70,000
	21 Accounts Receivable—Crescent Co.	112	2,300	
	Cash	110		2,300
	21 Cash	110	42,900	
	Accounts Receivable—Gee Co.	112		42,900
	21 Merchandise Inventory	115	88,000	
	Accounts Payable—Osterman Co.	210		88,000
	24 Accounts Payable—Osterman Co.	210	5,000	
	Merchandise Inventory	115		5,000
	26 Sales Returns and Allowances	411	7,500	
	Cash	110		7,500
	26 Merchandise Inventory	115	4,800	
	Cost of Merchandise Sold	510		4,800
	28 Sales Salaries Expense	520	56,000	
	Office Salaries Expense	530	29,000	
	Cash	110		85,000
	29 Store Supplies	117	2,400	
	Cash	110		2,400
	30 Accounts Receivable—Turner Co.	112	78,750	
	Sales	410		78,750
	30 Cost of Merchandise Sold	510	47,000	
	Merchandise Inventory	115		47,000
	30 Cash	110	111,200	
	Sales Discounts	412	1,100	
	Accounts Receivable—Crescent Co.	112		112,300
	31 Accounts Payable—Osterman Co.	210	83,000	
	Cash	110		82,170
	Merchandise Inventory	115		830

Comp. Problem 2 (Continued)

3.

PALISADE CREEK CO. Unadjusted Trial Balance May 31, 2014	Debit Balances	Credit Balances
Cash	84,500	
Accounts Receivable	247,450	
Merchandise Inventory	561,950	
Prepaid Insurance	16,800	
Store Supplies	13,800	
Store Equipment	569,500	
Accumulated Depreciation—Store Equipment		56,700
Accounts Payable		63,150
Salaries Payable		—
Lynn Tolley, Capital		685,300
Lynn Tolley, Drawing	135,000	
Sales		5,532,350
Sales Returns and Allowances	113,700	
Sales Discounts	61,600	
Cost of Merchandise Sold	3,000,200	
Sales Salaries Expense	720,800	
Advertising Expense	292,000	
Depreciation Expense	—	
Store Supplies Expense	—	
Miscellaneous Selling Expense	12,600	
Office Salaries Expense	411,100	
Rent Expense	88,700	
Insurance Expense	—	
Miscellaneous Administrative Expense	7,800	
	6,337,500	6,337,500

Comp. Problem 2 (Continued)

4. and 6.   **JOURNAL**   Page _____ **22**

Date			Post. Ref.	Debit	Credit
2014		**Adjusting Entries**			
May	31	Cost of Merchandise Sold	510	11,950	
		Merchandise Inventory	115		11,950
		Inventory shrinkage			
		($561,950 – $550,000).			
	31	Insurance Expense	532	12,000	
		Prepaid Insurance	116		12,000
		Insurance expired.			
	31	Store Supplies Expense	523	9,800	
		Store Supplies	117		9,800
		Supplies used ($13,800 – $4,000).			
	31	Depreciation Expense	522	14,000	
		Accum. Depr.—Store Equipment	124		14,000
		Store equipment depreciation.			
	31	Sales Salaries Expense	520	7,000	
		Office Salaries Expense	530	6,600	
		Salaries Payable	211		13,600
		Accrued salaries.			

Comp. Problem 2 (Continued)

7.

PALISADE CREEK CO. Adjusted Trial Balance May 31, 2014	Debit Balances	Credit Balances
Cash	84,500	
Accounts Receivable	247,450	
Merchandise Inventory	550,000	
Prepaid Insurance	4,800	
Store Supplies	4,000	
Store Equipment	569,500	
Accumulated Depreciation—Store Equipment		70,700
Accounts Payable		63,150
Salaries Payable		13,600
Lynn Tolley, Capital		685,300
Lynn Tolley, Drawing	135,000	
Sales		5,532,350
Sales Returns and Allowances	113,700	
Sales Discounts	61,600	
Cost of Merchandise Sold	3,012,150	
Sales Salaries Expense	727,800	
Advertising Expense	292,000	
Depreciation Expense	14,000	
Store Supplies Expense	9,800	
Miscellaneous Selling Expense	12,600	
Office Salaries Expense	417,700	
Rent Expense	88,700	
Insurance Expense	12,000	
Miscellaneous Administrative Expense	7,800	
	6,365,100	6,365,100

Comp. Problem 2 (Continued)

8.

PALISADE CREEK CO. Income Statement For the Year Ended May 31, 2014			
Revenue from sales:			
Sales		$5,532,350	
Less: Sales returns and allowances	$113,700		
Sales discounts	61,600	175,300	
Net sales			$5,357,050
Cost of merchandise sold			3,012,150
Gross profit			$2,344,900
Expenses:			
Selling expenses:			
Sales salaries expense	$727,800		
Advertising expense	292,000		
Depreciation expense	14,000		
Store supplies expense	9,800		
Miscellaneous selling expense	12,600		
Total selling expenses		$1,056,200	
Administrative expenses:			
Office salaries expense	$417,700		
Rent expense	88,700		
Insurance expense	12,000		
Miscellaneous administrative expense	7,800		
Total administrative expenses		526,200	
Total expenses			1,582,400
Net income			$ 762,500

PALISADE CREEK CO. Statement of Owner's Equity For the Year Ended May 31, 2014		
Lynn Tolley, capital, June 1, 2013		$ 685,300
Net income for the year	$762,500	
Less withdrawals	135,000	
Increase in owner's equity		627,500
Lynn Tolley, capital, May 31, 2014		$1,312,800

Comp. Problem 2 (Continued)

<table>
<tr><td colspan="3" align="center">PALISADE CREEK CO.
Balance Sheet
May 31, 2014</td></tr>
<tr><td colspan="3" align="center">Assets</td></tr>
<tr><td>Current assets:</td><td></td><td></td></tr>
<tr><td>Cash</td><td>$ 84,500</td><td></td></tr>
<tr><td>Accounts receivable</td><td>247,450</td><td></td></tr>
<tr><td>Merchandise inventory</td><td>550,000</td><td></td></tr>
<tr><td>Prepaid insurance</td><td>4,800</td><td></td></tr>
<tr><td>Store supplies</td><td>4,000</td><td></td></tr>
<tr><td>Total current assets</td><td></td><td>$ 890,750</td></tr>
<tr><td>Property, plant, and equipment:</td><td></td><td></td></tr>
<tr><td>Store equipment</td><td>$569,500</td><td></td></tr>
<tr><td>Less accumulated depreciation</td><td>70,700</td><td></td></tr>
<tr><td>Total property, plant, and equipment</td><td></td><td>498,800</td></tr>
<tr><td>Total assets</td><td></td><td>$1,389,550</td></tr>
<tr><td colspan="3" align="center">Liabilities</td></tr>
<tr><td>Current liabilities:</td><td></td><td></td></tr>
<tr><td>Accounts payable</td><td>$ 63,150</td><td></td></tr>
<tr><td>Salaries payable</td><td>13,600</td><td></td></tr>
<tr><td>Total liabilities</td><td></td><td>$ 76,750</td></tr>
<tr><td colspan="3" align="center">Owner's Equity</td></tr>
<tr><td>Lynn Tolley, capital</td><td></td><td>1,312,800</td></tr>
<tr><td>Total liabilities and owner's equity</td><td></td><td>$1,389,550</td></tr>
</table>

Comp. Problem 2 (Continued)

9.   **JOURNAL**   Page   23

Date			Post. Ref.	Debit	Credit
2014		Closing Entries			
May	31	Sales	410	5,532,350	
		Income Summary	312		5,532,350
	31	Income Summary	312	4,769,850	
		Sales Returns and Allowances	411		113,700
		Sales Discounts	412		61,600
		Cost of Merchandise Sold	510		3,012,150
		Sales Salaries Expense	520		727,800
		Advertising Expense	521		292,000
		Depreciation Expense	522		14,000
		Store Supplies Expense	523		9,800
		Miscellaneous Selling Expense	529		12,600
		Office Salaries Expense	530		417,700
		Rent Expense	531		88,700
		Insurance Expense	532		12,000
		Miscellaneous Administrative Exp.	539		7,800
	31	Income Summary	312	762,500	
		Lynn Tolley, Capital	310		762,500
	31	Lynn Tolley, Capital	310	135,000	
		Lynn Tolley, Drawing	311		135,000

Comp. Problem 2 (Continued)

10.

PALISADE CREEK CO. Post-Closing Trial Balance May 31, 2014	Debit Balances	Credit Balances
Cash	84,500	
Accounts Receivable	247,450	
Merchandise Inventory	550,000	
Prepaid Insurance	4,800	
Store Supplies	4,000	
Store Equipment	569,500	
Accumulated Depreciation—Store Equipment		70,700
Accounts Payable		63,150
Salaries Payable		13,600
Lynn Tolley, Capital		1,312,800
	1,460,250	1,460,250

Comp. Problem 2 (Concluded)

5.   Optional.

PALISADE CREEK CO.
End-of-Period Spreadsheet (Work Sheet)
For the Year Ended May 31, 2014

Account Title	Unadjusted Trial Balance Debit	Credit	Adjustments Debit	Credit	Adjusted Trial Balance Debit	Credit	Income Statement Debit	Credit	Balance Sheet Debit	Credit
Cash	84,500				84,500				84,500	
Accounts Receivable	247,450				247,450				247,450	
Merchandise Inventory	561,950			(a) 11,950	550,000				550,000	
Prepaid Insurance	16,800			(b) 12,000	4,800				4,800	
Store Supplies	13,800			(c) 9,800	4,000				4,000	
Store Equipment	569,500				569,500				569,500	
Accum. Depr.—Store Equip.		56,700		(d) 14,000		70,700				70,700
Accounts Payable		63,150				63,150				63,150
Salaries Payable				(e) 13,600		13,600				13,600
Lynn Tolley, Capital		685,300				685,300				685,300
Lynn Tolley, Drawing	135,000				135,000				135,000	
Sales		5,532,350				5,532,350		5,532,350		
Sales Returns and Allowances	113,700				113,700		113,700			
Sales Discounts	61,600				61,600		61,600			
Cost of Merchandise Sold	3,000,200		(a) 11,950		3,012,150		3,012,150			
Sales Salaries Expense	720,800		(e) 7,000		727,800		727,800			
Advertising Expense	292,000				292,000		292,000			
Depreciation Expense			(d) 14,000		14,000		14,000			
Store Supplies Expense			(c) 9,800		9,800		9,800			
Miscellaneous Selling Expense	12,600				12,600		12,600			
Office Salaries Expense	411,100		(e) 6,600		417,700		417,700			
Rent Expense	88,700				88,700		88,700			
Insurance Expense			(b) 12,000		12,000		12,000			
Miscellaneous Admin. Expense	7,800				7,800		7,800			
	6,337,500	6,337,500	61,350	61,350	6,365,100	6,365,100	4,769,850	5,532,350	1,595,250	832,750
Net income							762,500			762,500
							5,532,350	5,532,350	1,595,250	1,595,250

*This solution is applicable only if the end-of-period spreadsheet (work sheet) is used.

CASES & PROJECTS

CP 6–1

Standards of Ethical Conduct for Management Accountants requires management accountants to perform in a competent manner and to comply with relevant laws, regulations, and technical standards. If Shelby Davey intentionally subtracted the discount with knowledge that the discount period had expired, he would have behaved in an unprofessional manner. Such behavior could eventually jeopardize Bontanica Company's buyer/supplier relationship with Whitetail Seed Co.

CP 6–2

Cam Pfeifer is correct. The accounts payable due suppliers could be included on the balance sheet at an amount of $314,500 ($269,500 + $45,000). This is the amount that will be expected to be paid to satisfy the obligation (liability) to suppliers. However, this is proper only if Rustic Furniture Co. has a history of taking all purchases discounts, has a properly designed accounting system to identify available discounts, and has sufficient liquidity (cash) to pay the accounts payable within the discount period. In this case, Rustic Furniture Co. apparently meets these criteria, since it has a history of taking all available discounts, as indicated by Mitzi Wheeler. Thus, Rustic Furniture Co. could report total accounts payable of $314,500 on its balance sheet. Merchandise Inventory would also need to be reduced by the discount of $5,500 in order to maintain consistency in approach.

CP 6–3

1. If Mark doesn't need the stereo immediately (by the next day), Wholesale Stereo offers the best buy, as shown below.

Wholesale Stereo:

List price...	$1,200.00
Shipping and handling (not including next-day air).........................	49.99
Total...	$1,249.99

Tru-Sound Systems:

List price...	$1,175.00
Sales tax (9%)...	105.75
Total...	$1,280.75

Even if the 2% cash discount offered by Tru-Sound Systems is considered, Wholesale Stereo still offers the best buy, as shown below.

List price...	$1,175.00
Less 2% cash discount..	23.50
Subtotal..	$1,151.50
Sales tax (9%)...	103.64
Total...	$1,255.14

If Mark needs the stereo immediately (the next day), then Tru-Sound Systems has the best price. This is because a shipping and handling charge of $89.99 would be added to the Wholesale Stereo, as shown below.

Wholesale Stereo list price...	$1,200.00
Next-day freight charge..	89.99
Total...	$1,289.99

Since both Wholesale Stereo and Tru-Sound Systems will accept Mark's VISA, the ability to use a credit card would not affect the buying decision. Tru-Sound Systems will, however, allow Mark to pay his bill in three installments (the first due immediately). This would allow Mark to save some interest charges on his VISA for two months. If we assume that Mark would have otherwise used his VISA and that Mark's VISA carries an interest of 1.5% per month on the unpaid balance, the potential interest savings would be calculated as follows:

CP 6–3 (Concluded)

Tru-Sound Systems price (see previous page)...	$1,280.75
Less first installment (down payment)..	426.92
Remaining balance..	$ 853.83
Interest for first month at 1.5% ($853.83 × 1.5%).....................................	$ 12.81
Remaining balance ($853.83 + $12.81)...	$ 866.64
Less second installment...	426.92
Remaining balance..	$ 439.72
Interest for second month at 1.5% ($439.72 × 1.5%).................................	$ 6.60

The total interest savings would be $19.41 ($12.81 + $6.60). This interest savings would still not be enough to just offset the price advantage of Wholesale Stereo, as shown below.

Tru-Sound Systems price (see above)..	$1,280.75
Less interest savings..	19.41
Total...	$1,261.34

2. Other considerations in buying the stereo include the ability to have the stereo repaired locally. In addition, Tru-Sound Systems' employees would presumably be available to answer questions on the operation and installation of the stereo. In addition, if Mark purchased the stereo from Tru-Sound Systems, he would have the stereo the same day rather than the next day, which is the earliest that Wholesale Stereo could deliver the stereo.

CP 6–4

1.

WATERCRAFT SUPPLY COMPANY Projected Income Statement For the Year Ended October 31, 2015		
Revenues:		
Net sales (a)		$1,485,000
Interest revenue		15,000
Total revenues		$1,500,000
Expenses:		
Cost of merchandise sold (b)	$891,000	
Selling expenses (c)	129,800	
Administrative expenses (d)	90,550	
Interest expense	4,000	
Total expenses		1,115,350
Net income		$ 384,650

Notes:

a.   Projected net sales

[$1,350,000 + (10% × $1,350,000)]............................ $1,485,000

b.   Projected cost of merchandise sold

($1,485,000 × 60%).. $ 891,000

c.   Total selling expenses for year ended October 31, 2014.. $ 140,000

  Add: Increase in store supplies expense

($12,000 × 10%).. $1,200

  Increase in miscellaneous selling expense

($6,000 × 10%)..   600   1,800

  Less delivery expenses..   (12,000)

  Projected total selling expenses.................................. $ 129,800

d.   Total administrative expenses for year ended

October 31, 2014... $90,000

  Add: Increase in office supplies expense

($3,000 × 10%).. $ 300

  Increase in miscellaneous administrative

expense ($2,500 × 10%)..............................   250   550

  Projected total administrative expenses....................... $90,550

CP 6–4 (Concluded)

2. a. Yes. The proposed change will increase net income from $321,000 to $384,650, a change of $63,650.

    b. Possible concerns related to the proposed changes include the following:

        The primary concern is with the accuracy of the estimates used for projecting the effects of the proposed changes. If the increase in sales does not materialize, Watercraft Supply Company could incur significant costs of carrying excess inventory stocked in anticipation of increasing sales. At the same time it is incurring these additional inventory costs, cash collections from customers will be reduced by the amount of the discounts. This could create a liquidity problem for Watercraft Supply Company.

        Another concern arises from the proposed change in shipping terms so as to eliminate all shipments of merchandise FOB destination, thereby eliminating delivery expenses. Watercraft Supply Company assumes that this change will have no effect on sales. However, some (perhaps a significant number of) customers may object to this change and may seek other vendors with more favorable shipping terms. Hence, an unanticipated decline in sales could occur because of this change.

        As with any business decision, risks (concerns) such as those mentioned above must be thoroughly considered before final action is taken.

CP 6–5

Note to Instructors: The purpose of this activity is to familiarize students with the variety of possible purchase prices for a fairly common household item. Students should report several alternative prices when they consider the source of the purchase and the other factors that affect the purchase, e.g., delivery, financing, warranties, etc.

Consider going to www.cnet.com and entering a search for "55 inch LED TV." Pick one model of TV that offers a range of prices from different stores and compare shipping and payment differences among companies. For example, the Sony Bravia KDL-55EX720 TV as of August 2011 has a range of prices of $1,598 to $2,158 from 17 different stores. Some stores offer free shipping, while one store offers that no payment is required for six months. You might consider offering the student group(s) that comes up with the lowest price extra credit points for homework.

CHAPTER 7
INVENTORIES

DISCUSSION QUESTIONS

1. The receiving report should be reconciled to the initial purchase order and the vendor's invoice before recording or paying for inventory purchases. This procedure will verify that the inventory received matches the type and quantity of inventory ordered. It also verifies that the vendor's invoice is charging the company for the actual quantity of inventory received at the agreed-upon price.

2. A physical inventory should be taken periodically to test the accuracy of the perpetual records. In addition, a physical inventory will identify inventory shortages or shrinkage.

3. No, they are not techniques for determining physical quantities. The terms refer to cost flow assumptions, which affect the determination of the cost prices assigned to items in the inventory.

4.   **a.** LIFO   **c.** LIFO
     b. FIFO   **d.** FIFO

5. FIFO

6. LIFO. In periods of rising prices, the use of LIFO will result in the lowest net income and thus the lowest income tax expense.

7. Net realizable value (estimated selling price less any direct cost of disposition, such as sales commissions).

8.   **a.** Gross profit for the year was understated by $14,750.

     b. Merchandise inventory and owner's equity were understated by $14,750.

9. Bibbins Company. Since the merchandise was shipped FOB shipping point, title passed to Bibbins Company when it was shipped and should be reported in Bibbins Company's financial statements at May 31, the end of the fiscal year.

10. Manufacturer's. The manufacturer retains title until the goods are sold. Thus, any unsold merchandise at the end of the year is part of the manufacturer's (consignor's) inventory, even though the merchandise is in the hands of the retailer (consignee).

PRACTICE EXERCISES

PE 7–1A

	Gross Profit February	Ending Inventory February 28
a. First-in, first-out (FIFO)	$35 ($75 − $40)	$86 ($42 + $44)
b. Last-in, first-out (LIFO)	$31 ($75 − $44)	$82 ($40 + $42)
c. Weighted average cost	$33 ($75 − $42)	$84 ($42 × 2)

PE 7–1B

	Gross Profit June	Ending Inventory June 30
a. First-in, first-out (FIFO)	$60 ($110 − $50)	$130 ($60 + $70)
b. Last-in, first-out (LIFO)	$40 ($110 − $70)	$110 ($50 + $60)
c. Weighted average cost	$50 ($110 − $60)	$120 ($60 × 2)

PE 7–2A

a. Cost of merchandise sold (May 28):

15	units @ $120	$1,800
3	units @ $130	390
18		$2,190

b. Inventory, May 31: $7,410 = 57 units × $130

PE 7–2B

a. Cost of merchandise sold (July 24):

6	units @ $15	$ 90
34	units @ $18	612
40		$702

b. Inventory, July 31: $1,008 = 56 units × $18

PE 7–3A

a. **Cost of merchandise sold (June 26):**

   $5,400 = (90 units × $60)

b. **Inventory, June 30:**

20	units @ $50	$1,000
35	units @ $60	2,100
55		$3,100

PE 7–3B

a. **Cost of merchandise sold (March 27):**

   $4,800 = (240 units × $20)

b. **Inventory, March 31:**

45	units @ $18	$ 810
135	units @ $20	2,700
180		$3,510

PE 7–4A

a. **Weighted average unit cost: $71.25**

   Inventory total cost after purchase on July 15:

40	units @ $60	$ 2,400
120	units @ $75	9,000
160		$11,400

   Weighted average unit cost = $71.25 ($11,400 ÷ 160 units)

b. **Cost of merchandise sold (July 27): $5,985 (84 units × $71.25)**

c. **Inventory, July 31: $5,415 (76 units × $71.25)**

PE 7–4B

a. **Weighted average unit cost: $9.50**

   Inventory total cost after purchase on October 22:

125	units @ $8	$1,000
375	units @ $10	3,750
500		$4,750

   Weighted average unit cost = $9.50 ($4,750 ÷ 500 units)

b. **Cost of merchandise sold (October 29): $2,660 (280 units × $9.50)**

c. **Inventory, October 31: $2,090 (220 units × $9.50)**

PE 7–5A

a. First-in, first-out (FIFO) method: $3,726 = 23 units × $162

b. Last-in, first-out (LIFO) method: $3,105 = 23 units × $135

c. Weighted average cost method: $3,450 (23 units × $150), where average cost = $150 = $13,500 ÷ 90 units

PE 7–5B

a. First-in, first-out (FIFO) method: $20,094 = (40 units × $357) + (17 units × $342)

b. Last-in, first-out (LIFO) method: $19,854 = (20 units × $360) + (37 units × $342)

c. Weighted average cost method: $19,665 (57 units × $345), where average cost = $345 = $110,400 ÷ 320 units

PE 7–6A

Commodity	Inventory Quantity	Unit Cost Price	Unit Market Price	Total Cost	Total Market	Total Lower of C or M
1107B	450	$80	$78	$36,000	$35,100	$35,100
1110M	75	60	64	4,500	4,800	4,500
Total				$40,500	$39,900	$39,600

PE 7–6B

Commodity	Inventory Quantity	Unit Cost Price	Unit Market Price	Total Cost	Total Market	Total Lower of C or M
JFW1	6,330	$10	$11	$ 63,300	$ 69,630	$ 63,300
SAW9	1,140	36	34	41,040	38,760	38,760
Total				$104,340	$108,390	$102,060

PE 7–7A

	Amount of Misstatement Overstatement (Understatement)
Balance Sheet:	
Merchandise inventory understated*.....................	$(4,450)
Current assets understated................................	(4,450)
Total assets understated..................................	(4,450)
Owner's equity understated..............................	(4,450)
Income Statement:	
Cost of merchandise sold overstated....................	$ 4,450
Gross profit understated..................................	(4,450)
Net income understated..................................	(4,450)

* $118,350 – $113,900 = $4,450

PE 7–7B

	Amount of Misstatement Overstatement (Understatement)
Balance Sheet:	
Merchandise inventory overstated*.....................	$ 8,780
Current assets overstated................................	8,780
Total assets overstated..................................	8,780
Owner's equity overstated...............................	8,780
Income Statement:	
Cost of merchandise sold understated.................	$(8,780)
Gross profit overstated..................................	8,780
Net income overstated..................................	8,780

* $728,660 – $719,880 = $8,780

PE 7–8A

a.

Inventory Turnover	2014	2013
Cost of merchandise sold	$1,452,500	$1,120,000
Inventories:		
Beginning of year	$380,000	$320,000
End of year	$450,000	$380,000
Average inventory	$415,000	$350,000
	[($380,000 + $450,000) ÷ 2]	[($320,000 + $380,000) ÷ 2]
Inventory turnover	3.5	3.2
	($1,452,500 ÷ $415,000)	($1,120,000 ÷ $350,000)

b.

Number of Days' Sales in Inventory	2014	2013
Cost of merchandise sold	$1,452,500	$1,120,000
Average daily cost of merchandise sold	$3,979.5	$3,068.5
	($1,452,500 ÷ 365 days)	($1,120,000 ÷ 365 days)
Average inventory	$415,000	$350,000
	[($380,000 + $450,000) ÷ 2]	[($320,000 + $380,000) ÷ 2]
Number of days' sales in inventory	104.3 days	114.1 days
	($415,000 ÷ $3,979.5)	($350,000 ÷ $3,068.5)

c. The increase in the inventory turnover from 3.2 to 3.5 and the decrease in the number of days' sales in inventory from 114.1 days to 104.3 days indicate favorable trends in managing inventory.

PE 7–8B

a.

Inventory Turnover	2014	2013
Cost of merchandise sold	$3,864,000	$4,001,500
Inventories:		
Beginning of year	$770,000	$740,000
End of year	$840,000	$770,000
Average inventory	$805,000	$755,000
	[($770,000 + $840,000) ÷ 2]	[($740,000 + $770,000) ÷ 2]
Inventory turnover	4.8	5.3
	($3,864,000 ÷ $805,000)	($4,001,500 ÷ $755,000)

b.

Number of Days' Sales in Inventory	2014	2013
Cost of merchandise sold	$3,864,000	$4,001,500
Average daily cost of merchandise sold	$10,586.3	$10,963.0
	($3,864,000 ÷ 365 days)	($4,001,500 ÷ 365 days)
Average inventory	$805,000	$755,000
	[($770,000 + $840,000) ÷ 2]	[($740,000 + $770,000) ÷ 2]
Number of days' sales in inventory	76.0 days	68.9 days
	($805,000 ÷ $10,586.3)	($755,000 ÷ $10,963.0)

c. The decrease in the inventory turnover from 5.3 to 4.8 and the increase in the number of days' sales in inventory from 68.9 days to 76.0 days indicate unfavorable trends in managing inventory.

EXERCISES

Ex. 7–1

Switching to a perpetual inventory system will strengthen Triple Creek Hardware's internal controls over inventory, since the store managers will be able to keep track of how much of each item is on hand. This should minimize shortages of good-selling items and excess inventories of poor-selling items.

On the other hand, switching to a perpetual inventory system will not eliminate the need to take a physical inventory count. A physical inventory must be taken to verify the accuracy of the inventory records in a perpetual inventory system. In addition, a physical inventory count is needed to detect shortages of inventory due to damage or theft.

Ex. 7–2

a. Appropriate. The inventory tags will protect the inventory from customer theft.

b. Inappropriate. The control of using security measures to protect the inventory is violated if the stockroom is not locked.

c. Inappropriate. Good controls include a receiving report, prepared after all inventory items received have been counted and inspected. Inventory purchased should only be recorded and paid for after reconciling the receiving report, the initial purchase order, and the vendor's invoice.

Ex. 7–3

a.

Portable DVD Players

Date	Purchases			Cost of Merchandise Sold			Inventory		
	Quantity	Unit Cost	Total Cost	Quantity	Unit Cost	Total Cost	Quantity	Unit Cost	Total Cost
Apr. 1							120	39	4,680
6				90	39	3,510	30	39	1,170
14	140	40	5,600				30	39	1,170
							140	40	5,600
19				30	39	1,170	60	40	2,400
				80	40	3,200			
25				45	40	1,800	15	40	600
30	160	43	6,880				15	40	600
							160	43	6,880
30 Balances						9,680			7,480

b.   Since the prices rose from $39 for the April 1 inventory to $43 for the purchase on April 30, we would expect that under last-in, first-out the inventory would be lower.

Note to Instructors: Exercise 7–4 shows that the inventory is $7,465 under LIFO.

Ex. 7–4

Portable DVD Players

Date	Purchases			Cost of Merchandise Sold			Inventory		
	Quantity	Unit Cost	Total Cost	Quantity	Unit Cost	Total Cost	Quantity	Unit Cost	Total Cost
Apr. 1							120	39	4,680
6				90	39	3,510	30	39	1,170
14	140	40	5,600				30	39	1,170
							140	40	5,600
19				110	40	4,400	30	39	1,170
							30	40	1,200
25				30	40	1,200	15	39	585
				15	39	585			
30	160	43	6,880				15	39	585
							160	43	6,880
30 Balances						9,695			7,465

Ex. 7–5

a.

Prepaid Cell Phones

Date		Purchases			Cost of Merchandise Sold			Inventory		
		Quantity	Unit Cost	Total Cost	Quantity	Unit Cost	Total Cost	Quantity	Unit Cost	Total Cost
Aug.	1							775	44	34,100
	10	360	45	16,200				775	44	34,100
								360	45	16,200
	12				360	45	16,200	535	44	23,540
					240	44	10,560			
	14				415	44	18,260	120	44	5,280
	20	600	48	28,800				120	44	5,280
								600	48	28,800
	31				500	48	24,000	120	44	5,280
								100	48	4,800
	31	Balances					69,020			10,080

b.   Since the prices rose from $44 for the August 1 inventory to $48 for the purchase on August 20, we would expect that under first-in, first-out the inventory would be higher.

Note to Instructors: Exercise 7–6 shows that the inventory is $10,560 under FIFO.

Ex. 7–6

Prepaid Cell Phones

Date	Purchases Quantity	Purchases Unit Cost	Purchases Total Cost	Cost of Merchandise Sold Quantity	Cost of Merchandise Sold Unit Cost	Cost of Merchandise Sold Total Cost	Inventory Quantity	Inventory Unit Cost	Inventory Total Cost
Aug. 1							775	44	34,100
10	360	45	16,200				775	44	34,100
							360	45	16,200
12				600	44	26,400	175	44	7,700
							360	45	16,200
14				175	44	7,700			
				240	45	10,800	120	45	5,400
20	600	48	28,800				120	45	5,400
							600	48	28,800
31				120	45	5,400			
				380	48	18,240	220	48	10,560
31 Balances						68,540			10,560

Ex. 7–7

a. $22,880 ($440 × 52 units)

b. $22,000 [($400 × 12 units) + ($420 × 20 units) + ($440 × 20 units)] = $4,800 + $8,400 + $8,800

Ex. 7–8

Date		Purchases Quantity	Purchases Unit Cost	Purchases Total Cost	Cost of Merchandise Sold Quantity	Cost of Merchandise Sold Unit Cost	Cost of Merchandise Sold Total Cost	Inventory Quantity	Inventory Unit Cost	Inventory Total Cost
Jan.	1							1,000	150.00	150,000
Mar.	18				800	150.00	120,000	200	150.00	30,000
May	2	1,800	155.00	279,000				2,000	154.50	309,000
Aug.	9				1,500	154.50	231,750	500	154.50	77,250
Oct.	20	700	160.50	112,350				1,200	158.00	189,600
Dec.	31	Balances					351,750	1,200	158.00	189,600

Ex. 7–9

Date		Purchases Quantity	Purchases Unit Cost	Purchases Total Cost	Cost of Merchandise Sold Quantity	Cost of Merchandise Sold Unit Cost	Cost of Merchandise Sold Total Cost	Inventory Quantity	Inventory Unit Cost	Inventory Total Cost
Jan.	1							8,000	40.00	320,000
Apr.	19				5,000	40.00	200,000	3,000	40.00	120,000
June	30	12,000	48.00	576,000				15,000	46.40	696,000
Sept.	2				9,000	46.40	417,600	6,000	46.40	278,400
Nov.	15	2,000	50.00	100,000				8,000	47.30	378,400
Dec.	31	Balances					617,600	8,000	47.30	378,400

Ex. 7-10

Date		Purchases			Cost of Merchandise Sold			Inventory		
		Quantity	Unit Cost	Total Cost	Quantity	Unit Cost	Total Cost	Quantity	Unit Cost	Total Cost
Jan.	1							8,000	40.00	320,000
Apr.	19				5,000	40.00	200,000	3,000	40.00	120,000
June	30	12,000	48.00	576,000				3,000	40.00	120,000
								12,000	48.00	576,000
Sept.	2				3,000	40.00	120,000	6,000	48.00	288,000
					6,000	48.00	288,000			
Nov.	15	2,000	50.00	100,000				6,000	48.00	288,000
								2,000	50.00	100,000
Dec.	31	Balances					608,000			388,000

Ex. 7–11

Date	Purchases			Cost of Merchandise Sold			Inventory		
	Quantity	Unit Cost	Total Cost	Quantity	Unit Cost	Total Cost	Quantity	Unit Cost	Total Cost
Jan. 1							8,000	40.00	320,000
Apr. 19				5,000	40.00	200,000	3,000	40.00	120,000
June 30	12,000	48.00	576,000				3,000	40.00	120,000
							12,000	48.00	576,000
Sept. 2				9,000	48.00	432,000	3,000	40.00	120,000
							3,000	48.00	144,000
Nov. 15	2,000	50.00	100,000				3,000	40.00	120,000
							3,000	48.00	144,000
							2,000	50.00	100,000
Dec. 31 Balances						632,000			364,000

Ex. 7–12

a. $62,496 (24 units at $1,980 plus 8 units at $1,872) = $47,520 + $14,976

b. $49,104 (18 units at $1,440 plus 14 units at $1,656) = $25,920 + $23,184

c. $56,448 (32 units at $1,764; $211,680 ÷ 120 units = $1,764)

Cost of merchandise available for sale:

18	units @ $1,440	$ 25,920
36	units @ $1,656	59,616
42	units @ $1,872	78,624
24	units @ $1,980	47,520
120	units (at an average cost of $1,764)	$211,680

Ex. 7–13

	Inventory Method	Cost	
		Merchandise Inventory	Merchandise Sold
a.	FIFO	$39,888	$77,112
b.	LIFO	34,920	82,080
c.	Weighted average cost	37,440	79,560

Cost of merchandise available for sale:

42	units at $720..	$ 30,240
58	units at $780..	45,240
20	units at $816..	16,320
30	units at $840..	25,200
150	units (at an average cost of $780)...............	$117,000

a. **First-in, first-out:**

Merchandise inventory:

30	units at $840..	$25,200
18	units at $816..	14,688
48	units..	$39,888

Merchandise sold:

$117,000 – $39,888..	$77,112

b. **Last-in, first-out:**

Merchandise inventory:

42	units at $720..	$30,240
6	units at $780..	4,680
48	units..	$34,920

Merchandise sold:

$117,000 – $34,920..	$82,080

c. **Weighted average cost:**

Merchandise inventory:

48 units at $780 ($117,000 ÷ 150 units).....................	$37,440

Merchandise sold:

$117,000 – $37,440..	$79,560

Ex. 7–14

a. 1. FIFO inventory   > (greater than)   LIFO inventory
    2. FIFO cost of goods sold   < (less than)   LIFO cost of goods sold
    3. FIFO net income   > (greater than)   LIFO net income
    4. FIFO income taxes   > (greater than)   LIFO income taxes

b. In periods of rising prices, the income shown on the company's tax return
    would be lower if LIFO rather than FIFO were used; thus, there is a tax advantage of
    using LIFO.

Note to Instructors: The federal tax laws require that if LIFO is used for tax
purposes, LIFO must also be used for financial reporting purposes. This is
known as the LIFO conformity rule. Thus, selecting LIFO for tax purposes means
that the company's reported income will also be lower than if FIFO had been
used. Companies using LIFO believe the tax advantages from using LIFO
outweigh any negative impact of reporting a lower income to shareholders.

Ex. 7–15

Commodity	Inventory Quantity	Unit Cost Price	Unit Market Price	Total		
				Cost	Market	Lower of C or M
C300	77	$40	$39	$ 3,080	$ 3,003	$ 3,003
F679	115	8	9	920	1,035	920
K200	3,180	3	2	9,540	6,360	6,360
MN23	190	29	26	5,510	4,940	4,940
XX51	226	19	18	4,294	4,068	4,068
Total				$23,344	$19,406	$19,291

Ex. 7–16

The merchandise inventory would appear in the Current Assets section, as
follows:

Merchandise inventory—at lower of cost (FIFO) or market........................ $19,291

Alternatively, the details of the method of determining cost and the method of
valuation could be presented in a note.

Ex. 7–17

a.

	Balance Sheet	
Merchandise inventory*..	$13,850	understated
Current assets...	$13,850	understated
Total assets..	$13,850	understated
Owner's equity..	$13,850	understated

  * $13,850 = $338,500 − $324,650

b.

	Income Statement	
Cost of merchandise sold..	$13,850	overstated
Gross profit..	$13,850	understated
Net income...	$13,850	understated

c.

	Income Statement	
Cost of merchandise sold..	$13,850	understated
Gross profit..	$13,850	overstated
Net income...	$13,850	overstated

d. The December 31, 2015, balance sheet would be correct, since the 2014
   inventory error reverses itself in 2015.

Ex. 7–18

a.

	Balance Sheet	
Merchandise inventory*..	$21,600	overstated
Current assets...	$21,600	overstated
Total assets..	$21,600	overstated
Owner's equity..	$21,600	overstated

  * $21,600 = $640,500 − $618,900

b.

	Income Statement	
Cost of merchandise sold..	$21,600	understated
Gross profit..	$21,600	overstated
Net income...	$21,600	overstated

c.

	Income Statement	
Cost of merchandise sold..	$21,600	overstated
Gross profit..	$21,600	understated
Net income...	$21,600	understated

d. The December 31, 2015, balance sheet would be correct, since the 2014
   inventory error reverses itself in 2015.

Ex. 7–19

When an error is discovered affecting the prior period, it should be corrected. In this case, the merchandise inventory account should be debited and the owner's capital account credited for $33,000.

Failure to correct the error for 2013 and purposely misstating the inventory and the cost of merchandise sold in 2014 would cause the income statements for the two years to not be comparable. The balance sheet at the end of 2014 would be correct, however, since the 2013 inventory error reverses itself in 2014.

Ex. 7–20

a. Apple: 52.5 {$39,541,000 ÷ [($1,051,000 + $455,000) ÷ 2]}
    American Greetings: 4.0 {$682,368 ÷ [($179,730 + $163,956) ÷ 2]}

b. Lower. Although American Greetings' business is seasonal in nature, with most of its revenue generated during the major holidays, much of its nonholiday inventory may turn over very slowly. Apple, on the other hand, turns its inventory over very fast because it maintains a low inventory, which allows it to respond quickly to customer needs. Additionally, Apple's computer products can quickly become obsolete, so it cannot risk building large inventories.

Ex. 7–21

a.   Number of Days' Sales in Inventory $= \dfrac{\text{Average Inventory}}{\text{Cost of Goods Sold} \div 365}$

Kroger: $\dfrac{(\$4{,}966 + \$4{,}935) \div 2}{\$63{,}927 \div 365} = \dfrac{\$4{,}950.5}{175.1} = 28 \text{ days}$

Safeway: $\dfrac{(\$2{,}623 + \$2{,}509) \div 2}{\$29{,}443 \div 365} = \dfrac{\$2{,}566.0}{80.7} = 32 \text{ days}$

Winn-Dixie: $\dfrac{(\$658 + \$665) \div 2}{\$5{,}182 \div 365} = \dfrac{\$661.5}{14.2} = 47 \text{ days}$

Inventory Turnover $= \dfrac{\text{Cost of Goods Sold}}{\text{Average Inventory}}$

Kroger: $\dfrac{\$63{,}927}{(\$4{,}966 + \$4{,}935) \div 2} = 12.9$

Safeway: $\dfrac{\$29{,}443}{(\$2{,}623 + \$2{,}509) \div 2} = 11.5$

Winn-Dixie: $\dfrac{\$5{,}182}{(\$658 + \$665) \div 2} = 7.8$

b.   The number of days' sales in inventory and the inventory turnover ratios are relatively the same for Kroger and Safeway. Winn-Dixie has a significantly higher number of days' sales in inventory and a significantly lower inventory turnover than Kroger and Safeway. These results suggest that Kroger and Safeway are more efficient than Winn-Dixie in managing inventory.

c.   If Winn-Dixie matched Kroger's days' sales in inventory, then its hypothetical ending inventory would be determined as follows,

Number of Days' Sales in Inventory $= \dfrac{\text{Average Inventory}}{\text{Cost of Goods Sold} \div 365}$

$28 \text{ days} = \dfrac{X}{(\$5{,}182 \div 365)}$

$X = 28 \times (\$5{,}182 \div 365) = 28 \times \$14.2$

$X = \$397.6$

Thus, the additional cash flow that would have been generated is the difference between the actual average inventory and the hypothetical average inventory, as follows:

Actual average inventory.. $661.5 million
Hypothetical average inventory................................... 397.6 million
Positive cash flow potential.. $263.9 million

That is, a lower average inventory amount would have required less cash than actually was required.

Appendix Ex. 7–22

$666,900 ($1,235,000 × 54%)

Appendix Ex. 7–23

$241,804 ($396,400 × 61%)

Appendix Ex. 7–24

$511,500 ($775,000 × 66%)

Appendix Ex. 7–25

	Cost	Retail
Merchandise inventory, June 1	$ 165,000	$ 275,000
Purchases in June (net)	2,361,500	3,800,000
Merchandise available for sale	$2,526,500	$4,075,000
Ratio of cost to retail price: $\dfrac{\$2,526,500}{\$4,075,000}$ = 62%		
Sales for June (net)		3,550,000
Merchandise inventory, June 30, at retail price		$ 525,000
Merchandise inventory, June 30, at estimated cost ($525,000 × 62%)		$ 325,500

Appendix Ex. 7–26

a.

Merchandise inventory, January 1		$ 350,000
Purchases (net), January 1–December 31		2,950,000
Merchandise available for sale		$3,300,000
Sales (net), January 1–December 31	$4,440,000	
Less estimated gross profit ($4,440,000 × 35%)	1,554,000	
Estimated cost of merchandise sold		2,886,000
Estimated merchandise inventory, December 31		$ 414,000

b.   The gross profit method is useful for estimating inventories for monthly or quarterly financial statements. It is also useful in estimating the cost of merchandise destroyed by fire or other disasters.

Appendix Ex. 7–27

Merchandise available for sale..	$6,125,000
Less cost of merchandise sold [$9,250,000 × (100% – 36%)]................	5,920,000
Estimated ending merchandise inventory......................................	$ 205,000

Appendix Ex. 7–28

Merchandise available for sale..	$960,000
Less cost of merchandise sold [$1,450,000 × (100% – 42%)]................	841,000
Estimated ending merchandise inventory......................................	$119,000

PROBLEMS

Prob. 7–1A

1.

Date 2014	Purchases			Cost of Merchandise Sold			Inventory		
	Quantity	Unit Cost	Total Cost	Quantity	Unit Cost	Total Cost	Quantity	Unit Cost	Total Cost
June 1							500	30.00	15,000
10	1,500	34.00	51,000				500	30.00	15,000
							1,500	34.00	51,000
28				500	30.00	15,000	1,250	34.00	42,500
				250	34.00	8,500			
30				250	34.00	8,500	1,000	34.00	34,000
July 5				100	34.00	3,400	900	34.00	30,600
10	3,600	35.00	126,000				900	34.00	30,600
							3,600	35.00	126,000
16				900	34.00	30,600	2,700	35.00	94,500
				900	35.00	31,500			
28				1,700	35.00	59,500	1,000	35.00	35,000
Aug. 5	3,000	35.80	107,400				1,000	35.00	35,000
							3,000	35.80	107,400
14				1,000	35.00	35,000	2,000	35.80	71,600
				1,000	35.80	35,800			
25	500	36.00	18,000				2,000	35.80	71,600
							500	36.00	18,000
30				1,750	35.80	62,650	250	35.80	8,950
							500	36.00	18,000
31 Balances						290,450			26,950

Prob. 7–1A (Concluded)

2.

Accounts Receivable	483,800	
Sales		483,800*
Cost of Merchandise Sold	290,450	
Merchandise Inventory		290,450

*$483,800 = $37,500 + $13,000 + $5,500 + $100,800 + $102,000 + $120,000 + $105,000

3. $193,350 ($483,800 – $290,450)

4. $26,950 ($8,950 + $18,000)

5. Since the prices rose from $30 for the June 1 inventory to $36 for the purchase on August 25, we would expect that under the last-in, first-out method the inventory would be lower.

   Note to Instructors: Problem 7–2A shows that the inventory is $23,500 under LIFO.

Prob. 7–2A

1.

Date	Purchases			Cost of Merchandise Sold			Inventory		
	Quantity	Unit Cost	Total Cost	Quantity	Unit Cost	Total Cost	Quantity	Unit Cost	Total Cost
June 1							500	30.00	15,000
10	1,500	34.00	51,000				500	30.00	15,000
							1,500	34.00	51,000
28				750	34.00	25,500	500	30.00	15,000
							750	34.00	25,500
30				250	34.00	8,500	500	30.00	15,000
							500	34.00	17,000
July 5				100	34.00	3,400	500	30.00	15,000
							400	34.00	13,600
10	3,600	35.00	126,000				500	30.00	15,000
							400	34.00	13,600
							3,600	35.00	126,000
16				1,800	35.00	63,000	500	30.00	15,000
							400	34.00	13,600
							1,800	35.00	63,000
28				1,700	35.00	59,500	500	30.00	15,000
							400	34.00	13,600
							100	35.00	3,500
Aug. 5	3,000	35.80	107,400				500	30.00	15,000
							400	34.00	13,600
							100	35.00	3,500
							3,000	35.80	107,400
14				2,000	35.80	71,600	500	30.00	15,000
							400	34.00	13,600
							100	35.00	3,500
							1,000	35.80	35,800
25	500	36.00	18,000				500	30.00	15,000
							400	34.00	13,600
							100	35.00	3,500
							1,000	35.80	35,800
							500	36.00	18,000
30				500	36.00	18,000	500	30.00	15,000
				1,000	35.80	35,800	250	34.00	8,500
				100	35.00	3,500			
				150	34.00	5,100			
31	Balances					293,900			23,500

Prob. 7–2A (Concluded)

2.
Total sales..	$483,800 *
Total cost of merchandise sold......................................	293,900
Gross profit...	$189,900

*$483,800 = $37,500 + $13,000 + $5,500 + $100,800 + $102,000 + $120,000 + $105,000

3. $23,500 = [(500 units × $30) + (250 units × $34)]
            = $15,000 + $8,500

Prob. 7–3A

1.

Date	Purchases Quantity	Purchases Unit Cost	Purchases Total Cost	Cost of Merchandise Sold Quantity	Cost of Merchandise Sold Unit Cost	Cost of Merchandise Sold Total Cost	Inventory Quantity	Inventory Unit Cost	Inventory Total Cost
June 1							500	30.00	15,000
10	1,500	34.00	51,000				2,000	33.00	66,000
28				750	33.00	24,750	1,250	33.00	41,250
30				250	33.00	8,250	1,000	33.00	33,000
July 5				100	33.00	3,300	900	33.00	29,700
10	3,600	35.00	126,000				4,500	34.60	155,700
16				1,800	34.60	62,280	2,700	34.60	93,420
28				1,700	34.60	58,820	1,000	34.60	34,600
Aug. 5	3,000	35.80	107,400				4,000	35.50	142,000
14				2,000	35.50	71,000	2,000	35.50	71,000
25	500	36.00	18,000				2,500	35.60	89,000
30				1,750	35.60	62,300	750	35.60	26,700
31	Balances					290,700			26,700

2.

Total sales...	$483,800*
Total cost of merchandise sold......................................	290,700
Gross profit...	$193,100

*$483,800 = $37,500 + $13,000 + $5,500 + $100,800 + $102,000 + $120,000 + $105,000

3. $26,700 (750 units × $35.60)

Prob. 7–4A

1. **First-In, First-Out Method**

Merchandise inventory, August 31, 2014.....................................	$ 26,950
Cost of merchandise sold..	290,450

Supporting computations

Merchandise inventory:

500	units @ $36.00	$18,000
250	units @ $35.80	8,950
750	units	$26,950

Cost of merchandise sold:

Beginning inventory, June 1, 2014..	$ 15,000
Purchases...	302,400
Merchandise available for sale..	$317,400
Less ending inventory, August 31, 2014.....................................	26,950
Cost of merchandise sold...	$290,450

2. **Last-In, First-Out Method**

Merchandise inventory, August 31, 2014.....................................	$ 23,500
Cost of merchandise sold..	293,900

Supporting computations

Merchandise inventory:

500	units @ $30.00...	$15,000
250	units @ $34.00...	8,500
750	units...	$23,500

Cost of merchandise sold:

Beginning inventory, June 1, 2014..	$ 15,000
Purchases...	302,400
Merchandise available for sale..	$317,400
Less ending inventory, August 31, 2014.....................................	23,500
Cost of merchandise sold...	$293,900

Prob. 7–4A (Continued)

3. Weighted Average Cost Method

Merchandise inventory, August 31, 2014.....................	$ 26,160
Cost of merchandise sold.......................................	291,240

Supporting computations

Weighted Average Unit Cost = $\dfrac{\text{Total Cost of Merchandise Available for Sale}}{\text{Units Available for Sale}}$

$$= \frac{\$317,400}{9,100 \text{ units}} = \$34.88 \text{ per unit (rounded)}$$

Merchandise inventory:

750 units × $34.88 = $26,160

Cost of merchandise sold:

Beginning inventory, June 1, 2014............................	$ 15,000
Purchases..	302,400
Merchandise available for sale................................	$317,400
Less ending inventory, August 31, 2014....................	26,160
Cost of merchandise sold.......................................	$291,240

Prob. 7–4A (Concluded)

4.

	FIFO	LIFO	Weighted Average
Sales	$483,800	$483,800	$483,800
Cost of merchandise sold	290,450	293,900	291,240
Gross profit	$193,350	$189,900	$192,560
Inventory, August 31, 2014	$ 26,950	$ 23,500	$ 26,160

Prob. 7–5A

1. First-In, First-Out Method

Model	Quantity	Unit Cost	Total Cost
A10	4	$ 76	$ 304
	2	70	140
B15	6	184	1,104
	2	170	340
E60	5	70	350
G83	9	259	2,331
J34	15	270	4,050
M90	3	130	390
	2	128	256
Q70	7	180	1,260
	1	175	175
Total			$10,700

2. Last-In, First-Out Method

Model	Quantity	Unit Cost	Total Cost
A10	4	$ 64	$ 256
	2	70	140
B15	8	176	1,408
E60	3	75	225
	2	65	130
G83	7	242	1,694
	2	250	500
J34	12	240	2,880
	3	246	738
M90	2	108	216
	2	110	220
	1	128	128
Q70	5	160	800
	3	170	510
Total			$9,845

Prob. 7–5A (Concluded)

3. **Weighted Average Cost Method**

Model	Quantity	Unit Cost*	Total Cost
A10	6	$ 70	$ 420
B15	8	174	1,392
E60	5	69	345
G83	9	253	2,277
J34	15	258	3,870
M90	5	121	605
Q70	8	172	1,376
Total			$10,285

* Computations of unit costs:

A10: $70 = [(4 × $64) + (4 × $70) + (4 × $76)] ÷ (4 + 4 + 4)
B15: $174 = [(8 × $176) + (4 × $158) + (3 × $170) + (6 × $184)] ÷ (8 + 4 + 3 + 6)
E60: $69 = [(3 × $75) + (3 × $65) + (15 × $68) + (9 × $70)] ÷ (3 + 3 + 15 + 9)
G83: $253 = [(7 × $242) + (6 × $250) + (5 × $260) + (10 × $259)] ÷ (7 + 6 + 5 + 10)
J34: $258 = [(12 × $240) + (10 × $246) + (16 × $267) + (16 × $270)] ÷ (12 + 10 + 16 + 16)
M90: $121 = [(2 × $108) + (2 × $110) + (3 × $128) + (3 × $130)] ÷ (2 + 2 + 3 + 3)
Q70: $172 = [(5 × $160) + (4 × $170) + (4 × $175) + (7 × $180)] ÷ (5 + 4 + 4 + 7)

4. a. During periods of rising prices, the LIFO method will result in a lower cost of inventory, a greater amount of cost of merchandise sold, and a lesser amount of net income than the other two methods. For Dymac Appliances, the LIFO method would be preferred for the current year, since it would result in a lesser amount of income tax.

    b. During periods of declining prices, the FIFO method will result in a lesser amount of net income and would be preferred for income tax purposes.

Prob. 7–6A

Inventory Sheet
December 31, 2014

Description	Inventory Quantity		Unit Cost Price	Unit Market Price	Total Cost	Market	Lower of C or M
B12	38	30	$ 60	$ 57	$ 1,800	$ 1,710	
		8	59	57	472	456	
					2,272	2,166	$ 2,166
E41	18		178	180	3,204	3,240	3,204
G19	33	20	128	126	2,560	2,520	
		13	129	126	1,677	1,638	
					4,237	4,158	4,158
L88	18	10	563	550	5,630	5,500	
		8	560	550	4,480	4,400	
					10,110	9,900	9,900
N94	400		8	7	3,200	2,800	2,800
P24	90	80	22	18	1,760	1,440	
		10	21	18	210	180	
					1,970	1,620	1,620
R66	8	5	248	250	1,240	1,250	
		3	260	250	780	750	
					2,020	2,000	2,000
T33	140	100	21	20	2,100	2,000	
		40	19	20	760	800	
					2,860	2,800	2,800
Z16	15	10	750	752	7,500	7,520	
		5	745	752	3,725	3,760	
					11,225	11,280	11,225
Total					$41,098	$39,964	$39,873

Appendix Prob. 7–7A

1.

CELEBRITY TAN CO.		
	Cost	Retail
Merchandise inventory, August 1	$ 300,000	$ 575,000
Net purchases	2,149,000	3,375,000
Merchandise available for sale	$2,449,000	$3,950,000
Ratio of cost to retail price: $\dfrac{\$2,449,000}{\$3,950,000}$ = 62%		
Sales	$3,250,000	
Less sales returns and allowances	80,000	
Net sales		3,170,000
Merchandise inventory, August 31, at retail		$ 780,000
Merchandise inventory, at estimated cost ($780,000 × 62%)		$ 483,600

2.

RANCHWORKS CO.		
		Cost
a. Merchandise inventory, March 1		$ 880,000
Net purchases		9,500,000
Merchandise available for sale		$10,380,000
Sales	$15,900,000	
Less sales returns and allowances	100,000	
Net sales	$15,800,000	
Less estimated gross profit ($15,800,000 × 38%)	6,004,000	
Estimated cost of merchandise sold		9,796,000
Estimated merchandise inventory, November 30		$ 584,000
b. Estimated merchandise inventory, November 30		$ 584,000
Physical inventory count, November 30		369,750
Estimated loss due to theft or damage, March 1–November 30		$ 214,250

Prob. 7-1B

1.

Date		Purchases			Cost of Merchandise Sold			Inventory		
		Quantity	Unit Cost	Total Cost	Quantity	Unit Cost	Total Cost	Quantity	Unit Cost	Total Cost
Apr.	3							25	1,200	30,000
	8	75	1,240	93,000				25	1,200	30,000
								75	1,240	93,000
	11				25	1,200	30,000	60	1,240	74,400
					15	1,240	18,600			
	30				30	1,240	37,200	30	1,240	37,200
May	8	60	1,260	75,600				30	1,240	37,200
								60	1,260	75,600
	10				30	1,240	37,200	40	1,260	50,400
					20	1,260	25,200			
	19				20	1,260	25,200	20	1,260	25,200
	28	80	1,260	100,800				20	1,260	25,200
								80	1,260	100,800
June	5				20	1,260	25,200	60	1,260	75,600
					20	1,260	25,200			
	16				25	1,260	31,500	35	1,260	44,100
	21	35	1,264	44,240				35	1,260	44,100
								35	1,264	44,240
	28				35	1,260	44,100	26	1,264	32,864
					9	1,264	11,376			
	30	Balances					310,776			32,864

Prob. 7–1B (Concluded)

2.

Accounts Receivable	525,250	
Sales		525,250*
Cost of Merchandise Sold	310,776	
Merchandise Inventory		310,776

*$525,250 = $80,000 + $60,000 + $100,000 + $40,000 + $90,000 + $56,250 + $99,000

3. $214,474 ($525,250 – $310,776)

4. $32,864 ($26 units × $1,264)

5. Since the prices rose from $1,200 for the April 3 inventory to $1,264 for the purchase on June 21, we would expect that under last-in, first-out the inventory would be lower.

    Note to Instructors: Problem 7–2B shows that the inventory is $31,560 under LIFO.

Prob. 7–2B

CHAPTER 7 Inventories

1.

Date	Purchases Quantity	Purchases Unit Cost	Purchases Total Cost	Cost of Merchandise Sold Quantity	Cost of Merchandise Sold Unit Cost	Cost of Merchandise Sold Total Cost	Inventory Quantity	Inventory Unit Cost	Inventory Total Cost
Apr. 3							25	1,200	30,000
8	75	1,240	93,000				25	1,200	30,000
							75	1,240	93,000
11				40	1,240	49,600	25	1,200	30,000
							35	1,240	43,400
30				30	1,240	37,200	25	1,200	30,000
							5	1,240	6,200
May 8	60	1,260	75,600				25	1,200	30,000
							5	1,240	6,200
							60	1,260	75,600
10				50	1,260	63,000	25	1,200	30,000
							5	1,240	6,200
							10	1,260	12,600
19				10	1,260	12,600			
				5	1,240	6,200			
				5	1,200	6,000	20	1,200	24,000
28	80	1,260	100,800				20	1,200	24,000
							80	1,260	100,800
June 5				40	1,260	50,400	20	1,200	24,000
							40	1,260	50,400
16				25	1,260	31,500	20	1,200	24,000
							15	1,260	18,900
21	35	1,264	44,240				20	1,200	24,000
							15	1,260	18,900
							35	1,264	44,240
28				35	1,264	44,240	20	1,200	24,000
				9	1,260	11,340	6	1,260	7,560
30 Balances						312,080			31,560

Prob. 7–2B (Concluded)

2.   Total sales.. $525,250*

       Total cost of merchandise sold..   312,080

       Gross profit... $213,170

       *$525,250 = $80,000 + $60,000 + $100,000 + $40,000 + $90,000 + $56,250 + $99,000

3. $31,560   = [(20 units × $1,200) + (6 units × $1,260)]

                    = $24,000 + $7,560

Prob. 7–3B

1.

Date	Purchases Quantity	Purchases Unit Cost	Purchases Total Cost	Cost of Merchandise Sold Quantity	Cost of Merchandise Sold Unit Cost	Cost of Merchandise Sold Total Cost	Inventory Quantity	Inventory Unit Cost	Inventory Total Cost
Apr. 3							25	1,200	30,000
8	75	1,240	93,000				100	1,230	123,000
11				40	1,230	49,200	60	1,230	73,800
30				30	1,230	36,900	30	1,230	36,900
May 8	60	1,260	75,600				90	1,250	112,500
10				50	1,250	62,500	40	1,250	50,000
19				20	1,250	25,000	20	1,250	25,000
28	80	1,260	100,800				100	1,258	125,800
June 5				40	1,258	50,320	60	1,258	75,480
16				25	1,258	31,450	35	1,258	44,030
21	35	1,264	44,240				70	1,261	88,270
28				44	1,261	55,484	26	1,261	32,786
30	Balances					310,854			32,786

2. Total sales... $525,250*
    Total cost of merchandise sold...................................... 310,854
    Gross profit... $214,396

    *$525,250 = $80,000 + $60,000 + $100,000 + $40,000 + $90,000 + $56,250 + $99,000

3. $32,786 (26 units × $1,261)

Prob. 7–4B

1. **First-In, First-Out Method**

Merchandise inventory, June 30, 2014..	$ 32,864
Cost of merchandise sold...	310,776

Supporting computations

Merchandise inventory:

26 units @ $1,264..	$ 32,864

Cost of merchandise sold:

Beginning inventory, April 1, 2014...	$ 30,000
Purchases..	313,640
Merchandise available for sale..	$343,640
Less ending inventory, June 30, 2014..	32,864
Cost of merchandise sold..	$310,776

2. **Last-In, First-Out Method**

Merchandise inventory, June 30, 2014..	$ 31,240
Cost of merchandise sold...	312,400

Supporting computations

Merchandise inventory:

25 units @ $1,200..	$30,000
1 unit @ $1,240...	1,240
26 units..	$31,240

Cost of merchandise sold:

Beginning inventory, April 1, 2014...	$ 30,000
Purchases..	313,640
Merchandise available for sale..	$343,640
Less ending inventory, June 30, 2014..	31,240
Cost of merchandise sold..	$312,400

Prob. 7–4B (Continued)

3. Weighted Average Cost Method

Merchandise inventory, June 30, 2014.........................	$ 32,500
Cost of merchandise sold..	311,140

Supporting computations

Weighted Average Unit Cost $=$ $\dfrac{\text{Total Cost of Merchandise Available for Sale}}{\text{Units Available for Sale}}$

$$= \frac{\$343,640}{275 \text{ units}} = \$1,250 \text{ per unit (rounded)}$$

Merchandise inventory:

26 units × $1,250 = $32,500

Cost of merchandise sold:

Beginning inventory, April 1, 2014..............................	$ 30,000
Purchases...	313,640
Merchandise available for sale....................................	$343,640
Less ending inventory, June 30, 2014..........................	32,500
Cost of merchandise sold...	$311,140

Prob. 7–4B (Concluded)

4.

	FIFO	LIFO	Weighted Average
Sales	$525,250	$525,250	$525,250
Cost of merchandise sold	310,776	312,400	311,140
Gross profit	$214,474	$212,850	$214,110
Inventory, June 30, 2014	$ 32,864	$ 31,240	$ 32,500

Prob. 7–5B

1. First-In, First-Out Method

Model	Quantity	Unit Cost	Total Cost
C55	3	$1,070	$ 3,210
	1	1,060	1,060
D11	6	675	4,050
	5	666	3,330
F32	1	280	280
	1	260	260
H29	4	317	1,268
K47	6	542	3,252
	2	549	1,098
S33	2	232	464
X74	7	39	273
Total			$18,545

2. Last-In, First-Out Method

Model	Quantity	Unit Cost	Total Cost
C55	3	$1,040	$ 3,120
	1	1,054	1,054
D11	9	639	5,751
	2	645	1,290
F32	2	240	480
H29	4	305	1,220
K47	6	520	3,120
	2	531	1,062
S33	2	222	444
X74	4	35	140
	3	36	108
Total			$17,789

Prob. 7–5B (Concluded)

3. Weighted Average Cost Method

Model	Quantity	Unit Cost*	Total Cost
C55	4	$1,056	$ 4,224
D11	11	654	7,194
F32	2	252	504
H29	4	311	1,244
K47	8	534	4,272
S33	2	227	454
X74	7	37	259
Total			$18,151

* Computations of unit costs:

C55: $1,056 = [(3 × $1,040) + (3 × $1,054) + (3 × $1,060) + (3 × $1,070)] ÷ (3 + 3 + 3 + 3)
D11: $654 = [(9 × $639) + (7 × $645) + (6 × $666) + (6 × $675)] ÷ (9 + 7 + 6 + 6)
F32: $252 = [(5 × $240) + (3 × $260) + (1 × $260) + (1 × $280)] ÷ (5 + 3 + 1 + 1)
H29: $311 = [(6 × $305) + (3 × $310) + (3 × $316) + (4 × $317)] ÷ (6 + 3 + 3 + 4)
K47: $534 = [(6 × $520) + (8 × $531) + (4 × $549) + (6 × $542)] ÷ (6 + 8 + 4 + 6)
S33: $227 = [(4 × $222) + (4 × $232)] ÷ (4 + 4)
X74: $37 = [(4 × $35) + (6 × $36) + (8 × $37) + (7 × $39)] ÷ (4 + 6 + 8 + 7)

4. a. During periods of rising prices, the LIFO method will result in a lower cost of inventory, a greater amount of cost of merchandise sold, and a lesser amount of net income than the other two methods. For Pappa's Appliances, the LIFO method would be preferred for the current year, since it would result in a lesser amount of income tax.

   b. During periods of declining prices, the FIFO method will result in a lesser amount of net income and would be preferred for income tax purposes.

Prob. 7–6B

Inventory Sheet
December 31, 2014

Commodity	Inventory Quantity		Unit Cost Price	Unit Market Price	Total		
					Cost	Market	Lower of C or M
A54	37	30	$ 60	$ 56	$ 1,800	$ 1,680	
		7	58	56	406	392	
					2,206	2,072	$ 2,072
C77	24		174	178	4,176	4,272	4,176
F66	30	20	130	132	2,600	2,640	
		10	128	132	1,280	1,320	
					3,880	3,960	3,880
H83	21	6	547	545	3,282	3,270	
		15	540	545	8,100	8,175	
					11,382	11,445	11,382
K12	375		6	5	2,250	1,875	1,875
Q58	90	75	25	18	1,875	1,350	
		15	26	18	390	270	
					2,265	1,620	1,620
S36	8	5	256	235	1,280	1,175	
		3	260	235	780	705	
					2,060	1,880	1,880
V97	140	100	17	20	1,700	2,000	
		40	16	20	640	800	
					2,340	2,800	2,340
Y88	17	10	750	744	7,500	7,440	
		7	740	744	5,180	5,208	
					12,680	12,648	12,648
Total					$43,239	$42,572	$41,873

Appendix Prob. 7–7B

1.

JAFFE CO.		
	Cost	Retail
Merchandise inventory, February 1	$ 400,000	$ 615,000
Net purchases	4,055,000	5,325,000
Merchandise available for sale	$4,455,000	$5,940,000
Ratio of cost to retail price: $\dfrac{\$4,455,000}{\$5,940,000} = 75\%$		
Sales	$5,220,000	
Less sales returns and allowances	120,000	
Net sales		5,100,000
Merchandise inventory, February 28, at retail		$ 840,000
Merchandise inventory, at estimated cost ($840,000 × 75%)		$ 630,000

2.

CORONADO CO.		
		Cost
a. Merchandise inventory, May 1		$ 400,000
Net purchases		3,150,000
Merchandise available for sale		$3,550,000
Sales	$4,850,000	
Less sales returns and allowances	100,000	
Net sales	$4,750,000	
Less estimated gross profit ($4,750,000 × 35%)	1,662,500	
Estimated cost of merchandise sold		3,087,500
Estimated merchandise inventory, October 31		$ 462,500
b. Estimated merchandise inventory, October 31		$ 462,500
Physical inventory count, October 31		366,500
Estimated loss due to theft or damage, May 1–October 31		$ 96,000

CASES & PROJECTS

CP 7–1

Since the title to merchandise shipped FOB shipping point passes to the buyer when the merchandise is shipped, the shipments made before midnight, October 31, 2014, should properly be recorded as sales for the fiscal year ending October 31, 2014. Hence, Ryan Frazier is behaving in a professional manner. However, Ryan should realize that recording these sales in 2014 precludes them from being recognized as sales in 2015. Thus, accelerating the shipment of orders to increase sales of one period will have the effect of decreasing sales of the next period.

CP 7–2

In developing a response to Paula's concerns, you should probably first emphasize the practical need for an assumption concerning the flow of cost of goods purchased and sold. That is, when identical goods are frequently purchased, it may not be practical to specifically identify each item of inventory. If all the identical goods were purchased at the same price, it wouldn't make any difference for financial reporting purposes which goods we assumed were sold first, second, etc. However, in most cases, goods are purchased over time at different prices, and hence, a need arises to determine which goods are sold so that the price (cost) of those goods can be matched against the revenues to determine operating income.

Next, you should emphasize that accounting principles allow for the fact that the physical flow of the goods may differ from the flow of costs. Specifically, accounting principles allow for three cost flow assumptions: first-in, first-out; last-in, first-out; and weighted average. Each of these methods has advantages and disadvantages. One primary advantage of the last-in, first-out method is that it better matches current costs (the cost of goods purchased last) with current revenues. Therefore, the reported operating income is more reflective of current operations and what might be expected in the future. Another reason that the last-in, first-out method is often used is that it tends to minimize taxes during periods of price increases. Since for most businesses prices tend to increase, the LIFO method will generate lower taxes than will the alternative cost flow methods.

The preceding explanation should help Paula better understand LIFO and its impact on the financial statements and taxes.

CP 7–3

1. a. First-in, first-out method:

8,000	units at $48.00..	$ 384,000
8,000	units at $44.85..	358,800
12,800	units at $43.50..	556,800
3,200	units at $42.75...	136,800
32,000	units..	$1,436,400

b. Last-in, first-out method:

31,000	units at $36.60...	$1,134,600
1,000	units at $39.00..	39,000
32,000	units..	$1,173,600

c. Weighted average cost method:

32,000 units at $40.74*...	$1,303,680

* ($8,148,000 ÷ 200,000) = $40.74

2.

	FIFO	LIFO	Weighted Average Cost
Sales...	$10,000,000	$10,000,000	$10,000,000
Cost of merchandise sold*.................	6,711,600	6,974,400	6,844,320
Gross profit.....................................	$ 3,288,400	$ 3,025,600	$ 3,155,680
* Cost of merchandise available for sale......	$8,148,000	$8,148,000	$8,148,000
Less ending inventory.............................	1,436,400	1,173,600	1,303,680
Cost of merchandise sold........................	$6,711,600	$6,974,400	$6,844,320

3. a. The LIFO method is often viewed as the best basis for reflecting income from operations. This is because the LIFO method matches the most current cost of merchandise purchases against current sales. The matching of current costs with current sales results in a gross profit amount that many consider to best reflect the results of current operations. For Golden Eagle Company, the gross profit of $3,025,600 reflects the matching of the most current costs of the product of $6,974,400 against the current period sales of $10,000,000. This matching of current costs with current sales also tends to minimize the effects of price trends on the results of operations.

The LIFO method will not match current sales and the current cost of merchandise sold if the current-period quantity of sales exceeds the current-period quantity of purchases. In this case, the cost of merchandise sold will include a portion of the cost of the beginning inventory, which may have a unit cost from purchases made several years prior to the current period. The results of operations may then be distorted in the sense of the current matching concept. This situation occurs rarely in most businesses because of consistently increasing quantities of year-end inventory from year to year.

CP 7–3 (Continued)

While the LIFO method is often viewed as the best method for matching revenues and expenses, the FIFO method is often consistent with the physical movement of merchandise in a business, since most businesses tend to dispose of commodities in the order of their acquisition. To the extent that this is the case, the FIFO method approximates the results that will be attained by a specific identification of costs.

The weighted average cost method is, in a sense, a compromise between LIFO and FIFO. The effect of price trends is averaged, both in determining net income and in determining inventory cost.

Which inventory costing method best reflects the results of operations for Golden Eagle Company depends upon whether one emphasizes the importance of matching revenues and expenses (the LIFO method) or whether one emphasizes the physical flow of merchandise (the FIFO method). The average cost method might be considered best if one emphasizes the matching and physical flow of goods concepts equally.

b. The FIFO method provides the best reflection of the replacement cost of the ending inventory for the balance sheet. This is because the amount reported on the balance sheet for merchandise inventory will be assigned costs from the most recent purchases. For most businesses, these costs will reflect purchases made near the end of the period. For example, Golden Eagle Company's ending inventory on December 31, 2014, is assigned costs totaling $1,436,400 under the FIFO method. These costs represent purchases made during the period of August through December. This FIFO inventory amount ($1,436,400) more closely approximates the replacement cost of the ending inventory than either the LIFO ($1,173,600) or the average cost ($1,303,680) figures.

c. During periods of rising prices, such as shown for Golden Eagle Company, the LIFO method will result in a lesser amount of net income than the other two methods. Hence, for Golden Eagle Company, the LIFO method would be preferred for the current year, since it would result in a lesser amount of income tax.

During periods of declining prices, the FIFO method will result in a lesser amount of net income and would be preferred for income tax purposes.

CP 7–3 (Concluded)

d. The advantages of the perpetual inventory system include the following:

(1) A perpetual inventory system provides an effective means of control over inventory. A comparison of the amount of inventory on hand with the balance of the subsidiary account can be used to determine the existence and seriousness of any inventory shortages.

(2) A perpetual inventory system provides an accurate method for determining inventories used in the preparation of interim statements.

(3) A perpetual inventory system provides an aid for maintaining inventories at optimum levels. Frequent review of the perpetual inventory records helps management in the timely reordering of merchandise, so that loss of sales and excessive accumulation of inventory are avoided. An analysis of Golden Eagle Company's purchases and sales, as shown below, indicates that the company may have accumulated excess inventory from May through August because the amount of month-end inventory increased materially, while sales remained relatively constant for the period.

Month	Purchases	Sales	Increase (Decrease) in Inventory	Inventory at End of Month	Next Month's Sales
April	31,000 units	16,000 units	15,000 units	15,000 units	16,000 units
May	33,000	16,000	17,000	32,000	20,000
June	40,000	20,000	20,000	52,000	24,000
July	40,000	24,000	16,000	68,000	28,000
August	27,200	28,000	(800)	67,200	28,000
September	0	28,000	(28,000)	39,200	18,000
October	12,800	18,000	(5,200)	34,000	10,000
November	8,000	10,000	(2,000)	32,000	8,000
December	8,000	8,000	0	32,000	0

It appears that during April through July, the company ordered inventory without regard to the accumulation of excess inventory. A perpetual inventory system might have prevented this excess accumulation from occurring.

The primary disadvantage of the perpetual inventory system is the cost of maintaining the necessary inventory records. However, computers may be used to reduce this cost.

CP 7–4

a.

$$\text{Inventory Turnover} = \frac{\text{Cost of Goods Sold}}{\text{Average Inventory}}$$

$$\frac{\text{Number of Days'}}{\text{Sales in Inventory}} = \frac{\text{Average Inventory}}{\text{Cost of Goods Sold} \div 365}$$

Dell

$$\text{Inventory Turnover} = \frac{\$50,098}{(\$1,051 + \$1,301) \div 2} = \frac{\$50,098}{\$1,176.0} = 42.6$$

$$\frac{\text{Days' Sales in}}{\text{Inventory}} = \frac{(\$1,051 + \$1,301) \div 2}{\$50,098 \div 365} = \frac{\$1,176.0}{\$137.3} = 8.6 \text{ days}$$

Hewlett-Packard

$$\text{Inventory Turnover} = \frac{\$96,089}{(\$6,128 + \$6,466) \div 2} = \frac{\$96,089}{\$6,297.0} = 15.3$$

$$\frac{\text{Days' Sales in}}{\text{Inventory}} = \frac{(\$6,128 + \$6,466) \div 2}{\$96,089 \div 365} = \frac{\$6,297.0}{\$263.3} = 23.9 \text{ days}$$

b. Dell builds its computers primarily to a customer order, called a build-to-order strategy. Customers place their orders on the Internet. Dell then builds and delivers the computer, usually in a matter of days. HP, in contrast, builds computers before actual orders are received. This is called a build-to-stock strategy. HP must forecast the type of computers customers want before it receives the orders. This strategy results in greater inventory for HP, since the computers are built before there is a sale. HP has significant finished goods inventory, while Dell has less finished goods. It also explains the difference in their inventory efficiency ratios.

Note to Instructors: While Dell sells most of its computers online, it has also begun selling its computers through Best Buy. As a result, Dell's inventory turnover has decreased and its days' sales in inventory has increased from prior years.

CP 7–5

a.

	Inventory Turnover	Number of Days' Sales in Inventory
Tiffany Co.	0.83	441.15
Amazon.com	9.89	36.92

Computations:

<u>Tiffany Co.</u>

$$\text{Inventory Turnover} = \frac{\text{Cost of Goods Sold}}{\text{Average Inventory}}$$

$$\text{Inventory Turnover} = \frac{\$1,263}{(\$1,428 + \$1,625) \div 2} = 0.83$$

$$\frac{\text{Number of Days'}}{\text{Sales in Inventory}} = \frac{\text{Average Inventory}}{\text{Cost of Goods Sold} \div 365}$$

$$\frac{\text{Number of Days'}}{\text{Sales in Inventory}} = \frac{(\$1,428 + \$1,625) \div 2}{\$1,263 \div 365} = 441.19 \text{ days}$$
or 441 days (rounded)

<u>Amazon.com</u>

$$\text{Inventory Turnover} = \frac{\text{Cost of Goods Sold}}{\text{Average Inventory}}$$

$$\text{Inventory Turnover} = \frac{\$26,561}{(\$2,171 + \$3,202) \div 2} = 9.89$$

$$\frac{\text{Number of Days'}}{\text{Sales in Inventory}} = \frac{\text{Average Inventory}}{\text{Cost of Goods Sold} \div 365}$$

$$\frac{\text{Number of Days'}}{\text{Sales in Inventory}} = \frac{(\$2,171 + \$3,202) \div 2}{\$26,561 \div 365} = 36.92 \text{ days}$$
or 37 days (rounded)

b. Amazon.com has a smaller investment in inventory for its volume than does
Tiffany. Amazon.com's inventory turnover is faster (larger), and the number
of days' sales in inventory is shorter (smaller). This is due to the fact that
Amazon.com uses a different business model than Tiffany. That is,
Amazon.com sells through the Internet, while Tiffany uses the traditional
retail store model, which requires it to stock more inventory.

CP 7–6

a.

		Costco	Walmart	JCPenney
1.	Cost of merchandise sold...................	$67,995	$315,287	$10,799
	Merchandise inventory, beginning........	$ 5,405	$ 32,713	$ 3,024
	Merchandise inventory, ending............	5,638	36,318	3,213
	Total.......................................	$11,043	$ 69,031	$ 6,237
2.	Average merchandise inventory (Total ÷ 2).................................	$5,521.5	$34,515.5	$3,118.5
	Inventory turnover............................	12.3	9.1	3.5

b.

		Costco	Walmart	JCPenney
1.	Average merchandise inventory [from part (a)]...............................	$5,521.5	$34,515.5	$3,118.5
	Cost of merchandise sold...................	$ 67,995	$ 315,287	$ 10,799
	Average daily cost of merchandise sold (COMS ÷ 365)..........................	$ 186.3	$ 863.8	$ 29.6
	Number of day's sales in inventory.......	29.6	40.0	105.4

c. Both the inventory turnover ratio and the number of day's sales in inventory reflect the merchandising approaches of the three companies.

Costco is a club warehouse. Its approach is to hold only mass appeal items that are sold quickly off the shelf. Most items are sold in bulk quantities at very attractive prices. Costco couples thin margins with very fast inventory turnover.

Walmart has a traditional discounter approach. It has attractive pricing, but the inventory moves slower than would be the case at a club warehouse. For example, many purchases made at Walmart would not be packaged in the same bulk as would be the case at Costco.

JCPenney is a traditional department store with a wider assortment of goods that will not necessarily appeal to the mass market. That is, some of the merchandise items will be more specialized and unique. As such, its inventory moves slower, but at a higher price (and margin).

CHAPTER 8
SARBANES-OXLEY, INTERNAL CONTROL, AND CASH

DISCUSSION QUESTIONS

1. **a.** The five elements of internal control are the control environment, risk assessment, control procedures, monitoring, and information and communication. The control environment is the overall attitude of management and employees about the importance of controls. Risk assessment includes evaluating various risks facing the business, including competitive threats, regulatory changes, and changes in economic factors. Control procedures are established to provide reasonable assurance that business goals will be achieved. Monitoring is the evaluation of the internal control system. Information and communication provide management with feedback about internal control.

    b. No. One element of internal control is not more important than another element. All five elements are necessary for effective internal control.

2. To reduce the possibility of errors and embezzlement, the functions of operations and accounting should be separated. Thus, one employee should not be responsible for handling cash receipts (operations) and maintaining the accounts receivable records (accounting).

3. The control procedure requiring that responsibility for a sequence of related operations be divided among different persons is violated in this situation. This weakness in the internal control may permit irregularities. For example, the ticket seller, while acting as ticket taker, could admit friends without a ticket.

4. The responsibility for maintaining the accounting records should be separated from the responsibility for operations so that the accounting records can serve as an independent check on operations.

5. Controls that could have prevented or detected the fraud include (1) requiring supporting documentation such as receiving reports and purchase orders of all payments, (2) requiring approval by an independent party, and (3) allowing payments to only vendors who have been previously approved by upper management.

6. The three documents supporting the liability are the vendor's invoice, the purchase order, and the receiving report. The invoice should be compared with the receiving report to determine that the items billed have been received and with the purchase order to verify quantities, prices, and terms.

7. The cash balance and the bank statement balance are likely to differ because of (1) a delay by the bank or company in recording transactions or (2) errors by the bank or company in recording transactions.

8. The purpose of a bank reconciliation is to determine the reasons for the difference between the balance according to the company's records and the balance according to the bank statement and to correct those items representing errors in recording that may have been made by the bank or by the company.

DISCUSSION QUESTIONS (Continued)

9. a.   Yes. Even though the petty cash fund is only $750, if the fund is replenished frequently, a significant amount of cash could be stolen. For example, if the fund is replenished weekly, then $39,000 ($750 × 52 weeks) could be subject to theft.

    b.   Controls for petty cash include (1) designating one person who is responsible for the fund, (2) maintaining a written record of all payments, (3) requiring support (receipts) for payments from the fund, and (4) periodic review of the funds on hand and the payments by an independent person.

10. a.   Cash and cash equivalents are usually reported as one amount in the Current Assets section of the balance sheet.

    b.   Examples of cash equivalents include certificates of deposit, U.S. government securities, corporate notes and bonds, and commercial paper.

PRACTICE EXERCISES

PE 8–1A

1. (a) the control environment
2. (c) information and communication
3. (b) control procedures

PE 8–1B

1. (c) monitoring
2. (a) the control environment
3. (b) control procedures

PE 8–2A

Item No.	Appears on the Bank Statement as a Debit or Credit Memo	Increases or Decreases the Balance of the Company's Bank Account
1	debit memo	decreases
2	debit memo	decreases
3	credit memo	increases
4	debit memo	decreases

PE 8–2B

Item No.	Appears on the Bank Statement as a Debit or Credit Memo	Increases or Decreases the Balance of the Company's Bank Account
1	credit memo	increases
2	credit memo	increases
3	credit memo	increases
4	debit memo	decreases

PE 8–3A

a. **$9,810 as shown below.**

Bank section of reconciliation: $13,450 + $3,000 – $6,640 = $9,810
Company section of reconciliation: $11,655 – $45 – $1,800 = $9,810

b.

Accounts Receivable	1,800	
Miscellaneous Expense	45	
Cash		1,845

PE 8–3B

a. **$18,100 as shown below.**

Bank section of reconciliation: $23,900 + $5,500 – $11,300 = $18,100
Company section of reconciliation: $8,700 + $9,450 – $50 = $18,100

b.

Miscellaneous Expense	50	
Cash		50
Cash	9,450	
Notes Receivable		9,000
Interest Revenue		450

PE 8–4A

a.

Petty Cash	1,150	
Cash		1,150

b.

Repairs Expense	725	
Miscellaneous Selling Expense	150	
Cash Short and Over	25	
Cash		900

PE 8–4B

a.

Petty Cash	900	
Cash		900

b.

Store Supplies	550	
Miscellaneous Selling Expense	200	
Cash Short and Over	35	
Cash		785

PE 8–5A

a.   Monthly Cash Expenses $= \dfrac{\text{Negative Cash Flow from Operations}}{\text{12 months}}$

$$= \dfrac{\$114{,}000}{\text{12 months}} = \$9{,}500 \text{ per month}$$

$\dfrac{\text{Ratio of Cash to}}{\text{Monthly Cash Expenses}} = \dfrac{\text{Cash as of Year-End}}{\text{Monthly Cash Expenses}}$

$$= \dfrac{\$69{,}350}{\$9{,}500 \text{ per month}} = 7.3 \text{ months}$$

b.   The preceding computations indicate that Otto Company has 7.3 months of cash remaining as of December 31, 2014. Otto Company will need to generate positive cash flow from operations or raise additional financing from its owners or by issuing debt.

PE 8–5B

a.   Monthly Cash Expenses $= \dfrac{\text{Negative Cash Flow from Operations}}{\text{12 months}}$

$$= \dfrac{\$458{,}400}{\text{12 months}} = \$38{,}200 \text{ per month}$$

$\dfrac{\text{Ratio of Cash to}}{\text{Monthly Cash Expenses}} = \dfrac{\text{Cash as of Year-End}}{\text{Monthly Cash Expenses}}$

$$= \dfrac{\$187{,}180}{\$38{,}200 \text{ per month}} = 4.9 \text{ months}$$

b.   The preceding computations indicate that Bonita Company has 4.9 months of cash remaining as of December 31, 2014. Bonita Company will need to generate positive cash flow from operations or raise additional financing from its owners or by issuing debt.

EXERCISES

Ex. 8–1

Section 404 requires management's internal control report to:

(1) state the responsibility of management for establishing and maintaining an adequate internal control structure and procedures for financial reporting; and

(2) contain an assessment, as of the end of the issuer's fiscal year, of the effectiveness of the internal control structure and procedures of the issuer for financial reporting.

The complete AICPA summary of Section 404 of Sarbanes-Oxley is as follows:

Section 404: Management Assessment of Internal Controls.

Requires each annual report of an issuer to contain an "internal control report," which shall:

(1) state the responsibility of management for establishing and maintaining an adequate internal control structure and procedures for financial reporting; and

(2) contain an assessment, as of the end of the issuer's fiscal year, of the effectiveness of the internal control structure and procedures of the issuer for financial reporting.

Each issuer's auditor shall attest to, and report on, the assessment made by the management of the issuer. An attestation made under this section shall be in accordance with standards for attestation engagements issued or adopted by the Board. An attestation engagement shall not be the subject of a separate engagement.

The language in the report of the Committee which accompanies the bill to explain the legislative intent states, "…the Committee does not intend that the auditor's evaluation be the subject of a separate engagement or the basis for increased charges or fees."

Directs the SEC to require each issuer to disclose whether it has adopted a code of ethics for its senior financial officers and the contents of that code.

Directs the SEC to revise its regulations concerning prompt disclosure on Form 8-K to require immediate disclosure "of any change in, or waiver of," an issuer's code of ethics.

Ex. 8–2

a. Agree. Madonna has made one employee responsible for the cash drawer in accordance with the internal control principle of assignment of responsibility. In addition, Madonna has segregated the operations (preparing the orders) from the accounting (taking orders and payments).

b. Disagree. It is commendable that Madonna has given the employee a specific responsibility and is holding that employee accountable for it. However, after the cashier has counted the cash, another employee (or perhaps Madonna) should remove the cash register tape and compare the amount on the tape with the cash in the drawer. Also, Madonna's standard of no mistakes may encourage the cashiers to overcharge a few customers in order to cover any possible shortages in the cash drawer.

c. Disagree. Stealing is a serious issue. An employee who can justify taking a box of tea bags can probably justify "borrowing" cash from the cash register.

Ex. 8–3

a. The sales clerks could steal money by writing phony refunds and pocketing the cash supposedly refunded to these fictitious customers.

b. Ramona's Clothing suffers from inadequate separation of responsibilities for related operations, since the clerks issue refunds and restock all merchandise. In addition, there is a lack of proofs and security measures, since the supervisors authorize returns two hours after they are issued.

c. A store credit for any merchandise returned without a receipt would reduce the possibility of theft of cash. In this case, a clerk could only issue a phony store credit rather than taking money from the cash register. A store credit is not as tempting as cash. In addition, sales clerks could only use a few store credits to purchase merchandise for themselves without management getting suspicious.

An advantage of issuing a store credit for returns without a receipt is that the possibility of stealing cash is reduced. The store will also lose less revenue if customers must choose other store merchandise instead of getting a cash refund. The overall level of returns/exchanges may be reduced, since customers will not return an acceptable gift simply because they need cash more than the gift. The policy will also reduce the "cash drain" during the weeks immediately following the holidays, allowing Ramona's Clothing to keep more of its money earning interest or use that cash to purchase spring merchandise or pay creditors.

Ex. 8–3 (Concluded)

A disadvantage of issuing a store credit for returns without a receipt is that preholiday sales might drop as gift-givers realize that the return policy has tightened. After the holidays, customers wishing to return items for cash refunds may be frustrated when they learn the store policy has changed. The ill will may reduce future sales. It may take longer to explain the new policy and fill out the paperwork for a store credit, lengthening lines at the return counter after the holidays. Sales clerks will need to be trained to apply the new policy and write up a store credit. Sales clerks also will need to be trained to handle the redemption of the store credit on future merchandise purchases.

d.   The potential for abuse in the cash refund system could be eliminated if clerks were required to get a supervisor's authorization for a refund before giving the customer the cash. The supervisor should only authorize the refund after seeing both the customer and the merchandise that is being returned.

An alternative would be to use security measures that would detect a sales clerk attempting to ring up a refund and remove cash when a customer is not present at the sales desk. These security measures could include cameras or additional security personnel discreetly monitoring the sales desk.

Finally, an employee on the following work shift could be assigned the responsibility to restock returned merchandise and reconcile the returns to a refund list for the department.

Ex. 8–4

As an internal auditor, you would probably disagree with the change in policy. Pacific Bank has some normal business risk associated with default on bank loans. One way to help minimize this is to carefully evaluate loan applications. Large loans present greater risk in the event of default than do smaller loans. Thus, it is reasonable to have more than one person involved in making the decision to grant a large loan. In addition, loans should be granted on their merits, not on the basis of favoritism or mere association with the bank president. Allowing the bank president to have sole authority to grant large loans can lead to the president granting loans to friends and business associates, without the required due diligence. This can result in a bank becoming exposed to very poor credit risks. Indeed, this scenario is one of the causes of the savings and loan failures of the past.

Ex. 8–5

The Societe Generale trading losses show how small lapses in internal control can have large consequences. When the losses became so large that they could no longer be hidden, it was too late. The loss could have been avoided with a number of internal controls. First, the separation of duties control was overcome by the trader's intimate knowledge of the monitoring software. This knowledge of the monitoring system allowed the trader to effectively hide trades. The design of the monitoring software would need to be improved, and access prohibited by traders. If traders have access to the monitoring software, then the separation of duties control is violated. Second, the trader should be under managerial oversight. For example, trades that exceed a certain amount of exposure should require management approval. In this way, a trader would be forced to slow down or stop once trades have reached a certain limit. This would avoid the trader's tendency to try to "make up" losses with even larger bets. Lastly, required vacation time may have alerted managers to the hidden losses once the trader was unable to attend to the trading positions.

Ex. 8–6

This is an example of a fraud with significant collusion. Frauds that are perpetrated with multiple parties in different positions of control make detecting fraud more difficult. In this case, the fraud began with an employee responsible for authorizing claim payments. This is a sensitive position because his decisions would initiate payments. However, claims would need to be authorized and verified before payment would be made. Knowing this, the employee made sure each claim had a phony "victim." Thus, there was a verifiable story behind each claim. Only by tracking physical evidence of the accident could it be discovered that the claim was fictitious. However, the very nature of the process was to resolve small claims quickly without excessive control. Lastly, corrupt lawyers were brought into the fraud to act as attorneys for the claimants. This gave the claims even more credibility. In actuality, the lawyers had done legitimate business with the trucking company, so all appeared normal. This fraud was discovered when the fraudulent employee's bank noticed irregularities in his bank account and notified authorities. As the saying goes, "Follow the money!" As a side note, the corrupt claims administrator fell into this behavior due to gambling problems.

Ex. 8–7

All-Around Sound Co. should not have relied on the unusual nature of the vendors and delivery frequency to uncover this fraud. The purchase and payment cycle is one of the most critical business cycles to control, because the potential for abuse is so great. Purchases should be initiated by a requisition document. This document should be countersigned by a superior so that two people agree as to what is being purchased. The requisition should initiate a purchase order to a vendor for goods or services. The vendor responds to the purchase order by delivering the goods. The goods should be formally received using a receiving document. An accounts payable clerk matches the requisition, purchase order, and invoice before any payment is made. Such "triple matching" prevents unauthorized requests and payments. In this case, the requests were unauthorized, suggesting that the employee has sole authority to make a request. Second, this employee had access to the invoices. This access allowed the employee to change critical characteristics of the invoice to hide the true nature of the goods being received. The invoice should have been delivered directly to the accounts payable clerk to avoid corrupting the document. There apparently was no receiving document (common for smaller companies); thus, only the invoice provided proof of what was received and needed to be paid. If there had been a receiving report, the invoice could not have been doctored and gone undetected, because it would not have matched the receiving report.

Note to Instructors: This exercise is based on an actual fraud.

Ex. 8–8

a.   The most difficult frauds to detect are those that involve the senior management of a company that is in a conspiracy to commit the fraud. The senior managers have the power to access many parts of the accounting system, while the normal separation of duties is subverted by involving many people in the fraud. In addition, the authorization control is subverted because most of the authorization power resides in the senior management.

b.   Overall, this type of fraud can be stopped if there is a strong oversight of senior management, such as an audit committee of the board of directors. Individual "whistle blowers" in the company can make their concerns known to the independent or internal auditors who, in turn, can inform the audit committee. The audit committee should be independent of management and have the power to monitor the actions of management.

Ex. 8–9

a.   The sales clerks should not have access to the cash register tapes.

b.   The cash register tapes should be locked in the cash register and the key retained by the cashier. An employee of the cashier's office should remove the cash register tape, record the total on the memo form, and note discrepancies.

Ex. 8–10

Big & Bad Burgers suffers from a failure to separate responsibilities for related operations.

Big & Bad Burgers could stop this theft by limiting the drive-through clerk to taking customer orders, entering them on the cash register, accepting the customers' payments, returning customers' change, and handing customers their orders that another employee has assembled. By making another employee responsible for assembling orders, the drive-through clerk must enter the orders on the cash register. This will produce a printed receipt or an entry on a computer screen at the food bin area, specifying the items that must be assembled to fill each order. Once the drive-through clerk has entered the sale on the cash register, the clerk cannot steal the customer's payment because the clerk's cash drawer will not balance at the end of the shift. This change also makes the drive-through more efficient and could reduce the time it takes to service a drive-through customer.

If another employee cannot be added, the weakness in internal control could be improved with more thorough supervision. The restaurant manager should be directed to keep a watchful eye on the drive-through area in order to detect when a clerk takes an order without ringing up the sale.

Another option is for Big & Bad Burgers to implement a policy that any customer who does not receive a receipt is entitled to a free burger, and advertise this policy at the cash register and drive-in window. This approach uses the customer as an internal control.

Ex. 8–11

a.   The remittance advices should not be sent to the cashier.

b.   The remittance advices should be sent directly to the Accounting Department by the mailroom.

Ex. 8–12

Cash	114,850	
Cash Short or Over	125	
Sales		114,975

Ex. 8–13

Cash	32,730	
Sales		32,690
Cash Short or Over		40

Ex. 8–14

The use of the voucher system is appropriate, the essentials of which are outlined below. (Although invoices could be used instead of vouchers, the latter more satisfactorily provide for account distribution, signatures, and other significant data.)

1. Each voucher should be approved for payment by a designated official only after completion of the following verifications: (a) that prices, quantities, terms, etc., on the invoice are in accordance with the provisions of the purchase order, (b) that all quantities billed have been received in good condition, as indicated on a receiving report, and (c) that all arithmetic details are correct.

2. The file for unpaid vouchers should be composed of 31 compartments, one for each day of the month. Each voucher should be filed in the compartment representing the last day of the discount period or the due date if the invoice is not subject to a cash discount.

3. Each day, the vouchers should be removed from the appropriate section of the file and checks issued by the disbursing official. If the bank balance is insufficient to pay all of the vouchers, those that remain unpaid should be refiled according to the date when payment should next be considered.

4. At the time of payment, all vouchers and supporting documents should be stamped or perforated "Paid" to prevent their resubmission for payment. They should then be filed in numerical sequence for future reference. The implementation and use of a computerized system would also reduce the chance that any available cash discounts are missed. For example, when invoices are received and approved for payment, they would automatically be scheduled for payment within the discount period. However, even in a computerized system, the use of an approval process that requires supporting documents and indicating "paid" on these supporting documents is an important control for avoiding duplicate payments.

Ex. 8–15

To prevent the fraud scheme described, Paragon Tech must separate responsibilities for related operations. As in the past, all service requisitions should be submitted to the Purchasing Department. After receiving the service request, Purchasing should complete a Service Verification form, stating what service has been ordered and the name of the company that will provide the service. This form should be delivered via intercompany mail to the person responsible for verifying that the service was performed. This person should be someone who has firsthand knowledge of whether the service has been performed. This person, who must be someone other than the manager requesting the service, should fill in the date and time the service was received and sign the form. In addition, the vendor providing the service should sign the form before leaving the premises. When completed, the Service Verification form should be forwarded to the Accounting Department. Accounting will authorize payment of the vendor's invoice after the Service Verification form has been compared with the invoice.

Ex. 8–16

a. Addition to the balance per bank: (4), (5)
b. Deduction from the balance per bank: (6)
c. Addition to the balance per company's records: (3), (7)
d. Deduction from the balance per company's records: (1), (2)

Ex. 8–17

(1), (2), (3), (7)

The preceding additions and deductions to the cash balance according to the company's records require journal entries in the company's records. Additions and deductions to the cash balance according to the bank's records do not require the company to record journal entries.

Ex. 8–18

a.

ALLENBY CO. Bank Reconciliation August 31, 20—	
Cash balance according to bank statement	$38,280
Add deposit in transit, not recorded by bank	5,850
	$44,130
Deduct outstanding checks	12,460
Adjusted balance	$31,670
Cash balance according to company's records	$31,080
Add error in recording check as $810 instead of $180	630
	$31,710
Deduct bank service charge	40
Adjusted balance	$31,670

b. $31,670; the adjusted balance from the bank reconciliation should be reported on the August 31 balance sheet for Allenby Co.

c.   Yes, the bank reconciliation must always balance (reconcile) to an adjusted balance.

Ex. 8–19

Cash	630	
Accounts Payable		630
Miscellaneous Expense	40	
Cash		40

Ex. 8–20

Cash	18,200	
Notes Receivable		17,500
Interest Revenue		700

Ex. 8–21

a.

CHESNER CO. Bank Reconciliation July 31, 2014		
Cash balance according to bank statement		$20,300
Add: Deposit in transit on July 31		7,200
		$27,500
Deduct: Outstanding checks		3,585
Adjusted balance		$23,915
Cash balance according to company's records		$11,100
Add: Error in recording Check No. 1056 as $950		
instead of $590	$ 360	
Note for $12,000 collected by bank, including		
interest	12,480	12,840
		$23,940
Deduct: Bank service charges		25
Adjusted balance		$23,915

b. $23,915

Ex. 8–22

1.   The heading should be "June 30, 2014," and not "For the Month Ended June 30, 2014."

2.   The outstanding checks should be deducted from the balance per bank.

3.   The deposit of June 30, not recorded by the bank, should be added to the balance per bank.

4.   Service charges should be deducted from the balance per company's records.

5.   The error in recording the June 17 deposit of $7,150 as $1,750 should be added to the balance per company's records.

Ex. 8–22 (Concluded)

A correct bank reconciliation would be as follows:

POWAY CO. Bank Reconciliation June 30, 2014			
Cash balance according to bank statement			$16,185
Add deposit of June 30, not recorded			
by bank			6,600
			$22,785
Deduct outstanding checks:			
No. 1067		$ 575	
1106		470	
1110		1,050	
1113		910	3,005
Adjusted balance			$19,780
Cash balance according to company's records			$ 8,985
Add: Proceeds of note collected by bank:			
Principal	$6,000		
Interest	300	$6,300	
Error in recording June 17			
deposit as $1,750 instead of $7,150		5,400	11,700
			$20,685
Deduct: Check returned because			
of insufficient funds		$ 890	
Service charges		15	905
Adjusted balance			$19,780

Ex. 8–23

a. The amount of cash receipts stolen by the sales clerk can be determined by attempting to reconcile the bank account. The bank reconciliation will not reconcile by the amount of cash receipts stolen. The amount stolen by the sales clerk is $4,135, determined as shown below.

ALASKA IMPRESSIONS CO. Bank Reconciliation October 31, 2014	
Cash balance according to bank statement	$13,275
Deduct: Outstanding checks	3,670
Adjusted balance	$ 9,605
Cash balance according to company's records	$11,680
Add: Note collected by bank, including interest	2,100
	$13,780
Deduct: Bank service charges	40
Adjusted balance	$13,740

Amount stolen: $4,135 ($13,740 – $9,605)

b. The theft of the cash receipts might have been prevented by having more than one person make the daily deposit. Collusion between two individuals would then have been necessary to steal cash receipts. In addition, two employees making the daily cash deposits would tend to discourage theft of the cash receipts from the employees on the way to the bank.

Daily reconciliation of the amount of cash receipts—comparing the cash register tapes to a receipt from the bank as to the amount deposited (a duplicate deposit ticket)—would also discourage theft of the cash receipts. In this latter case, if the reconciliation were prepared by an employee independent of the cash function, any theft of cash receipts from the daily deposit would be discovered immediately. That is, the daily deposit would not reconcile against the daily cash receipts.

Ex. 8–24

a.

Petty Cash	900	
Cash		900

b.

Office Supplies	525	
Miscellaneous Selling Expense	190	
Miscellaneous Administrative Expense	85	
Cash Short and Over	30	
Cash		830

Ex. 8–25

Toy manufacturers and retailers experience a seasonal trend in cash flows from operating activities. Mattel, Inc., experiences negative cash flows during the periods when merchandise is ordered for the holiday season. Mattel, Inc., generates positive cash flows during the holiday season, November–December. As a result, Mattel, Inc., reports overall positive net cash flows from operating activities for the year.

Ex. 8–26

a.   8.4 months ($1,415,400 ÷ $168,500)

b.   At the current rate of operations, El Dorado has 8.4 months of cash remaining. El Dorado should either restructure its operations or begin planning on raising additional financing in order to continue in business.

Ex. 8–27

a. $1,824.9 ($21,899 ÷ 12)

b.   18.3 months ($33,456 ÷ $1,824.9)

c.   Capstone Turbine has cash to continue its operations for approximately 18.3 months.

    Note to Instructors: Capstone has credit agreements with Wells Fargo Bank that it can use (draw on) for short-term cash needs. Thus, it appears that Capstone will be able to continue to operate for the next several years. However, in the long-run Capstone Turbine will have to generate postive cash flows from operations in order to survive.

Ex. 8–28

a.   Year 3: $5,304.7 per month ($63,656 ÷ 12)
      Year 2: $5,183.3 per month ($62,199 ÷ 12)
      Year 1: $3,570.8 per month ($42,850 ÷ 12)

b.   Year 3: 9.1 months ($48,402 ÷ $5,304.7)
      Year 2: 27.3 months ($141,423 ÷ $5,183.3)
      Year 1: 8.6 months ($30,696 ÷ $3,570.8)

c.   Since Year 1, Allos Therapeutics monthly cash expenses have increased from $3,570.8 in Year 1 to $5,304.7 in Year 3. The ratio of cash to monthly cash expenses has increased from 8.6 months at the end of Year 1, to 27.3 months at the end of Year 2. Allos Therapeutics increased its monthly cash expenses in Year 3 to $5,304.7 per month and at the end of Year 3 it will run out of cash in just over nine months assuming it doesn't change its operations or raise additional financing. Unless the company improves its cash flows, it may have difficulty raising sufficient cash from investors or creditors to continue operations in the long term.

Note to Instructors: During Year 2, Allos Therapeutics sold additional stock, thus causing the increase in the ratio of cash to monthly cash expenses.

PROBLEMS

Prob. 8–1A

Strengths: a, b, e, and f

Weaknesses:

c. Employees should not be allowed to use the petty cash fund to cash personal checks. In any case, postdated checks should not be accepted. In effect, postdated checks represent a receivable from the employees.

d. Requiring cash register clerks to make up any cash shortages from their own funds gives the clerks an incentive to shortchange customers. That is, the clerks will want to make sure that they don't have a shortage at the end of the day. In addition, one might also assume that the clerks can keep any overages. This would again encourage clerks to shortchange customers. The shortchanging of customers will create customer complaints, etc. The best policy is to report any cash shortages or overages at the end of each day. If a clerk is consistently short or over, then corrective action (training, removal, etc.) could be taken.

g. The mail clerk should prepare an initial listing of cash remittances before forwarding the cash receipts to the cashier. This establishes initial accountability for the cash receipts. The mail clerk should forward a copy of the listing of remittances to the accounts receivable clerk for recording in the accounts.

h. The bank reconciliation should be prepared by someone not involved with the handling or recording of cash.

Prob. 8–2A

2014				
May	**1**	**Petty Cash**	800	
		Cash		800
	10	**Cash**	3,358	
		Cash Short and Over		13
		Sales		3,345
	31	**Store Supplies**	290	
		Delivery Expense	110	
		Office Supplies	65	
		Miscellaneous Administrative Expense	36	
		Cash Short and Over	24	
		Cash		525
	31	**Cash**	6,125	
		Cash Short and Over	30	
		Sales		6,155
	31	**Cash**	50	
		Petty Cash		50

Prob. 8–3A

1.

REMEDY MEDICAL CO. Bank Reconciliation April 30, 2014		
Cash balance according to bank statement		$23,775
Add: Deposit of April 30, not recorded by bank	$3,580	
Bank error in charging check as $3,300 instead of $330	2,970	6,550
		$30,325
Deduct outstanding checks		7,840
Adjusted balance		$22,485
Cash balance according to company's records		$18,885
Add proceeds of note collected by bank, including $180 interest		3,780
		$22,665
Deduct: Error in recording check	$ 70	
Bank service charges	110	180
Adjusted balance		$22,485

2.

Cash	3,780	
Notes Receivable		3,600
Interest Revenue		180
Accounts Payable—Copelin Co.	70	
Miscellaneous Expense	110	
Cash		180

3. $22,485; the adjusted balance from the bank reconciliation should be reported as cash on the April 30, 2014, balance sheet for Remedy Medical Co.

Prob. 8–4A

1.

FIT BIKE CO. Bank Reconciliation August 31, 2014			
Cash balance according to bank statement			$12,550
Add: Deposit of August 31, not recorded by bank		$2,880	
Bank error in charging check as $850 instead			
of $580		270	3,150
			$15,700
Deduct outstanding checks			7,440
Adjusted balance			$ 8,260
Cash balance according to company's records*			$ 7,280
Add proceeds of note collected by bank, including			
$80 interest			2,080
			$ 9,360
Deduct: Check returned because of insufficient funds		$ 900	
Bank service charges		20	
Error in recording check		180	1,100
Adjusted balance			$ 8,260

```
* Cash balance, August 1.....................................  $ 12,190
  Plus cash deposited in August.............................    28,100
  Less checks written in August.............................   (33,010)
  Balance per company's books, August 31...................  $  7,280
```

2.

Cash	2,080	
Notes Receivable		2,000
Interest Revenue		80
Accounts Payable—Brown Co.	180	
Accounts Receivable—Murdock Co.	900	
Miscellaneous Expense	20	
Cash		1,100

3. $8,260; the adjusted balance from the bank reconciliation should be reported as cash on the August 31, 2014, balance sheet for Fit Bike Co.

Prob. 8–5A

1.

BEELER FURNITURE COMPANY			
Bank Reconciliation			
June 30, 20—			
Cash balance according to bank statement			$13,624.71
Add deposit of June 30, not recorded			
by bank			1,117.74
			$14,742.45
Deduct outstanding checks:			
No. 738		$ 251.40	
756		113.95	
758		259.60	
759		901.50	1,526.45
Adjusted balance			$13,216.00
Cash balance according to company's			
records*			$10,145.50
Add: Proceeds of note collected by bank:			
Principal	$3,500.00		
Interest	210.00	$3,710.00	
Error in recording Check No. 743		90.00	3,800.00
			$13,945.50
Deduct: Check returned because of			
insufficient funds		$ 550.00	
Error in recording June 10 deposit		100.00	
Error in recording June 24 deposit		4.50	
Service charges		75.00	729.50
Adjusted balance			$13,216.00

* Balance per cash in bank account, June 1...............	$ 9,317.40	
Add June receipts...	9,223.76	
Deduct June disbursements.....................................	(8,395.66)	
Balance per cash in bank account, June 30.............	$10,145.50	

Prob. 8–5A (Concluded)

2.

Cash	3,800.00	
Notes Receivable		3,500.00
Interest Revenue		210.00
Accounts Payable		90.00
Sales ($100.00 + $4.50)	104.50	
Accounts Receivable	550.00	
Miscellaneous Expense	75.00	
Cash		729.50

3. $13,216.00

4.   The error of $540 ($930 – $390) in the canceled check should be added to the "balance according to bank statement" on the bank reconciliation. The canceled check should be presented to the bank with a request that the bank balance be corrected.

Prob. 8–1B

Strengths: a, b, e, and f

Weaknesses:

c. An independent person (for example, a supervisor) should count the cash in each cashier's cash register, unlock the record, and compare the amount of cash with the amount on the record to determine cash shortages or overages.

d. Cash receipts should not be handled by the accounts receivable clerk. This violates the segregation of duties between the handling of cash receipts and the recording of cash receipts.

g. The bank reconciliation should be prepared by someone not involved with the handling or recording of cash.

Prob. 8–2B

2014				
June	1	Petty Cash	1,000	
		Cash		1,000
	12	Cash	9,506	
		Cash Short and Over		66
		Sales		9,440
	30	Store Supplies	375	
		Merchandise Inventory	215	
		Office Supplies	208	
		Miscellaneous Administrative Expense	134	
		Cash Short and Over	22	
		Cash		954
	30	Cash	13,350	
		Cash Short and Over	40	
		Sales		13,390
	30	Petty Cash	200	
		Cash		200

Prob. 8–3B

1.

STONE SYSTEMS Bank Reconciliation July 31, 2014		
Cash balance according to bank statement		$33,650
Add deposit of July 31, not recorded by bank		9,150
		$42,800
Deduct: Outstanding checks	$17,865	
Bank error in charging check as $1,180 instead of $1,810	630	18,495
Adjusted balance		$24,305
Cash balance according to company's records		$17,750
Add: Proceeds of note collected by bank, including		
$345 interest	$ 6,095	
Error in recording check	540	6,635
		$24,385
Deduct bank service charges		80
Adjusted balance		$24,305

2.

Cash	6,635	
Notes Receivable		5,750
Interest Revenue		345
Accounts Payable—Holland Co.		540
Miscellaneous Expense	80	
Cash		80

3. $24,305; the adjusted balance from the bank reconciliation should be reported as cash on the July 31, 2014, balance sheet for Stone Systems.

Prob. 8–4B

1.

COLLEGIATE SPORTS CO. Bank Reconciliation November 30, 2014		
Cash balance according to bank statement		$112,675
Add deposit of November 30, not recorded by bank		12,200
		$124,875
Deduct: Outstanding checks	$41,840	
Bank error in charging check as $2,750 instead		
of $7,250	4,500	46,340
Adjusted balance		$ 78,535
Cash balance according to company's records*		$ 66,935
Add: Proceeds of note collected by bank, including		
$385 interest	$ 7,385	
Error in recording check as $7,600 instead of $760	6,840	14,225
		$ 81,160
Deduct: Check returned because of insufficient funds	$ 2,500	
Bank service charges	125	2,625
Adjusted balance		$ 78,535

* Cash balance, November 1...	$ 81,145
Plus cash deposited in November.....................................	293,150
Less checks written in November.....................................	(307,360)
Balance per company's records, November 30..................	$ 66,935

2.

Cash	14,225	
Notes Receivable		7,000
Interest Revenue		385
Accounts Payable—Ramirez Co.		6,840
Accounts Receivable—Hallen Academy	2,500	
Miscellaneous Expense	125	
Cash		2,625

3. $78,535; the adjusted balance from the bank reconciliation should be reported as cash on the November 30, 2014, balance sheet for Collegiate Sports Co.

Prob. 8–5B

1.

SUNSHINE INTERIORS		
Bank Reconciliation		
July 31, 20—		
Cash balance according to bank statement		$11,601.41
Add deposit of July 31, not recorded by bank		1,177.87
		$12,779.28
Deduct outstanding checks:		
No. 613	$ 137.50	
628	837.70	
633	310.08	1,285.28
Adjusted balance		$11,494.00
Cash balance according to company's records*		$ 7,664.00
Add proceeds of note collected by bank:		
Principal	$4,000.00	
Interest	160.00	
Add error in recording July 23 deposit	18.00	
Add error in recording Check No. 627	63.00	4,241.00
		$11,905.00
Deduct: Check returned because of insufficient funds	$ 375.00	
Service charges	36.00	411.00
Adjusted balance		$11,494.00

```
* Balance per cash in bank account, July 1................. $ 9,578.00
  Add July receipts...................................   6,465.42
  Deduct July disbursements...........................  (8,379.42)
  Balance per cash in bank account, July 31............. $ 7,664.00
```

Prob. 8–5B (Concluded)

2.

Cash	4,241.00	
Notes Receivable		4,000.00
Interest Revenue		160.00
Sales		18.00
Accounts Payable		63.00
Accounts Receivable	375.00	
Miscellaneous Expense	36.00	
Cash		411.00

3. $11,494.00

4.   The error of $1,620 ($1,800 – $180) in the canceled check should be added to the "balance according to bank statement" on the bank reconciliation. The canceled check should be presented to the bank, with a request that the bank balance be corrected.

CASES & PROJECTS

CP 8–1

Acceptable business and professional conduct requires Joel Kimmel to notify the bank of the error. *Note to Instructors:* Individuals may be criminally prosecuted for knowingly using funds that are erroneously credited to their bank accounts.

CP 8–2

Several control procedures could be implemented to prevent or detect the theft of cash from fictitious returns.

One procedure would be to establish a policy of "no cash refunds." That is, returns could only be exchanged for other merchandise. However, such a policy might not be popular with customers, and Turpin Meadows Electronics might lose sales from customers who would shop at other stores with a more liberal return policy.

Another procedure would be to allow returns only through a centralized location, such as a customer service desk. The customer service desk clerk would issue an approved refund slip, which the customer could then take to a cash register to receive a cash refund. Since the customer service clerk does not have access to cash, the customer service clerk could not steal cash through fictitious returns.

Yet another procedure would be to allow returns at the individual cash registers but require that all returns be approved by a supervisor. In this way, cash could be stolen through fictitious returns only with collusion of the supervisor and the cash register clerk.

CP 8–3

Several possible procedures for preventing or detecting the theft of grocery items by failing to scan their prices include the following:

a. Most scanning systems are designed so that an audible beep is heard each time an item is rung up on the cash register. This is intended to alert the cashier that the item has been properly rung up. Thus, observing whether a cashier is ringing up all merchandise can be accomplished by standing near the cash register and listening for the beeps. Such observations might be done on a periodic, surprise basis by supervisors.

b. Some grocery stores have their cash registers networked so that a monitor in a centralized office, usually high above the floor, can monitor any cash register's activity. In this way, a supervisor could monitor cash register activity on a periodic basis.

CP 8–3 (Concluded)

c.   Although this detection procedure would probably not be used in a grocery store, it is used by Sam's Clubs to detect this activity. Specifically, an employee is stationed at the exit to the store and checks each cash register receipt against the items with which the customer is leaving the store. This would not work well for a grocery store because of the large number of items that are usually placed in grocery bags at the checkout counter.

CP 8–4

Jo is clearly behaving in an unprofessional manner in intentionally shortchanging her customers.

At this point, Doris is in a difficult position. She is apparently adhering to Fuller's Organic Markets' policy of making up shortages out of her own pocket, but she is obviously upset about it. If Doris accepts Jo's advice, she will be engaging in unprofessional behavior. Doris is also faced with the dilemma of whether she should report Jo's behavior. If Doris continues to work for Fuller's Organic Markets, her best course of action is simply to try to do the best job possible in not making errors in ringing up sales and providing customers change.

One could argue that Tom is also acting in an unprofessional manner. First, allowing Jo to keep overages will simply encourage her to continue to shortchange customers. Second, since Jo has had no shortages in over a year, it should be obvious to Tom that Jo is shortchanging customers. Therefore, as store manager, Tom should take action to stop Jo's behavior. Better yet, Tom should consider revising Fuller's Organic Markets' control policy on shortages and overages. The cash register clerks should be required to report all shortages and overages without having to make up shortages from their own pockets. The cash register clerks could then be monitored for their effectiveness in making change for customers. Unusual amounts or trends could be investigated and corrective action taken, such as training, reassigning employees to other duties, etc. In any case, employees should not be allowed to keep overages at the end of each day.

CP 8–5

1. There are several methods that could be used to determine how much the cashier has stolen. The method described below is based on preparing a bank reconciliation as illustrated in this chapter. Because of the theft of the undeposited receipts, the bank reconciliation adjusted balances will not agree. The difference between the adjusted balances is the estimate of the amount stolen by the cashier.

PARKER COMPANY Bank Reconciliation July 31, 20—		
Balance according to bank statement		$10,575
Add undeposited cash receipts on hand		1,500
		$12,075
Deduct outstanding checks:		
No. 2670	$1,050	
3679	675	
3690	1,650	
5148	225	
5149	750	
5151	800	5,150
Adjusted balance		$ 6,925
Balance according to company's records		$10,400
Add note collected by bank, with interest		2,400
Adjusted balance		$12,800
Adjusted balance according to company's records		$12,800
Adjusted balance according to bank statement		6,925
Amount stolen by cashier		$ 5,875

Note to Instructors: The amount stolen by the cashier could also be computed directly from the cashier-prepared bank reconciliation as follows:

Outstanding checks omitted from the bank reconciliation prepared by the cashier:		
No. 2670...	$1,050	
3679...	675	
3690...	1,650	$3,375
Unrecorded note plus interest incorrectly recorded on the bank reconciliation prepared by the cashier.................		2,400
Addition error in the total of the outstanding checks in the bank reconciliation prepared by the cashier*.................		100
		$5,875

* *Note:* The cashier has altered the adding machine tape so that the total is not correct.

CP 8–5 (Concluded)

2.   The cashier attempted to conceal the theft by preparing an incorrect bank reconciliation. Specifically, the cashier (1) omitted outstanding checks on July 31 totaling $3,375, (2) added the list of outstanding checks shown on the bank reconciliation incorrectly so that the total is misstated by $100, and (3) incorrectly handled the treatment of the note and interest collected by the the bank.

3.   a.   Two major weaknesses in internal controls, which allowed the cashier to steal the undeposited cash receipts, are as follows:

   - First, large amounts of undeposited cash receipts were kept on hand during the month. For example, cash receipts for July 30 and 31 had yet to be deposited as of July 31. The large amount of undeposited cash receipts allowed the cashier to steal the cash without arousing suspicion that any cash was missing.

   - Second, the cashier prepared the bank reconciliation. This allowed the cashier to conceal the theft temporarily.

   b.   Two recommendations that would improve internal controls so that similar types of thefts of undeposited cash receipts could be prevented are as follows:

   - All cash receipts should be deposited daily. This would reduce the risk of significant cash losses. In addition, any missing cash would be more easily detected.

   - The bank reconciliation should be prepared by an independent individual who does not handle cash or the accounting records. One possibility would be for the owner of Parker Company to prepare the reconciliation.

Note to Instructors: In addition to the above recommendations, Parker Company should be counseled that it is standard practice for any disgruntled employees, fired employees, or employees who have announced quitting dates to be removed from sensitive positions (such as the cashier position) so that company assets or records will not be jeopardized. Finally, checks which have been outstanding for long periods of time (such as Nos. 2670, 3679, and 3690) should be voided (with stop payment instructions given to the bank) and reentered in the cash records. This establishes control over these items and prevents their misuse.

CP 8–6

Note to Instructors: The purpose of this activity is to familiarize students with the internal controls used by specific businesses. For example, when you order food at a McDonald's drive-through lane, your order is processed as follows:

1. The order is taken at a remote location by speaking with the cashier who rings up the order and indicates the amount you owe.

2. The order is simultaneously shown on a computer screen in the food preparation area.

3. You then drive up and pay the cashier the amount owed and are handed a receipt.

4. You drive further to where your order is delivered by an employee other than the cashier.

The preceding procedures separate the handling of cash from the delivery of the food order. If the cashier also delivered your order, the cashier could pocket your cash, not ring up your order, and deliver your food without anyone knowing.

CP 8–7

1. Year 3: $378.3 per month ($4,540 ÷ 12)
   Year 2: $341.5 per month ($4,098 ÷ 12)
   Year 1: $786.3 per month ($9,435 ÷ 12)

2. Year 3: 7.2 months ($2,726 ÷ $378.3)
   Year 2: 0.3 month ($106 ÷ $341.5)
   Year 1: 3.3 months ($2,565 ÷ $786.3)

3. At the end of Year 1, TearLab had less than four (3.3) months of cash remaining. During Year 2, the monthly cash expenses decreased from $786.3 to $341.5. However, by the end of Year 2 less than a month (0.3) of cash remained. In Year 3, TearLab slightly increased its monthly cash expenses from $341.5 to $378.3. At the end of Year 3, less than eight months (7.2) of cash remained unless TearLab changes its operations or raises additional financing. In the long term, unless the company improves its cash flows, it may have difficulty raising sufficient cash from investors or creditors to continue operations.

   Note to Instructors: During Year 2, TearLab raised additional cash by borrowing $1,750,000. In Year 3, TearLab raised additional cash of over $8,000,000 by issuing additional stock.

CHAPTER 9
RECEIVABLES

DISCUSSION QUESTIONS

1. Receivables are normally classified as (1) accounts receivable, (2) notes receivable, or (3) other receivables.

2. Dan's Hardware should use the direct write-off method because it is a small business that has a relatively small number and volume of accounts receivable.

3. Contra asset, credit balance

4. The accounts receivable and allowance for doubtful accounts may be reported at a net amount of $661,500 ($673,400 – $11,900) in the Current Assets section of the balance sheet. In this case, the amount of the allowance for doubtful accounts should be shown separately in a note to the financial statements or in parentheses on the balance sheet. Alternatively, the accounts receivable may be shown at the gross amount of $673,400 less the amount of the allowance for doubtful accounts of $11,900, thus yielding net accounts receivable of $661,500.

5. (1) The percentage rate used is excessive in relationship to the accounts written off as uncollectible; hence, the balance in the allowance is excessive.

   (2) A substantial volume of old uncollectible accounts is still being carried in the accounts receivable account.

6. An estimate based on analysis of receivables provides the most accurate estimate of the current net realizable value.

7. **a.** Sailfish Company
   b. Notes Receivable

8. The interest will amount to $5,100 ($85,000 × 6%) only if the note is payable one year from the date it was created. The usual practice is to state the interest rate in terms of an annual rate, rather than in terms of the period covered by the note.

9. Debit Accounts Receivable for $243,600
   Credit Notes Receivable for $240,000
   Credit Interest Revenue for $3,600

10.

Cash	245,427	
Accounts Receivable [$240,000 + ($240,000 × 6% × 90/360)]		243,600
Interest Revenue		1,827
($243,600 × 30/360 × 9% = $1,827).		

PRACTICE EXERCISES

PE 9–1A

Feb.	12	Cash	800	
		Bad Debt Expense	2,400	
		Accounts Receivable—Leo Jorgenson		3,200
May	3	Accounts Receivable—Leo Jorgenson	2,400	
		Bad Debt Expense		2,400
	3	Cash	2,400	
		Accounts Receivable—Leo Jorgenson		2,400

PE 9–1B

Oct.	2	Cash	600	
		Bad Debt Expense	1,350	
		Accounts Receivable—Rachel Elpel		1,950
Dec.	20	Accounts Receivable—Rachel Elpel	1,350	
		Bad Debt Expense		1,350
	20	Cash	1,350	
		Accounts Receivable—Rachel Elpel		1,350

PE 9–2A

Feb.	12	Cash	800	
		Allowance for Doubtful Accounts	2,400	
		Accounts Receivable—Leo Jorgenson		3,200
May	3	Accounts Receivable—Leo Jorgenson	2,400	
		Allowance for Doubtful Accounts		2,400
	3	Cash	2,400	
		Accounts Receivable—Leo Jorgenson		2,400

PE 9–2B

Oct.	2	Cash	600	
		Allowance for Doubtful Accounts	1,350	
		Accounts Receivable—Rachel Elpel		1,950
Dec.	20	Accounts Receivable—Rachel Elpel	1,350	
		Allowance for Doubtful Accounts		1,350
	20	Cash	1,350	
		Accounts Receivable—Rachel Elpel		1,350

PE 9–3A

a. $55,500 ($7,400,000 × 0.0075)

b.   Adjusted Balance

   Accounts Receivable.. $685,000
   Allowance for Doubtful Accounts ($9,000 + $55,500)..............   64,500
   Bad Debt Expense...   55,500

c. Net realizable value ($685,000 – $64,500)............................ $620,500

PE 9–3B

a. $231,500 ($46,300,000 × 0.0050)

b.   Adjusted Balance

   Accounts Receivable.. $3,460,000
   Allowance for Doubtful Accounts ($231,500 – $12,500)...........   219,000
   Bad Debt Expense...   231,500

c. Net realizable value ($3,460,000 – $219,000)......................... $3,241,000

PE 9–4A

a. $41,000 ($50,000 – $9,000)

b. | | Adjusted Balance |
|---|---|
| Accounts Receivable... | $685,000 |
| Allowance for Doubtful Accounts....................................... | 50,000 |
| Bad Debt Expense... | 41,000 |

c.   Net realizable value ($685,000 – $50,000)............................ $635,000

PE 9–4B

a. $257,500 ($245,000 + $12,500)

b. | | Adjusted Balance |
|---|---|
| Accounts Receivable... | $3,460,000 |
| Allowance for Doubtful Accounts....................................... | 245,000 |
| Bad Debt Expense... | 257,500 |

c.   Net realizable value ($3,460,000 – $245,000)........................ $3,215,000

PE 9–5A

a.   The due date for the note is September 6, determined as follows:

August	24 days (31 – 7)
September...	6 days
Total..	30 days

b. $210,875 [$210,000 + ($210,000 × 5% × 30/360)]

c.

Sept.	6	Cash	210,875	
		Notes Receivable		210,000
		Interest Revenue		875

PE 9–5B

a.   The due date for the note is August 7, determined as follows:

April...	21 days (30 – 9)
May...	31 days
June..	30 days
July..	31 days
August..	7 days
Total...	120 days

b. $462,000 [$450,000 + ($450,000 × 8% × 120/360)]

c.	Aug.	7	Cash	462,000	
			Notes Receivable		450,000
			Interest Revenue		12,000

PE 9–6A

a.	**Accounts Receivable Turnover**	**2014**	**2013**
	Net sales...................................	$2,912,000	$2,958,000
	Accounts receivable:		
	Beginning of year..................	$ 300,000	$ 280,000
	End of year..........................	$ 340,000	$ 300,000
	Average accts. receivable...........	$ 320,000	$ 290,000
		[($300,000 + $340,000) ÷ 2]	[($280,000 + $300,000) ÷ 2]
	Accts. receivable turnover..........	9.1	10.2
		($2,912,000 ÷ $320,000)	($2,958,000 ÷ $290,000)

b.	**Number of Days' Sales in Receivables**	**2014**	**2013**
	Net sales.................................	$2,912,000	$2,958,000
	Average daily sales....................	$ 7,978.1	$ 8,104.1
		($2,912,000 ÷ 365 days)	($2,958,000 ÷ 365 days)
	Average accts. receivable...........	$ 320,000	$ 290,000
		[($300,000 + $340,000) ÷ 2]	[($280,000 + $300,000) ÷ 2]
	Number of days' sales in receivables...........................	40.1 days	35.8 days
		($320,000 ÷ $7,978.1)	($290,000 ÷ $8,104.1)

c.   The decrease in the accounts receivable turnover from 10.2 to 9.1 and the increase in the number of days' sales in receivables from 35.8 days to 40.1 days indicate unfavorable trends in the efficiency of collecting receivables.

PE 9–6B

a.

Accounts Receivable Turnover	2014	2013
Net sales....................................	$7,906,000	$6,726,000
Accounts receivable:		
Beginning of year......................	$ 600,000	$ 540,000
End of year.............................	$ 580,000	$ 600,000
Average accts. receivable..............	$ 590,000	$ 570,000
	[($600,000 + $580,000) ÷ 2]	[($540,000 + $600,000) ÷ 2]
Accts. receivable turnover.............	13.4	11.8
	($7,906,000 ÷ $590,000)	($6,726,000 ÷ $570,000)

b.

Number of Days' Sales in Receivables	2014	2013
Net sales.....................................	$7,906,000	$6,726,000
Average daily sales.......................	$ 21,660.3	$ 18,427.4
	($7,906,000 ÷ 365 days)	($6,726,000 ÷ 365 days)
Average accts. receivable..............	$ 590,000	$ 570,000
	[($600,000 + $580,000) ÷ 2]	[($540,000 + $600,000) ÷ 2]
Number of days' sales in receivables...............................	27.2 days	30.9 days
	($590,000 ÷ $21,660.3)	($570,000 ÷ $18,427.4)

c.   The increase in the accounts receivable turnover from 11.8 to 13.4 and the decrease in the number of days' sales in receivables from 30.9 days to 27.2 days indicate favorable trends in the efficiency of collecting receivables.

EXERCISES

Ex. 9–1

Accounts receivable from the U.S. government are significantly different from receivables from commercial aircraft carriers such as Delta and United. Thus, Boeing should report each type of receivable separately. In its filing with the Securities and Exchange Commission, Boeing reports the receivables together on the balance sheet, but discloses each receivable separately in a note to the financial statements.

Ex. 9–2

a.   MGM Resorts International: 22.6% ($93,760,000 ÷ $415,654,000)

b.   Johnson & Johnson: 3.4% ($340,000,000 ÷ $10,114,000,000)

c.   Casino operations experience greater bad debt risk, since it is difficult to control the creditworthiness of customers entering the casino. In addition, individuals who may have adequate creditworthiness could overextend themselves and lose more than they can afford if they get caught up in the excitement of gambling. In contrast, Johnson & Johnson's customers are primarily other businesses such as grocery store chains.

Ex. 9–3

Jan.	30	Accounts Receivable—Dr. Cindy Mott	85,000	
		Sales		85,000
	30	Cost of Merchandise Sold	50,000	
		Merchandise Inventory		50,000
June	3	Cash	48,000	
		Bad Debt Expense	37,000	
		Accounts Receivable—Dr. Cindy Mott		85,000
Nov.	27	Accounts Receivable—Dr. Cindy Mott	37,000	
		Bad Debt Expense		37,000
	27	Cash	37,000	
		Accounts Receivable—Dr. Cindy Mott		37,000

Ex. 9–4

Mar.	19	Accounts Receivable—Midnight Delights Co.	37,500	
		Sales		37,500
	19	Cost of Merchandise Sold	23,000	
		Merchandise Inventory		23,000
Aug.	31	Cash	22,000	
		Allowance for Doubtful Accounts	15,500	
		Accounts Receivable—Midnight Delights Co.		37,500
Dec.	22	Accounts Receivable—Midnight Delights Co.	15,500	
		Allowance for Doubtful Accounts		15,500
	22	Cash	15,500	
		Accounts Receivable—Midnight Delights Co.		15,500

Ex. 9–5

a.	Bad Debt Expense	11,750	
	Accounts Receivable—Wil Treadwell		11,750

b.	Allowance for Doubtful Accounts	11,750	
	Accounts Receivable—Wil Treadwell		11,750

Ex. 9–6

a. $501,000 ($66,800,000 × 0.0075)   c. $334,000 ($66,800,000 × 0.0050)
b. $493,000 ($475,000 + $18,000)   d. $350,000 ($360,000 − $10,000)

Ex. 9–7

Account	Due Date	Number of Days Past Due
Avalanche Auto	August 8	84 (23 + 30 + 31)
Bales Auto	October 11	20 (31 − 11)
Derby Auto Repair	June 23	130 (7 + 31 + 31 + 30 + 31)
Lucky's Auto Repair	September 2	59 (28 + 31)
Pit Stop Auto	September 19	42 (11 + 31)
Reliable Auto Repair	July 15	108 (16 + 31 + 30 + 31)
Trident Auto	August 24	68 (7 + 30 + 31)
Valley Repair & Tow	May 17	167 (14 + 30 + 31 + 31 + 30 + 31)

Ex. 9–8

a.

Customer	Due Date	Number of Days Past Due
Color World Industries	March 13	171 days (18 + 30 + 31 + 30 + 31 + 31)
Hawks Company	June 29	63 days (1 + 31 + 31)
Osler Inc.	July 8	54 days (23 + 31)
Sather Sales Company	September 6	Not past due
Wisdom Company	August 25	6 days (31 – 25)

b.

Aging of Receivables Schedule August 31						
			Days Past Due			
Customer	Balance	Not Past Due	1–30	31–60	61–90	Over 90
Allied Industries Inc.	3,000	3,000				
Archer Company	4,500		4,500			
Zussman Company	5,000			5,000		
Subtotals	750,000	480,000	160,000	75,000	28,000	7,000
Color World Industries	33,000					33,000
Hawks Company	15,000				15,000	
Osler Inc.	21,000			21,000		
Sather Sales Company	8,000	8,000				
Wisdom Company	6,500		6,500			
Totals	833,500	488,000	166,500	96,000	43,000	40,000

Ex. 9–9

			Days Past Due			
	Balance	Not Past Due	1–30	31–60	61–90	Over 90
Total receivables	833,500	488,000	166,500	96,000	43,000	40,000
Percentage uncollectible		2%	6%	12%	30%	75%
Allowance for doubtful accounts	74,170	9,760	9,990	11,520	12,900	30,000

Ex. 9–10

Aug.	31	Bad Debt Expense	67,820	
		Allowance for Doubtful Accounts		67,820
		Uncollectible accounts estimate		
		($74,170 – $6,350).		

Ex. 9–11

Age Interval	Balance	Estimated Uncollectible Accounts Percent	Estimated Uncollectible Accounts Amount
Not past due	$ 740,000	0.5%	$ 3,700
1–30 days past due	390,000	2%	7,800
31–60 days past due	85,000	4%	3,400
61–90 days past due	28,000	14%	3,920
91–180 days past due	42,000	32%	13,440
Over 180 days past due	15,000	80%	12,000
Total	$1,300,000		$44,260

Ex. 9–12

2014				
Dec.	31	Bad Debt Expense	47,635	
		Allowance for Doubtful Accounts		47,635
		Uncollectible accounts estimate		
		($44,260 + $3,375).		

Ex. 9–13

a.

Apr.	13	Bad Debt Expense	8,450	
		Accounts Receivable—Dean Sheppard		8,450
May	15	Cash	500	
		Bad Debt Expense	6,600	
		Accounts Receivable—Dan Pyle		7,100
July	27	Accounts Receivable—Dean Sheppard	8,450	
		Bad Debt Expense		8,450
	27	Cash	8,450	
		Accounts Receivable—Dean Sheppard		8,450
Dec.	31	Bad Debt Expense	13,510	
		Accounts Receivable—Paul Chapman		2,225
		Accounts Receivable—Duane DeRosa		3,550
		Accounts Receivable—Teresa Galloway		4,770
		Accounts Receivable—Ernie Klatt		1,275
		Accounts Receivable—Marty Richey		1,690
	31	No entry		

Ex. 9–13 (Concluded)

b.

Apr.	13	Allowance for Doubtful Accounts		8,450	
		Accounts Receivable—Dean Sheppard			8,450
May	15	Cash		500	
		Allowance for Doubtful Accounts		6,600	
		Accounts Receivable—Dan Pyle			7,100
July	27	Accounts Receivable—Dean Sheppard		8,450	
		Allowance for Doubtful Accounts			8,450
	27	Cash		8,450	
		Accounts Receivable—Dean Sheppard			8,450
Dec.	31	Allowance for Doubtful Accounts		13,510	
		Accounts Receivable—Paul Chapman			2,225
		Accounts Receivable—Duane DeRosa			3,550
		Accounts Receivable—Teresa Galloway			4,770
		Accounts Receivable—Ernie Klatt			1,275
		Accounts Receivable—Marty Richey			1,690
	31	Bad Debt Expense		28,335	
		Allowance for Doubtful Accounts			28,335
		Uncollectible accounts estimate			
		($3,778,000 × 0.75% = $28,335).			

c. **Bad debt expense under:**

Allowance method.. $28,335

Direct write-off method ($8,450 + $6,600 – $8,450 + $13,510)............... 20,110

Difference ($28,335 – $20,110)... $ 8,225

Shipway Company's income would be $8,225 higher under the direct write-off method than under the allowance method.

Ex. 9–14

a.

June	8	Bad Debt Expense	8,440	
		Accounts Receivable—Kathy Quantel		8,440
Aug.	14	Cash	3,000	
		Bad Debt Expense	9,500	
		Accounts Receivable—Rosalie Oakes		12,500
Oct.	16	Accounts Receivable—Kathy Quantel	8,440	
		Bad Debt Expense		8,440
	16	Cash	8,440	
		Accounts Receivable—Kathy Quantel		8,440
Dec.	31	Bad Debt Expense	24,955	
		Accounts Receivable—Wade Dolan		4,600
		Accounts Receivable—Greg Gagne		3,600
		Accounts Receivable—Amber Kisko		7,150
		Accounts Receivable—Shannon Poole		2,975
		Accounts Receivable—Niki Spence		6,630
	31	No entry		

Ex. 9–14 (Continued)

b.

				Debit	Credit
June	8	Allowance for Doubtful Accounts		8,440	
			Accounts Receivable—Kathy Quantel		8,440
Aug.	14	Cash		3,000	
		Allowance for Doubtful Accounts		9,500	
			Accounts Receivable—Rosalie Oakes		12,500
Oct.	16	Accounts Receivable—Kathy Quantel		8,440	
			Allowance for Doubtful Accounts		8,440
	16	Cash		8,440	
			Accounts Receivable—Kathy Quantel		8,440
Dec.	31	Allowance for Doubtful Accounts		24,955	
			Accounts Receivable—Wade Dolan		4,600
			Accounts Receivable—Greg Gagne		3,600
			Accounts Receivable—Amber Kisko		7,150
			Accounts Receivable—Shannon Poole		2,975
			Accounts Receivable—Niki Spence		6,630
	31	Bad Debt Expense		45,545	
			Allowance for Doubtful Accounts		45,545
			Uncollectible accounts estimate		
			($47,090 – $1,545).		

Computations:

Aging Class (Number of Days Past Due)	Receivables Balance on December 31	Estimated Doubtful Accounts	
		Percent	Amount
0–30 days	$320,000	1%	$ 3,200
31–60 days	110,000	3%	3,300
61–90 days	24,000	10%	2,400
91–120 days	18,000	33%	5,940
More than 120 days	43,000	75%	32,250
Total receivables	$515,000		$47,090

Estimated balance of allowance account from aging schedule...................... $47,090

Unadjusted credit balance of allowance account*... 1,545

Adjustment... $45,545

* $36,000 – $8,440 – $9,500 + $8,440 – $24,955 = $1,545

Ex. 9–14 (Concluded)

c.   **Bad debt expense under:**

Allowance method...	$45,545
Direct write-off method ($8,440 + $9,500 – $8,440 + $24,955)...............	34,455
Difference...	$11,090

Rustic Tables' income would be $11,090 higher under the direct write-off method than under the allowance method.

Ex. 9–15

$482,800 [$487,500 + $27,800 – ($3,250,000 × 1%)]

Ex. 9–16

a. $593,000 [$600,000 + $34,000 – ($4,100,000 × 1%)]

b. $11,700 ($32,500 – $27,800) + ($41,000 – $34,000)

Ex. 9–17

a.

Bad Debt Expense	30,000	
Accounts Receivable—Shawn Brooke		4,650
Accounts Receivable—Eve Denton		5,180
Accounts Receivable—Art Malloy		11,050
Accounts Receivable—Cassie Yost		9,120

b.

Allowance for Doubtful Accounts	30,000	
Accounts Receivable—Shawn Brooke		4,650
Accounts Receivable—Eve Denton		5,180
Accounts Receivable—Art Malloy		11,050
Accounts Receivable—Cassie Yost		9,120
Bad Debt Expense	39,375	
Allowance for Doubtful Accounts		39,375
Uncollectible accounts estimate		
($5,250,000 × 0.75% = $39,375).		

c.   Net income would have been $9,375 higher in 2014 under the direct write-off method, because bad debt expense would have been $9,375 higher under the allowance method ($39,375 expense under the allowance method vs. $30,000 expense under the direct write-off method).

Ex. 9–18

a.

Bad Debt Expense	102,500	
Accounts Receivable—Kim Abel		21,550
Accounts Receivable—Lee Drake		33,925
Accounts Receivable—Jenny Green		27,565
Accounts Receivable—Mike Lamb		19,460

b.

Allowance for Doubtful Accounts	102,500	
Accounts Receivable—Kim Abel		21,550
Accounts Receivable—Lee Drake		33,925
Accounts Receivable—Jenny Green		27,565
Accounts Receivable—Mike Lamb		19,460
Bad Debt Expense	117,150	
Allowance for Doubtful Accounts		117,150
Uncollectible accounts estimate		
($109,650 + $7,500).		

Computations:

Aging Class (Number of Days Past Due)	Receivables Balance on December 31	Estimated Doubtful Accounts	
		Percent	Amount
0–30 days	$ 715,000	1%	$ 7,150
31–60 days	310,000	2%	6,200
61–90 days	102,000	15%	15,300
91–120 days	76,000	30%	22,800
More than 120 days	97,000	60%	58,200
Total receivables	$1,300,000		$109,650

Unadjusted debit balance of Allowance for Doubtful Accounts

($102,500 – $95,000)... $ 7,500

Estimated balance of Allowance for Doubtful Accounts

from aging schedule.. 109,650

Adjustment... $117,150

c.   Net income would have been $14,650 lower in 2014 under the allowance method, because bad debt expense would have been $14,650 higher under the allowance method ($117,150 expense under the allowance method versus $102,500 expense under the direct write-off method).

Ex. 9–19

	Due Date	Interest	
a.	Apr. 22	$1,100	[$55,000 × 0.08 × (90/360)]
b.	May 8	300	[$36,000 × 0.05 × (60/360)]
c.	July 30	390	[$78,000 × 0.04 × (45/360)]
d.	Nov. 3	161	[$13,800 × 0.07 × (60/360)]
e.	Jan. 29	1,160	[$58,000 × 0.06 × (120/360)]

Ex. 9–20

a.   June 18 (10 + 31 + 30 + 31 + 18)

b. $153,500 [($150,000 × 7% × 120/360) + $150,000]

c.   (1)

Notes Receivable	150,000	
Accounts Rec.—Dry Creek Interior Decorators		150,000

(2)

Cash	153,500	
Notes Receivable		150,000
Interest Revenue		3,500

Ex. 9–21

1.   Sale on account.

2.   Cost of merchandise sold for the sale on account.

3.   A sale return or allowance.

4.   Cost of merchandise returned.

5.   Note received from customer on account.

6.   Note dishonored and charged maturity value of note to customer's account receivable.

7.   Payment received from customer for dishonored note plus interest earned after due date.

Ex. 9–22

2013				
Dec.	16	Notes Receivable	21,000	
		Accounts Receivable—Lake Shore		
		Clothing & Bags Co.		21,000
	31	Interest Receivable	70	
		Interest Revenue		70
		Accrued interest		
		($21,000 × 0.08 × 15/360 = $70).		
	31	Interest Revenue	70	
		Income Summary		70
2014				
Mar.	16	Cash	21,420	
		Notes Receivable		21,000
		Interest Receivable		70
		Interest Revenue		350
		($21,000 × 0.08 × 75/360).		

Ex. 9–23

July	12	Notes Receivable	240,000	
		Accounts Receivable—Accolade Co.		240,000
Nov.	9	Accounts Receivable—Accolade Co.	245,600	
		Notes Receivable		240,000
		Interest Revenue		5,600
		($240,000 × 0.07 × 120/360).		
Dec.	9	Cash	247,442	
		Accounts Receivable—Accolade Co.		245,600
		Interest Revenue		1,842
		($245,600 × 0.09 × 30/360).		

Ex. 9–24

Apr.	18	Notes Receivable	60,000	
		Accounts Receivable—Glenn Cross		60,000
	30	Notes Receivable	42,000	
		Accounts Receivable—Rhoni Melville		42,000
May	18	Accounts Receivable—Glenn Cross	60,350	
		Notes Receivable		60,000
		Interest Revenue		350
		($60,000 × 7% × 30/360).		
June	29	Accounts Receivable—Rhoni Melville	42,560	
		Notes Receivable		42,000
		Interest Revenue		560
		($42,000 × 8% × 60/360).		
Aug.	16	Cash	61,557	
		Accounts Receivable—Glenn Cross		60,350
		Interest Revenue		1,207
		($60,350 × 8% × 90/360).		
Oct.	22	Allowance for Doubtful Accounts	42,560	
		Accounts Receivable—Rhoni Melville		42,560

Ex. 9–25

1. The interest receivable should be reported separately as a current asset. It should not be deducted from notes receivable.

2. The allowance for doubtful accounts should be deducted from accounts receivable.

   A corrected partial balance sheet would be as follows:

NAPA VINO COMPANY		
Balance Sheet		
December 31, 2014		
Assets		
Current assets:		
Cash		$ 78,500
Notes receivable		300,000
Accounts receivable	$1,200,000	
Less allowance for doubtful accounts	11,500	1,188,500
Interest receivable		4,500

Ex. 9–26

a. and b.

	Year 2	Year 1
Net sales..............................	$5,660,300	$4,978,900
Accounts receivable.................	$592,700	$486,200
Average accts. receivable..........	$539,450	$531,450
	[($592,700 + $486,200) ÷ 2]	[($486,200 + $576,700) ÷ 2]
Accts. receivable turnover.........	10.5	9.4
	($5,660,300 ÷ $539,450)	($4,978,900 ÷ $531,450)
Average daily sales..................	$15,507.7	$13,640.8
	($5,660,300 ÷ 365 days)	($4,978,900 ÷ 365 days)
Days' sales in receivables.........	34.8	39.0
	($539,450 ÷ $15,507.7)	($531,450 ÷ $13,640.8)

c.   The accounts receivable turnover indicates an increase in the efficiency of collecting accounts receivable by increasing from 9.4 to 10.5, a favorable trend. The days' sales in receivables also indicates an increase in the efficiency of collecting accounts receivable by decreasing from 39.0 to 34.8, which is a favorable trend. However, before reaching a final conclusion, the ratios should be compared with industry averages and similar firms.

Ex. 9–27

a. and b.

	Year 2	Year 1
Net sales..............................	$10,706,588	$10,494,983
Accounts receivable.................	$1,265,032	$1,045,338
Average accts. receivable..........	$1,155,185	$1,108,567.5
	[($1,265,032 + $1,045,338) ÷ 2]	[($1,045,338 + $1,171,797) ÷ 2]
Accts. receivable turnover.........	9.3	9.5
	($10,706,588 ÷ $1,155,185)	($10,494,983 ÷ $1,108,567.5)
Average daily sales..................	$29,333.1	$28,753.4
	($10,706,588 ÷ 365 days)	($10,494,983 ÷ 365 days)
Days' sales in receivables.........	39.4	38.6
	($1,155,185 ÷ $29,333.1)	($1,108,567.5 ÷ $28,753.4)

c.   The accounts receivable turnover indicates a decrease in the efficiency of collecting accounts receivable by decreasing from 9.5 to 9.3, an unfavorable trend. The number of days' sales in receivables increased from 38.6 to 39.4 days, also indicating an unfavorable trend in collections of receivables. These unfavorable trends are consistent with the economic downturn that occurred worldwide in Year 1 and Year 2. However, before reaching a final conclusion, both ratios should be compared with those of past years, industry averages, and similar firms.

Ex. 9–28

a. and b.

	Year 2	Year 1
Net sales............................	$9,613	$8,632
Accounts receivable............	$ 267	$ 249
Average accts. receivable.....	$ 258	$ 281
	[($267 + $249) ÷ 2]	[($249 + $313) ÷ 2]
Accts. receivable turnover....	37.3	30.7
	($9,613 ÷ $258)	($8,632 ÷ $281)
Average daily sales..............	$26.3	$23.6
	($9,613 ÷ 365 days)	($8,632 ÷ 365 days)
Days' sales in receivables.....	9.8	11.9
	($258 ÷ $26.3)	($281 ÷ $23.6)

c.   The accounts receivable turnover indicates an increase in the efficiency of collecting accounts receivable by increasing from 30.7 to 37.3, a favorable trend. The days' sales in receivables indicates an increase in the efficiency of collecting accounts receivable by decreasing from 11.9 to 9.8, also indicating a favorable trend. Before reaching a conclusion, however, the ratios should be compared with industry averages and similar firms.

Ex. 9–29

a. The average accounts receivable turnover ratios are as follows:

The Limited Brands Inc.: 34.0   [(37.3 + 30.7) ÷ 2]
H.J. Heinz Company: 9.4   [(9.3 + 9.5) ÷ 2]

Note: For computations of the individual ratios, see Ex. 9–27 and Ex. 9–28.

b. The Limited Brands has the higher average accounts receivable turnover ratio.

c. The Limited Brands operates a specialty retail chain of stores that sell directly to individual consumers. Many of these consumers (retail customers) pay with MasterCards or VISAs that are recorded as cash sales. In contrast, H.J. Heinz manufactures processed foods that are sold to food wholesalers, grocery store chains, and other food distributors that eventually sell Heinz products to individual consumers. Accordingly, because of the extended distribution chain, we would expect Heinz to have more accounts receivable than The Limited Brands. In addition, we would expect Heinz's business customers to take a longer period to pay their receivables. Thus, we would expect Heinz's average accounts receivable turnover ratio to be lower than The Limited Brands, as shown in (a).

PROBLEMS

Prob. 9–1A

2.

20—				
Feb.	8	Cash	7,200	
		Allowance for Doubtful Accounts	10,800	
		Accounts Receivable—DeCoy Co.		18,000
May	27	Accounts Receivable—Seth Nelsen	7,350	
		Allowance for Doubtful Accounts		7,350
	27	Cash	7,350	
		Accounts Receivable—Seth Nelsen		7,350
Aug.	13	Allowance for Doubtful Accounts	6,400	
		Accounts Receivable—Kat Tracks Co.		6,400
Oct.	31	Accounts Receivable—Crawford Co.	3,880	
		Allowance for Doubtful Accounts		3,880
	31	Cash	3,880	
		Accounts Receivable—Crawford Co.		3,880
Dec.	31	Allowance for Doubtful Accounts	23,200	
		Accounts Receivable—Newbauer Co.		7,190
		Accounts Receivable—Bonneville Co.		5,500
		Accounts Receivable—Crow Distributors		9,400
		Accounts Receivable—Fiber Optics		1,110
	31	Bad Debt Expense	38,870	
		Allowance for Doubtful Accounts		38,870
		Uncollectible accounts estimate		
		($35,700 + $3,170).		

Prob. 9–1A (Concluded)

1. and 2.

Allowance for Doubtful Accounts

Feb.	8		10,800	Jan.	1	Balance	26,000
Aug.	13		6,400	May	27		7,350
Dec.	31		23,200	Oct.	31		3,880
Dec.	31	Unadjusted Balance	3,170				
				Dec.	31	Adjusting Entry	38,870
				Dec.	31	Adj. Balance	35,700

Bad Debt Expense

Dec.	31	Adjusting Entry	38,870	

3. $1,749,300 ($1,785,000 – $35,700)

4. a. $45,500 ($18,200,000 × 0.0025)
    b. $42,330 ($45,500 – $3,170)
    c. $1,742,670 ($1,785,000 – $42,330)

Prob. 9–2A

1.

Customer	Due Date	Number of Days Past Due
Adams Sports & Flies	May 22, 2013	223 days (9 + 30 + 31 + 31 + 30 + 31 + 30 + 31)
Blue Dun Flies	Oct. 10, 2013	82 days (21 + 30 + 31)
Cicada Fish Co.	Sept. 29, 2013	93 days (1 + 31 + 30 + 31)
Deschutes Sports	Oct. 20, 2013	72 days (11 + 30 + 31)
Green River Sports	Nov. 7, 2013	54 days (23 + 31)
Smith River Co.	Nov. 28, 2013	33 days (2 + 31)
Western Trout Company	Dec. 7, 2013	24 days
Wolfe Sports	Jan. 20, 2014	Not past due

2. and 3.

Aging of Receivables Schedule December 31, 2013							
Customer	Balance	Not Past Due	1–30	31–60	61–90	91–120	Over 120
AAA Outfitters	20,000	20,000					
Brown Trout Fly Shop	7,500			7,500			
Zigs Fish Adventures	4,000		4,000				
Subtotals	1,300,000	750,000	290,000	120,000	40,000	20,000	80,000
Adams Sports & Flies	5,000						5,000
Blue Dun Flies	4,900				4,900		
Cicada Fish Co.	8,400					8,400	
Deschutes Sports	7,000				7,000		
Green River Sports	3,500			3,500			
Smith River Co.	2,400			2,400			
Western Trout Company	6,800		6,800				
Wolfe Sports	4,400	4,400					
Totals	1,342,400	754,400	296,800	125,900	51,900	28,400	85,000
Percentage uncollectible		1%	2%	10%	30%	40%	80%
Estimate of uncollectible accounts	121,000	7,544	5,936	12,590	15,570	11,360	68,000

Prob. 9–2A (Concluded)

4.

Bad Debt Expense	124,600	
Allowance for Doubtful Accounts		124,600
Uncollectible accounts estimate		
($121,000 + $3,600).		

5.   On the balance sheet, assets would be overstated by $124,600, since the allowance for doubtful accounts would be understated by $124,600. In addition, the owner's capital account would be overstated by $124,600, since bad debt expense would be understated and net income overstated by $124,600 on the income statement.

Prob. 9–3A

1.

| Year | Bad Debt Expense | | | |
	Expense Actually Reported	Expense Based on Estimate	Increase (Decrease) in Amount of Expense	Balance of Allowance Account, End of Year
1st	$ 4,500	$ 9,000	$4,500	$ 4,500
2nd	9,600	12,500	2,900	7,400
3rd	12,800	15,000	2,200	9,600
4th	16,550	22,000	5,450	15,050

2. Yes. The actual write-offs of accounts originating in the first two years are reasonably close to the expense that would have been charged to those years on the basis of 1% of sales. The total write-off of receivables originating in the first year amounted to $8,500 ($4,500 + $3,000 + $1,000), as compared with bad debt expense, based on the percentage of sales, of $9,000 ($900,000 × 1%). For the second year, the comparable amounts were $11,800 ($6,600 + $3,700 + $1,500) and $12,500 ($1,250,000 × 1%).

Prob. 9–4A

1.

	(a)		(b)
Note	Due Date		Interest Due at Maturity
1.	Apr. 20	$500	($80,000 × 45/360 × 5%)
2.	June 22	360	($24,000 × 60/360 × 9%)
3.	Nov. 17	840	($42,000 × 120/360 × 6%)
4.	Dec. 5	945	($54,000 × 90/360 × 7%)
5.	Jan. 28	270	($27,000 × 60/360 × 6%)
6.	Jan. 29	300	($72,000 × 30/360 × 5%)

2.

Nov.	17	Accounts Receivable		42,840	
		Notes Receivable			42,000
		Interest Revenue			840

3.

Dec.	31	Interest Receivable		154	
		Interest Revenue			154
		Accrued interest.			
		$27,000 × 6% × 32/360 = $144			
		$72,000 × 5% × 1/360 10			
		Total $154			

4.

Jan.	28	Cash		27,270	
		Notes Receivable			27,000
		Interest Receivable			144
		Interest Revenue			126
		($27,000 × 6% × 28/360).			
	29	Cash		72,300	
		Notes Receivable			72,000
		Interest Receivable			10
		Interest Revenue			290
		($72,000 × 5% × 29/360).			

Prob. 9–5A

Apr.	10	Notes Receivable	144,000	
		Accounts Receivable		144,000
May	15	Notes Receivable	270,000	
		Accounts Receivable		270,000
June	9	Cash	145,200	
		Notes Receivable		144,000
		Interest Revenue		1,200
Aug.	22	Notes Receivable	150,000	
		Accounts Receivable		150,000
Sept.	12	Cash	276,300	
		Notes Receivable		270,000
		Interest Revenue		6,300
	30	Notes Receivable	210,000	
		Accounts Receivable		210,000
Oct.	6	Cash	150,750	
		Notes Receivable		150,000
		Interest Revenue		750
	18	Notes Receivable	120,000	
		Accounts Receivable		120,000
Nov.	29	Cash	212,800	
		Notes Receivable		210,000
		Interest Revenue		2,800
Dec.	17	Cash	121,000	
		Notes Receivable		120,000
		Interest Revenue		1,000

Prob. 9–6A

Jan.	3	Notes Receivable	18,000	
		Cash		18,000
Feb.	10	Accounts Receivable—Bradford & Co.	24,000	
		Sales		24,000
	10	Cost of Merchandise Sold	14,400	
		Merchandise Inventory		14,400
	13	Accounts Receivable—Dry Creek Co.	60,000	
		Sales		60,000
	13	Cost of Merchandise Sold	54,000	
		Merchandise Inventory		54,000
Mar.	12	Notes Receivable	24,000	
		Accounts Receivable—Bradford & Co.		24,000
	14	Notes Receivable	60,000	
		Accounts Receivable—Dry Creek Co.		60,000
Apr.	3	Notes Receivable	18,000	
		Cash	360	
		Notes Receivable		18,000
		Interest Revenue		360
		($18,000 × 8% × 90/360).		
May	11	Cash	24,280	
		Notes Receivable		24,000
		Interest Revenue		280
		($24,000 × 7% × 60/360).		
	13	Accounts Receivable—Dry Creek Co.	60,900	
		Notes Receivable		60,000
		Interest Revenue		900
		($60,000 × 9% × 60/360).		
July	12	Cash	62,118	
		Accounts Receivable—Dry Creek Co.		60,900
		Interest Revenue		1,218
		($60,900 × 12% × 60/360).		

Prob. 9–6A (Concluded)

Aug.	1	Cash		18,540	
			Notes Receivable		18,000
			Interest Revenue		540
			($18,000 × 9% × 120/360).		
Oct.	5	Accounts Receivable—Halloran Co.		13,500	
			Sales		13,500
	5	Cost of Merchandise Sold		8,100	
			Merchandise Inventory		8,100
	15	Cash		13,230	
			Sales Discounts		270	
			Accounts Receivable—Halloran Co.		13,500

Prob. 9–1B

2.

20—				
Jan.	19	Accounts Receivable—Arlene Gurley	2,660	
		Allowance for Doubtful Accounts		2,660
	19	Cash	2,660	
		Accounts Receivable—Arlene Gurley		2,660
Apr.	3	Allowance for Doubtful Accounts	12,750	
		Accounts Receivable—Premier GS Co.		12,750
July	16	Cash	5,500	
		Allowance for Doubtful Accounts	16,500	
		Accounts Receivable—Hayden Co.		22,000
Nov.	23	Accounts Receivable—Harry Carr	4,000	
		Allowance for Doubtful Accounts		4,000
	23	Cash	4,000	
		Accounts Receivable—Harry Carr		4,000
Dec.	31	Allowance for Doubtful Accounts	24,000	
		Accounts Receivable—Cavey Co.		3,300
		Accounts Receivable—Fogle Co.		8,100
		Accounts Receivable—Lake Furniture		11,400
		Accounts Receivable—Melinda Shryer		1,200
	31	Bad Debt Expense	56,590	
		Allowance for Doubtful Accounts		56,590
		Uncollectible accounts estimate		
		($60,000 – $3,410).		

Prob. 9–1B (Concluded)

1. and 2.

Allowance for Doubtful Accounts

Apr.	3		12,750	Jan.	1	Balance	50,000
July	16		16,500	Jan.	19		2,660
Dec.	31		24,000	Nov.	23		4,000
				Dec.	31	Unadjusted Balance	3,410
				Dec.	31	Adjusting Entry	56,590
				Dec.	31	Adjusted Balance	60,000

Bad Debt Expense

Dec.	31	Adjusting Entry	56,590

3. $2,290,000 ($2,350,000 – $60,000)

4. a. $79,000 ($15,800,000 × 0.005)
    b. $82,410 ($79,000 + $3,410)
    c. $2,267,590 ($2,350,000 – $82,410)

Prob. 9–2B

1.

Customer	Due Date	Number of Days Past Due
Arcade Beauty	Aug. 17, 2013	136 days (14 + 30 + 31 + 30 + 31)
Creative Images	Oct. 30, 2013	62 days (1 + 30 + 31)
Excel Hair Products	July 3, 2013	181 days (28 + 31 + 30 + 31 + 30 + 31)
First Class Hair Care	Sept. 8, 2013	114 days (22 + 31 + 30 + 31)
Golden Images	Nov. 23, 2013	38 days (7 + 31)
Oh That Hair	Nov. 29, 2013	32 days (1 + 31)
One Stop Hair Designs	Dec. 7, 2013	24 days
Visions Hair & Nail	Jan. 11, 2014	Not past due

2. and 3.

Aging of Receivables Schedule December 31, 2013							
Customer	Balance	Not Past Due	1–30	31–60	61–90	91–120	Over 120
				Days Past Due			
ABC Beauty	15,000	15,000					
Angel Wigs	8,000			8,000			
Zodiac Beauty	3,000		3,000				
Subtotals	875,000	415,000	210,000	112,000	55,000	18,000	65,000
Arcade Beauty	10,000						10,000
Creative Images	8,500				8,500		
Excel Hair Products	7,500						7,500
First Class Hair Care	6,600					6,600	
Golden Images	3,600			3,600			
Oh That Hair	1,400			1,400			
One Stop Hair Designs	4,000		4,000				
Visions Hair & Nail	9,000	9,000					
Totals	925,600	424,000	214,000	117,000	63,500	24,600	82,500
Percentage uncollectible		1%	4%	16%	25%	40%	80%
Estimate of uncollectible accounts	123,235	4,240	8,560	18,720	15,875	9,840	66,000

Prob. 9–2B (Concluded)

4.

Bad Debt Expense	115,860	
Allowance for Doubtful Accounts		115,860
Uncollectible accounts estimate		
($123,235 – $7,375).		

5.   On the balance sheet, assets would be overstated by $115,860, since the allowance for doubtful accounts would be understated by $115,860. In addition, the owner's capital account would be overstated by $115,860, since bad debt expense would be understated and net income overstated by $115,860 on the income statement.

Prob. 9–3B

1.

Year	Bad Debt Expense			Balance of Allowance Account, End of Year
	Expense Actually Reported	Expense Based on Estimate	Increase (Decrease) in Amount of Expense	
1st	$18,000	$31,250	$13,250	$13,250
2nd	30,200	37,000	6,800	20,050
3rd	39,900	45,000	5,100	25,150
4th	52,600	60,000	7,400	32,550

2. Yes. The actual write-offs of accounts originating in the first two years are reasonably close to the expense that would have been charged to those years on the basis of 1/4% of sales. The total write-off of receivables originating in the first year amounted to $30,600 ($18,000 + $9,000 + $3,600), as compared with bad debt expense based on the percentage of sales, of $31,250 ($12,500,000 × 0.0025). For the second year, the comparable amounts were $35,600 ($21,200 + $9,300 + $5,100) and $37,000 ($14,800,000 × 0.0025).

Prob. 9–4B

1.

	(a)	(b)	
Note	**Due Date**	**Interest Due at Maturity**	
1.	Feb. 13	$110	($33,000 × 30/360 × 4%)
2.	Apr. 23	525	($60,000 × 45/360 × 7%)
3.	Oct. 10	600	($48,000 × 90/360 × 5%)
4.	Nov. 6	200	($16,000 × 75/360 × 6%)
5.	Jan. 14	480	($36,000 × 60/360 × 8%)
6.	Feb. 8	240	($24,000 × 60/360 × 6%)

2.

Oct.	10	Accounts Receivable		48,600	
		Notes Receivable			48,000
		Interest Revenue			600

3.

Dec.	31	Interest Receivable		452	
		Interest Revenue			452
		Accrued interest.			
		$36,000 × 8% × 46/360 = $368			
		$24,000 × 6% × 21/360 84			
		Total $452			

4.

Jan.	14	Cash		36,480	
		Notes Receivable			36,000
		Interest Receivable			368
		Interest Revenue			112
		($36,000 × 8% × 14/360).			
Feb.	8	Cash		24,240	
		Notes Receivable			24,000
		Interest Receivable			84
		Interest Revenue			156
		($24,000 × 6% × 39/360).			

Prob. 9–5B

Mar.	8	Notes Receivable	33,000	
		Accounts Receivable		33,000
	31	Notes Receivable	80,000	
		Accounts Receivable		80,000
May	7	Cash	33,275	
		Notes Receivable		33,000
		Interest Revenue		275
	16	Notes Receivable	72,000	
		Accounts Receivable		72,000
June	11	Notes Receivable	36,000	
		Accounts Receivable		36,000
	29	Cash	81,400	
		Notes Receivable		80,000
		Interest Revenue		1,400
July	26	Cash	36,270	
		Notes Receivable		36,000
		Interest Revenue		270
Aug.	4	Notes Receivable	48,000	
		Accounts Receivable		48,000
	14	Cash	73,260	
		Notes Receivable		72,000
		Interest Revenue		1,260
Dec.	2	Cash	49,440	
		Notes Receivable		48,000
		Interest Revenue		1,440

Prob. 9–6B

20—				
Jan.	21	Accounts Receivable—Black Tie Co.	28,000	
		Sales		28,000
	21	Cost of Merchandise Sold	16,800	
		Merchandise Inventory		16,800
Mar.	18	Notes Receivable	28,000	
		Accounts Receivable—Black Tie Co.		28,000
May	17	Cash	28,280	
		Notes Receivable		28,000
		Interest Revenue		280
		($28,000 × 6% × 60/360).		
June	15	Accounts Receivable—Pioneer Co.	17,700	
		Sales		17,700
	15	Cost of Merchandise Sold	10,600	
		Merchandise Inventory		10,600
	21	Notes Receivable	18,000	
		Cash		18,000
	25	Cash	17,523	
		Sales Discounts	177	
		Accounts Receivable—Pioneer Co.		17,700
July	21	Notes Receivable	18,000	
		Cash	120	
		Notes Receivable		18,000
		Interest Revenue		120
		($18,000 × 8% × 30/360).		
Sept.	19	Cash	18,270	
		Notes Receivable		18,000
		Interest Revenue		270
		($18,000 × 9% × 60/360).		
	22	Accounts Receivable—Wycoff Co.	20,000	
		Sales		20,000

Prob. 9–6B (Concluded)

Sept.	22	Cost of Merchandise Sold	12,000	
		Merchandise Inventory		12,000
Oct.	14	Notes Receivable	20,000	
		Accounts Receivable—Wycoff Co.		20,000
Nov.	13	Accounts Receivable—Wycoff Co.	20,100	
		Notes Receivable		20,000
		Interest Revenue		100
		($20,000 × 6% × 30/360).		
Dec.	28	Cash	20,301	
		Accounts Receivable—Wycoff Co.		20,100
		Interest Revenue		201
		($20,100 × 8% × 45/360).		

CASES & PROJECTS

CP 9–1

By computing interest using a 365-day year for depository accounts (liabilities), Bev is minimizing interest expense to the bank. By computing interest using a 360-day year for loans (assets), Bev is maximizing interest revenue to the bank. However, federal legislation (Truth in Lending Act) requires banks to compute interest on a 365-day year. Hence, Bev is behaving in an unprofessional manner.

CP 9–2

1.

Year	a. Addition to Allowance for Doubtful Accounts	b. Accounts Written Off During Year
2011	$20,000	$15,000 ($20,000 – $5,000)
2012	22,000	18,750 ($5,000 + $22,000 – $8,250)
2013	24,000	22,050 ($8,250 + $24,000 – $10,200)
2014	25,500	21,300 ($10,200 + $25,500 – $14,400)

2. a. The estimate of 1/2 of 1% of credit sales may be too large, since the allowance for doubtful accounts has steadily increased each year. The increasing balance of the allowance for doubtful accounts may also be due to the failure to write off a large number of uncollectible accounts. These possibilities could be evaluated by examining the accounts in the accounts receivable subsidiary ledger for collectibility and comparing the result with the balance in the allowance for doubtful accounts.

Note to Instructors: Since the allowance for doubtful accounts increased by 188% [($14,400 – $5,000) ÷ $5,000], while sales have increased by 27.5% [($5,100,000 – $4,000,000) ÷ $4,000,000], the increase cannot be explained by an expanding volume of sales.

CP 9–2 (Concluded)

b. The balance of Allowance for Doubtful Accounts that should exist at December 31, 2014, can only be determined after all attempts have been made to collect the receivables on hand at December 31, 2014. However, the account balances at December 31, 2014, could be analyzed, perhaps using an aging schedule, to determine a reasonable amount of allowance and to determine accounts that should be written off. Also, past write-offs of uncollectible accounts could be analyzed in depth in order to develop a reasonable percentage for future adjusting entries, based on past history. Caution, however, must be exercised in using historical percentages. Specifically, inquiries should be made to determine whether any significant changes between prior years and the current year may have occurred, which might reduce the accuracy of the historical data. For example, a recent change in credit-granting policies or changes in the general economy (entering a recessionary period, for example) could reduce the usefulness of analyzing historical data.

Based on the preceding analyses, a recommendation to decrease the annual rate charged as an expense may be in order (perhaps Xtreme Co. is experiencing a lower rate of uncollectibles than is the industry average), or perhaps a change to the "estimate based on analysis of receivables" method may be appropriate.

CP 9–3

1. and 2.

	Year 2	Year 1
Net sales..........................	$50,272	$49,694
Accounts receivable............	$2,348	$2,020
Average accts. receivable.....	$2,184.0	$1,944.0
	[($2,348 + $2,020) ÷ 2]	[($2,020 + $1,868) ÷ 2]
Accts. receivable turnover....	23.0	25.6
	($50,272 ÷ $2,184.0)	($49,694 ÷ $1,944.0)
Average daily sales..............	$137.7	$136.1
	($50,272 ÷ 365)	($49,694 ÷ 365)
Days' sales in receivables.....	15.9	14.3
	($2,184.0 ÷ $137.7)	($1,944.0 ÷ $136.1)

3. The accounts receivable turnover indicates a decrease in the efficiency of collecting accounts receivable by decreasing from 25.6 to 23.0, an unfavorable trend. The days' sales in receivables increased from 14.3 days to 15.9, an unfavorable trend. Thus, based on (1) and (2), Best Buy has decreased its efficiency in the collection of receivables.

CP 9–3 (Concluded)

4. We assumed that the percentage of credit sales to total sales remains constant from one period to the next and no major changes in operations occurred between years. For example, if the percentage of credit sales to total sales is not similar or if the percentage changes between years, then the ratios would be distorted and, thus, not comparable. Also, any major changes in operations could distort the comparison between years.

CP 9–4

1. Year 2: 14.7 {$65,225 ÷ [($5,510 + $3,361) ÷ 2]}
    Year 1: 14.8 {$42,905 ÷ [($3,361 + $2,422) ÷ 2]}

2. Year 2: 24.8 days [($5,510 + $3,361) ÷ 2] = $4,435.5; [$4,435.5 ÷ ($65,225 ÷ 365)]
    Year 1: 24.6 days [($3,361 + $2,422) ÷ 2] = $2,891.5; [$2,891.5 ÷ ($42,905 ÷ 365)]

3. The accounts receivable turnover indicates a slight decrease in the efficiency of collecting accounts receivable by decreasing from 14.8 to 14.7, an unfavorable trend. The days' sales in receivables increased from 24.6 days to 24.8, an unfavorable trend. Before reaching a more definitive conclusion, the ratios should be compared with industry averages and similar firms.

CP 9–5

1. and 2.

	Year 2	Year 1
Net sales..................................	$77,946	$71,422
Accounts receivable...................	$1,321	$1,205
Average accts. receivable............	$1,263.0	$1,107.0
	[($1,321 + $1,205) ÷ 2]	[($1,205 + $1,009) ÷ 2]
Accts. receivable turnover...........	61.7	64.5
	($77,946 ÷ $1,263.0)	($71,422 ÷ $1,107.0)
Average daily sales.....................	$213.6	$195.7
	($77,946 ÷ 365)	($71,422 ÷ 365)
Days' sales in receivables...........	5.9	5.7
	($1,263.0 ÷ $213.6)	($1,107.0 ÷ $195.7)

3. The accounts receivable turnover indicates a decrease in the efficiency of collecting accounts receivable by decreasing from 64.5 to 61.7, an unfavorable trend. The days' sales in receivables increased from 5.7 days to 5.9 days, an unfavorable trend. Before reaching a more definitive conclusion, the ratios should be compared with industry averages and similar firms.

4. Costco's accounts receivable turnover would normally be higher than that of a typical manufacturing company such as H.J. Heinz Company. This is because many of Costco's customers charge their purchases to American Express cards or pay with checks or cash. In contrast, the customers of H.J. Heinz Company are other businesses that pay their accounts receivable on a less timely basis. For a recent year, the accounts receivable turnover ratio for H.J. Heinz was 9.3 (see Ex. 9–27).

Note: Costco does not accept MasterCard or Visa, but only American Express.

CP 9–6

1. *Note to Instructors:* The turnover ratios will vary over time. Recently, the various turnover ratios (rounded to one decimal place) were as follows:

Alcoa Inc.	10.3
AutoZone, Inc.	58.4
Barnes & Noble, Inc.	54.5
Caterpillar	2.6
The Coca-Cola Company	8.6
Delta Air Lines	18.0
The Home Depot	66.4
IBM	3.4
Kroger	93.7
Procter & Gamble	12.0
Walmart	91.4
Whirlpool Corporation	7.0

Based on the above, the companies can be categorized as follows:

Accounts Receivable Turnover Ratio

Below 15	Above 15
Alcoa Inc.	AutoZone, Inc.
Caterpillar	Barnes & Noble, Inc.
The Coca-Cola Company	Delta Air Lines
IBM	The Home Depot
Procter & Gamble	Kroger
Whirlpool Corporation	Walmart

2. The companies with accounts receivable turnover ratios above 15 are all companies selling primarily to individual consumers. In contrast, companies with turnover ratios below 15 are companies selling primarily to other businesses. Generally, we would expect companies selling to individual consumers to have higher turnover ratios, since many customers will charge their purchases on credit cards. In contrast, companies selling to other businesses normally allow a credit period of at least 30 days or longer.

CHAPTER 10
FIXED ASSETS AND INTANGIBLE ASSETS

DISCUSSION QUESTIONS

1. **a.** Property, plant, and equipment or Fixed assets
    b. Current assets (merchandise inventory)

2. Real estate acquired as speculation should be listed in the balance sheet under the caption "Investments," below the Current Assets section.

3. $1,100,000

4. Capital expenditures include the cost of acquiring fixed assets and the cost of improving an asset. These costs are recorded by increasing (debiting) a fixed asset account. Capital expenditures also include the costs of extraordinary repairs, which are recorded by decreasing (debiting) the asset's accumulated depreciation account. Revenue expenditures are recorded as expenses and are costs that benefit only the current period and are incurred for normal maintenance and repairs of fixed assets.

5. Capital expenditure

6. 12 years

7. **a.** No
    b. No

8. **a.** An accelerated depreciation method is most appropriate for situations in which the decline in productivity or earning power of the asset is proportionately greater in the early years of use than in later years, and the repairs tend to increase with the age of the asset.

    b. An accelerated depreciation method reduces income tax payable to the IRS in the earlier periods of an asset's life. Thus, cash is freed up in the earlier periods to be used for other business purposes.

    c. MACRS was enacted by the Tax Reform Act of 1986. It is used for depreciation for fixed assets acquired after 1986.

9. **a.** No, the accumulated depreciation for an asset cannot exceed the cost of the asset. To do so would create a negative book value, which is meaningless.

    b. The cost and accumulated depreciation should be removed from the accounts when the asset is no longer useful and is removed from service. Presumably, the asset will then be sold, traded in, or discarded.

10. **a.** Over the shorter of its legal life or years of usefulness.
    b. Expense as incurred.
    c. Goodwill should not be amortized, but written down when impaired.

PRACTICE EXERCISES

PE 10–1A

Aug.		7	Delivery Truck	1,675	
			Cash		1,675
		7	Repairs and Maintenance Expense	40	
			Cash		40

PE 10–1B

Feb.		14	Accumulated Depreciation—Delivery Van	2,300	
			Cash		2,300
		14	Delivery Van	450	
			Cash		450

PE 10–2A

a. $415,000 ($440,000 – $25,000)

b.   12.5% = (1/8)

c. $51,875 ($415,000 × 12.5%), or ($415,000 ÷ 8 years)

PE 10–2B

a. $1,150,000 ($1,450,000 – $300,000)

b.   10% = (1/10)

c. $115,000 ($1,150,000 × 10%), or ($1,150,000 ÷ 10 years)

PE 10–3A

a. $236,000 ($275,000 – $39,000)

b. $5.90 per hour ($236,000 ÷ 40,000 hours)

c. $15,694 (2,660 hours × $5.90)

PE 10–3B

a. $57,000 ($69,000 – $12,000)

b. $0.19 per mile ($57,000 ÷ 300,000 miles)

c. $14,630 (77,000 miles × $0.19)

PE 10–4A

a.   12.5% = [(1/16) × 2]

b. $35,000 ($280,000 × 12.5%)

PE 10–4B

a.   5% = [(1/40) × 2]

b. $68,750 ($1,375,000 × 5%)

PE 10–5A

a. $5,500 [($82,000 – $16,000) ÷ 12]

b. $43,500 [$82,000 – ($5,500 × 7)]

c. $5,250 [($43,500 – $12,000) ÷ 6]

PE 10–5B

a. $10,350 [($180,000 – $14,400) ÷ 16]

b. $76,500 [$180,000 – ($10,350 × 10)]

c. $8,250 [($76,500 – $10,500) ÷ 8]

PE 10–6A

a. $28,000 [($465,000 – $45,000) ÷ 15]

b. $6,000 loss {$235,000 – [$465,000 – ($28,000 × 8)]}

c.

Cash	235,000	
Accumulated Depreciation—Equipment	224,000	
Loss on Sale of Equipment	6,000	
Equipment		465,000

PE 10–6B

a. $75,000 = $600,000 × [(1/16) × 2)] = $600,000 × 12.5%

b. $20,625 gain, computed as follows:

Cost...	$600,000
Less: First-year depreciation.........................	(75,000)
Second-year depreciation....................	(65,625) [($600,000 – $75,000) × 12.5%]
Book value at end of second year....................	$459,375

Gain on sale ($480,000 – $459,375) = $20,625

c.

Cash	480,000	
Accumulated Depreciation—Equipment	140,625	
Equipment		600,000
Gain on Sale of Equipment		20,625

PE 10–7A

a. $0.30 per ton = $127,500,000 ÷ 425,000,000 tons

b. $12,600,000 = 42,000,000 tons × $0.30 per ton

c.

Dec.	31	Depletion Expense	12,600,000	
		Accumulated Depletion		12,600,000
		Depletion of mineral deposit.		

PE 10–7B

a. $1.04 per ton = $494,000,000 ÷ 475,000,000 tons

b. $32,760,000 = 31,500,000 tons × $1.04 per ton

c.

Dec.	31	Depletion Expense	32,760,000	
		Accumulated Depletion		32,760,000
		Depletion of mineral deposit.		

PE 10–8A

a.	Dec.	31	Loss from Impaired Goodwill	4,000,000	
			Goodwill		4,000,000
			Impaired goodwill.		

b.	Dec.	31	Amortization Expense—Patents	25,000	
			Patents		25,000
			Amortized patent rights		
			[($900,000 ÷ 15) × 5/12].		

PE 10–8B

a.	Dec.	31	Loss from Impaired Goodwill	6,000,000	
			Goodwill		6,000,000
			Impaired goodwill.		

b.	Dec.	31	Amortization Expense—Patents	93,750	
			Patents		93,750
			Amortized patent rights		
			[($1,500,000 ÷ 12) × 9/12].		

PE 10–9A

a. **Fixed Asset Turnover:**

	2014	2013
Net sales..................................	$5,510,000	$4,880,000
Fixed assets:		
Beginning of year.................	$1,600,000	$1,450,000
End of year.........................	$2,200,000	$1,600,000
Average fixed assets.................	$1,900,000	$1,525,000
	[($1,600,000 + $2,200,000) ÷ 2]	[($1,450,000 + $1,600,000) ÷ 2]
Fixed asset turnover.................	2.9	3.2
	($5,510,000 ÷ $1,900,000)	($4,880,000 ÷ $1,525,000)

b. The decrease in the fixed asset turnover ratio from 3.2 to 2.9 indicates an unfavorable trend in the efficiency of using fixed assets to generate sales.

PE 10–9B

a. Fixed Asset Turnover:

	2014	2013
Revenue	$1,668,000	$1,125,000
Fixed assets:		
Beginning of year	$ 670,000	$ 580,000
End of year	$ 720,000	$ 670,000
Average fixed assets	$ 695,000	$ 625,000
	[($670,000 + $720,000) ÷ 2]	[($580,000 + $670,000) ÷ 2]
Fixed asset turnover	2.4	1.8
	($1,668,000 ÷ $695,000)	($1,125,000 ÷ $625,000)

b. The increase in the fixed asset turnover ratio from 1.8 to 2.4 indicates a favorable trend in the efficiency of using fixed assets to generate sales.

EXERCISES

Ex. 10–1

a.   New printing press: 1, 2, 3, 5, 6

b.   Used printing press: 7, 8, 9, 11

Ex. 10–2

a.   Yes. All expenditures incurred for the purpose of making the land suitable for its intended use should be debited to the land account.

b.   No. Land is not depreciated.

Ex. 10–3

Initial cost of land ($100,000 + $700,000)...............................			$800,000
Plus:	Legal fees..	$ 5,000	
	Delinquent taxes...	18,500	
	Demolition of building...	12,000	35,500
			$835,500
Less salvage of materials...			4,000
Cost of land...			$831,500

Ex. 10–4

Capital expenditures: 3, 4, 5, 6, 7, 9, 10

Revenue expenditures: 1, 2, 8

Ex. 10–5

Capital expenditures: 2, 3, 4, 8, 9, 10

Revenue expenditures: 1, 5, 6, 7

Ex. 10–6

Mar.	20	Accumulated Depreciation—Delivery Truck	1,890	
		Cash		1,890
June	11	Delivery Truck	1,350	
		Cash		1,350
Nov.	30	Repairs and Maintenance Expense	55	
		Cash		55

Ex. 10–7

a. No. The $44,500,000 represents the original cost of the equipment. Its replacement cost, which may be more or less than $44,500,000, is not reported in the financial statements.

b. No. The $29,800,000 is the accumulation of the past depreciation charges on the equipment. The recognition of depreciation expense has no relationship to the cash account or accumulation of cash funds.

Ex. 10–8

(a) 25% (1/4), (b) 12.5% (1/8), (c) 10% (1/10), (d) 6.25% (1/16), (e) 4% (1/25), (f) 2.5% (1/40), (g) 2% (1/50)

Ex. 10–9

$3,950 [($60,000 − $12,600) ÷ 12]

Ex. 10–10

$$\frac{\$214,000 - \$30,000}{50,000 \text{ hours}} = \$3.68 \text{ depreciation per hour}$$

175 hours at $3.68 = $644 depreciation for January

Ex. 10–11

a.   Depreciation Rate per Mile:

Truck #1   ($80,000 – $15,000)   ÷ 250,000 = $0.26
Truck #2   ($54,000 – $6,000)   ÷ 300,000 = $0.16
Truck #3   ($72,900 – $10,900)   ÷ 200,000 = $0.31
Truck #4   ($90,000 – $22,800)   ÷ 240,000 = $0.28

Truck No.	Rate per Mile	Miles Operated	Credit to Accumulated Depreciation
1	$0.26	21,000	$ 5,460
2	0.16	33,500	5,360
3	0.31	8,000	1,860*
4	0.28	22,500	6,300
Total..			$18,980

* Mileage depreciation of $2,480 (31 cents × 8,000) is limited to $1,860, which reduces the book value of the truck to $10,900, its residual value.

b.

Depreciation Expense—Trucks	18,980	
Accumulated Depreciation—Trucks		18,980
Truck depreciation.		

Ex. 10–12

First Year	Second Year
a. 5% of $90,000 = $4,500	5% of $90,000 = $4,500
or	or
$90,000 ÷ 20 = $4,500	$90,000 ÷ 20 = $4,500
b. 10% of $90,000 = $9,000	10% of ($90,000 – $9,000) = $8,100

Ex. 10–13

a.   4% of ($240,000 – $30,000) = $8,400 or [($240,000 – $30,000)/25]

b.   Year 1: 8% of $240,000 = $19,200
Year 2: 8% of ($240,000 – $19,200) = $17,664

Ex. 10–14

a.   Year 1: 9/12 × [($36,000 – $6,000) ÷ 10] = $2,250

     Year 2: ($36,000 – $6,000) ÷ 10 = $3,000

b.   Year 1: 9/12 × 20% of $36,000 = $5,400

     Year 2: 20% of ($36,000 – $5,400) = $6,120

Ex. 10–15

a. $17,250 [($780,000 – $90,000) ÷ 40]

b. $366,000 [$780,000 – ($17,250 × 24 yrs.)]

c. $29,600 [($366,000 – $70,000) ÷ 10 yrs.]

Ex. 10–16

a.

Apr.	30	Carpet	18,000	
		Cash		18,000

b.

Dec.	31	Depreciation Expense	800	
		Accumulated Depreciation—Carpet		800
		Carpet depreciation		
		[($18,000 ÷ 15 years) × 8/12].		

Ex. 10–17

a.

Cost of equipment...	$420,000
Accumulated depreciation at December 31, 2014	
(4 years at $26,000* per year)...	104,000
Book value at December 31, 2014...	$316,000

  * ($420,000 – $30,000) ÷ 15 = $26,000

b.

(1)	Depreciation Expense—Equipment		19,500	
	Accumulated Depreciation—Equipment			19,500
	Equipment depreciation ($26,000 × 9/12 = $19,500).			
(2)	Cash		275,000	
	Accumulated Depreciation—Equipment*		123,500	
	Loss on Sale of Equipment		21,500	
	Equipment			420,000

  * $104,000 + $19,500 = $123,500

Ex. 10–18

a. 2011 depreciation expense: $55,800 [($714,000 – $44,400) ÷ 12]

2012 depreciation expense: $55,800

2013 depreciation expense: $55,800

b. $546,600 [$714,000 – ($55,800 × 3)]

c.

Cash	525,000	
Accumulated Depreciation—Equipment	167,400	
Loss on Sale of Equipment	21,600	
Equipment		714,000

d.

Cash	560,000	
Accumulated Depreciation—Equipment	167,400	
Equipment		714,000
Gain on Sale of Equipment		13,400

Ex. 10–19

a. $21,750,000 ÷ 15,000,000 tons = $1.45 depletion per ton

3,600,000 tons × $1.45 = $5,220,000 depletion expense

b.

Depletion Expense	5,220,000	
Accumulated Depletion		5,220,000
Depletion of mineral deposit.		

Ex. 10–20

a. ($480,000 ÷ 8) + ($80,000 ÷ 5) = $76,000 total patent expense

b.

Amortization Expense—Patents	76,000	
Patents		76,000
Amortized patent rights ($60,000 + $16,000).		

Ex. 10–21

a.   **Property, Plant, and Equipment (in millions):**

	Current Year	Preceding Year
Land and buildings...	$1,471	$ 955
Machinery, equipment, and internal-use software................	3,589	1,932
Office furniture and equipment...	144	115
Other fixed assets related to leases.....................................	2,030	1,665
	$7,234	$4,667
Less accumulated depreciation and amortization.................	2,466	1,713
Book value..	$4,768	$2,954

A comparison of the book values of the current and preceding years indicates that they increased. A comparison of the total cost and accumulated depreciation reveals that Apple purchased $2,567 million ($7,234 – $4,667) of additional fixed assets, which was offset by the additional depreciation expense of $753 million ($2,466 – $1,713) taken during the current year.

b.   We would expect Apple's book value of fixed assets to increase during the year as its sales increase. Although additional depreciation expense will reduce the book value, most companies, such as Apple, invest in new assets in an amount that is at least equal to the depreciation expense. However, during periods of economic downturn, companies purchase fewer fixed assets, and the book value of their fixed assets may decline.

Ex. 10–22

1.   Fixed assets should be reported at cost and not replacement cost.

2.   Land does not depreciate.

3.   Patents and goodwill are intangible assets that should be listed in a separate section following the Fixed Assets section. Patents should be reported at their net book values (cost less amortization to date). Goodwill should not be amortized, but should be only written down upon impairment.

Ex. 10–23

a.   Fixed Asset Turnover Ratio = $\dfrac{\text{Revenue}}{\text{Average Book Value of Fixed Assets}}$

Fixed Asset Turnover Ratio = $\dfrac{\$106,565}{(\$87,711 + \$91,985) \div 2}$

Fixed Asset Turnover Ratio = 1.19

b.   Verizon earns $1.19 revenue for every dollar of fixed assets. This is a low fixed asset turnover ratio, reflecting the high fixed asset intensity in a telecommunications company. The industry average fixed asset turnover ratio is slightly lower at 1.10. Thus, Verizon is using its fixed assets more efficiently than the industry as a whole.

Ex. 10–24

a.   Best Buy: 12.74 ($50,272 ÷ $3,947)

RadioShack: 16.09 ($4,473 ÷ $278)

b.   RadioShack's fixed asset turnover ratio of 16.09 is higher than Best Buy's fixed asset turnover ratio of 12.74. Thus, RadioShack is generating $3.35 ($16.09 – $12.74) more revenue for each dollar of fixed assets than is Best Buy. On this basis, RadioShack is managing its fixed assets more efficiently than is Best Buy.

Appendix Ex. 10–25

a. Price (fair market value) of new equipment............................		$275,000
Trade-in allowance of old equipment......................................		90,000
Cash paid on the date of exchange.......................................		$185,000
b. Fair market value (trade-in allowance) of old equipment...........		$ 90,000
Less book value of old equipment..		68,000
Gain on exchange of equipment..		$ 22,000
or		
Price (fair market value) of new equipment............................		$275,000
Less assets given up in exchange:		
Book value of old equipment..	$ 68,000	
Cash paid on the exchange..	185,000	253,000
Gain on exchange of equipment..		$ 22,000

Appendix Ex. 10–26

a.	Price (fair market value) of new equipment............................	$275,000
	Trade-in allowance of old equipment....................................	90,000
	Cash paid on the date of exchange.......................................	$185,000

b.	Fair market value (trade-in allowance) of old equipment...........	$ 90,000
	Less book value of old equipment..	108,500
	Gain on exchange of equipment..	$ (18,500)

or

Price (fair market value) of new equipment............................			$275,000
Less assets given up in exchange:			
Book value of old equipment...		$108,500	
Cash paid on the exchange...		185,000	293,500
Loss on exchange of equipment..			$ (18,500)

Appendix Ex. 10–27

a.

Depreciation Expense—Equipment	6,000	
Accumulated Depreciation—Equipment		6,000
Equipment depreciation ($12,000 × 6/12).		

b.

Accumulated Depreciation—Equipment	126,000	
Equipment	220,000	
Loss on Exchange of Equipment	9,000	
Equipment		180,000
Cash		175,000

Appendix Ex. 10–28

a.

Depreciation Expense—Trucks	5,250	
Accumulated Depreciation—Trucks		5,250
Truck depreciation ($7,000 × 9/12).		

b.

Accumulated Depreciation—Trucks	40,250	
Trucks	75,000	
Trucks		56,000
Cash		51,000
Gain on Exchange of Trucks		8,250

PROBLEMS

Prob. 10–1A

1.

Item	Land	Land Improvements	Building	Other Accounts
a.	$ 2,500			
b.	340,000			
c.	15,500			
d.	5,000			
e.*	(4,000)			
f.	29,000			
g.			$ 60,000	
h.			6,000	
i.	12,000			
j.*				$(900,000)
k.				5,500
l.		$32,000		
m.		11,000		
n.		2,000		
o.				2,500
p.*				(7,500)
q.			800,000	
r.			34,500	
s.*			(500)	
2.	$400,000	$45,000	$900,000	

* Receipt.

3. Since land used as a plant site does not lose its ability to provide services, it is not depreciated. However, land improvements do lose their ability to provide services as time passes and are therefore depreciated.

4. Since Land Improvements are depreciated, depreciation expense of $1,200 ($12,000 × 1/20 × 2) would be overstated and net income would be understated by $1,200 on the income statement. On the balance sheet, Land would be understated by $12,000, Land Improvements would be overstated by $10,800 ($12,000 – $1,200), and Owner's Capital would be understated by $1,200.

Prob. 10–2A

1.

	Depreciation Expense		
Year	a. Straight-Line Method	b. Units-of-Output Method	c. Double-Declining-Balance Method
2012	$ 40,500	$ 58,050	$ 90,000
2013	40,500	35,775	30,000
2014	40,500	27,675	1,500
Total	$121,500	$121,500	$121,500

Calculations:

Straight-line method:

($135,000 − $13,500) ÷ 3 = $40,500 each year

Units-of-output method:

($135,000 − $13,500) ÷ 18,000 hours = $6.75 per hour

2012:   8,600 hours × $6.75 = $58,050
2013:   5,300 hours × $6.75 = $35,775
2014:   4,100 hours × $6.75 = $27,675

Double-declining-balance method:

2012: $135,000 × 2/3 = $90,000
2013:   ($135,000 − $90,000) × 2/3 = $30,000
2014:   ($135,000 − $90,000 − $30,000 − $13,500*) = $1,500

* Book value should not be reduced below the residual value of $13,500.

2. The double-declining-balance method yields the most depreciation expense in 2012 of $90,000.

3. Over the three-year life of the equipment, all three depreciation methods yield the same total depreciation, $121,500, which is the cost of the equipment of $135,000 less the residual value of $13,500.

Prob. 10–3A

a.   **Straight-line method:**

2012:	[($270,000 – $9,000) ÷ 3] × 9/12..	**$65,250**
2013:	($270,000 – $9,000) ÷ 3...	87,000
2014:	($270,000 – $9,000) ÷ 3...	87,000
2015:	[($270,000 – $9,000) ÷ 3] × 3/12..	21,750

b.   **Units-of-output method:**

2012:	7,500 hours × $14.50*..	**$108,750**
2013:	5,500 hours × $14.50..	79,750
2014:	4,000 hours × $14.50..	58,000
2015:	1,000 hours × $14.50..	14,500

* ($270,000 – $9,000) ÷ 18,000 hours = $14.50 per hour

c.   **Double-declining-balance method:**

2012:	$270,000 × 2/3 × 9/12...	**$135,000**
2013:	($270,000 – $135,000) × 2/3..	90,000
2014:	($270,000 – $135,000 – $90,000) × 2/3.....................................	30,000
2015:	($270,000 – $135,000 – $90,000 – $30,000 – $9,000*)...................	6,000

* Book value should not be reduced below $9,000, the residual value.

Prob. 10–4A

1.

Year		Depreciation Expense	Accumulated Depreciation, End of Year	Book Value, End of Year
a.	1..	$142,000 *	$142,000	$658,000
	2..	142,000	284,000	516,000
	3..	142,000	426,000	374,000
	4..	142,000	568,000	232,000
	5..	142,000	710,000	90,000

* [($800,000 – $90,000) ÷ 5]

			Depreciation Expense	Accumulated Depreciation, End of Year	Book Value, End of Year
b.	1	[$800,000 × (1/5) × 2].....................	$320,000	$320,000	$480,000
	2	[$480,000 × (1/5) × 2].....................	192,000	512,000	288,000
	3	[$288,000 × (1/5) × 2].....................	115,200	627,200	172,800
	4	[$172,800 × (1/5) × 2].....................	69,120	696,320	103,680
	5	($800,000 – $696,320 – $90,000)......	13,680 *	710,000	90,000

* Book value should not be reduced below $90,000, the residual value.

2.

Cash	135,000	
Accumulated Depreciation—Equipment	696,320	
Equipment		800,000
Gain on Sale of Equipment*		31,320

* $135,000 – $103,680

3.

Cash	88,750	
Accumulated Depreciation—Equipment	696,320	
Loss on Sale of Equipment*	14,930	
Equipment		800,000

* $103,680 – $88,750

Prob. 10–5A

2012					
Jan.	4	Delivery Truck		28,000	
		Cash			28,000
Nov.	2	Truck Repair Expense		675	
		Cash			675
Dec.	31	Depreciation Expense—Delivery Truck		14,000	
		Accum. Depreciation—Delivery Truck			14,000
		Delivery truck depreciation.			
		[$28,000 × (1/4 × 2)]			

2013					
Jan.	6	Delivery Truck		48,000	
		Cash			48,000
Apr.	1	Depreciation Expense—Delivery Truck		1,750	
		Accum. Depreciation—Delivery Truck			1,750
		Delivery truck depreciation.			
		[($28,000 – $14,000) × (1/4 × 2) × 3/12]			
	1	Accum. Depreciation—Delivery Truck		15,750	
		Cash		15,000	
		Delivery Truck			28,000
		Gain on Sale of Delivery Truck			2,750
June	11	Truck Repair Expense		450	
		Cash			450
Dec.	31	Depreciation Expense—Delivery Truck		19,200	
		Accum. Depreciation—Delivery Truck			19,200
		Delivery truck depreciation.			
		[$48,000 × (1/5 × 2)]			

Prob. 10–5A (Concluded)

2014					
July	1	Delivery Truck		54,000	
		Cash			54,000
Oct.	2	Depreciation Expense—Delivery Truck		8,640	
		Accum. Depreciation—Delivery Truck			8,640
		Delivery truck depreciation.			
		[($48,000 − $19,200) × (1/5 × 2) × 9/12]			
	2	Cash		16,750	
		Accum. Depreciation—Delivery Truck		27,840	
		Loss on Sale of Delivery Truck		3,410	
		Delivery Truck			48,000
Dec.	31	Depreciation Expense—Delivery Truck		6,750	
		Accum. Depreciation—Delivery Truck			6,750
		Delivery truck depreciation.			
		[$54,000 × (1/8 × 2) × 1/2]			

Prob. 10–6A

1. a. **$1,600,000 ÷ 5,000,000 board feet = $0.32 per board foot;**
      1,100,000 board feet × $0.32 per board foot = $352,000

   b. **Loss from impaired goodwill, $3,750,000**

   c. **$6,600,000 ÷ 12 years = $550,000;**
      3/4 of $550,000 = $412,500

2. a.

Depletion Expense	352,000	
Accumulated Depletion		352,000
Depletion of timber rights.		

   b.

Loss from Impaired Goodwill	3,750,000	
Goodwill		3,750,000
Impaired goodwill.		

   c.

Amortization Expense—Patents	412,500	
Patents		412,500
Patent amortization.		

Prob. 10–1B

1.

Item	Land	Land Improvements	Building	Other Accounts
a.	$ 3,600			
b.	780,000			
c.	23,400			
d.	15,000			
e.			$ 75,000	
f.	10,000			
g.*	(3,400)			
h.	18,000			
i.			8,400	
j.*				$(800,000)
k.	13,400			
l.				3,000
m.				2,000
n.		$14,000		
o.		21,600		
p.			40,000	
q.*				(4,500)
r.			800,000	
s.*			(1,400)	
2.	**$860,000**	**$35,600**	**$922,000**	

* Receipt.

3. Since land used as a plant site does not lose its ability to provide services, it is not depreciated. However, land improvements do lose their ability to provide services as time passes and are therefore depreciated.

4. Since Land Improvements are depreciated, depreciation expense of $4,320 ($21,600 × 1/10 × 2) would be understated and net income would be overstated by $4,320 on the income statement. On the balance sheet, Land would be overstated by $21,600, Land Improvements would be understated by $17,280 ($21,600 – $4,320), and Owner's Capital would be overstated by $4,320.

Prob. 10–2B

1.

Depreciation Expense

Year	a. Straight-Line Method	b. Units-of-Output Method	c. Double-Declining-Balance Method
2013	$ 71,250	$102,600	$160,000
2014	71,250	91,200	80,000
2015	71,250	62,700	40,000
2016	71,250	28,500	5,000
Total	$285,000	$285,000	$285,000

Calculations:

Straight-line method:

($320,000 – $35,000) ÷ 4 = $71,250 each year

Units-of-output method:

($320,000 – $35,000) ÷ 20,000 hours = $14.25 per hour

2013: 7,200 hours × $14.25 = $102,600
2014: 6,400 hours × $14.25 = $91,200
2015: 4,400 hours × $14.25 = $62,700
2016: 2,000 hours × $14.25 = $28,500

Double-declining-balance method:

2013: $320,000 × [(1/4) × 2] = $160,000
2014: ($320,000 – $160,000) × [(1/4) × 2] = $80,000
2015: ($320,000 – $160,000 – $80,000) × [(1/4) × 2] = $40,000
2016: ($320,000 – $160,000 – $80,000 – $40,000 – $35,000*) = $5,000

* Book value should not be reduced below the residual value of $35,000.

2. The double-declining-balance method yields the most depreciation expense in 2013 of $160,000.

3. Over the four-year life of the equipment, all three depreciation methods yield the same total depreciation, $285,000, which is the cost of the equipment of $320,000 less the residual value of $35,000.

Prob. 10–3B

a. Straight-line method:

2012:	[($108,000 – $7,200) ÷ 3] × 3/12...	$ 8,400
2013:	[($108,000 – $7,200) ÷ 3]...	33,600
2014:	[($108,000 – $7,200) ÷ 3]...	33,600
2015:	[($108,000 – $7,200) ÷ 3] × 9/12...	25,200

b. Units-of-output method:

2012:	1,350 hours × $8.40*..	$11,340
2013:	4,200 hours × $8.40...	35,280
2014:	3,650 hours × $8.40...	30,660
2015:	2,800 hours × $8.40...	23,520

* ($108,000 – $7,200) ÷ 12,000 hours = $8.40 per hour

c. Double-declining-balance method:

2012:	$108,000 × 2/3 × 3/12..	$18,000
2013:	($108,000 – $18,000) × 2/3...	60,000
2014:	($108,000 – $18,000 – $60,000) × 2/3..	20,000
2015:	($108,000 – $18,000 – $60,000 – $20,000 – $7,200*)...........................	2,800

* Book value should not be reduced below $7,200, the residual value.

Prob. 10–4B

1.

Year	Depreciation Expense	Accumulated Depreciation, End of Year	Book Value, End of Year
a. 1...	$25,625*	$ 25,625	$84,375
2...	25,625	51,250	58,750
3...	25,625	76,875	33,125
4...	25,625	102,500	7,500

* [($110,000 – $7,500) ÷ 4]

b.	1 [$110,000 × (1/4) × 2].........................	$55,000	$ 55,000	$55,000
	2 [$55,000 × (1/4) × 2].........................	27,500	82,500	27,500
	3 [$27,500 × (1/4) × 2].........................	13,750	96,250	13,750
	4 ($110,000 – $96,250 – $7,500).............	6,250*	102,500	7,500

* Book value should not be reduced below $7,500, the residual value.

2.

Cash	18,000	
Accumulated Depreciation—Equipment	96,250	
Equipment		110,000
Gain on Sale of Equipment*		4,250

* $18,000 – $13,750

3.

Cash	10,500	
Accumulated Depreciation—Equipment	96,250	
Loss on Sale of Equipment*	3,250	
Equipment		110,000

* $13,750 – $10,500

Prob. 10–5B

2012				
Jan.	8	Delivery Truck	24,000	
		Cash		24,000
Mar.	7	Truck Repair Expense	900	
		Cash		900
Dec.	31	Depreciation Expense—Delivery Truck	12,000	
		Accum. Depreciation—Delivery Truck		12,000
		Delivery truck depreciation.		
		[$24,000 × (1/4 × 2)]		

2013				
Jan.	9	Delivery Truck	50,000	
		Cash		50,000
Feb.	28	Truck Repair Expense	250	
		Cash		250
Apr.	30	Depreciation Expense—Delivery Truck	2,000	
		Accum. Depreciation—Delivery Truck		2,000
		Delivery truck depreciation.		
		[($24,000 – $12,000) × (1/4 × 2) × 4/12]		
	30	Accum. Depreciation—Delivery Truck	14,000	
		Cash	9,500	
		Loss on Sale of Delivery Truck	500	
		Delivery Truck		24,000
Dec.	31	Depreciation Expense—Delivery Truck	12,500	
		Accum. Depreciation—Delivery Truck		12,500
		Delivery truck depreciation.		
		[$50,000 × (1/8 × 2)]		

Prob. 10–5B (Concluded)

2014					
Sept.	1	Delivery Truck		58,500	
		Cash			58,500
	4	Depreciation Expense—Delivery Truck		6,250	
		Accum. Depreciation—Delivery Truck			6,250
		Delivery truck depreciation.			
		[($50,000 – $12,500) × (1/8 × 2) × 8/12]			
	4	Cash		36,000	
		Accum. Depreciation—Delivery Truck		18,750	
		Delivery Truck			50,000
		Gain on Sale of Delivery Truck			4,750
Dec.	31	Depreciation Expense—Delivery Truck		3,900	
		Accum. Depreciation—Delivery Truck			3,900
		Delivery truck depreciation.			
		[$58,500 × (1/10 × 2) × 4/12]			

Prob. 10–6B

1.   a.   **Loss from impaired goodwill, $3,400,000**

     b.   **$4,800,000 ÷ 8 years = $600,000;**
          1/4 of $600,000 = $150,000

     c.   **$2,975,000 ÷ 12,500,000 board feet = $0.238 per board foot;**
          4,150,000 board feet × $0.238 per board foot = $987,700

2.   a.

Loss from Impaired Goodwill	3,400,000	
Goodwill		3,400,000
Impaired goodwill.		

     b.

Amortization Expense—Patents	150,000	
Patents		150,000
Patent amortization.		

     c.

Depletion Expense	987,700	
Accumulated Depletion		987,700
Depletion of timber rights.		

CASES & PROJECTS

CP 10–1

It is considered unprofessional for employees to use company assets for personal reasons, because such use reduces the useful life of the assets for normal business purposes. Thus, it is unethical for Dave Elliott to use Lyric Consulting Co.'s computers and laser printers to service his part-time accounting business, even on an after-hours basis. In addition, it is improper for Dave's clients to call him during regular working hours. Such calls may interrupt or interfere with Dave's ability to carry out his assigned duties for Lyric Consulting Co.

CP 10–2

You should explain to Nolan and Stacy that it is acceptable to maintain two sets of records for tax and financial reporting purposes. This can happen when a company uses one method for financial statement purposes, such as straight-line depreciation, and another method for tax purposes, such as MACRS depreciation. This should not be surprising, since the methods for taxes and financial statements are established by two different groups with different objectives. That is, tax laws and related accounting methods are established by Congress. The Internal Revenue Service then applies the laws and, in some cases, issues interpretations of the law and congressional intent. The primary objective of the tax laws is to generate revenue in an equitable manner for government use. Generally accepted accounting principles, on the other hand, are established primarily by the Financial Accounting Standards Board. The objective of generally accepted accounting principles is the preparation and reporting of true economic conditions and results of operations of business entities.

You might note, however, that companies are required in their tax returns to reconcile differences in accounting methods. For example, income reported on the company's financial statements must be reconciled with taxable income.

Finally, you might also indicate to Nolan and Stacy that even generally accepted accounting principles allow for alternative methods of accounting for the same transactions or economic events. For example, a company could use straight-line depreciation for some assets and double-declining-balance depreciation for other assets.

CP 10–3

1. a. **Straight-line method:**

2012:	($400,000 ÷ 5) × 1/2	$40,000
2013:	($400,000 ÷ 5)	80,000
2014:	($400,000 ÷ 5)	80,000
2015:	($400,000 ÷ 5)	80,000
2016:	($400,000 ÷ 5)	80,000
2017:	($400,000 ÷ 5) × 1/2	40,000

   b. **MACRS:**

2012:	($400,000 × 20%)	$ 80,000
2013:	($400,000 × 32%)	128,000
2014:	($400,000 × 19.2%)	76,800
2015:	($400,000 × 11.5%)	46,000
2016:	($400,000 × 11.5%)	46,000
2017:	($400,000 × 5.8%)	23,200

CP 10–3 (Continued)

2.   a.   Straight-line method:

			Year			
	2012	2013	2014	2015	2016	2017
Income before depreciation..........	$750,000	$750,000	$750,000	$750,000	$750,000	$750,000
Depreciation expense...................	40,000	80,000	80,000	80,000	80,000	40,000
Income before income tax............	$710,000	$670,000	$670,000	$670,000	$670,000	$710,000
Income tax...................................	284,000	268,000	268,000	268,000	268,000	284,000
Net income..................................	$426,000	$402,000	$402,000	$402,000	$402,000	$426,000

b.   MACRS:

			Year			
	2012	2013	2014	2015	2016	2017
Income before depreciation..........	$750,000	$750,000	$750,000	$750,000	$750,000	$750,000
Depreciation expense...................	80,000	128,000	76,800	46,000	46,000	23,200
Income before income tax............	$670,000	$622,000	$673,200	$704,000	$704,000	$726,800
Income tax...................................	268,000	248,800	269,280	281,600	281,600	290,720
Net income..................................	$402,000	$373,200	$403,920	$422,400	$422,400	$436,080

CP 10–3 (Concluded)

3.   For financial reporting purposes, Tim should select the method that provides the net income figure that best represents the results of operations.

Note to Instructors: The concept of matching revenues and expenses is discussed in Chapter 3. However, for income tax purposes, Tim should consider selecting the method that will minimize taxes. Based on the analyses in (2), both methods of depreciation will yield the same total amount of taxes over the useful life of the equipment. MACRS results in fewer taxes paid in the early years of useful life and more in the later years. For example, in 2012 the income tax expense using MACRS is $268,000, which is $16,000 ($284,000 – $268,000) less than the income tax expense using the straight-line depreciation of $284,000. Tuttle Construction Co. can invest such differences in the early years and earn income.

In some situations, it may be more beneficial for a taxpayer not to choose MACRS. These situations usually occur when a taxpayer is expected to be subject to a low tax rate in the early years of use of an asset and a higher tax rate in the later years of the asset's useful life. In this case, the taxpayer may be better off to defer the larger deductions to offset the higher tax rate.

CP 10–4

Note to Instructors: The purpose of this activity is to familiarize students with the procedures involved in acquiring a patent, a copyright, and a trademark. You may wish to divide the class into three groups to report back on patents, copyrights, and trademarks separately.

The following is some information on patents, copyrights, and trademarks that you may find helpful in your discussions.

Patents

A patent is requested by filing a written application at the relevant patent office. The person or company filing the application is referred to as "the applicant." The applicant may be the inventor or its assignee. The application contains a description of how to make and use the invention that must provide sufficient detail for a person skilled in the art (i.e., the relevant area of technology) to make and use the invention. In some countries, there are requirements for providing specific information such as the usefulness of the invention, the best mode of performing the invention known to the inventor, or the technical problem or problems solved by the invention. Drawings illustrating the invention may also be provided.

CP 10–4 (Concluded)

The application also includes one or more claims, although it is not always a requirement to submit these when first filing the application. The claims set out what the applicant is seeking to protect in that they define what the patent owner has a right to exclude others from making, using, or selling, as the case may be. In other words, the claims define what a patent covers or the "scope of protection."

After filing, an application is often referred to as "patent pending." While this term does not confer legal protection, and a patent cannot be enforced until granted, it serves to provide warning to potential infringers that if the patent is issued, they may be liable for damages.

Source: http://en.wikipedia.org/wiki/Patent#Application_and_prosecution.

Copyright

While copyright in the United States automatically attaches upon the creation of an original work of authorship, registration with the Copyright Office puts a copyright holder in a better position if litigation arises over the copyright. A copyright holder desiring to register his or her copyright should do the following:

1. Obtain and complete appropriate form.
2. Prepare clear rendition of material being submitted for copyright.
3. Send both documents to the U.S. Copyright Office in Washington, D.C.

Source: http://en.wikipedia.org/wiki/United_States_copyright_law#Procedural_issues.

Trademark

The law considers a trademark to be a form of property. Proprietary rights in relation to a trademark may be established through actual use in the marketplace, or through registration of the mark with the trademarks office (or "trademarks registry") of a particular jurisdiction. In some jurisdictions, trademark rights can be established through either or both means. Certain jurisdictions generally do not recognize trademarks rights arising through use. In the United States, the only way to qualify for a federally registered trademark is to first use the trademark in commerce. If trademark owners do not hold registrations for their marks in such jurisdictions, the extent to which they will be able to enforce their rights through trademark infringement proceedings will therefore be limited. In cases of dispute, this disparity of rights is often referred to as "first to file" as opposed to "first to use." Other countries such as Germany offer a limited amount of common law rights for unregistered marks where, to gain protection, the goods or services must occupy a highly significant position in the marketplace—where this could be 40% or more market share for sales in the particular class of goods or services.

Source: http://en.wikipedia.org/wiki/Trademark#Maintaining_rights.

CP 10–5

a.   Fixed Asset Turnover Ratio $= \dfrac{\text{Revenue}}{\text{Average Book Value of Fixed Assets}}$

Walmart: $\dfrac{\$421,849}{\$105,093} = 4.01$

Occidental Petroleum: $\dfrac{\$19,045}{\$33,837} = 0.56$

Comcast Corporation: $\dfrac{\$37,937}{\$23,685} = 1.60$

b.   The fixed asset turnover measures the amount of revenue earned per dollar of fixed assets. Walmart earns $4.01 of revenue for every dollar of fixed assets, while Occidental earns $0.56 and Comcast Corporation earns $1.60 in revenue for every dollar of fixed assets. Occidental and Comcast require more fixed assets to operate their businesses than does Walmart, for a given level of revenue volume.

Does this mean that Walmart is a better company? Not necessarily. Revenue is not the same as earnings. More likely, Walmart has a smaller profit margin than do Occidental and Comcast. Although not required by the exercise, the income from operations before interest and taxes as a percent of sales (operating margin) for the three companies is Occidental, 39.2%; Comcast, 21.8%; and Walmart, 6.1%. Thus, the difference between the fixed asset turnovers seems reasonable. Generally, companies with very low fixed asset turnovers, such as gas and oil exploration and production (Occidental) and cable communications (Comcast), must be compensated with higher operating margins.

Note to Instructors: You may wish to consider the impact of different fixed asset turnover ratios across industries and the implications of these differences. This is a conceptual question designed to have students think about how competitive markets would likely reward the low fixed asset turnover companies for embracing high fixed asset commitments.

CHAPTER 11
CURRENT LIABILITIES AND PAYROLL

DISCUSSION QUESTIONS

1. No. A discounted note payable has no stated interest rate, but provides interest by discounting the note proceeds. The discount, which is the difference between the proceeds and the face of the note, is the interest and is accounted for as such.

2. **a.** Employee's federal income taxes, social security, and Medicare

   b. Employees Federal Income Tax Payable, Social Security Tax Payable, and Medicare Tax Payable

3. The deductions from employees' earnings are for amounts owed (liabilities) to others for such items as federal taxes, state and local income taxes, and contributions to pension plans.

4. **1.** a
   2. c
   3. c
   4. b
   5. b

5. An advantage of using a separate payroll bank account is that reconciling the bank statements is simplified. In addition, a payroll bank account establishes control over payroll checks and, thus, prevents their theft or misuse.

6. **a.** Constants are data that remain unchanged from payroll to payroll. These include employee names, social security numbers, marital status, number of income tax withholding allowances, rates of pay, tax rates, and withholding tables.

   b. Variables are data that change from payroll to payroll. These include number of hours or days worked for each employee, accrued days of sick leave, vacation credits, total earnings to date, and total taxes withheld.

7. The vacation pay expense should be recorded during the period in which the vacation privilege is earned.

8. In a defined contribution plan, the company invests contributions on behalf of the employee during the employee's working years. Normally, the employee and employer contribute to the plan. The employee's pension depends on the total contributions and the investment returns earned on those contributions.

9. To match revenues and expenses properly, the liability to cover product warranties should be recorded in the period during which the sale of the product is recorded.

10. When the defective product is repaired, the repair costs would be recorded by debiting Product Warranty Payable and crediting Cash, Supplies, or another appropriate account.

PRACTICE EXERCISES

PE 11–1A

a. $70,000

b. $69,650 [$70,000 – ($70,000 × 30/360 × 6%)]

PE 11–1B

a. $150,000

b. $148,125 [$150,000 – ($150,000 × 45/360 × 10%)]

PE 11–2A

Total wage payment		$2,600.00
One allowance (provided by IRS)	$70.00	
Multiplied by allowances claimed on Form W-4	× 2	140.00
Amount subject to withholding		$2,460.00
Initial withholding from wage bracket in Exhibit 3		$ 327.40
Plus additional withholding: 28% of excess over $1,648*		227.36
Federal income tax withholding		$ 554.76

*($2,460 – $1,648) × 28%

PE 11–2B

Total wage payment		$1,400.00
One allowance (provided by IRS)	$70.00	
Multiplied by allowances claimed on Form W-4	× 1	70.00
Amount subject to withholding		$1,330.00
Initial withholding from wage bracket in Exhibit 3		$ 91.40
Plus additional withholding: 25% of excess over $704*		156.50
Federal income tax withholding		$ 247.90

*($1,330 – $704) × 25%

PE 11–3A

Total wage payment...		$2,600.00
Less: Federal income tax withholding.....................	$554.76	
Social security tax ($2,600 × 6%)...................	156.00	
Medicare tax ($2,600 × 1.5%).......................	39.00	749.76
Net pay..		$1,850.24

PE 11–3B

Total wage payment...		$1,400.00
Less: Federal income tax withholding.....................	$247.90	
Social security tax ($1,400 × 6%)...................	84.00	
Medicare tax ($1,400 × 1.5%).......................	21.00	352.90
Net pay..		$1,047.10

PE 11–4A

Salaries Expense	220,000	
Social Security Tax Payable		13,200
Medicare Tax Payable		3,300
Employees Federal Income Tax Payable		43,560
Salaries Payable		159,940

PE 11–4B

Salaries Expense	90,000	
Social Security Tax Payable		5,400
Medicare Tax Payable		1,350
Employees Federal Income Tax Payable		17,820
Retirement Savings Deductions Payable		5,400
Salaries Payable		60,030

PE 11–5A

Payroll Tax Expense	18,670	
Social Security Tax Payable		13,200
Medicare Tax Payable		3,300
State Unemployment Tax Payable*		1,890
Federal Unemployment Tax Payable**		280

  * $35,000 × 5.4%
** $35,000 × 0.8%

PE 11–5B

Payroll Tax Expense	7,370	
Social Security Tax Payable		5,400
Medicare Tax Payable		1,350
State Unemployment Tax Payable*		540
Federal Unemployment Tax Payable**		80

  * $10,000 × 5.4%
** $10,000 × 0.8%

PE 11–6A

a.

Vacation Pay Expense	19,500	
Vacation Pay Payable		19,500
Vacation pay accrued for the period.		

b.

Pension Expense	15,600	
Cash		15,600
To record pension contribution,		
6% × $260,000.		

PE 11–6B

a.

Vacation Pay Expense	35,000	
Vacation Pay Payable		35,000
Vacation pay accrued for the period.		

b.

Pension Expense	201,250	
Cash		175,000
Unfunded Pension Liability		26,250
To record pension cost and funding.		

PE 11–7A

a.

				12,000	
Feb.	28	Product Warranty Expense		12,000	
		Product Warranty Payable			12,000
		To record warranty expense for February,			
		6% × $200,000.			

b.

July	24	Product Warranty Payable		92	
		Supplies			60
		Wages Payable			32

PE 11–7B

a.

July	31	Product Warranty Expense		14,625	
		Product Warranty Payable			14,625
		To record warranty expense for July,			
		4.5% × $325,000.			

b.

Nov.	11	Product Warranty Payable		220	
		Cash			220

PE 11–8A

a. December 31, 2014
Quick Ratio = Quick Assets ÷ Current Liabilities
Quick Ratio = ($650 + $1,500 + $700) ÷ $2,375
Quick Ratio = 1.2

December 31, 2013
Quick Ratio = Quick Assets ÷ Current Liabilities
Quick Ratio = ($680 + $1,550 + $770) ÷ $2,000
Quick Ratio = 1.5

b. The quick ratio of Nabors Company has declined from 1.5 in 2013 to 1.2 in 2014. This decrease is the result of a large increase in accounts payable compared to decreases in the three types of quick assets (cash, temporary investments, and accounts receivable).

PE 11–8B

a.   **December 31, 2014**
        Quick Ratio = Quick Assets ÷ Current Liabilities
        Quick Ratio = ($1,000 + $1,200 + $800) ÷ $1,875
        Quick Ratio = 1.6

        December 31, 2013
        Quick Ratio = Quick Assets ÷ Current Liabilities
        Quick Ratio = ($1,140 + $1,400 + $910) ÷ $2,300
        Quick Ratio = 1.5

b.   **The quick ratio of Adieu Company has improved from 1.5 in 2013 to 1.6 in
        2014. This increase is the result of a small decrease in the three types of quick
        assets (cash, temporary investments, and accounts receivable) compared to
        the larger decrease in the current liability, accounts payable.**

EXERCISES

Ex. 11–1

Current liabilities:

Federal income taxes payable*...	$ 336,000
Advances on magazine subscriptions**...	1,593,750
Total current liabilities...	$1,929,750

  * $840,000 × 40%

  ** 25,000 × $85 × 9/12 = $1,593,750

The nine months of unfilled subscriptions are a current liability because Bon Nebo received payment prior to providing the magazines.

Ex. 11–2

a. 1.

Merchandise Inventory	792,000	
Interest Expense*	8,000	
Notes Payable		800,000

2.

Notes Payable	800,000	
Cash		800,000

b. 1.

Notes Receivable	800,000	
Sales		792,000
Interest Revenue*		8,000

2.

Cash	800,000	
Notes Receivable		800,000

  * $800,000 × 6% × 60/360

Ex. 11–3

a. $240,000 × 8% × 60/360 = $3,200 for each alternative.

b.   (1) $240,000 simple-interest note: $240,000 proceeds
     (2) $240,000 discounted note: $240,000 – $3,200 interest = $236,800 proceeds

c.   Alternative (1) is more favorable to the borrower. This can be verified by comparing the effective interest rates for each loan as follows:

Situation (1): 8% effective interest rate
($3,200 × 360/60) ÷ $240,000 = 8%

Situation (2): 8.11% effective interest rate
($3,200 × 360/60) ÷ $236,800 = 8.11%

The effective interest rate is higher for the discounted note because the creditor lent only $236,800 in return for $3,200 interest over 60 days. In the undiscounted note, the creditor must lend $240,000 for 60 days to earn the same $3,200 interest.

Ex. 11–4

a.

Accounts Payable	150,000	
Notes Payable		150,000

b.

Notes Payable	150,000	
Interest Expense*	875	
Cash		150,875

* $150,000 × 7% × 30/360

Ex. 11–5

a.

Accounts Payable	89,100	
Interest Expense*	900	
Notes Payable		90,000

b.

Notes Payable	90,000	
Cash		90,000

* $90,000 × 8% × 45/360

Ex. 11–6

a.

June	30	Building	450,000	
		Land	350,000	
		Note Payable		400,000
		Cash		400,000

b.

Dec.	31	Note Payable	20,000	
		Interest Expense ($400,000 × 6% × 1/2)	12,000	
		Cash		32,000

c.

June	30	Note Payable	20,000	
		Interest Expense ($380,000 × 6% × 1/2)	11,400	
		Cash		31,400

Ex. 11–7

a. $1,276 is the amount disclosed as the current portion of long-term debt.

b. The current liabilities increased by $1,225 ($1,276 – $51).

c. $14,041 ($15,317 – $1,276)

Ex. 11–8

a.

Regular pay (40 hrs. × $50)...	$2,000
Overtime pay (10 hrs. × $100)..	1,000
Gross pay...	$3,000

b.

Gross pay...		$3,000
Less: Social security tax (6% × $3,000)...............................	$180	
Medicare tax (1.5% × $3,000)..................................	45	
Federal withholding..	686	911
Net pay..		$2,089

Ex. 11–9

	Consultant	Computer Programmer	Administrator
Regular earnings...............................	$3,800.00	$1,600.00	$1,760.00
Overtime earnings...............................		1,200.00	880.00
Gross pay...............................	$3,800.00	$2,800.00	$2,640.00
Less: Social security tax......................	$ 228.00[1]	$ 168.00[2]	$ 158.40[3]
Medicare tax...............................	57.00[4]	42.00[5]	39.60[6]
Federal income tax withheld..........	904.06	610.76	585.56
	$1,189.06	$ 820.76	$ 783.56
Net pay...............................	$2,610.94	$1,979.24	$1,856.44

[1] 6.0% × $3,800.00 = $228.00

[2] 6.0% × $2,800.00 = $168.00

[3] 6.0% × $2,640.00 = $158.40

[4] 1.5% × $3,800.00 = $57.00

[5] 1.5% × $2,800.00 = $42.00

[6] 1.5% × $2,640.00 = $39.60

Withholding supporting calculations:

	Consultant	Computer Programmer	Administrator
Gross weekly pay...................................	$3,800.00	$2,800.00	$2,640.00
Number of withholding allowances...........	2	2	1
Multiplied by: Value of one allowance.......	× $70.00	× $70.00	× $70.00
Amount to be deducted..........................	$ 140.00	$ 140.00	$ 70.00
Amount subject to withholding...............	$3,660.00	$2,660.00	$2,570.00
Initial withholding from wage bracket in Exhibit 3..	$ 816.28	$ 327.40	$ 327.40
Plus: Bracket percentage over bracket excess...................................	87.78[7]	283.36[8]	258.16[9]
Amount withheld..................................	$ 904.06	$ 610.76	$ 585.56

[7] 33% × ($3,660 – $3,394)

[8] 28% × ($2,660 – $1,648)

[9] 28% × ($2,570 – $1,648)

Ex. 11–10

a. Summary: (1) $460,000; (3) $540,000; (8) $6,750; (12) $135,000

	Net amount paid		$338,850
	Total deductions		201,150
(3)	Total earnings		$540,000
	Overtime		80,000
(1)	Regular		$460,000
	Total deductions		$201,150
	Social security tax	$ 32,400	
	Medicare tax	8,100	
	Income tax withheld	135,000	
	Medical insurance	18,900	194,400
(8)	Union dues		$ 6,750
	Total earnings		$540,000
	Factory wages	$285,000	
	Office salaries	120,000	405,000
(12)	Sales salaries		$135,000

b.

Factory Wages Expense	285,000	
Sales Salaries Expense	135,000	
Office Salaries Expense	120,000	
Social Security Tax Payable		32,400
Medicare Tax Payable		8,100
Employees Income Tax Payable		135,000
Medical Insurance Payable		18,900
Union Dues Payable		6,750
Salaries Payable		338,850

c.

Salaries Payable	338,850	
Cash		338,850

Ex. 11–11

a.

Social security tax (6% × $880,000)	$52,800
Medicare tax (1.5% × $880,000)	13,200
State unemployment tax (5.4% × $40,000)	2,160
Federal unemployment (0.8% × $40,000)	320
	$68,480

b.

Payroll Tax Expense	68,480	
Social Security Tax Payable		52,800
Medicare Tax Payable		13,200
State Unemployment Tax Payable		2,160
Federal Unemployment Tax Payable		320

Ex. 11–12

a.

Salaries Expense	1,250,000	
Social Security Tax Payable		58,750
Medicare Tax Payable		18,750
Employees Federal Income Tax Payable		250,000
Salaries Payable		922,500

b.

Payroll Tax Expense	91,450	
Social Security Tax Payable		58,750
Medicare Tax Payable		18,750
State Unemployment Tax Payable*		12,150
Federal Unemployment Tax Payable**		1,800

* 5.4% × $225,000
** 0.8% × $225,000

Ex. 11–13

a.

Wages Expense	240,000	
Social Security Tax Payable*		14,400
Medicare Tax Payable**		3,600
Employees Federal Income Tax Payable		48,000
Wages Payable		174,000

   * 6.0% × $240,000

  ** 1.5% × $240,000

b.

Payroll Tax Expense	20,170	
Social Security Tax Payable		14,400
Medicare Tax Payable		3,600
State Unemployment Tax Payable*		1,890
Federal Unemployment Tax Payable**		280

   * 5.4% × $35,000

  ** 0.8% × $35,000

Ex. 11–14

Big Howie's Hot Dog Stand does have an internal control procedure that should detect the payroll error. Before funds are transferred from the regular bank account to the payroll account, the owner authorizes the total amount of the week's payroll. The owner should catch the error, since the extra 60 hours will cause the weekly payroll to be substantially higher than usual. The owner should sign the paychecks, thereby restricting access to cash by employees who are responsible for record keeping.

Ex. 11–15

a. Appropriate. All changes to the payroll system, including wage rate increases, should be authorized by someone outside the Payroll Department.

b. Inappropriate. Each employee should record his or her own time out for lunch. Under the current procedures, one employee could clock in several employees who are still out to lunch. The company would be paying employees for more time than they actually worked.

c. Inappropriate. Payroll should be informed when any employee is terminated. A supervisor or other individual could continue to clock in and out for the terminated employee and collect the extra paycheck.

d. Inappropriate. Access to the check-signing machine should be restricted.

e. Appropriate. The use of a special payroll account assists in preventing fraud and makes it easier to reconcile the company's bank accounts.

Ex. 11–16

a.

Vacation Pay Expense	3,500	
Vacation Pay Payable		3,500
Vacation pay accrued for January, $42,000 × 1/12.		

b. Vacation pay is reported as a current liability on the balance sheet. If employees are allowed to accumulate their vacation pay, then the estimated vacation pay that will not be taken in the current year will be reported as a long-term liability. When employees take vacations, the liability for vacation pay is decreased.

Ex. 11–17

a.

Dec.	31	Pension Expense	365,000	
		Unfunded Pension Liability		365,000
		To record quarterly pension cost.		

Jan.	15	Unfunded Pension Liability	365,000	
		Cash		365,000

b. In a defined contribution plan, the company invests contributions on behalf of the employee during the employee's working years. Normally, the employee and employer contribute to the plan. The employee's pension depends on the total contributions and the investment return on those contributions. In a defined benefit plan, the company pays the employee a fixed annual amount based on a formula. The employer is obligated to pay for (fund) the employee's future pension benefits.

Ex. 11–18

The $4,267 million unfunded pension liability is the approximate amount of the pension obligation that exceeds the value of the net assets of the pension plan. Apparently, Procter & Gamble has underfunded its plan relative to the obligation that has accrued over time. This can occur when the company contributes less to the plan than the annual pension cost.

The obligation grows yearly by the amount of the periodic pension cost. Thus, the $538 million periodic pension cost is a measure of the amount of pension earned by employees during the year. The annual pension cost is determined by making assumptions about employee life expectancies, employee turnover, expected compensation levels, and interest.

Ex. 11–19

a.

Product Warranty Expense	22,400	
Product Warranty Payable		22,400
To record warranty expense for June,		
4% × $560,000.		

Product Warranty Payable	235	
Supplies		140
Wages Payable		95

Ex. 11–20

a. The warranty liability represents estimated outstanding automobile warranty claims. Of these claims, $2,965 million is estimated to be due during Year 2, while the remainder ($4,065 million) is expected to be paid after Year 2. The distinction between short- and long-term liabilities is important to creditors in order to accurately evaluate the near-term cash demands on the business, relative to the quick current assets and other longer-term demands.

b.

Product Warranty Expense	2,759,000,000	
Product Warranty Payable		2,759,000,000

$$\$7,030 + X - \$3,000 = \$6,789$$
$$X = \$6,789 - \$7,030 + \$3,000$$
$$X = \$2,759 \text{ million}$$

c. In order for a product warranty to be reported as a liability in the financial statements, it must qualify as a contingent liability. Contingent liabilities are only reported as liabilities on the balance sheet if it is *probable* that the liability will occur <u>and</u> the amount of the liability is *reasonably estimable*.

Ex. 11–21

a.

Damage Awards and Fines	365,000	
EPA Fines Payable		240,000
Litigation Claims Payable		125,000

Note to Instructors: The "damage awards and fines" would be disclosed on the income statement under "Other expenses."

b.   The company experienced a hazardous materials spill at one of its plants during the previous period. This spill has resulted in a number of lawsuits to which the company is a party. The Environmental Protection Agency (EPA) has fined the company $240,000, which the company is contesting in court. Although the company does not admit fault, legal counsel believes that the fine payment is probable. In addition, an employee has sued the company. A $125,000 out-of-court settlement has been reached with the employee. The EPA fine and out-of-court settlement have been recognized as an expense for the period. There is one other outstanding lawsuit related to this incident. Counsel does not believe that the lawsuit has merit. Other lawsuits and unknown liabilities may arise from this incident.

Ex. 11–22

a.

$$\text{Quick Ratio} = \frac{\text{Quick Assets}}{\text{Current Liabilities}}$$

December 31, 2013: $\dfrac{\$500,000 + \$200,000}{\$500,000} = 1.4$

December 31, 2014: $\dfrac{\$486,000 + \$210,000}{\$580,000} = 1.2$

b.   The quick ratio decreased between the two balance sheet dates. The major reason is a significant increase in inventory which likely drove the increase in accounts payable. Cash also declined, possibly to purchase the inventory. As a result, quick assets actually declined, while the current liabilities increased. The quick ratio for December 31, 2014, is not yet at an alarming level. However, the trend suggests that the firm's current asset (working capital) management should be watched closely.

Ex. 11–23

a.

	Apple Inc.	Dell, Inc.
Quick Ratio	1.8	1.3

$$\text{Quick Ratio} = \frac{\text{Quick Assets}}{\text{Current Liabilities}}$$

Apple Inc. (in millions):

$$\text{Quick Ratio} = \frac{\$11,261 + \$14,359 + \$11,560}{\$20,722} = \quad 1.8$$

Dell, Inc. (in millions):

$$\text{Quick Ratio} = \frac{\$13,913 + \$452 + \$10,136}{\$19,483} = \quad 1.3$$

b.   It is clear that Apple Inc.'s short-term liquidity is stronger than Dell's.
Apple's quick ratio is 38% [(1.8 – 1.3) ÷ 1.3] higher. Apple has a much stronger
relative cash and short-term investment position than does Dell. Apple's cash,
accounts receivable, and short-term investments are over 89% of total current
assets (180% of current liabilities), compared to Dell's 84% of total current assets
130% of current liabilities). In addition, Dell's relative accounts payable position is
larger than Apple's, indicating the possibility that Dell has longer supplier
payment terms than does Apple. A quick ratio of 1.8 for Apple suggests ample
flexibility to make strategic investments with its excess cash, while a quick
ratio of 1.3 for Dell indicates an efficient, but tight, quick asset management
policy.

PROBLEMS

Prob. 11–1A

1.

Feb.	3	Merchandise Inventory	410,000	
		Accounts Payable—Onifade Co.		410,000
Mar.	3	Accounts Payable—Onifade Co.	410,000	
		Notes Payable		410,000
Apr.	17	Notes Payable	410,000	
		Interest Expense ($410,000 × 45/360 × 6%)	3,075	
		Cash		413,075
June	1	Cash	250,000	
		Notes Payable		250,000
July	21	Tools	296,000	
		Interest Expense ($300,000 × 60/360 × 8%)	4,000	
		Notes Payable		300,000
	31	Notes Payable	250,000	
		Interest Expense ($250,000 × 60/360 × 7.5%)	3,125	
		Notes Payable		250,000
		Cash		3,125
Aug.	30	Notes Payable	250,000	
		Interest Expense ($250,000 × 30/360 × 9%)	1,875	
		Cash		251,875
Sept.	19	Notes Payable	300,000	
		Cash		300,000
Dec.	1	Office Equipment	340,000	
		Notes Payable		300,000
		Cash		40,000
	12	Litigation Loss	165,000	
		Litigation Claims Payable		165,000
	31	Notes Payable	30,000	
		Interest Expense ($30,000 × 30/360 × 8%)	200	
		Cash		30,200

Prob. 11–1A (Concluded)

2. a.

Product Warranty Expense	32,500	
Product Warranty Payable		32,500
Warranty expense for the current year.		

b.

Interest Expense	1,800	
Interest Payable		1,800
Interest on notes, $30,000 × 8.0% × 30/360 × 9.		

Prob. 11–2A

1. a.

Dec.	30	Sales Salaries Expense	350,000	
		Warehouse Salaries Expense	180,000	
		Office Salaries Expense	145,000	
		Employees Income Tax Payable		118,800
		Social Security Tax Payable		40,500
		Medicare Tax Payable		10,125
		Bond Deductions Payable		14,850
		Group Insurance Payable		12,150
		Salaries Payable		478,575

   b.

Dec.	30	Payroll Tax Expense	52,795	
		Social Security Tax Payable		40,500
		Medicare Tax Payable		10,125
		State Unemployment Tax Payable[1]		1,890
		Federal Unemployment Tax Payable[2]		280

[1] $35,000 × 5.4%

[2] $35,000 × 0.8%

2. a.

Dec.	30	Sales Salaries Expense	350,000	
		Warehouse Salaries Expense	180,000	
		Office Salaries Expense	145,000	
		Employees Income Tax Payable		118,800
		Social Security Tax Payable[1]		40,500
		Medicare Tax Payable[2]		10,125
		Bond Deductions Payable		14,850
		Group Insurance Payable		12,150
		Salaries Payable		478,575

[1] $675,000 × 6%

[2] $675,000 × 1.5%

   b.

Jan.	5	Payroll Tax Expense	92,475	
		Social Security Tax Payable		40,500
		Medicare Tax Payable		10,125
		State Unemployment Tax Payable[3]		36,450
		Federal Unemployment Tax Payable[4]		5,400

[3] $675,000 × 5.4%

[4] $675,000 × 0.8%

Prob. 11–3A

1.

Employee	Gross Earnings	Federal Income Tax Withheld	Social Security Tax Withheld	Medicare Tax Withheld
Arnett.....................	$ 8,250.00	$ 1,512.00	$ 495.00	$ 123.75
Cruz......................	57,600.00	9,996.00	3,456.00	864.00
Edwards.................	24,000.00	4,977.00	1,440.00	360.00
Harvin....................	6,000.00	1,133.00	360.00	90.00
Nicks.....................	110,000.00	24,409.00	6,600.00	1,650.00
Shiancoe................	116,000.00	26,670.00	6,960.00	1,740.00
Ward......................	7,830.00	1,407.00	469.80	117.45
			$19,780.80	$4,945.20

2. **a.** Social security tax paid by employer.. $19,780.80

   b. Medicare tax paid by employer... 4,945.20

   c. Earnings subject to unemployment compensation tax,
   $10,000 for all employees except Arnett, Harvin, and Ward.
   Thus, total earnings subject to SUTA and FUTA are
   $62,080 [(4 × $10,000) + $8,250 + $6,000 + $7,830].
   State unemployment compensation tax: $62,080 × 5.4%........................ 3,352.32

   d. Federal unemployment compensation tax: $62,080 × 0.8%..................... 496.64

   e. Total payroll tax expense.. $28,574.96

Prob. 11–4A

1.

PAYROLL FOR WEEK ENDING _December 7, 2014_

Employee	Total Hours	EARNINGS			DEDUCTIONS					PAID		ACCOUNT DEBITED	
		Regular	Overtime	Total	Social Security Tax	Medicare Tax	Federal Income Tax	U.S. Savings Bonds	Total	Net Pay	Ck. No.	Sales Salaries Expense	Office Salaries Expense
Aaron	46	2,720.00	612.00	3,332.00	199.92	49.98	766.36	100.00	1,116.26	2,215.74	901	3,332.00	
Cobb	41	2,480.00	93.00	2,573.00	154.38	38.60	553.20	110.00	856.18	1,716.82	902	2,573.00	
Clemente	48	2,800.00	840.00	3,640.00	218.40	54.60	691.60	120.00	1,084.60	2,555.40	903	3,640.00	
DiMaggio	35	1,960.00		1,960.00	117.60	29.40	411.60		558.60	1,401.40	904	1,960.00	
Griffey, Jr.	45	2,480.00	465.00	2,945.00	176.70	44.18	618.45	130.00	969.33	1,975.67	905	2,945.00	
Mantle				1,800.00	108.00	27.00	432.00	120.00	687.00	1,113.00	906		1,800.00
Robinson	36	1,944.00		1,944.00	116.64	29.16	291.60	130.00	567.40	1,376.60	907	1,944.00	
Williams				2,000.00	120.00	30.00	440.00	125.00	715.00	1,285.00	908		2,000.00
Vaughn	42	2,480.00	186.00	2,666.00	159.96	39.99	533.20	50.00	783.15	1,882.85	909	2,666.00	
		16,864.00	2,196.00	22,860.00	1,371.60	342.91	4,738.01	885.00	7,337.52	15,522.48		19,060.00	3,800.00

2.

Sales Salaries Expense	19,060.00
Office Salaries Expense	3,800.00
Social Security Tax Payable	1,371.60
Medicare Tax Payable	342.91
Employees Federal Income Tax Payable	4,738.01
Bond Deductions Payable	885.00
Salaries Payable	15,522.48

Prob. 11–5A

1.

	Dec.	2	Bond Deductions Payable	3,400	
			Cash		3,400
		2	Social Security Tax Payable	9,273	
			Medicare Tax Payable	2,318	
			Employees Federal Income Tax Payable	15,455	
			Cash		27,046
		13	Operations Salaries Expense	43,200	
			Officers Salaries Expense	27,200	
			Office Salaries Expense	6,800	
			Social Security Tax Payable		4,632
			Medicare Tax Payable		1,158
			Employees Federal Income Tax Payable		15,440
			Employees State Income Tax Payable		3,474
			Bond Deductions Payable		1,700
			Medical Insurance Payable		4,500
			Salaries Payable		46,296
		13	Salaries Payable	46,296	
			Cash		46,296
		13	Payroll Tax Expense	6,265	
			Social Security Tax Payable		4,632
			Medicare Tax Payable		1,158
			State Unemployment Tax Payable		350
			Federal Unemployment Tax Payable		125
		16	Social Security Tax Payable	9,264	
			Medicare Tax Payable	2,316	
			Employees Federal Income Tax Payable	15,440	
			Cash		27,020
		19	Medical Insurance Payable	31,500	
			Cash		31,500

Prob. 11–5A (Concluded)

Dec.	27	Operations Salaries Expense	42,800	
		Officers Salaries Expense	28,000	
		Office Salaries Expense	7,000	
		Social Security Tax Payable		4,668
		Medicare Tax Payable		1,167
		Employees Federal Income Tax Payable		15,404
		Employees State Income Tax Payable		3,501
		Bond Deductions Payable		1,700
		Salaries Payable		51,360
	27	Salaries Payable	51,360	
		Cash		51,360
	27	Payroll Tax Expense	6,135	
		Social Security Tax Payable		4,668
		Medicare Tax Payable		1,167
		State Unemployment Tax Payable		225
		Federal Unemployment Tax Payable		75
	27	Employees State Income Tax Payable	20,884	
		Cash		20,884
	31	Bond Deductions Payable	3,400	
		Cash		3,400
	31	Pension Expense	60,000	
		Cash		45,000
		Unfunded Pension Liability		15,000
		To record pension cost and unfunded		
		liability.		

2. a.	Dec.	31	Operations Salaries Expense	8,560	
			Officers Salaries Expense	5,600	
			Office Salaries Expense	1,400	
			Salaries Payable		15,560
			Accrued wages for the period.		
b.		31	Vacation Pay Expense	15,000	
			Vacation Pay Payable		15,000
			Vacation pay accrued for the period.		

11-24

Prob. 11–1B

1.

Apr.	15	Cash	225,000	
		Notes Payable		225,000
May	1	Equipment	310,400	
		Interest Expense ($320,000 × 180/360 × 6%)	9,600	
		Notes Payable		320,000
	15	Notes Payable	225,000	
		Interest Expense ($225,000 × 30/360 × 6%)	1,125	
		Notes Payable		225,000
		Cash		1,125
July	14	Notes Payable	225,000	
		Interest Expense ($225,000 × 60/360 × 8%)	3,000	
		Cash		228,000
Aug.	16	Merchandise Inventory	90,000	
		Accounts Payable—Exige Co.		90,000
Sept.	15	Accounts Payable—Exige Co.	90,000	
		Notes Payable		90,000
Oct.	28	Notes Payable	320,000	
		Cash		320,000
	30	Notes Payable	90,000	
		Interest Expense ($90,000 × 45/360 × 6%)	675	
		Cash		90,675
Nov.	16	Store Equipment	450,000	
		Notes Payable		400,000
		Cash		50,000
Dec.	16	Notes Payable	20,000	
		Interest Expense ($20,000 × 30/360 × 9%)	150	
		Cash		20,150
	28	Litigation Loss	87,500	
		Litigation Claims Payable		87,500

Prob. 11–1B (Concluded)

2. a.

Product Warranty Expense	26,800	
Product Warranty Payable		26,800
Warranty expense for the current year.		

b.

Interest Expense	4,275	
Interest Payable		4,275
Interest on notes, $20,000 × 9% × 45/360 × 19.		

Prob. 11–2B

1. a.

Dec.	30	Sales Salaries Expense	625,000	
		Warehouse Salaries Expense	240,000	
		Office Salaries Expense	320,000	
		Employees Income Tax Payable		232,260
		Social Security Tax Payable		71,100
		Medicare Tax Payable		17,775
		Bond Deductions Payable		35,500
		Group Insurance Payable		53,325
		Salaries Payable		775,040

b.

Dec.	30	Payroll Tax Expense	90,735	
		Social Security Tax Payable		71,100
		Medicare Tax Payable		17,775
		State Unemployment Tax Payable[1]		1,620
		Federal Unemployment Tax Payable[2]		240

[1] $30,000 × 5.4%

[2] $30,000 × 0.8%

2. a.

Dec.	30	Sales Salaries Expense	625,000	
		Warehouse Salaries Expense	240,000	
		Office Salaries Expense	320,000	
		Employees Income Tax Payable		232,260
		Social Security Tax Payable[1]		71,100
		Medicare Tax Payable[2]		17,775
		Bond Deductions Payable		35,500
		Group Insurance Payable		53,325
		Salaries Payable		775,040

[1] $1,185,000 × 6%

[2] $1,185,000 × 1.5%

b.

Jan.	4	Payroll Tax Expense	162,345	
		Social Security Tax Payable		71,100
		Medicare Tax Payable		17,775
		State Unemployment Tax Payable[3]		63,990
		Federal Unemployment Tax Payable[4]		9,480

[3] $1,185,000 × 5.4%

[4] $1,185,000 × 0.8%

11-27

Prob. 11–3B

1.

Employee	Gross Earnings*	Federal Income Tax Withheld	Social Security Tax Withheld	Medicare Tax Withheld
Addai......................	$44,880	$ 9,372	$ 2,692.80	$ 673.20
Kasay.....................	25,200	3,731	1,512.00	378.00
McGahee.................	67,410	12,999	4,044.60	1,011.15
Moss......................	55,200	9,396	3,312.00	828.00
Stewart...................	4,500	758	270.00	67.50
Tolbert....................	4,875	669	292.50	73.13
Wells.....................	84,000	18,872	5,040.00	1,260.00
			$17,163.90	$4,290.98

* The gross earnings are determined by multiplying the monthly earnings by the
number of months of employment based on the date of hire.

2.   a.   Social security tax paid by employer... $17,163.90

     b.   Medicare tax paid by employer... 4,290.98

     c.   Earnings subject to unemployment compensation tax,
         $10,000 for all employees except Stewart and Tolbert.
         Thus, total earnings subject to SUTA and FUTA are
         $59,375 [(5 × $10,000) + $4,500 + $4,875].
         State unemployment compensation tax: $59,375 × 5.4%................... 3,206.25

     d.   Federal unemployment compensation tax: $59,375 × 0.8%............... 475.00

     e.   Total payroll tax expense... $25,136.13

Prob. 11–4B

1.

PAYROLL FOR WEEK ENDING   December 7, 2014

Employee	Total Hours	EARNINGS			DEDUCTIONS					PAID		ACCOUNT DEBITED	
		Regular	Overtime	Total	Social Security Tax	Medicare Tax	Federal Income Tax	U.S. Savings Bonds	Total	Net Pay	Ck. No.	Sales Salaries Expense	Office Salaries Expense
Carlton	52	2,000.00	900.00	2,900.00	174.00	43.50	667.00	60.00	944.50	1,955.50	328	2,900.00	
Grove				4,000.00	240.00	60.00	860.00	100.00	1,260.00	2,740.00	329		4,000.00
Johnson	36	1,872.00		1,872.00	112.32	28.08	355.68		496.08	1,375.92	330	1,872.00	
Koufax	45	2,320.00	435.00	2,755.00	165.30	41.33	578.55	44.00	829.18	1,925.82	331	2,755.00	
Maddux	37	1,665.00		1,665.00	99.90	24.98	349.65	62.00	536.53	1,128.47	332	1,665.00	
Seaver				3,200.00	192.00	48.00	768.00	120.00	1,128.00	2,072.00	333		3,200.00
Spahn	46	2,080.00	468.00	2,548.00	152.88	38.22	382.20		573.30	1,974.70	334	2,548.00	
Winn	48	2,000.00	600.00	2,600.00	156.00	39.00	572.00	75.00	842.00	1,758.00	335	2,600.00	
Young	43	2,160.00	243.00	2,403.00	144.18	36.05	480.60	80.00	740.83	1,662.17	336	2,403.00	
		14,097.00	2,646.00	23,943.00	1,436.58	359.16	5,013.68	541.00	7,350.42	16,592.58		16,743.00	7,200.00

2.

Sales Salaries Expense	16,743.00	
Office Salaries Expense	7,200.00	
Social Security Tax Payable		1,436.58
Medicare Tax Payable		359.16
Employees Federal Income Tax Payable		5,013.68
Bond Deductions Payable		541.00
Salaries Payable		16,592.58

11-29

Prob. 11–5B

1.

Dec.		1	Medical Insurance Payable	2,520	
			Cash		2,520
		1	Social Security Tax Payable	2,913	
			Medicare Tax Payable	728	
			Employees Federal Income Tax Payable	4,490	
			Cash		8,131
		2	Bond Deductions Payable	2,300	
			Cash		2,300
		12	Sales Salaries Expense	14,500	
			Officers Salaries Expense	7,100	
			Office Salaries Expense	2,600	
			Social Security Tax Payable		1,452
			Medicare Tax Payable		363
			Employees Federal Income Tax Payable		4,308
			Employees State Income Tax Payable		1,089
			Bond Deductions Payable		1,150
			Medical Insurance Payable		420
			Salaries Payable		15,418
		12	Salaries Payable	15,418	
			Cash		15,418
		12	Payroll Tax Expense	2,220	
			Social Security Tax Payable		1,452
			Medicare Tax Payable		363
			State Unemployment Tax Payable		315
			Federal Unemployment Tax Payable		90
		15	Social Security Tax Payable	2,904	
			Medicare Tax Payable	726	
			Employees Federal Income Tax Payable	4,308	
			Cash		7,938

Prob. 11–5B (Concluded)

Dec.	26	Sales Salaries Expense	14,250	
		Officers Salaries Expense	7,250	
		Office Salaries Expense	2,750	
		Social Security Tax Payable		1,455
		Medicare Tax Payable		364
		Employees Federal Income Tax Payable		4,317
		Employees State Income Tax Payable		1,091
		Bond Deductions Payable		1,150
		Salaries Payable		15,873
	26	Salaries Payable	15,873	
		Cash		15,873
	26	Payroll Tax Expense	2,009	
		Social Security Tax Payable		1,455
		Medicare Tax Payable		364
		State Unemployment Tax Payable		150
		Federal Unemployment Tax Payable		40
	30	Employees State Income Tax Payable	6,258	
		Cash		6,258
	30	Bond Deductions Payable	2,300	
		Cash		2,300
	31	Pension Expense	65,500	
		Cash		55,400
		Unfunded Pension Liability		10,100
		To record pension cost and unfunded		
		liability.		

2.	Dec.	31	Sales Salaries Expense	4,275	
			Officers Salaries Expense	2,175	
			Office Salaries Expense	825	
			Salaries Payable		7,275
			Accrued wages for the period.		
		31	Vacation Pay Expense	13,350	
			Vacation Pay Payable		13,350
			Vacation pay accrued for the period.		

COMPREHENSIVE PROBLEM 3

1.	**Jan.**	3	Petty Cash	4,500	
			Cash		4,500
	Feb.	26	Office Supplies	1,680	
			Miscellaneous Selling Expense	570	
			Miscellaneous Administrative Expense	880	
			Cash		3,130
	Apr.	14	Merchandise Inventory	31,300	
			Accounts Payable		31,300
	May	13	Accounts Payable	31,300	
			Cash		31,300
		17	Cash	21,200	
			Cash Short and Over	40	
			Sales		21,240
	June	2	Notes Receivable	180,000	
			Accounts Receivable—Ryanair		180,000
	Aug.	1	Cash	182,400	
			Notes Receivable		180,000
			Interest Revenue		2,400
			($180,000 × 8% × 60/360 = $2,400).		
		24	Cash	7,600	
			Allowance for Doubtful Accounts	1,400	
			Accounts Receivable—Finley		9,000
	Sept.	15	Accounts Receivable—Finley	1,400	
			Allowance for Doubtful Accounts		1,400
			Cash	1,400	
			Accounts Receivable—Finley		1,400

Comp. Prob. 3 (Continued)

Sept.	15	Land	654,925	
		Interest Expense	15,075	
		Notes Payable		670,000
		($670,000 × 90/360 × 9%).		
Oct.	17	Cash	135,000	
		Notes Receivable	100,000	
		Accumulated Depreciation—Office Equipment	64,000	
		Loss on Sale of Office Equipment	21,000	
		Office Equipment		320,000
Nov.	30	Sales Salaries Expense	135,000	
		Office Salaries Expense	77,250	
		Employees Federal Income Tax Payable		39,266
		Social Security Tax Payable		12,735
		Medicare Tax Payable		3,184
		Salaries Payable		157,065
	30	Payroll Tax Expense	16,229	
		Social Security Tax Payable		12,735
		Medicare Tax Payable		3,184
		State Unemployment Tax Payable*		270
		Federal Unemployment Tax Payable**		40
		*$5,000 × 5.4%		
		**$5,000 × 0.8%		
Dec.	14	Notes Payable	670,000	
		Cash		670,000
	31	Pension Expense	190,400	
		Cash		139,700
		Unfunded Pension Liability		50,700
		Pension cost of $190,400 funded		
		at $139,700.		

Comp. Prob. 3 (Continued)

2.

KORNETT COMPANY Bank Reconciliation December 31, 2014	
Balance according to bank statement	$283,000
Add deposit in transit, not recorded by bank	29,500
	$312,500
Deduct outstanding checks	68,540
Adjusted balance	$243,960
Balance according to company's records	$245,410
Deduct:	
Bank service charges	750
Error in recording check	700
Adjusted balance	$243,960

3.

Miscellaneous Expense	750	
Accounts Payable	700	
Cash		1,450

4. a.

Bad Debt Expense	18,000	
Allowance for Doubtful Accounts		18,000
To record estimated uncollectible accounts,		
$16,000 + $2,000.		

b.

Cost of Merchandise Sold	3,300	
Merchandise Inventory		3,300
To record inventory shrinkage.		

c.

Insurance Expense	22,820	
Prepaid Insurance		22,820
To record expired insurance.		

d.

Office Supplies Expense	3,920	
Office Supplies		3,920
To record supplies used during the period.		

Comp. Prob. 3 (Continued)

e.

Depreciation Expense—Buildings		36,000	
Depreciation Expense—Office Equipment		44,000	
Depreciation Expense—Store Equipment		5,000	
Accumulated Depreciation—Buildings			36,000
Accumulated Depreciation—Office Equipment			44,000
Accumulated Depreciation—Store Equipment			5,000
To record depreciation for the period.			

Computations:

Buildings ($900,000 × 4.0%)...................... $36,000

Office Equipment

[20% × ($246,000 – $26,000)]................... 44,000

Store Equipment

[1/2 × 10% × ($112,000 – $12,000)]........... 5,000

f.

Amortization Expense—Patents		6,000	
Patents			6,000
To record patent amortization,			
$48,000 ÷ 8 years.			

g.

Depletion Expense		30,000	
Accumulated Depletion			30,000
To record depletion,			
($546,000 ÷ 910,000 tons) × 50,000 tons.			

h.

Vacation Pay Expense		10,500	
Vacation Pay Payable			10,500
To record vacation pay for the period.			

i.

Product Warranty Expense		76,000	
Product Warranty Payable			76,000
To record product warranty for the period,			
$1,900,000 × 4.0%.			

j.

Interest Receivable		1,875	
Interest Revenue			1,875
To record interest earned on note			
receivable, $100,000 × 75/360 × 9%.			

11-35

Comp. Prob. 3 (Continued)

5.

KORNETT COMPANY			
Balance Sheet			
December 31, 2014			
Assets			
Current assets:			
Petty cash		$ 4,500	
Cash		243,960	
Notes receivable		100,000	
Accounts receivable	$470,000		
Less allowance for doubtful accounts	16,000	454,000	
Merchandise inventory—at cost		320,000	
Interest receivable		1,875	
Prepaid insurance		45,640	
Office supplies		13,400	
Total current assets			$1,183,375
Property, plant, and equipment:			
Land		$654,925	
Buildings	$900,000		
Less accumulated depreciation	36,000	864,000	
Office equipment	$246,000		
Less accumulated depreciation	44,000	202,000	
Store equipment	$112,000		
Less accumulated depreciation	5,000	107,000	
Mineral rights	$546,000		
Less accumulated depletion	30,000	516,000	
Total property, plant, and equipment			2,343,925
Intangible assets:			
Patents			42,000
Total assets			$3,569,300

Comp. Prob. 3 (Concluded)

Liabilities			
Current liabilities:			
Social security tax payable		$ 25,470	
Medicare tax payable		4,710	
Employees federal income tax payable		40,000	
State unemployment tax payable		270	
Federal unemployment tax payable		40	
Salaries payable		157,000	
Accounts payable		131,600	
Interest payable		28,000	
Product warranty payable		76,000	
Vacation pay payable (current portion)		7,140	
Notes payable (current portion)		70,000	
Total current liabilities			$ 540,230
Long-term liabilities:			
Vacation pay payable		$ 3,360	
Unfunded pension liability		50,700	
Notes payable		630,000	
Total long-term liabilities			684,060
Total liabilities			$1,224,290
Owner's Equity			
J. Kornett, capital			2,345,010
Total liabilities and owner's equity			$3,569,300

CASES & PROJECTS

CP 11–1

The firm has no implicit or explicit contract to pay any bonus. The bonus is discretionary, even if the firm paid a two-week bonus for 10 straight years. The firm is not behaving unethically for reducing the bonus to one week—regardless of the reason. Tonya Latirno, on the other hand, has taken things into her own hands. Sensing that she is being cheated, she tries to rectify the situation to her own advantage by working overtime that isn't required. This behavior could be considered fraudulent, even though Tonya is actually present on the job during the overtime hours. The point is that the overtime is not required by the firm. Tonya is incorrect in thinking that her behavior is justified because she did not receive the full two-week bonus. In fact, this behavior would not be justified even if she had a legitimate claim against the company. If she had a claim or grievance against the firm, then it should be handled by other procedural or legal means.

CP 11–2

Sumana's interpretation of the pension issue is correct. The employee earns the pension during the working years. The pension is part of the employee's compensation that is deferred until retirement. Thus, Felton should record an expense equal to the amount of pension benefit earned by the employee for the period. This gives rise to the rather complex issue of estimating the amount of the pension expense. Francie indicates that the complexity of this calculation makes determining the annual pension expense impossible. This is not so. There are a number of mathematical and statistical approaches (termed "actuarial" approaches) that can reliably estimate the amount of benefits earned by the workforce for a given year.

As a side note, Francie's perspective can be summarized as "pay as you go." In her interpretation, there is no expense until a pension is paid to the retiree. Failing to account for pension promises when they are earned is not considered sound accounting.

CP 11–3

a. The so-called "underground economy" hides transactions from IRS scrutiny by conducting business with cash (not check or credit card, which leaves an audit trail). The intent in many such transactions is to evade income tax illegally. However, just because a transaction is in cash does not exempt it from taxation. Tina Song also appears to perform construction services on a cash basis to evade reporting income while paying employees with cash to avoid paying social security and Medicare payroll taxes. The IRS reports that nearly 86% of the persons convicted of evading employment taxes were sentenced to an average of 17 months in prison and ordered to make restitution to the government for the taxes evaded, plus interest and penalties.

b. Marvin should respond that he would rather receive a payroll check as a normal employee does. Receiving cash as an employee, rather than a payroll check, subverts the U.S. tax system. That is, such cash payments do not include deductions for payroll taxes, as required by law. That is why, for example, cash tips must be formally reported to the IRS and subjected to payroll tax deductions by the employer. In addition, if Marvin followed Tina's advice, Marvin not only would be avoiding payroll deductions, but would also be underreporting income. This would subject Marvin to potential fines and possible criminal prosecution for underreporting income.

CP 11–4

The purpose of this activity is to familiarize students with retrieving and using IRS forms. Students should be able to find the three required forms without much difficulty. Encourage students to retrieve the forms from the IRS Web site, since this is a useful source for any IRS form or publication that they might need. IRS Web site forms come in *.pdf* format, which means an Adobe Acrobat Reader is necessary to open and print the file. This software is available as a free plug-in on most Internet browser software. However, some students may need to download a free version in order to open the forms. This is also a useful exercise, since many sophisticated forms on the Web require an Acrobat Reader.

The W-2 form is the Annual Wage and Tax Statement transmitted by the employer to the IRS. The IRS uses this information to reconcile the taxpayer's reported income and withholding taxes with the taxpayer's tax return. Copies of the W-2 are provided for the employee's own records and for submitting with state and federal tax returns.

Form 940 is the Employer's Annual Federal Unemployment Tax Return. The FUTA tax is reported annually, while the 941 payroll taxes are reported quarterly to the IRS.

Form 941 is the Employer's Quarterly Federal Tax Return. This return is used to report federal withholding payroll taxes collected from employees and FICA taxes (both employee and employer portions) for the quarter.

CP 11–5

This activity does not require the student to research the contingency notes for Altria Group. The contingency disclosure is extensive and complicated. Rather, the student should identify Altria Group's main business, and from this information determine the likely cause of the contingency disclosures.

a. **Altria Group is a holding company for a number of businesses including Philip Morris. Thus, Altria's primary business is in the manufacture and distribution of tobacco products.**

b. **The health concerns surrounding tobacco products give rise to numerous lawsuits and legal actions against Altria. The notes to the financial statements include an extensive section describing the scope and status of these actions. As of December 31, 2011, Altria had over 109 cases pending, including 18 class actions and 1 health care recovery action (by state and federal governments). Altria's Form 10-K provides a section describing some of these actions.**

CHAPTER 12
ACCOUNTING FOR PARTNERSHIPS AND
LIMITED LIABILITY COMPANIES

DISCUSSION QUESTIONS

1. **a.** Proprietorship: Ease of formation and nontaxable entity.

   b. Partnership: Expanded owner expertise and capital, nontaxable entity, and moderate complexity of formation.

   c. Limited liability company: Limited liability to owners, expanded access to capital, nontaxable entity, and moderate complexity of formation.

2. The disadvantages of a partnership are that its life is limited, each partner has unlimited liability, one partner can bind the partnership to contracts, and raising large amounts of capital is more difficult for a partnership than a limited liability company.

3. Yes. A partnership may incur losses in excess of the total investment of all partners. The division of losses among the partners is made according to their agreement. In addition, because of the unlimited liability of each partner for partnership debts, a particular partner may actually lose a greater amount than his or her capital balance.

4. The partnership agreement (partnership) or operating agreement (LLC) establishes the income-sharing ratio among the partners (members), amounts to be invested, and admission and withdrawal of partners (members). In addition, for an LLC the operating agreement specifies if the LLC is owner-managed or manager-managed.

5. No. Maholic would have to bear his share of losses. In the absence of any agreement as to division of net income or net loss, his share would be one-third. In addition, because of the unlimited liability of each partner, Maholic may have to bear more than one-third of the losses if one partner is unable to absorb his share of the losses.

6. Yes. Partnership net income is divided according to the income-sharing ratio, regardless of the amount of the withdrawals by the partners. Therefore, it is very likely that the partners' monthly withdrawals from a partnership will not exactly equal their shares of net income.

7. **a.** Debit the partner's drawing account and credit Cash.

   b. No. Payments to partners and the division of net income are separate. The amount of one does not affect the amount of the other.

   c. Debit the income summary account for the amount of the net income and credit the partners' capital accounts for their respective shares of the net income.

8. **a.** By purchase of an interest, the capital interest of the new partner is obtained from the old partner, and neither the total assets nor the total equity of the partnership is affected.

   b. By investment, both the total assets and the total equity of the partnership are increased.

DISCUSSION QUESTIONS (Continued)

9. It is important to state all partnership assets in terms of current prices at the time of the admission of a new partner because failure to do so might result in participation by the new partner in gains or losses attributable to the period prior to admission to the partnership. To illustrate, assume that A and B share net income and net loss equally and operate a partnership that owns land recorded at and costing $20,000. C is admitted to the partnership, and the three partners share in income equally. The day after C is admitted to the partnership, the land is sold for $35,000 and, since the land was not revalued, C receives a one-third distribution of the $15,000 gain. In this case, C participates in the gain attributable to the period prior to admission to the partnership.

10. A new partner who is expected to improve the fortunes (income) of the partnership, through such things as reputation or skill, might be given equity in excess of the amount invested to join the partnership.

PRACTICE EXERCISES

PE 12–1A

Cash	51,000	
Accounts Receivable	65,000	
Patent	195,000	
Accounts Payable		12,000
Allowance for Doubtful Accounts		3,000
Rachel Bell, Capital		296,000

PE 12–1B

Cash	36,000	
Inventory	42,000	
Land	175,000	
Notes Payable		35,000
Austin Fisher, Capital		218,000

PE 12–2A

Distributed to Orr and Graham:

	Orr	Graham	Total
Annual salary......................	$28,000	$ 0	$28,000
Interest..............................	3,600[1]	9,000[2]	12,600
Remaining income...............	3,600[3]	1,800[4]	5,400
Total distributed to partners..	$35,200	$10,800	$46,000

[1] $60,000 × 6%

[2] $150,000 × 6%

[3] ($46,000 − $28,000 − $12,600) × 2/3

[4] ($46,000 − $28,000 − $12,600) × 1/3

Orr: $35,200

PE 12–2B

Distributed to Prado and Nicks:

	Prado	Nicks	Total
Annual salary..........................	$ 0	$38,000	$ 38,000
Interest.....................................	1,000[1]	2,500[2]	3,500
Remaining income................	35,250	35,250[3]	70,500
Total distributed to partners...	$36,250	$75,750	$112,000

[1] $20,000 × 5%

[2] $50,000 × 5%

[3] ($112,000 – $38,000 – $3,500) × 50%

Nicks: $75,750

PE 12–3A

a.	Land	45,000	
	Tony Vale, Capital		22,500
	Jordan Henry, Capital		22,500
	($125,000 – $80,000) × 50%.		

b.	Jordan Henry, Capital	26,250	
	Amar Harb, Capital		26,250
	($30,000 + $22,500) × 50%.		

PE 12–3B

a.	Equipment	9,000	
	Kevin Camden, Capital		6,000
	Chloe Sayler, Capital		3,000
	($39,000 – $30,000) × 2/3.		

b.	Cash	60,000	
	Demarco Lee, Capital		60,000

PE 12–4A

Equity of Bellows...	$200,000
Rodriguez's contribution..	360,000
Total equity after admitting Rodriguez.......................................	$560,000
Rodriguez's equity interest...	× 60%
Rodriguez's equity after admission...	$336,000
Rodriguez's contribution..	$360,000
Rodriguez's equity after admission...	336,000
Bonus paid to Bellows...	$ 24,000

PE 12–4B

Equity of Hiro...	$ 75,000
Marone's contribution..	25,000
Total equity after admitting Marone...	$100,000
Marone's equity interest..	× 40%
Marone's equity after admission...	$ 40,000
Marone's contribution..	25,000
Bonus paid to Marone..	$ 15,000

PE 12–5A

Morgan's equity prior to liquidation...............................		$32,000
Realization of asset sales..	$120,000	
Book value of assets		
($32,000 + $60,000 + $10,000).....................................	102,000	
Gain on liquidation...	$ 18,000	
Morgan's share of gain (50% × $18,000).........................		9,000
Morgan's cash distribution..		$41,000

PE 12–5B

Manning's equity prior to liquidation.............................		$240,000
Realization of asset sales..	$410,000	
Book value of assets		
($240,000 + $150,000 + $80,000).................................	470,000	
Loss on liquidation...	$ (60,000)	
Manning's share of loss (50% × $60,000).......................		30,000
Manning's cash distribution..		$270,000

PE 12–6A

a. Barns' equity prior to liquidation................... $55,000

Realization of asset sales...........................	$ 40,000
Book value of assets*................................	160,000
Loss on liquidation....................................	$(120,000)
Barns' share of loss (50% × –$120,000).........	(60,000)
Barns' deficiency.....................................	$ (5,000)

  * $105,000 + $55,000

b. $40,000. ($105,000 – $60,000 share of loss – $5,000 Barns' deficiency; also equals the amount realized from asset sales)

PE 12–6B

a. Bonilla's equity prior to liquidation............... $ 185,000

Realization of asset sales...........................	$ 30,000
Book value of assets*................................	430,000
Loss on liquidation....................................	$(400,000)
Bonilla's share of loss (50% × –$400,000)......	(200,000)
Bonilla's deficiency...................................	$ (15,000)

  * $185,000 + $245,000

b. $30,000. ($245,000 – $200,000 share of loss – $15,000 Bonilla's deficiency; also equals the amount realized from asset sales)

PE 12–7A

a. 2014: $\dfrac{\$12,375,000}{75 \text{ employees}}$ = $165,000 per employee

   2015: $\dfrac{\$15,400,000}{88 \text{ employees}}$ = $175,000 per employee

b. Niles and Cohen, CPAs grew revenues by $3,025,000 ($15,400,0000 – $12,375,000), or 24.4% ($3,025,000 ÷ $12,375,000). The number of employees expanded by 13, or 17.3% (13 ÷ 75). The growth in revenue was more than the growth in the number of employees; thus, the revenue per employee improved between the two years. The firm is more efficient in generating revenues from its staff resources between the two years.

PE 12–7B

a. 2014: $\dfrac{\$1,800,000}{12 \text{ employees}}$ = $150,000 per employee

   2015: $\dfrac{\$1,440,000}{9 \text{ employees}}$ = $160,000 per employee

b. Eclipse Architects reduced revenues by $360,000 ($1,800,000 – $1,440,000), or 20% ($360,000 ÷ $1,800,000). The number of employees declined by 3, or 25% (3 ÷ 12). The decline in revenue was less than the decline in the number of employees; thus, the revenue per employee improved between the two years. The firm is more efficient in generating revenues from its staff resources between the two years.

EXERCISES

Ex. 12–1

Cash	18,000	
Accounts Receivable*	141,000	
Merchandise Inventory	98,400	
Equipment	81,500	
Allowance for Doubtful Accounts		5,700
Beyonce Sheffield, Capital		333,200

*$146,000 – $5,000

Ex. 12–2

Cash	60,000	
Accounts Receivable	130,000	
Land	275,000	
Equipment	30,500	
Allowance for Doubtful Accounts		8,500
Accounts Payable		24,800
Notes Payable		90,000
Amanda Carcello, Capital		372,200

Ex. 12–3

	Murphy	Drake
a.	$175,000	$175,000
b.	262,500	87,500
c.	146,300	203,700
d.	170,000	180,000
e.	174,500	175,500

Details:	Murphy	Drake	Total
a. Net income (1:1)....................	$175,000	$175,000	$350,000
b. Net income (3:1)....................	$262,500	$ 87,500	$350,000
c. Interest allowance.................	$ 13,500[1]	$ 4,500[2]	$ 18,000
Remaining income (2:3).........	132,800	199,200	332,000
Net income..........................	$146,300	$203,700	$350,000
d. Salary allowance...................	$ 40,000	$ 50,000	$ 90,000
Remaining income (1:1).........	130,000	130,000	260,000
Net income..........................	$170,000	$180,000	$350,000
e. Interest allowance.................	$ 13,500[1]	$ 4,500[2]	$ 18,000
Salary allowance...................	40,000	50,000	90,000
Remaining income (1:1).........	121,000	121,000	242,000
Net income..........................	$174,500	$175,500	$350,000

[1]$270,000 × 5%

[2]$90,000 × 5%

Ex. 12–4

	Murphy	Drake
a.	$63,000	$63,000
b.	94,500	31,500
c.	56,700	69,300
d.	58,000	68,000
e.	62,500	63,500

Details:	Murphy	Drake	Total
a. Net income (1:1)..........	$63,000	$63,000	$126,000
b. Net income (3:1)..........	$94,500	$31,500	$126,000
c. Interest allowance..........	$13,500[1]	$ 4,500[2]	$ 18,000
Remaining income (2:3)..........	43,200	64,800	108,000
Net income..........	$56,700	$69,300	$126,000
d. Salary allowance..........	$40,000	$50,000	$ 90,000
Remaining income (1:1)..........	18,000	18,000	36,000
Net income..........	$58,000	$68,000	$126,000
e. Interest allowance..........	$13,500[1]	$ 4,500[2]	$ 18,000
Salary allowance..........	40,000	50,000	90,000
Remaining income (1:1)..........	9,000	9,000	18,000
Net income..........	$62,500	$63,500	$126,000

[1]$270,000 × 5%

[2]$90,000 × 5%

Ex. 12–5

	Megan West	Jon Sokolov	Total
Salary allowances..........	$ 45,000	$ 35,000	$ 80,000
Remainder (net loss, $40,000 plus $80,000 salary allowances) divided equally..........	(60,000)	(60,000)	(120,000)
Net loss..........	$(15,000)	$(25,000)	$ (40,000)

Ex. 12–6

a. The partners can divide net income in any ratio that they wish. However, in the absence of an agreement, net income is divided equally between the partners. Therefore, Wanda's conclusion was correct, but for the wrong reasons. In addition, note that the monthly drawings have no impact on the division of income. These drawings are not the same as a salary allowance, which is part of a formal income-sharing agreement.

b. An income-sharing agreement could be designed to credit each partner's capital account for his or her respective share of income. For example, an income-sharing agreement could be designed to credit Wanda for interest on her capital contribution, while a salary allowance could be designed to credit Ava for the greater effort she puts into the partnership. After deducting for these items, the remaining income could be divided equally.

Ex. 12–7

a. Net income: $112,000

	Neel	Tate	Total
Salary allowance......................	$45,000	$30,000	$ 75,000
Remaining income..................	22,200	14,800	37,000
Net income............................	$67,200	$44,800	$112,000

Neel's remaining income: ($112,000 – $75,000) × 3/5
Tate's remaining income: ($112,000 – $75,000) × 2/5

b. (1)

Income Summary	112,000	
Zachery Neel, Member Equity		67,200
Lauren Tate, Member Equity		44,800

(2)

Zachery Neel, Member Equity	45,000	
Lauren Tate, Member Equity	30,000	
Zachery Neel, Drawing		45,000
Lauren Tate, Drawing		30,000

Note: The reduction in members' equity from withdrawals would be disclosed on the statement of members' equity.

c. If the net income of the LLC were less than the sum of the salary allowances, both members would still be credited with their salary allowances. From this amount, each partner would deduct his or her share of the excess of the total salary allowance over the net income. Thus, the difference between the net income and total salary allowances would be allocated to each partner as a deduction, according to the income-sharing ratio.

Ex. 12–8

a.

	WLKT Partners	Madison Sanders	Observer Newspaper, LLC	Total
Salary allowance.................		$ 55,000		$ 55,000
Interest allowance..............	$ 20,000[1]	4,000[2]	$16,000[3]	40,000
Remaining income (4:3:3)...	106,000	79,500	79,500	265,000
Net income........................	$126,000	$138,500	$95,500	$360,000

[1] 10% × $200,000

[2] 10% × $40,000

[3] 10% × $160,000

b.

2014				
Dec.	31	Income Summary	360,000	
		WLKT Partners, Member Equity		126,000
		Madison Sanders, Member Equity		138,500
		Observer Newspaper, LLC,		
		Member Equity		95,500
2014				
Dec.	31	WLKT Partners, Member Equity	20,000	
		Madison Sanders, Member Equity*	59,000	
		Observer Newspaper, LLC,		
		Member Equity	16,000	
		WLKT Partners, Drawing		20,000
		Madison Sanders, Drawing		59,000
		Observer Newspaper, LLC,		
		Drawing		16,000

* $55,000 + $4,000

Ex. 12–8 (Concluded)

c.

	WLKT Partners	Madison Sanders	Observer Newspaper, LLC	Total
MARVEL MEDIA, LLC				
Statement of Members' Equity				
For the Year Ended December 31, 2014				
Members' equity, January 1, 2014	$200,000	$ 40,000	$160,000	$400,000
Additional investment during the year	50,000			50,000
	$250,000	$ 40,000	$160,000	$450,000
Net income for the year	126,000	138,500	95,500	360,000
	$376,000	$178,500	$255,500	$810,000
Withdrawals during the year	20,000	59,000	16,000	95,000
Members' equity, December 31, 2014	$356,000	$119,500	$239,500	$715,000

d. An income-sharing agreement provides flexibility and fairness. Without an income-sharing agreement, each member would be credited with an equal proportion of the total earnings, or one-third each. However, the members provide different capital and effort to the LLC. WLKT is a large contributor of capital (funds), while Madison Sanders is providing ongoing effort and expertise. These separate contributions should be acknowledged in the income-sharing formula. Thus, the agreement credits member equity for both interest on capital and a salary allowance for Sanders. Any remaining income is credited to capital according to a negotiated allocation, which in this case is not an equal amount to each member.

Ex. 12–9

a.	Jan.	31	Partner, Drawing	50,000,000	
			Cash		50,000,000

b.	Dec.	31	Income Summary	740,000,000	
			Partner, Capital		740,000,000

c.	Dec.	31	Partner, Capital*	600,000,000	
			Partner, Drawing		600,000,000

* 12 months × £50 million

d. Partner drawings are not the same as a salary. The drawings represent a distribution of the profits of the partnership that has been credited to the partners' capital accounts. In this case, the drawings occur during the year prior to the final accounting for profit distribution. Thus, the drawings could end up greater than the final partner net income. If this were the case, the partner would be liable to the partnership for returning the excess drawings over the income earned for the year.

Ex. 12–10

a. and b.

May Cheng, Capital	69,000	
Michael Cross, Capital		69,000
$207,000 × 1/3.		

Note: The sale to Cross is not a transaction of the partnership, so the sales price is not considered in this journal entry.

Ex. 12–11

a. (1)	Aaron Garner, Capital (20% × $180,000)	36,000	
	Ricardo Fernandez, Capital (25% × $120,000)	30,000	
	Aisha Carpenter, Capital		66,000

(2)	Cash	90,000	
	Isabel Diaz, Capital		90,000

b. Aaron Garner, Capital ($180,000 – $36,000)............... $144,000
Ricardo Fernandez, Capital ($120,000 – $30,000)....... 90,000
Aisha Carpenter.. 66,000
Isabel Diaz.. 90,000

12-14

Ex. 12–12

a.	Cash	70,000	
	Alex Jensen, Capital	4,000	
	Elon Craig, Capital	4,000	
	Marco Vega, Capital		78,000

b. Alex Jensen... $116,000
   Elon Craig.. 176,000
   Marco Vega.. 78,000

c. Tangible assets should be adjusted to current market prices so that the new partner does not share in any gains or losses from changes in market prices prior to being admitted. For example, if the market price of land doubled prior to admitting a new partner, the existing partners should realize the increase in the value of the land in their capital accounts prior to the new partner's admission. Otherwise, the new partner would share in the increase in the market value of the land.

Ex. 12–13

a. Bonus received by Solano:

   Cody Jenkins, capital.................................... $ 72,000
   Jun Ito, capital... 38,000
   Solano's contribution.................................... 30,000
   Total partners' capital after admitting Solano... $140,000
   Solano's equity interest after admission.......... × 30%
   Valeria Solano, capital.................................. $ 42,000
   Solano's contribution.................................... 30,000
   Bonus paid to Solano.................................... $ 12,000

b.	Cash	30,000	
	Cody Jenkins, Capital	6,000	
	Jun Ito, Capital	6,000	
	Valeria Solano, Capital		42,000

c. Apparently, Jenkins and Ito value the expertise offered by Solano. Solano is able to use the computer to design and render landscape designs. It is likely that this type of skill is very useful for both selling and implementing landscape ideas. Her skills can help the partnership sell ideas to clients by providing computer renderings of the designs. In this way, a client can see the design on the computer before agreeing to work. In addition, the computer-aided landscapes provide materials plans, labor estimates, and other cost estimates for a particular design. Thus, the partners may be better able to control their costs by using Solano's skills. Overall, they value her skills sufficiently to provide a partner bonus upon her admittance to the partnership.

Ex. 12–14

a.

Medical Equipment	40,000	
Abrams, Member Equity*		16,000
Lipscomb, Member Equity**		24,000

　* $40,000 × 2/5 = $16,000

** $40,000 × 3/5 = $24,000

b. (1)

Cash	228,000	
Abrams, Member Equity*		15,600
Lipscomb, Member Equity**		23,400
Lin, Member Equity		189,000

　* $39,000 × 2/5 = $15,600

** $39,000 × 3/5 = $23,400

Supporting calculations for the bonus:

Abrams, member equity ($154,000 + $16,000).....	$170,000
Lipscomb, member equity ($208,000 + $24,000)..	232,000
Contribution by Lin...	228,000
Total equity after admitting Lin........................	$630,000
Lin's equity interest after admission.................	× 30%
Lin, member equity...	$189,000
Contribution by Lin...	$228,000
Lin's equity interest after admission.................	189,000
Bonus paid to Abrams and Lipscomb...............	$ 39,000

(2)

Cash	124,000	
Abrams, Member Equity*	3,000	
Lipscomb, Member Equity**	4,500	
Lin, Member Equity		131,500

　* $7,500 × 2/5 = $3,000

** $7,500 × 3/5 = $4,500

Supporting calculations for the bonus:

Abrams, member equity...................................	$170,000
Lipscomb, member equity...............................	232,000
Contribution by Lin...	124,000
Total equity after admitting Lin........................	$526,000
Lin's equity interest after admission.................	× 25%
Lin, member equity...	$131,500
Contribution by Lin...	124,000
Bonus paid to Lin...	$ 7,500

Ex. 12–15

a.	G. Ferris, Capital	9,000	
	T. Martinez, Capital	9,000	
	Equipment		18,000

b. (1)	Cash	40,000	
	G. Ferris, Capital*	4,000	
	T. Martinez, Capital	4,000	
	D. Perez, Capital		48,000

* $8,000 × 1/2 = $4,000

Supporting calculations for the bonus:

G. Ferris, capital ($133,000 – $9,000)......	$124,000
T. Martinez, capital ($85,000 – $9,000)....	76,000
Contribution by Perez.........................	40,000
Total equity after admitting Perez..........	$240,000
Perez's equity interest after admission..	× 20%
D. Perez, capital...............................	$ 48,000
Contribution by Perez.........................	40,000
Bonus paid to Perez..........................	$ 8,000

(2)	Cash	112,000	
	G. Ferris, Capital*		9,200
	T. Martinez, Capital		9,200
	D. Perez, Capital		93,600

* $18,400 × 1/2 = $9,200

Supporting calculations for the bonus:

G. Ferris, capital...............................	$124,000
T. Martinez, capital...........................	76,000
Contribution by Perez.........................	112,000
Total equity after admitting Perez..........	$312,000
Perez's equity interest after admission..	× 30%
D. Perez, capital...............................	$ 93,600
Contribution by Perez.........................	$112,000
D. Perez, capital...............................	93,600
Bonus paid to Ferris and Martinez	$ 18,400

**The bonus to Ferris and Martinez is credited equally between Ferris'
and Martinez's capital accounts.**

Ex. 12–16

	Dennis Overton, Capital	Ben Testerman, Capital	Randy Campbell, Capital	Total Partner-ship Capital
ANGEL INVESTOR ASSOCIATES Statement of Partnership Equity For the Year Ended December 31, 2014				
Partnership capital, January 1, 2014	$180,000	$120,000		$300,000
Admission of Randy Campbell	—	—	$ 75,000	75,000
Salary allowance	40,000			40,000
Remaining income	52,800	35,200	22,000	110,000
Less: Partner withdrawals	(46,400)[1]	(17,600)[2]	(11,000)[3]	(75,000)
Partnership capital, December 31, 2014	$226,400	$137,600	$ 86,000	$450,000

[1] ($52,800 + $40,000) ÷ 2
[2] $35,200 ÷ 2
[3] $22,000 ÷ 2

Admission of Randy Campbell:

Equity of initial partners prior to admission......................... $300,000
Contribution by Campbell... 75,000
Total... $375,000
Campbell's equity interest after admission......................... × 20%
Campbell's equity after admission..................................... $ 75,000
Contribution by Campbell... 75,000
Bonus... $ 0

Net income distribution:

The income-sharing ratio is equal to the proportion of the capital balances after admitting Campbell according to the partnership agreement:

$$\text{Dennis Overton: } \frac{\$180,000}{\$375,000} = 48\%$$

$$\text{Ben Testerman: } \frac{\$120,000}{\$375,000} = 32\%$$

$$\text{Randy Campbell: } \frac{\$75,000}{\$375,000} = 20\%$$

These ratios can be multiplied by the $110,000 remaining income after the salary allowance to Overton ($150,000 – $40,000). These amounts are credited to the respective partner capital accounts. For example, Dennis Overton: $52,800 = $110,000 × 48%.

Ex. 12–16 (Concluded)

<u>Withdrawals:</u>

Half of the remaining income is distributed to the three partners. Overton need not take the salary allowance as a withdrawal but may allow it to accumulate in the member equity account. He is taking half of the allowance as a withdrawal.

Ex. 12–17

a.	Merchandise Inventory	24,000	
	Allowance for Doubtful Accounts		3,000
	Nick Rawls, Capital*		9,000
	Sarah Fitzpatrick, Capital**		6,000
	Antoine Faber, Capital**		6,000

* ($24,000 – $3,000) × 3/7

** ($24,000 – $3,000) × 2/7

b.	Nick Rawls, Capital*	274,000	
	Cash		104,000
	Notes Payable		170,000

* $265,000 + $9,000

Ex. 12–18

a. The income-sharing ratio is determined by dividing the net income for each member by the total net income. Thus, in 2014, the income-sharing ratio is as follows:

Idaho Properties, LLC: $\dfrac{\$57,000}{\$190,000} = 30\%$

Silver Streams, LLC: $\dfrac{\$133,000}{\$190,000} = 70\%$

Or a 3:7 ratio

Ex. 12–18 (Concluded)

b. Following the same procedure as in (a):

Idaho Properties, LLC: $\dfrac{\$62,500}{\$250,000}$ = 25%

Silver Streams, LLC: $\dfrac{\$137,500}{\$250,000}$ = 55%

Thomas Dunn: $\dfrac{\$50,000}{\$250,000}$ = 20%

c. Thomas Dunn provided a $230,000 cash contribution to the business. The amount credited to his member equity account is this amount less a $10,000 bonus paid to the other two members, or $220,000.

d. The positive entries to Idaho Properties and Silver Streams are the result of a bonus paid by Thomas Dunn.

e. Thomas Dunn acquired a 22% interest in the business on January 1, 2015, computed as follows:

Thomas Dunn, member equity...............................	$ 220,000
Idaho Properties, LLC, member equity....................	333,000
Silver Streams, LLC, member equity......................	447,000
Total...	$1,000,000
Thomas' ownership interest after admission	
($220,000 ÷ $1,000,000)..	22%

f. Withdrawals need not be the same as the income credited to the members' equity accounts. Withdrawals will be less than the amounts credited when the members wish to retain capital in the business to support business growth or otherwise strengthen the business.

Ex. 12–19

a. Cash balance...	$19,000	
Sum of capital accounts.................................	35,000	
Loss on realization.......................................	$16,000	

	Manley	Singh
Capital balances before realization.........................	$20,000	$15,000
b. Division of loss on realization*.............................	8,000	8,000
Balances...	$12,000	$ 7,000
c. Cash distributed to partners.................................	12,000	7,000
Final balances...	$ 0	$ 0

* $16,000 ÷ 2

Ex. 12–20

	Oliver	Ansari	Total
Capital balances before realization...........	$28,000	$35,000	$63,000
Division of gain on realization			
[($67,000 – $63,000) ÷ 2]........................	2,000	2,000	
Capital balances after realization..............	$30,000	$37,000	
Cash distributed to partners....................	30,000	37,000	
Final balances.......................................	$ 0	$ 0	

Ex. 12–21

a. Deficiency

b. $97,500 ($73,500 + $41,000 – $17,000)

c.	Cash		17,000	
	Fowler, Capital			17,000

Support for entry:	Lewis	Zapata	Fowler
Capital balances after realization..........	$73,500	$41,000	$(17,000) Dr.
Receipt of partner deficiency...............			17,000
Capital balances after eliminating			
deficiency..	$73,500	$41,000	$ 0

Ex. 12–22

a. Cash should be distributed as indicated in the following tabulation:

	Bray	Lincoln	Mapes	Total
Capital invested.......	$225	$300	$ —	$ 525
Net income.............	+325	+325	+325	+ 975*
Capital balances and cash distribution.....	$550	$625	$325	$1,500

* $1,500 – $225 – $300

b. Mapes has a capital deficiency of $75, as indicated in the following tabulation:

	Bray	Lincoln	Mapes	Total
Capital invested.......	$225	$300	$—	$525
Net loss..................	– 75	– 75	–75	–225*
Capital balances.......	$150	$225	$(75) Dr.	$300

* $300 – $525

Ex. 12–23

	Nettles	King	Tanaka
Capital balances after realization.....	$(15,000)	$ 46,000	$71,000
Distribution of partner deficiency....	15,000	(10,000)*	(5,000)**
Capital balances after deficiency distribution.................	$ 0	$ 36,000	$66,000

* $15,000 × 2/3
** $15,000 × 1/3

Ex. 12–24

GOLD, PORTER, AND SIMS
Statement of Partnership Liquidation
For the Period Ending July 1–29, 2014

	Cash	+	Noncash Assets	=	Liabilities	+	Gold (3/6)	+	Porter (2/6)	+	Sims (1/6)
Balances before realization	$ 56,000		$ 96,000		$32,000		$55,000		$45,000		$20,000
Sale of assets and division of loss	+90,000		–96,000		—		–3,000		–2,000		–1,000
Balances after realization	$146,000		$ 0		$32,000		$52,000		$43,000		$19,000
Payment of liabilities	–32,000		—		–32,000		—		—		—
Balances after payment of liabilities	$114,000		$ 0		$ 0		$52,000		$43,000		$19,000
Cash distributed to partners	–114,000		—		—		–52,000		–43,000		–19,000
Final balances	$ 0		$ 0		$ 0		$ 0		$ 0		$ 0

Ex. 12–25

a.

ARCADIA SALES, LLC
Statement of LLC Liquidation
For the Period August 1–31, 2014

	Cash	+	Noncash Assets	=	Liabilities	+	Lester (2/5)	+	Torres (2/5)	+	Hearst (1/5)
							Member Equity				
Balances before realization	$ 26,000		$146,000		$35,000		$49,000		$61,000		$27,000
Sale of assets and division of gain	+158,000		–146,000		—		+4,800		+4,800		+2,400
Balances after realization	$184,000		$ 0		$35,000		$53,800		$65,800		$29,400
Payment of liabilities	–35,000		—		–35,000		—		—		—
Balances after payment of liabilities	$149,000		$ 0		$ 0		$53,800		$65,800		$29,400
Cash distributed to members	–149,000		—		—		–53,800		–65,800		–29,400
Final balances	$ 0		$ 0		$ 0		$ 0		$ 0		$ 0

b.

Lester, Member Equity	53,800
Torres, Member Equity	65,800
Hearst, Member Equity	29,400
Cash	149,000

c. The income- and loss-sharing ratio is only used to distribute the gain or loss on the realization of asset sales. It is not used for the final distribution. The final distribution is based upon the credit balances in the member equity accounts after all gains and losses on realization have been divided and any partner deficiencies have been paid or allocated.

Ex. 12–26

a. (1)

Income Summary	62,000	
Angel Alvarez, Capital		31,000
Emma Allison, Capital		31,000

(2)

Angel Alvarez, Capital	32,000	
Emma Allison, Capital	39,000	
Angel Alvarez, Drawing		32,000
Emma Allison, Drawing		39,000

b.

ALVAREZ AND ALLISON			
Statement of Partnership Equity			
For the Year Ended December 31, 2014			
	Angel Alvarez	Emma Allison	Total
Capital, January 1, 2014	$47,000	$ 73,000	$120,000
Additional investment during the year	8,000	—	8,000
	$55,000	$ 73,000	$128,000
Net income for the year	31,000	31,000	62,000
	$86,000	$104,000	$190,000
Withdrawals during the year	32,000	39,000	71,000
Capital, December 31, 2014	$54,000	$ 65,000	$119,000

Ex. 12–27

a. Revenue per professional staff, current yr.: $\dfrac{\$10,900,000,000}{36,571} = \$298,050$

Revenue per professional staff, previous yr.: $\dfrac{\$10,700,000,000}{33,605} = \$318,405$

b. The revenues increased between the two years from $10.7 billion to $10.9 billion, or 1.9% [($10.9 – $10.7) ÷ $10.7]. Revenues have increased slowly during this period. The number of employees has grown, from 33,605 to 36,571, or 8.8% [(36,571 – 33,605) ÷ 33,605]. As a result, the revenue per professional staff employee has declined by approximately $20,000, from $318,405 to $298,050. There is a decline in efficiency during this time. It is interesting that Deloitte expanded staff during this period, even while revenues increased slowly. There is some risk, because there is a near-term loss of efficiency from this strategy.

Ex. 12–28

a. Revenue per employee, 2015: $\dfrac{\$16,200,000}{150} = \$108,000$

Revenue per employee, 2014: $\dfrac{\$18,400,000}{200} = \$92,000$

b. Revenues decreased between the two years; however, the number of employees has decreased at a faster rate. Thus, the revenue per employee increased from $92,000 in 2014 to $108,000 in 2015. This indicates that the efficiency of the firm has increased in the two years, even though revenues declined. This is likely the result of the termination of the two contracts. That is, the large decrease in the employment base is the likely result of the reduction in business. Thus, the business was able to reduce the workforce faster than the revenue base. This suggests that the contracts were not very efficient from a revenue per employee perspective, and were thus likely good candidates for termination.

PROBLEMS

Prob. 12–1A

1.

Mar.	1	Cash		21,100	
		Merchandise Inventory		55,900	
		Eric Keene, Capital			77,000
	1	Cash		39,600	
		Accounts Receivable		18,000	
		Equipment		54,900	
		Allowance for Doubtful Accounts			1,500
		Accounts Payable			15,000
		Notes Payable			36,000
		Abigail McKee, Capital			60,000

2.

KEENE AND MCKEE			
Balance Sheet			
March 1, 2014			
Assets			
Current assets:			
Cash		$60,700	
Accounts receivable	$18,000		
Less allowance for doubtful accounts	1,500	16,500	
Merchandise inventory		55,900	
Total current assets			$133,100
Plant assets:			
Equipment			54,900
Total assets			$188,000
Liabilities			
Current liabilities:			
Accounts payable		$15,000	
Notes payable		36,000	
Total liabilities			$ 51,000
Partners' Equity			
Eric Keene, capital		$77,000	
Abigail McKee, capital		60,000	
Total partners' equity			137,000
Total liabilities and partners' equity			$188,000

Prob. 12–1A (Concluded)

3.	Feb.	28	Income Summary	90,000	
			Eric Keene, Capital*		41,900
			Abigail McKee, Capital*		48,100
		28	Eric Keene, Capital	28,000	
			Abigail McKee, Capital	30,400	
			Eric Keene, Drawing		28,000
			Abigail McKee, Drawing		30,400

* Computations:

	Keene	McKee	Total
Interest allowance.................	$ 7,700[1]	$ 6,000[2]	$13,700
Salary allowance..................	22,500	30,400	52,900
Remaining income (1:1).........	11,700[3]	11,700[3]	23,400
Net income.........................	$41,900	$48,100	$90,000

[1] 10% × $77,000

[2] 10% × $60,000

[3] ($90,000 – $13,700 – $52,900) × 1/2

Prob. 12–2A

Plan	(1) $90,000 Lawford	Delgado	(2) $135,000 Lawford	Delgado
a.	$45,000	$45,000	$ 67,500	$67,500
b.	67,500	22,500	101,250	33,750
c.	30,000	60,000	45,000	90,000
d.	48,600	41,400	71,100	63,900
e.	32,600	57,400	55,100	79,900
f.	32,400	57,600	50,400	84,600

Details:

	$90,000 Lawford	Delgado	$135,000 Lawford	Delgado
a. Net income (1:1)....................	$45,000	$45,000	$ 67,500	$67,500
b. Net income (3:1)....................	$67,500	$22,500	$101,250	$33,750
c. Net income (1:2)....................	$30,000	$60,000	$ 45,000	$90,000
d. Interest allowance.................	$10,800	$ 3,600	$ 10,800	$ 3,600
Remaining income (1:1)..........	37,800	37,800	60,300	60,300
Net income..........................	$48,600	$41,400	$ 71,100	$63,900
e. Interest allowance.................	$10,800	$ 3,600	$ 10,800	$ 3,600
Salary allowance...................	28,000	60,000	28,000	60,000
Excess of allowances over				
income (1:1)........................	(6,200)	(6,200)		
Remaining income (1:1)..........			16,300	16,300
Net income..........................	$32,600	$57,400	$ 55,100	$79,900
f. Interest allowance.................	$10,800	$ 3,600	$ 10,800	$ 3,600
Salary allowance...................	28,000	60,000	28,000	60,000
Bonus allowance...................		400*		9,400**
Excess of allowances over				
income (1:1)........................	(6,400)	(6,400)		
Remaining income (1:1)..........			11,600	11,600
Net income..........................	$32,400	$57,600	$ 50,400	$84,600

* 20% × [$90,000 – ($28,000 + $60,000)]

** 20% × [$135,000 – ($28,000 + $60,000)]

Prob. 12–3A

1.

LAMBERT AND YOST Income Statement For the Year Ended December 31, 2014		
Professional fees		$395,300
Operating expenses:		
Salary expense	$154,500	
Depreciation expense—building	15,700	
Property tax expense	12,000	
Heating and lighting expense	8,500	
Supplies expense	6,000	
Depreciation expense—office equipment	5,000	
Miscellaneous expense	3,600	
Total operating expenses		205,300
Net income		$190,000

	Tyler Lambert	Jayla Yost	Total
Division of net income:			
Salary allowance.....................	$45,000	$54,700	$ 99,700
Interest allowance...................	13,500*	7,800**	21,300
Remaining income (1:1)............	34,500	34,500	69,000
Net income...............................	$93,000	$97,000	$190,000

* $135,000 × 10%

** ($88,000 – $10,000) × 10%

2.

LAMBERT AND YOST Statement of Partnership Equity For the Year Ended December 31, 2014			
	Tyler Lambert	Jayla Yost	Total
Capital, January 1, 2014	$135,000	$ 78,000	$213,000
Additional investment during the year	—	10,000	10,000
	$135,000	$ 88,000	$223,000
Net income for the year	93,000	97,000	190,000
	$228,000	$185,000	$413,000
Withdrawals during the year	50,000	60,000	110,000
Capital, December 31, 2014	$178,000	$125,000	$303,000

Prob. 12–3A (Concluded)

3.

LAMBERT AND YOST Balance Sheet December 31, 2014			
Assets			
Current assets:			
Cash		$ 34,000	
Accounts receivable		47,800	
Supplies		2,000	
Total current assets			$ 83,800
Plant assets:			
Land		$120,000	
Building	$157,500		
Less accumulated depreciation	67,200	90,300	
Office equipment	$ 63,600		
Less accumulated depreciation	21,700	41,900	
Total plant assets			252,200
Total assets			$336,000
Liabilities			
Current liabilities:			
Accounts payable		$ 27,900	
Salaries payable		5,100	
Total liabilities			$ 33,000
Partners' Equity			
Tyler Lambert, capital		$178,000	
Jayla Yost, capital		125,000	
Total partners' equity			303,000
Total liabilities and partners' equity			$336,000

Prob. 12–4A

1.

June	30	Asset Revaluations		2,900	
		Accounts Receivable			2,500
		Allowance for Doubtful Accounts			400
		[($42,500 – $2,500) × 5%] – $1,600.			

	30	Merchandise Inventory		4,600	
		Asset Revaluations			4,600
		$76,600 – $72,000.			

	30	Accumulated Depreciation—Equipment		43,100	
		Equipment			24,800
		Asset Revaluations			18,300
		$155,700 – $180,500.			

	30	Asset Revaluations		20,000	
		Musa Moshref, Capital			10,000
		Shaniqua Hollins, Capital			10,000

2.

July	1	Shaniqua Hollins, Capital		70,000	
		Taylor Anderson, Capital			70,000

	1	Cash		45,000	
		Taylor Anderson, Capital			45,000

Prob. 12–4A (Concluded)

3.

MOSHREF, HOLLINS, AND ANDERSON Balance Sheet July 1, 2014			
Assets			
Current assets:			
Cash[1]		$ 53,000	
Accounts receivable	$40,000		
Less allowance for doubtful accounts	2,000	38,000	
Merchandise inventory		76,600	
Prepaid insurance		3,000	
Total current assets			$170,600
Plant assets:			
Equipment			155,700
Total assets			$326,300
Liabilities			
Current liabilities:			
Accounts payable		$ 21,300	
Notes payable		35,000	
Total liabilities			$ 56,300
Partners' Equity			
Musa Moshref, capital[2]		$130,000	
Shaniqua Hollins, capital[3]		25,000	
Taylor Anderson, capital		115,000	
Total partners' equity			270,000
Total liabilities and partners' equity			$326,300

[1] $8,000 + $45,000

[2] $120,000 + $10,000

[3] $85,000 + $10,000 – $70,000

Prob. 12–5A

1.

GERLOFF, CHU, AND JEWETT
Statement of Partnership Liquidation
For Period February 3–28, 2014

		Cash	+	Noncash Assets	=	Liabilities	+	Gerloff (2/4)	+	Chu (1/4)	+	Jewett (1/4)
										Capital		
	Balances before realization	$ 5,200		$55,900		$15,000		$19,300		$4,500		$22,300
a.	Sale of assets and division of loss	+34,300		−55,900		—		−10,800		−5,400		−5,400
	Balances after realization	$39,500		$ 0		$15,000		$ 8,500		$ (900)		$16,900
b.	Payment of liabilities	−15,000		—		−15,000		—		—		—
	Balances after payment of liabilities	$24,500		$ 0		$ 0		$ 8,500		$ (900)		$16,900
c.	Receipt of deficiency	+900		—		—		—		+900		—
	Balances	$25,400		$ 0		$ 0		$ 8,500		$ 0		$16,900
d.	Cash distributed to partners	−25,400		—		—		−8,500		—		−16,900
	Final balances	$ 0		$ 0		$ 0		$ 0		$ 0		$ 0

2 a.

William Gerloff, Capital	600
Courtney Jewett, Capital	300
Joshua Chu, Capital	900

The $900 deficiency of Chu would be divided between the other partners, Gerloff and Jewett, in their income-sharing ratio (2:1, respectively). Therefore, Gerloff would absorb 2/3 of the $900 deficiency, or $600, and Jewett would absorb 1/3 of the $900 deficiency, or $300.

b.

William Gerloff, Capital*	7,900
Courtney Jewett, Capital**	16,600
Cash	24,500

*$8,500 − $600
**$16,900 − $300

12-34

Prob. 12–6A

1. a.

SAILS, WELCH, AND GREENBERG
Statement of Partnership Liquidation
For Period November 1–30, 2014

	Cash	+	Noncash Assets	=	Liabilities	+	Capital		
							Sails (2/5)	Welch (2/5)	Greenberg (1/5)
Balances before realization	$ 32,000		$128,000		$20,000		$58,000	$72,000	$10,000
Sale of assets and division of gain	+156,000		−128,000		—		+11,200	+11,200	+5,600
Balances after realization	$188,000		$ 0		$20,000		$69,200	$83,200	$15,600
Payment of liabilities	−20,000		—		−20,000		—	—	—
Balances after payment of liabilities	$168,000		$ 0		$ 0		$69,200	$83,200	$15,600
Cash distributed to partners	−168,000		—		—		−69,200	−83,200	−15,600
Final balances	$ 0		$ 0		$ 0		$ 0	$ 0	$ 0

Prob. 12–6A (Concluded)

1. b.

SAILS, WELCH, AND GREENBERG
Statement of Partnership Liquidation
For Period November 1–30, 2014

	Cash	+	Noncash Assets	=	Liabilities	+	Capital Sails (2/5)	+	Welch (2/5)	+	Greenberg (1/5)
Balances before realization	$32,000		$128,000		$20,000		$58,000		$72,000		$10,000
Sale of assets and division of loss	+55,000		–128,000		—		–29,200		–29,200		–14,600
Balances after realization	$87,000		$ 0		$20,000		$28,800		$42,800		$ (4,600)
Payment of liabilities	–20,000		—		–20,000		—		—		—
Balances after payment of liabilities	$67,000		$ 0		$ 0		$28,800		$42,800		$ (4,600)
Receipt of deficiency	+4,600		—		—		—		—		+4,600
Balances	$71,600		$ 0		$ 0		$28,800		$42,800		$ 0
Cash distributed to partners	–71,600		—		—		–28,800		–42,800		—
Final balances	$ 0		$ 0		$ 0		$ 0		$ 0		$ 0

2. a.

Sails, Capital	2,300	
Welch, Capital	2,300	
Greenberg, Capital		4,600

The $4,600 deficiency of Greenberg would be divided between the other partners, Sails and Welch, in their income-sharing ratio (1:1, respectively). Therefore, Sails would absorb 1/2 of the $4,600 deficiency, or $2,300, and Welch would absorb 1/2 of the $4,600 deficiency, or $2,300.

b.

Sails, Capital*	26,500	
Welch, Capital**	40,500	
Cash		67,000

*$28,800 – $2,300

**$42,800 – $2,300

12-36

Prob. 12–1B

1.

Apr.	1	Cash		18,000	
		Merchandise Inventory		50,000	
		Whitney Lang, Capital			68,000
	1	Cash		26,200	
		Accounts Receivable		43,400	
		Merchandise Inventory		28,900	
		Equipment		63,400	
		Allowance for Doubtful Accounts			3,500
		Accounts Payable			23,400
		Notes Payable			15,000
		Eli Capri, Capital			120,000

2.

<table>
<tr><td colspan="4" align="center">LANG AND CAPRI
Balance Sheet
April 1, 2013</td></tr>
<tr><td colspan="4" align="center">Assets</td></tr>
<tr><td>Current assets:</td><td></td><td></td><td></td></tr>
<tr><td>Cash</td><td></td><td>$ 44,200</td><td></td></tr>
<tr><td>Accounts receivable</td><td>$43,400</td><td></td><td></td></tr>
<tr><td>Less allowance for doubtful accounts</td><td>3,500</td><td>39,900</td><td></td></tr>
<tr><td>Merchandise inventory</td><td></td><td>78,900</td><td></td></tr>
<tr><td>Total current assets</td><td></td><td></td><td>$163,000</td></tr>
<tr><td>Plant assets:</td><td></td><td></td><td></td></tr>
<tr><td>Equipment</td><td></td><td></td><td>63,400</td></tr>
<tr><td>Total assets</td><td></td><td></td><td>$226,400</td></tr>
<tr><td colspan="4" align="center">Liabilities</td></tr>
<tr><td>Current liabilities:</td><td></td><td></td><td></td></tr>
<tr><td>Accounts payable</td><td></td><td>$ 23,400</td><td></td></tr>
<tr><td>Notes payable</td><td></td><td>15,000</td><td></td></tr>
<tr><td>Total liabilities</td><td></td><td></td><td>$ 38,400</td></tr>
<tr><td colspan="4" align="center">Partners' Equity</td></tr>
<tr><td>Whitney Lang, capital</td><td></td><td>$ 68,000</td><td></td></tr>
<tr><td>Eli Capri, capital</td><td></td><td>120,000</td><td></td></tr>
<tr><td>Total partners' equity</td><td></td><td></td><td>188,000</td></tr>
<tr><td>Total liabilities and partners' equity</td><td></td><td></td><td>$226,400</td></tr>
</table>

CHAPTER 12   Accounting for Partnerships and Limited Liability Companies

Prob. 12–1B (Concluded)

3.	Mar.	31	Income Summary	118,000	
			Whitney Lang, Capital*		63,400
			Eli Capri, Capital*		54,600
		31	Whitney Lang, Capital	40,000	
			Eli Capri, Capital	30,000	
			Whitney Lang, Drawing		40,000
			Eli Capri, Drawing		30,000

* Computations:

	Lang	Capri	Total
Interest allowance.................	$ 6,800[1]	$ 12,000[2]	$ 18,800
Salary allowance...................	36,000	22,000	58,000
Remaining income (1:1).........	20,600[3]	20,600[3]	41,200
Net income..........................	$63,400	$54,600	$118,000

[1] 10% × $68,000

[2] 10% × $120,000

[3] ($118,000 – $18,800 – $58,000) × 1/2

Prob. 12–2B

Plan	(1) $420,000 Howell	Nickles	(2) $150,000 Howell	Nickles
a.	$210,000	$210,000	$ 75,000	$75,000
b.	168,000	252,000	60,000	90,000
c.	280,000	140,000	100,000	50,000
d.	249,500	170,500	87,500	62,500
e.	218,250	201,750	83,250	66,750
f.	254,550	165,450	92,550	57,450

Details:

	$420,000 Howell	Nickles	$150,000 Howell	Nickles
a. Net income (1:1)......................	$210,000	$210,000	$ 75,000	$75,000
b. Net income (2:3)......................	$168,000	$252,000	$ 60,000	$90,000
c. Net income (2:1)......................	$280,000	$140,000	$100,000	$50,000
d. Interest allowance....................	$ 5,000	$ 7,500	$ 5,000	$ 7,500
Remaining income (3:2).............	244,500	163,000	82,500	55,000
Net income...............................	$249,500	$170,500	$ 87,500	$62,500
e. Interest allowance....................	$ 5,000	$ 7,500	$ 5,000	$ 7,500
Salary allowance......................	38,000	19,000	38,000	19,000
Remaining income (1:1).............	175,250	175,250	40,250	40,250
Net income..............................	$218,250	$201,750	$ 83,250	$66,750
f. Interest allowance....................	$ 5,000	$ 7,500	$ 5,000	$ 7,500
Salary allowance......................	38,000	19,000	38,000	19,000
Bonus allowance......................	72,600*		18,600**	
Remaining income (1:1).............	138,950	138,950	30,950	30,950
Net income..............................	$254,550	$165,450	$ 92,550	$57,450

* 20% × [$420,000 – ($38,000 + $19,000)]

** 20% × [$150,000 – ($38,000 + $19,000)]

Prob. 12–3B

1.

RAMIREZ AND XUE Income Statement For the Year Ended December 31, 2014		
Professional fees		$555,300
Operating expenses:		
Salary expense	$384,900	
Depreciation expense—building	12,900	
Heating and lighting expense	10,500	
Depreciation expense—office equipment	6,300	
Property tax expense	3,200	
Supplies expense	3,000	
Miscellaneous expense	2,500	
Total operating expenses		423,300
Net income		$132,000

	Camila Ramirez	Ping Xue	Total
Division of net income:			
Salary allowance	$50,000	$65,000	$115,000
Interest allowance	15,000 *	16,200 **	31,200
Remaining income (loss) (1:1)	(7,100)	(7,100)	(14,200)
Net income	$57,900	$74,100	$132,000

* $125,000 × 12%
** ($155,000 − $20,000) × 12%

2.

RAMIREZ AND XUE Statement of Partnership Equity For the Year Ended December 31, 2014			
	Camila Ramirez	Ping Xue	Total
Capital, January 1, 2014	$125,000	$135,000	$260,000
Additional investment during the year	—	20,000	20,000
	$125,000	$155,000	$280,000
Net income for the year	57,900	74,100	132,000
	$182,900	$229,100	$412,000
Withdrawals during the year	35,000	50,000	85,000
Capital, December 31, 2014	$147,900	$179,100	$327,000

Prob. 12–3B (Concluded)

3.

RAMIREZ AND XUE Balance Sheet December 31, 2014			
Assets			
Current assets:			
Cash		$ 70,300	
Accounts receivable		33,600	
Supplies		5,800	
Total current assets			$ 109,700
Plant assets:			
Land		$128,000	
Building	$175,000		
Less accumulated depreciation	80,000	95,000	
Office equipment	$ 42,000		
Less accumulated depreciation	25,300	16,700	
Total plant assets			239,700
Total assets			$349,400
Liabilities			
Current liabilities:			
Accounts payable		$ 12,400	
Salaries payable		10,000	
Total liabilities			$ 22,400
Partners' Equity			
Camila Ramirez, capital		$147,900	
Ping Xue, capital		179,100	
Total partners' equity			327,000
Total liabilities and partners' equity			$349,400

Prob. 12–4B

1.

Aug.	31	Asset Revaluations		1,800	
		Accounts Receivable			1,500
		Allowance for Doubtful Accounts			300
		[($19,500 − $1,500) × 5%] − $600.			

	31	Merchandise Inventory		4,300	
		Asset Revaluations			4,300
		$46,800 − $42,500.			

	31	Accumulated Depreciation—Equipment		15,500	
		Equipment			3,000
		Asset Revaluations			12,500
		$64,500 − $67,500.			

	31	Asset Revaluations		15,000	
		Brian Caldwell, Capital			7,500
		Adriana Estrada, Capital			7,500

2.

Sept.	1	Adriana Estrada, Capital		26,000	
		Kris Mays, Capital			26,000

	1	Cash		32,000	
		Kris Mays, Capital			32,000

Prob. 12–4B (Concluded)

3.

CALDWELL, ESTRADA, AND MAYS Balance Sheet September 1, 2014			
Assets			
Current assets:			
Cash[1]		$44,300	
Accounts receivable	$18,000		
Less allowance for doubtful accounts	900	17,100	
Merchandise inventory		46,800	
Prepaid insurance		1,200	
Total current assets			$109,400
Plant assets:			
Equipment			64,500
Total assets			$173,900
Liabilities			
Current liabilities:			
Accounts payable		$ 8,900	
Notes payable		15,000	
Total liabilities			$ 23,900
Partners' Equity			
Brian Caldwell, capital[2]		$62,500	
Adriana Estrada, capital[3]		29,500	
Kris Mays, capital		58,000	
Total partners' equity			150,000
Total liabilities and partners' equity			$173,900

[1] $12,300 + $32,000

[2] $55,000 + $7,500

[3] $48,000 + $7,500 – $26,000

12-43

Prob. 12–5B

1.

FAIRCHILD, LOWES, AND HOWARD
Statement of Partnership Liquidation
For the Period April 10–30, 2014

		Cash	+	Noncash Assets	=	Liabilities	+	Capital Fairchild (1/4)	+	Lowes (1/4)	+	Howard (2/4)
	Balances before realization	$23,500		$84,500		$22,000		$42,000		$ 7,500		$36,500
a.	Sale of assets and division of loss	+48,500		–84,500		—		–9,000		–9,000		–18,000
b.	Balances after realization	$72,000		$ 0		$22,000		$33,000		$(1,500)		$18,500
	Payment of liabilities	–22,000		—		–22,000		—		—		—
c.	Balances after payment of liabilities	$50,000		$ 0		$ 0		$33,000		$(1,500)		$18,500
	Receipt of deficiency	+1,500		—		—		—		+1,500		—
d.	Balances	$51,500		$ 0		$ 0		$33,000		$ 0		$18,500
	Cash distributed to partners	–51,500		—		—		–33,000		—		–18,500
	Final balances	$ 0		$ 0		$ 0		$ 0		$ 0		$ 0

2. a.

Zach Fairchild, Capital	500
Amber Howard, Capital	1,000
Austin Lowes, Capital	1,500

The $1,500 deficiency of Lowes would be divided between the other partners, Fairchild and Howard, in their income-sharing ratio (1:2 respectively). Therefore, Fairchild would absorb 1/3 of the $1,500 deficiency, or $500, and Howard would absorb 2/3 of the $1,500 deficiency, or $1,000.

b.

Zach Fairchild, Capital*	32,500
Amber Howard, Capital**	17,500
Cash	50,000

*$33,000 – $500

**$18,500 – $1,000

Prob. 12–6B

1. a.

CHAPELLE, ROCK, AND PRYOR
Statement of Partnership Liquidation
For Period August 3–29, 2014

	Cash	+	Noncash Assets	=	Liabilities	+	Capital Chapelle (1/5)	+	Capital Rock (2/5)	+	Capital Pryor (2/5)
Balances before realization	$ 65,000		$167,000		$30,000		$14,000		$102,000		$ 86,000
Sale of assets and division of gain	+217,000		−167,000		—		+10,000		+20,000		+20,000
Balances after realization	$282,000		$ 0		$30,000		$24,000		$122,000		$106,000
Payment of liabilities	−30,000		—		−30,000		—		—		—
Balances after payment of liabilities	$252,000		$ 0		$ 0		$24,000		$122,000		$106,000
Cash distributed to partners	−252,000		—		—		−24,000		−122,000		−106,000
Final balances	$ 0		$ 0		$ 0		$ 0		$ 0		$ 0

Prob. 12–6B (Concluded)

1. b.

CHAPELLE, ROCK, AND PRYOR
Statement of Partnership Liquidation
For Period August 3–29, 2014

	Cash	+	Noncash Assets	=	Liabilities	+	Capital Chapelle (1/5)	+	Capital Rock (2/5)	+	Capital Pryor (2/5)
Balances before realization	$ 65,000		$167,000		$30,000		$14,000		$102,000		$86,000
Sale of assets and division of loss	+72,000		–167,000		—		–19,000		–38,000		–38,000
Balances after realization	$137,000		$ 0		$30,000		$ (5,000)		$ 64,000		$48,000
Payment of liabilities	–30,000		—		–30,000		—		—		—
Balances after payment of liabilities	$107,000		$ 0		$ 0		$ (5,000)		$ 64,000		$48,000
Receipt of deficiency	+5,000		—		—		+5,000		—		—
Balances	$112,000		$ 0		$ 0		$ 0		$ 64,000		$48,000
Cash distributed to partners	–112,000		—		—		—		–64,000		–48,000
Final balances	$ 0		$ 0		$ 0		$ 0		$ 0		$ 0

2. a.

Rock, Capital	2,500
Pryor, Capital	2,500
Chapelle, Capital	5,000

The $5,000 deficiency of Chapelle would be divided between the other partners, Rock and Pryor, in their income-sharing ratio (1:1, respectively). Therefore, Rock would absorb 1/2 of the $5,000 deficiency, or $2,500, and Pryor would absorb 1/2 of the $5,000 deficiency, or $2,500.

b.

Rock, Capital*	61,500
Pryor, Capital**	45,500
Cash	107,000

*$64,000 – $2,500
**$48,000 – $2,500

CASES & PROJECTS

CP 12–1

This scenario highlights one of the problems that arises in partnerships: attempting to align contribution with income division. Often, disagreements are based on honest differences of opinion. However, in this scenario, there is evidence that Robbins was acting unethically. Robbins apparently made no mention of his plans to "scale back" once the partnership was consummated. As a result, Barrow agreed to an equal division of income based on the assumption that Robbins' past efforts would project into the future, while in fact, Robbins had no intention of this. As a result, Barrow is now providing more effort, while receiving the same income as Robbins. This is clearly not sustainable in the long term. Robbins does not appear to be concerned about this inequity. Thus, the evidence points to some duplicity on Robbins' part. Essentially, he knows that he is riding on Barrow's effort and had planned it that way.

Barrow could respond to this situation by either withdrawing from the partnership or changing the partnership agreement. One possible change would be to provide a partner salary based on the amount of patient billings. This salary would be highly associated with the amount of revenue brought into the partnership, thus avoiding disputes associated with unequal contributions to the firm.

CP 12–2

A good solution to this problem would be to divide income in three steps:

1. Provide interest on each partner's capital balance.
2. Provide a monthly salary for each partner.
3. Divide the remainder according to a partnership formula.

With this approach, the return on capital and effort will be separately calculated in the income division formula before applying the percentage formula. Thus, Willard will receive a large interest distribution based on the large capital balance, while Hill should receive a large salary distribution based on the larger service contribution. The return on capital and salary allowances should be based on prevailing market rates. If both partners are pleased with their return on capital and effort, then the remaining income could be divided equally between them.

CP 12–3

a.

	Revenue per Partner*	Revenue per Professional Staff**
Deloitte & Touche..	$3,795,281	$324,685
PwC..	3,645,191	370,897
Ernst & Young..	3,086,957	405,714
KPMG..	2,779,420	331,188

PwC is PricewaterhouseCoopers

* Revenue per partner is determined by dividing the total revenue by the number of partners for each firm, adjusting the revenues for the fact that they are expressed in millions in the table. For example, revenue per partner is determined for Deloitte & Touche as follows:

Deloitte & Touche revenue per partner: $\dfrac{\$10,938,000,000}{2,882} = \$3,795,281$

** Likewise, the revenue per professional staff is determined by dividing the total revenue by the number of professional staff, adjusting the revenues for the fact that they are expressed in millions in the table. For example, revenue per professional staff is determined for Deloitte & Touche as follows:

Deloitte & Touche revenue per professional staff: $\dfrac{\$10,938,000,000}{33,688} = \$324,685$

b. The amount of revenue earned per partner can be compared across the four firms by setting each firm's revenue per partner as a percent of the highest revenue per partner firm, as follows:

	Revenue per Partner	Percent of Deloitte & Touche
Deloitte & Touche...	$3,795,281	100%
PwC...	3,645,191	96%*
Ernst & Young...	3,086,957	81%
KPMG...	2,779,420	73%

* $3,645,191 ÷ $3,795,281

As can be seen, Deloitte & Touche has the highest revenue per partner relative to the other three firms, while KPMG has the lowest. KPMG's revenue per partner is 73% of Deloitte & Touche's. These data suggest that Deloitte & Touche has a somewhat smaller partner base supporting its revenues than do the other three firms.

CP 12–3 (Concluded)

The amount of revenue earned per professional staff can be compared across the four firms by setting each firm's revenue per professional staff as a percent of the highest revenue per professional staff firm, as follows:

	Revenue per Professional Staff	Percent of Ernst & Young
Deloitte & Touche............................	$324,685	80%*
PwC..	370,897	91%
Ernst & Young.................................	405,714	100%
KPMG...	331,188	82%

* $324,685 ÷ $405,714

As can be seen, Ernst & Young has the highest revenue per professional staff of the four firms. PwC, for example, has revenue per professional staff equal to 91% of Ernst & Young. Ernst & Young appears to be the most efficient firm in the use of professional staff compared to the other three firms.

Taken together, both tables indicate that Deloitte & Touche provides more revenue per partner (and possibly more profit per partner) than the other three firms, but does not have the operating efficiency of Ernst & Young in terms of the use of professional staff. In contrast, Ernst & Young appears to have the most efficient use of professional staff of all the firms, but provides less revenue per partner (and possibly less profit per partner) than does Deloitte & Touche.

CP 12–4

When developing an LLC (or partnership), the operating (or partnership) agreement is a critical part of establishing a business. Each party must consider the various incentives of each individual in the LLC. For example, in this case, one party, Lindsey Wilson, is providing all of the funding, while the other two parties are providing expertise and talent. This type of arrangement can create some natural conflicts because the interests of an investor might not be exactly the same as those operating the LLC. Specifically, you would want to advise Wilson that not all matters should be settled by majority vote. Such a provision would allow the two noninvesting members to vote as a block to the detriment of Wilson. For example, the salaries for the two working members could be set by their vote, so that little profit would be left to be distributed. This would essentially keep Wilson's return limited to the 10% preferred return. Wilson should insist that salary allowances require unanimous approval of all members.

CP 12–4 (Concluded)

A second issue is the division of partnership income. The suggested agreement is for all the partners to share the remaining income, after the 10% preferred return, equally. Wilson should be counseled to consider all aspects of the LLC contribution to determine if this division is equitable. There are many considerations including the amount of investment, risk of the venture, degree of expertise of noninvesting partners, and degree of exclusivity of noninvesting members' effort contribution (unique skills or business connections, for example). Often, the simple assumption of equal division is not appropriate.

In addition, it is sometimes best to require even working members to have an investment in the LLC, even if it is small, so that they are sensitive to the perspective of financial loss.

CP 12–5

a. Chrysler Group LLC produces and sells Chrysler, Jeep, and Dodge vehicles.

b. A transaction selling a majority interest of Chrysler from DaimlerChrysler to Cerberus Capital Management to form Chrysler LLC was announced on May 14, 2007, and completed on August 3, 2007. Since that time, Chrysler LLC went into Chapter 11 bankruptcy and emerged in late 2009 as Chrysler Group LLC. The new entity has an alliance with Fiat. In 2011, Fiat exercised options to increase its ownership stake.

c. Chrysler Group LLC went through significant changes during the recession of 2009. The U.S. government provided bailout funds that were turned into an equity interest in the firm. As of June 30, 2011, Chrysler Group LLC was 47% owned by Fiat, 45% by the United Auto Workers union, 6.5% by the U.S. government, and 1.5% by the Canadian government.

d. Chrysler Group LLC is not a public company. Its major owners, Fiat, UAW, U.S. and Canadian governments, and private equity funds hold their ownership interests privately. The LLC form is well suited to Chrysler Group because there are a few large private owners to the firm.

Note to Instructors: The ownership details of part (c) change over time as Fiat continues to exercise options to buy out other members. Students may have more current details than provided here. The point of the case is to see that the ownership structure is limited to a few members. Wikipedia provides dated ownership information which should be satisfactory for the purposes of the case.

CHAPTER 13
CORPORATIONS: ORGANIZATION, STOCK
TRANSACTIONS, AND DIVIDENDS

DISCUSSION QUESTIONS

1. No. Common stock with a higher par is not necessarily a better investment than common stock with a lower par because par is an amount assigned to the shares.

2. The broker is not correct. Corporations are not legally liable to pay dividends until the dividends are declared. If the company that issued the preferred stock has operating losses, it could omit dividends, first, on its common stock and, later, on its preferred stock.

3. The company may not have had enough cash on hand to pay a dividend on the common stock, or resources may be needed for plant expansion, replacement of facilities, payment of liabilities, etc.

4. a. No change.
   b. Total equity is the same.

5. a. Current liability
   b. Stockholders' equity

6. a. It has no effect on revenue or expense.
   b. It reduces stockholders' equity by $3,000,000.

7. a. It has no effect on revenue.
   b. It increases stockholders' equity by $3,750,000.

8. The three classifications of restrictions on retained earnings are legal, contractual, and discretionary. Restrictions are normally reported in the notes to the financial statements.

9. Such prior period adjustments should be reported as an adjustment to the beginning balance of retained earnings.

10. The primary purpose of a stock split is to bring about a reduction in the market price per share and thus to encourage more investors to buy the company's shares.

PRACTICE EXERCISES

PE 13–1A

	Year 1	Year 2	Year 3
Amount distributed....................................	$30,000	$90,000	$125,000
Preferred dividend (40,000 shares)...............	30,000	66,000*	48,000
Common dividend (50,000 shares)...............	$ 0	$24,000	$ 77,000

* $18,000 + $48,000

Dividends per share:			
Preferred stock......................................	$0.75	$1.65	$1.20
Common stock.......................................	None	$0.48	$1.54

PE 13–1B

	Year 1	Year 2	Year 3
Amount distributed....................................	$21,600	$4,000	$100,800
Preferred dividend (16,000 shares)...............	6,400	4,000	8,800*
Common dividend (80,000 shares)...............	$15,200	$ 0	$ 92,000

* $2,400 + $6,400

Dividends per share:			
Preferred stock......................................	$0.40	$0.25	$0.55
Common stock.......................................	$0.19	None	$1.15

PE 13–2A

May	10	Cash (90,000 shares × $42)	3,780,000	
		Common Stock (90,000 shares × $30)		2,700,000
		Paid-In Capital in Excess of Stated Value—		
		Common Stock [90,000 shares × ($42 – $30)]		1,080,000

Sept.	3	Cash	900,000	
		Preferred Stock (36,000 shares × $25)		900,000

Dec.	1	Cash (14,000 shares × $33)	462,000	
		Preferred Stock (14,000 shares × $25)		350,000
		Paid-In Capital in Excess of Par—		
		Preferred Stock [14,000 shares × ($33 – $25)]		112,000

PE 13–2B

Jan.	22	Cash	720,000	
		Common Stock (180,000 shares × $4)		720,000
Feb.	14	Cash	2,420,000	
		Preferred Stock (44,000 shares × $55)		2,420,000
Aug.	30	Cash (9,000 shares × $60)	540,000	
		Preferred Stock (9,000 shares × $55)		495,000
		Paid-In Capital in Excess of Par—		
		Preferred Stock [9,000 shares × ($60 – $55)]		45,000

PE 13–3A

Aug.	1	Cash Dividends	1,250,000	
		Cash Dividends Payable		1,250,000
Oct.	15	No entry required.		
Nov.	14	Cash Dividends Payable	1,250,000	
		Cash		1,250,000

PE 13–3B

Feb.	1	Cash Dividends	480,000	
		Cash Dividends Payable		480,000
Mar.	18	No entry required.		
May	1	Cash Dividends Payable	480,000	
		Cash		480,000

PE 13–4A

Feb.	15	Stock Dividends (250,000 shares × 2% × $52)	260,000	
		Stock Dividends Distributable (5,000 shares × $40)		200,000
		Paid-In Capital in Excess of Par—		
		Common Stock [$5,000 shares × ($52 – $40)]		60,000
Mar.	27	No entry required.		
May	2	Stock Dividends Distributable	200,000	
		Common Stock		200,000

PE 13–4B

June	8	Stock Dividends (820,000 shares × 5% × $63)	2,583,000	
		Stock Dividends Distributable (41,000 shares × $35)		1,435,000
		Paid-In Capital in Excess of Par—		
		Common Stock [41,000 shares × ($63 – $35)]		1,148,000
July	13	No entry required.		
Aug.	12	Stock Dividends Distributable	1,435,000	
		Common Stock		1,435,000

PE 13–5A

Jan.	31	Treasury Stock (22,500 shares × $31)	697,500	
		Cash		697,500
Apr.	20	Cash (12,800 shares × $40)	512,000	
		Treasury Stock (12,800 shares × $31)		396,800
		Paid-In Capital from Sale of		
		Treasury Stock [12,800 shares × ($40 – $31)]		115,200
Oct.	4	Cash (9,700 shares × $28)	271,600	
		Paid-In Capital from Sale of		
		Treasury Stock [9,700 shares × ($31 – $28)]	29,100	
		Treasury Stock (9,700 shares × $31)		300,700

PE 13–5B

May	27	Treasury Stock (75,000 shares × $8)	600,000	
		Cash		600,000
Aug.	3	Cash (54,000 shares × $11)	594,000	
		Treasury Stock (54,000 shares × $8)		432,000
		Paid-In Capital from Sale of		
		Treasury Stock [54,000 shares × ($11 – $8)]		162,000
Nov.	14	Cash (21,000 shares × $7)	147,000	
		Paid-In Capital from Sale of		
		Treasury Stock [21,000 shares × ($8 – $7)]	21,000	
		Treasury Stock (21,000 shares × $8)		168,000

PE 13–6A

Stockholders' Equity		
Paid-in capital:		
Common stock, $60 par (250,000 shares		
authorized, 200,000 shares issued)	$12,000,000	
Excess of issue price over par	3,200,000	$15,200,000
From sale of treasury stock		320,000
Total paid-in capital		$15,520,000
Retained earnings		18,500,000
Total		$34,020,000
Deduct treasury stock (17,500 shares at cost)		1,137,500
Total stockholders' equity		$32,882,500

PE 13–6B

Stockholders' Equity		
Paid-in capital:		
Common stock, $120 par (500,000 shares		
authorized, 400,000 shares issued)	$48,000,000	
Excess of issue price over par	6,400,000	$ 54,400,000
From sale of treasury stock		4,500,000
Total paid-in capital		$ 58,900,000
Retained earnings		63,680,000
Total		$122,580,000
Deduct treasury stock (40,000 shares at cost)		5,200,000
Total stockholders' equity		$117,380,000

PE 13–7A

ROCKWELL INC. Retained Earnings Statement For the Year Ended June 30, 2014		
Retained earnings, July 1, 2013		$3,900,000
Net income	$714,000	
Less dividends declared	150,000	
Increase in retained earnings		564,000
Retained earnings, June 30, 2014		$4,464,000

PE 13–7B

NORIC CRUISES INC. Retained Earnings Statement For the Year Ended October 31, 2014		
Retained earnings, November 1, 2013		$12,400,000
Net income	$2,350,000	
Less dividends declared	475,000	
Increase in retained earnings		1,875,000
Retained earnings, October 31, 2014		$14,275,000

PE 13–8A

a.   2014: Earnings per Share $= \dfrac{\text{Net Income – Preferred Dividends}}{\text{Avg. Number of Common Shares Outstanding}}$

$= \dfrac{\$448,750 - \$40,000}{75,000 \text{ shares}}$

$= \dfrac{\$408,750}{75,000 \text{ shares}} = \$5.45$

2013: Earnings per Share $= \dfrac{\text{Net Income – Preferred Dividends}}{\text{Avg. Number of Common Shares Outstanding}}$

$= \dfrac{\$376,000 - \$40,000}{60,000 \text{ shares}}$

$= \dfrac{\$336,000}{60,000 \text{ shares}} = \$5.60$

b.   The decrease in the earnings per share from $5.60 to $5.45 indicates an unfavorable trend in the company's profitability.

PE 13–8B

a.   2014: Earnings per Share $= \dfrac{\text{Net Income – Preferred Dividends}}{\text{Avg. Number of Common Shares Outstanding}}$

$= \dfrac{\$2,485,700 - \$50,000}{115,000 \text{ shares}}$

$= \dfrac{\$2,435,700}{115,000 \text{ shares}} = \$21.18$

2013: Earnings per Share $= \dfrac{\text{Net Income – Preferred Dividends}}{\text{Avg. Number of Common Shares Outstanding}}$

$= \dfrac{\$1,538,000 - \$50,000}{80,000 \text{ shares}}$

$= \dfrac{\$1,488,000}{80,000 \text{ shares}} = \$18.60$

b.   The increase in the earnings per share from $18.60 to $21.18 indicates a favorable trend in the company's profitability.

EXERCISES

Ex. 13–1

		1st Year	2nd Year	3rd Year	4th Year
a.	Total dividend declared..............	$24,000	$81,000	$92,000	$139,000
	Preferred dividend (current)........	$24,000	$51,000*	$54,000	$ 54,000
	Preferred dividend in arrears.......	—	30,000	3,000	—
b.	Total preferred dividends............	$24,000	$81,000	$57,000	$ 54,000
	Preferred shares outstanding......	÷ 30,000	÷ 30,000	÷ 30,000	÷ 30,000
	Preferred dividend per share.......	$ 0.80	$ 2.70	$ 1.90	$ 1.80

  * $51,000 = $81,000 − $30,000

		1st Year	2nd Year	3rd Year	4th Year
	Dividend for common shares (a. − b.)...................................	$ —	$ —	$ 35,000	$ 85,000
	Common shares outstanding......			÷ 125,000	÷ 125,000
	Common dividend per share.......			$ 0.28	$ 0.68

Ex. 13–2

		1st Year	2nd Year	3rd Year	4th Year
a.	Total dividend declared..............	$36,000	$58,000	$75,000	$124,000
	Preferred dividend (current)........	$36,000	$44,000*	$50,000	$ 50,000
	Preferred dividend in arrears.......	—	14,000	6,000	—
b.	Total preferred dividends............	$36,000	$58,000	$56,000	$ 50,000
	Preferred shares outstanding......	÷ 40,000	÷ 40,000	÷ 40,000	÷ 40,000
	Preferred dividend per share.......	$ 0.90	$ 1.45	$ 1.40	$ 1.25

  * $44,000 = $58,000 − $14,000

		1st Year	2nd Year	3rd Year	4th Year
	Dividend for common shares (a. − b.)...................................	$ —	$ —	$ 19,000	$ 74,000
	Common shares outstanding......			÷ 100,000	÷ 100,000
	Common dividend per share.......			$ 0.19	$ 0.74

Ex. 13–3

a.

Feb.	25	Cash (120,000 shares × $40)	4,800,000	
		Common Stock (120,000 shares × $36)		4,320,000
		Paid-In Capital in Excess of Par—		
		Common Stock [120,000 shares × ($40 – $36)]		480,000
June	3	Cash (50,000 shares × $9)	450,000	
		Preferred Stock (50,000 shares × $8)		400,000
		Paid-In Capital in Excess of Par—		
		Preferred Stock [50,000 shares × ($9 – $8)]		50,000

b. $5,250,000 ($4,800,000 + $450,000)

Ex. 13–4

a.

Aug.	5	Cash (500,000 shares × $3)	1,500,000	
		Common Stock (500,000 shares × $1)		500,000
		Paid-In Capital in Excess of Stated Value—		
		Common Stock [500,000 shares × ($3 – $1)]		1,000,000
Dec.	17	Cash (5,000 shares × $200)	1,000,000	
		Preferred Stock (5,000 shares × $180)		900,000
		Paid-In Capital in Excess of Par—		
		Preferred Stock [5,000 shares × ($200 – $180)]		100,000

b. $2,500,000 ($1,500,000 + $1,000,000)

Ex. 13–5

May	10	Land (3,600 shares × $28)	100,800	
		Common Stock (3,600 shares × $4)		14,400
		Paid-In Capital in Excess of Par—		
		Common Stock [3,600 shares × ($28 – $4)]		86,400

Ex. 13–6

a.

Cash	900,000	
Common Stock (45,000 shares × $20)		900,000

b.

Organizational Expenses	8,000	
Common Stock (400 shares × $20)		8,000
Cash	1,200,000	
Common Stock (60,000 shares × $20)		1,200,000

c.

Land	150,000	
Building	600,000	
Interest Payable*		1,500
Mortgage Note Payable		450,000
Common Stock (14,925 shares × $20)		298,500

* An acceptable alternative would be to credit Interest Expense.

Ex. 13–7

Oct.	1	Cash (120,000 shares × $31.50)	3,780,000	
		Common Stock (120,000 shares × $30.00)		3,600,000
		Paid-In Capital in Excess of Par—		
		Common Stock [120,000 shares × ($31.50 – $30.00)]		180,000
Oct.	1	Buildings	2,380,000	
		Land	840,000	
		Preferred Stock (35,000 shares × $80)		2,800,000
		Paid-In Capital in Excess of Par—		
		Preferred Stock [35,000 shares × ($92 – $80)]		420,000

Ex. 13–8

Feb.	1	Cash	4,500,000	
		Common Stock (180,000 shares × $25)		4,500,000
	1	Organizational Expenses	10,000	
		Common Stock (400 shares × $25)		10,000
Mar.	9	Land	200,000	
		Buildings	550,000	
		Equipment	135,000	
		Common Stock (30,000 shares × $25.00)		750,000
		Paid-In Capital in Excess of Par—		
		Common Stock [30,000 shares × ($29.50 – $25.00)]		135,000
Apr.	13	Cash (8,500 shares × $131)	1,113,500	
		Preferred Stock (8,500 shares × $120)		1,020,000
		Paid-In Capital in Excess of Par—		
		Preferred Stock [8,500 shares × ($131 – $120)]		93,500

Ex. 13–9

July	10	Cash Dividends	187,500	
		Cash Dividends Payable		187,500
Aug.	9	No entry required.		
Sept.	18	Cash Dividends Payable	187,500	
		Cash		187,500

Ex. 13–10

a. (1)

Stock Dividends [(300,000 shares × 5%) × $40]	600,000	
Stock Dividends Distributable (15,000 shares × $18)		270,000
Paid-In Capital in Excess of Par—		
Common Stock [15,000 shares × ($40 – $18)]		330,000

(2)

Stock Dividends Distributable	270,000	
Common Stock		270,000

b. (1) $6,900,000 ($5,400,000 + $1,500,000)

(2) $78,000,000

(3) $84,900,000 ($6,900,000 + $78,000,000)

c. (1) $7,500,000 ($5,400,000 + $1,500,000 + $270,000 + $330,000)

(2) $77,400,000 ($78,000,000 – $600,000)

(3) $84,900,000 ($7,500,000 + $77,400,000)

Ex. 13–11

a.

Mar.	4	Treasury Stock (33,000 shares × $84)	2,772,000	
		Cash		2,772,000
Aug.	27	Cash (25,000 shares × $90)	2,250,000	
		Treasury Stock (25,000 shares × $84)		2,100,000
		Paid-In Capital from Sale of Treasury		
		Stock [25,000 shares × ($90 – $84)]		150,000
Nov.	11	Cash (8,000 shares × $80)	640,000	
		Paid-In Capital from Sale of Treasury		
		Stock [8,000 shares × ($84 – $80)]	32,000	
		Treasury Stock (8,000 shares × $84)		672,000

b. $118,000 ($150,000 – $32,000) credit

c.   Crystal Lake may have purchased the stock to support the market price of the stock, to provide shares for resale to employees, or for reissuance to employees as a bonus according to stock purchase agreements.

Ex. 13–12

a.

Feb.	17	Treasury Stock (50,000 shares × $12)	600,000	
		Cash		600,000
Apr.	29	Cash (31,000 shares × $15)	465,000	
		Treasury Stock (31,000 shares × $12)		372,000
		Paid-In Capital from Sale of Treasury		
		Stock [31,000 shares × ($15 – $12)]		93,000
July	31	Cash (12,000 shares × $17)	204,000	
		Treasury Stock (12,000 shares × $12)		144,000
		Paid-In Capital from Sale of Treasury		
		Stock [12,000 shares × ($17 – $12)]		60,000

b. $153,000 ($93,000 + $60,000) credit

c. $84,000 (7,000 shares × $12) debit

d.   The balance in the treasury stock account is reported as a deduction from the total of the paid-in capital and retained earnings.

Ex. 13–13

a.

May	14	Treasury Stock (23,500 shares × $75)	1,762,500	
		Cash		1,762,500
Sept.	6	Cash (14,000 shares × $81)	1,134,000	
		Treasury Stock (14,000 shares × $75)		1,050,000
		Paid-In Capital from Sale of Treasury		
		Stock [14,000 shares × ($81 – $75)]		84,000
Nov.	30	Cash (9,500 shares × $72)	684,000	
		Paid-In Capital from Sale of Treasury		
		Stock [9,500 shares × ($75 – $72)]	28,500	
		Treasury Stock (9,500 shares × $75)		712,500

b. $55,500 ($84,000 – $28,500) credit

c. Stockholders' equity section

d. Biscayne Bay Water Inc. may have purchased the stock to support the market price of the stock, to provide shares for resale to employees, or for reissuance to employees as a bonus according to stock purchase agreements.

Ex. 13–14

Stockholders' Equity			
Paid-in capital:			
Preferred 2% stock, $120 par			
(85,000 shares authorized,			
70,000 shares issued)	$8,400,000		
Excess of issue price over par	210,000	$ 8,610,000	
Common stock, no par, $14 stated			
value (375,000 shares authorized,			
320,000 shares issued)	$4,480,000		
Excess of issue price over par	480,000	4,960,000	
From sale of treasury stock		45,000	
Total paid-in capital		$13,615,000	

Ex. 13–15

Stockholders' Equity			
Paid-in capital:			
Common stock, $45 par			
(80,000 shares authorized,			
68,000 shares issued)	$3,060,000		
Excess of issue price over par	272,000	$ 3,332,000	
From sale of treasury stock		115,000	
Total paid-in capital		$ 3,447,000	
Retained earnings		20,553,000	
Total		$24,000,000	
Deduct treasury stock			
(9,000 shares at cost)		324,000	
Total stockholders' equity			$23,676,000

Ex. 13–16

Stockholders' Equity			
Paid-in capital:			
Preferred 1% stock, $150 par			
(50,000 shares authorized,			
48,000 shares issued)	$ 7,200,000		
Excess of issue price over par	384,000	$ 7,584,000	
Common stock, $36 par			
(300,000 shares authorized,			
280,000 shares issued)	$10,080,000		
Excess of issue price over par	420,000	10,500,000	
From sale of treasury stock		340,000	
Total paid-in capital		$18,424,000	
Retained earnings		71,684,000	
Total		$90,108,000	
Deduct treasury common stock			
(24,000 shares at cost)		1,008,000	
Total stockholders' equity			$89,100,000

Ex. 13–17

ATLAS PUMPS CORPORATION		
Retained Earnings Statement		
For the Year Ended January 31, 2014		
Retained earnings, February 1, 2013		$48,110,000
Net income	$9,330,000	
Less dividends declared	2,400,000	
Increase in retained earnings		6,930,000
Retained earnings, January 31, 2014		$55,040,000

Ex. 13–18

1. Retained earnings is not part of paid-in capital.

2. The cost of treasury stock should be *deducted* from the *total* stockholders' equity.

3. Dividends payable should be included as part of current liabilities and not as part of stockholders' equity.

4. Common stock should be included as part of paid-in capital.

5. The amount of shares of common stock issued of 825,000 times the par value per share of $20 should be extended as $16,500,000, not $17,655,000. The difference, $1,155,000, probably represents paid-in capital in excess of par.

6. Organizing costs should be expensed as Organizational Expenses when incurred and not included as a part of stockholders' equity.

One possible corrected Stockholders' Equity section of the balance sheet using Method 1 of Exhibit 4 is as follows:

Stockholders' Equity		
Paid-in capital:		
Preferred 2% stock, $80 par (125,000		
shares authorized and issued)	$10,000,000	
Excess of issue price over par	500,000	$ 10,500,000
Common stock, $20 par (1,000,000 shares		
authorized, 825,000 shares issued)	$16,500,000	
Excess of issue price over par	1,155,000	17,655,000
Total paid-in capital		$ 28,155,000
Retained earnings*		96,400,000
Total		$124,555,000
Deduct treasury stock (75,000 shares at cost)		1,755,000
Total stockholders' equity		$122,800,000

* $96,700,000 – $300,000. Since the organizing costs should have been expensed, the retained earnings should be $300,000 less.

Ex. 13–19

	Common Stock, $40 par	Paid-In Capital in Excess of Par	Treasury Stock	Retained Earnings	Total
I-CARDS INC. **Statement of Stockholders' Equity** **For the Year Ended December 31, 2014**					
Balance, Jan. 1, 2014	$4,800,000	$ 960,000	—	$11,375,000	$17,135,000
Issued 30,000 shares					
of common stock	1,200,000	300,000			1,500,000
Purchased 12,000 shares					
as treasury stock			$(552,000)		(552,000)
Net income				3,780,000	3,780,000
Dividends				(276,000)	(276,000)
Balance, Dec. 31, 2014	$6,000,000	$1,260,000	$(552,000)	$14,879,000	$21,587,000

Ex. 13–20

a.   160,000 shares (40,000 × 4)

b. $75 per share ($300 ÷ 4)

Ex. 13–21

	Assets	Liabilities	Stockholders' Equity
(1) Authorizing and issuing stock certificates in a stock split	0	0	0
(2) Declaring a stock dividend	0	0	0
(3) Issuing stock certificates for the stock dividend declared in (2)	0	0	0
(4) Declaring a cash dividend	0	+	–
(5) Paying the cash dividend declared in (4)	–	–	0

Ex. 13–22

Jan.	8	No entry required. The stockholders' ledger would be revised to		
		record the increased number of shares held by each stockholder.		
Apr.	30	Cash Dividends {[(18,000 shares × $0.75) +	55,500	
		(150,000 shares × $0.28)] = $13,500 + $42,000 = $55,500}		
		Cash Dividends Payable		55,500
July	1	Cash Dividends Payable	55,500	
		Cash		55,500
Oct.	31	Cash Dividends {[(18,000 shares × $0.75) +	34,500	
		(150,000 shares × $0.14)] = $13,500 + $21,000 = $34,500}		
		Cash Dividends Payable		34,500
	31	Stock Dividends [(150,000 shares × 5% × $52) = $390,000]	390,000	
		Stock Dividends Distributable (7,500 shares × $40)		300,000
		Paid-In Capital in Excess of Par—Common Stock		90,000
		[7,500 shares × ($52 – $40)]		
Dec.	31	Cash Dividends Payable	34,500	
		Cash		34,500
	31	Stock Dividends Distributable	300,000	
		Common Stock		300,000

Ex. 13–23

$$\text{Earnings per Share} = \frac{\text{Net Income – Preferred Dividends}}{\text{Avg. Number of Common Shares Outstanding}}$$

$$\text{Earnings per Share} = \frac{\$316,000 – (\$1.60 × 15,000 \text{ shares})}{40,000 \text{ shares}}$$

$$\text{Earnings per Share} = \$7.30 \text{ per share}$$

Ex. 13–24

a.

$$\text{Earnings per Share} = \frac{\text{Net Income} - \text{Preferred Dividends}}{\text{Avg. Number of Common Shares Outstanding}}$$

$$\text{Year 3 Earnings per Share} = \frac{\$1,105 - \$14}{382 \text{ shares}}$$

$$= \$2.86 \text{ per share}$$

$$\text{Year 2 Earnings per Share} = \frac{\$1,208 - \$14}{368 \text{ shares}}$$

$$= \$3.24 \text{ per share}$$

$$\text{Year 1 Earnings per Share} = \frac{\$1,312 - \$14}{357 \text{ shares}}$$

$$= \$3.64 \text{ per share}$$

b.

	Year 3	Year 2	Year 1
Earnings per share..	$2.86	$3.24	$3.64
Growth as a percent of Year 1 (base year)................	79%	89%	100%
Net income..	$1,105	$1,208	$1,312
Growth as a percent of Year 1 (base year)................	84%	92%	100%

Net income has declined over the three-year period. Year 2 net income declined 8% (100% – 92%) of Year 1, while Year 3 earnings declined 16% (100% – 84%) of Year 1. The decline in earnings per share is slightly more than the decline in earnings. Year 2 earnings per share declined 11% (100% – 89%) of Year 1, while Year 3 earnings per share declined 21% (100% – 79%) of Year 1.

Ex. 13–25

a. <u>**OfficeMax:**</u>

$$\text{Earnings per Share } = \frac{\text{Net Income} - \text{Preferred Dividends}}{\text{Avg. Number of Common Shares Outstanding}}$$

$$\text{Earnings per Share } = \frac{\$71{,}155{,}000 - \$2{,}527{,}000}{84{,}908{,}000 \text{ shares}}$$

$$= \$0.81 \text{ per share}$$

<u>**Staples**</u>:

$$\text{Earnings per Share } = \frac{\text{Net Income} - \text{Preferred Dividends}}{\text{Avg. Number of Common Shares Outstanding}}$$

$$\text{Earnings per Share } = \frac{\$881{,}948{,}000}{715{,}596{,}000 \text{ shares}}$$

$$= \$1.23 \text{ per share}$$

b. Staples' net income of $881,948,000 is much greater than OfficeMax's net income of $71,155,0000. This is because Staples is a much larger business than OfficeMax. Staples also has over 8 times more shares of common stock outstanding than does OfficeMax. Regardless of these size differences, however, earnings per share can be used to compare their relative earnings. As shown above, Staples has a better earnings per share of $1.23 than does OfficeMax, which has earnings per share of $0.81.

PROBLEMS

Prob. 13–1A

1.

Year	Total Dividends	Preferred Dividends Total	Preferred Dividends Per Share	Common Dividends Total	Common Dividends Per Share
2009.............	$ 18,000	$18,000	$0.45	$ 0	$0.00
2010.............	40,000	40,000	1.00	0	0.00
2011.............	80,000	32,000*	0.80	48,000	0.24
2012.............	120,000	30,000	0.75	90,000	0.45
2013.............	150,000	30,000	0.75	120,000	0.60
2014.............	228,000	30,000	0.75	198,000	0.99
			$4.50		$2.28

* $32,000 =   (2010 dividends in arrears of $2,000) + (2011 current dividend of $30,000)

2.   Average annual dividend for preferred: $0.75 per share ($4.50 ÷ 6)
     Average annual dividend for common: $0.38 per share ($2.28 ÷ 6)

3.   a.   0.60% ($0.75 ÷ $125)
     b.   5.0% ($0.38 ÷ $7.60)

Prob. 13–2A

May	11	Building	3,375,000	
		Land	1,500,000	
		Common Stock (125,000 shares × $35)		4,375,000
		Paid-In Capital in Excess of Par—		
		Common Stock [125,000 shares × ($39 – $35)]		500,000
	20	Cash (40,000 shares × $52)	2,080,000	
		Preferred Stock (40,000 shares × $50)		2,000,000
		Paid-In Capital in Excess of Par—		
		Preferred Stock [40,000 shares × ($52 – $50)]		80,000
	31	Cash	4,000,000	
		Mortgage Note Payable		4,000,000

Prob. 13–3A

a.	Cash (360,000 shares × $22)	7,920,000	
	Common Stock (360,000 shares × $12)		4,320,000
	Paid-In Capital in Excess of Par—Common		
	Stock [360,000 shares × ($22 – $12)]		3,600,000
b.	Cash (14,000 shares × $43)	602,000	
	Preferred Stock (14,000 shares × $40)		560,000
	Paid-In Capital in Excess of Par—Preferred		
	Stock [14,000 shares × ($43 – $40)]		42,000
c.	Treasury Stock (66,000 shares × $18)	1,188,000	
	Cash		1,188,000
d.	Cash (51,000 shares × $21)	1,071,000	
	Treasury Stock (51,000 shares × $18)		918,000
	Paid-In Capital from Sale of Treasury Stock		153,000
	[51,000 shares × ($21 – $18)]		
e.	Cash (10,000 shares × $16)	160,000	
	Paid-In Capital from Sale of Treasury Stock	20,000	
	[10,000 shares × ($18 – $16)]		
	Treasury Stock (10,000 shares × $18)		180,000
f.	Cash Dividends {(59,000 shares × $0.40) + [(1,250,000 shares +	71,750	
	360,000 shares – 66,000 shares + 51,000 shares +		
	10,000 shares) × 0.03]}		
	Cash Dividends Payable		71,750
g.	Cash Dividends Payable	71,750	
	Cash		71,750

Prob. 13–4A

1. and 2.

Common Stock

			Jan.	1	Bal.	7,500,000
			Apr.	10		1,500,000
			Aug.	15		360,000
			Dec.	31	Bal.	9,360,000

Paid-In Capital in Excess of Stated Value—Common Stock

			Jan.	1	Bal.	825,000
			Apr.	10		300,000
			July	5		90,000
			Dec.	31	Bal.	1,215,000

Retained Earnings

Dec.	31		493,800	Jan.	1	Bal.	33,600,000
				Dec.	31		1,125,000
				Dec.	31	Bal.	34,231,200

Treasury Stock

Jan.	1	Bal.	450,000	June	6		450,000
Nov.	23		570,000				
Dec.	31	Bal.	570,000				

Paid-In Capital from Sale of Treasury Stock

			June	6	200,000

Stock Dividends Distributable

Aug.	15	360,000	July	5	360,000

Stock Dividends

July	5	450,000	Dec.	31	450,000

Cash Dividends

Dec.	28	43,800	Dec.	31	43,800

Prob. 13–4A (Continued)

2.

Jan.	22	Cash Dividends Payable [(375,000 shares – 25,000 shares) × $0.08]	28,000	
		Cash		28,000
Apr.	10	Cash (75,000 shares × $24)	1,800,000	
		Common Stock (75,000 shares × $20)		1,500,000
		Paid-In Capital in Excess of Stated Value—Common Stock		300,000
		[75,000 shares × ($24 – $20)]		
June	6	Cash (25,000 shares × $26)	650,000	
		Treasury Stock (25,000 shares × $18)		450,000
		Paid-In Capital from Sale of Treasury Stock		200,000
		[25,000 shares × ($26 – $18)]		
July	5	Stock Dividends [(375,000 shares + 75,000 shares) × 4% × $25]	450,000	
		Stock Dividends Distributable (18,000 shares × $20)		360,000
		Paid-In Capital in Excess of Stated Value—Common Stock		90,000
		[18,000 shares × ($25 – $20)]		
Aug.	15	Stock Dividends Distributable	360,000	
		Common Stock		360,000
Nov.	23	Treasury Stock (30,000 shares × $19)	570,000	
		Cash		570,000
Dec.	28	Cash Dividends [(375,000 shares + 75,000 shares + 18,000 shares – 30,000 shares) × $0.10]	43,800	
		Cash Dividends Payable		43,800
	31	Income Summary	1,125,000	
		Retained Earnings		1,125,000
	31	Retained Earnings	493,800	
		Stock Dividends		450,000
		Cash Dividends		43,800

Prob. 13–4A (Concluded)

3.

MORROW ENTERPRISES INC. Retained Earnings Statement For the Year Ended December 31, 2014		
Retained earnings, January 1, 2014		$33,600,000
Net income	$1,125,000	
Less: Cash dividends	(43,800)	
Stock dividends	(450,000)	
Increase in retained earnings		631,200
Retained earnings, December 31, 2014		$34,231,200

4.

Stockholders' Equity		
Paid-in capital:		
Common stock, $20 stated value (500,000 shares authorized, 468,000 shares issued)	$9,360,000	
Excess of issue price over stated value	1,215,000	
From sale of treasury stock	200,000	
Total paid-in capital		$10,775,000
Retained earnings		34,231,200
Total		$45,006,200
Deduct treasury stock (30,000 shares at cost)		570,000
Total stockholders' equity		$44,436,200

Prob. 13–5A

Jan.	9	No entry required. The stockholders' ledger would be revised to		
		record the increased number of shares held by each stockholder and new par value.		
Feb.	28	Treasury Stock (40,000 shares × $28)	1,120,000	
		Cash		1,120,000
May	1	Cash Dividends {(75,000 shares × $0.80) + [(1,200,000 shares –	199,200	
		40,000 shares) + $0.12]}		
		Cash Dividends Payable		199,200
July	10	Cash Dividends Payable	199,200	
		Cash		199,200
Sept.	7	Cash (30,000 shares × $34)	1,020,000	
		Treasury Stock (30,000 shares × $28)		840,000
		Paid-In Capital from Sale of Treasury		
		Stock [30,000 shares × ($34 – $28)]		180,000
Oct.	1	Cash Dividends {(75,000 shares × $0.80) + [(1,200,000 shares –	202,800	
		10,000 shares) × $0.12]}		
		Cash Dividends Payable		202,800
	1	Stock Dividends [(1,200,000 shares – 10,000 shares) × 2% × $36]	856,800	
		Stock Dividends Distributable (23,800 shares × $25)		595,000
		Paid-In Capital in Excess of Par—		
		Common Stock [23,800 shares × ($36 – $25)]		261,800
Dec.	1	Cash Dividends Payable	202,800	
		Cash		202,800
	1	Stock Dividends Distributable	595,000	
		Common Stock		595,000

Prob. 13–1B

1.

Year	Total Dividends	Preferred Dividends		Common Dividends	
		Total	Per Share	Total	Per Share
2009.............	$ 24,000	$ 24,000	$ 0.96	$ 0	$0.00
2010.............	10,000	10,000	0.40	0	0.00
2011.............	126,000	101,000*	4.04	25,000	0.25
2012.............	100,000	45,000	1.80	55,000	0.55
2013.............	125,000	45,000	1.80	80,000	0.80
2014.............	125,000	45,000	1.80	80,000	0.80
			$10.80		$2.40

* $101,000 = (2009 dividends in arrears of $11,000) +
  (2010 dividends in arrears of $45,000) +
  (2011 current dividend of $45,000)

2. Average annual dividend for preferred: $1.80 per share ($10.80 ÷ 6)
   Average annual dividend for common: $0.40 per share ($2.40 ÷ 6)

3. a.   1.8% ($1.80 ÷ $100)
    b.   8.0% ($0.40 ÷ $5.00)

Prob. 13–2B

Oct.	9	Cash	1,500,000	
		Mortgage Note Payable		1,500,000
	17	Cash (20,000 shares × $126)	2,520,000	
		Preferred Stock (20,000 shares × $120)		2,400,000
		Paid-In Capital in Excess of Par—		
		Preferred Stock [20,000 shares × ($126 – $120)]		120,000
	28	Building	4,150,000	
		Land	800,000	
		Common Stock (300,000 shares × $15)		4,500,000
		Paid-In Capital in Excess of Par—		
		Preferred Stock [300,000 shares × ($16.50 – $15.00)]		450,000

Prob. 13–3B

a.	Treasury Stock (87,500 shares × $8)	700,000	
	Cash		700,000
b.	Cash (55,000 shares × $11)	605,000	
	Treasury Stock (55,000 shares × $8)		440,000
	Paid-In Capital from Sale of Treasury Stock		165,000
	[55,000 shares × ($11 – $8)]		
c.	Cash (20,000 shares × $84)	1,680,000	
	Preferred Stock (20,000 shares × $80)		1,600,000
	Paid-In Capital in Excess of Par—Preferred		
	Stock [20,000 shares × ($84 – $80)]		80,000
d.	Cash (400,000 shares × $13)	5,200,000	
	Common Stock (400,000 shares × $9)		3,600,000
	Paid-In Capital in Excess of Par—Common		
	Stock [400,000 shares × ($13 – $9)]		1,600,000
e.	Cash (18,000 shares × $7.50)	135,000	
	Paid-In Capital from Sale of Treasury Stock	9,000	
	[18,000 shares × ($8.00 – $7.50)]		
	Treasury Stock (18,000 shares × $8)		144,000
f.	Cash Dividends {(80,000 shares × $1.60) + [(1,750,000 shares –	234,775	
	87,500 shares + 55,000 shares + 400,000 shares +		
	18,000 shares) × $0.05]}		
	Cash Dividends Payable		234,775
g.	Cash Dividends Payable	234,775	
	Cash		234,775

Prob. 13–4B

1. and 2.

Common Stock

					Jan.	1	Bal.	3,100,000
					Apr.	13		1,000,000
					July	16		123,000
					Dec.	31	Bal.	4,223,000

Paid-In Capital in Excess of Stated Value—Common Stock

					Jan.	1	Bal.	1,240,000
					Apr.	13		600,000
					June	14		61,500
					Dec.	31	Bal.	1,901,500

Retained Earnings

Dec.	31		248,068	Jan.	1	Bal.	4,875,000
				Dec.	31		775,000
				Dec.	31	Bal.	5,401,932

Treasury Stock

Jan.	1	Bal.	288,000	Mar.	15		288,000
Oct.	30		300,000				
Dec.	31	Bal.	300,000				

Paid-In Capital from Sale of Treasury Stock

			Mar.	15	36,000

Stock Dividends Distributable

July	16	123,000	June	14	123,000

Stock Dividends

June	14	184,500	Dec.	31	184,500

Cash Dividends

Dec.	30	63,568	Dec.	31	63,568

Prob. 13–4B (Continued)

2.

Jan.	15	Cash Dividends Payable [(620,000 shares – 48,000 shares) × $0.06]	34,320	
		Cash		34,320
Mar.	15	Cash (48,000 shares × $6.75)	324,000	
		Treasury Stock (48,000 shares × $6.00)		288,000
		Paid-In Capital from Sale of Treasury Stock		36,000
		[48,000 shares × ($6.75 – $6.00)]		
Apr.	13	Cash (200,000 shares × $8)	1,600,000	
		Common Stock (200,000 shares × $5)		1,000,000
		Paid-In Capital in Excess of Stated Value—Common Stock		600,000
		[200,000 shares × ($8 – $5)]		
June	14	Stock Dividends [(620,000 shares + 200,000 shares) × 3% × $7.50]	184,500	
		Stock Dividends Distributable (24,600 shares × $5)		123,000
		Paid-In Capital in Excess of Stated Value—Common Stock		61,500
		[24,600 shares × ($7.50 – $5.00)]		
July	16	Stock Dividends Distributable	123,000	
		Common Stock		123,000
Oct.	30	Treasury Stock (50,000 shares × $6)	300,000	
		Cash		300,000
Dec.	30	Cash Dividends [(620,000 shares + 200,000 shares + 24,600 shares – 50,000 shares) × $0.08]	63,568	
		Cash Dividends Payable		63,568
	31	Income Summary	775,000	
		Retained Earnings		775,000
	31	Retained Earnings	248,068	
		Stock Dividends		184,500
		Cash Dividends		63,568

13-33

Prob. 13–4B (Concluded)

NAV-GO ENTERPRISES INC. Retained Earnings Statement For the Year Ended December 31, 2014		
Retained earnings, January 1, 2014		$4,875,000
Net income	$ 775,000	
Less: Cash dividends	(63,568)	
Stock dividends	(184,500)	
Increase in retained earnings		526,932
Retained earnings, December 31, 2014		$5,401,932

4.

Stockholders' Equity		
Paid-in capital:		
Common stock, $5 stated value (900,000 shares		
authorized, 844,600 shares issued)	$4,223,000	
Excess of issue price over stated value	1,901,500	
From sale of treasury stock	36,000	
Total paid-in capital		$ 6,160,500
Retained earnings		5,401,932
Total		$11,562,432
Deduct treasury stock (50,000 shares at cost)		300,000
Total stockholders' equity		$11,262,432

Prob. 13–5B

Jan.	15	No entry required. The stockholders' ledger would be revised to record the increased number of shares held by each stockholder and new par value.		
Mar.	1	Cash Dividends [(100,000 shares × $0.25) + (800,000 shares × $0.07)]	81,000	
		Cash Dividends Payable		81,000
Apr.	30	Cash Dividends Payable	81,000	
		Cash		81,000
May	31	Treasury Stock (60,000 shares × $32)	1,920,000	
		Cash		1,920,000
Aug.	17	Cash (40,000 shares × $38)	1,520,000	
		Treasury Stock (40,000 shares × $32)		1,280,000
		Paid-In Capital from Sale of Treasury Stock [40,000 shares × ($38 – $32)]		240,000
Sept.	1	Cash Dividends {(100,000 shares × $0.25) + [(800,000 shares – 60,000 shares + 40,000 shares) × $0.09]}	95,200	
		Cash Dividends Payable		95,200
	1	Stock Dividends [(800,000 shares – 60,000 shares + 40,000 shares) × 1% × $40]	312,000	
		Stock Dividends Distributable (7,800 shares × $30)		234,000
		Paid-In Capital in Excess of Par— Common Stock [7,800 shares × ($40 – $30)]		78,000
Oct.	31	Cash Dividends Payable	95,200	
		Cash		95,200
	31	Stock Dividends Distributable	234,000	
		Common Stock		234,000

CASES & PROJECTS

CP 13–1

At the time of this decision, the WorldCom board had come under intense scrutiny. This was the largest loan by a company to its CEO in history. The SEC began an investigation into this loan, and Bernie Ebbers was eventually terminated as the CEO, with this loan being cited as part of the reason. The board indicated that the decision to lend Ebbers this money was to keep him from selling his stock and depressing the share price. Thus, it claimed that it was actually helping shareholders by keeping these shares from being sold. However, this argument wasn't well received, given that the share price dropped from around $15 per share at the time of the loan to about $2.50 per share when Ebbers was terminated. In addition, critics were scornful of the low "sweetheart" interest rate given to Ebbers for this loan. In addition, many critics viewed the loan as risky, given that it was not supported by any personal assets. WorldCom has since entered bankruptcy proceedings, Ebbers has gone to prison, and the Ebbers loan went uncollected.

Some press comments:

1. *When he borrowed money personally, he used his WorldCom stock as collateral. As these loans came due, he was unwilling to sell at "depressed prices" of $10 to $15 (it's now around $2.50). So WorldCom lent him the money to consolidate his loans, to the tune of $366 million. How a board of directors, representing you and me at the table, allowed this to happen is beyond comprehension. They should resign with Bernie.* (Source: Andy Kessler, "Bernie Bites the Dust," *The Wall Street Journal,* May 1, 2002, p. A18.)

2. *It was astonishing to read the other day that the board of directors of the United States' second-largest telecommunications company claims to have had its shareholders' interests in mind when it agreed to grant more than $430 million in low-interest loans to the company's CEO, mainly to meet margin calls on his stock.*

   Yet that's the level to which fiduciary responsibility seems to have sunk on the board of Clinton, Mississippi-based WorldCom, the deeply troubled telecom giant, as it sought to bail Bernard Ebbers out of the folly of speculating in shares of WorldCom itself. Sadly, WorldCom is hardly alone.

   "The very essence of why Mr. Ebbers was granted a loan was to protect shareholder value," said a WorldCom spokesman in mid-March, just as the U.S. Securities & Exchange Commission was unfurling a probe of the loan and 23 other matters related to WorldCom's finances.

   Yes, folks, you read that right. On March 14, 2002, a spokesman for a publicly traded, $20 billion company actually stood up and declared that of all the uses to which the company could have put almost half-a-billion dollars, the

CP 13–1 (Concluded)

> *best one by far—at least from the point of view of the shareholders—was to spend it on some sort of stock-parking scheme in order to keep the CEO out of bankruptcy court*. (Source: Christopher Byron, "Bernie's Bad Idea," *Red Herring*, April 16, 2002.)

> *Note to Instructors:* Bernie Ebbers is currently serving a 25-year prison sentence for conspiracy, securities fraud, and making false statements to securities regulators.

CP 13–2

Lou and Shirley are behaving in a professional manner as long as full and complete information is provided to potential investors in accordance with federal regulations for the sale of securities to the public. If such information is provided, the marketplace will determine the fair value of the company's stock.

CP 13–3

1. This case involves a transaction in which a security has been issued that has characteristics of both stock and debt. The primary argument for classifying the issuance of the common stock as debt is that the investors have a legal right to an amount equal to the purchase price (face value) of the security. This is similar to a note payable or a bond payable. The additional $120 payment could be argued to be equivalent to an interest payment, whose payment has been deferred until a later date.

    Arguments against classifying the security as debt include the fact that the investors will not receive fixed "annual" interest payments. In fact, if Epstein Engineering Inc. does not generate any net sales, the investors do not have a right to receive any payments. One could argue that the payments of 5% of net sales are, in substance, a method of redeeming the stock. As indicated in the case, the stockholders must surrender their stock for $120 per share after the $25 million payment has been made. Overall, the arguments would seem to favor classifying the security as common stock.

2. In practice, the $25 million stock issuance would probably be classified as common stock. However, full disclosure should be made of the 5% of net sales and $120 per share payment obligations in the notes to the financial statements. In addition, as Epstein Engineering Inc. generates net sales, a current liability should be recorded for the payment to stockholders. Such payments would be classified as dividend payments rather than as interest payments. Dan Fisher should also investigate whether such payments might violate any loan agreements with the banks. Banks often restrict dividend payments in loan agreements. If such an agreement has been violated, Epstein Engineering Inc. should notify the bank immediately and request a waiver of the violation.

CP 13–4

a.   **500 shares × ($0.80 ÷ 4) = $100**

b.   **(0.4)% = ($31.74 – $31.87) ÷ $31.87**

c.   **34.8% = ($31.87 – $23.65) ÷ $23.65**

d.   **500 shares × $31.74 = $15,870 plus brokerage commission**

e.   **The $15,870 paid for 500 shares of Microsoft common stock goes to the seller of the common stock (another shareholder).**

CP 13–5

1.   **Before a cash dividend is declared, there must be sufficient retained earnings and cash. On December 31, 2014, the retained earnings balance of $4,630,000 is available for use in declaring a dividend. This balance is sufficient for the payment of the normal quarterly cash dividend of $0.50 per share, which would amount to $90,000 ($0.50 × 180,000).**

Motion Designs Inc.'s cash balance at December 31, 2014, is $250,000, of which $100,000 is committed as the compensating balance under the loan agreement. This leaves only $150,000 to pay the dividend of $90,000 and to finance normal operations in the future. Unless the cash balance can be expected to increase significantly in early 2015, it is questionable whether sufficient cash will be available to pay a cash dividend and to provide for future cash needs.

Other factors that should be considered include the company's working capital (current assets – current liabilities) position and the loan provision pertaining to the current ratio, resources needed for plant expansion or replacement of facilities, future business prospects of the company, and forecasts for the industry and the economy in general. The working capital is $5,000,000 ($7,000,000 – $2,000,000) on December 31, 2014. The current ratio is therefore 3.5:1 ($7,000,000 ÷ $2,000,000) on December 31, 2014. However, after deducting the $3,000,000 committed to store modernization and product-line expansion, the ratio drops to 2:1 ($4,000,000 ÷ $2,000,000). If the cash dividend were declared and paid and the other current assets and current liabilities remain unchanged, the current ratio would drop to 1.955:1 ($3,910,000 ÷ $2,000,000), and this would violate the loan agreement. Further, working capital commitments for 2015 and any additional funds that might be required, such as funds for the replacement of fixed assets, would suggest that the declaration of a cash dividend for the fourth quarter of 2014 might not be wise.

2.   **Given the cash and working capital position of Motion Designs Inc. on December 31, 2014, a stock dividend might be an appropriate alternative to a cash dividend.**

CP 13–5 (Concluded)

a.   From the point of view of a stockholder, the declaration of a stock dividend would continue the dividend declaration trend of Motion Designs Inc. In addition, although the amount of the stockholders' equity and proportional interest in the corporation would remain unchanged, the stockholders might benefit from an increase in the fair market value of their total holdings of Motion Designs Inc. stock after distribution of the dividend.

b.   From the point of view of the board of directors, a stock dividend would continue the dividend trend, while the cash and working capital position of the company would not be jeopardized. Many corporations use stock dividends as a way to "plow back" retained earnings for use in acquiring new facilities or for expanding their operations. Motion Designs Inc. has sufficient unissued common stock to declare a stock dividend without changing the amount authorized.

CP 13–6

Note to Instructors: The purpose of this activity is to familiarize students with sources of information about corporations and how that information is useful in evaluating the corporation's activities.

The following information was prepared for Google Inc. based upon the SEC 10-K filing for the year ending December 31, 2011.

1.   Google Inc.

2.   Delaware

3.   The following is taken from Google's 10-K:

"Google is a global technology leader focused on improving the ways people connect with information. We aspire to build products that improve the lives of billions of people globally. Our mission is to organize the world's information and make it universally accessible and useful. Our innovations in web search and advertising have made our website a top internet property and our brand one of the most recognized in the world.

We generate revenue primarily by delivering relevant, cost-effective online advertising. Businesses use our AdWords program to promote their products and services with targeted advertising. In addition, the third parties that comprise the Google Network use our AdSense program to deliver relevant ads that generate revenue and enhance the user experience."

CP 13–6 (Continued)

4. $72,574,000,000

5. $37,905,000,000

6. $9,737,000,000

7. Convertible preferred stock, $0.001 par value, 100,000 shares authorized; no shares issued and outstanding.

Class A and Class B common stock and additional paid-in capital, $0.001 par value per share: 9,000,000 shares authorized; 321,301 (Class A 250,413, Class B 70,888) and par value of $321 (Class A $250, Class B $71) and 324,895 (Class A 257,553, Class B 67,342) and par value of $325 (Class A $258, Class B $67) shares issued and outstanding.

Note to Instructors: The rights of Class A and Class B common stock are identical except for voting rights. Specifically, each share of Class A common stock is entitled to one vote per share. Each share of Class B common stock is entitled to 10 votes per share. Shares of Class B common stock may be converted at any time at the option of the stockholder and automatically convert upon sale or transfer to Class A common stock. The Class A common stock is the stock that is actively traded on the New York Stock Exchange. The Class B common stock allows the founders of Google (Sergery Brin and Larry Page) and Executive Chairman (Eric Schmidt) to maintain control of the corporation. Specifically, the following stated in Google's 10-K:

"… As of December 31, 2011, Larry, Sergey, and Eric beneficially owned approximately 92% of our outstanding Class B common stock, representing approximately 66% of the voting power of our outstanding capital stock. Larry, Sergey, and Eric therefore have significant influence over management and affairs and over all matters requiring stockholder approval, including the election of directors and significant corporate transactions, such as a merger or other sale of our company or our assets, for the foreseeable future."

8. $618.39 as of close on February 28, 2012.

9. $642.96 – $473.02

CP 13–6 (Concluded)

10. **Google Inc. does not pay dividends. In its SEC 10-K filing for the year ending December 31, 2011, Google states:**

    "We have never declared or paid any cash dividend on our common stock. We intend to retain any future earnings and do not expect to pay any dividends in the foreseeable future."

Note to Instructors: The preceding information, which may be updated as needed, can be used as a basis for class discussion. Some issues that you may want to raise in class are (1) the high price of Google's Class A stock; (2) control of the corporation by the founders, using the voting rights of their Class B stock; (3) the no dividend policy; and (4) future prospects for Google, including appreciation in value of the Class A stock.

CHAPTER 14
LONG-TERM LIABILITIES: BONDS AND NOTES

DISCUSSION QUESTIONS

1. (1) To pay the face (maturity) amount of the bonds at a specified date. (2) To pay periodic interest at a specified percentage of the face amount.

2. a. Bonds that may be exchanged for other securities under specified conditions.

   b. The issuing corporation reserves the right to redeem the bonds before the maturity date.

   c. Bonds issued on the basis of the general credit of the corporation.

3. More than face amount. Because comparable bonds provide a market interest rate (11%) that is less than the rate on the bond being issued (12%), the bond will sell at a premium as the market's means of equalizing the two interest rates.

4. a. Greater than $26,000,000

   b. 1. $26,000,000
      2. 7%
      3. 9%
      4. $26,000,000

5. Less than the contract rate

6. a. Premium

   b. $593,454

   c. Premium on Bonds Payable

7. A loss of $50,000 [($5,000,000 × 0.98) − ($5,000,000 − $150,000)]

8. A mortgage note is an installment note that is secured by a pledge of the borrower's assets. If the borrower fails to pay the note, the lender has the right to take possession of the pledged asset and sell it to pay off the debt.

9. A bond is an interest-bearing note that requires periodic interest payments and repayment of the face amount of the bonds at maturity. Bonds consist of two different components: (1) interest payments made periodically over the life of the bond and (2) the face amount that must be repaid at maturity. The periodic payments consist entirely of interest, and the final payment at maturity consists entirely of principal. Installment notes, on the other hand, have periodic payments that consist partially of interest and partially of principal. Each payment reduces the principal on the note so that at maturity the entire amount borrowed will have been repaid.

10. a. As a current liability on the balance sheet.

    b. As a long-term liability on the balance sheet.

PRACTICE EXERCISES

PE 14–1A

	Plan 1	Plan 2
Earnings before bond interest and income tax.............	$1,200,000	$1,200,000
Deduct interest on bonds.......................................	360,000[1]	300,000[3]
Income before income tax.....................................	$ 840,000	$ 900,000
Deduct income tax..	336,000[2]	360,000[4]
Net income...	$ 504,000	$ 540,000
Dividends on preferred stock...............................	0	300,000[5]
Available for dividends on common stock................	$ 504,000	$ 240,000
Shares of common stock outstanding.....................	÷ 300,000	÷ 200,000
Earnings per share on common stock.....................	$ 1.68	$ 1.20

[1] $6,000,000 × 6%

[2] $840,000 × 40%

[3] $5,000,000 × 6%

[4] $900,000 × 40%

[5] ($3,000,000 ÷ $30) × $3.00

PE 14–1B

	Plan 1	Plan 2
Earnings before bond interest and income tax.............	$2,000,000	$2,000,000
Deduct interest on bonds.......................................	400,000[1]	250,000[3]
Income before income tax.....................................	$1,600,000	$1,750,000
Deduct income tax..	640,000[2]	700,000[4]
Net income...	$ 960,000	$1,050,000
Dividends on preferred stock...............................	0	300,000[5]
Available for dividends on common stock................	$ 960,000	$ 750,000
Shares of common stock outstanding.....................	÷ 400,000	÷ 250,000
Earnings per share on common stock.....................	$ 2.40	$ 3.00

[1] $4,000,000 × 10%

[2] $1,600,000 × 40%

[3] $2,500,000 × 10%

[4] $1,750,000 × 40%

[5] ($3,000,000 ÷ $25) × $2.50

PE 14–2A

Cash	1,920,873	
Discount on Bonds Payable	79,127	
Bonds Payable		2,000,000

PE 14–2B

Cash	2,889,599	
Discount on Bonds Payable	110,401	
Bonds Payable		3,000,000

PE 14–3A

Interest Expense	87,913	
Discount on Bonds Payable*		7,913
Cash		80,000

* $79,127 ÷ 10 semiannual payments

PE 14–3B

Interest Expense	176,040	
Discount on Bonds Payable*		11,040
Cash		165,000

* $110,401 ÷ 10 semiannual payments

PE 14–4A

Cash	4,175,041	
Premium on Bonds Payable		175,041
Bonds Payable		4,000,000

PE 14–4B

Cash	8,308,869	
Premium on Bonds Payable		308,869
Bonds Payable		8,000,000

PE 14–5A

Interest Expense	102,496	
Premium on Bonds Payable*	17,504	
Cash		120,000

  * $175,041 ÷ 10 semiannual payments

PE 14–5B

Interest Expense	409,113	
Premium on Bonds Payable*	30,887	
Cash		440,000

  * $308,869 ÷ 10 semiannual payments

PE 14–6A

Bonds Payable	900,000	
Loss on Redemption of Bonds	42,000	
Discount on Bonds Payable		87,000
Cash		855,000

PE 14–6B

Bonds Payable	500,000	
Premium on Bonds Payable	67,000	
Gain on Redemption of Bonds		77,000
Cash		490,000

PE 14–7A

a.

Cash	80,000	
Notes Payable		80,000
Issued installment notes for cash.		

b.

Interest Expense	5,600	
Notes Payable	9,244	
Cash		14,844
Paid principal and interest on installment notes.		

PE 14–7B

a.

Cash	45,000	
Notes Payable		45,000
Issued installment notes for cash.		

b.

Interest Expense	3,600	
Notes Payable	6,134	
Cash		9,734
Paid principal and interest on installment		
notes.		

PE 14–8A

a.   Number of times interest charges earned:

$$2014: \frac{\$3,200,000 + \$320,000}{\$320,000} = 11.0$$

$$2013: \frac{\$3,600,000 + \$300,000}{\$300,000} = 13.0$$

b.   The number of times interest charges are earned has decreased from 13.0 in 2013 to 11.0 in 2014. Although the company has adequate earnings to pay interest, the decline in this ratio may cause concern among debtholders.

PE 14–8B

a.   Number of times interest charges earned:

$$2014: \frac{\$5,544,000 + \$440,000}{\$440,000} = 13.6$$

$$2013: \frac{\$4,400,000 + \$400,000}{\$400,000} = 12.0$$

b.   The number of times interest charges are earned has increased from 12.0 in 2013 to 13.6 in 2014. The increase in this ratio increases debtholders' confidence in the company's ability to make its interest payments.

EXERCISES

Ex. 14–1

		Rhett Co.
a.	Earnings before bond interest and income tax...............................	$15,000,000
	Bond interest...	2,250,000
	Balance..	$12,750,000
	Income tax..	5,100,000
	Net income...	$ 7,650,000
	Dividends on preferred stock..	4,500,000
	Earnings available for common stock......................................	$ 3,150,000
	Shares of common stock outstanding......................................	÷ 1,500,000
	Earnings per share on common stock......................................	$ 2.10*
b.	Earnings before bond interest and income tax...............................	$17,500,000
	Bond interest...	2,250,000
	Balance..	$15,250,000
	Income tax..	6,100,000
	Net income...	$ 9,150,000
	Dividends on preferred stock..	4,500,000
	Earnings available for common stock......................................	$ 4,650,000
	Shares of common stock outstanding......................................	÷ 1,500,000
	Earnings per share on common stock......................................	$ 3.10**
c.	Earnings before bond interest and income tax...............................	$20,000,000
	Bond interest...	2,250,000
	Balance..	$17,750,000
	Income tax..	7,100,000
	Net income...	$10,650,000
	Dividends on preferred stock..	4,500,000
	Earnings available for common stock......................................	$ 6,150,000
	Shares of common stock outstanding......................................	÷ 1,500,000
	Earnings per share on common stock......................................	$ 4.10***

Ex. 14–2

Factors other than earnings per share that should be considered in evaluating financing plans include: bonds represent a fixed annual interest requirement, while dividends on stock do not; bonds require the repayment of principal, while stock does not; and common stock represents a voting interest in the ownership of the corporation, while bonds do not.

Ex. 14–3

Nike's major source of financing is common stock. It has relatively little long-term debt compared to stockholders' equity.

Ex. 14–4

The bonds were selling at a premium. This is indicated by the selling price of 115.948, which is stated as a percentage of the face amount and is more than par (100%). The market rate of interest for similar quality bonds was lower than 7.25%, and this is why the bonds were selling at a premium.

Ex. 14–5

Apr.	1	Cash	7,500,000	
		Bonds Payable		7,500,000
Oct.	1	Interest Expense	375,000	
		Cash		375,000
Dec.	31	Interest Expense*	187,500	
		Interest Payable		187,500

* $7,500,000 × 10% × 3/12

Ex. 14–6

a.	1.	Cash	10,504,541	
		Discount on Bonds Payable	1,495,459	
		Bonds Payable		12,000,000
	2.	Interest Expense	480,000	
		Cash		480,000
	3.	Interest Expense	480,000	
		Cash		480,000
	4.	Interest Expense	149,546	
		Discount on Bonds Payable		149,546

Ex. 14–6 (Concluded)

b.	Annual interest paid..	$ 960,000
	Plus discount amortized..	149,546
	Interest expense for first year..	$1,109,546

c. The bonds sell for less than their face amount because the market rate of interest is greater than the contract rate of interest. Investors are not willing to pay the full face amount for bonds that pay a lower contract rate of interest than the rate they could earn on similar bonds (market rate).

Ex. 14–7

a.

Cash	22,842,560	
Premium on Bonds Payable		2,842,560
Bonds Payable		20,000,000

b.

Interest Expense	757,872	
Premium on Bonds Payable*	142,128	
Cash**		900,000

* $2,842,560 ÷ 20 semiannual payments

** $20,000,000 × 9% × 6/12

c. The bonds sell for more than their face amount because the market rate of interest is less than the contract rate of interest. Investors are willing to pay more for bonds that pay a higher rate of interest (contract rate) than the rate they could earn on similar bonds (market rate).

Ex. 14–8

2014					
Apr.	1	Cash		40,000,000	
		Bonds Payable			40,000,000
Oct.	1	Interest Expense		1,600,000	
		Cash			1,600,000
2018					
Oct.	1	Bonds Payable		40,000,000	
		Loss on Redemption of Bonds		1,600,000	
		Cash*			41,600,000

* $40,000,000 × 1.04

Ex. 14–9

2014				
Mar.	1	Cash	30,000,000	
		Bonds Payable		30,000,000
Sept.	1	Interest Expense	1,500,000	
		Cash		1,500,000
2020				
Sept.	1	Bonds Payable	30,000,000	
		Gain on Redemption of Bonds		600,000
		Cash*		29,400,000

* $30,000,000 × 0.98

Ex. 14–10

a. 1.

	Cash	50,000	
	Notes Payable		50,000

2.

	Interest Expense*	2,500	
	Notes Payable	7,351	
	Cash		9,851

* $50,000 × 0.05

b. Notes payable are reported as liabilities on the balance sheet. The portion of the note payable that is due within one year is reported as a current liability. The remaining portion of the note payable that is not due within one year is reported as a long-term liability. For this company, the current and noncurrent portions of the note payable would be reported as follows:

Ex. 14–10 (Concluded)

Current liabilities:

Notes payable*.. $ 7,719

* The principal repayment portion of the next installment payment. See computation below.

Noncurrent liabilities:

Notes payable**.. $34,930

** Original note payable..	$50,000	
Less principal repayment from year 1..	7,351	
Note payable balance at the end of year 1......................................	$42,649	
Annual payment on note...	$ 9,851	
Second year interest payment ($42,649 × 0.05).............................	2,132	
Principal repayment portion of next installment.............................	$ 7,719	
Note payable balance at the end of year 1......................................	$42,649	
Current portion of note payable (due within one year).....................	7,719	
Noncurrent portion of note payable..	$34,930	

Ex. 14–11

2014					
Jan.	1	Cash		210,000	
		Notes Payable			210,000
Dec.	31	Interest Expense		18,900	
		Notes Payable		27,913	
		Cash			46,813
2017					
Dec.	31	Interest Expense		10,665	
		Notes Payable*		36,148	
		Cash			46,813

*$46,813 – $10,665

Ex. 14–12

a.

Amortization of Installment Notes

For the Year Ending	A January 1 Carrying Amount	B Note Payment (Cash Paid)	C Interest Expense (6% of January 1 Note Carrying Amount)		D Decrease in Notes Payable (B – C)	E Dec. 31 Carrying Amount (A – D)
Dec. 31, 2014	$125,000	$ 36,074	$ 7,500	(6% of $125,000)	$ 28,574	$96,426
Dec. 31, 2015	96,426	36,074	5,786	(6% of $96,426)	30,288	66,138
Dec. 31, 2016	66,138	36,074	3,968	(6% of $66,138)	32,106	34,032
Dec. 31, 2017	34,032	36,074	2,042	(6% of $34,032)	34,032	0
		$144,296	$19,296		$125,000	

b.

2014				
Jan.	1	Cash	125,000	
		Notes Payable		125,000
Dec.	31	Interest Expense	7,500	
		Notes Payable	28,574	
		Cash		36,074
2015				
Dec.	31	Interest Expense	5,786	
		Notes Payable	30,288	
		Cash		36,074
2016				
Dec.	31	Interest Expense	3,968	
		Notes Payable	32,106	
		Cash		36,074
2017				
Dec.	31	Interest Expense	2,042	
		Notes Payable	34,032	
		Cash		36,074

c.   Interest expense of $7,500 would be reported on the income statement.

Ex. 14–13

1. The significant loss on redemption of the Simmons Industries bonds should be reported in the Other Income and Expense section of the income statement, rather than as an extraordinary loss.

2. The Hunter Corporation bonds outstanding at the end of the current year should be reported as a current liability on the balance sheet because they mature within one year.

Ex. 14–14

a. Number of times interest charges earned:

$$\text{Current year: } \frac{\$745,000,000 + \$167,000,000}{\$167,000,000} = 5.5$$

$$\text{Preceding year: } \frac{\$164,000,000 + \$186,000,000}{\$186,000,000} = 1.9$$

b. The number of times interest charges are earned has increased from 1.9 in the prior year to 5.5 in the current year. Although Southwest Airlines had enough earnings to pay interest in the preceding year, the improvement in this ratio will be welcomed by the debtholders.

Ex. 14–15

a. Number of times interest charges earned:

$$\text{2014: } \frac{\$310,500,000 + \$13,500,000}{\$13,500,000} = 24.0$$

$$\text{2013: } \frac{\$432,000,000 + \$16,000,000}{\$16,000,000} = 28.0$$

b. The number of times interest charges are earned has decreased from 28.0 in 2013 to 24.0 in 2014. Although Loomis has adequate earnings to pay interest, the decline in this ratio may cause concern among debtholders.

Ex. 14–16

a.   **Number of times interest charges earned:**

$$2014: \frac{\$3,500,000 + \$5,000,000}{\$5,000,000} = 1.7$$

$$2013: \frac{\$6,000,000 + \$5,000,000}{\$5,000,000} = 2.2$$

b.   **The number of times interest charges are earned has decreased from 2.2 in 2013 to 1.7 in 2014. Although the company has enough earnings to pay interest in 2014, the deterioration in this ratio is a cause for concern to debtholders.**

Appendix 1 Ex. 14–17

$1,000,000 × 0.75131 = $751,310

Cash on hand today can be invested to earn income. If $751,315 is invested at 10%, it will be worth $1,000,000 at the end of three years.

Appendix 1 Ex. 14–18

a. | First Year: | $200,000 × 0.93458 | = | $186,916 |
Second Year:	$200,000 × 0.87344	=	$174,688
Third Year:	$200,000 × 0.81630	=	$163,260
Fourth Year:	$200,000 × 0.76290	=	$152,580
Total present value			$677,444

b. $200,000 × 3.38721 = $677,442*

   *$2 difference between a. and b. is due to rounding.

c.   Cash on hand today can be invested to earn income. If each of the $200,000 of cash receipts is invested at 7%, it will be worth $677,444 at the end of four years.

Appendix 1 Ex. 14–19

$7,500,000 × 7.02358 = $52,676,850

Appendix 1 Ex. 14–20

No. The present value of your winnings using an interest rate of 12% is $42,376,650 ($7,500,000 × 5.65022), which is less than the present value of your winnings using an interest rate of 7% ($52,676,865; see Appendix 1 Ex. 14–19). This is because the winnings are affected by the higher interest rate.

Appendix 1 Ex. 14–21

Present value of $1 for 10 semiannual periods at 4.5% semiannual rate.............................	**0.64393**	
Face amount of bonds...	**× $25,000,000**	**$16,098,250**
Present value of an annuity of $1 for 10 periods at 4.5%..	**7.91272**	
Semiannual interest payment.................................	**× $ 875,000***	**6,923,630**
Total present value (proceeds).............................		**$23,021,880**

   * $25,000,000 × 3.5%

Appendix 1 Ex. 14–22

Present value of $1 for 8 semiannual periods at 4.0% semiannual rate.............................	**0.73069**	
Face amount of bonds...	**× $30,000,000**	**$21,920,700**
Present value of an annuity of $1 for 8 semiannual periods at 4.0% semiannual rate.......	**6.73274**	
Semiannual interest payment.................................	**× $ 1,500,000***	**10,099,110**
Total present value (proceeds).............................		**$32,019,810**

   * $30,000,000 × 5%

Appendix 2 Ex. 14–23

a. 1.

Cash	**43,495,895**	
Discount on Bonds Payable	**6,504,105**	
Bonds Payable		**50,000,000**

   2.

Interest Expense*	**1,957,315**	
Discount on Bonds Payable		**207,315**
Cash**		**1,750,000**

   * $43,495,895 × 4.5%

   ** $50,000,000 × 3.5%

Appendix 2 Ex. 14–23 (Concluded)

3.	Interest Expense*	1,966,644	
	Discount on Bonds Payable		216,644
	Cash		1,750,000

* ($43,495,895 + $207,315) × 4.5%

Note: **The following data in support of the proceeds of the bond issue stated in the exercise are presented for the instructor's information. Students are not required to make the computations.**

Present value of $1 for 20 semiannual periods at 4.5% semiannual rate..................................	0.41464	
Face amount of bonds... ×	$50,000,000	$20,732,000
Present value of annuity of $1 for 20 semiannual periods at 4.5% semiannual rate........	13.00794	
Semiannual interest payment....................................... ×	$ 1,750,000*	22,763,895
Total present value (proceeds).....................................		$43,495,895

* $50,000,000 × 3.5%

b.	Annual interest paid..	$ 3,500,000
	Plus discount amortized*..	423,959
	Interest expense for first year.......................................	$ 3,923,959

* $207,315 + $216,644

c. The bonds sell for less than their face amount because the market rate of interest is greater than the contract rate of interest. Investors are not willing to pay the full face amount for bonds that pay a lower contract rate of interest than the rate they could earn on similar bonds (market rate).

Appendix 2 Ex. 14–24

a.	1.	Cash	23,829,684	
		Premium on Bonds Payable		1,829,684
		Bonds Payable		22,000,000

	2.	Interest Expense*	834,039	
		Premium on Bonds Payable	155,961	
		Cash**		990,000

* $23,829,684 × 3.5%
** $22,000,000 × 4.5%

	3.	Interest Expense*	828,580	
		Premium on Bonds Payable	161,420	
		Cash		990,000

* ($23,829,684 – $155,961) × 3.5%

Appendix 2 Ex. 14–24 (Concluded)

b.	Annual interest paid...	$1,980,000
	Less premium amortized*.....................................	317,381
	Interest expense for first year...............................	$1,662,619

* $155,961 + $161,420

c. The bonds sell for more than their face amount because the market rate of interest is less than the contract rate of interest. Investors are willing to pay more for bonds that pay a higher rate of interest (contract rate) than the rate they could earn on similar bonds (market rate).

Appendix 1 and 2 Ex. 14–25

a.	Present value of $1 for 10 semiannual periods at 5% semiannual rate...........................	0.61391	
	Face amount of bonds..	× $35,000,000	$21,486,850
	Present value of an annuity of $1 for 10 semiannual periods at 5% semiannual rate...........	7.72173	
	Semiannual interest payment...............................	× $ 2,100,000	16,215,633
	Proceeds of bond sale...		$37,702,483
b.	First semiannual interest payment........................		$ 2,100,000
	5% of carrying amount of $37,702,483....................		1,885,124
	Premium amortized...		$ 214,876
c.	Second semiannual interest payment....................		$ 2,100,000
	5% of carrying amount of $37,487,607*..................		1,874,380
	Premium amortized...		$ 225,620

* $37,702,483 – $214,876

d.	Annual interest paid...	$ 4,200,000
	Less premium amortized*.....................................	440,495
	Interest expense for first year...............................	$ 3,759,505

* $214,876 + $225,620

Appendix 1 and 2 Ex. 14–26

a. Present value of $1 for 10 semiannual

periods at 6.0% semiannual rate................................ 0.55839

Face amount of bonds... × $80,000,000 $44,671,200

Present value of an annuity of $1 for 10 semiannual

periods at 6.0% semiannual rate............................... 7.36009

Semiannual interest payment..................................... × $ 3,600,000*   26,496,324

Proceeds of bond sale.. $71,167,524

* $80,000,000 × 4.5%

b. 6.0% of carrying amount of $71,167,524......................... $ 4,270,051

First semiannual interest payment...............................   3,600,000

Discount amortized.. $ 670,051

c. 6.0% of carrying amount of $71,837,575*........................ $ 4,310,255

Second semiannual interest payment...........................   3,600,000

Discount amortized.. $ 710,255

* $71,167,524 + $670,051

d. Annual interest paid... $ 7,200,000

Plus discount amortized*...   1,380,306

Interest expense for first year..................................... $ 8,580,306

* $670,051 + $710,255

PROBLEMS

Prob. 14–1A

1.

	Plan 1	Plan 2	Plan 3
Earnings before interest and income tax.....	$2,100,000	$2,100,000	$2,100,000
Deduct interest on bonds.........................	0	0	720,000
Income before income tax.........................	$2,100,000	$2,100,000	$1,380,000
Deduct income tax...................................	840,000	840,000	552,000
Net income...	$1,260,000	$1,260,000	$ 828,000
Dividends on preferred stock....................	0	360,000	180,000
Available for dividends on common stock...	$1,260,000	$ 900,000	$ 648,000
Shares of common stock outstanding.........	÷1,800,000	÷ 900,000	÷ 450,000
Earnings per share on common stock.........	$ 0.70	$ 1.00	$ 1.44

2.

	Plan 1	Plan 2	Plan 3
Earnings before interest and income tax.....	$1,050,000	$1,050,000	$1,050,000
Deduct interest on bonds.........................	0	0	720,000
Income before income tax.........................	$1,050,000	$1,050,000	$ 330,000
Deduct income tax...................................	420,000	420,000	132,000
Net income...	$ 630,000	$ 630,000	$ 198,000
Dividends on preferred stock....................	0	360,000	180,000
Available for dividends on common stock...	$ 630,000	$ 270,000	$ 18,000
Shares of common stock outstanding.........	÷1,800,000	÷ 900,000	÷ 450,000
Earnings per share on common stock.........	$ 0.35	$ 0.30	$ 0.04

3.   The principal advantage of Plan 1 is that it involves only the issuance of common stock, which does not require a periodic interest payment or return of principal, and a payment of preferred dividends is not required. It is also more attractive to common shareholders than is Plan 2 or 3 if earnings before interest and income tax is $1,050,000. In this case, it has the largest EPS ($0.35). The principal disadvantage of Plan 1 is that, if earnings before interest and income tax is $2,100,000, it offers the lowest EPS ($0.70) on common stock.

The principal advantage of Plan 3 is that less investment would need to be made by common shareholders. Also, it offers the largest EPS ($1.44) if earnings before interest and income tax is $2,100,000. Its principal disadvantage is that the bonds carry a fixed annual interest charge and require the payment of principal. It also requires a dividend payment to preferred stockholders before a common dividend can be paid. Finally, Plan 3 provides the lowest EPS ($0.04) if earnings before interest and income tax is $1,050,000.

Plan 2 provides a middle ground in terms of the advantages and disadvantages described in the preceding paragraphs for Plans 1 and 3.

Prob. 14–2A

1.

Cash	91,420,905	
Discount on Bonds Payable	8,579,095	
Bonds Payable		100,000,000

2.   a.

Interest Expense	4,714,477	
Discount on Bonds Payable*		214,477
Cash		4,500,000

   * $8,579,095 ÷ 40 semiannual payments

   b.

Interest Expense	4,714,477	
Discount on Bonds Payable*		214,477
Cash		4,500,000

   * $8,579,095 ÷ 40 semiannual payments

3. $4,714,477

4.   Yes. Investors will not be willing to pay the face amount of the bonds when the interest payments they will receive from the bonds are less than the amount of interest that they could receive from investing in other bonds.

5.   Present value of $1 for 40 semiannual

periods at 5.0% semiannual rate............................	0.14205	
Face amount of bonds..	× $100,000,000	$14,205,000
Present value of annuity of $1 for 40		
semiannual periods at 5.0% semiannual rate...........	17.15909	
Semiannual interest payment..................................	× $ 4,500,000	77,215,905
Proceeds of bond issue.......................................		$91,420,905

Prob. 14–3A

1.

Cash	191,403,720	
Premium on Bonds Payable		41,403,720
Bonds Payable		150,000,000

2. a.

Interest Expense	7,964,907	
Premium on Bonds Payable*	1,035,093	
Cash		9,000,000

 * $41,403,720 ÷ 40 semiannual payments

   b.

Interest Expense	7,964,907	
Premium on Bonds Payable*	1,035,093	
Cash		9,000,000

 * $41,403,720 ÷ 40 semiannual payments

3. $7,964,907

4. Yes. Investors will be willing to pay more than the face amount of the bonds
when the interest payments they will receive from the bonds exceed the amount
of interest that they could receive from investing in other bonds.

5.

Present value of $1 for 40 semiannual		
periods at 4.5% semiannual rate...................................	0.17193	
Face amount of bonds...	× $150,000,000	$ 25,789,500
Present value of annuity of $1		
for 40 semiannual periods at 4.5% semiannual rate........	18.40158	
Semiannual interest payment...	× $ 9,000,000	165,614,220
Proceeds of bond issue..		$191,403,720

Prob. 14–4A

1.

	2014				
	July	1	Cash	77,906,048	
			Discount on Bonds Payable	10,093,952	
			Bonds Payable		88,000,000
	Oct.	1	Cash	240,000	
			Notes Payable		240,000
	Dec.	31	Interest Expense	3,000	
			Interest Payable		3,000
		31	Interest Expense	4,400,000	
			Cash		4,400,000
		31	Interest Expense	504,698	
			Discount on Bonds Payable		504,698
		31	Income Summary	4,907,698	
			Interest Expense		4,907,698
	2015				
	June	30	Interest Expense	4,400,000	
			Cash		4,400,000
	Sept.	30	Interest Expense	9,000	
			Interest Payable	3,000	
			Notes Payable	43,434	
			Cash		55,434
	Dec.	31	Interest Expense	2,457	
			Interest Payable		2,457
		31	Interest Expense	4,400,000	
			Cash		4,400,000
		31	Interest Expense	1,009,395	
			Discount on Bonds Payable		1,009,395
		31	Income Summary	9,820,852	
			Interest Expense		9,820,852
	2016				
	June	30	Bonds Payable	88,000,000	
			Loss on Redemption of Bonds	5,435,160	
			Discount on Bonds Payable		8,075,160
			Cash*		85,360,000

* $88,000,000 × 0.97

Prob. 14–4A (Concluded)

2016					
Sept.	30	Interest Expense		7,371	
		Interest Payable		2,457	
		Notes Payable		45,606	
		Cash			55,434

2. a. 2014: $4,907,698
   b. 2015: $9,820,853

3. Initial carrying amount of bonds.. $77,906,048
   Discount amortized on December 31, 2014.. 504,698
   Discount amortized on December 31, 2015.. 1,009,395
   Carrying amount of bonds, December 31, 2015.................................... $79,420,141

Appendix 1 and 2 Prob. 14–5A

1.

2014				
July	1	Cash	91,420,905	
		Discount on Bonds Payable	8,579,095	
		Bonds Payable		100,000,000

2. a.

2014				
Dec.	31	Interest Expense*	4,571,045	
		Discount on Bonds Payable		71,045
		Cash		4,500,000

*$91,420,905 × 5.0%

b.

2015				
June	30	Interest Expense*	4,574,598	
		Discount on Bonds Payable		74,598
		Cash		4,500,000

*($91,420,905 + $71,045) × 5.0%

3. $4,571,045

Appendix 1 and 2 Prob. 14–6A

1.

2014				
July	1	Cash	191,403,720	
		Premium on Bonds Payable		41,403,720
		Bonds Payable		150,000,000

2. a.

2014				
Dec.	31	Interest Expense*	8,613,167	
		Premium on Bonds Payable	386,833	
		Cash		9,000,000

*$191,403,720 × 4.5%

b.

2015				
June	30	Interest Expense*	8,595,760	
		Premium on Bonds Payable	404,240	
		Cash		9,000,000

*($191,403,720 – $386,833) × 4.5%

3. $8,613,167

Prob. 14–1B

1.

	Plan 1	Plan 2	Plan 3
Earnings before interest and income tax.........	$10,000,000	$10,000,000	$10,000,000
Deduct interest on bonds.............................	0	0	3,600,000
Income before income tax............................	$10,000,000	$10,000,000	$ 6,400,000
Deduct income tax.......................................	4,000,000	4,000,000	2,560,000
Net income...	$ 6,000,000	$ 6,000,000	$ 3,840,000
Dividends on preferred stock.........................	0	2,000,000	1,000,000
Available for dividends on common stock.......	$ 6,000,000	$ 4,000,000	$ 2,840,000
Shares of common stock outstanding.............	÷ 4,000,000	÷ 2,000,000	÷ 1,000,000
Earnings per share on common stock.............	$ 1.50	$ 2.00	$ 2.84

2.

	Plan 1	Plan 2	Plan 3
Earnings before interest and income tax.........	$6,000,000	$6,000,000	$6,000,000
Deduct interest on bonds.............................	0	0	3,600,000
Income before income tax............................	$6,000,000	$6,000,000	$2,400,000
Deduct income tax.......................................	2,400,000	2,400,000	960,000
Net income...	$3,600,000	$3,600,000	$1,440,000
Dividends on preferred stock.........................	0	2,000,000	1,000,000
Available for dividends on common stock.......	$3,600,000	$1,600,000	$ 440,000
Shares of common stock outstanding.............	÷4,000,000	÷2,000,000	÷1,000,000
Earnings per share on common stock.............	$ 0.90	$ 0.80	$ 0.44

3.   The principal advantage of Plan 1 is that it involves only the issuance of
common stock, which does not require a periodic interest payment or return of
principal, and a payment of preferred dividends is not required. It is also more
attractive to common shareholders than is Plan 2 or 3 if earnings before interest
and income tax is $6,000,000. In this case, it has the largest EPS ($0.90). The
principal disadvantage of Plan 1 is that, if earnings before interest and income tax
is $10,000,000, it offers the lowest EPS ($1.50) on common stock.

The principal advantage of Plan 3 is that less investment would need to be made
by common shareholders. Also, it offers the largest EPS ($2.84) if earnings before
interest and income tax is $10,000,000. Its principal disadvantage is that the bonds
carry a fixed annual interest charge and require the payment of principal. It also
requires a dividend payment to preferred stockholders before a common dividend
can be paid. Finally, Plan 3 provides the lowest EPS ($0.44) if earnings before interest
and income tax is $6,000,000.

Plan 2 provides a middle ground in terms of the advantages and disadvantages
described in the preceding paragraphs for Plans 1 and 3.

Prob. 14–2B

1.

Cash	42,309,236	
Discount on Bonds Payable	3,690,764	
Bonds Payable		46,000,000

2. a.

Interest Expense	2,392,269	
Discount on Bonds Payable*		92,269
Cash		2,300,000

*$3,690,764 ÷ 40 semiannual payments

b.

Interest Expense	2,392,269	
Discount on Bonds Payable*		92,269
Cash		2,300,000

*$3,690,764 ÷ 40 semiannual payments

3. $2,392,269

4. Yes. Investors will not be willing to pay the face amount of the bonds when the interest payments they will receive from the bonds are less than the amount of interest that they could receive from investing in other bonds.

5. Present value of $1 for 40 semiannual
periods at 5.5% semiannual rate.................................... 0.11746
Face amount of bonds.. × $46,000,000 $ 5,403,160

Present value of an annuity of $1
for 40 semiannual periods at 5.5% semiannual rate.......... 16.04612
Semiannual interest payment.. × $ 2,300,000   36,906,076
Proceeds of bond issue... $42,309,236

Prob. 14–3B

1.

Cash	73,100,469	
Premium on Bonds Payable		8,100,469
Bonds Payable		65,000,000

2. a.

Interest Expense	3,494,977	
Premium on Bonds Payable*	405,023	
Cash		3,900,000

*$8,100,469 ÷ 20 semiannual periods

b.

Interest Expense	3,494,977	
Premium on Bonds Payable*	405,023	
Cash		3,900,000

*$8,100,469 ÷ 20 semiannual periods

3. $3,494,977

4. Yes. Investors will be willing to pay more than the face amount of the bonds when the interest payments they will receive from the bonds exceed the amount of interest that they could receive from investing in other bonds.

5.

Present value of $1 for 20 semiannual		
periods at 5% semiannual rate....................................	0.37689	
Face amount of bonds..................................... ×	$65,000,000	$24,497,850
Present value of annuity of $1		
for 20 semiannual periods at 5% semiannual rate............	12.46221	
Semiannual interest payment........................... ×	$ 3,900,000	48,602,619
Proceeds of bond issue...................................		$73,100,469

Prob. 14—4B

1.

2014					
July	1	Cash		62,817,040	
		Premium on Bonds Payable			7,817,040
		Bonds Payable			55,000,000
Oct.	1	Cash		450,000	
		Notes Payable			450,000
Dec.	31	Interest Expense		9,000	
		Interest Payable			9,000
	31	Interest Expense		2,475,000	
		Cash			2,475,000
	31	Premium on Bonds Payable		390,852	
		Interest Expense			390,852
	31	Income Summary		2,093,148	
		Interest Expense			2,093,148
2015					
June	30	Interest Expense		2,475,000	
		Cash			2,475,000
Sept.	30	Interest Expense		27,000	
		Interest Payable		9,000	
		Notes Payable		61,342	
		Cash			97,342
Dec.	31	Interest Expense		7,773	
		Interest Payable			7,773
	31	Interest Expense		2,475,000	
		Cash			2,475,000
	31	Premium on Bonds Payable		781,704	
		Interest Expense			781,704
	31	Income Summary		4,203,069	
		Interest Expense			4,203,069
2016					
June	30	Bonds Payable		55,000,000	
		Premium on Bonds Payable		6,253,632	
		Gain on Redemption of Bonds			4,603,632
		Cash*			56,650,000

*$55,000,000 × 1.03

Prob. 14–4B (Concluded)

2016				
Sept.	30	Interest Expense	23,320	
		Interest Payable	7,773	
		Notes Payable	66,249	
		Cash		97,342

2. a. 2014: $2,093,148
    b. 2015: $4,203,069

3. Initial carrying amount of bonds.. $62,817,040
    Premium amortized on December 31, 2014... (390,852)
    Premium amortized on December 31, 2015... (781,704)
    Carrying amount of bonds, December 31, 2015................................... $61,644,484

Appendix 1 and 2 Prob. 14–5B

1.

2014					
July	1	Cash		42,309,236	
		Discount on Bonds Payable		3,690,764	
		Bonds Payable			46,000,000

2. a.

2014					
Dec.	31	Interest Expense*		2,327,008	
		Discount on Bonds Payable			27,008
		Cash			2,300,000

*$42,309,236 × 5.5%

b.

2015					
June	30	Interest Expense*		2,328,493	
		Discount on Bonds Payable			28,493
		Cash			2,300,000

*($42,309,236 + $27,008) × 5.5%

3. $2,327,008

Appendix 1 and 2 Prob. 14–6B

1.

2014					
July	1	Cash		73,100,469	
		Premium on Bonds Payable			8,100,469
		Bonds Payable			65,000,000

2. a.

2014					
Dec.	31	Interest Expense*		3,655,023	
		Premium on Bonds Payable		244,977	
		Cash			3,900,000

*$73,100,469 × 5%

b.

2015					
June	30	Interest Expense*		3,642,775	
		Premium on Bonds Payable		257,225	
		Cash			3,900,000

*($73,100,469 – $244,977) × 5%

3. $3,655,023

CASES & PROJECTS

CP 14-1

GE Capital's action was legal, but caused a great public relations stir at the time. Some quotes:

"A lot of people feel like they have been sorely used," said one bond fund manager. *"There was nothing illegal about it, but it was nasty."*

The fund manager said that GE Capital's decision to upsize its bond issue to $11 billion from $6 billion midway through the offering ordinarily wouldn't have upset bondholders.

"But then to find out two days later that they had filed a $50 billion shelf?" he said. *"People buy GE because it's like buying Treasuries, not because they want to get jerked around."*

GE Capital's action was probably ethical, even though it caused some stir. In its own defense, it stated:

In a statement released late Thursday, GE Capital said "with the $11 billion bond issuance of March 13, GE Capital exhausted its existing debt shelf registration; consequently, on March 20, GE Capital filed a $50 billion shelf registration."

The release said the shelf filing was not an offering and that it would be used in part to roll over $31 billion in maturing long-term debt.

In retrospect, GE Capital could have been a little more forthcoming about its financing plans prior to selling the $11 billion of bonds, but there was nothing unethical or illegal about its disclosures.

Source: "GE Capital Timing on $50B Shelf Filing Added to Backlash," *Dow Jones Capital Markets Report*, March 22, 2002, Copyright (c) 2002, Dow Jones & Company, Inc.

CP 14-2

Without the consent of the bondholders, Bob's use of the sinking fund cash to temporarily alleviate the shortage of funds would violate the bond indenture contract and the trust of the bondholders. It would therefore be unprofessional. In addition, the use of Bob's brother-in-law as trustee of the sinking fund is a potential conflict of interest that could be considered unprofessional.

CP 14–3

Receive $100,000,000 today:

Present value of $100,000,000 today = $100,000,000

Receive $25,000,000 today, plus $9,000,000 per year for 8 years:

Present value of $25,000,000 today = $25,000,000

Present value of annual payments = $9,000,000 × 5.97130 (Present value of an annuity of $1 for 8 periods at 7%) = $53,741,700

Total value = Present value of $25,000,000 + Present value of annual payments

Total value = $25,000,000 + $53,741,700 = $78,741,700

Receive $15,000,000 per year for 10 years:

Present value of annual payments = $15,000,000 × 7.02358 (Present value of an annuity of $1 for 10 periods at 7%) = $105,353,700

The option that has the highest value in terms of present value is to receive $15,000,000 a year for 10 years.

CP 14–4

The primary advantage of issuing preferred stock rather than bonds is that the preferred stock does not obligate Xentec to pay dividends, while interest on bonds must be paid. The issuance of bonds will require annual interest payments, necessitating a periodic (probably semiannual) cash outflow. Given Sweeping Sweeping Bluff Golf Course's volatility of operating cash flows, the required interest payments might strain Xentec's liquidity. In the extreme, this could even lead to a bankruptcy of Xentec.

The issuance of bonds has the advantage of providing a tax deduction for interest expense. This would tend to reduce the net (after-tax) cost of the bonds. Probably the safest alternative is for Xentec to issue preferred stock. Of course, another alternative might be to issue a combination of preferred stock and bonds.

CP 14–5

1.

	Plan 1	Plan 2
Shares of common stock................................	400,000	950,000
Earnings before bond interest and income tax.........	$5,000,000	$5,000,000
Deduct interest on bonds....................................	2,080,000	1,200,000
Income before income tax....................................	$2,920,000	$3,800,000
Deduct income tax...	1,168,000	1,520,000
Net income...	$1,752,000	$2,280,000
Earnings per share on common stock....................	$ 4.38*	$ 2.40**

  * $1,752,000 ÷ 400,000
 ** $2,280,000 ÷ 950,000

2. a.   Factors to be considered in addition to earnings per share:

   1.   There is a definite legal obligation to pay interest on bonds, but there is
        no definite commitment to pay dividends on common stock. Therefore, if
        net income should drop substantially, bonds would be less desirable
        than common stock.

   2.   If the bonds are issued, there is a definite commitment to repay the
        principal in 20 years. In case of liquidation, the claims of the bondholders
        would rank ahead of the claims of the common stockholders.

   3.   Present stockholders must purchase the new stock if they are to retain
        their proportionate control and financial interest in the corporation.

   b.   Since the net income has been relatively stable in the past and anticipated
        earnings under Plan 1 offer earnings per share of $4.38 for each share of
        common stock, Plan 1 appears to be somewhat more advantageous for
        stockholders.

CP 14–6

1. Year 3: $7.3 = \dfrac{\$214,824 + \$1,356,595}{\$214,824}$

    Year 2: $5.9 = \dfrac{\$237,025 + \$1,155,894}{\$237,025}$

    Year 1: $9.3 = \dfrac{\$149,774 + \$1,243,084}{\$149,774}$

2. The number of times interest charges are earned has decreased from Year 1 to Year 3. This was due to the company's increasing interest expense during this period.

CHAPTER 15
INVESTMENTS AND FAIR VALUE ACCOUNTING

DISCUSSION QUESTIONS

1. A company may temporarily have excess cash that is not needed for use in its current operations. Instead of letting excess cash remain idle in a checking account, most companies invest their excess cash in temporary investments. The primary objective of investing in temporary investments is to:
   a. earn interest revenue.
   b. receive dividends.
   c. realize gains from increases in the market price of the securities.

2. A gain or loss can occur when the selling price of the bond differs from the book value (cost) of the bond. The price of bond investments can change due to changes in the market rate of interest. If the proceeds from the sale exceed the book value (cost) of the bonds, then a gain is recorded.

3. The equity method is used for equity investments representing more than 20% and less than 50% of the outstanding shares of the investee.

4. Under the cost method, a dividend received is treated as dividend revenue. Under the equity method, a dividend received is *not* treated as dividend revenue, but is treated as a reduction in the book value of the investment.

5. An investment greater than 50% of the investee is considered to be an investment that exerts control. Thus, the financial statements of the investee (subsidiary) are consolidated (combined) with that of the investor (parent company).

6. Both portfolios are reported at fair value. However, changes in the fair value of trading securities during a period are reported as an unrealized gain or loss on the income statement. For available-for-sale securities, changes in the fair value of the securities are reported in stockholders' equity and, thus, are not recognized as part of net income.

7. A credit balance in Valuation Allowance for Available-for-Sale Investments is subtracted from Available-for-Sale Investments (at cost). The net reported amount is the available-for-sale securities at fair value.

8. A debit balance in Unrealized Gain (Loss) on Available-for-Sale Investments would be reported as a reduction in the Stockholders' Equity section of the balance sheet, after Retained Earnings.

9. Current GAAP requires fair value accounting for impaired assets. Current GAAP allows financial assets and liabilities to be reported at fair value. The assets and liabilities reported at fair value are becoming a more significant portion of many companies' balance sheets. International Financial Reporting Standards are also moving more aggressively toward fair value accounting. As a result of the desire to converge U.S. and international standards, the United States is also moving toward fair value reporting.

10. Fair values may not be readily obtainable for some assets or liabilities, which causes financial statement valuations to become more subjective. In addition, comparability between financial statements among different companies may be hampered by different methods of determining fair value. Lastly, using fair value can result in greater fluctuations in reported results, making predictions of future trends potentially more difficult.

PRACTICE EXERCISES

PE 15–1A

a.

Investments—Tyler City Bonds	400,000	
Interest Receivable	2,000	
Cash		402,000

b.

Cash*	12,000	
Interest Receivable		2,000
Interest Revenue		10,000

* $400,000 × 6% × 1/2

c.

Cash*	197,000	
Loss on Sale of Investments	4,000	
Interest Revenue		1,000
Investments—Tyler City Bonds		200,000

* Sales proceeds ($200,000 × 98%)............................ $196,000
Accrued interest..   1,000
Total proceeds from sale....................................... $197,000

PE 15–1B

a.

Investments—Iceline Inc. Bonds	120,000	
Interest Receivable	1,000	
Cash		121,000

b.

Cash*	3,000	
Interest Receivable		1,000
Interest Revenue		2,000

* $120,000 × 5% × 1/2

c.

Cash*	61,100	
Interest Revenue		500
Gain on Sale of Investments		600
Investments—Iceline Inc. Bonds		60,000

* Sales proceeds ($60,000 × 101%)........................... $60,600
Accrued interest..   500
Total proceeds from sale....................................... $61,100

PE 15–2A

Mar.	20	Investments—Thorlite Company Stock*	300,250	
		Cash		300,250
		*(10,000 shares × $30 per share) + $250		
May	30	Cash*	2,500	
		Dividend Revenue		2,500
		*$0.25 per share × 10,000 shares		
June	15	Cash*	179,800	
		Gain on Sale of Investments		29,675
		Investments—Thorlite Company Stock**		150,125
		*(5,000 shares × $36) – $200		
		**5,000 shares × ($300,250 ÷ 10,000 shares)		

PE 15–2B

Sept.	12	Investments—Aspen Company Stock*	100,200	
		Cash		100,200
		*(2,000 shares × $50 per share) + $200		
Oct.	15	Cash*	1,000	
		Dividend Revenue		1,000
		*$0.50 per share × 2,000 shares		
Nov.	10	Cash*	50,250	
		Loss on Sale of Investments	9,870	
		Investments—Aspen Company Stock**		60,120
		*(1,200 shares × $42) – $150		
		**1,200 shares × ($100,200 ÷ 2,000 shares)		

PE 15–3A

Jan.	2	Investment in ARO Company Stock	300,000	
		Cash		300,000
Dec.	31	Investment in ARO Company Stock	18,000	
		Income of ARO Company		18,000
		Recorded 30% of ARO Company		
		income, 30% × $60,000.		
	31	Cash*	4,500	
		Investment in ARO Company Stock		4,500
		*30% × $15,000		

PE 15–3B

Jan.	2	Investment in Fain Company Stock	500,000	
		Cash		500,000
Dec.	31	Investment in Fain Company Stock	56,000	
		Income of Fain Company		56,000
		Recorded 40% of Fain Company income,		
		40% × $140,000.		
	31	Cash*	20,000	
		Investment in Fain Company Stock		20,000
		*40% × $50,000		

PE 15–4A

2014				
Dec.	31	Unrealized Loss on Trading Investments*	8,900	
		Valuation Allowance for Trading Investments		8,900
		To record decrease in fair value of		
		trading investments.		

* Trading investments at fair value, December 31, 2014............. $203,600
Trading investments at cost, December 31, 2014.................... 212,500
Unrealized loss on trading investments.............................. $ (8,900)

PE 15–4B

2014					
Dec.	31	Valuation Allowance for Trading Investments*	4,800	
		Unrealized Gain on Trading Investments		4,800
		To record increase in fair value of		
		trading investments.		

* Trading investments at fair value, December 31, 2014........................... $46,300
  Trading investments at cost, December 31, 2014................................ 41,500
  Unrealized gain on trading investments... $ 4,800

PE 15–5A

2014					
Dec.	31	Unrealized Gain (Loss) on Available-for-Sale		
		Investments*	5,800	
		Valuation Allowance for Available-for-Sale		
		Investments		5,800
		To record decrease in fair value of		
		available-for-sale securities.		

* Available-for-sale investments at fair value,
  December 31, 2014... $72,600
  Available-for-sale investments at cost, December 31, 2014................... 78,400
  Unrealized gain (loss) on available-for-sale investments...................... $ (5,800)

PE 15–5B

2014					
Dec.	31	Valuation Allowance for Available-for-Sale		
		Investments*	2,090	
		Unrealized Gain (Loss) on Available-for-Sale		
		Investments		2,090
		To record increase in fair value of		
		available-for-sale securities.		

* Available-for-sale investments at fair value,
  December 31, 2014... $26,350
  Available-for-sale investments at cost, December 31, 2014................... 24,260
  Unrealized gain (loss) on available-for-sale investments...................... $ 2,090

PE 15–6A

$$\text{Dividend Yield} = \frac{\text{Dividends per Share of Common Stock}}{\text{Market Price per Share of Common Stock}}$$

$$\text{Dividend Yield} = \frac{\$4.00}{\$100} = 0.04, \text{ or } 4\%$$

PE 15–6B

$$\text{Dividend Yield} = \frac{\text{Dividends per Share of Common Stock}}{\text{Market Price per Share of Common Stock}}$$

$$\text{Dividend Yield} = \frac{\$1.20}{\$40} = 0.03, \text{ or } 3\%$$

EXERCISES

Ex. 15–1

a.

2014				
Apr.	1	Investments—Clayton Co. Bonds	75,000	
		Cash		75,000

b.

2014				
Oct.	1	Cash	2,250	
		Interest Revenue		2,250
		$75,000 × 6% × 6/12.		

c.

2014				
Oct.	1	Cash*	24,500	
		Loss on Sale of Investments	500	
		Investments—Clayton Co. Bonds		25,000
		*$25,000 × 98%		

d.

2014				
Dec.	31	Interest Receivable	750	
		Interest Revenue		750
		Accrued interest.		

Ex. 15–2

a.

2014				
Sept.	1	Investments—Pluto Corp. Bonds	150,000	
		Cash		150,000

b.

2014				
Dec.	31	Interest Receivable	4,000	
		Interest Revenue		4,000
		Accrued interest, $150,000 × 8%		
		× 4/12.		

c.

2015				
Mar.	1	Cash	6,000	
		Interest Receivable		4,000
		Interest Revenue*		2,000
		*$150,000 × 8% × 2/12		

d.

2015				
Mar.	1	Cash*	76,500	
		Gain on Sale of Investments		1,500
		Investments—Pluto Corp. Bonds		75,000
		*$75,000 × 102%		

Ex. 15–3

a.

2014				
June	20	Investments—Thomas County Bonds	60,000	
		Interest Receivable*	500	
		Cash		60,500

  * $60,000 × 6% × 50/360

b.

Nov.	1	Cash*	1,800	
		Interest Receivable		500
		Interest Revenue		1,300

  * $60,000 × 6% × 1/2

c.

Dec.	1	Cash*	14,475	
		Loss on Sale of Investments	600	
		Interest Revenue		75
		Investments—Thomas County Bonds		15,000

  * Bond sale ($15,000 × 0.97).. $14,550
  Accrued interest... 75
  Less brokerage commission................................... (150)
  Total proceeds.. $14,475

d.

Dec.	31	Interest Receivable	450	
		Interest Revenue		450

Ex. 15–4

a.

2014				
Jan.	31	Investments—Government Bonds	75,000	
		Interest Receivable*	375	
		Cash		75,375

* $75,000 × 6% × 30/360

July	1	Cash*	2,250	
		Interest Receivable		375
		Interest Revenue		1,875

* $75,000 × 6% × 1/2

Aug.	29	Cash*	34,650	
		Loss on Sale of Investments	700	
		Interest Revenue		350
		Investments—Government Bonds		35,000

* Bond sale ($35,000 × 98%).. $34,300
Accrued interest... 350
Total proceeds from sale...................................... $34,650

b.

2014				
Dec.	31	Interest Receivable	1,200	
		Interest Revenue		1,200
		Accrued interest, $40,000 ×		
		6% × 1/2.		

Ex. 15–5

Interest earned (April 1 to September 1)[1]...	$1,500
Interest earned on sold bonds (September 1 to November 1)[2]......................	225
Interest earned on remaining bonds (September 1 to December 31)[3]...........	750
Total interest earned in 2014..	$2,475

[1] $80,000 × 4.5% × 5/12
[2] $30,000 × 4.5% × 2/12
[3] $50,000 × 4.5% × 4/12

Ex. 15–6

a.	Mar.	10	Investments—Dickson Co. Stock*	192,240	
			Cash		192,240
			*(6,000 shares × $32.00) + $240		
b.	July	23	Cash*	8,400	
			Dividend Revenue		8,400
			*$1.40 × 6,000 shares		
c.	Nov.	22	Cash*	91,000	
			Gain on Sale of Investments		14,104
			Investments—Dickson Co. Stock**		76,896
			*(2,400 shares × $38.00) – $200		
			**($192,240 ÷ 6,000 shares) × 2,400 shares		

Ex. 15–7

Feb.	8	Investments—Tybee Company Stock*	148,920	
		Cash		148,920
		*(2,400 shares × $62.00) + $120		
Apr.	22	Cash*	1,440	
		Dividend Revenue		1,440
		*$0.60 per share × 2,400 shares		
May	26	Cash*	51,940	
		Loss on Sale of Investments	10,110	
		Investments—Tybee Company Stock**		62,050
		*(1,000 shares × $52.00) – $60		
		**1,000 shares × ($148,920 ÷ 2,400 shares)		

Ex. 15–8

Jan.	16	Investments—McDowell Inc. Stock*	75,140	
		Cash		75,140

* (3,000 shares × $25) + $140

Mar.	23	Cash*	1,380	
		Dividend Revenue		1,380

* 3,000 shares × $0.46

May	25	Investments—McDowell Inc. Stock*	35,160	
		Cash		35,160

* (1,000 shares × $35) + $160

July	10	Cash*	127,800	
		Gain on Sale of Investments		45,628
		Investments—McDowell Inc. Stock**		82,172

* (3,200 shares × $40) – $200

** 3,000 shares purchased.................................. $75,140
200 shares × ($35,160 ÷ 1,000 shares)..............   7,032
Total cost... $82,172

Oct.	12	Cash*	408	
		Dividend Revenue		408

* 800 shares × $0.51

Ex. 15–9

Feb.	24	Investments—Tett Co. Stock*	85,150	
		Cash		85,150
		*(1,000 shares × $85) + $150		
May	16	Investments—Issacson Co. Stock*	90,100	
		Cash		90,100
		*(2,500 shares × $36) + $100		
July	14	Cash*	39,925	
		Gain on Sale of Investments		5,865
		Investments—Tett Co. Stock**		34,060
		*(400 shares × $100) – $75		
		**400 shares × ($85,150 ÷ 1,000 shares)		
Aug.	12	Cash*	24,295	
		Loss on Sale of Investments	2,735	
		Investments—Issacson Co. Stock**		27,030
		*(750 shares × $32.50) – $80		
		**750 shares × ($90,100 ÷ 2,500 shares)		
Oct.	31	Cash*	240	
		Dividend Revenue		240
		*(1,000 shares – 400 shares) × $0.40		

Ex. 15–10

a. 1.

Investment in Larson Corp. Stock	480,000	
Income of Larson Corp.		480,000
Record 40% share of Larson Corp.		
net income, $1,200,000 × (160,000 shares ÷		
400,000 shares).		

2.

Cash*	320,000	
Investment in Larson Corp. Stock		320,000
*160,000 shares × $2.00		

b.   Stieg's investment in Larson Corp. represents 40% of the outstanding shares of Larson Corp. An investment amount between 20% and 50% of the outstanding common stock of the investee is presumed to represent significant influence. The equity method is appropriate when the investor can exercise significant influence over the investee.

Ex. 15–11

a.

2014				
Jan.	4	Investment in Hi Energy Co. Stock*	5,456,000	
		Cash		5,456,000
		*124,000 shares × $44 per share		
July	2	Cash*	136,400	
		Investment in Hi Energy Co. Stock		136,400
		*$440,000 × ($124,000 ÷ 400,000 shares)		
Dec.	31	Investment in Hi Energy Co. Stock	248,000	
		Income of Hi Energy Co.		248,000
		Record 31% share of Hi Energy		
		Co. net income, $800,000 ×		
		(124,000 shares ÷ 400,000 shares).		

b.
Initial acquisition cost..	$5,456,000
Equity earnings for 2014..	248,000
Cash dividends received...	(136,400)
Investment in Hi Energy Co. Stock balance, December 31, 2014.............	$5,567,600

Ex. 15–12

a.

2014				
Jan.	6	Investment in Gator Co. Stock	212,000	
		Cash		212,000
June	30	Cash*	8,160	
		Investment in Gator Co. Stock		8,160
		*$24,000 × 34%		
Dec.	31	Loss of Gator Co.	19,040	
		Investment in Gator Co. Stock		19,040
		Record 34% share of Gator Co.		
		net loss, $56,000 × 34%.		

b.
Initial acquisition cost..	$212,000
Equity loss for 2014..	(19,040)
Cash dividends received...	(8,160)
Investment in Gator Co. Stock balance, December 31, 2014..................	$184,800

Ex. 15–12 (Concluded)

c. Under the equity method, the investor will record their proportionate share of the net increase (or decrease) of the book value of the investee resulting from earnings and dividend distributions. The fair value method uses market price information to value the investment in the investee. These two methods result in different valuations because the equity method is based upon book accounting, while the fair value approach uses market information. The two methods need not be related to each other over time. While changes in book value can influence market prices, many other variables can influence the market price of a stock.

Ex. 15–13

	(in millions)
Investment in Raven Company stock, December 31, 2014............................	$264
Plus equity earnings in Raven Company..	25
Less dividends received*...	(8)
Investment in Raven Company stock, December 31, 2015............................	$281

  * The Raven Company investment is accounted for under the equity method. Since there were no purchases or sales of Raven Company stock, a dividend must have been received. This would explain how the ending balance of the investment account went from $264 to $281, with $25 million in equity earnings. Since the investment is accounted for under the equity method, the fair value is not used for valuation purposes.

Ex. 15–14

a.	$6,000	$35,000 [from (c)] – $29,000 [from (b)]
b.	$29,000	$17,000 – (– $12,000)
c.	$35,000	$245,000 – $210,000
d.	$132,000	$144,000 – $12,000
e.	$39,000	$28,000 + $11,000
f.	$185,000	$168,000 + $17,000
g.	$6,000	$17,000 – $11,000
h.	$211,000	$205,000 + $6,000
i.	$273,000	$245,000 + $28,000

Ex. 15–15

a.

2014				
Feb.	24	Investments—Raiders, Inc. Stock	551,000	
		Cash		551,000
		14,500 shares × $38 per share.		
Dec.	31	Valuation Allowance for Trading		
		Investments	58,000	
		Unrealized Gain on Trading		
		Investments		58,000
		To record increase in fair value of		
		trading investments, 14,500 shares ×		
		($42 per share – $38 per share).		

b.   The unrealized gain or unrealized loss for trading investments is disclosed in the income statement as "other income" (or a separate item if significant). Unrealized losses would be deducted in determining net income, while unrealized gains would be added in determining net income.

Ex. 15–16

a.

2014				
Dec.	31	Unrealized Loss on Trading Investments	1,200	
		Valuation Allowance for Trading		
		Investments		1,200
		To record decrease in fair value		
		of trading investments, $84,800 –		
		$86,000.		

b.

2015				
May	10	Investments—Giants, Inc.*	24,150	
		Cash		24,150
		*(1,000 shares × $24 per share) + $150		

Ex. 15–17

a.

2014				
Dec.	31	Valuation Allowance for Trading		
		Investments*	17,500	
		Unrealized Gain on Trading Investments		17,500

* $337,500 – $320,000, as determined from the following schedule:

	Cost	Fair Value (Dec. 31, 2014)
Arden Enterprises, Inc.	$150,000	$170,000[1]
French Broad Industries, Inc.	66,000	71,500[2]
Pisgah Construction, Inc.	104,000	96,000[3]
Total..	$320,000	$337,500

[1] 5,000 shares × $34 per share

[2] 2,750 shares × $26 per share

[3] 1,600 shares × $60 per share

b. **There would be no adjusting entry for December 31, 2015, if the market prices remained unchanged from December 31, 2014. This is because the unrealized gain from the difference between the cost and market has already been recognized on December 31, 2014. Only *changes* in market prices would be recognized subsequent to December 31, 2014.**

Ex. 15–18

a.

Retained earnings, December 31, 2013..	**$ 825,000**
Plus net income..	**245,000**
	$1,070,000
Less dividends...	**65,000**
Retained earnings, December 31, 2014...	**$1,005,000**

b.

Trading investments (at cost)*..	**$ 280,000**
Less valuation allowance for trading investments...............................	**72,500**
Trading investments (at fair value)...	**$ 207,500**

* $346,000 – $66,000

Ex. 15–19

a.	$37,100	$44,600 – $7,500
b.	$44,600	$220,000 – $175,400
c.	$102,000	$90,000 + $12,000
d.	$12,000	Same as valuation allowance for available-for-sale investments
e.	$75,000	$86,000 – $11,000
f.	($11,000)	Same as valuation allowance for available-for-sale investments
g.	($9,000)	($21,000) + $12,000
h.	($16,400)	Same as unrealized gain (loss) from available-for-sale investments
i.	$85,600	$102,000 – $16,400
j.	$199,000	$220,000 – $21,000

Ex. 15–20

a.

2014				
Sept.	12	Investments—Bengals Inc. Stock	430,300	
		Cash		430,300
		33,100 shares × $13 per share.		
Dec.	31	Unrealized Gain (Loss) on Available-for-		
		Sale Investments	66,200	
		Valuation Allowance for Available-for-Sale		
		Investments		66,200
		33,100 shares × ($11 per share – $13 per		
		share).		

b.   Unrealized Gain (Loss) on Available-for-Sale Investments is reported in the Stockholde Equity section of the balance sheet, separately from the retained earnings or paid-in capital accounts. On December 31, 2014, the account would show a debit balance of $66,200, which would be subtracted from stockholders' equity.

Ex. 15–21

a. 1.

2014				
Dec.	31	Valuation Allowance for Available-for-		
		Sale Investments	4,280	
		Unrealized Gain (Loss) on Available-		
		for-Sale Investments		4,280
		$93,400 – $89,120.		

2.

2015				
June	12	Investments—Rogue Wave Inc.*	65,350	
		Cash		65,350
		*(1,450 shares × $45 per share) + $100		

b.   Unrealized gains and losses for available-for-sale securities are accumulated over time and reported as a credit (positive) or debit (negative) balance in the Stockholders' Equity section. As a result, the changes in fair value are not reflected on the income statement, as is the case with trading securities. Bypassing the income statement is supported on the grounds that available-for-sale securities will be held for a longer time than trading securities; thus, fluctuations in market prices have a greater opportunity to "cancel out" over time.

Ex. 15–22

a.

2014					
Dec.		31	Unrealized Gain (Loss) on Available-for-		
			Sale Investments	4,250	
			Valuation Allowance for Available-for-		
			Sale Investments*		4,250

* $259,450 – $263,700, as determined from the following schedule:

	Cost	Fair Value (Dec. 31, 2014)
Dust Devil, Inc.	$ 81,700	$ 76,000[1]
Gale Co.	68,000	63,750[2]
Whirlwind Co.	114,000	119,700[3]
Total..	$263,700	$259,450

[1] 1,900 shares × $40 per share

[2] 850 shares × $75 per share

[3] 2,850 shares × $42 per share

b.   There is no income statement impact from the December 31, 2014, adjusting
entry. Unrealized Gain (Loss) on Available-for-Sale Investments is reported
in the Stockholders' Equity section of the balance sheet. On December 31,
2014, Unrealized Gain or Loss on Available-for-Sale Investments would be
disclosed as follows:

Unrealized gain (loss) on available-for-sale investments...................... $(4,250)

Ex. 15–23

a.

GALILEO COMPANY Balance Sheet (selected items) December 31, 2014		
Assets		
Current assets:		
Available-for-sale investments, at cost	$82,000	
Plus valuation allowance for available-for-sale		
investments*	5,720	$87,720

* Computation:

Market:

Hawking Inc.: 900 shares × $50...	$45,000
Pavlov Co.: 1,780 shares × $24...	42,720
	$87,720
Cost ($44,000 + $38,000)..	82,000
Unrealized gain..	$ 5,720

b.

GALILEO COMPANY Balance Sheet (selected items) December 31, 2014	
Stockholders' Equity	
Retained earnings	$300,000
Unrealized gain (loss) on available-for-sale	
investments	5,720

Ex. 15–24

COPERNICUS CORPORATION Balance Sheet (selected Stockholders' Equity items) December 31, 2014	
Common stock	$ 50,000
Paid-in capital in excess of par	250,000
Retained earnings*	520,000
Unrealized gain (loss) on available-for-sale investments**	(25,000)
Total	$795,000

* $340,000 + $180,000

** $40,000 + ($160,000 – $225,000), or $160,000 – $185,000

Ex. 15–25

$$\text{Dividend Yield} = \frac{\text{Cash Dividends per Share of Common Stock}}{\text{Market Price per Share of Common Stock}}$$

$$\text{Dividend Yield} = \frac{\$2.44}{\$93.49} = 2.6\%$$

Ex. 15–26

a.   Year 1: Dividend Yield = $0.52 ÷ $30.48 = 1.71%
     Year 2: Dividend Yield = $0.52 ÷ $27.91 = 1.86%

b.   Dividends per share remained constant from Year 1 to Year 2. In addition, the dividend yield increased from 1.71% in Year 1 to 1.86% in Year 2. The increase in the dividend yield is a result of a slight decrease in the stock price. Microsoft provides a small return to the shareholder in terms of a dividend yield and an additional return in terms of price appreciation of the stock.

Ex. 15–27

The investor would receive a return on the investment through share price appreciation as internally generated funds are used to fund growth and earnings opportunities. Thus, investors in eBay would likely approve of this policy, because the company is able to earn superior returns with internally generated earnings beyond what investors could likely earn on their own by investing dividend distributions.

Appendix Ex. 15–28

CHEWCO CO. For the Year Ended December 31, 2014	
Net income	$50,000
Other comprehensive income (loss):	
Unrealized gain on available-for-sale investments*	24,000
Comprehensive income	$74,000

  * 2,000 shares × ($124 per share – $112 per share)

Appendix Ex. 15–29

VALUR CO. For the Year Ended December 31, 2014	
Net income	$210,000
Other comprehensive income (loss):	
Unrealized gain on available-for-sale investments*	15,000
Comprehensive income	$225,000

  * $200,000 – $185,000

PROBLEMS

Prob. 15–1A

1.

2014				
Mar.	1	Investments—Buncombe Co. Bonds	50,000	
		Interest Receivable	250	
		Cash		50,250
	16	Investments—French Broad Bonds	84,000	
		Interest Receivable	175	
		Cash		84,175
Aug.	1	Cash*	1,500	
		Interest Receivable		250
		Interest Revenue		1,250
		*$50,000 × 6% × 1/2		
	31	Cash*	19,900	
		Loss on Sale of Investment	200	
		Interest Revenue		100
		Investments—Buncombe Co. Bonds		20,000
		*($20,000 × 0.99) + $100		
Sept.	1	Cash*	2,100	
		Interest Receivable		175
		Interest Revenue		1,925
		*$84,000 × 5% × 1/2		
Dec.	31	Interest Receivable	750	
		Interest Revenue		750
	31	Interest Receivable	1,400	
		Interest Revenue		1,400

Prob. 15–1A (Concluded)

2015				
Feb.	1	Cash*	900	
		Interest Receivable		750
		Interest Revenue		150
		*$30,000 × 6% × 1/2		
Mar.	1	Cash*	2,100	
		Interest Receivable		1,400
		Interest Revenue		700
		*$84,000 × 5% × 1/2		

2. If the bonds are classified as available-for-sale securities, then the portfolio of bonds would need to be adjusted to fair value. This would be accomplished by using a valuation allowance account and an unrealized gain (loss) account as part of stockholders' equity. If the fair value were greater than the cost of the bond portfolio, the two accounts would be positive, and thus added to investments and stockholders' equity, respectively. If the fair value were less than the cost of the bond portfolio, the two accounts would be negative, and thus subtracted from investments and stockholders' equity, respectively.

Prob. 15–2A

1.

2014				
Mar.	14	Investments—Wilkomm Inc.*	200,500	
		Cash		200,500
		*(5,000 shares × $40 per share) + $500		
Apr.	24	Investments—McMarsh Inc.*	90,198	
		Cash		90,198
		*(1,800 shares × $50 per share) + $198		
June	1	Cash*	98,700	
		Loss on Sale of Investments	5,560	
		Investments—Wilkomm Inc.**		104,260
		*(2,600 shares × $38.00 per share) – $100		
		**2,600 shares × ($200,500 ÷ 5,000 shares)		
	30	Cash*	840	
		Dividend Revenue		840
		*(5,000 shares – 2,600 shares) × $0.35		
Dec.	31	Unrealized Loss on Trading Investments	7,038	
		Valuation Allowance for Trading		
		Investments*		7,038

* $179,400 – $186,438, in table below

	Number of Shares	Cost per Share	Fair Value per Share	Cost	Fair Value
Wilkomm Inc.	2,400	$40.10[1]	$38	$ 96,240	$ 91,200
McMarsh Inc.	1,800	$50.11[2]	$49	90,198	88,200
Total...........................				$186,438	$179,400

[1] $200,500 ÷ 5,000 shares = $40.10 per share

[2] $90,198 ÷ 1,800 shares = $50.11 per share

Prob. 15–2A (Concluded)

2015				
Apr.	4	Investments—Daley Inc.*	105,175	
		Cash		105,175
		*(3,500 shares × $30 per share) + $175		
June	28	Cash*	960	
		Dividend Revenue		960
		*2,400 shares × $0.40 per share		
Sept.	9	Cash*	22,350	
		Gain on Sale of Investments		1,315
		Investments—Daley Inc.**		21,035
		*(700 shares × $32 per share) – $50		
		**700 shares × ($105,175 ÷ 3,500 shares)		
Dec.	31	Valuation Allowance for Trading Investments*	86,460	
		Unrealized Gain on Trading Investments		86,460
		*$7,038 + $79,422		

2.

SCOFIELD FINANCIAL CO. Balance Sheet (selected items) December 31, 2015		
Current assets:		
Trading investments (at cost)	$270,578	
Plus valuation allowance for trading investments	79,422	
Trading investments (at fair value)		$350,000

3. Unrealized gains or losses are reported on the income statement, often as "Other Income (Losses)." For 2014, Scofield Financial Co. would have reported an unrealized loss of $7,038 as "Other Losses." For 2015, Scofield Financial Co. would have reported an unrealized gain of $86,460 as "Other Income." If unrealized gains and losses were significant for Scofield Financial, then they would be separately disclosed on the income statement.

Prob. 15–3A

1.

2014				
Feb.	1	Investments—Acuity Inc.*	324,000	
		Cash		324,000
		*12,000 shares × $27 per share		
Mar.	18	Cash*	2,160	
		Dividend Revenue		2,160
		*12,000 shares × $0.18 per share		
Sept.	12	Cash*	2,880	
		Dividend Revenue		2,880
		*12,000 shares × $0.24 per share		
	28	Cash*	20,950	
		Loss on Sale of Investments	6,050	
		Investments—Acuity Inc.**		27,000
		*(1,000 shares × $21.00) – $50		
		**1,000 shares × $27 per share		
Dec.	31	Valuation Allowance for Available-for-		
		Sale Investments	66,000	
		Unrealized Gain (Loss) on Available-for-		
		Sale Investments		66,000
		11,000 shares × ($33.00 – $27.00).		
2015				
Jan.	23	Investment in Shouse Inc. Stock	376,000	
		Cash		376,000
Mar.	16	Cash*	2,640	
		Dividend Revenue		2,640
		*(12,000 shares – 1,000 shares) × $0.24 per share		

Prob. 15–3A (Concluded)

Sept.	16	Cash*	3,300	
		Dividend Revenue		3,300
		*11,000 shares × ($0.24 + $0.06)		
Dec.	31	Cash	30,100	
		Investment in Shouse Inc. Stock		30,100
	31	Investment in Shouse Inc. Stock	53,200	
		Income of Shouse Inc.		53,200
		To record 28% of Shouse Inc.		
		income $190,000 × (70,000 shares ÷		
		250,000 shares).		
	31	Unrealized Gain (Loss) on Available-for-		
		Sale Investments	33,000	
		Valuation Allowance for Available-for-		
		Sale Investments*		33,000
		*($30.00 – $33.00) × 11,000 shares		

2.

DAFFITAR INC. Balance Sheet (selected items) December 31, 2015		
Current assets:		
Available-for-sale investments (at cost)[1]	$297,000	
Plus valuation allowance for available-for-		
sale investments	33,000	
Available-for-sale investments (at fair value)[2]		$330,000
Investments:		
Investment in Shouse Inc. stock[3]		$399,100
Stockholders' equity:		
Retained earnings		$465,000
Unrealized gain (loss) on available-for-sale		
investments		33,000

[1] 11,000 shares × $27 per share

[2] 11,000 shares × $30 per share

[3] $376,000 + $53,200 – $30,100

Prob. 15–4A

a. $236,170   (see table below)

b. $(5,800)   ($230,370 – $236,170, from table)

c. $230,370   (from table)

Investments	No. of Shares (or face amount)	Cost per Share (or $100 of face amount)	Market Value per Share (or $100 of face amount)	Total Cost	Fair Value
Bernard Co. stock......	2,250	$17.00	$15.40	$ 38,250	$ 34,650
Chadwick Co. stock....	1,260	52.00	46.00	65,520	57,960
Gozar Inc. stock.........	3,080	30.00	32.00	92,400	98,560
Nightline Co. bonds....	$40,000	100	98	40,000	39,200
				$236,170	$230,370

d. $600   ($40,000 × 6% × 3/12)

e. $98,100   [$77,000 + ($112,000 × 30%) – $12,500]

f. $813,600   ($233,000 + $136,530 + $230,370 + $600 + $98,100 + $115,000)

g. $455,000   ($308,770 + $146,230)

h. $(5,800)   [same as (b)]

i. $813,600   ($69,400 + $70,000 + $225,000 + $455,000 – $5,800)

Prob. 15–4A (Continued)

The completed comparative unclassified balance sheets are as follows:

O'BRIEN INDUSTRIES, INC. Balance Sheet December 31, 2015 and 2014		
	Dec. 31, 2015	Dec. 31, 2014
Cash	$233,000	$220,000
Accounts receivable (net)	136,530	138,000
Available-for-sale investments (at cost)—Note 1	$236,170	$103,770
Less valuation allowance for available-for-sale		
investments	5,800	2,500
Available-for-sale investments (fair value)	$230,370	$101,270
Interest receivable	$ 600	—
Investment in Jolly Roger Co. stock—Note 2	98,100	$ 77,000
Office equipment (net)	115,000	130,000
Total assets	$813,600	$666,270
Accounts payable	$ 69,400	$ 60,000
Common stock	70,000	70,000
Excess of issue price over par	225,000	225,000
Retained earnings	455,000	308,770
Unrealized gain (loss) on available-for-sale		
investments	(5,800)	2,500
Total liabilities and stockholders' equity	$813,600	$666,270

Note 1. Investments are classified as available for sale. The investments at cost and fair value on December 31, 2014, are as follows:

	No. of Shares	Cost per Share	Total Cost	Total Fair Value
Bernard Co. stock.............................	2,250	$17.00	$ 38,250	$ 37,500
Chadwick Co. stock...........................	1,260	52.00	65,520	63,770
			$103,770	$101,270

Prob. 15–4A (Concluded)

For December 31, 2015:

	No. of Shares (or face amount)	Cost per Share (or $100 of face amount)	Market Value per Share (or $100 of face amount)	Total Cost	Fair Value
Bernard Co. stock....	2,250	$17.00	$15.40	$ 38,250	$ 34,650
Chadwick Co. stock..	1,260	52.00	46.00	65,520	57,960
Gozar Inc. stock.......	3,080	30.00	32.00	92,400	98,560
Nightline Co. bonds..	$40,000	100	98	40,000	39,200
				$236,170	$230,370

Note 2. The investment in Jolly Roger Co. stock is an equity method investment representing 30% of the outstanding shares of Jolly Roger Co.

Prob. 15–1B

1.

2014					
Apr.	1	Investments—Smoke Bay Bonds	90,000		
		Interest Receivable	900		
		Cash			90,900
May	16	Investments—Geotherma Co. Bonds	42,000		
		Interest Receivable	70		
		Cash			42,070
Aug.	1	Cash*	2,700		
		Interest Receivable			900
		Interest Revenue			1,800
		*$90,000 × 6% × 1/2			
Sept.	1	Cash*	12,180		
		Interest Revenue			60
		Gain on Sale of Investment			120
		Investments—Smoke Bay Bonds			12,000
		*($12,000 × 1.01) + $60			
Nov.	1	Cash*	840		
		Interest Receivable			70
		Interest Revenue			770
		*$42,000 × 4% × 1/2			
Dec.	31	Interest Receivable	1,950		
		Interest Revenue			1,950
		Accrued interest.			
	31	Interest Receivable	280		
		Interest Revenue			280
		Accrued interest.			

Prob. 15–1B (Concluded)

2015				
Feb.	1	Cash*	2,340	
		Interest Receivable		1,950
		Interest Revenue		390
		*$78,000 × 6% × 1/2		
May	1	Cash*	840	
		Interest Receivable		280
		Interest Revenue		560
		*$42,000 × 4% × 1/2		

2. If the bonds are classified as available-for-sale securities, then the portfolio of bonds would need to be adjusted to fair value. This would be accomplished by using a valuation allowance account and an unrealized gain (loss) account. If the fair value were greater than the cost of the bond portfolio, the two accounts would be positive, and thus added to investments and stockholders' equity, respectively. If the fair value were less than the cost of the bond portfolio, the two accounts would be negative, and thus subtracted from investments and stockholders' equity, respectively.

Prob. 15–2B

1.

2014				
Feb.	14	Investments—Apollo Inc.*	124,992	
		Cash		124,992
		*(4,800 shares × $26 per share) + $192		
Apr.	1	Investments—Ares Inc.*	43,792	
		Cash		43,792
		*(2,300 shares × $19 per share) + $92		
June	1	Cash*	19,100	
		Gain on Sale of Investments		3,476
		Investments—Apollo Inc.**		15,624
		*(600 shares × $32 per share) – $100		
		**600 shares × ($124,992 ÷ 4,800 shares)		
	27	Cash*	840	
		Dividend Revenue		840
		*(4,800 shares – 600 shares) × $0.20		
Dec.	31	Valuation Allowance for Trading Investments*	27,990	
		Unrealized Gain on Trading Investments		27,990

* $181,150 – $153,160, in table below

	Number of Shares	Cost per Share	Fair Value per Share	Cost	Fair Value
Apollo Inc.	4,200	$26.04[1]	$33.00	$109,368	$138,600
Ares Co.	2,300	$19.04[2]	$18.50	43,792	42,550
Total......................................				$153,160	$181,150

[1] $124,992 ÷ 4,800 shares = $26.04 per share

[2] $43,792 ÷ 2,300 shares = $19.04 per share

Prob. 15–2B (Concluded)

2015				
Mar.	14	Investments—Athena Inc.*	78,120	
		Cash		78,120
		*(1,200 shares × $65 per share) + $120		
June	26	Cash*	882	
		Dividend Revenue		882
		*4,200 shares × $0.21 per share		
July	30	Cash*	28,750	
		Loss on Sale of Investments	2,498	
		Investments—Athena Inc.**		31,248
		*(480 shares × $60 per share) – $50		
		**480 shares × ($78,120 ÷ 1,200 shares)		
Dec.	31	Unrealized Loss on Trading Investments*	40,022	
		Valuation Allowance for Trading Investments*		40,022
		*$27,990 + $12,032		

2.

ZEUS INVESTMENTS INC. Balance Sheet (selected items) December 31, 2015		
Current assets:		
Trading investments (at cost)*	$200,032	
Less valuation allowance for trading investments	12,032	
Trading investments (at fair value)		$188,000

*$153,160 (from Dec. 31, 2014) + $78,120 – $31,248

3. Unrealized gains or losses are reported in the income statement, often as "Other Income (Losses)." For 2014, Zeus Investments Inc. would have reported an unrealized gain of $27,990 as "Other Income." For 2015, Zeus Investments Inc. would have reported an unrealized loss of $40,022 as "Other Losses." If unrealized gains and losses were significant for Zeus Investments, then they would be separately disclosed on the income statement.

Prob. 15–3B

1.

2014				
Jan.	18	Investments—Malmo Inc.*	360,000	
		Cash		360,000
		*9,000 shares × $40 per share		
July	22	Cash*	27,000	
		Dividend Revenue		27,000
		*9,000 shares × $3.00 per share		
Oct.	5	Cash*	28,900	
		Gain on Sale of Investments		8,900
		Investments—Malmo Inc.**		20,000
		*(500 shares × $58.00) − $100		
		**500 shares × $40 per share		
Dec.	18	Cash*	25,500	
		Dividend Revenue		25,500
		*(9,000 shares − 500 shares) × $3.00		
	31	Unrealized Gain (Loss) on Available-for-Sale Investments	34,000	
		Valuation Allowance for Available-for-Sale Investments		34,000
		8,500 shares × ($36.00 − $40).		
2015				
Jan.	25	Investment in Helsi Co. Stock	800,000	
		Cash		800,000
July	16	Cash*	25,500	
		Dividend Revenue		25,500
		*8,500 shares × $3.00 per share		

15-36

Prob. 15–3B (Concluded)

Dec.				
	16	Cash*	27,200	
		Dividend Revenue		27,200
		*8,500 shares × ($3.00 + $0.20)		
	31	Cash	38,000	
		Investment in Helsi Co. Stock		38,000
	31	Investment in Helsi Co. Stock	51,000	
		Income of Helsi Co.		51,000
		To record 30% of Helsi Co. income		
		$170,000 × (75,000 shares ÷ 250,000		
		shares).		
	31	Valuation Allowance for Available-for-		
		Sale Investments*	68,000	
		Unrealized Gain (Loss) on Available-for-		
		Sale Investments		68,000
		*8,500 × ($44 − $36.00)		

2.

GLACIER PRODUCTS, INC.		
Balance Sheet (selected items)		
December 31, 2015		
Current assets:		
Available-for-sale investments (at cost)[1]	$340,000	
Plus valuation allowance for available-for-		
sale investments	34,000	
Available-for-sale investments (at fair value)[2]		$374,000
Investments:		
Investment in Helsi Co. stock[3]		$813,000
Stockholders' equity:		
Retained earnings		$700,000
Unrealized gain (loss) on available-for-sale		
investments		34,000

[1] 8,500 shares × $40 per share

[2] 8,500 shares × $44 per share

[3] $800,000 + $51,000 − $38,000

Prob. 15–4B

a. $147,200   (from table)
b. $4,680   ($151,880 – $147,200, from table)
c. $151,880   (from table)

	No. of Shares (or face amount)	Cost per Share (or $100 of face amount)	Market Value per Share (or $100 of face amount)	Total Cost	Fair Value
Alvarez Inc. stock......	960	$38.00	$41.50	$ 36,480	$ 39,840
Hirsch Inc. stock........	1,900	28.80	26.00	54,720	49,400
Richter Inc. stock......	800	40.00	48.00	32,000	38,400
Toon Co. bonds.........	$24,000	100	101	24,000	24,240
				$147,200	$151,880

d. $240   ($24,000 × 4% × 3/12)
e. $81,200   [$69,200 + ($80,000 × 30%) – $12,000]
f. $604,320   ($160,000 + $115,000 + $151,880 + $240 + $81,200 + $96,000)
g. $178,640   ($127,400 + $51,240)
h. $4,680   [same as (b)]
i. $604,320   ($91,000 + $80,000 + $250,000 + $178,640 + $4,680)

Prob. 15–4B (Continued)

The completed comparative unclassified balance sheets are as follows:

TEASDALE, INC. Balance Sheet December 31, 2015 and 2014	Dec. 31, 2015	Dec. 31, 2014
Cash	$160,000	$156,000
Accounts receivable (net)	115,000	108,000
Available-for-sale investments (at cost)—Note 1	$147,200	$ 91,200
Plus valuation allowance for available-for-sale		
investments	4,680	8,776
Available-for-sale investments (fair value)	$151,880	$ 99,976
Interest receivable	$ 240	$ —
Investment in Wright Co. stock—Note 2	81,200	69,200
Office equipment (net)	96,000	105,000
Total assets	$604,320	$538,176
Accounts payable	$ 91,000	$ 72,000
Common stock	80,000	80,000
Excess of issue price over par	250,000	250,000
Retained earnings	178,640	127,400
Unrealized gain (loss) on available-for-sale		
investments	4,680	8,776
Total liabilities and stockholders' equity	$604,320	$538,176

Note 1. Investments are classified as available for sale. The investments at cost and fair value on December 31, 2014, are as follows:

	No. of Shares	Cost per Share	Total Cost	Total Fair Value
Alvarez Inc. stock........................	960	$38.00	$36,480	$39,936
Hirsch Inc. stock.........................	1,900	$28.80	54,720	60,040
			$91,200	$99,976

Prob. 15–4B (Concluded)

For December 31, 2015:

	No. of Shares (or face amount)	Cost per Share (or $100 of face amount)	Market Value per Share (or $100 of face amount)	Total Cost	Fair Value
Alvarez Inc. stock...	960	$38.00	$41.50	$ 36,480	$ 39,840
Hirsch Inc. stock.....	1,900	28.80	26.00	54,720	49,400
Richter Inc. stock....	800	40.00	48.00	32,000	38,400
Toon Co. bonds......	$24,000	100	101	24,000	24,240
				$147,200	$151,880

Note 2. The Investment in Wright Co. stock is an equity method investment representing 30% of the outstanding shares of Wright Co.

COMPREHENSIVE PROBLEM 4

1.	a.	Cash	450,000	
		Common Stock		300,000
		Paid-In Capital in Excess of Par—		
		Common Stock		150,000
	b.	Cash	400,000	
		Preferred Stock		320,000
		Paid-In Capital in Excess of Par—		
		Preferred Stock		80,000
	c.	Cash*	520,000	
		Bonds Payable		500,000
		Premium on Bonds Payable		20,000
		*$500,000 × 1.04		
	d.	Cash Dividends*	50,000	
		Cash Dividends Payable		50,000
		*100,000 shares × $0.50 per share		
		Cash Dividends*	20,000	
		Cash Dividends Payable		20,000
		*20,000 shares × $1.00 per share		
	e.	Cash Dividends Payable	70,000	
		Cash		70,000
	f.	Investments—Solstice Corp.*	300,150	
		Cash		300,150
		*(7,500 shares × $40 per share) + $150		
	g.	Treasury Stock*	264,000	
		Cash		264,000
		*8,000 shares × $33 per share		
	h.	Investment in Pinkberry Co. Stock*	960,000	
		Cash		960,000
		*40,000 shares × $24 per share		

Comp. Prob. 4 (Continued)

i.	Cash Dividends	20,000	
	Cash Dividends Payable		20,000
j.	Cash Dividends Payable	20,000	
	Cash		20,000
k.	Cash	27,500	
	Investment in Pinkberry Co. Stock		27,500
l.	Investments—Dream Inc. Bonds	90,000	
	Interest Receivable	375	
	Cash		90,375
m.	Cash*	98,800	
	Treasury Stock**		85,800
	Paid-In Capital from Sale of Treasury Stock		13,000
	* 2,600 shares × $38 per share		
	** 2,600 shares × $33 per share		
n.	Cash*	4,500	
	Dividend Revenue		4,500
	* 7,500 shares × $0.60 per share		
o.	Cash*	45,000	
	Gain on Sale of Investment		4,980
	Investments—Solstice Corp.**		40,020
	* 1,000 shares × $45.00 per share		
	** 1,000 shares × ($300,150 ÷ 7,500 shares)		

Comp. Prob. 4 (Continued)

p.

Interest Expense	11,500	
Premium on Bonds Payable	1,000	
Cash		12,500

Computations:

Semiannual interest payment ($500,000 × 5% × 1/2)...................	$12,500
Less amortization premium [($20,000 ÷ 10 years) × 1/2].............	1,000
Interest expense..	$11,500

q.

Interest Receivable	1,125	
Interest Revenue		1,125
Interest accrued for three months.		

Computation: $90,000 × 5% × 3/12 = $1,125

r.

Investment in Pinkberry Co. Stock*	76,800	
Income from Pinkberry Co.		76,800
Recorded 32% share of Pinkberry Co.		
net income.		
* $240,000 × 32%, 32% = 40,000 shares ÷ 125,000 shares		

s.

Unrealized Gain (Loss) on Available-for-Sale		
Investments	6,500	
Valuation Allowance for Available-for-Sale		
Investments		6,500
6,500 shares × ($39.02 – $40.02*).		
* $40.02 = $300,150 ÷ 7,500 shares		

Comp. Prob. 4 (Continued)

2.   a.

EQUINOX PRODUCTS INC. Income Statement For the Year Ended December 31, 2014			
Sales			$5,254,000
Cost of merchandise sold			3,700,000
Gross profit			$1,554,000
Operating expenses:			
Selling expenses:			
Sales salaries expense	$385,000		
Sales commissions	185,000		
Advertising expense	150,000		
Depreciation expense—store buildings and equipment	100,000		
Delivery expense	30,000		
Store supplies expense	21,000		
Miscellaneous selling expense	14,000	$885,000	
Administrative expenses:			
Office salaries expense	$170,000		
Office rent expense	50,000		
Depreciation expense—office buildings and equipment	30,000		
Office supplies expense	10,000		
Miscellaneous administrative expense	7,500	267,500	
Total operating expenses			1,152,500
Income from operations			$ 401,500
Other expenses and income:			
Dividend revenue		$ 4,500	
Interest revenue		2,720	
Income from Pinkberry Co. investment		76,800	
Gain on sale of investment		4,980	
Interest expense		(21,000)	68,000
Income before income tax			$ 469,500
Income tax			140,500
Net income			$ 329,000
Earnings per common share:			
Net income*		$2.29	

* ($329,000 – $100,000 preferred dividends) ÷ 100,000 common shares, rounded

Comp. Prob. 4 (Continued)

b.

EQUINOX PRODUCTS INC. Retained Earnings Statement For the Year Ended December 31, 2014			
Retained earnings, January 1, 2014			$9,319,725
Net income for year		$329,000	
Less cash dividends:			
Common	$155,120		
Preferred	100,000	255,120	
Increase in retained earnings			73,880
Retained earnings, December 31, 2014			$9,393,605

c.

EQUINOX PRODUCTS INC. Balance Sheet For the Year Ended December 31, 2014			
Assets			
Current assets:			
Cash		$ 246,000	
Available-for-sale investments	$ 260,130		
Less valuation allowance for			
available-for-sale investment	6,500	253,630	
Accounts receivable	$ 545,000		
Less allowance for doubtful accounts	8,450	536,550	
Merchandise inventory, at lower of			
cost (FIFO) or market		778,000	
Interest receivable		1,125	
Prepaid expenses		27,400	
Total current assets			$ 1,842,705
Investments:			
Investment in Pinkberry Co. stock			1,009,300
Investment in Dream Inc. bonds			90,000
Property, plant, and equipment:			
Store buildings and equipment	$12,560,000		
Less accumulated depreciation	4,126,000	$8,434,000	
Office buildings and equipment	$ 4,320,000		
Less accumulated depreciation	1,580,000	2,740,000	
Total property, plant, and			
equipment			11,174,000
Intangible assets:			
Goodwill			500,000
Total assets			$14,616,005

Comp. Prob. 4 (Concluded)

EQUINOX PRODUCTS INC. Balance Sheet For the Year Ended December 31, 2014			
Liabilities			
Current liabilities:			
Accounts payable		$ 194,300	
Income tax payable		44,000	
Total current liabilities			$ 238,300
Long-term liabilities:			
Bonds payable, 5%, due 2022		$ 500,000	
Add premium on bonds payable		19,000	519,000
Total liabilities			$ 757,300
Stockholders' Equity			
Paid-in capital:			
Preferred 5% stock, $80 par			
(30,000 shares authorized;			
20,000 shares issued)	$1,600,000		
Excess of issue price over par	150,000	$ 1,750,000	
Common stock, $20 par (400,000			
shares authorized; 100,000 shares			
issued, 94,600 shares outstanding)	$2,000,000		
Excess of issue price over par	886,800	2,886,800	
From sale of treasury stock		13,000	
Total paid-in capital		$ 4,649,800	
Retained earnings		9,393,605	
Unrealized gain (loss) on available-			
for-sale investments		(6,500)	
Total		$14,036,905	
Deduct treasury common stock			
(5,400 shares at cost)		178,200	
Total stockholders' equity			13,858,705
Total liabilities and stockholders' equity			$14,616,005

CASES & PROJECTS

CP 15–1

1. Under generally accepted accounting principles, the land would be reported at $350,000 for Wyatt Corp. and $2,000,000 for TexoPete Inc. These valuations reflect their historical costs.

2. The historical cost valuation reduces the ability to compare the two companies. In this scenario, both companies have nearly identical land holdings. Wyatt Corp. purchased its land in 1996; thus, the land is valued according to a 1996 valuation. TexoPete Inc., purchased its land in 2014, reflecting a more current valuation. Thus, both companies have a similar asset; however, the balance sheet reports very different valuations (Wyatt's valuation is approximately 17.5% of TexoPete's). Therefore, comparability is reduced. If the land were valued at fair value, then both companies would report the land at nearly identical valuations, which is a better reflection of reality.

CP 15–2

1. There is an emerging trend toward more uniform accounting standards worldwide. This is caused by companies participating in multiple capital markets. For example, many companies not only have their stock trade on the New York Stock Exchange, but might also have their stock trade in London or Japan. In these cases, companies must provide financial reports that conform to the laws of the country in which their stock trades. Lack of accounting uniformity causes unnecessary reporting expenses for companies that wish to broaden the market for their stock worldwide, while making financial statements less comparable for users around the world. Thus, the United States and the European Union are working to align their financial accounting standards. When the International Accounting Standards Board (IASB, European Union) releases a standard such as *IAS No. 16*, it influences U.S. GAAP. In this case, the United States does not embrace *IAS No. 16*, so it is not U.S. GAAP. However, as the United States and Europe work to converge standards, we might see the substance of *IAS No. 16* reflected in a future FASB pronouncement.

2. Fair value reporting for property, plant, and equipment is a very aggressive fair value position. This is because property, plant, and equipment fair values are usually very subjective. Given this subjectivity, there is concern that the reported balance sheet amounts for property, plant, and equipment would be subject to manipulation and possible abuse. Moreover, the lack of objective fair values for these types of assets could reduce the comparability of financial statements across companies, depending on the subjective assumptions selected in the valuation.

CP 15–2 (Concluded)

3. The accounting treatment for increases in fair value for property, plant, and equipment under International Accounting Standards is similar to the treatment for unrealized gains and losses from available-for-sale investments. Increases in fair value bypass the income statement and are reported directly in stockholders' equity. Thus, increases in property, plant, and equipment fair values would not be reported in earnings. Decreases in fair value are reported on the income statement as an expense. Income statement treatment is similar to the treatment for unrealized gains and losses from trading securities. If the property, plant, and equipment fair value declines, the income statement impact of this decline is fully disclosed.

CP 15–3

Since many complex and exotic investment vehicles do not have ready market values, management must value these investments using mathematical models, subjective inputs, and risk assessments. These mathematically determined valuations are subject to wide variation, depending on the assumptions. Therein lies the ethical challenge. Since the valuation is subjective, it is possible for managers to over- or underestimate fair values to meet their personal objectives. Moreover, the ability for auditors to verify these values independently is difficult, since there is a lack of agreed-upon objectivity.

CP 15–4

1. Look-through earnings is a Warren Buffett term. It is the GAAP net income plus an adjustment for the equity earnings (the "forgotten-but-not-gone" earnings) in investments where less than 20% of the outstanding shares are owned. Thus, look-through earnings would be significantly greater than GAAP net income for a company that held a large portfolio of these types of investments (which Berkshire does). These are supplemental disclosures that Buffet provides his shareholders in addition to GAAP disclosures. Essentially, he is treating these investments as if they were being accounted for under the equity method.

2. Buffett makes the case that there is no reason for the equity method to be used only for 20%–50% investees, but that the rationale for the equity method applies equally well for investments of less than 20%. Thus, Berkshire Hathaway provides an additional non-GAAP disclosure to its investors, which essentially adds the after-tax equity earnings of its less than 20% investees to its net income. In so doing, Buffett argues that the earning power of all of his investments is properly disclosed in look-through earnings. He argues that the dividends that he receives from his less than 20%-owned investees do not reflect the earning power of his investment, even though that is what is required by GAAP.

CP 15–5

The following are portions of Notes 3 and 4 from the financial statements dated June 30, 2011, for Microsoft.

NOTE 4   INVESTMENTS

Investment Components, Including Associated Derivatives

(In millions)	Cost Basis	Unrealized Gains	Unrealized Losses	Recorded Basis	Cash and Cash Equivalents	Short-Term Investments	Equity and Other Investments
June 30, 2011							
Cash	$ 1,648	$ —	$ —	$ 1,648	$1,648	$ —	$ —
Mutual funds	1,752	—	—	1,752	1,752	—	—
Commercial paper	639	—	—	639	414	225	—
Certificates of deposit	598	—	—	598	372	226	—
U.S. Government and Agency securities	33,607	162	(7)	33,762	2,049	31,713	—
Foreign government bonds	658	11	(2)	667	—	667	—
Mortgage-backed securities	2,307	121	(4)	2,424	—	2,424	—
Corporate notes and bonds	10,575	260	(11)	10,824	3,375	7,449	—
Municipal securities	441	15	(2)	454	—	454	—
Common and preferred stock	7,925	2,483	(193)	10,215	—	—	10,215
Other investments	654	—	—	654	—	4	650
Total	**$60,804**	**$3,052**	**$(219)**	**$63,637**	**$9,610**	**$43,162**	**$10,865**

CP 15–5 (Concluded)

NOTE 3   OTHER INCOME (EXPENSE)

The components of other income (expense) were as follows:

(In millions) Year Ended June 30,	2011	2010	2009
Dividends and interest	$ 900	$ 843	$ 744
Net recognized gains (losses) on investments	(295)	(151)	(38)
Net gains (losses) on derivatives	439	348	(125)
Net gains (losses) on foreign currency	(77)	(140)	(558)
remeasurements	(26)	1	(509)
Other	(31)	14	(56)
Total	$ 910	$ 915	$(542)

Note to Instructors: **This solution is provided as a guide. Students may have different numbers, depending on the date of the financial statements.**

Answers in millions.

1. $60,804
2. $63,637 (termed, "recorded basis" by Microsoft)
3. $3,052
4. ($219)
5. a. $9,610 ÷ $63,637 = 15.1%
    b. $43,162 ÷ $63,637 = 67.8%
    c. $10,865 ÷ $63,637 = 17.1%
6. $900
7. ($295)

CHAPTER 16
STATEMENT OF CASH FLOWS

DISCUSSION QUESTIONS

1. It is costly to accumulate the data needed and to prepare the statement of cash flows.

2. It focuses on the differences between net income and cash flows from operating activities, and the data needed are generally more readily available and less costly to obtain than is the case for the direct method.

3. In a separate schedule of noncash investing and financing activities accompanying the statement of cash flows.

4. The $30,000 increase must be added to income from operations because the amount of cash paid to merchandise creditors was $30,000 less than the amount of purchases included in the cost of goods sold.

5. The $25,000 decrease in salaries payable should be deducted from income to determine the amount of cash flows from operating activities. The effect of the decrease in the amount of salaries owed was to pay $25,000 more cash during the year than had been recorded as an expense.

6. a. $100,000 gain

   b. Cash inflow of $600,000

   c. The gain of $100,000 would be deducted from net income in determining net cash flow from operating activities; $600,000 would be reported as cash flows from investing activities.

7. Cash flows from financing activities—issuance of bonds, $1,960,000

8. a. Cash flows from investing activities—Cash received from the disposal of fixed assets, $15,000

   The $15,000 gain on asset disposal should be deducted from net income in determining net cash flow from operating activities under the indirect method.

   b. No effect

9. The same. The amount reported as the net cash flow from operating activities is not affected by the use of the direct or indirect method.

10. Cash received from customers, cash payments for merchandise, cash payments for operating expenses, cash payments for interest, cash payments for income taxes.

PRACTICE EXERCISES

PE 16–1A

a.	Operating	d.	Financing
b.	Operating	e.	Financing
c.	Investing	f.	Operating

PE 16–1B

a.	Investing	d.	Operating
b.	Investing	e.	Operating
c.	Operating	f.	Financing

PE 16–2A

Net income..	$107,500
Adjustments to reconcile net income to net cash flow from operating activities:	
Depreciation..	7,500
Amortization of patents...	2,750
Loss from sale of land...	4,000
Net cash flow from operating activities...	$121,750

PE 16–2B

Net income..	$175,000
Adjustments to reconcile net income to net cash flow from operating activities:	
Depreciation..	8,750
Amortization of patents...	3,250
Gain from sale of investments...	(18,750)
Net cash flow from operating activities...	$168,250

PE 16–3A

Net income...	$253,000
Adjustments to reconcile net income to net cash flow from operating activities:	
Changes in current operating assets and liabilities:	
Decrease in accounts receivable...	6,600
Increase in inventory...	(3,080)
Increase in accounts payable..	2,420
Net cash flow from operating activities..	$258,940

Note: The change in dividends payable impacts the cash paid for dividends, which is disclosed under financing activities.

PE 16–3B

Net income...	$160,000
Adjustments to reconcile net income to net cash flow from operating activities:	
Changes in current operating assets and liabilities:	
Increase in accounts receivable...	(3,600)
Increase in inventory...	(5,100)
Increase in accounts payable..	6,900
Net cash flow from operating activities..	$158,200

Note: The change in dividends payable impacts the cash paid for dividends, which is disclosed under financing activities.

PE 16–4A

Cash flows from operating activities:		
Net income...	$270,000	
Adjustments to reconcile net income to net cash flow from operating activities:		
Depreciation...	30,000	
Gain on disposal of equipment......................	(24,600)	
Changes in current operating assets and liabilities:		
Decrease in accounts receivable...................	16,800	
Decrease in accounts payable.......................	(4,320)	
Net cash flow from operating activities.............		$287,880

PE 16–4B

Cash flows from operating activities:

Net income...	$280,000	
Adjustments to reconcile net income to net cash flow		
from operating activities:		
Depreciation...	48,000	
Loss on disposal of equipment...........................	19,520	
Changes in current operating assets and liabilities:		
Increase in accounts receivable................................	(17,280)	
Increase in accounts payable.....................................	8,960	
Net cash flow from operating activities......................................		$339,200

PE 16–5A

The loss on the sale of land is added to net income in the Operating Activities section.

Loss on sale of land...	$ 60,000

The purchase and sale of land is reported as part of cash flows from investing activities as shown below.

Cash received from sale of land...	120,000
Cash paid for purchase of land..	(360,000)

PE 16–5B

The gain on the sale of land is subtracted from net income in the Operating Activities section.

Gain on sale of land...	$ (40,000)

The purchase and sale of land is reported as part of cash flows from investing activities as shown below.

Cash received from sale of land...	240,000
Cash paid for purchase of land..	(400,000)

PE 16–6A

Sales..	$480,000
Deduct increase in accounts receivable................................	54,000
Cash received from customers..	$426,000

PE 16–6B

Sales..	$112,000
Add decrease in accounts receivable.....................................	10,500
Cash received from customers..	$122,500

PE 16–7A

Cost of merchandise sold...	$770,000
Deduct decrease in inventories...	(66,000)
Add decrease in accounts payable..	44,000
Cash paid for merchandise..	$748,000

PE 16–7B

Cost of merchandise sold...	$240,000
Add increase in inventories..	19,200
Deduct increase in accounts payable..	(12,000)
Cash paid for merchandise..	$247,200

PE 16–8A

a. Net cash flow from operating activities......................	$ 294,000	$ 280,000
Less: Investments in fixed assets		
to replace existing capacity...........................	(156,800)*	(176,400)**
Free cash flow...	$ 137,200	$ 103,600

      * 70% × $224,000
    ** 70% × $252,000

b. The change from $103,600 to $137,200 indicates a positive trend.

PE 16–8B

a. Net cash flow from operating activities......................	$ 476,000	$ 455,000
Less: Investments in fixed assets		
to replace existing capacity...........................	(341,600)*	(302,400)**
Free cash flow...	$ 134,400	$ 152,600

      * 80% × $427,000
    ** 80% × $378,000

b. The change from $152,600 to $134,400 indicates a negative trend.

EXERCISES

Ex. 16–1

There were net additions to the net loss reported on the income statement to convert the net loss from the accrual basis to the cash basis. For example, depreciation is an expense in determining net income, but it does not result in a cash outflow. Thus, depreciation is added back to the net loss in order to determine net cash flow from operations. A second large item that is added to the net loss is the increase in air traffic liability of $225 million. This represents an increase in unused, but paid, tickets (unearned revenue) between the two balance sheet dates. This is a significant item that is largely unique to the airline industry.

The cash flows from operating activities detail is provided as follows for class discussion:

CONTINENTAL AIRLINES, INC. Cash Flows from Operating Activities (Selected from Statement of Cash Flows) (in millions)	
CASH FLOWS FROM OPERATING ACTIVITIES	
Net income (loss)	$ (471)
Adjustments to reconcile net income (loss) to net cash flow	
provided by operating activities:	
Depreciation and amortization	1,093
Special charges	279
Gain on disposition of investments	—
Undistributed equity in the income of other companies	—
Other, net	(45)
Changes in certain assets and liabilities:	
Decrease (increase) in accounts receivable	29
Decrease (increase) in spare parts and supplies	(81)
Decrease (increase) in prepaid expenses	87
Increase (decrease) in accounts payable	(19)
Increase (decrease) in air traffic liability	225
Increase (decrease) in other liabilities	144
Net cash flows from (used for) operating activities	$1,241

Ex. 16–2

a. Cash receipt, $94,000
b. Cash receipt, $255,000
c. Cash payment, $475,000
d. Cash payment, $120,000

e. Cash receipt, $200,000
f. Cash payment, $52,500
g. Cash payment, $287,000
h. Cash payment, $60,000

Ex. 16–3

a. financing
b. investing
c. investing
d. financing
e. investing
f. financing

g. financing
h. financing
i. operating
j. financing
k. investing

Ex. 16–4

a. added
b. added
c. deducted
d. added
e. added
f. deducted

g. deducted
h. deducted
i. added
j. added
k. deducted

© 2014 Cengage Learning. All Rights Reserved. May not be scanned, copied or duplicated, or posted to a publicly accessible website, in whole or in part.

Ex. 16–5

a.

Net income	$600,000
Adjustments to reconcile net income to net cash flow from operating activities:	
Depreciation	24,000
Changes in current operating assets and liabilities:	
Increase in accounts receivable	(3,600)
Decrease in merchandise inventory	6,000
Increase in prepaid expenses	(1,800)
Increase in accounts payable	6,000
Decrease in wages payable	(4,200)
Net cash flow from operating activities	$626,400

b.   Cash flows from operating activities shows the cash inflow or outflow from a company's day-to-day operations. Net income reports the excess of revenues over expenses for a company using the accrual basis of accounting. Revenues are recorded when they are earned, not necessarily when cash is received. Expenses are recorded when they are incurred and matched against revenue, not necessarily when cash is paid. As a result, the cash flows from operating activities differs from net income because it does not use the accrual basis of accounting.

Ex. 16–6

a.   Cash flows from operating activities:

Net income	$240,000
Adjustments to reconcile net income to net cash flow from operating activities:	
Depreciation	72,000
Changes in current operating assets and liabilities:	
Decrease in accounts receivable	4,800
Increase in inventories	(18,000)
Decrease in prepaid expenses	1,200
Decrease in accounts payable	(6,000)
Increase in salaries payable	1,800
Net cash flow from operating activities	$295,800

b.   Yes. The amount of cash flows from operating activities reported on the statement of cash flows is not affected by the method of reporting such flows.

Ex. 16–7

a.   Cash flows from operating activities:

Net income..	$635,000	
Adjustments to reconcile net income to net cash		
flow from operating activities:		
Depreciation..	72,000	
Gain on disposal of equipment.....................................	(42,000)	
Changes in current operating assets and liabilities:		
Increase in accounts receivable...............................	(11,200)	
Decrease in inventory...	6,400	
Decrease in prepaid insurance.................................	2,400	
Decrease in accounts payable..................................	(7,600)	
Increase in income taxes payable.............................	2,400	
Net cash flow from operating activities................................		$657,400

Note: The change in dividends payable would be used to adjust the dividends declared in obtaining the cash paid for dividends in the Financing Activities section of the statement of cash flows.

b.   Cash flows from operating activities reports the cash inflow or outflow from a company's day-to-day operations. Net income reports the excess of revenues over expenses for a company using the accrual basis of accounting. Revenues are recorded when they are earned, not necessarily when cash is received. Expenses are recorded when they are incurred and matched against revenue, not necessarily when cash is paid. As a result, the cash flows from operating activities differs from net income because it does not use the accrual basis of accounting.

Ex. 16–8

Dividends declared...	$364,000
Add decrease in dividends payable..	13,300
Dividends paid to stockholders during the year........................	$377,300

Ex. 16–9

Cash flows from investing activities:
Cash received from sale of equipment.. $72,000

The loss on the sale, $12,000 ($72,000 proceeds from sale less $84,000 book value), would be added to net income in determining the cash flows from operating activities if the indirect method of reporting cash flows from operations is used.

Ex. 16–10

Cash flows from investing activities:
Cash received from sale of equipment.. $37,200

The loss on the sale, $6,800 ($37,200 proceeds from sale less $44,000 book value), would be added to net income in determining the cash flows from operating activities if the indirect method of reporting cash flows from operations is used.

Ex. 16–11

Cash flows from investing activities:
Cash received from sale of land... $54,600
Less: Cash paid for purchase of land... 60,200

The gain on the sale of land, $18,120, would be deducted from net income in determining the cash flows from operating activities if the indirect method of reporting cash flows from operations is used.

Ex. 16–12

Cash flows from financing activities:
Cash received from sale of common stock... $4,875,000
Less: Cash paid for dividends... 723,750

Note: The stock dividend is not disclosed on the statement of cash flows.

Ex. 16–13

Cash flows from investing activities:

Cash paid for purchase of land.. $246,000

A separate schedule of noncash investing and financing activities would report the purchase of $324,000 land with a long-term mortgage note, as follows:

Purchase of land by issuing long-term mortgage note................................. $324,000

Ex. 16–14

Cash flows from financing activities:

Cash received from issuing bonds payable... $224,000

Less: Cash paid to redeem bonds payable... 73,600

Note: The discount amortization of $1,400 would be shown as an adjusting item (increase) in the Cash Flows from Operating Activities section under the indirect method.

Ex. 16–15

a.	Net cash flow from operating activities..............................		$357,500
	Add: Increase in accounts receivable.............................	$14,300	
	Increase in prepaid expenses....................................	2,970	
	Decrease in income taxes payable..........................	7,700	
	Gain on sale of investments	13,200	38,170
			$395,670
	Deduct: Depreciation..	$29,480	
	Decrease in inventories......................................	19,140	
	Increase in accounts payable...............................	5,280	53,900
	Net income, per income statement......................................		$341,770

Note to Instructors: The net income must be determined by working backward through the Cash Flows from Operating Activities section of the statement of cash flows. Hence, those items that were added (deducted) to determine net cash flow from operating activities must be deducted (added) to determine net income.

Ex. 16–15 (Concluded)

b. Curwen's net income differed from cash flows from operations because of:

- $29,480 of depreciation expense which has no effect on cash flows from operating activities,

- a $13,200 gain on the sale of investments. The proceeds from this sale, which include the gain, are reported in the Investing Activities section of the statement of cash flows.

- Changes in current operating assets and liabilities that are added or deducted, depending on their effect on cash flows:

    Increase in accounts receivable, $14,300
    Increase in prepaid expenses, $2,970
    Decrease in income taxes payable, $7,700
    Decrease in inventories, $19,140
    Increase in accounts payable, $5,280

Ex. 16–16

a.

JONES SODA CO. Cash Flows from Operating Activities (in thousands)		
Cash flows from operating activities:		
Net loss	$(6,106)	
Adjustments to reconcile net loss to net		
cash flow from operating activities:		
Depreciation	799	
Loss on inventory write-down and fixed assets	379	
Stock-based compensation expense (noncash)	830	
Changes in current operating assets and		
liabilities:		
Increase in accounts receivable	(278)	
Decrease in inventory	1,252	
Decrease in prepaid expenses	131	
Decrease in accounts payable	(472)	
Net cash flow from operating activities		$(3,465)

b. Jones Soda is struggling financially. The company has negative earnings and negative net cash flow from operating activities. The company had grown quickly in prior years, but the company has struggled in recent years. The increase in accounts receivable is a positive sign, indicating an increase in sales. However, the dramatic decrease in inventory and accounts payable suggests that the company is reducing the units sold and reducing its size (i.e., going into a period of negative growth). This is not a healthy trend.

Ex. 16–17

a.

WEDGE INDUSTRIES INC. Statement of Cash Flows For the Year Ended December 31, 2014		
Cash flows from operating activities:		
Net income	$260	
Adjustments to reconcile net income to net		
cash flow from operating activities:		
Depreciation	24	
Gain on sale of land	(60)	
Changes in current operating assets and		
liabilities:		
Increase in accounts receivable	(64)	
Increase in inventories	(52)	
Increase in accounts payable	12	
Net cash flow from operating activities		$120
Cash flows from investing activities:		
Cash received from sale of land	$100	
Less cash paid for purchase of equipment	40	
Net cash flow from investing activities		60
Cash flows from financing activities:		
Cash received from sale of common stock	$140	
Less cash paid for dividends*	56	
Net cash flow from financing activities		84
Increase in cash		$264
Cash at the beginning of the year		128
Cash at the end of the year		$392

* $80 – $24 = $56

b.   Wedge Industries Inc.'s net income was more than the cash flows from operations because of:

  • $24 of depreciation expense which has no effect on cash.

  • A $60 gain on the sale of land. The proceeds from this sale of $100, which include the gain, are reported in the Investing Activities section of the statement of cash flows.

  • Changes in current operating assets and liabilities that are added or deducted, depending on their effect on cash flows:

    Increase in accounts receivable, $64 deducted
    Increase in inventories, $52 deducted
    Increase in accounts payable, $12 added

16-13

Ex. 16–18

1. The increase in accounts receivable should be deducted from net income in the Cash Flows from Operating Activities section.

2. The gain on the sale of investments should be deducted from net income in the Cash Flows from Operating Activities section.

3. The increase in accounts payable should be added to net income in the Cash Flows from Operating Activities section.

4. The correct amount of cash at the beginning of the year, $240,000, should be added to the increase in cash.

5. The final amount should be the amount of cash at the end of the year, $350,160.

6. The final amount of net cash flow from operating activities is $381,360.

7. The "cash paid for dividends" should be preceded by "Less:".

Ex. 16–18 (Concluded)

A correct statement of cash flows would be as follows:

SHASTA INC. Statement of Cash Flows For the Year Ended December 31, 2014			
Cash flows from operating activities:			
Net income		$360,000	
Adjustments to reconcile net income to			
net cash flow from operating activities:			
Depreciation		100,800	
Gain on sale of investments		(17,280)	
Changes in current operating assets			
and liabilities:			
Increase in accounts receivable		(27,360)	
Increase in inventories		(36,000)	
Increase in accounts payable		3,600	
Decrease in accrued expenses			
payable		(2,400)	
Net cash flow from operating activities			$ 381,360
Cash flows from investing activities:			
Cash received from sale of investments		$240,000	
Less: Cash paid for purchase of land	$259,200		
Cash paid for purchase of equip.	432,000	691,200	
Net cash flow used for investing activities			(451,200)
Cash flows from financing activities:			
Cash received from sale of common stock		$312,000	
Less: Cash paid for dividends		132,000	
Net cash flow from financing activities			180,000
Increase in cash			$ 110,160
Cash at the beginning of the year			240,000
Cash at the end of the year			$ 350,160

Ex. 16–19

a. Sales... $753,500
   Plus decrease in accounts receivable balance....................................... 48,400
   Cash received from customers.. $801,900

b. Income tax expense.. $ 50,600
   Plus decrease in income tax payable.. 5,500
   Cash payments for income taxes.. $ 56,100

c. Because the customer paid more than the amount of sales for the period, cash received from customers exceeded sales made on account by $48,400 during the current year.

Ex. 16–20

Cost of merchandise sold*.. $15,480
Add increase in merchandise inventories.. 630
Deduct increase in accounts payable.. (234)
Cash paid for merchandise.. $15,876

*In millions

Ex. 16–21

a. Cost of merchandise sold.. $1,031,550
   Add decrease in accounts payable... 9,660
                                                                                    $1,041,210
   Deduct decrease in inventories.. (15,410)
   Cash payments for merchandise.. $1,025,800

b. Operating expenses other than depreciation... $179,400
   Add decrease in accrued expenses payable.. 1,380
                                                                                    $180,780
   Deduct decrease in prepaid expenses... (1,610)
   Cash payments for operating expenses... $179,170

Ex. 16–22

a.   **Cash flows from operating activities:**

Cash received from customers......................		$522,760[1]	
Deduct: Cash payments for merchandise....	$302,400[2]		
Cash payments for operating expenses....................................	99,960[3]		
Cash payments for income taxes....	24,360[4]	426,720	
Net cash flow from operating activities.........			$ 96,040

Computations:

1.
Sales...		$511,000
Add decrease in accounts receivable........................		11,760
Cash received from customers....................................		$522,760

2.
Cost of merchandise sold...		$290,500
Add: Increase in inventories......................................	$3,920	
Decrease in accounts payable..........................	7,980	11,900
Cash payments for merchandise.................................		$302,400

3.
Operating expenses other than depreciation................		$105,000
Deduct: Decrease in prepaid expenses......................	$3,780	
Increase in accrued expenses payable..	1,260	5,040
Cash payments for operating expenses......................		$ 99,960

4.
Income tax expense...		$ 21,700
Add decrease in income tax payable..........................		2,660
Cash payments for income taxes...............................		$ 24,360

b.   The *direct method* directly reports cash receipts and payments. The cash received less the cash payments is the net cash flow from operating activities. Individual cash receipts and payments are reported in the Cash Flows from Operating Activities section.

The *indirect method* adjusts accrual-basis net income for revenues and expenses that do not involve the receipt or payment of cash to arrive at cash flows from operating activities.

Ex. 16–23

Cash flows from operating activities:

Cash received from customers..........................		$440,440 [1]	
Deduct: Cash payments for merchandise...........	$161,260 [2]		
Cash payments for operating			
expenses.......................................	115,720 [3]		
Cash payments for income taxes...........	39,600	316,580	
Net cash flow from operating activities..............			$123,860

Computations:

1.	Sales...	$445,500
	Deduct increase in accounts receivable..	5,060
	Cash received from customers..	$440,440
2.	Cost of merchandise sold..	$154,000
	Add increase in inventories...	12,100
		$166,100
	Deduct increase in accounts payable..	4,840
	Cash payments for merchandise...	$161,260
3.	Operating expenses other than depreciation..	$115,280
	Add decrease in accrued expenses payable...	1,760
		$117,040
	Deduct decrease in prepaid expenses..	1,320
	Cash payments for operating expenses..	$115,720

Ex. 16–24

a.	Cash flows from investment in PPE...	$210,000
	Replacement percentage...	75%
	Cash paid for maintaining property, plant, and equipment........................	$157,500
	Cash flows from operating activities..	$539,000
	Less cash paid for maintaining property, plant, and equipment.................	157,500
	Free cash flow..	$381,500

b. Free cash flow is often used to measure the financial strength of a business. The more free cash flow that a business has, the easier it will be for the company to pay the interest on the loan and repay the loan principal. Sweeter's free cash flow is $381,500, which is very strong.

Ex. 16–25

a.

	Recent Fiscal Year End (all numbers in thousands)
Cash flows from investment in PPE...................................	$432
Replacement percentage...	90%
Cash paid for maintaining PPE..	$389
Cash flows from operating activities...............................	$1,812
Less cash paid for maintaining PPE................................	(389)
	$1,423

b.   Free cash flow is often used to measure the financial strength of a business. The more free cash flow that a business has, the easier it will be for the company to pay the interest on the loan and repay the loan principal.

c.   Yes. Nike's free cash flow is extremely strong, and is 3.7 times greater than the capital expenditures necessary to maintain capacity.

Ex. 16–26

Cash flows from investment in PPE..	$440,000
Replacement percentage...	85%
Cash paid for maintaining PPE...	$374,000
Net cash flow from operating activities...	$720,000
Less investments in fixed assets to maintain current production...	374,000
Free cash flow..	$346,000

PROBLEMS

Prob. 16–1A

CHARLES INC.			
Statement of Cash Flows			
For the Year Ended December 31, 2014			
Cash flows from operating activities:			
Net income		$ 190,280	
Adjustments to reconcile net income to			
net cash flow from operating activities:			
Depreciation		13,800	
Gain on sale of investments		(30,000)	
Changes in current operating assets			
and liabilities:			
Increase in accounts receivable		(14,160)	
Increase in inventories		(18,480)	
Increase in accounts payable		14,640	
Decrease in accrued expenses			
payable		(7,800)	
Net cash flow from operating activities			$ 148,280
Cash flows from investing activities:			
Cash received from sale of investments		$ 210,000	
Less: Cash paid for purchase of land	$(246,000)		
Cash paid for purchase of			
equipment	(114,000)	(360,000)	
Net cash flow used for investing activities			(150,000)
Cash flows from financing activities:			
Cash received from sale of common stock		$ 100,000	
Less cash paid for dividends*		(68,400)	
Net cash flow from financing activities			31,600
Increase in cash			$ 29,880
Cash at the beginning of the year			439,440
Cash at the end of the year			$ 469,320

*$72,000 + $14,400 – $18,000 = $68,400

Prob. 16–1A (Concluded)

(Optional)

Account Title	Balance Dec. 31, 2013	Transactions Debit	Transactions Credit	Balance Dec. 31, 2014
CHARLES INC. Spreadsheet (Work Sheet) for Statement of Cash Flows For the Year Ended December 31, 2014				
Cash	439,440	(m) 29,880		469,320
Accounts receivable (net)	156,720	(l) 14,160		170,880
Inventories	462,840	(k) 18,480		481,320
Investments	180,000		(j) 180,000	0
Land	0	(i) 246,000		246,000
Equipment	414,840	(h) 114,000		528,840
Accum. depr.—equipment	(111,000)		(g) 13,800	(124,800)
Accounts payable	(303,720)		(f) 14,640	(318,360)
Accrued expenses payable	(39,480)	(e) 7,800		(31,680)
Dividends payable	(14,400)		(d) 3,600	(18,000)
Common stock, $2 par	(75,000)		(c) 20,000	(95,000)
Paid-in capital in excess of par—common stock	(210,000)		(c) 80,000	(290,000)
Retained earnings	(900,240)	(b) 72,000	(a) 190,280	(1,018,520)
Totals	0	502,320	502,320	0
Operating activities:				
Net income		(a) 190,280		
Depreciation		(g) 13,800		
Gain on sale of investments			(j) 30,000	
Increase in accounts receivable			(l) 14,160	
Increase in inventories			(k) 18,480	
Increase in accounts payable		(f) 14,640		
Decrease in accrued expenses payable			(e) 7,800	
Investing activities:				
Purchase of equipment			(h) 114,000	
Purchase of land			(i) 246,000	
Sale of investments		(j) 210,000		
Financing activities:				
Declaration of cash dividends			(b) 72,000	
Sale of common stock		(c) 100,000		
Increase in dividends payable		(d) 3,600		
Net increase in cash			(m) 29,880	
Totals		532,320	532,320	

The letters in the debit and credit columns are included for reference purposes. They do not correspond to the letters in the additional data section of this problem.

Prob. 16–2A

LANKAU ENTERPRISES INC. Statement of Cash Flows For the Year Ended December 31, 2014			
Cash flows from operating activities:			
Net income		$ 198,000	
Adjustments to reconcile net income to			
net cash flow from operating activities:			
Depreciation		125,100	
Changes in current operating assets			
and liabilities:			
Decrease in accounts receivable		26,100	
Increase in inventory		(33,600)	
Increase in prepaid expenses		(5,700)	
Increase in accounts payable		18,900	
Net cash flow from operating activities			$ 328,800
Cash flows from investing activities:			
Cash paid for equipment		$(244,200)	
Net cash flow used for investing			
activities			(244,200)
Cash flows from financing activities:			
Cash received from sale of common stock		$ 600,000	
Less: Cash paid for dividends	$(230,400)		
Cash paid to retire mortgage			
note payable	(504,000)	(734,400)	
Net cash flow used for financing			
activities			(134,400)
Decrease in cash			$ (49,800)
Cash at the beginning of the year			269,700
Cash at the end of the year			$ 219,900

Note to Instructors: The disposal of fully depreciated equipment is not included in the cash flow statement because there is no associated cash flow. This transaction strictly involves the removal of $67,200 from the equipment and accumulated depreciation—equipment accounts.

Prob. 16–2A (Concluded)

(Optional)

Account Title	Balance Dec. 31, 2013	Debit		Credit		Balance Dec. 31, 2014
			Transactions			
Cash	269,700			(l)	49,800	219,900
Accounts receivable (net)	363,000			(k)	26,100	336,900
Merchandise inventory	448,800	(j)	33,600			482,400
Prepaid expenses	14,400	(i)	5,700			20,100
Equipment	805,500	(h)	244,200	(g)	67,200	982,500
Accum. depr.—equipment	(198,300)	(g)	67,200	(f)	125,100	(256,200)
Accounts payable	(356,400)			(e)	18,900	(375,300)
Mortgage note payable	(504,000)	(d)	504,000			0
Common stock, $25 par	(36,000)			(c)	375,000	(411,000)
Paid-in capital in excess						
of par—common stock	(480,000)			(c)	225,000	(705,000)
Retained earnings	(326,700)	(b)	230,400	(a)	198,000	(294,300)
Totals	0		1,085,100		1,085,100	0
Operating activities:						
Net income		(a)	198,000			
Depreciation		(f)	125,100			
Decrease in accts. receivable		(k)	26,100			
Increase in merchandise						
inventory				(j)	33,600	
Increase in prepaid expenses				(i)	5,700	
Increase in accounts payable		(e)	18,900			
Investing activities:						
Purchase of equipment				(h)	244,200	
Financing activities:						
Payment of cash dividends				(b)	230,400	
Sale of common stock		(c)	600,000			
Payment of mortgage note						
payable				(d)	504,000	
Net decrease in cash		(l)	49,800			
Totals			1,017,900		1,017,900	

LANKAU ENTERPRISES INC.
Spreadsheet (Work Sheet) for Statement of Cash Flows
For the Year Ended December 31, 2014

The letters in the debit and credit columns are included for reference purposes. They do not correspond to the letters in the additional data section of this problem.

16-23

Prob. 16–3A

WHITMAN CO. Statement of Cash Flows For the Year Ended December 31, 2014			
Cash flows from operating activities:			
Net loss		$ (35,320)	
Adjustments to reconcile net loss to			
net cash flow from operating activities:			
Depreciation*		55,620	
Loss on sale of land**		12,600	
Changes in current operating assets			
and liabilities:			
Increase in accounts receivable		(66,960)	
Increase in inventories		(105,480)	
Decrease in prepaid expenses		5,760	
Decrease in accounts payable		(35,820)	
Net cash flow used for operating activities			$(169,600)
Cash flows from investing activities:			
Cash received from land sold		$151,200	
Less: Cash paid for acquisition			
of building	$561,600		
Cash paid for purchase			
of equipment	104,400	666,000	
Net cash flow used for investing activities			(514,800)
activities			
Cash flows from financing activities:			
Cash received from issuance of			
bonds payable	$270,000		
Cash received from issuance of			
common stock	400,000	$670,000	
Less cash paid for dividends		32,400	
Net cash flow from financing activities			637,600
Decrease in cash			$ (46,800)
Cash at the beginning of the year			964,800
Cash at the end of the year			$ 918,000

* $26,280 + $29,340

** $151,200 – $163,800

Prob. 16–3A (Concluded)

(Optional)

		WHITMAN CO.					
		Spreadsheet (Work Sheet) for Statement of Cash Flows					
		For the Year Ended December 31, 2014					
Account Title	Balance Dec. 31, 2013		Debit		Credit	Balance Dec. 31, 2014	
Cash	964,800			(o)	46,800	918,000	
Accounts receivable	761,940	(g)	66,960			828,900	
Inventories	1,162,980	(h)	105,480			1,268,460	
Prepaid expenses	35,100			(f)	5,760	29,340	
Land	479,700			(l)	163,800	315,900	
Buildings	900,900	(k)	561,600			1,462,500	
Accum. depr.—buildings	(382,320)			(e)	26,280	(408,600)	
Equipment	454,680	(i)	104,400	(j)	46,800	512,280	
Accum. depr.—equipment	(158,760)	(j)	46,800	(d)	29,340	(141,300)	
Accounts payable	(958,320)	(c)	35,820			(922,500)	
Bonds payable	0			(m)	270,000	(270,000)	
Common stock, $25 par	(117,000)			(n)	200,000	(317,000)	
Paid-in capital in excess of							
par—common stock	(558,000)			(n)	200,000	(758,000)	
Retained earnings	(2,585,700)	(a)	35,320			(2,517,980)	
		(b)	32,400				
Totals	0		988,780		988,780	0	
Operating activities:							
Net loss				(a)	35,320		
Depreciation—equipment		(d)	29,340				
Depreciation—buildings		(e)	26,280				
Loss on sale of land		(l)	12,600				
Increase in accts. receivable				(g)	66,960		
Increase in inventories				(h)	105,480		
Decrease in prepaid expenses		(f)	5,760				
Decrease in accounts payable				(c)	35,820		
Investing activities:							
Purchase of equipment				(i)	104,400		
Acquisition of building				(k)	561,600		
Sale of land		(l)	151,200				
Financing activities:							
Payment of cash dividends				(b)	32,400		
Issuance of bonds payable		(m)	270,000				
Issuance of common stock		(n)	400,000				
Net decrease in cash		(o)	46,800				
Totals			941,980		941,980		

Prob. 16–4A

CANACE PRODUCTS INC. Statement of Cash Flows For the Year Ended December 31, 2014			
Cash flows from operating activities:			
Cash received from customers[1]		$5,960,600	
Deduct: Cash payments for merchandise[2]	$2,456,800		
Cash payments for operating expenses[3]	3,107,400		
Cash payments for income taxes	102,800	5,667,000	
Net cash flow from operating activities			$ 293,600
Cash flows from investing activities:			
Cash received from sale of investments		$ 176,000	
Less: Cash paid for purchase of land	$ (520,000)		
Cash paid for purchase of equipment	(200,000)	(720,000)	
Net cash flow used for investing activities			(544,000)
Cash flows from financing activities:			
Cash received from sale of common stock		$ 240,000	
Less cash paid for dividends*		25,600	
Net cash flow from financing activities			214,400
Decrease in cash			$ (36,000)
Cash at the beginning of the year			679,400
Cash at the end of the year			$ 643,400

Reconciliation of Net Income with Cash Flows from Operating Activities:

Net income..	$217,200
Adjustments to reconcile net income to net cash flow from operating activities:	
Depreciation..	44,000
Loss on sale of investments...	64,000
Changes in current operating assets and liabilities:	
Increase in accounts receivable..	(19,400)
Increase in inventories...	(28,200)
Increase in accounts payable..	23,400
Decrease in accrued expenses payable............................	(7,400)
Net cash flow from operating activities..................................	$293,600

* Dividends paid: $28,000 + $6,400 – $8,800 = $25,600

Prob. 16–4A (Concluded)

Computations:

1. Sales.. $5,980,000
    Deduct increase in accounts receivable............................. 19,400
    Cash received from customers....................................... $5,960,600

2. Cost of merchandise sold.. $2,452,000
    Add increase in inventories.. 28,200
                                                                        $2,480,200
    Deduct increase in accounts payable................................ 23,400
    Cash payments for merchandise...................................... $2,456,800

3. Operating expenses other than depreciation......................... $3,100,000
    Add decrease in accrued expenses payable........................... 7,400
    Cash payments for operating expenses............................... $3,107,400

Prob. 16–5A

CHARLES INC. Statement of Cash Flows For the Year Ended December 31, 2014			
Cash flows from operating activities:			
Cash received from customers[1]		$5,247,541	
Deduct: Cash payments for merchandise[2]	$3,241,810		
Cash payments for operating expenses[3]	1,730,598		
Cash payments for income taxes	126,853	5,099,261	
Net cash flow from operating activities			$ 148,280
Cash flows from investing activities:			
Cash received from sale of investments		$ 210,000	
Less: Cash paid for purchase of land	$ 246,000		
Cash paid for purchase of equipment	114,000	360,000	
Net cash flow used for investing activities			(150,000)
Cash flows from financing activities:			
Cash received from sale of common stock		$ 100,000	
Less: Cash paid for dividends[4]		68,400	
Net cash flow from financing activities			31,600
Increase in cash			$ 29,880
Cash at the beginning of the year			439,440
Cash at the end of the year			$ 469,320

Reconciliation of Net Income with Cash Flows from Operating Activities:

Net income.. $190,280

Adjustments to reconcile net income to net cash flow
from operating activities:

  Depreciation.. 13,800

  Gain on sale of investments.. (30,000)

  Changes in current operating assets and liabilities:

    Increase in accounts receivable.. (14,160)

    Increase in inventories... (18,480)

    Increase in accounts payable.. 14,640

    Decrease in accrued expenses payable.................................. (7,800)

Net cash flow from operating activities.. $148,280

Prob. 16–5A (Concluded)

Computations:

1. Sales... $5,261,701
    Deduct increase in accounts receivable............................... 14,160
    Cash received from customers.. $5,247,541

2. Cost of merchandise sold.. $3,237,970
    Add increase in inventories.. 18,480
    _____
    $3,256,450
    Deduct increase in accounts payable................................... 14,640
    Cash payments for merchandise.. $3,241,810

3. Operating expenses other than depreciation......................... $1,722,798
    Add decrease in accrued expenses payable.......................... 7,800
    Cash payments for operating expenses............................... $1,730,598

4. Cash dividends declared.. $ 72,000
    Deduct increase in dividends payable.................................. 3,600
    Cash payments for dividends... $ 68,400

Prob. 16–1B

MERRICK EQUIPMENT CO.			
Statement of Cash Flows			
For the Year Ended December 31, 2014			
Cash flows from operating activities:			
Net income		$141,680	
Adjustments to reconcile net income to			
net cash flow from operating activities:			
Depreciation		14,790	
Loss on sale of investments		10,200	
Changes in current operating assets			
and liabilities:			
Increase in accounts receivable		(19,040)	
Increase in inventories		(8,670)	
Increase in accounts payable		11,560	
Increase in accrued expenses			
payable		3,740	
Net cash flow from operating activities			$ 154,260
Cash flows from investing activities:			
Cash received from sale of investments		$ 91,800	
Less: Cash paid for purchase of land	$295,800		
Cash paid for purchase of			
equipment	80,580	376,380	
Net cash flow used for investing activities			(284,580)
Cash flows from financing activities:			
Cash received from sale of common stock		$250,000	
Less: Cash paid for dividends*		(96,900)	
Net cash flow from financing activities			153,100
Increase in cash			$ 22,780
Cash at the beginning of the year			47,940
Cash at the end of the year			$ 70,720

*$102,000 + $20,400 – $25,500 = $96,900

Prob. 16–1B (Concluded)

(Optional)

	Balance	Transactions					Balance
Account Title	**Dec. 31, 2013**		**Debit**		**Credit**		**Dec. 31, 2014**
Cash	47,940	(m)	22,780				70,720
Accounts receivable (net)	188,190	(l)	19,040				207,230
Inventories	289,850	(k)	8,670				298,520
Investments	102,000			(j)	102,000		0
Land	0	(i)	295,800				295,800
Equipment	358,020	(h)	80,580				438,600
Accum. depr.—equipment	(84,320)			(g)	14,790		(99,110)
Accounts payable	(194,140)			(f)	11,560		(205,700)
Accrued expenses payable	(26,860)			(e)	3,740		(30,600)
Dividends payable	(20,400)			(d)	5,100		(25,500)
Common stock, $1 par	(102,000)			(c)	100,000		(202,000)
Paid-in capital in excess							
of par—common stock	(204,000)			(c)	150,000		(354,000)
Retained earnings	(354,280)	(b)	102,000	(a)	141,680		(393,960)
Totals	0		528,870		528,870		0
Operating activities:							
Net income		(a)	141,680				
Depreciation		(g)	14,790				
Loss on sale of investments		(j)	10,200				
Increase in accounts							
receivable				(l)	19,040		
Increase in inventories				(k)	8,670		
Increase in accounts payable		(f)	11,560				
Increase in accrued expenses							
payable		(e)	3,740				
Investing activities:							
Purchase of equipment				(h)	80,580		
Purchase of land				(i)	295,800		
Sale of investments		(j)	91,800				
Financing activities:							
Declaration of cash dividends				(b)	102,000		
Sale of common stock		(c)	250,000				
Increase in dividends payable		(d)	5,100				
Net increase in cash				(m)	22,780		
Totals			528,870		528,870		

Title block:

MERRICK EQUIPMENT CO.
Spreadsheet (Work Sheet) for Statement of Cash Flows
For the Year Ended December 31, 2014

The letters in the debit and credit columns are included for reference purposes. They do not correspond to the letters in the additional data section of this problem.

Prob. 16–2B

HARRIS INDUSTRIES INC. Statement of Cash Flows For the Year Ended December 31, 2014		
Cash flows from operating activities:		
Net income	$ 524,580	
Adjustments to reconcile net income to		
net cash flow from operating activities:		
Depreciation	74,340	
Patent amortization	5,040	
Changes in current operating assets		
and liabilities:		
Increase in accounts receivable	(73,080)	
Decrease in inventories	134,680	
Increase in prepaid expenses	(6,440)	
Decrease in accounts payable	(89,600)	
Decrease in salaries payable	(8,120)	
Net cash flow from operating activities		$ 561,400
Cash flows from investing activities:		
Cash paid for construction of building	$(579,600)	
Net cash flow used for investing activities		(579,600)
Cash flows from financing activities:		
Cash received from issuance of mortgage note	$ 224,000	
Less: Cash paid for dividends*	(123,480)	
Net cash flow from financing activities		100,520
Increase in cash		$ 82,320
Cash at the beginning of the year		360,920
Cash at the end of the year		$ 443,240
Schedule of Noncash Financing and Investing Activities:		
Issuance of common stock to retire bonds		$ 390,000

*$131,040 + $25,200 – $32,760 = $123,480

16-32

Prob. 16–2B (Continued)

(Optional)

Account Title	Balance Dec. 31, 2013	Transactions Debit		Transactions Credit		Balance Dec. 31, 2014
Cash	360,920	(p)	82,320			443,240
Accounts receivable (net)	592,200	(o)	73,080			665,280
Inventories	1,022,560			(n)	134,680	887,880
Prepaid expenses	25,200	(m)	6,440			31,640
Land	302,400					302,400
Buildings	1,134,000	(l)	579,600			1,713,600
Accum. depr.—buildings	(414,540)			(k)	51,660	(466,200)
Machinery and equipment	781,200					781,200
Accum. depr.—machinery and equipment	(191,520)			(j)	22,680	(214,200)
Patents	112,000			(i)	5,040	106,960
Accounts payable	(927,080)	(h)	89,600			(837,480)
Dividends payable	(25,200)			(g)	7,560	(32,760)
Salaries payable	(87,080)	(f)	8,120			(78,960)
Mortgage note payable	0			(e)	224,000	(224,000)
Bonds payable	(390,000)	(d)	390,000			0
Common stock, $5 par	(50,400)			(c)	150,000	(200,400)
Paid-in capital in excess of par—common stock	(126,000)			(c)	240,000	(366,000)
Retained earnings	(2,118,660)	(b)	131,040	(a)	524,580	(2,512,200)
Totals	0		1,360,200		1,360,200	0

Table title (above): **HARRIS INDUSTRIES INC.** / **Spreadsheet (Work Sheet) for Statement of Cash Flows** / **For the Year Ended December 31, 2014**

The letters in the debit and credit columns are included for reference purposes. They do not correspond to the letters in the additional data section of this problem.

Prob. 16–2B (Concluded)

	HARRIS INDUSTRIES INC. Spreadsheet (Work Sheet) for Statement of Cash Flows For the Year Ended December 31, 2014				
Account Title	**Balance** **Dec. 31, 2013**	**Transactions**			**Balance** **Dec. 31, 2014**
		Debit		**Credit**	
Operating activities:					
Net income		(a)	524,580		
Depreciation—buildings		(k)	51,660		
Depreciation—machinery					
and equipment		(j)	22,680		
Amortization of patents		(i)	5,040		
Increase in accounts					
receivable				(o) 73,080	
Decrease in inventories		(n)	134,680		
Increase in prepaid expenses				(m) 6,440	
Decrease in accounts payable				(h) 89,600	
Decrease in salaries payable				(f) 8,120	
Investing activities:					
Construction of building				(l) 579,600	
Financial activities:					
Declaration of cash dividends				(b) 131,040	
Issuance of mortgage note					
payable		(e)	224,000		
Increase in dividends payable		(g)	7,560		
Schedule of noncash investing					
and financing activities:					
Issuance of common stock					
to retire bonds		(c)	390,000	(d) 390,000	
Net increase in cash				(p) 82,320	
Totals			1,360,200	1,360,200	

Prob. 16–3B

	COULSON INC. Statement of Cash Flows For the Year Ended December 31, 2014		
Cash flows from operating activities:			
Net income		$ 326,600	
Adjustments to reconcile net income to			
net cash flow from operating activities:			
Depreciation		68,400	
Gain on sale of land		(60,000)	
Changes in current operating assets			
and liabilities:			
Increase in accounts receivable		(94,800)	
Increase in inventories		(52,800)	
Decrease in prepaid expenses		7,800	
Decrease in accounts payable		(37,200)	
Increase in income taxes payable		4,800	
Net cash flow from operating activities			$ 162,800
Cash flows from investing activities:			
Cash received from sale of land		$ 456,000	
Less: Cash paid for acquisition			
of building	$990,000		
Cash paid for purchase			
of equipment	196,800	1,186,800	
Net cash flow used for investing activities			(730,800)
Cash flows from financing activities:			
Cash received from issuance of			
bonds payable	$330,000		
Cash received from issuance of			
common stock	280,000	$ 610,000	
Less cash paid for dividends		79,200	
Net cash flow from financing activities			530,800
Decrease in cash			$ (37,200)
Cash at the beginning of the year			337,800
Cash at the end of the year			$ 300,600

Prob. 16–3B (Concluded)

(Optional)

COULSON INC.							
Spreadsheet (Work Sheet) for Statement of Cash Flows							
For the Year Ended December 31, 2014							
	Balance	Transactions					Balance
Account Title	Dec. 31, 2013	Debit			Credit		Dec. 31, 2014
Cash	337,800			(p)	37,200		300,600
Accounts receivable (net)	609,600	(i)	94,800				704,400
Inventories	865,800	(h)	52,800				918,600
Prepaid expenses	26,400			(g)	7,800		18,600
Land	1,386,000			(m)	396,000		990,000
Buildings	990,000	(l)	990,000				1,980,000
Accum. depr.—buildings	(366,000)			(f)	31,200		(397,200)
Equipment	529,800	(j)	196,800	(k)	66,000		660,600
Accum. depr.—equipment	(162,000)	(k)	66,000	(e)	37,200		(133,200)
Accounts payable	(631,200)	(d)	37,200				(594,000)
Income taxes payable	(21,600)			(c)	4,800		(26,400)
Bonds payable	0			(n)	330,000		(330,000)
Common stock, $20 par	(180,000)			(o)	140,000		(320,000)
Paid-in capital in excess of							
par—common stock	(810,000)			(o)	140,000		(950,000)
Retained earnings	(2,574,600)	(b)	79,200	(a)	326,600		(2,822,000)
Totals	0		1,516,800		1,516,800		0
Operating activities:							
Net income		(a)	326,600				
Depreciation—equipment		(e)	37,200				
Depreciation—buildings		(f)	31,200				
Gain on sale of land				(m)	60,000		
Increase in accts. receivable				(i)	94,800		
Increase in inventories				(h)	52,800		
Decrease in prepaid expenses		(g)	7,800				
Decrease in accounts payable				(d)	37,200		
Increase in income taxes							
payable		(c)	4,800				
Investing activities:							
Purchase of equipment				(j)	196,800		
Acquisition of building				(l)	990,000		
Sale of land		(m)	456,000				
Financing activities:							
Payment of cash dividends				(b)	79,200		
Issuance of bonds payable		(n)	330,000				
Issuance of common stock		(o)	280,000				
Net decrease in cash		(p)	37,200				
Totals			1,510,800		1,510,800		

Prob. 16–4B

MARTINEZ INC. Statement of Cash Flows For the Year Ended December 31, 2014			
Cash flows from operating activities:			
Cash received from customers[1]		$4,433,760	
Deduct: Cash payments for merchandise[2]	$2,269,200		
Cash payments for operating expenses[3]	1,356,240		
Cash payments for income tax	299,100	3,924,540	
Net cash flow from operating activities			$ 509,220
Cash flows from investing activities:			
Cash received from sale of investments		$ 588,000	
Less: Cash paid for land	$ 960,000		
Cash paid for equipment	240,000	1,200,000	
Net cash flow used for investing activities			(612,000)
Cash flows from financing activities:			
Cash received from sale of common stock		$ 600,000	
Less: Cash paid for dividends*		518,400	
Net cash flow from financing activities			81,600
Decrease in cash			$ (21,180)
Cash at the beginning of the year			683,100
Cash at the end of the year			$ 661,920

Reconciliation of Net Income with Cash Flows from Operating Activities:

Net income...	$ 558,960
Adjustments to reconcile net income to net cash flow from operating activities:	
Depreciation expense...	113,100
Gain on sale of investments..	(156,000)
Changes in current operating assets and liabilities:	
Increase in accounts receivable...	(78,240)
Increase in inventories..	(30,600)
Increase in accounts payable...	113,400
Decrease in accrued expenses payable..............................	(11,400)
Net cash flow from operating activities...................................	$ 509,220

* Dividends paid: $528,000 + $91,200 – $100,800 = $518,400

Prob. 16–4B (Concluded)

Computations:

1. Sales.. $4,512,000
    Deduct increase in accounts receivable...   78,240
    Cash received from customers... $4,433,760

2. Cost of merchandise sold... $2,352,000
    Add increase in inventories..   30,600
                                                                                        $2,382,600
    Deduct increase in accounts payable...   113,400
    Cash payments for merchandise.. $2,269,200

3. Operating expenses other than depreciation.. $1,344,840
    Add decrease in accrued expenses payable...   11,400
    Cash payments for operating expenses... $1,356,240

Prob. 16–5B

MERRICK EQUIPMENT CO.
Statement of Cash Flows
For the Year Ended December 31, 2014

Cash flows from operating activities:			
Cash received from customers¹		$2,004,858	
Deduct: Cash payments for merchandise²	$1,242,586		
Cash payments for operating expenses³	513,559		
Cash payments for income taxes	94,453	1,850,598	
Net cash flow from operating activities			$ 154,260
Cash flows from investing activities:			
Cash received from sale of investments		$ 91,800	
Less: Cash paid for purchase of land	$ 295,800		
Cash paid for purchase of equipment	80,580	376,380	
Net cash flow used for investing activities			(284,580)
Cash flows from financing activities:			
Cash received from sale of common stock		$ 250,000	
Less: Cash paid for dividends*		96,900	
Net cash flow from financing activities			153,100
Increase in cash			$ 22,780
Cash at the beginning of the year			47,940
Cash at the end of the year			$ 70,720

Reconciliation of Net Income with Cash Flows from Operating Activities:

Net income...	$141,680
Adjustments to reconcile net income to net cash flow from operating activities:	
Depreciation...	14,790
Loss on sale of investments......................................	10,200
Changes in current operating assets and liabilities:	
Increase in accounts receivable...............................	(19,040)
Increase in inventories...	(8,670)
Increase in accounts payable....................................	11,560
Increase in accrued expenses payable......................	3,740
Net cash flow from operating activities..........................	$154,260

* Dividends paid: $102,000 + $20,400 − $25,500 = $96,900

Prob. 16–5B (Concluded)

Computations:

1. | Sales.. | $2,023,898 |
    |---|---|
    | Deduct increase in accounts receivable............................. | 19,040 |
    | Cash received from customers.. | $2,004,858 |

2. | Cost of merchandise sold.. | $1,245,476 |
    |---|---|
    | Add increase in inventories.. | 8,670 |
    | | $1,254,146 |
    | Deduct increase in accounts payable................................ | 11,560 |
    | Cash payments for merchandise...................................... | $1,242,586 |

3. | Operating expenses other than depreciation....................... | $ 517,299 |
    |---|---|
    | Deduct increase in accrued expenses payable..................... | 3,740 |
    | Cash payments for operating expenses.............................. | $ 513,559 |

CASES & PROJECTS

CP 16–1

Although this situation might seem harmless at first, it is, in fact, a violation of generally accepted accounting principles. The operating cash flow per share figure should not be shown on the face of the income statement. The income statement is constructed under accrual accounting concepts, while operating cash flow "undoes" the accounting accruals. Thus, unlike Lucas's assertion that this information would be useful, more likely the information could be confusing to users. Some users might not be able to distinguish between earnings and operating cash flow per share—or how to interpret the difference. By agreeing with Lucas, John has breached his professional ethics because the disclosure would violate generally accepted accounting principles. On a more subtle note, Lucas is being somewhat disingenuous. Apparently, Lucas is not pleased with this year's operating performance and would like to cover the earnings "bad news" with some cash flow "good news" disclosures. An interesting question is: Would Lucas be as interested in the dual per share disclosures in the opposite scenario—with earnings per share improving and cash flow per share deteriorating? Probably not.

CP 16–2

Start-up companies are unique in that they frequently will have negative retained earnings and operating cash flows. The negative retained earnings are often due to losses from high start-up expenses. The negative operating cash flows are typical because growth requires cash. Growth must be financed with cash before the cash returns. For example, a company must expend cash to provide the service in Period 1 before selling it and receiving cash in Period 2. The start-up company constantly faces the problem of spending cash today for the next period's growth. For Giraffe Inc., the money spent on salaries to develop the business is a cash outflow that must occur before the service provides revenues. In addition, the company must use cash to market its service to potential customers. In this situation, the only way the company stays in business is from the capital provided by the owners. This owner-supplied capital is the lifeblood of a start-up company. Banks will not likely lend money on this type of venture (except with assets as security). Giraffe Inc. could be a good investment. It all depends on whether the new service has promise. The financial figures will not reveal this easily. Only actual sales will reveal if the service is a hit. Until this time, the company is at risk. If the service is not popular, the company will have no cash to fall back on—it will likely go bankrupt. If, however, the service is successful, then Giraffe Inc. should become self-sustaining and provide a good return for the shareholders.

CP 16–3

a. 1. Normal practice for determining the amount of cash flows from operating activities during the year is to begin with the reported net income. This net income must ordinarily be adjusted upward and/or downward to determine the amount of cash flows. Although many operating expenses decrease cash, depreciation does not. The amount of net income understates the amount of cash flows provided by operations to the extent that depreciation expense is deducted from revenue. The associated cash outflow occurs when the asset is purchased and is reported as a cash outflow from investing activities. Accordingly, the depreciation expense for the year must be added back to the reported net income in arriving at cash flows from operating activities.

2. Generally accepted accounting principles require that significant transactions affecting future cash flows should be reported in a separate schedule to the statement, even though they do not affect cash. Accordingly, even though the issuance of the common stock for land does not affect cash, the transaction affects future cash flows and must be reported.

3. The $180,000 cash received from the sale of the investments is reported in the Cash Flows from Investing Activities section. Since the net income included a gain of $30,000, the gain is deducted from net income to avoid double reporting this amount and to remove it from the determination of cash flows from operating activities.

4. The balance sheets for the last two years will indicate the increase in cash but will not indicate the firm's activities in meeting its financial obligations, paying dividends, and maintaining and expanding operating capacity. Such information, as provided by the statement of cash flows, assists creditors in assessing the firm's solvency and profitability—two very important factors bearing on the evaluation of a potential loan.

b. The statement of cash flows indicates a strong liquidity position for Argon Inc. The increase in cash of $291,000 for the past year is more than adequate to cover the $150,000 of new building and store equipment costs that will not be provided by the loan. Thus, the statement of cash flows most likely will enhance the company's chances of receiving a loan. However, other information, such as a projection of future earnings, a description of collateral pledged to support the loan, and an independent credit report, would normally be considered before a final loan decision is made.

CP 16–4

The senior vice president is very focused on profitability but has been bleeding cash. The increase in accounts receivable and inventory is striking. Apparently, the new credit card campaign has found many new customers, since the accounts receivable is growing. Unfortunately, it appears as though the new campaign has done a poor job of screening creditworthiness in these new customers. In other words, there are many new credit card purchasers—unfortunately, they do not appear to be paying off their balances. The new merchandise purchases appear to be backfiring. The company has received some "good deals," except that they are only "good deals" if it can resell the merchandise. If the merchandise has no customer appeal, then that would explain the inventory increase. In other words, the division is purchasing merchandise that sits on the shelf, regardless of pricing. The reduction in payables is the result of the division becoming overdue on payments. The memo reports that most of the past due payables have been paid. This situation is critical in the retailing business. A retailer cannot afford a poor payment history, or it will be denied future merchandise shipments. This is a signal of severe cash problems. Overall, the picture is of a retailer having severe operating cash flow difficulties.

Note to Instructors: This scenario is essentially similar to Kmart's path to eventual bankruptcy. It reported earnings, while having significant negative cash flows from operations due to expanding credit too liberally (increases in accounts receivable) and purchasing too much unsaleable inventory (increases in inventory). Eventually, Kmart's inventory write-down resulted in significant losses about the time it entered bankruptcy.

CP 16–5

a. and b.

Recent statements of cash flows for Johnson & Johnson and JetBlue Airways Corp. are shown on the following pages. The actual analysis may be different due to updated information. However, this answer shows the structure for a possible response.

<u>Johnson & Johnson</u>

Johnson & Johnson (J&J) is a powerful generator of cash flows from operating activities, with almost $14.3 billion in cash flow from operations. This is enough to support over $4.6 billion in investing activities, with the remainder available for dividends, repurchases of common stock, and retirement of debt, while still adding $5.2 billion to the company's cash balance. Overall, the statement of cash flows indicates very favorable cash flows for J&J. J&J's free cash flow is approximately $11.4 billion for the year ($14.3 – $2.9).

<u>JetBlue Airways Corp.</u>

JetBlue is weaker than J&J. JetBlue had cash flows from operating activities of around $614 million. In addition, JetBlue had net negative cash flows from investing activities of $502 million. The net cash inflows from financing activities was $96 million, which primarily came from the issuance of short-term debt. JetBlue did not generate enough cash flow from operations to maintain the necessary investment in its fixed assets. Free cash flow is approximately $89 million ($614 – $525). JetBlue is in a much weaker cash flow position than Johnson & Johnson.

CP 16–5 (Continued)

JOHNSON & JOHNSON Consolidated Statements of Cash Flows	
In Millions For Period Ended December 31, 2011	**12/31/11**
CASH FLOWS FROM OPERATING ACTIVITIES:	
Net earnings	$ 9,672
Adjustments to reconcile net earnings to cash flows:	
Depreciation and amortization of property and intangibles	3,158
Stock based compensation	621
Deferred tax provision	(836)
Accounts receivable allowances	32
Changes in assets and liabilities, net of effects from acquisitions:	
Increase in accounts receivable	(915)
(Increase)/decrease in inventories	(715)
(Decrease)/increase in accounts payable and accrued liabilities	493
(Decrease)/increase in other current and noncurrent assets	(1,625)
(Decrease)/increase in other current and noncurrent liabilities	4,413
NET CASH FLOWS FROM OPERATING ACTIVITIES	$ 14,298
CASH FLOWS FROM INVESTING ACTIVITIES:	
Additions to property, plant and equipment	$ (2,893)
Proceeds from the disposal of assets	1,342
Acquisitions, net of cash acquired (Note 17)	(2,797)
Purchases of investments	(29,882)
Sales of investments	30,396
Other (primarily intangibles)	(778)
NET CASH USED BY INVESTING ACTIVITIES	$ (4,612)
CASH FLOWS FROM FINANCING ACTIVITIES:	
Dividends to shareholders	$ (6,156)
Repurchase of common stock	(2,525)
Proceeds from short-term debt	9,729
Retirement of short-term debt	(11,200)
Proceeds from long-term debt	4,470
Retirement of long-term debt	(16)
Proceeds from the exercise of stock options	1,246
NET CASH USED BY FINANCING ACTIVITIES	$ (4,452)
Effect of exchange rate changes on cash and cash equivalents	$ (47)
Increase in cash and cash equivalents	$ 5,187
Cash and cash equivalents, beginning of year (Note 1)	19,355
CASH AND CASH EQUIVALENTS, END OF YEAR (NOTE 1)	$ 24,542
SUPPLEMENTAL SCHEDULE OF NONCASH INVESTING AND	
FINANCING ACTIVITIES	
Treasury stock issued for employee compensation and	
stock option plans, net of cash proceeds	433
Conversion of debt	1

CP 16–5 (Concluded)

JETBLUE AIRWAYS CORP. Consolidated Statements of Cash Flows 31-Dec-11	
In Millions For Period Ended December 31, 2011	12/31/11
Cash Flow from Operating Activities:	
Net income	$ 86
Adjustments to reconcile net loss to net cash provided (used) by operating activities:	
Depreciation	213
Amortization	34
Stock-based compensation	13
Losses (Gains) on sale of flight equipment and extinguishment of debt	6
Deferred income taxes	58
Collateral returned (deposits) for derivative instruments	10
Changes in certain operating assets and liabilities:	
Decrease (increase) in receivables	(10)
Increase (decrease) in inventories, prepaid and other	4
Increase (decrease) in air traffic liability	113
Increase (decrease) accounts payable and other accrued liabilities	26
Other, net	61
Net cash (used) provided by operating activities	$ 614
Cash Flow from Investing Activities:	
Capital expenditures, including purchase deposits on flight equipment	$(525)
Net decrease in short-term investments	24
Proceeds from sale of equipment and property and other investments	2
Other	(3)
Net cash used for investing activities	$(502)
Cash Flow from Financing Activities:	
Proceeds from:	
Issuance of common stock	$ 10
Issuance of long-term debt	245
Short-term borrowings	128
Other	6
Repayment of:	
Long-term debt and capital lease obligations	(238)
Short-term borrowings	(40)
Other	(15)
Net cash provided by financing activities	$ 96
Net increase in cash	$ 208
Cash at beginning of year	465
Cash at end of year	$ 673

CHAPTER 17
FINANCIAL STATEMENT ANALYSIS

DISCUSSION QUESTIONS

1. Horizontal analysis is the percentage analysis of increases and decreases in corresponding statements. The percent change in the cash balances at the end of the preceding year from the end of the current year is an example. Vertical analysis is the percentage analysis showing the relationship of the component parts to the total in a single statement. The percent of cash as a portion of total assets at the end of the current year is an example.

2. Comparative statements provide information as to changes between dates or periods. Trends indicated by comparisons may be far more significant than the data for a single date or period.

3. Before this question can be answered, the increase in net income should be compared with changes in sales, expenses, and assets devoted to the business for the current year. The return on assets for both periods should also be compared. If these comparisons indicate favorable trends, the operating performance has improved; if not, the apparent favorable increase in net income may be offset by unfavorable trends in other areas.

4. Generally, the two ratios would be very close, because most service businesses sell services and hold very little inventory.

5. a. A high inventory turnover minimizes the amount invested in inventories, thus freeing funds for more advantageous use. Storage costs, administrative expenses, and losses caused by obsolescence and adverse changes in prices are also kept to a minimum.

   b. Yes. The inventory turnover relates to the "turnover" of inventory during the year, while the number of days' sales in inventory relates to the amount of inventory on hand at the beginning and end of the year. Therefore, a business could have a high inventory turnover during the year, yet have a high number of days' sales in inventory based on the beginning and end-of-year inventory amounts.

6. The ratio of fixed assets to long-term liabilities increased from 3.4 for the preceding year to 4.2 for the current year, indicating that the company is in a stronger position now than in the preceding year to borrow additional funds on a long-term basis.

7. a. The rate earned on total assets adds interest expense to the net income, which is divided by average total assets. It measures the profitability of the total assets, without regard for how the assets are financed. The rate earned on stockholders' equity divides net income by the average total stockholders' equity. It measures the profitability of the stockholders' investment.

   b. The rate earned on stockholders' equity is normally higher than the rate earned on total assets. This is because of leverage, which compensates stockholders for the higher risk of their investments.

DISCUSSION QUESTIONS (Concluded)

8. a.   Due to leverage, the rate on stockholders' equity will often be greater than the rate on total assets. This occurs because the amount earned on assets acquired through the use of funds provided by creditors exceeds the interest charges paid to creditors.

    b.   Higher. The concept of leverage applies to preferred stock as well as debt. The rate earned on common stockholders' equity ordinarily exceeds the rate earned on total stockholders' equity because the amount earned on assets acquired through the use of funds provided by preferred stockholders normally exceeds the dividends paid to preferred stockholders.

9.   The earnings per share in the preceding year were $3 per share ($6/2), adjusted for the stock split in the latest year. McCants' earnings per share has deteriorated.

10. One report is the Report on Internal Control, which verifies management's conclusions on internal control. Another report is the Report on Fairness of the Financial Statements of Independent Registered Public Accounting Firm, where the Certified Public Accounting (CPA) firm that conducts the audit renders an opinion on the fairness of the statements.

PRACTICE EXERCISES

PE 17–1A

Temporary investments........	$6,400 increase ($46,400 – $40,000), or 16%
Inventory...........................	$6,400 decrease ($73,600 – $80,000), or –8%

PE 17–1B

Accounts payable.................	$11,000 increase ($111,000 – $100,000), or 11%
Long-term debt....................	$8,680 increase ($132,680 – $124,000), or 7%

PE 17–2A

	Amount	Percentage	
Sales..................................	$850,000	100%	($850,000 ÷ $850,000)
Cost of goods sold..............	493,000	58%	($493,000 ÷ $850,000)
Gross profit........................	$357,000	42%	($357,000 ÷ $850,000)

PE 17–2B

	Amount	Percentage	
Sales..................................	$1,200,000	100%	($1,200,000 ÷ $1,200,000)
Cost of goods sold..............	780,000	65%	($780,000 ÷ $1,200,000)
Gross profit........................	$ 420,000	35%	($420,000 ÷ $1,200,000)

PE 17–3A

a. Current Ratio = Current Assets ÷ Current Liabilities

Current Ratio = ($130,000 + $50,000 + $60,000 + $120,000) ÷ $150,000

Current Ratio = 2.4

b. Quick Ratio = Quick Assets ÷ Current Liabilities

Quick Ratio = ($130,000 + $50,000 + $60,000) ÷ $150,000

Quick Ratio = 1.6

PE 17–3B

a.　**Current Ratio　=　Current Assets ÷ Current Liabilities**

　　Current Ratio　=　($210,000 + $120,000 + $110,000 + $160,000) ÷ $200,000

　　Current Ratio　=　3.0

b.　**Quick Ratio　=　Quick Assets ÷ Current Liabilities**

　　Quick Ratio　=　($210,000 + $120,000 + $110,000) ÷ $200,000

　　Quick Ratio　=　2.2

PE 17–4A

a.　**Accounts Receivable Turnover　=　Net Sales ÷ Average Accounts Receivable**

　　Accounts Receivable Turnover　=　$1,200,000 ÷ $100,000

　　Accounts Receivable Turnover　=　12.0

b.　**Number of Days' Sales in Receivables**　　=　$\dfrac{\text{Average Accounts Receivable}}{\text{Average Daily Sales}}$

　　Number of Days' Sales in Receivables　　=　**$100,000 ÷ ($1,200,000 ÷ 365)**

　　　　　　　　　　　　　　　　　　　　　=　**$100,000 ÷ $3,288**

　　Number of Days' Sales in Receivables　　=　**30.4 days**

PE 17–4B

a.　**Accounts Receivable Turnover　=　Net Sales ÷ Average Accounts Receivable**

　　Accounts Receivable Turnover　=　$3,150,000 ÷ $210,000

　　Accounts Receivable Turnover　=　15.0

b.　**Number of Days' Sales in Receivables**　　=　$\dfrac{\text{Average Accounts Receivable}}{\text{Average Daily Sales}}$

　　Number of Days' Sales in Receivables　　=　**$210,000 ÷ ($3,150,000 ÷ 365)**

　　　　　　　　　　　　　　　　　　　　　=　**$210,000 ÷ $8,630**

　　Number of Days' Sales in Receivables　　=　**24.3 days**

PE 17–5A

a. **Inventory Turnover = Cost of Goods Sold ÷ Average Inventory**

   Inventory Turnover = $630,000 ÷ $90,000

   Inventory Turnover = 7.0

b. **Number of Days' Sales in Inventory** $=\dfrac{\textbf{Average Inventory}}{\textbf{Average Daily Cost of Goods Sold}}$

   Number of Days' Sales in Inventory   = $90,000 ÷ ($630,000 ÷ 365)

   = $90,000 ÷ $1,726

   Number of Days' Sales in Inventory   = 52.1 days

PE 17–5B

a. **Inventory Turnover = Cost of Goods Sold ÷ Average Inventory**

   Inventory Turnover = $435,000 ÷ $72,500

   Inventory Turnover = 6.0

b. **Number of Days' Sales in Inventory** $=\dfrac{\textbf{Average Inventory}}{\textbf{Average Daily Cost of Goods Sold}}$

   Number of Days' Sales in Inventory   = $72,500 ÷ ($435,000 ÷ 365)

   = $72,500 ÷ $1,192

   Number of Days' Sales in Inventory   = 60.8 days

PE 17–6A

a. Ratio of Fixed Assets to Long-Term Liabilities $= \dfrac{\text{Fixed Assets}}{\text{Long-Term Liabilities}}$

Ratio of Fixed Assets to Long-Term Liabilities $= \$1{,}800{,}000 \div \$600{,}000$

Ratio of Fixed Assets to Long-Term Liabilities $= 3.0$

b. Ratio of Liabilities to Stockholders' Equity $= \dfrac{\text{Total Liabilities}}{\text{Total Stockholders' Equity}}$

Ratio of Liabilities to Stockholders' Equity $= \$900{,}000 \div \$750{,}000$

Ratio of Liabilities to Stockholders' Equity $= 1.2$

PE 17–6B

a. Ratio of Fixed Assets to Long-Term Liabilities $= \dfrac{\text{Fixed Assets}}{\text{Long-Term Liabilities}}$

Ratio of Fixed Assets to Long-Term Liabilities $= \$2{,}000{,}000 \div \$800{,}000$

Ratio of Fixed Assets to Long-Term Liabilities $= 2.5$

b. Ratio of Liabilities to Stockholders' Equity $= \dfrac{\text{Total Liabilities}}{\text{Total Stockholders' Equity}}$

Ratio of Liabilities to Stockholders' Equity $= \$1{,}000{,}000 \div \$625{,}000$

Ratio of Liabilities to Stockholders' Equity $= 1.6$

PE 17–7A

$\dfrac{\text{Number of Times}}{\text{Interest Charges Are Earned}} = \dfrac{\text{Income Before Income Tax} + \text{Interest Expense}}{\text{Interest Expense}}$

$\dfrac{\text{Number of Times}}{\text{Interest Charges Are Earned}} = \dfrac{\$4{,}000{,}000 + \$400{,}000}{\$400{,}000}$

$\dfrac{\text{Number of Times}}{\text{Interest Charges Are Earned}} = 11.0$

PE 17–7B

$\dfrac{\text{Number of Times}}{\text{Interest Charges Are Earned}} = \dfrac{\text{Income Before Income Tax} + \text{Interest Expense}}{\text{Interest Expense}}$

$\dfrac{\text{Number of Times}}{\text{Interest Charges Are Earned}} = \dfrac{\$8{,}000{,}000 + \$500{,}000}{\$500{,}000}$

$\dfrac{\text{Number of Times}}{\text{Interest Charges Are Earned}} = 17.0$

17-6

PE 17–8A

> Ratio of Net Sales to Assets = Net Sales ÷ Average Total Assets
>
> Ratio of Net Sales to Assets = $1,800,000 ÷ $1,125,000
>
> Ratio of Net Sales to Assets = 1.6

PE 17–8B

> Ratio of Net Sales to Assets = Net Sales ÷ Average Total Assets
>
> Ratio of Net Sales to Assets = $4,400,000 ÷ $2,000,000
>
> Ratio of Net Sales to Assets = 2.2

PE 17–9A

$$\text{Rate Earned on Total Assets} = \frac{\text{Net Income + Interest Expense}}{\text{Average Total Assets}}$$

$$\text{Rate Earned on Total Assets} = \frac{\$250,000 + \$100,000}{\$2,500,000}$$

$$\text{Rate Earned on Total Assets} = \frac{\$350,000}{\$2,500,000}$$

> Rate Earned on Total Assets = 14.0%

PE 17–9B

$$\text{Rate Earned on Total Assets} = \frac{\text{Net Income + Interest Expense}}{\text{Average Total Assets}}$$

$$\text{Rate Earned on Total Assets} = \frac{\$410,000 + \$90,000}{\$5,000,000}$$

$$\text{Rate Earned on Total Assets} = \frac{\$500,000}{\$5,000,000}$$

> Rate Earned on Total Assets = 10.0%

PE 17–10A

a. **Rate Earned on Stockholders' Equity** $= \dfrac{\text{Net Income}}{\text{Average Stockholders' Equity}}$

   Rate Earned on Stockholders' Equity $= \$375,000 \div \$2,500,000$

   Rate Earned on Stockholders' Equity $= 15.0\%$

b. **Rate Earned on Common Stockholders' Equity** $= \dfrac{\text{Net Income – Preferred Dividends}}{\text{Average Common Stockholders' Equity}}$

   Rate Earned on Common Stockholders' Equity $= \dfrac{\$375,000 - \$75,000}{\$1,875,000}$

   Rate Earned on Common Stockholders' Equity $= 16.0\%$

PE 17–10B

a. **Rate Earned on Stockholders' Equity** $= \dfrac{\text{Net Income}}{\text{Average Stockholders' Equity}}$

   Rate Earned on Stockholders' Equity $= \$1,000,000 \div \$6,250,000$

   Rate Earned on Stockholders' Equity $= 16.0\%$

b. **Rate Earned on Common Stockholders' Equity** $= \dfrac{\text{Net Income – Preferred Dividends}}{\text{Average Common Stockholders' Equity}}$

   Rate Earned on Common Stockholders' Equity $= \dfrac{\$1,000,000 - \$50,000}{\$3,800,000}$

   Rate Earned on Common Stockholders' Equity $= 25.0\%$

PE 17–11A

a. **Earnings per Share on Common Stock** $= \dfrac{\text{Net Income} - \text{Preferred Dividends}}{\text{Shares of Common Stock Outstanding}}$

Earnings per Share on Common Stock $= (\$185{,}000 - \$25{,}000) \div \$100{,}000$

Earnings per Share on Common Stock $= \$1.60$

b. **Price-Earnings Ratio** $= \dfrac{\text{Market Price per Share of Common Stock}}{\text{Earnings per Share on Common Stock}}$

Price-Earnings Ratio $= \$20.00 \div \$1.60$

Price-Earnings Ratio $= 12.5$

PE 17–11B

a. **Earnings per Share on Common Stock** $= \dfrac{\text{Net Income} - \text{Preferred Dividends}}{\text{Shares of Common Stock Outstanding}}$

Earnings per Share on Common Stock $= (\$410{,}000 - \$60{,}000) \div \$50{,}000$

Earnings per Share on Common Stock $= \$7.00$

b. **Price-Earnings Ratio** $= \dfrac{\text{Market Price per Share of Common Stock}}{\text{Earnings per Share on Common Stock}}$

Price-Earnings Ratio $= \$84.00 \div \$7.00$

Price-Earnings Ratio $= 12.0$

EXERCISES

Ex. 17–1

a.

SOLDNER, Inc.				
Comparative Income Statement				
For the Years Ended December 31, 2014 and 2013				
	2014		2013	
	Amount	Percent	Amount	Percent
Sales	$1,500,000	100%	$1,450,000	100%
Cost of goods sold	930,000	62%	812,000	56%
Gross profit	$ 570,000	38%	$ 638,000	44%
Selling expenses	210,000	14%	261,000	18%
Administrative expenses	255,000	17%	232,000	16%
Total operating expenses	$ 465,000	31%	$ 493,000	34%
Income from operations	105,000	7%	145,000	10%
Income tax expense	52,500	3.5%	72,500	5%
Net income	$ 52,500	3.5%	$ 72,500	5%

b.   The vertical analysis indicates that the cost of goods sold as a percent of sales
      increased by 6 percentage points (62% – 56%), while selling expenses decreased
      by 4 percentage points (14% – 18%), and administrative expenses increased by 1%
      (17% – 16%). Thus, net income as a percent of sales dropped by 1.5% (5% – 3.5%).

Ex. 17–2

a.

SPEEDWAY MOTORSPORTS, INC.				
Comparative Income Statement (in thousands of dollars)				
For the Years Ended December 31				
	Current Year		Prior Year	
	Amount	Percent	Amount	Percent
Revenues:				
Admissions	$139,125	27.7%	$163,087	29.6%
Event-related revenue	156,691	31.2%	178,805	32.5%
NASCAR broadcasting				
revenue	178,722	35.6%	173,803	31.6%
Other operating revenue	27,705	5.5%	34,827	6.3%
Total revenue	$502,243	100.0%	$550,522	100.0%
Expenses and other:				
Direct expense of events	$100,843	20.1%	$100,922	18.3%
NASCAR purse and				
sanction fees	120,273	23.9%	123,078	22.4%
Other direct expenses	21,846	4.3%	26,208	4.8%
General and administrative	188,196	37.5%	266,252	48.3%
Total expenses and other	$431,158	85.8%	$516,460	93.8%
Income from continuing				
operations	$ 71,085	14.2%	$ 34,062	6.2%

b. While overall revenue decreased some between the two years, the overall mix of revenue sources did change somewhat. The NASCAR broadcasting revenue increased as a percent of total revenue by 4 percentage points, while the percent of admissions revenue to total revenue decreased by almost 2%. Two of the major expense categories (direct expense of events and NASCAR purse and sanction fees) as a percent of total revenue increased by approximately 4%. Other direct expenses, however, decreased by 0.5%, and general and administrative expenses decreased by about 11%. Overall, the income from continuing operations increased by 8% of total revenue between the two years, which is a favorable trend. The income from continuing operations as a percent of sales exceeds 14% in the current year, which is excellent. Apparently, owning and operating motor speedways is a business that produces high operating profit margins.

Note to Instructors: The high operating margin is probably necessary to compensate for the extensive investment in speedway assets.

Ex. 17–3

a.

	BULL RUN COMPANY Common-Sized Income Statement For the Year Ended December 31, 20—		Electronics Industry Average
	Bull Run Company		
	Amount	Percent	
Sales	$2,100,000	105%	105%
Sales returns and allowances	100,000	5%	5%
Net sales	$2,000,000	100%	100%
Cost of goods sold	1,040,000	52%	60%
Gross profit	$ 960,000	48%	40%
Selling expenses	560,000	28%	22%
Administrative expenses	300,000	15%	12%
Total operating expenses	$ 860,000	43%	34%
Operating income	100,000	5%	6%
Other income	60,000	3%	3%
	$ 160,000	8%	9%
Other expense	40,000	2%	2%
Income before income tax	$ 120,000	6%	7%
Income tax expense	60,000	3%	6%
Net income	$ 60,000	3%	1%

b.   The cost of goods sold is 8% lower than the industry average, but the selling expenses and administrative expenses are 6% and 3% higher than the industry average. The combined impact causes net income as a percent of sales to be 2% better than the industry average. Apparently, the company is managing the cost of manufacturing product better than the industry, but has slightly higher selling and administrative expenses relative to the industry. The cause of the higher selling and administrative expenses as a percent of sales, relative to the industry, can be investigated further.

Ex. 17–4

PEACOCK COMPANY				
Comparative Balance Sheet				
December 31, 2014 and 2013				
	2014		2013	
	Amount	Percent	Amount	Percent
Current assets	$1,050,000	30%	$ 750,000	25%
Property, plant, and equipment	1,960,000	56%	2,100,000	70%
Intangible assets	490,000	14%	150,000	5%
Total assets	$3,500,000	100%	$3,000,000	100%
Current liabilities	$ 630,000	18%	$ 420,000	14%
Long-term liabilities	1,260,000	36%	1,200,000	40%
Common stock	350,000	10%	300,000	10%
Retained earnings	1,260,000	36%	1,080,000	36%
Total liabilities and				
stockholders' equity	$3,500,000	100%	$3,000,000	100%

Ex. 17–5

a.

BEZOS COMPANY				
Comparative Income Statement				
For the Years Ended December 31, 2014 and 2013				
	2014	2013	Increase (Decrease)	
	Amount	Amount	Amount	Percent
Sales	$840,000	$600,000	$240,000	40.0%
Cost of goods sold	724,500	525,000	199,500	38.0%
Gross profit	$115,500	$ 75,000	$ 40,500	54.0%
Selling expenses	52,500	37,500	15,000	40.0%
Administrative expenses	41,400	30,000	11,400	38.0%
Total operating expenses	$ 93,900	$ 67,500	$ 26,400	39.1%
Income before income tax	21,600	7,500	14,100	188.0%
Income tax expense	10,800	2,700	8,100	300.0%
Net income	$ 10,800	$ 4,800	$ 6,000	125.0%

b.   The net income for Bezos Company increased by approximately 125% from 2013
   to 2014. This increase was the combined result of an increase in sales of 40%
   and lower percentage increases in cost of goods sold and administrative expenses.
   The cost of goods sold increased at a slower rate than the increase in sales, thus
   causing the percentage increase in gross profit to exceed the percentage increase
   in sales.

Ex. 17–6

a. (1) **Working Capital = Current Assets – Current Liabilities**

2014: $2,420,000 = $3,520,000 – $1,100,000

2013: $2,000,000 = $3,000,000 – $1,000,000

(2) Current Ratio $= \dfrac{\text{Current Assets}}{\text{Current Liabilities}}$

2014: $\dfrac{\$3,520,000}{\$1,100,000}$ = 3.2   2013: $\dfrac{\$3,000,000}{\$1,000,000}$ = 3.0

(3) Quick Ratio $= \dfrac{\text{Quick Assets}}{\text{Current Liabilities}}$

2014: $\dfrac{\$2,420,000}{\$1,100,000}$ = 2.2   2013: $\dfrac{\$2,000,000}{\$1,000,000}$ = 2.0

b. The liquidity of Mossberg has improved from the preceding year to the current year. The working capital, current ratio, and quick ratio have all increased. Most of these changes are the result of an increase in current assets relative to current liabilities.

Ex. 17–7

a. (1) Current Ratio $= \dfrac{\text{Current Assets}}{\text{Current Liabilities}}$

Current Year: $\dfrac{\$17,569}{\$15,892}$ = 1.1   Prior Year: $\dfrac{\$12,571}{\$8,756}$ = 1.4

(2) Quick Ratio $= \dfrac{\text{Quick Assets}}{\text{Current Liabilities}}$

Current Year: $\dfrac{\$12,692}{\$15,892}$ = 0.8   Prior Year: $\dfrac{\$8,759}{\$8,756}$ = 1.0

b. The solvency of PepsiCo has decreased some over this time period. Both the current and quick ratios have decreased. The current ratio decreased from 1.4 to 1.1, and the quick ratio decreased from 1.0 to 0.8. While PepsiCo is a strong company with ample resources for meeting short-term obligations, its solvency as measured by the current and quick ratios has deteriorated during this period.

Ex. 17–8

a.   The working capital, current ratio, and quick ratio are calculated incorrectly. The working capital and current ratio incorrectly include intangible assets and property, plant, and equipment as a part of current assets. Both are noncurrent. The quick ratio has both an incorrect numerator and denominator. The numerator of the quick ratio is incorrectly calculated as the sum of inventories, prepaid expenses, and property, plant, and equipment ($36,000 + $24,000 + $55,200). The denominator is also incorrect, as it does not include accrued liabilities. The denominator of the quick ratio should be total current liabilities.

The correct calculations are as follows:

Working Capital = Current Assets – Current Liabilities
$30,000 = $330,000 – $300,000

$$\text{Current Ratio} = \frac{\text{Current Assets}}{\text{Current Liabilities}}$$

$$\frac{\$330,000}{\$300,000} = 1.1$$

$$\text{Quick Ratio} = \frac{\text{Quick Assets}}{\text{Current Liabilities}}$$

$$\frac{\$102,000 + \$48,000 + \$120,000}{\$300,000} = 0.9$$

b.   Unfortunately, the working capital, current ratio, and quick ratio are below the minimum threshold required by the bond indenture. This may require the company to renegotiate the bond contract, including a possible unfavorable change in the interest rate.

Ex. 17–9

a. (1)   Accounts Receivable Turnover $=\dfrac{\text{Net Sales}}{\text{Average Accounts Receivable}}$

2014: $\dfrac{\$3,412,500}{\$487,500^{*}} = 7.0$ 2013: $\dfrac{\$2,836,500}{\$457,500^{**}} = 6.2$

*$487,500 = ($475,000 + $500,000) ÷ 2   **$457,500 = ($440,000 + $475,000) ÷ 2

(2)   Number of Days' Sales in Receivables $=\dfrac{\text{Average Accounts Receivable}}{\text{Average Daily Sales}}$

2014: $\dfrac{\$487,500^{1}}{\$9,349^{2}} = 52.1$ days   2013: $\dfrac{\$457,500^{3}}{\$7,771^{4}} = 58.9$ days

[1] $487,500 = ($475,000 + $500,000) ÷ 2
[2] $9,349 = $3,412,500 ÷ 365 days
[3] $457,500 = ($440,000 + $475,000) ÷ 2
[4] $7,771 = $2,836,500 ÷ 365 days

b.   The collection of accounts receivable has improved. This can be seen in both the increase in accounts receivable turnover and the reduction in the collection period. The credit terms require payment in 55 days. In 2013, the collection period exceeded these terms. However, the company apparently became more aggressive in collecting accounts receivable or more restrictive in granting credit to customers. Thus, in 2014, the collection period is within the credit terms of the company.

Ex. 17–10

a. (1)   Accounts Receivable Turnover $=$ $\dfrac{\text{Net Sales}}{\text{Average Accounts Receivable}}$

Xavier: $\dfrac{\$8,500,000}{(\$820,000 + \$880,000) \div 2}$ $=$ 10.0

Lestrade: $\dfrac{\$4,585,000}{(\$600,000 + \$710,000) \div 2}$ $=$ 7.0

(2)   Number of Days' Sales in Receivables $=$ $\dfrac{\text{Average Accounts Receivable}}{\text{Average Daily Sales}}$

Xavier: $\dfrac{(\$820,000 + \$880,000) \div 2}{\$23,287.7^{*}}$ $=$ 36.5 days

Lestrade: $\dfrac{(\$600,000 + \$710,000) \div 2}{\$12,561.6^{**}}$ $=$ 52.1 days

* $\$23,287.7 = \$8,500,000 \div 365 \text{ days}$
** $\$12,561.6 = \$4,585,000 \div 365 \text{ days}$

b. Xavier's accounts receivable turnover is much higher than Lestrade's (10.0 for Xavier vs. 7.0 for Lestrade). The number of days' sales in receivables is lower for Xavier than for Lestrade (36.5 days for Xavier vs. 52.1 days for Lestrade). These differences indicate that Xavier is able to turn over its receivables more quickly than Lestrade. As a result, it takes Xavier less time to collect its receivables.

Ex. 17–11

a. (1) $\text{Inventory Turnover} = \dfrac{\text{Cost of Goods Sold}}{\text{Average Inventory}}$

Current Year: $\dfrac{\$6,375,000}{(\$860,000 + \$840,000) \div 2} = 7.5$

Preceding Year: $\dfrac{\$7,380,000}{(\$840,000 + \$800,000) \div 2} = 9.0$

(2) $\text{Number of Days' Sales in Inventory} = \dfrac{\text{Average Inventory}}{\text{Average Daily Cost of Goods Sold}}$

Current Year: $\dfrac{(\$860,000 + \$840,000) \div 2}{\$17,466^{*}} = 48.7 \text{ days}$

Preceding Year: $\dfrac{(\$840,000 + \$800,000) \div 2}{\$20,219^{**}} = 40.6 \text{ days}$

* $\$17,466 = \$6,375,000 \div 365 \text{ days}$

** $\$20,219 = \$7,380,000 \div 365 \text{ days}$

b. The inventory position of the business has deteriorated. The inventory turnover has decreased, while the number of days' sales in inventory has increased. The sales volume has declined faster than the inventory has declined, thus resulting in the deteriorating inventory position.

Ex. 17–12

a. (1)   Inventory Turnover $= \dfrac{\text{Cost of Goods Sold}}{\text{Average Inventory}}$

Dell: $\dfrac{\$50,098}{(\$1,051 + \$1,301) \div 2} = 42.6$

HP: $\dfrac{\$96,089}{(\$6,128 + \$6,466) \div 2} = 15.3$

(2)   Number of Days' Sales in Inventory $= \dfrac{\text{Average Inventory}}{\text{Average Daily Cost of Goods Sold}}$

Dell: $\dfrac{(\$1,051 + \$1,301) \div 2}{\$137.3^{*}} = 8.6 \text{ days}$

HP: $\dfrac{(\$6,128 + \$6,466) \div 2}{\$263.3^{**}}$ 23.9 days

* $\$137.3 = \$50,098 \div 365 \text{ days}$
** $\$263.3 = \$96,089 \div 365 \text{ days}$

b.   Dell has a much higher inventory turnover ratio than does HP (42.6 vs. 15.3). Likewise, Dell has a much smaller number of days' sales in inventory (8.6 days vs. 23.9 days). These significant differences are a result of Dell's make-to-order strategy. Dell has successfully developed a manufacturing process that is able to fill a customer order quickly. As a result, Dell does not pre-build as many computers to inventory. HP, in contrast, pre-builds computers, printers, and other equipment to be sold by retail stores and other retail channels. In this industry, there is great obsolescence risk in holding computers in inventory. New technology can make an inventory of computers difficult to sell; therefore, inventory is costly and risky. Dell's operating strategy is considered revolutionary and is now being adopted by many both in and out of the computer industry.

Ex. 17–13

a.   Ratio of Liabilities to Stockholders' Equity $=$ $\dfrac{\text{Total Liabilities}}{\text{Total Stockholders' Equity}}$

Dec. 31, 2014: $\dfrac{\$2,124,000}{\$2,360,000}$ $=$ 0.9

Dec. 31, 2013: $\dfrac{\$2,200,000}{\$2,000,000}$ $=$ 1.1

b. $\dfrac{\text{Number of Times Bond}}{\text{Interest Charges Are Earned}}$ $=$ $\dfrac{\text{Income Before Income Tax + Interest Expense}}{\text{Interest Expense}}$

Dec. 31, 2014: $\dfrac{\$480,000 + \$120,000\ ^*}{\$120,000}$ $=$ 5.0

Dec. 31, 2013: $\dfrac{\$420,000 + \$140,000\ ^{**}}{\$140,000}$ $=$ 4.0

   *   ($1,000,000 + $200,000) × 10% = $120,000
   ** ($1,200,000 + $200,000) × 10% = $140,000

c.   Both the ratio of liabilities to stockholders' equity and the number of times bond interest charges were earned have improved from 2013 to 2014. These results are the combined result of a larger income before income taxes and lower serial bonds payable in the year 2014 compared to 2013.

Ex. 17–14

a.   **Ratio of Liabilities to Stockholders' Equity** $= \dfrac{\text{Total Liabilities}}{\text{Total Stockholders' Equity}}$

Hasbro: $\dfrac{\$2,477,806}{\$1,615,420} = 1.5$

Mattel, Inc.: $\dfrac{\$2,789,149}{\$2,628,584} = 1.1$

b. $\dfrac{\text{Number of Times}}{\text{Interest Charges Are Earned}} = \dfrac{\text{Income Before Income Tax + Interest Expense}}{\text{Interest Expense}}$

Hasbro: $\dfrac{\$397,752 + \$82,112}{\$82,112} = 5.8$

Mattel, Inc.: $\dfrac{\$684,863 + \$64,839}{\$64,839} = 11.6$

c.   Both companies carry a moderate proportion of debt to the stockholders' equity, with Hasbro carrying slightly more debt than Mattel (1.5 and 1.1 times stockholders' equity). Therefore, the companies' debt as a percent of stockholders' equity is similar. Both companies also have very strong interest coverage; however, Mattel's ratio is stronger than Hasbro's. Together, these ratios indicate that both companies provide creditors with a margin of safety, and that earnings appear more than enough to make interest payments.

Ex. 17–15

a.

$$\text{Ratio of Liabilities to Stockholders' Equity} = \frac{\text{Total Liabilities}}{\text{Total Stockholders' Equity}}$$

H.J. Heinz: $\dfrac{\$4,161,460 + \$3,078,128 + \$1,757,426}{\$3,108,962} = 2.9$

Hershey: $\dfrac{\$1,298,845 + \$1,541,825 + \$529,746}{\$902,316} = 3.7$

b.

$$\text{Ratio of Fixed Assets to Long-Term Liabilities} = \frac{\text{Fixed Assets (net)}}{\text{Long-Term Liabilities}}$$

H.J. Heinz: $\dfrac{\$2,505,083}{\$4,835,554} = 0.5$

Hershey: $\dfrac{\$1,437,702}{\$2,071,571} = 0.7$

c.   Hershey uses more debt than does H.J. Heinz. As a result, Hershey's total liabilities to stockholders' equity ratio is higher than H.J. Heinz's (3.7 vs. 2.9). H.J. Heinz has a lower ratio of fixed assets to long-term liabilities than Hershey. This ratio divides the property, plant, and equipment (net) by the long-term debt. The ratio for H.J. Heinz is aggressive, with fixed assets covering only 50% of the long-term debt. That is, the creditors of H.J. Heinz have 50 cents of property, plant, and equipment covering every dollar of long-term debt. The same ratio for Hershey shows fixed assets covering 70% of the long-term debt. That is, Hershey's creditors have $0.70 of property, plant, and equipment covering every dollar of long-term debt. This would suggest that Hershey has slightly stronger creditor protection and borrowing capacity than does H.J. Heinz.

Ex. 17–16

a. $\text{Ratio of Net Sales to Total Assets} = \dfrac{\text{Net Sales}}{\text{Average Total Assets}}$

$$\text{YRC Worldwide:} \quad \dfrac{\$4,334,640}{\$2,812,504} = 1.5$$

$$\text{Union Pacific:} \quad \dfrac{\$16,965,000}{\$42,636,000} = 0.4$$

$$\text{C.H. Robinson Worldwide Inc.:} \quad \dfrac{\$9,274,305}{\$1,914,974} = 4.8$$

b.   The ratio of net sales to assets measures the number of sales dollars earned for each dollar of assets. The greater the number of sales dollars earned for every dollar of assets, the more efficient a firm is in using assets. Thus, the ratio is a measure of the efficiency in using assets. The three companies are different in their efficiency in using assets, because they are different in the nature of their operations. Union Pacific earns only 40 cents for every dollar of assets. This is because Union Pacific is very asset intensive. That is, Union Pacific must invest in locomotives, railcars, terminals, tracks, right-of-way, and information systems in order to earn revenues. These investments are significant. YRC Worldwide is able to earn $1.50 for every dollar of assets, and thus is able to earn more revenue for every dollar of assets than does the railroad. This is because the motor carrier invests in trucks, trailers, and terminals, which require less investment per dollar of revenue than does the railroad. Moreover, the motor carrier does not invest in the highway system, because the government owns the highway system. Thus, the motor carrier has no investment in the transportation network itself, unlike the railroad. C.H. Robinson Worldwide Inc., the transportation arranger, hires transportation services from motor carriers and railroads, but does not own these assets itself. The transportation arranger has assets in accounts receivable and information systems but does not require transportation assets; thus, it is able to earn the highest revenue per dollar of assets.

Note to Instructors: Students may wonder how asset-intensive companies overcome their asset efficiency disadvantages to competitors with better asset efficiencies, as in the case between railroads and motor carriers. Asset efficiency is part of the financial equation; the other part is the profit margin made on each dollar of sales. Thus, companies with high asset efficiency often operate on thinner margins than do companies with lower asset efficiency. For example, the motor carrier must pay highway taxes, which lowers its operating margins when compared to railroads that own their right-of-way, and thus do not have the tax expense of the highway. While not required in this exercise, the railroad has the highest profit margins, the motor carrier is in the middle, while the transportation arranger operates on very thin margins.

Ex. 17–17

a.   **Rate Earned on Total Assets** $=$ $\dfrac{\text{Net Income + Interest Expense}}{\text{Average Total Assets}}$

2014: $\dfrac{\$372,000 + \$180,000^{1}}{\$4,600,000^{2}}$ $=$ **12.0%**

2013: $\dfrac{\$492,000 + \$180,000^{3}}{\$4,200,000^{4}}$ $=$ **16.0%**

[1] $2,250,000 × 8%

[2] ($4,800,000 + $4,400,000) ÷ 2

[3] $2,250,000 × 8%

[4] ($4,400,000 + $4,000,000) ÷ 2

Rate Earned on Stockholders' Equity $=$ $\dfrac{\text{Net Income}}{\text{Average Total Stockholders' Equity}}$

2014: $\dfrac{\$372,000}{\$2,148,000\ *}$ $=$ **17.3%**

2013: $\dfrac{\$492,000}{\$1,736,000\ **}$ $=$ **28.3%**

* ($2,324,000 + $1,972,000) ÷ 2

** ($1,972,000 + $1,500,000) ÷ 2

Rate Earned on Common Stockholders' Equity $=$ $\dfrac{\text{Net Income − Preferred Dividends}}{\text{Average Common Stockholders' Equity}}$

2014: $\dfrac{\$372,000 - \$20,000^{1}}{\$1,648,000^{2}}$ $=$ **21.4%**

2013: $\dfrac{\$492,000 - \$20,000^{3}}{\$1,236,000^{4}}$ $=$ **38.2%**

[1] $500,000 × 4%

[2] ($1,824,000 + $1,472,000) ÷ 2

[3] $500,000 × 4%

[4] ($1,472,000 + $1,000,000) ÷ 2

b.   **The profitability ratios indicate that Robinson Inc.'s profitability has deteriorated. Most of this change is from net income falling from $492,000 in 2013 to $372,000 in 2014. Since the rate of return on assets exceeds this amount in both years, there is positive leverage from the use of debt. However, this leverage is greater in 2013 because the rate of return on assets exceeds the cost of debt by a greater amount in 2013.**

17-24

Ex. 17–18

a.   Rate Earned on Total Assets $= \dfrac{\text{Net Income + Interest Expense}}{\text{Average Total Assets}}$

Fiscal Year 3: $\dfrac{\$567,600 + \$18,300}{(\$4,981,100 + \$4,648,900) \div 2} = 12.2\%$

Fiscal Year 2: $\dfrac{\$479,500 + \$22,200}{(\$4,648,900 + \$4,356,500) \div 2} = 11.1\%$

b.   Rate Earned on Stockholders' Equity $= \dfrac{\text{Net Income}}{\text{Average Total Stockholders' Equity}}$

Fiscal Year 3: $\dfrac{\$567,600}{(\$3,304,700 + \$3,116,600) \div 2} = 17.7\%$

Fiscal Year 2: $\dfrac{\$479,500}{(\$3,116,600 + \$2,735,100) \div 2} = 16.4\%$

c.   Both the rate earned on total assets and the rate earned on stockholders' equity have increased over the two-year period. The rate earned on total assets increased from 11.1% to 12.2%, and the rate earned on stockholders' equity increased from 16.4% to 17.7%. The rate earned on stockholders' equity exceeds the rate earned on total assets due to the positive use of leverage.

d.   During fiscal Year 3, Polo Ralph Lauren's results were strong compared to the industry average. The rate earned on total assets for Polo Ralph Lauren was more than the industry average (12.2% vs. 8.0%). The rate earned on stockholders' equity was more than the industry average (17.7% vs. 10.0%). These relationships suggest that Polo Ralph Lauren has more leverage than the industry, on average.

Ex. 17–19

a.
$$\text{Ratio of Fixed Assets to Long-Term Liabilities} = \frac{\text{Fixed Assets (net)}}{\text{Long-Term Liabilities}}$$

$$\frac{\$3,200,000}{\$2,000,000} = 1.6$$

b.
$$\text{Ratio of Liabilities to Stockholders' Equity} = \frac{\text{Total Liabilities}}{\text{Total Stockholders' Equity}}$$

$$\frac{\$3,000,000}{\$5,000,000} = 0.6$$

c.
$$\text{Ratio of Net Sales to Assets} = \frac{\text{Net Sales}}{\text{Average Total Assets (excluding long-term investments)}}$$

$$\frac{\$18,900,000}{\$4,500,000 \ *} = 4.2$$

* [($7,000,000 + $8,000,000) ÷ 2] – $3,000,000. The end-of-period total assets are equal to the sum of total liabilities ($3,000,000) and stockholders' equity ($5,000,000).

d.
$$\text{Rate Earned on Total Assets} = \frac{\text{Net Income + Interest Expense}}{\text{Average Total Assets}}$$

$$\frac{\$930,000 + \$120,000^*}{\$7,500,000^{**}} = 14.0\%$$

* $2,000,000 × 6%

** ($7,000,000 + $8,000,000) ÷ 2

e.
$$\text{Rate Earned on Stockholders' Equity} = \frac{\text{Net Income}}{\text{Average Total Stockholders' Equity}}$$

$$\frac{\$930,000}{\$4,785,000^*} = 19.4\%$$

* [($1,570,000 + $2,000,000 + $1,000,000) + $5,000,000] ÷ 2

f.
$$\text{Rate Earned on Common Stockholders' Equity} = \frac{\text{Net Income – Preferred Dividends}}{\text{Average Common Stockholders' Equity}}$$

$$\frac{\$930,000 - \$100,000 \ ^*}{\$3,785,000^{**}} = 21.9\%$$

* ($1,000,000 ÷ $100) × $10

** [($2,000,000 + $1,570,000) + ($2,000,000 + $2,000,000)] ÷ 2

17-26

Ex. 17–20

a. $$\text{Number of Times Bond Interest Charges Are Earned} = \frac{\text{Income Before Income Tax} + \text{Interest Expense}}{\text{Interest Expense}}$$

$$\frac{\$3,000,000 + \$400,000 \;^{*}}{\$400,000} = 8.5 \text{ times}$$

* $5,000,000 bonds payable × 8%

b. $$\text{Number of Times Preferred Dividends Are Earned} = \frac{\text{Net Income}}{\text{Preferred Dividends}}$$

$$\frac{\$1,800,000^{*}}{\$200,000^{**}} = 9.0 \text{ times}$$

* $3,000,000 income before income tax – $1,200,000 income taxes
** ($2,500,000 ÷ $50 par value per share) × $4

c. $$\text{Earnings per Share on Common Stock} = \frac{\text{Net Income} - \text{Preferred Dividends}}{\text{Common Stock Outstanding}}$$

$$\frac{\$1,800,000 - \$200,000}{500,000 \text{ shares}} = \$3.20$$

d. $$\text{Price-Earnings Ratio} = \frac{\text{Market Price per Share of Common Stock}}{\text{Earnings per Share}}$$

$$\frac{\$32.00}{\$3.20} = 10.0$$

e. $$\text{Dividends per Share of Common Stock} = \frac{\text{Dividends on Common Stock}}{\text{Shares of Common Stock Outstanding}}$$

$$\frac{\$1,200,000}{500,000 \text{ shares}^{*}} = \$2.40$$

* $5,000,000 ÷ $10 par value per share

f. $$\text{Dividend Yield} = \frac{\text{Dividends per Share of Common Stock}}{\text{Market Price per Share of Common Stock}}$$

$$\frac{\$2.40}{\$32.00} = 7.5\%$$

Ex. 17–21

a.

$$\text{Earnings per Share} = \frac{\text{Net Income} - \text{Preferred Dividends}}{\text{Shares of Common Stock Outstanding}}$$

$$\frac{\$1,750,000 - \$250,000^*}{500,000^{**} \text{ shares}} = \$3.00$$

* ($2,500,000 ÷ $40) × $4
** $10,000,000 ÷ $20

b.

$$\text{Price-Earnings Ratio} = \frac{\text{Market Price per Share of Common Stock}}{\text{Earnings per Share of Common Stock}}$$

$$\frac{\$45.00}{\$3.00} = 15.0$$

c.

$$\text{Dividends per Share} = \frac{\text{Common Dividends}}{\text{Shares of Common Stock Outstanding}}$$

$$\frac{\$1,125,000}{500,000 \text{ shares}} = \$2.25$$

d.

$$\text{Dividend Yield} = \frac{\text{Dividends per Share of Common Stock}}{\text{Market Price per Share of Common Stock}}$$

$$\frac{\$2.25}{\$45.00} = 5.0\%$$

Ex. 17–22

a.

$$\text{Price-Earnings Ratio} = \frac{\text{Market Price per Share of Common Stock}}{\text{Earnings per Share}}$$

Deere & Co.: $\dfrac{\$65.70}{\$4.40} = 14.9$

Google: $\dfrac{\$528.33}{\$27.72} = 19.1$

The Coca-Cola Company: $\dfrac{\$69.05}{\$5.37} = 12.9$

$$\text{Dividend Yield} = \frac{\text{Dividends per Share of Common Stock}}{\text{Market Price per Share of Common Stock}}$$

Deere & Co.: $\dfrac{\$1.16}{\$65.70} = 1.8\%$

Google: $\dfrac{\$0.00}{\$528.33} = 0.0\%$

The Coca-Cola Company: $\dfrac{\$1.88}{\$69.05} = 2.7\%$

b. Coca-Cola has a large dividend yield, but the smallest price-earnings ratio. Stock market participants value Coca-Cola common stock on the basis of its dividend. The dividend is an attractive yield at this date. Because of this attractive yield, stock market participants do not expect the share price to grow significantly, hence the low price-earnings valuation. This is a typical pattern for companies that pay high dividends. Google shows the opposite extreme. Google pays no dividend, and thus has no dividend yield. However, Google has the largest price-earnings ratio of the three companies. Stock market participants are expecting a return on their investment from appreciation in the stock price. Deere & Co. is priced in between the other two companies. Deere & Co has a moderate dividend, producing a yield of 1.8%. The price-earnings ratio is 14.9. Thus, Deere & Co. is expected to produce shareholder returns through a combination of some share price appreciation and a moderate dividend.

Appendix Ex. 17–23

a. **Earnings per share on income before extraordinary items:**

Net income..	$4,000,000
Less gain on condemnation....................................	(800,000)
Plus loss from flood damage..................................	400,000
Income before extraordinary items.........................	$3,600,000

$$\text{Earnings Before Extraordinary Items per Share on Common Stock} = \frac{\text{Income Before Extraordinary Items} - \text{Preferred Dividends}}{\text{Shares of Common Stock Outstanding}}$$

$$\frac{\$3,600,000 - \$200,000 \,^*}{500,000 \text{ shares}} = \$6.80 \text{ per share}$$

* 100,000 shares × $2.00 per share

b. $$\text{Earnings per Share on Common Stock} = \frac{\text{Net Income} - \text{Preferred Dividends}}{\text{Shares of Common Stock Outstanding}}$$

$$\frac{\$4,000,000 - \$200,000}{500,000 \text{ shares}} = \$7.60 \text{ per share}$$

Appendix Ex. 17–24

a. NR

b. E

c. E

d. NR

e. NR

f. NR

g. NR

Appendix Ex. 17–25

a.

CRUZ, INC. Partial Income Statement For the Year Ended December 31, 2014	
Income from continuing operations before income tax	$1,000,000
Income tax expense*	400,000
Income from continuing operations	$ 600,000
Loss on discontinued operations	240,000
Income before extraordinary item	$ 360,000
Extraordinary item:	
Loss due to hurricane	140,000
Net income	$ 220,000

* $1,000,000 × 40%

b.

CRUZ, INC. Partial Income Statement For the Year Ended December 31, 2014	
Earnings per common share:	
Income from continuing operations	$30.00[1]
Loss from discontinued operations	12.00[2]
Income before extraordinary item	$18.00
Extraordinary item:	
Loss due to hurricane	7.00[3]
Net income	$11.00

[1] $30.00 = $600,000 ÷ 20,000

[2] $12.00 = $240,000 ÷ 20,000

[3] $7.00 = $140,000 ÷ 20,000

Appendix Ex. 17–26

a. Colston Company reported this item correctly in the financial statements. This item is an error in the recognition, measurement, or presentation in the financial statements, which is correctly handled by retroactively restating prior-period earnings.

b. Colston Company did not report this item correctly. This item is a change from one generally accepted accounting principle to another, which is correctly handled by retroactively restating prior-period earnings. In this case, Colston reports this change cumulatively in the current period, which is incorrect.

PROBLEMS

Prob. 17–1A

1.

LINDELL COMPANY Comparative Income Statement For the Years Ended December 31, 2014 and 2013				
			Increase (Decrease)	
	2014	2013	Amount	Percent
Sales	$1,092,500	$950,000	$142,500	15.0%
Sales returns and allowances	57,500	50,000	7,500	15.0%
Net sales	$1,035,000	$900,000	$135,000	15.0%
Cost of goods sold	625,000	500,000	125,000	25.0%
Gross profit	$ 410,000	$400,000	$ 10,000	2.5%
Selling expenses	153,600	120,000	33,600	28.0%
Administrative expenses	97,600	80,000	17,600	22.0%
Total operating expenses	$ 251,200	$200,000	$ 51,200	25.6%
Income from operations	$ 158,800	200,000	$ (41,200)	–20.6%
Other income	15,000	10,000	5,000	50.0%
Income before income tax	$ 173,800	$210,000	$ (36,200)	–17.2%
Income tax expense	23,000	20,000	3,000	15.0%
Net income	$ 150,800	$190,000	$ (39,200)	–20.6%

2.   Net income has declined from 2013 to 2014. Net sales have increased by 15.0%; however, the cost of goods sold has increased by 25.0%, causing the gross profit to increase at a slower pace than net sales. In addition, total operating expenses have increased at a faster rate than sales (25.6% increase vs. 15.0% net sales increase). Increases in costs and expenses that are higher than the increase in sales have caused the net income to decline by 20.6%.

Prob. 17–2A

1.

KASAY COMPANY Comparative Income Statement For the Years Ended December 31, 2014 and 2013				
	2014		2013	
	Amount	Percent	Amount	Percent
Sales	$922,500	102.5%	$820,000	102.5%
Sales returns and allowances	22,500	2.5%	20,000	2.5%
Net sales	$900,000	100.0%	$800,000	100.0%
Cost of goods sold	360,000	40.0%	340,000	42.5%
Gross profit	$540,000	60.0%	$460,000	57.5%
Selling expenses	216,000	24.0%	176,000	22.0%
Administrative expenses	81,000	9.0%	72,000	9.0%
Total operating expenses	$297,000	33.0%	$248,000	31.0%
Income from operations	$243,000	27.0%	$212,000	26.5%
Other income	135,000	15.0%	92,000	11.5%
Income before income tax	$378,000	42.0%	$304,000	38.0%
Income tax expense	270,000	30.0%	240,000	30.0%
Net income	$108,000	12.0%	$ 64,000	8.0%

2. The vertical analysis indicates that the costs other than selling expenses (cost of goods sold and administrative expenses) improved as a percentage of sales. As a result, net income as a percentage of sales increased from 8.0% to 12.0%. The sales promotion campaign appears to have been successful. While selling expenses as a percent of sales increased slightly (2.0%), the increased cost was more than made up for by increased sales.

Prob. 17–3A

1. a.   Working Capital = Current Assets – Current Liabilities

$1,650,000 – $750,000 = $900,000

b. $$\text{Current Ratio} = \frac{\text{Current Assets}}{\text{Current Liabilities}}$$

$$\frac{\$1,650,000}{\$750,000} = 2.2$$

c. $$\text{Quick Ratio} = \frac{\text{Quick Assets}}{\text{Current Liabilities}}$$

$$\frac{\$412,500 + \$187,500 + \$300,000}{\$750,000} = 1.2$$

2.

Transaction	Working Capital	Current Ratio	Quick Ratio	Supporting Data		
				Current Assets	Quick Assets	Current Liabilities
a.	$ 900,000	2.2	1.2	$1,650,000	$ 900,000	$750,000
b.	900,000	2.4	1.2	1,525,000	775,000	625,000
c.	900,000	2.0	1.0	1,760,000	900,000	860,000
d.	900,000	2.4	1.2	1,550,000	800,000	650,000
e.	750,000	1.8	1.0	1,650,000	900,000	900,000
f.	900,000	2.2	1.2	1,650,000	900,000	750,000
g.	1,125,000	2.5	1.5	1,875,000	1,125,000	750,000
h.	900,000	2.2	1.2	1,650,000	900,000	750,000
i.	1,500,000	3.0	2.0	2,250,000	1,500,000	750,000
j.	900,000	2.2	1.2	1,650,000	890,000	750,000

Prob. 17–4A

1. Working Capital: $1,100,000 – $440,000 = $660,000

Ratio	Numerator	Denominator	Calculated Value
2. Current ratio	$1,100,000	$440,000	2.5
3. Quick ratio	$880,000	$440,000	2.0
4. Accounts receivable turnover	$1,200,000	($130,000 + $110,000) ÷ 2	10.0
5. Number of days' sales in receivables	($130,000 + $110,000) ÷ 2	$1,200,000 ÷ 365	36.5
6. Inventory turnover	$500,000	($67,000 + $58,000) ÷ 2	8.0
7. Number of days' sales in inventory	($67,000 + $58,000) ÷ 2	$500,000 ÷ 365	45.6
8. Ratio of fixed assets to long-term liabilities	$1,320,000	$1,100,000	1.2
9. Ratio of liabilities to stockholders' equity	$1,540,000	$3,230,000	0.5
10. Number of times interest charges are earned	$380,000 + $66,000	$66,000	6.8
11. Number of times preferred dividends are earned	$300,000	$15,000	20.0
12. Ratio of net sales to assets	$1,200,000	($2,420,000 + $2,155,000) ÷ 2	0.5 or 52.5%
13. Rate earned on total assets	$300,000 + $66,000	($4,770,000 + $4,355,000) ÷ 2	8.0%
14. Rate earned on stockholders' equity	$300,000	($3,230,000 + $2,955,000) ÷ 2	9.7%
15. Rate earned on common stockholders' equity	$300,000 – $15,000	($3,030,000 + $2,755,000) ÷ 2	9.9%
16. Earnings per share on common stock	$300,000 – $15,000	10,000	$28.50
17. Price-earnings ratio	71.25	28.50	2.5
18. Dividends per share of common stock	$10,000	10,000	$1.00
19. Dividend yield	$1.00	$71.25	1.4%

Prob. 17–5A

1. a.

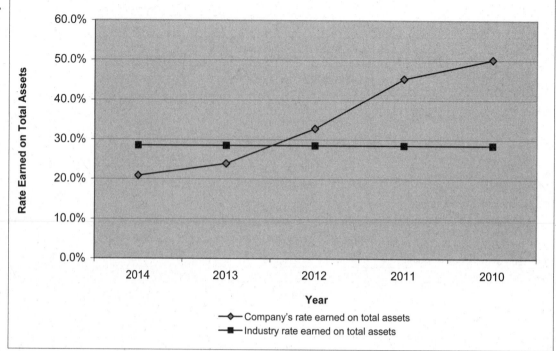

$$\text{Rate Earned on Total Assets} = \frac{\text{Net Income} + \text{Interest Expense}}{\text{Average Total Assets}}$$

2014: $\dfrac{\$889,453}{\$4,270,764} = 20.8\%$ 2011: $\dfrac{\$1,379,000}{\$3,044,250} = 45.3\%$

2013: $\dfrac{\$939,979}{\$3,928,396} = 23.9\%$ 2010: $\dfrac{\$1,240,000}{\$2,475,000} = 50.1\%$

2012: $\dfrac{\$1,159,341}{\$3,535,472} = 32.8\%$

Prob. 17–5A (Continued)

1. b.

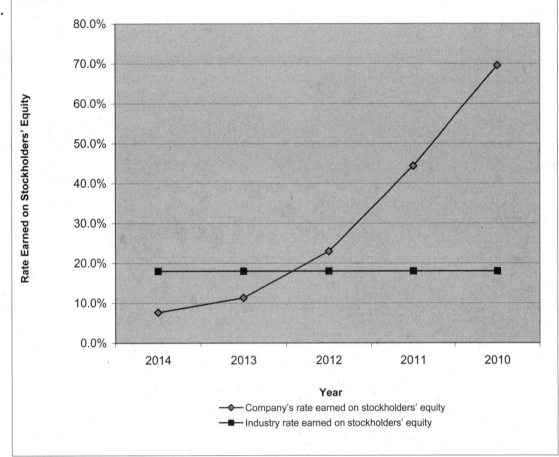

$$\text{Rate Earned on Stockholders' Equity} = \frac{\text{Net Income}}{\text{Average Total Stockholders' Equity}}$$

2014: $\dfrac{\$273,406}{\$3,569,855} = 7.7\%$ 2011: $\dfrac{\$884,000}{\$1,992,000} = 44.4\%$

2013: $\dfrac{\$367,976}{\$3,249,164} = 11.3\%$ 2010: $\dfrac{\$800,000}{\$1,150,000} = 69.6\%$

2012: $\dfrac{\$631,176}{\$2,749,588} = 23.0\%$

Prob. 17–5A (Continued)

1.   c.

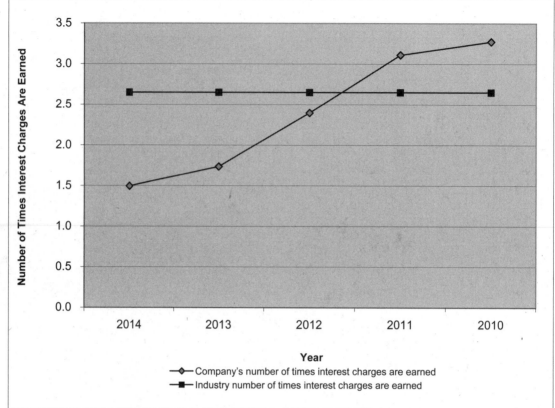

$$\text{Number of Times Interest Charges Are Earned} = \frac{\text{Net Income + Income Tax Expense + Interest Expense}}{\text{Interest Expense}}$$

2014: $\dfrac{\$921,202}{\$616,047} = 1.5$ 2011: $\dfrac{\$1,539,000}{\$495,000} = 3.1$

2013: $\dfrac{\$993,539}{\$572,003} = 1.7$ 2010: $\dfrac{\$1,440,000}{\$440,000} = 3.3$

2012: $\dfrac{\$1,266,061}{\$528,165} = 2.4$

Prob. 17–5A (Continued)

1. d.

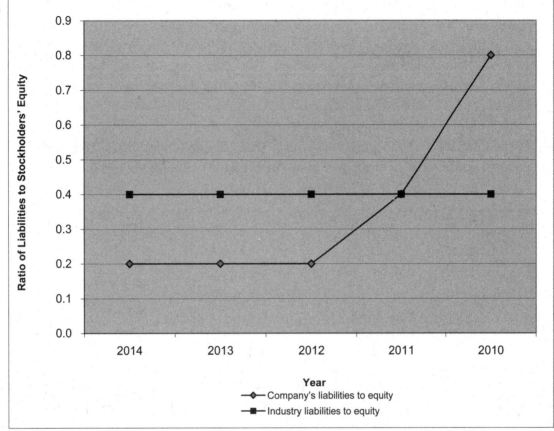

Ratio of Liabilities to Stockholders' Equity	=	Total Liabilities
		Total Stockholders' Equity

2014: $\dfrac{\$710,621}{\$3,706,557}$ = 0.2   2011: $\dfrac{\$904,500}{\$2,434,000}$ = 0.4

2013: $\dfrac{\$691,198}{\$3,433,152}$ = 0.2   2010: $\dfrac{\$1,200,000}{\$1,550,000}$ = 0.8

2012: $\dfrac{\$667,267}{\$3,065,176}$ = 0.2

Note: The total liabilities are the difference between the total assets and total stockholders' equity ending balances.

Prob. 17–5A (Concluded)

2. Both the rate earned on total assets and the rate earned on stockholders' equity have been moving in a negative direction in the last five years. Both measures have moved below the industry average over the last two years. The cause of this decline is driven by a rapid decline in earnings. The use of debt can be seen from the ratio of liabilities to stockholders' equity. The ratio has declined over the time period and has declined below the industry average. Thus, the level of debt relative to the stockholders' equity has gradually improved over the five years. The number of times interest charges were earned has been falling below the industry average for several years. This is the result of low profitability combined with high interest costs. The number of times interest is earned has fallen to a dangerously low level in 2014.

Prob. 17–1B

1.

MACKLIN INC. Comparative Income Statement For the Years Ended December 31, 2014 and 2013			Increase (Decrease)	
	2014	2013	Amount	Percent
Sales	$936,000	$720,000	$216,000	30.0%
Sales returns and allowances	26,000	20,000	6,000	30.0%
Net sales	$910,000	$700,000	$210,000	30.0%
Cost of goods sold	441,000	350,000	91,000	26.0%
Gross profit	$469,000	$350,000	$119,000	34.0%
Selling expenses	139,150	115,000	24,150	21.0%
Administrative expenses	99,450	85,000	14,450	17.0%
Total operating expenses	$238,600	$200,000	$ 38,600	19.3%
Income from operations	$230,400	$150,000	$ 80,400	53.6%
Other income	65,000	50,000	15,000	30.0%
Income before income tax	$295,400	$200,000	$ 95,400	47.7%
Income tax expense	65,000	50,000	15,000	30.0%
Net income	$230,400	$150,000	$ 80,400	53.6%

2.   The profitability has significantly improved from 2013 to 2014. Net sales have increased by 30% over the 2013 base year. However, the cost of goods sold, selling expenses, and administrative expenses grew at a slower rate. Increasing sales combined with costs that increase at a slower rate results in strong earnings growth. In this case, net income grew 53.6% over the base year.

Prob. 17–2B

1.

FIELDER INDUSTRIES INC. Comparative Income Statement For the Years Ended December 31, 2014 and 2013				
	2014		2013	
	Amount	Percent	Amount	Percent
Sales	$1,325,000	101.9%	$1,200,000	101.7%
Sales returns and allowances	25,000	1.9%	20,000	1.7%
Net sales	$1,300,000	100.0%	$1,180,000	100.0%
Cost of goods sold	682,500	52.5%	613,600	52.0%
Gross profit	$ 617,500	47.5%	$ 566,400	48.0%
Selling expenses	260,000	20.0%	188,800	16.0%
Administrative expenses	169,000	13.0%	177,000	15.0%
Total operating expenses	$ 429,000	33.0%	$ 365,800	31.0%
Income from operations	$ 188,500	14.5%	$ 200,600	17.0%
Other income	78,000	6.0%	70,800	6.0%
Income before income tax	$ 266,500	20.5%	$ 271,400	23.0%
Income tax expense	117,000	9.0%	106,200	9.0%
Net income	$ 149,500	11.5%	$ 165,200	14.0%

2.   The net income as a percent of sales has declined. All the costs and expenses, other than selling expenses, have maintained their approximate cost as a percent of sales relationship between 2013 and 2014. Selling expenses as a percent of sales, however, have grown from 16.0% to 20.0% of sales. Apparently, the new advertising campaign has not been successful. The increased expense has not produced sufficient sales to maintain relative profitability. Thus, selling expenses as a percent of sales have increased.

Prob. 17–3B

1. a.   **Working Capital = Current Assets – Current Liabilities**

$3,200,000 – $2,000,000 = $1,200,000

b. $$\text{Current Ratio} = \frac{\text{Current Assets}}{\text{Current Liabilities}}$$

$$\frac{\$3,200,000}{\$2,000,000} = 1.6$$

c. $$\text{Quick Ratio} = \frac{\text{Quick Assets}}{\text{Current Liabilities}}$$

$$\frac{\$800,000 + \$550,000 + \$850,000}{\$2,000,000} = 1.1$$

2.

				Supporting Data		
Transaction	Working Capital	Current Ratio	Quick Ratio	Current Assets	Quick Assets	Current Liabilities
a.	$1,200,000	1.6	1.1	$3,200,000	$2,200,000	$2,000,000
b.	1,200,000	1.7	1.1	2,912,500	1,912,500	1,712,500
c.	1,200,000	1.5	0.9	3,600,000	2,200,000	2,400,000
d.	1,200,000	1.6	1.1	3,075,000	2,075,000	1,875,000
e.	875,000	1.4	0.9	3,200,000	2,200,000	2,325,000
f.	1,200,000	1.6	1.1	3,200,000	2,200,000	2,000,000
g.	2,200,000	2.1	1.6	4,200,000	3,200,000	2,000,000
h.	1,200,000	1.6	1.1	3,200,000	2,200,000	2,000,000
i.	3,200,000	2.6	2.1	5,200,000	4,200,000	2,000,000
j.	1,200,000	1.6	1.0	3,200,000	2,000,000	2,000,000

Prob. 17–4B

1. Working Capital: $3,690,000 – $900,000 = $2,790,000

Ratio	Numerator	Denominator	Calculated Value
2. Current ratio	$3,690,000	$900,000	4.1
3. Quick ratio	$2,250,000	$900,000	2.5
4. Accounts receivable turnover	$10,000,000	($740,000 + $510,000) ÷ 2	16.0
5. Number of days' sales in receivables	($740,000 + $510,000) ÷ 2	$10,000,000 ÷ 365	22.8
6. Inventory turnover	$5,350,000	($1,190,000 + $950,000) ÷ 2	5.0
7. Number of days' sales in inventory	($1,190,000 + $950,000) ÷ 2	$5,350,000 ÷ 365	73.0
8. Ratio of fixed assets to long-term liabilities	$3,740,000	$1,700,000	2.2
9. Ratio of liabilities to stockholders' equity	$2,600,000	$7,180,000	0.4
10. Number of times interest charges are earned	$1,130,000 + $170,000	$170,000	7.6
11. Number of times preferred dividends are earned	$900,000	$45,000	20.0
12. Ratio of net sales to assets	10,000,000	($7,430,000 + $6,455,000) ÷ 2	1.4
13. Rate earned on total assets	$900,000 + $170,000	($9,780,000 + $8,755,000) ÷ 2	11.5%
14. Rate earned on stockholders' equity	$900,000	($7,180,000 + $6,375,000) ÷ 2	13.3%
15. Rate earned on common stockholders' equity	$900,000 – $45,000	($6,680,000 + $5,875,000) ÷ 2	13.6%
16. Earnings per share on common stock	$900,000 – $45,000	100,000	$8.55
17. Price-earnings ratio	119.70	8.55	14.0
18. Dividends per share of common stock	$50,000	100,000	$0.50
19. Dividend yield	$0.50	$119.70	0.4%

Prob. 17–5B

1. a.

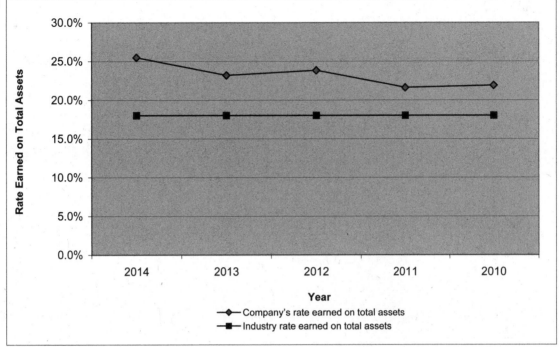

$$\text{Rate Earned on Total Assets} = \frac{\text{Net Income + Interest Expense}}{\text{Average Total Assets}}$$

2014: $\dfrac{\$6,623,780}{\$25,988,665}$ = 25.5%   2011: $\dfrac{\$2,458,000}{\$11,370,240}$ = 21.6%

2013: $\dfrac{\$4,606,056}{\$19,859,586}$ = 23.2%   2010: $\dfrac{\$1,900,000}{\$8,676,000}$ = 21.9%

2012: $\dfrac{\$3,540,600}{\$14,854,406}$ = 23.8%

17-45

Prob. 17–5B (Continued)

1.   b.

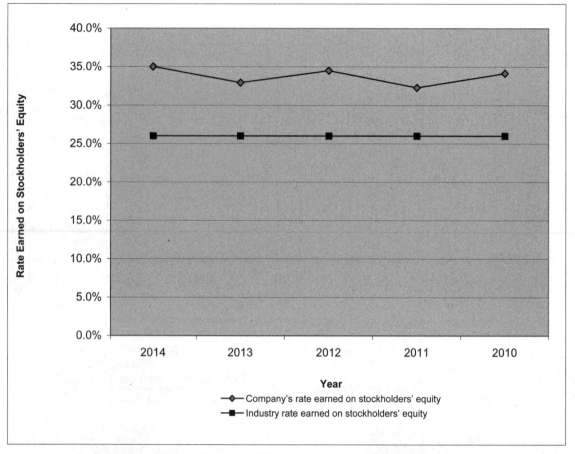

$$\begin{array}{c}\textbf{Rate Earned on}\\ \textbf{Stockholders' Equity}\end{array} = \frac{\textbf{Net Income}}{\textbf{Average Total Stockholders' Equity}}$$

2014: $\dfrac{\$5,571,720}{\$15,920,340}$ = 35.0%

2013: $\dfrac{\$3,714,480}{\$11,277,240}$ = 32.9%

2012: $\dfrac{\$2,772,000}{\$8,034,000}$ = 34.5%

2011: $\dfrac{\$1,848,000}{\$5,724,000}$ = 32.3%

2010: $\dfrac{\$1,400,000}{\$4,100,000}$ = 34.1%

Prob. 17–5B (Continued)

1. c.

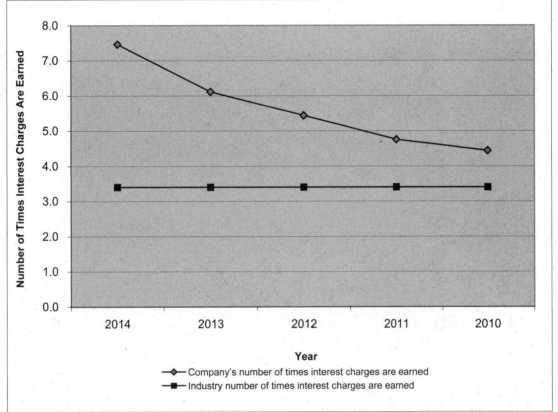

$$\frac{\text{Number of Times}}{\text{Interest Charges Are Earned}} = \frac{\text{Net Income + Income Tax Expense + Interest Expense}}{\text{Interest Expense}}$$

2014: $\dfrac{\$7,849,352}{\$1,052,060} = 7.5$ 2011: $\dfrac{\$2,899,600}{\$610,000} = 4.8$

2013: $\dfrac{\$5,451,278}{\$891,576} = 6.1$ 2010: $\dfrac{\$2,220,000}{\$500,000} = 4.4$

2012: $\dfrac{\$4,180,920}{\$768,600} = 5.4$

Prob. 17–5B (Continued)

1. d.

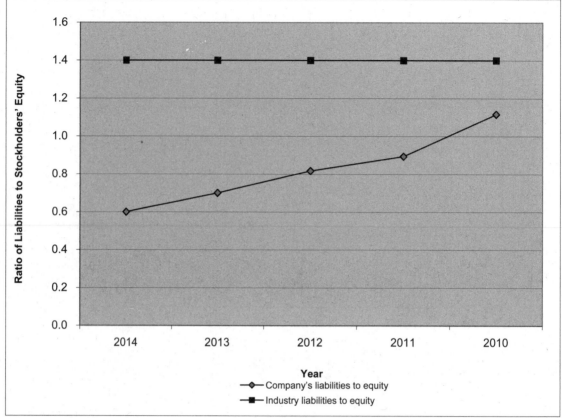

Ratio of Liabilities to Stockholders' Equity	=	Total Liabilities
		Total Stockholders' Equity

2014: $\dfrac{\$10,672,291}{\$18,706,200}$ = 0.6   2011: $\dfrac{\$5,940,480}{\$6,648,000}$ = 0.9

2013: $\dfrac{\$9,464,359}{\$13,134,480}$ = 0.7   2010: $\dfrac{\$5,352,000}{\$4,800,000}$ = 1.1

2012: $\dfrac{\$7,700,333}{\$9,420,000}$ = 0.8

Note: Total liabilities are determined by subtracting stockholders' equity (ending balance) from the total assets (ending balance).

Prob. 17–5B (Concluded)

2. Both the rate earned on total assets and the rate earned on stockholders' equity are above the industry average for all five years. The rate earned on total assets is actually improving gradually. The rate earned on stockholders' equity exceeds the rate earned on total assets, providing evidence of the positive use of leverage. The company is clearly growing earnings as fast as the asset and equity base. In addition, the ratio of liabilities to stockholders' equity indicates that the proportion of debt to stockholders' equity has been declining over the period. The firm is adding to debt at a slower rate than the assets are growing from earnings. The number of times interest charges were earned is improving during this time period. Again, the firm is increasing earnings faster than the increase in interest charges. Overall, these ratios indicate excellent financial performance coupled with appropriate use of debt (leverage).

NIKE, INC., PROBLEM

			Fiscal 2010	Fiscal 2009
1.	a.	Total current assets..................................	$11,297.0	$10,959.0
		Total current liabilities............................	3,958.0	3,364.0
		Working capital......................................	$ 7,339.0	$ 7,595.0
	b.	Total current assets..................................	$11,297.0	$10,959.0
		÷ Total current liabilities........................	3,958.0	3,364.0
		Current ratio..	2.9	3.3
	c.	Cash...	$ 1,955.0	$ 3,079.0
		Short-term investments...........................	2,583.0	2,067.0
		Accounts receivable...............................	3,138.0	2,650.0
		Total quick assets..................................	$ 7,676.0	$ 7,796.0
		÷ Total current liabilities........................	3,958.0	3,364.0
		Quick ratio..	1.9	2.3
	d.	Net sales..	$20,862.0	$19,014.0
		Accounts receivable (net):		
		Beginning of year................................	$ 2,650.0	$ 2,884.0
		End of year..	3,138.0	2,650.0
		Total..	$ 5,788.0	$ 5,534.0
		Average (Total ÷ 2)...............................	2,894.0	2,767.0
		Accounts receivable turnover		
		(Net sales ÷ Average accounts receivable)...........	7.2	6.9
	e.	Accounts receivable (average):		
		Net sales...	$20,862.0	$19,014.0
		Average daily sales (Sales ÷ 365)...................	57.2	52.1
		Number of days' sales in receivables..................	50.6	53.1
	f.	Cost of goods sold..................................	$11,354.0	$10,214.0
		Inventories:		
		Beginning of year................................	$ 2,041.0	$ 2,357.0
		End of year..	2,715.0	2,041.0
		Total..	$ 4,756.0	$ 4,398.0
		Average (Total ÷ 2)...............................	2,378.0	2,199.0
		Inventory turnover		
		(Cost of goods sold ÷ Average inventory)...........	4.8	4.6

NIKE, INC., PROBLEM (Continued)

		Fiscal 2010	Fiscal 2009
g.	Inventory (average)...	$ 2,378.0	$ 2,199.0
	Cost of goods sold...	11,354.0	10,214.0
	Average daily cost of goods sold................................	31.1	28.0
	Number of days' sales in inventory (Average inventory ÷ Average daily cost of goods sold)................	76.5	78.5
h.	Total liabilities..	$ 5,155.0	$ 4,665.0
	÷ Total stockholders' equity...	9,843.0	9,754.0
	Ratio of liabilities to stockholders' equity......................	0.5	0.5
i.	Net sales..	$20,862.0	$19,014.0
	Total assets (excluding long-term investments):		
	Beginning of year..	$14,419.0	$13,249.0
	End of year..	14,998.0	14,419.0
	Total..	$29,417.0	$27,668.0
	Average total assets...	14,708.5	13,834.0
	Ratio of net sales to assets..	1.4	1.4
j.	Net income...	$ 2,133.0	$ 1,907.0
	Plus interest expense*...	4.0	6.0
	Total..	$ 2,137.0	$ 1,913.0
	Total assets:		
	Beginning of year..	$14,419.0	$13,249.0
	End of year..	14,998.0	14,419.0
	Total..	$29,417.0	$27,668.0
	Average total assets...	14,708.5	13,834.0
	Rate earned on total assets [(Net income + Interest expense) ÷ Average total assets]..	14.5%	13.8%

* See Nike note 6

		Fiscal 2010	Fiscal 2009
k.	Net income...	$ 2,133.0	$ 1,907.0
	Stockholders' equity:		
	Beginning of year..	$ 9,754.0	$ 8,693.0
	End of year..	9,843.0	9,754.0
	Total..	$19,597.0	$18,447.0
	Average common stockholders' equity...........................	9,798.5	9,223.5
	Rate earned on common stockholders' equity...................	21.8%	20.7%
l.	Market price per share of common stock.........................	$75.70	$73.50
	Earnings per share on common stock.............................	4.48	3.93
	Price-earnings ratio...	16.9	18.7

NIKE, INC., PROBLEM (Concluded)

		Fiscal 2010	Fiscal 2009
m.	Net income...	$ 2,133.0	$ 1,907.0
	Net sales...	20,862.0	19,014.0
	Net income to net sales...........................	$　10.2%	$　10.0%

2. Before reaching definitive conclusions, each measure should be compared with past years, industry averages, and similar firms in the industry.

   a. The working capital decreased somewhat.

   b. and c. The current and quick ratios decreased during 2010.

   d. and e. The accounts receivable turnover and the number of days' sales in receivable indicate a slight increase in the efficiency of collecting accounts receivable. The accounts receivable turnover increased from 6.9 to 7.2. The number of days' sales in receivables decreased slightly from 53.1 to 50.6. Thus, it takes the company less than two months to collect its accounts receivable from credit sales. These numbers should be compared to their competitors, industry averages, and Nike's credit policy to draw definitive conclusions.

   f. and g. The results of these two analyses show a very slight increase in inventory turnover and a decrease in the number of days' sales in inventory. Both trends are small. Inventory management is critical to Nike, so this indicates a favorable trend.

   h. The margin of protection to creditors remained the same. Overall, Nike provides sound protection to its creditors.

   i. These analyses indicate that the effectiveness in the use of assets to generate revenues was very similar in both years.

   j. The rate earned on total assets increased during 2010. This increase was due to Nike's strong earnings performance in 2010 relative to 2009. Overall, rates earned on assets that exceed 10% are usually considered good performance.

   k. The rate earned on common stockholders' equity increased. This increase was due to Nike's strong earnings performance in 2010 relative to 2009.

   l. The price-earnings ratio decreased somewhat from 2010 to 2011. This decrease was driven by an increase in Nike's earnings per share (from $3.93 in fiscal 2009 to $4.48 in fiscal 2010) combined with a relatively small increase in stock price during the same period.

   m. The percent of net income to sales improved during 2010 as Nike's growth in earnings outpaced its growth in sales.

CASES & PROJECTS

CP 17–1

This position does not allow the shareholders to take advantage of leverage. As a result, the return on shareholders' equity cannot be improved by using debt. In contrast, a low or no debt load does provide the company great flexibility in the case of a national calamity. However, the "no debt" position only makes sense within the "national calamity" scenario. Within normal business operations, most companies can assume some debt without much loss of flexibility or control. Freeman Industries is competing against companies that will not be so inclined to avoid debt. As a result, they will likely be able to grow faster than Freeman Industries. The Freeman Industries management should consider the risk of not being able to keep up with the competition because of their conservative financing policies.

CP 17–2

Josh is concerned about the inventory and accounts receivable levels because he must determine their value. Inventory that cannot be sold (or sold at a large discount) or accounts receivable that cannot be collected must be written down to reflect their reduced value. Josh has conducted the ratio analysis and interviewed Aaron to help make this determination. The inventory and accounts receivable levels have grown alarmingly. Aaron's response to Josh is not reassuring. The inventory represents obsolete technology that is left over after the holiday season. The accounts receivable have apparently grown from loosening the credit standards. Josh may need to insist on write-downs of the inventory and accounts receivable balances to reflect their net realizable values. Aaron is correct in pointing out that the current ratio has probably improved. Thus, although Aaron calls this "good," it is only such if the current assets in the numerator are fairly valued. Under these circumstances, the current ratio is probably overstated because the inventory and accounts receivable balances are inflated relative to their net realizable values.

CP 17–3

DELL INC. AND APPLE INC. Common-Sized Statements		
	Dell Inc.	Apple Inc.
Sales (net)	100.0%	100.0%
Cost of sales	81.5%	60.6%
Gross profit	18.5%	39.4%
Operating expenses:		
Selling, general, and administrative	11.9%	8.5%
Research and development	1.1%	2.7%
Total operating expenses	13.0%	11.2%*
Income from operations	5.6%	28.2%

* Rounded to the nearest tenth of a percent.

The common-sized analysis indicates that Dell and Apple are very different computer companies. Dell's income from operations was 5.6% of sales, while Apple's was 28.2% of sales. There is almost a 23 percentage point difference between the two companies. What explains this difference? The gross profit for Dell was 18.5% of sales, which is fairly narrow. Apple, in contrast, had a gross profit of 39.4% of sales, which is over 20% better than Dell's. This suggests that Apple is able to charge higher prices than Dell for its products (assuming that they are both equally efficient in making products). Apple's selling, general, and administrative expenses were at about 8.5% of sales, while Dell's are 11.9% of sales. Apple has larger research expenses as a percent of sales. It attempts to sell a unique array of products to a wide audience. This requires significant research and development. Dell's R&D was a narrow 1.1% of sales, while Apple's was 2.7% of sales. Essentially, Dell focuses its R&D effort on the final assembly of computers. Dell relies on its suppliers to develop innovation in the components and operating system software (Microsoft). Apple, on the other hand, must constantly spend R&D on computers, peripherals, and its own operating system software. This is because Apple chooses not to follow the industry standards and thus must pave its own way on both hardware and software. The higher gross profit as a percentage of sales for Apple carries through to its income from operations, generating a significantly higher operating income as a percentage of sales compared to Dell.

CP 17–4

a. $$\text{Rate Earned on Total Assets} = \frac{\text{Net Income} + \text{Interest Expense}}{\text{Average Total Assets}}$$

Year 3: $\dfrac{\$1,865 + \$811}{\$42,200} = 6.3\%$

Year 2: $\dfrac{\$874 + \$1,042}{\$39,934} = 4.8\%$

Year 1: $\dfrac{\$2,053 + \$1,137}{\$38,655} = 8.3\%$

b. $$\text{Rate Earned on Total Stockholders' Equity} = \frac{\text{Net Income}}{\text{Average Total Stockholders' Equity}}$$

Year 3: $\dfrac{\$1,865}{\$5,555} = 33.6\%$

Year 2: $\dfrac{\$874}{\$5,676} = 15.4\%$

Year 1: $\dfrac{\$2,053}{\$6,844} = 30.0\%$

c. $$\text{Earnings per Share} = \frac{\text{Net Income} - \text{Preferred Dividends}}{\text{Shares of Common Stock Outstanding}}$$

Year 3: $\dfrac{\$1,865 - \$0}{424} = \$4.40$

Year 2: $\dfrac{\$874 - \$0}{423} = \$2.07$

Year 1: $\dfrac{\$2,053 - \$0}{431} = \$4.76$

CP 17–4 (Continued)

d. $$\text{Dividend Yield} = \frac{\text{Dividend per Share of Common Stock}}{\text{Market Price per Share of Common Stock}}$$

Year 3: $\dfrac{\$1.16}{\$60.95}$ = 1.9%

Year 2: $\dfrac{\$1.12}{\$47.06}$ = 2.4%

Year 1: $\dfrac{\$1.06}{\$58.01}$ = 1.8%

e. $$\text{Price-Earnings Ratio} = \frac{\text{Market Price per Share of Common Stock}}{\text{Earnings per Share}}$$

Year 3: $\dfrac{\$60.95}{\$4.40}$ = 13.9

Year 2: $\dfrac{\$47.06}{\$2.07}$ = 22.7

Year 1: $\dfrac{\$58.01}{\$4.76}$ = 12.2

2. $$\text{Ratio of Average Liabilities to Average Stockholders' Equity} = \frac{\text{Average Liabilities}}{\text{Average Stockholders' Equity}}$$

Year 3: $\dfrac{\$42,200 - \$5,555}{\$5,555}$ = 6.6

CP 17–4 (Concluded)

3. Deere & Co.'s profitability, as measured by earnings per share, has fluctuated significantly during the three-year period presented. The rates earned on total assets and total stockholders' equity have also fluctuated significantly during this period. This is most likely due to the significant deterioration in the overall economy, as well as in the construction industry, which was primarily concentrated during Year 2. The rebound in these metrics in Year 3 can be attributed to improved capital equipment spending, and a jump in commodity prices that fueled increases in the sales of farm equipment. The dividend yield and the price-earnings ratio increased significantly in Year 2 due to a large drop in the company's stock price, which was likely due to the drop in earnings per share during Year 2. The share price returned to the Year 1 level by the end of fiscal Year 3, reducing the dividend yield and price-earnings ratio.

CP 17–5

1. a.   Rate Earned on Total Assets $= \dfrac{\text{Net Income + Interest Expense}}{\text{Average Total Assets}}$

Marriott: $\dfrac{\$458 + \$180}{\$8,458} = 7.5\%$

Hyatt: $\dfrac{\$66 + \$54}{\$7,199} = 1.7\%$

b.   Rate Earned on Stockholders' Equity $= \dfrac{\text{Net Income}}{\text{Average Total Stockholders' Equity}}$

Marriott: $\dfrac{\$458}{\$1,364} = 33.6\%$

Hyatt: $\dfrac{\$66}{\$5,067} = 1.3\%$

c.   Number of Times Interest Charges Are Earned $= \dfrac{\text{Income Before Income Tax + Interest Expense}}{\text{Interest Expense}}$

Marriott: $\dfrac{\$551 + \$180}{\$180} = 4.1$

Hyatt: $\dfrac{\$103 + \$54}{\$54} = 2.9$

d.   Ratio of Liabilities to Stockholders' Equity $= \dfrac{\text{Total Liabilities}}{\text{Total Stockholders' Equity}}$

Marriott: $\dfrac{\$7,398}{\$1,585} = 4.7$

Hyatt: $\dfrac{\$2,125}{\$5,118} = 0.4$

Summary Table:

	Marriott	Hyatt
Rate earned on total assets	7.5%	1.7%
Rate earned on stockholders' equity	33.6%	1.3%
Number of times interest charges are earned	4.1	2.9
Ratio of liabilities to stockholders' equity	4.7	0.4

CP 17–5 (Concluded)

2. Marriott has a higher rate earned on total assets (7.5% vs. 1.7%), and a higher rate on stockholders' equity (33.6% vs. 1.3%), compared to Hyatt. Hyatt's weaker performance relative to Marriott appears to be due to its weak earnings relative to its debt level. Hyatt has less leverage than Marriott. This is confirmed by the the ratio of liabilities to stockholders' equity, which shows the relative debt held by Marriott is 4.7 times stockholders' equity, compared to 0.4 time for Hyatt. The number of times interest charges are earned shows that Marriott covers its interest charges 4.1 times. The comparable number for Hyatt is 2.9, which is marginally sufficient. Hyatt is not covering the interest expense on its debt as well as Marriott, which is negatively affecting the rate earned on total assets and stockholders' equity. In summary, Hyatt's weak earnings and low debt levels are affecting the company's ability to earn returns for stockholders.

MORNIN' JOE INTERNATIONAL

DISCUSSION QUESTIONS

1.

U.S. GAAP Term	IFRS International Term
Statement of comprehensive income*	Statement of comprehensive income
Balance sheet	Statement of financial position
Interest expense	Finance costs
Net income	Profit for the year
Trading investments	Financial assets at fair value through profit or loss
Excess of issue price over par	Share premium
Examples: Accumulated other comprehensive income, treasury stock, unrealized gain (loss) on available-for-sale investments	Reserves
Notes payable	Loans
Wages and salaries payable, payroll taxes payable	Employee provisions

*Note: U.S. GAAP and IFRS have converged on the title and disclosure requirements for other comprehensive income items, such as Unrealized Gain (Loss) on Available-for-Sale Investments.

2. The *nature* of an expense is how the expense would naturally be recorded in a journal entry reflecting the economic benefit received for that expense. An example is wages expense. The *function* of an expense identifies the purpose of the expense, such as selling expense or administrative expense.

3. If an expense is classified by function on the income statement, then the natural classification must be disclosed in the footnotes. Both classifications cannot be comingled on the income statement.

4. Under U.S. practice, the term "provision" usually denotes an expense, as in provision for income taxes (income tax expense). International practice uses the term "provision" to denote a liability. Thus, an income tax provision would be income taxes payable.

5. First, under IFRS, LIFO is prohibited, whereas it is acceptable under U.S. GAAP. Second, in using a lower-of-cost-or-market valuation, IFRS define "market" as net realizable value. U.S. GAAP, in contrast, defines "market" as replacement cost in most circumstances.

6. A biological asset is an agricultural asset, such as a forest, a vineyard, a farm, or livestock. These assets must be separately identified and valued using fair value. They can be separately disclosed in a footnote.

7. IFRS allow property, plant, and equipment to be valued at either historical cost or fair value. This is in contrast to U.S. GAAP, which requires historical cost for property, plant, and equipment.

8. A share premium is an international term for "excess of issue price over par value."

9. A reserve under IFRS denotes an element of stockholders' equity. Most reserve items are accumulated other comprehensive income. An example would be the revaluation reserve for the accumulated unrealized gains and losses from plant and equipment revaluation or unrealized gain (loss) from available-for-sale investments. The term "reserve" typically denotes a liability in the United States, such as "reserve for restructuring."

10. Treasury stock need not be disclosed on an IFRS balance sheet as a separate line item. It may be included as a reduction within reserves or share premium. U.S. GAAP favors disclosure of treasury stock as a separate line item, often as the last item in the stockholders' equity section.

IFRS ACTIVITIES

IFRS Activity 1

a. Turnover is a European and British term for "Sales" or "Revenue." It is commonly the first line of the income statement.

b. The most striking aspect of this income statement is the lack of detail. The statement begins with "Turnover," and the second line is "Operating profit." None of the operating expenses that appear in a GAAP statement, including cost of goods sold, are shown on the statement. These items of expense are provided in the footnotes under both functional and natural classifications. There is wide latitude in the choice of subtotals and items included, or not included, in the income statement under IFRS. The items that are shown are financing costs and investment income, affiliate earnings, and unique charges and credits. These are required disclosures on the face of the statement. This income statement nearly represents the minimal disclosure allowed on the face of the statement under IFRS.

c. The subtotal for net finance costs is presented at the top of the column. This is a European presentation approach that would not be found in most U.S. financial statements. In U.S. financial statements, subtotals are at the bottom of the column.

IFRS Activity 2

a. The statement of financial position (balance sheet) of LVMH is clearly ordered differently than a U.S. company statement of financial position (balance sheet) would be. On the asset side of the statement of financial position prepared under IFRS (balance sheet), the non-current items are listed prior to the current items. Within the non-current items, intangible assets are listed first, followed by property, plant, and equipment. On Mornin' Joe's statement of financial position (balance sheet), the intangible assets are listed last, not first.

Within the current assets, the least liquid current assets are listed first. Thus, inventories are identified first, followed by accounts receivable and cash. On Mornin' Joe's statement of financial position (balance sheet), the current assets begin with cash, followed by accounts receivable and inventories.

IFRS Activity 2   (Concluded)

For LVMH, the equities are listed first on the liabilities and equity side of the statement of financial position (balance sheet). The liabilities are listed after the equities. The liabilities begin with non-current liabilities, followed by current liabilities. So again, the statement of financial position (balance sheet) is listing long-term elements first. On Mornin' Joe's statement of financial position (balance sheet), the liabilities precede the stockholders' equity, and the current liabilities precede the noncurrent liabilities.

In the stockholders' equity section of the statement of financial position for LVMH (balance sheet), treasury shares (treasury stock) are separately identified, but are not placed as the last line of the stockholders' equity section, as would be the case under U.S. GAAP.

Retained earnings do not appear to be separately identified on the LVMH statement. "Other reserves" clearly includes retained earnings, as can be determined by the size of the balance. The current period's "net profit, group share" (synonymous with net income under GAAP) is included as a separate line item in the stockholders' equity section, rather than being included in the ending balance of retained earnings.

b.

LVMH Term	Mornin' Joe U.S. GAAP Term
Statement of financial position	Balance sheet
Share capital	Common stock
Share premium	Excess of issue price over par
Other reserves	Retained earnings
Provisions	Accrued liabilities, such as wages and salaries payable

c. The revaluation reserve is the adjustment to stockholders' equity for accumulated unrealized gains and losses from changes in fair market value for selected assets, such as available-for-sale investments. This account is similar to "Unrealized gain (loss) on available-for-sale investments," which is discussed in the Investments chapter. However, under IFRS, fair market valuation is available for a wider selection of assets than under U.S. GAAP. For example, LVMH values its vineyards at fair value.

IFRS Activity 3

a and b.

	(1) FIFO less LIFO	(2) IFRS Net Income	(3) (FIFO less LIFO) Total Current Assets	(4) IFRS Net Income Col. (2) Reported Net Income
Exxon Mobil	$21,348	$30,143	36%	99%
Kroger	827	1,173	11%	105%
Ford Motor	865	4,686	3%	100%

c. Exxon Mobil has the largest difference between FIFO and LIFO inventory valuation as a percent of current assets. This is because Exxon Mobil has significant inventories of oil, gasoline, and other oil-related products in proportion to its current assets. In addition, the difference between FIFO and LIFO valuation is large because of the difference between the current price of oil and the historical average price for oil reflected in the LIFO inventory.

d. A change to IFRS would cause Kroger's net income to increase to 105% of its LIFO-reported net income. This is the largest relative impact among the three firms. Kroger's net income, as a percent of its inventory, is small. This is because the percent of net income to sales is smaller for Kroger than for the other two firms. Thus, the earnings impact of a change from LIFO to FIFO is large, relative to its reported net income.

e. In periods of rising prices, net income reported under LIFO would normally be less than as reported under FIFO. This is because LIFO matches current period costs with sales. If the net income reported under LIFO is greater than what would be reported under FIFO, then there are two possible explanations. First, the company experienced declining purchase prices during the period, relative to prior periods. Second, the company sold from (liquidated) inventory and, hence, matched older cost layers to revenues. Crude oil prices fluctuate; thus, Exxon Mobil may have operated in a period of declining crude oil prices during this reporting period, causing its LIFO net income to exceed FIFO net income. Ford reduced operations and liquidated inventory. Thus, it used old historical cost layers that were established at lower costs than current replacement cost. As Ford stated in its annual report:

At December 31, 2010, inventory quantities were reduced, resulting in a liquidation of LIFO inventory quantities carried at lower costs prevailing in prior years as compared with the cost of 2010 purchases, the effect of which decreased Automotive cost of sales by about $4 million.

APPENDIX B
REVERSING ENTRIES

Ex. B–1

a. (1) Sales Salaries Expense... 7,050

        Salaries Payable..   7,050

             Accrued salaries ($11,750 ÷ 5 days = $2,350;
             $2,350 × 3 days).

   (2) Accounts Receivable 51,300

        Fees Earned..   51,300

             Accrued fees earned.

b. (1) Salaries Payable 7,050

        Sales Salaries Expense   7,050

             Reversing entry.

   (2) Fees Earned 51,300

        Accounts Receivable   51,300

             Reversing entry.

Ex. B–2

a. (1) Wages Expense 13,200

        Wages Payable...   13,200

             Accrued wages ($66,000 ÷ 5 days).

   (2) Accounts Receivable 25,000

        Fees Earned..   25,000

             Accrued fees earned.

b. (1) Wages Payable 13,200

        Wages Expense..   13,200

             Reversing entry.

   (2) Fees Earned 25,000

        Accounts Receivable   25,000

             Reversing entry.

Ex. B–3

a. (1) Payment (last payday in year)

    (2) Adjusting (accrual of wages at end of year)

    (3) Closing

    (4) Reversing

    (5) Payment (first payday in following year)

b.			
(1)	Wages Expense	15,400	
	Cash		15,400
(2)	Wages Expense	9,250	
	Wages Payable		9,250
	Accrued wages.		
(3)	Income Summary	809,250	
	Wages Expense		809,250
(4)	Wages Payable	9,250	
	Wages Expense		9,250
	Reversing entry.		
(5)	Wages Expense	14,800	
	Cash		14,800

Ex. B–4

a. (1) Payment (last payday in year)

   (2) Adjusting (accrual of wages at end of year)

   (3) Closing

   (4) Reversing

   (5) Payment (first payday in following year)

b. (1) Salaries Expense 22,000
         Cash   22,000

   (2) Salaries Expense 13,200
         Salaries Payable   13,200
            Accrued salaries.

   (3) Income Summary 1,213,200
         Salaries Expense   1,213,200

   (4) Salaries Payable 13,200
         Salaries Expense   13,200
            Reversing entry.

   (5) Salaries Expense 24,000
         Cash   24,000

APPENDIX D

INTERNATIONAL FINANCIAL REPORTING STANDARDS

DISCUSSION QUESTIONS

1. In recent years, the removal of trade barriers and the growth in cross-border equity and debt issuances have led to a dramatic increase in international commerce. As a result, companies are often reporting financial results to users outside of the United States. Historically, accounting standards have varied considerably across countries. These differences have been driven by cultural, legal, and political differences and resulted in financial statements that were not easily comparable and difficult to interpret. A global set of accounting standards can reduce cross-country differences in accounting standards, making it easier for users to compare and use financial statement information.

2. International Financial Reporting Standards (IFRS) are a set of global accounting standards. IFRS applies to companies that issue publicly traded debt or equity securities, called public companies, in countries that have adopted IFRS as their accounting standards. Since 2005, all 27 countries in the European Union (EU) require public companies to prepare financial statements using IFRS. In addition, over 100 other countries have adopted IFRS for public companies.

3. The International Accounting Standards Board (IASB) is the body charged with developing International Financial Reporting Standards. Like the FASB, the IASB is an independent entity that establishes accounting rules. Unlike the FASB, the IASB does not establish accounting rules for any specific country. Rather, it develops accounting rules that can be used by a variety of countries, with the goal of developing a single set of global accounting standards.

4. a. Convergence is the alignment of IFRS and U.S. GAAP one topic at a time, slowly merging IFRS and U.S. GAAP into two broadly uniform sets of accounting standards. The FASB and IASB have agreed to work together on a number of difficult and high-profile accounting issues. These issues frame a large portion of the disagreement between the two sets of standards, and if accomplished, will significantly reduce the differences between U.S. GAAP and IFRS.

   b. Adoption would entail the U.S. Securities and Exchange Commission formally deciding to adopt IFRS as the accounting standard framework for U.S. GAAP. Only the SEC has the authority to adopt IFRS as GAAP for U.S. public companies.

5. a. U.S. GAAP is considered to be a "rules-based" approach to accounting standard setting. The accounting standards provide detailed and specific rules on the accounting for business transactions. There are few exceptions or varying interpretations of the accounting for a business event.

   b. IFRS is a "principles-based" approach that must be broad enough to capture cross-country legal and cultural differences, while still presenting comparable financial statements. This approach provides greater opportunity for different interpretations of the accounting treatment of a business event across different business entities. It also provides more latitude for professional judgment than typically found in comparable U.S. GAAP.

6. Under IFRS, a company may select between historical cost or revalued amount (a form of fair value). If impaired, the impairment loss may be reversed in future periods.

   U.S. GAAP requires the use of historical cost. If the asset is impaired, the impairment loss may NOT be reversed in future periods.

7. IFRS prohibits the use of LIFO. U.S. GAAP allows the use of LIFO.

James Herriot's

Dog Stories

Also by James Herriot

All Creatures Great and Small
All Things Bright and Beautiful
All Things Wise and Wonderful
The Lord God Made Them All
Every Living Thing
James Herriot's Yorkshire
The Best of James Herriot
James Herriot's Cat Stories
James Herriot's Favorite Dog Stories

For Children

Moses the Kitten
Only One Woof
The Christmas Day Kitten
Bonny's Big Day
Blossom Comes Home
The Market Square Dog
Oscar, Cat-About-Town
Smudge, the Little Lost Lamb
James Herriot's Treasury for Children

James Herriot's
Dog Stories

Warm and Wonderful Stories About the
Animals Herriot Loves Best

St. Martin's Griffin
New York

Chapter opener illustrations by Victor Ambrus.

www.stmartins.com

Library of Congress Cataloging-in-Publication Data

Herriot, James.
    James Herriot's dog stories.
        p. cm.
    ISBN 978-0-312-36452-6 (trade paperback)
        1. Dogs—England—Yorkshire—Anecdotes. 2. Dogs—
England—Yorkshire—Biography. 3. Herriot, James. 4.
Veterinarians—England—Yorkshire—Biography. I. Title.
    SF426.2.H47 2006
    636.7—dc23

                                        2007274677

ISBN 978-1-250-06189-8 (trade paperback)

Second St. Martin's Griffin Edition: April 2015

11

To my youngest grandchild,
Katrina, with love

Contents

Introduction

As I look through the pages of this book I have the impression of a wheel turning full circle. As a child, I was fascinated by dogs and had a burning ambition to be a dog doctor, then I spent a lifetime treating the ailments of cows, horses, sheep and pigs, yet here I am, in my twilight years, bringing out a volume of my dog stories. I feel that an explanation rather than an introduction is necessary.

The story is quite a simple one. My boyhood in Glasgow was very much involved with dogs—my own and other people's. Living in the extreme west where the city sprawl thinned out into the countryside, I could look from my windows on to the Kilpatrick Hills and Campsie Fells in the north and over the Clyde to Neilston Pad and the hills beyond Barrhead to the south. Those green hills beckoned to me and though they were far away I walked to them. Through the last straggle of houses to the summits from which I could see the lochs and mountains of Argyll. When I look back now, they seem to be immense distances—often making over thirty miles in a day—and Don was always with me. He was an Irish setter, lean, glossy and beautiful, and he shared my joy in the countryside.

Usually my school friends came with me and on those long sunny days much of the pleasure came from watching our dogs enjoying themselves and playing together. And even at that early age, I was intrigued by the character and behaviour of these animals. I could never quite take dogs for granted. Why were they so devoted to the human race? Why should they delight in our company and welcome us home in transports of joy? Why should their greatest pleasure lie in being with us in our homes and wherever we were? They were just animals after all and it seemed to me that their main preoccupation ought to be in seeking food and protection; instead they dispensed a flow of affection and loyalty which appeared to be limitless.

And another thing. There were so many different shapes, sizes and colours, yet they all had the same fundamental characteristics. Why, why?

I consulted my favourite reference book, Arthur Mee's *Children's Encyclopaedia,* and I wasn't surprised to learn that dogs had been cherished friends of man for thousands of years. The Egyptians loved them and it is probable that they were a happy part of family life in Stone Age caves. I noted, too, that they were thought to be descended from wolves or jackals. All this was interesting but it did not fully explain their appeal and I still marvelled. Behind it all was a vague desire to be always with dogs, to spend my life working with them if possible, but I could never see just how I was going to manage it.

It was when I saw the article in the *Meccano Magazine* that everything began to crystallise out. VETERINARY SURGERY AS A CAREER. As a vet, I could be with dogs all the time, attending to them, curing their illnesses, saving their lives. It made my head swim.

I was still trying to come to terms with this totally new conception when old Dr Whitehouse, the Principal of the Glasgow Veterinary College, came to my school to talk to us. It must be heartbreaking to the hundreds of young people who now are struggling in vain to gain entry to a veterinary school to know that in those days these institutions were going round begging the boys and girls to come to them. The reasons were simple. In 1930, the country was in the grip of a terrible economic depression, people could not afford to keep pets on anything like the present day scale and, perhaps most important of all, the draught horse, once the glory and mainstay of the veterinary profession, was rapidly disappearing from the streets and fields. Nobody wanted vets.

Dr Whitehouse, however, refused to accept that the profession was in its death throes. He told us that if we became veterinary surgeons we would never be rich, but we would have a life of infinite variety, fulfilling in many different ways.

I was hooked. I knew now exactly what I wanted to do with my life, but the obstacles seemed enormous. This was a scientific profession and I was certainly not a scientific type. The things I was good at in school were English and languages and I had already split off from the pupils who were doing such things as physics and chemistry. And I was nearly fourteen years old—in about eighteen months I would be taking my 'highers' which were the A-level examinations in Scotland. It was too late to change now.

There was only one thing to do. I went up to the College to talk to Dr Whitehouse. He was a wonderful old man, a strong, benign personality with a gentle sense of humour. He listened patiently as I poured out my problems.

'I love dogs,' I told him. 'I want to work with them. I want to be a vet. But the subjects I am taking at school are English, French and Latin. No science at all. Can I get into the college?'

He smiled. 'Of course you can. If you get two highers and two lowers you have the matriculation standard. It doesn't matter what the subjects are. You can do physics, chemistry and biology in your first year.'

This again must seem incredible to modern students, but it was a lifeline to me. 'Oh, I'm pretty sure I can get three highers.'

'That's fine, then,' he said. 'You've nothing to worry about.'

I hesitated: 'I'll have to try hard to get lower maths. I'm terrible at maths—will I need them to be a vet?'

His smile widened 'Only to add up your day's takings,' he replied.

That was it, then. My goal was fixed and clearly in front of me. I worked hard in my fourth and fifth year and it is wryly amusing to me now to think of the hours I spent boning up on those apparently useless subjects. Particularly Latin. I loved Latin and most nights I sat poring happily over Virgil, Ovid and Cicero. Towards the end, I think I could have carried on an intelligent conversation with an Ancient Roman, but the thought kept obtruding—what possible use is all this going to be to me as a veterinary student. Some people were encouraging. 'Oh, it will help you to understand a lot of the medical terms,' they said.

I believe it did, but I'd have been a lot better learning about biology.

As I hoped, I got my three highers and actually managed lower maths. I am such a total numbskull at the subject that I can't believe I really passed, but they used to say that if you got higher Latin they would give you anything, so maybe that is what happened. At the time, I wasn't worried. My foot was on the ladder. I was a student at the Glasgow Veterinary College. I was on my way to being a dog doctor.

And I knew exactly what kind of a dog doctor I would be. During the summer holidays between leaving school and going to the College, I carried a vision with me. I could see myself quite clearly, standing masked and gowned in a gleaming operating theatre. I was surrounded by nurses and on the table lay a dog which I was restoring to health by brilliant surgery. Or sometimes I was in a white coat under the spotless walls of a consulting room, ministering to a series of dogs, large, small, tail-wagging, woebegone, but all enchanting and all in need of my services. It was a heavenly prospect.

However, when I rolled up to the college with the new students to start the autumn term, I found that the authorities had no intention of encouraging me in my ambition. They had other plans for me. They were going to make me into a horse doctor.

Veterinary education had stood still despite the fundamental changes which were taking place and all our studies were geared to the horse. The order of priorities, as set out, was quite clear. Horse, ox, sheep, pig, dog. It was a little jingle, repeated over and over and pumped into us as we read our text books. Sisson's great tome, *The Anatomy of the Domestic Animals*, provided exhaustive descriptions of the bones, muscles, digestive system, etc. of the horse, then perhaps about a fifth of the space to the ox and so on down sheep, pig, to the poor dog pushed in at the end.

It was the same with the important subject of Animal Husbandry. When I look through the yellowing pages of my text book of more than fifty years ago, I see that nearly all of it deals with the casting of horses, conformation, stable management, grooming, clipping, harness and saddlery and an enormous amount of shoeing. We had to learn how to shoe a horse, how to remove the old shoe and hammer on a new one. We spent hours in the acrid smoke of blacksmiths' forges. And we were expected to know how to harness a cart horse without making a mistake; collar, hames, harness—saddle and breeching, bridle and reins and belly band.

All this was a surprise to me but another surprise was the totally different attitude towards working and learning. At Hill-head High School, I had been accustomed to a strict regime.

Academic standards were high and the teachers there took their job seriously. They were quite determined that we would master our subjects and any slackness was quickly followed by a few strokes of the leather 'tawse'. But now I found I had been transported into a world where nobody seemed to care whether we learned anything or not.

The present day Veterinary School of Glasgow University is rightly regarded as one of the best in the world with every modern amenity and many brilliant men among its professors. The Glasgow Veterinary College of fifty years ago was very different.

It was a long, low, dilapidated building in a raffish quarter of the city and I was told that it was once used as the stables for the horses when the Glasgow tram-cars were horse-drawn. It certainly looked like that. In an attempt to improve its appearance it had been painted a sickly yellow, but it didn't help.

In the late twenties, the government, faced with the declining demand for vets, had decided to close the Glasgow College and had withdrawn the financial grant. However, a board of governors banded together in an attempt to keep the place going and when I arrived they were still just hanging on, doing everything on a shoe string.

Our teachers, with a few exceptions, were old, retired practitioners. Some of them were very old indeed—deaf, short-sighted, not particularly interested in what they were doing. The professor of Botany and Zoology did his job simply by reading aloud from a text book. Quite often he would turn over two pages by mistake but never noticed until the class drew his attention to it by a series of yells, when he would look over his spectacles at us, smile indulgently and turn the page back, quite unabashed. We were very fond of him and cheered him to the echo at the end of every lecture when he never failed to make the same little joke.

'Well, gentlemen,' he would murmur, forgetting that there was actually one girl among us. 'I see by my gold watch and chain that our time is up.' He always accepted our standing ovation graciously.

The students, too, were different. Many of them were farmers' sons, some from the far north and the Hebrides. I really took to these highland boys, polite, earnest, hairy-tweeded lads whose softly accented voices dropped easily into the Gaelic when they were talking together. The rest were city boys like myself from all over Britain.

My biggest shock was to find that some of them had been at the College for a surprising length of time without making much progress. One chap, McAloon by name, had been there for fourteen years but had managed to get only as far as the second year in the curriculum. He held the record at the time but many others were into double figures. The explanation was simple. The College was desperate for money. There were no student grants and no question of being thrown out after failing an exam, so as long as their parents would cough up the fees regularly, these veterans were valued members of the community. The fourteen-year man was held in particularly high esteem and when he finally left to join the police force, he was sadly missed. Old Dr Whitehouse, who lectured in anatomy, was visibly moved at the time.

'Mr McAloon,' he said, putting down a horse's skull and pointing with his probe at an empty place, 'has sat on that stool for eleven years. It is going to be very strange without him.'

The long-stay students formed a happy group and appeared to spend much of their time playing poker on top of a cut-down grand piano in the common-room. Incidentally, there were never any highlanders among them. The boys from the far north attended all the lectures, lived in Glasgow tenements on porridge and salt herrings and won medals at the end of the year.

As part of our equine education, we were initiated into the 'principles of horse-mastership', which comprised proficiency in handling the animals and also in riding them. Our class was transported once a week to Motherwell where we galloped around the fields on an assortment of nags, thundering down narrow lanes between steelworks like a raggle-taggle cavalry charge, getting mixed up with the traffic in the main streets. Few of the students had ridden before, and since there was not the slightest attempt to break us in gently, we were thrown off in all directions and we bounced around on our unhelmeted heads, concussions were frequent. My own bout of amnesia lasted several days and really worried my parents who thought everything I had learned at school had gone forever.

In the anatomy lab the main dissection was, of course, done on the horse and the same atmosphere prevailed in the vast and complicated subject of Materia Medica. This is the study of the actions and uses of all the drugs used in the treatment of animal diseases. It is now called Pharmacology and deals largely with antibiotics, sulpha drugs and steroids. But there was not a word about such things in my text book of the thirties. They hadn't been invented. Instead, as I turn the pages, gently lifting the many pressed flowers my little daughter placed in there thirty years ago, I find an almost endless list of medicaments which are never used now. The Alkalies, the Metals, the Non-metallic Elements, the Acids, Carbon and its Compounds, the Vegetable Kingdom and, in each group, a frightening catalogue of individual drugs with their Latin names, then a description of their actions on the horse, then on cattle, then on sheep and pigs and finally on dogs.

Doctors of humans have to learn only one dosage rate for their patients, but a vet has to know five. And the order of importance is there to see in my ancient book, the same depressing litany. Horse, ox, sheep, pig, dog.

But there was nothing depressing in the general ambience of the College. Instead, there was a glorious insouciance. Nobody seemed to mind whether we attended lectures or not. It was pretty well left to us to decide. Many preferred to play cards on the grand piano and if they did go to a class they took their game with them. At times it was difficult to hear the droning of the old professors for the chink of coins at the back.

I'm afraid we really plagued these poor old men, shouting, laughing, throwing things around, playing practical jokes. Our professor of Histology was almost totally deaf but he didn't appear to mind in the least as he mumbled contentedly through his lecture with the hubbub raging round him.

I found all this wonderfully beguiling. It had a warm appeal to me after my strict school days and I was soon drifting happily into the new ways. Since the old stagers round the grand piano welcomed newcomers I began to be a frequent attender at the card games and I very soon decided that poker was the most fascinating of occupations. The only snag was that I lost money. Not only that, but I ran into debt. Besotted by the game, I asked for credit after my travel and dinner money had run out, and after some time I found I owed everybody several shillings with no means of paying.

Ridden with guilt, I studied my position. At the age of sixteen, the cautionary novels of my childhood were fresh in my memory. *Eric or Little by Little, The Adventures of a Three Guinea Watch.* They told the story of a boy's slide to perdition through gambling and other evil ways and when I thought of the way I was repaying my hard-working parents by frittering away my youth round that piano, I could so easily apply it all to me. I avoided the card school and started a strict regime of financial economy. I saved bus and tram fares by walking part of the way to the College and lunched exclusively off a single slice of a leaden comestible called apple cake which the canteen purveyed. It cost a penny and successfully killed my appetite for the rest of the day. At length I was able to pay off my dues.

The recipients seemed surprised and not a little amused when I meticulously handed over the money. Their feelings were probably expressed by one big Glaswegian as he pocketed his few shillings. 'Payin' gambling debts!' he chuckled. 'You'll come tae a bad end!'

The card playing went on unabated without me, but I still watched from a distance. Indeed, I felt an attachment to these genial characters, veterans of a thousand failed exams, and I still look back on them with affection because you would not find their like today. As the years passed and I progressed through the veterinary course, it saddened me to see most of them gradually fall away. Several left to become salesmen of the new-fangled vacuum cleaners and I often wondered how they had fared. McAloon, the doyen of them all, was obviously nicely settled in the police force because I frequently gave him a wave as he directed the traffic at George's Cross.

As I have said, much of the tuition at the old College was a joke and, indeed, the whole curriculum was steeped in the dark ages, but there was a bright side. We saw a lot of practice. We had no clinic, as we had to go out and observe animal treatment in the real world. In fact, in our final year we had only one lecture in the morning and then we were out with one of the local practitioners for the rest of the day. The real world contained very few horses and a lot of dogs.

I was lucky, I was a student with Donald Campbell of Rutherglen, a fine man and an outstanding veterinarian but, being dog-oriented, my biggest break was being able to work at the surgery of the great Weipers in the heart of the city. Bill Weipers, now Sir William Weipers and in later life Dean of the new Veterinary School Glasgow University was a man ahead of his time by many years. He set up a purely small animal practice and established it on a standard which was undreamed of at that time. He was a brilliant, immensely likeable man of boundless energy and his students worshipped at his shrine. As for me, I was spellbound. It was just dogs and cats all day long and when I saw the fine operating theatre, the top class surgical procedures, the X-ray machine and the laboratory where blood, bacterial and other examinations were carried out, one thought hammered away in my head. This was what I would do some day.

This practical experience was a Godsend and there was another advantage about those old days. There was no Veterinary Surgeons Act then and it was quite legal for students to work on their own. Some of us helped out the local vets at weekends and I actually did a complete fortnight's locum at the age of nineteen. The vet went off on holiday and left me, wet behind the ears as I was, to run his practice. That fortnight seemed to last a year, but it did me a world of good.

It was deeply satisfying to be able to apply our scientific knowledge to practical things, because we did glean some vital information from the college tuition. For instance we really did learn pathology. The redoubtable Professor Emslie insisted on it. He was no broken-down old practitioner, he was a dynamic intellectual in the prime of life with a passion for his subject and an awesome personality. Burly, black-browed, smouldering-eyed, he could cower every one of us with a single look. The bunch of hell-raisers with the poor old men were frightened little mice with Emslie. And he taught us pathology. With a savage wit and terrifying outbursts of rage, he rammed it into us.

I was as scared as the rest but grateful to him, too, because pathology lies at the heart of all animal treatment and in those early days when I was seeing animals with pneumonia, renal and cardiac conditions and struggling to understand what was behind them, it was like the lifting of a veil.

When I qualified and walked out of the door of the college for the last time I felt an acute sense of loss, an awareness of something good gone forever. Some of my happiest years were spent in that seedy old building and though my veterinary course was out of date and inefficient in many ways, there was a carefree, easy-going charm about that whole time which has held it in my mind in a golden glow.

When, many years later, I saw my son, Jimmy, on to the train in York to begin his new life as a veterinary student, I said only one thing to him—'Have a good time.'

I know he did, but nobody had a better time than me.

With MRCVS after my name, I was now out in the big world, but it soon turned out to be cold and hard. I must have been blinkered during my years of training because my boyhood vision had remained unchanged. I was still in my white coat or in an operating gown under the brilliant lights with the nurses around me. I could see no impediment to my ambition. I would take an assistantship in a small animal practice, then after I had gained experience and earned some money I would look for a partnership or possibly put up my plate in Glasgow. The future seemed rosy. There were dogs everywhere, just waiting for me.

But when I qualified I came up against harsh reality. The depression of the thirties was still lying over our profession like a dark blanket and jobs were desperately scarce. For every vacant appointment advertised in the *Veterinary Record,* there were eighty applicants and for those who did manage to find a post, the remuneration was often pitiful. Qualified veterinary surgeons were working for thirty shillings a week plus bed and board and it was terrible to read in the 'appointments required' column the dread phrase 'Will work for keep'. These words cropped up again and again, a heart cry from many who, like me, would do anything to get off their parents' hands.

I saw my colleagues taking jobs in shops or in the Clydeside shipyards and I was just beginning to despair when I was offered an interview for a post in the Yorkshire Dales. I could hardly believe my luck when I was taken on. It was a lifeline, but even in my euphoria a sad little thought intruded. This was a large animal practice, dealing almost entirely with farm horses, cows, sheep and pigs. Where was my dream now?

But I had no time to worry about such things and the vision of the immaculate young vet in his sterile surroundings soon melted away. I spent my time in shirt sleeves and wellingtons, trudging through mud and muck, wrestling with huge beasts, being kicked, knocked down and trodden on. As a city boy, thrown headlong into the kind of remote rural community I had only read about in books, I was like a poor swimmer trying to keep afloat in the deep end. I was acutely aware that I had no agricultural background and that I had to establish myself among farmers who had spent a lifetime with livestock and often had a jaundiced attitude to what they called 'book-learn'. Life was very full.

And yet, among the hurly burly, there was a magical element. I was working outside all the time, in the sunshine and clean air, and around me was a countryside which was all the more enchanting for being unexpected. I was amazed that nobody had ever told me about Yorkshire. The majestic grassy fells soaring high above the pebbly rivers and the grey villages, the airy distances of the moors with their billowing sea of purple heather. I had stumbled on a wonderland which appeared to be undiscovered because often I was quite alone in those wide landscapes. There was a sense of solitude here, a nearness of the wild which was exciting and I realised that if fate had decreed that I was going to be a farm physician instead of a dog doctor, the compensations were enormous.

As the months passed this feeling deepened into a conviction. This was the life for me. I would never go back to a city again.

It was a pity I would never realise my ambition. It had been with me for a long time, but I pushed it to the back of my mind. Then it began to come through to me that, even here, there was dog work all around—a whole charming little world of it among the scattered villages of the Dales. People had pets there, just as in the cities. Not in such large numbers but enough to make a refreshing sideline to my large animal duties. And to my surprise I found that these people were ready and eager for my services. The main reason was that among the tough, hard-bitten horse- and farm-doctors of that period, it was considered slightly cissy to attend to the needs of dogs and cats. I remember one old practitioner looking down his nose at me when I described a small animal case. 'That's not veterinary surgery,' he grunted.

But it was to me. Very much so. And I found that I had a

pretty free rein in my practice, because my boss, later to be my partner, was a dedicated horseman who seized on every equine problem, leaving the dogs and cats to me. So it happened that after a year or so I had what amounted to my own small animal practice, with clients coming from far around to our little town to seek the services of a vet who actually wanted to treat their pets.

This part of my work was like a bright thread running through the stern fabric of my daily round. Country practice is hard, but it was a lot harder half a century ago, before the modern drugs, the metal crushes and tranquillisers which make the handling of the big, struggling beasts so much easier. I was a young, fit man and I gladly accepted the rough life, but it was still a magical relief to step out of the dirt, the cold, and the bruising routine to treat the ailments of gentle little animals in drawing-rooms.

It wasn't the kind of dog practice I had dreamed of as a boy. There was no operating room, no white-coated nurses. Memories come back of anaesthetising a broken-legged yellow Labrador on the floor of a village post office, of delivering puppies in a dark corner of a cow shed, of carrying out all sorts of surgical procedures on the kitchen tables and draining boards of lonely cottages. Since I spent ninety-nine per cent of my time driving round the farms, I could not have set surgery hours so people brought their pets to me when they knew I would probably be at home, at meal times or first thing in the morning. My wife often had to leave her cooking to hang on to a reluctant patient.

As I say, the reality was nothing like the dream, but there was one tremendous bonus. My dog practice, though widely scattered, was never big enough to become impersonal. Whereas a city practice could consist of a never-ending canine wave flowing through the consulting rooms, that never happened to me. I knew every patient by name. I could remember all their ailments and it was one of my rewards to be able to pick them out in the village streets as I drove through and to see how well they had recovered.

Over the years, our practice, like country practices all over the world, has gradually changed. The pet population has vastly increased so that something like fifty per cent of our work is with small animals. We now have the operating theatre, the X-ray equipment, the consulting rooms I dreamed of as a boy. And, of course, we also have all the modern drugs which were not available to me in those early days. To me, as to all vets, it is a source of great satisfaction to be able to do so many things for our patients which were impossible a few years ago.

I know I am lucky in my job because I get a kick out of just seeing the dogs and cats come into our surgery. Apart from the medical aspect, there is a constant pleasure for the animal lover in observing the differing personalities of people's pets. Because vets are animal lovers—that's why they become vets in the first place. A lot of people think we are detached and have only a clinical interest in our patients, but it is not so. Ours is a caring profession.

This attitude of mind is often borne out in our relationship with our own pets, and I have often detected in some of the most macho of my colleagues, a thoroughly sentimental streak. As for myself, I am as soppy over my dogs as any old lady and it is a trait which has always stood me in good stead in my dealings with clients. So many people are embarrassed when they have to reveal to the vet their affection for their pets, their worries over their welfare, the anguish when their too-short lives come to an end. They needn't be diffident with me. In the words of the old song, they don't have to tell me, I know.

I realise when I look back over the years that I have been so fortunate with my own dogs. Everyone who acquires a dog has to face the fact that they do not live long enough and that there is sadness ahead and in the course of my work I have had to witness so many little tragedies when even that short span is cruelly curtailed by illness or accident. But all my dogs have lived into their teens and, though the final break was possibly even harder, I have always felt thankful that I have been able to keep them for so long.

I often think of them all, of their different characters and the happiness I had with them. The beautiful Irish setter with whom I walked the Scottish hills during my boyhood, the little white mongrel who baffled all attempts to pinpoint his ancestry but who bulged with character and intelligence, my beloved beagle whose big liquid eyes still seem to look out at me from so many birthday cards. Then came Hector and Dan.

Introduction

I dedicated my book *All Things Wise and Wonderful* 'To my dogs, Hector and Dan, faithful companions of the daily round'. That is what they were. Their life was mine. Every morning after breakfast, they rushed outside and leaped into the car, eager to start the day's work. Hector was a Jack Russell terrier and Dan a black Labrador and they made a sharp contrast of perkiness and dignity.

Hector was the elder by two years. When my beagle died, I followed the advice I had given to so many people—to get another dog immediately. Twenty-four hours of enquiries produced nothing, then I noticed an entry in an evening paper advertising a litter of Jack Russell puppies. Strangely, I had been speaking to a friend a few days before and he had warned me never to get a Jack Russell. 'They're snappy little devils,' he said. 'Take the hand off you as soon as look at you.' And in truth, I had dealt with some very tough specimens in my surgery and had come to the conclusion that the Darrowby Jack Russells had to be watched carefully.

Nevertheless, I drove out to the farm and asked to see the litter. There were five puppies, seven weeks old, grouped around their mother. Four of them looked at me impassively but the fifth trotted out to me, wagged his stumpy tail and licked my hand furiously.

'I'll have this one,' I said, and Hector and I started our fifteen-year association.

He turned out to be the soul of good nature, a dog who loved all people and all other dogs. Everybody fell for him on sight, too, and he was exposed to a wide section of the community, because, in those days, I drove only convertible cars and he was on show all the time. When I arrived on the farms, the farmers' children used to run out to stroke the friendly little animal craning out of the roofless vehicle. Their parents, in turn, were invariably intrigued by the sight of an amiable Jack Russell and one phrase cropped up again and again. 'Hey, that's a grand little dog. Can I use him when my bitch comes into season?'

Over the years, Hector's fame as a stud dog grew steadily and he produced a long series of happy, good-natured puppies. These puppies in turn had puppies of their own, all seemingly stamped with Hector's temperament and so it went on in great widening ripples. It is not too much to say that by his own efforts, he changed the character of the Jack Russell breed in the entire district.

Even now, many years after his death, my heart lifts when I see little Hector look-alikes walk into our surgery. He had an unusually long, sharp-pointed face and lean body with the classical 'Chippendale legs' and sometimes his progeny's progeny remind me almost painfully of the happy years I spent with him.

Dan came to me by accident. When my son, Jimmy, qualified as a veterinary surgeon, he received various gifts from family and friends. One of my colleagues gave him a five pound note. With this money, he bought a black Labrador pup and named him Dan. Jimmy's first job was as assistant to the famous Eddie Straiton, the TV vet, and Dan was his companion in the night and day slog of this busy practice.

When he came to join our practice, he brought Dan with him, so we had two dogs in the house. It was an instant friendship between them, Hector frisking around, gnawing playfully at the big dog's legs, Dan submitting happily.

Dan was truly beautiful with his noble head, serene expression and the glossiest black coat I had ever seen. Jimmy declared that his superb lustre was due to the vast quantities of milk he consumed at the Straiton establishment. There was a large cat colony at Eddie's animal hospital and Dan used to raid their bowls shamelessly. I loved to watch him bounding along after a stick with his muscles rippling under that shiny skin. It was his greatest joy and it is how I always think of him now.

When Jimmy left home to be married, he left Dan with me. He knew I had become attached to the big dog and he was being kind to me and kind to Hector. I consoled myself with the thought that his unselfishness would not be too hard on him because his new home was only a mile away, he was working with me in the practice and he would see Dan every day. He bought himself a lovely little Lancashire Heeler bitch which he mated and kept one of the pups, so that in Sophie and Chloe he had his own car dogs.

As for me, I settled down to an era which I cherish in my memory as the Hector and Dan time. To a country vet like myself whose life was spent on the roads and lanes these dogs were very important. The pattern was always the same, Dan stretched on the passenger seat with his head on my knee, Hector peering through the windshield, his paws balanced on my hand as it rested on the gear lever. Dan wasn't worried about what went on outside but Hector hated to miss a thing. His head bobbed around erratically as I changed gear but his feet never slipped off my hand.

One great bonus in my life was that I was able to take occasional breaks between visits, and since I worked among some of the finest dog-walking country in England those breaks were special. I do feel for the thousands of dog owners who live in cities. They labour under so many difficulties and disadvantages, but my walks took me along grassy tracks on the hilltops and among the heather. There was an endless multitude of these little paths, soft on paws and feet, free of cars and people and noise, remote and peaceful.

I could hardly believe my good fortune at being able to call a halt in the day and step from the car into a tranquil world. Within seconds I was out in the beauty of Yorkshire, wandering along in the sunshine and the clean air with my two companions trotting ahead of me. Lucky dogs, I often thought, and lucky, lucky me.

One thing Dan insisted on during these walks was a stick to carry. If he didn't have one in his mouth he was miserable, and since we were usually up on the high, treeless country where wood was difficult to find, he used to spend his time ferreting about in frustration. Sometimes I was compelled to break off a strong stem of heather for him to carry, but he accepted it with poor grace. He didn't just like sticks, he liked big ones, so very early in our association I took to carrying a supply in my car boot.

One day a farmer was standing by me as I fished out my wellingtons and syringe, and he looked wonderingly at the stout branches reclining among my drugs.

'What the 'ell have you got them great shillelaghs for?' he asked.

Though Hector wasn't at all stick-minded, he did love to grab hold of Dan's and try to pull it from his mouth. Innumerable contests of tug-of-war ensued in this way and it amused me to see the different reactions of the two dogs. To Hector, it was deadly serious as he hung on with terrier pertinacity, growling fiercely as he was swung around. All his attention was fixed desperately on the business in hand, but to Dan, the thing was a game, mere light relaxation, and he kept glancing at me with a 'how'm I doing?' expression as he gripped his stick.

He would carry his stick for many miles and the first sign of his deterioration in his fourteenth year was when he occasionally returned from a walk without it. I knew something was wrong then. Another sign was that, as he aged, he no longer insisted on very large sticks. In fact, his tastes gradually tended towards smaller and smaller ones.

There is a silhouetted photograph on the cover of this book. It shows Dan looking up at me. He was an old dog then, a year after Hector had gone, and his eyes are fixed on something in my hand. It is a very small stick . . .

I have the same feeling about the wheel turning full circle when I look at my present dog, Bodie. He is a Border terrier and I always wanted one since I first arrived in Yorkshire nearly fifty years ago.

Siegfried had a partner in Leyburn called Frank Bingham. Leyburn stands at the gate of Wensleydale and I used to go up there several days a week to do Frank's tuberculin testing. Every time I entered the house a little Border terrier, Toby by name, trotted up to me, rolled on his back and looked up at me solemnly, waiting for me to scratch his chest. I have always liked little dogs who roll over like that—I think it is an unfailing sign of good-nature—and I took a tremendous fancy to Toby. Besides, there was something greatly appealing in his whiskery face, topped by little black ears.

'Some day I'll have a Border,' I said to Frank.

I said that to many people, especially to myself, over the years, but each time I lost one of my own dogs there was never one of the breed available. When Hector went and then Dan within a year, I must have been somewhat numbed because I did not follow my own precept of getting another dog immediately. Perhaps I felt that I could never replace those two. They had been such a wonderful combination in their contrasting ways, filling that side of my life to overflowing, and I was in my mid sixties by then, less resilient, less willing to accept the possibility that I could feel for another dog as I felt for them.

I seemed to be in a state of limbo for several months—the only time in my life that I can remember being without a dog—and my walks would have lost their savour but for the fact that my daughter, Rosie, who lived next door, acquired a beautiful yellow Labrador puppy. She called her Polly and I found to my delight that I had another companion. But my car seemed very empty as I went on my rounds.

It was a Saturday lunchtime when Rosie came in and said excitedly, 'There's an advertisement in the *Darlington and Stockton Times* about some Border puppies. It's a Mrs Mason in Bedale.'

The announcement burst on me like a bombshell and I was all for immediate action, but my wife's response surprised me.

'It says here,' she said, studying the newspaper, 'that these pups are eight weeks old, so they'd be born around Christmas. Remember you said that after waiting all this time we'd be better with a spring puppy.'

'Yes, that's right,' I replied. 'But Helen, these are Borders! We might not get another chance for ages!'

She shrugged. 'Oh, I'm sure we'll find one at the right time if only we're patient.'

'But . . . but . . .' I found I was talking to Helen's back. She was bending over a pan of potatoes.

'Lunch will be ready in ten minutes,' she said. 'You and Rosie can take Polly for a little walk.'

As we strolled along the lane outside our house, Rosie turned to me. 'What a funny thing. I can't understand it. Mum is as keen as you to get another dog and yet here is a litter of Borders—the very thing you've been waiting for. They're so scarce. It seems such a pity to miss them.'

'I don't think we will miss them,' I murmured.

'What do you mean? You heard what she said.'

I smiled indulgently. 'You've often heard your mother say that she knows me inside out. She can tell in advance every single thing I'm going to do?'

'Yes but . . .'

'Well, what she forgets is that I know her inside out, too. I'll lay a small bet that when we get back to the house, she'll have changed her mind.'

Rosie raised her eyebrows. 'I very much doubt it. She seemed very definite to me.'

On our return I opened the front door and saw Helen speaking into the telephone.

She turned to me and spoke agitatedly. 'I've got Mrs Mason on the line now. There's only one pup left out of the litter and there are people coming from as far as eighty miles away to see it. We'll have to hurry. What a long time you've been out there!'

We bolted our lunch and Helen, Rosie, granddaughter Emma and I drove out to Bedale. Mrs Mason led us into the kitchen and pointed to a tiny brindle creature twisting and writhing under the table.

'That's him,' she said.

I reached down and lifted the puppy as he curled his little body round, apparently trying to touch his tail with his nose. But that tail wagged furiously and the pink tongue was busy at my hand. I knew he was ours before my quick examination for hernia and overshot jaw.

The deal was quickly struck and we went outside to inspect the puppy's relations. His mother and grandmother were out there. They lived in little barrels which served as kennels and both of them darted out and stood up at our legs, tails lashing, mouths panting in delight. I felt vastly reassured. With happy, healthy ancestors like those I knew we had every chance of a first rate dog.

As we drove home with the puppy in Emma's arms, the warm thought came to me. The wheel had indeed turned. After nearly fifty years I had my Border terrier.

The choice of a name exercised our minds for many days with arguments, suggestions and counter-suggestions. We finally decided on 'Bodie'. Helen and I were great fans of the TV series, 'The Professionals', and our particular hero was Lewis Collins who took the part of Bodie. We have met Lewis a few times and were at first a little hesitant about telling him that we had named our dog after him, but he doesn't mind, knowing us and understanding the honoured place a dog occupies in our household.

Helen and I settled down happily with Bodie. We had been lost without a dog in the house and it was a lovely relief to have filled that awful gap. It was extraordinary that the gap was filled by a grizzled, hairy-faced little creature about nine inches long, but Bodie effortlessly performed the miracle. Helen had a dog to feed again and see to his in-house care and bedding, and I had a companion in my car and on my bed-time walk even though he was almost invisible on the end of his lead.

Introduction

His first meeting with Polly was a tremendous event. I mentioned the instant friendship between Hector and Dan. It was different with Bodie. He fell in love.

This is no exaggeration. Polly became and is to this day the most important living creature in his world. Since she lived next door he was able to watch her house from our sitting-room window and a wild yapping was always the sign that the adored one had appeared in her garden. Fortunately for his peace of mind, he had a walk with her every day and at the weekends several times a day and, as he grew up, it was clear that this routine was the most significant thing in his life.

It was when he was about a year old that I was walking down a lane with the two of them trotting ahead. Memories stirred in me as I watched them—the noble Labrador and the scruffy little terrier side by side. Suddenly Polly picked up a stick, Bodie seized one end of it, and in a flash a hectic tug-of-war was raging. The little Border grumbled and growled in fierce concentration and as Polly glanced at me with amusement in her eyes, I had the uncanny impression that I had got Hector and Dan back again.

As Bodie approached the adult stage, I was able to assess his various qualities. My Dog Encyclopaedia, describing the Border, uses words like 'tough', 'honest', 'down to earth'. It does not say that it is pretty; in fact, it states that it has 'not quite the elegance of the more fashionable members of the terrier group'. I would have to admit all that. Bodie's shaggy, whiskered little face is almost comic, but it has certainly grown on me. When I look at it now, I can find great depths of character and expression.

The book also describes the breed as 'intensely loyal and gentle with children'. Again, right on both counts, but Bodie obviously regards himself as a tough guy and, as such, seems a little embarrassed about showing his affection. If I am sitting on a sofa, he will flop down almost apologetically by my side as though doing so by accident, but lying very close all the same, and he has a particular habit of creeping unobtrusively between my feet at mealtimes or when I am writing. He is down there at this moment and since this is a swivel chair I have to be careful about sudden turns.

One unfortunate result of his infatuation with Polly is that he has become insanely jealous. His possessiveness is such that he will hurl himself unhesitatingly at any male dog, however large, who might be a possible suitor, and this invariably leads to an embarrassing fracas followed by profuse apologies to the irate owner.

Such behavior is very unwise in one so small because he usually comes off second best. Yet he never surrenders. Only last week I removed the stitches from his shoulder after an encounter with an enormous cross-bred Alsatian. By the time I dived in after Bodie's attack, this dog was waving him round in the air by one leg, but the Border, his mouth full of hair, was still looking for more trouble.

He may be foolish, but he is also very brave. My Encyclopaedia points out that these little terriers have been for centuries in the Border country between Scotland and England to hunt and destroy foxes, and maybe that accounts for his total lack of fear. But, be that as it may, I have to scan the horizon carefully every time I am out with him and Polly.

However, he is by no means entirely aggressive. With lady dogs he is all charm, swaggering round them, tail high, smirking through his whiskers. And if they will consent to play with him, he behaves with the utmost gallantry as they roll him over in happy rough and rumbles. They can knock him down and jump on him at will, but he submits cheerfully, a silly half-smile on his face.

The strange twisting of his body which I observed when I first saw him has remained with him. Whenever he is pleased to see anybody, he sidles up to them almost crab-wise, his tail almost touching his nose. I have never seen this characteristic in any other dog.

Since Dan was his immediate predecessor, the difference in obedience was acutely evident. The big Labrador, like most of his breed, was born with the desire to obey. He watched me anxiously all the time, longing to do my bidding, and even little things like getting out of the car or moving from one room to another had to wait for my gesture. Not so with Bodie. After prolonged effort, I have managed to get him to respond to such simple commands as 'stay' or 'here' and even then he does so in his own good time, but if he is really engrossed in something which interests him, he pays very little attention to me. After hearing me bawl at him about ten times he may look up at me with an expression of mild enquiry and I find this disconcerting because people expect vets to have well-trained dogs. Recently, a little five-year-old boy, a near neighbour, informed me solemnly, 'You're always shouting "Bodie! Bodie! Bodie!"' so I fear it is part of the local pattern to hear my despairing cries echoing round our village.

And yet . . . and yet . . . the little fellow has a charisma all of his own, a scruffy appeal which seems to get under the skin of all Border owners. There aren't all that many of the breed around and I find myself staring with the keenest interest whenever I see one in the street. I know I am not alone in this, because other owners seem to be similarly fascinated with Bodie. There is certainly a bond between us all.

Last summer I was walking Bodie outside a motel half way between here and Glasgow when a man pushed his head out of his car window as he drew out of the park.

'That's a nice little Border!' he cried.

I swelled with unimaginable pride. 'Yes, have you got one?' I called back.

'We have indeed!' He waved and was gone, but the feeling of comradeship remained.

There was another warming encounter during our spring holiday this year. I had just parked my car in the vehicle deck of the ferry which plies between Oban and the Isle of Barra in the Outer Hebrides when I noticed a silver-haired American gentleman gazing at Bodie who was stretched out in his favourite position on the back shelf.

He was another devotee and told me about his own Border. It seems they are even scarcer on the other side of the Atlantic and he said he knew of only three kennels of the breed in that vast country. Before he left he took another long look into my car.

'Magnificent little dogs,' he murmured reverently.

He was voicing my own feelings, but when I think of Bodie I am not concerned with the merits of his breed. The thing which warms and fills me with gratitude is that he has completely taken the place of the loved animals which have gone before him. It is a reaffirmation of the truth which must console all dog owners; that those short lives do not mean unending emptiness; that the void can be filled while the good memories remain.

That is how it is with our family and Bodie. He is just as dear to us as all the others.

It is here that I will finish my introduction. I started with the intention of explaining how a cow doctor came to bring out a book of dog stories, but it reads rather like the many letters which come to me from my readers all over the world. They tell me about their dogs, about their funny ways, the things they do which bring joy into their homes. They tell me, too, about their troubles and sorrows, in fact about the whole range of experiences which go into the keeping of a dog.

Perhaps this is a good way of replying to them all. Because these are the things which happened to me.

James Herriot's

Dog Stories

1. *Tricki Woo*

As autumn wore into winter and the high tops were streaked with the first snows, the discomforts of practice in the Dales began to make themselves felt.

Driving for hours with frozen feet, climbing to the high barns in biting winds which seared and flattened the wiry hill grass; the interminable stripping off in draughty buildings and the washing of hands and chest in buckets of cold water, using scrubbing soap and often a piece of sacking for a towel.

I really found out the meaning of chapped hands. When there was a rush of work, my hands were never quite dry, and the little red fissures crept up almost to my elbows.

This was when some small animal work came as a blessed relief. To step out of the rough, hard routine for a while; to walk into a warm drawing-room instead of a cow house and tackle something less formidable than a horse or a bull. And among all those comfortable drawing-rooms there was none so beguiling as Mrs Pumphrey's.

Mrs Pumphrey was an elderly widow. Her late husband, a beer baron whose breweries and pubs were scattered widely over the broad bosom of Yorkshire, had left her a vast fortune and a beautiful house on the outskirts of Darrowby. Here she lived with a large staff of servants, a gardener, a chauffeur, and Tricki Woo. Tricki Woo was a Pekingese and the apple of his mistress's eye.

Standing now in the magnificent doorway, I furtively rubbed the toes of my shoes on the backs of my trousers and blew on my cold hands. I could almost see the deep armchair drawn close to the leaping flames, the tray of cocktail biscuits, the bottle of excellent sherry. Because of the sherry, I was always careful to time my visits for half an hour before lunch.

A maid answered my ring, beaming on me as an honoured guest, and led me to the room, crammed with expensive furniture and littered with glossy magazines and the latest novels. Mrs Pumphrey, in the high-backed chair by the fire, put down her book with a cry of delight. 'Trick! Tricki! Here is your uncle Herriot.' I had been made an uncle very early and, sensing the advantages of the relationship, had made no objection.

Tricki, as always, bounded from his cushion, leaped on to the back of a sofa and put his paws on my shoulders. He then licked my face thoroughly before retiring, exhausted. He was soon exhausted because he was given roughly twice the amount of food needed for a dog of his size. And it was the wrong kind of food.

'Oh, Mr Herriot,' Mrs Pumphrey said, looking at her pet anxiously, 'I'm so glad you've come. Tricki has gone flop-bott again.'

This ailment, not to be found in any text book, was her way of describing the symptoms of Tricki's impacted anal glands. When the glands filled up, he showed discomfort by sitting down suddenly in mid-walk and his mistress would rush to the phone in great agitation.

'Mr Herriot! Please come, he's going flop-bott again!'

I hoisted the little dog on to a table and, by pressure on the anus with a pad of cotton wool, I evacuated the glands.

It baffled me that the Peke was always so pleased to see me. Any dog who could still like a man who grabbed him and squeezed his bottom hard every time they met had to have an incredibly forgiving nature. But Tricki never showed any resentment; in fact he was an outstandingly equable little animal, bursting with intelligence, and I was genuinely attached to him. It was a pleasure to be his personal physician.

The squeezing over, I lifted my patient from the table, noticing the increased weight, the padding of extra flesh over the ribs. 'You know, Mrs Pumphrey, you're overfeeding him again. Didn't I tell you to cut out all those pieces of cake and give him more protein?'

'Oh yes, Mr Herriot,' Mrs Pumphrey wailed. 'But what can I do? He's so tired of chicken.'

I shrugged; it was hopeless. I allowed the maid to lead me to the palatial bathroom where I always performed a ritual handwashing after the operation. It was a huge room with a fully stocked dressing table, massive green ware and rows of glass shelves laden with toilet preparations. My private guest towel was laid out next to the slab of expensive soap.

Then I returned to the drawing-room, my sherry glass was filled, and I settled down by the fire to listen to Mrs Pumphrey. It couldn't be called a conversation because she did all the talking, but I always found it rewarding.

Mrs Pumphrey was likeable, gave widely to charities and would help anybody in trouble. She was intelligent and amusing and had a lot of waffling charm; but most people have a blind spot and her's was Tricki Woo. The tales she told about her darling ranged far into the realms of fantasy, and I waited eagerly for the next instalment.

'Oh Mr Herriot, I have the most exciting news. Tricki has a pen pal! Yes, he wrote a letter to the editor of *Doggy World* enclosing a donation, and told him that even though he was descended from a long line of Chinese emperors, he had decided to come down and mingle freely with the common dogs. He asked the editor to seek out a pen pal for him among the dogs he knew so that they could correspond to their mutual benefit. And for this purpose, Tricki said he would adopt the name of Mr Utterbunkum. And, do you know, he received the most beautiful letter from the editor' (I could imagine the sensible man leaping upon this potential gold mine) 'who said he would like to introduce Bonzo Fotheringham, a lonely Dalmatian who would be delighted to exchange letters with a new friend in Yorkshire.'

I sipped the sherry. Tricki snored on my lap. Mrs Pumphrey went on.

'But I'm so disappointed about the new summerhouse – you know I got it specially for Tricki so we could sit out together on warm

3

afternoons. It's such a nice little rustic shelter, but he's taken a passionate dislike to it. Simply loathes it – absolutely refuses to go inside. You should see the dreadful expression on his face when he looks at it. And do you know what he called it yesterday? Oh, I hardly dare tell you.' She looked around the room before leaning over and whispering: 'He called it "the bloody hut"!'

The maid struck fresh life into the fire and refilled my glass. The wind hurled a handful of sleet against the window. This, I thought, was the life. I listened for more.

'And did I tell you, Mr Herriot, Tricki had another good win yesterday? You know, I'm sure he must study the racing columns, he's such a tremendous judge of form. Well, he told me to back Canny Lad in the three o'clock at Redcar yesterday and, as usual, it won. He put on a shilling each way and got back nine shillings.'

These bets were always placed in the name of Tricki Woo and I thought with compassion of the reactions of the local bookies. The Darrowby turf accountants were a harassed and fugitive body of men. A board would appear at the end of some alley urging the population to invest with Joe Downs and enjoy perfect security. Joe would live for a few months on a knife edge while he pitted his wits against the knowledgeable citizens, but the end was always the same: a few favourites would win in a row and Joe would be gone in the night, taking his board with him. Once I asked a local inhabitant about the sudden departure of one of these luckless nomads. He replied unemotionally: 'Oh, we brok 'im.'

Losing a regular flow of shillings to a dog must have been a heavy cross for these unfortunate men to bear.

'I had such a frightening experience last week,' Mrs Pumphrey continued. 'I was sure I would have to call you out. Poor little Tricki – he went completely crackerdog!'

I mentally lined this up with flop-bott among the new canine diseases and asked for more information.

'It was awful. I was terrified. The gardener was throwing rings for Tricki – you know he does this for half an hour every day.' I had witnessed this spectacle several times. Hodgkin, a dour, bent old Yorkshireman who looked as though he hated all dogs and Tricki in particular, had to go out on the lawn every day and throw little rubber rings over and over again. Tricki bounded after them and brought them back, barking madly till the process was repeated. The bitter lines on the old man's face deepened as the game progressed.

4

His lips moved continually, but it was impossible to hear what he was saying.

Mrs Pumphrey went on: 'Well, he was playing his game, and he does adore it so, when suddenly, without warning, he went cracker-dog. He forgot all about his rings and began to run around in circles, barking and yelping in such a strange way. Then he fell over on his side and lay like a little dead thing. Do you know, Mr Herriot, I really thought he was dead, he lay so perfectly still. And what hurt me most was that Hodgkin began to laugh. He has been with me for twenty-four years and I have never even seen him smile, and yet, when he looked down at that still form, he broke into a queer, high-pitched cackle. It was horrid. I was just going to rush to the telephone when Tricki got up and walked away – he seemed perfectly normal.'

Hysteria, I thought, brought on by wrong feeding and over-excitement. I put down my glass and fixed Mrs Pumphrey with a severe glare. 'Now look, this is just what I was talking about. If you persist in feeding all that fancy rubbish to Tricki you are going to ruin his health. You really must get him on to a sensible dog diet of one or, at the most, two small meals a day of meat and brown bread or a little biscuit. And nothing in between.'

Mrs Pumphrey shrank into her chair, a picture of abject guilt. 'Oh, please don't speak to me like that. I do try to give him the right things, but it is so difficult. When he begs for his little titbits, I can't refuse him.' She dabbed her eyes with a handkerchief.

But I was unrelenting. 'All right, Mrs Pumphrey, it's up to you, but I warn you that if you go on as you are doing, Tricki will go crackerdog more and more often.'

I left the cosy haven with reluctance, pausing on the gravelled drive to look back at Mrs Pumphrey waving and Tricki, as always, standing against the window, his wide-mouthed face apparently in the middle of a hearty laugh.

Driving home, I mused on the many advantages of being Tricki's uncle. When he went to the seaside he sent me boxes of oak-smoked kippers; and when the tomatoes ripened in his greenhouse, he sent a pound or two every week. Tins of tobacco arrived regularly, some-times with a photograph carrying a loving inscription.

But it was when the Christmas hamper arrived from Fortnum and Mason's that I decided that I was on a really good thing which should be helped along a bit. Hitherto, I had merely rung up and thanked Mrs Pumphrey for the gifts, and she had been rather cool, pointing out that it was Tricki who had sent the things and he was the one who should be thanked.

With the arrival of the hamper it come to me, blindingly, that I had been guilty of a grave error of tactics. I set myself to compose a letter to Tricki. Avoiding Siegfried's sardonic eye, I thanked my doggy nephew for his Christmas gifts and for all his generosity in the past. I expressed my sincere hopes that the festive fare had not upset his delicate digestion and suggested that if he did experience any discomfort he should have recourse to the black powder his uncle always prescribed. A vague feeling of professional shame was easily swamped by floating visions of kippers, tomatoes and hampers. I addressed the envelope to Master Tricki Pumphrey, Barlby Grange, and slipped it into the post-box with only a slight feeling of guilt.

On my next visit, Mrs Pumphrey drew me to one side. 'Mr Herriot,' she whispered, 'Tricki adored your charming letter and he will keep it always, but he was very put out about one thing – you addressed it to Master Tricki and he does insist upon Mister. He was dreadfully affronted at first, quite beside himself, but when he saw it was from you he soon recovered his good temper. I can't think why he should have these little prejudices. Perhaps it is because he is an only dog – I do think an only dog develops more prejudices than one from a large family.'

Entering Skeldale House was like returning to a colder world. Siegfried bumped into me in the passage. 'Ah, who have we here? Why I do believe it's dear Uncle Herriot. And what have you been doing, Uncle? Slaving away at Barlby Grange, I expect. Poor fellow, you must be tired out. Do you really think it's worth it, working your fingers to the bone for another hamper?'

*

Even in the most high-powered small-animal practice with a wide spectrum of clients, Mrs Pumphrey would have been remarkable, but to me, working daily with earthy farmers in rough conditions, she was almost unreal. Her drawing-room was a warm haven in my hard life and Tricki Woo a lovable patient. The little Peke with his eccentric ailments has captured the affection of people all over the world, and I have received countless letters about him. He lived to a great age, flop-botting but happy right to the end. Mrs Pumphrey was eighty-eight when she died. She was one of the few who recognised herself in my books, and I know she appreciated the fun because when I stopped writing about her she wrote to me, saying, 'There's nuffin' to larf at now.' I wonder if she had her tongue in her cheek all the time?

2. *Tristan's Vigil*

I dropped the suture needle into the tray and stepped back to survey the finished job. 'Well though I say it myself, that looks rather nice.'

Tristan leaned over the unconscious dog and examined the neat incision with its row of regular stiches. 'Very pretty indeed, my boy. Couldn't have done better myself.'

The big black Labrador lay peacefully on the table, his tongue lolling, his eyes glazed and unseeing. He had been brought in with an ugly growth over his ribs and I had decided that it was a simple lipoma, quite benign and very suitable for surgery. And so it had turned out. The tumour had come away with almost ridiculous ease,

8

round, intact and shining, like a hard boiled egg from its shell. No haemorrhage, no fear of recurrence.

The unsightly swelling had been replaced by this tidy scar which would be invisible in a few weeks. I was pleased.

'We'd better keep him here till he comes round,' I said. 'Give me a hand to get him on to these blankets.' We made the dog comfortable in front of an electric stove and I left to start my morning round.

It was during lunch that we first heard the strange sound. It was something between a moan and a howl, starting quite softly but rising to a piercing pitch before shuddering back down the scale to silence.

Siegfried looked up, startled, from his soup. 'What in God's name is that?'

'Must be that dog I operated on this morning,' I replied. 'The odd one does that coming out of barbiturates. I expect he'll stop soon.'

Siegfried looked at me doubtfully. 'Well, I hope so – I could soon get tired of that. Gives me the creeps.'

We went through and looked at the dog. Pulse strong, respirations deep and regular, mucous membranes a good colour. He was still stretched out, immobile, and the only sign of returning consciousness was the howl which seemed to have settled down into a groove of one every ten seconds.

'Yes, he's perfectly all right,' Siegfried said. 'But what a bloody noise! Let's get out of here.'

Lunch was finished hastily and in silence except for the ceaseless background wailing. Siegfried had scarcely swallowed his last mouthful before he was on his feet. 'Well, I must fly. Got a lot on this afternoon. Tristan, I think it would be a good idea to bring that dog through to the sitting-room and put him by the fire. Then you could stay by him and keep an eye on him.'

Tristan was stunned. 'You mean I have to stay in the same room as that noise all afternoon?'

'Yes, I mean just that. We can't send him home as he is and I don't want anything to happen to him. He needs care and attention.'

'Maybe you'd like me to hold his paw or perhaps wheel him round the market-place?'

'Don't give me any of your bloody cheek. You stay with the dog and that's an order!'

Tristan and I stretchered the heavy animal along the passage on the blankets, then I had to leave for the afternoon round. I paused and looked back at the big black form by the fire and Tristan crouched miserably in his chair. The noise was overpowering. I closed the door hurriedly.

It was dark when I got back and the old house hung over me, black and silent against the frosty sky. Silent, that is, except for the howling which still echoed along the passage and filtered eerily into the deserted street.

I glanced at my watch as I slammed the car door. It was six o'clock, so Tristan had had four hours of it. I ran up the steps and along the passage and when I opened the sitting-room door the noise jarred in my head. Tristan was standing with his back to me, looking through the french window into the darkness of the garden. His hands were deep in his pockets; tufts of cotton wool drooped from his ears.

'Well, how is it going?' I asked.

There was no reply so I walked over and tapped him on the shoulder. The effect was spectacular. Tristan leaped into the air and corkscrewed round. His face was ashen and he was trembling violently.

'God help us, Jim, you nearly killed me there. I can't hear a damn thing through these ear plugs – except the dog, of course. Nothing keeps that out.'

I knelt by the Labrador and examined him. The dog's condition was excellent but, except for a faint eye reflex, there was no sign that he was regaining consciousness. And all the time there were the piercing, evenly spaced howls.

'He's taking a hell of a time to come out of it,' I said. 'Has he been like this all afternoon?'

'Yes, just like that. Not one bit different. And don't waste any sympathy on him, the yowling devil. He's as happy as a sandboy down by the fire – doesn't know a thing about it. But how about me? My nerves are about shot to bits listening to him hour after hour. Much more of it and you'll have to give me a shot too.' He ran a shaking hand through his hair and a twitching started in his cheek.

I took his arm. 'Well, come through and eat. You'll feel better after some food.' I led him unresisting into the dining-room.

Siegfried was in excellent form over the meal. He seemed to be in a mood of exhilaration and monopolised the conversation, but he did not once refer to the shrill obligato from the other room. There was no doubt, however, that it was still getting through to Tristan.

Tristan's Vigil

As they were leaving the room, Siegfried put his hand on my shoulder. 'Remember we've got that meeting in Brawton tonight, James. Old Reeves on diseases of sheep – he's usually very good. Pity you can't come too, Tristan, but I'm afraid you'll have to stay with the dog till he comes round.'

Tristan flinched as if he had been struck. 'Oh not another session with that bloody animal! He's driving me mad!'

'I'm afraid there's nothing else for it. James or I could have taken over tonight but we have to show up at this meeting. It would look bad if we missed it.'

Tristan stumbled back into the room and I put on my coat. As I went out into the street I paused for a moment and listened. The dog was still howling.

The meeting was a success. It was held in one of Brawton's lush hotels and, as usual, the best part was the get-together of the vets in the bar afterwards. It was infinitely soothing to hear the other man's problems and mistakes – especially the mistakes.

It amused me to look round the crowded room and try to guess what the little knots of men were talking about. That man over there, bent double and slashing away at the air with one hand – he was castrating a colt in the standing position. And the one with his arm out at full stretch, his fingers working busily at nothing – almost certainly foaling a mare; probably correcting a carpal flexion. And doing it effortlessly too. Veterinary surgery was a childishly simple matter in a warm bar with a few drinks inside you.

It was eleven o'clock before we all got into our cars and headed for our own particular niche in Yorkshire – some to the big industrial towns of the West Riding, others to the seaside places of the east coast and Siegfried and I hurrying thankfully back on the narrow road which twisted between its stone walls into the Northern Pennines.

I thought guiltily that for the last few hours I had completely forgotten about Tristan and his vigil. Still, it must have been better tonight. The dog would surely have quietened down by now. But, jumping from the car in Darrowby, I froze in mid-stride as a thin wail came out faintly from Skeldale House. This was incredible; it was after midnight and the dog was still at it. And what of Tristan? I hated to think what kind of shape he'd be in. Almost fearfully I turned the knob on the sitting-room door.

Tristan's chair made a little island in a sea of empty beer bottles.

An upturned crate lay against the wall and Tristan was sitting very upright and looking solemn. I picked my way over the debris.

'Well, has it been rough, Triss? How do you feel now?'

'Could be worse, old lad, could be worse. Soon as you'd gone I slipped over to the Drovers for a crate of pint Magnets. Made all the difference. After three or four the dog stopped worrying me – matter of fact, I've been yowling back at him for hours now. We've had quite an interesting evening. Anyway, he's coming out now. Look at him.'

The big dog had his head up and there was recognition in his eyes. The howling had stopped. I went over and patted him and the long black tail jerked in a fair attempt at a wag.

'That's better, old boy,' I said. 'But you'd better behave yourself now. You've given your uncle Tristan one hell of a day.'

The Labrador responded immediately by struggling to his feet. He took a few swaying steps and collapsed among the bottles.

Siegfried appeared in the doorway and looked distastefully at Tristan, still very upright and wearing a judicial expression, and at the dog scrabbling among the bottles. 'What an infernal mess! Surely you can do a little job without making an orgy out of it.'

At the sound of his voice the Labrador staggered up and, in a flush of over-confidence, tried to run towards him, wagging his tail unsteadily. He didn't get very far and went down in a heap, sending a Magnet empty rolling gently up to Siegfried's feet.

Siegfried bent over and stroked the shining black head. 'Nice friendly animal that. I should think he's a grand dog when he's got his senses about him. He'll be normal in the morning, but the problem is what to do with him now. We can't leave him staggering about down here – he could break a leg.' He glanced at Tristan who had not moved a muscle. He was sitting up straighter than ever, stiff and motionless like a Prussian general. 'You know, I think the best thing would be for you to take him up to your room tonight. Now we've got him so far, we don't want him to hurt himself. Yes, that's it, he can spend the night with you.'

'Thank you, thank you very much indeed,' Tristan said in a flat voice, still looking straight to his front.

Siegfried looked at him narrowly for a moment, then turned away. 'Right then, clear away this rubbish and let's get to bed.'

My bedroom and Tristan's were connected by a door. Mine was the main room, huge, square, with a high ceiling, pillared fireplace and graceful alcoves like the ones downstairs. I always felt a little like a duke lying there.

Tristan's had been the old dressing-room and was long and narrow with his small bed crouching at one end as if trying to hide. There were no carpets on the smooth, varnished boards so I laid the dog on a heap of blankets and talked down soothingly at Tristan's wan face on the pillow.

'He's quiet now – sleeping like a baby and looks as though he's going to stay that way. You'll be able to have a well earned rest now.'

I went back to my own room, undressed quickly and got into bed. I went to sleep immediately and I couldn't tell just when the noises started next door, but I came suddenly wide awake with an angry yell ringing in my ears. Then there was a slithering and a bump followed by another distracted cry from Tristan.

I quailed at the idea of going into the dressing-room – there was nothing I could do, anyway – so I huddled closer into the sheets and listened. I kept sliding into a half sleep then starting into wakefulness as more bumping and shouting came through the wall.

After about two hours the noises began to change. The Labrador seemed to have gained mastery over his legs and was marching up and down the room, his claws making a regular tck-a-tck, tck-a-tck, tck-a-tck on the wooden floor. It went on and on, interminably. At intervals, Tristan's voice, hoarse now, burst out. 'Stop it, for Christ's sake! Sit down, you bloody dog!'

I must have fallen into a deeper sleep because when I awoke the room was grey with the cold light of morning. I rolled on to my back and listened. I could still hear the tck-a-tck of the claws but it had become irregular as though the Labrador was strolling about instead of blundering blindly from one end of the room to the other. There was no sound from Tristan.

I got out of bed, shivering as the icy air of the room gripped me, and pulled on my shirt and trousers. Tiptoeing across the floor, I opened the connecting door and was almost floored as two large feet were planted on my chest. The Labrador was delighted to see me and appeared to be thoroughly at home. His fine brown eyes shone with intelligence and well-being and he showed rows of glittering teeth and a flawlessly pink tongue in a wide, panting grin. Far below, the tail lashed ecstatically.

'Well, you're all right, chum,' I said. 'Let's have a look at that wound.' I removed the horny paws from my chest and explored the line of stitches over the ribs. No swelling, no pain, no reaction at all.

'Lovely!' I cried. 'Beautiful. You're as good as new again.' I gave the dog a playful slap on the rump which sent him into a transport of joy. He leaped all over me, clawing and licking.

I was fighting him off when I heard a dismal groan from the bed. In the dim light Tristan looked ghastly. He was lying on his back, both hands clutching the quilt, and there was a wild look in his eyes. 'Not a wink of sleep, Jim,' he whispered. 'Not a bloody wink. He's got a wonderful sense of humour, my brother, making me spend the night with this animal. It'll really make his day when he hears what I've been through. Just watch him – I'll bet you anything you like he'll look pleased.'

Later, over breakfast, Siegfried heard the details of his brother's harrowing night and was very sympathetic. He condoled with him at length and apologised for all the trouble the dog had given him. But Tristan was right. He did look pleased.

*

I keep stressing the fact that animals are unpredictable things, and, indeed, this unpredictability is at the heart of much of my writing. One aspect of this is their varied reaction to anaesthetics. I understand that some human patients burst into song or come out with unprintable language. This dog just howled, and, of course, the incident is etched particularly deeply in my memory because poor Tristan was so closely involved. It is one of the things he and I laugh about now. The whole story gives me a nostalgic twinge with the recollection that in those days we would bring a patient into our sitting-room and even into our bedroom to look after him. We still like to think that we give personal attention, but I doubt if it will ever go as far as that again.

3. *A Triumph of Surgery*

I was really worried about Tricki this time. I had pulled up my car when I saw him in the street with his mistress and I was shocked at his appearance. He had become hugely fat, like a bloated sausage with a leg at each corner. His eyes, bloodshot and rheumy, stared straight ahead and his tongue lolled from his jaws.

Mrs Pumphrey hastened to explain. 'He was so listless, Mr Herriot. He seemed to have no energy. I thought he must be suffering from malnutrition, so I have been giving him some little extras between meals to build him up. Some calf's foot jelly and malt and cod liver oil and a bowl of Horlick's at night to make him sleep – nothing much really.'

'And did you cut down on the sweet things as I told you?'

'Oh, I did for a bit, but he seemed to be so weak I had to relent.

He does love cream cakes and chocolates so. I can't bear to refuse him.'

I looked down again at the little dog. That was the trouble. Tricki's only fault was greed. He had never been known to refuse food; he would tackle a meal at any hour of the day or night. And I wondered about all the things Mrs Pumphrey hadn't mentioned: the pâté on thin biscuits, the fudge, the rich trifles – Tricki loved them all.

'Are you giving him plenty of exercise?'

'Well, he has his little walks with me as you can see, but Hodgkin has been down with lumbago, so there has been no ring-throwing lately.'

I tried to sound severe. 'Now I really mean this. If you don't cut his food right down and give him more exercise he is going to be really ill. You must harden your heart and keep him on a very strict diet.'

Mrs Pumphrey wrung her hands. 'Oh I will, Mr Herriot. I'm sure you are right, but it is so difficult, so very difficult.' She set off, head down, along the road, as if determined to put the new regime into practice immediately.

I watched their progress with growing concern. Tricki was tottering along in his little tweed coat; he had a whole wardrobe of these coats – warm tweed or tartan ones for the cold weather and macintoshes for the wet days. He struggled on, drooping in his harness. I thought it wouldn't be long before I heard from Mrs Pumphrey.

The expected call came within a few days. Mrs Pumphrey was distraught. Tricki would eat nothing. Refused even his favourite dishes; and besides, he had bouts of vomiting. He spent all his time lying on a rug, panting. Didn't want to go walks, didn't want to do anything.

I had made my plans in advance. The only way was to get Tricki out of the house for a period. I suggested that he be hospitalised for about a fortnight to be kept under observation.

The poor lady almost swooned. She had never been separated from her darling before; she was sure he would pine and die if he did not see her every day.

But I took a firm line. Tricki was very ill and this was the only way to save him; in fact, I thought it best to take him without delay and, followed by Mrs Pumphrey's wailings, I marched out to the car carrying the little dog wrapped in a blanket.

The entire staff was roused and maids rushed in and out bringing his day bed, his night bed, favourite cushions, toys and rubber rings, breakfast bowl, lunch bowl, supper bowl. Realising that my car would never hold all the stuff, I started to drive away. As I moved off, Mrs Pumphrey, with a despairing cry, threw an armful of the little coats through the window. I looked in the mirror before I turned the corner of the drive; everybody was in tears.

Out on the road, I glanced down at the pathetic little animal gasping on the seat by my side. I patted the head and Tricki made a brave effort to wag his tail. 'Poor old lad,' I said, 'you haven't a kick in you but I think I know a cure for you.'

At the surgery, the household dogs surged round me. Tricki looked down at the noisy pack with dull eyes and, when put down, lay motionless on the carpet. The other dogs, after sniffing round him for a few seconds, decided he was an uninteresting object and ignored him.

I made up a bed for him in a warm loose box next to the one where the other dogs slept. For two days I kept an eye on him, giving him no food but plenty of water. At the end of the second day he started to show some interest in his surroundings and on the third he began to whimper when he heard the dogs in the yard.

When I opened the door, Tricki trotted out and was immediately engulfed by Joe the Greyhound and his friends. After rolling him over and thoroughly inspecting him, the dogs moved off down the garden. Tricki followed them, rolling slightly with his surplus fat but obviously intrigued.

Later that day, I was present at feeding time. I watched while Tristan slopped the food into the bowls. There was the usual headlong rush followed by the sounds of high-speed eating; every dog knew that if he fell behind the others he was liable to have some competition for the last part of his meal.

When they had finished, Tricki took a walk round the shining bowls, licking casually inside one or two of them. Next day, an extra bowl was put out for him and I was pleased to see him jostling his way towards it.

From then on, his progress was rapid. He had no medicinal treat-ment of any kind but all day he ran about with the dogs, joining in their friendly scrimmages. He discovered the joys of being bowled over, trampled on and squashed every few minutes. He became an accepted member of the gang, an unlikely, silky little object among the shaggy crew, fighting like a tiger for his share at meal times and hunting rats in the old hen house at night. He had never had such a time in his life.

All the while, Mrs Pumphrey hovered anxiously in the background, ringing a dozen times a day for the latest bulletins. I dodged the questions about whether his cushions were being turned regularly or his correct coat worn according to the weather; but I was able to tell her that the little fellow was out of danger and convalescing rapidly.

The word 'convalescing' seemed to do something to Mrs Pumphrey. She started to bring round fresh eggs, two dozen at a time, to build up Tricki's strength. For a happy period there were two eggs each for breakfast, but when the bottles of sherry began to arrive, the real possibilities of the situation began to dawn on the household.

It was the same delicious vintage that I knew so well and it was to enrich Tricki's blood. Lunch became a ceremonial occasion with two glasses before and several during the meal. Siegfried and Tristan took turns at proposing Tricki's health and the standard of speech-making improved daily. As the sponsor, I was always called upon to reply.

We could hardly believe it when the brandy came. Two bottles of Cordon Bleu, intended to put a final edge on Tricki's constitution. Siegfried dug out some balloon glasses belonging to his mother. I had never seen them before, but for a few nights they saw constant service as the fine spirit was rolled around, inhaled and reverently drunk.

They were days of deep content, starting well with the extra egg in the morning, bolstered up and sustained by the midday sherry and finishing luxuriously round the fire with the brandy.

It was a temptation to keep Tricki on as a permanent guest, but I knew Mrs Pumphrey was suffering and after a fortnight, felt compelled to phone and tell her that the little dog had recovered and was awaiting collection.

Within minutes, about thirty feet of gleaming black metal drew up outside the surgery. The chauffeur opened the door and I could just make out the figure of Mrs Pumphrey almost lost in the interior. Her hands were tightly clasped in front of her; her lips trembled. 'Oh, Mr Herriot, do tell me the truth. Is he really better?'

'Yes, he's fine. There's no need for you to get out of the car – I'll go and fetch him.'

I walked through the house into the garden. A mass of dogs was hurtling round and round the lawn and in their midst, ears flapping, tail waving, was the little golden figure of Tricki. In two weeks he had been transformed into a lithe, hard-muscled animal; he was keeping up well with the pack, stretching out in great bounds, his chest almost brushing the ground.

I carried him back along the passage to the front of the house. The chauffeur was still holding the car door open and when Tricki saw his mistress he took off from my arms in a tremendous leap and sailed into Mrs Pumphrey's lap. She gave a startled 'Ooh!' and then had to defend herself as he swarmed over her, licking her face and barking.

During the excitement, I helped the chauffeur to bring out the beds, toys, cushions, coats and bowls, none of which had been used. As the car moved away, Mrs Pumphrey leaned out of the window. Tears shone in her eyes. Her lips trembled.

'Oh, Mr Herriot,' she cried, 'how can I ever thank you? This is a triumph of surgery!'

*

Tricki Woo again and a delightful example of treating the individual animal with time to enjoy the rewards. The story also brings back one of the warmest memories of the camaraderie at Skeldale House when we shared out Mrs Pumphrey's goodies. Readers will be pleased to learn that from that time on, Tricki's diet was kept on a sensible basis so that there was no more obesity or cracker-dog.

4. *Have a Cigar*

I looked again at the slip of paper where I had written my visits. 'Dean, 3 Thompson's Yard. Old dog ill.'

There were a lot of these 'yards' in Darrowby. They were, in fact, tiny streets, like pictures from a Dickens novel. Some of them opened off the market-place and many more were scattered behind the main thoroughfares in the old part of the town. From the outside you could see only an archway, and it was always a surprise to me to go down a narrow passage and come suddenly upon the uneven rows of little houses with no two alike, looking into each other's windows across eight feet of cobbles.

In front of some of the houses a strip of garden had been dug out and marigolds and nasturtiums straggled over the rough stones; but at the far end the houses were in a tumbledown condition and some were abandoned with their windows boarded up.

Number three was down at this end and looked as though it wouldn't be able to hold out much longer.

The flakes of paint quivered on the rotten wood of the door as I knocked; above, the outer wall bulged dangerously on either side of a long crack in the masonry.

A small, white-haired man answered. His face, pinched and lined, was enlivened by a pair of cheerful eyes; he wore a much-darned woollen cardigan, patched trousers and slippers.

'I've come to see your dog,' I said, and the old man smiled.

'Oh, I'm so glad you've come, sir,' he said. 'I'm getting a bit worried about the old chap. Come inside, please.'

He led me into the tiny living-room. 'I'm alone now, sir. Lost my missus over a year ago. She used to think the world of the old dog.'

The grim evidence of poverty was everywhere. In the worn out lino, the fireless hearth, the dank, musty smell of the place. The wallpaper hung away from the damp patches and on the table the old man's solitary dinner was laid: a fragment of bacon, a few fried potatoes and a cup of tea. This was life on the old age pension.

In the corner, on a blanket, lay my patient, a cross-bred Labrador. He must have been a big, powerful dog in his time, but the signs of age showed in the white hairs round his muzzle and the pale opacity in the depth of his eyes. He lay quietly and looked at me without hostility.

'Getting on a bit, isn't he, Mr Dean?'

'Aye he is that. Nearly fourteen, but he's been like a pup galloping about until these last few weeks. Wonderful dog for his age is old Bob, and he's never offered to bite anybody in his life. Children can do anything with him. He's my only friend now – I hope you'll soon be able to put him right.'

'Is he off his food, Mr Dean?'

'Yes, clean off, and that's a strange thing because by gum, he could eat. He always sat by me and put his head on my knee at meal times, but he hasn't been doing it lately.'

I looked at the dog with growing uneasiness. The abdomen was grossly distended and I could read the tell-tale symptoms of pain: the catch in the respirations, the retracted commissures of the lips, the anxious, preoccupied expression in the eyes.

When his master spoke, the tail thumped twice on the blankets and a momentary interest showed in the white old eyes; but it quickly disappeared and the blank, inward look returned.

I passed my hand carefully over the dog's abdomen. Ascites was pronounced and the dropsical fluid had gathered till the pressure was intense. 'Come on, old chap,' I said, 'let's see if we can roll you over.' The dog made no resistance as I eased him slowly on to his other side, but, just as the movement was completed, he whimpered and looked round. The cause of the trouble was now only too easy to find.

I palpated gently. Through the thin muscle of the flank I could feel a hard, corrugated mass; certainly a splenic or hepatic carcinoma, enormous and completely inoperable. I stroked the old dog's head as I tried to collect my thoughts. This wasn't going to be easy.

'Is he going to be ill for long?' the old man asked, and again came the thump, thump of the tail at the sound of the loved voice. 'It's miserable when Bob isn't following me round the house when I'm doing my little jobs.'

'I'm sorry, Mr Dean, but I'm afraid this is something very serious. You see this large swelling. It is caused by an internal growth.'

'You mean . . . cancer?' the little man said faintly.

'I'm afraid so, and it has progressed too far for anything to be done. I wish there was something I could do to help him, but there isn't.'

The old man looked bewildered and his lips trembled. 'Then he's going to die?'

I swallowed hard. 'We really can't just leave him to die, can we? He's in some distress now, but it will soon be an awful lot worse. Don't you think it would be kindest to put him to sleep? After all, he's had a good, long innings.' I always aimed at a brisk, matter-of-fact approach, but the old clichés had an empty ring.

The old man was silent, then he said, 'Just a minute,' and slowly and painfully knelt down by the side of the dog. He did not speak, but ran his hand again and again over the grey muzzle and the ears, while the tail thump, thump, thumped on the floor.

He knelt there a long time while I stood in the cheerless room, my eyes taking in the faded pictures on the walls, the frayed, grimy curtains, the broken-springed armchair.

At length the old man struggled to his feet and gulped once or twice. Without looking at me, he said huskily, 'All right, will you do it now?'

I filled the syringe and said the things I always said. 'You needn't worry, this is absolutely painless. Just an overdose of an anaesthetic. It is really an easy way out for the old fellow.'

The dog did not move as the needle was inserted, and, as the barbiturate began to flow into the vein, the anxious expression left his face and the muscles began to relax. By the time the injection was finished, the breathing had stopped.

'Is that it?' the old man whispered.

'Yes, that's it,' I said. 'He is out of his pain now.'

The old man stood motionless except for the clasping and unclasping of his hands. When he turned to face me his eyes were bright. 'That's right, we couldn't let him suffer, and I'm grateful for what you've done. And now, what do I owe you for your services, sir?'

'Oh, that's all right, Mr Dean,' I said quickly. 'It's nothing – nothing at all. I was passing right by here – it was no trouble.'

The old man was astonished. 'But you can't do that for nothing.'

'Now please say no more about it, Mr Dean. As I told you, I was passing right by your door.' I said goodbye and went out of the house, through the passage and into the street. In the bustle of people and the bright sunshine, I could still see only the stark, little room, the old man and his dead dog.

As I walked towards my car, I heard a shout behind me. The old man was shuffling excitedly towards me in his slippers. His cheeks were streaked and wet, but he was smiling. In his hand he held a small, brown object.

'You've been very kind, sir. I've got something for you.' He held out the object and I looked at it. It was tattered but just recognisable as a precious relic of a bygone celebration.

'Go on, it's for you,' said the old man. 'Have a cigar.'

*

This incident, which happened so early in my veterinary career, haunted me for many weeks afterwards, and it still remains as one of my most vivid and poignant memories. Putting old people's precious pets to sleep is sadly a common duty in veterinary practice, and the fact that it can be done humanely and peacefully with barbiturates makes it tolerable. But there was something about the Mr Dean episode that made it stand out, and I remember it as the very first time I said to myself, 'If ever I write a book, I'll put that in.' Maybe it was that cigar . . .

5. *Maternal Instincts*

There didn't seem much point in a millionaire filling up football pools coupons but it was one of the motive forces in old Harold Denham's life. It made a tremendous bond between us because, despite his devotion to the pools, Harold knew nothing about football, had never seen a match and was unable to name a single player in league football; and when he found that I could discourse knowledgeably not only about Everton and Preston North End, but even about Arbroath and Cowdenbeath, the respect with which he had always treated me deepened into a wide-eyed deference.

Maternal Instincts

Of course we had first met over his animals. He had an assortment of dogs, cats, rabbits, budgies and goldfish which made me a frequent visitor to the dusty mansion whose Victorian turrets peeping above their sheltering woods could be seen for miles around Darrowby. When I first knew him, the circumstances of my visits were entirely normal – his Fox Terrier had cut its pad or the old grey tabby was having trouble with its sinusitis, but later on I began to wonder. He called me out so often on a Wednesday and the excuse was at times so trivial that I began seriously to suspect that there was nothing wrong with the animal but that Harold was in difficulties with his Nine Results or the Easy Six.

I could never be quite sure, but it was funny how he always received me with the same words. 'Ah, Mr Herriot, how are your pools?' He used to say the word in a long-drawn, loving way – poools. This enquiry had been unvarying ever since I had won sixteen shillings one week on the Three Draws. I can never forget the awe with which he fingered the little slip from Littlewoods, looking unbelievingly from it to the postal order. That was the only time I was a winner but it made no difference – I was still the oracle, unchallenged, supreme. Harold never won anything, ever.

The Denhams were a family of note in North Yorkshire. The immensely wealthy industrialists of the last century had become leaders in the world of agriculture. They were 'gentlemen farmers' who used their money to build up pedigree herds of dairy cows or pigs; they ploughed out the high, stony moorland and fertilised it and made it grow crops; they drained sour bogs and made them yield potatoes and turnips; they were the chairmen of committees, masters of fox hounds, leaders of the county society.

But Harold had opted out of all that at an early age. He had refuted the age-old dictum that you can't be happy doing absolutely nothing; all day and every day he pottered around his house and his few untidy acres, uninterested in the world outside, not entirely aware of what was going on in his immediate vicinity, but utterly content. I don't think he ever gave a thought to other people's opinions, which was just as well because they were often unkind; his brother, the eminent Basil Denham, referred to him invariably as 'that bloody fool' and with the country people it was often 'nobbut ninepence in t'shillin''.

Personally I always found something appealing in him. He was kind, friendly, with a sense of fun and I enjoyed going to his house.

25

He and his wife ate all their meals in the kitchen and in fact seemed to spend most of their time there, so I usually went round the back of the house.

On this particular day it was to see his Great Dane bitch which had just had pups and seemed unwell; since it wasn't Wednesday I felt that there really might be something amiss with her and hurried round. Harold gave me his usual greeting; he had the most attractive voice – round, fruity, mellow, like a bishop's, and for the hundredth time I thought how odd it was to hear those organ-like vocal chords intoning such incongruities as Mansfield Town or Bradford City.

'I wonder if you could advise me, Mr Herriot,' he said as we left the kitchen and entered a long, ill-lit passage. 'I'm searching for an away winner and I wondered about Sunderland at Aston Villa?'

I stopped and fell into an attitude of deep thought while Harold regarded me anxiously. 'Well, I'm not sure, Mr Denham,' I replied. 'Sunderland are a good side but I happen to know that Raich Carter's auntie isn't too well at present and it could easily affect his game this Saturday.'

Harold looked crestfallen and he nodded his head gravely a few times; then he looked closely at me for a few seconds and broke into a shout of laughter. 'Ah, Mr Herriot, you're pulling my leg again.' He seized my arm, gave it a squeeze and shuffled off along the passage, chuckling deeply.

We traversed a labyrinth of gloomy, cobwebbed passages before he led the way into a little gun room. My patient was lying on a raised wooden dog bed and I recognised her as the enormous Dane I had seen leaping around at previous visits. I had never treated her, but my first sight of her had dealt a blow at one of my new-found theories – that you didn't find big dogs in big houses. Times without number I had critically observed Bull Mastiffs, Alsatians and Old English Sheepdogs catapulting out of the tiny, back-street dwellings of Darrowby, pulling their helpless owners on the end of a lead, while in the spacious rooms and wide acres of the stately homes I saw nothing but Border Terriers and Jack Russells. But Harold would have to be different.

He patted the bitch's head. 'She had the puppies yesterday and she's got a nasty dark discharge. She's eating well, but I'd like you to look her over.'

Great Danes, like most of the big breeds, are usually placid animals and the bitch didn't move as I took her temperature. She lay on her side, listening contentedly to the squeals of her family as the little blind creatures climbed over each other to get at the engorged teats. 'Yes, she's got a slight fever and you're right about the discharge.' I gently palpated the long hollow of the flank. 'I don't think there's another pup there but I'd better have a feel inside her to make sure. Could you bring me some warm water, soap and towel please?'

As the door closed behind Harold I looked idly around the gun room. It wasn't much bigger than a cupboard and, since another of Harold's idiosyncrasies was that he never killed anything, was devoid of guns. The glass cases contained only musty bound volumes of *Blackwood's Magazine* and *Country Life*. I stood there for maybe ten minutes, wondering why the old chap was taking so long, then I turned to look at an old print on the wall; it was the usual hunting scene and I was peering through the grimy glass and wondering why they always drew those horses flying over the stream with such impossible long legs when I heard a sound behind me.

It was a faint growl, a deep rumble, soft but menacing. I turned and saw the bitch rising very slowly from her bed. She wasn't getting to her feet in the normal way of dogs, it was as though she were being lifted up by strings somewhere in the ceiling, the legs straightening almost imperceptibly, the body rigid, every hair bristling. All the time she glared at me unblinkingly and for the first time in my life I realised the meaning of blazing eyes. I had only once seen anything like this before and it was on the cover of an old copy of *The Hound of the Baskervilles*. At the time I had thought the artist ridiculously fanciful but here were two eyes filled with the same yellow fire and fixed unwaveringly on mine.

She thought I was after her pups, of course. After all, her master had gone and there was only this stranger standing motionless and silent in the corner of the room, obviously up to no good. One thing was sure – she was going to come at me any second, and I blessed the luck that had made me stand right by the door. Carefully I inched my left hand towards the handle as the bitch still rose with terrifying slowness, still rumbling deep in her chest. I had almost reached the handle when I made the mistake of making a quick grab for it. Just as I touched the metal the bitch came out of the bed like a rocket and sank her teeth into my wrist.

I thumped her over the head with my right fist and she let go and seized me high up on the inside of the left thigh. This really made me yell out and I don't know just what my immediate future would have been if I hadn't bumped up against the only chair in the room; it was old and flimsy but it saved me. As the bitch, apparently tiring of gnawing my leg, made a sudden leap at my face, I snatched the chair up and fended her off.

The rest of my spell in the gun room was a sort of parody of a lion-taming act and would have been richly funny to an impartial observer. In fact, in later years I have often wished I could have a ciné film of the episode; but at the time, with that great animal stalking me round those few cramped yards of space, the blood trickling down my leg and only a rickety chair to protect me, I didn't feel a bit like laughing. There was a dreadful dedication in the way she followed me and those maddened eyes never left my face for an instant.

The pups, furious at the unceremonious removal of their delightful source of warmth and nourishment, were crawling blindly across the bed and bawling, all nine of them, at the top of their voices. The din acted as a spur to the bitch and the louder it became the more she pressed home her attack. Every few seconds she would launch herself at me and I would prance about, stabbing at her with my chair in best circus fashion. Once she bore me back against the wall, chair and all; on her hind legs she was about as tall as me and I had a disturbing close-up of the snarling gaping jaws.

My biggest worry was that my chair was beginning to show signs of wear; the bitch had already crunched two of the spars effortlessly away and I tried not to think of what would happen if the whole thing finally disintegrated. But I was working my way back to the door and when I felt the handle at my back I knew I had to do something about it. I gave a final, intimidating shout, threw the remains of the chair at the bitch and dived out into the corridor. As I slammed the door behind me and leaned against it I could feel the panels quivering as the big animal threw herself against the wood.

I was sitting on the floor with my back against the passage wall, pants round my ankles, examining my wounds, when I saw Harold pass across the far end, pottering vaguely along with a basin of steaming water held in front of him and a towel over his shoulder. I could understand now why he had been so long – he had been wandering around like that all the time; being Harold it was just possible he had been lost in his own house. Or maybe he was just worrying about his Four Aways.

Back at Skeldale House I had to endure some unkind remarks

about my straddling gait, but later, in my bedroom, the smile left Siegfried's face as he examined my leg.

'Right up there, by God.' He gave a low, awed whistle. 'You know, James, we've often made jokes about what a savage dog might do to us one day. Well, I tell you boy, it damn nearly happened to you.'

*

Shortly after this happened, I went walking in Scotland with the rough inside of my khaki shorts rubbing against the semi-circle of tooth marks on my thigh. A constant reminder that even small-animal practice can be dangerous, and a little lesson that even docile bitches are sometimes alarmingly protective towards their pups. Of course, the opposite can be the case. Quite often when I approach a bitch with her puppies nestling close to her I can see that she is bursting with pride, and when I lift out one of the little creatures she wags her tail in obvious delight. You just never know. It is one of the many uncertainties of our job.

6. *Dan – and Helen*

'Could Mr Herriot see my dog, please?'

Familiar enough words coming from the waiting-room but it was the voice that brought me to a slithering halt just beyond the door.

It couldn't be, no of course it couldn't, but it sounded just like Helen. I tiptoed back and applied my eye without hesitation to the crack in the door. Tristan was standing there looking down at somebody just beyond my range of vision. All I could see was a hand resting on the head of a patient sheepdog, the hem of a tweed skirt and two silk stockinged legs.

They were nice legs – not skinny – and could easily belong to a big girl like Helen. My cogitations were cut short as a head bent over to speak to the dog and I had a close-up in profile of the small straight nose and the dark hair falling across the milky smoothness of the cheek.

I was still peering, bemused, when Tristan shot out of the room and collided with me. Stifling an oath, he grabbed my arm and hauled me along the passage into the dispensary. He shut the door and spoke in a hoarse whisper.

'It's her! The Alderson woman! And she wants to see you! Not Siegfried, not me, but you, Mr Herriot himself!'

He looked at me wide-eyed for a few moments then, as I stood hesitating, he opened the door and tried to propel me into the passage.

'What the hell are you waiting for?' he hissed.

'Well, it's a bit embarrassing, isn't it? After that dance, I mean. Last time she saw me I was a lovely sight – so pie-eyed I couldn't even speak.'

Tristan struck his forehead with his hand. 'God help us! You worry about details, don't you? She's asked to see you – what more do you want? Go on, get in there!'

I was shuffling off irresolutely when he raised a hand. 'Just a minute. Stay right there.' He trotted off and returned in a few seconds holding out a white lab coat.

'Just back from the laundry,' he said as he began to work my arms into the starched sleeves. 'You'll look marvellous in this, Jim – the immaculate young surgeon.'

I stood unresisting as he buttoned me into the garment but struck away his hand when he started to straighten my tie. As I left him he gave me a final encouraging wave before heading for the back stairs.

I didn't give myself any more time to think but marched straight into the waiting-room. Helen looked up and smiled. And it was just the same smile. Nothing behind it. Just the same friendly, steady-eyed smile as when I first met her.

We faced each other in silence for some moments, then when I didn't say anything she looked down at the dog.

'It's Dan in trouble this time,' she said. 'He's our sheepdog but we're so fond of him that he's more like one of the family.'

The dog wagged his tail furiously at the sound of his name but yelped as he came towards me. I bent down and patted his head. 'I see he's holding up a hind leg.'

'Yes, he jumped over a wall this morning and he's been like that ever since. I think it's something quite bad – he can't put any weight on the leg.'

'Right, bring him through to the other room and I'll have a look at him. But take him on in front of me, will you, and I'll be able to watch how he walks.'

I held the door open and she went through ahead of me with the dog.

Watching how Helen walked distracted me over the first few yards, but it was a long passage and by the time we had reached the second bend I had managed to drag my attention back to my patient.

And glory be, it was a dislocated hip. It had to be with that shortening of the limb and the way he carried it underneath his body with the paw just brushing the ground.

My feelings were mixed. This was a major injury, but on the other hand the chances were I could put it right quickly and look good in the process. Because I had found, in my brief experience, that one of the most spectacular procedures in practice was the reduction of a dislocated hip. Maybe I had been lucky, but with the few I had seen I had been able to convert an alarmingly lame animal into a completely sound one as though by magic.

In the operating room I hoisted Dan on to the table. He stood without moving as I examined the hip. There was no doubt about it at all – the head of the femur was displaced upwards and backwards, plainly palpable under my thumb.

The dog looked round only once – when I made a gentle attempt to flex the limb – but turned away immediately and stared resolutely ahead. His mouth hung open a little as he panted nervously, but like a lot of the placid animals which arrived on our surgery table he seemed to have resigned himself to his fate. I had the strong impression that I could have started to cut his head off and he wouldn't have made much fuss.

'Nice, good-natured dog,' I said. 'And a bonny one, too.'

Helen patted the handsome head with the broad blaze of white down the face; the tail waved slowly from side to side.

'Yes,' she said. 'He's just as much a family pet as a working dog. I do hope he hasn't hurt himself too badly.'

'Well, he has a dislocated hip. It's a nasty thing but with a bit of luck I ought to be able to put it back.'

'What happens if it won't go back?'

'He'd have to form a false joint up there. He'd be very lame for several weeks and probably always have a slightly short leg.'

'Oh dear, I wouldn't like that,' Helen said. 'Do you think he'll be all right?'

I looked at the docile animal still gazing steadfastly to his front. 'I think he's got a good chance, mainly because you haven't hung about for days before bringing him in. The sooner these things are tackled the better.'

'Oh good. When will you be able to start on him?'

'Right now.' I went over to the door. 'I'll just give Tristan a shout. This is a two-man job.'

'Couldn't I help?' Helen said. 'I'd very much like to if you wouldn't mind.'

I looked at her doubtfully. 'Well I don't know. You mightn't like playing tug of war with Dan in the middle. He'll be anaesthetised of course, but there's usually a lot of pulling.'

Helen laughed. 'Oh, I'm quite strong. And not a bit squeamish. I'm used to animals, you know, and I like working with them.'

'Right,' I said. 'Slip on this spare coat and we'll begin.'

The dog didn't flinch as I pushed the needle into his vein and, as the Nembutal flowed in, his head began to slump against Helen's arm and his supporting paw to slide along the smooth top of the table. Soon he was stretched unconscious on his side.

I held the needle in the vein as I looked down at the sleeping animal. 'I might have to give him a bit more. They have to be pretty deep to overcome the muscular resistance.'

Another cc. and Dan was as limp as any rag doll. I took hold of the affected leg and spoke across the table. 'I want you to link your hands underneath his thigh and try to hold him there when I pull. O.K.? Here we go, then.'

It takes a surprising amount of force to pull the head of a displaced femur over the rim of the acetabulum. I kept up a steady traction with my right hand, pressing on the head of the femur at the same time with my left. Helen did her part efficiently, leaning back against the pull, her lips pushed forward in a little pout of concentration.

I suppose there must be a foolproof way of doing this job – a method which works the very first time – but I have never been able to find it. Success has always come to me only after a fairly long period of trial and error and it was the same today. I tried all sorts of angles, rotations and twists on the flaccid limb, trying not to think of how it would look if this just happened to be the one I couldn't put back. I was wondering what Helen, still hanging on determinedly to her end, must be thinking of this wrestling match when I heard the muffled click. It was a sweet and welcome sound.

I flexed the hip joint once or twice. No resistance at all now. The femoral head was once more riding smoothly in its socket.

'Well, that's it,' I said. 'Hope it stays put – we'll have to keep our fingers crossed. The odd one does pop out again but I've got a feeling this is going to be all right.'

Helen ran her hand over the silky ears and neck of the sleeping dog. 'Poor old Dan. He wouldn't have jumped over that wall this morning if he'd known what was in store for him. How long will it be before he comes round?'

'Oh, he'll be out for the rest of the day. When he starts to wake up tonight I want you to be around to steady him in case he falls and puts the thing out again. Perhaps you'd give me a ring. I'd like to know how things are.'

I gathered Dan up in my arms and was carrying him along the passage, staggering under his weight, when I met Mrs Hall. She was carrying a tray with two cups.

'I was just having a drink of tea, Mr Herriot,' she said. 'I thought you and the young lady might fancy a cup.'

I looked at her narrowly. This was unusual. Was it possible she had joined Tristan in playing Cupid? But the broad, dark-skinned face was as unemotional as ever. It told me nothing.

'Well, thanks very much, Mrs Hall. I'll just put this dog outside first.' I went out and settled Dan on the back seat of Helen's car; with only his eyes and nose sticking out from under a blanket he looked at peace with the world.

Helen was already sitting with a cup in her lap and I thought of the other time I had drunk tea in this room with a girl. On the day I had arrived in Darrowby. She had been one of Siegfried's followers and surely the toughest of them all.

This was a lot different. During the struggle in the operating room I had been able to observe Helen at close range and I had discovered that her mouth turned up markedly at the corners as though she was just going to smile or had just been smiling; also that the deep warm blue of the eyes under the smoothly arching brows made a dizzying partnership with the rich black-brown of her hair.

And this time the conversation didn't lag. Maybe it was because

I was on my own ground – perhaps I never felt fully at ease unless there was a sick animal involved somewhere, but at any rate I found myself prattling effortlessly just as I had done up on that hill when we had first met.

Mrs Hall's teapot was empty and the last of the biscuits gone before I finally saw Helen off and started on my round.

The same feeling of easy confidence was on me that night when I heard her voice on the phone.

'Dan is up and walking about,' she said. 'He's still a bit wobbly but he's perfectly sound on that leg.'

'Oh great, he's got the first stage over. I think everything's going to be fine.'

There was a pause at the other end of the line, then: 'Thank you so much for what you've done. We were terribly worried about him, especially my young brother and sister. We're very grateful.'

'Not at all, I'm delighted too. He's a grand dog.' I hesitated for a moment – it had to be now. 'Oh, you remember we were talking about Scotland today. Well, I was passing the Plaza this afternoon and I see they're showing a film about the Hebrides. I thought maybe . . . I wondered if perhaps, er . . . you might like to come and see it with me.'

Another pause and my heart did a quick thud-thud.

'All right,' Helen said. 'Yes, I'd like that. When? Friday night? Well, thank you – goodbye till then.'

I replaced the receiver with a trembling hand. Why did I make such heavy weather of these things? But it didn't matter – I was back in business.

*

It so often happens that spectacular cures go unnoticed and unappreciated, but how wonderful that this one should further my courtship so beautifully. Reducing a dislocated hip is truly dramatic and it couldn't have happened at a better time. It is surprising how easily a hip can pop out of place. Just as it is deeply satisfying to a vet to convert a lame dog to a sound one with one quick click, it is similarly alarming to an owner to see a pet suddenly transformed into a three-legged cripple for no apparent reason. It can happen so simply. Jumping for a ball. Falling off a chair. It must be one of the worst panic-instigators.

7. *Tip*

It looked as though I was going to make it back to the road all right. And I was thankful for it because seven o'clock in the morning with the wintry dawn only just beginning to lighten the eastern rim of the moor was no time to be digging my car out of the snow.

This narrow, unfenced road skirted a high tableland and gave on to a few lonely farms at the end of even narrower tracks. It hadn't actually been snowing on my way out to this early call – a uterine haemorrhage in a cow – but the wind had been rising steadily and whipping the top surface from the white blanket which had covered the fell-tops for weeks. My headlights had picked out the creeping drifts; pretty, pointed fingers feeling their way inch by inch across the strip of tarmac.

This was how all blocked roads began, and at the farm as I injected pituitrin and packed the bleeding cervix with a clean sheet I could hear the wind buffeting the byre door and wondered if I would win the race home.

On the way back the drifts had stopped being pretty and lay across the road like white bolsters; but my little car had managed to cleave through them, veering crazily at times, wheels spinning, and now I could see the main road a few hundred yards ahead, reassuringly black in the pale light.

But just over there on the left, a field away, was Cote House. I was treating a bullock there – he had eaten some frozen turnips – and a visit was fixed for today. I didn't fancy trailing back up here if I could avoid it and there was a light in the kitchen window. The family were up, anyway. I turned and drove down into the yard.

The farmhouse door lay within a small porch and the wind had driven the snow inside, forming a smooth, two-foot heap against the timbers. As I leaned across to knock, the surface of the heap trembled a little, then began to heave. There was something in there, something quite big. It was eerie standing in the half-light watching the snow parting to reveal a furry body. Some creature of the wild must have strayed in, searching for warmth – but it was bigger than a fox or anything else I could think of.

Just then the door opened and the light from the kitchen streamed out. Peter Trenholm beckoned me inside and his wife smiled at me from the bright interior. They were a cheerful young couple.

'What's that?' I gasped, pointing at the animal which was shaking the snow vigorously from its coat.

'That?' Peter grinned. 'That's awd Tip.'

'Tip? Your dog? But what's he doing under a pile of snow?'

'Just blew in on him, I reckon. That's where he sleeps, you know, just outside back door.'

I stared at the farmer. 'You mean he sleeps there, out in the open, every night?'

'Aye, allus. Summer and winter. But don't look at me like that Mr Herriot – it's his own choice. The other dogs have a warm bed in the cow house but Tip won't entertain it. He's fifteen now and he's been sleeping out there since he were a pup. I remember when me father was alive he tried all ways to get t'awd feller to sleep inside but it was no good.'

I looked at the old dog in amazement. I could see him more clearly now; he wasn't the typical sheepdog type, he was bigger boned, longer in the hair, and he projected a bursting vitality that didn't go with his fifteen years. It was difficult to believe that any animal living in these bleak uplands should choose to sleep outside – and thrive on it. I had to look closely to see any sign of his great age. There was the slightest stiffness in his gait as he moved around, perhaps a fleshless look about his head and face, and of course the tell-tale lens opacity in the depths of his eyes. But the general impression was of an unquenchable jauntiness.

He shook the last of the snow from his coat, pranced jerkily up to the farmer and gave a couple of reedy barks. Peter Trenholm laughed. 'You see he's ready to be off – he's a beggar for work is Tip.' He led the way towards the buildings and I followed, stumbling over the frozen ruts, like iron under the snow, and bending my head against the knife-like wind. It was a relief to open the byre door and escape into the sweet bovine warmth.

There was a fair mixture of animals in the long building. The dairy cows took up most of the length, then there were a few young heifers, some bullocks, and finally, in an empty stall deeply bedded with straw, the other farm dogs. The cats were there too, so it had to be warm. No animal is a better judge of comfort than a cat and they were just visible as furry balls in the straw. They had the best place, up against the wooden partition where the warmth came through from the big animals.

Tip strode confidently among his colleagues – a young dog and a bitch with three half-grown pups. You could see he was boss.

One of the bullocks was my patient and he was looking a bit better. When I had seen him yesterday his rumen (the big first stomach) had been completely static and atonic following an over-eager consumption of frozen turnips. He had been slightly bloated and groaning with discomfort. But today as I leaned with my ear against his left side I could hear the beginnings of the surge and rumble of the normal rumen instead of the deathly silence of yesterday. My gastric lavage had undoubtedly tickled things up and I felt that another of the same would just about put him right. Almost lovingly I got together the ingredients of one of my favourite treatments, long since washed away in the flood of progress: the ounce of formalin, the half pound of common salt, the can of black treacle from the barrel which you used to find in most cow houses, all mixed up in a bucket with two gallons of hot water.

I jammed the wooden gag into the bullock's mouth and buckled it behind the horns, then as Peter held the handles I passed the stomach tube down into the rumen and pumped in the mixture. When I had finished the bullock opened his eyes wide in surprise and began to paddle his hind legs. Listening again at his side, I could hear the reassuring bubbling of the stomach contents. I smiled to myself in satisfaction. It worked; it always worked.

Wiping down the tube I could hear the hiss-hiss as Peter's brother got on with the morning's milking, and as I prepared to leave he came down the byre with a full bucket on the way to the cooler. As he passed the dogs' stall he tipped a few pints of the warm milk into their dishes and Tip strolled forward casually for his breakfast. While he was drinking, the young dog tried to push his way in, but a soundless snap from Tip's jaws missed his nose by a fraction and he retired to another dish. I noticed, however, that the old dog made no protest as the bitch and pups joined him. The cats, black and white, tortoise-shell, tabby grey, appeared, stretching, from the straw and advanced in a watchful ring. Their turn would come.

Mrs Trenholm called me in for a cup of tea and when I came out it was full daylight. But the sky was a burdened grey and the sparse trees near the house strained their bare branches against the wind which drove in long, icy gusts over the white empty miles of moor. It was what the Yorkshiremen called a 'thin wind' or sometimes a 'lazy wind' – the kind that couldn't be bothered to blow round you but went straight through instead. It made me feel that the best place on earth was by the side of that bright fire in the farmhouse kitchen.

Most people would have felt like that, but not old Tip. He was capering around as Peter loaded a flat cart with some hay bales for the young cattle in the outside barns; and as Peter shook the reins and the cob set off over the fields, he leapt on to the back of the cart.

As I threw my tackle into the boot I looked back at the old dog, legs braced against the uneven motion, tail waving, barking defiance at the cold world. I carried away the memory of Tip who scorned the softer things and slept in what he considered the place of honour – at his master's door.

*

Dear old Tip. So typical of the thousands of hardy farm dogs who joyfully earn their keep in the high country of North Yorkshire. Bursting with energy, tough and stringy. You never see a fat one. They know little of comfort, leisure or balanced diets – many of them live on flaked maize and milk – but they are wonderfully healthy. Perhaps their life-span is a little shorter because of their constant work and activity, but that doesn't always hold good; I can remember one old fellow of twenty tottering out of a stable on shaky limbs to welcome me on to a farm. His waving tail told me that he was still enjoying life. Tip, however, remains as the only dog I have ever known who slept under the snow.

8. *The Card over the Bed*

The card dangled above the old lady's bed. It read 'God is Near' but it wasn't like the usual religious text. It didn't have a frame or ornate printing. It was just a strip of cardboard about eight inches long with plain lettering which might have said 'No smoking' or 'Exit' and it was looped carelessly over an old gas bracket so that Miss Stubbs from where she lay could look up at it and read 'God is Near' in square black capitals.

There wasn't much more Miss Stubbs could see; perhaps a few feet of privet hedge through the frayed curtains but mainly it was just the cluttered little room which had been her world for so many years.

The room was on the ground floor and in the front of the cottage, and as I came up through the wilderness which had once been a garden I could see the dogs watching me from where they had jumped on to the old lady's bed. And when I knocked on the door the place almost erupted with their barking. It was always like this. I had been visiting regularly for over a year and the pattern never changed; the furious barking, then Mrs Broadwith who looked after Miss Stubbs would push all the animals but my patient into the back kitchen and open the door and I would go in and see Miss Stubbs in the corner in her bed with the card hanging over it.

She had been there for a long time and would never get up again. But she never mentioned her illness and pain to me; all her concern was for her three dogs and two cats.

Today it was old Prince and I was worried about him. It was his heart – just about the most spectacular valvular incompetence I had ever heard. He was waiting for me as I came in, pleased as ever to see me, his long, fringed tail waving gently.

The sight of that tail used to make me think there must be a lot of Irish Setter in Prince, but I was inclined to change my mind as I worked my way forward over the bulging black and white body to the shaggy head and upstanding Alsatian ears. Miss Stubbs often used to call him 'Mr Heinz', and though he may not have had 57 varieties in him his hybrid vigour had stood him in good stead. With his heart he should have been dead long ago.

'I thought I'd best give you a ring, Mr Herriot,' Mrs Broadwith said. She was a comfortable, elderly widow with a square, ruddy face contrasting sharply with the pinched features on the pillow. 'He's been coughing right bad this week and this morning he was a bit staggery. Still eats well, though.'

'I bet he does.' I ran my hands over the rolls of fat on the ribs. 'It would take something really drastic to put old Prince off his grub.'

Miss Stubbs laughed from the bed and the old dog, his mouth wide, eyes dancing, seemed to be joining in the joke. I put my stethoscope over his heart and listened, knowing well what I was going to hear. They say the heart is supposed to go 'lub-dup, lub-dup', but Prince's went 'swish-swoosh, swish-swoosh'. There seemed to be nearly as much blood leaking back as was being pumped into the circulatory system. And another thing, the 'swish-swoosh' was a good bit faster than last time; he was on oral digitalis but it wasn't quite doing its job.

The Card over the Bed

Gloomily I moved the stethoscope over the rest of the chest. Like all old dogs with a chronic heart weakness he had an ever-present bronchitis and I listened without enthusiasm to the symphony of whistles, rales, squeaks and bubbles which signalled the workings of Prince's lungs. The old dog stood very erect and proud, his tail still waving slowly. He always took it as a tremendous compliment when I examined him and there was no doubt he was enjoying himself now. Fortunately his was not a very painful ailment.

Straightening up, I patted his head and he responded immediately by trying to put his paws on my chest. He didn't quite make it and even that slight exertion started his ribs heaving and his tongue lolling. I gave him an intramuscular injection of digitalin and another of morphine hydrochloride which he accepted with apparent pleasure as part of the game.

'I hope that will steady his heart and breathing, Miss Stubbs. You'll find he'll be a bit dopey for the rest of the day and that will help, too. Carry on with the tablets, and I'm going to leave you some more medicine for his bronchitis.' I handed over a bottle of my old standby mixture of ipecacuanha and ammonium acetate.

The next stage of the visit began now as Mrs Broadwith brought in a cup of tea and the rest of the animals were let out of the kitchen. There were Ben, a Sealyham, and Sally, a Cocker Spaniel, and they started a deafening barking contest with Prince. They were closely followed by the cats, Arthur and Susie, who stalked in gracefully and began to rub themselves against my trouser legs.

It was the usual scenario for the many cups of tea I had drunk with Miss Stubbs under the little card which dangled above her bed.

'How are you today?' I asked.

'Oh, much better,' she replied and immediately, as always, changed the subject.

Mostly she liked to talk about her pets and the ones she had known right back to her girlhood. She spoke a lot, too, about the days when her family were alive. She loved to describe the escapades of her three brothers and today she showed me a photograph which Mrs Broadwith had found at the bottom of a drawer.

I took it from her and three young men in the knee breeches and little round caps of the nineties smiled up at me from the yellowed old print; they all held long church warden pipes and the impish humour in their expressions came down undimmed over the years.

'My word, they look really bright lads, Miss Stubbs,' I said.

43

'Oh, they were young rips!' she exclaimed. She threw back her head and laughed, and for a moment her face was radiant, transfigured by her memories.

The things I had heard in the village came back to me; about the prosperous father and his family who lived in the big house many years ago. Then the foreign investments which crashed and the sudden change in circumstances. 'When t'owd feller died he was about skint,' one old man had said. 'There's not much brass there now.'

Probably just enough brass to keep Miss Stubbs and her animals alive and to pay Mrs Broadwith. Not enough to keep the garden dug or the house painted or for any of the normal little luxuries.

And, sitting there, drinking my tea, with the dogs in a row by the bedside and the cats making themselves comfortable on the bed itself, I felt as I had often felt before – a bit afraid of the responsibility I had. The one thing which brought some light into the life of the brave old woman was the transparent devotion of this shaggy bunch whose eyes were never far from her face. And the snag was that they were all elderly.

There had, in fact, been four dogs originally, but one of them, a truly ancient Golden Labrador, had died a few months previously. And now I had the rest of them to look after and none of them less than ten years old.

They were perky enough but all showing some of the signs of old age; Prince with his heart, Sally beginning to drink a lot of water which made me wonder if she was starting with a pyometra, Ben growing steadily thinner with his nephritis. I couldn't give him new kidneys and I hadn't much faith in the hexamine tablets I had prescribed. Another peculiar thing about Ben was that I was always having to clip his claws; they grew at an extraordinary rate.

The cats were better, though Susie was a bit scraggy and I kept up a morbid kneading of her furry abdomen for signs of lymphosarcoma. Arthur was the best of the bunch; he never seemed to ail anything beyond a tendency for his teeth to tartar up.

This must have been in Miss Stubbs's mind because, when I had finished my tea, she asked me to look at him. I hauled him across the bedspread and opened his mouth.

'Yes, there's a bit of the old trouble there. Might as well fix it while I'm here.'

Arthur was a huge, grey, neutered tom, a living denial of all those

44

theories that cats are cold-natured, selfish and the rest. His fine eyes, framed in the widest cat face I have ever seen, looked out on the world with an all-embracing benevolence and tolerance. His every movement was marked by immense dignity.

As I started to scrape his teeth his chest echoed with a booming purr like a distant outboard motor. There was no need for anybody to hold him; he sat there placidly and moved only once – when I was using forceps to crack off a tough piece of tartar from a back tooth and accidentally nicked his gum. He casually raised a massive paw as if to say 'Have a care, chum', but his claws were sheathed.

My next visit was less than a month later and was in response to an urgent summons from Mrs Broadwith at six o'clock in the evening. Ben had collapsed. I jumped straight into my car and in less than ten minutes was threading my way through the overgrown grass in the front garden with the animals watching from their window. The barking broke out as I knocked, but Ben's was absent. As I went into the little room I saw the old dog lying on his side, very still, by the bed.

D.O.A. is what we write in the day book. Dead on arrival. Just three words but they covered all kinds of situations – the end of milk fever cows, bloated bullocks, calves in fits. And tonight they meant that I wouldn't be clipping old Ben's claws any more.

It wasn't often these nephritis cases went off so suddenly but his urine albumen had been building up dangerously lately.

'Well, it was quick, Miss Stubbs. I'm sure the old chap didn't suffer at all.' My words sounded lame and ineffectual.

The old lady was in full command of herself. No tears, only a fixity of expression as she looked down from the bed at her companion for so many years. My idea was to get him out of the place as quickly as possible and I pulled a blanket under him and lifted him up. As I was moving away, Miss Stubbs said, 'Wait a moment.' With an effort she turned on to her side and gazed at Ben. Still without changing expression, she reached out and touched his head lightly. Then she lay back calmly as I hurried from the room.

In the back kitchen I had a whispered conference with Mrs Broadwith. 'I'll run down t'village and get Fred Manners to come and bury him,' she said. 'And if you've got time could you stay with the old lady while I'm gone. Talk to her, like, it'll do her good.'

I went back and sat down by the bed. Miss Stubbs looked out of the window for a few moments then turned to me. 'You know, Mr Herriot,' she said casually, 'it will be my turn next.'

'What do you mean?'

'Well, tonight Ben has gone and I'm going to be the next one. I just know it.'

'Oh, nonsense! You're feeling a bit low, that's all. We all do when something like this happens.' But I was disturbed. I had never heard her even hint at such a thing before.

'I'm not afraid,' she said. 'I know there's something better waiting for me. I've never had any doubts.' There was silence between us as she lay calmly looking up at the card on the gas bracket.

Then the head on the pillow turned to me again. 'I have only one fear.' Her expression changed with startling suddenness as if a mask had dropped. The brave face was almost unrecognisable. A kind of terror flickered in her eyes and she quickly grasped my hand.

'It's my dogs and cats, Mr Herriot. I'm afraid I might never see them when I'm gone and it worries me so. You see, I know I'll be reunited with my parents and my brothers but . . . but . . .'

'Well, why not with your animals?'

'That's just it.' She rocked her head on the pillow and for the first time I saw tears on her cheeks. 'They say animals have no souls.'

'Who says?'

'Oh, I've read it and I know a lot of religious people believe it.'

'Well I don't believe it.' I patted the hand which still grasped mine. 'If having a soul means being able to feel love and loyalty and gratitude, then animals are better off than a lot of humans. You've nothing to worry about there.'

'Oh, I hope you're right. Sometimes I lie at night thinking about it.'

'I know I'm right, Miss Stubbs, and don't you argue with me. They teach us vets all about animals' souls.'

The tension left her face and she laughed with a return of her old spirit. 'I'm sorry to bore you with this and I'm not going to talk about it again. But before you go, I want you to be absolutely honest with me. I don't want reassurance from you – just the truth. I know you are very young but please tell me – what are your beliefs? Will my animals go with me?'

She stared intently into my eyes. I shifted in my chair and swallowed once or twice.

'Miss Stubbs, I'm afraid I'm a bit foggy about all this,' I said.

'But I'm absolutely certain of one thing. Wherever you are going, they are going too.'

She still stared at me but her face was calm again. 'Thank you, Mr Herriot. I know you are being honest with me. That is what you really believe, isn't it?'

'I do believe it,' I said. 'With all my heart I believe it.'

It must have been about a month later and it was entirely by accident that I learned I had seen Miss Stubbs for the last time. When a lonely, penniless old woman dies people don't rush up to you in the street to tell you. I was on my rounds and a farmer happened to mention that the cottage in Corby village was up for sale.

'But what about Miss Stubbs?' I asked.

'Oh, went off sudden about three weeks ago. House is in a bad state, they say – nowt been done at it for years.'

'Mrs Broadwith isn't staying on, then?'

'Nay, I hear she's staying at t'other end of village.'

'Do you know what's happened to the dogs and cats?'

'What dogs and cats?'

I cut my visit short. And I didn't go straight home though it was nearly lunch time. Instead I urged my complaining little car at top speed to Corby and asked the first person I saw where Mrs Broadwith was living. It was a tiny house but attractive and Mrs Broadwith answered my knock herself.

'Oh, come in, Mr Herriot. It's right good of you to call.' I went inside and we sat facing each other across a scrubbed table top.

'Well, it was sad about the old lady,' she said.

'Yes, I've only just heard.'

'Any road, she had a peaceful end. Just slept away at finish.'

'I'm glad to hear that.'

Mrs Broadwith looked round the room. 'I was real lucky to get this place – it's just what I've always wanted.'

I could contain myself no longer. 'What's happened to the animals?' I blurted out.

'Oh, they're in t'garden,' she said calmly. 'I've got a grand big stretch at back.' She got up and opened the door and with a surge of relief I watched my old friends pour in.

Arthur was on my knee in a flash, arching himself ecstatically against my arm while his outboard motor roared softly above the barking of the dogs. Prince, wheezy as ever, tail fanning the air, laughed up at me delightedly between barks.

'They look great, Mrs Broadwith. How long are they going to be here?'

'They're here for good. I think just as much about them as t'old lady ever did and I couldn't be parted from them. They'll have a good home with me as long as they live.'

I looked at the typical Yorkshire country face, at the heavy cheeks with their grim lines belied by the kindly eyes. 'This is wonderful,' I said. 'But won't you find it just a bit . . . er . . . expensive to feed them?'

'Nay, you don't have to worry about that. I 'ave a bit put away.'

'Well fine, fine, and I'll be looking in now and then to see how they are. I'm through the village every few days.' I got up and started for the door.

Mrs Broadwith held up her hand. 'There's just one thing I'd like you to do before they start selling off the things at the cottage. Would you please pop in and collect what's left of your medicines. They're in t'front room.'

I took the key and drove along to the other end of the village. As I pushed open the rickety gate and began to walk through the tangled grass the front of the cottage looked strangely lifeless without the faces of the dogs at the window; and when the door creaked open and I went inside the silence was like a heavy pall.

Nothing had been moved. The bed with its rumpled blankets was still in the corner. I moved around, picking up half-empty bottles, a jar of ointment, the cardboard box with old Ben's tablets – a lot of good they had done him.

When I had got everything I looked slowly round the little room. I wouldn't be coming here any more and at the door I paused and read for the last time the card which hung over the empty bed.

*

Old people and their attachment to their beloved animals. It shone with a quiet radiance in the case of Miss Stubbs. Her courage and faith were inspiring. So many people write to me voicing the same worry as Miss Stubbs: 'Do dogs have souls?' I can say that I am as sure now as I was then that her pets have gone where she has gone. Another thing which worries old people is what will happen to their pets when they die. Who will look after them? Will they be treated kindly? I know from my experiences in practice that some of these old folk are less concerned about their own welfare than with the unbearable thought that their animals might be neglected after they are gone. This is a dread which will continue to haunt people, but I have found that it is very often groundless. We live in a compassionate country and there are a lot of Mrs Broadwiths about.

9. *Clancy*

As the faint rumbling growl rolled up from the rib cage into the ear pieces of my stethoscope the realisation burst upon me with uncomfortable clarity that this was probably the biggest dog I had ever seen. In my limited past experience some Irish Wolfhounds had undoubtedly been taller and a certain number of Bull Mastiffs had possibly been broader, but for sheer gross poundage this one had it. His name was Clancy.

It was a good name for an Irishman's dog and Joe Mulligan was very Irish despite his many years in Yorkshire. Joe had brought him in to the afternoon surgery and as the huge hairy form ambled along, almost filling the passage, I was reminded of the times I had seen him out in the fields around Darrowby enduring the frisking attentions of smaller animals with massive benignity. He looked like a nice friendly dog.

But now there was this ominous sound echoing round the great thorax like a distant drum roll in a subterranean cavern, and as the chest piece of the stethoscope bumped along the ribs the sound swelled in volume and the lips fluttered over the enormous teeth as though a gentle breeze had stirred them. It was then that I became aware not only that Clancy was very big indeed but that my position, kneeling on the floor with my right ear a few inches from his mouth, was infinitely vulnerable.

I got to my feet and as I dropped the stethoscope into my pocket the dog gave me a cold look – a sideways glance without moving his head; and there was a chilling menace in his very immobility. I didn't mind my patients snapping at me but this one, I felt sure, wouldn't snap. If he started something it would be on a spectacular scale.

I stepped back a pace. 'Now what did you say his symptoms were, Mr Mulligan?'

'Phwaat's that?' Joe cupped his ear with his hand. I took a deep breath. 'What's the trouble with him?' I shouted.

The old man looked at me with total incomprehension from beneath the straightly adjusted cloth cap. He fingered the muffler knotted immediately over his larynx and the pipe which grew from the dead centre of his mouth puffed blue wisps of puzzlement.

Then, remembering something of Clancy's past history, I moved close to Mr Mulligan and bawled with all my power into his face. 'Is he vomiting?'

The response was immediate. Joe smiled in great relief and removed his pipe. 'Oh aye, he's womitin' sorr. He's womitin' bad.' Clearly he was on familiar ground.

Over the years Clancy's treatment had all been at long range. My young boss, Siegfried Farnon, had told me on the first day I had arrived in Darrowby two years ago that there was nothing wrong with the dog, which he had described as a cross between an Airedale and a donkey, but his penchant for eating every bit of rubbish in his path had the inevitable result. A large bottle of bismuth–mag carb mixture had been dispensed at regular intervals. He had also told me that Clancy, when bored, used occasionally to throw Joe to the ground and worry him like a rat just for a bit of light relief. But his master still adored him.

.Prickings of conscience told me I should carry out a full examination. Take his temperature, for instance. All I had to do was to grab hold of that tail, lift it and push a thermometer into his rectum. The dog turned his head and met my eye with a blank stare; again I heard the low booming drum roll and the upper lip lifted a fraction to show a quick gleam of white.

'Yes, yes, right, Mr Mulligan,' I said briskly. 'I'll get you a bottle of the usual.'

In the dispensary, under the rows of bottles with their Latin names and glass stoppers, I shook up the mixture in a ten-ounce bottle, corked it, stuck on a label and wrote the directions. Joe seemed well satisfied as he pocketed the familiar white medicine but as he turned to go my conscience smote me again. The dog did look perfectly fit but maybe he ought to be seen again.

'Bring him back again on Thursday afternoon at two o'clock,' I yelled into the old man's ear. 'And please come on time if you can. You were a bit late today.'

I watched Mr Mulligan going down the street, preceded by his pipe from which regular puffs rose upwards as though from a departing railway engine. Behind him ambled Clancy, a picture of massive calm. With his all-over covering of tight brown curls he did indeed look like a gigantic Airedale.

Thursday afternoon, I ruminated. That was my half-day and at two o'clock I'd probably be watching the afternoon cinema show in Brawton.

The following Friday morning Siegfried was sitting behind his desk, working out the morning rounds. He scribbled a list of visits on a pad, tore out the sheet and handed it to me.

'Here you are, James, I think that'll just about keep you out of mischief till lunch time.' Then something in the previous day's entries caught his eye and he turned to his younger brother who was at his morning task of stoking the fire.

'Tristan, I see Joe Mulligan was in yesterday afternoon with his dog and you saw it. What did you make of it?'

Tristan put down his bucket. 'Oh, I gave him some of the bismuth mixture.'

'Yes, but what did your examination of the patient disclose?'

'Well now, let's see.' Tristan rubbed his chin. 'He looked pretty lively, really.'

'Is that all?'

'Yes . . . yes . . . I think so.'

Siegfried turned back to me. 'And how about you, James? You saw the dog the day before. What were your findings?'

'Well it was a bit difficult,' I said. 'That dog's as big as an elephant and there's something creepy about him. He seemed to me to be just

52

waiting his chance and there was only old Joe to hold him. I'm afraid I wasn't able to make a close examination but I must say I thought the same as Tristan – he did look pretty lively.'

Siegfried put down his pen wearily. On the previous night, fate had dealt him one of the shattering blows which it occasionally reserves for vets – a call at each end of his sleeping time. He had been dragged from his bed at 1 a.m. and again at 6 a.m. and the fires of his personality were temporarily damped.

He passed a hand across his eyes. 'Well God help us. You, James, a veterinary surgeon of two years experience and you, Tristan, a final year student can't come up with anything better between you than the phrase "pretty lively". It's a bloody poor thing! Hardly a worthy description of clinical findings is it? When an animal comes in here I expect you to record pulse, temperature and respiratory rate. To auscultate the chest and thoroughly palpate the abdomen. To open his mouth and examine teeth, gums and pharynx. To check the condition of the skin. To catheterise him and examine the urine if necessary.'

'Right,' I said.

'O.K.,' said Tristan.

My employer rose from his seat. 'Have you fixed another appointment?'

'I have, yes.' Tristan drew his packet of Woodbines from his pocket. 'For Monday. And since Mr Mulligan's always late for the surgery I said we'd visit the dog at his home in the evening.'

'I see.' Siegfried made a note on the pad, then he looked up suddenly. 'That's when you and James are going to the young farmers' meeting, isn't it?'

The young man drew on his cigarette. 'That's right. Good for the practice for us to mix with the young clients.'

'Very well,' Siegfried said as he walked to the door. 'I'll see the dog myself.'

On the following Tuesday I was fairly confident that Siegfried would have something to say about Mulligan's dog, if only to point out the benefits of a thorough clinical examination. But he was silent on the subject.

It happened that I came upon old Joe in the market-place sauntering over the cobbles with Clancy inevitably trotting at his heels.

I went up to him and shouted in his ear. 'How's your dog?'

Mr Mulligan removed his pipe and smiled with slow benevolence. 'Oh foine, sorr, foine. Still womitin' a bit, but not bad.'

'Mr Farnon fixed him up, then?'

'Aye, gave him some more of the white medicine. It's wonderful stuff, sorr, wonderful stuff.'

'Good, good,' I said. 'He didn't find anything else when he examined him?'

Joe took another suck at his pipe. 'No he didn't now, he didn't. He's a clever man, Mr Farnon – I've niver seen a man work as fast, no I haven't.'

'What do you mean?'

'Well now he saw all he wanted in tree seconds, so he did.'

I was mystified. 'Three seconds?'

'Yis,' said Mr Mulligan firmly. 'Not a moment more.'

'Amazing. What happened?'

Joe tapped out his pipe on his heel and without haste took out a knife and began to carve a refill from an evil looking coil of black twist. 'Well now I'll tell ye. Mr Farnon is a man who moves awful sudden, and that night he banged on our front door and jumped into the room.' (I knew those cottages. There was no hall or lobby – you walked straight from the street into the living room.) 'And as he came in he was pullin' his thermometer out of its case. Well now Clancy was lyin' by the fire and he rose up in a flash and he gave a bit of a wuff, so he did.'

'A bit of a wuff, eh?' I could imagine the hairy monster leaping up and baying into Siegfried's face. I could see the gaping jaws, the gleaming teeth.

'Aye, just a bit of a wuff. Well, Mr Farnon just put the thermometer straight back in its case, turned round and went out the door.'

'Didn't he say anything?' I asked.

'No, divil a word. Just turned about like a soldier and marched out the door, so he did.'

It sounded authentic. Siegfried was a man of instant decision. I put my hand out to pat Clancy but something in his eyes made me change my mind.

'Well, I'm glad he's better,' I shouted.

The old man ignited his pipe with an ancient brass lighter, puffed a cloud of choking blue smoke into my face and tapped a little metal lid on to the bowl. 'Aye, Mr Farnon sent round a big bottle of the

54

white stuff and it's done 'im good. Mind yous,' he gave a beatific smile, 'Clancy's allus been one for the womitin', so he has.'

Nothing more was said about the big dog for over a week, but Siegfried's professional conscience must have been niggling at him because he came into the dispensary one afternoon when Tristan and I were busy at the tasks which have passed into history – making up fever drinks, stomach powders, boric acid pessaries. He was elaborately casual.

'Oh by the way, I dropped a note to Joe Mulligan. I'm not entirely convinced that we have adequately explored the causes of his dog's symptoms. This womiting . . . er, vomiting is almost certainly due to depraved appetite but I just want to make sure. So I have asked him to bring him round tomorrow afternoon between two and two thirty when we'll all be here.'

No cries of joy greeted his statement, so he continued. 'I suppose you could say that this dog is to some degree a difficult animal and I think we should plan accordingly.' He turned to me. 'James, when he arrives you get hold of his back end, will you?'

'Right,' I replied without enthusiasm.

He faced his brother. 'And you, Tristan, can deal with the head. O.K.?'

'Fine, fine,' the young man muttered, his face expressionless.

His brother continued. 'I suggest you get a good grip with your arms round his neck and I'll be ready to give him a shot of sedative.'

'Splendid, splendid,' said Tristan.

'Ah well, that's capital.' My employer rubbed his hands together. 'Once I get the dope into him the rest will be easy. I do like to satisfy my mind about these things.'

It was a typical Dales practice at Darrowby; mainly large animal and we didn't have packed waiting rooms at surgery times. But on the following afternoon we had nobody in at all, and it added to the tension of waiting. The three of us mooched about the office, making aimless conversation, glancing with studied carelessness into the front street, whistling little tunes to ourselves. By two twenty-five we had all fallen silent. Over the next five minutes we consulted our watches about every thirty seconds, then at exactly two thirty Siegfried spoke up.

'This is no damn good. I told Joe he had to be here before half past but he's taken not a bit of notice. He's always late and there doesn't seem to be any way to get him here on time.' He took a last look out of the window at the empty street. 'Right, we're not waiting any longer. You and I, James, have got that colt to cut and you, Tristan, have to see that beast of Wilson's. So let's be off.'

Up till then, Laurel and Hardy were the only people I had ever seen getting jammed together in doorways but there was a moment when the three of us gave a passable imitation of the famous comics as we all fought our way into the passage at the same time. Within seconds we were in the street and Tristan was roaring off in a cloud of exhaust smoke. My employer and I proceeded almost as rapidly in the opposite direction.

At the end of Trengate we turned into the market-place and I looked around in vain for signs of Mr Mulligan. It wasn't until we had reached the outskirts of the town that we saw him. He had just left his house and was pacing along under a moving pall of blue smoke with Clancy as always bringing up the rear.

'There he is!' Siegfried exclaimed. 'Would you believe it? At the rate he's going he'll get to the surgery around three o'clock. Well we won't be there and it's his own fault.' He looked at the great curly-coated animal tripping along, a picture of health and energy. 'Well, I suppose we'd have been wasting our time examining that dog in any case. There's nothing really wrong with him.'

For a moment he paused, lost in thought, then he turned to me. 'He does look pretty lively, doesn't he?'

*

Formidable dogs come in many forms, but Clancy with his quiet menace was unique in my experience. And Joe Mulligan was memorable in his own right. His favourite word has stuck in my mind, and to this day when I am examining a dog with stomach trouble, I often only just stop myself asking, 'Is he womiting?'

10. *Mrs Donovan*

The silvery-haired old gentleman with the pleasant face didn't look the type to be easily upset but his eyes glared at me angrily and his lips quivered with indignation.

'Mr Herriot,' he said, 'I have come to make a complaint. I strongly object to your callousness in subjecting my dog to unnecessary suffering.'

'Suffering? What suffering?' I was mystified.

'I think you know, Mr Herriot. I brought my dog in a few days ago. He was very lame and I am referring to your treatment on that occasion.'

I nodded. 'Yes, I remember it well . . . but where does the suffering come in?'

'Well, the poor animal is going around with his leg dangling and I have it on good authority that the bone is fractured and should

57

have been put in plaster immediately.' The old gentleman stuck his chin out fiercely.

'All right, you can stop worrying,' I said. 'Your dog has a radial paralysis caused by a blow on the ribs and if you are patient and follow my treatment he'll gradually improve. In fact I think he'll recover completely.'

'But he trails his leg when he walks.'

'I know – that's typical, and to the layman it does give the appearance of a broken leg. But he shows no sign of pain, does he?'

'No, he seems quite happy, but this lady seemed to be absolutely sure of her facts. She was adamant.'

'Lady?' ·

'Yes,' said the old gentleman. 'She is clever with animals and she came round to see if she could help in my dog's convalescence. She brought some excellent condition powders with her.'

'Ah!' A blinding shaft pierced the fog in my mind. All was suddenly clear. 'It was Mrs Donovan, wasn't it?'

'Well . . . er, yes. That was her name.'

Old Mrs Donovan was a woman who really got around. No matter what was going on in Darrowby – weddings, funerals, house-sales – you'd find the dumpy little figure and walnut face among the spectators, the darting, black-button eyes taking everything in. And always, on the end of its lead, her terrier dog.

When I say 'old', I'm only guessing, because she appeared ageless; she seemed to have been around a long time but she could have been anything between fifty-five and seventy-five. She certainly had the vitality of a young woman because she must have walked vast distances in her dedicated quest to keep abreast of events. Many people took an uncharitable view of her acute curiosity but whatever the motivation, her activities took her into almost every channel of life in the town. One of these channels was our veterinary practice.

Because Mrs Donovan, among her other widely ranging interests, was an animal doctor. In fact I think it would be safe to say that this facet of her life transcended all the others.

She could talk at length on the ailments of small animals and she had a whole armoury of medicines and remedies at her command, her two specialities being her miracle working condition powders and a dog shampoo of unprecedented value for improving the coat. She had an uncanny ability to sniff out a sick animal, and it was not uncommon when I was on my rounds to find Mrs Donovan's dark gipsy face poised intently over what I had thought was my patient while she administered calf's foot jelly or one of her own patent nostrums.

I suffered more than Siegfried because I took a more active part in the small animal side of our practice. I was anxious to develop this aspect and to improve my image in this field and Mrs Donovan didn't help at all. 'Young Mr Herriot,' she would confide to my clients, 'is all right with cattle and such like, but he don't know nothing about dogs and cats.'

And of course they believed her and had implicit faith in her. She had the irresistible mystic appeal of the amateur and on top of that there was her habit, particularly endearing in Darrowby, of never charging for her advice, her medicines, her long periods of diligent nursing.

Older folk in the town told how her husband, an Irish farm worker, had died many years ago and how he must have had a 'bit put away' because Mrs Donovan had apparently been able to indulge all her interests over the years without financial strain. Since she inhabited the streets of Darrowby all day and every day I often encountered her and she always smiled up at me sweetly and told me how she had been sitting up all night with Mrs So-and-so's dog that I'd been treating. She felt sure she'd be able to pull it through.

There was no smile on her face, however, on the day when she rushed into the surgery while Siegfried and I were having tea.

'Mr Herriot!' she gasped. 'Can you come? My little dog's been run over!'

I jumped up and ran out to the car with her. She sat in the passenger seat with her head bowed, her hands clasped tightly on her knees.

'He slipped his collar and ran in front of a car,' she murmured. 'He's lying in front of the school half-way up Cliffend Road. Please hurry.'

I was there within three minutes but as I bent over the dusty little body stretched on the pavement I knew there was nothing I could do. The fast-glazing eyes, the faint, gasping respirations, the ghastly pallor of the mucous membranes all told the same story.

'I'll take him back to the surgery and get some saline into him, Mrs Donovan,' I said. 'But I'm afraid he's had a massive internal haemorrhage. Did you see what happened exactly?'

She gulped. 'Yes, the wheel went right over him.'

Ruptured liver, for sure. I passed my hands under the little animal and began to lift him gently, but as I did so the breathing stopped and the eyes stared fixedly ahead.

Mrs Donovan sank to her knees and for a few moments she gently stroked the rough hair of the head and chest. 'He's dead, isn't he?' she whispered at last.

'I'm afraid he is,' I said.

She got slowly to her feet and stood bewilderedly among the little group of bystanders on the pavement. Her lips moved but she seemed unable to say any more.

I took her arm, led her over to the car and opened the door. 'Get in and sit down,' I said. 'I'll run you home. Leave everything to me.'

I wrapped the dog in my calving overall and laid him in the boot before driving away. It wasn't until we drew up outside Mrs Donovan's house that she began to weep silently. I sat there without speaking till she had finished. Then she wiped her eyes and turned to me.

'Do you think he suffered at all?'

'I'm certain he didn't. It was all so quick – he wouldn't know a thing about it.'

She tried to smile. 'Poor little Rex, I don't know what I'm going to do without him. We've travelled a few miles together, you know.'

'Yes, you have. He had a wonderful life, Mrs Donovan. And let me give you a bit of advice – you must get another dog. You'd be lost without one.'

She shook her head. 'No, I couldn't. That little dog meant too much to me. I couldn't let another take his place.'

'Well I know that's how you feel just now but I wish you'd think about it. I don't want to seem callous – I tell everybody this when they lose an animal and I know it's good advice.'

'Mr Herriot, I'll never have another one.' She shook her head again, very decisively. 'Rex was my faithful friend for many years and I just want to remember him. He's the last dog I'll ever have.'

I often saw Mrs Donovan around the town after this and I was glad to see she was still as active as ever, though she looked strangely incomplete without the little dog on its lead. But it must have been over a month before I had the chance to speak to her.

It was on the afternoon that Inspector Halliday of the RSPCA rang me.

'Mr Herriot,' he said, 'I'd like you to come and see an animal with me. A cruelty case.'

'Right, what is it?'

'A dog, and it's pretty grim. A dreadful case of neglect.' He gave me the name of a row of old brick cottages down by the river and said he'd meet me there.

Halliday was waiting for me, smart and business-like in his dark uniform, as I pulled up in the back lane behind the houses. He was a big, blond man with cheerful blue eyes but he didn't smile as he came over to the car.

'He's in here,' he said, and led the way towards one of the doors in the long, crumbling wall. A few curious people were hanging around and with a feeling of inevitability I recognised a gnome-like brown face. Trust Mrs Donovan, I thought, to be among those present at a time like this.

We went through the door into the long garden. I had found that even the lowliest dwellings in Darrowby had long strips of land at the back as though the builders had taken it for granted that the country people who were going to live in them would want to occupy themselves with the pursuits of the soil; with vegetable and fruit growing, even stock keeping in a small way. You usually found a pig there, a few hens, often pretty beds of flowers.

But this garden was a wilderness. A chilling air of desolation hung over the few gnarled apple and plum trees standing among a tangle of rank grass as though the place had been forsaken by all living creatures.

Halliday went over to a ramshackle wooden shed with peeling paint and a rusted corrugated iron roof. He produced a key, unlocked the padlock and dragged the door partly open. There was no window and it wasn't easy to identify the jumble inside: broken gardening tools, an ancient mangle, rows of flower pots and partly used paint tins. And right at the back, a dog sitting quietly.

I didn't notice him immediately because of the gloom and because the smell in the shed started me coughing, but as I drew closer I saw that he was a big animal, sitting very upright, his collar secured by a chain to a ring in the wall. I had seen some thin dogs but this advanced emaciation reminded me of my text books on anatomy; nowhere else did the bones of pelvis, face and rib cage stand out with such horrifying clarity. A deep, smoothed out hollow in the earth floor showed where he had lain, moved about, in fact lived for a very long time.

The sight of the animal had a stupefying effect on me; I only half took in the rest of the scene – the filthy shreds of sacking scattered nearby, the bowl of scummy water.

'Look at his back end,' Halliday muttered.

I carefully raised the dog from his sitting position and realised that the stench in the place was not entirely due to the piles of excrement. The hindquarters were a welter of pressure sores which had turned gangrenous, and strips of sloughing tissue hung down from them. There were similar sores along the sternum and ribs. The coat, which seemed to be a dull yellow, was matted and caked with dirt.

The Inspector spoke again. 'I don't think he's ever been out of here. He's only a young dog – about a year old – but I understand he's been in this shed since he was an eight-week-old pup. Somebody out in the lane heard a whimper or he'd never have been found.'

I felt a tightening of the throat and a sudden nausea which wasn't due to the smell. It was the thought of this patient animal sitting starved and forgotten in the darkness and filth for a year. I looked again at the dog and saw in his eyes only a calm trust. Some dogs would have barked their heads off and soon been discovered, some would have become terrified and vicious, but this was one of the totally undemanding kind, the kind which had complete faith in people and accepted all their actions without complaint. Just an occasional whimper perhaps as he sat interminably in the empty blackness which had been his world and at times wondered what it was all about.

'Well, Inspector, I hope you're going to throw the book at whoever's responsible,' I said.

Halliday grunted. 'Oh, there won't be much done. It's a case of diminished responsibility. The owner's definitely simple. Lives with an aged mother who hardly knows what's going on either. I've seen the fellow and it seems he threw in a bit of food when he felt like it and that's about all he did. They'll fine him and stop him keeping an animal in the future but nothing more than that.'

'I see.' I reached out and stroked the dog's head and he immediately responded by resting a paw on my wrist. There was a pathetic dignity about the way he held himself erect, the calm eyes regarding me, friendly and unafraid. 'Well, you'll let me know if you want me in court.'

'Of course, and thank you for coming along.' Halliday hesitated for a moment. 'And now I expect you'll want to put this poor thing out of his misery right away.'

I continued to run my hand over the head and ears while I thought for a moment. 'Yes . . . yes, I suppose so. We'd never find a home for him in this state. It's the kindest thing to do. Anyway, push the door wide open will you so that I can get a proper look at him.'

In the improved light I examined him more thoroughly. Perfect teeth, well-proportioned limbs with a fringe of yellow hair. I put my stethoscope on his chest and as I listened to the slow, strong thudding of the heart the dog again put his paw on my hand.

I turned to Halliday. 'You know, Inspector, inside this bag of bones there's a lovely healthy Golden Retriever. I wish there was some way of letting him out.'

As I spoke I noticed there was more than one figure in the door opening. A pair of black pebble eyes were peering intently at the big dog from behind the Inspector's broad back. The other spectators had remained in the lane but Mrs Donovan's curiosity had been too much for her. I continued conversationally as though I hadn't seen her.

'You know, what this dog needs first of all is a good shampoo to clean up his matted coat.'

'Huh?' said Halliday.

'Yes. And then he wants a long course of some really strong condition powders.'

'What's that?' The Inspector looked startled.

'There's no doubt about it,' I said. 'It's the only hope for him, but where are you going to find such things? Really powerful enough, I mean.' I sighed and straightened up. 'Ah well, I suppose there's nothing else for it. I'd better put him to sleep right away. I'll get the things from my car.'

When I got back to the shed Mrs Donovan was already inside examining the dog despite the feeble remonstrances of the big man.

'Look!' she said excitedly, pointing to a name roughly scratched on the collar. 'His name's Roy.' She smiled up at me. 'It's a bit like Rex, isn't it, that name?'

'You know, Mrs Donovan, now you mention it, it is. It's very like Rex, the way it comes off your tongue.' I nodded seriously.

She stood silent for a few moments, obviously in the grip of a deep emotion, then she burst out.

'Can I have 'im? I can make him better, I know I can. Please, please let me have 'im!'

'Well I don't know,' I said. 'It's really up to the Inspector. You'll have to get his permission.'

Halliday looked at her in bewilderment, then he said: 'Excuse me, Madam,' and drew me to one side. We walked a few yards through the long grass and stopped under a tree.

'Mr Herriot,' he whispered, 'I don't know what's going on here, but I can't just pass over an animal in this condition to anybody who has a casual whim. The poor beggar's had one bad break already – I think it's enough. This woman doesn't look a suitable person . . .'

I held up a hand. 'Believe me, Inspector, you've nothing to worry about. She's a funny old stick but she's been sent from heaven today. If anybody in Darrowby can give this dog a new life it's her.'

Halliday still looked very doubtful. 'But I still don't get it. What was all that stuff about him needing shampoos and condition powders?'

'Oh never mind about that. I'll tell you some other time. What he needs is lots of good grub, care and affection, and that's just what he'll get. You can take my word for it.'

'All right, you seem very sure.' Halliday looked at me for a second or two then turned and walked over to the eager little figure by the shed.

I had never before been deliberately on the look out for Mrs Donovan: she had just cropped up wherever I happened to be, but now I scanned the streets of Darrowby anxiously day by day without sighting her. I didn't like it when Gobber Newhouse got drunk and drove his bicycle determinedly through a barrier into a ten-foot hole where they were laying the new sewer and Mrs Donovan was not in evidence among the happy crowd who watched the council workmen and two policemen trying to get him out; and when she was nowhere to be seen when they had to fetch the fire engine to the fish and chip shop the night the fat burst into flames I became seriously worried.

Maybe I should have called round to see how she was getting on with that dog. Certainly I had trimmed off the necrotic tissue and dressed the sores before she took him away, but perhaps he needed something more than that. And yet at the time I had felt a strong conviction that the main thing was to get him out of there and clean him and feed him and nature would do the rest. And I had a lot of faith in Mrs Donovan – far more than she had in me – when it came to animal doctoring; it was hard to believe I'd been completely wrong.

It must have been nearly three weeks and I was on the point of calling at her home when I noticed her stumping briskly along the far side of the market-place, peering closely into every shop window exactly as before. The only difference was that she had a big yellow dog on the end of the lead.

I turned the wheel and sent my car bumping over the cobbles till I was abreast of her. When she saw me getting out she stopped and smiled impishly, but she didn't speak as I bent over Roy and examined him. He was still a skinny dog but he looked bright and happy, his wounds were healthy and granulating and there was not a speck of dirt in his coat or on his skin. I knew then what Mrs Donovan had been doing all this time; she had been washing and combing and teasing at that filthy tangle till she had finally conquered it.

As I straightened up she seized my wrist in a grip of surprising strength and looked up into my eyes.

'Now Mr Herriot,' she said, 'haven't I made a difference to this dog!'

'You've done wonders, Mrs Donovan,' I said. 'And you've been at him with that marvellous shampoo of yours, haven't you?'

She giggled and walked away and from that day I saw the two of them frequently but at a distance and something like two months went by before I had a chance to talk to her again. She was passing by the surgery as I was coming down the steps and again she grabbed my wrist.

'Mr Herriot,' she said, just as she had done before, 'haven't I made a difference to this dog!'

I looked down at Roy with something akin to awe. He had grown and filled out and his coat, no longer yellow but a rich gold, lay in luxuriant shining swathes over the well-fleshed ribs and back. A new, brightly studded collar glittered on his neck and his tail, beautifully fringed, fanned the air gently. He was now a Golden Retriever in full magnificence. As I stared at him he reared up, plunked his fore paws on my chest and looked into my face, and in his eyes I read plainly the same calm affection and trust I had seen back in that black, noisome shed.

'Mrs Donovan,' I said softly, 'he's the most beautiful dog in Yorkshire.' Then, because I knew she was waiting for it, 'It's those wonderful condition powders. Whatever do you put in them?'

'Ah, wouldn't you like to know!' She bridled and smiled up at me coquettishly and indeed she was nearer being kissed at that moment than for many years.

I suppose you could say that that was the start of Roy's second life. And as the years passed I often pondered on the beneficent providence which had decreed that an animal which had spent his first twelve months abandoned and unwanted, staring uncomprehendingly into that unchanging, stinking darkness, should be whisked in a moment into an existence of light and movement and love. Because I don't think any dog had it quite so good as Roy from then on.

His diet changed dramatically from odd bread crusts to best stewing steak and biscuit, meaty bones and a bowl of warm milk every evening. And he never missed a thing. Garden fêtes, school sports, evictions, gymkhanas – he'd be there. I was pleased to note that as time went on Mrs Donovan seemed to be clocking up an even greater daily mileage. Her expenditure on shoe leather must have been phenomenal, but of course it was absolute pie for Roy – a busy round in the morning, home for a meal, then straight out again; it was all go.

Mrs Donovan didn't confine her activities to the town centre; there was a big stretch of common land down by the river where there were seats and people used to take their dogs for a gallop, and she liked to get down there fairly regularly to check on the latest developments on the domestic scene. I often saw Roy loping majestically over the grass among a pack of assorted canines, and when he wasn't doing that he was submitting to being stroked or patted or generally fussed over. He was handsome and he just liked people; it made him irresistible.

It was common knowledge that his mistress had bought a whole selection of brushes and combs of various sizes with which she laboured over his coat. Some people said she had a little brush for his teeth, too, and it might have been true, but he certainly wouldn't need his nails clipped – his life on the roads would keep them down.

Mrs Donovan, too, had her reward; she had a faithful companion by her side every hour of the day and night. But there was more to it than that; she had always had the compulsion to help and heal animals and the salvation of Roy was the high point of her life – a blazing triumph which never dimmed.

I know the memory of it was always fresh because many years

later I was sitting on the sidelines at a cricket match and I saw the two of them; the old lady glancing keenly around her, Roy gazing placidly out at the field of play, apparently enjoying every ball. At the end of the match I watched them move away with the dispersing crowd; Roy would have been about twelve then and heaven only knows how old Mrs Donovan must have been, but the big golden animal was trotting along effortlessly and his mistress, a little more bent perhaps and her head rather nearer the ground, was going very well.

When she saw me she came over and I felt the familiar tight grip on my wrist.

'Mr Herriot,' she said, and in the dark probing eyes the pride was still as warm, the triumph still as bursting new as if it had all happened yesterday.

'Mr Herriot, haven't I made a difference to this dog!'

*

Mrs Donovan's dedicated care was rewarded with many years of loyal companionship and Roy, despite his bad start in life, lived well into his teens. After his death, Mrs Donovan went to live in an old folks' home in our town. I always tried to disguise my characters, but she recognised herself and rejoiced. She was so proud to be in my book. The salvation of Roy and the wonderful transformation in his appearance and in his entire life is one of my warmest memories, and, of course, a triumph by an amateur healer has a special glamour.

11. *The Darrowby Show*

'How would you like to officiate at Darrowby Show, James?' Siegfried threw the letter he had been reading on to the desk and turned to me.

'I don't mind, but I thought you always did it.'

'I do, but it says in that letter that they've changed the date this year and it happens I'm going to be away that weekend.'

'Oh well, fine. What do I have to do?'

Siegfried ran his eye down his list of calls. 'It's a sinecure, really. More a pleasant day out than anything else. You have to measure the ponies and be on call in case any animals are injured. That's about all. Oh, and they want you to judge the Family Pets.'

'Family Pets?'

'Yes, they run a proper dog show but they have an expert judge for that. This is just a bit of fun – all kinds of pets. You've got to find a first, second and third.'

'Right,' I said. 'I think I should just about be able to manage that.'

'Splendid.' Siegfried tipped up the envelope in which the letter had come. 'Here are your car park and luncheon tickets for self and friend if you want to take somebody with you. Also your vet's badge. O.K.?'

The Saturday of the show brought the kind of weather that must have had the organisers purring with pleasure: a sky of wide, unsullied blue, hardly a whiff of wind and the kind of torrid, brazen sunshine you don't often find in North Yorkshire.

As I drove down towards the show ground I felt I was looking at a living breathing piece of old England: the group of tents and marquees vivid against the green of the riverside field, the women and children in their bright summer dresses, the cattle with their smocked attendants, a line of massive Shire horses parading in the ring.

I parked the car and made for the stewards' tent with its flag hanging limply from the mast. Tristan parted from me there. With the impecunious student's unerring eye for a little free food and entertainment he had taken up my spare tickets. He headed purposefully for the beer tent as I went in to report to the show secretary.

Leaving my measuring stick there, I looked around for a while.

A country show is a lot of different things to a lot of different people. Riding horses of all kinds from small ponies to hunters were being galloped up and down and in one ring the judges hovered around a group of mares and their beautiful little foals.

In a corner four men armed with buckets and brushes were washing and grooming a row of young bulls with great concentration, twiddling and crimping the fuzz over the rumps like society hairdressers.

Wandering through the marquees I examined the bewildering variety of produce from stalks of rhubarb to bunches of onions, the flower displays, embroidery, jams, cakes, pies. And the children's section: a painting of 'The Beach at Scarborough' by Annie Heseltine, aged nine; rows of wobbling copperplate handwriting – 'A thing of beauty is a joy for ever', Bernard Peacock, aged twelve.

But my attention was jerked away as a group of people walked across on the far side of the band. It was Helen with Richard Edmundson and behind them Mr Alderson and Richard's father deep in conversation. The young man walked very close to Helen, his shining, plastered-down fair hair hovering possessively over her dark head, his face animated as he talked and laughed.

There were no clouds in the sky but it was as if a dark hand had reached across and smudged away the brightness of the sunshine. I turned quickly and went in search of Tristan.

I soon picked out my colleague as I hurried into the marquee with 'Refreshments' over the entrance. He was leaning with an elbow on the makeshift counter of boards and trestles, chatting contentedly with a knot of cloth-capped locals, a Woodbine in one hand, a pint glass in the other. There was a general air of earthy bonhomie. Drinking of a more decorous kind would be taking place at the president's bar behind the stewards' headquarters with pink gins or sherry as the main tipple but here it was beer, bottled and draught, and the stout ladies behind the counter were working with the fierce concentration of people who knew they were in for a hard day.

'Yes, I saw her,' Tristan said when I gave him my news. 'In fact there she is now.' He nodded in the direction of the family group as they strolled past the entrance. 'I've had my eye on them for some time – I don't miss much from in here you know, Jim.'

'Ah well.' I accepted a half of bitter from him. 'It all looks pretty cosy. The two dads like blood brothers and Helen hanging on to that bloke's arm.'

Tristan squinted over the top of his pint at the scene outside and shook his head. 'Not exactly. He's hanging on to HER arm.' He looked at me judicially. 'There's a difference, you know.'

'I don't suppose it makes much difference to me either way,' I grunted.

'Well don't look so bloody mournful.' He took an effortless swallow which lowered the level in his glass by about six inches. 'What do you expect an attractive girl to do? Sit at home waiting for you to call? If you've been pounding on her door every night you haven't told me about it.'

'It's all right you talking. I think old man Alderson would set his dogs on me if I showed up there. I know he doesn't like me hanging around Helen and on top of that I've got the feeling he thinks I killed his cow on my last visit.'

'And did you?'

'No, I didn't. But I walked up to a living animal, gave it an injection and it promptly died, so I can't blame him.'

I took a sip at my beer and watched the Alderson party who had changed direction and were heading away from our retreat. Helen was wearing a pale blue dress and I was thinking how well the colour went with the deep brown of her hair and how I liked the way she walked with her legs swinging easily and her shoulders high and straight when the loudspeaker boomed across the show ground.

'Will Mr Herriot, Veterinary Surgeon, please report to the stewards immediately.'

It made me jump but at the same time I felt a quick stab of pride. It was the first time I had heard myself and my profession publicly proclaimed.

A glow of importance filled me as I hurried over the grass, my official badge with 'Veterinary Surgeon' in gold letters dangling from my lapel. A steward met me on the way.

'It's one of the cattle. Had an accident, I think.' He pointed to a row of pens along the edge of the field.

A curious crowd had collected around my patient which had been entered in the in-calf heifers class. The owner, a stranger from outside the Darrowby practice, came up to me, his face glum.

'She tripped coming off the cattle wagon and went 'ead first into the wall. Knocked one of 'er horns clean off.'

The heifer, a bonny little light roan, was a pathetic sight. She had been washed, combed, powdered and primped for the big day and there she was with one horn dangling drunkenly down the side of her face and an ornamental fountain of bright arterial blood climbing gracefully in three jets from the broken surface high into the air.

The broken horn was connected to the head only by a band of skin and I quickly snipped it away with scissors; then, with the farmer holding the heifer's nose, I began to probe with my forceps for the severed vessels. In the bright sunshine it was surprisingly difficult to see the spurting blood and as the little animal threw her head about I repeatedly felt the warm spray across my face and heard it spatter on my collar.

71

It was when I was beginning to lose heart with my ineffectual groping that I looked up and saw Helen and her boy friend watching me from the crowd. Young Edmundson looked mildly amused as he watched my unavailing efforts but Helen smiled encouragingly as she caught my eye. I did my best to smile back at her through my bloody mask but I don't suppose it showed.

I gave it up when the heifer gave a particularly brisk toss which sent my forceps flying on to the grass. I did what I should probably have done at the beginning – clapped a pad of cotton wool and antiseptic powder on to the stump and secured it with a figure of eight bandage round the other horn.

'That's it, then,' I said to the farmer as I tried to blink the blood out of my eyes. 'The bleeding's stopped, anyway. I'd advise you to have her properly de-horned soon or she's going to look a bit odd.'

Just then Tristan appeared from among the spectators.

'What's got you out of the beer tent?' I enquired with a touch of bitterness.

'It's lunch time, old lad,' Tristan replied equably. 'But we'll have to get you cleaned up a bit first. I can't be seen with you in that condition. Hang on, I'll get a bucket of water.'

The show luncheon was so excellent that it greatly restored me. Although it was taken in a marquee the committee men's wives had somehow managed to conjure up a memorable cold spread. There was fresh salmon and home-fed ham and slices of prime beef with mixed salads and apple pie and the big brimming jugs of cream you only see at farming functions. One of the ladies was a noted cheese-maker and we finished with some delicious goat cheese and coffee. The liquid side was catered for too with a bottle of Magnet Pale Ale and a glass at every place.

I didn't have the pleasure of Tristan's company at lunch because he had strategically placed himself well down the table between two strict Methodists so that his intake of Magnet was trebled.

I had hardly emerged into the sunshine when a man touched me on the shoulder.

'One of the dog show judges wants you to examine a dog. He doesn't like the look of it.'

He led me to where a thin man of about forty with a small dark moustache was standing by his car. He held a wire-haired Fox Terrier on a leash and he met me with an ingratiating smile.

'There's nothing whatever the matter with my dog,' he declared, 'but the chap in there seems very fussy.'

I looked down at the terrier. 'I see he has some matter in the corner of his eyes.'

The man shook his head vigorously. 'Oh no, that's not matter. I've been using some white powder on him and a bit's got into his eyes, that's all.'

'Hmm, well let's see what his temperature says, shall we?'

The little animal stood uncomplaining as I inserted the thermometer. When I took the reading my eyebrows went up.

'It's a hundred and four. I'm afraid he's not fit to go into the show.'

'Wait a minute.' The man thrust out his jaw. 'You're talking like that chap in there. I've come a long way to show this dog and I'm going to show him.'

'I'm sorry but you can't show him with a temperature of a hundred and four.'

'But he's had a car journey. That could put up his temperature.'

I shook my head. 'Not as high as that it couldn't. Anyway he looks sick to me. Do you see how he's half closing his eyes as though he's frightened of the light? It's possible he could have distemper.'

'What? That's rubbish and you know it. He's never been fitter!' The man's mouth trembled with anger.

I looked down at the little dog. He was crouching on the grass miserably. Occasionally he shivered, he had a definite photophobia, and there was that creamy blob of pus in the corner of each eye. 'Has he been inoculated against distemper?'

'Well no, he hasn't, but why do you keep on about it?'

'Because I think he's got it now and for his sake and for the sake of the other dogs here you ought to take him straight home and see your own vet.'

He glared at me. 'So you won't let me take him into the show tent?'

'That's right. I'm very sorry, but it's out of the question.' I turned and walked away.

I had gone only a few yards when the loudspeaker boomed again.

'Will Mr Herriot please go to the measuring stand where the ponies are ready for him.'

I collected my stick and trotted over to a corner of the field where a group of ponies had assembled: Welsh, Dales, Exmoor, Dartmoor – all kinds of breeds were represented.

For the uninitiated, horses are measured in hands which consist of four inches, and a graduated stick is used with a cross piece and a spirit level which rests on the withers, the highest point of the shoulders. I had done a fair bit of it in individual animals but this was the first time I had done the job at a show. With my stick at the ready I stood by the two wide boards which had been placed on the turf to give the animals a reasonably level standing surface.

A smiling young woman led the first pony, a smart chestnut, on to the boards.

'Which class?' I asked.

'Thirteen hands.'

I tried the stick on him. He was well under.

'Fine, next please.'

A few more came through without incident, then there was a lull before the next group came up. The ponies were arriving on the field all the time in their boxes and being led over to me, some by their young riders, others by the parents. It looked as though I could be here quite a long time.

During one of the lulls a little man who had been standing near me spoke up.

'No trouble yet?' he asked.

'No, everything's in order,' I replied.

He nodded expressionlessly and as I took a closer look at him his slight body, dark, leathery features and high shoulders seemed to give him the appearance of a little brown gnome. At the same time there was something undeniably horsy about him.

'You'll 'ave some awkward 'uns,' he grunted. 'And they allus say the same thing. They allus tell you the vet at some other show passed their pony.' His swarthy cheeks crinkled in a wry smile.

'Is that so?'

'Aye, you'll see.'

Another candidate, led by a beautiful blonde, was led on to the platform. She gave me the full blast of two big greenish eyes and flashed a mouthful of sparkling teeth at me.

'Twelve two,' she murmured seductively.

I tried the stick on the pony and worked it around, but try as I might I couldn't get it down to that.

'I'm afraid he's a bit big,' I said.

The blonde's smile vanished. 'Have you allowed half an inch for his shoes?'

'I have indeed, but you can see for yourself, he's well over.'

'But he passed the vet without any trouble at Hickley,' she snapped, and out of the corner of my eye I saw the gnome nodding sagely.

'I can't help that,' I said. 'I'm afraid you'll have to put him into the next class.'

For a moment two green pebbles from the cold sea bed fixed me with a frigid glare, then the blonde was gone taking her pony with her.

Next, a little bay animal was led on to the stand by a hard-faced gentleman in a check suit and I must say I was baffled by its behaviour. Whenever the stick touched the withers it sank at the knees so that I couldn't be sure whether I was getting the right reading or not. Finally I gave up and passed him through.

The gnome coughed. 'I know that feller.'

'You do?'

'Aye, he's pricked that pony's withers with a pin so many times that it drops down whenever you try to measure 'im.'

'Never!'

'Sure as I'm standing here.'

I was staggered, but the arrival of another batch took up my attention for a few minutes.

The last pony in this group was a nice grey led by a bouncy man wearing a great big matey smile.

'How are you, all right?' he enquired courteously. 'This 'un's thirteen two.'

The animal went under the stick without trouble but after he had trotted away the gnome spoke up again.

'I know that feller, too.'

'Really?'

'Not 'alf. Weighs down 'is ponies before they're measured. That grey's been standing in 'is box for the last hour with a twelve-stone sack of corn on 'is back. Knocks an inch off.'

'Good God! Are you sure?'

'Don't worry, I've seen 'im at it.'

My mind was beginning to reel just a little. Was the man making it all up or were there really these malign forces at work behind all this innocent fun?

'That same feller,' continued the gnome, 'I've seen 'im bring a pony to a show and get half an inch knocked off for shoes when it never 'ad no shoes on.'

I wished he'd stop. And just then there was an interruption. It was the man with the moustache. He sidled up to me and whispered confidentially in my ear.

'Now I've just been thinking. My dog must have got over his journey by now and I expect his temperature will be normal. I wonder if you'd just try him again. I've still got time to show him.'

I turned wearily. 'Honestly, it'll be a waste of time. I've told you, he's ill.'

'Please! Just as a favour.' He had a desperate look and a fanatical light flickered in his eye.

'All right.' I went over to the car with him and produced my thermometer. The temperature was still a hundred and four.

'Now I wish you'd take this poor little dog home,' I said. 'He shouldn't be here.'

For a moment I thought the man was going to strike me. 'There's nothing wrong with him!' he hissed, his whole face working with emotion.

'I'm sorry,' I said, and went back to the measuring stand.

A boy of about fifteen was waiting for me with his pony. It was supposed to be in the thirteen two class but was nearly one and a half inches over.

'Much too big, I'm afraid,' I said. 'He can't go in that class.'

The boy didn't answer. He put his hand inside his jacket and produced a sheet of paper. 'This is a veterinary certificate to say he's under thirteen two.'

'No good, I'm sorry,' I replied. 'The stewards have told me not to accept any certificates. I've turned down two others today. Everything has to go under the stick. It's a pity, but there it is.'

His manner changed abruptly. 'But you've GOT to accept it!' he shouted in my face. 'There doesn't have to be any measurements when you have a certificate.'

'You'd better see the stewards. Those are my instructions.'

'I'll see my father about this, that's what!' he shouted and led the animal away.

Father was quickly on the scene. Big, fat, prosperous-looking, confident. He obviously wasn't going to stand any nonsense from me.

'Now look here, I don't know what this is all about but you have no option in this matter. You have to accept the certificate.'

'I don't, I assure you,' I answered. 'And anyway, it's not as though your pony was slightly over the mark. He's miles over – nowhere near the height.'

Father flushed dark red. 'Well let me tell you he was passed through by the vet at . . .'

'I know, I know,' I said, and I heard the gnome give a short laugh. 'But he's not going through here.'

There was a brief silence, then both father and son began to scream at me. And as they continued to hurl abuse I felt a hand on my arm. It was the man with the moustache again.

'I'm going to ask you just once more to take my dog's temperature,' he whispered with a ghastly attempt at a smile. 'I'm sure he'll be all right this time. Will you try him again?'

I'd had enough. 'No, I bloody well won't!' I barked. 'Will you kindly stop bothering me and take that poor animal home.'

It's funny how the most unlikely things motivate certain people. It didn't seem a life and death matter whether a dog got into a show or not but it was to the man with the moustache. He started to rave at me.

'You don't know your job, that's the trouble with you! I've come all this way and you've played a dirty trick on me. I've got a friend who's a vet, a proper vet, and I'm going to tell him about you, yes I am. I'm going to tell him about you!'

At the same time the father and son were still in full cry, snarling and mouthing at me, and I became suddenly aware that I was in the centre of a hostile circle. The blonde was there too, and some of the others whose ponies I had outed, and they were all staring at me belligerently, making angry gestures.

I felt very much alone because the gnome, who had seemed an ally, was nowhere to be seen. I was disappointed in the gnome; he was a big talker but had vanished at the first whiff of danger. As I surveyed the threatening crowd I moved my measuring stick round in front of me; it wasn't much of a weapon but it might serve to fend them off if they rushed me.

And just at that moment, as the unkind words were thick upon the air, I saw Helen and Richard Edmundson on the fringe of the circle, taking it all in. I wasn't worried about him but again it struck me as strange that it should be my destiny always to be looking a bit of a clown when Helen was around.

Anyway, the measuring was over and I felt in need of sustenance. I retreated and went to find Tristan.

*

The memory of Darrowby Show has stayed with me and it has left me with a deep respect and sympathy for the many veterinarians who have the thankless task of adjudicating at these functions. People just don't like it when you have to turn their animals down. Of course I have had many trouble-free occasions since then, and I sometimes think it was my youth and inexperience which made me such a target for disapproval. I didn't mention it in the story, but things got so bad on that day that I was glad to see the local police sergeant strolling round the field. I quite seriously thought that I would ultimately have to ask for police protection.

12. *A Momentous Birth*

The occasion was the Daffodil Ball at the Drovers' Arms and we were dressed in our best. This was a different kind of function from the usual village institute hop with the farm lads in their big boots and music from a scraping fiddle and piano. It was a proper dance with a popular local band – Lenny Butterfield and His Hot Shots – and was an annual affair to herald the arrival of spring.

I watched Tristan dispensing the drinks.

'Nice little gathering, Jim,' he said, appearing at my elbow. 'A few more blokes than girls but that won't matter much.'

I eyed him coldly. I knew why there were extra men. It was so that Tristan wouldn't have to take the floor too often. It fitted in with his general dislike of squandering energy that he was an unenthusiastic dancer; he didn't mind walking a girl round the floor now and again during the evening, but he preferred to spend most of the time in the bar.

So, in fact, did a lot of the Darrowby folk. When we arrived at the Drovers' the bar was congested while only a dedicated few circled round the ballroom. But as time went on more and more couples ventured out and by ten o'clock the dance floor was truly packed.

And I soon found I was enjoying myself. Tristan's friends were an effervescent bunch, likeable young men and attractive girls; I just couldn't help having a good time.

Butterfield's famed band in their short red jackets added greatly to the general merriment. Lenny himself looked about fifty-five and indeed all four of the Hot Shots ensemble were rather elderly, but they made up for their grey hairs by sheer vivacity. Not that Lenny's hair was grey; it was dyed a determined black and he thumped the piano with dynamic energy, beaming out at the company through his horn-rimmed glasses, occasionally bawling a chorus into the microphone by his side, announcing the dances, making throaty wisecracks. He gave value for money.

There was no pairing off in our party and I danced with all the girls in turn. At the peak of the evening I was jockeying my way around the floor with Daphne and the way she was constructed made it a rewarding experience. I never have been one for skinny women but I suppose you could say that Daphne's development had strayed a little too far in the other direction. She wasn't fat, just lavishly endowed.

Battling through the crush, colliding with exuberant neighbours, bouncing deliciously off Daphne, with everybody singing as they danced and the Hot Shots pouring out an insistent boom-boom beat, I felt I hadn't a care in the world. And then I saw Helen.

She was dancing with the inevitable Richard Edmundson, his shining gold head floating above the company like an emblem of doom. And it was uncanny how in an instant my cosy little world disintegrated, leaving a chill gnawing emptiness.

When the music stopped I returned Daphne to her friends and went to find Tristan. The comfortable little bar in the Drovers' was overflowing and the temperature like an oven. Through an almost impenetrable fog of cigarette smoke I discerned my colleague on a high stool holding court with a group of perspiring revellers. Tristan himself looked cool and, as always, profoundly content. He drained his glass, smacked his lips gently as though it had been the best pint of beer he'd ever tasted, then, as he reached across the counter and courteously requested a refill, he spotted me struggling towards him.

When I reached his stool he laid an affable hand on my shoulder. 'Ah, Jim, nice to see you. Splendid dance, this, don't you think?'

A Momentous Birth

I didn't bring up the fact that I hadn't seen him on the floor yet, but making my voice casual I mentioned that Helen was there.

Tristan nodded benignly. 'Yes, saw her come in. Why don't you go and dance with her?'

'I can't do that. She's with a partner – young Edmundson.'

'Not at all.' Tristan surveyed his fresh pint with a critical eye and took an exploratory sip. 'She's with a party, like us. No partner.'

'How do you know that?'

'I watched all the fellows hang their coats out there while the girls went upstairs. No reason at all why you shouldn't have a dance with her.'

'I see.' I hesitated for a few moments then made my way back to the ballroom.

But it wasn't as easy as that. I had to keep doing my duty with the girls in our group, and whenever I headed for Helen she was whisked away by one of her men friends before I got near her. At times I fancied she was looking over at me but I couldn't be sure; the only thing I knew for certain was that I wasn't enjoying myself any more; the magic and gaiety had gone and I felt a rising misery at the thought that this was going to be another of my frustrating contacts with Helen when all I could do was look at her hopelessly. Only this time was worse – I hadn't even spoken to her.

I was almost relieved when the manager came up and told me there was a call for me. I went to the phone and spoke to Mrs Hall. There was a bitch in trouble whelping and I had to go. I looked at my watch – after midnight, so that was the end of the dance for me.

I stood for a moment listening to the muffled thudding from the dance floor, then slowly pulled on my coat before going in to say goodbye to Tristan's friends. I exchanged a few words with them, waved, then turned back and pushed the swing door open.

Helen was standing there, about a foot away from me. Her hand was on the door, too. I didn't wonder whether she was going in or out but stared dumbly into her smiling blue eyes.

'Leaving already, Jim?' she said.

'Yes, I've got a call, I'm afraid.'

'Oh what a shame. I hope it's nothing very serious.'

I opened my mouth to speak, but her dark beauty and the very nearness of her suddenly filled my world and a wave of hopeless longing swept over and submerged me. I slid my hand a few inches down the door and gripped hers as a drowning man might, and wonderingly I felt her fingers come round and entwine themselves tightly in mine.

And in an instant there was no band, no noise, no people, just the two of us standing very close in the doorway.

'Come with me,' I said.

Helen's eyes were very large as she smiled that smile I knew so well.

'I'll get my coat,' she murmured.

This wasn't really me, I thought, standing on the hall carpet watching Helen trotting quickly up the stairs, but I had to believe it as she reappeared on the landing pulling on her coat. Outside, on the cobbles of the market-place my car, too, appeared to be taken by surprise because it roared into life at the first touch of the starter.

I had to go back to the surgery for my whelping instruments and in the silent moonlit street we got out and I opened the big white door to Skeldale House.

And once in the passage it was the most natural thing in the world to take her in my arms and kiss her gratefully and unhurriedly. I had waited a long time for this and the minutes flowed past unnoticed as we stood there, our feet on the black and red eighteenth-century tiles, our heads almost touching the vast picture of the Death of Nelson which dominated the entrance.

We kissed again at the first bend of the passage under the companion picture of the Meeting of Wellington and Blücher at Waterloo. We kissed at the second bend by the tall cupboard where Siegfried kept his riding coats and boots. We kissed in the dispensary in between searching for my instruments. Then we tried it out in the garden and this was the best of all, with the flowers still and expectant in the moonlight and the fragrance of the moist earth and grass rising about us.

I have never driven so slowly to a case. About ten miles an hour, with Helen's head on my shoulder and all the scents of spring drifting in through the open window. And it was like sailing from stormy seas into a sweet, safe harbour, like coming home.

The light in the cottage window was the only one showing in the sleeping village, and when I knocked at the door Bert Chapman answered. Bert was a council roadman – one of the breed for whom I felt an abiding affinity.

The council men were my brethren of the roads. Like me they spent most of their lives on the lonely by-ways around Darrowby and

I saw them most days of the week, repairing the tarmac, cutting back the grass verges in the summer, gritting and snow ploughing in the winter. And when they spotted me driving past they would grin cheerfully and wave as if the very sight of me had made their day. I don't know whether they were specially picked for good nature, but I don't think I have ever met a more equable body of men.

One old farmer remarked sourly to me once, 'There's no wonder the buggers are 'appy, they've got nowt to do.' An exaggeration, of course, but I knew how he felt; compared with farming every other job was easy.

I had seen Bert Chapman just a day or two ago, sitting on a grassy bank, his shovel by his side, a vast sandwich in his hand. He had raised a corded forearm in salute, a broad smile bisecting his round, sun-reddened face. He had looked eternally carefree but tonight his smile was strained.

'I'm sorry to bother you this late, Mr Herriot,' he said as he ushered us into the house, 'but I'm gettin' a bit worried about Susie. Her pups are due and she's been making a bed for them and messing about all day but nowt's happened. I was goin' to leave her till morning but about midnight she started panting like 'ell – I don't like the look of her.'

Susie was one of my regular patients. Her big, burly master was always bringing her to the surgery, a little shame-faced at his solicitude, and when I saw him sitting in the waiting room looking strangely out of place among the ladies with their pets, he usually said, 'T'missus asked me to bring Susie.' But it was a transparent excuse.

'She's nobbut a little mongrel, but very faithful,' Bert said, still apologetic, but I could understand how he felt about Susie, a shaggy little ragamuffin whose only wile was to put her paws on my knees and laugh up into my face with her tail lashing. I found her irresistible.

But she was a very different character tonight. As we went into the living room of the cottage the little animal crept from her basket, gave a single indeterminate wag of her tail, then stood miserably in the middle of the floor, her ribs heaving. As I bent to examine her she turned a wide panting mouth and anxious eyes up to me.

I ran my hands over her abdomen. I don't think I have ever felt a more bloated little dog; she was as round as a football, absolutely bulging with pups, ready to pop, but nothing was happening.

'What do you think?' Bert's face was haggard under his sunburn and he touched the dog's head briefly with a big calloused hand.

'I don't know yet, Bert,' I said. 'I'll have to have a feel inside. Bring me some hot water, will you?'

I added some antiseptic to the water, soaped my hand and with one finger carefully explored the vagina. There was a pup there, all right; my fingertip brushed across the nostrils, the tiny mouth and tongue; but he was jammed in that passage like a cork in a bottle.

Squatting back on my heels I turned to the Chapmans.

'I'm afraid there's a big pup stuck fast. I have a feeling that if she could get rid of this chap the others would come away. They'd probably be smaller.'

'Is there any way of shiftin' him, Mr Herriot?' Bert asked.

I paused for a moment. 'I'm going to put forceps on his head and see if he'll move. I don't like using forceps but I'm going to have one careful try, and if it doesn't work I'll have to take her back to the surgery for a caesarian.'

'An operation?' Bert said hollowly. He gulped and glanced fearfully at his wife. Like many big men he had married a tiny woman and at this moment Mrs Chapman looked even smaller than her four foot eleven inches as she huddled in her chair and stared at me with wide eyes.

'Oh I wish we'd never had her mated,' she wailed, wringing her hands. 'I told Bert five year old was too late for a first litter but he wouldn't listen. And now we're maybe going to lose 'er.'

I hastened to reassure her. 'No, she isn't too old, and everything may be all right. Let's just see how we get on.'

I boiled the instrument for a few minutes on the stove then kneeled behind my patient again. I poised the forceps for a moment and at the flash of steel a grey tinge crept under Bert's sunburn and his wife coiled herself into a ball in her chair. Obviously they were non-starters as assistants so Helen held Susie's head while I once more reached in towards the pup. There was desperately little room but I managed to direct the forceps along my finger till they touched the nose. Then very gingerly I opened the jaws and pushed them forward with the very gentlest pressure until I was able to clamp them on either side of the head.

I'd soon know now. In a situation like this you can't do any pulling, you can only try to ease the thing along. This I did and I fancied I felt just a bit of movement; I tried again and there was no doubt

84

about it, the pup was coming towards me. Susie, too, appeared to sense that things were taking a turn for the better. She cast off her apathy and began to strain lustily.

It was no trouble after that and I was able to draw the pup forth almost without resistance.

'I'm afraid this one'll be dead,' I said, and as the tiny creature lay across my palm there was no sign of breathing. But, pinching the chest between the thumb and forefinger I could feel the heart pulsing steadily, and I quickly opened his mouth and blew softly down into his lungs.

I repeated this a few times then laid the pup on his side in the basket. I was just thinking it was going to be no good when the little rib cage gave a sudden lift, then another and another.

'He's off!' Bert exclaimed happily. 'That's champion! We want these puppies alive tha knows. They're by Jack Dennison's terrier and he's a grand 'un.'

'That's right,' Mrs Chapman put in. 'No matter how many she has, they're all spoken for. Everybody wants a pup out of Susie.'

'I can believe that,' I said. But I smiled to myself. Jack Dennison's terrier was another hound of uncertain ancestry, so this lot would be a right mixture. But none the worse for that.

I gave Susie half a c.c. of pituitrin. 'I think she needs it after pushing against that fellow for hours. We'll wait and see what happens now.'

And it was nice waiting. Mrs Chapman brewed a pot of tea and began to slap butter on to home-made scones. Susie, partly aided by my pituitrin, pushed out a pup in a self-satisfied manner about every fifteen minutes. The pups themselves soon set up a bawling of surprising volume for such minute creatures. Bert, relaxing visibly with every minute, filled his pipe and regarded the fast-growing family with a grin of increasing width.

'Ee, it is kind of you young folks to stay with us like this.' Mrs Chapman put her head on one side and looked at us worriedly. 'I should think you've been dying to get back to your dance all this time.'

I thought of the crush at the Drovers'. The smoke, the heat, the non-stop boom-boom of the Hot Shots, and I looked around the peaceful little room with the old-fashioned black grate, the low, varnished beams, Mrs Chapman's sewing box, the row of Bert's pipes on the wall. I took a firmer grasp of Helen's hand which I had been holding under the table for the last hour.

'Not at all, Mrs Chapman,' I said. 'We haven't missed it in the least.' And I have never been more sincere.

It must have been about half past two when I finally decided that Susie had finished. She had six fine pups which was a good score for a little thing like her and the noise had abated as the family settled down to feast on her abundant udder.

I lifted the pups out one by one and examined them. Susie didn't mind in the least but appeared to be smiling with modest pride as I handled her brood. When I put them back with her she inspected them and sniffed them over busily before rolling on to her side again.

'Three dogs and three bitches,' I said. 'Nice even litter.'

Before leaving I took Susie from her basket and palpated her abdomen. The degree of deflation was almost unbelievable; a pricked balloon could not have altered its shape more spectacularly and she had made a remarkable metamorphosis to the lean, scruffy little extrovert I knew so well.

When I released her she scurried back and curled herself round her new family who were soon sucking away with total absorption.

Bert laughed. 'She's fair capped wi' them pups.' He bent over and prodded the first arrival with a horny forefinger. 'I like the look o' this big dog pup. I reckon we'll keep this 'un for ourselves, mother. He'll be company for t'awd lass.'

It was time to go. Helen and I moved over to the door and little Mrs Chapman with her fingers on the handle looked up at me.

'Well, Mr Herriot,' she said, 'I can't thank you enough for comin' out and putting our minds at rest. I don't know what I'd have done wi' this man of mine if anything had happened to his little dog.'

Bert grinned sheepishly. 'Nay,' he muttered. 'Ah was never really worried.'

His wife laughed and opened the door and as we stepped out into the silent scented night she gripped my arm and looked up at me roguishly.

'I suppose this is your young lady,' she said.

I put my arm round Helen's shoulders.

'Yes,' I said firmly, 'this is my young lady.'

*

A Momentous Birth

That night marked the birth not only of Susie's new family but of my whole married life, because up till then everything had gone wrong in my courtship of Helen. From that time on my course was set for the most important of all things, and as I look back over nearly forty-five years of our life together I am thankful for the happy fate which worked for me at the Daffodil Ball. It is good, too, to be reminded of the very personal way in which we dealt with our patients in those days – sitting in a cottage throughout a whelping. This is a romantic story and technical things seem to be of no great matter, but I must just mention that we very rarely use whelping forceps now.

13. *Jock*

I had only to sit up in bed to look right across Darrowby to the hills beyond.

I got up and walked to the window. It was going to be a fine morning and the early sun glanced over the weathered reds and greys of the jumbled roofs, some of them sagging under their burden of ancient tiles, and brightened the tufts of green where trees pushed upwards from the gardens among the bristle of chimney pots. And behind everything the calm bulk of the fells.

It was my good fortune that this was the first thing I saw every morning; after Helen, of course, which was better still.

Jock

Following our unorthodox tuberculin testing honeymoon we had set up our first home on the top of Skeldale House. Siegfried, my boss up to my wedding and now my partner, had offered us free use of these empty rooms on the third storey and we had gratefully accepted; and though it was a makeshift arrangement there was an airy charm, an exhilaration in our high perch that many would have envied.

The front room was our bed-sitter and though it was not luxuriously furnished it did have an excellent bed, a carpet, a handsome side table which had belonged to Helen's mother and two armchairs. It had an ancient wardrobe, too, but the lock didn't work and the only way we kept the door closed was by jamming one of my socks in it. The toe always dangled outside but it never seemed of any importance.

I went out and across a few feet of landing to our kitchen-dining room at the back. This apartment was definitely spartan. I clumped over bare boards to a bench we had rigged against the wall by the window. This held a gas ring and our crockery and cutlery. I seized a tall jug and began my long descent to the main kitchen downstairs because one minor snag was that there was no water at the top of the house. Down two flights to the three rooms on the first storey, then down two more and a final gallop along the passage to the big stone-flagged kitchen at the end.

I filled the jug and returned to our eyrie two steps at a time. I wouldn't like to do this now whenever I needed water, but at that time I didn't find it the least inconvenience.

Helen soon had the kettle boiling and we drank our first cup of tea by the window looking down on the long garden. From up here we had an aerial view of the unkempt lawns, the fruit trees, the wistaria climbing the weathered brick towards our window, and the high walls with their old stone copings stretching away to the cobbled yard under the elms. Every day I went up and down that path to the garage in the yard but it looked so different from above.

'Wait a minute, Helen,' I said. 'Let me sit on that chair.'

She had laid the breakfast on the bench where we ate and this was where the difficulty arose. Because it was a tall bench and our recently acquired high stool fitted it but our chair didn't.

'No, I'm all right, Jim, really I am.' She smiled at me reassuringly from her absurd position, almost at eye-level with her plate.

'You can't be all right,' I retorted. 'Your chin's nearly in among your cornflakes. Please let me sit there.'

She patted the seat of the stool. 'Come on, stop arguing. Sit down and have your breakfast.'

This, I felt, just wouldn't do. I tried a different tack.

'Helen!' I said severely. 'Get off that chair!'

'No!' she replied without looking at me, her lips pushed forward in a characteristic pout which I always found enchanting but which also meant she wasn't kidding.

I was at a loss. I toyed with the idea of pulling her off the chair, but she was a big girl. We had had a previous physical try-out when a minor disagreement had escalated into a wrestling match and though I thoroughly enjoyed the contest and actually won in the end, I had been surprised by her sheer strength. At this time in the morning I didn't feel up to it. I sat on the stool.

After breakfast Helen began to boil water for the washing-up, the next stage in our routine. Meanwhile I went downstairs, collected my gear, including suture material for a foal which had cut its leg, and went out the side door into the garden. Just about opposite the rockery I turned and looked up at our window. It was open at the bottom and an arm emerged holding a dishcloth. I waved and the dishcloth waved back furiously. It was the start to every day.

And, driving from the yard, it seemed a good start. In fact everything was good. The raucous cawing of the rooks in the elms above as I closed the double doors, the clean fragrance of the air which greeted me every morning, and the challenge and interest of my job.

The injured foal was at Robert Corner's farm and I hadn't been there long before I spotted Jock, his sheepdog. And I began to watch the dog because behind a vet's daily chore of treating his patients there is always the fascinating kaleidoscope of animal personality and Jock was an interesting case.

A lot of farm dogs are partial to a little light relief from their work. They like to play and one of their favourite games is chasing cars off the premises. Often I drove off with a hairy form galloping alongside, and the dog would usually give a final defiant bark after a few hundred yards to speed me on my way. But Jock was different.

He was really dedicated. Car chasing to him was a deadly serious art which he practised daily without a trace of levity. Corner's farm was at the end of a long track, twisting for nearly a mile between its stone walls down through the gently sloping fields to the road below, and Jock didn't consider he had done his job properly until he had escorted his chosen vehicle right to the very foot. So his hobby was an exacting one.

I watched him now as I finished stitching the foal's leg and began to tie on a bandage. He was slinking about the buildings, a skinny little creature who, without his mass of black and white hair, would have been an almost invisible mite, and he was playing out a transparent charade of pretending he was taking no notice of me – wasn't the least bit interested in my presence, in fact. But his furtive glances in the direction of the stable, his repeated criss-crossing of my line of vision gave him away. He was waiting for his big moment.

When I was putting on my shoes and throwing my wellingtons into the boot I saw him again. Or rather part of him; just a long nose and one eye protruding from beneath a broken door. It wasn't till I had started the engine and begun to move off that he finally declared himself, stealing out from his hiding place, body low, tail trailing, eyes fixed intently on the car's front wheels, and as I gathered speed and headed down the track he broke into an effortless lope.

I had been through this before and was always afraid he might run in front of me, so I put my foot down and began to hurtle downhill. This was where Jock came into his own. I often wondered how he'd fare against a racing Greyhound because by golly he could run. That sparse frame housed a perfect physical machine and the slender limbs reached and flew again and again, devouring the stony ground beneath, keeping up with the speeding car with joyful ease.

There was a sharp bend about half-way down and here Jock invariably sailed over the wall and streaked across the turf, a little dark blur against the green, and having craftily cut off the corner he reappeared like a missile zooming over the grey stones lower down. This put him into a nice position for the run to the road and when he finally saw me on to the tarmac, my last view of him was of a happy panting face looking after me. Clearly he considered it was a job well done and he would wander contentedly back up to the farm to await the next session, perhaps with the postman or the baker's van.

And there was another side to Jock. He was an outstanding performer at the sheepdog trials and Mr Corner had won many trophies with him. In fact the farmer could have sold the little animal for a lot of money but couldn't be persuaded to part with him. Instead he purchased a bitch, a scrawny little female counterpart of

Jock and a trial winner in her own right. With this combination Mr
Corner thought he could breed some world-beating types for sale.
On my visits to the farm the bitch joined in the car-chasing, but it
seemed as though she was doing it more or less to humour her new
mate and she always gave up at the first bend leaving Jock in
command. You could see her heart wasn't in it.

When the pups arrived, seven fluffy black balls tumbling about
the yard and getting under everybody's feet, Jock watched indulgently
as they tried to follow him in his pursuit of my vehicle and you could
almost see him laughing as they fell over their feet and were left
trailing far behind.

It happened that I didn't have to go there for about ten months,
but I saw Robert Corner in the market occasionally and he told me
he was training the pups and they were shaping well. Not that they
needed much training; it was in their blood and he said they had
tried to round up the cattle and sheep nearly as soon as they could
walk. When I finally saw them they were like seven Jocks – meagre,
darting little creatures flitting noiselessly about the buildings – and
it didn't take me long to find out that they had learned more than
sheep herding from their father. There was something very evocative
about the way they began to prowl around in the background as I
prepared to get into my car, peeping furtively from behind straw
bales, slinking with elaborate nonchalance into favourable positions
for a quick getaway. And as I settled in my seat I could sense they
were all crouched in readiness for the off.

I revved my engine, let in the clutch with a bump and shot across
the yard, and in a second the immediate vicinity erupted in a mass
of hairy forms. I roared on to the track and put my foot down and
on either side of me the little animals pelted along shoulder to
shoulder, their faces all wearing the intent fanatical expression I knew
so well. When Jock cleared the wall the seven pups went with him
and when they reappeared and entered the home straight I noticed
something different. On past occasions Jock had always had one eye
on the car – this was what he considered his opponent; but now on
that last quarter mile as he hurtled along at the head of a shaggy
phalanx he was glancing at the pups on either side as though they
were the main opposition.

And there was no doubt he was in trouble. Superbly fit though he
was, these stringy bundles of bone and sinew which he had fathered
had all his speed plus the newly minted energy of youth, and it was

Jock

taking every shred of his power to keep up with them. Indeed there was one terrible moment when he stumbled and was engulfed by the bounding creatures around him; it seemed that all was lost but there was a core of steel in Jock. Eyes popping, nostrils dilated, he fought his way through the pack until by the time we reached the road he was once more in the lead.

But it had taken its toll. I slowed down before driving away and looked down at the little animal standing with lolling tongue and heaving flanks on the grass verge. It must have been like this with all the other vehicles and it wasn't a merry game any more. I suppose it sounds silly to say you could read a dog's thoughts but everything in his posture betrayed the mounting apprehension that his days of supremacy were numbered. Just round the corner lay the unthinkable ignominy of being left trailing in the rear of that litter of young upstarts, and as I drew away Jock looked after me and his expression was eloquent.

'How long can I keep this up?'

I felt for the little dog and on my next visit to the farm about two months later I wasn't looking forward to witnessing the final degradation which I felt was inevitable. But when I drove into the yard I found the place strangely unpopulated.

Robert Corner was forking hay into the cows' racks in the byre. He turned as I came in.

'Where are all your dogs?' I asked.

He put down his fork. 'All gone. By gaw, there's a market for good workin' sheepdogs. I've done right well out of t'job.'

'But you've still got Jock?'

'Oh aye, ah couldn't part with t'awd lad. He's over there.'

And so he was, creeping around as of old, pretending he wasn't watching me. And when the happy time finally arrived and I drove away, it was like it used to be with the lean little animal haring along by the side of the car, but relaxed, enjoying the game, winging effortlessly over the wall and beating the car down to the tarmac with no trouble at all.

I think I was as relieved as he was that he was left alone with his supremacy unchallenged; that he was still top dog.

*

93

There are many Jocks in Yorkshire, many dogs who lurk in corners until I am ready to drive away from the farm. But none that I can recall had such an airy race-track like Jock, winding for such a long way down that green hillside, and none had his utter dedication to his job. Most of them consider they have done their duty if they chase me off the premises for a short distance, then stand barking till I am out of sight. Whether that barking means 'good riddance' or 'nice to have seen you' I have never been able to decide. However, one of these little animals, Matty by name, had me worried. He worried the farmer too, because he didn't only chase cars, he nibbled at the speeding tyres. It was obvious that it was only a matter of time till he was run over. It was my twelve-year-old son, Jimmy, who cured the dog of his habit and probably saved his life. He came with me on my rounds whenever possible and on Matty's farm he filled a 100 c.c. syringe with water and when we drove away and the dog homed in on our tyres, he leaned out and squirted the water in his face. The effect was dramatic. Matty pulled up immediately, and as I looked in the mirror I could see him watching us in silence, an expression of deep puzzlement on his face. It had such a lasting effect that the farmer asked us to repeat the procedure another day. We did so and Matty was cured. He never went for tyres again.

14. *Sexual Harassment*

You could hardly expect to find a more unlikely character in Darrowby than Roland Partridge. The thought came to me for the hundredth time as I saw him peering through the window which looked on to Trengate just a little way up the other side of the street from our surgery.

He was tapping the glass and beckoning to me and the eyes behind the thick spectacles were wide with concern. I waited, and when he opened the door I stepped straight from the street into his living room, because these were tiny dwellings with only a kitchen in the rear and a single small bedroom overlooking the street above. But when I went in I had the familiar feeling of surprise. Because most of the other occupants of the row were farmworkers and their furnishings were orthodox; but this place was a studio.

An easel stood in the light from the window and the walls were covered from floor to ceiling with paintings. Unframed canvases were stacked everywhere and the few ornate chairs and the table with its load of painted china and other bric-à-brac added to the artistic atmosphere.

The simple explanation was, of course, that Mr Partridge was in fact an artist. But the unlikely aspect came into it when you learned that this middle-aged velvet-jacketed aesthete was the son of a small farmer, a man whose forebears had been steeped in the soil for generations.

'I happened to see you passing there, Mr Herriot,' he said. 'Are you terribly busy?'

'Not too busy, Mr Partridge. Can I help you?'

He nodded gravely. 'I wonder whether you could spare a moment to look at Percy. I'd be most grateful.'

'Of course,' I replied. 'Where is he?'

He was ushering me towards the kitchen when there was a bang on the outer door and Bert Hardisty the postman burst in. Bert was a rough-hewn character and he dumped a parcel unceremoniously on the table.

'There y'are, Rolie!' he shouted and turned to go.

Mr Partridge gazed with unruffled dignity at the retreating back. 'Thank you very much indeed, Bertram, good day to you.'

Here was another thing. The postman and the artist were both Darrowby born and bred, had the same social background, had gone to the same school, yet their voices were quite different. Roland Partridge, in fact, spoke with the precise, well-modulated syllables of a barrister-at-law.

We went into the kitchen. This was where he cooked for himself in his bachelor state. When his father died many years ago he had sold the farm immediately. Apparently his whole nature was appalled by the earthy farming scene and he could not get out quickly enough. At any rate he had got sufficient money from the sale to indulge his interests and he had taken up painting and lived ever since in this humble cottage, resolutely doing his own thing. This had all happened long before I came to Darrowby, and the dangling lank hair was silver now. I always had the feeling that he was happy in his way because I couldn't imagine that small, rather exquisite figure plodding round a muddy farmyard.

It was probably in keeping with his nature that he had never married. There was a touch of asceticism in the thin cheeks and pale blue eyes and it was possible that his self-contained imperturbable personality might denote a lack of warmth. But that didn't hold good with regard to his dog, Percy.

He loved Percy with a fierce protective passion and as the little animal trotted towards him he bent over him, his face alight with tenderness.

'He looks pretty bright to me,' I said. 'He's not sick, is he?'

'No . . . no . . .' Mr Partridge seemed strangely ill at ease. 'He's perfectly well in himself, but I want you to look at him and see if you notice anything.'

I looked. And I saw only what I had always seen, the snow-white, shaggy-haired little object regarded by local dog breeders and other *cognoscenti* as a negligible mongrel but nevertheless one of my favourite patients. Mr Partridge, looking through the window of a pet shop in Brawton about five years ago, had succumbed immediately to the charms of two soulful eyes gazing up at him from a six-week-old tangle of white hair and had put down his five bob and rushed the little creature home. Percy had been described in the shop somewhat vaguely as a 'terrier', and Mr Partridge had flirted fearfully with the idea of having his tail docked; but such was his infatuation that he couldn't bring himself to cause such a mutilation and the tail had grown in a great fringed curve almost full circle over the back.

To me, the tail nicely balanced the head which was undoubtedly a little too big for the body, but Mr Partridge had been made to suffer for it. His old friends in Darrowby who, like all country folks, considered themselves experts with animals, were free with their comments. I had heard them at it. When Percy was young it was:

'Time ye had that tail off, Rolie. Ah'll bite it off for ye if ye like.' And later, again and again: 'Hey, Rolie, you should've had that dog's tail off when he were a pup. He looks bloody daft like that.'

When asked Percy's breed Mr Partridge always replied haughtily, 'Sealyham Cross', but it wasn't as simple as that; the tiny body with its luxuriant bristling coat, the large, rather noble head with high, pricked ears, the short, knock-kneed legs and that tail made him a baffling mixture.

Mr Partridge's friends again were merciless, referring to Percy as a 'tripe-'ound' or a 'mouse-'ound', and though the little artist received these railleries with a thin smile I knew they bit deep. He had a high regard for me based simply on the fact that the first time I saw Percy I exclaimed quite spontaneously, 'What a beautiful little dog!' And since I have never had much time for the points and fads of dog breeding I really meant it.

'Just what is wrong, Mr Partridge?' I asked. 'I can't see anything unusual.'

Again the little man appeared to be uneasy. 'Well now, watch as he walks across the floor. Come, Percy my dear.' He moved away from me and the dog followed him.

'No . . . no . . . I don't quite understand what you mean.'

'Watch again.' He set off once more. 'It's at his . . . his er . . . back end.'

I crouched down. 'Ah now, yes, wait a minute. Just hold him there, will you?'

I went over and had a close look. 'I see it now. One of his testicles is slightly enlarged.'

'Yes . . . yes . . . quite.' Mr Partridge's face turned a shade pinker. 'That is . . . er . . . what I thought.'

'Hang on to him a second while I examine it.' I lifted the scrotum and palpated gently. 'Yes, the left one is definitely bigger and it is harder too.'

'Is it . . . anything serious?'

I paused. 'No, I shouldn't think so. Tumours of the testicles are not uncommon in dogs and fortunately they aren't inclined to metastasise – spread through the body – very readily. So I shouldn't worry too much.'

I added the last bit hastily because at the mention of the word 'tumour' the colour had drained from his face alarmingly.

'That's a growth, isn't it?' he stammered.

'Yes, but there are all kinds and a lot of them are not malignant. So don't worry but please keep an eye on him. It may not grow much, but if it does you must let me know immediately.'

'I see . . . and if it does grow?'

'Well the only thing would be to remove the testicle.'

'An operation?' The little man stared at me and for a moment I thought he would faint.

'Yes, but not a serious one. Quite straightforward, really.' I bent down and felt the enlargement again. It was very slight. From the front end, Percy kept up a continuous musical growling. I grinned. He always did that – when I took his temperature, cut his nails, anything; a nonstop grumble – and it didn't mean a thing. I knew him well enough to realise there was no viciousness in him; he was merely asserting his virility, reminding me what a tough fellow he was, and it was not idle boasting because for all his lack of size he was a proud, mettlesome little dog, absolutely crammed with character.

After I had left the house I looked back and saw Mr Partridge standing there watching me. He was clasping and unclasping his hands.

And even when I was back in the surgery half of me was still in that odd little studio. I had to admire Mr Partridge for doing exactly what he wanted to do, because in Darrowby he would never get any credit for it. A good horseman or cricketer would be revered in the town but an artist . . . never. Not even if he became famous, and Mr Partridge would never be famous. A few people bought his paintings but he could not have lived on the proceeds. I had one of them hanging in our bed-sitter and to my mind he had a definite gift. In fact I would have tried to afford more of them but for the fact that he obviously shrank from that aspect of the Yorkshire Dales which I loved most.

If I had been able to paint I would have wanted to show how the walls climbed everywhere over the stark fell-sides. I would have tried to capture the magic of the endless empty moors with the reeds trembling over the black bog pools. But Mr Partridge went only for the cosy things: willows hanging by a rustic bridge, village churches, rose-covered cottages.

Since Percy was a near neighbour I saw him nearly every day, either from our bed-sitter at the top of the house or from the surgery below. His master exercised him with great zeal and regularity and it was a common sight to see the artist passing on the other side of the road with the little animal trotting proudly beside him. But from that distance it was impossible to see if the tumour was progressing, and since I heard nothing from Mr Partridge I assumed that all was well. Maybe that thing had grown no more. Sometimes it happened that way.

Keeping a close watch on the little dog reminded me of other incidents connected with him, particularly the number of times he was involved in a fight. Not that Percy ever started a brawl – at ten inches high he wasn't stupid enough for that – but somehow big dogs when they saw that dainty white figure prancing along were inclined to go for him on sight. I witnessed some of these attacks from our windows and the same thing happened every time: a quick flurry of limbs, a snarling and yelping and then the big dog retreated bleeding.

Percy never had a mark on him – that tremendous thick coat gave him complete protection – but he always got a nip in from underneath. I had stitched up several of the local street fighters after Percy had finished with them.

It must have been about six weeks later when Mr Partridge came in again. He looked tense.

'I'd like you to have a look at Percy again, Mr Herriot.'

I lifted the dog on to the surgery table and I didn't need to examine him very closely.

'It's quite a lot bigger, I'm afraid.' I looked across the table at the little man.

'Yes, I know.' He hesitated. 'What do you suggest?'

'Oh there's no doubt at all he'll have to come in for an operation. That thing must come off.'

Horror and despair flickered behind the thick spectacles.

'An operation!' He leaned on the table with both hands.

'I hate the idea, I just can't bear the thought of it!'

I smiled reassuringly. 'I know how you feel, but honestly there's nothing to worry about. As I told you before, it's quite a simple procedure.'

'Oh I know, I know,' he moaned. 'But I don't want him to be . . . cut about, you understand . . . it's just the idea of it.'

And I couldn't persuade him. He remained adamant and marched resolutely from the surgery with his pet. I watched him crossing the road to his house and I knew he had let himself in for a load of worry, but I didn't realise just how bad it was going to be.

It was to be a kind of martyrdom.

I do not think martyrdom is too strong a word for what Mr Partridge went through over the next few weeks, because with the passage of time that testicle became more and more massive and due to the way Percy carried his tail the thing was lamentably conspicuous.

People used to turn and stare as man and dog made their way down the street, Percy trotting bravely, his master, eyes rigidly to the front, putting up a magnificent pretence of being quite unaware of anything unusual. It really hurt me to see them and I found the sight of the smart little dog's disfigurement particularly hard to bear.

Mr Partridge's superior facade had always made him a natural target for a certain amount of legpulling which he bore stoically; but the fact that it now involved his pet pierced him to the soul.

One afternoon he brought him over to the surgery and I could see that the little man was almost in tears. Gloomily I examined the offending organ which was now about six inches long; gross, pendulous, undeniably ludicrous.

'You know, Mr Herriot,' the artist gasped, 'some boys chalked on my window, "Roll up and see the famous Chinese dog, Wun Hung Lo." I've just been wiping it off.'

I rubbed my chin. 'Well that's an ancient joke, Mr Partridge. I shouldn't worry about that.'

'But I do worry! I can't sleep because of the thing!'

'For heaven's sake, then, why don't you let me operate? I could put the whole business right for you.'

'No! No! I can't do that!' His head rolled on his shoulders; he was the very picture of misery as he stared at me. 'I'm frightened, that's what it is. I'm frightened he'll die under the anaesthetic.'

'Oh come now! He's a strong little animal. There's no reason at all for such fears.'

'But there is a risk, isn't there?'

I looked at him helplessly. 'Well there's a slight risk in all operations if you come right down to it, but honestly in this case . . .'

'No! That's enough. I won't hear of it,' he burst out and seizing Percy's lead he strode away.

Things went from bad to worse after that. The tumour grew steadily, easily visible now from my vantage point in the surgery window as the dog went by on the other side of the street, and I could see too that the stares and occasional ridicule were beginning to tell on Mr Partridge. His cheeks had hollowed and he had lost some of his high colour.

But I didn't have words with him till one market day several weeks later. It was early afternoon – the time the farmers often came in to pay their bills. I was showing one of them out when I saw Percy and his master coming out of the house. And I noticed immediately that the little animal now had to swing one hind leg slightly to clear the massive obstruction.

On an impulse I called out and beckoned to Mr Partridge.

'Look,' I said as he came across to me, 'you've just got to let me take that thing off. It's interfering with his walking – making him lame. He can't go on like this.'

The artist didn't say anything but stared back at me with hunted eyes. We were standing there in silence when Bill Dalton came round the corner and marched up to the surgery steps, cheque book in hand. Bill was a large beefy farmer who spent most of market day in the bar of the Black Swan, and he was preceded by an almost palpable wave of beer fumes.

'Nah then, Rolie lad, how ista?' he roared, slapping the little man violently on the back.

'I am quite well, William, thank you, and how are you?'

But Bill didn't answer. His attention was all on Percy who had strolled a few paces along the pavement. He watched him intently for a few moments then, repressing a giggle, he turned back to Mr Partridge with a mock-serious expression.

'Tha knows, Rolie,' he said, 'that blood 'ound of your reminds me of the young man of Devizes, whose balls were of different sizes. The one was so small it was no ball at all, but the other one won several prizes.' He finished with a shout of laughter which went on and on till he collapsed weakly against the iron railings.

For a moment I thought Mr Partridge was going to strike him. He glared up at the big man and his chin and mouth trembled with rage, then he seemed to gain control of himself and turned to me.

'Can I have a word with you, Mr Herriot?'

'Certainly.' I walked a few yards with him down the street.

'You're right,' he said. 'Percy will have to have that operation. When can you do him?'

'Tomorrow,' I replied. 'Don't give him any more food and bring him in at two in the afternoon.'

It was with a feeling of intense relief that I saw the little dog stretched on the table the next day. With Tristan as anaesthetist I quickly removed the huge testicle, going well up the spermatic cord to ensure the complete excision of all tumour tissue. The only thing which troubled me was that the scrotum itself had become involved due to the long delay in operating. This is the sort of thing that can lead to a recurrence, and as I carefully cut away the affected parts of the scrotal wall I cursed Mr Partridge's procrastination. I put in the last stitch with my fingers crossed.

The little man was in such transports of joy at seeing his pet alive after my efforts and rid of that horrid excrescence that I didn't want to spoil everything by voicing my doubts; but I wasn't entirely happy. If the tumour did recur, I wasn't sure just what I could do about it.

But in the meantime I enjoyed my own share of pleasure at my patient's return to normality. I felt a warm rush of satisfaction whenever I saw him tripping along, perky as ever and free from the disfigurement which had bulked so large in his master's life. Occasionally I used to stroll casually behind him on the way down Trengate into the market place, saying nothing to Mr Partridge but shooting some sharp glances at the region beneath Percy's tail.

In the meantime I had sent the removed organ off to the pathology department at Glasgow Veterinary College and their report told me that it was a Sertoli Cell Tumour. They also added the comforting information that this type was usually benign and that metastasis into the internal organs occurred in only a very small proportion of cases. Maybe this lulled me into a deeper security than was warranted because I stopped following Percy around and in fact, in the non-stop rush of new cases, forgot all about his spell of trouble.

So that when Mr Partridge brought him round to the surgery I thought it was for something else, and when his master lifted him on to the table and turned him round to show his rear end I stared uncomprehendingly for a moment. But I leaned forward anxiously when I spotted the ugly swelling on the left side of the scrotum. I palpated quickly, with Percy's growls and grousings providing an irritable obligato, and there was no doubt about it, the tumour was growing again. It meant business, too, because it was red, angry-looking, painful; a dangerously active growth if ever I had seen one.

'It's come up quite quickly, has it?' I asked.

Mr Partridge nodded. 'Yes, indeed. I can almost see it getting bigger every day.'

We were in trouble. There was no hope of trying to cut this lot away; it was a great diffuse mass without clear boundaries and I wouldn't have known where to start. Anyway, if I began any more poking about it would be just what was needed to start a spread into the internal organs, and that would be the end of Percy.

'It's worse this time, isn't it?' The little man looked at me and gulped.

'Yes . . . yes . . . I'm afraid so.'

'Is there anything at all you can do about it?' he asked.

I was trying to think of a painless way of telling him that there wasn't, when I remembered something I had read in the *Veterinary*

Record a week ago. It was about a new drug, Stilboestrol, which had just come out and was supposed to be useful for hormonal therapy in animals; but the bit I was thinking about was a small print extract which said it had been useful in cancer of the prostate in men. I wondered . . .

'There's one thing I'd like to try,' I said, suddenly brisk. 'I can't guarantee anything, of course, because it's something new. But we'll see what a week or two's course does.'

'Oh good, good,' Mr Partridge breathed, snatching gratefully at the straw.

I rang May and Baker's and they sent the Stilboestrol to me immediately.

I injected Percy with 10 mg of the oily suspension and put him on to 10 mg tablets daily. They were big doses for a little dog but in a desperate situation I felt they were justified. Then I sat back and waited.

For about a week the tumour continued to grow and I nearly stopped the treatment, then there was a spell lasting several days during which I couldn't be sure; but then with a surge of relief I realised there could be no further doubt – the thing wasn't getting any bigger. I wasn't going to throw my hat in the air and I knew anything could still happen, but I had done something with my treatment; I had halted that fateful progress.

The artist's step acquired a fresh spring as he passed on his daily walk and then as the ugly mass actually began to diminish he would wave towards the surgery window and point happily at the little white animal trotting by his side.

Poor Mr Partridge. He was on the crest of the wave but just ahead of him was the second and more bizarre phase of his martyrdom.

At first neither I nor anybody else realised what was going on. All we knew was there suddenly seemed to be a lot of dogs in Trengate – dogs we didn't usually see, from other parts of the town; big ones, small ones, shaggy mongrels and sleek aristocrats all hanging around apparently aimlessly, but then it was noticed that there was a focal point of attraction. It was Mr Partridge's house.

And it hit me blindingly one morning as I looked out of our bedroom window. They were after Percy. For some reason he had taken on the attributes of a bitch in heat. I hurried downstairs and got out my pathology book. Yes, there it was. The Sertoli Cell tumour occasionally made dogs attractive to other male dogs. But why should it be happening now when the thing was reducing and not when it was at its height? Or could it be the Stilboestrol? The new drug was said to have a feminising effect, but surely not to that extent.

Anyway, whatever the cause, the undeniable fact remained that Percy was under siege, and as the word got around the pack increased, being augmented by several of the nearby farm dogs, a Great Dane who had made the journey from Houlton, and Magnus, the little Dachshund from the Drovers' Arms. The queue started forming almost at first light and by ten o'clock there would be a milling throng almost blocking the street. Apart from the regulars, the odd canine visitor passing through would join the company, and no matter what his breed or size he was readily accepted into the club, adding one more to the assortment of stupid expressions, lolling tongues and waving tails; because, motley crew though they were, they were all happily united in the roisterous, bawdy camaraderie of lust.

The strain on Mr Partridge must have been almost intolerable. At times I noticed the thick spectacles glinting balefully at the mob through his window, but most of the time he kept himself in hand, working calmly at his easel as though he were oblivious that every one of the creatures outside had evil designs on his treasure.

Only rarely did his control snap. I witnessed one of these occasions when he rushed screaming from his doorway, laying about him with a walking stick; and I noticed that the polished veneer slipped from him and his cries rang out in broadest Yorkshire.

'Gerrout, ye bloody rotten buggers! Gerrout of it!'

He might as well have saved his energy because the pack scattered only for a few seconds before taking up their stations again.

I felt for the little man but there was nothing I could do about it. My main feeling was of relief that the tumour was going down, but I had to admit to a certain morbid fascination at the train of events across the street.

Percy's walks were fraught with peril. Mr Partridge always armed himself with his stick before venturing from the house and kept Percy on a short lead, but his precautions were unavailing as the wave of dogs swept down on him. The besotted creatures, mad with passion, leapt on top of the little animal as the artist beat vainly on the shaggy backs and yelled at them; and the humiliating procession usually continued right across the market-place to the great amusement of the inhabitants.

At lunch time most of the dogs took a break and at nightfall they all went home to bed, but there was one little brown spaniel type who, with the greatest dedication, never left his post. I think he must have gone almost without food for about two weeks because he dwindled practically to a skeleton, and I think he might have died if Helen hadn't taken pieces of meat over to him when she saw him huddled trembling in the doorway in the cold darkness of the evening. I know he stayed there all night because every now and then a shrill yelping wakened me in the small hours and I deduced that Mr Partridge had got home on him with some missile from his bedroom window. But it made no difference; he continued his vigil undaunted.

I don't quite know how Mr Partridge would have survived if this state of affairs had continued indefinitely; I think his reason might have given way. But mercifully signs began to appear that the nightmare was on the wane. The mob began to thin as Percy's condition improved and one day even the little brown dog reluctantly left his beat and slunk away to his unknown home.

That was the very day I had Percy on the table for the last time. I felt a thrill of satisfaction as I ran a fold of the scrotal skin between my fingers.

'There's nothing there now, Mr Partridge. No thickening, even. Not a thing.'

The little man nodded. 'Yes, it's a miracle, isn't it! I'm very grateful to you for all you've done. I've been so terribly worried.'

'Oh, I can imagine. You've been through a bad time. But I'm really as pleased as you are yourself – it's one of the most satisfying things in practice when an experiment like this comes off.'

But often over the subsequent years, as I watched dog and master pass our window, Mr Partridge with all his dignity restored, Percy as trim and proud as ever, I wondered about that strange interlude.

Did the Stilboestrol really reduce that tumour or did it regress naturally? And were the extraordinary events caused by the treatment or the condition or both?

I could never be quite sure of the answer, but of the outcome I could be happily certain. That unpleasant growth never came back . . . and neither did all those dogs.

*

Veterinarians and physicians have contacted me from all over the world about this case of a cancerous testicle in the hope that I might be able to help in similar problems. Sadly I have to record that stilboestrol does not always work; but I am glad it did with Percy, especially after his harrowing spell as a bitch in heat. On another note, the memory of the queue of dogs outside Mr Partridge's house brings home to me the fact that we very rarely see such a thing in our town now. Those amorous throngs used to be quite commonplace years ago but they are almost a thing of the past. Partly responsible, of course, is the spaying of bitches which we now do on a wide scale, and the various injections and tablets which can suppress or prevent a heat period. Many people prefer bitches for pets, but there is always that snag which happily can now be overcome.

15. *Granville Bennett*

This was one for Granville Bennett. I liked a bit of small animal surgery and was gradually doing more as time went on, but this one frightened me. A twelve-year-old spaniel bitch in the last stages of pyometritis, pus dripping from her vulva on to the surgery table, temperature a hundred and four, panting, trembling, and, as I held my stethoscope against her chest I could hear the classical signs of valvular insufficiency. A dicky heart was just what I needed on top of everything else.

'Drinking a lot of water, is she?' I asked.

Old Mrs Barker twisted the strings of her shopping bag anxiously. 'Aye, she never seems to be away from the water bowl. But she won't eat – hasn't had a bite for the last four days.'

'Well I don't know.' I took off my stethoscope and stuffed it in my pocket. 'You should have brought her in long ago. She must have been ill for weeks.'

'Not rightly ill, but a bit off it. I thought there was nothing to worry about as long as she was eating.'

I didn't say anything for a few moments. I had no desire to upset the old girl but she had to be told.

'I'm afraid this is rather serious, Mrs Barker. The condition has been building up for a long time. It's in her womb, you see, a bad infection, and the only cure is an operation.'

'Well, will you do it, please?' The old lady's lips quivered.

I came round the table and put my hand on her shoulder.

'I'd like to, but there are snags. She's in poor shape and twelve years old. Really a poor operation risk. I'd like to take her through to the Veterinary Hospital at Hartington and let Mr Bennett operate on her.'

'All right,' she said, nodding eagerly. 'I don't care what it costs.'

'Oh we'll keep it down as much as possible.' I walked along the passage with her and showed her out of the door. 'Leave her with me – I'll look after her, don't worry. What's her name, by the way?'

'Dinah,' she replied huskily, still peering past me down the passage.

I went through and lifted the phone. Thirty years ago country practitioners had to turn to the small animal experts when anything unusual cropped up in that line. It is different nowadays when our practices are more mixed. In Darrowby now we have the staff and equipment to tackle any type of small animal surgery, but it was different then. I had heard it said that sooner or later every large animal man had to scream for help from Granville Bennett and now it was my turn.

'Hello, is that Mr Bennett?'

'It is indeed.' A big voice, friendly, full of give.

'Herriot here. I'm with Farnon in Darrowby.'

'Of course! Heard of you, laddie, heard of you.'

'Oh . . . er . . . thanks. Look, I've got a bit of a sticky job here. I wonder if you'd take it on for me.'

'Delighted, laddie, what is it?'

'A real stinking pyo.'

'Oh lovely!'

'The bitch is twelve years old.'

'Splendid!'

'And toxic as hell.'

'Excellent!'

'And one of the worst hearts I've heard for a long time.'

'Fine, fine! When are you coming through?'

'This evening, if it's O.K. with you. About eight.'

'Couldn't be better, laddie. See you.'

Hartington was a fair-sized town – about 200,000 inhabitants – but as I drove into the centre the traffic had thinned and only a few cars rolled past the rows of shop fronts. I hoped my twenty-five mile journey had been worth it. Dinah, stretched out on a blanket in the back, looked as if she didn't care either way. I glanced behind me at the head drooping over the edge of the seat, at the white muzzle and the cataracts in her eyes gleaming palely in the light from the dash. She looked so old. Maybe I was wasting my time, placing too much faith in this man's reputation.

There was no doubt Granville Bennett had become something of a legend in northern England. In those days when specialisation was almost unknown he had gone all out for small animal work – never looked at farm stock – and had set a new standard by the modern procedures in his animal hospital which was run as nearly as possible on human lines. It was, in fact, fashionable for veterinary surgeons of that era to belittle dog and cat work; a lot of the older men who had spent their lives among the teeming thousands of draught horses in city and agriculture would sneer, 'Oh I've no time to bother with those damn things.' Bennett had gone dead in the opposite direction.

I had never met him but I knew he was a young man in his early thirties. I had heard a lot about his skill, his business acumen, and about his reputation as a *bon viveur*. He was, they said, a dedicated devotee of the work-hard-play-hard school.

The Veterinary Hospital was a long low building near the top of a busy street. I drove into a yard and knocked at a door in the corner. I was looking with some awe at a gleaming Bentley dwarfing my own battered little Austin when the door was opened by a pretty receptionist.

'Good evening,' she murmured with a dazzling smile which I thought must be worth another half crown on the bill for a start. 'Do come in; Mr Bennett is expecting you.'

I was shown into a waiting room with magazines and flowers on a corner table and many impressive photographs of dogs and cats on the walls – taken, I learned later, by the principal himself. I was looking closely at a superb study of two white poodles when I heard a footstep behind me. I turned and had my first view of Granville Bennett.

He seemed to fill the room. Not over tall but of tremendous bulk. Fat, I thought at first, but as he came nearer it seemed to me that the tissue of which he was composed wasn't distributed like fat. He wasn't flabby, he didn't stick out in any particular place, he was just a big, wide, solid, hard-looking man. From the middle of a pleasant blunt-featured face the most magnificent pipe I had ever seen stuck forth shining and glorious, giving out delicious wisps of expensive smoke. It was an enormous pipe, in fact it would have looked downright silly with a smaller man, but on him it was a thing of beauty. I had a final impression of a beautifully cut dark suit and sparkling shirt cuffs as he held out a hand.

'James Herriot!' He said it as somebody else might have said 'Winston Churchill', or 'Stanley Matthews'.

'That's right.'

'Well, this is grand. Jim, is it?'

'Well yes, usually.'

'Lovely. We've got everything laid on for you, Jim. The girls are waiting in the theatre.'

'That's very kind of you, Mr Bennett.'

'Granville, Granville please! He put his arm through mine and led me to the operating room.

Dinah was already there, looking very woebegone. She had had a sedative injection and her head nodded wearily. Bennett went over to her and gave her a swift examination.

'Mm, yes, let's get on, then.'

The two girls went into action like cogs in a smooth machine. Bennett kept a large lay staff and these animal nurses, both attractive, clearly knew what they were about. While one of them pulled up the anaesthetic and instrument trolleys, the other seized Dinah's foreleg expertly above the elbow, raised the radial vein by pressure and quickly clipped and disinfected the area.

The big man strolled up with a loaded needle and effortlessly slipped the needle into the vein.

'Pentothal,' he said as Dinah slowly collapsed and lay unconscious on the table. It was one of the new short-acting anaesthetics which I had never seen used.

While Bennett scrubbed up and donned sterilised gown and cap the girls rolled Dinah on her back and secured her there with ties to loops on the operating table. They applied the ether and oxygen mask to her face then shaved and swabbed the operation site. The big man returned in time to have a scalpel placed in his hand.

With almost casual speed he incised skin and muscle layers and when he went through the peritoneum the horns of the uterus which in normal health would have been two slim pink ribbons now welled into the wound like twin balloons, swollen and turgid with pus. No wonder Dinah had felt ill, carrying that lot around with her.

The stubby fingers tenderly worked round the mass, ligated the ovarian vessels and uterine body, then removed the whole thing and dropped it into an enamel bowl. It wasn't till he had begun to stitch that I realised that the operation was nearly over though he had been at the table for only a few minutes. It would all have looked childishly easy except that his total involvement showed in occasional explosive commands to the nurses.

And as I watched him working under the shadowless lamp with the white tiled walls around him and the rows of instruments gleaming by his side, it came to me with a rush of mixed emotions that this was what I had always wanted to do myself. My dreams when I had first decided on veterinary work had been precisely of this. Yet here I was, a somewhat shaggy cow doctor; or perhaps, more correctly, a farm physician, but certainly something very different. The scene before me was a far cry from my routine of kicks and buffets, of muck and sweat. And yet I had no regrets; the life which had been forced on me by circumstances had turned out to be a thing of magical fulfilment. It came to me with a flooding certainty that I would rather spend my days driving over the unfenced roads of the high country than stooping over that operating table.

And anyway I couldn't have been a Bennett. I don't think I could have matched his technique, and this whole set up was eloquent of a lot of things like business sense, foresight and driving ambition which I just didn't possess.

My colleague was finished now and was fitting up an intravenous saline drip. He taped the needle down in the vein then turned to me.

'That's it, then, Jim. It's up to the old girl now.' He began to lead me from the room and it struck me how very pleasant it must be to finish your job and walk away from it like this. In Darrowby I'd have been starting now to wash the instruments, scrub the table, and the final scene would have been of Herriot the great surgeon swilling the floor with mop and bucket. This was a better way.

Granville Bennett

Back in the waiting room Bennett pulled on his jacket and extracted from a side pocket the immense pipe which he inspected with a touch of anxiety as if he feared mice had been nibbling at it in his absence. He wasn't satisfied with his examination because he brought forth a soft yellow cloth and began to polish the briar with intense absorption. Then he held the pipe high, moving it slightly from side to side, his eyes softening at the play of the light on the exquisite grain. Finally he produced a pouch of mammoth proportions, filled the bowl, applied a match with a touch of reverence and closed his eyes as a fragrant mist drifted from his lips.

'That baccy smells marvellous,' I said. 'What is it?'

'Navy Cut De Luxe.' He closed his eyes again. 'You know, I could eat the smoke.'

I laughed. 'I use the ordinary Navy Cut myself.'

He gazed at me like a sorrowing Buddha. 'Oh you mustn't, laddie, you mustn't. This is the only stuff. Rich . . . fruity . . .' His hand made languid motions in the air. 'Here, you can take some away with you.'

He pulled open a drawer. I had a brief view of a stock which wouldn't have disgraced a fair-sized tobacconist's shop; innumerable tins, pipes, cleaners, reamers, cloths.

'Try this,' he said, 'and tell me if I'm not right.'

I looked down at the first container in my hand. 'Oh, but I can't take all this. It's a four-ounce tin!'

'Rubbish, my boy. Put it in your pocket.' He became suddenly brisk. 'Now I expect you'll want to hang around till old Dinah comes out of the anaesthetic so why don't we have a quick beer? I'm a member of a nice little club just across the road.'

'Well fine, sounds great.'

He moved lightly and swiftly for a big man and I had to hurry to keep up with him as he left the surgery and crossed to a building on the other side of the street.

Inside the club was masculine comfort, hails of welcome from some prosperous looking members and a friendly greeting from the man behind the bar.

'Two pints, Fred,' murmured Bennett absently, and the drinks appeared with amazing speed. My colleage poured his down apparently without swallowing and turned to me.

'Another, Jim?'

I had just tried a sip at mine and began to gulp anxiously at the bitter ale. 'Right, but let me get this one.'

'No can do, laddie.' He glanced at me with mild severity. 'Only members can buy drinks. Same again, Fred.'

I found I had two glasses at my elbow and with a tremendous effort I got the first one down. Gasping slightly I was surveying the second one timidly when I noticed that Bennett was three-quarters down his. As I watched he drained it effortlessly.

'You're slow, Jim,' he said, smiling indulgently. 'Just set them up again will you, Fred.'

In some alarm I watched the barman ply his handle and attacked my second pint resolutely. I surprised myself by forcing it over my tonsils then, breathing heavily, I got hold of the third one just as Bennett spoke again.

'We'll just have one for the road, Jim,' he said pleasantly. 'Would you be so kind, Fred?'

This was ridiculous but I didn't want to appear a piker at our first meeting. With something akin to desperation I raised the third and began to suck feebly at it. When my glass was empty I almost collapsed against the counter. My stomach was agonisingly distended and a light perspiration had broken out on my brow. As I almost lay there I saw my colleague moving across the carpet towards the door.

'Time we were off, Jim,' he said. 'Drink up.'

It's wonderful what the human frame can tolerate when put to the test. I would have taken bets that it was impossible for me to drink that fourth pint without at least half an hour's rest, preferably in the prone position, but as Bennett's shoe tapped impatiently I tipped the beer a little at a time into my mouth, feeling it wash around my back teeth before incredibly disappearing down my gullet. I believe the water torture was a favourite with the Spanish Inquisition and as the pressure inside me increased I knew just how their victims felt.

When I at last blindly replaced my glass and splashed my way from the bar, the big man was holding the door open. Outside in the street he placed an arm across my shoulder.

'The old Spaniel won't be out of it yet,' he said. 'We'll just slip to my house and have a bite – I'm a little peckish.

Sunk in the deep upholstery of the Bentley, cradling my swollen abdomen in my arms I watched the shop fronts flicker past the windows and give way to the darkness of the open countryside. We drew up outside a fine grey stone house in a typical Yorkshire village and Bennett ushered me inside.

He pushed me towards a leather armchair. 'Make yourself at home, laddie. Zoe's out at the moment but I'll get some grub.' He bustled through to the kitchen and reappeared in seconds with a deep bowl which he placed on a table by my side.

'You know, Jim,' he said, rubbing his hands. 'There's nothing better after beer than a few pickled onions.'

I cast a timorous glance into the bowl. Everything in this man's life seemed to be larger than life, even the onions. They were bigger than golf balls, brownish-white, glistening.

'Well thanks, Mr Ben . . . Granville.' I took one of them, held it between finger and thumb and stared at it helplessly. The beer hadn't even begun to sort itself out inside me; the idea of starting on this potent-looking vegetable was unthinkable.

Granville reached into the bowl, popped an onion into his mouth, crunched it quickly, swallowed and sank his teeth into a second. 'By God, that's good. You know, my little wife's a marvellous cook. She even makes pickled onions better than anyone.'

Munching happily he moved over to the sideboard and clinked around for a few moments before placing in my hand a heavy cut-glass tumbler about two-thirds full of neat whisky. I couldn't say anything because I had taken the plunge and put the onion in my mouth; and as I bit boldly into it the fumes rolled in a volatile wave into my nasal passages, making me splutter. I took a gulp at the whisky and looked up at Granville with watering eyes.

He was holding out the onion bowl again and when I declined he regarded it for a moment with hurt in his eyes. 'It's funny you don't like them, I always thought Zoe did them marvellously.'

'Oh you're wrong, Granville, they're delicious. I just haven't finished this one.'

He didn't reply but continued to look at the bowl with gentle sorrow. I realised there was nothing else for it; I took another onion.

Immensely gratified, Granville hurried through to the kitchen again. This time when he came back he bore a tray with an enormous cold roast, a loaf of bread, butter and mustard.

'I think a beef sandwich would go down rather nicely, Jim,' he murmured, as he stropped his carving knife on a steel. Then he noticed my glass of whisky still half full.

'C'mon, c'mon, c'mon!' he said with some asperity. 'You're not touching your drink.' He watched me benevolently as I drained the glass then he refilled it to its old level. 'That's better. And have another onion.'

I stretched my legs out and rested my head on the back of the chair in an attempt to ease my internal turmoil. My stomach was a lake of volcanic lava bubbling and popping fiercely in its crater with each additional piece of onion, every sip of whisky setting up a fresh violent reaction. Watching Granville at work, a great wave of nausea swept over me. He was sawing busily at the roast, carving off slices which looked to be an inch thick, slapping mustard on them and enclosing them in the bread. He hammered with contentment as the pile grew. Every now and then he had another onion.

'Now then, laddie,' he cried at length, putting a heaped plate at my elbow. 'Get yourself round that lot.' He took his own supply and collapsed with a sigh into another chair.

He took a gargantuan bite and spoke as he chewed. 'You know, Jim, this is something I enjoy – a nice little snack. Zoe always leaves me plenty to go at when she pops out.' He engulfed a further few inches of sandwich. 'And I'll tell you something, though I say it myself, these are bloody good, don't you think so?'

'Yes indeed.' Squaring my shoulders I bit, swallowed and held my breath as another unwanted foreign body slid down to the ferment below.

Just then I heard the front door open.

'Ah, that'll be Zoe,' Granville said, and was about to rise when a disgracefully fat Staffordshire Bull Terrier burst into the room, waddled across the carpet and leapt into his lap.

'Phoebles, my dear, come to Daddykins!' he shouted. 'Have you had nice walkies with Mummy?'

The Staffordshire was closely followed by a Yorkshire Terrier which was also enthusiastically greeted by Granville.

'Yoo-hoo, Victoria, yoo-hoo!'

The Yorkie, an obvious smiler, did not jump up but contented herself with sitting at her master's feet, baring her teeth ingratiatingly every few seconds.

I smiled through my pain. Another myth exploded; the one about these specialist small animal vets not being fond of dogs themselves. The big man crooned over the two little animals. The fact that he called Phoebe 'Phoebles' was symptomatic.

I heard light footsteps in the hall and looked up expectantly. I had

Granville's wife taped neatly in my mind; domesticated, devoted, homely; many of these dynamic types had wives like that, willing slaves content to lurk in the background. I waited confidently for the entrance of a plain little hausfrau.

When the door opened I almost let my vast sandwich fall. Zoe Bennett was a glowing warm beauty who would make any man alive stop for another look. A lot of soft brown hair, large grey-green friendly eyes, a tweed suit sitting sweetly on a slim but not too slim figure; and something else, a wholesomeness, an inner light which made me wish suddenly that I was a better man or at least that I looked better than I did.

In an instant I was acutely conscious of the fact that my shoes were dirty, that my old jacket and corduroy trousers were out of place here. I hadn't troubled to change but had rushed straight out in my working clothes, and they were different from Granville's because I couldn't go round the farms in a suit like his.

'My love, my love!' he carolled joyously as his wife bent over and kissed him fondly. 'Let me introduce Jim Herriot from Darrowby.'

The beautiful eyes turned on me.

'How d'you do, Mr Herriot!' She looked as pleased to see me as her husband had done, and again I had the desperate wish that I was more presentable; that my hair was combed, that I didn't have this mounting conviction that I was going to explode into a thousand pieces at any moment.

'I'm going to have a cup of tea, Mr Herriot. Would you like one?'

'No-no, no no, thank you very much but no, no, not at the moment.' I backed away slightly.

'Ah well, I see you've got one of Granville's little sandwiches.' She giggled and went to get her tea.

When she came back she handed a parcel to her husband. 'I've been shopping today, darling. Picked up some of those shirts you like so much.'

'My sweet! How kind of you!' He began to tear at the brown paper like a schoolboy and produced three elegant shirts in cellophane covers. 'They're marvellous, my pet, you spoil me.' He looked up at me. 'Jim! These are the most wonderful shirts, you must have one.' He flicked a shining package across the room on to my lap.

I looked down at it in amazement. 'No, really I can't . . .'

'Of course you can. You keep it.'

'But Granville, not a shirt . . . it's too . . .'

'It's a very good shirt.' He was beginning to look hurt again. I subsided.

They were both so kind. Zoe sat right by me with her tea cup, chatting pleasantly, while Granville beamed at me from his chair as he finished the last of the sandwiches and started again on the onions.

The proximity of the attractive woman was agreeable but embarrassing. My corduroys in the warmth of the room had begun to give off the unmistakable bouquet of the farmyard where they spent most of their time. And though it was one of my favourite scents there was no doubt it didn't go with these elegant surroundings.

And worse still, I had started a series of internal rumblings and musical tinklings which resounded only too audibly during every lull in the conversation. The only other time I have heard such sounds was in a cow with an advanced case of displacement of the abomasum. My companions delicately feigned deafness even when I produced a shameful, explosive belch which made the little fat dog start up in alarm, but when another of these mighty borborygmi escaped me and almost made the windows rattle I thought it time to go.

In any case I wasn't contributing much else. The alcohol had taken hold and I was increasingly conscious that I was just sitting there with a stupid leer on my face. In striking contrast to Granville, who looked just the same as when I first met him back at the surgery. He was cool and possessed, his massive urbanity unimpaired. It was a little hard.

So, with the tin of tobacco bumping against my hip and the shirt tucked under my arm, I took my leave.

Back at the hospital I looked down at Dinah. The old dog had come through wonderfully well and she lifted her head and gazed at me sleepily. Her colour was good and her pulse strong. The operative shock had been dramatically minimised by my colleague's skilful speedy technique and by the intravenous drip.

I knelt down and stroked her ears. 'You know, I'm sure she's going to make it, Granville.'

Above me the great pipe nodded with majestic confidence.

'Of course, laddie, of course.'

And he was right. Dinah was rejuvenated by her hysterectomy and lived to delight her mistress for many more years.

On the way home that night she lay by my side on the passenger seat, her nose poking from a blanket. Now and then she rested her chin on my hand as it gripped the gear lever and occasionally she licked me lazily.

I could see she felt better than I did.

*

A momentous occasion in my life. Not just because it was my first meeting with a gifted man who showed me small animal surgery at its best, but it was also the beginning of a lasting friendship. I am always grateful when I run into a larger-than-life character. There aren't so many of them about and they throw a splash of brilliant colour into the lives of ordinary mortals like me. Granville Bennett was such a man. He had a devastating effect on me in other ways but my admiration for him remains unimpaired.

16. *Abandoned*

You often see dogs running along a road but there was something about this one which made me slow down and take a second look.

It was a small brown animal and it was approaching on the other side; and it wasn't just ambling by the grass verge but galloping all out on its short legs, head extended forward as though in desperate pursuit of something unseen beyond the long empty curve of tarmac ahead. As the dog passed I had a brief glimpse of two staring eyes and a lolling tongue, then he was gone.

My car stalled and lurched to a halt but I sat unheeding, still gazing into the mirror at the small form receding rapidly until it was almost invisible against the browns and greens of the surrounding moor. As I switched on the engine I had difficulty in dragging my thoughts back to the job in hand; because I had seen something chilling there, a momentary but vivid impression of frantic effort, despair, blind terror. And driving away, the image stayed with me. Where had that dog come from? There were no roadside farms on this high, lonely by-way, not a parked car anywhere. And in any case he wasn't just casually going somewhere; there was a frenzied urgency in his every movement.

It was no good, I had to find out. I backed off the unfenced road among the sparse tufts of heather and turned back in the direction I had come. I had to drive a surprisingly long way before I saw the little animal, still beating his solitary way, and at the sound of the approaching car he halted, stared for a moment, then trotted on again. But his labouring limbs told me he was near exhaustion and I pulled up twenty yards ahead of him, got out and waited.

He made no protest as I knelt on the roadside turf and caught him gently as he came up to me. He was a Border Terrier, and after another quick glance at the car his eyes took on their terrified light as he looked again at the empty road ahead.

He wasn't wearing a collar but there was a ring of flattened hair on his neck as though one had recently been removed. I opened his mouth and looked at his teeth; he wasn't very old – probably around two or three. There were rolls of fat along his ribs so he hadn't been starved. I was examining his skin when suddenly the wide panting mouth closed and the whole body stiffened as another car approached. For a moment he stared at it with fierce hope, but when the vehicle flashed by he sagged and began to pant again.

So that was it. He had been dumped. Some time ago the humans he had loved and trusted had opened their car door, hurled him out into an unknown world and driven merrily away. I began to feel sick – physically sick – and a murderous rage flowed through me. Had they laughed, I wondered, these people, at the idea of the bewildered little creature toiling vainly behind them?

I passed my hand over the rough hairs of the head. I could forgive anybody for robbing a bank but never for this. 'Come on, fella,' I said, lifting him gently, 'you're coming home with me.'

Sam was used to strange dogs in the car and he sniffed incuriously at the newcomer. The terrier huddled on the passenger seat trembling violently and I kept my hand on him as I drove.

Back in our bed-sitter Helen pushed a bowl of meat and biscuit under his nose but the little animal showed no interest.

'How could anybody do this?' she murmured. 'And anyway, why? What reason could they have?'

I stroked the head again. 'Oh, you'd be surprised at some of the reasons. Sometimes they do it because a dog turns savage, but that can't be so in this case.' I had seen enough of dogs to interpret the warm friendly light behind the fear in those eyes. And the way the terrier had submitted unquestioningly as I had prised his mouth open, lifted him, handled him, all pointed to one thing: he was a docile little creature.

'Or sometimes,' I continued, 'they dump dogs just because they're tired of them. They got them when they were charming puppies and have no interest in them when they grow up. Or maybe the licence is due to be paid – that's a good enough reason for some people to take a drive into the country and push their pets out into the unknown.'

I didn't say any more. There was quite a long list and why should I depress Helen with tales of the other times when I had seen it happen? People moving to another house where they couldn't keep a dog. A baby arriving and claiming all the attention and affection. And dogs were occasionally abandoned when a more glamorous pet superseded them.

I looked at the little terrier. This was the sort of thing which could have happened to him. A big dashing Alsatian, an eye-catching Saluki – anything like that would take over effortlessly from a rather roly-poly Border Terrier with some people. I had seen it in the past. The little fellow was definitely running to fat despite his comparative youth; in fact when he had been running back there his legs had splayed out from his shoulders. That was another clue; it was possible he had spent most of his time indoors without exercise.

Anyway I was only guessing. I rang the police. No reports of a lost dog in the district. I hadn't really expected any.

During the evening we did our best to comfort the terrier, but he lay trembling, his head on his paws, his eyes closed. The only time he showed interest was when a car passed along the street outside, then he would raise his head and listen, ears pricked, for a few seconds till the sound died away. Helen hoisted him on to her lap and held him there for over an hour, but he was too deeply sunk in his misery to respond to her caresses and soft words.

I finally decided it would be the best thing to sedate him and gave him a shot of morphine. When we went to bed he was stretched out sound asleep in Sam's basket with Sam himself curled up philosophically on the rug by his side.

Next morning he was still unhappy but sufficiently recovered to look around him and take stock. When I went up and spoke to him he rolled over on his back, not playfully but almost automatically as though it was a normal mannerism. I bent and rubbed his chest while he looked up at me non-committally. I liked dogs which rolled over like this; they were usually good-natured and it was a gesture of trust.

'That's better, old lad,' I said. 'Come on, cheer up!'

For a moment his mouth opened wide. He had a comical little monkey face and briefly it seemed to be split in two by a huge grin, making him look extraordinarily attractive.

Helen spoke over my shoulder. 'He's a lovely little dog, Jim! He's so appealing – I could get really fond of him.'

Yes, that was the trouble. So could I. I could get too fond of all the unwanted animals which passed through our hands; not just the abandoned ones but the dogs which came in for euthanasia with the traumatic addendum 'unless you can find him a home'. That put the pressure on me. Putting an animal to sleep when he was incurably ill, in pain, or so old that life had lost its savour was something I could tolerate. In fact often it seemed as though I were doing the suffering creature a favour. But when a young, healthy, charming animal was involved, then it was a harrowing business.

What does a vet do in these circumstances? Refuse and send the owner away with the lurking knowledge that the man might go round to the chemist and buy a dose of poison? That was far worse than our humane, painless barbiturate. One thing a vet can't do is take in all those animals himself. If I had given way to all my impulses I would have accumulated a positive menagerie by now.

It was a hell of a problem which had always troubled me and now I had a soft-hearted wife which made the pull twice as strong.

I turned to her now and voiced my thoughts.

'Helen, we can't keep him, you know. One dog in a bed-sitter is enough.' I didn't add that we ourselves probably would not be in the bed-sitter much longer; that was another thing I didn't want to bring up.

She nodded. 'I suppose so. But I have the feeling that this is one of the sweetest little dogs I've seen for a long time. When he gets over his fear, I mean. What on earth can we do with him?'

'Well, he's a stray.' I bent again and rubbed the rough hair over the chest. 'So he should really go to the kennels at the police station. But if he isn't claimed in ten days we are back where we started.' I put my hand under the terrier's body and lifted him, limp and unresisting, into the crook of my arm. He liked people, this one; liked and trusted them. 'I could ask around the practice, of course, but nobody seems to want a dog when there's one going spare.' I thought for a moment or two. 'Maybe an advert in the local paper.'

'Wait a minute,' Helen said. 'Talking about the paper – didn't I read something about an animal shelter last week?'

I looked at her uncomprehendingly, then I remembered.

'That's right. Sister Rose from the Topley Banks hospital. They were interviewing her about the stray animals she had taken in. It would be worth a try.' I replaced the terrier in Sam's basket. 'We'll keep this little chap today and I'll ring Sister Rose when I finish work tonight.'

At teatime I could see that things were getting out of hand. When I came in the little dog was on Helen's knee and it looked as though he had been there for a long time. She was stroking his head and looking definitely broody.

Not only that, but as I looked down at him I could feel myself weakening. Little phrases were creeping unbidden into my mind . . . 'I wonder if we could find room for him . . .', 'Not much extra trouble . . .', 'Perhaps if we . . .'

I had to act quickly or I was sunk. Reaching for the phone I dialled the hospital number. They soon found Sister Rose and I listened to a cheerful, businesslike voice. She didn't seem to find anything unusual in the situation and the matter-of-fact way she asked questions about the terrier's age, appearance, temperament etc. gave the impression that she had seen a lot of unwanted animals through her hands.

I could hear the firm pencilling sounds as she took notes then, 'Well now that sounds fine. He's the sort we can usually find a home for. When can you bring him along?"

'Now,' I replied.

The misty look in Helen's eyes as I marched out with the dog under my arm told me I was only just in time. And as I drove along the road I couldn't put away the thought that if things had been different – the future settled and a proper home – this little brown creature rolling on his back on the passenger seat with his wide mouth half open and the friendly eyes fixed questioningly on mine would never have got away from me. Only when the occasional car flashed by did he spring upright and look from the window with the old despairing expression. Would he ever forget?

Sister Louisa Rose was a rather handsome woman in her late forties with the sort of healthy smiling face I had imagined at the other end of the phone. She reached out and took the terrier from me with the eager gesture of the animal lover.

'Oh, he looks rather a dear, doesn't he?' she murmured.

Behind her house, a modern bungalow in the open country near the hospital, she led me to a row of kennels with outside runs. Some of them housed single dogs but there was one large one with an assortment of mixed breeds playing happily together on the grass.

'I think we'll put him in here,' she said. 'It'll cheer him up quicker than anything and I'm sure he'll mix in well.' She opened a door in the wire netting surround and pushed the little animal in. The other dogs surrounded him and there was the usual ceremonious sniffing and leg-cocking.

Sister Rose cupped her chin with her hand and looked down thoughtfully through the wire. 'A name, we must have a name . . . let me see . . . no . . . no . . . yes . . . Pip! We'll call him Pip!'

She looked at me with raised eyebrows and I nodded vigorously. 'Yes, definitely – just right. He looks like a Pip.'

She smiled impishly. 'I think so, too, but I've had a lot of practice, you know. I've become rather good at it.'

'I'll bet you have. I suppose you've named all this lot?'

'Of course.' She began to point them out one by one. 'There's Bingo – he was a badly neglected puppy. And Fergus – just lost. That bigger retriever is Griff – he was the survivor of a car crash where his owners were killed. And Tessa, badly injured when she was thrown from a fast-moving vehicle. Behind her over there is Sally Anne who really started me in the business of Animal Sheltering. She was found heavily pregnant with her paws bleeding so she must have run for many miles. I took her in and managed to find homes for all her puppies and she's still here. Placing those pups got me into contact with a lot of pet owners and before I knew what was happening everybody had the idea that I regularly took in stray animals. So I started and you can see the result. I shall have to expand these premises soon.'

Pip didn't look so lonely now and after the preliminary courtesies he joined a group watching interestedly a fierce tug-of-war on a stick between a Collie and a crossed Labrador.

I laughed. 'You know I had no idea you had all these dogs. How long do you keep them?'

'Till I can find a home for them. Some are only here a day, others stay for weeks or months. And there are one or two like Sally Anne who seem to be permanent boarders now.'

'But how on earth do you feed them all? It must be an expensive business.'

She nodded and smiled. 'Oh I run little dog shows, coffee mornings, raffles, jumble sales, anything, but whatever my efforts I'm afraid the strays keep munching their way into the red. But I manage.'

She managed, I guessed, by dipping deeply into her own pocket. Around me the abandoned and rejected dogs barked and ran around happily. I had often thought when I encountered cruelty and neglect that there was a whole army of people who did these unspeakable things, a great unheeding horde who never spared a thought for the feelings of the helpless creatures who depended on them. It was frightening in a way, but thank heavens there was another army ranged on the other side, an army who fought for the animals with everything they had – with their energy, their time, their money.

I looked at Sister Rose, at the steady eyes in the clear-skinned, scrubbed, nurse's face. I would have thought her profession of dedication to the human race would have filled her life utterly with no room for anything else, but it was not so.

'Well, I'm very grateful to you, Sister,' I said. 'I hope somebody will take Pip off your hands soon and if there's anything else I can do, please let me know.'

She smiled. 'Oh don't worry, I have a feeling this little chap won't be here very long.'

Before leaving I leaned on the wire and took another look at the Border Terrier. He seemed to be settling all right but every now and then he stopped and looked up at me with those questioning eyes which pulled so hard. I had the nasty feeling that I, too, was letting him down. His owners, then me, then Sister Rose, all in a couple of days . . . I hoped it would work out for him.

I found it difficult to get that dog out of my mind and I lasted only a week before dropping in at the Animal Shelter. Sister Rose in an old mackintosh and wellingtons was filling the feeding bowls in one of the kennels.

'You've come about Pip, I expect,' she said, putting down her bucket. 'Well he went yesterday. I thought I'd have no trouble. A very nice couple called round. They wanted to give a home to a stray and they picked him out straight away.' She pushed the hair back from her forehead. 'In fact I've had a good week. I've found excellent homes for Griff and Fergus too.'

'Fine, fine. That's great.' I paused for a moment. 'I was wondering . . . er . . . about Pip. Has he gone out of the district?'

'Oh, no, he's right here in Darrowby. The people are called Plenderleith – he's a retired civil servant, quite high up I believe, and he gave a generous donation to the centre though I didn't expect one. They've bought one of those nice little houses on the Houlton Road and there's a lovely garden for Pip to play. I gave them your name, by the way, so no doubt they'll be coming round to see you.'

A wave of totally irrational pleasure swept over me.

'Ah well, I'm glad to hear that. I'll be able to see how he's getting on.'

I didn't have long to wait. It was less than a week later that I opened the waiting-room door and saw an elderly couple sitting there with Pip on the end of a very new lead. He adopted his usual gambit of rolling on to his back as soon as he saw me, but this time there was no helpless appeal in his expression but sheer joyous abandon with the comical little face split across by a wide panting grin. As I went through the ritual of chest rubbing I noticed he was wearing a new collar, too; expensive looking, with a shining medallion bearing his name, address and telephone number. I lifted him and we all went through to the consulting room.

'Well now, what's the trouble?' I asked.

'No trouble, really,' the man replied. He was plump, and the pink face, grave eyes and immaculate dark suit accorded perfectly with my idea of a top civil servant.

'I have recently acquired this small animal and should be grateful for your advice about him. By the way, my name is Plenderleith and may I introduce my wife.'

Mrs Plenderleith was plump too, but it was a giggly plumpness. She didn't look such a solid citizen as her husband.

'Firstly,' he continued, 'I should like you to give him a thorough check-up.'

I had already done this, but went through it again, though Pip made things difficult by rolling over every time I got the stethoscope on his chest. And as I took his temperature I noticed that Mr Plenderleith ran his hand repeatedly over the brown hair of the back while his wife, looking over his shoulder, made encouraging noises and nodded reassuringly at the little dog.

'Absolutely sound in wind and limb,' I pronounced as I finished.
'Splendid,' the man said. 'Er . . . there was this little brown mark
on his abdomen . . .' A touch of anxiety showed in his eyes.

'Just a patch of pigment. Nothing, I assure you.'

'Ah yes, good, good.' Mr Plenderleith cleared his throat. 'I have
to confess, Mr Herriot, that my wife and I have never owned an
animal before. Now I believe in doing things thoroughly, so in order
to give him proper care and attention I have decided to study the
matter. With this in view I have purchased some books on the
subject.' He produced some shiny volumes from under his arm. *Care
of the Dog, The Dog in Sickness and Health,* and finally *The Border Terrier.*

'Good idea,' I replied. Normally I would have shied away from this
imposing battery but in this case I liked the way things were going.
I had the growing conviction that Pip was on a good wicket here.

'I have already gleaned a considerable amount from my reading,'
Mr Plenderleith went on, 'and I believe it is desirable that he be
inoculated against distemper. As you know, he is a stray, so there is
no means of ascertaining whether or not this has been done.'

I nodded. 'Quite right. In fact I was going to suggest that.' I
produced a phial of the vaccine and began to fill a syringe.

Pip was much less concerned than his owners as I gently injected
the contents under his skin. Mr Plenderleith, his face rigid with
apprehension, kept patting the dog's head while his wife at the other
end stroked the hind limbs and adjured her pet to be brave.

After I had put the syringe away, Mr Plenderleith, visibly relieved,
recommenced his investigations. 'Let me see now.' He put on his
spectacles, produced a gold pencil and snapped open a leather-bound
pad where I could see a long list of neatly written notes. 'I have one
or two queries here.'

And he had indeed. He grilled me at length on feeding, housing,
exercise, the relative values of wicker dog baskets and metal frame
beds, the salient features of the common ailments, often referring to
his shiny books. 'I have a note here concerning page 143, line 9. It
says . . .'

I answered him patiently, leaning across the table. I had a waiting
list of farm visits including several fairly urgent jobs but I listened
with growing contentment. I had hoped for concerned and responsible persons to take this little animal over and these people were
right out of the blueprint.

When at length Mr Plenderleith had finished he put away his notepad and pencil and removed his spectacles with the firm precise movements which seemed part of him.

'One of the reasons I desired a dog, Mr Herriot,' he went on, 'was to provide myself with exercise. Don't you think that is a good idea?'

'It certainly is. One of the surest ways to keep fit is to own an active little animal like this. You simply *have* to take him out and just think of all the lovely grassy tracks over the hills around here. On Sunday afternoons when other people are lying asleep in their chairs under their newspapers you'll be out there striding the fells, rain, hail or snow.'

Mr Plenderleith squared his shoulders and his jaw jutted as though he already saw himself battling through a blizzard.

'And another thing,' his wife giggled, 'it'll take some of this off.' She thumped him irreverently on his bulging waistline.

'Now now, my dear,' he admonished her gravely, but I had seen the makings of a sheepish grin which completely belied his stuffed shirt image. Mr Plenderleith, I felt, was all right.

He put his books under his arm and reached out for the little dog. 'Come, Pip, we mustn't delay Mr Herriot any longer.' But his wife was too quick for him. She gathered the terrier into her arms and as we walked along the passage she held the rough face against her own.

Outside the surgery door I saw them installed in a spotless little family saloon and as they drove away Mr Plenderleith inclined his head gravely, his wife gave a gay wave, but Pip, his hind legs on her knee, feet on the dashboard, gazing eagerly through the windscreen, was too busy and interested to look at me.

As they rounded the corner I had the impression of a little cycle coming to a happy end. And of course the main cog in the sequence of events had been Sister Rose. This was just one of the helpless creatures she had salvaged. Her Animal Shelter would grow and expand and daily she would work harder without gain to herself. There were other people like her all over the country, other Shelters; and I felt I had been given a privileged glimpse of that selfless army which battled ceaselessly and untiringly on the side of the great throng of dependent animals.

But right now I was concerned only with one thing. Pip had come home for good.

*

I was grateful for the opportunity to write about these two things – the abhorrent practice of 'dumping' unwanted dogs and the humanitarian work of Sister Rose and people like her. Those two armies have always been very real to me: the great throng of uncaring humans on the one hand who do these despicable things, and the brave group of compassionate people on the other who devote their lives to the abandoned creatures. Sister Rose is still immersed in her great work and there is now a Sister Rose branch of the Jerry Green Dog Sanctuary just outside our town. Every stray and rejected dog is taken in and cared for until a good home is found for it. The thousands of visitors who come to my surgery give generously to this cause when I sign their books and every penny goes to help the dogs. The good army is winning in Darrowby.

17. *Penny*

It was lambing time and I was delivering twin lambs in a stable on Mr Kitson's farm when I heard another ewe panting and moaning in a dark corner. She was in great pain and apparently dying after a 'rough' lambing, and in effort to give her a peaceful end I administered what I thought was a lethal dose of barbiturate. To my amazement she made a miraculous recovery after sleeping deeply for a full two days.

I found it difficult to get Mr Kitson's ewe out of my mind but I had to make the effort, because while all the sheep work was going on the rest of the practice problems rolled along unabated. One of these concerned the Flaxtons' Poodle, Penny.

Penny's first visit to the surgery was made notable by the attractiveness of her mistress. When I stuck my head round the waiting-room door and said, 'Next please,' Mrs Flaxton's little round face with its shining tight cap of blue-black hair seemed to illumine the place like a beacon. It is possible that the effect was heightened by the fact that she was sitting between fifteen stone Mrs Barmby, who had brought her canary to have its claws clipped, and old Mr Spence who was nearly ninety and had called round for some flea powder for his cat, but there was no doubt she was good to look at.

And it wasn't just that she was pretty; there was a round-eyed, innocent appeal about her and she smiled all the time. Penny, sitting on her knee, seemed to be smiling from under the mound of brown curls on her forehead.

In the consulting room I lifted the little dog on to the table. 'Well now, what's the trouble?'

'She has a touch of sickness and diarrhoea,' Mrs Flaxton replied. 'It started yesterday.'

'I see.' I turned and lifted the thermometer from the trolley. 'Has she had a change of food?'

'No, nothing like that.'

'Is she inclined to eat rubbish when she's out?'

Mrs Flaxton shook her head. 'No, not as a rule. But I suppose even the nicest dog will have a nibble at a dead bird or something horrid like that now and then.' She laughed and Penny laughed back at her.

'Well, she has a slightly raised temperature but she seems bright enough.' I put my hand round the dog's middle. 'Let's have a feel at your tummy, Penny.'

The little animal winced as I gently palpated the abdomen, and there was a tenderness throughout the stomach and intestines.

'She has gastroenteritis,' I said. 'But it seems fairly mild and I think it should clear up quite soon. I'll give you some medicine for her and you'd better keep her on a light diet for a few days.'

'Yes, I'll do that. Thank you very much.' Mrs Flaxton's smile deepened as she patted her dog's head. She was about twenty-three and she and her young husband had only recently come to Darrowby. He was a representative of one of the big agricultural firms which supplied meal and cattle cake to the farms and I saw him occasionally on my rounds. Like his wife, and indeed his dog, he gave off an ambience of eager friendliness.

Penny

I sent Mrs Flaxton off with a bottle of bismuth, kaolin and chloro-dyne mixture which was one of our cherished treatments. The little dog trotted down the surgery steps, tail wagging, and I really didn't expect any more trouble.

Three days later, however, Penny was in the surgery again. She was still vomiting and the diarrhoea had not taken up in the least.

I got the dog on the table again and carried out a further examin-ation, but there was nothing significant to see. She had now had five days of this weakening condition but though she had lost a bit of her perkiness she still looked remarkably bright. The Toy Poodle is small but tough and very game, and this one wasn't going to let anything get her down easily.

But I still didn't like it. She couldn't go on like this. I decided to alter the treatment to a mixture of carbon and astringents which had served me well in the past.

'This stuff looks a bit messy,' I said, as I gave Mrs Flaxton a powder box full of the black granules, 'but I have had good results with it. She's still eating, isn't she, so I should mix it in her food.'

'Oh thank you.' She gave me one of her marvellous smiles as she put the box in her bag and I walked along the passage with her to the door. She had left her pram at the foot of the steps and I knew before I looked under the hood what kind of baby I would find. Sure enough the chubby face on the pillow gazed at me with round friendly eyes and then split into a delighted grin.

They were the kind of people I liked to see, but as they moved off down the street I hoped for Penny's sake that I wouldn't be seeing them for a long time. However, it was not to be. A couple of days later they were back, and this time the Poodle was showing signs of strain. As I examined her she stood motionless and dead-eyed with only the occasional twitch of her tail as I stroked her head and spoke to her.

'I'm afraid she's just the same, Mr Herriot,' her mistress said. 'She's not eating much now and whatever she does goes straight through her. And she has a terrific thirst – always at her water bowl and then she brings it back.'

I nodded. 'I know. This inflammation inside her gives her a raging desire for water and of course the more she drinks the more she vomits. And this is terribly weakening.'

Again I changed the treatment. In fact over the next few days I ran through just about the entire range of available drugs. I look back with a wry smile at the things I gave that little dog, powdered epicacuanha and opium, sodium salicylate and tincture of camphor, even way-out exotics like decoction of haematoxylin and infusion of caryophyllum which, thank heavens, have been long forgotten. I might have done a bit of good if I had had access to a gut-active antibiotic like neomycin, but as it was I got nowhere.

I was visiting Penny daily as she was unfit to bring to the surgery. I had her on a diet of arrowroot and boiled milk but that, like my medical treatment, achieved nothing. And all the time the little dog was slipping away.

The climax came about three o'clock one morning. As I lifted the bedside phone Mr Flaxton's voice, with a tremor in it, came over the line.

'I'm terribly sorry to get you out of your bed at this hour, Mr Herriot, but I wish you'd come round to see Penny.'

'Why, is she worse?'

'Yes, and she's . . . well . . . she's suffering now, I'm afraid. You saw her this afternoon didn't you? Well since then she's been drinking and vomiting and this diarrhoea running away from her all the time till she's about at the far end. She's just lying in her basket crying. I'm sure she's in great pain.'

'Right, I'll be there in a few minutes.'

'Oh thank you.' He paused for a moment. 'And Mr Herriot . . . you'll come prepared to put her down won't you?'

My spirits, never very high at that time in the morning, plummeted to the depths. 'As bad as that, is it?'

'Well honestly we can't bear to see her. My wife is so upset . . . I don't think she can stand any more.'

'I see.' I hung up the phone and threw the bedclothes back with a violence which brought Helen wide awake. Being disturbed in the small hours was one of the crosses a vet's wife has to bear, but normally I crept out as quietly as I could. This time, however, I stamped about the bedroom, dragging on my clothes and muttering to myself; and though she must have wondered what this latest crisis meant she wisely watched me in silence until I turned out the light and left.

I had not far to go. The Flaxtons lived in one of the new bungalows on the Brawton Road, less than a mile away. The young couple, in their dressing gowns, led me into the kitchen, and before I reached the dog basket in the corner I could hear Penny's whimperings. She was not lying comfortably curled up, but on her chest, head forward, obviously acutely distressed. I put my hands under her and lifted her and she was almost weightless. A Toy Poodle in its prime is fairly insubstantial, but after her long illness Penny was like a bedraggled little piece of thistledown, her curly brown coat wet and soiled by vomit and diarrhoea.

Mrs Flaxton's smile for once was absent. I could see she was keeping back the tears as she spoke.

'It really would be the kindest thing . . .'

'Yes . . . yes . . .' I replaced the tiny animal in her basket and crouched over her, chin in hand. 'Yes, I suppose you're right.'

But still I didn't move but stayed, squatting there, staring down in disbelief at the evidence of my failure. This dog was only two years old – a lifetime of running and jumping and barking in front of her; all she was suffering from was gastroenteritis and now I was going to extinguish the final spark in her. It was a bitter thought that this would be just about the only positive thing I had done right from the start.

A weariness swept over me that was not just due to the fact that I had been snatched from sleep. I got to my feet with the slow stiff movements of an old man and was about to turn away when I noticed something about the little animal. She was on her chest again, head extended, mouth open, tongue lolling as she panted. There was something there I had seen before somewhere . . . that posture . . . and the exhaustion, pain and shock . . . it slid almost imperceptibly into my sleepy brain that she looked exactly like Mr Kitson's ewe in its dark corner. A different species, yes, but all the other things were there.

'Mrs Flaxton,' I said, 'I want to put Penny to sleep. Not the way you think, but to anaesthetise her. Maybe if she has a rest from this non-stop drinking and vomiting and straining it will give nature a chance.'

The young couple looked at me doubtfully for a few moments, then it was the husband who spoke.

'Don't you think she has been through enough, Mr Herriot?'

'She has, yes she has.' I ran a hand through my rumpled uncombed hair. 'But this won't cause her any more distress. She won't know a thing about it.'

When they still hesitated, I went on. 'I would very much like to try it – it's just an idea I've got.'

They looked at each other, then Mrs Flaxton nodded. 'All right, go ahead, but this will be the last, won't it?'

Out into the night air to my car for the same bottle of nembutal and a very small dose for the little creature. I went back to my bed with the same feeling I had had about the ewe: come what may there would be no more suffering.

Next morning Penny was still stretched peacefully on her side and when, about four o'clock in the afternoon, she showed signs of awakening I repeated the injection.

Like the ewe she slept for forty-eight hours and when she finally did stagger to her feet she did not head immediately for her water bowl as she had done for so many days. Instead she made her feeble way outside and had a walk round the garden.

From then on, recovery, as they say in the case histories, was uneventful. Or as I would rather write it, she wonderfully and miraculously just got better and never ailed another thing throughout her long life.

Helen and I used to play tennis on the grass courts near the Darrowby cricket ground. So did the Flaxtons, and they always brought Penny along with them. I used to look through the wire at her romping with other dogs and later with the Flaxtons' fast growing young son and I marvelled.

I do not wish to give the impression that I advocate wholesale anaesthesia for all animal ailments but I do know that sedation has a definite place. Nowadays we have a sophisticated range of sedatives and tranquillisers to choose from, and when I come up against an acute case of gastroenteritis in dogs I use one of them as an adjunct to the normal treatment; because it puts a brake on the deadly exhausting cycle and blots out the pain and fear which go with it.

And over the years, whenever I saw Penny running around, barking, bright-eyed, full of the devil, I felt a renewed welling of thankfulness for the cure which I discovered in a dark corner of a stable by accident.

*

Fleming discovered penicillin by accident and on a much smaller scale many vets in practice stumble on things which are of inestimable value to them in their work. My own priceless find was that relief from pain can aid an animal's recovery to a magical extent and I have used it happily for over forty years. When the pain disappears, so does the fear. A sick animal doesn't know what has happened to it and the unknown is terrifying.

18. *Cindy*

The name was on the garden gate – Lilac Cottage. I pulled out my list of visits and checked the entry again. 'Cook, Lilac Cottage, Marston Hall. Bitch overdue for whelping.' This was the place all right, standing in the grounds of the Hall, a nineteenth-century mansion house whose rounded turrets reared above the fringe of pine trees less than half a mile away.

The door was opened by a heavy-featured dark woman of about sixty who regarded me unsmilingly.

'Good morning, Mrs Cook,' I said. 'I've come to see your bitch.'

She still didn't smile. 'Oh, very well. You'd better come in.'

She led me into the small living room and as a little Yorkshire Terrier jumped down from an armchair her manner changed.

'Come here, Cindy my darlin',' she cooed. 'This gentleman's come

138

to make you better.' She bent down and stroked the little animal, her face radiant with affection.

I sat down in another armchair. 'Well what's the trouble, Mrs Cook?'

'Oh, I'm worried to death.' She clasped her hands anxiously. 'She should have had her pups yesterday and there's nothing happenin'. Ah couldn't sleep all night – I'd die if anything happened to this dog.'

I looked at the terrier, tail wagging, gazing up, bright-eyed under her mistress's caress. 'She doesn't seem distressed at all. Has she shown any signs of labour?'

'What d'you mean?'

'Well, has she been panting or uneasy in any way? Is there any discharge?'

'No, nothing like that.'

I beckoned to Cindy and spoke to her and she came timidly across the lino till I was able to lift her on to my lap. I palpated the distended abdomen; there was a lot of pups in there but everything appeared normal. I took her temperature – normal again.

'Bring me some warm water and soap, Mrs Cook, will you please?' I said. The terrier was so small that I had to use my little finger, soaped and disinfected, to examine her, and as I felt carefully forward the walls of the vagina were dry and clinging and the cervix, when I reached it, tightly closed.

I washed and dried my hands. 'This little bitch isn't anywhere near whelping, Mrs Cook. Are you sure you haven't got your dates wrong?'

'No, I 'aven't, it was sixty-three days yesterday.' She paused in thought for a moment. 'Now ah'd better tell you this, young man. Cindy's had pups before and she did self and same thing – wouldn't get on with t'job. That was two years ago when I was livin' over in Listondale. I got Mr Broomfield the vet to her and he just gave her an injection. It was wonderful – she had the pups half an hour after it.'

I smiled. 'Yes, that would be pituitrin. She must have been actually whelping when Mr Broomfield saw her.'

'Well whatever it was, young man, I wish you'd give her some now. Ah can't stand all this suspense.'

'I'm sorry,' I lifted Cindy from my lap and stood up, 'I can't do that. It would be very harmful at this stage.'

She stared at me and it struck me that that dark face could look very forbidding. 'So you're not goin' to do anything at all?'

'Well . . .' There are times when it is a soothing procedure to give a client something to do even if it is unnecessary. 'Yes, I've got some tablets in the car. They'll help to keep the little dog fit until she whelps.'

'But I'd far rather have that injection. It was just a little prick. Didn't take Mr Broomfield more than a second to do.'

'I assure you, Mrs Cook, it can't be done at the moment. I'll get the tablets from the car.'

Her mouth tightened. I could see she was grievously disappointed in me. 'Oh well if you won't you won't, so you'd better get them things.' She paused: 'And me name isn't Cook!'

'It isn't?'

'No it isn't, young man.' She didn't seem disposed to offer further information so I left in some bewilderment.

Out in the road, a few yards from my car, a farm man was trying to start a tractor. I called over to him.

'Hey, the lady in there says her name isn't Cook.'

'She's right an' all. She's the cook over at the Hall. You've gotten a bit mixed up.' He laughed heartily.

It all became suddenly clear; the entry in the day book, everything. 'What's her right name, then?'

'Booby,' he shouted just as the tractor roared into life.

Funny name, I thought, as I produced my harmless vitamin tablets from the boot and returned to the cottage. Once inside I did my best to put things right with plenty of 'Yes, Mrs Booby' and 'No, Mrs Booby' but the lady didn't thaw. I told her not to worry and that I was sure nothing would happen for several days, but I could tell I wasn't impressing her.

I waved cheerfully as I went down the path.

'Goodbye, Mrs Booby,' I cried. 'Don't hesitate to ring me if you're in doubt about anything.'

She didn't appear to have heard.

'Oh I wish you'd do as I say,' she wailed. 'It was just a little prick.'

The good lady certainly didn't hesitate to ring. She was at me again the next day and I had to rush out to her cottage. Her message was the same as before: she wanted the wonderful injection which would

Cindy

make those pups pop out and she wanted it right away. Mr Broomfield hadn't messed about and wasted time like I had. And on the third and fourth and fifth mornings she had me out at Marston examining the little bitch and reciting the same explanations. Things came to a head on the sixth day.

In the room at Lilac Cottage the dark eyes held a desperate light as they stared into mine. 'I'm about at the end of my tether, young man. I tell you I'll die if anything happens to this dog. I'll die. Don't you understand?'

'Of course I know how you feel about her, Mrs Booby. Believe me, I fully understand.'

'Then why don't you do something?' she snapped.

I dug my nails into my palms. 'Look, I've told you. A pituitrin injection works by contracting the muscular walls of the uterus so it can only be given when labour has started and the cervix is open. If I find it is indicated I will do it, but if I give this injection now it could cause rupture of the uterus. It could cause death.' I stopped because I fancied little bubbles were beginning to collect at the corners of my mouth.

But I don't think she had listened to a word. She sunk her head in her hands. 'All this time, I can't stand it.'

I was wondering if I could stand much more of it myself. Bulging Yorkshire Terriers had begun to prance through my dreams at night and I greeted each new day with a silent prayer that the pups had arrived. I held out my hand to Cindy and she crept reluctantly towards me. She was heartily sick of this strange man who came every day and squeezed her and stuck fingers into her, and she submitted again with trembling limbs and frightened eyes to the indignity.

'Mrs Booby,' I said, 'are you absolutely sure that dog didn't have access to Cindy after the service date you gave me?'

She sniffed. 'You keep askin' me that and ah've been thinking about it. Maybe he did come a week after, now I think on.'

'Well, that's it, then!' I spread my hands. 'She's held to the second mating, so she should be due tomorrow.'

'Ah would still far rather you would get it over with today like Mr Broomfield did . . . it was just a little prick.'

'But Mrs Booby . . . !'

'And let me tell you another thing, me name's not Booby!'

I clutched at the back of the chair. 'It's not?'

141

'Naw!'

'Well . . . what is it, then?'

'It's Dooley . . . Dooley!' She looked very cross.

'Right . . . right . . .' I stumbled down the garden path and drove away. It was not a happy departure.

Next morning I could hardly believe it when there was no call from Marston. Maybe all was well at last. But I turned cold when an urgent call to go to Lilac Cottage was passed on to one of the farms on my round. I was right at the far end of the practice area and was in the middle of a tough calving, and it was well over three hours before I got out at the now familiar garden gate. The cottage door was open and as I ventured up the path a little brown missile hurtled out at me. It was Cindy, but a transformed Cindy, a snarling, barking little bundle of ferocity; and though I recoiled she fastened her teeth in my trouser cuff and hung on grimly.

I was hopping around on one leg trying to shake off the growling little creature when a peal of almost girlish laughter made me look round.

Mrs Dooley, vastly amused, was watching me from the doorway. 'My word, she's different since she had them pups. Just shows what a good little mother she is, guarding them like that.' She gazed fondly at the tiny animal dangling from my ankle.

'Had the pups . . . ?'

'Aye, when they said you'd be a long time I rang Mr Farnon. He came right away and d'you know he gave Cindy that injection I've wanted all along. And I tell you 'e wasn't right out of t'garden gate before the pups started. She's had seven – beauties they are.'

'Ah well that's fine, Mrs Dooley . . . splendid.' Siegfried had obviously felt a pup in the passage. I finally managed to rid myself of Cindy and when her mistress lifted her up I went into the kitchen to inspect the family.

They certainly were grand pups and I lifted the squawking little morsels one by one from their basket while their mother snarled from Mrs Dooley's arms like a starving wolfhound.

'They're lovely, Mrs Dooley,' I murmured.

She looked at me pityingly. 'I told you what to do, didn't I, but you wouldn't 'ave it. It only needed a little prick. Ooo, that Mr Farnon's a lovely man – just like Mr Broomfield.'

Cindy

That was a bit much. 'But you must realise, Mrs Dooley, he just happened to arrive at the right time. If I had come . . .'

'Now, now, young man, be fair. Ah'm not blamin' you, but some people have had more experience. We all 'ave to learn.' She sighed reminiscently. 'It was just a little prick – Mr Farnon'll have to show you how to do it. I tell you he wasn't right out of t'garden gate . . .'

Enough is enough. I drew myself up to my full height. 'Mrs Dooley, madam,' I said frigidly, 'let me repeat once and for all . . .'

'Oh, hoity toity, hoity toity, don't get on your high horse wi' me!' she exclaimed. 'We've managed very nicely without you so don't complain.' Her expression became very severe. 'And one more thing – me name's not Mrs Dooley.'

My brain reeled for a moment. The world seemed to be crumbling about me. 'What did you say?'

'I said me name's not Mrs Dooley.'

'It isn't?'

'Naw!' She lifted her left hand and as I gazed at it dully I realised it must have been all the mental stress which had prevented me from noticing the total absence of rings.

'Naw!' she said. 'It's Miss!'

*

Points up the fact that sometimes you feel you are a loser from the start. When you can't even get a client's name right it is no use trying to prove you are using the correct treatment. When I first came to Darrowby Siegfried told me that veterinary practice offered unrivalled opportunities for making a fool of yourself. He was right.

19. *Only One Woof*

'Is this the thing you've been telling me about?' I asked.

Mr Wilkin nodded. 'Aye, that's it, it's always like that.'

I looked down at the helpless convulsions of the big dog lying at my feet; at the staring eyes, the wildly pedalling limbs. The farmer had told me about the periodic attacks which had begun to affect his sheepdog, Gyp, but it was coincidence that one should occur when I was on the farm for another reason.

'And he's all right afterwards, you say?'

'Right as a bobbin. Seems a bit dazed, maybe, for about an hour, then he's back to normal.' The farmer shrugged. 'I've had lots o' dogs through my hands as you know and I've seen plenty of dogs with fits. I thought I knew all the causes – worms, wrong feeding, distemper – but this has me beat. I've tried everything.'

'Well you can stop trying, Mr Wilkin,' I said. 'You won't be able to do much for Gyp. He's got epilepsy.'

'Epilepsy? But he's a grand, normal dog most of t'time.'

'Yes, I know. That's how it goes. There's nothing actually wrong with his brain – it's a mysterious condition. The cause is unknown but it's almost certainly hereditary.'

Mr Wilkin raised his eyebrows. 'Well that's a rum 'un. If it's hereditary why hasn't it shown up before now? He's nearly two years old and he didn't start this till a few weeks ago.'

'That's typical,' I replied. 'Eighteen months to two years is about the time it usually appears.'

Gyp interrupted us by getting up and staggering towards his master, wagging his tail. He seemed untroubled by his experience. In fact the whole thing had lasted less than two minutes.

Mr Wilkin bent and stroked the rough head briefly. His craggy features were set in a thoughtful cast. He was a big powerful man in his forties and now as the eyes narrowed in that face which rarely smiled he looked almost menacing. I had heard more than one man say he wouldn't like to get on the wrong side of Sep Wilkin and I could see what they meant. But he had always treated me right and since he farmed nearly a thousand acres I saw quite a lot of him.

His passion was sheepdogs. A lot of farmers like to run dogs at the trials but Mr Wilkin was one of the top men. He bred and trained dogs which regularly won at the local events and occasionally at the national trials. And what was troubling me was that Gyp was his main hope.

He had picked out the two best pups from a litter – Gyp and Sweep – and had trained them with the dedication that had made him a winner. I don't think I have ever seen two dogs enjoy each other quite as much; whenever I was on the farm I would see them together, sometimes peeping nose by nose over the half-door of the loose box where they slept, occasionally slinking devotedly round the feet of their master but usually just playing together. They must have spent hours rolling about in ecstatic wrestling matches, growling and panting, gnawing gently at each other's limbs.

A few months ago George Crossley, one of Mr Wilkin's oldest friends and a keen trial man, had lost his best dog with nephritis and Mr Wilkin had let him have Sweep. I was surprised at the time because Sweep was shaping better than Gyp in his training and looked like turning out a real champion. But it was Gyp who remained. He must have missed his friend but there were other dogs on the farm and if they didn't quite make up for Sweep he was never really lonely.

As I watched, I could see the dog recovering rapidly. It was extraordinary how soon normality was restored after that frightening convulsion. And I waited with some apprehension to hear what his master would say.

The cold, logical decision for him to make would be to have Gyp put down and, looking at the friendly, tail-wagging animal, I didn't like the idea at all. There was something very attractive about him. The big-boned, well-marked body was handsome but his most distinctive feature was his head, where one ear somehow contrived to stick up while the other lay flat, giving him a lop-sided, comic appeal. Gyp, in fact, looked a bit of a clown. But a clown who radiated goodwill and camaraderie.

Mr Wilkin spoke at last. 'Will he get any better as he grows older?'

'Almost certainly not,' I replied.

'Then he'll always 'ave these fits?'

'I'm afraid so. You say he has them every two or three weeks – well it will probably carry on more or less like that with occasional variations.'

'But he could have one any time?'

'Yes.'

'In the middle of a trial, like.' The farmer sunk his head on his chest and his voice rumbled deep. 'That's it, then.'

In the long silence which followed, the fateful words became more and more inevitable. Sep Wilkin wasn't the man to hesitate in a matter which concerned his ruling passion. Ruthless culling of any animal which didn't come up to standard would be his policy. When he finally cleared his throat I had a sinking premonition of what he was going to say.

But I was wrong.

'If I kept him, could you do anything for him?' he asked.

'Well I could give you some pills for him. They might decrease the frequency of the fits.' I tried to keep the eagerness out of my voice.

'Right ... right ... I'll come into t'surgery and get some,' he muttered.

'Fine. But ... er ... you won't ever breed from him, will you?' I said.

'Naw, naw, naw,' the farmer grunted with a touch of irritability as though he didn't want to pursue the matter further.

And I held my peace because I felt intuitively that he did not want to be detected in a weakness; that he was prepared to keep the dog simply as a pet. It was funny how events began to slot into place and suddenly make sense. That was why he had let Sweep, the superior trial dog, go. He just liked Gyp. In fact Sep Wilkin, hard man though he may be, had succumbed to that off-beat charm.

So I shifted to some light chatter about the weather as I walked back to the car, but when I was about to drive off the farmer returned to the main subject.

'There's one thing about Gyp I never mentioned,' he said, bending to the window. 'I don't know whether it has owt to do with the job or not. He has never barked in his life.'

I looked at him in surprise. 'You mean never, ever?'

'That's right. Not a single bark. T'other dogs make a noise when strangers come on the farm but I've never heard Gyp utter a sound since he was born.'

'Well that's very strange,' I said. 'But I can't see that it is connected with his condition in any way.'

And as I switched on the engine I noticed for the first time that while a bitch and two half-grown pups gave tongue to see me on my way, Gyp merely regarded me in his comradely way, mouth open, tongue lolling, but made no noise. A silent dog.

The thing intrigued me. So much so that whenever I was on the farm over the next few months I made a point of watching the big sheepdog at whatever he was doing. But there was never any change. Between the convulsions which had settled down to around three-week intervals he was a normal active happy animal. But soundless.

I saw him, too, in Darrowby when his master came in to market. Gyp was often seated comfortably in the back of the car, but if I happened to speak to Mr Wilkin on these occasions I kept off the subject because, as I said, I had the feeling that he more than most farmers would hate to be exposed in keeping a dog for other than working purposes.

And yet I have always entertained a suspicion that most farm dogs were more or less pets. The dogs on sheep farms were of course indispensable working animals and on other establishments they no doubt performed a function in helping to bring in the cows. But watching them on my daily rounds I often wondered. I saw them rocking along on carts at haytime, chasing rats among the stooks at harvest, pottering around the buildings or roaming the fields at the side of the farmer; and I wondered . . . what did they really do?

My suspicions were strengthened at other times – as when I was trying to round up some cattle into a corner and the dog tried to get into the act by nipping at a hock or tail. There was invariably a hoarse yell of 'Siddown, dog!' or 'Gerrout, dog!'

So right up to the present day I still stick to my theory: most farm dogs are pets and they are there mainly because the farmer just likes to have them around. You would have to put a farmer on the rack to get him to admit it but I think I am right. And in the process those dogs have a wonderful time. They don't have to beg for walks, they are out all day long, and in the company of their masters. If I want to find a man on a farm I look for his dog, knowing the man won't be far away. I try to give my own dogs a good life but it cannot compare with the life of the average farm dog.

There was a long spell when Sep Wilkin's stock stayed healthy and I didn't see either him or Gyp, then I came across them both by accident at a sheepdog trial. It was a local event run in conjunction with the Mellerton Agricultural Show and since I was in the district I decided to steal an hour off.

I took Helen with me, too, because these trials have always fascinated us. The wonderful control of the owners over their animals, the intense involvement of the dogs themselves, the sheer skill of the whole operation always held us spellbound.

She put her arm through mine as we went in at the entrance gate to where a crescent of cars was drawn up at one end of a long field. The field was on the river's edge and through a fringe of trees the afternoon sunshine glinted on the tumbling water of the shallows and turned the long beach of bleached stones to a dazzling white. Groups of men, mainly competitors, stood around chatting as they watched. They were quiet, easy, bronzed men and as they seemed to be drawn from all social strata from prosperous farmers to working men their garb was varied: cloth caps, trilbies, deerstalkers or no hat at all; tweed jackets, stiff best suits, open-necked shirts, fancy ties, sometimes neither collar nor tie. Nearly all of them leaned on long crooks with the handles fashioned from rams' horns.

Snatches of talk reached us as we walked among them.

'You got 'ere, then, Fred.' 'That's a good gather.' 'Nay, 'e's missed one, 'e'll get nowt for that.' 'Them sheep's a bit flighty.' 'Aye they're buggers.' And above it all the whistles of the man running a dog; every conceivable level and pitch of whistle with now and then a shout. 'Sit!' 'Get by!' Every man had his own way with his dog.

The dogs waiting their turn were tied up to a fence with a hedge growing over it. There were about seventy of them and it was rather wonderful to see that long row of waving tails and friendly expressions. They were mostly strangers to each other but there wasn't even the semblance of disagreement, never mind a fight. It seemed that the natural obedience of these little creatures was linked to an amicable disposition.

This appeared to be common to their owners, too. There was no animosity, no resentment at defeat, no unseemly display of triumph in victory. If a man overran his time he ushered his group of sheep quietly in the corner and returned with a philosophical grin to his colleagues. There was a little quiet leg-pulling but that was all.

We came across Sep Wilkin leaning against his car at the best vantage point about thirty yards away from the final pen. Gyp, tied to the bumper, turned and gave me his crooked grin while Mrs Wilkin on a camp stool by his side rested a hand on his shoulder. Gyp, it seemed, had got under her skin too.

Helen went over to speak to her and I turned to her husband. 'Are you running a dog today, Mr Wilkin?'

'No, not this time, just come to watch. I know a lot o' the dogs.'

I stood near him for a while watching the competitors in action, breathing in the clean smell of trampled grass and plug tobacco. In front of us next to the pen the judge stood by his post.

I had been there for about ten minutes when Mr Wilkin lifted a pointing finger. 'Look who's there!'

George Crossley with Sweep trotting at his heels was making his way unhurriedly to the post. Gyp suddenly stiffened and sat up very straight, his cocked ears accentuating the lop-sided look. It was many months since he had seen his brother and companion; it seemed unlikely, I thought, that he would remember him. But his interest was clearly intense, and as the judge waved his white handkerchief and the three sheep were released from the far corner he rose slowly to his feet.

A gesture from Mr Crossley sent Sweep winging round the perimeter of the field in a wide, joyous gallop and as he neared the sheep a whistle dropped him on his belly. From then on it was an object lesson in the cooperation of man and dog. Sep Wilkin had always said Sweep would be a champion and he looked the part, darting and falling at his master's commands. Short piercing whistles, shrill plaintive whistles; he was in tune with them all.

No dog all day had brought his sheep through the three lots of gates as effortlessly as Sweep did now and as he approached the pen near us it was obvious that he would win the cup unless some disaster struck. But this was the touchy bit; more than once with other dogs the sheep had broken free and gone bounding away within feet of the wooden rails.

George Crossley held the gate wide and extended his crook. You could see now why they all carried those long sticks. His commands to Sweep, huddled flat along the turf, were now almost inaudible but the quiet words brought the dog inching first one way then the other. The sheep were in the entrance to the pen now but they still looked around them irresolutely and the game was not over yet. But as Sweep wriggled towards them almost imperceptibly they turned and entered and Mr Crossley crashed the gate behind them.

As he did so he turned to Sweep with a happy cry of '*Good lad!*' and the dog responded with a quick jerking wag of his tail.

At that, Gyp, who had been standing very tall, watching every move with the most intense concentration, raised his head and emitted a single resounding bark.

'*Woof!*' went Gyp as we all stared at him in astonishment.

'Did you hear that?' gasped Mrs Wilkin.

'Well, by gaw!' her husband burst out, looking open-mouthed at his dog.

Gyp didn't seem to be aware that he had done anything unusual. He was too preoccupied by the reunion with his brother and within seconds the two dogs were rolling around, chewing playfully at each other as of old.

I suppose the Wilkins as well as myself had the feeling that this event might start Gyp barking like any other dog, but it was not to be.

Six years later I was on the farm and went to the house to get some hot water. As Mrs Wilkin handed me the bucket she looked down at Gyp who was basking in the sunshine outside the kitchen window.

'There you are, then, funny fellow,' she said to the dog.

I laughed. 'Has he ever barked since that day?'

Mrs Wilkin shook her head. 'No he hasn't, not a sound. I waited a long time but I know he's not going to do it now.'

'Ah well, it's not important. But still, I'll never forget that afternoon at the trial,' I said.

Only One Woof

'Nor will I!' She looked at Gyp again and her eyes softened in reminiscence. 'Poor old lad, eight years old and only one woof!'

*

One of those quirks of animal behaviour which are delightful but inexplicable. I will never know how it happened, and if I had not witnessed the whole thing I would have found it difficult to believe. Many children write to me about my books and this story is one which particularly seemed to capture their imagination. As a result, it has been specially adapted for my young readers and illustrated by Peter Barrett. This story of a dog who gave one single bark throughout his long life just had to be called *Only One Woof*. It was published last September.

20. *The Dimmocks*

A full surgery! But the ripple of satisfaction as I surveyed the packed rows of heads waned quickly as realisation dawned. It was only the Dimmocks again.

I first encountered the Dimmocks one evening when I had a call to a dog which had been knocked down by a car. The address was down in the old part of the town and I was cruising slowly along the row of decaying cottages looking for the number when a door burst open and three shock-headed little children ran into the street and waved me down frantically.

'He's in ere, Mister!' they gasped in unison as I got out, and then began immediately to put me in the picture.

'It's Bonzo!' 'Aye, a car 'it 'im!' 'We 'ad to carry 'im in, Mister!' They all got their words in as I opened the garden gate and struggled up the path with the three of them hanging on to my arms and tugging at my coat; and en route I gazed in wonder at the window of the house where a mass of other young faces mouthed at me and a tangle of arms gesticulated.

Once through the door which opened directly into the living room

I was swamped by a rush of bodies and borne over to the corner where I saw my patient.

Bonzo was sitting upright on a ragged blanket. He was a large shaggy animal of indeterminate breed and though at a glance there didn't seem to be much ailing him he wore a pathetic expression of self-pity. Since everybody was talking at once I decided to ignore them and carry out my examination. I worked my way over legs, pelvis, ribs and spine; no fractures. His mucous membranes were a good colour, there was no evidence of internal injury. In fact the only thing I could find was slight bruising over the left shoulder. Bronzo had sat like a statue as I felt over him, but as I finished he toppled over on to his side and lay looking up at me apologetically, his tail thumping on the blanket.

'You're a big soft dog, that's what you are,' I said and the tail thumped faster.

I turned and viewed the throng and after a moment or two managed to pick out the parents. Mum was fighting her way to the front while at the rear, Dad, a diminutive figure, was beaming at me over the heads. I did a bit of shushing and when the babel died down I addressed myself to Mrs Dimmock.

'I think he's been lucky,' I said. 'I can't find any serious injury. I think the car must have bowled him over and knocked the wind out of him for a minute, or he may have been suffering from shock.'

The uproar broke out again. 'Will 'e die, Mister?' 'What's the matter with 'im?' 'What are you going to do?'

I gave Bonzo an injection of a mild sedative while he lay rigid, a picture of canine suffering, with the tousled heads looking down at him with deep concern and innumerable little hands poking out and caressing him.

Mrs Dimmock produced a basin of hot water and while I washed my hands I was able to make a rough assessment of the household. I counted eleven little Dimmocks from a boy in his early teens down to a grubby-faced infant crawling around the floor; and judging by the significant bulge in Mum's midriff the number was soon to be augmented. They were clad in a motley selection of hand-me downs, darned pullovers, patched trousers, tattered dresses, yet the general atmosphere in the house was of unconfined *joie de vivre*.

Bonzo wasn't the only animal and I stared in disbelief as another biggish dog and a cat with two half-grown kittens appeared from among the crowding legs and feet. I would have thought that the problem of filling the human mouths would have been difficult enough without importing several animals.

But the Dimmocks didn't worry about such things; they did what they wanted to do, and they got by. Dad, I learned later, had never done any work within living memory. He had a 'bad back' and lived what seemed to me a reasonably gracious life, roaming interestedly around the town by day and enjoying a quiet beer and a game of dominoes in a corner of the Four Horse Shoes by night.

I saw him quite often; he was easy to pick out because he invariably carried a walking stick which gave him an air of dignity and he always walked briskly and purposefully as though he were going somewhere important.

I took a final look at Bonzo, still stretched on the blanket, looking up at me with soulful eyes, then I struggled towards the door.

'I don't think there's anything to worry about,' I shouted above the chattering which had speedily broken out again, 'but I'll look in tomorrow and make sure.'

When I drew up outside the house next morning I could see Bonzo lolloping around the garden with several of the children. They were passing a ball from one to the other and he was leaping ecstatically high in the air to try to intercept it.

He was clearly none the worse for his accident but when he saw me opening the gate his tail went down and he dropped almost to his knees and slunk into the house. The children received me rapturously.

'You've made 'im better, Mister!' 'He's all right now, isn't he?' 'He's 'ad a right big breakfast this mornin', Mister!'

I went inside with little hands clutching at my coat. Bonzo was sitting bolt upright on his blanket in the same attitude as the previous evening, but as I approached he slowly collapsed on to his side and lay looking up at me with a martyred expression.

I laughed as I knelt by him. 'You're the original old soldier, Bonzo, but you can't fool me. I saw you out there.'

I gently touched the bruised shoulder and the big dog tremblingly closed his eyes as he resigned himself to his fate. Then when I stood up and he realised he wasn't going to have another injection he leapt to his feet and bounded away into the garden.

There was a chorus of delighted cries from the Dimmocks and they turned and looked at me with undisguised admiration. Clearly they considered that I had plucked Bonzo from the jaws of death. Mr Dimmock stepped forward from the mass.

'You'll send me a bill, won't you,' he said, with the dignity that was peculiar to him.

My first glance last night had decided me that this was a no-charging job and I hadn't even written it in the book, but I nodded solemnly.

'Very well, Mr Dimmock, I'll do that.'

And throughout our long association, though no money ever changed hands, he always said the same thing – 'You'll send me a bill, won't you.'

This was the beginning of my close relationship with the Dimmocks. Obviously they had taken a fancy to me and wanted to see as much as possible of me. Over the succeeding weeks and months they brought in a varied selection of dogs, cats, budgies, rabbits at frequent intervals, and when they found that my services were free they stepped up the number of visits; and when one came they all came. I was anxiously trying to expand the small animal side of the practice and increasingly my hopes were raised momentarily then dashed when I opened the door and saw a packed waiting room.

And it increased the congestion when they started bringing their auntie, Mrs Pounder, from down the road with them to see what a nice chap I was. Mrs Pounder, a fat lady who always wore a greasy velour hat perched on an untidy mound of hair, evidently shared the family tendency to fertility and usually brought a few of her own ample brood with her.

That is how it was this particular morning. I swept the assembled company with my eye but could discern only beaming Dimmocks and Pounders; and this time I couldn't even pick out my patient. Then the assembly parted and spread out as though by a prearranged signal and I saw little Nellie Dimmock with a tiny puppy on her knee.

Nellie was my favourite. Mind you, I liked all the family; in fact they were such nice people that I always enjoyed their visits after that first disappointment. Mum and Dad were always courteous and cheerful and the children, though boisterous, were never ill-mannered; they were happy and friendly and if they saw me in the street they would wave madly and go on waving till I was out of sight. And I saw them often because they were continually scurrying around the town doing odd jobs – delivering milk or papers. Best of all, they loved their animals and were kind to them.

But as I say, Nellie was my favourite. She was about nine and had suffered an attack of 'infantile paralysis', as it used to be called, when very young. It had left her with a pronounced limp and a frailty which set her apart from her robust brothers and sisters. Her painfully thin legs seemed almost too fragile to carry her around but above the pinched face her hair, the colour of ripe corn, flowed to her shoulders and her eyes, though slightly crossed, gazed out calm and limpid blue through steel-rimmed spectacles.

'What's that you've got, Nellie?' I asked.

'It's a little dog,' she almost whispered. "e's mine.'

'You mean he's your very own?'

She nodded proudly. 'Aye, 'e's mine.'

'He doesn't belong to your brothers and sisters, too?'

'Naw, 'e's mine.'

Rows of Dimmock and Pounder heads nodded in eager acquiescence as Nellie lifted the puppy to her cheek and looked up at me with a smile of a strange sweetness. It was a smile that always tugged at my heart; full of a child's artless happiness and trust but with something else which was poignant and maybe had to do with the way Nellie was.

'Well, he looks a fine dog to me," I said. 'He's a Spaniel, isn't he?'

She ran a hand over the little head. 'Aye, a Cocker. Mr Brown said 'e was a Cocker.'

There was a slight disturbance at the back and Mr Dimmock appeared from the crush. He gave a respectful cough.

'He's a proper pure bred, Mr Herriot,' he said. 'Mr Brown from the bank's bitch had a litter and 'e gave this 'un to Nellie.' He tucked his stick under his arm and pulled a long envelope from an inside pocket. He handed it to me with a flourish. 'That's 'is pedigree.'

I read it through and whistled softly. 'He's a real blue-blooded hound, all right, and I see he's got a big long name. Darrowby Tobias the Third. My word, that sounds great.'

I looked down at the little girl again. 'And what do *you* call him, Nellie?'

'Toby,' she said softly. 'I calls 'im Toby.'

I laughed. 'All right, then. What's the matter with Toby anyway? Why have you brought him?'

The Dimmocks

'He's been sick, Mr Herriot.' Mrs Dimmock spoke from somewhere among the heads. 'He can't keep nothin' down.'

'Well I know what that'll be. Has he been wormed?'

'No, don't think so.'

'I should think he just needs a pill,' I said. 'But bring him through and I'll have a look at him.'

Other clients were usually content to send one representative through with their animals but the Dimmocks all had to come. I marched along with the crowd behind me filling the passage from wall to wall. Our consulting-cum-operating room was quite small and I watched with some apprehension as the procession filed in after me. But they all got in, Mrs Pounder, her velour hat slightly askew, squeezing herself in with some difficulty at the rear.

My examination of the puppy took longer than usual as I had to fight my way to the thermometer on the trolley then struggle in the other direction to get the stethoscope from its hook on the wall. But I finished at last.

'Well I can't find anything wrong with him,' I said. 'So I'm pretty sure he just has a tummy full of worms. I'll give you a pill now and you must give it to him first thing tomorrow morning.'

Like a football match turning out, the mass of people surged along the passage and into the street and another Dimmock visit had come to an end.

I forgot the incident immediately because there was nothing unusual about it. The pot-bellied appearance of the puppy made my diagnosis a formality; I didn't expect to see him again.

But I was wrong. A week later my surgery was once more overflowing and I had another squashed-in session with Toby in the little back room. My pill had evacuated a few worms but he was still vomiting, still distended.

'Are you giving him five very small meals a day as I told you?' I asked.

I received emphatic affirmative and I believed them. The Dimmocks really took care of their animals. There was something else here, yet I couldn't find it. Temperature normal, lungs clear, abdomen negative on palpation; I couldn't make it out. I dispensed a bottle of our antacid mixture with a feeling of defeat. A young puppy like this shouldn't need such a thing.

This was the beginning of a frustrating period. There would be a span of two or three weeks when I would think the trouble had righted

157

itself, then without warning the place would be full of Dimmocks and Pounders and I'd be back where I started.

And all the time Toby was growing thinner.

I tried everything: gastric sedatives, variations of diet, quack remedies. I interrogated the Dimmocks repeatedly about the character of the vomiting – how long after eating, what were the intervals between, and I received varying replies. Sometimes he brought his food straight back, at others he retained it for several hours. I got nowhere.

It must have been over eight weeks later – Toby would be about four months old – when I again viewed the assembled Dimmocks with a sinking heart. Their visits had become depressing affairs and I could not foresee anything better today as I opened the waiting-room door and allowed myself to be almost carried along the passage. This time it was Dad who was the last to wedge himself into the consulting room, then Nellie placed the little dog on the table.

I felt an inward lurch of sheer misery. Toby had grown despite his disability and was now a grim caricature of a Cocker Spaniel, the long silky ears drooping from an almost fleshless skull, the spindly legs pathetically feathered. I had thought Nellie was thin but her pet had outdone her. And he wasn't just thin, he was trembling slightly as he stood arch-backed on the smooth surface, and his face had the dull inward look of an animal which has lost interest.

The little girl ran her hand along the jutting ribs and the pale, squinting eyes looked up at me through the steel spectacles with that smile which pulled at me more painfully than ever before. She didn't seem worried. Probably she had no idea how things were, but whether she had or not I knew I'd never be able to tell her that her dog was slowly dying.

I rubbed my eyes wearily. 'What has he had to eat today?'

Nellie answered herself. 'He's 'ad some bread and milk.'

'How long ago was that?' I asked, but before anybody could reply the little dog vomited, sending the half-digested stomach contents soaring in a graceful arc to land two feet away on the table.

I swung round on Mrs Dimmock. 'Does he always do it like that?'

'Aye he mostly does – sends it flying out, like.'

'But why didn't you tell me?'

The poor lady looked flustered. 'Well . . . I don't know . . . I . . .'

I held up a hand. 'That's all right, Mrs Dimmock, never mind.'

It occurred to me that all the way through my totally ineffectual treatment of this dog not a single Dimmock or Pounder had uttered a word of criticism so why should I start to complain now?

But I knew what Toby's trouble was now. At last, at long last, I knew.

And in case my present-day colleagues reading this may think I had been more than usually thick-headed in my handling of the case, I would like to offer in my defence that such limited text books as there were in those days made only a cursory reference to pyloric stenosis (narrowing of the exit of the stomach where it joins the small intestine) and if they did they said nothing about treatment.

But surely, I thought, somebody in England was ahead of the books. There must be people who were actually doing this operation . . . and if there were I had a feeling one might not be too far away . . .

I worked my way through the crush and trotted along the passage to the phone.

'Is that you, Granville?'

'*Jim!*' A bellow of pure unalloyed joy. 'How are you laddie?'

'Very well, how are you?'

'Ab-so-lutely tip top, old son! Never better!'

'Granville, I've got a four-month-old spaniel pup I'd like to bring through to you. It's got pyloric stenosis.'

'Oh lovely!'

'I'm afraid the little thing's just about on its last legs – a bag of bones.'

'Splendid, splendid!'

'This is because I've been mucking about for four weeks in ignorance.'

'Fine, just fine!'

'And the owners are a very poor family. They can't pay anything, I'm afraid.'

'Wonderful!'

I hesitated a moment. 'Granville, you do . . . er . . . you have . . . operated on these cases before?'

'Did five yesterday.'

'What!'

A deep rumble of laughter. 'I do but jest, old son, but you needn't worry, I've done a few. And it isn't such a bad job.'

'Well that's great.' I looked at my watch. 'It's half past nine now.

I'll get Siegfried to take over my morning round and I'll see you before eleven.'

Granville had been called out when I arrived and I hung around his surgery till I heard the expensive sound of the Bentley purring into the yard. Through the window I saw yet another magnificent pipe glinting behind the wheel then my colleague, in an impeccable pin-striped suit which made him look like the Governor of the Bank of England, paced majestically towards the side door.

'Good to see you, Jim!' he exclaimed, wringing my hand warmly. Then before removing his jacket he took his pipe from his mouth and regarded it with a trace of anxiety for a second before giving it a polish with his yellow cloth and placing it tenderly in a drawer.

It wasn't long before I was under the lamp in the operating room bending over Toby's small outstretched form while Granville – the other Granville Bennett – worked with fierce concentration inside the abdomen of the little animal.

'You see the gross gastric dilatation,' he murmured. 'Classical lesion.' He gripped the pylorus and poised his scalpel. 'Now I'm going through the serous coat.' A quick deft incision. 'A bit of blunt dissection here for the muscle fibres . . . down . . . down . . . a little more . . . ah, there it is, can you see it – the mucosa bulging into the cleft. Yes . . . yes . . . just right. That's what you've got to arrive at.'

I peered down at the tiny tube which had been the site of all Toby's troubles. 'Is that all, then?'

'That's all, laddie.' He stepped back with a grin. 'The obstruction is relieved now and you can take bets that this little chap will start to put weight on now.'

'That's wonderful, Granville. I'm really grateful.'

'Nonsense, Jim, it was a pleasure. You can do the next one yourself now, eh?' He laughed, seized needle and sutures and sewed up the abdominal muscles and skin at an impossible pace.

A few minutes later he was in his office pulling on his jacket, then as he filled his pipe he turned to me.

'I've got a little plan for the rest of the morning, laddie.'

I shrank away from him and threw up a protective hand. 'Well now, er . . . it's kind of you, Granville, but I really . . . I honestly must get back . . . we're very busy, you know . . . can't leave Siegfried too long . . . work'll be piling up . . .' I stopped because I felt I was beginning to gibber.

My colleague looked wounded. 'All I meant, old son, was that we want you to come to lunch. Zoe is expecting you.'

'Oh . . . oh, I see. Well that's very kind. We're not going . . . anywhere else, then?'

'Anywhere else?' He blew out his cheeks and spread his arms wide. 'Of course not. I just have to call in at my branch surgery on the way.'

'Branch surgery? I didn't know you had one.'

'Oh yes, just a stone's throw from my house.' He put an arm round my shoulders. 'Well let's go, shall we?'

As I lay back, cradled in the Bentley's luxury, I dwelt happily on the thought that at last I was going to meet Zoe Bennett when I was my normal self. She would learn this time that I wasn't a perpetually drunken oaf. In fact the next hour or two seemed full of rosy promise; an excellent lunch illumined by my witty conversation and polished manners, then back with Toby, magically resuscitated, to Darrowby.

I smiled to myself when I thought of Nellie's face when I told her her pet was going to be able to eat and grow strong and playful like any other pup. I was still smiling when the car pulled up on the outskirts of Granville's home village. I glanced idly through the window at a low stone building with leaded panes and a wooden sign dangling over the entrance. It read 'Old Oak Tree Inn'. I turned quickly to my companion.

'I thought we were going to your branch surgery?'

Granville gave me a smile of childish innocence. 'Oh that's what I call this place. It's so near home and I transact quite a lot of business here.' He patted my knee. 'We'll just pop in for an appetiser, eh?'

'Now wait a minute,' I stammered, gripping the sides of my seat tightly. 'I just can't be late today. I'd much rather . . .'

Granville raised a hand. 'Jim, laddie, we won't be in for long.' He looked at his watch. 'It's exactly twelve thirty and I promised Zoe we'd be home by one o'clock. She's cooking roast beef and Yorkshire pudding and it would take a braver man than me to let her pudding go flat. I guarantee we'll be in that house at one o'clock on the dot – O.K.?'

I hesitated. I couldn't come to much harm in half an hour. I climbed out of the car.

As we went into the pub a large man, who had been leaning on the counter, turned and exchanged enthusiastic greetings with my colleague.

'Albert!' cried Granville. 'Meet Jim Herriot from Darrowby. Jim, this is Albert Wainright, the landlord of the Wagon and Horses over in Matherley. In fact he's the president of the Licensed Victuallers' Association this year, aren't you, Albert?'

The big man grinned and nodded and for a moment I felt overwhelmed by the two figures on either side of me. It was difficult to describe the hard, bulky tissue of Granville's construction but Mr Wainright was unequivocally fat. A checked jacket hung open to display an enormous expanse of striped shirted abdomen overflowing the waistband of his trousers. Above a gay bow tie cheerful eyes twinkled at me from a red face and when he spoke his tone was rich and fruity. He embodied the rich ambience of the term 'Licensed Victualler'.

I began to sip at the half pint of beer I had ordered but when another appeared in two minutes I saw I was going to fall hopelessly behind and switched to the whiskies and sodas which the others were drinking. And my undoing was that both my companions appeared to have a standing account here; they downed their drinks, tapped softly on the counter and said, 'Yes please, Jack,' whereupon three more glasses appeared with magical speed. I never had a chance to buy a round. In fact no money ever changed hands.

It was a quiet, friendly little session with Albert and Granville carrying on a conversation of the utmost good humour punctuated by the almost soundless taps on the bar. And as I fought to keep up with the two virtuosos the taps came more and more frequently till I seemed to hear them every few seconds.

Granville was as good as his word. When it was nearly one o'clock he looked at his watch.

'Got to be off now, Albert. Zoe's expecting us right now.'

And as the car rolled to a stop outside the house dead on time I realised with a dull despair that it had happened to me again. Within me a witch's brew was beginning to bubble, sending choking fumes into my brain. I felt terrible and I knew for sure I would get rapidly worse.

Granville, fresh and debonair as ever, leaped out and led me into the house.

'Zoe, my love!' he warbled, embracing his wife as she came through from the kitchen.

When she disengaged herself she came over to me. She was wearing a flowered apron which made her look if possible even more attractive.

'Hel-*lo!*' she cried and gave me that look which she shared with her husband as though meeting James Herriot was an unbelievable boon. 'Lovely to see you again. I'll get lunch now.' I replied with a foolish grin and she skipped away.

Flopping into an armchair I listened to Granville pouring steadily over at the sideboard. He put a glass in my hand and sat in another chair. Immediately the obese Staffordshire Terrier bounded on to his lap.

'Phoebles, my little pet!' he sang joyfully. 'Daddykins is home again.' And he pointed playfully at the tiny Yorkie who was sitting at his feet, baring her teeth repeatedly in a series of ecstatic smiles. 'And I see you, my little Victoria, I see you!'

By the time I was ushered to the table I was like a man in a dream, moving sluggishly, speaking with slurred deliberation. Granville poised himself over a vast sirloin, stropped his knife briskly, then began to hack away ruthlessly. He was a prodigal server and piled about two pounds of meat on my plate, then he started on the Yorkshire puddings. Instead of a single big one, Zoe had made a large number of little round ones as the farmers' wives often did, delicious golden cups, crisply brown round the sides. Granville heaped about six of these by the side of the meat as I watched stupidly. Then Zoe passed me the gravy boat.

With an effort I took a careful grip on the handle, closed one eye and began to pour. For some reason I felt I had to fill up each of the little puddings with gravy and owlishly directed the stream into one then another till they were all overflowing. Once I missed and spilled a few drops of the fragrant liquid on the tablecloth. I looked up guiltily at Zoe and giggled.

Zoe giggled back, and I had the impression that she felt that though I was a peculiar individual there was no harm in me. I just had this terrible weakness that I was never sober day or night, but I wasn't such a bad fellow at heart.

It usually took me a few days to recover from a visit to Granville and by the following Saturday I was convalescing nicely. It happened that I was in the market-place and saw a large concourse of people crossing the cobbles. At first I thought from the mixture of children

and adults that it must be a school outing but on closer inspection
I realised it was only the Dimmocks and Pounders going shopping.

When they saw me they diverted their course and I was engulfed
by a human wave.

'Look at 'im now, Mister!' 'He's eatin' like a 'oss now!' 'He's goin'
to get fat soon, Mister!' The delighted cries rang around me.

Nellie had Toby on a lead and as I bent over the little animal I
could hardly believe how a few days had altered him. He was still
skinny but the hopeless look had gone; he was perky, ready to play.
It was just a matter of time now.

His little mistress ran her hand again and again over the smooth
brown coat.

'You are proud of your little dog, aren't you, Nellie,' I said, and
the gentle squinting eyes turned on me.

'Yes, I am.' She smiled that smile again. 'Because 'e's mine.'

*

I am so glad I got the Dimmock family down on paper. They were
some of the truest animal lovers I have ever known, and dealing with
the crowd of them at one time as I always did gave a richness and
warmth to every consultation. After seeing them I used to feel strangely alone when meeting a solitary client. And of course I had my
wings singed as always when I came into contact with the immortal
Granville Bennett, but to this day I have never found a better way
of relieving pyloric stenosis than the one he showed me.

21. *Magnus and Company*

There was one marvellous thing about the set-up in Darrowby. I had the inestimable advantage of being a large animal practitioner with a passion for dogs and cats. So that although I spent most of my time in the wide outdoors of Yorkshire there was always the captivating background of the household pets to make a contrast.

I treated some of them every day and it made an extra interest in my life; interest of a different kind, based on sentiment instead of commerce, and because of the way things were it was something I could linger over and enjoy. I suppose with a very intensive small animal practice it would be easy to regard the thing as a huge sausage machine, an endless procession of hairy forms to prod with hypodermic needles. But in Darrowby we got to know them all as individual entities.

Driving through the town I was able to identify my ex-patients without difficulty: Rover Johnson, recovered from his ear canker, coming out of the ironmongers with his mistress; Patch Walker, whose broken leg had healed beautifully, balanced happily on the back of his owner's coal wagon or Spot Briggs, who was a bit of a rake anyway and would soon be tearing himself again on barbed wire, ambling all alone across the market-place cobbles in search of adventure. I got quite a kick out of recalling their ailments and mulling over their characteristics. Because they all had their own personalities and they were manifested in different ways.

One of these was their personal reaction to me and my treatment. Most dogs and cats appeared to bear me not the slightest ill will despite the fact that I usually had to do something disagreeable to them.

But there were exceptions and one of these was Magnus, the Miniature Dachshund from the Drovers' Arms.

He was in my mind now as I leaned across the bar counter.

'A pint of Smiths, please, Danny,' I whispered.

The barman grinned. 'Coming up, Mr Herriot.' He pulled at the lever and the beer hissed gently into the glass and as he passed it over the froth stood high and firm on the surface.

'That ale looks really fit tonight,' I breathed almost inaudibly.

'Fit? It's beautiful!' Danny looked fondly at the brimming glass. 'In fact it's a shame to sell it.'

I laughed, but pianissimo. 'Well it's nice of you to spare me a drop.' I took a deep pull and turned to old Mr Fairburn who was as always sitting at the far corner of the bar with his own fancy flower-painted glass in his hand.

'It's been a grand day, Mr Fairburn,' I murmured *sotto voce*.

The old man put his hand to his ear. 'What's that you say?'

'Nice warm day it's been.' My voice was like a soft breeze sighing over the marshes.

I felt a violent dig at my back. 'What the heck's the matter with you, Jim? Have you got laryngitis?'

I turned and saw the tall bald-headed figure of Dr Allinson, my medical adviser and friend. 'Hello, Harry,' I cried. 'Nice to see you.' Then I put my hand to my mouth.

But it was too late. A furious yapping issued from the manager's office. It was loud and penetrating and it went on and on.

'Damn, I forgot,' I said wearily. 'There goes Magnus again.'

'Magnus? What are you talking about?'

'Well, it's a long story.' I took another sip at my beer as the din continued from the office. It really shattered the peace of the comfortable bar and I could see the regulars fidgeting and looking out into the hallway.

Would that little dog ever forget? It seemed a long time now since Mr Beckwith, the new young manager at the Drovers', had brought Magnus into the surgery. He had looked a little apprehensive.

'You'll have to watch him, Mr Herriot.'

'What do you mean?'

'Well, be careful. He's very vicious.'

I looked at the sleek little form, a mere brown dot on the table. He would probably turn the scale at around six pounds. And I couldn't help laughing.

'Vicious? He's not big enough, surely.'

'Don't you worry!' Mr Beckwith raised a warning finger. 'I took him to the vet in Bradford where I used to manage the White Swan and he sank his teeth into the poor chap's finger.'

'He did?'

'He certainly did! Right down to the bone! By God I've never heard such language but I couldn't blame the man. There was blood all over the place. I had to help him to put a bandage on.'

'Mm, I see.' It was nice to be told before you had been bitten and not after. 'And what was he trying to do to the dog? Must have been something pretty major.'

'It wasn't you know. All I wanted was his nails clipping.'

'Is that all? And why have you brought him today?'

'Same thing.'

'Well honestly, Mr Beckwith,' I said, 'I think we can manage to cut his nails without bloodshed. If he'd been a Bull Mastiff or an Alsatian we might have had a problem, but I think that you and I between us can control a Miniature Dachshund.'

The manager shook his head. 'Don't bring me into it. I'm sorry, but I'd rather not hold him, if you don't mind.'

'Why not?'

'Well, he'd never forgive me. He's a funny little dog.'

I rubbed my chin. 'But if he's as difficult as you say and you can't hold him, what do you expect me to do?'

'I don't know, really . . . maybe you could sort of dope him . . . knock him out?'

'You mean a general anaesthetic? To cut his claws . . . ?'

'It'll be the only way, I'm afraid.' Mr Beckwith stared gloomily at the tiny animal. 'You don't know him.'

It was difficult to believe but it seemed pretty obvious that this canine morsel was the boss in the Beckwith home. In my experience many dogs had occupied this position but none as small as this one. Anyway, I had no more time to waste on this nonsense.

'Look,' I said, 'I'll put a tape muzzle on his nose and I'll have this job done in a couple of minutes.' I reached behind me for the nail clippers and laid them on the table, then I unrolled a length of bandage and tied it in a loop.

'Good boy, Magnus,' I said ingratiatingly as I advanced towards him.

The little dog eyed the bandage unwinkingly until it was almost touching his nose then, with a surprising outburst of ferocity, he made a snarling leap at my hand. I felt the draught on my fingers as a row of sparkling teeth snapped shut half an inch away, but as he turned to have another go my free hand clamped on the scruff of his neck.

'Right, Mr Beckwith,' I said calmly, 'I have him now. Just pass me that bandage again and I won't be long.'

But the young man had had enough. 'Not me!' he gasped. 'I'm off!' He turned the door handle and I heard his feet scurrying along the passage.

Ah well, I thought, it was probably best. With boss dogs my primary move was usually to get the owner out of the way. It was surprising how quickly these tough guys calmed down when they found themselves alone with a no-nonsense stranger who knew how to handle them. I could recite a list who were raving tearaways in their own homes but apologetic tail-waggers once they crossed the surgery threshold. And they were all bigger than Magnus.

Retaining my firm grip on his neck I unwound another foot of bandage and as he fought furiously, mouth gaping, lips retracted like a scaled-down Siberian wolf, I slipped the loop over his nose, tightened it and tied the knot behind his ears. His mouth was now clamped shut and just to make sure, I applied a second bandage so that he was well and truly trussed.

This was when they usually packed in and I looked confidently at the dog for signs of submission. But above the encircling white coils the eyes glared furiously and from within the little frame an enraged growling issued, rising and falling like the distant droning of a thousand bees.

Sometimes a stern word or two had the effect of showing them who was boss.

'Magnus!' I barked at him. 'That's enough! Behave yourself!' I gave his neck a shake to make it clear that I wasn't kidding but the only response was a sidelong squint of pure defiance from the slightly bulging eyes.

I lifted the clippers. 'All right,' I said wearily, 'if you won't have it one way you'll have it the other.' And I tucked him under one arm, seized a paw and began to clip.

He couldn't do a thing about it. He fought and wriggled but I had him as in a vice. And as I methodically trimmed the overgrown nails, wrathful bubbles escaped on either side of the bandage along with his splutterings. If dogs could swear I was getting the biggest cursing in history.

I did my job with particular care, taking pains to keep well away from the sensitive core of the claw so that he felt nothing, but it made no difference. The indignity of being mastered for once in his life was insupportable.

Towards the conclusion of the operation I began to change my tone. I had found in the past that once dominance has been established it is quite easy to work up a friendly relationship, so I started to introduce a wheedling note.

'Good little chap,' I cooed. 'That wasn't so bad, was it?'

I laid down the clippers and stroked his head as a few more resentful bubbles forced their way round the bandage. 'All right, Magnus, we'll take your muzzle off now.' I began to loosen the knot. 'You'll feel a lot better then, won't you?'

So often it happened that when I finally removed the restraint the dog would apparently decide to let bygones be bygones and in some cases would even lick my hand. But not so with Magnus. As the last turn of bandage fell from his nose he made another very creditable attempt to bite me.

'All right, Mr Beckwith,' I called along the passage, 'you can come and get him now.'

My final memory of the visit was of the little dog turning at the top of the surgery steps and giving me a last dirty look before his master led him down the street.

It said very clearly, 'Right, mate, I won't forget you.'

That had been weeks ago but ever since that day the very sound of my voice was enough to set Magnus yapping his disapproval. At first the regulars treated it as a big joke but now they had started to look at me strangely. Maybe they thought I had been cruel to the animal or something. It was all very embarrassing because I didn't want to abandon the Drovers'; the bar was always cosy even on the coldest night and the beer very consistent.

Anyway if I had gone to another pub I would probably have started to do my talking in whispers and people would have looked at me even more strangely then.

How different it was with Mrs Hammond's Irish Setter. This started with an urgent phone call one night when I was in the bath. Helen knocked on the bathroom door and I dried off quickly and threw on my dressing gown. I ran upstairs and as soon as I lifted the receiver an anxious voice burst in my ear.

'Mr Herriot, it's Rock! He's been missing for two days and a man has just brought him back now. He found him in a wood with his foot in a gin trap. He must . . .' I heard a half sob at the end of the line. 'He must have been caught there all this time.'

'Oh, I'm sorry! Is it very bad?'

'Yes it is.' Mrs Hammond was the wife of one of the local bank managers and a capable, sensible woman. There was a pause and I imagined her determinedly gaining control of herself. When she spoke her voice was calm.

'Yes, I'm afraid it looks as though he'll have to have his foot amputated.'

'Oh, I'm terribly sorry to hear that.' But I wasn't really surprised. A limb compressed in one of those barbarous instruments for forty-eight hours would be in a critical state. These traps are now mercifully illegal but in those days they often provided me with the kind of jobs I didn't want and the kind of decisions I hated to make. Did you take a limb from an uncomprehending animal to keep it alive or did you bring down the merciful but final curtain of euthanasia? I was responsible for the fact that there were several three-legged dogs and cats running around Darrowby and though they seemed happy enough and their owners still had the pleasure of their pets, the thing, for me, was clouded with sorrow.

Anyway, I would do what had to be done.

'Bring him straight round, Mrs Hammond,' I said.

Rock was a big dog but he was the lean type of Setter and seemed very light as I lifted him on to the surgery table. As my arms encircled the unresisting body I could feel the rib cage sharply ridged under the skin.

'He's lost a lot of weight,' I said.

His mistress nodded. 'It's a long time to go without food. He ate ravenously when he came in, despite his pain.'

I put a hand beneath the dog's elbow and gently lifted the leg. The vicious teeth of the trap had been clamped on the radius and ulna but what worried me was the grossly swollen state of the foot. It was at least twice its normal size.

'What do you think, Mr Herriot?' Mrs Hammond's hands twisted anxiously at the handbag which every woman seemed to bring to the surgery irrespective of the circumstances.

I stroked the dog's head. Under the light, the rich sheen of the coat glowed red and gold. 'This terrific swelling of the foot. It's partly due to inflammation but also to the fact that the circulation was pretty well cut off for the time he was in the trap. The danger is gangrene – that's when the tissue dies and decomposes.'

'I know,' she replied. 'I did a bit of nursing before I married.'

Carefully I lifted the enormous foot. Rock gazed calmly in front of him as I felt around the metacarpals and phalanges, working my way up to the dreadful wound.

'Well, it's a mess,' I said, 'but there are two good things. First, the leg isn't broken. The trap has gone right down to the bone but there is no fracture. And second and more important, the foot is still warm.'

'That's a good sign?'

'Oh yes. It means there's still some circulation. If the foot had been cold and clammy the thing would have been hopeless. I would have had to amputate.'

'You think you can save his foot, then?'

I held up my hand. 'I don't know, Mrs Hammond. As I say, he

still has some circulation but the question is how much. Some of this tissue is bound to slough off and things could look very nasty in a few days. But I'd like to try.'

I flushed out the wound with a mild antiseptic in warm water and gingerly explored the grisly depths. As I snipped away the pieces of damaged muscle and cut off the shreds and flaps of dead skin the thought was uppermost that it must be extremely unpleasant for the dog; but Rock held his head high and scarcely flinched. Once or twice he turned his head towards me enquiringly as I probed deeply and at times I felt his moist nose softly brushing my face as I bent over the foot, but that was all.

The injury seemed a desecration. There are few more beautiful dogs than an Irish Setter and Rock was a picture: sleek coated and graceful with silky feathers on legs and tail and a noble, gentle-eyed head. As the thought of how he would look without a foot drove into my mind I shook my head and turned quickly to lift the sulphanilamide powder from the trolley behind me. Thank heavens this was now available, one of the new revolutionary drugs, and I packed it deep into the wound with the confidence that it would really do something to keep down the infection. I applied a layer of gauze then a light bandage with a feeling of fatalism. There was nothing else I could do.

Rock was brought in to me every day. And every day he endured the same procedure: the removal of the dressing which was usually adhering to the wound to some degree, then the inevitable trimming of the dying tissues and the rebandaging. Yet, incredibly, he never showed any reluctance to come. Most of my patients came in very slowly and left at top speed, dragging their owners on the end of the leads; in fact some turned tail at the door, slipping their collar, and sped down Trengate with their owners in hot pursuit. Dogs aren't so daft and there is doubtless a dentist's chair type of association about a vet's surgery.

Rock, however, always marched in happily with a gentle waving of his tail. In fact when I went into the waiting room and saw him sitting there he usually offered me his paw. This had always been a characteristic gesture of his but there seemed something uncanny about it when I bent over him and saw the white-swathed limb outstretched towards me.

After a week the outlook was grim. All the time the dead tissue had been sloughing and one night when I removed the dressing Mrs

Hammond gasped and turned away. With her nursing training she had been very helpful, holding the foot this way and that intuitively as I worked, but tonight she didn't want to look.

I couldn't blame her. In places the white bones of the metacarpals could be seen like the fingers of a human hand with only random strands of skin covering them.

'Is it hopeless, do you think?' she whispered, still looking away.

I didn't answer for a moment as I felt my way underneath the foot. 'It does look awful, but do you know, I think we have reached the end of the road and are going to turn the corner soon.'

'How do you mean?'

'Well, all the under surface is sound and warm. His pads are perfectly intact. And do you notice, there's no smell tonight? That's because there is no more dead stuff to cut away. I really think this foot is going to start granulating.'

She stole a look. 'And do you think those . . . bones . . . will be covered over?'

'Yes, I do.' I dusted on the faithful sulphanilamide. 'It won't be exactly the same foot as before but it will do.'

And it turned out just that way. It took a long time but the new healthy tissue worked its way upwards as though determined to prove me right and when, many months later, Rock came into the surgery with a mild attack of conjunctivitis he proffered a courteous paw as was his wont. I accepted the civility and as we shook hands I looked at the upper surface of the foot. It was hairless, smooth and shining, but it was completely healed.

'You'd hardly notice it, would you?' Mrs Hammond said.

'That's right, it's marvellous. Just this little bare patch. And he walked in without a limp.'

Mrs Hammond laughed. 'Oh, he's quite sound on that leg now. And do you know, I really think he's grateful to you – look at him.'

I suppose the animal psychologists would say it was ridiculous even to think that the big dog realised I had done him a bit of good; that lolling-tongued open mouth, warm eyes and outstretched paw didn't mean anything like that.

Maybe they are right, but what I do know and cherish is the certainty that after all the discomforts I had put him through Rock didn't hold a thing against me.

I have to turn back to the other side of the coin to discuss Timmy

Butterworth. He was a wire-haired Fox Terrier who resided in Gimber's Yard, one of the little cobbled alleys off Trengate, and the only time I had to treat him was one lunch time.

I had just got out of the car and was climbing the surgery steps when I saw a little girl running along the street, waving frantically as she approached. I waited for her and when she panted up to me her eyes were wide with fright.

'Ah'm Wendy Butterworth,' she gasped. 'Me mam sent me. Will you come to our dog?'

'What's wrong with him?'

'Me mam says he's et summat!'

'Poison?'

'Ah think so.'

It was less than a hundred yards away, not worth taking the car. I broke into a trot with Wendy by my side and within seconds we were turning into the narrow archway of the 'yard'. Our feet clattered along the tunnel-like passage then we emerged into one of the unlikely scenes which had surprised me so much when I first came to Darrowby: the miniature street with its tiny crowded houses, strips of garden, bow windows looking into each other across a few feet of cobbles. But I had no time to gaze around me today because Mrs Butterworth, stout, red-faced and very flustered was waiting for me.

'He's in 'ere, Mr Herriot!' she cried and threw wide the door of one of the cottages. It opened straight into the living room and I saw my patient sitting on the hearth rug looking somewhat thoughtful.

'What's happened, then?' I asked.

The lady clasped and unclasped her hands. 'I saw a big rat run down across t'yard yesterday and I got some poison to put down for 'im.' She gulped agitatedly. 'I mixed it in a saucer full o' porridge then somebody came to t'door and when ah came back, Timmy was just finishin' it off!'

The terrier's thoughtful expression had deepened and he ran his tongue slowly round his lips with the obvious reflection that that was the strangest porridge he had ever tasted.

I turned to Mrs Butterworth. 'Have you got the poison tin there?'

'Yes, here it is.' With a violently trembling hand she passed it to me.

I read the label. It was a well-known name and the very look of it sounded a knell in my mind recalling the many dead and dying animals with which it was associated. Its active ingredient was zinc phosphide and even today with our modern drugs we are usually helpless once a dog has absorbed it.

I thumped the tin down on the table. 'We've got to make him vomit immediately! I don't want to waste time going back to the surgery – have you got any washing soda? If I push a few crystals down it'll do the trick.'

'Oh dear!' Mrs Butterworth bit her lip. 'We 'aven't such a thing in the house . . . is there anything else we could . . .'

'Wait a minute!' I looked across the table, past the piece of cold mutton, the tureen of potatoes and a jar of pickles. 'Is there any mustard in that pot?'

'Aye, it's full.'

Quickly I grabbed the pot, ran to the tap and diluted the mustard to the consistency of milk.

'Come on!' I shouted. 'Let's have him outside.'

I seized the astonished Timmy, whisked him from the rug, shot through the door and dumped him on the cobbles. Holding his body clamped tightly between my knees and his jaws close together with my left hand I poured the liquid mustard into the side of his mouth whence it trickled down to the back of his throat. There was nothing he could do about it, he had swallowed the disgusting stuff, and when about a tablespoon had gone down I released him.

After a single affronted glare at me the terrier began to retch, then to lurch across the smooth stones. Within seconds he had deposited his stolen meal in a quiet corner.

'Do you think that's the lot?' I asked.

'That's it,' Mrs Butterworth replied firmly. 'I'll fetch a brush and shovel.'

Timmy, his short tail tucked down, slunk back into the house and I watched him as he took up his favourite position on the hearthrug. He coughed, snorted, pawed at his mouth, but he just couldn't rid himself of that dreadful taste; and increasingly it was obvious that he had me firmly tagged as the cause of all the trouble. As I left he flashed me a glance which said quite plainly, 'You rotten swine!'

There was something in that look which reminded me of Magnus from the Drovers', but the first sign that Timmy, unlike Magnus, wasn't going to be satisfied with vocal disapproval came within a few days. I was strolling meditatively down Trengate when a white missile issued from Gimber's Yard, nipped me on the ankle and disappeared as silently as it had come. I caught only a glimpse of the little form speeding on its short legs down the passage.

I laughed. Fancy his remembering! But it happened again and again and I realised that the little dog was indeed lying in wait for me. He never actually sank his teeth into me – it was a gesture more than anything – but it seemed to satisfy him to see me jump as he snatched briefly at my calf or trouser leg. I was a sitting bird because I was usually deep in thought as I walked down the street.

And when I thought about it, I couldn't blame Timmy. Looking at it from his point of view, he had been sitting by his fireside digesting an unusual meal and minding his own business when a total stranger had pounced on him, hustled him from the comfort of his rug and poured mustard into him. It was outrageous and he just wasn't prepared to let the matter rest there.

For my part there was a certain satisfaction in being the object of a vendetta waged by an animal who would have been dead without my services. And unpleasantly dead, because the victims of phosphorus poisoning had to endure long days and sometimes weeks of jaundice, misery and creeping debility before the inevitable end.

So I suffered the attacks with good grace. But when I remembered I crossed to the other side of the street to avoid the hazard of Gimber's Yard; and from there I could often see the little white dog peeping round the corner waiting for the moment when he would make me pay for that indignity.

Timmy, I knew, was one who would never forget.

*

These stories illustrate the different reactions one receives from different dogs, a subject which has always fascinated me. It is interesting that the sulphanilamide used on Rock's injury is still a useful wound dressing but would probably be replaced nowadays by an antibiotic powder. Thank heaven we no longer see that zinc phosphide rat poison which Timmy Butterworth swallowed. Modern rodent pesticides such as warfarin have to be used with care, but their effects are not so drastic and we do not have to witness the slow deaths of those horribly jaundiced dogs. I used to feel so helpless in those cases.

22. *Last Visit*

I suppose there was a wry humour in the fact that my call-up papers
arrived on my birthday, but I didn't see the joke at the time.

The event is preserved in my memory in a picture which is as clear
to me today as when I walked into our 'dining room' that morning.
Helen perched away up on her high stool at the end of the table,
very still, eyes downcast. By the side of my plate my birthday present,
a tin of Dobie's Blue Square tobacco, and next to it a long envelope.
I didn't have to ask what it contained.

I had been expecting it for some time but it still gave me a jolt to find I had only a week before presenting myself at Lord's Cricket Ground, St John's Wood, London. And that week went by at frightening speed as I made my final plans, tidying up the loose ends in the practice, getting my Ministry of Agriculture forms sent off, arranging for our few possessions to be taken to Helen's old home where she would stay while I was away.

Having decided that I would finish work at teatime on Friday, I had a call from old Arnold Summergill at about three o'clock that afternoon; and I knew that would be my very last job because it was always an expedition rather than a visit to his smallholding which clung to a bracken-strewn slope in the depths of the hills. I didn't speak directly to Arnold but to Miss Thompson, the postmistress in Hainby village.

'Mr Summergill wants you to come and see his dog,' she said over the phone.

'What's the trouble?' I asked.

I heard a muttered consultation at the far end.

'He says its leg's gone funny.'

'Funny? What d'you mean, funny?'

Again the quick babble of voices. 'He says it's kind of stickin' out.'

'All right,' I said. 'I'll be along very soon.'

It was no good asking for the dog to be brought in. Arnold had never owned a car. Nor had he ever spoken on a telephone – all our conversations had been carried on through the medium of Miss Thompson. Arnold would mount his rusty bicycle, pedal to Hainby and tell his troubles to the postmistress. And the symptoms, they were typically vague and I didn't suppose there would be anything either 'funny' or 'sticking out' about that leg when I saw it.

Anyway, I thought, as I drove out of Darrowby, I wouldn't mind having a last look at Benjamin. It was a fanciful name for a small farmer's dog and I never really found out how he had acquired it. But after all he was an unlikely breed for such a setting, a massive Old English Sheepdog who would have looked more in place decorating the lawns of a stately home than following his master round Arnold's stony pastures. He was a classical example of the walking hearthrug and it took a second look to decide which end of him was which. But when you did manage to locate his head you found two of the most benevolent eyes imaginable glinting through the thick fringe of hair.

Last Visit

Benjamin was in fact too friendly at times, especially in winter when he had been strolling in the farmyard mud and showed his delight at my arrival by planting his huge feet on my chest. He did the same thing to my car, too, usually just after I had washed it, smearing clay lavishly over windows and bodywork while exchanging pleasantries with Sam inside. When Benjamin made a mess of anything he did it right.

But I had to interrupt my musings when I reached the last stage of my journey. And as I hung on to the kicking, jerking wheel and listened to the creaking and groaning of springs and shock absorbers, the thought forced its way into my mind as it always did around here that it cost us money to come to Mr Summergill's farm. There could be no profit from the visit because this vicious track must knock at least five pounds off the value of the car on every trip. Since Arnold did not have a car himself he saw no reason why he should interfere with the primeval state of his road.

It was simply a six-foot strip of earth and rock and it wound and twisted for an awful long way. The trouble was that to get to the farm you had to descend into a deep valley before climbing through a wood towards the house. I think going down was worse because the vehicle hovered agonisingly on the top of each ridge before plunging into the yawning ruts beyond; and each time, listening to the unyielding stone grating on sump and exhaust, I tried to stop myself working out the damage in pounds shillings and pence.

And when at last, mouth gaping, eyes popping, tyres sending the sharp pebbles flying, I ground my way upwards in bottom gear over the last few yards leading to the house I was surprised to see Arnold waiting for me there alone. It was unusual to see him without Benjamin.

He must have read my questioning look because he jerked his thumb over his shoulder.

'He's in t'house,' he grunted, and his eyes were anxious.

I got out of the car and looked at him for a moment as he stood there in a typical attitude, wide shoulders back, head high. I have called him 'old' and indeed he was over seventy, but the features beneath the woollen tammy which he always wore pulled down over his ears were clean and regular and the tall figure lean and straight. He was a fine looking man and must have been handsome in his youth, yet he had never married. I often felt there was a story there but he seemed content to live here alone, a 'bit of a 'ermit' as they said in the village. Alone, that is, except for Benjamin.

As I followed him into the kitchen he casually shooed out a couple of hens who had been perching on a dusty dresser. Then I saw Benjamin and pulled up with a jerk.

The big dog was sitting quite motionless by the side of the table and this time the eyes behind the overhanging hair were big and liquid with fright. He appeared to be too terrified to move and when I saw his left fore leg I couldn't blame him. Arnold had been right after all; it was indeed sticking out with a vengeance, at an angle which made my heart give a quick double thud; a complete lateral dislocation of the elbow, the radius projecting away out from the humerus at an almost impossible obliquity.

I swallowed carefully. 'When did this happen, Mr Summergill?'

'Just an hour since.' He tugged worriedly at his strange headgear. 'I was changing the cows into another field and awd Benjamin likes to have a nip at their heels when he's behind 'em. Well he did it once ower often and one of them lashed out and got 'im on the leg.'

'I see.' My mind was racing. This thing was grotesque. I had never seen anything like it, in fact thirty years later I still haven't seen anything like it. How on earth was I going to reduce the thing away up here in the hills? By the look of it I would need general anaesthesia and a skilled assistant.

'Poor old lad,' I said, resting my hand on the shaggy head as I tried to think. 'What are we going to do with you?'

The tail whisked along the flags in reply and the mouth opened in a nervous panting, giving a glimpse of flawlessly white teeth.

Arnold cleared his throat. 'Can you put 'im right?'

Well it was a good question. An airy answer might give the wrong impression yet I didn't want to worry him with my doubts. It would be a mammoth task to get the enormous dog down to Darrowby; he nearly filled the kitchen, never mind my little car. And with that leg sticking out and with Sam already in residence. And would I be able to get the joint back in place when I got him there? And even if I did manage it I would still have to bring him all the way back up here. It would just about take care of the rest of the day.

Gently I passed my fingers over the dislocated joint and searched my memory for details of the anatomy of the elbow. For the leg to be in this position the processus anconeus must have been completely disengaged from the supracondyloid fossa where it normally lay; and to get it back the joint would have to be flexed until the anconeus was clear of the epicondyles.

'Now let's see,' I murmured to myself. 'If I had this dog anaesthetised and on the table I would have to get hold of him like this.' I grasped the leg just above the elbow and began to move the radius slowly upwards. Benjamin gave me a quick glance then turned his head away, a gesture typical of good-natured dogs, conveying the message that he was going to put up with whatever I thought it necessary to do.

I flexed the joint still further until I was sure the anconeus was clear, then carefully rotated the radius and ulna inwards.

'Yes . . . yes . . .' I muttered again. 'This must be about the right position . . .' But my soliloquy was interrupted by a sudden movement of the bones under my hand; a springing, flicking sensation.

I looked incredulously at the leg. It was perfectly straight.

Benjamin, too, seemed unable to take it in right away, because he peered cautiously round through his shaggy curtain before lowering his nose and sniffing around the elbow. Then he seemed to realise all was well and ambled over to his master.

And he was perfectly sound. Not a trace of a limp.

A slow smile spread over Arnold's face. 'You've mended him, then.'

'Looks like it, Mr Summergill.' I tried to keep my voice casual, but I felt like cheering or bursting into hysterical laughter. I had only been making an examination, feeling things out a little, and the joint had popped back into place. A glorious accident.

'Aye well, that's grand,' the farmer said. 'Isn't it, awd lad?' He bent and tickled Benjamin's ear.

I could have been disappointed by this laconic reception of my performance, but I realised it was a compliment to me that he wasn't surprised that I, James Herriot, his vet, should effortlessly produce a miracle when it was required.

A theatre-full of cheering students would have rounded off the incident or it would be nice to do this kind of thing to some millionaire's animal in a crowded drawing room, but it never happened that way. I looked around the kitchen, at the cluttered table, the pile of unwashed crockery in the sink, a couple of Arnold's ragged shirts drying before the fire, and I smiled to myself. This was the sort of setting in which I usually pulled off my spectacular cures. The only spectators here, apart from Arnold, were the two hens who had made their way back on to the dresser and they didn't seem particularly impressed.

'Well, I'll be getting back down the hill,' I said. And Arnold walked with me across the yard to the car.

'I hear you're off to join up,' he said as I put my hand on the door.

'Yes, I'm away tomorrow, Mr Summergill.'

'Tomorrow, eh?' he raised his eyebrows.

'Yes, to London. Ever been there?'

'Nay, nay, be damned!' The woollen cap quivered as he shook his head. 'That'd be no good to me.'

I laughed. 'Why do you say that?'

'Well now, I'll tell ye.' He scratched his chin ruminatively. 'Ah nobbut went once to Brawton and that was enough. Ah couldn't walk on t'street!'

'Couldn't walk?'

'Nay. There were that many people about. I 'ad to take big steps and little 'uns, then big steps and little 'uns again. Couldn't get goin'.'

I had often seen Arnold stalking over his fields with the long, even stride of the hillman with nothing in his way and I knew exactly what he meant. 'Big steps and little 'uns.' That put it perfectly.

I started the engine and waved and as I moved away the old man raised a hand.

'Tek care, lad,' he murmured.

I spotted Benjamin's nose just peeping round the kitchen door. Any other time he would have been out with his master to see me off the premises but it had been a strange day for him culminating with my descending on him and mauling his leg about. He wasn't taking any more chances.

I drove gingerly down through the wood and before starting up the track on the other side I stopped the car and got out with Sam leaping eagerly after me.

This was a little lost valley in the hills, a green cleft cut off from the wild country above. One of the bonuses in a country vet's life is that he sees these hidden places. Apart from old Arnold nobody ever came down here, not even the postman who left the infrequent mail in a box at the top of the track, and nobody saw the blazing scarlets and golds of the autumn trees nor heard the busy clucking and murmuring of the beck among its clean-washed stones.

Last Visit

I walked along the water's edge watching the little fish darting and flitting in the cool depths. In the spring these banks were bright with primroses and in May a great sea of bluebells flowed among the trees but today, though the sky was an untroubled blue, the clean air was touched with the sweetness of the dying year.

I climbed a little way up the hillside and sat down among the bracken now fast turning to bronze. Sam, as was his way, flopped by my side and I ran a hand over the silky hair of his ears. The far side of the valley rose steeply to where, above the gleaming ridge of limestone cliffs, I could just see the sunlit rim of the moor.

I looked back to where the farm chimney sent a thin tendril of smoke from behind the brow of the hill, and it seemed that the episode with Benjamin, my last job in veterinary practice before I left Darrowby, was a fitting epilogue. A little triumph, intensely satisfying but by no means world shaking; like all the other little triumphs and disasters which make up a veterinary surgeon's life but go unnoticed by the world.

Last night, after Helen had packed my bag, I had pushed Black's *Veterinary Dictionary* in among the shirts and socks. It was a bulky volume but I had been gripped momentarily by a fear that I might forget the things I had learned, and conceived on an impulse the scheme of reading a page or two each day to keep my memory fresh. And here among the bracken the thought came back to me: that it was the greatest good fortune not only to be fascinated by animals but to know about them. Suddenly the knowing became a precious thing.

I went back and opened the car door. Sam jumped on to the seat and before I got in I looked away down in the other direction from the house to the valley's mouth, where the hills parted to give a glimpse of the plain below. And the endless wash of pale tints, the gold of the stubble, the dark smudges of wood, the mottled greens of the pasture land were like a perfect water-colour. I found myself staring greedily as if for the first time at the scene which had so often lifted my heart, the great wide clean-blown face of Yorkshire.

I would come back to it all, I thought as I drove away; back to my work . . . how was it that book had described it? . . . my hard, honest and fine profession.

*

I keep telling my young assistants that they must not become frustrated when receiving no credit for doing a brilliant job, because they will often get disproportionate praise for something easy. It is a strange thing, but I have reduced several dislocated elbows during my career and in every case there was only one unimpressed person to see it. A pity, because it does look so good. And yet, this single-handed piece of work seemed to epitomise my life before entering the RAF. It was a very fitting last visit.

23. *Cedric*

The voice at the other end of the phone was oddly hesitant.

'Mr Herriot . . . I should be grateful if you would come and see my dog.' It was a woman, obviously upper class.

'Certainly. What's the trouble?'

'Well . . . he . . . er . . . he seems to suffer from . . . a certain amount of flatus.'

'I beg your pardon?'

There was a long pause. 'He has . . . excessive flatus.'

'In what way, exactly?'

'Well . . . I suppose you'd describe it as . . . windiness.' The voice had begun to tremble.

I thought I could see a gleam of light. 'You mean his stomach . . . ?'

'No, not his stomach. He passes . . . er . . . a considerable quantity of . . . wind from his . . . his . . .' A note of desperation had crept in.

'Ah, yes!' All became suddenly clear. 'I quite understand. But that doesn't sound very serious. Is he ill?'

'No, he's very fit in other ways.'

'Well then, do you think it's necessary for me to see him?'

'Oh yes, indeed, Mr Herriot. I wish you would come as soon as possible. It has become quite . . . quite a problem.'

'All right,' I said. 'I'll look in this morning. Can I have your name and address, please?'

'It's Mrs Rumney, The Laurels.'

The Laurels was a very nice house on the edge of the town standing back from the road in a large garden. Mrs Rumney herself let me in and I felt a shock of surprise at my first sight of her. It wasn't just that she was strikingly beautiful; there was an unworldly air about her. She would be around forty but had the appearance of a heroine in a Victorian novel – tall, willowy, ethereal. And I could understand immediately her hesitation on the phone. Everything about her suggested fastidiousness and delicacy.

'Cedric is in the kitchen,' she said. 'I'll take you through.'

I had another surprise when I saw Cedric. An enormous Boxer hurled himself on me in delight, clawing at my chest with the biggest, horniest feet I had seen for a long time. I tried to fight him off but he kept at me, panting ecstatically into my face and wagging his entire rear end.

'Sit down, boy!' the lady said sharply, then, as Cedric took absolutely no notice, she turned to me nervously. 'He's so friendly.'

'Yes,' I said breathlessly, 'I can see that.' I finally managed to push the huge animal away and backed into a corner for safety. 'How often does this . . . excessive flatus occur?'

As if in reply an almost palpable sulphurous wave arose from the dog and eddied around me. It appeared that the excitement of seeing me had activated Cedric's weakness. I was up against the wall and unable to obey my first instinct to run for cover so I held my hand over my face for a few moments before speaking.

'Is that what you meant?'

Mrs Rumney waved a lace handkerchief under her nose and the faintest flush crept into the pallor of her cheeks.

'Yes,' she replied almost inaudibly 'Yes . . . that is it.'

'Oh well,' I said briskly, 'there's nothing to worry about. Let's go into the other room and we'll have a word about his diet and a few other things.'

It turned out that Cedric was getting rather a lot of meat and I drew up a little chart cutting down the protein and adding extra carbohydrates. I prescribed a kaolin antacid mixture to be given night and morning and left the house in a confident frame of mind.

It was one of those trivial things and I had entirely forgotten it when Mrs Rumney phoned again.

'I'm afraid Cedric is no better, Mr Herriot.'

'Oh I'm sorry to hear that. He's still . . . er . . . still . . . yes . . . yes . . .' I spent a few moments in thought. 'I tell you what – I don't think I can do any more by seeing him at the moment, but I think you should cut out his meat completely for a week or two. Keep him on biscuits and brown bread rusked in the oven. Try him with that and vegetables and I'll give you some powder to mix in his food. Perhaps you'd call round for it.'

The powder was a pretty strong absorbent mixture and I felt sure it would do the trick, but a week later Mrs Rumney was on the phone again.

'There's absolutely no improvement, Mr Herriot.' The tremble was back in her voice. 'I . . . I do wish you'd come and see him again.'

I couldn't see much point in viewing this perfectly healthy animal again but I promised to call. I had a busy day and it was after six o'clock before I got round to The Laurels. There were several cars in the drive and when I went into the house I saw that Mrs Rumney had a few people in for drinks; people like herself – upper class and of obvious refinement. In fact I felt rather a lout in my working clothes among the elegant gathering.

Mrs Rumney was about to lead me through to the kitchen when the door burst open and Cedric bounded delightedly into the midst of the company. Within seconds an aesthetic-looking gentleman was frantically beating off the attack as the great feet ripped down his waistcoat. He got away at the cost of a couple of buttons and the Boxer turned his attention to one of the ladies. She was in imminent danger of losing her dress when I pulled the dog off her.

Pandemonium broke out in the graceful room. The hostess's plaintive appeals rang out above the cries of alarm as the big dog charged around, but very soon I realised that a more insidious element had crept into the situation. The atmosphere in the room became rapidly charged with an unmistakable effluvium and it was clear that Cedric's unfortunate malady had reasserted itself.

I did my best to shepherd the animal out of the room but he didn't seem to know the meaning of obedience and I chased him in vain. And as the embarrassing minutes ticked away I began to realise for the first time the enormity of the problem which confronted Mrs Rumney. Most dogs break wind occasionally but Cedric was different: he did it all the time. And while his silent emanations were perhaps more treacherous, there was no doubt that the audible ones were painfully distresssing in company like this.

Cedric made it worse, because at each rasping expulsion he would look round enquiringly at his back end, then gambol about the room as though the fugitive zephyr was clearly visible to him and he was determined to corner it.

It seemed a year before I got him out of there. Mrs Rumney held the door wide as I finally managed to steer him towards it but the big dog wasn't finished yet. On his way out he cocked a leg swiftly and directed a powerful jet against an immaculate trouser leg.

After that night I threw myself into the struggle on Mrs Rumney's behalf. I felt she desperately needed my help, and I made frequent visits and tried innumerable remedies. I consulted my colleague Siegfried on the problem and he suggested a diet of charcoal biscuits. Cedric ate them in vast quantities and with evident enjoyment but they, like everything else, made not the slightest difference to his condition.

And all the time I pondered upon the enigma of Mrs Rumney. She had lived in Darrowby for several years but the townsfolk knew little about her. It was a matter of debate whether she was a widow or separated from her husband. But I was not interested in such things; the biggest mystery to me was how she ever got involved with a dog like Cedric.

It was difficult to think of any animal less suited to her personality. Apart from his regrettable affliction he was in every way the opposite to herself; a great thick-headed rumbustious extrovert totally out of place in her gracious ménage. I never did find out how they came together but on my visits I found that Cedric had one admirer at least.

He was Con Fenton, a retired farm worker who did a bit of jobbing gardening and spent an average of three days a week at The Laurels. The Boxer romped down the drive after me as I was leaving and the old man looked at him with undisguised admiration.

'By gaw,' he said, 'he's a fine dog, is that!'

'Yes, he is, Con, he's a good chap, really.' And I meant it. You couldn't help liking Cedric when you got to know him. He was utterly amiable and without vice and he gave off a constant aura not merely of noxious vapours but of bonhomie. When he tore off people's buttons or sprinkled their trousers he did it in a spirit of the purest amity.

'Just look at them limbs!' breathed Con, staring rapturously at the dog's muscular thighs. 'By heck, 'e can jump ower that gate as if it weren't there. He's what ah call a dog!'

As he spoke it struck me that Cedric would be likely to appeal to him because he was very like the Boxer himself: not over-burdened with brains, built like an ox with powerful shoulders and a big constantly-grinning face – they were two of a kind.

'Aye, ah allus likes it when t'missus lets him out in t'garden,' Con went on. He always spoke in a peculiar snuffling manner. 'He's grand company.'

I looked at him narrowly. No, he wouldn't be likely to notice Cedric's complaint since he always saw him out of doors.

On my way back to the surgery I brooded on the fact that I was achieving absolutely nothing with my treatment. And though it seemed ridiculous to worry about a case like this, there was no doubt the thing had begun to prey on my mind. In fact I began to transmit my anxieties to Siegfried. As I got out of the car he was coming down the steps of Skeldale House and he put a hand on my arm.

'You've been to The Laurels, James? Tell me,' he enquired solicitously, 'how is your farting Boxer today?'

'Still at it, I'm afraid,' I replied, and my colleague shook his head in commiseration.

We were both defeated. Maybe if chlorophyll tablets had been available in those days they might have helped, but as it was I had tried everything. It seemed certain that nothing would alter the situation. And it wouldn't have been so bad if the owner had been anybody else but Mrs Rumney; I found that even discussing the thing with her had become almost unbearable.

Siegfried's student brother Tristan didn't help, either. When seeing practice he was very selective in the cases he wished to observe, but he was immediately attracted to Cedric's symptoms and insisted on coming with me on one occasion. I never took him again because as we went in the big dog bounded from his mistress's side and produced a particularly sonorous blast as if in greeting.

Tristan immediately threw out a hand in a dramatic gesture and declaimed: 'Speak on, sweet lips that never told a lie!' That was his only visit. I had enough trouble without that.

I didn't know it at the time but a greater blow awaited me. A few days later Mrs Rumney was on the phone again.

'Mr Herriot, a friend of mine has such a sweet little Boxer bitch. She wants to bring her along to be mated with Cedric.'

'Eh?'

'She wants to mate her bitch with my dog.'

'With Cedric . . . ?' I clutched at the edge of the desk. It couldn't be true! 'And . . . and are you agreeable?'

'Yes, of course.'

I shook my head to dispel the feeling of unreality. I found it incomprehensible that anyone should want to reproduce Cedric, and as I gaped into the receiver a frightening vision floated before me of eight little Cedrics all with his complaint. But of course such a thing wasn't hereditary. I took a grip of myself and cleared my throat.

'Very well, then, Mrs Rumney, you'd better go ahead.'

There was a pause. 'But Mr Herriot, I want you to supervise the mating.'

'Oh really, I don't think that's necessary.' I dug my nails into my palm. 'I think you'll be all right without me.'

'Oh but I would be much happier if you were there. Please come,' she said appealingly.

Instead of emitting a long-drawn groan I took a deep breath.

'Right,' I said. 'I'll be along in the morning.'

All that evening I was obsessed by a feeling of dread. Another acutely embarrassing session was in store with this exquisite woman. Why was it I always had to share things like this with her? And I really feared the worst. Even the daftest dog, when confronted with a bitch in heat, knows instinctively how to proceed, but with a really ivory-skulled animal like Cedric I wondered . . .

And next morning all my fears were realised. The bitch, Trudy, was a trim little creature and showed every sign of willingness to cooperate. Cedric, on the other hand, though obviously delighted to meet her, gave no hint of doing his part. After sniffing her over, he

danced around her a few times, goofy-faced, tongue lolling. Then he
had a roll on the lawn before charging at her and coming to a full
stop, big feet outsplayed, head down, ready to play. I sighed. It was
as I thought. The big chump didn't know what to do.

This pantomime went on for some time and, inevitably, the
emotional strain brought on a resurgence of his symptoms. Frequently
he paused to inspect his tail as though he had never heard noises
like that before.

He varied his dancing routine with occasional headlong gallops
round the lawn and it was after he had done about ten successive
laps that he seemed to decide he ought to do something about the
bitch. I held my breath as he approached her but unfortunately he
chose the wrong end to commence operations. Trudy had put up
with his nonsense with great patience but when she found him busily
working away in the region of her left ear it was too much. With a
shrill yelp she nipped him in the hind leg and he shot away in alarm.

After that whenever he came near she warned him off with bared
teeth. Clearly she was disenchanted with her bridegroom and I
couldn't blame her.

'I think she's had enough, Mrs Rumney,' I said.

I certainly had had enough and so had the poor lady, judging by
her slight breathlessness, flushed cheeks and waving handkerchief.

'Yes . . . yes . . . I suppose you're right,' she replied.

So Trudy was taken home and that was the end of Cedric's career
as a stud dog.

This last episode decided me. I had to have a talk with Mrs
Rumney and a few days later I called in at The Laurels.

'Maybe you'll think it's none of my business,' I said, 'but I honestly
don't think Cedric is the dog for you. In fact he's so wrong for you
that he is upsetting your life.'

Mrs Rumney's eyes widened. 'Well . . . he is a problem in some
ways . . . but what do you suggest?'

'I think you should get another dog in his place. Maybe a poodle
or a corgi – something smaller, something you could control.'

'But Mr Herriot, I couldn't possibly have Cedric put down.' Her
eyes filled quickly with tears. 'I really am fond of him despite his . . .
despite everything.'

'No, no, of course not!' I said. 'I like him too. He has no malice
in him. But I think I have a good idea. Why not let Con Fenton
have him?'

'Con . . . ?'

'Yes, he admires Cedric tremendously and the big fellow would have a good life with the old man. He has a couple of fields behind his cottage and keeps a few beasts. Cedric could run to his heart's content out there and Con would be able to bring him along when he does the garden. You'd still see him three times a week.'

Mrs Rumney looked at me in silence for a few moments and I saw in her face the dawning of relief and hope.

'You know, Mr Herriot, I think that could work very well. But are you sure Con would take him?'

'I'd like to bet on it. An old bachelor like him must be lonely. There's only one thing worries me. Normally they only meet outside and I wonder how it would be when they were indoors and Cedric started to . . . when the old trouble . . .'

'Oh, I think that would be all right,' Mrs Rumney broke in quickly. 'When I go on holiday Con always takes him for a week or two and he has never mentioned any . . . anything unusual . . . in that way.'

I got up to go. 'Well, that's fine. I should put it to the old man right away.'

Mrs Rumney rang within a few days. Con had jumped at the chance of taking on Cedric and the pair had apparently settled in happily together. She had also taken my advice and acquired a poodle puppy.

I didn't see the new dog till it was nearly six months old and its mistress asked me to call to treat it for a slight attack of eczema. As I sat in the graceful room looking at Mrs Rumney, cool, poised, tranquil, with the little white creature resting on her knee, I couldn't help feeling how right and fitting the whole scene was. The lush carpet, the trailing velvet curtains, the fragile tables with their load of expensive china and framed miniatures. It was no place for Cedric.

Con Fenton's cottage was less than half a mile away and on my way back to the surgery, on an impulse, I pulled up at the door. The old man answered my knock and his big face split into a delighted grin when he saw me.

'Come in, young man!' he cried in his strange snuffly voice. 'I'm right glad to see tha!'

I had hardly stepped into the tiny living room when a hairy form hurled itself upon me. Cedric hadn't changed a bit and I had to battle my way to the broken armchair by the fireside. Con settled down opposite and when the Boxer leaped to lick his face he clumped him companionably on the head with his fist.

'Siddown, ye great daft bugger,' he murmured with affection. Cedric sank happily on to the tattered hearthrug at his feet and gazed up adoringly at his new master.

'Well, Mr Herriot,' Con went on as he cut up some villainous-looking plug tobacco and began to stuff it into his pipe. 'I'm right grateful to ye for gettin' me this grand dog. By gaw, he's a topper and ah wouldn't sell 'im for any money. No man could ask for a better friend.'

'Well that's great, Con,' I said. 'And I can see that the big chap is really happy here.'

The old man ignited his pipe and a cloud of acrid smoke rose to the low, blackened beams. 'Aye, he's 'ardly ever inside. A gurt strong dog like 'im wants to work 'is energy off, like.'

But just at that moment Cedric was obviously working something else off because the familiar pungency rose from him even above the billowings from the pipe. Con seemed oblivious of it but in the enclosed space I found it overpowering.

'Ah well,' I gasped. 'I just looked in for a moment to see how you were getting on together. I must be on my way.' I rose hurriedly and stumbled towards the door but the redolence followed me in a wave. As I passed the table with the remains of the old man's meal I saw what seemed to be the only form of ornament in the cottage, a cracked vase holding a magnificent bouquet of carnations. It was a way of escape and I buried my nose in their fragrance.

Con watched me approvingly. 'Aye, they're lovely flowers, aren't they? T'missus at Laurels lets me bring 'ome what I want and I reckon them carnations is me favourite.'

'Yes, they're a credit to you.' I still kept my nose among the blooms.

'There's only one thing,' the old man said pensively. 'Ah don't get t'full benefit of 'em.'

'How's that, Con?'

He pulled at his pipe a couple of times. 'Well, you can hear ah speak a bit funny, like?'

'No . . . no . . . not really.'

'Oh aye, ye know ah do. I've been like it since I were a lad. I 'ad a operation for adenoids and summat went wrong.'

'Oh, I'm sorry to hear that,' I said.

'Well, it's nowt serious, but it's left me lackin' in one way.'

'You mean . . . ?' A light was beginning to dawn in my mind, an elucidation of how man and dog had found each other, of why their relationship was so perfect, of the certainty of their happy future together. It seemed like fate.

'Aye,' the old man went on sadly. 'I 'ave no sense of smell.'

*

The acute embarrassment I felt about Cedric's unfortunate weakness was due mainly to the fact that Mrs Rumney was so exquisite and unworldly. It was agony to try to discuss such an earthy matter with her. But there is another thing. Forty years ago this subject was considered unmentionable in polite society. It is very different now, and this fact was brought home to me forcibly when a charming old lady came up to me in a shop in Harrogate and put her hand on my arm. 'Oh, Mr Herriot,' she said, 'I did so love your story about the farting Boxer.'

24. *Wes*

It was Wesley Binks who put the firework through the surgery letter-box.

It was what they used to call a 'banger' and it exploded at my feet as I hurried along the dark passage in answer to the door bell's ring, making me leap into the air in terror.

I threw open the front door and looked into the street. It was empty, but at the corner where the lamplight was reflected in Robson's shop window I had a brief impression of a fleeing form and a faint echo of laughter. I couldn't do anything about it but I knew Wes was out there somewhere.

Wearily I trailed back into the house. Why did this lad persecute me? What could a ten-year-old boy possibly have against me? I had never done him any harm, yet I seemed to be the object of a deliberate campaign.

Or maybe it wasn't personal. It could be that he felt I represented authority or the establishment in some way, or perhaps I was just convenient.

I was certainly the ideal subject for his little tricks of ringing the door bell and running away, because I dared not ignore the summons in case it might be a client, and also the consulting and operating rooms were such a long way from the front of the house. Sometimes I was dragged down from our bed-sitter under the tiles. Every trip to the door was an expedition and it was acutely exasperating to arrive there and see only a little figure in the distance dancing about and grimacing at me.

He varied this routine by pushing rubbish through the letter-box, pulling the flowers from the tiny strip of garden we tried to cultivate between the flagstones, and chalking rude messages on my car.

I knew I wasn't the only victim because I had heard complaints from others: the fruiterer who saw his apples disappear from the box in front of the shop, the grocer who unwillingly supplied him with free biscuits.

He was the town naughty boy all right, and it was incongruous that he should have been named Wesley. There was not the slightest sign in his behaviour of any strict Methodist upbringing. In fact I knew nothing of his family life – only that he came from the poorest part of the town, a row of 'yards' containing tumbledown cottages, some of them evacuated because of their condition.

I often saw him wandering about in the fields and lanes or fishing in quiet reaches of the river when he should have been in school. When he spotted me on these occasions he invariably called out some mocking remark and if he happened to be with some of his cronies they all joined in the laughter at my expense. It was annoying but I used to tell myself that there was nothing personal in it. I was an adult and that was enough to make me a target.

Wes's greatest triumph was undoubtedly the time he removed the grating from the coal cellar outside Skeldale House. It was on the left of the front steps and underneath it was a steep ramp down which the coalmen tipped their bags.

I don't know whether it was inspired intuition but he pinched the grating on the day of the Darrowby Gala. The festivities started with a parade through the town led by the Houlton Silver Band, and as I looked down from the windows of our bed-sitter I could see them all gathering in the street below.

'Look, Helen,' I said, 'they must be starting the march from Trengate. Everybody I know seems to be down there.'

Helen leaned over my shoulder and gazed at the long lines of boy scouts, girl guides, ex-servicemen, with half the population of the town packed on the pavements, watching. 'Yes, it's quite a sight, isn't it? Let's go down and see them move off.'

We trotted down the long flights of stairs and I followed her out through the front door. And as I appeared in the entrance I was suddenly conscious that I was the centre of attention. The citizens on the pavements, waiting patiently for the parade to start, had something else to look at now. The little Brownies and Wolf Cubs waved at me from their ranks and there were nods and smiles from the people across the road and on all sides.

I could divine their thoughts. 'There's t'young vitnery coming out of his house. Not long married, too. That's his missus next to him.'

A feeling of wellbeing rose in me. I don't know whether other newly married men feel the same, but in those early days I was aware of a calm satisfaction and fulfilment. And I was proud to be the 'vitnery' and part of the life of the town. There was my plate on the wall beside me, a symbol of my solid importance. I was a man of substance now, I had arrived.

Looking around me, I acknowledged the greeting with a few dignified little smiles, raising a gracious hand now and then rather like a royal personage on view. Then I noticed that Helen hadn't much room by my side, so I stepped to the left to where the grating should have been and slid gracefully down into the cellar.

It would be a dramatic touch to say I disappeared from view; in fact I wish I had, because I would have stayed down there and avoided further embarrassment. But as it was I travelled only so far down the ramp and stuck there with my head and shoulders protruding into the street.

My little exhibition caused a sensation among the spectators. Nothing in the Gala parade could compete with this. One or two of the surrounding faces expressed alarm but loud laughter was the general response. The adults were almost holding each other up but the little Brownies and Wolf Cubs made my most appreciative audience, breaking their ranks and staggering about helplessly in the roadway while their leaders tried to restore order.

I caused chaos, too, in the Houlton Silver Band, who were hoisting their instruments prior to marching off. If they had any ideas about bursting into tune they had to abandon them temporarily because I don't think any of them had breath to blow.

It was, in fact, two of the bandsmen who extricated me by linking their hands under my armpits. My wife was of no service at all in the crisis and I could only look up at her reproachfully as she leaned against the doorpost dabbing at her eyes.

It all became clear to me when I reached street level. I was flicking the coal dust from my trousers and trying to look unconcerned when I saw Wesley Binks doubled up with mirth, pointing triumphantly at me and at the hole over the cellar. He was quite near, jostling among the spectators, and I had my first close look at the wild-eyed little goblin who had plagued me. I may have made an unconscious movement towards him because he gave me a last malevolent grin and disappeared into the crowd.

Later I asked Helen about him. She could only tell me that Wesley's father had left home when he was about six years old, that his mother had remarried and the boy now lived with her and his stepfather.

Strangely, I had another opportunity to study him quite soon afterwards. It was about a week later and my feathers were still a little ruffled after the grating incident when I saw him sitting all alone in the waiting room. Alone, that is, except for a skinny black dog in his lap.

I could hardly believe it. I had often rehearsed the choice phrases which I would use on this very occasion but the sight of the animal restrained me; if he had come to consult me professionally I could hardly start pitching into him right away. Maybe later.

I pulled on a white coat and went in.

'Well, what can I do for you?' I asked coldly.

The boy stood up and his expression of mixed defiance and desperation showed that it had cost him something to enter this house.

'Summat matter wi' me dog,' he muttered.

'Right, bring him through.' I led the way along the passage to the consulting room.

'Put him on the table please,' I said, and as he lifted the little animal I decided that I couldn't let this opportunity pass. While I was carrying out my examination I would quite casually discuss recent events. Nothing nasty, no clever phrases, just a quiet probe into the situation. I was just about to say something like 'What's the idea of all those tricks you play on me?' when I took my first look at the dog and everything else fled from my mind.

He wasn't much more than a big puppy and an out-and-out mongrel. His shiny black coat could have come from a Labrador and there was a suggestion of terrier in the pointed nose and pricked ears, but the long string-like tail and the knock-kneed fore limbs baffled me. For all that he was an attractive little creature with a sweetly expressive face.

But the things that seized my whole attention were the yellow blobs of pus in the corners of the eyes, the muco-purulent discharge from the nostrils, and the photophobia which made the dog blink painfully at the light from the surgery window.

Classical canine distemper is so easy to diagnose but there is never any satisfaction in doing so.

'I didn't know you had a dog,' I said. 'How long have you had him?'

'A month. Feller got 'im from t'dog and cat home at Hartington and sold 'im to me.'

'I see.' I took the temperature and was not surprised to find it was 104°F.

'How old is he?'

'Nine months.'

I nodded. Just about the worst age.

I went ahead and asked all the usual questions but I knew the answers already.

Yes, the dog had been slightly off colour for a week or two. No, he wasn't really ill, but listless and coughing occasionally. And of course it was not until the eyes and nose began to discharge that the boy became worried and brought him to see me. That was when we usually saw these cases – when it was too late.

Wesley imparted the information defensively, looking at me under lowered brows as though he expected me to clip his ear at any moment. But as I studied him any aggressive feelings I may have harboured evaporated quickly. The imp of hell appeared on closer examination to be a neglected child. His elbows stuck out through holes in a filthy jersey, his shorts were similarly ragged, but what

appalled me most was the sour smell of his unwashed little body. I
hadn't thought there were children like this in Darrowby.

When he had answered my questions he made an effort and blurted
out one of his own.

'What's matter with 'im?'

I hesitated a moment. 'He's got distemper, Wes.'

'What's that?'

'Well, it's a nasty infectious disease. He must have got it from
another sick dog.'

'Will 'e get better?'

'I hope so. I'll do the best I can for him.' I couldn't bring myself
to tell a small boy of his age that his pet was probably going to die.

I filled a syringe with a 'mixed macterin' which we used at that
time against the secondary invaders of distemper. It never did much
good and even now with all our antibiotics we cannot greatly
influence the final outcome. If you can catch a case in the early viral
phase then a shot of hyperimmune serum is curative, but people
rarely bring their dogs in until that phase is over.

As I gave the injection the dog whimpered a little and the boy
stretched out a hand and patted him.

'It's awright, Duke,' he said.

'That's what you call him, is it – Duke?'

'Aye.' He fondled the ears and the dog turned, whipped his strange
long tail about and licked the hand quickly. Wes smiled and looked
up at me and for a moment the tough mask dropped from the grubby
features and in the dark wild eyes I read sheer delight. I swore under
my breath. This made it worse.

I tipped some boracic crystals into a box and handed it over. 'Use
this dissolved in water to keep his eyes and nose clean. See how his
nostrils are all caked and blocked up – you can make him a lot more
comfortable.'

He took the box without speaking and almost with the same movement dropped three and sixpence on the table. It was about our
average charge and resolved my doubts on that score.

'When'll ah bring 'im back?' he asked.

I looked at him doubtfully for a moment. All I could do was repeat
the injections, but was it going to make the slightest difference?

The boy misread my hesitation.

'Ah can pay!' he burst out. 'Ah can get t'money!'

'Oh I didn't mean that, Wes. I was just wondering when it would be suitable. How about bringing him in on Thursday?'

He nodded eagerly and left with his dog.

As I swabbed the table with disinfectant I had the old feeling of helplessness. The modern veterinary surgeon does not see nearly as many cases of distemper as we used to, simply because most people immunise their puppies at the earliest possible moment. But back in the thirties it was only the few fortunate dogs who were inoculated. The disease is so easy to prevent but almost impossible to cure.

The next three weeks saw an incredible change in Wesley Binks's character. He had built up a reputation as an idle scamp but now he was transformed into a model of industry, delivering papers in the mornings, digging people's gardens, helping to drive the beasts at the auction mart. I was perhaps the only one who knew he was doing it for Duke.

He brought the dog in every two or three days and paid on the nail. I naturally charged him as little as possible but the money he earned went on other things – fresh meat from the butcher, extra milk and biscuits.

'Duke's looking very smart today,' I said on one of the visits. 'I see you've been getting him a new collar and lead.'

The boy nodded shyly then looked up at me, dark eyes intent. 'Is 'e any better?'

'Well, he's about the same, Wes. That's how it goes – dragging on without much change.'

'When . . . when will ye know?'

I thought for a moment. Maybe he would worry less if he understood the situation. 'The thing is this. Duke will get better if he can avoid the nervous complications of distemper.'

'Wot's them?'

'Fits, paralysis and a thing called chorea which makes the muscles twitch.'

'Wot if he gets them?'

'It's a bad lookout in that case. But not all dogs develop them.' I tried to smile reassuringly. 'And there's one thing in Duke's favour – he's not a pure bred. Cross-bred dogs have a thing called hybrid vigour which helps them to fight disease. After all, he's eating fairly well and he's quite lively, isn't he?'

'Aye, not bad.'

'Well then, we'll carry on. I'll give him another shot now.'

The boy was back in three days and I knew by his face he had momentous news.

'Duke's a lot better – 'is eyes and nose 'ave dried up and he's eatin' like a 'oss!' He was panting with excitement.

I lifted the dog on to the table. There was no doubt he was enormously improved and I did my best to join in the rejoicing.

'That's great, Wes,' I said, but a warning bell was tinkling in my mind. If nervous symptoms were going to supervene, this was the time – just when the dog was apparently recovering.

I forced myself to be optimistic. 'Well now, there's no need to come back any more but watch him carefully and if you see anything unusual bring him in.'

The ragged little figure was overjoyed. He almost pranced along the passage with his pet and I hoped fervently that I would not see them in there again.

That was on the Friday evening and by Monday I had put the whole thing out of my head and into the category of satisfying memories when the boy came in with Duke on the lead.

I looked up from the desk where I was writing in the day book. 'What is it, Wes?'

'He's dotherin'.'

I didn't bother going through to the consulting room but hastened from behind the desk and crouched on the floor, studying the dog intently. At first I saw nothing, then as I watched I could just discern a faint nodding of the head. I placed my hand on the top of the skull and waited. And it was there: the slight but regular twitching of the temporal muscles which I had dreaded.

'I'm afraid he's got chorea, Wes,' I said.

'What's that?'

'It's one of the things I was telling you about. Sometimes they call it St Vitus' Dance. I was hoping it wouldn't happen.'

The boy looked suddenly small and forlorn and he stood there silent twisting the new leather lead between his fingers. It was such an effort for him to speak that he almost closed his eyes.

'Will 'e die?'

'Some dogs do get over it, Wes.' I didn't tell him that I had seen it happen only once. 'I've got some tablets which might help him. I'll get you some.'

I gave him a few of the arsenical tablets I had used in my only cure. I didn't even know if they had been responsible but I had nothing more to offer.

Duke's chorea pursued a text book course over the next two weeks. All the things which I had feared turned up in a relentless progression. The twitching spread from his head to his limbs, then his hindquarters began to sway as he walked.

His young master brought him in repeatedly and I went through the motions, trying at the same time to make it clear that it was all hopeless. The boy persisted doggedly, rushing about meanwhile with his paper deliveries and other jobs, insisting on paying though I didn't want his money. Then one afternoon he called in.

'Ah couldn't bring Duke,' he muttered. 'Can't walk now. Will you come and see 'im?'

We got into my car. It was a Sunday, about three o'clock, and the streets were quiet. He led me up the cobbled yard and opened the door of one of the houses.

The stink of the place hit me as I went in. Country vets aren't easily sickened but I felt my stomach turning. Mrs Binks was very fat and a filthy dress hung shapelessly on her as she slumped, cigarette in mouth, over the kitchen table. She was absorbed in a magazine which lay in a clearing among mounds of dirty dishes and her curlers nodded as she looked up briefly at us.

On a couch under the window her husband sprawled asleep, open-mouthed, snoring out the reek of beer. The sink, which held a further supply of greasy dishes, was covered in a revolting green scum. Clothes, newspapers and nameless rubbish littered the floor, and over everything a radio blasted away at full strength.

The only clean new thing was the dog basket in the corner. I went across and bent over the little animal. Duke was now prostrate and helpless, his body emaciated and jerking uncontrollably. The sunken eyes had filled up again with pus and gazed apathetically ahead.

'Wes,' I said, 'you've got to let me put him to sleep.'

He didn't answer, and as I tried to explain, the blaring radio drowned my words. I looked over at his mother.

'Do you mind turning the radio down?' I asked.

She jerked her head at the boy and he went over and turned the knob. In the ensuing silence I spoke to him again.

'It's the only thing, believe me. You can't let him die by inches like this.'

He didn't look at me. All his attention was fixed desperately on his dog. Then he raised a hand and I heard his whisper.

'Awright.'

I hurried out to the car for the Nembutal.

'I promise you he'll feel no pain,' I said as I filled the syringe. And indeed the little creature merely sighed before lying motionless, the fateful twitching stilled at last.

I put the syringe in my pocket. 'Do you want me to take him away, Wes?'

He looked at me bewilderedly and his mother broke in.

'Aye, get 'im out. Ah never wanted t'bloody thing 'ere in t'first place.' She resumed her reading.

I quickly lifted the little body and went out. Wes followed me and watched as I opened the boot and laid Duke gently on top of my black working coat.

As I closed the lid he screwed his knuckles into his eyes and his body shook. I put my arm across his shoulders, and as he leaned against me for a moment and sobbed I wondered if he had ever been able to cry like this – like a little boy with somebody to comfort him.

But soon he stood back and smeared the tears across the dirt on his cheeks.

'Are you going back into the house, Wes?' I asked.

He blinked and looked at me with a return of his tough expression.

'Naw!' he said and turned and walked away. He didn't look back and I watched him cross the road, climb a wall and trail away across the fields towards the river.

And it has always seemed to me that at that moment Wes walked back into his old life. From then on there were no more odd jobs or useful activities. He never played any more tricks on me but in other ways he progressed into more serious misdemeanours. He set barns on fire, was up before the magistrates for theft, and by the time he was thirteen he was stealing cars.

Finally he was sent to an approved school and then he disappeared from the district. Nobody knew where he went and most people forgot him. One person who didn't was the police sergeant.

'That young Wesley Binks,' he said to me ruminatively. 'He was a wrong 'un if ever I saw one. You know, I don't think he ever cared a damn for anybody or any living thing in his life.'

Wes

'I know how you feel, sergeant,' I replied, 'but you're not entirely right. There was one living thing . . .'

*

It is so true that having an animal to love and care for can greatly influence the lives of young people. This story also highlights the horrors of canine distemper, and when I see the stream of people coming into our surgery to have their puppies inoculated I feel thankful that we now have the means to push this dreadful disease into the background.

25. *The Bandaged Finger*

I was castrating pigs and Rory was holding them. There were several litters to do and I was in a hurry and failed to notice the Irish farm worker's mounting apprehension. His young boss was catching the little animals and handing them to Rory who held them upside down, gripped between his thighs with their legs apart, and as I quickly incised the scrotums and drew out the testicles my blade almost touched the rough material of his trouser crutch.

'For God's sake, have a care, Mr Herriot!' he gasped at last.

I looked up from my work. 'What's wrong, Rory?'

'Watch what you're doin' with that bloody knife! You're whippin'

The Bandaged Finger

it round between me legs like a bloody Red Indian. You'll do me a mischief afore you've finished!'

'Aye, be careful, Mr Herriot,' the young farmer cried. 'Don't geld Rory instead of the pig. His missus ud never forgive ye.' He burst into a loud peal of laughter, the Irishman grinned sheepishly and I giggled.

That was my undoing, because the momentary inattention sent the blade slicing across my left forefinger. The razor-sharp edge went deep and in an instant the entire neighbourhood seemed flooded with my blood. I thought I would never staunch the flow. The red ooze continued, despite a long session of self-doctoring from the car boot, and when I finally drove away my finger was swathed in the biggest, clumsiest dressing I had ever seen. I had finally been forced to apply a large pad of cotton wool held in place with an enormous length of three-inch bandage.

It was dark when I left the farm. About five o'clock on a late December day, the light gone early and the stars beginning to show in a frosty sky. I drove slowly, the enormous finger jutting upwards from the wheel, pointing the way between the headlights like a guiding beacon. I was within half a mile of Darrowby, with the lights of the little town beginning to wink between the bare roadside branches, when a car approached, went past, then I heard a squeal of brakes as it stopped and began to double back.

It passed me again, drew into the side and I saw a frantically waving arm. I pulled up and a young man jumped from the driving seat and ran towards me.

He pushed his head in at the window. 'Are you the vet?' His voice was breathless, panic-stricken.

'Yes, I am.'

'Oh thank God! We're passing through on the way to Manchester and we've been to your surgery . . . they said you were out this way . . . described your car. Please help us!'

'What's the trouble?'

'It's our dog . . . in the back of the car. He's got a ball stuck in his throat. I . . . I think he might be dead.'

I was out of my seat and running along the road before he had finished. It was a big white saloon and in the darkness of the back seat a wailing chorus issued from several little heads silhouetted against the glass.

I tore open the door and the wailing took on words.

'Oh Benny, Benny, Benny . . . !'
I dimly discerned a large dog spread over the knees of four small children. 'Oh Daddy, he's dead, he's dead!'
'Let's have him out,' I gasped, and as the young man pulled on the forelegs I supported the body, which slid and toppled on to the tarmac with a horrible limpness.
I pawed at the hairy form. 'I can't see a bloody thing! Help me pull him round.'
We dragged the unresisting bulk into the headlights' glare and I could see it all. A huge, beautiful Collie in his luxuriant prime, mouth gaping, tongue lolling, eyes staring lifelessly at nothing. He wasn't breathing.
The young father took one look, then gripped his head with both hands. 'Oh God, oh God . . .' From within the car I heard the quiet sobbing of his wife and the piercing cries from the back. 'Benny . . . Benny . . .'
I grabbed the man's shoulder and shouted at him. 'What did you say about a ball?'
'It's in his throat . . . I've had my fingers in his mouth for ages but I couldn't move it.' The words came mumbling up from beneath the bent head.
I pushed my hand into the mouth and I could feel it all right. A sphere of hard solid rubber not much bigger than a golf ball and jammed like a cork in the pharynx, effectively blocking the trachea. I scrabbled feverishly at the wet smoothness but there was nothing to get hold of. It took me about three seconds to realise that no human agency would ever get the ball out that way and without thinking I withdrew my hands, braced both thumbs behind the angle of the lower jaw and pushed.
The ball shot forth, bounced on the frosty road and rolled sadly on to the grass verge. I touched the corneal surface of the eye. No reflex. I slumped to my knees, burdened by the hopeless regret that I hadn't had the chance to do this just a bit sooner. The only function I could perform now was to take the body back to Skeldale House for disposal. I couldn't allow the family to drive to Manchester with a dead dog. But I wished fervently that I had been able to do more, and as I passed my hand along the richly coloured coat over the ribs the vast bandaged finger stood out like a symbol of my helplessness.
It was when I was gazing dully at the finger, the heel of my hand

resting in an intercostal space, that I felt the faintest flutter from below.

I jerked upright with a hoarse cry. 'His heart's still beating! He's not gone yet!' I began to work on the dog with all I had. And out there in the darkness of that lonely country road it wasn't much. No stimulant injections, no oxygen cylinders or intratracheal tubes. But I depressed his chest with my palms every three seconds in the old-fashioned way, willing the dog to breathe as the eyes still stared at nothing. Every now and then I blew desperately down the throat or probed between the ribs for that almost imperceptible beat.

I don't know which I noticed first, the slight twitch of an eyelid or the small lift of the ribs which pulled the icy Yorkshire air into his lungs. Maybe they both happened at once, but from that moment everything was dreamlike and wonderful. I lost count of time as I sat there while the breathing became deep and regular and the animal began to be aware of his surroundings; and by the time he started to look around him and twitch his tail tentatively I realised suddenly that I was stiff-jointed and almost frozen to the spot.

With some difficulty I got up and watched in disbelief as the Collie staggered to his feet. The young father ushered him round to the back where he was received with screams of delight.

The man seemed stunned. Throughout the recovery he had kept muttering, 'You just flicked that ball out . . . just flicked it out. Why didn't I think of that . . . ?' And when he turned to me before leaving he appeared to be still in a state of shock.

'I don't . . . I don't know how to thank you,' he said huskily. 'It's a miracle.' He leaned against the car for a second. 'And now what is your fee? How much do I owe you?'

I rubbed my chin. I had used no drugs. The only expenditure had been time.

'Five bob,' I said. 'And never let him play with such a little ball again.'

He handed the money over, shook my hand and drove away. His wife, who had never left her place, waved as she left, but my greatest reward was in the last shadowy glimpse of the back seat where little arms twined around the dog, hugging him ecstatically, and in the cries, thankful and joyous, fading into the night.

'Benny . . . Benny . . . Benny . . .'

Vets often wonder after a patient's recovery just how much credit they might take. Maybe it would have got better without treatment – it happened sometimes; it was difficult to be sure.

But when you know without a shadow of a doubt that, even without doing anything clever, you have pulled an animal back from the brink of death into the living, breathing world, it is a satisfaction which lingers, flowing like balm over the discomforts and frustrations of veterinary practice, making everything right.

Yet, in the case of Benny, the whole thing had an unreal quality. I never even glimpsed the faces of those happy children nor that of their mother huddled in the front seat. I had a vague impression of their father, but he had spent most of the time with his head in his hands. I wouldn't have known him if I met him in the street. Even the dog, in the unnatural glare of the headlights, was a blurred memory.

It seemed the family had the same feeling, because a week later I had a pleasant letter from the mother. She apologised for skulking out of the way so shamelessly, she thanked me for saving the life of their beloved dog who was now prancing around with the children as though nothing had happened, and she finished with the regret that she hadn't even asked me my name.

Yes, it had been a strange episode, and not only were those people unaware of my name but I'd like to bet they would fail to recognise me if they saw me again.

In fact, looking back at the affair, the only thing which stood out unequivocal and substantial was my great white-bound digit which had hovered constantly over the scene, almost taking on a personality and significance of its own. I am sure that is what the family remembered best about me because of the way the mother's letter began.

'Dear Vet with the bandaged finger . . .'

*

It was nice to have that letter all those years ago, but nicer still to hear from a lady quite recently. She wrote to tell me that she had been in exactly the same predicament with a ball stuck in her dog's throat. She, too, had tried in vain to remove the ball by the mouth, then, just as she was giving up hope, she remembered the incident in my book and pushed from behind the jaw. She thanked me for saving her dog's life, and the thought struck me that though my books were not intended primarily to instruct, perhaps they had helped other people in this way.

26. *Shep's Hobby*

Mr Bailes's little place was situated about half-way along Highburn Village, and to get into the farmyard you had to walk twenty yards or so between five-foot walls. On the left was the neighbouring house, on the right the front garden of the farm. In this garden Shep lurked for most of the day.

He was a huge dog, much larger than the average Collie. In fact I am convinced he was part Alsatian, because though he had a luxuriant black and white coat there was something significant in the massive limbs and in the noble brown-shaded head with its upstanding ears. He was quite different from the stringy little animals I saw on my daily round.

As I walked between the walls my mind was already in the byre, just visible at the far end of the yard. Because one of the Bailes's cows, Rose by name, had the kind of obscure digestive ailment which interferes with veterinary surgeons' sleep. They are so difficult to diagnose. This animal had begun to grunt and go off her milk two days ago, and when I had seen her yesterday I had flitted from one possibility to the other. Could be a wire? But the fourth stomach was contracting well and there were plenty of rumenal sounds. Also she was eating a little hay in a half-hearted way.

Could it be impaction . . . ? Or a partial torsion of the gut . . . ? There was abdominal pain without a doubt and that nagging temperature of 102.5° – that was damn like a wire. Of course I could settle the whole thing by opening the cow up, but Mr Bailes was an old-fashioned type and didn't like the idea of my diving into his animal unless I was certain of my diagnosis. And I wasn't – there was no getting away from that.

I was half-way down the alley between the walls with the hope bright before me that my patient would be improved, when from nowhere an appalling explosion of sound blasted into my right ear. It was Shep again.

The wall was just the right height for the dog to make a leap and bark into the ear of the passers-by. It was a favourite gambit of his and I had been caught before; but never so successfully as now. My attention had been so far away and the dog had timed his jump to a split second so that his bark came at the highest point, his teeth only inches from my face. And his voice befitted his size, a great bull bellow surging from the depths of his powerful chest and booming from his gaping jaws.

I rose several inches into the air and when I descended, heart thumping, head singing, I glared over the wall. But as usual all I saw was the hairy form bounding away out of sight round the corner of the house.

That was what puzzled me. Why did he do it? Was he a savage creature with evil designs on me, or was it his idea of a joke? I never got near enough to him to find out.

I wasn't in the best of shape to receive bad news and that was what awaited me in the byre. I had only to look at the farmer's face to know that the cow was worse.

'Ah reckon she's got a stoppage,' Mr Bailes muttered gloomily.

I gritted my teeth. The entire spectrum of abdominal disorders were lumped as 'stoppages' by the older race of farmers. 'The oil hasn't worked, then?'

'Nay, she's nobbut passin' little hard bits. It's a proper stoppage, ah tell you.'

'Right, Mr Bailes,' I said with a twisted smile. 'We'll have to try something stronger.' I brought in from my car the gastric lavage outfit I loved so well and which has so sadly disappeared from my life. The long rubber stomach tube, the wooden gag with its leather straps to buckle behind the horns. As I pumped in the two gallons of warm water rich in formalin and sodium chloride I felt like Napoleon sending in the Old Guard at Waterloo. If this didn't work, nothing would.

Next morning I was driving down the single village street when I saw Mrs Bailes coming out of the shop. I drew up and pushed my head out of the window.

'How's Rose this morning, Mrs Bailes?'

She rested her basket on the ground and looked down at me gravely. 'Oh, she's bad, Mr Herriot. Me husband thinks she's goin' down fast. If you want to find him you'll have to go across the field there. He's mindin' the door in that little barn.'

A sudden misery enveloped me as I drove over to the gate leading into the field. I left the car in the road and lifted the latch.

'Damn! Damn! Damn!' I muttered as I trailed across the green. I had a nasty feeling that a little tragedy was building up here. If this animal died it would be a sickening blow to a small farmer with ten cows and a few pigs. I should be able to do something about it and it was a depressing thought that I was getting nowhere.

And yet, despite it all, I felt peace stealing into my soul. It was a large field and I could see the barn at the far end as I walked with the tall grass brushing my knees. It was a meadow ready for cutting and suddenly I realised that it was high summer, the sun was hot and that every step brought the fragrance of clover and warm grass rising about me into the crystal freshness of the air. Somewhere nearby a field of broad beans was in full flower, and as the exotic scent drifted across I found myself inhaling with half-closed eyes as though straining to discern the ingredients of the glorious melange.

And then there was the silence; it was the most soothing thing of all. That and the feeling of being alone. I looked drowsily around at the empty green miles sleeping under the sunshine. Nothing stirred, there was no sound.

Then without warning the ground at me feet erupted in an incredible blast of noise. For a dreadful moment the blue sky was obscured by an enormous hairy form and a red mouth went 'WAAAHH!' in my face. Almost screaming, I staggered back, and as I glared wildly I saw Shep disappearing at top speed towards the gate. Concealed in the deep herbage right in the middle of the field he had waited till he saw the whites of my eyes before making his assault.

Whether he had been there by accident or whether he had spotted me arriving and slunk into position I shall never know, but from his point of view the result must have been eminently satisfactory because it was certainly the worst fright I have ever had. I live a life which is well larded with scares and alarms, but this great dog rising bellowing from that empty landscape was something on its own. I have heard of cases where sudden terror and stress has caused involuntary evacuation of the bowels, and I know without question that this was the occasion when I came nearest to suffering that unhappy fate.

I was still trembling when I reached the barn and hardly said a word as Mr Bailes led me back across the road to the farm.

And it was like rubbing it in when I saw my patient. The flesh had melted from her and she stared at the wall apathetically from sunken eyes. The doom-laden grunt was louder.

I decided to have one last go with the lavage. It was still the strongest weapon in my armoury but this time I added two pounds of black treacle to the mixture. Nearly every farmer had a barrel of the stuff in his cow house in those days and I had only to go into the corner and turn the tap.

It was not till the following afternoon that I drove into Highburn. I left the car outside the farm and was about to walk between the walls when I paused and stared at a cow in the field on the other side of the road. It was a pasture next to the hayfield of yesterday and that cow was Rose. There could be no mistake – she was a fine deep red with a distinctive white mark like a football on her left flank.

I opened the gate and within seconds my cares dropped from me. She was wonderfully, miraculously improved, in fact she looked like a normal animal. I walked up to her and scratched the root of her tail. She was a docile creature and merely looked round at me as she cropped the grass; and her eyes were no longer sunken but bright and full.

As the wave of relief flooded through me I saw Mr Bailes climbing over the wall from the next field. He would still be mending that barn door.

As he approached I felt a pang of commiseration. I had to guard against any display of triumph – after all the poor chap had been worried. No, it wouldn't do to preen myself unduly.

'Ah, good morning to you, Mr Bailes,' I said expansively. 'Rose looks fine today, doesn't she?'

The farmer took off his cap and wiped his brow. 'Aye, she's a different cow, all right.'

'I don't think she needs any more treatment,' I said. I hesitated. Perhaps one little dig would do no harm. 'But it's a good thing I gave her that extra lavage yesterday.'

'Yon pumpin' job?' Mr Bailes raised his eyebrows. 'Oh that had nowt to do with it.'

'What . . . what do you mean? It cured her, surely.'

'Nay, lad, nay, Jim Oakley cured her.'

'Jim . . . what on earth . . . ?'

'Aye, Jim was round 'ere last night. He often comes in of an evenin' and he took one look at the cow and told me what to do. Ah'll tell you she was like dyin' – that pumpin' job hadn't done no good at all. He told me to give her a bloody good gallop round t'field.'

'What!'

'Aye, that's what he said. He'd seen 'em like that afore and a good gallop put 'em right. So we got Rose out here and did as he said and by gaw it did the trick. She looked better right away.'

I drew myself up. 'And who,' I asked frigidly, 'is Jim Oakley?'

'He's t'postman, of course.'

'The postman!'

'Aye, but he used to keep a few beasts years ago. He's a very clever man wi' stock, is Jim.'

'No doubt, but I assure you, Mr Bailes . . .'

The farmer raised a hand. 'Say no more, lad. Jim put 'er right and there's no denyin' it. I wish you'd seen 'im chasin' 'er round. He's as awd as me, but by gaw 'e did go. He can run like 'ell, can Jim.' He chuckled reminiscently.

I had had about enough. During the farmer's eulogy I had been distractedly scratching the cow's tail and had soiled my hand in the process. Mustering the remains of my dignity I nodded to Mr Bailes.

'Well, I must be on my way. Do you mind if I go into the house to wash my hands?'

'You go right in,' he replied. 'T'missus will get you some hot water.'

It seemed to take a long time to reach the end of the wall and I was about to turn right towards the door of the farm kitchen when from my left I heard the sudden rattle of a chain, then a roaring creature launched itself at me, bayed once, mightily, into my face and was gone.

This time I thought my heart would stop. With my defences at their lowest I was in no state to withstand Shep. I had quite forgotten that Mrs Bailes occasionally tethered him in the kennel at the entrance to discourage unwelcome visitors, and as I half lay against the wall, the blood thundering in my ears, I looked dully at the long coil of chain on the cobbles.

I have no time for people who lose their temper with animals but something snapped in my mind then. All my frustration burst from me in a torrent of incoherent shouts and I grabbed the chain and began to pull on it frenziedly. That dog which had tortured me was there in that kennel. For once I knew where to get at him and this time I was going to have the matter out with him. The kennel would be about ten feet away and at first I saw nothing. There was only the dead weight on the end of the chain. Then as I hauled inexorably a nose appeared, then a head, then all of the big animal hanging limply by his collar. He showed no desire to get up and greet me but I was merciless and dragged him inch by inch over the cobbles till he was lying at my feet.

Beside myself with rage, I crouched, shook my fist under his nose and yelled at him from a few inches' range.

'You big bugger! If you do that to me again I'll knock your bloody head off! Do you hear me, I'll knock your bloody head clean off!'

Shep rolled frightened eyes at me and his tail flickered apologetically between his legs. When I continued to scream at him he bared his upper teeth in an ingratiating grin and finally rolled on his back where he lay inert with half-closed eyes.

So now I knew. He was a softie. All his ferocious attacks were just a game. I began to calm down but for all that I wanted him to get the message.

'Right, mate,' I said in a menacing whisper. 'Remember what I've said!' I let go the chain and gave a final shout. 'Now get back in there!'

Shep, almost on his knees, tail tucked well in, shot back into his kennel and I turned toward the farmhouse to wash my hands.

* * *

Shep's Hobby

I was surprised when, about a month later, I received another call to one of Mr Bailes's cows. I felt that after my performance with Rose he would have called on the services of Jim Oakley for any further trouble. But no, his voice on the phone was as polite and friendly as ever, with not a hint that he had lost faith. It was strange . . .

Leaving my car outside the farm I looked warily into the front garden before venturing between the walls. A faint tinkle of metal told me that Shep was lurking there in his kennel and I slowed my steps; I wasn't going to be caught again. At the end of the alley I paused, waiting, but all I saw was the end of a nose which quietly withdrew as I stood there. So my outburst had got through to the big dog – he knew I wasn't going to stand any more nonsense from him.

And yet, as I drove away after the visit, I didn't feel good about it. A victory over an animal is a hollow one and I had the uncomfortable feeling that I had deprived him of his chief pleasure. After all, every creature is entitled to some form of recreation and though Shep's hobby could result in the occasional heart failure it was, after all, his thing and part of him. The thought that I had crushed something out of his life was a disquieting one. I wasn't proud.

So that when, later that summer, I was driving through Highburn, I paused in anticipation outside the Bailes's farm. The village street, white and dusty, slumbered under the afternoon sun. In the blanketing silence nothing moved – except for one small man strolling towards the opening between the walls. He was fat and very dark – one of the tinkers from a camp outside the village – and he carried an armful of pots and pans.

From my vantage point I could see through the railings into the front garden where Shep was slinking noiselessly into position beneath the stones. Fascinated, I watched as the man turned unhurriedly into the opening and the dog followed the course of the disembodied head along the top of the wall.

As I expected it all happened half-way along. The perfectly timed leap, the momentary pause at the summit, then the tremendous 'WOOF!' into the unsuspecting ear.

It had its usual effect. I had a brief view of flailing arms and flying pans followed by a prolonged metallic clatter, then the little man reappeared like a projectile, turned right and sped away from me up the street. Considering his almost round physique he showed an

217

astonishing turn of speed, his little legs pistoning, and he did not pause till he disappeared into the shop at the far end of the village.

I don't know why he went in there because he wouldn't find any stronger restorative than ginger pop.

Shep, apparently well satisfied, wandered back over the grass and collapsed in a cool patch where an apple tree threw its shade over the grass; head on paws, he waited in comfort for his next victim.

I smiled to myself as I let in the clutch and moved off. I would stop at the shop and tell the little man that he could collect his pans without the slightest fear of being torn limb from limb, but my overriding emotion was one of relief that I had not cut the sparkle out of the big dog's life.

Shep was still having his fun.

*

The fact that dogs clearly love to play or have some source of amusement makes me feel that people should really keep two dogs so that they would never be lonely. However, this is often inconvenient or impossible, so the more often an owner can play with his pet the better. It is surprising what can be done in this way – tug-of-war, retrieving, even hide-and-seek! Sometimes, of course, the dog will find his own entertainment – as Shep did.

27. *Mick*

It was nine o'clock on a filthy wet night and I was still at work. I gripped the steering wheel more tightly and shifted in my seat, groaning softly as my tired muscles complained.

Why had I entered this profession? I could have gone in for something easier and gentler – like coalmining or lumberjacking. I had started feeling sorry for myself three hours ago, driving across Darrowby market-place on the way to a calving. The shops were shut and even through the wintry drizzle there was a suggestion of repose, of work done, of firesides and books and drifting tobacco

219

smoke. I had all those things, plus Helen, back there in our bed-sitter.

I think the iron really entered when I saw the carload of young people setting off from the front of the Drovers': three girls and three young fellows, all dressed up and laughing and obviously on their way to a dance or party. Everybody was set for comfort and a good time; everybody except Herriot, rattling towards the cold wet hills and the certain prospect of toil.

And the case did nothing to raise my spirits. A skinny little heifer stretched on her side in a ramshackle open-fronted shed littered with old tin cans, half bricks and other junk; it was difficult to see what I was stumbling over since the only light came from a rusty oil lamp whose flame flickered and dipped in the wind.

I was two hours in that shed, easing out the calf inch by inch. It wasn't a malpresentation, just a tight fit, but the heifer never rose to her feet and I spent the whole time on the floor, rolling among the bricks and tins, getting up only to shiver my way to the water bucket while the rain hurled itself icily against the shrinking flesh of my chest and back.

And now here I was, driving home frozen-faced with my skin chafing under my clothes and feeling as though a group of strong men had been kicking me enthusiastically from head to foot for most of the evening. I was almost drowning in self-pity when I turned into the tiny village of Copton. In the warm days of summer it was idyllic, reminding me always of a corner of Perthshire, with its single street hugging the lower slopes of a green hillside and a dark drift of trees spreading to the heathery uplands high above.

But tonight it was a dead black place with the rain sweeping across the headlights against the tight-shut houses; except for a faint glow right in the middle where the light from the village pub fell softly on the streaming roadway. I stopped the car under the swinging sign of the Fox and Hounds and on an impulse opened the door. A beer would do me good.

A pleasant warmth met me as I went into the pub. There was no bar counter, only high-backed settles and oak tables arranged under the whitewashed walls of what was simply a converted farm kitchen. At one end a wood fire crackled in an old black cooking range and above it the tick of a wall clock sounded above the murmur of voices. It wasn't as lively as the modern places but it was peaceful.

Mick

'Now then, Mr Herriot, you've been workin',' my neighbour said as I sank into the settle.

'Yes, Ted, how did you know?'

The man glanced over my soiled mackintosh and the wellingtons which I hadn't bothered to change on the farm. 'Well, that's not your Sunday suit, there's blood on your nose end and cow shit on your ear.' Ted Dobson was a burly cowman in his thirties and his white teeth showed suddenly in a wide grin.

I smiled too and plied my handkerchief. 'It's funny how you always want to scratch your nose at times like that.'

I looked around the room. There were about a dozen men drinking from pint glasses, some of them playing dominoes. They were all farm workers, the people I saw when I was called from my bed in the darkness before dawn; hunched figures they were then, shapeless in old greatcoats, cycling out to the farms, heads down against the wind and rain, accepting the facts of their hard existence. I often thought at those times that this happened to me only occasionally, but they did it every morning.

And they did it for thirty shillings a week; just seeing them here made me feel a little ashamed.

Mr Waters, the landlord, whose name let him in for a certain amount of ribbing, filled my glass, holding his tall jug high to produce the professional froth.

'There y'are, Mr Herriot, that'll be sixpence. Cheap at 'alf the price.'

Every drop of beer was brought up in that jug from the wooden barrels in the cellar. It would have been totally impracticable in a busy establishment, but the Fox and Hounds was seldom bustling and Mr Waters would never get rich as a publican. But he had four cows in the little byre adjoining this room, fifty hens pecked around in his long back garden, and he reared a few litters of pigs every year from his two sows.

'Thank you, Mr Waters.' I took a deep pull at the glass. I had lost some sweat despite the cold and my thirst welcomed the flow of rich nutty ale. I had been in here a few times before and the faces were all familiar. Especially old Albert Close, a retired shepherd who sat in the same place every night at the end of the settle hard against the fire.

He sat as always, his hands and chin resting on the tall crook which he had carried through his working days, his eyes blank.

Stretched half under the seat, half under the table lay his dog, Mick, old and retired like his master. The animal was clearly in the middle of a vivid dream; his paws pedalled the air spasmodically, his lips and ears twitched, and now and then he emitted a stifled bark.

Ted Dobson nudged me and laughed. 'Ah reckon awd Mick's still rounding up them sheep.'

I nodded. There was little doubt the dog was reliving the great days, crouching and darting, speeding in a wide arc round the perimeter of the field at his master's whistle. And Albert himself. What lay behind those empty eyes? I could imagine him in his youth, striding the windy uplands, covering endless miles over moor and rock and beck, digging that same crook into the turf at every step. There were no fitter men than the Dales shepherds, living in the open in all weathers, throwing a sack over their shoulders in snow and rain.

And there was Albert now, a broken, arthritic old man gazing apathetically from beneath the ragged peak of an ancient tweed cap. I noticed he had just drained his glass and I walked across the room.

'Good evening, Mr Close,' I said.

He cupped an ear with his hand and blinked up at me. 'Eh?'

I raised my voice to a shout. 'How are you, Mr Close?'

'Can't complain, young man,' he murmured. 'Can't complain.'

'Will you have a drink?'

'Aye, thank ye.' He directed a trembling finger at his glass. 'You can put a drop i' there, young man.'

I knew a drop meant a pint and beckoned to the landlord who plied his jug expertly. The old shepherd lifted the recharged glass and looked up at me.

'Good 'ealth,' he grunted.

'All the best,' I said and was about to return to my seat when the old dog sat up. My shouts at his master must have wakened him from his dream because he stretched sleepily, shook his head a couple of times and looked around him. And as he turned and faced me I felt a sudden sense of shock.

His eyes were terrible. In fact I could hardly see them as they winked painfully at me through a sodden fringe of pus-caked lashes. Rivulets of discharge showed dark and ugly against the white hair on either side of the nose.

I stretched my hand out to him and the dog wagged his tail briefly

Mick

before closing his eyes and keeping them closed. It seemed he felt better that way.

I put my hand on Albert's shoulder. 'Mr Close, how long has he been like this?'

'Eh?'

I increased my volume. 'Mick's eyes. They're in a bad state.'

'Oh aye.' The old man nodded in comprehension. 'He's got a bit o' caud in 'em. He's allus been subjeck to it ever since 'e were a pup.'

'No, it's more than cold, it's his eyelids.'

'Eh?'

I took a deep breath and let go at the top of my voice.

'He's got turned-in eyelids. It's rather a serious thing.'

The old man nodded again. 'Aye, 'e lies a lot wi' his head at foot of t'door. It's draughty there.'

'No, Mr Close!' I bawled. 'It's got nothing to do with that. It's a thing called entropion and it needs an operation to put it right.'

'That's right, young man.' He took a sip at his beer. 'Just a bit o' caud. Ever since he were a pup he's been subjeck . . .'

I turned away wearily and returned to my seat. Ted Dobson looked at me enquiringly.

'What was that about?'

'Well, it's a nasty thing, Ted. Entropion is when the eyelids are turned in and the lashes rub against the eyeball. Causes a lot of pain, sometimes ulceration or even blindness. Even a mild case is damned uncomfortable for a dog.'

'I see,' Ted said ruminatively. 'Ah've noticed awd Mick's had mucky eyes for a long time but they've got worse lately.'

'Yes, sometimes it happens like that, but often it's congenital. I should think Mick has had a touch of it all his life but for some reason it's suddenly developed to this horrible state.' I turned again towards the old dog, sitting patiently under the table, eyes still tight shut.

'He's sufferin' then?'

I shrugged my shoulders. 'Well, you know what it's like if you have a speck of dust in your eyes or even one lash turned in. I should say he feels pretty miserable.'

'Poor awd beggar. Ah never knew it was owt like that.' He drew on his cigarette. 'And could an operation cure it?'

223

'Yes, Ted, it's one of the most satisfying jobs a vet can do. I always feel I've done a dog a good turn when I've finished.'

'Aye, ah bet you do. It must be a nice feelin'. But it'll be a costly job, ah reckon?'

I smiled wryly. 'It depends how you look at it. It's a fiddly business and takes time. We usually charge about a pound for it.' A human surgeon would laugh at a sum like that, but it would still be too much for old Albert.

For a few moments we were both silent, looking across the room at the old man, at the threadbare coat, the long tatter of trouser bottoms falling over the broken boots. A pound was two weeks of the old age pension. It was a fortune.

Ted got up suddenly. 'Any road, somebody ought to tell 'im. Ah'll explain it to 'im.'

He crossed the room. 'Are ye ready for another, Albert?'

The old shepherd glanced at him absently then indicated his glass, empty again. 'Aye, ye can put a drop i' there, Ted.'

The cowman waved to Mr Waters then bent down. 'Did ye understand what Mr Herriot was tellin' ye, Albert?' he shouted.

'Aye . . . aye . . . Mick's got a bit o' caud in 'is eyes.'

'Nay, 'e hasn't! It's nowt of t'soart! It's a en . . . a en . . . summat different.'

'Keeps gettin' caud in 'em,' Albert mumbled, nose in glass.

Ted yelled in exasperation. 'Ye daft awd divil! Listen to what ah'm sayin' – ye've got to take care of 'im and . . .'

But the old man was far away. 'Ever sin 'e were a pup . . . allus been subjeck to it . . .'

Though Mick took my mind off my own troubles at the time, the memory of those eyes haunted me for days. I yearned to get my hands on them. I knew an hour's work would transport the old dog into a world he perhaps had not known for years, and every instinct told me to rush back to Copton, throw him in the car and bear him back to Darrowby for surgery. I wasn't worried about the money but you just can't run a practice that way.

I regularly saw lame dogs on farms, skinny cats on the streets, and it would have been lovely to descend on each and every one and minister to them out of my knowledge. In fact I had tried a bit of it and it didn't work.

It was Ted Dobson who put me out of my pain. He had come in

to the town to see his sister for the evening and he stood leaning on his bicycle in the surgery doorway, his cheerful, scrubbed face gleaming as if it would light up the street.

He came straight to the point. 'Will ye do that operation on awd Mick, Mr Herriot?'

'Yes, of course, but . . . how about . . . ?'

'Oh that'll be right. T'lads at Fox and Hounds are seein' to it. We're takin' it out of the club money.'

'Club money?'

'Aye, we put in a bit every week for an outin' in t'summer. Trip to t'seaside or summat like.'

'Well it's extremely kind of you, Ted, but are you quite sure? Won't any of them mind?'

Ted laughed. 'Nay, it's nowt, we won't miss a quid. We drink ower much on them do's anyway.' He paused. 'All t'lads want this job done – it's been gettin' on our bloody nerves watchin' t'awd dog ever since you told us about 'im.'

'Well, that's great,' I said. 'How will you get him down?'

'Me boss is lendin' me 'is van. Wednesday night be all right?'

'Fine.' I watched him ride away then turned back along the passage. It may seem to modern eyes that a lot of fuss had been made over a pound, but in those days it was a very substantial sum, and some idea may be gained from the fact that four pounds a week was my commencing salary as a veterinary surgeon.

When Wednesday night arrived it was clear that Mick's operation had become something of a gala occasion. The little van was crammed with regulars from the Fox and Hounds and others rolled up on their bicycles.

The old dog slunk fearfully down the passage to the operating room, nostrils twitching at the unfamiliar odours of ether and antiseptic. Behind him trooped the noisy throng of farm men, their heavy boots clattering on the tiles.

Tristan, who was doing the anaesthesia, hoisted the dog on the table and I looked around at the unusual spectacle of rows of faces regarding me with keen anticipation. Normally I am not in favour of lay people witnessing operations but since these men were sponsoring the whole thing they would have to stay.

Under the lamp I got my first good look at Mick. He was a handsome, well-marked animal except for those dreadful eyes. As he sat there he opened them a fraction and peered at me for a painful moment before closing them against the bright light; that, I felt, was how he spent his life, squinting carefully and briefly at his surroundings. Giving him the intravenous barbiturate was like doing him a favour, ridding him of his torment for a while.

And when he was stretched unconscious on his side I was able to carry out my first examination. I parted the lids, wincing at the matted lashes, awash with tears and discharge; there was a long standing keratitis and conjunctivitis but with a gush of relief I found that the cornea was not ulcerated.

'You know,' I said, 'this is a mess, but I don't think there's any permanent damage.'

The farm men didn't exactly break into a cheer but they were enormously pleased. The carnival air was heightened as they chattered and laughed, and when I poised my scalpel it struck me that I had never operated in such a noisy environment.

But I felt almost gleeful as I made the first incision; I had been looking forward so much to this moment. Starting with the left eye I cut along the full length parallel to the margin of the lid then made a semicircular sweep of the knife to include half an inch of the tissue above the eye. Seizing the skin with forceps I stripped it away, and as I drew the lips of the bleeding wound together with stitches I noticed with intense gratification how the lashes were pulled high and away from the corneal surface they had irritated, perhaps for years.

I cut away less skin from the lower lid – you never need to take so much there – then started on the right eye. I was slicing away happily when I realised that the noise had subsided; there were a few mutterings, but the chaff and laughter had died. I glanced up and saw big Ken Appleton, the horseman from Laurel Grove; it was natural that he should catch my eye, because he was six feet four and built like the Shires he cared for.

'By gaw, it's 'ot in 'ere,' he whispered, and I could see he meant it because sweat was streaming down his face.

I was engrossed in my work or I would have noticed that he wasn't only sweating but deadly pale. I was stripping the skin from the eyelid when I heard Tristan's yell.

'Catch him!'

The big man's surrounding friends supported him as he slid gently to the floor and he stayed there, sleeping peacefully, till I had inserted the last stitch. Then as Tristan and I cleaned up and put the instruments away he began to look around him and his companions helped him to his feet. Now that the cutting was over the life had returned to the party and Ken came in for some leg-pulling; but his was not the only white face.

'I think you could do with a drop of whisky, Ken,' Tristan said. He left the room and returned with a bottle which, with typical hospitality, he dispensed to all. Beakers, measuring glasses and test tubes were pressed into service, and soon there was a boisterous throng around the sleeping dog. When the van finally roared off into the night the last thing I heard was the sound of singing from the packed interior.

They brought Mick back in ten days for removal of the stitches. The wounds had healed well but the keratitis had still not cleared and the old dog was still blinking painfully. I didn't see the final result of my work for another month.

It was when I was again driving home through Copton from an evening call that the lighted doorway of the Fox and Hounds recalled me to the little operation which had been almost forgotten in the rush of new work. I went in and sat down among the familiar faces.

Things were uncannily like before. Old Albert Close in his usual place, Mick stretched under the table, his twitching feet testifying to another vivid dream. I watched him closely until I could stand it no longer. As if drawn by a magnet I crossed the room and crouched by him.

'Mick!' I said. 'Hey, wake up, boy!'

The quivering limbs stilled and there was a long moment when I held my breath as the shaggy head turned towards me. Then with a kind of blissful disbelief I found myself gazing into the wide, clear, bright eyes of a young dog.

Warm wine flowed richly through my veins as he faced me, mouth open in a panting grin, tail swishing along the stone flags. There was no inflammation, no discharge, and the lashes, clean and dry, grew in a soft arc well clear of the corneal surface which they had chafed and rasped for so long. I stroked his head and as he began to look around him eagerly I felt a thrill of utter delight at the sight of the old animal exulting in his freedom, savouring the new world which had opened to him. I could see Ted Dobson and the other men smiling conspiratorially as I stood up.

'Mr Close,' I shouted. 'Will you have a drink?'

'Aye, you can put a drop i' there, young man.'

'Mick's eyes are a lot better.'

The old man raised his glass. 'Good 'ealth. Aye, it were nobbut a bit o' caud.'

'But Mr Close . . . !'

'Nasty thing, is caud in t'eyes. T'awd feller keeps lyin' in that door'ole and ah reckon he'll get it again. Ever since 'e were a pup 'e's been subjeck . . .'

*

I do love writing about those surgical procedures which bring an animal quick and blissful relief. The entropion operation does just that and it is one which we perform regularly in our practice, though not under the colourful circumstances of that night with Mick on the table and the kindly farm men crowding round. There is one thing, however – we get more appreciation from our present-day clients than I got from dear old Albert Close.

28. *Strychnine*

The man was distraught and gasping on the surgery steps. 'I's no good, I can't bring him in. He's as stiff as a board!'

My stomach lurched. It was another one. 'Jasper, you mean?'

'Yes, he's in the back of my car, right here.'

I ran across the pavement and opened the car door. It was as I feared: a handsome Dalmatian stretched in a dreadful tetanic spasm, spine arched, head craning desperately backward, legs like four wooden rods groping at nothing.

I didn't wait to talk but dashed back into the house for syringe and drugs.

I leaned into the car, tucked some papers under the dog's head, injected the apomorhphine and waited.

The man looked at me with anxious eyes. 'What is it?'

'Strychnine poisoning, Mr Bartle. I've just given an emetic to make him vomit.' As I spoke, the animal brought up the contents of his stomach on to the paper.

'Will that put him right?'

'It depends on how much of the poison has been absorbed.' I didn't feel like telling him that it was almost invariably fatal, that in fact I had treated six dogs in the last week with the same condition and they had all died. 'We'll just have to hope.'

He watched me as I filled another syringe with barbiturate. 'What are you doing now?'

'Anaesthetising him.' I slipped the needle into the radial vein and as I slowly trickled the fluid into the dog's bloodstream the taut muscles relaxed and he sank into a deep slumber.

'He looks better already,' Mr Bartle said.

'Yes, but the trouble is when the injection wears off he may go back into a spasm. As I say, it all depends on how much of the strychnine has got into his system. Keep him in a quiet place with as little noise as possible. Any sound can bring on a spasm. When he shows signs of coming out of it give me a ring.'

I went back into the house. Seven cases in a week! It was tragic and scarcely believable, but there was no doubt left in my mind now. This was malicious. Some psychopath in our little town was deliberately putting down poison to kill dogs. Strychnine poisoning was something that cropped up occasionally. Gamekeepers and other people used the deady drug to kill vermin, but usually it was handled with great care and placed out of reach of domestic pets. Trouble started when a burrowing dog came across the poison by accident. But this was different.

I had to warn pet owners somehow. I lifted the phone and spoke to one of the reporters on the *Darrowby and Houlton Times*. He promised to put the story in the next edition, along with advice to keep dogs on their leads and otherwise supervise pets more carefully.

Then I rang the police. The sergeant listened to my account.

Strychnine

'Right, Mr Herriot, I agree with you that there's some crackpot going around and we'll certainly investigate this matter. If you'll just give me the names of the dog owners involved . . . thank you . . . thank you. We'll see these people and check round the local chemists to see if anybody has been buying strychnine lately. And of course we'll keep our eyes open for anybody acting suspiciously.'

I came away from the phone feeling that I might have done something to halt the depressing series of events, but I couldn't rid myself of a gloomy apprehension that more trouble was round the corner. But my mood lightened when I saw Johnny Clifford in the waiting room.

Johnny always made me feel better because he was invariably optimistic and wore a cheerful grin which never altered, even though he was blind. He was about my own age, and he sat there in his habitual pose, one hand on the head of his guide dog, Fergus.

'Is it inspection time again already, Johnny?' I asked.

'Aye, it is that, Mr Herriot, it's come round again. It's been a quick six months.' He laughed and held out his card.

I squatted and looked into the face of the big Alsatian sitting motionless and dignified by his master's side. 'Well, and how's Fergus these days?'

'Oh he's in grand fettle. Eatin' well and full of life.' The hand on the head moved round to the ears and at the other end the tail did a bit of sweeping along the waiting-room floor.

As I looked at the young man, his face alight with pride and affection, I realised afresh what this dog meant to him. He had told me that when his failing sight progressed to total blindness in his early twenties he was filled with a despair which did not lessen until he was sent to train with a guide dog and met Fergus; because he found something more than another living creature to act as his eyes, he found a friend and companion to share every moment of his days.

'Well, we'd better get started,' I said. 'Stand up a minute, old lad, while I take your temperature.' That was normal and I went over the big animal's chest with a stethoscope, listening to the reassuringly steady thud of the heart. As I parted the hair along the neck and back to examine the skin, I laughed.

'I'm wasting my time here, Johnny. You've got his coat in perfect condition.'

'Aye, never a day goes by but he gets a good groomin'.'

I had seen him at it, brushing and combing tirelessly to bring extra

231

lustre to the sleek swathes of hair. The nicest thing anybody could say to Johnny was, 'That's a beautiful dog you've got.' His pride in that beauty was boundless, even though he had never seen it himself.

Treating guide dogs for the blind has always seemed to me to be one of a veterinary surgeon's most rewarding tasks. To be in a position to help and care for these magnificent animals is a privilege, not just because they are highly trained and valuable but because they represent in the ultimate way something which has always lain near the core and centre of my life: the mutually depending, trusting and loving association between man and animal.

Meeting these blind people was a humbling experience which sent me about my work with a new appreciation of my blessings.

I opened the dog's mouth and peered at the huge gleaming teeth. It was dicing with danger to do this with some Alsatians, but with Fergus you could haul the great jaws apart and nearly put your head in and he would only lick your ear. In fact he was at it now. My cheek was nicely within range and he gave it a quick wipe with his large wet tongue.

'Hey, just a minute, Fergus!' I withdrew and plied my handkerchief. 'I've had a wash this morning. And anyway, only little dogs lick – not big tough Alsatians.'

Johnny threw back his head and gave a great peal of laughter. 'There's nowt tough about him, he's the softest dog you could ever meet.'

'Well, that's the way I like them,' I said. I reached for a tooth scaler. 'There's just a bit of tartar on one of his back teeth. I'll scrape it off right now.'

When I had finished I looked in the ears with an auroscope. There was no canker but I cleaned out a little wax.

Then I went round the feet, examining paws and claws. They always fascinated me, these feet: wide, enormous, with great spreading toes. They had to be that size to support the big body and the massive bones of the limbs.

'All correct except that one funny claw, Johnny.'

'Aye, you allus have to trim that 'un don't you? I could feel it was growin' long again.'

'Yes, that toe seems to be slightly crooked or it would wear down like the others with all the walking he does. You have a great time going walks all day, don't you, Fergus?'

I dodged another attempted lick and closed my clippers around the claw. I had to squeeze till my eyes popped before the overgrown piece shot away with a loud crack.

'By gosh, we'd go through some clippers if all dogs had claws like that,' I gasped. 'It just about does them in every time he calls.'

Johnny laughed again and dropped his hand on the great head with that gesture which said so much.

I took the card and entered my report on the dog's health along with the things I had done. Then I dated it and handed it back. 'That's it for this time, Johnny. He's in excellent order and there's nothing more I need do to him.'

'Thank you, Mr Herriot. See you next time round, then.' The young man took hold of the harness and I followed the two of them along the passage and out of the front door. I watched as Fergus halted by the kerb and waited till a car had passed before crossing the road.

They hadn't gone very far along the road when a woman with a shopping bag stopped them. She began to chatter animatedly, looking down repeatedly at the big dog. She was talking about Fergus and Johnny rested his hand on the noble head and nodded and smiled. Fergus was his favourite topic.

Shortly after midday Mr Bartle rang to say Jasper showed signs of returning spasms and before sitting down to lunch I rushed round to his house and repeated the barbiturate injection. Mr Bartle owned one of the local mills, producing cattle food for the district. He was a very bright man indeed.

'Mr Herriot,' he said, 'please don't misunderstand me. I have every faith in you, but isn't there anything else you can do? I am so very fond of this dog.'

I shrugged helplessly. 'I'm sorry, but I can't do any more.'

'But is there no antidote to this poison?'

'No, I'm afraid there isn't.'

'Well . . .' He looked down with drawn face at the unconscious animal. 'What's going on? What's happening to Jasper when he goes stiff like he did? I'm only a layman, but I like to understand things.'

'I'll try to explain it,' I said. 'Strychnine is absorbed into the nervous system and it increases the conductivity of the spinal cord.'

'What does that mean?'

'It means that the muscles become more sensitive to outside stimuli

233

so that the slightest touch or sound throws them into violent contractions.'

'But why does a dog stretch out like that?'

'Because the extensor muscles are stronger than the flexors, causing the back to be arched and the legs extended.'

He nodded. 'I see, but . . . I believe it is usually fatal. What is it that . . . that kills them?'

'They die of asphyxia due to paralysis of the respiratory centre or contraction of the diaphragm.'

Maybe he wanted to ask more, but it was painful for him and he stayed silent.

'There's one thing I'd like you to know, Mr Bartle,' I said. 'It is almost certainly not a painful condition.'

'Thank you.' He bent and briefly stroked the sleeping dog. 'So nothing more can be done?'

I shook my head. 'The barbiturate keeps the spasms in abeyance and we'll go on hoping he hasn't absorbed too much strychnine. I'll call back later, or you can ring me if he gets worse. I can be here in a few minutes.'

Driving away, I pondered on the irony that made Darrowby a paradise for dog killers as well as dog lovers. There were grassy tracks everywhere: wandering by the river's edge, climbing the fell-sides and coiling green and tempting among the heather on the high tops. I often felt sympathy for pet owners in the big cities, trying to find places to walk their dogs. Here in Darrowby we could take our pick. But so could the poisoner. He could drop his deadly bait unobserved in a hundred different places.

I was finishing the afternoon surgery when the phone rang. It was Mr Bartle.

'Has he started the spasms again?' I asked.

There was a pause. 'No, I'm afraid Jasper is dead. He never regained consciousness.'

'Oh . . . I'm very sorry.' I felt a dull despair. That was the seventh death in a week.

'Well, thank you for your treatment, Mr Herriot. I'm sure nothing could have saved him.'

I hung up the phone wearily. He was right. Nothing or nobody could have done any good in this case, but it didn't help. If you finish up with a dead animal there is always the feeling of defeat.

Strychnine

Next day I was walking on to a farm when the farmer's wife called to me. 'I have a message for you to ring back to the surgery.'

I heard Helen's voice at the other end. 'Jack Brimham has just come in with his dog. I think it's another strychnine case.'

I excused myself and drove back to Darrowby at top speed. Jack Brimham was a builder. He ran a one-man business and whatever job he was on – repairing roofs or walls or chimneys – his little white rough-haired terrier went with him, and you could usually see the little animal nosing among the piles of bricks, exploring in the surrounding fields.

Jack was a friend, too. I often had a beer with him at the Drovers' Arms and I recognised his van outside the surgery. I trotted along the passage and found him leaning over the table in the consulting room. His dog was stretched there in that attitude which I dreaded.

'He's gone, Jim,' he muttered.

I looked at the shaggy little body. There was no movement, the eyes stared silently. The legs, even in death, strained across the smooth surface of the table. It was pointless, but I slipped my hand inside the thigh and felt for the femoral artery. There was no pulse.

'I'm sorry, Jack,' I said.

He didn't answer for a moment. 'I've been readin' about this in the paper, Jim, but I never thought it would happen to me. It's a bugger, isn't it?'

I nodded. He was a craggy-faced man, a tough Yorkshireman with a humour and integrity which I liked and a soft place inside which his dog had occupied. I did not know what to say to him.

'Who's doin' this?' he said, half to himself.

'I don't know, Jack. Nobody knows.'

'Well I wish I could have five minutes with him, that's all.' He gathered the rigid little form into his arms and went out.

My troubles were not over for that day. It was about 11 p.m. and I had just got into bed when Helen nudged me.

'I think there's somebody knocking at the front door, Jim.'

I opened the window and looked out. Old Boardman, the lame veteran of the First War who did odd jobs for us, was standing on the steps.

'Mr Herriot,' he called up to me, 'I'm sorry to bother you at this hour, but Patch is ill.'

I leaned further out. 'What's he doing?'

'He's like a bit o' wood – stiff like, and laid on 'is side.'

I didn't bother to dress, just pulled my working corduroys over my pyjamas and went down the stairs two at a time. I grabbed what I needed from the dispensary and opened the front door. The old man, in shirt sleeves, caught at my arm.

'Come quickly, Mr Herriot!' He limped ahead of me to his little house about twenty yards away in the lane round the corner.

Patch was like all the others. The fat spaniel I had seen so often waddling round the top yard with his master was in that nightmare position on the kitchen floor, but he had vomited, which gave me hope. I administered the intravenous injection but as I withdrew the needle the breathing stopped.

Mrs Boardman, in nightgown and slippers, dropped on her knees and stretched a trembling hand towards the motionless animal.

'Patch . . .' She turned and stared at me, wide-eyed. 'He's dead!'

I put my hand on the old woman's shoulder and said some sympathetic words. I thought grimly that I was getting good at it. As I left I looked back at the two old people. Boardman was kneeling now by his wife and even after I had closed the door I could hear their voices: 'Patch . . . oh Patch.'

I almost reeled over the few steps to Skeldale House and before going in I stood in the empty street breathing the cool air and trying to calm my racing thoughts. With Patch gone, this thing was getting very near home. I saw that dog every day. In fact all the dogs that had died were old friends – in a little town like Darrowby you came to know your patients personally. Where was it going to end?

I didn't sleep much that night and over the next few days I was obsessed with apprehension. I expected another poisoning with every phone call and took care never to let my own dog, Sam, out of the car in the region of the town. Thanks to my job I was able to exercise him miles away on the summits of the fells, but even there I kept him close to me.

By the fourth day I was beginning to feel more relaxed. Maybe the nightmare was over. I was driving home in the late afternoon past the row of grey cottages at the end of the Houlton Road when a woman ran waving into the road.

'Oh, Mr Herriot,' she cried when I stopped, 'I was just goin' to t'phone box when I saw you.'

I pulled up by the kerb. 'It's Mrs Clifford, isn't it?'

'Yes, Johnny's just come in and Fergus 'as gone queer. Collapsed and laid on t'floor.'

Strychnine

'Oh no!' An icy chill drove through me and for a moment I stared at her, unable to move. Then I threw open the car door and hurried after Johnny's mother into the end cottage. I halted abruptly in the little room and stared down in horror. The very sight of the splendid dignified animal scrabbling helplessly on the linoleum was a desecration, but strychnine is no respecter of such things.

'Oh God!' I breathed. 'Has he vomited, Johnny?'

'Aye, me mum said he was sick in t'back garden when we came in.' The young man was sitting very upright in a chair by the side of his dog. Even now there was a half smile on his face, but he looked strained as he put out his hand in the old gesture and failed to find the head that should have been there.

The bottle of barbiturate wobbled in my shaking hand as I filled the syringe. I tried to put away the thought that I was doing what I had done to all the others – all the dead ones. At my feet Fergus panted desperately, then as I bent over him he suddenly became still and went into the horrible distinctive spasm, the great limbs I knew so well straining frantically into space, the head pulled back grotesquely over the spine.

This was when they died, when the muscles were at full contraction. As the barbiturate flowed into the vein I waited for signs of relaxation but saw none. Fergus was about twice as heavy as any of the other victims I had treated and the plunger went to the end of the syringe without result.

Quickly I drew in another dose and began to inject it, my tension building as I saw how much I was administering. The recommended dose was 1 cc per 5 lb body weight and beyond that you could kill the animal. I watched the gradations on the glass barrel of the syringe and my mouth went dry when the dose crept far beyond the safety limit. But I knew I had to relieve this spasm and continued to depress the plunger relentlessly.

I did it in the grim knowledge that if he died now I would never know whether to blame the strychnine or myself for his death.

The big dog had received more than a lethal amount before peace began to return to the taut body and even then I sat back on my heels, almost afraid to look in case I had brought about his end. There was a long agonising moment when he lay still and apparently lifeless, then the rib cage began to move almost imperceptibly as the breathing recommenced.

Even then I was in suspense. The anaesthesia was so deep that he was only just alive, yet I knew that the only hope was to keep him that way. I sent Mrs Clifford out to phone Siegfried that I would be tied up here for a while, then I pulled up a chair and settled down to wait.

The hours passed as Johnny and I sat there, the dog stretched between us. The young man discussed the case calmly and without self-pity. There was no suggestion that this was anything more than a pet animal lying at his feet – except for the tell-tale reaching for the head that was no longer there.

Several times Fergus showed signs of going into another spasm and each time I sent him back into his deep, deep insensibility, pushing him repeatedly to the brink with a fateful certainty that it was the only way.

It was well after midnight when I came sleepily out into the darkness. I felt drained. Watching the life of the friendly, clever, face-licking animal flicker as he lay inert and unheeding had been a tremendous strain, but I had left him sleeping – still anaesthetised but breathing deeply and regularly. Would he wake up and start the dread sequence again? I didn't know and I couldn't stay any longer. There was a practice with other animals to attend to.

But my anxiety jerked me into early wakefulness next morning. I tossed around till seven thirty telling myself this wasn't the way to be a veterinary surgeon, that you couldn't live like this. But my worry was stronger than the voice of reason and I slipped out before breakfast to the roadside cottage.

My nerves were like a bowstring as I knocked on the door. Mrs Clifford answered, and I was about to blurt out my enquiries when Fergus trotted from the inner room.

He was still a little groggy from the vast dosage of barbiturate but he was relaxed and happy, the symptoms had gone, he was himself again. With a gush of pure joy I knelt and took the great head between my hands. He slobbered at me playfully with his wet tongue and I had to fight him off.

He followed me into the living room where Johnny was seated at the table, drinking tea. He took up his usual position, sitting upright and proud by his master's side.

'You'll have a cup, Mr Herriot?' Mrs Clifford asked, poising the teapot.

'Thanks, I'd love one, Mrs Clifford,' I replied.

No tea ever tasted better, and as I sipped I watched the young man's smiling face.

'What a relief, Mr Herriot! I sat up with him all night, listenin' to the chimes of the church clock. It was just after four when I knew we'd won because I heard 'im get to his feet and sort o' stagger about. I stopped worryin' then, just listened to 'is feet patterin' on the linoleum. It was lovely!'

He turned his head to me and I looked at the slightly upturned eyes in the cheerful face.

'I'd have been lost without Fergus,' he said softly. 'I don't know how to thank you.'

But as he unthinkingly rested his hand on the head of the big dog who was his pride and delight I felt that the gesture alone was all the thanks I wanted.

That was the end of the strychnine poisoning outbreak in Darrowby. The older people still talk about it, but nobody ever had the slightest clue as to the identity of the killer and it is a mystery to this day.

I feel that the vigilance of the police and the publicity in the press frightened this twisted person off, but anyway it just stopped and the only cases since then have been accidental ones.

To me it is a sad memory of failure and frustration. Fergus was my only cure, and I'm not sure why he recovered. Maybe the fact that I pushed the injection to dangerous levels because I was desperate had something to do with it, or maybe he just didn't pick up as much poison as the others. I'll never know.

But over the years when I saw the big dog striding majestically in his harness, leading his master unerringly around the streets of Darrowby, I always had the same feeling.

If there had to be just one saved, I'm glad it was him.

*

Only yesterday I opened my newspaper and read of an outbreak of deliberate strychnine poisoning in a country district. So it still goes on. There are still such people around. And, sadly, we have never found an antidote. My only successes have been by anaesthetising the victims and keeping them asleep for a prolonged period. Strychnine is so deadly that in order to obtain it a permit has to be obtained from the Ministry of Agriculture. This permit, which specifies the amount of the drug and the purpose for which it is to be used, has to be presented to the chemist, but despite all precautions tragedies still occur.

29. *Locum*

Siegfried and I were at breakfast in the big dining-room. My colleague looked up from a letter he was reading.

'James, do you remember Stewie Brannan?'

I smiled. 'I could hardly forget. That was quite a day at Brawton races.' I would always carry a vivid recollection of Siegfried's amiable college chum with me.

'Yes ... yes, it was.' Siegfried nodded briefly. 'Well I've got a letter from him here. He's got six kids now, and though he doesn't complain, I don't think life is exactly a picnic working in a dump like Hensfield. Especially when he knocks a bare living out of it.' He pulled thoughtfully at the lobe of his ear. 'You know, James, it would be rather nice if he could have a break. Would you be willing to go through there and run his practice for a couple of weeks so that he could take his family on holiday?'

'Certainly. Glad to. But you'll be a bit pushed here on your own, won't you?'

Siegfried waved a hand. 'It'll do me good. Anyway it's the quiet time for us. I'll write back today.'

Stewie grasped the opportunity eagerly and within a few days I was on the road to Hensfield. Yorkshire is the biggest county in England and it must be the most varied. I could hardly believe it when, less than two hours after leaving the clean grassy fells and crystal air of Darrowby, I saw the forest of factory chimneys sprouting from the brown pall of grime.

This was the industrial West Riding and I drove past mills as dark and satanic as any I had dreamed of, past long rows of dreary featureless houses where the workers lived. Everything was black: houses, mills, walls, trees, even the surrounding hillsides, smeared and soiled from the smoke which drifted across the town from a hundred belching stacks.

Stewie's surgery was right in the heart of it, a gloomy edifice in a terrace of sooty stone. As I rang the bell I read the painted board: 'Stewart Brannan MRCVS, Veterinary Surgeon and Canine Specialist.' I was wondering what the Royal College would think about the last part when the door opened and my colleague stood before me.

He seemed to fill the entrance. If anything he was fatter than before, but that was the only difference. Since it was August I couldn't expect him to be wearing his navy nap overcoat, but otherwise he was as I remembered him in Darrowby: the big, meaty, good-natured face, the greasy black hair slicked across the brow which always seemed to carry a gentle dew of perspiration.

He reached out, grabbed my hand and pulled me delightedly through the doorway.

'Jim! Great to see you!' He put an arm round my shoulders as we crossed a dark hallway. 'It's good of you to help me out like this. The family are thrilled – they're all in the town shopping for the holiday. We've got fixed up in a flat at Blackpool.' His permanent smile widened.

We went into a room at the back where a rickety kitchen-type table stood on brown linoleum. I saw a sink in one corner, a few shelves with bottles and a white-painted cupboard. The atmosphere held a faint redolence of carbolic and cat's urine.

'This is where I see the animals,' Stewie said contentedly. He looked at his watch. 'Twenty past five – I have a surgery at five thirty. I'll show you round till then.'

It didn't take long because there wasn't much to see. I knew there was a more fashionable veterinary firm in Hensfield and that Stewie made his living from the poor people of the town; the whole set-up was an illustration of practice on a shoestring. There didn't seem to be more than one of anything – one straight suture needle, one curved needle, one pair of scissors, one syringe. There was a sparse selection of drugs and an extraordinary array of dispensing bottles and jars. These bottles were of many strange shapes – weird things which I had never seen in a dispensary before.

Stewie seemed to read my thoughts. 'It's nothing great, Jim. I haven't a smart practice and I don't make a lot, but we manage to clear the housekeeping and that's the main thing.'

The phrase was familiar. 'Clear the housekeeping' – that was how he had put it when I first met him at Brawton races. It seemed to be the lodestar of his life.

The end of the room was cut off by a curtain which my colleague drew to one side.

'This is what you might call the waiting room.' He smiled as I looked in some surprise at half a dozen wooden chairs arranged round the three walls. 'No high-powered stuff, Jim, no queues into the streets, but we get by.'

Some of Stewie's clients were already filing in: two little girls with a black dog, a cloth-capped old man with a terrier on a string, a teenage boy carrying a rabbit in a basket.

'Right,' the big man said, 'we'll get started.' He pulled on a white coat, opened the curtain and said, 'First, please.'

The little girls put their dog on the table. He was a long-tailed mixture of breeds and he stood trembling with fear, rolling his eyes apprehensively at the white coat.

'All right, lad,' Stewie murmured, 'I'm not going to hurt you.' He stroked and patted the quivering head before turning to the girls. 'What's the trouble, then?'

'It's 'is leg, 'e's lame,' one of them replied.

As if in confirmation the little dog raised a fore leg and held it up with a pitiful expression. Stewie engulfed the limb with his great hand and palpated it with the utmost care. And it struck me immediately – the gentleness of this shambling bear of a man.

'There's nothing broken,' he said. 'He's just sprained his shoulder. Try to rest it for a few days and rub this in night and morning.'

He poured some whitish liniment from a winchester bottle into one of the odd-shaped bottles and handed it over.

One of the little girls held out her hand and unclasped her fingers to reveal a shilling in her palm.

'Thanks,' said Stewie without surprise. 'Goodbye.'

He saw several other cases, then as he was on his way to the curtain two grubby urchins appeared through the door at the other end of the room. They carried a clothes basket containing a widely varied assortment of glassware.

Stewie bent over the basket, lifting out HP sauce bottles, pickle jars, ketchup containers and examining them with the air of a connoisseur. At length he appeared to come to a decision.

'Threepence,' he said.

'Sixpence,' said the urchins in unison.

'Fourpence,' grunted Stewie.

'Sixpence,' chorused the urchins.

'Fivepence,' my colleague muttered doggedly.

'Sixpence!' There was a hint of triumph in the cry.

Stewie sighed. 'Go on then.' He passed over the coin and began to stack the bottles under the sink.

'I just scrape off the labels and give them a good boil up, Jim.'

'I see.'

'It's a big saving.'

'Yes, of course.' The mystery of the strangely shaped dispensing bottles was suddenly resolved.

It was six thirty when the last client came through the curtain. I had watched Stewie examining each animal carefully, taking his time and treating their conditions ably within the confines of his limited resources. His charges were all around a shilling to two shillings and it was easy to see why he only just cleared the housekeeping.

One other thing I noticed: the people all seemed to like him. He had no 'front' but he was kind and concerned. I felt there was a lesson there.

The last arrival was a stout lady with a prim manner and a very correct manner of speech.

'My dog was bit last week,' she announced, 'and I'm afraid the wound is goin' antiseptic.'

'Ah yes,' Stewie nodded gravely. The banana fingers explored the tumefied area on the animal's neck with a gossamer touch. 'It's quite nasty, really. He could have an abscess there if we're not careful.'

He took a long time over clipping the hair away, swabbing out the deep puncture with peroxide of hydrogen. Then he puffed in some dusting powder, applied a pad of cotton wool and secured it with a bandage. He followed with an antistaphylococcal injection and finally handed over a sauce bottle filled to the rim with acriflavine solution.

'Use as directed on the label,' he said, then stood back as the lady opened her purse expectantly.

A long inward struggle showed in the occasional twitches of his cheeks and flickerings of his eyelids but finally he squared his shoulders. 'That,' he said resolutely, 'will be three and sixpence.'

It was a vast fee by Stewie's standards, but probably the minimum in other veterinary establishments, and I couldn't see how he could make any profit from the transaction.

As the lady left, a sudden uproar broke out within the house. Stewie gave me a seraphic smile.

'That'll be Meg and the kids. Come and meet them.'

We went out to the hall and into an incredible hubbub. Children shouted, screamed and laughed, spades and pails clattered, a large ball thumped from wall to wall and above it all a baby bawled relentlessly.

Stewie moved into the mob and extracted a small woman. 'This,' he murmured with quiet pride, 'is my wife.' He gazed at her like a small boy admiring a film star.

'How do you do,' I said.

Meg Brannan took my hand and smiled. Any glamour about her existed only in her husband's eye. A ravaged prettiness still remained but her face bore the traces of some tough years. I could imagine her life of mother, housewife, cook, secretary, receptionist and animal nurse.

'Oh, Mr Herriot, it is good of you and Mr Farnon to help us out like this. We're so looking forward to going away.' Her eyes held a faintly desperate gleam but they were kind.

I shrugged. 'Oh, it's a pleasure, Mrs Brannan. I'm sure I'll enjoy it and I hope you all have a marvellous holiday.' I really meant it – she looked as though she needed one.

I was introduced to the children but I never really got them sorted out. Apart from the baby, who yelled indefatigably from leather lungs, I think there were three little boys and two little girls, but I couldn't be sure – they moved around too quickly.

The only time they were silent was for a brief period at supper when Meg fed them and us from a kind of cauldron in which floated chunks of mutton, potatoes and carrots. It was very good, too, and was followed by a vast blancmange with jam on top.

The tumult broke out again very soon as the youngsters raced through their meal and began to play in the room. One thing I found disconcerting was that the two biggest boys kept throwing a large, new, painted ball from one to the other across the table as we ate. The parents said nothing about it – Meg, I felt, because she had stopped caring, and Stewie because he never had cared.

Only once when the ball whizzed past my nose and almost carried away a poised spoonful of blancmange did their father remonstrate.

'Now then, now then,' he murmured absently, and the throwing was re-sited more towards the middle of the table.

Next morning I saw the family off. Stewie had changed his dilapidated Austin Seven for a large rust-encrusted Ford V Eight. Seated at the wheel he waved and beamed through the cracked side windows with serene contentment. Meg, by his side, managed a harassed smile, and at the other windows an assortment of dogs and children fought for a vantage point. As the car moved away a pram, several suitcases and a cot swayed perilously on the roof, the children yelled, the dogs barked, the baby bawled, then they were gone.

As I re-entered the house the unaccustomed silence settled around me, and with the silence came a faint unease. I had to look after this practice for two weeks and the memory of the thinly furnished surgery was not reassuring. I just didn't have the tools to tackle any major problem.

But it was easy to comfort myself. From what I had seen this wasn't the sort of place where dramatic things happened. Stewie had once said he made most of his living by castrating tom cats, and I supposed if you threw in a few ear cankers and minor ailments that would be about it.

The morning surgery seemed to confirm this impression; a few humble folk led in nondescript pets with mild conditions and I happily dispensed a series of Bovril bottles and meat paste jars containing Stewie's limited drug store.

I had only one difficulty and that was with the table, which kept collapsing when I lifted the animals on to it. For some obscure reason it had folding legs held by metal struts underneath, and these were apt to disengage at crucial moments, causing the patient to slide abruptly to the floor. After a while I got the hang of the thing and kept one leg jammed against the struts throughout the examination.

Locum

It was about 10.30 a.m. when I finally parted the curtains and found the waiting room empty and only the distinctive cat–dog smell lingering on the air. As I locked the door it struck me that I had very little to do till the afternoon surgery. At Darrowby I would have been dashing out to start the long day's driving round the country-side, but here almost all the work was done at the practice house.

I was wondering how I would put the time in after the single outside visit on the book when the door bell rang. Then it rang again followed by a frantic pounding on the wood. I hurried through the curtain and turned the handle. A well-dressed young couple stood on the step. The man held a Golden Labrador in his arms and behind them a caravan drawn by a large gleaming car stood by the kerb.

'Are you the vet?' the girl gasped. She was in her twenties, auburn-haired, extremely attractive, but her eyes were terrified.

I nodded. 'Yes – yes, I am. What's the trouble?'

'It's our dog.' The young man's voice was hoarse, his face deathly pale. 'A car hit him.'

I glanced over the motionless yellow form. 'Is he badly hurt?'

There were a few moments of silence then the girl spoke almost in a whisper. 'Look at his hind leg.'

I stepped forward and as I peered into the crook of the man's arm a freezing wave drove through me. The limb was hanging off at the hock. Not fractured but snapped through the joint and dangling from what looked like a mere shred of skin. In the bright morning sunshine the white ends of naked bones glittered with a sickening lustre.

It seemed a long time before I came out of my first shock and found myself staring stupidly at the animal. And when I spoke the voice didn't sound like my own.

'Bring him in,' I muttered, and as I led the way back through the odorous waiting room the realisation burst on me that I had been wrong when I thought that nothing ever happened here.

*

Doing locums is a fascinating way of seeing how the other man lives. There are an infinite number of ways of running a small animal practice and Stewie Brannan's was one of the more bizarre ones. It was a strange quirk of fate that one of the most traumatic and demanding cases I can remember should crop up in Stewie's surgery where drugs and equipment were frighteningly minimal . . .

30. *Kim*

I held the curtains apart as the young man staggered in and placed his burden on the table.

Now I could see the whole thing: the typical signs of a road accident; the dirt driven savagely into the glossy gold of the coat, the multiple abrasions. But that mangled leg wasn't typical. I had never seen anything like it before.

I dragged my eyes round to the girl. 'How did it happen?'

'Oh, just in a flash.' The tears welled in her eyes. 'We are on a caravanning holiday. We had no intention of staying in Hensfield' – (I could understand that) – 'but we stopped for a newspaper, Kim jumped out of the car, and that was it.'

I looked at the big dog stretched motionless on the table. I reached out a hand and gently ran my fingers over the noble outlines of the head.

Kim

'Poor old lad,' I murmured and for an instant the beautiful hazel eyes turned to me and the tail thumped briefly against the wood.

'Where have you come from?' I asked.

'Surrey,' the young man replied. He looked rather like the prosperous young stockbroker that the name conjured up.

I rubbed my chin. 'I see . . .' A way of escape shone for a moment in the tunnel. 'Perhaps if I patch him up you could get him back to your own vet there.'

He looked at his wife for a moment then back at me. 'And what would they do there? Amputate his leg?'

I was silent. If an animal in this condition arrived in one of those high-powered southern practices with plenty of skilled assistance and full surgical equipment, that's what they probably would do. It would be the only sensible thing.

The girl broke in on my thoughts. 'Anyway, if it's at all possible to save his leg something has to be done right now. Isn't that so?' She gazed at me appealingly.

'Yes,' I said huskily. 'That's right.' I began to examine the dog. The abrasions on the skin were trivial. He was shocked, but his mucous membranes were pink enough to suggest that there was no internal haemorrhage. He had escaped serious injury except for that terrible leg.

I stared at it intently, appalled by the smooth glistening articular surfaces of the tibio-tarsal joint. There was something obscene in its exposure in a living animal. It was as though the hock had been broken open by brutal inquisitive hands.

I began a feverish search of the premises, pulling open drawers, cupboards, opening tins and boxes. My heart leaped at each little find: a jar of catgut in spirit, a packet of lint, a sprinkler tin of iodoform, and – treasure trove indeed – a bottle of barbiturate anaesthetic.

Most of all I needed antibiotics, but it was pointless looking for those because they hadn't been discovered yet. But I did hope fervently for just an ounce or two of sulphanilamide, and there I was disappointed, because Stewie's menage didn't stretch to that. It was when I came upon the box of plaster of paris bandages that something seemed to click.

At that time in the late thirties the Spanish Civil War was vivid in people's minds. In the chaos of the later stages there had been no proper medicaments to treat the terrible wounds. They had often been encased in plaster and left, in the grim phrase, to 'stew in their own juice'. Sometimes the results were surprisingly good.

I grabbed the bandages. I knew what I was going to do. Gripped by a fierce determination, I inserted the needle into the radial vein and slowly injected the anaesthetic. Kim blinked, yawned lazily and went to sleep. I quickly laid out my meagre armoury, then began to shift the dog into a better position. But I had forgotten about the table, and as I lifted the hind quarters the whole thing gave way and the dog slithered helplessly towards the floor.

'Catch him!' At my frantic shout the man grabbed the inert form, then I reinserted the slots in their holes and got the wooden surface back on the level.

'Put your leg under there,' I gasped, then turned to the girl. 'And would you please do the same at the other end. This table mustn't fall over once I get started.'

Silently they complied and as I looked at them, each with a leg jammed against the underside, I felt a deep sense of shame. What sort of place did they think this was?

But for a long time after I forgot everything. First I put the joint back in place, slipping the ridges of the tibial-tarsal trochlea into the grooves at the distal end of the tibia as I had done so often in the anatomy lab at college. And I noticed with a flicker of hope that some of the ligaments were still intact and, most important, that a few good blood vessels still ran down to the lower part of the limb.

I never said a word as I cleaned and disinfected the area, puffed iodoform into every crevice and began to stitch. I stitched interminably, pulling together shattered tendons, torn joint capsule and fascia. It was a warm morning and as the sun beat on the surgery window the sweat broke out on my forehead. By the time I had sutured the skin a little river was flowing down my nose and dripping from the tip. Next, more iodoform, then the lint, and finally two of the plaster bandages, making a firm cast above the hock down over the foot.

I straightened up and faced the young couple. They had never moved from their uncomfortable postures as they held the table upright, but I gazed at them as though seeing them for the first time.

I mopped my brow and drew a long breath. 'Well, that's it. I'd be inclined to leave it as it is for a week, then wherever you are let a vet have a look at it.'

Kim

They were silent for a moment, then the girl spoke. 'I would rather you saw it yourself.' Her husband nodded agreement.

'Really?' I was amazed. I had thought they would never want to see me, my smelly waiting room or my collapsible table again.

'Yes, of course we would,' the man said. 'You have taken such pains over him. Whatever happens we are deeply grateful to you, Mr Brannan.'

'Oh, I'm not Mr Brannan, he's on holiday. I'm his locum, my name is Herriot.'

He held out his hand. 'Well thank you again, Mr Herriot. I am Peter Gillard and this is my wife, Marjorie.'

We shook hands and he took the dog in his arms and went out to the car.

For the next few days I couldn't keep Kim's leg out of my mind. At times I felt I was crazy trying to salvage a limb that was joined to the dog only by a strip of skin. I had never met anything remotely like it before, and in unoccupied moments that hock joint with all its imponderables would float across my vision.

There were plenty of these moments because Stewie's was a restful practice. Apart from the three daily surgeries there was little activity, and in particular the uncomfortable pre-breakfast call so common in Darrowby was unknown here.

The Brannans had left the house and me in the care of Mrs Holroyd, an elderly widow of raddled appearance who slouched around in a flowered overall down which ash cascaded from a permanently dangling cigarette. She wasn't a good riser but she soon had me trained, because after a few mornings when I couldn't find her, I began to prepare my own breakfast and that was how it stayed.

However, at other times she looked after me very well. She was what you might call a good rough cook and pushed large tasty meals at me regularly with a 'There y'are, luv,' watching me impassively till I started to eat. The only thing that disturbed me was the long trembling finger of ash which always hung over my food from the cigarette that was part of her.

Mrs Holroyd also took telephone messages when I wasn't around. There weren't many outside visits but two have stuck in my memory.

The first was when I looked on the pad and read, 'Go to Mr Pimmarov to see Bulldog,' in Mrs Holroyd's careful back-sloped script.

'Pimmarov?' I asked her. 'Was he a Russian gentleman?'

'Dunno, luv, never asked 'im.'

'Well – did he sound foreign? I mean did he speak broken English?'

'Nay, luv, Yorkshire as me, 'e were.'

'Ah well, never mind, Mrs Holroyd. What's his address?'

She gave me a surprised look. 'How should ah know? He never said.'

'But . . . but, Mrs Holroyd. How can I visit him when I don't know where he lives?'

'Well you'll know best about that, luv.'

I was baffled. 'But he must have told you.'

'Now then, young man, Pimmarov was all 'e told me. Said you would know.' She stuck out her chin, her cigarette quivered and she regarded me stonily. Maybe she had had similar sessions with Stewie, but she left me in no doubt that the interview was over.

During the day I tried not to think about it, but the knowledge that somewhere in the neighbourhood there was an ailing Bulldog that I could not succour was worrying. I just hoped it was nothing fatal.

A phone call at seven p.m. resolved my fears.

'Is that t'vet?' The voice was gruff and grumpy.

'Yes . . . speaking.'

'Well, ah've been waitin' all day for tha. When are you comin' to see ma flippin' Bulldog?'

A light glimmered. But still . . . that accent . . . no suggestion of the Kremlin . . . not a hint of the Steppes.

'Oh, I'm terribly sorry,' I gabbled. 'I'm afraid there's been a little misunderstanding. I'm doing Mr Brannan's work and I don't know the district. I do hope your dog isn't seriously ill.'

'Nay, nay, nobbut a bit o' cough, but ah want 'im seein' to.'

'Certainly, certainly, I'll be right out, Mr . . . er . . .'

'Pym's ma name and ah live next to t'post office in Roff village.'

'Roff?'

'Aye, two miles outside Hensfield.'

I sighed with relief. 'Very good, Mr Pym, I'm on my way.'

'Thank ye.' The voice sounded mollified. 'Well, tha knows me now, don't tha – Pym o' Roff.'

The light was blinding. 'Pym o' Roff!' Such a simple explanation.

A lot of Mrs Holroyd's messages were eccentric, but I could usually interpret them after some thought. However, one bizarre entry jolted me later in the week. It read simply: 'Johnson, 12, Back Lane, Smiling Harry Syphilis.'

I wrestled with this for a long time before making a diffident approach to Mrs Holroyd.

She was kneading dough for scones and didn't look up as I entered the kitchen.

'Ah, Mrs Holroyd,' I rubbed my hands nervously, 'I see you have written down that I have to go to Mr Johnson's.'

'That's right, luv.'

'Well, er . . . fine, but I don't quite understand the other part – the Smiling Harry Syphilis.'

She shot a sidelong glance at me. 'Well that's 'ow you spell that word, isn't it? Ah looked it up once in a doctor's book in our 'ouse,' she said defensively.

'Oh yes, of course, yes, you've spelled it correctly. It's just the Smiling . . . and the Harry.'

Her eyes glinted dangerously and she blew a puff of smoke at me. 'Well, that's what t'feller said. Repeated it three times. Couldn't make no mistake.'

'I see. But did he mention any particular animal?'

'Naw, 'e didn't. That was what 'e said. That and no more.' A grey spicule of ash toppled into the basin and was immediately incorporated in the scones. 'Ah do ma best, tha knows!'

'Of course you do, Mrs Holroyd,' I said hastily. 'I'll just pop round to Back Lane now.'

And Mr Johnson put everything right within seconds as he led me to a shed on his allotment.

'It's me pig, guvnor. Covered wi' big red spots. Reckon it's Swine Erysipelas.'

Only he pronounced it arrysipelas and he did have a slurring mode of speech. I really couldn't blame Mrs Holroyd.

Little things like that enlivened the week, but the tension still mounted as I awaited the return of Kim. And even when the seventh day came round I was still in suspense because the Gillards did not appear at the morning surgery. When they failed to show up at the afternoon session I began to conclude that they had had the good sense to return south to a more sophisticated establishment. But at five thirty they were there.

I knew it even before I pulled the curtains apart. The smell of doom was everywhere, filling the premises, and when I went through the curtains it hit me: the sickening stink of putrefaction.

Gangrene. It was the fear which had haunted me all week and now it was realised.

There were about half a dozen other people in the waiting room, all keeping as far away as possible from the young couple, who looked up at me with strained smiles. Kim tried to rise when he saw me, but I had eyes only for the dangling useless hind limb where my once stone-hard plaster hung in sodden folds.

Of course it had to happen that the Gillards were last in and I was forced to see all the other animals first. I examined them and prescribed treatment in a stupor of misery and shame. What had I done to that beautiful dog out there? I had been crazy to try that experiment. A gangrenous leg meant that even amputation might be too late to save his life. Death from septicaemia was likely now and what the hell could I do for him in this ramshackle surgery?

When at last it was their turn, the Gillards came in with Kim limping between them, and it was an extra stab to realise afresh what a handsome animal he was. I bent over the great golden head and for a moment the friendly eyes looked into mine and the tail waved.

'Right,' I said to Peter Gillard, putting my arms under the chest. 'You take the back end and we'll lift him up.'

As we hoisted the heavy dog on to the table the flimsy structure disintegrated immediately, but this time the young people were ready for it and thrust their legs under the struts like a well-trained team till the surface was level again.

With Kim stretched on his side I fingered the bandage. It usually took time and patience with a special saw to remove a plaster, but this was just a stinking pulp. My hand shook as I cut the bandage lengthways with scissors and removed it.

I had steeled myself against the sight of the cold dead limb with its green flesh, but though there was pus and serous fluid everywhere the exposed flesh was a surprising, healthy pink. I took the foot in my hand and my heart gave a great bound. It was warm and so was the leg, right up to the hock. There was no gangrene.

Feeling suddenly weak I leaned against the table. 'I'm sorry about the terrible smell. All the pus and discharge have been decomposing under the bandage for a week, but despite the mess it's not as bad as I feared.'

'Do you . . . do you think you can save his leg?' Marjorie Gillard's voice trembled.

'I don't know. I honestly don't know. So much has to happen. But I'd say it was a case of so far so good.'

I cleaned the area thoroughly with spirit, gave a dusting of iodoform, and applied fresh lint and two more plaster bandages.

'You'll feel a lot more comfortable now, Kim,' I said, and the big dog flapped his tail against the wood at the sound of his name.

I turned to his owners. 'I want him to have another week in plaster, so what would you like to do?'

'Oh, we'll stay around Hensfield,' Peter Gillard replied. 'We've found a place for our caravan by the river – it's not too bad.'

'Very well, till next Saturday, then.' I watched Kim hobble out, holding his new white cast high, and as I went back into the house relief flowed over me in a warm wave.

But at the back of my mind the voice of caution sounded. There was still a long way to go . . .

*

How lucky I was that in those days the Spanish Civil War was still fresh in my memory. I would never have dared to encase Kim's leg in plaster if I had not read of the miraculous recoveries of the soldiers whose terrible wounds had no other means of treatment.

31. *The Flapping Track and Success Against the Odds*

The second week went by without incident. I had a mildly indecent postcard from Stewie and a view of Blackpool Tower from his wife. The weather was scorching and they were having the best holiday of their lives. I tried to picture them enjoying themselves but I had to wait a few weeks for the evidence – a snap taken by a beach photographer. The whole family were standing in the sea, grinning delightedly into the camera as the wavelets lapped round their ankles. The children brandished buckets and spades, the baby dangled bandy legs towards the water, but it was Stewie who fascinated me. A smile of blissful contentment beamed from beneath a knotted handkerchief, sturdy braces supported baggy flannel trousers rolled decorously calf-high. He was the archetype of the British father on holiday.

The last event of my stay in Hensfield was a visit to the local greyhound track. Stewie had an appointment there every other Friday to inspect the dogs.

The Hensfield stadium was not prepossessing from the outside. It had been built in a natural hollow in the sooty hills and was surrounded by ramshackle hoardings.

It was a cool night, and as I drove down to the entrance I could hear the tinny blaring from the loudspeakers. It was George Formby singing 'When I'm Cleaning Windows' and strumming on his famous ukelele.

There are all kinds of greyhound tracks. My own experience had been as a student, accompanying vets who officiated under the auspices of the National Greyhound Racing Club, but this was an unlicensed or 'flapping' track, and vastly different. I know there are many highly reputable flapping tracks but this one had a seedy air. It was, I thought wryly, just the sort of place that would be under the care of Stewie.

First I had to go to the manager's office. Mr Coker was a hard-eyed man in a shiny pin-striped suit, and he nodded briefly before giving me a calculating stare.

'Your duties here are just a formality,' he said, twisting his features into a smile. 'There'll be nothing to trouble you.'

I had the impression that he was assessing me with quiet satisfaction, looking me up and down, taking in my rumpled jacket and slacks, savouring my obvious youth and inexperience. He kept the smile going as he stubbed out his cigar. 'Well, I hope you'll have a pleasant evening.'

'Thank you,' I replied, and left.

I met the judge, timekeeper and other officials, then went down to a long glass-fronted bar overlooking the track. Quite suddenly I felt I was in an alien environment. The place was rapidly filling up and the faces around me were out of a different mould from the wholesome rural countenances of Darrowby. There seemed to be a large proportion of fat men in camel coats with brassy blondes in two. Shifty-looking characters studied race cards and glared intently at the flickering numbers on the tote board.

I looked at my watch. It was time to inspect the dogs for the first race. 'When I'm cleanin' winders!' bawled George Formby as I made my way round the edge of the track to the paddock, a paved enclosure with a wire-netting surround. Five dogs were being led round the perimeter and I stood in the centre and watched them for a minute or two. Then I halted them and went from one to the other, looking at their eyes, examining their mouths for salivation and finally palpating their abdomens.

They all appeared bright and normal except number four, which seemed rather full in the stomach region. A greyhound should only have a light meal on the morning of a race and nothing thereafter, and I turned to the man who was holding the animal.

'Has this dog been fed within the last hour or two?' I asked.

'No,' he replied. 'He's had nothing since breakfast.'

As I passed my fingers over the abdomen again I had the feeling that several of the onlookers were watching me with unusual intentness. But I dismissed it as imagination and passed on to the next animal.

Number four was second favourite, but from the moment it left its trap it was flagging. It finished last and from the darkness on the far side of the track a storm of booing broke out. I was able to make out some of the remarks which came across on the night air. 'Open your bloody eyes, vet!' was one of them. And here, in the long, brightly lit bar, I could see people nudging each other and looking at me.

I felt a thrill of anger. Maybe some of those gentlemen down there thought they could cash in on Stewie's absence. I probably looked a soft touch to them.

My next visit to the paddock was greeted with friendly nods and grins from all sides. In fact there was a strong atmosphere of joviality. When I went round the dogs all was well until I came to number five, and this time I couldn't be mistaken. Under my probing fingers the stomach bulged tensely and the animal gave a soft grunt as I squeezed.

'You'll have to take this dog out of the race,' I said. 'He's got a full stomach.'

The owner was standing by the kennel lad.

'Can't 'ave!' he burst out. 'He's had nowt!'

258

I straightened up and looked him full in the face, but his eyes were reluctant to meet mine. I knew some of the tricks: a couple of pounds of steak before the race; a bowlful of bread crumbs and two pints of milk – the crumbs swelled beautifully within a short time.

'Would you like me to vomit him?' I began to move away. 'I've got some washing soda in my car – we'll soon find out.'

The man held up a hand. 'Naw, naw, I don't want you messin' about with me dog.' He gave me a malevolent glare and trailed sulkily away.

I had only just got back to the bar when I heard the announcement over the loudspeakers. 'Will the vet please report to the manager's office.'

Mr Coker looked up from his desk and glared at me through a haze of cigar smoke. 'You've taken a dog out of the race!'

'That's right. I'm sorry, but his stomach was full.'

'But damn it . . . !' He stabbed a finger at me, then subsided and forced a tortured smile across his face. 'Now, Mr Herriot, we have to be reasonable in these matters. I've no doubt you know your job, but don't you think there's just a chance you could be wrong?' He waved his cigar expansively. 'After all, anybody can make a mistake, so perhaps you would be kind enough to reconsider.' He stretched his smile wider.

'No, I'm sorry, Mr Coker, but that would be impossible.'

There was a long pause. 'That's your last word, then?'

'It is.'

The smile vanished and he gave me a threatening stare.

'Now look,' he said, 'you've mucked up that race and it's a serious matter. I don't want any repetition, do you understand?' He ground his cigar out savagely and his jaw jutted. 'So I hope we won't have any more trouble like this.'

'I hope so, too, Mr Coker,' I said as I went out.

It seemed a long way down to the paddock on my next visit. It was very dark now and I was conscious of the hum of the crowd, the shouts of the bookies, and George and his ukelele still going full blast. 'Oh, don't the wind blow cold!' he roared.

This time it was dog number two. I could feel the tension as I examined him and found the same turgid belly.

'This one's out,' I said, and apart from a few black looks there was no argument.

They say bad news travels fast, and I had hardly started my return

journey when George was switched off and the loudspeaker asked me
to report to the manager's office.

Mr Coker was no longer at his desk. He was pacing up and down
agitatedly, and when he saw me he did another length of the room
before coming to a halt. His expression was venomous and it was
clear he had decided that the tough approach was best.

'What the bloody hell do you think you're playing at?' he barked.
'Are you trying to ruin this meeting?'

'No,' I replied. 'I've just taken out another dog which was unfit
to run. That's my job. That's what I'm here for.'

His face flushed deep red. 'I don't think you know what you're
here for. Mr Brannan goes off on holiday and leaves us at the mercy
of a young clever clogs like you, throwing your weight about and
spoiling people's pleasure. Wait till I see him!'

'Mr Brannan would have done just the same as I have. Any
veterinary surgeon would.'

'Rubbish! Don't tell me what it's all about – you're still wet behind
the ears.' He advanced slowly towards me. 'But I'll tell you this, I've
had enough! So get it straight, once and for all – no more of this
nonsense. Cut it out!'

I felt my heart thudding as I went down to see the dogs for the
next race. As I examined the five animals the owners and kennel lads
fixed me with a hypnotic stare as though I were some strange freak.
My pulse began to slow down when I found there were no full
stomachs this time, and I glanced back in relief along the line. I was
about to walk away when I noticed that number one looked a little
unusual. I went back and bent over him, trying to decide what it
was about him that had caught my attention. Then I realised what
it was – he looked sleepy. The head was hanging slightly and he had
an air of apathy.

I lifted his chin and looked into his eyes. The pupils were dilated
and every now and then there was a faint twitch of nystagmus. There
was absolutely no doubt about it – he had received some kind of
sedative. He had been doped.

The men in the paddock were very still as I stood upright. For a
few moments I gazed through the wire netting at the brightly lit
green oval, feeling the night air cold on my cheeks. George was still
at it on the loudspeakers.

'Oh Mr Wu,' he trilled. 'What can I do?'

Well I knew what I had to do, anyway. I tapped the dog on the back.

'This one's out,' I said.

I didn't wait for the announcement and was half-way up the steps to the manager's office before I heard the request for my presence blared across the stadium.

When I opened the door I half-expected Mr Coker to rush at me and attack me, and I was surprised when I found him sitting at his desk, his head buried in his hands. I stood there on the carpet for some time before he raised a ghastly countenance to me.

'Is it true?' he whispered despairingly. 'Have you done it again?'

I nodded. 'Afraid so.'

His lips trembled but he didn't say anything, and after a brief, disbelieving scrutiny he sank his head in his hands again.

I waited for a minute or two but when he stayed like that, quite motionless, I realised that the audience was at an end and took my leave.

I found no fault with the dogs for the next race and as I left the paddock an unaccustomed peace settled around me. I couldn't understand it when I heard the loudspeaker again – 'Will the vet please report . . .' But this time it was to the paddock, and I wondered if a dog had been injured. Anyway, it would be a relief to do a bit of real vetting for a change.

But when I arrived there were no animals to be seen; only two men cradling a fat companion in their arms.

'What's this?' I asked one of them.

'Ambrose 'ere fell down the steps in the stand and skinned 'is knee.'

I stared at him. 'But I'm a vet, not a doctor.'

'Ain't no doctor on the track,' the man mumbled. 'We reckoned you could patch 'im up.'

Ah well, it was a funny night. 'Put him over on that bench,' I said.

I rolled up the trouser to reveal a rather revolting fat dimpled knee. Ambrose emitted a hollow groan as I touched a very minor abrasion on the patella.

'It's nothing much,' I said. 'You've just knocked a bit of skin off.'

Ambrose looked at me tremblingly. 'Aye, but it could go t'wrong way, couldn't it? I don't want no blood poisonin'.'

'All right, I'll put something on it.' I looked inside Stewie's medical bag. The selection was limited, but I found some tincture of iodine and I poured a little on a pad of cotton wool and dabbed the wound.

Ambrose gave a shrill yelp. 'Bloody 'ell, that 'urts! What are you doin' to me?' His foot jerked up and rapped me sharply on the elbow.

Even my human patients kicked me, it seemed. I smiled reassuringly. 'Don't worry, it won't sting for long. I'll put a bandage on now.'

I bound up the knee, rolled down the trouser and patted the fat man's shoulder. 'There you are – good as new.'

He got off the bench, nodded, then grimacing painfully, prepared to leave. But an afterthought appeared to strike him and he pulled a handful of change from his pocket. He rummaged among it with a forefinger before selecting a coin which he pressed into my palm.

'There y'are,' he said.

I looked at the coin. It was a sixpence, the fee for my only piece of doctoring of my own species. I stared stupidly at it for a long time, and when I finally looked up with the half-formed idea of throwing Ambrose's honorarium back at his head the man was limping into the crowd and was soon lost to sight.

Back in the bar I was gazing apathetically through the glass at the dogs parading round the track when I felt a hand on my arm. I turned and recognised a man I had spotted earlier in the evening. He was one of a group of three men and three women, the men dark, tight-suited, foreign-looking, the women loud and over-dressed. There was something sinister about them, and I remembered thinking they could have passed without question as members of the Mafia.

The man put his face close to mine and I had a brief impression of black, darting eyes and a predatory smile.

'Is number three fit?' he whispered.

I couldn't understand the question. He seemed to know I was the vet and surely it was obvious that if I had passed the dog I considered him fit.

'Yes,' I replied. 'Yes, he is.'

The man nodded vigorously and gave me a knowing glance from hooded eyes. He returned and held a short, intimate conversation with his friends, then they all turned and looked over at me approvingly.

I was bewildered, then it struck me that they may have thought I was giving them an inside tip. To this day I am not really sure, but I think that was it because when number three finished nowhere in the race their attitude changed dramatically and they flashed me some black glares which made them look more like the Mafia than ever.

Anyway I had no more trouble down at the paddock for the rest of the evening. No more dogs to take out, which was just as well, because I had made enough enemies for one night.

After the last race I looked around the long bar. Most of the tables were occupied by people having a final drink, but I noticed an empty one and sank wearily into a chair. Stewie had asked me to stay for half an hour after the finish to make sure all the dogs got away safely, and I would stick to my bargain even though what I wanted most in the world was to get away from here and never come back.

George was still in splendid voice on the loudspeakers. 'I always get to bed by half past nine,' he warbled, and I felt strongly that he had a point there.

Along the bar counter were assembled most of the people with whom I had clashed: Mr Coker and other officials and dog owners. There was a lot of nudging and whispering and I didn't have to be told the subject of their discussion. The Mafia, too, were doing their bit with fierce side glances, and I could almost feel the waves of antagonism beating against me.

My gloomy thoughts were interrupted by the arrival of a bookie and his clerk. The bookie dropped into a chair opposite me and tipped out a huge leather bag on to the table. I had never seen so much money in my life. I peered at the man over a mountain of fivers and pounds and ten-shilling notes while little streams and tributaries of coins ran down its flanks.

The two of them began a methodical stacking and counting of the loot while I watched hypnotically. They had eroded the mountain to about half its height when the bookie caught my eye. Maybe he thought I looked envious or poverty-stricken or just miserable, because he put his finger behind a stray half-crown and flicked it expertly across the smooth surface in my direction.

'Get yourself a drink, son,' he said.

It was the second time I had been offered money during the last hour and I was almost as much taken aback as the first time. The bookie looked at me expressionlessly for a moment then he grinned. He had an attractively ugly, good-natured face that I liked instinctively, and suddenly I felt grateful to him, not for the money but for the sight of a friendly face. It was the only one I had seen all evening.

I smiled back. 'Thanks,' I said. I lifted the half-crown and went over to the bar.

I awoke next morning with the knowledge that it was my last day at Hensfield. Stewie was due back at lunch time.

When I parted the now familiar curtains at the morning surgery I still felt a vague depression, a hangover from my unhappy night at the dog track.

But when I looked into the waiting room my mood lightened immediately. There was only one animal among the odd assortment of chairs but that animal was Kim, massive, golden and beautiful, sitting between his owners, and when he saw me he sprang up with swishing tail and laughing mouth.

There was none of the smell which had horrified me before, but as I looked at the dog I could sniff something else – the sweet, sweet scent of success. Because he was touching the ground with that leg; not putting any weight on it but definitely dotting it down as he capered around me.

In an instant I was back in my world again and Mr Coker and the events of last night were but the dissolving mists of a bad dream.

I could hardly wait to get started.

'Get him on the table,' I cried, then began to laugh as the Gillards automatically pushed their legs against the collapsible struts. They knew the drill now.

I had to restrain myself from doing a dance of joy when I got the plaster off. There was a bit of discharge, but when I cleaned it away I found healthy granulation tissue everywhere. Pink new flesh binding the shattered joint together, smoothing over and hiding the original mutilation.

'Is his leg safe now?' Marjorie Gillard asked softly.

I looked at her and smiled. 'Yes, it is. There's no doubt about it now.' I rubbed my hand under the big dog's chin and the tail beat ecstatically on the wood. 'He'll probably have a stiff joint but that won't matter, will it?'

I applied the last of Stewie's bandages then we hoisted Kim off the table.

'Well, that's it,' I said. 'Take him to your own vet in another fortnight. After that I don't think he'll need a bandage at all.'

The Gillards left on their journey back to the south, and a couple of hours later Stewie and his family returned. The children were very brown; even the baby, still bawling resolutely, had a fine tan. The skin had peeled off Meg's nose but she looked wonderfully relaxed. Stewie, in open-necked shirt and with a face like a boiled lobster, seemed to have put on weight.

'That holiday saved our lives, Jim,' he said. 'I can't thank you enough, and please tell Siegfried how grateful we are.' He looked fondly at his turbulent brood flooding through the house, then as an afterthought he turned to me.

'Is everything all right in the practice?'

'Yes, Stewie, it is. I had my ups and downs of course.'

He laughed. 'Don't we all.'

'We certainly do, but everything's fine now.'

And everything did seem fine as I drove away from the smoke. I watched the houses thin and fall away behind me till the whole world opened out clean and free and I saw the green line of the fells rising over Darrowby.

I suppose we all tend to remember the good things, but as it turned out I had no option. The following Christmas I had a letter from the Gillards with a packet of snapshots showing a big golden dog clearing a gate, leaping high for a ball, strutting proudly with a stick in his mouth. There was hardly any stiffness in the leg, they said; he was perfectly sound.

So even now when I think of Hensfield the thing I remember best is Kim.

*

I know I was unfortunate in having to officiate at an unlicensed 'flapping' track, but the experience cured me for ever of any desire to earn my living that way. But the end of the story records one of my happiest triumphs – the saving of Kim's leg. How strange and wonderful that there should be such an outcome. If that dog came into our surgery today, with all our antibiotics and equipment to hand I could not possibly hope that the mangled limb would heal more perfectly. The ancient surgeons used to talk about 'laudable pus'. It means something to me now.

32. *Mr Pinkerton's Problem*

Mr Pinkerton, a smallholder, was sitting in the office next to Miss
Harbottle's desk. By his side sat his farm Collie.

'Well, what can I do for you, Mr Pinkerton?' I asked as I closed
the door behind me.

The farmer hesitated. 'It's me dog – 'e isn't right.'

'What do you mean? Is he ill?' I bent down and stroked the shaggy
head and as the dog leaped up in delight his tail began to beat a
booming tom-tom rhythm against the side of the desk.

'Nay, nay, he's right enough in 'imself.' The man was clearly ill at ease.

'Well, what's the trouble? He looks the picture of health to me.'

'Aye, but ah'm a bit worried. Ye see it's 'is ...' He glanced furtively towards Miss Harbottle. 'It's 'is pencil.'

'What d'you say?'

A faint flush mounted in Mr Pinkerton's thin cheeks. Again he shot a terrified glance at Miss Harbottle. 'It's 'is ... pencil. There's summat matter with 'is pencil.' He indicated by the merest twitch of his forefinger somewhere in the direction of the animal's belly.

I looked. 'I'm sorry, but I can't see anything unusual.'

'Ah, but there is.' The farmer's face twisted in an agony of embarrassment and he pushed his face close to mine. 'There's summat there,' he said in a hoarse whisper. 'Summat comin' from 'is ... 'is pencil.'

I got down on my knees and had a closer look, and suddenly all became clear.

'Is that what you mean?' I pointed to a tiny blob of semen on the end of the prepuce.

He nodded dumbly, his face a study in woe.

I laughed. 'Well you can stop worrying. That's nothing abnormal. You might call it an overflow. He's just a young dog, isn't he?'

'Aye, nobbut eighteen months.'

'Well, that's it. He's just too full of the joys. Plenty of good food and maybe not a lot of work to do, eh?'

'Aye, he gets good grub. Nowt but the best. And you're right – I 'aven't much work for him.'

'Well, there you are.' I held out a hand. 'Just cut down his diet and see he gets more exercise and this thing will sort itself out.'

Mr Pinkerton stared at me. 'But aren't you goin' to do anything to 'is ... 'is ...' Again he cast an anguished glance at our secretary.

'No, no,' I said. 'I assure you there's nothing wrong with his ... er ... pencil. No local trouble at all.'

I could see he was still totally unconvinced so I threw in another ploy. 'I tell you what. I'll give you some mild sedative tablets for him. They'll help a bit.'

I went through to the dispensary and counted the tablets into a box. Back in the office I handed them to the farmer with a confident smile, but his face registered only a deepening misery. Obviously I hadn't explained the thing clearly enough and as I led him along the passage to the front door I talked incessantly, putting the whole business into simple words which I was sure he would understand.

As he stood on the doorstep I gave him a final comforting pat on the shoulder and though I was almost breathless with my own babbling I thought it best to sum up the entire oration before he left.

'So there you are,' I said with a light laugh. 'Reduce his food, see that he gets plenty of work and exercise, and give him one of the tablets night and morning.'

The farmer's mouth drooped until I thought he would burst into tears, then he turned and trailed down the steps into the street. He took a couple of indeterminate strides then swung round and his voice rose in a plaintive wail.

'But Mr Herriot . . . 'ow about 'is pencil?'

*

A happy reminder of the days when, among the farming community, even remotely sexual matters were either unmentionable or were referred to with the utmost delicacy. 'Pencil' was only one of the many euphemisms. How different it is now when the young farmers' wives often make me gulp with their recital of explicit anatomical details.

33. *Kind Hearts and Country Vets*

It was one of the many times Siegfried had to take me to task. An old-age pensioner was leading a small mongrel dog along the passage on the end of a piece of string. I patted the consulting room table.

'Put him up here, will you?' I said.

The old man bent over slowly, groaning and puffing.

'Wait a minute.' I tapped his shoulder. 'Let me do it.' I hoisted the little animal on to the smooth surface.

'Thank ye, sir.' The man straightened up and rubbed his back and leg. 'I 'ave arthritis bad and I'm not much good at liftin'. My name's Bailey and I live at t'council houses.'

'Right, Mr Bailey, what's the trouble?'

'It's this cough. He's allus at it. And 'e kind of retches at t'end of it.'

'I see. How old is he?'

'He were ten last month.'

'Yes . . .' I took the temperature and carefully auscultated the chest. As I moved the stethoscope over the ribs Siegfried came in and began to rummage in the cupboard.

'It's a chronic bronchitis, Mr Bailey,' I said. 'Many older dogs suffer from it just like old folks.'

He laughed. 'Aye, ah'm a bit wheezy meself sometimes.'

'That's right, but you're not so bad, really, are you?'

'Naw, naw.'

'Well neither is your little dog. I'm going to give him an injection and a course of tablets and it will help him quite a bit. I'm afraid he'll never quite get rid of this cough, but bring him in again if it gets very bad.'

He nodded vigorously. 'Very good, sir. Thank ye kindly, sir.'

As Siegfried banged about in the cupboard I gave the injection and counted out twenty of the new M&B 693 tablets.

The old man gazed at them with interest, then put them in his pocket. 'Now what do ah owe ye, Mr Herriot?'

I looked at the ragged tie knotted carefully over the frayed shirt collar, at the threadbare antiquity of the jacket. His trouser knees had been darned but on one side I caught a pink glimpse of the flesh through the material.

'No, that's all right, Mr Bailey. Just see how he goes on.'

'Eh?'

'There's no charge.'

'But . . .'

'Now don't worry about it – it's nothing, really. Just see he gets his tablets regularly.'

'I will, sir, and it's very kind of you. I never expected . . .'

'I know you didn't, Mr Bailey. Goodbye for now and bring him back if he's not a lot better in a few days.'

The sound of the old man's footsteps had hardly died away when Siegfried emerged from the cupboard. He brandished a pair of horse tooth forceps in my face. 'God, I've been ages hunting these down. I'm sure you deliberately hide things from me, James.'

I smiled but made no reply and as I was replacing my syringe on the trolley my colleague spoke again.

'James, I don't like to mention this, but aren't you rather rash, doing work for nothing?'

I looked at him in surprise. 'He was an old-age pensioner. Pretty hard up I should think.'

'Maybe so, but really, you know, you just cannot give your services free.'

'Oh but surely occasionally, Siegfried – in a case like this . . .'

'No, James, not even occasionally. It's just not practical.'

'But I've seen you do it – time and time again!'

'Me?' His eyes widened in astonishment. 'Never! I'm too aware of the harsh realities of life for that. Everything has become so frightfully expensive. For instance, weren't those M&B 693 tablets you were dishing out? Heaven help us, do you know those things are threepence each? It's no good – you must never work without charging.'

'But dammit, you're always doing it!' I burst out. 'Only last week there was that . . .'

Siegfried held up a restraining hand. 'Please, James, please. You imagine things, that's your trouble.'

I must have given him one of my most exasperated stares because he reached out and patted my shoulder.

'Believe me, my boy, I do understand. You acted from the highest possible motives and I have often been tempted to do the same. But you must be firm. These are hard times and one must be hard to survive. So remember in future – no more Robin Hood stuff, we can't afford it.'

I nodded and went on my way somewhat bemusedly, but I soon forgot the incident and would have thought no more about it had I not seen Mr Bailey about a week later.

His dog was once more on the consulting room table and Siegfried was giving it an injection. I didn't want to interfere so I went back along the passage to the front office and sat down to write in the day book. It was a summer afternoon, the window was open and through a parting in the curtain I could see the front steps.

As I wrote I heard Siegfried and the old man passing on their way to the front door. They stopped on the steps. The little dog, still on the end of its string, looked much as it did before.

'All right, Mr Bailey,' my colleague said. 'I can only tell you the same as Mr Herriot. I'm afraid he's got that cough for life, but when it gets bad you must come and see us.'

'Very good, sir.' The old man put his hand in his pocket. 'And what is the charge, please?'

'The charge, oh yes . . . the charge . . .' Siegfried cleared his throat a few times but seemed unable to articulate. He kept looking from the mongrel dog to the old man's tattered clothing and back again. Then he glanced furtively into the house and spoke in a hoarse whisper.

'It's nothing, Mr Bailey.'

'But Mr Farnon, I can't let ye . . .'

'Shh! Shh!' Siegfried waved a hand agitatedly in the old man's face. 'Not a word now! I don't want to hear any more about it.'

Having silenced Mr Bailey he produced a large bag.

'There's about a hundred M&B tablets in here,' he said, throwing an anxious glance over his shoulder. 'He's going to keep needing them, so I've given you a good supply.'

I could see my colleague had spotted the hole in the trouser knee because he gazed down at it for a long time before putting his hand in his jacket pocket.

'Hang on a minute.' He extracted a handful of assorted chattels. A few coins fell and rolled down the steps as he prodded in his palm among scissors, thermometers, pieces of string, bottle openers. Finally his search was rewarded and he pulled out a bank note.

'Here's a quid,' he whispered and again nervously shushed the man's attempts to speak.

Mr Bailey, realising the futility of argument, pocketed the money.

'Well, thank ye, Mr Farnon. Ah'll take t'missus to Scarborough wi' that.'

'Good lad, good lad,' muttered Siegfried, still looking around him guiltily. 'Now off you go.'

The old man solemnly raised his cap and began to shuffle painfully down the street.

'Hey, hold on, there,' my colleague called after him. 'What's the matter? You're not going very well.'

'It's this dang arthritis. Ah go a long way in a long time.'

'And you've got to walk all the way to the council houses?' Siegfried rubbed his chin irresolutely. 'It's a fair step.' He took a last wary peep down the passage then beckoned with his hand.

'Look, my car's right here,' he whispered. 'Nip in and I'll run you home.'

*

I must admit that I am rather attached to this little vignette. There isn't much of it, but it illustrates quite a few things: the very common syndrome of chronic bronchitis in old dogs and, more particularly, Siegfried's glorious inconsistency along with the generosity and compassion which he tried so hard to conceal.

34. *Jingo and Skipper*

Animals need friends. Have you ever watched two animals in a field?
They may be of different species – a pony and a sheep – but they
hang together. This comradeship between animals has always fascinated me, and I often think of Jack Sanders's two dogs as a perfect
example of mutual devotion.

One of them was called Jingo, and as I injected the local anaesthetic alongside the barbed wire tear in his skin the powerful white
Bull Terrier whimpered just once. Then he decided to resign himself
to his fate and looked stolidly to the front as I depressed the plunger.

Jingo and Skipper

Meanwhile his inseparable friend, Skipper the Corgi, gnawed gently at Jingo's hind leg. It was odd to see two dogs on the table at once, but I knew the relationship between them and made no comment as their master hoisted them both up.

After I had infiltrated the area around the wound I began to stitch and Jingo relaxed noticeably when he found that he could feel nothing.

'Maybe this'll teach you to avoid barbed wire fences in future, Jing,' I said.

Jack Sanders laughed. 'I doubt if it will, Mr Herriot. I thought the coast was clear when I took him down the lane this morning, but he spotted a dog on the other side of the fence and he was through like a bullet. Fortunately it was a Greyhound and he couldn't catch it.'

'You're a regular terror, Jing.' I patted my patient, and the big Roman-nosed face turned to me with an ear-to-ear grin and at the other end the tail whipped delightedly.

'Yes, it's amazing, isn't it?' his master said. 'He's always looking for a fight, yet people and children can do anything with him. He's the best natured dog in the world.'

I finished stitching and dropped the suture needle into a kidney dish on the trolley. 'Well, you've got to remember that the Bull Terrier is the original English fighting dog and Jing is only obeying an age-old instinct.'

'Oh I realise that. I'll just have to go on scanning the horizon every time I let him off the lead. No dog is safe from him.'

'Except this one, Jack.' I laughed and pointed to the little Corgi who had tired of his companion's leg and was now chewing his ear.

'Yes, isn't it marvellous. I think he could bite Jing's ear off without reprisal.'

It was indeed rather wonderful. The Corgi was eleven years old and beginning to show his age in stiffness of movement and impairment of sight, while the Bull Terrier was only three, at the height of his strength and power. A squat, barrel-chested bundle of bone and muscle, he was a formidable animal. But when the ear-chewing became too violent, all he did was turn and gently engulf Skipper's head in his huge jaws till the little animal desisted. Those jaws could be as merciless as a steel trap but they held the tiny head in a loving embrace.

Ten days later their master brought both dogs back to the surgery for the removal of the stitches. He looked worried as he lifted the animals on to the table.

'Jingo isn't at all well, Mr Herriot,' he said. 'He's been off his food for a couple of days and he looks miserable. Could that wound make him ill if it turned septic?'

'Yes it could, of course.' I looked down anxiously at the area of the flank where I had stitched, and my fingers explored the long scar. 'But there's not the slightest sign of infection here. No swelling, no pain. He's healed beautifully.'

I stepped back and looked at the Bull Terrier. He was strangely disconsolate, tail tucked down, eyes gazing ahead with total lack of interest. Not even the busy nibbling of his friend at one of his paws relieved his apathy.

Clearly Skipper didn't like being ignored in this fashion. He transferred his operations to the front end and started on the big dog's ear. As his efforts still went unnoticed he began to chew and tug harder, dragging the massive head down to one side, but as far as Jingo was concerned he might as well not have been there.

'Hey, that's enough, Skipper,' I said. 'Jing isn't in the mood for rough stuff today.' I lifted him gently to the floor where he paced indignantly around the table legs.

I examined the Bull Terrier thoroughly and the only significant finding was an elevated temperature.

'It's a hundred and five, Jack. He's very ill, there's no doubt about that.'

'But what's the matter with him?'

'With a high fever like that he must have some acute infection. But at the moment it's difficult to pinpoint.' I reached out and stroked the broad skull, running my fingers over the curving white face as my thoughts raced.

For an instant the tail twitched between his hocks and the friendly eyes rolled round to me and then to his master. It was that movement of the eyes which seized my whole attention. I quickly raised the upper lid. The conjunctiva appeared to be a normal pink, but in the smooth white sclera I could discern the faintest tinge of yellow.

'He's got jaundice,' I said. 'Have you noticed anything peculiar about his urine?'

Jack Sanders nodded. 'Yes, now you mention it. I saw him cock his leg in the garden and his water looked a bit dark.'

'Those are bile pigments.' I gently squeezed the abdomen and the dog winced slightly. 'Yes, he's definitely tender in there.'

'Jaundice?' His master stared at me across the table. 'Where would he get that?'

I rubbed my chin. 'Well, when I see a dog like this I think firstly of two things – phosphorus poisoning and leptospirosis. In view of the high temperature I go for the leptospirosis.'

'Would he catch it from another dog?'

'Possibly, but more likely from rats. Does he come into contact with any rats?'

'Yes, now and then. There's a lot of them in an old hen house at the foot of the lane and Jing sometimes gets in there after them.'

'Well that's it.' I shrugged. 'I don't think we need to look any further for the cause.'

He nodded slowly. 'Anyway, it's something to know what's wrong with him. Now you can set about putting him right.'

I looked at him for a moment in silence. It wasn't like that at all. I didn't want to upset him, but on the other hand he was a highly intelligent and sensible man in his forties, a teacher at the local school. I felt I had to tell him the whole truth.

'Jack,' I said, 'this is a terrible condition to treat. If there's one thing I hate to see it's a jaundiced dog.'

'You mean it's serious?'

'I'm afraid so. In fact the mortality rate is very high.'

I felt for him when I saw the sudden pain and concern in his face, but a warning now was better than a shock later, because I knew that Jingo could be dead within a few days. Even now, thirty years later, I quail when I see that yellowish discoloration in a dog's eyes. Penicillin and other antibiotics have some effect against the causal organism of leptospirosis, but the disease is still very often fatal.

'I see ... I see ...' He was collecting his thoughts. 'But surely you can do something?'

'Yes, yes, of course,' I said briskly. 'I'm going to give him a big shot of antileptospiral serum and some medicine to administer by the mouth. It isn't completely hopeless.'

I injected the serum in the knowledge that it didn't have much effect at this stage, but I had nothing else to offer. I gave Skipper a shot, too, with the happier feeling that it would protect him against the infection.

'One thing more, Jack,' I added. 'This desease also affects humans, so please take all hygienic precautions when handling Jingo. All right?'

He nodded and lifted the Bull Terrier from the table. The big dog, as most of my patients do, tried to hurry away from the disturbing white-coat-and-antispetic atmosphere of the surgery. As he trotted along the passage his master turned to me eagerly.

'Look at that! He doesn't seem too bad, does he?'

I didn't say anything. I hoped with all my heart that he was right, but I was fighting off the conviction that this nice animal was doomed. At any rate I would soon know.

I knew, in fact, next day. Jack Sanders was on the phone before nine o'clock in the morning.

'Jing's not so good,' he said, but the tremor in his voice belied the lightness of his words.

'Oh.' I experienced the familiar drooping of the spirits. 'What is he doing?'

'Nothing, I'm afraid. Won't eat a thing . . . lying around . . . just lifeless. And every now and then he vomits.'

It was what I expected, but I still felt like kicking the desk by my side. 'Very well, I'll be right round.'

There were no tail wags from Jing to-day. He was crouched before the fire, gazing listlessly into the coals. The yellow in his eyes had deepened to a rich orange and his temperature still soared. I repeated the serum injection, but the big dog did not heed the entry of the needle. Before I left I ran my hand over the smooth white body and Skipper as ever kept burrowing in on his friend, but Jingo's thoughts were elsewhere, sunk in his inner misery.

I visited him daily and on the fourth day I found him stretched almost comatose on his side. The conjunctiva, sclera, and the mucous membranes of the mouth were a dirty chocolate colour.

'Is he suffering?' Jack Sanders asked.

I hesitated for a moment. 'I honestly don't think he's in pain. Sickness, nausea, yes, but I'd say that's all.'

'Well I'd like to keep on trying,' he said. 'I don't want to put him down even though you think it's hopeless. You do . . . don't you?'

I made a non-committal gesture. I was watching Skipper who seemed bewildered. He had given up his worrying tactics and was sniffing round his friend in a puzzled manner. Only once did he pull very gently at the unresponsive ear.

I went through the motions with a feeling of helplessness and left with the unpleasant intuition that I would never see Jingo alive again.

And even though I was waiting for it, Jack Sanders's phone call next morning was a bad start to the day.

'Jing died during the night, Mr Herriot. I thought I'd better let you know. You said you were coming back this morning.' He was trying to be matter-of-fact.

'I'm sorry, Jack,' I said. 'I did rather expect . . .'

'Yes, I know. And thank you for what you did.'

It made it worse when people were nice at these times. The Sanders were a childless couple and devoted to their animals. I knew how he was feeling.

I stood there with the receiver in my hand. 'Anyway, Jack, you've still got Skipper.' It sounded a bit lame, but it did help to have the comfort of one remaining dog, even though he was old.

'That's right,' he replied. 'We're very thankful for Skipper.'

I went on with my work. Patients died sometimes and once it was over it was almost a relief, especially when I knew in Jingo's case that the end was inevitable.

But this thing wasn't over. Less than a week later Jack Sanders was on the phone again.

'It's Skipper,' he said. 'He seems to be going the same way as Jing.'

A cold hand took hold of my stomach and twisted it.

'But . . . but . . . he can't be! I gave him the protective injection!'

'Well, I don't know, but he's hanging around miserably and hardly eats a thing. He seems to be going down fast.'

I ran out and jumped into my car. And as I drove to the edge of the town where the Sanders lived my heart thudded and panicky thoughts jostled around in my mind. How could he have got the infection? I had little faith in the serum as a cure but as a prevention I felt it was safe. I had even given him a second shot to make sure. The idea of these people losing both their dogs was bad enough, but I couldn't bear the thought that the second one might be my fault.

The little Corgi trailed unhappily across the carpet when he saw me and I lifted him quickly on to the kitchen table. I almost snatched at his eyelids in my anxiety but there was no sign of jaundice in the sclera nor in the mucous membranes of the mouth. The temperature was dead normal and I felt a wave of relief.

'He hasn't got leptospirosis, anyway,' I said.

Mrs Sanders clasped her hands. 'Oh thank God for that. We were sure it was the same thing. He looks so awful.'

I examined the little animal meticulously and when I finished I put my stethoscope in my pocket. 'Well, I can't find much wrong here. He's got a bit of a heart murmur but you've known about that for some time. He's old, after all.'

'Do you think he could be fretting for Jing?' Jack Sanders asked.

'Yes, I do. They were such friends. He must feel lost.'

'But he'll get over that, won't he?'

'Oh of course he will. I'll leave some mild sedative tablets for him and I'm sure they'll help.'

I met Jack a few days later in the market-place.

'How is Skipper?' I asked.

He blew out his cheeks. 'About the same. Maybe a bit worse. The trouble is he eats practically nothing – he's getting very thin.'

I didn't see what else I could do, but on the following day I looked in at the Sanders's as I was passing.

I was shocked at the little Corgi's appearance. Despite his age he had been so cocky and full of bounce, and when Jing was alive he had been indisputably the boss dog. But now he was utterly deflated. He looked at me with lack-lustre eyes as I came in, then crept stiffly to his basket where he curled himself as though wishing to shut out the world.

I examined him again. The heart murmur seemed a little more pronounced but there was nothing else except that he looked old and decrepit and done.

'You know, I'm beginning to wonder if he really is fretting,' I said. 'It could be just his age catching up on him. After all, he'll be twelve in the spring, won't he?'

Mrs Sanders nodded. 'That's right. Then you think . . . this could be the end?'

'It's possible.' I knew what she was thinking. A couple of weeks ago two healthy dogs rolling around and playing in this house and now there could soon be none.

'But isn't there anything else you can do?'

'Well I can give him a course of digitalis for his heart. And perhaps you would bring in a sample of his urine. I want to see how his kidneys are functioning.'

I tested the urine. There was a little albumen, but no more than you would expect in a dog of his age. I ruled out nephritis as a cause.

As the days passed I tried other things: vitamins, iron tonics, organo-phosphates, but the little animal declined steadily. It was about a month after Jing's death that I was called to the house again.

Skipper was in his basket and when I called to him he slowly raised his head. His face was pinched and fleshless and the filmed eyes regarded me without recognition.

'Come on, lad,' I said encouragingly. 'Let's see you get out of there.'

Jack Sanders shook his head. 'It's no good, Mr Herriot. He never leaves his basket now and when we lift him out he's almost too weak to walk. Another thing . . . he makes a mess down here in the kitchen during the night. That's something he's never done.'

It was like the tolling of a sad bell. Everything he said pointed to a dog in the last stages of senility. I tried to pick my words.

'I'm sorry, Jack, but it all sounds as if the old chap has come to the end of the road. I don't think fretting could possibly cause all this.'

He didn't speak for a moment. He looked at his wife then down at the forlorn little creature. 'Well of course this has been in the back of our minds. But we've kept hoping he would start to eat. What . . . what do you suggest?'

I could not bring myself to say the fateful words. 'It seems to me that we can't stand by and let him suffer. He's just a little skeleton and I can't think he's getting any pleasure out of his life now.'

'I see,' he said. 'And I agree. He lies there all day – he has no interest in anything.' He paused and looked at his wife again. 'I tell you what, Mr Herriot. Let us think it over till tomorrow. But you do think there's no hope?'

'Yes, Jack, I do. Old dogs often go this way at the end. Skipper has just cracked up . . . he's finished, I'm afraid.'

He drew a long breath. 'Right, if you don't hear from me by eight o'clock tomorrow morning, please come and put him to sleep.'

I had small hope of the call coming and it didn't. In those early days of our marriage Helen worked as a secretary for one of the local millers. We often started our day together by descending the long flights of stairs from our bed-sitter and I would see her out of the front door before getting ready for my round.

This morning she gave me her usual kiss before going out into the street, but then she looked at me searchingly. 'You've been quiet all through breakfast, Jim. What's the matter?'

'It's nothing, really. Just part of the job,' I said. But when she kept her steady gaze on me I told her quickly about the Sanders.

She touched my arm. 'It's such a shame, Jim, but you can't let your sad cases depress you. You'd never survive.'

'Aagh, I know that. But I'm a softy, that's my trouble. Sometimes I think I should never have been a vet.'

'You're wrong there,' she said. 'I couldn't imagine you as anything else. You'll do what you have to do, and you'll do it the right way.' She kissed me again, turned and ran down the steps.

It was mid-morning before I drew up outside the Sanders's home. I opened the car boot and took out the syringe and the bottle of concentrated anaesthetic which would give the old dog a peaceful and painless end.

The first thing I saw when I went into the kitchen was a fat little white puppy waddling across the floor.

I looked down in astonishment. 'What's this . . . ?'

Mrs Sanders gave me a strained smile. 'Jack and I had a talk yesterday. We couldn't bear the idea of not having a dog at all, so we went round to Mrs Palmer who bred Jing and found she had a litter for sale. It seemed like fate. We've called him Jingo, too.'

'What a splendid idea!' I lifted the pup which squirmed in my hand, grunted in an obese manner and tried to lick my face. This, I felt, would make my unpleasant task easier. 'I think you've been very sensible.'

I lifted the bottle of anaesthetic unobtrusively from my pocket and went over to the basket in the corner. Skipper was still curled in the unheeding ball of yesterday and the comforting thought came to me that all I was going to do was push him a little further along the journey he had already begun.

I pierced the rubber diaphragm on the bottle with my needle and was about to withdraw the barbiturate when I saw that Skipper had raised his head. Chin resting on the edge of the basket, he seemed to be watching the pup. Wearily his eyes followed the tiny creature as it made its way to a dish of milk and began to lap busily. And there was something in his intent expression which had not been there for a long time.

I stood very still as the Corgi made a couple of attempts then heaved himself to a standing position. He almost fell out of the basket and staggered on shaking legs across the floor. When he came alongside the pup he remained there, swaying, for some time, a gaunt caricature of his former self, but as I watched in disbelief, he reached forward and seized the little white ear in his mouth.

Stoicism is not a characteristic of pups and Jingo the Second yelped shrilly as the teeth squeezed. Skipper, undeterred, continued to gnaw with rapt concentration.

I dropped bottle and syringe back in my pocket. 'Bring him some food,' I said quietly.

Mrs Sanders hurried to the pantry and came back with a few pieces of meat on a saucer. Skipper continued his ear-nibbling for a few moments then sniffed the pup unhurriedly from end to end before turning to the saucer. He hardly had the strength to chew but he lifted a portion of meat and his jaws moved slowly.

'Good heavens!' Jack Sanders burst out. 'That's the first thing he's eaten for days!'

His wife seized my arm. 'What's happened, Mr Herriot? We only got the puppy because we couldn't have a house without a dog.'

'Well, it looks to me as though you've got two again.' I went over to the door and smiled back at the two people watching fascinated as the Corgi swallowed, then started determinedly on another piece of meat. 'Good morning, I'm going now.'

About eight months later, Jack Sanders came into the surgery and put Jingo Two on the table. He was growing into a fine animal with the wide chest and powerful legs of the breed. His good-natured face and whipping tail reminded me strongly of his predecessor.

'He's got a bit of eczema between his pads,' Jack said, then he bent and lifted Skipper up.

At that moment I had no eyes for my patient. All my attention was on the Corgi, plump and bright-eyed, nibbling at the big white dog's hind limbs with all his old bounce and vigour.

'Just look at that!' I murmured. 'It's like turning the clock back.'

Jack Sanders laughed. 'Yes, isn't it. They're tremendous friends – just like before.'

'Come here, Skipper.' I grabbed the little Corgi and looked him over. When I had finished I held him for a moment as he tried to wriggle his way back to his friend. 'Do you know, I honestly think he'll go on for years yet.'

'Really?' Jack Sanders looked at me with a mischievous light in his eyes. 'But I seem to remember you saying quite a long time ago that his days were over – he was finished.'

I held up a hand. 'I know, I know. But sometimes it's lovely to be wrong.'

*

One of my warm memories about the importance of animal relationships. The psychological side of animal doctoring is deeply interesting. If they feel they have nothing to live for they will very often die, and this holds good in all animal species, as in the case of a ewe who will usually survive a tough lambing if she has a lamb to care for. Skipper's case was proof of the most satisfying kind. Of course, losing a companion affects different dogs in different ways. Some of them just fret briefly, but others mourn the loss for a very long time.

35. *Seth Pilling and His Little Knowledge*

'That young Herriot's a bloody thick-'ead.'

It wasn't the sort of statement to raise one's morale and for a moment the good ale turned to vinegar in my mouth. I was having a quiet pint all alone in the 'snug' of the Crown and Anchor on my way home from an evening colic case, and the words came clearly through the hatch from the public bar.

I shifted my position slightly so that I could see into the brightly lit room. The speaker was Seth Pilling, a casual labourer and a well-known character in Darrowby. He was designated a labourer, but in truth he didn't labour unduly and his burly frame and red meaty face was a common sight around the Labour Exchange where he signed for his unemployment pay.

'Aye, 'e's got no idea. Knaws nowt about dogs.' The big man tipped about half a pint over his throat in one swallow.

'He's not a bad hand wi' cows,' another voice broke in.

'Aye, maybe, but I'm not talkin' about bloody awd cows,' Seth retorted witheringly. 'I'm talkin' about dogs. Ye need skill to doctor dogs.'

A third man spoke up. 'Well, 'e's a vitnery, isn't he?'

'Aye, a knaw he is, but there's all kind o' vitneries and this 'un's a dead loss. Ah could tell ye some tales about this feller.'

They say an eavesdropper never hears anything good about himself, and I knew the sensible thing would be to get out of there immediately rather than hear this man vilifying me in a crowded bar. But of course I didn't get out. I stayed, morbidly fascinated, listening with every nerve and fibre.

'What sort o' tales, Seth?' The company was as interested as I was.

'Well,' he replied, 'there's many a time folks 'ave brought dogs to me that he's made a mess of.'

'Tha knaws all about dogs, doesn't tha, Seth?'

It was perhaps wishful thinking that made me imagine a touch of sarcasm in the last remark, but if it were so it was lost on Mr Pilling. His big, stupid face creased into a self-satisfied smirk.

'Ah'll tell ye there's not a lot ah don't know about 'em. I've been among 'em all me life and I've studied t'job, too.' He slurped down more beer. 'I've got a houseful o' books and read 'em all. Ah ken everythin' about them diseases and the remedies.'

Another of the men in the bar spoke. 'Have ye never been beat wi' a dog job, Seth?'

There was a pause. 'Well ah'm not goin' to say I never 'ave,' he said judicially. 'It's very rare I'm beat, but if I am I don't go to Herriot.' He shook his head. 'Nay, nay, ah slip through to Brawton and consult wi' Dennaby Broome. He's a big friend o' mine.'

In the quiet of the snug I sipped at my glass. Dennaby Broome was one of the many 'quacks' who flourished in those days. He had started in the building trade – as a plasterer to be exact – and had gravitated mysteriously and without formal training into the field of veterinary science, where he now made a comfortable living.

I had nothing against him for that – we all have to live. In any case he rarely bothered me because Brawton was mainly outside our practice orbit, but my colleagues around there used some unkind words about him. I had a private conviction that a lot of his success was due to his resounding name. To me, the very words 'Dennaby Broome' were profoundly imposing.

'Aye, that's what ah do,' Seth continued. 'Dennaby and me's big friends and we oft consult about dogs. Matter of fact ah took me own dog to 'im once – he looks well, eh?'

I stood on tiptoe and peered into the bar. I could just see Seth's Keeshond sitting at his feet. A handsome creature with a luxuriant glossy coat. The big man leaned over and patted the fox-like head. 'He's a vallible animal is that. Ah couldn't trust 'im to a feller like Herriot.'

'What's the matter wi' Herriot, any road?' somebody asked.

'Well, ah'll tell tha.' Seth tapped his head. 'He hasn't got ower much up 'ere.'

I didn't want to hear any more. I put down my glass and stole out into the night.

After that experience I took more notice of Seth Pilling. He was often to be seen strolling round the town because, despite his vast store of knowledge on many subjects, he was frequently out of work. He wasn't an expert only on dogs – he pontificated in the Crown and Anchor on politics, gardening, cage birds, agriculture, the state of the economy, cricket, fishing and many other matters. There were few topics which his wide intellect did not effortlessly embrace, so that it was surprising that employers seemed to dispense with his services after a very brief period.

He usually took his dog with him on his strolls, and the attractive animal began to appear to me as a symbol of my shortcomings. Instinctively I kept out of his way but one morning I came right up against him.

It was at the little shelter in the market-place and a group of people were waiting for the Brawton bus. Among them was Seth Pilling and the Keeshond, and as I passed within a few feet of them on my way to the post office I stopped involuntarily and stared. The dog was almost unrecognisable.

The dense, off-standing ash-grey coat I knew so well had become sparse and lustreless. The thick ruff, so characteristic of the breed, had shrunk to nothing.

'You're lookin' at me dog?' Mr Pilling tightened the lead and pulled the little animal towards him protectively as though he feared I might put my contaminating hand on him.

'Yes . . . I'm sorry, but I couldn't help noticing. He has a skin condition . . . ?'

The big man looked down his nose at me. 'Aye, 'e has, a bit. I'm just takin' him through to Brawton to see Dennaby Broome.'

'I see.'

'Yes, ah thought ah'd better take 'im to somebody as knows summat about dogs.' He smirked as he looked around at the people in the shelter who were listening with interest. 'He's a vallible dog is that.'

'I'm sure he is,' I said.

He raised his voice further. 'Mind you, ah've been givin' him some of me own treatment.' He didn't have to tell me. There was a strong smell of tar, and the dog's hair was streaked with some oily substance. 'But it's maybe better to make sure. We're lucky to 'ave a man like Dennaby Broome to turn to.'

'Quite.'

He looked around his audience appreciatively. 'Especially with a vallible dog like this. You can't 'ave any Tom, Dick or Harry muckin' around with 'im.'

'Well,' I said, 'I hope you get him put right.'

'Oh, ah will.' The big man was enjoying the interlude, and he laughed. 'Don't *you* worry about *that*.'

This little session did not enliven my day, but it gave me more reason to watch out for Mr Pilling. For the next two weeks I observed his movements with the deepest interest because his dog was losing its hair at an alarming rate. Not only that, but the animal's whole demeanour had changed, and instead of tripping along in his old sprightly way he dragged one foot after another as though he were on the point of death.

Towards the end of the period I was horrified to see the big man with something like a shorn ewe on the end of the lead. It was all that was left of the beautiful Keeshond, but as I started to walk towards him his master spotted me and hurried off in the opposite direction, dragging the unfortunate animal behind him.

Seth Pilling and His Little Knowledge

I did, however, succeed in having a look at the dog a few days afterwards. He was in the waiting room at Skeldale House, and this time he was accompanied by his mistress instead of his master.

Mrs Pilling was sitting very upright, and when I asked her to come through to the consulting room she jumped to her feet, marched past me and stumped quickly along the passage in front of me.

She was quite small, but broad hipped and stocky, and she always walked rapidly, her head nodding forward aggressively at each step, her jaw thrust out. She never smiled.

I had heard it said that Seth Pilling was a big talker outside, but under his own roof he was scared to death of his little wife. And as the tight-mouthed fiery-eyed face turned to me I could believe it.

She bent, pushed powerful arms under the Keeshond and hoisted him on to the table.

'Just look at me good dog, Mr Herriot!' she rapped out.

I looked. 'Good heavens!' I gasped.

The little animal was almost completely bald. His skin was dry, scaly and wrinkled, and his head hung down as though he were under sedation.

'Aye, you're surprised, aren't you?' she barked. 'And no wonder. He's in a terrible state, isn't he?'

'I'm afraid so. I wouldn't have known him.'

'No, nobody would. Ah think the world 'o this dog and just look at 'im!' She paused and snorted a few times. 'And I know who's responsible, don't you?'

'Well . . .'

'Oh, you do. It's that husband o' mine.' She paused and glared at me, breathing rapidly. 'What d'you think of my husband, Mr Herriot?'

'I really don't know him very well. I . . .'

'Well ah know 'im and he's a gawp. He's a great gawp. Knows everything and knows nowt. He's played around wi' me good dog till he's ruined 'im.'

I didn't say anything. I was studying the Keeshond. It was the first time I had been able to observe him closely and I was certain I knew the cause of his trouble.

Mrs Pilling stuck her jaw out further and continued.

'First me husband said it was eczema. Is it?'

'No.'

'Then 'e said it was mange. Is it?'

289

'No.'

'D'you know what it is?'

'Yes.'

'Well, will you tell me please?'

'It's myxoedema.'

'Myx . . . ?'

'Wait a minute,' I said. 'I'll just make absolutely sure.' I reached for my stethoscope and put it on the dog's chest. And the bradycardia was there as I expected, the slow, slow heartbeat of hypothyroidism. 'Yes, that's it. Not a shadow of a doubt about it.'

'What did you call it?'

'Myxoedema. It's a thyroid deficiency – there's a gland in his neck which isn't doing its job properly.'

'And that makes 'is hair fall out?'

'Oh yes. And it also causes this typical scaliness and wrinkling of the skin.'

'Aye, but he's half asleep all t'time. How about that?'

'Another classical symptom. Dogs with this condition become very lethargic – lose all their energy.'

She reached out and touched the dog's skin, bare and leathery where once the coat had grown in bushy glory. 'And can you cure it?'

'Yes.'

'Now Mr Herriot, don't take this the wrong way, but could you be mistaken? Are ye positive it's this myxi-whatever-it-is?'

'Of course I am. It's a straightforward case.'

'Straightforward to you, maybe.' She flushed and appeared to be grinding her teeth. 'But not straightforward to that clever husband o' mine. The great lubbert! When ah think what he's put me good dog through – ah could kill 'im.'

'Well, I suppose he thought he was acting for the best, Mrs Pilling.'

'Ah don't care what he thought, he's made this poor dog suffer, the big fool. Wait till ah get hold of 'im.'

I gave her a supply of tablets. 'These are thyroid extract, and I want you to give him one night and morning.' I also handed her a bottle of potassium iodide which I had found helpful in these cases.

She looked at me doubtfully. 'But surely he'll want summat rubbed on 'is skin.'

'No,' I replied. 'Applications to the skin do no good at all.'

'Then you mean,' she turned a dark purple colour and began

snorting again, 'you mean all them bottles o' filthy stuff me husband put on 'im were a waste o' time?'

'Afraid so.'

'Oh ah'll murder 'im!' she burst out. 'Mucky, oily rubbish, it was. And that fancy feller in Brawton sent some 'orrible lotion – yeller it was, and stank the place out. Ruined me carpets and good chair covers an' all!'

Sulphur, whale oil and creosote, I thought. Splendid old-fashioned ingredients, but quite useless in this case and definitely antisocial.

Mrs Pilling heaved the Keeshond to the floor and strode along the passage, head down, powerful shoulders hunched. I could hear her muttering to herself as she went.

'By gaw, just wait till ah get home. Ah'll sort 'im, by gaw ah will!'

I was naturally interested in the progress of my patient, and when I failed to see him around for the next fortnight I could only conclude that Seth Pilling was keeping out of my way. Indeed there was one occasion when I thought I saw him and the dog disappearing down an alley, but I couldn't be sure.

When I did see them both it was by accident. I was driving round the corner into the market-place and I came upon a man and dog coming away from one of the stalls on the cobbles.

And as I peered through the window I caught my breath. Even in that short space of time the animal's skin was covered with a healthy down of new hair, and he was stepping out with something very like his old vitality.

His master swung round as I slowed down. He gave me a single hunted look then tugged on the lead and scuttled away.

I could only imagine the turmoil in his mind, the conflict of emotions. No doubt he wanted to see his dog recover, but not this way. And as it turned out, the dice were loaded against the poor man because this was an unbelievably rapid recovery. I have seen some spectacular cures in myxoedema, but none so dramatic as that Keeshond.

Mr Pilling's sufferings were communicated to me in various ways. For instance I heard he had changed his pub and now went to the Red Bear of an evening. In a little place like Darrowby, news fairly crackles around, and I had a good idea that the farm men in the Crown and Anchor would have had a bit of quiet Yorkshire sport with the expert.

But his main martyrdom was at home. It was about six weeks after I had finished treating the dog that Mrs Pilling brought him to the surgery.

As before, she lifted him easily on to the table and looked at me, her face as always grim and unsmiling.

'Mr Herriot,' she said, 'ah've just come to say thank ye, and ah thought you'd be interested to see me dog now.'

'I am indeed, Mrs Pilling. It's nice of you to come.' I gazed wonderingly at the thick coat, bushy, shining and new, and at the sparkling eyes and alert expression. 'I think you can say he's about back to normal.'

She nodded. 'That's what I thought and ah'm grateful to ye for what you've done.'

I walked with her to the front door and as she led her dog onto the street she turned her tough little face to me again. As the stern eyes met mine she looked very menacing.

'There's one thing,' she said. 'Ah'll never forgive that man o' mine for what he did to me dog. By gum, I've given 'im some stick, the great goof! He'll never hear the last of it from me.'

As she made off down the street, the little animal trotting briskly by her side, I brimmed with pleasant emotions. It is always warming to see a case recover so well, but in this instance there was an additional bonus.

For a long time little Mrs Pilling was going to give her husband pure hell.

*

There are not many unpleasant characters in my books, but Seth Pilling is one of them. And yet, although I took an unholy delight in his discomfiture, I can find it in my heart to feel sorry for him. It was incredibly bad luck for a professional know-all like him to come across a condition like myxoedema which is comparatively rare but which is easily and dramatically curable if you REALLY know.

36. *The Stray*

It was when Siegfried and I were making one of our market day
sorties that we noticed the little dog among the stalls.

When things were quiet in the surgery we often used to walk
together across the cobbles and have a word with the farmers gathered round the doorway of the Drovers' Arms. Sometimes we
collected a few outstanding bills or drummed up a bit of work for
the forthcoming week – and if nothing like that happened we still
enjoyed the fresh air.

The thing that made us notice the dog was that he was sitting up
begging in front of the biscuit stall.

'Look at that little chap,' Siegfried said. 'I wonder where he's
sprung from.'

As he spoke, the stallholder threw a biscuit which the dog devoured eagerly, but when the man came round and stretched out a hand the little animal trotted away.

He stopped, however, at another stall which sold produce: eggs, cheese, butter, cakes and scones. Without hesitation he sat up again in the begging position, rock steady, paws dangling, head pointing expectantly.

I nudged Siegfried. 'There he goes again.'

My colleague nodded. 'Yes, he's an engaging little thing, isn't he? What breed would you call him?'

'A cross, I'd say. He's like a little brown Sheepdog, but there's a touch of something else – maybe terrier.'

It wasn't long before he was munching a bun, and this time we walked over to him. And as we drew near I spoke gently.

'Here, boy,' I said, squatting down a yard away. 'Come on, let's have a look at you.'

He faced me and for a moment two friendly brown eyes gazed at me from a singularly attractive little face. The fringed tail waved in response to my words, but as I inched nearer he turned and ambled unhurriedly among the market day crowd till he was lost to sight. I didn't want to make a thing out of the encounter because I could never quite divine Siegfried's attitude to the small animals. He was eminently wrapped up in his horse work and often seemed amused at the way I rushed around after dogs and cats.

At that time, in fact, Siegfried was strongly opposed to the whole idea of keeping animals as pets. He was quite vociferous on the subject – said it was utterly foolish – despite the fact that five assorted dogs travelled everywhere with him in his car. Now, thirty-five years later, he is just as strongly in favour of keeping pets, though he now carries only one dog in his car. So, as I say, it was difficult to assess his reactions in this field and I refrained from following the little animal.

I was standing there when a young policeman came up to me.

'I've been watching that little dog begging among the stalls all morning,' he said. 'But like you, I haven't been able to get near him.'

'Yes, it's strange. He's obviously friendly, yet he's afraid. I wonder who owns him.'

'I reckon he's a stray, Mr Herriot. I'm interested in dogs myself and I fancy I know just about all of them around here. But this 'un's a stranger to me.'

I nodded. 'I bet you're right. So anything could have happened to him. He could have been ill-treated by somebody and run away, or he could have been dumped from a car.'

'Yes,' he replied. 'There's some lovely people around. It beats me how anybody can leave a helpless animal to fend for itself like that. I've had a few goes at catching him myself but it's no good.'

The memory stayed with me for the rest of the day, and even when I lay in bed that night I was unable to dispel the disturbing image of the little brown creature wandering in a strange world, sitting up asking for help in the only way he knew.

I was still a bachelor at that time and on the Friday night of the same week Siegfried and I were arraying ourselves in evening dress in preparation for the Hunt Ball at East Hirdsley, about ten miles away.

It was a tortuous business because those were the days of starched shirt fronts and stiff high collars and I kept hearing explosions of colourful language from Siegfried's room as he wrestled with his studs.

I was in an even worse plight because I had outgrown my suit, and even when I had managed to secure the strangling collar I had to fight my way into the dinner jacket which nipped me cruelly under the arms. I had just managed to don the complete outfit and was trying out a few careful breaths when the phone rang.

It was the same young policeman I had been speaking to earlier in the week.

'We've got that dog round here, Mr Herriot. You know – the one that was begging in the market-place.'

'Oh yes? Somebody's managed to catch him, then?'

There was a pause. 'No, not really. One of our men found him lying by the roadside about a mile out of town and brought him in. He's been in an accident.'

I told Siegfried. He looked at his watch. 'Always happens, doesn't it, James. Just when we're ready to go out. It's nine o'clock now and we should be on our way.' He thought for a moment. 'Anyway, slip round there and have a look and I'll wait for you. It would be better if we could go to this affair together.'

As I drove round to the Police Station I hoped fervently that there wouldn't be much to do. This Hunt Ball meant a lot to my boss because it would be a gathering of the horse-loving fraternity of the district and he would have a wonderful time just chatting and drinking with so many kindred spirits, even though he hardly danced at all. Also, he maintained, it was good for business to meet the clients socially.

The kennels were at the bottom of a yard behind the Station and the policeman led me down and opened one of the doors. The little dog was lying very still under the single electric bulb and when I bent and stroked the brown coat his tail stirred briefly among the straw of his bed.

'He can still manage a wag, anyway,' I said.

The policeman nodded. 'Aye, there's no doubt he's a good-natured little thing.'

I tried to examine him as much as possible without touching. I didn't want to hurt him and there was no saying what the extent of his injuries might be. But even at a glance certain things were obvious: he had multiple lacerations, one hind leg was crooked in the unmistakeable posture of a fracture and there was blood on his lips.

This could be from damaged teeth, and I gently raised the head with a view to looking into his mouth. He was lying on his right side and as the head came round it was as though somebody had struck me in the face.

The right eye had been violently dislodged from its socket and it sprouted like some hideous growth from above the cheek bone, a great glistening orb with the eyelids tucked behind the white expanse of sclera.

I seemed to squat there for a long time, stunned by the obscenity, and as the seconds dragged by I looked into the little dog's face and he looked back at me – trustingly from one soft brown eye, glaring meaninglessly from the grotesque ball on the other side.

The policeman's voice broke my thoughts. 'He's a mess, isn't he?'

'Yes . . . yes . . . must have been struck by some vehicle – maybe dragged along by the look of all those wounds.'

'What d'you think, Mr Herriot?'

I knew what he meant. It was the sensible thing to ease this lost unwanted creature from the world. He was grievously hurt and he didn't seem to belong to anybody. A quick overdose of anaesthetic – his troubles would be over and I'd be on my way to the dance.

But the policeman didn't say anything of the sort. Maybe, like me, he was looking into the soft depths of that one trusting eye.

I stood up quickly. 'Can I use your phone?'

At the other end of the line Siegfried's voice crackled with impatience. 'Hell, James, it's half-past nine! If we're going to this thing we've got to go now or we might as well not bother. A stray dog, badly injured. It doesn't sound such a great problem.'

'I know, Siegfried. I'm sorry to hold you up, but I can't make up my mind. I wish you'd come round and tell me what you think.'

There was a silence then a long sigh. 'All right, James. See you in five minutes.'

He created a slight stir as he entered the Station. Even in his casual working clothes Siegfried always managed to look distinguished, but as he swept into the station newly bathed and shaved, a camel coat thrown over the sparkling white shirt and black tie, there was something ducal about him.

He drew respectful glances from the men sitting around, then my young policeman stepped forward.

'This way, sir,' he said, and we went back to the kennels.

Siegfried was silent as he crouched over the dog, looking him over as I had done without touching him. Then he carefully raised the head and the monstrous eye glared.

'My God!' he said softly, and at the sound of his voice the long fringed tail moved along the ground.

For a few seconds he stayed very still looking fixedly at the dog's face, while in the silence the whisking tail rustled the straw.

Then he straightened up. 'Let's get him round there,' he murmured.

In the surgery we anaesthetised the little animal and as he lay unconscious on the table we were able to examine him thoroughly. After a few minutes Siegfried stuffed his stethoscope into the pocket of his white coat and leaned both hands on the table.

'Luxated eyeball, fractured femur, umpteen deep lacerations, broken claws. There's enough here to keep us going till midnight, James.'

I didn't say anything.

My boss pulled the knot from his black tie and undid the front stud. He peeled off the stiff collar and hung it on the cross bar of the surgery lamp.

'By God, that's better,' he muttered, and began to lay out suture materials.

I looked at him across the table. 'How about the Hunt Ball?'

'Oh bugger the Hunt Ball,' Siegfried said. 'Let's get busy.'

We were busy, too, for a long time. I hung up my collar next to my colleague's and we began on the eye. I know we both felt the same – we wanted to get rid of that horror before we did anything else.

I lubricated the great ball and pulled the eyelids apart while Siegfried gently manoeuvred it back into the orbital cavity. I sighed as everything slid out of sight, leaving only the cornea visible.

Siegfried chuckled with satisfaction. 'Looks like an eye again, doesn't it.' He seized an ophthalmoscope and peered into the depths.

'And there's no major damage – could be as good as new again. But we'll just stitch the lids together to protect it for a few days.'

The broken ends of the fractured tibia were badly displaced and we had a struggle to bring them into apposition before applying the plaster of paris. But at last we finished and started on the long job of stitching the many cuts and lacerations.

We worked separately for this, and for a long time it was quiet in the operating room except for the snip of scissors as we clipped the brown hair away from the wounds. I knew and Siegfried knew that we were almost certainly working without payment, but the most disturbing thought was that after all our efforts we might still have to put him down. He was still in the care of the police and if nobody claimed him within ten days it meant euthanasia. And if his late owners were really interested in his fate, why hadn't they tried to contact the police before now . . .

By the time we had completed our work and washed the instruments it was after midnight. Siegfried dropped the last suture needle into its tray and looked at the sleeping animal.

'I think he's beginning to come round,' he said. 'Let's take him through to the fire and we can have a drink while he recovers.'

We stretchered the dog through to the sitting-room on a blanket and laid him on the rug before the brightly burning coals. My colleague reached a long arm up to the glass-fronted cabinet above the mantelpiece and pulled down the whisky bottle and two glasses. Drinks in hand, collarless, still in shirt sleeves, with our starched white fronts and braided evening trousers to remind us of the lost dance, we lay back in our chairs on either side of the fireplace and between us our patient stretched peacefully.

He was a happier sight now. One eye was closed by the protecting stiches and his hind leg projected stiffly in its white cast, but he was tidy, cleaned up, cared for. He looked as though he belonged to somebody – but then there was a great big doubt about that.

The Stray

It was nearly one o'clock in the morning and we were getting well down the bottle when the shaggy brown head began to move.

Siegfried leaned forward and touched one of the ears and immediately the tail flapped against the rug and a pink tongue lazily licked his fingers.

'What an absolutely grand little dog,' he murmured, but his voice had a distant quality. I knew he was worried too.

I took the stitches out of the eyelids in two days and was delighted to find a normal eye underneath.

The young policeman was as pleased as I was. 'Look at that!' he exclaimed. 'You'd never know anything had happened there.'

'Yes, it's done wonderfully well. All the swelling and inflammation has gone.' I hesitated for a moment. 'Has anybody enquired about him?'

He shook his head. 'Nothing yet. But there's another eight days to go and we're taking good care of him here.'

I visited the Police Station several times and the little animal greeted me with undisguised joy, all his fear gone, standing upright against my legs on his plastered limb, his tail swishing.

But all the time my sense of foreboding increased, and on the tenth day I made my way almost with dread to the police kennels. I had heard nothing. My course of action seemed inevitable. Putting down old or hopelessly ill dogs was often an act of mercy, but when it was a young healthy dog it was terrible. I hated it, but it was one of the things veterinary surgeons had to do.

The young policeman was standing in the doorway.

'Still no news?' I asked, and he shook his head.

I went past him into the kennel and the shaggy little creature stood up against my legs as before, laughing into my face, mouth open, eyes shining.

I turned away quickly. I'd have to do this right now or I'd never do it.

'Mr Herriot.' The policeman put his hand on my arm. 'I think I'll take him.'

'You?' I stared at him.

'Aye, that's right. We get a lot o' stray dogs in here and though I feel sorry for them you can't give them all a home, can you?'

'No, you can't,' I said. 'I have the same problem.'

He nodded slowly. 'But somehow this 'un's different, and it seems to me he's just come at the right time. I have two little girls and they've been at me for a bit to get 'em a dog. This little bloke looks just right for the job.'

Warm relief began to ebb through me. 'I couldn't agree more. He's the soul of good nature. I bet he'll be wonderful with children.'

'Good. That's settled then. I thought I'd ask your advice first.' He smiled happily.

I looked at him as though I had never seen him before. 'What's your name?'

'Phelps,' he replied. 'P.C. Phelps.'

He was a good-looking young fellow, clear-skinned, with cheerful blue eyes and a solid dependable look about him. I had to fight against an impulse to wring his hand and thump him on the back. But I managed to preserve the professional exterior.

'Well, that's fine.' I bent and stroked the little dog. 'Don't forget to bring him along to the surgery in ten days for removal of the stitches, and we'll have to get that plaster off in about a month.'

It was Siegfried who took out the stitches, and I didn't see our patient again until four weeks later.

P.C. Phelps had his little girls, aged four and six, with him as well as the dog.

'You said the plaster ought to come off about now,' he said, and I nodded.

He looked down at the children. 'Well, come on, you two, lift him on the table.'

Eagerly the little girls put their arms around their new pet and as they hoisted him the tail wagged furiously and the wide mouth panted in delight.

'Looks as though he's been a success,' I said.

He smiled. 'That's an understatement. He's perfect with these two. I can't tell you what pleasure he's given us. He's one of the family.'

I got out my little saw and began to hack at the plaster.

'It's worked both ways, I should say. A dog loves a secure home.'

'Well, he couldn't be more secure.' He ran his hand along the brown coat and laughed as he addressed the little dog. 'That's what you get for begging among the stalls on market day, my lad. You're in the hands of the law now.'

*

The Stray

This story covers a lot of the things which make veterinary surgery a beguiling life. The appeal of the begging dog, the total unpredictability, as when we finished up operating in starched evening shirts, and the kindness of people as epitomised by the young policeman. And, of course, the recurring situation of an attractive little animal finding a good home. The fact that children were involved at the end completed a happy story.

37. *The Stolen Car*

'Oh Mr Herriot!' Mrs Ridge said delightedly. 'Somebody stole our car last night.' She looked at me with a radiant smile.

I stopped in the doorway of her house. 'Mrs Ridge, I'm terribly sorry. How . . . ?'

'Yes, yes, oh I can't wait to tell you!' Her voice trembled with excitement and joy. 'There must have been some prowlers around here last night, and I'm such a silly about leaving the car unlocked.'

'I see . . . how unfortunate.'

'But do come in,' she giggled. 'Forgive me for keeping you standing on the step, but I'm all of a dither!'

I went past her into the lounge. 'Well, it's very understandable. It must have been quite a shock.'

'Shock? Oh, but you don't see what I mean. It's wonderful!'

'Eh?'

'Yes, of course!' She clasped her hands and looked up at the ceiling. 'Do you know what happened?'

'Well yes,' I said. 'You've just told me.'

'No, I haven't told you half.'

'You haven't?'

'No, but do sit down. I know you'll want to hear all about it.'

To explain this I have to go back ten days to the afternoon when Mrs Ridge ran tearfully up the steps of Skeldale House.

'My little dog's had an accident,' she gasped.

I looked past her. 'Where is he?'

'In the car. I didn't know whether I should move him.'

I crossed the pavement and opened the door. Her Cairn Terrier, Joshua, lay very still on a blanket on the back seat.

'What happened?' I asked.

She put a hand over her eyes. 'Oh it was terrible. You know he often plays in the farmer's field opposite our house – well about half an hour ago he started to chase a rabbit and ran under the wheels of a tractor.'

I looked from her face to the motionless animal and back again. 'Did the wheels go over him?'

She nodded as the tears streamed down her cheeks.

I took her by the arm. 'Mrs Ridge, this is important. Are you absolutely sure that wheel passed right over his body?'

'Yes, I am – quite certain. I saw it happen. I couldn't believe he'd be alive when I ran to pick him up.' She took a long breath. 'I don't suppose he can live after that, can he?'

I didn't want to depress her but it seemed impossible that a small dog like this could survive being crushed under that great weight. Massive internal damage would be inevitable apart altogether from broken bones. It was sad to see the little sandy form lying still and unheeding when I had watched him so often running and leaping in the fields.

'Let's have a look at him,' I said.

I climbed into the car and sat down on the seat beside him. With the utmost care I felt my way over the limbs, expecting every moment to feel the crepitus which would indicate a fracture. I put my hand underneath him very slowly, supporting his weight every inch of the way. The only time Joshua showed any reaction was when I moved the pelvic girdle.

The best sign of all was the pinkness of the mucous membranes of eye and mouth and I turned to Mrs Ridge rather more hopefully.

'Miraculously he doesn't seem to have any internal haemorrhage and there are no limb bones broken. I'm pretty sure he has a fractured pelvis, but that's not so bad.'

She drew her fingers over the smears on her cheeks and looked at me, wide-eyed. 'You really think he has a chance?'

'Well I don't want to raise your hopes unduly, but at this moment I can't find any sign of severe injury.'

'But it doesn't seem possible.'

I shrugged. 'I agree, it doesn't, but if he has got away with it I can only think it was because he was on soft ground which yielded as the wheel squeezed him down. Anyway, let's get him X-rayed to make sure.'

At that time, in common with most large animal practices, we didn't have an X-ray machine, but the local hospital helped us out in times of need. I took Joshua round there and the picture confirmed my diagnosis of pelvic fracture.

'There's not much I can do,' I said to his mistress. 'This type of injury usually heals itself. He'll probably have difficulty in standing on his hind legs for a while and for several weeks he'll be weak in the rear end, but with rest and time he ought to recover.'

'Oh marvellous!' She watched me place the little animal back on the car seat. 'I suppose it's just a matter of waiting, then?'

'That's what I hope.'

My fears that Joshua might have some internal damage were finally allayed when I saw him two days later. His membranes were a rich deep pink and all natural functions were operating.

Mrs Ridge, however, was still worried. 'He's such a sorrowful little thing,' she said. 'Just look at him – he's lifeless.'

'Well you know he must be bruised and sore after that squashing he had. And he was very shocked, too. You must be patient.'

As I spoke, the little dog stood up, wobbled a few feet across the carpet and flopped down again. He showed no interest in me or his surroundings.

Before I left I gave his mistress some salicylate tablets to give him. 'These will ease his discomfort,' I said. 'Let me know if he doesn't improve.'

She did let me know – within forty-eight hours. 'I wish you'd come and see Joshua again,' she said on the phone. 'I'm not at all happy about him.'

The little animal was as before. I looked down at him as he lay dejectedly on the rug, head on his paws, looking into the fireplace.

'Come on, Joshua, old lad,' I said. 'You must be feeling better now.' I bent and rubbed my fingers along the wiry coat, but neither word or gesture made any impression. I might as well not have been there.

Mrs Ridge turned to me worriedly. 'That's what he's like all the time. And you know how he is normally.'

'Yes, he's always been a ball of fire.' Again I recalled him jumping round my legs, gazing up at me eagerly. 'It's very strange.'

'And another thing,' she went on. 'He never utters a sound. And you know, that worries me more than anything because he's always been such a good little watch dog. We used to hear him barking when the early post came, he barked at the milk boy, the dustman, everybody. He was never a yappy dog, but he let us know when anybody was around.'

'Yes . . .' That was another thing I remembered. The tumult of sound from within whenever I rang the door bell.

'And now there's just this dreadful silence. People come and go but he never even looks up.' She shook her head slowly. 'Oh, if only he'd bark! Just once! I think it would mean he was getting better.'

'It probably would,' I said.

'Is there something else wrong with him, do you think?' she asked.

I thought for a moment or two. 'No, I'm convinced there isn't. Not physically, anyway. He's had a tremendous fright and he has withdrawn within himself. He'll come out of it in time.'

As I left I had the feeling I was trying to convince myself as much as Mrs Ridge. And as, over the next few days, she kept phoning me with bad reports about the little dog my confidence began to ebb.

It was a week after the accident that she begged me to come to the house again. Joshua was unchanged. Apathetic, tail tucked down, sad-eyed – and still soundless.

His mistress was obviously under strain.

'Mr Herriot,' she said, 'what are we going to do? I can't sleep for thinking about him.'

I produced stethoscope and thermometer and examined the little animal again. Then I palpated him thoroughly from head to tail. When I had finished I squatted on the rug and looked up at Mrs Ridge.

'I can't find anything new. You'll just have to be patient.'

'But that's what you said before, and I feel I can't go on much longer like this.'

'Still no barking?'

She shook her head. 'No, and that's what I'm waiting for. He eats a little, walks around a little, but we never hear a sound from him. I know I'd stop worrying if I heard him bark, just once, but otherwise I have a horrible feeling he's going to die . . .'

I had hoped that my next visit would be more cheerful, but though I was greatly relieved at Mrs Ridge's high spirits I was surprised, too.

I sat down in one of the comfortable chairs in the lounge.

'Well I hope you'll soon recover your car,' I said.

She waved a hand negligently. 'Oh, it'll turn up somewhere, I'm sure.'

'But still – you must be very upset.'

'Upset? Not a bit! I'm so happy!'

'Happy? About losing the car . . . ?'

'No, not about that. About Joshua.'

'Joshua?'

'Yes.' She sat down in the chair opposite and leaned forward. 'Do you know what he did when those people were driving the car away?'

'No, tell me.'

'He *barked*, Mr Herriot! Joshua *barked*!'

*

I suppose I wrote this story simply because it is the only time I have known a person to be delighted at having a car stolen. And yet, I shouldn't have been too surprised. Again and again I have noticed that the recovery of a pet can lift people away from their troubles. Everybody knows that the first bark is often a sign that the worst is over and that their dog will soon be restored to health. And what is a lost car compared with that?

38. *Theo the 'Pub Terrier'*

I was in the Drovers' Arms and George Wilks, the auctioneer, was speaking.

'I reckon that's the best pub terrier I've ever seen.' He bent down from the bar counter and patted Theo's shaggy head as it protruded from beneath his master's stool.

It struck me that 'pub terrier' wasn't a bad description. Theo was small and mainly white, though there were odd streaks of black on his flanks, and his muzzle had a bushy outgrowth of hair which made him undeniably attractive but still more mysterious.

I warmed to a Scottish colleague recently who, when pressed by a lady client to diagnose her dog's breed and lineage, replied finally, 'Madam, I think it would be best just to call him a wee broon dug.'

By the same token Theo could safely be described as a wee white dug, but in Yorkshire the expression 'pub terrier' would be more easily understood.

His master, Paul Cotterell, looked down from his high perch.

'What's he saying about you, old chap?' he murmured languidly, and at the sound of his voice the little animal leaped, eager and wagging, from his retreat.

Theo spent a considerable part of his life between the four metal legs of that stool, as did his master on the seat. And it often seemed to me to be a waste of time for both of them. I often took my own dog, Sam, into pubs, and he would squat beneath my seat, but whereas it was an occasional thing with me – maybe once or twice a week – with Paul Cotterell it was an unvarying ritual. Every night from eight o'clock onwards he could be found sitting there at the end of the bar of the Drovers' Arms, pint glass in front of him, little curly pipe drooping over his chin.

For a young man like him – he was a bachelor in his late thirties – and a person of education and intelligence, it seemed a sterile existence.

He turned to me as I approached the counter. 'Hello, Jim, let me get you a drink.'

'That's very kind of you, Paul,' I replied. 'I'll have a pint.'

'Splendid.' He turned to the barmaid with easy courtesy. 'Could I trouble you, Moyra?'

We sipped our beer and we chatted. This time it was about the music festival at Brawton and then we got on to music in general. As with any other topic I had discussed with him, he seemed to know a lot about it.

'So you're not all that keen on Bach?' he enquired lazily.

'No, not really. Some of it, yes, but on the whole I like something a bit more emotional. Elgar, Beethoven, Mozart. Even Tchaikovsky – I suppose you highbrows look down your noses at him?'

He shrugged, puffed his little pipe and regarded me with a half-smile, one eyebrow raised. He often looked like that and it made me feel he ought to wear a monocle. But he didn't enthuse about Bach, though it seemed he was his favourite composer. He never enthused about anything, and he listened with that funny look on his face while I rhapsodised about the Elgar violin concerto.

Paul Cotterell was from the south of England, but the locals had long since forgiven him for that because he was likeable, amusing, and always ready to buy anybody a drink from his corner in the Drovers'. To me, he had a charm which was very English: casual, effortless. He never got excited; he was always polite and utterly self-contained.

'While you're here, Jim,' he said, 'I wonder if you'd have a look at Theo's foot?'

'Of course.' It is one of a vet's occupational hazards that wherever he goes socially it is taken for granted that there is nothing he would rather do than dole out advice or listen to symptoms. 'Let's have him up.'

'Here, boy, come on.' Paul patted his knee and the little dog jumped up and sat there, eyes sparkling with pleasure. And I thought as I always did that Theo should be in pictures. He was the perfect film dog with that extraordinarily fuzzy laugh-face. People paid good money to see dogs just like him in cinemas all over the world.

'All right, Theo,' I said, scooping him from his master's knee, 'where's the trouble?'

Paul indicated the right fore foot with the stem of his pipe. 'It's that one. He's been going a bit lame off and on for the last few days.'

'I see.' I rolled the little animal on his back and then laughed. 'Oh, he's only got a broken claw. There's a little bit hanging off here. He must have caught it on a stone. Hang on a minute.' I delved in my pocket for the scissors which always dwelt there. A quick snip and the job was done.

'Is that all?' asked Paul.

'Yes, that's it.'

One eyebrow went up mockingly as he looked at Theo. 'So that's what you were making all the fuss about, eh? Silly old trout.' He snapped his fingers. 'Back you go.'

The little dog obediently leaped to the carpet and disappeared into his sanctuary beneath the stool. And at that moment I had a flash of intuition about Paul – about his charm which I had often admired and envied. He didn't really care. He was fond of his dog, of course. He took him everywhere with him, exercised him regularly by the river, but there was none of the anxiety, the almost desperate concern which I had so often seen in the eyes of my clients when I dealt with even the most trivial of their ailments. They cared too much – as I have always done with my own animals.

And of course he was right. It was an easier and more comfortable way to live. Caring made you vulnerable, while Paul cruised along, impregnable. That attractive casualness, the nonchalant good manners, the imperturbability – they all had their roots in the fact that nothing touched him very deeply.

And despite my snap diagnosis of his character I still envied him. I have always been blown around too easily by my emotions; it must be lovely to be like Paul. And the more I thought about it the more I realised how everything fitted in. He had never cared enough to get married. Even Bach, with his mathematical music, was part of the pattern.

'I think that major operation deserves another pint, Jim.' He smiled his lop-sided smile. 'Unless you demand a higher fee?'

I laughed. I would always like him. We are all different and we have to act as we are made, but as I started my second glass I thought again of his carefree life. He had a good job in the government offices in Brawton, no domestic responsibilities, and every night he sat on that same stool drinking beer with his dog underneath. He hadn't a worry in the world.

Anyway, he was part of the Darrowby scene, part of something I liked, and since I have always hated change it was in a sense reassuring to know that no matter what night you went into the Drovers' you would find Paul Cotterell in the corner and Theo's shaggy muzzle peeping from below.

I felt like that one night when I dropped in near closing time.

'D'you think he's got worms?' The question was typically off-hand.

'I don't know, Paul. Why do you ask?'

He drew on his pipe. 'Oh I just thought he looked a bit thin lately. Come up, Theo!'

The little dog, perched on his master's knee, looked as chirpy as ever, and when I reached over and lifted him he licked my hand. But his ribs did feel rather prominent.

'Mmmm, yes,' I said. 'Maybe he has lost a bit of weight. Have you noticed him passing any worms?'

'I haven't, actually.'

'Not even little bits – whitish segments sticking round his rear?'

'No, Jim.' He shook his head and smiled. 'But I haven't looked all that closely, old boy.'

'Okay,' I said. 'Let's worm him, just in case. I'll bring in some tablets tomorrow night. You'll be here . . . ?'

The eyebrow went up. 'I think that's highly probable.'

Theo duly got his worm tablets and after that there was a space of several weeks when I was too busy to visit the Drovers'. When I finally did get in it was a Saturday night and the Athletic Club dance was in full spate. A rhythmic beat drifted from the ballroom, the little bar was packed, and the domino players were under pressure, squashed into a corner by the crush of dinner jackets and backless dresses.

In the noise and heat I struggled towards the bar, thinking that the place was unrecognisable. But there was one feature unchanged – Paul Cotterell on his stool at the far end of the counter.

I squeezed in next to him and saw he was wearing his usual tweed jacket. 'Not dancing, Paul?'

He half-closed his eyes, shook his head slowly and smiled at me over his bent little pipe. 'Not for me, old boy,' he murmured. 'Too much like work.'

I glanced down and saw that something else hadn't changed. Theo was there, too, keeping his nose well clear of the milling feet. I ordered two beers and we tried to converse, but it was difficult to shout above the babel. Arms kept poking between us towards the counter, red faces pushed into ours and shouted greetings. Most of the time we just looked around us.

Then Paul leaned close and spoke into my ear. 'I gave Theo those pills but he's still getting thinner.'

'Really?' I shouted back. 'That's unusual.'

'Yes . . . perhaps you'd have a look at him?'

I nodded, he snapped his fingers and the little dog was on his knee in an instant. I reached and lifted him onto mine and I noticed immediately that he was lighter in my hands.

'You're right,' I said. 'He's still losing weight.'

Balancing the dog in my lap, I pulled down an eyelid and saw that the conjunctiva was pale.

I shouted again. 'He's anaemic.' I felt my way back over his face and behind the angle of the jaw I found that the post pharyngeal lymph glands were greatly enlarged. This was strange. Could he have some form of mouth or throat infection? I looked helplessly around me, wishing fervently that Paul wouldn't invariably consult me about his dog in a pub. I wanted to examine the animal, but I couldn't very well deposit him among the glasses on the bar.

I was trying to get a better grip with a view to looking down his throat when my hand slipped behind his fore leg and my heart gave a sudden thump as I encountered the axillary gland. It, too, was grossly enlarged. I whipped my fingers back into his groin and there was the inguinal gland, prominent as an egg. The prescapular was the same, and as I groped feverishly I realised that every superficial lymph gland was several times its normal size.

Hodgkin's disease. For a few moments I was oblivious of the shouting and laughter, the muffled blare of music. Then I looked at Paul who was regarding me calmly as he puffed his pipe. How could I tell him in these surroundings? He would ask me what Hodgkin's disease was and I would have to explain that it was a cancer of the lymphatic system and that his dog was surely going to die.

As my thoughts raced I stroked the shaggy head and Theo's comic whiskered face turned towards me. People jostled past, hands reached out and bore gins and whiskies and beers past my face, a fat man threw his arm round my neck.

I leaned across. 'Paul,' I said.

'Yes, Jim?'

'Will you . . . will you bring Theo round to the surgery tomorrow morning. It's ten o'clock on a Sunday.'

Momentarily the eyebrow twitched upwards, then he nodded.

'Right, old boy.'

I didn't bother to finish my drink. I began to push my way towards the door and as the crush closed around me I glanced back. The little dog's tail was just disappearing under the stool.

Next day I had one of those early waking mornings when I started tossing around at six o'clock and finished by staring at the ceiling.

Even after I had got my feet on the ground and brought Helen a cup of tea the waiting was interminable until the moment arrived which I had been dreading – when I faced Paul across the surgery table with Theo standing between us.

I told him straight away. I couldn't think of any easy way to lead up to it.

His expression did not change, but he took his pipe out of his mouth and looked steadily at me, then at the dog and back again at me.

'Oh,' he said at last, 'I see.'

I didn't say anything and he slowly ran his hand along the little animal's back. 'Are you quite sure, Jim?'

'Absolutely. I'm terribly sorry.'

'Is there no treatment?'

'There are various palliatives, Paul, but I've never seen any of them do any good. The end result is always the same.'

'Yes . . .' He nodded slowly. 'But he doesn't look so bad. What will happen if we don't do anything?'

I paused. 'Well, as the internal glands enlarge, various things will happen. Ascites – dropsy – will develop in the abdomen. In fact you see he's a little bit pot-bellied now.'

'Yes . . . I do see, now you mention it. Anything else?'

'As the thoracic glands get bigger he'll begin to pant.'

'I've noticed that already. He's breathless after a short walk.'

'And all the time he'll get thinner and thinner and more debilitated.'

Paul looked down at his feet for a few moments then faced me. 'So what it amounts to is that he's going to be pretty miserable for the rest of his life.' He swallowed. 'And how long is that going to be?'

'A few weeks. It varies. Maybe up to three months.'

'Well, Jim,' he smoothed back his hair, 'I can't let that happen. It's my responsibility. You must put him to sleep now, before he really starts to suffer. Don't you agree?'

'Yes, Paul, it's the kindest thing to do.'

'Will you do it immediately – as soon as I am out of that door?'

'I will,' I replied. 'And I promise you he won't know a thing.'

His face held a curious fixity of expression. He put his pipe in his mouth, but it had gone out so he stuffed it into his pocket. Then he leaned forward and patted his dog once on the head. The bushy face with the funny shock of hair round the muzzle turned to him and for a few seconds they looked at each other.

Then, 'Goodbye, old chap,' he muttered and strode quickly from the room.

I kept my promise.

'Good lad, good old Theo,' I murmured, and stroked the face and ears again and again as the little creature slipped peacefully away. Like all vets I hated doing this, painless though it was, but to me there has always been a comfort in the knowledge that the last thing these helpless animals knew was the sound of a friendly voice and the touch of a gentle hand.

Sentimental, maybe. Not like Paul. He had been practical and utterly rational in the way he had acted. He had been able to do the right thing because he was not at the mercy of his emotions.

313

Later, over a Sunday lunch which I didn't enjoy as much as usual, I told Helen about Theo.

I had to say something because she had produced a delicious pot roast on the gas ring which was our only means of cooking and I wasn't doing justice to her skill.

Sitting at our bench I looked down at her. It was my turn for the high stool.

'You know, Helen,' I said, 'that was an object lesson for me. The way Paul acted, I mean. If I'd been in his position I'd have shilly-shallied – tried to put off something which was inevitable.'

She thought for a moment. 'Well, a lot of people would.'

'Yes, but he didn't.' I put down my knife and fork and stared at the wall. 'He behaved in a mature way. I suppose Paul has one of those personalities you read about. Well-adjusted, completely adequate.'

'Come on, Jim, eat your lunch. I know it was a sad thing but it had to be done and you mustn't start criticising yourself. Paul is Paul and you are you.'

I started again on the meat but I couldn't repress the rising sense of my own inadequacy. Then as I glanced to one side I saw that my wife was smiling up at me.

I felt suddenly reassured. It seemed that she at least didn't seem to mind that I was me.

That was on the Sunday, and on Tuesday morning I was handing out some wart lotion to Mr Sangster who kept a few dairy cows down by the station.

'Dab that on the udder night and morning after milking,' I said. 'I think you'll find that the warts will start to drop off after a week or two.'

'Thank ye.' He handed over half a crown and I was dropping it into the desk drawer when he spoke again.

'Bad job about Paul Cotterell, wasn't it?'

'What do you mean?'

'Ah thought you'd have heard,' he said. 'He's dead.'

'Dead!' I stared at him stupidly. 'How . . . what . . . ?'

'Found 'im this mornin'. He did away with 'isself.'

I leaned with both hands on the desk. 'Do you mean . . . suicide?'

'Aye, that's what they say. Took a lot o' pills. It's all ower t'town.'

I found myself hunching over the day book, sightlessly scanning the list of calls while the farmer's voice seemed to come from far away.

'It's a bad job, right enough. He were a nice feller. Reckon everybody liked 'im.'

Later that day I was passing Paul's lodgings when I saw his landlady, Mrs Clayton, in the doorway. I pulled up and got out of the car.

'Mrs Clayton,' I said, 'I still can't believe this.'

'Nor can I, Mr Herriot, it's terrible.' Her face was pale, her eyes red. 'He was with me six years, you know – he was like a son.'

'But why on earth . . . ?'

'Oh, it was losin' his dog that did it. He just couldn't stand it.'

A great wave of misery rose and engulfed me and she put her hand on my arm.

'Don't look like that, Mr Herriot. It wasn't your fault. Paul told me all about it and nobody could have saved Theo. People die of that, never mind dogs.'

I nodded dumbly and she went on.

'But I'll tell you something in confidence, Mr Herriot. Paul wasn't able to stand things like you or me. It was the way he was made – you see he suffered from depression.'

'Depression! Paul . . . ?'

'Oh yes, he's been under the doctor for a long time and takin' pills regular. He allus put a brave face on, but he's had nervous trouble off and on for years.'

'Nervous trouble . . . I'd never have dreamed . . .'

'No, nobody would, but that's how it was. He had an unhappy childhood from what I made out. Maybe that's why he was so fond of his dog. He got too attached to him, really.'

'Yes . . . yes . . .'

She took out a screwed up handkerchief and blew her nose. 'Well, as I said, the poor lad had a rough time most of his life, but he was brave.'

There didn't seem anything else to say. I drove away out of the town and the calm green hills offered a quiet contrast to the turmoil which can fill a man's mind. So much for Herriot as a judge of character. I couldn't have been more wrong, but Paul had fought his secret battle with a courage which had deceived everybody.

I reflected on the object lesson which I thought he had given me, but in fact it was a lesson of another kind and one which I have never forgotten: that there are countless people like Paul who are not what they seem.

*

Not very pleasant to look back on this and it saddened me to write about it. But it happened. It was a unique and unhappy episode in my life and highlighted in a particularly tragic way the vital part a pet can play in the life of a troubled person. I can still see Paul in the corner of the Drovers' Arms with his little dog peeping out from under his stool. This picture of ease and contentment was such an unexpected prelude to tragedy.

39. *Digger*

The shock of Paul Cotterell's death stayed with me for a long time, and in fact I know I have never quite got over it because even now when the company in the bar of the Drovers' has changed and I am one of the few old faces left from thirty-five years ago I can still see the jaunty figure on the corner stool and the bushy face peeping from beneath.

It was the kind of experience I didn't want repeated in my lifetime yet, uncannily, I ran into the same sort of thing almost immediately afterwards.

It couldn't have been more than a week after Paul's funeral that Andrew Vine brought his fox terrier to the surgery.

I put the little dog on the table and examined each of his eyes carefully in turn.

'I'm afraid he's getting worse,' I said.

Without warning the man slumped across the table and buried his face in his hands.

I put my hand on his shoulder. 'What is it, Andrew? What on earth's the matter?'

At first he did not answer but stayed there, huddled grotesquely by the side of his dog as great sobs shook his body.

When he spoke at last it was into his hands and his voice was hoarse and desperate. 'I can't stand it! If Digger goes blind I'll kill myself!'

I looked down at the bowed head in horrified disbelief. It couldn't be happening again. Not so soon after Paul. And yet there were similarities. Andrew was another bachelor in his thirties and the terrier was his constant companion. He lived in lodgings and appeared to have no worries though he was a shy, diffident man with a fragile look about his tall stooping frame and pallid face.

He had first consulted me about Digger several months ago.

'I call him that because he's dug large holes in the garden ever since his puppy days,' he said with a half-smile, looking at me almost apprehensively from large dark eyes.

I laughed. 'I hope you haven't brought him to me to cure that, because I've never read anything in the books about it.'

'No, no, it's about something else -- his eyes. And he's had that trouble since he was a pup, too.'

'Really? Tell me.'

'Well, when I first got him he had sort of mattery eyes, but the breeder said he'd probably just got some irritant in them and it would soon clear up. And in fact it did. But he's never been quite right. He always seems to have a little discomfort in his eyes.'

'How do you mean?'

'He rubs the side of his face along the carpet and he blinks in bright light.'

'I see.' I pulled the little animal's face round towards me and looked intently at the eyelids. My mind had been busy as he spoke

Digger

and I was fairly sure I should find either entropion (inversion of the eyelids) or distichiasis (an extra row of lashes rubbing against the eyeball) but there was no sign of either. The surface of the cornea, too, looked normal, except perhaps that the deeper structure of lens and iris was not as easy to define as usual.

I moved over to a cupboard for the ophthalmoscope. 'How old is he now?'

'About a year.'

'So he's had this for about ten months?'

'Yes, about that. But it varies a lot. Most of the time he seems normal, then there are days when he goes and lies in his basket with his eyes half-closed and you can tell there's something wrong. Not pain, really. More like discomfort, as I said.'

I nodded and hoped I was looking wise but none of this added up to anything familiar. I switched on the little light on the ophthalmoscope and peered into the depths of that most magical and delicate of all organs, down through the lens to the brilliant tapestry of the retina with its optic papilla and branching blood vessels. I couldn't find a thing wrong.

'Does he still dig holes?' I asked. When baffled I often snatch at straws and I wondered if the dog was suffering from a soil irritation.

Andrew shook his head. 'No, very seldom now, and anyway, his bad days are never associated with his digging.'

'Is that so?' I rubbed my chin. The man was obviously ahead of me with his thinking and I had an uncomfortable feeling of bewilderment. People were always bringing their dogs in with 'bad eyes' and there was invariably something to be seen, some cause to be found. 'And would you say that this was one of his bad days?'

'Well I thought so this morning, but he seems a bit better now. Still, he's a bit blinky, don't you think?'

'Yes . . . maybe so.' Digger did appear to be reluctant to open his eyes fully to the sunshine streaming through the surgery window. And occasionally he kept them closed for a second or two as though he wasn't very happy. But damn it, nothing gave me the slightest clue.

I didn't tell the owner that I hadn't the faintest idea what was wrong with his dog. Such remarks do not inspire confidence. Instead, I took refuge in businesslike activity.

'I'm going to give you some lotion,' I said briskly. 'Put a few drops

319

into his eyes three times daily. And let me know how he goes on. It's possible he has some long-standing infection in there.'

I handed over a bottle of 2 per cent boric acid solution and patted Digger's head. 'I hope that will clear things up for you, lad,' I said, and the stumpy tail wagged in reply. He was a sharp looking little animal, attractive and good-natured and a fine specimen of the smooth-haired breed with his long head and neck, pointed nose and beautifully straight limbs.

He jumped from the table and leaped excitedly around his master's legs.

I laughed. 'He's eager to go, like most of my patients.' I bent and slapped him playfully on the rump. 'My word, doesn't he look fit!'

'He is fit.' Andrew smiled proudly. 'In fact I often think that apart from those eyes he's a perfect little physical machine. You should see him out in the fields – he can run like a whippet.'

'I'll bet he can. Keep in touch, will you?' I waved them out of the door and turned to my other work, mercifully unaware that I had just embarked on one of the most frustrating and traumatic cases of my career.

After that first time I took special notice of Digger and his owner. Andrew, a sensitive likeable man, was a representative for a firm of agricultural chemists and, like myself, spent most of his time driving around the Darrowby district. His dog was always with him and I had been perfunctorily amused by the fact that the little animal was invariably peering intently through the windscreen, his paws either on the dash or balanced on his master's hand as he operated the gear lever.

But now that I was personally interested I could discern the obvious delight which the little animal derived from taking in every detail of his surroundings. He missed nothing in his daily journeys. The road ahead, the houses and people, trees and fields which flashed by the windows – these made up his world.

I met him one day when I was exercising Sam up on the high moors which crown the windy summits of the fells. But this was May, the air was soft and a week's hot sunshine had dried the green paths which wandered among the heather. I saw Digger flashing like a white streak over the velvet turf and when he spotted Sam he darted up to him, set himself teasingly for a moment, then shot back to Andrew who was standing in a natural circular glade among the harsh brown growth.

Digger

Here gorse bushes blazed in full yellow glory and the little dog hurtled round and round the arena, exulting in his health and speed.

'That's what I'd call sheer joy of living,' I said.

Andrew smiled shyly. 'Yes, isn't he beautiful,' he murmured.

'How are the eyes?' I asked.

He shrugged. 'Sometimes good, sometimes not so good. Much the same as before. But I must say he seems easier whenever I put the drops in.'

'But he still has days when he looks unhappy?'

'Yes . . . I have to say yes. Some days they bother him a lot.'

Again the frustration welled in me. 'Let's walk back to the car,' I said. 'I might as well have a look at him.'

I lifted Digger on to the bonnet and examined him again. There wasn't a single abnormality in the eyelids – I had wondered if I had missed something last time – but as the bright sunshine slanted across the eyeballs I could just discern the faintest cloudiness in the cornea. There was a slight keratitis there which hadn't been visible before. But why . . . why?

'He'd better have some stronger lotion.' I rummaged in the car boot. 'I've got some here. We'll try silver nitrate this time.'

Andrew brought him in about a week later. The corneal discoloration had gone – probably the silver nitrate had moved it – but the underlying trouble was unchanged. There was still something sadly wrong. Something I couldn't diagnose.

That was when I started to get really worried. As the weeks passed I bombarded those eyes with everything in the book: oxide of mercury, chinosol, zinc sulphide, ichthyol and a host of other things which are now buried in history.

I had none of the modern sophisticated antibiotic and steroid applications, but it would have made no difference if I had. I know that now.

The real nightmare started when I saw the first of the pigment cells beginning to invade the cornea. Sinister brown specks gathering at the limbus and pushing out dark tendrils into the smooth membrane which was Digger's window on the world. I had seen cells like them before. When they came they usually stayed. And they were opaque.

Over the next month I fought them with my pathetic remedies, but they crept inwards, slowly but inexorably, blurring and narrowing Digger's field of vision. Andrew noticed them too, and when he brought the little dog into the surgery he clasped and unclasped his hands anxiously.

'You know, he's seeing less all the time, Mr Herriot. I can tell. He still looks out of the car windows but he used to bark at all sorts of things he didn't like – other dogs for instance – and now he just doesn't spot them. He's – he's losing his sight.'

I felt like screaming or kicking the table, but since that wouldn't have helped I just looked at him.

'It's that brown stuff, isn't it?' he said. 'What is it?'

'It's called pigmentary keratitis, Andrew. It sometimes happens when the cornea – the front of the eyeball – has been inflamed over a long period, and it is very difficult to treat. I'll do the best I can.'

My best wasn't enough. That slow, creeping tide was pitiless, and as the pigment cells were laid down thicker and thicker the resulting layer was almost black, lowering a dingy curtain between Digger and all the things he had gazed at so eagerly.

And all the time I suffered a long gnawing worry, a helpless wretchedness as I contemplated the inevitable.

It was when I examined the eyes five months after I had first seen them that Andrew broke down. There was hardly anything to be seen of the original corneal structure now; just a brown-black opacity which left only minute chinks for moments of sight. Blindness was not far away.

I patted the man's shoulder again. 'Come on, Andrew. Come over here and sit down.' I pulled over the single wooden chair in the consulting room.

He staggered across the floor and almost collapsed on the seat. He sat there, head in hands, for some time, then raised a tearstained face to me. His expression was distraught.

'I can't bear the thought of it,' he gasped. 'A friendly little thing like Digger – he loves everybody. What has he ever done to deserve this?'

'Nothing, Andrew. It's just one of the sad things which happen. I'm terribly sorry.'

He rolled his head from side to side. 'Oh God, but it's worse for him. You've seen him in the car – he's so interested in everything. Life wouldn't be worth living for him if he lost his sight. And I don't want to live any more either!'

'You mustn't talk like that, Andrew,' I said. 'That's going too far.'

I hesitated. 'Please don't be offended, but you ought to see your doctor.'

'Oh I'm always at the doctor,' he replied dully. 'I'm full of pills right now. He tells me I have a depression.'

The word was like a mournful knell. Coming so soon after Paul it sent a wave of panic through me.

'How long have you been like this?'

'Oh, weeks. I seem to be getting worse.'

'Have you ever had it before?'

'No, never.' He wrung his hands and looked at the floor. 'The doctor says that if I keep on taking the pills I'll get over it, but I'm reaching the end of my tether now.'

'But the doctor is right, Andrew. You've got to stick it and you'll be as good as new.'

'I don't believe it,' he muttered. 'Every day lasts a year. I never enjoy anything. And every morning when I wake up I dread having to face the world again.'

I didn't know what to say or how to help. 'Can I get you a glass of water?'

'No . . . no thanks.'

He turned his deathly pale face up to me again and the dark eyes held a terrible blankness. 'What's the use of going on? I know I'm going to be miserable for the rest of my life.'

I am no psychiatrist but I knew better than to tell somebody in Andrew's condition to snap out of it. And I had a flash of intuition.

'All right,' I said. 'Be miserable for the rest of your life, but while you're about it you've got to look after this dog.'

'Look after him? What can I do? He's going blind. There's nothing anybody can do for him now.'

'You're wrong, Andrew. This is where you start doing things for him. He's going to be lost without your help.'

'How do you mean?'

'Well, you know all those walks you take him – you've got to get him used to the same tracks and paths so that he can trot along on familiar ground without fear. Keep him clear of holes and ditches.'

He screwed up his face. 'Yes, but he won't enjoy the walks any more.'

'He will,' I said. 'You'll be surprised.'

'Oh, but . . .'

'And that nice big lawn at the back of your house where he runs.

You'll have to be on the lookout all the time in case there are things left lying around on the grass that he might bump into. And the eye drops – you say they make him more comfortable. Who's going to put them in if you don't?'

'But Mr Herriot . . . you've seen how he always looks out of the car when he's with me . . .'

'He'll still look out.'

'Even if he can't see?'

'Yes.' I put my hand on his arm. 'You must understand, Andrew, when an animal loses his sight he doesn't realise what's happened to him. It's a terrible thing, I know, but he doesn't suffer the mental agony of a human being.'

He stood up and took a long shuddering breath. 'But I'm having the agony. I've been dreading this happening for so long. I haven't been able to sleep for thinking about it. It seems so cruel and unjust for this to strike a helpless animal – a little creature who's never done anybody any harm.' He began to wring his hands again and pace about the room.

'You're just torturing yourself!' I said sharply. 'That's part of your trouble. You're using Digger to punish yourself instead of doing something useful.'

'Oh but what can I do that will really help? All those things you talked about – they can't give him a happy life.'

'Oh but they can. Digger can be happy for years and years if you really work at it. It's up to you.'

Like a man in a dream he bent and gathered his dog into his arms and shuffled along the passage to the front door. As he went down the steps into the street I called out to him.

'Keep in touch with your doctor, Andrew. Take your pills regularly – and remember.' I raised my voice to a shout. 'Remember you've got a job to do with that dog!'

After Paul I was on a knife edge of apprehension, but this time there was no tragic news to shatter me. Instead I saw Andrew Vine frequently, sometimes in the town with Digger on a lead, occasionally in his car with the little white head framed always in the windscreen, and most often in the fields by the river where he seemed to be carrying out my advice by following the good open tracks again and again.

It was by the river that I stopped him one day. 'How are things going, Andrew?'

He looked at me unsmilingly. 'Oh, he's finding his way around not too badly. I keep my eye on him. I always avoid that field over there – there's a lot of boggy places in it.'

'Good, that's the idea. And how are you yourself?'

'Do you really want to know?'

'Yes, of course.'

He tried to smile. 'Well this is one of my good days. I'm just tense and dreadfully unhappy. On my bad days I'm terror-stricken, despairing, utterly desolate.'

'I'm sorry, Andrew.'

He shrugged. 'Don't think I'm wallowing in self-pity. You asked me. Anyway, I have a system. Every morning I look at myself in the mirror and I say, "Okay, Vine, here's another bloody awful day coming up, but you're going to do your job and you're going to look after your dog."'

'That's good, Andrew. And it will all pass. The whole thing will go away and you'll be all right one day.'

'That's what the doctor says.' He gave me a sidelong glance. 'But in the meantime . . .' He looked down at his dog. 'Come on, Digger.'

He turned and strode away abruptly with the little dog trotting after him, and there was something in the set of the man's shoulders and the forward thrust of his head which gave me hope. He was a picture of fierce determination.

My hopes were fulfilled. Both Andrew and Digger won through. I knew that within months, but the final picture in my mind is of a meeting I had with the two of them about two years later. It was on the flat table-land above Darrowby where I had first seen Digger hurtling joyously among the gorse bushes.

He wasn't doing so badly now, running freely over the smooth green turf, sniffing among the herbage, cocking a leg now and then with deep contentment against the drystone wall which ran along the hillside.

Andrew laughed when he saw me. He had put on weight and looked a different person. 'Digger knows every inch of this walk,' he said. 'I think it's just about his favourite spot – you can see how he's enjoying himself.'

I nodded. 'He certainly looks a happy little dog.'

'Yes, he's happy all right. He has a good life and honestly I often forget that he can't see.' He paused. 'You were right, that day in your surgery. You said this would happen.'

'Well that's great, Andrew,' I said. 'And you're happy, too, aren't you?'

'I am, Mr Herriot. Thank God, I am.' A shadow crossed his face. 'When I think how it was then, I can't believe my luck. It was like being in a dark valley, and bit by bit I've climbed out into the sunshine.'

'I can see that. You're as good as new, now.'

He smiled. 'I'm better than that – better than I was before. That terrible experience did me good. Remember you said I was torturing myself? I realised I had spent all my days doing that. I used to take every little mishap of life and beat myself over the head with it.'

'You don't have to tell me, Andrew,' I said ruefully. 'I've always been pretty good at that myself.'

'Well yes, I suppose a lot of us are. But I became an expert and see where it got me. It helped so much to have Digger to look after.' His face lit up and he pointed over the grass. 'Just look at that!'

The little dog had been inspecting an ancient fence, a few rotting planks which were probably part of an old sheep fold, and as we watched he leaped effortlessly between the spars to the other side.

'Marvellous!' I said delightedly. 'You'd think there was nothing wrong with him.'

Andrew turned to me. 'Mr Herriot, when I see a thing like that it makes me wonder. Can a blind dog do such a thing? Do you think . . . do you think there's a chance he can see just a little?'

I hesitated. 'Maybe he can see a bit through that pigment, but it can't be much – a flicker of light and shade, perhaps. I really don't know. But in any case, he's become so clever in his familiar surroundings that it doesn't make much difference.'

'Yes . . . yes.' He smiled philosophically. 'Anyway, we must get on our way. Come on, Digger!'

He snapped his fingers and set off along a track which pushed a vivid green finger through the heather, pointing clean and unbroken to the sunny skyline. His dog bounded ahead of him, not just at a trot but at a gallop.

I have made no secret of the fact that I never really knew the cause of Digger's blindness, but in the light of modern developments in eye surgery I believe it was a condition called keratitis sicca. This was simply not recognised in those early days and anyway, if I had known, I could have done little about it. The name means 'dryness of the cornea', and it occurs when the dog is not producing enough tears. At the present time it is treated by instilling artificial tears or by an intricate operation whereby the salivary ducts are transferred to the eyes. But even now, despite these things, I have seen that dread pigmentation taking over in the end.

When I look back on the whole episode my feeling is of thankfulness. All sorts of things help people to pull out of a depression. Mostly it is their family – the knowledge that wife and children are dependent on them – sometimes it is a cause to work for, but in Andrew Vine's case it was a dog.

I often think of the dark valley which closed around him at that time and I am convinced he came out of it on the end of Digger's lead.

*

This is a glorious contrast with the other story and a good example of the therapeutic benefit of owning a pet. I know beyond doubt that just being with a dog and talking to it has a cheering and soothing effect – my morning chat with my own dog sets me up for the day – and when Andrew had the responsibility of looking after Digger it was a life-saver. This story also gave me the opportunity of recording a case of a dog going blind. It is a heartbreaking thing to observe and, in a way, worse for the owner. I hope that I have been able to point out that animals can adjust in a miraculous way to this affliction, because it is a great comfort to people to realise that their pet can still be very happy in its way.

40. *The Great Escape*

I poised my knife over a swollen ear. Tristan, one elbow leaning wearily on the table, was holding an anaesthetic mask over the nose of the sleeping dog when Siegfried came into the room.

He glanced briefly at the patient. 'Ah yes, that haematoma you were telling me about, James.' Then he looked across the table at his brother. 'Good God, you're a lovely sight this morning! When did you get in last night?'

Tristan raised a pallid countenance. His eyes were bloodshot slits between puffy lids. 'Oh, I don't quite know. Fairly late, I should think.'

'Fairly late! I got back from a farrowing at four o'clock and you hadn't arrived then. Where the hell were you, anyway?'

'I was at the Licensed Victuallers' Ball. Very good do, actually.'

'I bet it was!' Siegfried snorted. 'You don't miss a thing, do you? Darts Team Dinner, Bellringers' Outing, Pigeon Club Dance, and now it's the Licensed Victuallers' Ball. If there's a good booze-up going on anywhere you'll find it.'

When under fire Tristan always retained his dignity and he drew it around him now like a threadbare cloak.

'As a matter of fact,' he said, 'many of the Licensed Victuallers are my friends.'

His brother flushed. 'I believe you. I should think you're the best bloody customer they've ever had!'

Tristan made no reply but began to make a careful check of the flow of oxygen into the ether bottle.

'And another thing,' Siegfried continued. 'I keep seeing you slinking around with about a dozen different women. And you're supposed to be studying for an exam.'

'That's an exaggeration.' The young man gave him a pained look. 'I admit I enjoy a little female company now and then – just like yourself.'

Tristan believed in attack as the best form of defence, and it was a telling blow, because there was a constant stream of attractive girls laying siege to Siegfried at Skeldale House.

But the elder brother was only temporarily halted. 'Never mind me!' he shouted. 'I've passed all my exams. I'm talking about you! Didn't I see you with that new barmaid from the Drovers' the other night? You dodged rapidly into a shop doorway but I'm bloody sure it was you.'

Tristan cleared his throat. 'It quite possibly was. I have recently become friendly with Lydia – she's a very nice girl.'

'I'm not saying she isn't. What I am saying is that I want to see you indoors at night with your books instead of boozing and chasing women. Is that clear?'

'Quite.' The young man inclined his head gracefully and turned down the knob on the anaesthetic machine.

His brother regarded him balefully for a few moments, breathing deeply. These remonstrations always took it out of him. Then he turned away quickly and left.

Tristan's facade crumbled as soon as the door closed.

'Watch the anaesthetic for a minute, Jim,' he croaked. He went over to the basin in the corner, filled a measuring jar with cold water and drank it at a long gulp. Then he soaked some cotton wool under the tap and applied it to his brow.

'I wish he hadn't come in just then. I'm in no mood for the raised voices and angry words.' He reached up to a large bottle of aspirins, swallowed a few and washed them down with another gargantuan draught. 'All right then, Jim,' he murmured as he returned to the table and took over the mask again. 'Let's go.'

I bent once more over the sleeping dog. He was a Scottie called

Hamish and his mistress, Miss Westerman, had brought him in two days ago.

She was a retired schoolteacher and I always used to think she must have had little trouble in keeping her class in order. The chilly pale eyes looking straight into mine reminded me that she was as tall as I was and the square jaw between the muscular shoulders completed a redoubtable presence.

'Mr Herriot,' she barked, 'I want you to have a look at Hamish. I do hope it's nothing serious but his ear has become very swollen and painful. They don't get – er – cancer there, do they?' For a moment the steady gaze wavered.

'Oh that's most unlikely.' I lifted the little animal's chin and looked at the left ear which was drooping over the side of his face. His whole head, in fact, was askew, as though dragged down by pain.

Carefully I lifted the ear and touched the tense swelling with a forefinger. Hamish looked round at me and whimpered.

'Yes, I know, old chap. It's tender, isn't it?' As I turned to Miss Westerman I almost bumped into the close-cropped iron-grey head which was hovering close over the little dog.

'He's got an aural haematoma,' I said.

'What on earth is that?'

'It's when the little blood vessels between the skin and cartilage of the ear rupture and the blood flows out and causes this acute distension.'

She patted the jet black shaggy coat. 'But what causes it?'

'Canker, usually. Has he been shaking his head lately?'

'Yes, now you mention it he has. Just as though he had got something in his ear and was trying to get rid of it.'

'Well, that's what bursts the blood vessels. I can see he has a touch of canker, though it isn't common in this breed.'

She nodded. 'I see. And how can you cure it?'

'Only by an operation, I'm afraid.'

'Oh dear!' She put her hand to her mouth. 'I'm not keen on that.'

'There's nothing to worry about,' I said. 'It's just a case of letting the blood out and stitching the layers of the ear together. If we don't do this soon he'll suffer a lot of pain and finish up with a cauliflower ear, and we don't want that because he's a bonny little chap.'

I meant it, too. Hamish was a proud-strutting, trim little dog. The Scottish Terrier is an attractive creature and I often lament that there are so few around in these modern days.

After some hesitation Miss Westerman agreed and we fixed a date two days from then. When she brought him in for the operation she deposited Hamish in my arms, stroked his head again and again, then looked from Tristan to me and back again.

'You'll take care of him, won't you,' she said, and the jaw jutted and the pale blue eyes stabbed. For a moment I felt like a little boy caught in mischief, and I think my colleague felt the same because he blew out his breath as the lady departed.

'By gum, Jim, that's a tough baby,' he muttered. 'I wouldn't like to get on the wrong side of her.'

I nodded. 'Yes, and she thinks all the world of this dog, so let's make a good job of him.'

After Siegfried's departure I lifted the ear which was now a turgid cone and made an incision along the inner skin. As the pent up blood gushed forth I caught it in an enamel dish, then I squeezed several big clots through the wound.

'No wonder the poor little chap was in pain,' I said softly. 'He'll feel a lot better when he wakes up.'

I filled the cavity between skin and cartilage with sulphanilamide, then began to stitch the layers together, using a row of buttons. You had to do something like this or the thing filled up again within a few days. When I first began to operate on aural haematomata I used to pack the interior with gauze, then bandage the ear to the head. The owners often made little granny-hats to try to keep the bandage in place, but a frisky dog usually had it off very soon.

The buttons were a far better idea and kept the layers in close contact, lessening the chance of distortion.

By lunchtime Hamish had come round from the anaesthetic and though still slightly dopey he already seemed to be relieved that his bulging ear had been deflated. Miss Westerman had gone away for the day and was due to pick him up in the evening. The little dog, curled in his basket, waited philosophically.

At tea-time, Siegfried glanced across the table at his brother. 'I'm going off to Brawton for a few hours, Tristan,' he said. 'I want you to stay in the house and give Miss Westerman her dog when she arrives. I don't know just when she'll come.' He scooped out a spoonful of jam. 'You can keep an eye on the patient and do a bit of studying, too. It's about time you had a night at home.'

Tristan nodded. 'Right, I'll do that.' But I could see he wasn't enthusiastic.

When Siegfried had driven away Tristan rubbed his chin and gazed reflectively through the french window into the darkening garden. 'This is distinctly awkward, Jim.'

'Why?'

'Well, Lydia has tonight off and I promised to see her.' He whistled a few bars under his breath. 'It seems a pity to waste the opportunity just when things are building up nicely. I've got a strong feeling that girl fancies me. In fact she's nearly eating out of my hand.'

I looked at him wonderingly. 'My God, I thought you'd want a bit of peace and quiet and an early bed after last night!'

'Not me,' he said. 'I'm raring to go again.'

And indeed he looked fresh and fit, eyes sparkling, roses back in his cheeks.

'Look, Jim,' he went on, 'I don't suppose you could stick around with this dog?'

I shrugged. 'Sorry, Triss. I'm going back to see that cow of Ted Binns – right at the top of the Dale. I'll be away for nearly two hours.'

For a few moments he was silent, then he raised a finger. 'I think I have the solution. It's quite simple, in fact it's perfect. I'll bring Lydia in here.'

'What! Into the house?'

'Yes, into this very room. I can put Hamish in his basket by the fire and Lydia and I can occupy the sofa. Marvellous! What could be nicer on a cold winter's night. Cheap, too.'

'But Triss! How about Siegfried's lecture this morning? What if he comes home early and catches the two of you here?'

Tristan lit a Woodbine and blew out an expansive cloud. 'Not a chance. You worry about such tiny things, Jim. He's always late when he goes to Brawton. There's no problem at all.'

'Well, please yourself,' I said. 'But I think you're asking for trouble. Anyway, shouldn't you be doing a bit of bacteriology? The exams are getting close.'

He smiled seraphically through the smoke. 'Oh, I'll have a quick read through it all in good time.'

I couldn't argue with him there. I always had to go over a thing about six times before it finally sank in, but with his brain the quick read would no doubt suffice. I went out on my call.

I got back about eight o'clock and as I opened the front door my mind was far from Tristan. Ted Binns's cow wasn't responding to my treatment and I was beginning to wonder if I was on the right track. When in doubt I liked to look the subject up, and the books were on the shelves in the sitting room. I hurried along the passage and threw open the door.

For a moment I stood there bewildered, trying to reorientate my thoughts. The sofa was drawn close to the bright fire, the atmosphere was heavy with cigarette smoke and the scent of perfume, but there was nobody to be seen.

The most striking feature was the long curtain over the french window. It was wafting slowly downwards as though some object had just hurtled through it at great speed. I trotted over the carpet and peered out into the dark garden. From somewhere in the gloom I heard a scuffling noise, a thud and a muffled cry, then there was a pitter-patter followed by a shrill yelping. I stood for some time listening, then as my eyes grew accustomed to the darkness I walked down the long path under the high brick wall to the yard at the foot. The yard door was open as were the big double doors into the back lane, but there was no sign of life.

Slowly I retraced my steps to the warm oblong of light at the foot of the tall old house. I was about to close the french window when I heard a stealthy movement and an urgent whisper.

'Is that you, Jim?'

'Triss! Where the hell have you sprung from?'

The young man tiptoed past me into the room and looked around him anxiously. 'It was you, then, not Siegfried?'

'Yes, I've just come in.'

He flopped on the sofa and sunk his head in his hands. 'Oh damn! I was just lying here a few minutes ago with Lydia in my arms. At peace with the world. Everything was wonderful. Then I heard the front door open.'

'But you knew I was coming back.'

'Yes, and I'd have given you a shout, but for some reason I thought, "God help us, it's Siegfried!" It sounded like his step in the passage.'

'Then what happened?'

He churned his hair around with his fingers. 'Oh, I panicked. I was whispering lovely things into Lydia's ear, then the next second I grabbed her, threw her off the couch and out of the french window.'

'I heard a thud . . .'

333

'Yes, that was Lydia falling into the rockery.'

'And then some sort of high-pitched cries . . .'

He sighed and closed his eyes. 'That was Lydia in the rose bushes. She doesn't know the geography of the place, poor lass.'

'Gosh, Triss,' I said, 'I'm really sorry. I shouldn't have burst in on you like that. I was thinking of something else.'

He rose wearily and put a hand on my shoulder. 'Not your fault, Jim, not your fault. You did warn me.' He reached for his cigarettes. 'I don't know how I'm going to face that girl again. I just chucked her out into the lane and told her to beat it home with all speed. She must think I'm stone balmy.' He gave a hollow groan.

I tried to be cheerful. 'Oh, you'll get round her again. You'll have a laugh about it later.'

But he wasn't listening. His eyes, wide with horror, were staring past me. Slowly he raised a trembling finger and pointed towards the fireplace. His mouth worked for a few seconds before he spoke.

'Christ, Jim, it's gone!' he gasped.

For a moment I thought the shock had deranged him. 'Gone . . . ? What's gone?'

'The bloody dog! He was there when I dashed outside. Right there!'

I looked down at the empty basket and a cold hand clutched at me. 'Oh no! He must have got out through the open window. We're in trouble.'

We rushed into the garden and searched in vain. We came back for torches and searched once more, prowling around the yard and back lane, shouting the little dog's name with diminishing hope.

After ten minutes we trailed back to the brightly lit room and stared at each other.

Tristan was the first to voice our thoughts. 'What do we tell Miss Westerman when she calls?'

I shook my head. My mind fled from the thought of informing that lady that we had lost her dog.

Just at that moment the front door bell pealed in the passage and Tristan almost leaped in the air.

'Oh God!' he quavered. 'That'll be her now. Go and see her, Jim. Tell her it was my fault – anything you like – but I daren't face her.'

I squared my shoulders, marched over the long stretch of tiles and opened the door. It wasn't Miss Westerman, it was a well-built platinum blonde, and she glared at me angrily.

'Where's Tristan?' she rasped in a voice which told me we had more than one tough female to deal with tonight.

'Well, he's – er – '

'Oh, I know he's in there!' As she brushed past me I noticed she had a smear of soil on her cheek and her hair was sadly disarranged. I followed her into the room where she stalked up to my friend.

'Look at my bloody stockings!' she burst out. 'They're ruined!'

Tristan peered nervously at the shapely legs. 'I'm sorry, Lydia. I'll get you another pair. Honestly, love, I will.'

'You'd better, you bugger!' she replied. 'And don't "love" me – I've never been so insulted in my life. What did you think you were playing at?'

'It was all a misunderstanding. Let me explain . . .' Tristan advanced on her with a brave attempt at a winning smile, but she backed away.

'Keep your distance,' she said frigidly. 'I've had enough of you for one night.'

She swept out and Tristan leaned his head against the mantelpiece. 'The end of a lovely friendship, Jim.' Then he shook himself. 'But we've got to find that dog. Come on.'

I set off in one direction and he went in the other. It was a moonless night of impenetrable darkness and we were looking for a jet black dog. I think we both knew it was hopeless but we had to try.

In a little town like Darrowby you are soon out on the country roads where there are no lights, and as I stumbled around peering vainly over invisible fields the utter pointlessness of the activity became more and more obvious.

Occasionally I came within Tristan's orbit and heard his despairing cries echoing over the empty landscape. 'Haamiish! Haamiish! Haamiish . . . !'

After half an hour we met at Skeldale House. Tristan faced me and as I shook my head he seemed to shrink within himself. His chest heaved as he fought for breath. Obviously he had been running while I had been walking and I suppose that was natural enough. We were both in an awkward situation but the final devastating blow would inevitably fall on him.

'Well, we'd better get out on the road again,' he gasped, and as he spoke the front door bell rang again.

The colour drained rapidly from his face and he clutched my arm.

'That must be Miss Westerman this time. God almighty, she's coming in!'

Rapid footseps sounded in the passage and the sitting room door opened. But it wasn't Miss Westerman, it was Lydia again. She strode over to the sofa, reached underneath and extracted her handbag. She didn't say anything but merely shrivelled Tristan with a sidelong glance before leaving.

'What a night!' he moaned, putting a hand to his forehead. 'I can't stand much more of this.'

Over the next hour we made innumerable sorties but we couldn't find Hamish and nobody else seemed to have seen him. I came in to find Tristan collapsed in an armchair. His mouth hung open and he showed every sign of advanced exhaustion. I shook my head and he shook his, then I heard the telephone.

I lifted the receiver, listened for a minute and turned to the young man. 'I've got to go out, Triss. Mr Drew's old pony has colic again.'

He reached out a hand from the depths of his chair. 'You're not going to leave me, Jim?'

'Sorry, I must. But I won't be long. It's only a mile away.'

'But what if Miss Westerman comes?'

I shrugged. 'You'll just have to apologise. Hamish is bound to turn up – maybe in the morning.'

'You make it sound easy . . .' He ran a hand inside his collar. 'And another thing – how about Siegfried? What if he arrives and asks about the dog? What do I tell him?'

'Oh, I shouldn't worry about that,' I replied airily. 'Just say you were too busy on the sofa with the Drovers' barmaid to bother about such things. He'll understand.'

But my attempt at jocularity fell flat. The young man fixed me with a cold eye and ignited a quivering Woodbine. 'I believe I've told you this before, Jim, but there's a nasty cruel streak in you.'

Mr Drew's pony had almost recovered when I got there but I gave it a mild sedative injection before turning for home. On the way back a thought struck me and I took a road round the edge of the town to the row of modern bungalows where Miss Westerman lived. I parked the car and walked up the path of number ten.

And there was Hamish in the porch, coiled up comfortably on the mat, looking up at me with mild surprise as I hovered over him.

'Come on, lad,' I said. 'You've got more sense than we had. Why didn't we think of this before?'

I deposited him on the passenger seat and as I drove away he hoisted his paws on to the dash and gazed out interestedly at the road unfolding in the headlights. Truly a phlegmatic little hound.

Outside Skeldale House I tucked him under my arm and was about to turn the handle of the front door when I paused. Tristan had notched up a long succession of successful pranks against me – fake telephone calls, the ghost in my bedroom and many others – and in fact, good friends as we were, he never neglected a chance to take the mickey out of me. In this situation, with the positions reversed, he would be merciless. I put my finger on the bell and leaned on it for several long seconds.

For some time there was neither sound nor movement from within and I pictured the cowering figure mustering his courage before marching to his doom. Then the light came on in the passage and as I peered expectantly through the glass a nose appeared round the far corner followed very gingerly by a wary eye. By degrees the full face inched into view and when Tristan recognised my grinning countenance he unleashed a cry of rage and bounded along the passage with upraised fist.

I really think that in his distraught state he would have attacked me, but the sight of Hamish banished all else. He grabbed the hairy creature and began to fondle him.

'Good little dog, nice little dog,' he crooned as he trotted through to the sitting room. 'What a beautiful thing you are.' He laid him lovingly in the basket, and Hamish, after a 'heigh-ho, here we are again' glance around him, put his head along his side and promptly went to sleep.

Tristan fell limply into the armchair and gazed at me with glazed eyes.

'Well, we're saved, Jim,' he whispered. 'But I'll never be the same after tonight. I've run bloody miles and I've nearly lost my voice with shouting. I tell you I'm about knackered.'

I too was vastly relieved, and the nearness of catastrophe was brought home to us when Miss Westerman arrived within ten minutes.

'Oh, my darling!' she cried as Hamish leaped at her, mouth open, short tail wagging furiously. 'I've been so worried about you all day.'

She looked tentatively at the ear with its rows of buttons. 'Oh, it does look a lot better without that horrid swelling – and what a nice neat job you have made. Thank you, Mr Herriot, and thank you, too, young man.'

Tristan, who had staggered to his feet, bowed slightly as I showed the lady out.

'Bring him back in six weeks to have the stitches out,' I called to her as she left, then I rushed back into the room.

'Siegfried's just pulled up outside! You'd better look as if you've been working.'

He rushed to the bookshelves, pulled down Gaiger and Davis's *Bacteriology* and a notebook and dived into a chair. When his brother came in he was utterly engrossed.

Siegfried moved over to the fire and warmed his hands. He looked pink and mellow.

'I've just been speaking to Miss Westerman,' he said. 'She's really pleased. Well done, both of you.'

'Thank you,' I said, but Tristan was too busy to reply, scanning the pages anxiously and scribbling repeatedly in the notebook.

Siegfried walked behind the young man's chair and looked down at the open volume.

'Ah yes, Clostridium septique,' he murmured, smiling indulgently. 'That's a good one to study. Keeps coming up in exams.' He rested a hand briefly on his brother's shoulder. 'I'm glad to see you at work. You've been raking about too much lately and it's getting you down. A night at your books will have been good for you.'

He yawned, stretched, and made for the door. 'I'm off to bed. I'm rather sleepy.' He paused with his hand on the door. 'You know, Tristan, I quite envy you – there's nothing like a nice restful evening at home.'

*

The situation of a patient escaping is by no means unique. It is something which has happened to many vets, particularly in the thirties when small animal work was very much a sideline and there were few organised arrangements for hospitalisation. It was especially traumatic when formidable people like Miss Westerman and Siegfried were involved. It is interesting to record another of the satisfying little operations – the treatment of an aural haematoma. A very quick relief from pain. I also relished the chance to chronicle a typical vignette from Tristan's love life.

41. *Roddy Travers and Jake*

I suppose it isn't unusual to see a man pushing a pram in a town, but on a lonely moorland road the sight merits a second glance. Especially when the pram contains a large dog.

That was what I saw in the hills above Darrowby one morning and I slowed down as I drove past. I had noticed the strange combination before – on several occasions over the last few weeks – and it was clear that man and dog had recently moved into the district.

As the car drew abreast of him the man turned, smiled and raised his hand. It was a smile of rare sweetness in a very brown face. A forty-year-old face, I thought, above a brown neck which bore neither collar nor tie, and a faded striped shirt lying open over a bare chest despite the coldness of the day.

I couldn't help wondering who or what he was. The outfit of

scuffed suede golf jacket, corduroy trousers and sturdy boots didn't give much clue. Some people might have put him down as an ordinary tramp, but there was a businesslike energetic look about him which didn't fit the term.

I wound the window down and the thin wind of a Yorkshire March bit at my cheeks.

'Nippy this morning,' I said.

The man seemed surprised. 'Aye,' he replied after a moment. 'Aye, reckon it is.'

I looked at the pram, ancient and rusty, and at the big animal sitting upright inside it. He was a lurcher, a cross-bred Greyhound, and he gazed back at me with unruffled dignity.

'Nice dog,' I said.

'Aye, that's Jake.' The man smiled again, showing good regular teeth. 'He's a grand 'un.'

I waved and drove on. In the mirror I could see the compact figure stepping out briskly, head up, shoulders squared, and, rising like a statue from the middle of the pram, the huge brindled form of Jake.

I didn't have to wait long to meet the unlikely pair again. I was examining a carthorse's teeth in a farmyard when on the hillside beyond the stable I saw a figure kneeling by a dry stone wall. And by his side, a pram and a big dog sitting patiently on the grass.

'Hey, just a minute.' I pointed at the hill. 'Who is that?'

The farmer laughed. 'That's Roddy Travers. D'you ken 'im?'

'No, no I don't. I had a word with him on the road the other day, that's all.'

'Aye, on the road.' He nodded knowingly. 'That's where you'd see Roddy, right enough.'

'But what is he? Where does he come from?'

'He comes from somewhere in Yorkshire, but ah don't rightly know where and ah don't think anybody else does. But I'll tell you this – he can turn 'is hand to anything.'

'Yes,' I said, watching the man expertly laying the flat slabs of stone as he repaired a gap in the wall. 'There's not many can do what he's doing now.'

'That's true. Wallin' is a skilled job and it's dying out, but Roddy's a dab hand at it. But he can do owt – hedgin', ditchin', lookin' after stock, it's all the same to him.'

I lifted the tooth rasp and began to rub a few sharp corners off the horse's molars. 'And how long will he stay here?'

'Oh, when he's finished that wall he'll be off. Ah could do with 'im stoppin' around for a bit, but he never stays in one place for long.'

'But hasn't he got a home anywhere?'

'Nay, nay.' The farmer laughed again. 'Roddy's got nowt. All 'e has in the world is in that there pram.'

Over the next weeks as the harsh spring began to soften and the sunshine brought a bright speckle of primroses on to the grassy banks I saw Roddy quite often, sometimes on the road, occasionally wielding a spade busily on the ditches around the fields. Jake was always there, either loping by his side or watching him at work. But we didn't actually meet again till I was inoculating Mr Pawson's sheep for pulpy kidney.

There were three hundred to do and they drove them in batches into a small pen where Roddy caught and held them for me. And I could see he was an expert at this, too. The wild hill sheep whipped past him like bullets but he seized their fleece effortlessly, sometimes in mid-air, and held the fore leg up to expose that bare clean area of skin behind the elbow that nature seemed to provide for the veterinary surgeon's needle.

Outside, on the windy slopes, the big lurcher sat upright in typical pose, looking with mild interest at the farm dogs prowling intently around the pens, but not interfering in any way.

'You've got him well trained,' I said.

Roddy smiled. 'Yes, ye'll never find Jake dashin' about, annoyin' people. He knows 'e has to sit there till I'm finished and there he'll sit.'

'And quite happy to do so, by the look of him.' I glanced again at the dog, a picture of contentment. 'He must live a wonderful life, travelling everywhere with you.'

'You're right there,' Mr Pawson broke in as he ushered another bunch of sheep into the pen. 'He hasn't a care in t'world, just like his master.'

Roddy didn't say anything, but as the sheep ran in he straightened up and took a long steady breath. He had been working hard and a little trickle of sweat ran down the side of his forehead, but as he gazed over the wide sweep of moor and fell I could read utter serenity in his face. After a few moments he spoke.

'I reckon that's true. We haven't much to worry us, Jake and me.'

Mr Pawson grinned mischievously. 'By gaw, Roddy, you never spoke a truer word. No wife, no kids, no life insurance, no overdraft at t'bank – you must have a right peaceful existence.'

'Ah suppose so,' Roddy said. 'But then ah've no money either.'

The farmer gave him a quizzical look. 'Aye, how about that, then? Wouldn't you feel a bit more secure, like, if you had a bit o' brass put by?'

'Nay, nay. Ye can't take it with you and any road, as long as a man can pay 'is way, he's got enough.'

There was nothing original about the words, but they have stayed with me all my life because they came from his lips and were spoken with such profound assurance.

When I had finished the inoculations and the ewes were turned out to trot back happily over the open fields, I turned to Roddy. 'Well, thanks very much. It makes my job a lot quicker when I have a good catcher like you.' I pulled out a packet of Gold Flake. 'Will you have a cigarette?'

'No, thank ye, Mr Herriot. I don't smoke.'

'You don't?'

'No – don't drink either.' He gave me his gentle smile and again I had the impression of physical and mental purity. No drinking, no smoking, a life of constant movement in the open air without material possessions or ambitions – it all showed in the unclouded eyes, the fresh skin and the hard muscular frame. He wasn't very big but he looked indestructible.

'C'mon, Jake, it's dinner time,' he said and the big lurcher bounded around him in delight. I went over and spoke to the dog and he responded with tremendous body-swaying wags, his handsome face looking up at me, full of friendliness.

I stroked the long pointed head and tickled the ears. 'He's a beauty, Roddy – a grand 'un, as you said.'

I walked to the house to wash my hands and before I went inside I glanced back at the two of them. They were sitting in the shelter of a wall and Roddy was laying out a thermos flask and a parcel of food while Jake watched eagerly. The hard bright sunshine beat on them as the wind whistled over the top of the wall. They looked supremely comfortable and at peace.

'He's independent, you see,' the farmer's wife said as I stood at the kitchen sink. 'He's welcome to come in for a bit o' dinner but he'd rather stay outside with his dog.'

I nodded. 'Where does he sleep when he's going round the farms like this?'

'Oh, anywhere,' she replied. 'In hay barns or granaries or some-times out in the open, but when he's with us he sleeps upstairs in one of our rooms. Ah know for a fact any of the farmers would be willin' to have him in the house because he allus keeps himself spotless clean.'

'I see.' I pulled the towel from behind the door. 'He's quite a character, isn't he?'

She smiled ruminatively. 'Aye, he certainly is. Just him and his dog!' She lifted a fragrant dishful of hot roast ham from the oven and set it on the table. 'But I'll tell you this. The feller's all right. Everybody likes Roddy Travers – he's a very nice man.'

Roddy stayed around the Darrowby district throughout the summer and I grew used to the sight of him on the farms or pushing his pram along the roads. When it was raining he wore a tattered over-long gaberdine coat, but at other times it was always the golf jacket and corduroys. I don't know where he had accumulated his wardrobe. It was a safe bet he had never been on a golf course in his life and it was just another of the little mysteries about him.

I saw him early one morning on a hill path in early October. It had been a night of iron frost and the tussocky pastures beyond the walls were held in a pitiless white grip with every blade of grass stiffly ensheathed in rime.

I was muffled to the eyes and had been beating my gloved fingers against my knees to thaw them out, but when I pulled up and wound down the window the first thing I saw was the bare chest under the collarless unbuttoned shirt.

'Mornin', Mr Herriot,' he said. 'Ah'm glad I've seen ye.' He paused and gave me his tranquil smile. 'There's a job along t'road for a couple of weeks, then I'm movin' on.'

'I see.' I knew enough about him now not to ask where he was going. Instead I looked down at Jake who was sniffling the herbage. 'I see he's walking this morning.'

Roddy laughed. 'Yes, sometimes 'e likes to walk, sometimes 'e likes to ride. He pleases 'imself.'

'Right, Roddy,' I said. 'No doubt we'll meet again. All the best to you.'

He waved and set off jauntily over the icebound road and I felt that a little vein of richness had gone from my life.

But I was wrong. That same evening about eight o'clock the front door bell rang. I answered it and found Roddy on the front door steps. Behind him, just visible in the frosty darkness, stood the ubiquitous pram.

'I want you to look at me dog, Mr Herriot,' he said.

'Why, what's the trouble?'

'Ah don't rightly know. He's havin' sort of . . . faintin' fits.'

'Fainting fits? That doesn't sound like Jake. Where is he, anyway?'

He pointed behind him. 'In t'pram, under t'cover.'

'All right.' I threw the door wide. 'Bring him in.'

Roddy adroitly manhandled the rusty old vehicle up the steps and pushed it, squeaking and rattling, along the passage to the consulting room. There, under the bright lights, he snapped back the fasteners and threw off the cover to reveal Jake stretched beneath.

His head was pillowed on the familiar gaberdine coat and around him lay his master's worldly goods: a string-tied bundle of spare shirt and socks, a packet of tea, a thermos, knife and spoon and an ex-army haversack.

The big dog looked up at me with terrified eyes and as I patted him I could feel his whole frame quivering.

'Let him lie there a minute, Roddy,' I said. 'And tell me exactly what you've seen.'

He rubbed his palms together and his fingers trembled. 'Well it only started this afternoon. He was right as rain, larkin' about on the grass, then he went into a sort o'fit.'

'How do you mean?'

'Just kind of seized up and toppled over on 'is side. He lay there for a bit, gaspin' and slaverin'. Ah'll tell ye, I thought he was a goner.' His eyes widened and a corner of his mouth twitched at the memory.

'How long did that last?'

'Nobbut a few seconds. Then he got up and you'd say there was nowt wrong with 'im.'

'But he did it again?'

'Aye, time and time again. Drove me near daft. But in between 'e was normal. Normal, Mr Herriot!'

Roddy Travers and Jake

It sounded ominously like the onset of epilepsy. 'How old is he?' I asked.

'Five gone last February.'

Ah well, it was a bit old for that. I reached for a stethoscope and auscultated the heart. I listened intently but heard only the racing beat of a frightened animal. There was no abnormality. My thermometer showed no rise in temperature.

'Let's have him on the table, Roddy. You take the back end.'

The big animal was limp in our arms as we hoisted him on to the smooth surface, but after lying there for a moment he looked timidly around him then sat up with a slow and careful movement. As we watched he reached out and licked his master's face while his tail flickered between his legs.

'Look at that!' the man exclaimed. 'He's all right again. You'd think he didn't ail a thing.'

And indeed Jake was recovering his confidence rapidly. He peered tentatively at the floor a few times then suddenly jumped down, trotted to his master and put his paws against his chest.

I looked at the dog standing there, tail wagging furiously. 'Well, that's a relief, anyway. I didn't like the look of him just then, but whatever's been troubling him seems to have righted itself. I'll . . .'

My happy flow was cut off. I stared at the lurcher. His fore legs were on the floor again and his mouth was gaping as he fought for breath. Frantically he gasped and retched then he blundered across the floor, collided with the pram wheels and fell on his side.

'What the hell . . . ! Quick, get him up again!' I grabbed the animal round the middle and we lifted him back on to the table.

I watched in disbelief as the huge form lay there. There was no fight for breath now – he wasn't breathing at all, he was unconscious. I pushed my fingers inside his thigh and felt the pulse. It was still going, rapid and feeble, but yet he didn't breathe.

He could die any moment and I stood there helpless, all my scientific training useless. Finally my frustration burst from me and I struck the dog on the ribs with the flat of my hand.

'Jake!' I yelled. 'Jake, what's the matter with you?'

As though in reply, the lurcher immediately started to take great wheezing breaths, his eyelids twitched back to consciousness and he began to look about him. But he was still mortally afraid and he lay prone as I gently stroked his head.

There was a long silence while the animal's terror slowly subsided, then he sat up on the table and regarded us placidly.

'There you are,' Roddy said softly. 'Same thing again. Ah can't reckon it up and ah thought ah knew summat about dogs.'

I didn't say anything. I couldn't reckon it up either, and I was supposed to be a veterinary surgeon.

I spoke at last. 'Roddy, that wasn't a fit. He was choking. Something was interfering with his air flow.' I took my hand torch from my breast pocket. 'I'm going to have a look at his throat.'

I pushed Jake's jaws apart, depressed his tongue with a forefinger and shone the light into the depths. He was the kind of good-natured dog who offered no resistance as I prodded around, but despite my floodlit view of the pharynx I could find nothing wrong. I had been hoping desperately to come across a bit of bone stuck there somewhere but I ranged feverishly over pink tongue, healthy tonsils and gleaming molars without success. Everything looked perfect.

I was tilting his head a little further when I felt him stiffen and heard Roddy's cry.

'He's goin' again!'

And he was, too. I stared in horror as the brindled body slid away from me and lay prostrate once more on the table. And again the mouth strained wide and froth bubbled round the lips. As before, the breathing had stopped and the rib cage was motionless. As the seconds ticked away I beat on the chest with my hand but it didn't work this time. I pulled the lower eyelid down from the staring orb – the conjunctiva was blue, Jake hadn't long to live. The tragedy of the thing bore down on me. This wasn't just a dog, he was this man's family and I was watching him die.

It was at that moment that I heard the faint sound. It was a strangled cough which barely stirred the dog's lips.

'Damn it!' I shouted. 'He *is* choking. There must be something down there.'

Again I seized the head and pushed my torch into the mouth and I shall always be thankful that at that very instant the dog coughed again, opening the cartilages of the larynx and giving me a glimpse of the cause of all the trouble. There, beyond the drooping epiglottis, I saw for a fleeting moment a smooth round object no bigger than a pea.

'I think it's a pebble,' I gasped. 'Right inside his larynx.'

'You mean, in 'is Adam's apple?'

'That's right, and it's acting like a ball valve, blocking his windpipe every now and then.' I shook the dog's head. 'You see, look, I've dislodged it for the moment. He's coming round again.'

Once more Jake was reviving and breathing steadily.

Roddy ran his hand over the head, along the back and down the great muscles of the hind limbs. 'But . . . but . . . it'll happen again, won't it?'

I nodded. 'I'm afraid so.'

'And one of these times it isn't goin' to shift and that'll be the end of 'im?' He had gone very pale.

'That's about it, Roddy. I'll have to get that pebble out.'

'But how . . . ?'

'Cut into the larynx. And right now – it's the only way.'

'All right.' He swallowed. 'Let's get on. I don't think ah could stand it if he went down again.'

I knew what he meant. My knees had begun to shake, and I had a strong conviction that if Jake collapsed once more then so would I.

I seized a pair of scissors and clipped away the hair from the ventral surface of the larynx. I dared not use a general anaesthetic and infiltrated the area with local before swabbing with antiseptic. Mercifully there was a freshly boiled set of instruments lying in the steriliser and I lifted out the tray and set it on the trolley by the side of the table.

'Hold his head steady,' I said hoarsely, and gripped a scalpel.

I cut down through skin, fascia and the thin layers of the sterno-hyoid and omo-hyoid muscles till the ventral surface of the larynx was revealed. This was something I had never done to a live dog before, but desperation abolished any hesitancy and it took me only another few seconds to incise the thin membrane and peer into the interior.

And there it was. A pebble right enough – grey and glistening and tiny, but big enough to kill.

I had to fish it out quickly and cleanly without pushing it into the trachea. I leaned back and rummaged in the tray till I found some broad-bladed forceps, then I poised them over the wound. Great surgeons' hands, I felt sure, didn't shake like this, nor did such men pant as I was doing. But I clenched my teeth, introduced the forceps, and my hand magically steadied as I clamped them over the pebble.

I stopped panting, too. In fact I didn't breathe at all as I bore the shining little object slowly and tenderly through the opening and dropped it with a gentle rat-tat on the table.

'Is that it?' asked Roddy, almost in a whisper.

'That's it.' I reached for needle and suture silk. 'All is well now.'

The stitching took only a few minutes and by the end of it Jake was bright-eyed and alert, paws shifting impatiently, ready for anything. He seemed to know his troubles were over.

Roddy brought him back in ten days to have the stitches removed. It was, in fact, the very morning he was leaving the Darrowby district, and after I had picked the few loops of silk from the nicely healed wound I walked with him to the front door while Jake capered round our feet.

On the pavement outside Skeldale House the ancient pram stood in all its high, rusted dignity. Roddy pulled back the cover.

'Up, boy,' he murmured, and the big dog leaped effortlessly into his accustomed place.

Roddy took hold of the handle with both hands and as the autumn sunshine broke suddenly through the clouds it lit up a picture which had grown familiar and part of the daily scene. The golf jacket, the open shirt and brown chest, the handsome animal sitting up, looking around him with natural grace.

'Well, so long, Roddy,' I said. 'I suppose you'll be round these parts again.'

He turned and I saw that smile again. 'Aye, reckon ah'll be back.'

He gave a push and they were off, the strange vehicle creaking, Jake swaying gently as they went down the street. The memory came back to me of what I had seen under the cover that night in the surgery. The haversack, which would contain his razor, towel, soap and a few other things. The packet of tea and the thermos. And something else – a tiny dog collar. Could it have belonged to Jake as a pup or to another loved animal? It added a little more mystery to the man . . . and explained other things, too. That farmer had been right – all Roddy possessed was in that pram.

And it seemed it was all he desired, too, because as he turned the corner and disappeared from my view I could hear him whistling.

*

A journalist came to me recently and asked me to introduce him to some of the local characters. 'There aren't any.' I replied. Maybe too sweeping a statement, but it is true that the wonderful old rural types who provided such a fertile field for my writing are no longer around. You don't hear the real old Yorkshire dialect and expressions any more. Education, television, radio and ease of transport have smoothed the people out till they are like people anywhere. There isn't a Roddy Travers to be found. Old people in Darrowby still talk about him with affection, recalling the memory of the sunburned man who pushed that big dog in the pram along the country roads. Jake was a fitting companion for him, and whenever I see a lurcher it reminds me of the only time in my veterinary experience that I ever removed a foreign body from a larynx.

42. *Nip and Sam*

'How are you, Mr Herriot?'

Ordinary words, but the eagerness, almost desperation in the old man's voice made them urgent and meaningful.

I saw him nearly every day. In my unpredictable life it was difficult to do anything regularly but I did like a stroll by the river before lunch and so did my beagle, Sam. That was when we met Mr Potts and Nip, his elderly sheepdog – they seemed to have the same habits as us. His house backed on to the riverside fields and he spent a lot of time just walking around with his dog.

Many retired farmers kept a bit of land and a few stock to occupy their minds and ease the transition from their arduous existence to day-long leisure, but Mr Potts had bought a little bungalow with a scrap of garden and it was obvious that time dragged.

Probably his health had dictated this. As he faced me he leaned on his stick and his bluish cheeks rose and fell with his breathing. He was a heart case if ever I saw one.

'I'm fine, Mr Potts,' I replied. 'And how are things with you?'

Nip and Sam

'Nobbut middlin', lad. Ah soon get short o' wind.' He coughed a couple of times then asked the inevitable question.

'And what have you been doin' this mornin'?' That was when his eyes grew intent and wide. He really wanted to know.

I thought for a moment. 'Well now, let's see.' I always tried to give him a detailed answer because I knew it meant a lot to him and brought back the life he missed so much. 'I've done a couple of cleansings, seen a lame bullock, treated two cows with mastitis and another with milk fever.'

He nodded eagerly at every word.

'By gaw!' he exclaimed. 'It's a beggar, that milk fever. When I were a lad, good cows used to die like flies with it. Allus good milkers after their third or fourth calf. Couldn't get to their feet and we used to dose 'em with all sorts, but they died, every one of 'em.'

'Yes,' I said. 'It must have been heartbreaking in those days.'

'But then,' he smiled delightedly, digging a forefinger into my chest, 'then we started blowin' up their udders wi' a bicycle pump, and d'you know – they jumped up and walked away. Like magic it were.' His eyes sparkled at the memory.

'I know, Mr Potts, I've blown up a few myself, only I didn't use a bicycle pump – I had a special little inflation apparatus.'

That black box with its shining cylinders and filter is now in my personal museum, and it is the best place for it. It had got me out of some difficult situations but in the background there had always been the gnawing dread of transmitting tuberculosis. I had heard of it happening and was glad that calcium borogluconate had arrived.

As we spoke, Sam and Nip played on the grass beside us. I watched as the Beagle frisked round the old animal while Nip pawed at him stiff-jointedly, his tail waving with pleasure. You could see that he enjoyed these meetings as much as his master, and for a brief time the years fell away from him as he rolled on his back with Sam astride him, nibbling gently at his chest.

I walked with the old farmer as far as the little wooden bridge, then I had to turn for home. I watched the two of them pottering slowly over the narrow strip of timber to the other side of the river. Sam and I had our work pressing, but they had nothing else to do.

I used to see Mr Potts at other times, too. Wandering aimlessly among the stalls on market days or standing on the fringe of the group of farmers who always gathered in front of the Drovers' Arms to meet cattle dealers, cow feed merchants, or just to talk business among themselves.

Or I saw him at the auction mart, leaning on his stick, listening to the rapid-fire chanting of the auctioneer, watching listlessly as the beasts were bought and sold. And all the time I knew there was an emptiness in him, because there were none of his cattle in the stalls, none of his sheep in the long rows of pens. He was out of it all, old and done.

I saw him the day before he died. It was in the usual place and I was standing at the river's edge watching a heron rising from a rush-lined island and flapping lazily away over the fields.

The old man stopped as he came abreast of me and the two dogs began their friendly wrestling.

'Well now, Mr Herriot.' He paused and bowed his head over the stick which he had dug into the grass of his farm for half a century. 'What have you been doin' today?'

Perhaps his cheeks were a deeper shade of blue and the breath whistled through his pursed lips as he exhaled, but I can't recall that he looked any worse than usual.

'I'll tell you, Mr Potts,' I said. 'I'm feeling a bit weary. I ran into a real snorter of a foaling this morning – took me over two hours and I ache all over.'

'Foaling, eh? Foal would be laid wrong, I reckon?'

'Yes, cross-ways on, and I had a struggle to turn it.'

'By gaw, yes, it's hard work is that.' He smiled reminiscently. 'Doesta remember that Clydesdale mare you foaled at ma place? Must 'ave been one of your first jobs when you came to Darrowby.'

'Of course I do,' I replied. And I remembered, too, how kind the old man had been. Seeing I was young and green and unsure of myself he had taken pains, in his quiet way, to put me at my ease and give me confidence. 'Yes,' I went on, 'it was late on a Sunday night and we had a right tussle with it. There was just the two of us but we managed, didn't we?'

He squared his shoulders and for a moment his eyes looked past me at something I couldn't see. 'Aye, that's right. We made a job of 'er, you and me. Ah could push and pull a bit then.'

'You certainly could. There's no doubt about that.'

He sucked the air in with difficulty and blew it out again with that peculiar pursing of the lips. Then he turned to me with a strange dignity.

Nip and Sam

'They were good days, Mr Herriot, weren't they?'

'They were, Mr Potts, they were indeed.'

'Aye, aye.' He nodded slowly. 'Ah've had a lot o' them days. Hard but good.' He looked down at his dog. 'And awd Nip shared 'em with me, didn't ye, lad?'

His words took me back to the very first time I had seen Mr Potts. He was perched on a stool, milking one of his few cows, his cloth-capped head thrusting into the hairy flank, and as he pulled at the teats old Nip dropped a stone on the toe of his boot. The farmer reached down, lifted the stone between two fingers and flicked it out through the open door into the yard. Nip scurried delightedly after it and was back within seconds, dropping the stone on the boot and panting hopefully.

He wasn't disappointed. His master repeated the throw automatically as if it was something he did all the time, and as I watched it happening again and again I realised that this was a daily ritual between the two. I had a piercing impression of infinite patience and devotion.

'Right, then, Mr Herriot, we'll be off,' Mr Potts said, jerking me back to the present. 'Come on, Nip.' He waved his stick and I watched him till a low-hanging willow branch hid man and dog from my sight.

That was the last time I saw him. Next day the man at the petrol pumps mumbled casually, 'See old Mr Potts got his time in, eh?'

And that was it. There was no excitement, and only a handful of his old friends turned up at the funeral.

For me it was a stab of sorrow. Another familiar face gone, and I should miss him as my busy life went on. I knew our daily conversations had cheered him but I felt with a sad finality that there was nothing else I could do for Mr Potts.

It was about a fortnight later and as I opened the gate to let Sam into the riverside fields I glanced at my watch. Twelve thirty – plenty of time for our pre-lunch walk and the long stretch of green was empty. Then I noticed a single dog away on the left. It was Nip, and as I watched he got up, took a few indeterminate steps over the grass, then turned and sat down again at the gate of his back garden.

Instead of taking my usual route I cut along behind the houses till I reached the old dog. He had been looking around him aimlessly, but when we came up to him he seemed to come to life, sniffing Sam over and wagging his tail at me.

On the other side of the gate Mrs Potts was doing a bit of weeding, bending painfully as she plied her trowel.

'How are you, Mrs Potts?' I said.

With an effort she straightened up. 'Oh, not too bad, thank you, Mr Herriot.' She came over and leaned on the gate. 'I see you're lookin' at the awd dog. My word he's missin' his master.'

I didn't say anything and she went on. 'He's eating all right and I can give him plenty of good food, but what I can't do is take 'im for walks.' She rubbed her back. 'I'm plagued with rheumaticks, Mr Herriot, and it takes me all my time to get around the house and garden.'

'I can understand that,' I said. 'And I don't suppose he'll walk by himself.'

'Nay, he won't. There's the path he went along every day.' She pointed to the winding strip of beaten earth among the grass. 'But he won't go more'n a few yards.'

'Ah well, dogs like a bit of company just the same as we do.' I bent and ran my hand over the old animal's head and ears. 'How would you like to come with us, Nip?'

I set off along the path and he followed unhesitatingly, trotting alongside Sam with swinging tail.

'Eee, look!' the old lady cried. 'Isn't that grand to see!'

I followed his usual route down to the river where the water ran dark and silent under the branches of the gnarled willows. Then we went over the bridge and in front of us the river widened into pebbly shallows and murmured and chattered among the stones.

It was peaceful down there with only the endless water sound and the piping of birds in my ears and the long curtain of leaves parting here and there to give glimpses of the green flanks of the fells.

I watched the two dogs frisking ahead of me and the decision came to me quite naturally: I would do this regularly. From that day I altered my route and went along behind the houses first. Nip was happy again, Sam loved the whole idea, and for me there was a strange comfort in the knowledge that there was still something I could do for Mr Potts.

*

Dogs do love a regular programme. One of their greatest pleasures is to look forward to something and then to see that something come about. It may be a meal or the arrival home of one of the household. With Nip it was his daily walk by the river with his master. I have always had a warm feeling for my farmer friends who shared my early struggles, and this feeling has strengthened over the years now that I myself can look back on more than half a century of this association. In the case of Mr Potts, I was glad to be able to show that veterinary services could embrace many things.

43. *Judy the Nurse Dog*

I first met Judy the Sheepdog when I was treating Eric's bullock for wooden tongue. The bullock was only a young one and the farmer admitted ruefully that he had neglected it because it was almost a walking skeleton.

'Damn!' Eric grunted. 'He's been runnin' out with that bunch in the far fields and I must have missed 'im. I never knew he'd got to this state.'

When actinobacillosis affects the tongue it should be treated right at the start, when the first symptoms of salivation and swelling beneath the jaw appear. Otherwise the tongue becomes harder and harder till finally it sticks out of the front of the mouth, as unyielding as the wood which gives the disease its ancient name.

This skinny little creature had reached that state, so that he not only looked pathetic but also slightly comic, as though he were making a derisive gesture at me. But with a tongue like that he just couldn't eat and was literally starving to death. He lay quietly as though he didn't care.

'There's one thing, Eric,' I said. 'Giving him an intravenous injection won't be any problem. He hasn't the strength to resist.'

The great new treatment at that time was sodium iodide into the vein – modern and spectacular. Before that the farmers used to paint the tongue with tincture of iodine, a tedious procedure which sometimes worked and sometimes didn't. The sodium iodide was a magical improvement and showed results within a few days.

I inserted the needle into the jugular and tipped up the bottle of clear fluid. Two drachms of iodide I used to use, in eight ounces of distilled water, and it didn't take long to flow in. In fact the bottle was nearly empty before I noticed Judy.

I had been aware of a big dog sitting near me all the time, but as I neared the end of the injection a black nose moved ever closer till it was almost touching the needle. Then the nose moved along the rubber tube up to the bottle and back again, sniffing with the utmost concentration. When I removed the needle the nose began a careful inspection of the injection site. Then a tongue appeared and began to lick the bullock's neck methodically.

I squatted back on my heels and watched. This was something more than mere curiosity; everything in the dog's attitude suggested intense interest and concern.

'You know, Eric,' I said, 'I have the impression that this dog isn't just watching me. She's supervising the whole job.'

The farmer laughed. 'You're right there. She's a funny old bitch is Judy – sort of a nurse. If there's anything amiss she's on duty. You can't keep her away.'

Judy looked up quickly at the sound of her name. She was a handsome animal; not the usual colour, but a variegated brindle with waving lines of brown and grey mingling with the normal black and white of the farm collie. Maybe there was a cross somewhere, but the result was very attractive and the effect was heightened by her bright-eyed, laughing-mouthed friendliness.

I reached out and tickled the backs of her ears and she wagged mightily – not just her tail but her entire rear end. 'I suppose she's just good-natured.'

'Oh aye, she is,' the farmer said. 'But it's not only that. It sounds daft but I think Judy feels a sense of responsibility to all the stock on t'farm.'

I nodded. 'I believe you. Anyway, let's get this beast on to his chest.'

We got down in the straw and with our hands under the back bone, rolled the bullock till he was resting on his sternum. We balanced him there with straw bales on either side, then covered him with a horse rug.

In that position he didn't look as moribund as before, but the emaciated head with the useless jutting tongue lolled feebly on his shoulders and the saliva drooled uncontrolled on to the straw. I wondered if I'd ever see him alive again.

Judy, however, didn't appear to share my pessimism. After a thorough sniffing examination of rug and bales she moved to the front, applied an encouraging tongue to the shaggy forehead, then stationed herself comfortably facing the bullock, very like a night nurse keeping an eye on her patient.

'Will she stay there?' I closed the half-door and took a last look inside.

'Aye, nothing'll shift her till he's dead or better,' Eric replied. 'She's in her element now.'

'Well, you never know, she may give him an interest in life, just sitting there. He certainly needs some help. You must keep him alive with milk or gruel till the injection starts to work. If he'll drink it it'll do him most good, but otherwise you'll have to bottle it into him. But be careful – you can choke a beast that way.'

A case like this had more than the usual share of the old fascination because I was using a therapeutic agent which really worked – something that didn't happen too often at that time. So I was eager to get back to see if I had been able to pull that bullock from the brink of death. But I knew I had to give the drug a chance and kept away for five days.

When I walked across the yard to the box I knew there would be no further doubts. He would either be dead or on the road to recovery.

The sound of my steps on the cobbles hadn't gone unnoticed. Judy's head, ears cocked, appeared above the half-door. A little well of triumph brimmed in me. If the nurse was still on duty then the patient must be alive. And I felt even more certain when the big dog disappeared for a second, then came soaring effortlessly over the door and capered up to me, working her hind end into convolutions of delight. She seemed to be doing her best to tell me all was well.

Inside the box the bullock was still lying down but he turned to look at me and I noticed a strand of hay hanging from his mouth. The tongue itself had disappeared behind the lips.

'Well, we're winnin', aren't we?' Eric Abbot came in from the yard.

'Without a doubt,' I said. 'The tongue's much softer and I see he's been trying to eat hay.'

'Aye, can't quite manage it yet, but he's suppin' the milk and gruel like a good 'un. He's been up a time or two but he's very wobbly on his pins.'

I produced another bottle of sodium iodide and repeated the injection with Judy's nose again almost touching the needle as she sniffed avidly. Her eyes were focused on the injection site with fierce concentration and so intent was she on extracting the full savour that she occasionally blew out her nostrils with a sharp blast before recommencing her inspection.

When I had finished she took up her position at the head and as I prepared to leave I noticed a voluptuous swaying of her hips which were embedded in the straw. I was a little puzzled until I realised she was wagging in the sitting position.

'Well, Judy's happy at the way things are going,' I said.

The farmer nodded. 'Yes, she is. She likes to be in charge. Do you know, she gives every new-born calf a good lick over as soon as it comes into t'world and it's the same whenever one of our cats 'as kittens.'

'Bit of a midwife, too, eh?'

'You could say that. And another funny thing about 'er – she lives with the livestock in the buildings. She's got a nice warm kennel but she never bothers with it – sleeps with the beasts in the straw every night.'

I revisited the bullock a week later and this time he galloped round the box like a racehorse when I approached him. When I finally trapped him in a corner and caught his nose I was breathless but happy. I slipped my fingers into his mouth; the tongue was pliable and almost normal.

'One more shot, Eric,' I said. 'Wooden tongue is the very devil for recurring if you don't get it cleared up thoroughly.' I began to unwind the rubber tube. 'By the way, I don't see Judy around.'

'Oh, I reckon she feels he's cured now, and anyway, she has summat else on her plate this mornin'. Can you see her over there?'

I looked through the doorway. Judy was stalking importantly across the yard. She had something in her mouth – a yellow, fluffy object.

I craned out further. 'What is she carrying?'

'It's a chicken.'

'A chicken?'

'Aye, there's a brood of them runnin' around just now. They're only a month old and t'awd bitch seems to think they'd be better off in the stable. She's made a bed for them in there and she keeps tryin' to curl herself round them. But the little things won't 'ave it.'

I watched Judy disappear into the stable. Very soon she came out, trotted after a group of tiny chicks which were pecking happily among the cobbles and gently scooped one up. Busily she made her way back to the stable but as she entered, the previous chick reappeared in the doorway and pottered over to rejoin his friends.

She was having a frustrating time but I knew she would keep at it because that was the way she was.

Judy the nurse dog was still on duty.

*

The caring instinct in animals is manifested most obviously in the maternal feeling, surely one of the most powerful and most commonly observed characteristics, but Judy is the only animal I have ever known whose concern embraced all her fellow creatures. As Eric Abbot said, she was in her element when there was any sickness among his livestock. She was a natural canine nurse, and so unique in my experience that I have often wondered if anybody else has encountered one like her.

44. *Myrtle*

'Ooh . . . ooh-hoo-hooo!' The broken-hearted sobbing jerked me into full wakefulness. It was one a.m. and after the familiar jangling of the bedside phone I expected the gruff voice of a farmer with a calving cow. Instead, there was this terrible sound.

'Who is this?' I asked a little breathlessly. 'What on earth is the trouble?'

I heard a gulping at the other end and then a man's voice pleading between sobs. 'It's Humphrey Cobb. For God's sake come out and see Myrtle. I think she's dyin'.'

'Myrtle?'

'Aye, me poor little dog. She's in a 'ell of a state! Oooh-hooo!'

The receiver trembled in my grasp. 'What is she doing?'

'Oh, pantin' and gaspin'. I think it's nearly all over with 'er. Come quick!'

'Where do you live?'

'Cedar House. End of Hill Street.'

'I know it. I'll be there very soon.'

'Oh, thank ye, thank ye. Myrtle hasn't got long. Hurry, hurry!'

I leaped from the bed and rushed at my clothes, draped over a chair against the wall. In my haste, in the darkness, I got both feet down one leg of my working corduroys and crashed full length on the floor.

Helen was used to nocturnal calls and often she only half woke. For my part I always tried to avoid disturbing her by dressing without switching on the light; there was always a glow from the nightlight we kept burning on the landing for young Jimmy.

However, the system broke down this time. The thud of my falling body brought her into a sitting position.

'What is it, Jim? What's happening?'

I struggled to my feet. 'It's all right, Helen, I just tripped over.' I snatched my shirt from the chair back.

'But what are you dashing about for?'

'Desperately urgent case. I have to hurry.'

'All right, Jim, but you won't get there any sooner by going on like this. Just calm down.'

My wife was right, of course. I have always envied those vets who can stay relaxed under pressure. But I wasn't made that way.

I galloped down the stairs and through the long back garden to the garage. Cedar House was only a mile away and I didn't have much time to think about the case, but by the time I arrived I had pretty well decided that an acute dyspnoea like this would probably be caused by a heart-attack or some sudden allergy.

In answer to my ring the porch light flashed on and Humphrey Cobb stood before me. He was a little round man in his sixties and his humpty-dumpty appearance was accentuated by his gleaming bald head.

'Oh, Mr Herriot, come in, come in,' he cried brokenly as the tears streamed down his cheeks. 'Thank ye for gettin' out of your bed to help me poor little Myrtle.'

As he spoke, the blast of whisky fumes almost made my head spin and I noticed that as he preceded me across the hall he staggered slightly.

My patient was lying in a basket by the side of an Aga cooker in a large, well-appointed kitchen. I felt a warm surge when I saw that

362

Myrtle

she was a Beagle like my own dog, Sam. I knelt down and looked at her closely. Her mouth was open and her tongue lolled, but she did not seem to be in acute distress. In fact, as I patted her head her tail flapped against the blanket.

A heart-rending wail sounded in my ear. 'What d'ye make of her, Mr Herriot? It's her heart, isn't it? Oh, Myrtle, Myrtle!' The little man crouched over his pet and the tears flowed unchecked.

'You know, Mr Cobb,' I said, 'she doesn't seem all that bad to me, so don't upset yourself too much. Just give me a chance to examine her.'

I placed my stethoscope over the ribs and listened to the steady thudding of a superbly strong heart. The temperature was normal and I was palpating the abdomen when Mr Cobb broke in again.

'The trouble is,' he gasped, 'I neglect this poor little animal.'

'What do you mean?'

'Well, ah've been all day at Catterick at the races, gamblin' and drinkin' with never a thought for me dog.'

'You left her alone all that time in the house?'

'Nay, nay, t'missus has been with her.'

'Well, then.' I felt I was getting out of my depth. 'She would feed Myrtle and let her out in the garden?'

'Oh aye,' he said, wringing his hands. 'But I shouldn't leave 'er. She thinks such a lot about me.'

As he spoke, I could feel one side of my face tingling with heat. My problem was suddenly solved.

'You've got her too near the Aga,' I said. 'She's panting because she's uncomfortably hot.'

He looked at me doubtfully. 'We just shifted 'er basket today. We've been gettin' some new tiles put down on the floor.'

'Right,' I said. 'Shift it back again and she'll be fine.'

'But Mr Herriot.' His lips began to tremble again. 'It's more than that. She's sufferin'. Look at her eyes.'

Myrtle had the lovely big liquid eyes of her breed and she knew how to use them. Many people think the Spaniel is number one when it comes to looking soulful but I personally plump for the Beagle. And Myrtle was an expert.

'Oh, I shouldn't worry about that, Mr Cobb,' I said. 'Believe me, she'll be all right.'

He still seemed unhappy. 'But aren't ye going to do something?'

It was one of the great questions in veterinary practice. If you

363

didn't 'do something' they were not satisfied. And in this case Mr Cobb was in greater need of treatment than his pet. Still, I wasn't going to stick a needle into Myrtle just to please him, so I produced a vitamin tablet from my bag and pushed it over the back of the little animal's tongue.

'There you are,' I said. 'I'm sure that will do her good.' And after all, I thought, I wasn't a complete charlatan – it wouldn't do her any harm.

Mr Cobb relaxed visibly. 'Eee, that's champion. You've set me mind at rest.' He led the way into a luxurious drawing-room and tacked unsteadily towards a cocktail cabinet. 'You'll 'ave a drink before you go?'

'No really, thanks,' I said. 'I'd rather not, if you don't mind.'

'Well, I'll 'ave a drop. Just to steady me nerves. I was that upset.' He tipped a lavish measure of whisky into a glass and waved me to a chair.

My bed was calling me, but I sat down and watched as he drank. He told me that he was a retired bookmaker from the West Riding and that he had come to Darrowby only a month ago. Although no longer directly connected with horse racing, he still loved the sport and never missed a meeting in the north of England.

'I allus get a taxi to take me and I have a right good day.' His face was radiant as he recalled the happy times, then for a moment his cheeks quivered and his woebegone expression returned.

'But I neglect me dog. I leave her at home.'

'Oh nonsense,' I said. 'I've seen you out in the fields with Myrtle. You give her plenty of exercise, don't you?'

'Oh aye, lots of walks every day.'

'Well, then she really has a good life. This is just a silly little notion you've got.'

He beamed at me and sloshed out another few fingers of whisky.

'Eee, you're a good lad. Come on, you'll just have one before you go.'

'Oh, all right, just a small one, then.'

As we drank he became more and more benign until he was gazing at me with something like devotion.

'James Herriot,' he slurred. 'I suppose it'll be Jim, eh?'

'Well, yes.'

'I'll call you Jim, then, and you can call me Humphrey.'

'Okay, Humphrey,' I said, and swallowed the last of my whisky. 'But I really must go now.'

Out in the street again he put a hand on my arm and his face became serious again. 'Thank ye, Jim. Myrtle was right bad tonight and I'm grateful.'

Driving away, I realised that I had failed to convince him that there was nothing wrong with his dog. He was sure I had saved her life. It had been an unusual visit and as my 2 a.m. whisky burned in my stomach I decided that Humphrey Cobb was a very funny little man. But I liked him.

After that night I saw him quite frequently exercising Myrtle in the fields. With his almost spherical build he seemed to bounce over the grass, but his manner was always self-contained and rational except that he kept thanking me for pulling his dog back from the jaws of death.

Then quite suddenly I was back at the beginning again. It was shortly after midnight and as I lifted the bedside phone I could hear the distraught weeping before the receiver touched my ear.

'Oooh . . . oooh . . . Jim, Jim. Myrtle's in a terrible bad way. Will ye come?'

'What . . . what is it this time?'

'She's twitchin'.'

'Twitching?'

'Aye, twitchin' summat terrible. Oh, come on, Jim, lad, don't keep me waiting. I'm worried to death. I'm sure she's got distemper.' He broke down again.

My head began to reel. 'She can't have distemper, Humphrey. Not in a flash, like that.'

'I'm beggin' you Jim,' he went on as though he hadn't heard. 'Be a pal. Come and see Myrtle.'

'All right,' I said wearily. 'I'll be there in a few minutes.'

'Oh, you're a good lad, Jim, you're a good lad . . .' The voice trailed away as I replaced the phone.

I dressed at normal speed with none of the panic of the first time. It sounded like a repetition, but why after midnight again? On my way to Cedar House I decided it must be another false alarm – but you never knew.

The same dizzying wave of whisky fumes enveloped me in the porch. Humphrey, sniffling and moaning, fell against me once or twice as he ushered me into the kitchen. He pointed to the basket in the corner.

'There she is,' he said, wiping his eyes. 'I've just got back from Ripon and found 'er like this.'

'Racing again, eh?'

'Aye, gamblin' on them 'osses and drinkin' and leavin' me poor dog pining at home. I'm a rotter, Jim, that's what I am.'

'Rubbish, Humphrey! I've told you before. You're not doing her any harm by having a day out. Anyway, how about this twitching? She looks all right now.'

'Yes, she's stopped doing it, but when I came in her back leg was goin' like this.' He made a jerking movement with his hand.

I groaned inwardly. 'But she could have been scratching or flicking away a fly.'

'Nay, there's summat more than that. I can tell she's sufferin'. Just look at them eyes.'

I could see what he meant. Myrtle's beagle eyes were pools of emotion and it was easy to read a melting reproach in their depths.

With a feeling of futility I examined her. I knew what I would find – nothing. But when I tried to explain to the little man that his pet was normal he wouldn't have it.

'Oh, you'll give her one of them wonderful tablets,' he pleaded. 'It cured her last time.'

I felt I had to pacify him, so Myrtle received another instalment of vitamins.

Humphrey was immensely relieved and weaved his way to the drawing-room and the whisky bottle.

'I need a little pick-me-up after that shock,' he said. 'You'll 'ave one too, won't you, Jim lad?'

This pantomime was enacted frequently over the next few months, always after race meetings and always between midnight and 1 a.m. I had ample opportunity to analyse the situation and I came to a fairly obvious conclusion.

Most of the time Humphrey was a normal conscientious pet owner, but after a large intake of alcohol his affectionate feelings degenerated into a glutinous sentimentality and guilt. I invariably went out when he called me because I knew that he would be deeply distressed if I refused. I was treating Humphrey, not Myrtle.

It amused me that not once did he accept my protestations that my visit was unnecessary. Each time he was sure that my magic tablets had saved his dog's life.

Mind you, I did not discount the possibility that Myrtle was deliberately working on him with those eyes. The canine mind is quite capable of disapproval. I took my own dog almost everywhere with me but if I left him at home to take Helen to the cinema he would lie under our bed, sulking, and when he emerged, would studiously ignore us for an hour or two.

I quailed when Humphrey told me he had decided to have Myrtle mated because I knew that the ensuing pregnancy would be laden with harassment for me.

That was how it turned out. The little man flew into a series of alcoholic panics, all of them unfounded, and he discovered imaginary symptoms in Myrtle at regular intervals throughout the nine weeks.

I was vastly relieved when she gave birth to five healthy pups. Now, I thought, I would get some peace. The fact was that I was just about tired of Humphrey's nocturnal nonsense. I have always made a point of never refusing to turn out at night but Humphrey had stretched this principle to breaking point. One of these times he would have to be told.

The crunch came when the pups were a few weeks old. I had had a terrible day, starting with a prolapsed uterus in a cow at 5 a.m. and progressing through hours of road-slogging, missed meals and a late-night wrestle with Ministry forms, some of which I suspected I had filled up wrongly.

My clerical incompetence has always infuriated me and when I crawled, dog tired, into bed, my mind was still buzzing with frustration. I lay for a long time trying to put those forms away from me, and it was well after midnight when I fell asleep.

I have always had a silly fancy that our practice knows when I desperately want a full night's sleep. It knows and gleefully steps in. When the phone exploded in my ear I wasn't really surprised.

As I stretched a weary hand to the receiver the luminous dial of the alarm clock read 1.15 a.m.

'Hello,' I grunted.

'Oooh . . . oooh . . . oooh!' The reply was only too familiar.

I clenched my teeth. This was just what I needed. 'Humphrey! What is it this time?'

'Oh Jim, Myrtle's really dyin', I know she is. Come quick, lad, come quick!'

'Dying?' I took a couple of rasping breaths. 'How do you make that out?'

'Well . . . she's stretched out on 'er side, tremblin'.'

'Anything else?'

'Aye, t'missus said Myrtle's been looking worried and walkin' stiff when she let her out in the garden this afternoon. I'm not long back from Redcar, ye see?'

'So you've been to the races, eh?'

'That's right . . . neglectin' me dog. I'm a scamp, nothing but a scamp.'

I closed my eyes in the darkness. There was no end to Humphrey's imaginary symptoms. Trembling, this time, looking worried, walking stiff. We'd had panting and twitching and head-nodding and ear-shaking – what would it be next?

But enough was enough. 'Look, Humphrey,' I said, 'there's nothing wrong with your dog. I've told you again and again . . .'

'Oh, Jim, lad, don't be long. Oooh-hooo!'

'I'm not coming, Humphrey.'

'Nay, nay, don't say that! She's goin' fast, I tell ye!'

'I really mean it. It's just wasting my time and your money, so go to bed. Myrtle will be fine.'

As I lay quivering between the sheets I realised that refusing to go out was an exhausting business. There was no doubt in my mind that it would have taken less out of me to get up and attend another charade at Cedar House than to say 'no' for the first time in my life. But this couldn't go on. I had to make a stand.

I was still tormented by remorse when I fell into an uneasy slumber and it is a good thing that the subconscious mind works on during sleep, because with the alarm clock reading 2.30 a.m. I came suddenly wide awake.

'My God!' I cried, staring at the dark ceiling. 'Myrtle's got eclampsia!'

I scrambled from the bed and began to throw on my clothes. I must have made some commotion because I heard Helen's sleepy voice.

'What is it? What's the matter?'

'Humphrey Cobb!' I gasped, tying a shoe lace.

'Humphrey . . . but you said there was never any hurry . . .'

'There is this time. His dog's dying.' I glared again at the clock.

'In fact she could be dead now.' I lifted my tie, then hurled it back on the chair. 'Damn it! I don't need that!' I fled from the room.

Down the long garden and into the car with my brain spelling out the concise case history which Humphrey had given me. Small bitch nursing five puppies, signs of anxiety and stiff gait this afternoon and now prostrate and trembling. Classical puerperal eclampsia. Rapidly fatal without treatment. And it was nearly an hour and a half since he had phoned. I couldn't bear to think about it.

Humphrey was still up. He had obviously been consoling himself with the bottle because he could barely stand.

'You've come, Jim lad,' he mumbled, blinking at me.

'Yes, how is she?'

'Just t'same . . .'

Clutching my calcium and my intravenous syringe I rushed past him into the kitchen.

Myrtle's sleek body was extended in a tetanic spasm. She was gasping for breath, quivering violently, and bubbles of saliva dripped from her mouth. Those eyes had lost their softness and were fixed in a frantic stare. She looked terrible, but she was alive . . . she was alive.

I lifted the squealing pups on to a rug nearby and quickly clipped and swabbed the area over the radial vein. I inserted the needle into the blood vessel and began to depress the plunger with infinite care and very slowly. Calcium was the cure for this condition but a quick blast would surely kill the patient.

I took several minutes to empty the syringe then sat back on my heels and watched. Some of these cases needed narcotics as well as calcium and I had nembutal and morphine ready to hand. But as the time passed Myrtle's breathing slowed down and the rigid muscles began to relax. When she started to swallow her saliva and look round at me I knew she would live.

I was waiting for the last tremors to disappear from her limbs when I felt a tap on my shoulder. Humphrey was standing there with the whisky bottle in his hand.

'You'll 'ave one, won't you, Jim?'

I didn't need much persuading. The knowledge that I had almost been responsible for Myrtle's death had thrown me into a mild degree of shock.

My hand was still shaking as I raised the glass and I had barely taken the first sip when the little animal got up from the basket and walked over to inspect her pups. Some eclampsias were slow to respond but others were spectacularly quick and I was grateful for the sake of my nervous system that this was one of the quick ones.

In fact the recovery was almost uncanny because, after sniffing her family over, Myrtle walked across to the table to greet me. Her eyes brimmed with friendliness and her tail waved high in the true Beagle fashion.

I was stroking her ears when Humphrey broke into a throaty giggle.

'You know, Jim, I've learned summat tonight.' His voice was a slow drawl but he was still in possession of his wits.

'What's that, Humphrey?'

'I've learned . . . hee-hee-hee . . . I've learned what a silly feller I've been all these months.'

'How do you mean?'

He raised a forefinger and wagged it sagely. 'Well, you've allus been tellin' me that I got you out of your bed for nothing and I was imagining things when I thought me dog was ill.'

'Yes,' I said. 'That's right.'

'And I never believed you, did I? I wouldn't be told. Well, now I know you were right all the time. I've been nobbut a fool and I'm right sorry for botherin' you all those nights.'

'Oh, I shouldn't worry about that, Humphrey.'

'Aye, but it's not right.' He waved a hand towards his bright-faced, tail-wagging little dog. 'Just look at her. Anybody can see there was never anythin' wrong with Myrtle tonight.'

*

Thank heaven for people like Humphrey Cobb. He drove me to distraction all those years ago, but just to think about him now makes me smile. Nice to write about eclampsia, too. Another rapidly fatal condition which can be just as quickly and easily cured. Calcium still does the trick – we have never found anything better. It is interesting, too, that despite Humphrey's apparent flash of insight into his irrational behaviour he still continued his tearful nocturnal phone calls for many years thereafter.

45. *Venus*

The farm man moved between the cows and took hold of my patient's tail, and when I saw his haircut I knew immediately that Josh Anderson had been on the job again. It was a Sunday morning and everything fitted into place. I really didn't have to ask.

'Were you in the Hare and Pheasant last night?' I enquired carelessly as I inserted my thermometer.

He ran a hand ruefully over his head. 'Aye, bugger it, ah was. Ye can see straight off, can't ye? T'missus has been playin' 'ell with me ever since.'

'I suppose Josh had had one too many, eh?'

'Aye he had. I should've known better, pickin' a Saturday night. It's me own fault.'

Josh Anderson was one of the local barbers. He liked his job, but he also liked his beer. In fact he was devoted to it, even to the extent of taking his scissors and clippers to the pub with him every night. For the price of a pint he would give anybody a quick trim in the gents' lavatory.

Habitués of the Hare and Pheasant were never surprised to find one of the customers sitting impassively on the toilet seat with Josh snip-snipping round his head. With beer at sixpence a pint it was good value, but Josh's clients knew they were taking a chance. If the barber's intake had been moderate they would escape relatively unscathed because the standard of hair-styling in the Darrowby district was not very fastidious, but if he had imbibed beyond a certain point terrible things could happen.

Josh had not as yet been known to cut off anybody's ear, but if you strolled around the town on Sundays and Mondays you were liable to come across some very strange coiffures.

I looked again at the farm man's head. From my experience I judged that Josh would be around the ten-pint mark when he did that one. The right sideburn had been trimmed off meticulously just below eye-level while the left was non-existent. The upper hair seemed to have been delved into at random, leaving bare patches in some parts and long dangling wisps in others. I couldn't see the back but I had no doubt it would be interesting, too. There could be a pigtail or anything lurking behind there.

Yes, I decided, definitely a ten-pinter. After twelve to fourteen pints Josh was inclined to cast away all caution and simply run over his victim's head with the clippers, leaving a tuft in front. The classical convict's crop, which necessitated wearing a cap well pulled down at all times for several weeks thereafter.

I always played safe, and when my hair needed cutting I went to Josh's shop, where he operated in a state of strict sobriety.

I was sitting there a few days later waiting my turn, with my dog Sam under my seat, and as I watched the barber at work the wonder of human nature seemed to glow with a particular radiance. There was a burly man in the chair and his red face, reflected in the mirror above the enveloping white sheet, was contorted every few seconds with spasms of pain. Because the simple fact was that Josh didn't cut hair, he pulled it out.

He did this not only because his equipment was antiquated and needed sharpening but because he had perfected a certain flick of the wrist with his hand clippers which wrenched the hairs from their follicles at the end of each stroke. He had never got round to buying electric clippers, but with his distinctive technique I doubt whether it would have made any difference.

One wonder was that anybody went to Josh for a haircut, because there was another barber in the town. My own opinion was that it was because everybody liked him.

Sitting there in his shop I looked at him as he worked. He was a tiny man in his fifties with a bald head which made a mockery of the rows of hair restorer on his shelves, and on his face rested the gentle smile which never seemed to leave him. That smile and the big, curiously unworldly eyes gave him an unusual attraction.

And then there was his obvious love of his fellow men. As his client rose from the chair, patently relieved that his ordeal was over, Josh fussed around him, brushing him down, patting his back and chattering gaily. You could see that he hadn't been just cutting this man's hair, he had been enjoying a happy social occasion.

Next to the big farmer, Josh looked smaller than ever, a minute husk of humanity, and I marvelled as I had often done at how he managed to accommodate all that beer.

Of course foreigners are often astonished at the Englishman's ability to consume vast quantities of ale. Even now, after forty years in Yorkshire, I cannot compete. Maybe it is my Glasgow upbringing, but after two or three pints discomfort sets in. The remarkable thing is that throughout the years I can hardly recall seeing a Yorkshireman drunk. Their natural reserve relaxes and they become progressively jovial as the long cascade goes down their throats, but they seldom fall about or do anything silly.

Josh, for instance. He would swallow around eight pints every night of the week except Saturday, when he stepped up his intake to between ten and fourteen, yet he never looked much different. His professional skill suffered, but that was all.

He was turning to me now. 'Well, Mr Herriot, it's good to see you again.' He warmed me with his smile and those wide eyes with their almost mystic depths caressed me as he ushered me to the chair. 'Are you very well?'

'I'm fine, thank you, Mr Anderson,' I replied. 'And how are you?'

'Nicely, sir, nicely.' He began to tuck the sheet under my chin, then laughed delightedly as my little Beagle trotted in under the folds.

'Hullo, Sam, you're there as usual, I see.' He bent and stroked the sleek ears. 'By gum, Mr Herriot, he's a faithful friend. Never lets you out of 'is sight if he can help it.'

'That's right,' I said. 'And I don't like to go anywhere without him.' I screwed round in my chair. 'By the way, didn't I see you with a dog the other day?'

Josh paused, scissors in hand. 'You did an' all. A little bitch. A stray – got 'er from the Cat and Dog Home at York. Now that our kids have all left home, t'missus and I fancied gettin' a dog and we think the world of her. I tell ye, she's a grand 'un.'

'What breed is she?'

'Eee, now you're askin'. Nobbut a mongrel, I reckon. I can't see any pedigree about her but money wouldn't buy 'er.'

I was about to agree with him when he held up a hand. 'Hang on a minute and I'll bring 'er down.'

He lived above the shop and his feet clumped on the stairs as he returned with a little bitch in his arms.

'There you are, Mr Herriot. What d'you think of that?' He stood her on the floor for my inspection.

I looked at the little animal. She was a light grey in colour with very long crinkled hair. In fact at a quick glance she looked like a miniature Wensleydale sheep. Definitely a hound of baffling lineage, but the panting mouth and swishing tail bore witness to her good nature.

'I like her,' I said. 'I think you've picked a winner there.'

'That's what we think.' He stopped and fondled his new pet and I noticed that he kept picking up the long hairs and rubbing them gently between finger and thumb again. It looked a little odd, then it occurred to me that was what he was used to doing with his human customers. 'We've called her Venus,' he said.

'Venus?'

'Aye, because she's so beautiful.' His tone was very serious.

'Ah yes,' I said. 'I see.'

He washed his hands, took up his scissors again and grasped a few strands of my hair. Again I saw that he went through the same procedure of rubbing the hairs between his fingers before cutting them.

I couldn't understand why he did this but my mind was too preoccupied to give the matter much thought. I was steeling myself.

Still, it wasn't too bad with the scissors – just an uncomfortable tug as the blunt edges came together.

It was when he reached for the clippers that I gripped the arms of the chair as though I were at the dentist. It was all right as long as he was running the things up the back of my neck; it was that jerk at the end, plucking the last tuft from its roots, which set my face grimacing at me in the mirror. Once or twice an involuntary 'Ooh!' or 'Aah!' escaped me but Josh gave no sign of having heard.

I remember that for years I had sat in that shop listening to the half-stilled cries of pain from the customers, but at no time had the barber shown any reaction.

The thing was that, although he was the least arrogant or conceited of men, he did consider himself a gifted hairdresser. Even now as he gave me a final combing, I could see the pride shining from his face. Head on one side, he patted my hair repeatedly, circling the chair and viewing me from all angles, making a finicky snip here and there before holding up the hand mirror for my inspection.

'All right, Mr Herriot?' he enquired with the quiet satisfaction which comes from a job well done.

'Lovely, Mr Anderson, just fine.' Relief added warmth to my voice.

He bowed slightly, well pleased. 'Aye, you know, it's easy enough to cut hair off. The secret is knowin' what to leave on.'

I had heard him say it a hundred times before, but I laughed dutifully as he whisked his brush over the back of my coat.

My hair used to grow pretty fast in those days, but I didn't have time to pay another visit to the barber before he arrived on my front door step. I was having tea at the time and I trotted to the door in answer to the insistent ringing of the bell.

He was carrying Venus in his arms but she was a vastly different creature from the placid little animal I had seen in his shop. She was bubbling saliva from her mouth, retching and pawing frantically at her face.

Josh looked distraught. 'She's chokin', Mr Herriot. Look at 'er! She'll die if you don't do summat quick!'

'Wait a minute, Mr Anderson. Tell me what's happened. Has she swallowed something?'

'Aye, she's 'ad a chicken bone.'

'A chicken bone! Don't you know you should never give a dog chicken bones?'

'Aye, ah know, ah know, everybody knows that, but we'd had a bird for our dinner and she pinched the frame out of the dustbin, the little beggar. She had a good crunch at it afore I spotted 'er and now she's goin' to choke!' He glared at me, lips quivering. He was on the verge of tears.

'Now just calm down,' I said. 'I don't think Venus is choking. By the way she's pawing, I should say there's something stuck in her mouth.'

I grabbed the little animal's jaws with finger and thumb and forced them apart. And I saw with a surge of relief the sight familiar to all vets – a long spicule of bone jammed tightly between the back molars and forming a bar across the roof of the mouth.

As I say, it is a common occurrence in practice and a happy one, because it is harmless and easily relieved by a flick of the forceps. Recovery is instantaneous, skill minimal and the kudos most warming. I loved it.

I put my hand on the barber's shoulder. 'You can stop worrying, Mr Anderson, it's just a bone stuck in her teeth. Come through to the consulting-room and I'll have it out in a jiffy.'

I could see the man relaxing as we walked along the passage to the back of the house. 'Oh, thank God for that, Mr Herriot. I thought she'd had it, honest, I did. And we've grown right fond of the little thing. I couldn't bear to lose 'er.'

I gave a light laugh, put the dog on the table and reached for a strong pair of forceps. 'No question of that, I assure you. This won't take a minute.'

Jimmy, aged five, had left his tea and trailed after us. He watched with mild interest as I poised the instrument. Even at his age he had seen this sort of thing many a time and it wasn't very exciting. But you never knew in veterinary practice; it was worth hanging around because funny things could happen. He put his hands in his pockets and rocked back and forth on his heels, whistling softly as he watched me.

Usually it is simply a matter of opening the mouth, clamping the forceps on the bone and removing it. But Venus recoiled from the gleaming metal and so did the barber. The terror in the dog's eyes was reproduced fourfold in those of its owner.

I tried to be soothing. 'This is nothing, Mr Anderson. I'm not going to hurt her in the least, but you'll just have to hold her head firmly for a moment.'

Venus

The little man took a deep breath, grasped the dog's neck, screwed his eyes tight shut and turned his head as far away as he could.

'Now, little Venus,' I cooed, 'I'm going to make you better.'

Venus clearly didn't believe me. She struggled violently, pawing at my hand, to the accompaniment of strange moaning sounds from her owner. When I did get the forceps into her mouth she locked her front teeth on the instrument and hung on fiercely. And as I began to grapple with her, Mr Anderson could stand it no longer and let go.

The little dog leaped to the floor and resumed her inner battle there while Jimmy watched appreciatively.

I looked at the barber more in sorrow than in anger. This was just not his thing. He was manually ham-fisted, as his hairdressing proved, and he seemed quite incapable of holding a wriggling dog.

'Let's have another go,' I said cheerfully. 'We'll try it on the floor this time. Maybe she's frightened of the table. It's a trifling little job, really.'

The little man, lips tight, eyes like slits, bent and extended trembling hands towards his dog, but each time he touched her she slithered away from him until with a great shuddering sigh he flopped face down on the tiles. Jimmy giggled. Things were looking up.

I helped the barber to his feet. 'I tell you what, Mr Anderson, I'll give her a short-acting anaesthetic. That will cut out all this fighting and struggling.'

Josh's face paled. 'An anaesthetic? Put her to sleep, you mean?' Anxiety flickered in his eyes. 'Will she be all right?'

'Of course, of course. Just leave her to me and come back for her in about an hour. She'll be able to walk then.' I began to steer him through the door into the passage.

'Are you sure?' He glanced back pitifully at his pet. 'We're doing the right thing?'

'Without a doubt. We'll only upset her if we go on this way.'

'Very well, then, I'll go along to me brother's for an hour.'

'Splendid.' I waited till I heard the front door close behind him then quickly made up a dose of pentothal.

Dogs do not put on such a tough front when their owners are not present and I scooped Venus easily from the floor on to the table. But her jaws were still clamped tight and her front feet at the ready. She wasn't going to stand for any messing with her mouth.

'Okay, old girl, have it your own way,' I said. I gripped her leg

377

above the elbow and clipped an area from the raised radial vein. In those days Siegfried or myself were often left to anaesthetise dogs without assistance. It is wonderful what you can do when you have to.

Venus didn't seem to care what I was about as long as I kept away from her face. I slid the needle into the vein, depressed the plunger and within seconds her fighting pose relaxed, her head dropped and her whole body sagged on to the table. I rolled her over. She was fast asleep.

'No trouble now, Jimmy, lad,' I said. I pushed the teeth apart effortlessly with finger and thumb, gripped the bone with the forceps and lifted it from the mouth. 'Nothing left in there – lovely. All done.'

I dropped the piece of chicken bone into the waste bin. 'Yes, that's how to do it, my boy. No undignified scrambling. That's the professional way.'

My son nodded briefly. Things had gone dull again. He had been hoping for great things when Mr Anderson draped himself along the surgery floor, but this was tame stuff. He had stopped smiling.

My own satisfied smile, too, had become a little fixed. I was watching Venus carefully and she wasn't breathing. I tried to ignore the lurch in my stomach, because I have always been a nervous anaesthetist and am not very proud of it. Even now when I come upon one of my younger colleagues operating, I have a nasty habit of placing my hand over the patient's chest wall over the heart and standing wide-eyed and rigid for a few seconds. I know the young surgeons hate to have me spreading alarm and despondency, and one day I am going to be told to get out in sharp terms, but I can't help it.

As I watched Venus I told myself as always that there was no danger. She had received the correct dose and, anyway, you often did get this period of apnoea with pentothal. Everything was normal, but just the same I wished to God she would start breathing.

The heart was still going all right. I depressed the ribs a few times – nothing. I touched the unseeing eyeball – no corneal reflex. I began to rap my fingers on the table and stare closely at the little animal and I could see that Jimmy was watching me just as keenly. His deep interest in veterinary practice was built upon a fascination for animals, farmers and the open air, but it was given extra colour by something else: he never knew when his father might do something funny or something funny might happen to him.

Venus

The unpredictable mishaps of the daily round were all good for a laugh, and my son, with his unerring instinct, had a feeling that something of the sort was going to happen now.

His hunch was proved right when I suddenly lifted Venus from the table, shook her vainly a few times above my head, then set off at full gallop along the passage. I could hear the eager shuffle of the little slippers just behind me.

I threw open the side door and shot into the back garden. I halted at the narrow part – no, there wasn't enough room there – and continued my headlong rush till I reached the big lawn.

Here I dropped the little dog on to the grass and fell down on my knees by her side in an attitude of prayer. I waited and watched as my heart hammered, but those ribs were not moving and the eyes stared sightlessly ahead.

Oh, this just couldn't happen! I seized Venus by a hind leg in either hand and began to whirl her round my head. Sometimes higher, sometimes lower, but attaining a remarkable speed as I put all my strength into the swing. This method of resuscitation seems to have gone out of fashion now, but it was very much in vogue then. It certainly met with the full approval of my son. He laughed so much that he fell down and sprawled on the grass.

When I stopped and glared at the still immobile ribs he cried, 'Again, Daddy, again.' And he didn't have to wait more than a few seconds before Daddy was in full action once more with Venus swooping through the air like a bird on the wing.

It exceeded all Jimmy's expectations. He probably had wondered about leaving his jam sandwiches to see the old man perform, but how gloriously he had been rewarded. To this day the whole thing is so vivid: my tension and misery lest my patient should die for no reason at all, and in the background the helpless, high-pitched laughter of my son.

I don't know how many times I stopped, dropped the inert form on the grass, then recommenced my whirling, but at last at one of the intervals the chest wall gave a heave and the eyes blinked.

With a gasp of relief I collapsed face down on the cool turf and peered through the green blades as the breathing became regular and Venus began to lick her lips and look around her.

I dared not get up immediately because the old brick walls of the garden were still dancing around me and I am sure I would have fallen.

Jimmy was disappointed. 'Aren't you going to do any more, Daddy?'

'No, son, no.' I sat up and dragged Venus on to my lap. 'It's all over now.'

'Well, that was funny. Why did you do it?'

'To make the dog breathe.'

'Do you always do that to make them breathe?'

'No, thank heaven, not often.' I got slowly to my feet and carried the little animal back to the consulting-room.

By the time Josh Anderson arrived, his pet was looking almost normal.

'She's still a little unsteady from the anaesthetic,' I said. 'But that won't last long.'

'Eee, isn't that grand. And that nasty bone, is it . . . ?'

'All gone, Mr Anderson.'

He shrank back as I opened the mouth. 'You see?' I said. 'Not a thing.'

He smiled happily. 'Did ye have any bother with her?'

Well, my parents brought me up to be honest rather than clever and the whole story almost bubbled out of me. But why should I worry this sensitive little man? To tell him that his dog had been almost dead for a considerable time would not cheer him nor would it bolster his faith in me.

I swallowed. 'Not a bit, Mr Anderson. A quite uneventful operation.' The whitest of lies, but it nearly choked me and the after-taste of guilt was strong.

'Wonderful, wonderful. I am grateful, Mr Herriot.' He bent over the dog and again I noticed the strange rolling of the strands of hair between his fingers.

'Have ye been floatin' through the air, Venus?' he murmured absently.

The back of my neck prickled. 'What . . . what makes you say that?'

He turned his eyes up to me, those eyes with their unworldly depths. 'Well . . . I reckon she'd think she was floatin' while she was asleep. Just a funny feeling I had.'

'Ah, yes, well, er . . . right.' I had a very funny feeling myself. 'You'd better take her home now and keep her quiet for the rest of the day.'

I was very thoughtful as I finished my tea. Floating . . . floating.

A fortnight later I was again seated in Josh's barber's chair, bracing myself for the ordeal. To my alarm he started straight in with the dread clippers. Usually he began with the scissors and worked up gradually, but he was throwing me in at the deep end this time.

In an attempt to alleviate the pain I began to chatter with an edge of hysteria in my voice.

'How is – ouch – Venus going on?'

'Oh fine, fine.' Josh smiled at me tenderly in the mirror. 'She was neither up nor down after that job.'

'Well – ooh, aah – I really didn't expect any trouble. As I said, it was – ow – just a trifling thing.'

The barber whipped out another tuft with that inimitable flick of his. 'The thing is, Mr Herriot, it's a grand thing to 'ave faith in your vet. I knew our little pet was in good 'ands.'

'Well, thank you very much, Mr Anderson, it's – aaah – very nice to hear that.' I was gratified, but that guilt feeling was still there.

I got tired of trying to speak while watching my twitching features in the mirror, so I tried to concentrate on something else. It is a trick I adopt at the dentist's and it doesn't work very well, but as the little man tugged away I thought as hard as I could about my garden at Skeldale House.

The lawns really did want mowing and there were all those weeds to get at when I had a minute to spare. I had got round to considering whether it was time to put some fertiliser on my outdoor tomatoes when Josh laid down the clippers and lifted his scissors.

I sighed and relaxed. The next part was only mildly uncomfortable and who knows, he may have had the scissors sharpened since last time. My mind was wandering over the fascinating subject of tomatoes when the barber's voice pulled me back to reality.

'Mr Herriot.' He was twiddling away at a wisp of my hair with his fingers. 'I like gardening, too.'

I almost jumped from the chair. 'That's remarkable. I was just thinking about my garden.'

'Aye, ah know.' There was a faraway look in his eyes as he rolled and rolled with finger and thumb. 'It comes through the hair, ye know.'

'Eh?'

'Your thoughts. They come through to me.'

'What!'

'Yes, just think about it. Them hairs go right down into your head and they catch summat from your brain and send it up to me.'

'Oh really, you're kidding me.' I gave a loud laugh which nevertheless had a hollow ring.

Josh shook his head. 'I'm not jokin' nor jestin', Mr Herriot. I've been at this game for nearly forty years and it keeps happenin' to me. You'd be flabbergasted if I told ye some of the thoughts that's come up. Couldn't repeat 'em, I tell ye.'

I slumped lower in my white sheet. Absolute rubbish and nonsense, of course, but I made a firm resolve never to think of Venus's anaesthetic during a haircut.

*

One of my most enjoyable pieces of writing, because there are so many unusual things in it. For instance, you don't find barbers like Josh Anderson any more. One thing I omitted to mention in the story was that Josh was also a tobacconist, and it was a regular thing for him to put down his clippers in the middle of a haircut to serve a customer with cigarettes and return unabashed after a long conversation about the weather, cricket and other matters. Also, Venus was a dog of most unusual appearance; in fact I've never seen one like her before or since. And what about my thoughts going through my hair? Preposterous, but I still wonder about it . . .

46. *Amber*

'This is Amber,' Sister Rose said. 'The one I wanted you to examine.'

I looked at the pale, almost honey-coloured shading of the hair on the dog's ears and flanks. 'I can see why you've given her that name. I bet she'd really glow in the sunshine.'

The nurse laughed. 'Yes, funnily enough it was sunny when I first saw her and the name just jumped into my mind.' She gave me a sideways glance. 'I'm good at names, as you know.'

'Oh yes, without a doubt,' I said, smiling. It was a little joke between us. Sister Rose had to be good at christening the endless stream of unwanted animals which passed through the little dog sanctuary which lay behind her house and which she ran and maintained by organising small shows, jumble sales, etc., and by spending her own money.

And she didn't only give her money, she also gave her precious time, because as a nursing sister she led a full life of service to the human race. I often asked myself how she found the time to fight for the animals, too. It was a mystery to me, but I admired her.

'Where did this one come from?' I asked.

Sister Rose shrugged. 'Oh, found wandering in the streets of Hebbleton. Nobody knows her and there have been no enquiries to the police. Obviously abandoned.'

I felt the old tightening of anger in my throat. 'How could they do this to such a beautiful dog? Just turn it away to fend for itself.'

'Oh, people like that have some astonishing reasons. In this case I think it's because Amber has a little skin disease. Perhaps it frightened them.'

'They could at least have taken her to a vet,' I grunted as I opened the door of the pen.

I noticed some bare patches around the toes and as I knelt and examined the feet, Amber nuzzled my cheek and wagged her tail. I looked up at her, at the flopping ears, the pronounced jowls and the trusting eyes which had been betrayed.

'It's a hound's face,' I said. 'But how about the rest of her? What breed would you call her?'

Sister Rose laughed. 'Oh, she's a puzzle. I get a lot of practice at guessing, but this one beats me. I wondered if a Fox Hound had got astray and mated with something like a Labrador or Dalmatian, but I don't know.'

I didn't know, either. The body, dappled with patches of brown, black and white, was the wrong shape for a hound. She had very large feet, a long thin tail in constant motion, and everywhere on her coat the delicate sheen of gold.

'Well,' I said. 'Whatever she is, she's a bonny one, and good-natured, too.'

'Oh yes, she's a darling. We'll have no difficulty in finding a home for her. She's the perfect pet. How old do you think she is?'

I smiled. 'You can never tell for sure, but she's got a juvenile look about her.' I opened the mouth and looked at the rows of untainted teeth. 'I'd say nine or ten months. She's just a big pup.'

'That's what I thought. She'll be really large when she reaches full size.'

As if to prove the sister's words, the young bitch reared up and planted her forefeet on my chest. I looked again at the laughing mouth and those eyes. 'Amber,' I said, 'I really like you.'

'Oh, I'm so glad,' Sister Rose said. 'We must get this skin trouble cleared up as quickly as possible and then I can start finding her a home. It's just a bit of eczema, isn't it?'

'Probably . . . probably . . . I see there's some bareness around the eyes and cheeks, too.' Skin diseases in dogs, as in humans, are tricky things, often baffling in origin and difficult to cure. I fingered the hairless areas. I didn't like the combination of feet and face, but the skin was dry and sound. Maybe it was nothing much. I banished to the back of my mind a spectre which appeared for a brief instant. I didn't want to think of that and I had no intention of worrying Sister Rose. She had enough on her mind.

'Yes, probably eczema,' I said briskly. 'Rub this ointment well into the parts night and morning.' I handed over the box of zinc oxide and lanoline. A bit old-fashioned, maybe, but it had served me well for a few years and ought to do the trick in combination with the nurse's good feeding.

When two weeks passed without news of Amber I was relieved. I was happy, too, at the thought that she would now be in a good home among people who appreciated her.

I was brought back to reality with a bump when Sister Rose phoned one morning.

'Mr Herriot, those bare patches aren't any better. In fact they're spreading.'

'Spreading? Where?'

'Up her legs and on the face.'

The spectre leaped up, mouthing and gesticulating. Oh not that, please. 'I'll come right out, Sister,' I said, and on my way to the car I picked up the microscope.

Amber greeted me as she had before, with dancing eyes and lashing tail, but I felt sick when I saw the ragged denudation of the face and the naked skin staring at me on the legs.

I got hold of the young animal and held her close, sniffing at the hairless areas.

Sister Rose looked at me in surprise. 'What are you doing?'

'Trying to detect a mousy smell.'

'Mousy smell? And is it there?'

'Yes.'

'And what does that mean?'

'Mange.'

'Oh dear.' The nurse put a hand to her mouth. 'That's rather nasty, isn't it.' Then she put her shoulders back in a characteristic gesture. 'Well, I've had experience of mange before and I can tackle it. I've always been able to clear it up with sulphur baths, but there's such a danger of infection to the other dogs. It really is a worry.'

I put Amber down and stood up, feeling suddenly weary. 'Yes, but you're thinking of sarcoptic mange, Sister. I'm afraid this is something rather worse.'

'Worse? In what way?'

'Well, the whole look of the thing suggests demodectic mange.'

She nodded. 'I've heard of that – and it's more serious?'

'Yes . . .' I may as well bite the bullet. 'Very often incurable.'

'Goodness me, I had no idea. She wasn't scratching much, so I didn't worry.'

'Yes, that's just it,' I said wryly. 'Dogs scratch almost non-stop with sarcoptic mange and we can cure it, but they often show only mild discomfort with demodectic which usually defeats us.'

The spectre was very large in my mind now and I use the word literally, because this skin disease had haunted me ever since I had qualified. I had seen many fine dogs put to sleep after the most prolonged attempts to treat them.

I lifted the microscope from the back of the car. 'Anyway, I may be jumping the gun. I hope I am. This is the only way to find out.'

There was a patch on Amber's left foreleg which I squeezed and scraped with a scalpel blade. I deposited the debris and serum on a glass slide, added a few drops of potassium hydroxide and put a cover-slip on top.

Sister Rose gave me a cup of coffee while I waited, then I rigged up the microscope in the light from the kitchen window and looked down the eyepiece. And there it was. My stomach tightened as I saw what I didn't want to see – the dread mite, *Demodex canis:* the head, the thorax with its eight stumpy legs and the long, cigar-shaped body. And there wasn't just one. The whole microscopic field was teeming with them.

'Ah well, that's it, Sister,' I said. 'There's no doubt about it. I'm very sorry.'

The corners of her mouth drooped. 'But . . . isn't there anything we can do?'

'Oh yes, we can try. And we're going to try like anything, because I've taken a fancy to Amber. Don't worry too much. I've cured a few demodex cases in my time, always by using the same stuff.' I

went to the car and fished around in the boot. 'Here it is – Odylen.'
I held up the can in front of her. 'I'll show you how to apply it.'

It was difficult to rub the lotion into the affected patches as Amber
wagged and licked, but I finished at last.

'Now do that every day,' I said, 'and let me know in about a week.
Sometimes that Odylen really does work.'

Sister Rose stuck out her jaw with the determination which had
saved so many animals. 'I assure you I'll do it most carefully. I'm
sure we can succeed. It doesn't look so bad.'

I didn't say anything and she went on, 'But how about my other
dogs? Won't they become infected?'

I shook my head. 'Another odd thing about demodex. It very
rarely spreads to another animal. It is nothing like as contagious as
the sarcops, so you have very little cause for worry in that way.'

'That's something, anyway. But how on earth does a dog get the
disease in the first place?'

'Mysterious again,' I said. 'The veterinary profession are pretty
well convinced that all dogs have a certain number of demodex mites
in their skins, but why they should cause mange in some and not in
others has never been explained. Heredity has got something to do
with it because it sometimes occurs in several dogs in the same litter.
But it's a baffling business.'

I left Sister Rose with her can of Odylen. Maybe this would be
one of the exceptions to my experiences with this condition. I had to
hope so.

I heard from the nurse within a week. She had been applying the
Odylen religiously but the disease was spreading further up the legs.

I hurried out there and my fears were confirmed when I saw
Amber's face. It was disfigured by the increasing hairlessness and
when I thought of the beauty which had captivated me on my first
visit the sight was like a blow. Her tail-wagging cheerfulness was
undiminished, and that seemed to make the whole thing worse.

I had to try something else, and in view of the fact that a secondary
subcutaneous invasion of *staphylococci* was an impediment to recovery,
I gave the dog an injection of staph toxoid. I also started her on a
course of Fowler's solution of arsenic which at that time was popular
in the treatment of skin conditions.

When ten days passed I had begun to hope, and it was a bitter
disappointment when Sister Rose telephoned just after breakfast.

Her voice trembled as she spoke. 'Mr Herriot, she really is deteriorating all the time. Nothing seems to do any good. I'm beginning to think that . . .'

I cut her off in mid-sentence. 'All right, I'll be out there within an hour. Don't give up hope yet. These cases sometimes take months to recover.'

I knew as I drove to the sanctuary that my words were only meant to comfort. They had no real substance. But I had tried to say something helpful because there was nothing Sister Rose hated more than putting a dog to sleep. Of all the hundreds of animals which had passed through her hands I could remember only a handful which had defeated her. Very old dogs with chronic kidney or heart conditions which were in a hopeless plight, or young ones with distemper. With all the others she had battled until they were fit to go to their new homes. And it wasn't only Sister Rose – I myself recoiled from the idea of doing such a thing to Amber. There was something about that dog which had taken hold of me.

When I arrived I still had no idea what I was going to do, and when I spoke I was half-surprised at the things I said.

'Sister, I've come to take Amber home with me. I'll be able to treat her myself every day, then. You've got enough to do, looking after your other dogs. I know you have done everything possible but I'm going to take on this job myself.'

'But . . . you are a busy man. How will you find the time?'

'I can treat her in the evenings and any other spare moments. This way I'll be able to check on her progress all the time. I'm determined to get her right.'

And, driving back to the surgery, I was surprised at the depth of my feeling. Throughout my career I have often had this compulsive desire to cure an animal, but never stronger than with Amber. The young bitch was delighted to be in the car with me. Like everything else she seemed to regard this as just another game, and she capered around, licking my ear, resting her paws on the dash and peering through the windscreen. I looked at her happy face, scarred by the disease and smeared with Odylen, and thumped my hand on the wheel. Demodectic mange was hell, but this was one case which was going to get better.

It was the beginning of a strangely vivid episode in my life, as fresh now as it was then, more than thirty years ago. We had no facilities for boarding dogs – very few vets had at that time – but I made up a comfortable billet for her in the old stable in the yard. I penned off one of the stalls with a sheet of plywood and put down a bed of straw. Despite its age the stable was a substantial building and free from draughts. She would be snug in there.

I made sure of one thing. I kept Helen out of the whole business. I remembered how stricken she had been when we adopted Oscar the cat and then lost him to his rightful owner, and I knew she would soon grow too fond of this dog. But I had forgotten about myself.

Veterinary surgeons would never last in their profession if they became too involved with their patients. I knew from experience that most of my colleagues were just as sentimental over animals as the owners, but before I knew what was happening I became involved with Amber.

I fed her myself, changed her bedding, and carried out the treatment. I saw her as often as possible during the day, but when I think of her now it is always night. It was late November, when darkness came in soon after four o'clock, and the last few visits were a dim-sighted fumbling in cow byres, and when I came home I always drove round to the yard at the back of Skeldale House and trained my headlights on the stable.

When I threw open the door Amber was always there, waiting to welcome me, her forefeet resting on the plywood sheet, her long yellow ears gleaming in the bright beam. That is my picture of her to this day. Her temperament never altered and her tail swished the straw unceasingly as I did all the uncomfortable things to her, rubbing the tender skin with the lotion, injecting her with the staph toxoid, taking further skin scrapings to check progress.

As the days and the weeks went by and I saw no improvement I became a little desperate. I gave her sulphur baths, and derris baths, although I had done no good with such things in the past, and I also began to go through all the proprietary things on the market. In veterinary practice every resistant disease spawns a multitude of quack 'cures' and I lost count of the shampoos and washes I swilled over the young animal in the hope that there might be some magic element in them despite my misgivings.

These nightly sessions under the headlights became part of my life, and I think I might have gone on blindly for an indefinite period until one very dark evening with the rain beating on the cobbles of the yard I seemed to see the young dog for the first time.

The condition had spread over the entire body, leaving only tufts and straggling wisps of hair. The long ears were golden no longer.

They were almost bald, as was the rest of her face and head. Everywhere her skin was thickened and wrinkled and had assumed a bluish tinge. And when I squeezed it a slow ooze of pus and serum came up around my fingers.

I flopped back and sat down in the straw while Amber leaped around me, licking and wagging. Despite her terrible state, her nature was unchanged.

But this couldn't go on. I knew now that she and I had come to the end of the road. As I tried to think, I stroked her head, and her cheerful eyes were pathetic in the scarecrow face. My misery was compounded of various things: I had grown too fond of her, I had failed, and she had nobody, only Sister Rose and myself. And that was another thing – what was I going to tell that good lady after all my brave words?

It took me until the following lunchtime to summon the will to telephone her. In my effort to be matter-of-fact about the thing I fear I was almost brusque.

'Sister,' I said, 'I'm afraid it's all over with Amber. I've tried everything and she has got worse all the time. I do think it would be the kindest thing to put her to sleep.'

Shock was evident in her voice. 'But . . . it seems so awful. Just for a skin disease.'

'I know, that's what everybody thinks. But this is a dreadful thing. In its worst form it can ruin an animal's life. Amber must be very uncomfortable now and soon she is going to be in pain. We can't let her go on.'

'Oh . . . well, I trust in your judgement, Mr Herriot. I know you wouldn't do anything that wasn't necessary.' There was a long pause and I knew she was trying to control her voice. Then she spoke calmly. 'I think I would like to come out and see her when I can get away from the hospital.'

'Please, Sister,' I said gently, 'I'd much rather you didn't.'

Again the pause, then, 'Very well, Mr Herriot. I leave everything to you.'

I had an urgent visit immediately afterwards and a rush of work kept me going all afternoon. I never really stopped thinking about what I had to do later but at least the other pressures stopped it from obsessing me. It was as always pitch dark when I drove into the yard and opened the garage doors.

And it was like all the other times. Amber was there in the beam, paws on the plywood, body swinging with her wagging, mouth open and panting with delight, welcoming me.

I put the barbiturate and syringe into my pocket before climbing into the pen. For a long time I made a fuss of her, patting her and talking to her as she leaped up at me. Then I filled the syringe.

'Sit, girl,' I said, and she flopped obediently on to her hind-quarters. I gripped her right leg above the elbow to raise the radial vein. There was no need for clipping – all the hair had gone. Amber looked at me interestedly, wondering what new game this might be as I slipped the needle into the vein. I realised that there was no need to say the things I always said. 'She won't know a thing.' 'This is just an overdose of anaesthetic.' 'It's as easy way out for her.' There was no sorrowing owner to hear me. There were just the two of us.

And as I murmured, 'Good girl, Amber, good lass,' as she sank down on the straw, I had the conviction that if I had said those things they would have been true. She didn't know a thing between her playfulness and oblivion and it was indeed an easy way out from that prison which would soon become a torture chamber.

I stepped from the pen and switched off the car lights and in the cold darkness the yard had never seemed so empty. After the weeks of struggle the sense of loss and of failure was overpowering, but at the end I was at least able to spare Amber the ultimate miseries: the internal abscesses and septicaemia which await a dog suffering from a progressive and incurable demodectic mange.

For a long time I carried a weight around with me, and I feel some of it now after all these years. Because the tragedy of Amber was that she was born too soon. At the present time we can cure most cases of demodectic mange by a long course of organo-phosphates and antibiotics, but neither of these things were available then when I needed them.

It is still a dread condition, but we have fought patiently with our modern weapons and won most of the battles over the past few years. I know several fine dogs in Darrowby who have survived, and when I see them in the streets, healthy and glossy-coated, the picture of Amber comes back into my mind. It is always dark and she is always in the headlights' beam.

*

Even in these modern times my heart sinks when I see a dog with bare patches on its legs and face and a mousy smell, although the prognosis is rather better than it used to be. But demodectic mange is a dreaded condition because it is an appalling, almost unacceptable thought that an animal can lose its life because of a skin condition. I often wonder why the memory of Amber should be so vivid and painful. She was a cheerful and loveable little creature throughout her illness, but I have known many dogs like that. Perhaps she would not have stayed in my memory so clearly if I had treated her in one of the steel kennels in our present-day surgery and not under the primitive conditions which were available then. That old stable is never used now, but whenever I wander up to the yard, I look into the dark doorway and remember that long struggle which Amber and I both lost.

47. *Counting Blessings*

'Was there no peace in a vet's life?' I wondered fretfully as I hurried my car along the road to Gilthorpe village. Eight o'clock on a Sunday evening and here I was trailing off to visit a dog ten miles away which, according to Helen who had taken the message, had been ailing for more than a week.

I had worked all morning, then spent an afternoon in the hills with the children and some of their friends, a long-standing weekly even during which we had managed to explore nearly every corner of the district over the years. Jimmy had set a brisk pace with his hardy young pals and I had had to carry Rosie on my shoulders up the steepest slopes. After tea there was the usual routine of baths, story-reading and bed for the two of them, then I was ready to settle down with the Sunday papers and listen to the radio.

Yet here I was back on the treadmill, staring through the wind-screen at the roads and the walls which I saw day in, day out. When I left Darrowby the streets of the little town were empty in the gathering dusk and the houses had that tight-shut, comfortable look which raised images of armchairs and pipes and firesides, and now as I saw the lights of the farms winking on the fell-sides I could picture the stocksmen dozing contentedly with their feet up.

I had not passed a single car on the darkening road. There was nobody out but Herriot.

I was really sloshing around in my trough of self-pity when I drew up outside a row of greystone cottages at the far end of Gilthorpe. Mrs Cundall, Number 4, Chestnut Row, Helen had written on the slip of paper, and as I opened the gate and stepped through the tiny strip of garden my mind was busy with half-formed ideas of what I was going to say.

My few years' experience in practice had taught me that it did no good at all to remonstrate with people for calling me out at unreasonable times. I knew perfectly well that my words never seemed to get through to them and that they would continue to do exactly as they had done before, but for all that I had to say something if only to make me feel better.

No need to be rude or ill-mannered, just a firm statement of the position, that vets liked to relax on Sunday evenings just like other people; that we did not mind at all coming out for emergencies but that we did object to having to visit animals which had been ill for a week.

I had my speech fairly well prepared when a little middle-aged woman opened the door.

'Good evening, Mrs Cundall,' I said, slightly tight-lipped.

'Oh, it's Mr Herriot.' She smiled shyly. 'We've never met but I've seen you walkin' round Darrowby on market days. Come inside.'

The door opened straight into the little low-beamed living-room and my first glance took in the shabby furniture and some pictures framed in tarnished gilt, when I noticed that the end of the room was partly curtained off.

Mrs Cundall pulled the curtain aside. In a narrow bed a man was lying, a skeleton-thin man whose eyes looked up at me from hollows in a yellowed face.

'This is my husband, Ron,' she said cheerfully, and the man smiled and raised a bony arm from the quilt in greeting.

'And here is your patient, Hermann,' she went on, pointing to a little Dachshund who sat by the side of the bed.

'Hermann?'

'Yes, we thought it was a good name for a German sausage dog.' They both laughed.

'Of course,' I said. 'Excellent name. He looks like a Hermann.'

The little animal gazed up at me, bright-eyed and welcoming. I bent down and stroked his head and the pink tongue flickered over my fingers.

I ran my hand over the glossy skin. 'He looks very healthy. What's the trouble?'

'Oh, he's fine in himself,' Mrs Cundall replied. 'Eats well and everything, but over the last week he's been goin' funny on 'is legs. We weren't all that worried, but tonight he sort of flopped down and couldn't get up again.'

'I see. I noticed he didn't seem keen to rise when I patted his head.' I put my hand under the little dog's body and gently lifted him on to his feet. 'Come on, lad,' I said. 'Come on, Hermann, let's see you walk.'

As I encouraged him he took a few hesitant steps, but his hind end swayed progressively and he soon dropped into the sitting position again.

'It's his back, isn't it?' Mrs Cundall said. 'He's strong enough on 'is forelegs.'

'That's ma trouble, too,' Ron murmured in a soft husky voice, but he was smiling and his wife laughed and patted the arm on the quilt.

I lifted the dog on to my knee. 'Yes, the weakness is certainly in the back.' I began to palpate the lumbar vertebrae, feeling my way along, watching for any sign of pain.

'Has he hurt 'imself?' Mrs Cundall asked. 'Has somebody hit 'im? We don't usually let him out alone but sometimes he sneaks through the garden gate.'

'There's always the possibility of an injury,' I said. 'But there are other causes.' There were indeed – a host of unpleasant possibilities. I did not like the look of this little dog at all. This syndrome was one of the things I hated to encounter in canine practice.

'Can you tell me what you really think?' she said. 'I'd like to know.'

'Well, an injury could cause haemorrhage or concussion or oedema

– that's fluid – all affecting his spinal cord. He could even have a fractured vertebra, but I don't think so.'

'And how about the other causes.'

'There's quite a lot. Tumours, bony growths, abscesses or discs can press on the cord.'

'Discs?'

'Yes, little pads of cartilage and fibrous tissue between the vertebrae. In long-bodied dogs like Hermann they sometimes protrude into the spinal canal. In fact I think that is what is causing his symptoms.'

Ron's husky voice came again from the bed. 'And what's 'is prospects, Mr Herriot?'

Oh, that was the question. Complete recovery or incurable paralysis. It could be anything. 'Very difficult to say at this moment,' I replied. 'I'll give him an injection and some tablets and we'll see how he goes over the next few days.'

I injected an analgesic and some antibiotic and counted out some salicylate tablets into a box. We had no steroids at that time. It was the best I could do.

'Now then, Mr Herriot,' Mrs Cundall smiled at me eagerly. 'Ron has a bottle o' beer every night about this time. Would you like to join 'im?'

'Well . . . it's very kind of you but I don't want to intrude . . .'

'Oh, you're not doing that. We're glad to see you.'

She poured two glasses of brown ale, propped her husband up with pillows and sat down by the bed.

'We're from South Yorkshire, Mr Herriot,' she said.

I nodded. I had noticed the difference from the local accent.

'Aye, we came up here after Ron's accident, eight years ago.'

'What was that?'

'I were a miner,' Ron said. 'Roof fell in on me. I got a broken back, crushed liver and a lot o' other internal injuries, but two of me mates were killed in the same fall so ah'm lucky to be 'ere.' He sipped his beer 'I've survived, but doctor says I'll never walk no more.'

'I'm terribly sorry.'

'Nay, nay,' the husky voice went on, 'I count me blessings and I've got a lot to be thankful for. Ah suffer very little and I've got t'best wife in the world.'

Mrs Cundall laughed. 'Oh, listen to 'im. But I'm right glad we came to Gilthorpe. We used to spend all our holidays in the Dales.

We were great walkers and it was lovely to get away from the smoke and the chimneys. The bedroom in our old house just looked out on a lot o'brick walls but Ron has this big window right by 'im and he can see for miles.'

'Yes, of course,' I said. 'This is a lovely situation.' The village was perched on a high ridge on the fell-side and that window would command a wide view of the green slopes running down to the river and climbing high to the wildness of the moor on the other side. This sight had beguiled me so often on my rounds and the grassy paths climbing among the airy tops seemed to beckon to me. But they would beckon in vain to Ron Cundall.

'Gettin' Hermann was a good idea, too,' he said. 'Ah used to feel a bit lonely when t'missus went into Darrowby for shoppin' but the little feller's made all the difference. You're never alone when you've got a dog.'

I smiled. 'How right you are. What is his age now, by the way?'

'He's six,' Ron replied. 'Right in the prime o'life, aren't you, old lad.' He let his arm fall by the bedside and his hand fondled the sleek ears.

'That seems to be his favourite place.'

'Aye, it's a funny thing, but 'e allus sits there. T'missus is the one who has to take 'im walks and feeds 'im but he's very faithful to me. He has a basket over there but this is 'is place. I only have to reach down and he's there.'

This was something that I had seen on many occasions with disabled people: that their pets stayed close by them as if conscious of their role of comforter and friend.

I finished my beer and got to my feet. Ron looked up at me. 'Reckon I'll spin mine out a bit longer.' He glanced at his half-full glass. 'Ah used to shift about six pints some nights when I went out wi' the lads but you know, I enjoy this one bottle just as much. Strange how things turn out.'

His wife bent over him, mock-scolding. 'Yes, you've had to right your ways. You're a reformed character, aren't you?'

They both laughed as though it were a stock joke between them.

'Well, thank you for the drink, Mrs Cundall. I'll look in to see Hermann on Tuesday.' I moved towards the door.

As I left I waved to the man in the bed and his wife put her hand on my arm. 'We're very grateful to you for comin' out at this time on a Sunday night, Mr Herriot. We felt awful about callin' you, but you understand it was only today that the little chap started going off his legs like that.'

'Oh, of course, of course, please don't worry. I didn't mind in the least.'

And as I drove through the darkness I knew that I didn't mind – now. My petty irritation had evaporated within two minutes of my entering that house and I was left only with a feeling of humility. If that man back there had a lot to be thankful for, how about me? I had everything. I only wished I could dispel the foreboding I felt about his dog. There was a hint of doom about those symptoms of Hermann's and yet I knew I just had to get him right . . .

On Tuesday he looked much the same, possibly a little worse.

'I think I'd better take him back to the surgery for X-ray,' I said to Mrs Cundall. 'He doesn't seem to be improving with the treatment.'

In the car Hermann curled up happily on Rosie's knee, submitting with good grace to her petting.

I had no need to anaesthetise him or sedate him when I placed him on our newly acquired X-ray machine. Those hind quarters stayed still all by themselves. A lot too still for my liking.

I was no expert at interpreting X-ray pictures but at least I could be sure there was no fracture of the vertebrae. Also, there was no sign of bony extoses, but I thought I could detect a narrowing of the space between a couple of the vertebrae which would confirm my suspicions of a protrusion of a disc.

Laminectomy or fenestration had not even been heard of in those days so I could do nothing more than continue with my treatment and hope.

By the end of the week hope had grown very dim. I had supplemented the salycilates with long-standing remedies like tincture of nux vomica and other ancient stimulant drugs, but when I saw Hermann on the Saturday he was unable to rise. I tweaked the toes of his hind limbs and was rewarded by a faint reflex movement, but with a sick certainty I knew that complete posterior paralysis was not far away.

A week later I had the unhappy experience of seeing my prognosis confirmed in the most classical way. When I entered the door of the Cundall's cottage Hermann came to meet me, happy and welcoming in his front end but dragging his hind limbs helplessly behind him.

'Hello, Mr Herriot.' Mrs Cundall gave me a wan smile and looked down at the little creature stretched frog-like on the carpet. 'What d'you think of him now?'

I bent and tried the reflexes. Nothing. I shrugged my shoulders, unable to think of anything to say. I looked at the gaunt figure in the bed, the arm outstretched as always on the quilt.

'Good morning, Ron,' I said as cheerfully as I could, but there was no reply. The face was averted, looking out of the window. I walked over to the bed. Ron's eyes were staring fixedly at the glorious panorama of moor and fell, at the pebbles of the river, white in the early sunshine, at the criss-cross of the grey walls against the green. His face was expressionless. It was as though he did not know I was there.

I went back to his wife. I don't think I have ever felt more miserable.

'Is he annoyed with me?' I whispered.

'No, no, no, it's this.' She held out a newspaper. 'It's upset him something awful.'

I looked at the printed page. There was a large picture at the top, a picture of a dachshund exactly like Hermann. This dog, too, was paralysed, but its hind end was supported my a little four-wheeled bogie. On the picture it appeared to be sporting with its mistress. In fact it looked quite happy and normal except for those wheels.

Ron seemed to hear the rustle of the paper because his head came round quickly. 'What d'ye think of that, Mr Herriot? D'ye agree with it?'

'Well . . . I don't really know, Ron. I don't like the look of it, but I suppose the lady in the picture thought it was the only thing to do.'

'Aye, maybe.' The husky voice trembled. 'But ah don't want Hermann to finish up like that.' The arm dropped by the side of the bed and his fingers felt around on the carpet, but the little dog was still splayed out near the door. 'It's 'opeless now, Mr Herriot, isn't it?'

'Well, it was a black look-out from the beginning,' I said. 'These cases are so difficult. I'm very sorry.'

'Nay, I'm not blamin' you,' he said. 'You've done what ye could, same as vet for that dog in the picture did what 'e could. But is was no good, was it? What do we do now – put 'im down?'

'No, Ron, forget about that just now. Sometimes paralysis cases just recover on their own after many weeks. We must carry on. At this moment I honestly cannot say there is no hope.'

I paused for a moment, then turned to Mrs Cundall. 'One of the problems is the dog's natural functions. You'll have to carry him out into the garden for that. If you gently squeeze each side of his abdomen you'll encourage him to pass water. I'm sure you'll soon learn how to do that.'

'Oh, of course, of course,' she replied. 'I'll do anything. As long as there's some hope.'

'There is, I assure you, there is.'

But on the way back to the surgery the thought hammered in my brain. That hope was very slight. Spontaneous recovery did sometimes occur, but Hermann's condition was extreme. I repressed a groan as I thought of the nightmarish atmosphere which had begun to surround my dealings with the Cundalls. The paralysed man and the paralysed dog. And why did that picture have to appear in the paper just at this very time? Every veterinary surgeon knows the feeling that fate has loaded the scales against him, and it weighed on me despite the bright sunshine spreading into the car.

However, I kept going back every few days. Sometimes I took a couple of bottles of brown ale along in the evening and drank them with Ron. He and his wife were always cheerful but the little dog never showed the slightest sign of improvement. He still had to pull his useless hind limbs after him when he came to greet me, and though he always returned to his station by his master's bed, nuzzling up into Ron's hand, I was beginning to resign myself to the certainty that one day that arm would come down from the quilt and Hermann would not be there.

It was on one of these visits that I noticed an unpleasant smell as I entered the house. There was something familiar about it.

I sniffed and the Cundalls looked at each other guiltily. There was a silence and then Ron spoke.

'It's some medicine ah've been givin' Hermann. Stinks like 'ell but it's supposed to be good for dogs.'

'Oh yes?'

'Aye, well . . .' His fingers twitched uncomfortably on the bed-clothes. 'It was Bill Noakes put me on to it. He's an old mate o' mine – we used to work down t'pit together – and he came to visit me last weekend. Keeps a few whippets, does Bill. Knows a lot about dogs and 'e sent me this stuff along for Hermann.'

Mrs Cundall went to the cupboard and sheepishly presented me with a plain bottle. I removed the cork and as the horrid stench rose up to me my memory became suddenly clear. Asafoetida, a common constituent of quack medicines before the war and still lingering on the shelves of occasional chemist shops and in the medicine chests of people who liked to doctor their own animals.

I had never prescribed the stuff myself but it was supposed to be beneficial in horses with colic and dogs with digestive troubles. My own feeling had always been that its popularity had been due solely to the assumption that anything which stank as badly as that must have some magical properties, but one thing I knew for sure was that it could not possibly do anything for Hermann.

I replaced the cork. 'So you're giving him this, eh?'

Ron nodded. 'Aye, three times a day. He doesn't like it much, but Bill Noakes has great faith in it. Cured hundreds o' dogs with it, 'e says.' The deep-sunk eyes looked at me with a silent appeal.

'Well, fine, Ron,' I said. 'You carry on. Let's hope it does the trick.'

I knew the asafoetida couldn't do any harm and since my treatment had proved useless I was in no position to turn haughty. But my main concern was that these two nice people had been given a glimmer of hope, and I wasn't going to blot it out.

Mrs Cundall smiled and Ron's expression relaxed. 'That's grand, Mr Herriot,' he said. 'Ah'm glad ye don't mind. I can dose the little feller myself. It's summat for me to do.'

It was about a week after the commencement of the new treatment that I called in at the Cundalls as I was passing through Gilthorpe.

'How are you today, Ron?' I asked.

'Champion, Mr Herriot, champion.' He always said that, but today there was a new eagerness in his face. He reached down and lifted his dog on to the bed. 'Look 'ere.'

He pinched the little paw betweeen his fingers and there was a faint but definite retraction of the leg. I almost fell over in my haste to grab at the other foot. The result was the same.

'My God, Ron,' I gasped, 'the reflexes are coming back.'

He laughed his soft husky laugh. 'Bill Noakes's stuff's working, isn't it?'

A gush of emotions, mainly professional shame and wounded pride, welled in me, but it was only for a moment. 'Yes, Ron,' I replied, 'it's working. No doubt about it.'

He stared up at me. 'Then Hermann's going to be all right?'

'Well, it's early days yet, but that's the way it looks to me.'

It was several weeks more before the little dachshund was back to normal and of course it was a fairly typical case of spontaneous recovery with nothing whatever to do with the asafoetida or indeed with my own efforts. Even now, thirty years later, when I treat these puzzling back conditions with steroids, broad spectrum antibiotics and sometimes colloidal calcium, I wonder how many of them would have recovered without my aid. Quite a number, I imagine.

Sadly, despite the modern drugs, we still have our failures and I always regard a successful termination with profound relief.

But that feeling of relief has never been stronger than it was with Hermann and I can recall vividly my final call at the cottage in Gilthorpe. As it happened it was around the same time as my first visit, eight o'clock in the evening, and when Mrs Cundall ushered me in, the little dog bounded joyously up to me before returning to his post by the bed.

'Well, that's a lovely sight,' I said. 'He can gallop like a racehorse now.'

Ron dropped his hand down and stroked the sleek head. 'Aye, isn't it grand. By heck, it's been a worryin' time.'

'Well, I'll be going.' I gave Hermann a farewell pat. 'I just looked in on my way home to make sure all was well. I don't need to come any more now.'

'Nay, nay,' Ron said. 'Don't rush off. You've time to have a bottle o' beer with me before ye go.'

I sat down by the bed and Mrs Cundall gave us our glasses before pulling up a chair for herself. It was exactly like that first night. I poured my beer and looked at the two of them. Their faces glowed with friendliness and I marvelled because my part in Hermann's salvation had been anything but heroic.

In their eyes everything I had done must have seemed bumbling and ineffectual, and in fact they must be convinced that all would have been lost if Ron's old chum from the coal-face had not stepped in and effortlessly put things right.

At best they could only regard me as an amiable fathead and all the explanations and protestations in the world would not alter that. But though my ego had been bruised, I did not really care. I was witnessing a happy ending instead of a tragedy and that was more important than petty self-justification. I made a mental resolve never to say anything which might spoil their picture of this triumph.

I was about to take my first sip when Mrs Cundall spoke up. 'This is your last visit, Mr Herriot, and all's ended well. I think we ought to drink some sort o' toast.'

'I agree,' I said. 'Let's see, what shall it be? Ah yes, I've got it.' I raised my glass. 'Here's to Bill Noakes.'

*

The sight of a long-bodied dog losing the power in its hind limbs is another thing which can spoil a veterinary surgeon's day. The outlook is always poor. It was especially worrying for me when it happened to Hermann who occupied such a vital place in the life of his brave master. I didn't learn much from his recovery because it seemed to be mainly spontaneous, but I did learn a lesson in counting my blessings from Ron Cundall.

48. *Rip*

I winced as Jack Scott's slender frame crashed against the cow's ribs, but Jack himself didn't seem unduly troubled. His eyes popped a little and his cap slid over one ear, but he took a fresh grip on the tail, braced his boots once more against the cobbles and prepared himself for further action.

I was trying to irrigate the cow's uterus with Lugol's iodine. This was the common post-war treatment for infertility in cattle caused by endometritis, but it involved the insertion of the long metal Nielsen catheter through the uterine cervix and this animal didn't seem to appreciate it. Every time I attempted to work the catheter through the cervical folds she swung round violently, and since the farmer weighed only about eight stones he was whirled repeatedly against the neighbouring cow.

But this time I had the feeling I was winning. The tube was sliding nicely into the uterus and if only she would stand still for a few seconds the job would be over.

'Hang on, Jack,' I gasped as I began to pump in the Lugol's. As soon as the cow felt the fluid trickling in she veered over again, and the farmer's mouth fell open as he was squashed between the big creatures. And when a hoof descended on his toes a soft groan escaped him.

'Lovely, that's it.' I withdrew the catheter and stepped back, thinking at the same time that this had been a singularly uncooperative patient.

Jack, however, didn't seem to share my view. Hobbling on his bruised foot he went up to the front of the cow and put his arms round her neck.

'Ah, you're a grand awd lass,' he murmured, resting his cheek against the craggy jaw.

I looked at him wonderingly. It was always like this with Jack. He had a deep affection for every creature, human and animal, on his farm and, with an occasional exception such as the cow I had just treated, the feeling seemed to be returned.

When he had concluded his embrace he pushed his way out and hopped over the dung channel. His face wore its usual smile. It was not the ruddy face of the typical farmer, in fact it was always pale and haggard as though its owner hadn't slept for a few nights, and the deep wrinkles on the cheeks and forehead made Jack look older than his forty years. But the smile was radiant, like an inner light.

'Ah've one or two other jobs for ye, Mr Herriot,' he said. 'First I want you to give a bullock a shot. He's got a bit of a cough.'

We walked across the yard with Jack's sheepdog, Rip, gambolling around his master in delight. Often these farm dogs were slinking, furtive little creatures, but Rip behaved like a happy pet.

The farmer bent and patted him. 'Hello, feller, are you comin' too?' As the dog went into further transports a little boy and girl, the two youngest of the Scott family, trotted along with us.

'Dad, where are ye goin'?' 'Dad, what are ye doin'?' they cried. There were usually children mixed up with the visits on this farm, getting in between the cows' legs, often hindering the work, but it never worried Jack.

The bullock was lying in deep straw in a loose box. He was a huge animal and obviously not very ill because he was placidly chewing his cud as we entered.

'There's nowt much wrong with 'im,' Jack said. 'Maybe just a bit o'cold. But I've heard 'im cough a few times and I reckon he'd be better with an injection.'

The temperature was slightly elevated and I filled a syringe with the penicillin suspension which the veterinary profession had recently acquired. I leaned over, gave the hairy rump the usual quick thump with my hand and plunged the needle in.

On any farm an animal of this size could have been something of a problem to inject, perhaps involving a chase round the box, but this one did not even rise to his feet. Nobody was restraining him in any way but he continued to chew, merely looking round with mild interest as I drove the needle deep into his muscle.

'Champion. Good lad, good lad.' Jack scratched the hairy poll for a few moments before we left.

'There's some lambs ah want you to look at,' he said, and led me into a Nissen hut. 'Ah've never seen owt like them.'

There were a number of ewes and lambs in the hut but it was not difficult to see what the farmer meant. Several of the lambs were wobbling on their hind legs as they walked and two could take only a few faltering steps before collapsing on their sides.

Jack turned to me. 'What's matter wi' them, Mr Herriot?'

'They've got swayback,' I replied.

'Swayback. What's that?'

'Well, it's a copper deficiency. Causes degeneration of the brain which makes them weak on their hindquarters. That's the typical form, but sometimes they become paralysed or take fits. It's a funny disease.'

'That's strange,' the farmer said. 'Them ewes have had copper licks to go at all the time.'

'I'm afraid that's not enough. If you get many cases you ought to inject the ewes with copper halfway through pregnancy to prevent it for next time.'

He sighed. 'Ah well, now we know what it is you'll be able to put these lambs right.'

'Sorry, Jack,' I replied. 'There's no cure. Only prevention.'

'Well, that's a beggar.' The farmer tipped back his cap. 'What's goin' to happ.n to this lot, then?'

'Well, the ones that are just wobbly have a good chance of making fat lambs, but I haven't much hope for those two.' I pointed to the pair lying on their sides. 'They are already partially paralysed. I honestly think the kindest thing would be . . .'

That was when the smile left Jack's face. It always did at the merest suggestion of putting an animal down. It is a country vet's duty to advise his clients when treatment is obviously unprofitable. He must always have the farmer's commercial interest in mind.

This system worked at most places but not at Jack Scott's. Tell him to get rid of a cow which had lost a couple of quarters with mastitis and the curtain would come down over that smiling face. He had various animals on the farm which could not possibly be making him any money, but they were his friends and he was happy to see them pottering about.

He dug his hands deep in his pockets and looked down at the prostrate lambs. 'Are they sufferin', Mr Herriot?'

'No, Jack, no. It doesn't seem to be a painful disease.'

'Awright, I'll keep them two. If they can't suck, I'll feed 'em meself. Ah like to give things a chance.'

He didn't have to tell me. He gave everything a chance. No farmer likes to have the extra work of lamb feeding, especially when the little creatures are abnormal, but I knew it was no use arguing with Jack. It was his way.

Out in the yard again, he leaned against the half-door of a loose box. 'Any road, I'll have to remember to do them ewes with copper next time.'

As he spoke an enormous head poked over the door. This was the bull box and the great Shorthorn inside clearly wished to pay his respects.

He began to lick the back of Jack's neck, and as the rasping tongue repeatedly knocked his cap over his eyes the farmer remonstrated gently. 'Give over, George, ye daft thing. What d'you think you're doing'?' But he reached back and tickled the animal's chin at the same time.

The expression on George's face made him look more like a dog than a bull. Goofy-eyed and anxious to please, he licked and nuzzled faster than ever despite the farmer's protests. On many farms a bull that size would be a potential killer, but George was just another of Jack's pets.

As lambing time was left behind and the summer wore on, I was glad to see that Jack's dedication had paid off. The two semi-para-lysed lambs were surviving and doing well. They still flopped down after a few steps but they were able to nibble the fast-growing grass and the demyelination of their brains had mercifully not progressed.

It was in October, when the trees around the Scott farm were bursting into a blaze of warm colour, that he hailed me as I drove past his gate.

'Will ye stop for a minute and see Rip?' His face was anxious.

'Why, is he ill?'

'Naw, naw, just lame, but I can't mek it out.'

I didn't have to go far to find Rip – he was never far from his master – and I experienced a shock of surprise when I saw him because his right foreleg was trailing uselessly.

'What's happened to him?' I asked.

'He was roundin' up t'cows when one of 'em lashed out and got him on the chest. He's been gettin' lamer ever since. The funny thing is, ah can't find a thing wrong with his leg. It's a mystery.'

Rip wagged vigorously as I felt my way up his leg from foot to shoulder. There was no pain in the limb, no wound or injury, but he winced as I passed my hand over his first rib. Diagnosis was not difficult.

'It's radial paralysis,' I said.

'Radial . . . what's that?'

'The radial nerve passes over the first rib and the kick must have damaged rib and nerve. This has put the extensor muscles out of action so that he can't bring his leg forward.'

'Well, that's a rum 'un.' The farmer passed a hand over the shaggy head and down the fine white markings of the cheeks. 'Will he get better?'

'It's usually a long job,' I replied. 'Nervous tissue is slow to regenerate and it could take weeks or months. Treatment doesn't seem to make much difference.'

The farmer nodded. 'Awright, we'll just have to wait. There's one thing,' and again the bright smile flooded his face, 'he can still get round them cows, lame or not. It 'ud break 'is heart if he couldn't work. Loves 'is job, does Rip.'

On the way back to the car he nudged me and opened the door of a shed. In the corner, in a nest of straw, a cat was sitting with her family of tiny kittens. He lifted two out, holding one in each of his roughened hands. 'Look at them little fellers, aren't they lovely!' He held them against his cheeks and laughed.

As I started the engine I felt I ought to say something encouraging.

Rip

'Don't worry too much about Rip, Jack. These cases usually recover in time.'

But Rip did not recover. After several months his leg was as useless as ever and the muscles had wasted greatly. The nerve must have been irreparably damaged and it was an unhappy thought that this attractive little animal was going to be three-legged for the rest of his life.

Jack was undismayed and maintained stoutly that Rip was still a good working dog.

The real blow fell one Sunday morning as Siegfried and I were arranging the rounds in the office. I answered the door bell and found Jack on the step with his dog in his arms.

'What's wrong?' I asked. 'Is he worse?'

'No, Mr Herriot.' The farmer's voice was husky. 'It's summat different. He's been knocked down.'

We examined the dog on the surgery table. 'Fracture of the tibia,' Siegfried said. 'But there's no sign of internal damage. Do you know exactly what happened?'

Jack shook his head. 'Nay, Mr Farnon. He ran on to the village street and a car caught 'im. He dragged 'imself back into t'yard.'

'Dragged?' Siegfried was puzzled.

'Aye, the broken leg's on the same side as t'other thing.'

My partner blew out his cheeks. 'Ah yes, the radial paralysis. I remember you told me about it, James.' He looked at me across the table and I knew he was thinking the same thing as I was. A fracture and a paralysis on the same side was a forbidding combination.

'Right, let's get on,' Siegfried murmured.

We set the leg in plaster and I held open the door of Jack's old car as he laid Rip on the back seat.

The farmer smiled out at me through the window. 'I'm takin' the family to church this mornin' and I'll say a little prayer for Rip while I'm there.'

I watched until he drove round the corner of the street and when I turned I found Siegfried at my elbow.

'I just hope that job goes right,' he said thoughtfully. 'Jack would take it hard if it didn't.' He turned and carelessly dusted his old brass plate on its new place on the wall. 'He's a truly remarkable chap. He says he's going to say a prayer for his dog and there's nobody better qualified. Remember what Coleridge said? "He prayeth best who loveth best all things both great and small." '

'Yes,' I said. 'That's Jack, all right.'

The farmer brought his dog into the surgery six weeks later for the removal of the plaster.

'Taking a cast off is a much longer job than putting it on,' I said as I worked away with my little saw.

Jack laughed. 'Aye, ah can see that. It's hard stuff to get through.'

I have never liked this job and it seemed a long time before I splayed open the white roll with my fingers and eased it away from the hair of the leg.

I felt at the site of the fracture and my spirits plummeted. Hardly any healing had taken place. There should have been a healthy callus by now but I could feel the loose ends of the broken bones moving against each other, like a hinge. We were no further forward.

I could hear Siegfried pottering among the bottles in the dispensary and I called to him.

He palpated the limb. 'Damn! One of those! And just when we didn't want it.' He looked at the farmer. 'We'll have to try again, Jack, but I don't like it.'

We applied a fresh plaster and the farmer grinned confidently. 'Just wanted a bit more time, I reckon. He'll be right next time.'

But it was not to be. Siegfried and I worked together to strip off the second cast but the situation was practically unchanged. There was little or no healing tissue around the fracture.

We didn't know what to say. Even at the present time, after the most sophisticated bone-pinning procedures, we still find these cases where the bones just will not unite. They are as frustrating now as they were that afternoon when Rip lay on the surgery table.

I broke the silence. 'It's just the same, I'm afraid, Jack.'

'You mean it 'asn't joined up?'

'That's right.'

The farmer rubbed a finger along his upper lip. 'Then 'e won't be able to take any weight on that leg?'

'I don't see how he possibly can.'

'Aye . . . aye . . . well, we'll just have to see how he goes on, then.'

'But Jack,' Siegfried said gently, 'he can't go on. There's no way a dog can get around with two useless legs on the same side.'

The silence set in again and I could see the familiar curtain coming down over the farmer's face. He knew what was in our minds and he wasn't going to have it. In fact I knew what he was going to say next.

Rip

'Is he sufferin'?'

'No, he isn't,' Siegfried replied. 'There's no pain in the fracture now and the paralysis is painless anyway, but he won't be able to walk, don't you see?'

But Jack was already gathering his dog into his arms. 'Well, we'll give him a chance, any road,' he said, and walked from the room.

Siegfried leaned against the table and looked at me, wide-eyed. 'Well, what do you make of that, James?'

'Same as you,' I replied gloomily. 'Poor old Jack. He always gives everything a chance, but he's got no hope this time.'

But I was wrong. Several weeks later I was called to the Scott farm to see a sick calf and the first thing I saw was Rip bringing the cows in for milking. He was darting to and fro around the rear of the herd, guiding them through the gate from the field, and I watched him in amazement.

He still could not bear any appreciable weight on either of his right limbs, yet he was running happily. Don't ask me how he was doing it because I'll never know, but somehow he was supporting his body with his two strong left legs and the paws of the stricken limbs merely brushing the turf. Maybe he had perfected some balancing feat like a one-wheel bicycle rider but, as I say, I just don't know. The great thing was that he was still the old friendly Rip, his tail swishing when he saw me, his mouth panting with pleasure.

Jack didn't say anything about 'I told you so', and I wouldn't have cared, because it thrilled me to see the little animal doing the job he loved.

*

I suppose the things I pick out to write about are the unusual ones. Jack Scott is the only farmer I have known who resolutely refused to have any animal put down, and Rip was the only dog in my experience who could run about despite two useless legs on one side. I always think of Jack as the man who had faith, and it was good to see that faith rewarded in the case of Rip.

49. *Ruffles and Muffles*

What horrible little dogs!

It was a sentiment which rarely entered my mind, because I could find something attractive in nearly all my canine patients.

I had to make an exception in the cases of Ruffles and Muffles Whithorn. Try as I might I could find no lovable traits, only unpleasant ones – like their unvarying method of welcoming me into their home.

'Down! Down!' I yelped, as I always did. The two little animals – West Highland Whites – were standing on their hind limbs clawing furiously at my trouser legs with their front paws. I don't know whether I have unusually tender shins but the effect was agonising.

As I backed away on tiptoe like a ballet dancer going into reverse the room resounded to Mr and Mrs Whithorn's delighted laughter. They found this unfailingly amusing.

'Aren't they little pets!' Mr Whithorn gasped between paroxysms. 'Don't they give you a lovely greeting, bless them!'

I wasn't so sure about that. Apart from excoriating my flesh through my grey flannels, the dogs were glaring up at me balefully, their mouths half-open, lips quivering, teeth chattering in a characteristic manner. It wasn't exactly a snarl, but it wasn't friendly either.

'Come, my darlings.' The man gathered the dogs into his arms and kissed them both fondly on the cheeks. He was still giggling. 'You know, Mr Herriot, isn't it priceless that they welcome you into our house so lovingly, and then try to stop you from leaving?'

I didn't say anything, but massaged my trousers in silence. The truth was that these animals invariably clawed me on my entry, then did their best to bite my ankles on the way out. In between, they molested me in whatever ways they could devise. The strange thing was that they were both old – Ruffles fourteen and Muffles twelve – and one might have expected some mellowness in their characters, but it was not so.

'Well,' I said, after reassuring myself that my wounds were superficial, 'I understand Ruffles is lame.'

'Yes.' Mrs Whithorn took the dog and placed him on the table where she had spread some newspapers. 'It's his left front paw. Just started this morning. He's in agony, poor dear.'

Gingerly I took hold of the foot, then whipped my hand away as the teeth snapped shut less than an inch from my fingers.

'Oh, my precious!' Mrs Whithorn exclaimed 'It's so painful. Do be careful, Mr Herriot, he's so nervous and I think you're hurting him.'

I breathed deeply. This dog should have had a tape muzzle applied right at the start, but I had previously caused shock and dismay in the Whithorns by suggesting such a thing, so I had to manage as best I could. Anyway, I wasn't a novice at the business. It would take a very smart biter to catch me.

I curled my forefinger round the leg and had another look, and I was able to see what I wanted in the fleeting instant before the next snap. A reddish swelling pouting from between the toes.

An interdigital cyst! How ridiculous that a vet should be making a house call for such a trivial ailment. But the Whithorns had always

413

firmly refused to bring their dogs to the surgery. It frightened the darlings, they said.

I stood back from the table. 'This is just a harmless cyst, but I agree that it is painful, so I'd advise you to bathe it in hot water until it bursts, and that will relieve the pain. Many dogs burst these things themselves by nibbling at them but you can hasten the process.'

I drew some antibiotic into a syringe. 'Nobody knows exactly what causes an interdigital cyst. No specific causal organisms have been found, but I'll give him this shot in case of infection.'

I achieved the injection by holding the little animal by the scruff of the neck, then Mrs Whithorn lifted the other dog on to the table.

'You'd better give him a check-up while you're here,' she said.

This usually happened, and I palpated the snarling bundle of white hair and went over him with stethoscope and thermometer. He had most of the afflictions which beset old dogs – arthritis, nephritis and other things, including a heart murmur which was difficult to hear among the bad-tempered rumblings which echoed round his thorax.

My examination completed, I replenished his various medicaments and prepared to leave. This was when the exit phase of my visit started and it was relished by Mr and Mrs Whithorn even more than the entry.

The ritual never changed. As their owners tittered gleefully, the two little dogs stationed themselves in the doorway, effectively barring my way out. Their lips were drawn back from their teeth. They were the very picture of venom. To draw them away from their posts I feinted to the right, then made a rush for the door, but with my fingers on the handle I had to turn and fend off the hungry jaws snapping at my ankles, and as I skipped around on my heels my previous dainty ballet steps were superseded by the coarser hoppings of a clog dance.

But I escaped. A final couple of quick pushes with my feet and I was out in the fresh air, crashing the door thankfully behind me.

I was regaining my breath when Doug Watson the milkman drew up in his blue van. He kept a few dairy cows on a smallholding on the edge of the town and augmented his income by operating a retail round among the citizens of Darrowby.

'Mornin', Mr Herriot.' He gestured towards the house. 'You been in to see them dogs?'

'Yes.'

'Proper little sods, aren't they?'

I laughed. 'Not very sweet-tempered.'

'By gaw, that's the truth. I've got to watch meself when I deliver t'milk. If that door happens to be open they're straight out at me.'

'I'll bet they are.'

His eyes widened. 'They go for me feet. Sometimes I feel a right bloody Charlie, jumpin' about like a daft thing in front of everybody.'

I nodded. 'I know exactly how you feel.'

'You've got to keep movin' or you've 'ad it,' he said, 'Look 'ere.' He pushed his leg out of the van and pointed to the heel of one of the wellington boots he always wore on his rounds. I could see a neat puncture hole on either side. 'One of 'em got me there, just t'other day. Went right through to me skin.'

'Good heavens, which one did that?'

'Don't rightly know – what's their names, anyway?'

'Ruffles and Muffles,' I replied.

'Bloody 'ell!' Doug looked at me wonderingly. His own dog was called Spot. He spent a few moments in thought, then raised a finger. 'But ah'll tell tha summat and maybe ye won't believe me. Them dogs used to be real nice little things.'

'What!'

'I'm not jokin' or jestin'. When they fust came here they were as friendly as any dogs I've ever seen. It was afore your time, but it's true.'

'Well, that's remarkable,' I said. 'I wonder what happened.'

Doug shrugged his shoulders. 'God knows, but each of 'em turned nasty after a few months and they've got wuss and wuss ever since.'

Doug's words stayed with me until I got back to the surgery. I was puzzled. Westies, in my experience, were a particularly amiable breed. Siegfried was in the dispensary, writing directions on a bottle of colic mixture. I mentioned the situation to him.

'Yes,' he said. 'I've heard the same thing. I've been to the Whithorns a couple of times and I know why those dogs are so objectionable.'

'Really? Why is it?'

'Their owners make them that way. They never correct them and they slobber over them all the time.'

'You could be right,' I said. 'I've always made a fuss of my own dogs, but all that kissing and cuddling is a bit sickening.'

'Quite. Too much of that is bad for a dog. And another thing, those two animals are the bosses in that home. A dog likes to obey. It gives them security. Believe me, Ruffles and Muffles would be happy and good-tempered if they had been controlled right from the start.'

'There's no doubt they rule the roost now.'

'Absolutely,' Siegfried said. 'And really, they hate it. If only the Whithorns would take off the rose-tinted spectacles and treat them normally. But it's too late now, I'm afraid.' He pocketed the colic mixture and left.

The months passed, I had a few more visits to the Whithorns and went through the usual dancing routine, then, oddly, both the old dogs died within a few weeks of each other. And despite their tempestuous lives they had peaceful ends. Ruffles was found dead in his basket one morning and Muffles wandered down the garden for a sleep under the apple tree and never woke up.

That was merciful, anyway. They hadn't treated me very well but I was glad they had been spared the things which upset me most in small animal practice. The road accident, the lingering illness, the euthanasia. It was like a chapter in my life closing, but shortly afterwards Mr Whithorn rang me.

'Mr Herriot,' he said, 'we have acquired another pair of Westies and I wonder if you would call and give them their distemper inoculations.'

It was a delightful change to go into the room and be met by two tail-wagging puppies. They were twelve weeks old and they looked up at me with benevolent eyes.

'They're beautiful,' I said. 'What have you called them?'

'Ruffles and Muffles,' Mr Whithorn replied.

'Same again, eh?'

'Yes, we wanted to keep the memory of our other darlings alive.' He seized the puppies and showered kisses on them.

After the inoculations it was a long time before I saw the little dogs again. They seemed to be singularly healthy. It must have been nearly a year later when I was called to the house to give them a check-up.

When I went into the sitting-room, Ruffles and Muffles Mark 2 were seated side by side on the sofa. There was an odd immobility in their attitude. As I approached, they stared at me coldly and as if responding to a signal they bared their teeth and growled softly but menacingly.

A chill ran through me. It couldn't be happening all over again. But as Mr Whithorn lifted Ruffles on to the table and I took the auroscope from its box I quickly realised that fate had turned the clock back. The little animal stood there, regarding me with a bristling mistrust.

'Hold his head, will you, please,' I said, 'I want to examine his ears first.' I took the ear between finger and thumb and gently inserted the auroscope. I applied my eye to the instrument and was inspecting the external meatus when the dog exploded into action. I heard a vicious snarl and as I jerked my head back, the draught of the crunching teeth fanned my face.

Mr Whithorn leaned back and abandoned himself to mirth.

'Oh, isn't he a little monkey! Ha-ha-ha, he just won't stand any nonsense.' He rested his hands on the table for some time, shaking with merriment, then he wiped his eyes. 'Dear, oh dear, what a character he is.'

I stared at the man. The fact that he might easily have been confronted by a noseless veterinary surgeon did not seem to weigh with him. I looked, too, at his wife standing behind him. She was laughing just as merrily. What was the use of trying to instil reason into these people? They were utterly besotted. All I could do was get on with the job.

'Mr Whithorn,' I said tautly, 'will you please hold him again, and this time take a tight grip with your hands on either side of the neck.'

He looked at me anxiously. 'But I won't hurt the little pet?'

'No, no, of course not.'

'All right.' He placed his cheek against the dog's face and whispered lovingly, 'Daddy promises to be gentle, my angel. Don't worry, sweetheart.'

He grasped the loose skin of the neck as I directed and I warily recommenced operations. Peering at the interior of the ear, listening to Mr Whithorn's murmured endearments, I was tensed in readiness for another explosion. But when it came with a ferocious yap I found I was in no danger because Ruffles had turned his attention elsewhere.

As I dropped the auroscope and jumped back I saw that the dog had sunk his teeth into the ball of his master's thumb. And it wasn't an ordinary bite. He was hanging on, grinding deeply into the flesh.

Mr Whithorn emitted a piercing yell of agony before shaking himself free.

'*You rotten little bugger!*' he screamed, dancing around the room, holding the stricken hand. He looked at the blood pouring from the two deep holes, then glared at Ruffles. '*Oh, you bloody little swine!*'

I thought of Siegfried's words and of his wish that these people might take a more sensible view of their dogs. Well, this could be a start.

*

It is an extraordinary fact that some owners always have nice dogs and others nasty ones. The vast majority of our clients produce generation after generation of friendly little tail-waggers, while others, down through the years, have brought dogs into our surgery whose only ambition seems to be to take a piece out of the vet. And these latter owners do not always spoil their pets – it isn't as simple as that. I do wish I knew the reason.

50. *The Dustbin Dog*

In the semi-darkness of the surgery passage I thought it was a hideous growth dangling from the side of the dog's face, but as he came closer I saw that it was only a condensed milk can. Not that condensed milk cans are commonly found sprouting from dogs' cheeks, but I was relieved because I knew I was dealing with Brandy again.

I hoisted him on to the table. 'Brandy, you've been at the dustbin again.'

The big golden Labrador gave me an apologetic grin and did his best to lick my face. He couldn't manage it since his tongue was jammed inside the can, but he made up for it by a furious wagging of tail and rear end.

'Oh, Mr Herriot, I am sorry to trouble you again.' Mrs Westby, his attractive young mistress, smiled ruefully. 'He just won't keep out of that dustbin. Sometimes the children and I can get the cans off ourselves but this one is stuck fast. His tongue is trapped under the lid.'

'Yes . . . yes . . .' I eased my finger along the jagged edge of the metal. 'It's a bit tricky, isn't it? We don't want to cut his mouth.'

As I reached for a pair of forceps I thought of the many other occasions when I had done something like this for Brandy. He was one of my patients, a huge, lolloping, slightly goofy animal, but this dustbin raiding was becoming an obsession.

He liked to fish out a can and lick out the tasty remnants, but his licking was carried out with such dedication that he burrowed deeper and deeper until he got stuck. Again and again he had been freed by his family or myself from fruit salad cans, corned beef cans, baked bean cans, soup cans. There didn't seem to be any kind of can he didn't like.

I gripped the edge of the lid with my forceps and gently bent it back along its length till I was able to lift it away from the tongue. An instant later, that tongue was slobbering all over my cheek as Brandy expressed his delight and thanks.

'Get back, you daft dog!' I said, laughing, as I held the panting face away from me.

'Yes, come down, Brandy.' Mrs Westby hauled him from the table and spoke sharply. 'It's all very fine making a fuss now, but you're becoming a nuisance with this business. It will have to stop.'

The scolding had no effect on the lashing tail and I saw that his mistress was smiling. You just couldn't help liking Brandy, because he was a great ball of affection and tolerance without an ounce of malice in him.

I had seen the Westby children – there were three girls and a boy – carrying him around by the legs, upside down, or pushing him in a pram, sometimes dressed in baby clothes. Those youngsters played all sorts of games with him, but he suffered them all with good humour. In fact I am sure he enjoyed them.

Brandy had other idiosyncrasies apart from his fondness for dustbins.

I was attending the Westby cat at their home one afternoon when I noticed the dog acting strangely. Mrs Westby was sitting knitting in an armchair while the oldest girl squatted on the hearth rug with me and held the cat's head.

It was when I was searching my pockets for my thermometer that I noticed Brandy slinking into the room. He wore a furtive air as he moved across the carpet and sat down with studied carelessness in front of his mistress. After a few moments he began to work his rear end gradually up the front of the chair towards her knees. Absently she took a hand away from her knitting and pushed him down, but he immediately restarted his backward ascent. It was an extraordinary mode of progression, his hips moving in a very slow rumba rhythm as he elevated them inch by inch, and all the time the golden face was blank and innocent as though nothing at all was happening.

Fascinated, I stopped hunting for my thermometer and watched. Mrs Westby was absorbed in an intricate part of her knitting and didn't seem to notice that Brandy's bottom was now firmly parked on her shapely knees which were clad in blue jeans. The dog paused as though acknowledging that phase one had been successfully completed, then ever so gently he began to consolidate his position, pushing his way up the front of the chair with his fore limbs till at one time he was almost standing on his head.

It was at that moment, just when one final backward heave would have seen the great dog ensconced on her lap, that Mrs Westby finished the tricky bit of knitting and looked up.

'Oh, really, Brandy, you are silly!' She put a hand on his rump and sent him slithering disconsolately to the carpet where he lay and looked at her with liquid eyes.

'What was all that about?' I asked.

Mrs Westby laughed. 'Oh, it's these old blue jeans. When Brandy first came here as a tiny puppy I spent hours nursing him on my knee and I used to wear the jeans a lot then. Ever since, even though he's a grown dog, the very sight of the things makes him try to get on my knee.'

'But he doesn't just jump up?'

'Oh no,' she said. 'He's tried it and got ticked off. He knows perfectly well I can't have a huge Labrador in my lap.'

'So now it's the stealthy approach, eh?'

She giggled. 'That's right. When I'm preoccupied – knitting or reading – sometimes he manages to get nearly all the way up, and if he's been playing in the mud he makes an awful mess and I have to go and change. That's when he really does receive a scolding.'

A patient like Brandy added colour to my daily round. When I was walking my own dog I often saw him playing in the fields by the river. One particularly hot day, many of the dogs were taking to the water either to chase sticks or just to cool off, but whereas they glided in and swam off sedately, Brandy's approach was unique.

I watched as he ran up to the river bank, expecting him to pause before entering. But instead he launched himself outwards, legs splayed in a sort of swallow dive, and hung for a moment in the air rather like a flying fox before splashing thunderously into the depths. To me it was the action of a completely happy extrovert.

On the following day in those same fields I witnessed something even more extraordinary. There is a little children's playground in one corner – a few swings, a roundabout and a slide. Brandy was disporting himself on the slide.

For this activity he had assumed an uncharacteristic gravity of expression and stood calmly in the queue of children. When his turn came he mounted the steps, slid down the metal slope, all dignity and importance, then took a staid walk round to rejoin the queue.

The little boys and girls who were his companions seemed to take him for granted, but I found it difficult to tear myself away. I could have watched him all day.

I often smiled to myself when I thought of Brandy's antics, but I didn't smile when Mrs Westby brought him into the surgery a few months later. His bounding ebullience had disappeared and he dragged himself along the passage to the consulting-room.

As I lifted him on to the table I noticed that he had lost a lot of weight.

'Now, what is the trouble, Mrs Westby?' I asked.

She looked at me worriedly. 'He's been off colour for a few days now, listless and coughing and not eating very well, but this morning he seems quite ill and you can see he's starting to pant.'

'Yes . . . yes . . .' As I inserted the thermometer I watched the rapid rise and fall of the rib cage and noted the gaping mouth and anxious eyes. 'He does look very sorry for himself.'

His temperature was 104°F. I took out my stethoscope and auscultated his lungs. I have heard of an old Scottish doctor describing a seriously ill patient's chest as sounding like a 'kist o' whustles' and that just about described Brandy's. Râles, wheezes, squeaks and bubblings – they were all there against a background of laboured respiration.

I put the stethoscope back in my pocket. 'He's got pneumonia.'

'Oh dear.' Mrs Westby reached out and touched the heaving chest. 'That's bad, isn't it?'

'Yes, I'm afraid so.'

'But . . .' She gave me an appealing glance. 'I understand it isn't so fatal since the new drugs came out.'

I hesitated. 'Yes, that's quite right. In humans and most animals the sulpha drugs and now penicillin have changed the picture completely, but dogs are still very difficult to cure.'

Thirty years later it is still the same. Even with all the armoury of antibiotics which followed penicillin – streptomycin, the tetracyclines, and synthetics, and the new non-antibiotic drugs and steroids – I still hate to see pneumonia in a dog.

'But you don't think it's hopeless?' Mrs Westby asked.

'No, no, not at all. I'm just warning you that so many dogs don't respond to treatment when they should. But Brandy is young and strong. He must stand a fair chance. I wonder what started this off, anyway.'

'Oh, I think I know, Mr Herriot. He had a swim in the river about a week ago. I try to keep him out of the water in this cold weather but if he sees a stick floating he just takes a dive into the middle. You've seen him – it's one of the funny little things he does.'

'Yes, I know. And was he shivery afterwards?'

'He was. I walked him straight home, but it was such a freezing cold day. I could feel him trembling as I dried him down.'

I nodded. 'That would be the cause, all right. Anyway, let's start his treatment. I'm going to give him this injection of penicillin and I'll call at your house tomorrow to repeat it. He's not well enough to come to the surgery.'

'Very well, Mr Herriot. And is there anything else?'

'Yes, there is. I want you to make him what we call a pneumonia jacket. Cut two holes in an old blanket for his forelegs and stitch him into it along his back. You can use an old sweater if you like, but he must have his chest warmly covered. Only let him out in the garden for necessities.'

I called and repeated the injection on the following day. There wasn't much change. I injected him for four more days and the realisation came to me sadly that Brandy was like so many of the others – he wasn't responding. The temperature did drop a little but he hardly ate anything and grew gradually thinner. I put him on sulphapyridine tablets, but they didn't seem to make any difference.

As the days passed and he continued to cough and pant and to sink deeper into a blank-eyed lethargy, I was forced more and more to a conclusion which, a few weeks ago, would have seemed impossible: that this happy, bounding animal was going to die.

But Brandy didn't die. He survived. You couldn't put it any higher than that. His temperature came down and his appetite improved and he climbed on to a plateau of twilight existence where he seemed content to stay.

'He isn't Brandy any more,' Mrs Westby said one morning a few weeks later when I called in. Her eyes filled with tears as she spoke.

I shook my head. 'No, I'm afraid he isn't. Are you giving him the halibut-liver oil?'

'Yes, every day. But nothing seems to do him any good. Why is he like this, Mr Herriot?'

'Well, he has recovered from a really virulent pneumonia, but it's left him with a chronic pleurisy, adhesions and probably other kinds of lung damage. It looks as though he's just stuck there.'

She dabbed at her eyes. 'It breaks my heart to see him like this. He's only five, but he's like an old, old dog. He was so full of life, too.' She sniffed and blew her nose. 'When I think of how I used to scold him for getting into the dustbins and muddying up my jeans. How I wish he would do some of his funny old tricks now.'

I thrust my hands deep into my pockets. 'Never does anything like that now, eh?'

'No, no, just hangs about the house. Doesn't even want to go for a walk.'

As I watched, Brandy rose from his place in the corner and pottered slowly over to the fire. He stood there for a moment, gaunt and dead-eyed, and he seemed to notice me for the first time because the end of his tail gave a brief twitch before he coughed, groaned and flopped down on the hearth rug.

Mrs Westby was right. He was like a very old dog.

'Do you think he'll always be like this?' she asked.

I shrugged. 'We can only hope.'

But as I got into my car and drove away I really didn't have much hope. I had seen calves with lung damage after bad pneumonias. They recovered but were called 'bad doers' because they remained thin and listless for the rest of their lives. Doctors, too, had plenty of 'chesty' people on their books; they were, more or less, in the same predicament.

Weeks and then months went by and the only time I saw the Labrador was when Mrs Westby was walking him on his lead. I

The Dustbin Dog

always had the impression that he was reluctant to move and his mistress had to stroll along very slowly so that he could keep up with her. The sight of him saddened me when I thought of the lolloping Brandy of old, but I told myself that at least I had saved his life. I could do no more for him now and I made a determined effort to push him out of my mind.

In fact I tried to forget Brandy and managed to do so fairly well until one afternoon in February. On the previous night I felt I had been through the fire. I had treated a colicky horse until 4 a.m. and was crawling into bed, comforted by the knowledge that the animal was settled down and free from pain when I was called to a calving. I had managed to produce a large live calf from a small heifer, but the effort had drained the last of my strength and when I got home it was too late to return to bed.

Ploughing through the morning round I was so tired that I felt disembodied, and at lunch Helen watched me anxiously as my head nodded over my food. There were a few dogs in the waiting-room at two o'clock and I dealt with them mechanically, peering through half-closed eyelids. By the time I reached my last patient I was almost asleep on my feet. In fact I had the feeling that I wasn't there at all.

'Next, please,' I mumbled as I pushed open the waiting-room door and stood back waiting for the usual sight of a dog being led out to the passage.

But this time there was a big difference. There was a man in the doorway all right and he had a little poodle with him, but the thing that made my eyes snap wide open was that the dog was walking upright on his hind limbs.

I knew I was half-asleep but surely I wasn't seeing things. I stared down at the dog, but the picture hadn't changed – the little creature strutted through the doorway, chest out, head up, as erect as a soldier.

'Follow me, please,' I said hoarsely and set off over the tiles to the consulting-room. Halfway along I just had to turn round to check the evidence of my eyes and it was just the same – the poodle, still on his hind legs, marching along unconcernedly at his master's side.

The man must have seen the bewilderment in my face because he burst suddenly into a roar of laughter.

'Don't worry, Mr Herriot,' he said, 'this little dog was circus

425

trained before I got him as a pet. I like to show off his little tricks. This one really startles people.'

'You can say that again,' I said breathlessly. 'It nearly gave me heart failure.'

The poodle wasn't ill, he just wanted his nails clipping. I smiled as I hoisted him on to the table and began to ply the clippers.

'I suppose he won't want his hind claws doing,' I said. 'He'll have worn them down himself.' I was glad to find I had recovered sufficiently to attempt a little joke.

However, by the time I had finished, the old lassitude had taken over again and I felt ready to fall down as I showed man and dog to the front door.

I watched the little animal trotting away down the street – in the orthodox manner this time – and it came to me suddenly that it had been a long time since I had seen a dog doing something unusual and amusing. Like the things Brandy used to do.

A wave of gentle memories flowed through me as I leaned wearily against the door post and closed my eyes. When I opened them I saw Brandy coming round the corner of the street with Mrs Westby. His nose was entirely obscured by a large red tomato-soup can and he strained madly at the leash and whipped his tail when he saw me.

It was certainly a hallucination this time. I was looking into the past. I really ought to go to bed immediately. But I was still rooted to the door post when the Labrador bounded up the steps, made an attempt, aborted by the soup can, to lick my face and contented himself with cocking a convivial leg against the bottom step.

I stared into Mrs Westby's radiant face. 'What . . . what . . . ?'

With her sparkling eyes and wide smile she looked more attractive than ever. 'Look, Mr Herriot, look! He's better, he's better!'

In an instant I was wide awake. 'And I . . . I suppose you'll want me to get that can off him?'

'Oh yes, yes, please!'

It took all my strength to lift him on to the table. He was heavier now than before his illness. I reached for the familiar forceps and began to turn the jagged edges of the can outwards from the nose and mouth. Tomato soup must have been one of his favourites because he was really deeply embedded and it took some time before I was able to slide the can from his face.

The Dustbin Dog

I fought off his slobbering attack. 'He's back in the dustbins, I see.'

'Yes, he is, quite regularly. I've pulled several cans off him myself. And he goes sliding with the children, too.' She smiled happily.

Thoughtfully I took my stethoscope from the pocket of my white coat and listened to his lungs. They were wonderfully clear. A slight roughness here and there, but the old cacophony had gone.

I leaned on the table and looked at the great dog with a mixture of thankfulness and incredulity. He was as before, boisterous and full of the joy of living. His tongue lolled in a happy grin and the sun glinted through the surgery window on his sleek golden coat.

'But Mr Herriot,' Mrs Westby's eyes were wide, 'how on earth has this happened? How has he got better?'

'*Vis medicatrix naturae*,' I replied in tones of deep respect.

'I beg your pardon?'

'The healing power of nature. Something no veterinary surgeon can compete with when it decides to act.'

'I see. And you can never tell when this is going to happen?'

'No.'

For a few seconds we were silent as we stroked the dog's head, ears and flanks.

'Oh, by the way,' I said, 'has he shown any renewed interest in the blue jeans?'

'Oh my word, yes! They're in the washing-machine at this very moment. Absolutely covered in mud. Isn't it marvellous!'

*

Dogs like Brandy have always lightened my life. The ones who do funny things and make me laugh. He was a natural comedian and even his troubles with dustbins had their funny side, but his pneumonia did wipe the smile off my face for quite a long time. It is good to end my book with a story about a genuine doggy character like Brandy, and a story, too, with a happy ending. To this day I really don't know why he got better, but it doesn't matter.